Foreign & Commonwealth Office

GW00692100

The Diplomatic Service List 2002

THIRTY-SEVENTH EDITION

London: The Stationery Office

Preface

Her Majesty's Diplomatic Service provides the staffs of British Diplomatic and Consular posts overseas in Commonwealth and Foreign countries, as well as in the Foreign & Commonwealth Office in London.

The organisation of the Service and the careers of its members are described in this List, which will be published each year. It is based on information available in August 2001 but includes details of some later changes.

The Diplomatic Service was established on 1 January, 1965, by the merger of the former Foreign, Commonwealth and Trade Commissioner Services. Subsequently, it incorporated the staffs of the Colonial Office in London, which merged with the Commonwealth Relations Office on 1 August, 1966, to form the Commonwealth Office.

The Foreign Office and Commonwealth Office continued as separate Departments of State responsible to separate Secretaries of State until 17 October, 1968. On that day they combined to form the Foreign and Commonwealth Office responsible to one Secretary of State. The Permanent Under-Secretary of the Office and the Head of the Diplomatic Service is Sir Michael Jay, KCMG.

Representatives of Commonwealth countries and foreign states serving in London are shown in a separate publication, the London Diplomatic List, published by The Stationery Office every six months.

Every effort has been made to ensure that the information given in this edition is correct at the time of going to press. Amendments and new entries to the Diplomatic Service List should be sent to the Editor to arrive no later than Friday, 23rd August 2002:-

> Lisa T. Gamandi (Editor)
> Foreign and Commonwealth Office
> Publications Section
> Room WH. MZ. 11,
> King Charles St,
> LONDON SW1A 2AH.

November 2001.

Table of Contents

Part I

Part II

Part III

Part IV

Table of Contents

Home Departments

List of Ministers, Senior Officers and
Home Departments in the
Foreign Commonwealth Office

Part I: Home Departments

Accommodation

Ministers, Senior Officers and most geographical departments are accommodated in the Main Building, Downing Street, London SW1. Departments are also accommodated in other buildings.

Foreign and Commonwealth Office, Downing Street (West) SW1A 2AL	020 7270 1500
Foreign and Commonwealth Office, Downing Street (East) SW1A 2AL	020 7270 1500
Foreign and Commonwealth Office, Whitehall SW1A 2AP	020 7270 1500
Foreign and Commonwealth Office, King Charles St, SW1A 2AH	020 7270 1500
Apollo House, 36 Wellesley Road, Croydon, CR9 3 RR	020 8686 5622
3 Carlton Gardens SW1Y 5AA	020 7270 1500
Vauxhall Cross 85 Albert Embankment, SE1 7TP	020 7270 0850
Cromwell House, Dean Stanley Street, SW1P 3JG	020 7276 7676
94 Victoria Street, SW1E 5JL	020 7917 7000
Hanslope Park, Hanslope, Milton Keynes MK19 7BH	01908 510444
Old Admiralty Building, Whitehall, London, SW1A 2AF	020 7008 1500
British Trade International, Kingsgate House, 66-74 Victoria Street. London SW1E 6SW	020 7215 5000

TELEPHONE ENQUIRIES
If the number, department or building is not known, callers should ring 020 7270 3000 and ask to be connected to the Central Enquiry point.

TELEGRAPHIC ADDRESS
PRODROME LONDON

TELEX 297711 (a/b PRDRME G)

Internet World Wide Web Address: www.fco.gov.uk

The Foreign & Commonwealth Office provides, through its staff in the UK and through its diplomatic missions abroad, the means of communication between the British Government and other governments and international governmental organisations on all matters falling within the field of international relations. It is responsible for alerting the British Government to the implications of developments overseas; for promoting British interests overseas; for protecting British citizens abroad; for explaining British policies to, and cultivating relationships with, governments overseas; for the discharge of British responsibilities to the overseas territories; for entry clearance (through the Joint Entry Clearance Unit, with the Home Office) and for promoting British business overseas (jointly with the Department of Trade and Industry through British Trade International).

MINISTERS AND THEIR STAFFS

Secretary of State for Foreign & Commonwealth Affairs
The Rt Hon Jack Straw, MP
Principal Private Secretary: Simon McDonald
Private Secretaries: Mark Sedwill, Patrick Davies
Diary Secretary: Lynne Rossiter
Telephone: 020 7270 2061
GTN 270 2061

Minister of State for Europe
Peter Hain MP
Private Secretary: James Morrison
Assistant Private Secretary: Sarah Lyons
Telephone: 020 7270 3367
GTN 270 3367

Minister of State for Trade (also DTI)
Baroness Symons
Private Secretary: Robin Gwynn
Assistant Private Secretary: Nick Allen
Telephone: 020 7270 2091
GTN 270 2091

Parliamentary Under-Secretary of State
Ben Bradshaw MP
Private Secretary: Nick Astbury
Assistant Private Secretary: Kara Owen
Telephone: 020 7270 2129/2128
GTN 270 2129/2128

Parliamentary Under-Secretary of State
Denis MacShane, MP
Private Secretary/Assistant Private Secretary:
Fionna Gibb
Telephone: 020 7008 8294
GTN: 7008 8294

Parliamentary Under-Secretary of State
Baroness Amos
Private Secretary: David Cairns
Telephone: 020 7270 2173
GTN 270 2173

SENIOR OFFICERS AND THEIR STAFFS

Permanent Under-Secretary of State & Head of the Diplomatic Service
Sir Michael Jay KCMG
Private Secretary: Susan Hyland
Assistant Private Secretary: Fiona Morrison
Diary Secretary: Fiona Butters
Telephone: 020 7270 2150
GTN 270 2150
Email: PSPUS@fco.gov.uk

Group Chief Executive British Trade International
Sir David Wright KCMG LVO
Telephone: 020 7270 2142
GTN 270 2142
Private Secretary: Gavin Scott
Telephone: 020 7215 4300
GTN 215 4300

Deputy Under-Secretaries of State
Peter Collecott (*Chief Clerk*)
Peter Ricketts CMG (*Political Director*)
Michael Arthur CMG (*Economic Director*)
Stephen Wright CMG (*Defence/Intelligence*)
Peter Westmacott CMG LVO (*Wider World*)
Michael Wood CMG (*Legal Adviser*)

Directors
Mark Lyall Grant (*Director, Africa*)
Richard D Wilkinson CVO (*Director, Americas/Overseas Territories*)
William Ehrman CMG (*Director, International Security*)
John Macgregor CVO (*Director, Wider Europe*)
Kim Darroch CMG (*Director, European Union*)
Stephen Sage (*Chief Executive, FCO Services*)
Nicola Brewer (*Director, Global Issues*)
Alan Charlton CMG (*Director South East Europe*)
Alan Goulty CMG (*Director, Middle East/North Africa*)
Rosalind Marsden (*Director, Asia Pacific*)
Denise Holt (*Director, Personnel*)
David Reddaway CMG MBE (*Director, Public Services*)
Simon Gass CMG (*Director, Resources*)

DEPARTMENTS IN THE FOREIGN AND COMMONWEALTH OFFICE

African Department (Equatorial)
Political and economic relations with Nigeria, Ghana, Sierra Leone, The Gambia, Kenya, Tanzania, Uganda, Ethiopia, Eritrea, Somalia, Djibouti, Liberia, Senegal, Guinea, Mali, Burkina Faso, Côte d'Ivoire, Togo, Benin, Niger, Chad, Cameroon, Gabon, Congo, Democratic Republic of Congo, Burundi, Rwanda, Central African Republic, Equatorial Guinea, Guinea Bissau, Cape Verde, ECOWAS and EAC.

King Charles Street,
LONDON SW1A 2AH
Enquiries: 020 7270 2903
GTN 270 2903
Superintending Director: Mark Lyall Grant
Head of Department: Frank Baker OBE
Deputy Head of Department: Ian Whitting

African Department (Southern)
Political and economic relations with Angola, Botswana, The Comoros, Lesotho, Madagascar, Malawi, Mauritius, Mozambique, Namibia, São Tomé and Principe, Seychelles, South Africa, Swaziland, Zambia and Zimbabwe; Southern African Development Community (SADC).

King Charles Street,
LONDON SW1A 2AH
Enquiries: 020 7270 2535
GTN 270 2535
Superintending Director: Mark Lyall Grant
Head of Department: Andrew Pocock
Deputy Head: Janet Douglas

Aviation, Maritime & Energy Department
Civil aviation and bilateral air services agreements; ICAO; Aerospace industry and civil aircraft exports; Law of the Sea; Maritime Delimitation; Shipping; Fisheries; IMO; Channel Tunnel; Inland Transport; multilateral and bilateral science and technology collaboration; large scientific facilities; relations with Royal Society and Research Councils; international space, broadcasting, postal and telecommunications issues; global and multilateral energy policy and collaboration; fossil fuels; nuclear, new and renewable energy technologies; electricity.

King Charles Street,
LONDON SW1A 2AH
Enquiries: 020 7270 2625
GTN: 270 2625
Superintending Director: Nicola Brewer
Head of Department: Christopher Segar
Deputy Head of Department: Nick Griffiths

British Trade International
British Trade International has lead responsibility within Government for trade and investment development and promotion. It is responsible to both FCO and DTI Ministers, bringing together the work of both departments in those areas.
Within British Trade International, trade and outward investment activities on behalf of British business are delivered by Trade Partners UK. Inward investment promotion activity is delivered by Invest UK, which aims to attract, retain and add value to foreign direct investment in the UK

Kingsgate House, 66-74 Victoria Street,
LONDON SW1E 6SW
Enquiries: 020 7215 5000
GTN: 215 5000
Chairman: Baroness Symons
Group Chief Executive: Sir David Wright KCMG LVO
Deputy Chief Executive: David Hall

Central Services Group
Group Director: David Hall

Regional Group
Group Director: Ian Jones

International Group
Group Director: Quinton Quayle

Business Group
Group Director: David Warren

Strategy and Communications Group
Group Director: John Reynolds

INVEST UK
Chief Executive: William Pedder

Central and North West European Department
Political and bilateral economic relations with Bulgaria, the Czech Republic, Estonia, Latvia, Lithuania, Hungary, Poland, Romania, Slovakia, Slovenia, Switzerland, Liechtenstein, Iceland and Norway.

Downing Street West,
LONDON SW1A 2AL
Enquiries: Bulgaria, Norway, Switzerland, Iceland and Liechtenstein 020 7270 3608
GTN: 270 3608
Enquiries: Baltic States and Romania 020 7270 2363
GTN: 270 2363
Enquiries: Czech Republic, Slovenia and Slovakia 020 7270 3429
GTN: 270 3429
Enquiries: Hungary and Poland 020 7270 3805
GTN: 270 3805
Superintending Director: John Macgregor CVO
Head of Department: Sir John Ramsden Bt
Deputy Head of Department: Julian Evans

Change Management Unit
To work with all staff, stimulating and drawing on creative ideas to ensure the FCO's structure, practices and processes continue to equip it to deliver its targets effectively in a changing world.

Old Admiralty Building
LONDON SW1A 2PA
Enquiries: 020 7008 0074
GTN 7008 0074
Email: cmu.fco@gtnet.gov.uk
Deputy Under-Secretary: Peter Collecott
Head of Unit: Sheena Matthews

China Hong Kong Department
Relations between the United Kingdom and China, including the Hong Kong Special Administrative Region.

FCO,
Whitehall,
LONDON SW1A 2AP
Enquiries: 020 7270 3074
GTN 270 3074
Superintending Director: Rosalind Marsden
Head of Department: Andrew Seaton
Deputy Head of Department: Rod Wye

Common Foreign and Security Policy Department
Co-ordination of foreign policy among EU member states and implementation of Common Foreign and Security Policy.

Downing Street East,
LONDON SW1A 2AH
Enquiries: 020 7270 2807
GTN 270 2807
Political Director: Peter Ricketts CMG
Superintending Director: Kim Darroch CMG
Head of Department: Tim Barrow LVO, MBE
Deputy Head of Department: Martin Shearman

Commonwealth Co-ordination Department
Policy, procedures and practices relating to the Commonwealth as a whole. Commonwealth Heads of Government Meetings. Commonwealth Ministerial Action Group meetings. Liaison with the Commonwealth Secretariat, Commonwealth Foundation, and a wide range of pan-

Commonwealth NGO's professional associations, organisations and societies. Commonwealth constitutional questions.

Downing Street East,
LONDON SW1A 2AL
Enquiries: 020 7270 2962
GTN 270 2962
Email: CCD@mail.fco.gov.uk
Superintending Director: Nicola Brewer
Head of Department: Colin Bright
Deputy Head of Department: Tony Humphries OBE

Consular Division
Consular Policy, Supervision of Consular Services. Protection and assistance for British nationals abroad, including financial assistance, relief and repatriation. Worldwide travel advice, nationality matters, FCO passport policy and co-ordination of Posts' passport operations, birth and death registration and marriages abroad. Legalisation of documents in the UK and overseas; Notarial acts, taking of evidence (civil) and service of process (civil), estates of deceased persons abroad; setting of Consular Fees, liaison with the Home Office on extradition matters. Claims for compensation from other Governments in respect of loss, injury or damage suffered overseas by individuals or companies; electoral Registration Overseas.

Old Admiralty Building,
LONDON SW1A 2PA
Enquiries: 020 7008 0218
GTN 7008 0218
Superintending Director: David Reddaway CMG MBE
Head of Division: James Watt CVO
Deputy Heads of Division: David Clegg MVO,
Matthew Gould MBE

Counter Terrorism Policy Department
Counter-terrorism policy, bilaterally and in international fora. Crisis management.

Downing Street
LONDON SW1A 2AL
Enquiries: 020 7270 2077
GTN 270 2077
Superintending Director: William Ehrman CMG
Head of Department: Keith Bloomfield
Deputy Head of Department: Sian MacLeod

Cultural Relations Department
Cultural relations, bilateral and multilateral, other than EU; British Council policy; scholarship programmes for overseas students; international education; international sport; youth affairs.

King Charles Street,
LONDON SW1A 2AH
Enquiries: 020 7270 6199/6200
GTN 270 6199/6200
Superintending Director: David Reddaway CMG MBE
Head of Department: Michael Reilly
Deputy Head of Department: Rob Holland

Diplomatic Service Families Association
Promotes the interests and welfare of all its members.

FCO
Old Admiralty Building
LONDON SW1A 2PA
Enquiries: 020 7008 0286
GTN 7008 0286
DSFA Chairman: Emilie Salvesen
Vice Chairman and Community Liaison Officer Co-ordinator: Fiona Davies
Executive Secretary: Christine Easter

Diplomatic Service Trade Union Side (DSTUS)
Representing the interests of all FCO Diplomatic and Home Civil Service staff, in all aspects of terms and conditions of service.

FCO,
King Charles Street
LONDON SW1A 2AH
Enquiries: 020 7238 0064
GTN 238 0064
DSTUS Chair: Stephen Watson
DSTUS Deputy Chairs: Alan Bubbear, Robert Streeton
DSTUS Vice Chairs: Rod Baker, Patrick Holditch, John Hudson-Peat
DSTUS Secretary: Pauline Abrams
DSTUS Assistant Secretary and Treasurer: (Vacant)

Drugs & International Crime Department
Co-ordination of Government policies to counter the international drugs trade, both bilateral and in international fora; foreign policy implications; foreign policy relating to wider organised crime.

King Charles Street
LONDON SW1A 2AH
Enquiries: 020 7238 0243/0244
Superintending Director: William Ehrman CMG
Head of Department and Special Representative for International Drugs Issues: Michael Ryder
Deputy Head of Department: Jon Benjamin

Eastern Adriatic Department
Relations with Croatia, Federal Republic of Yugoslavia (including Kosovo), Bosnia and Herzegovina, Macedonia and Albania.

Downing Street West,
LONDON SW1A 2AL
Enquiries: 020 7270 0254/2756/2372/3433/3459
GTN 270 0254/2756/2372/3433/3459
Superintending Director: Alan Charlton CMG
Head of Department: Stephen Wordsworth LVO
Deputy Head of Department: Andrew Levi

Eastern Department
Policy on Russia, Ukraine, the South Caucasus (Armenia, Azerbaijan, Georgia), Central Asia (Kazakhstan, Kyrgyzstan, Tajikistan, Turkmenistan, Uzbekistan), Moldova, Belarus and Caspian energy issues.

Downing Street West,
LONDON SW1A 2AL
Enquiries: 020 7270/2427/2423/3831/1499
GTN 270 /2427/3423/3831/1499
Superintending Director: John Macgregor CVO

Head of Department: Simon Butt
Deputy Head of Department: Paul Brummell

Economic Policy Department

Analysis of global economic trends and world economic conjuncture. Country economic analysis for the Americas, Asia, Australasia, Middle East, Africa, CIS and South-east Europe. Economic analysis of commodities markets. Emerging market issues, including financial sector reform, exchange rate regimes. Development issues, including debt relief (Paris Club) and export credits. Support for UK G8 Sherpa. Policy on the G8. Policy on and liaison with international economic organisations (IMF, IBRD, OECD, EBRD, UN Economic Commission for Europe). Financial sector relations, including Financial Action Task Force, mutual legal assistance, money laundering, financial fraud, asset confiscation, international tax issues, banking regulation and secrecy. Corporate sector issues, including global citizenship, investment protection and promotion agreements.

FCO,
Whitehall,
LONDON SW1A 2AP
Enquiries: 020 7270 2735
GTN 270 2735
Deputy Under Secretary: Michael Arthur
Chief Economist and Head of Department: Creon Butler
Deputy Head of Department (IFIs, Non-European Economies, Development Issues): Harold Freeman
Deputy Head of Department (Summits and Institutions, Business, Finance and Tax, Global Citizenship Unit): Hugh Salvesen

Environment Policy Department

International environment policy; climate change; wildlife protection; biodiversity; marine pollution; nuclear safety and environment.

FCO,
King Charles Street,
LONDON SW1A 2AH
Enquiries: 020 7270 4131/4112
GTN: 270 4131/4112
Superintending Director: Nicola Brewer
Head of Department: John Ashton
Deputy Head of Department: Dr Helen Marquard

Estate Strategy Unit

Formulation and implementation of strategy for the FCO's estate in the UK and overseas.

Apollo House,
36 Wellesley Road,
CROYDON CR0 9YA
Enquiries: 020 8253 6377/6378
GTN: 3822 6377/6378
Superintending Director: Peter Collecott
Head of Unit: Julian Metcalfe
Deputy Head of Unit: Jeremy Neate

European Union Department (Bilateral)

Political and economic relations with Andorra, Austria, Belgium, Denmark, Finland, France, Germany, Greece, the Holy See, Ireland, Italy, Luxembourg, Monaco, the Netherlands, Portugal, San Marino, Spain, Sweden, non-devolved Northern Ireland matters affecting relations with Ireland and other countries; and post-Holocaust issues.

Downing Street (East),
LONDON,
SW1A 2AL
Director EU: Kim Darroch CMG
Head of Department: Karen Pierce
Deputy Head of Department: James Kidner

European Union Department (External)

Relations between the European Union and third countries; international trade and development matters; enlargement of the Union.

Downing Street East,
LONDON SW1A 2AL
Enquiries: 020 7270 3770/2293
GTN 270 3770/2293
Superintending Director: Kim Darroch CMG
Head of Department: Simon Featherstone
Deputy Heads of Department: Alex Ellis, Paul Johnston

European Union Department (Internal)

The internal economic and institutional policies of the European Union.

Downing Street East,
LONDON SW1A 2AL
Enquiries: 020 7270 3388/3391
GTN 270 3388/3391
Superintending Director: Kim Darroch CMG
Head of Department: James Bevan
Deputy Heads of Department: (Vacant), Richard Jones

Financial Compliance Unit

Whitehall,
LONDON SW1A 2AH
Enquiries: 020 7008 8275
GTN 7008 8275
Superintending Director: Simon Gass CMG
Head of Unit: David Major

FCO Association

Old Admiralty Building
LONDON SW1A 2PA
Enquiries: 020 7008 0967
GTN 7008 0967
Chairman: David Burns CMG
Hon. Secretary: Maureen Howley

FCO Services

FCO Services provides the main support services for the FCO at home and overseas.
Chief Executive: Stephen Sage

CONFERENCE AND VISITS GROUP
King Charles Street
LONDON SW1A 2AH
Head of Group: James Clark
Deputy Head of Group: Richard Lyne

CONSULTANCY GROUP
Old Admiralty Building,
LONDON SW1A 2PA
Head of Group: Vivien Life

ESTATE GROUP
Apollo House,
36 Wellesley Road,
CROYDON CR0 9YA
Head of Group: John Elgie
Deputy Head of Group: Nigel Morris

FINANCE GROUP
Hanslope Park,
Hanslope,
MILTON KEYNES MK19 7BH
Acting Head of Group: Roy Coombs

HUMAN RESOURCE GROUP
Hanslope Park,
Hanslope,
MILTON KEYNES MK19 7BH
Head of Group: Elaine Kennedy

INFORMATION MANAGEMENT GROUP
King Charles Street,
LONDON SW1A 2AH
Head of Group: Roger French

LANGUAGE GROUP (DIPLOMATIC SERVICE
LANGUAGE CENTRE)
Old Admiralty Building,
LONDON SW1A 2PA
Head of Group: Dr Vanessa L Davies

SUPPORT GROUP
Hanslope Park,
Hanslope,
MILTON KEYNES MK19 7BH
Head of Group: Michael Carr
Deputy Head of Group: Paul Bell

TECHNICAL GROUP
Hanslope Park,
Hanslope,
MILTON KEYNES MK19 7BH
Head of Group: Nigel Stickells

Human Rights Policy Department
The FCO point of advice on human rights policy
questions in all international organisations,
including obligations and commitments at the UN,
Council of Europe, OSCE and Commonwealth.
Responsible, in co-operation with geographical
departments, for: developing and co-ordinating
HMG's human rights policy and ensuring
consistency of application in the UK's overseas
bilateral relations; liaison with Department for
International Development on human rights aspects
of bilateral and multilateral development policy;
liaison with Whitehall departments, ensuring that
the development of domestic policy takes account
of HMG's international human rights obligations
and objectives; supervision of UK and Overseas
Territory periodic reports under international treaty
obligations; FCO point of contact and liaison for
NGOs and other bodies on general (ie non-country
specific) human rights matters. Manages FCO's
Human Rights Project Fund and produces the
Human Rights Annual Report.

King Charles Street,
LONDON SW1A 2AH
Enquiries: 020 7270 2501
GTN 270 2501
Superintending Director: Nicola Brewer
Head of Department: Carolyn Browne
Deputy Head of Department: Barbara Woodward

**Internal Audit Department (FCO/DFID
Department)**
King Charles Street,
LONDON SW1A 2AH
Enquiries: FCO 020 7008 8028
Enquiries: DFID GTN 3535 0788
Superintending Directors: Simon Gass CMG (FCO),
Richard Manning (DFID)
Head of Internal Audit Dept (FCO/DFID): Roger
Elias
Audit Manager FCO: Trevor Jarvis
Audit Manager DFID: Mike Noronha

I T Strategy Unit
Responsible for ICT investment policy and budgets
and co-ordination with central government
Departments on ICT issues.

Old Admiralty Building
Whitehall
LONDON SW1A 2PA
Enquiries: 020 7008 0520/0521
GTN: 7008 0520/0521
Superintending Deputy Under-Secretary: Peter
Collecott
Head of Unit: Matthew Kirk
Deputy Head of Unit: Nick Clouting

**Joint Entry Clearance Unit (Joint FCO/Home
Office Unit)**
Management of the visa operation at British
missions overseas in accordance with UK
Immigration Rules. Liaison with other interested
departments on matters arising from immigration
legislation and policy.
Replies to letters from MPs and members of the
public on individual visa cases.

89 Albert Embankment,
LONDON SE1 7TP
Enquiries: 020 7238 3838
GTN 7238 3838
Superintending Directors: David Reddaway CMG
MBE (FCO), Peter Wrench (Home Office),
Steve O'Leary (Cabinet Office)
Head of Unit: Robert Brinkley
Deputy Heads of Unit: Tony Mercer, Keith Moss

Latin America and Caribbean Department
Political and economic bilateral relations with all
Latin American and independent Caribbean
countries, and Latin American and Caribbean
regional organisations.

FCO,
King Charles Street,
LONDON SW1A 2AH
Enquiries: 020 7270 2481
GTN 270 2481
Email: LACD.FCO@gtnet.gov.uk

Superintending Director: Richard D Wilkinson cvo
Head of Department: John Dew
Deputy Heads of Department: Georgina Butler,
Syd Maddicott

Legal Advisers
Advice on international, EU and UK law and
practice in connection with HMG's foreign
relations, including treaties and international
litigation, and with the work of the FCO generally.
Legal advice concerning the governance of UK
overseas territories.

King Charles Street,
LONDON SW1A 2AH
Enquiries: 020 7270 3080/3081
GTN 270 3080/3081
Legal Adviser: Michael Wood cmg
Deputy Legal Advisers: Ian Hendry cmg, Elizabeth
Wilmshurst cmg, Tony Aust cmg
Legal Counsellors: Catherine Adams, Diana
Brookes, Huw Llewellyn, John Grainger,
Nigel Parker, Christopher Whomersley

Middle East Department
Relations with Bahrain, Iran, Iraq, Kuwait, Oman,
Qatar, Republic of Yemen, Saudi Arabia, United
Arab Emirates.

Downing Street West,
LONDON SW1A 2AL
Enquiries: 020 7270 2996
GTN 270 2996
Superintending Director: Alan Goulty cmg
Head of Department: William Patey
Deputy Head of Department: Barry Lowen

Near East & North Africa Department
Political and bilateral economic relations with
Algeria, Egypt, the West Bank and Gaza Strip,
Israel, Jordan, Lebanon, Mauritania, Libya,
Morocco, Sudan, Syria and Tunisia. Arab/Israel
relations. EU Mediterranean relations.

Downing Street West and King Charles Street,
LONDON SW1A 2AL
Enquiries: 020 7270 3751
GTN 270 3751
Superintending Director: Alan Goulty cmg
Head of Department: Christopher Prentice
Deputy Head of Department: Pat Phillips

News Department
Advises the Secretary of State and departments of
the FCO on questions of presentation relating to
the British Government's foreign policy. It is the
authorised contact between the FCO and the
British media.

Downing Street West,
LONDON SW1A 2AH
Enquiries: 020 7270 3100
GTN 270 3100
Superintending Director: David Reddaway cmg mbe
Head of Department: John Williams
Deputy Head of Department: Raymond Kyles

Non-Proliferation Department
Nuclear non-proliferation issues, including the
Non-Proliferation Treaty, CTBT, IAEA and
Nuclear Suppliers Group. Missile proliferation
issues and MTCR. Chemical and Biological
Weapons Conventions, Australia Group and
CW/BW proliferation issues. UNMOVIC. Policy
on conventional arms sales, small arms and exports
of Dual-Use Goods. UN Arms Register. Wassenaar
Arrangement. Arms Control and Disarmament
Research Unit.

Downing Street West,
LONDON SW1A 2AH
Enquiries: 020 7270 2261/2751
GTN 270 2261/2751
Superintending Director: William Ehrman cmg
Head of Department: Tim Dowse
Deputy Heads of Department: Patrick Lamb,
Andrew Turner

North America Department
Relations with Canada and the United States
(including the US Virgin Islands).

FCO,
Whitehall,
LONDON SW1A 2AH
Enquiries: 020 7270 2663/3332
GTN 270 2663/3332
Superintending Director: Richard D Wilkinson cvo
Head of Department: Nicholas Armour
Deputy Head of Department: Jonathan Darby

North East Asia and Pacific Department
Relations with Japan, Democratic People's
Republic of Korea, Republic of Korea, Mongolia,
Australia, New Zealand, Samoa, Fiji, Kiribati,
Republic of the Marshall Islands, Federated States
of Micronesia, Nauru, Palau, Papua New Guinea,
Solomon Islands, Tonga, Tuvalu, Vanuatu and
French and US territories in the South Pacific.

King Charles Street,
LONDON SW1A 2AH
Enquiries: 020 7270 2960/3296/3264/2952
GTN 270 2960/3296/3264/2952
Superintending Director: Rosalind Marsden
Head of Department: Nicholas Archer

**Organisation for Security & Co-operation in
Europe (OSCE) & the Council of Europe
Department**
UK Policy on the Organisation for Security & Co-
operation in Europe and on the Council of Europe.

Whitehall,
LONDON SW1A 2AH
Enquiries: 020 7270 2426
GTN 270 2426
Superintending Director: John Macgregor cvo
Head of Department: Peter January
Deputy Head of Department: Richard Tauwhare

Overseas Territories Department
HMG's responsibilities for the Overseas Territories
of Anguilla, Bermuda, the British Antarctic
Territory, the British Indian Ocean Territory, the

British Virgin Islands, the Cayman Islands, the Falkland Islands, Montserrat, Pitcairn, South Georgia and the South Sandwich Islands, St Helena and its dependencies, Ascension and Tristan da Cunha and the Turks and Caicos Islands. Co-ordination of policy on the Overseas Territories and organisation the Overseas Consultative Council; liaison on subjects of common interest to the Overseas Territories; interpretation of Colonial Regulations; South Atlantic matters and HMG's responsibilities under the Antarctic Treaty.

King Charles Street,
LONDON SW1A 2AH
Enquiries: 020 7270 2643
GTN 270 2643
Superintending Director: Richard D Wilkinson cvo
Head of Department: Alan Huckle
Deputy Head of Department: Roy Osborne

Parliamentary Relations & Devolution Department

Advice and guidance to FCO Ministers and officials on parliamentary procedures. Monitoring of all parliamentary business of interest to the FCO. Contact with Select Committees of both Houses of Parliament. Liaison with the British Group of the Inter-Parliamentary Union. Liaison with the Parliamentary Commissioner for Administration. Responsibility for FCO relations with the devolved administrations and legislatures in Scotland, Wales and Northern Ireland.

King Charles Street,
LONDON SW1A 2AH
Enquiries: 020 7270 2236/5/4
GTN 270 2236
Superintending Director: David Reddaway cmg, mbe
Head of Department: Mark Hutton
Deputy Head of Department: Mark Capes
Parliamentary Clerk: Charles Hill

Personnel Command

Recruitment, development, motivation, deployment and support of staff.

Old Admiralty Building,
LONDON SW1A 2PA
Superintending Director: Denise Holt

MEDICAL AND WELFARE
Health, safety and welfare of staff at home and overseas.

Joint FCO/DFID Department,
Old Admiralty Building,
LONDON SW1A 2PA
Superintending Directors: Denise Holt (FCO), Richard Manning (DFID)
Assistant Director: Tony Millson
Clinical Services Manager and Deputy: Lin Cargill
Principal Welfare Officer and Deputy: Ruth Wills

PERFORMANCE AND DEVELOPMENT
All aspects of staff performance management including core competences, staff appraisal and assessment, promotion competitions and Assessment and Development Centres.
Assistant Director: Gerry Reffo

PERSONNEL MANAGEMENT
Career planning, individual personnel movements, appointments, probation, promotions, secondments, loans, recruitment and transfers to and from other services.
Assistant Director: Peter Jones
Assistant Director (Senior Management Structure): Nigel Haywood
Heads of Personnel Management Units: Andy Heyn, Judi Garstang, Martyn Warr, Marilia Astle

PERSONNEL POLICY
Policy aspects of personnel, management questions including implementation of employment legislation and relations with the trade union side, organisation and structure of the FCO's Personnel, conduct and discipline, diversity and equal opportunities. Human resource planning, personnel statistics, sick absence and diplomatic status.
Assistant Director: Scott Wightman

PERSONNEL SERVICES
Pay, allowances, conditions of service, superannuation.
Assistant Director: Richard White mbe
Head of Pay, Superannuation and Local Staff Section: Brian Bennett
Head of Allowances Section: John Brook

PROSPER (ADVICE ON RETIREMENT/OUTPLACEMENT)
Assistant Directors: Colin Edgerton, Tom Malcomson

RECRUITMENT
Head: Alison Cookson-Hall

INTERCHANGE
Head: Debbie Clare

TRAINING
Assistant Director: Christine Dharwarkar
Deputy Head of Training Wing: Karen Smith

Policy Planning Staff

Innovative policy thinking. Contacts with non-governmental opinion on policy issues

Downing Street West,
LONDON SW1A 2AL
Enquiries: 020 7270 2913
GTN 270 2913
Superintending Under-Secretary: Sir Michael Jay kcmg
Head of Policy Planning Staff: Dianna Melrose
Deputy Head: Nick Kay

Prism Programme

Prism is the FCO's business change management programme. Prism will provide the Office with a global on-line management information system (covering personnel, pay, finance and procurement), which will assist decision making.

Old Admiralty Building,
Whitehall
LONDON SW1A 2PA
Superintending Director: Simon Gass cmg
Programme Manager (Business): Fiona Moore
Deputy Programme Manager: Giles Whitaker

Protocol Division

Diplomatic Missions:
Policy on handling of appointments, privileges, immunities and security of the Diplomatic Corps and International Organisations in Britain. Diplomatic and International Organisations lists. Organisation of ceremonial events, and policy and advice on protocol and precedence. VIP facilities at London's airports.
Honours Secretariat:
FCO aspects of honours policy. Diplomatic Service and Overseas Honours Lists, British honorary awards, Foreign and Commonwealth honours for British citizens. Investitures, presentation of insignia.
Royal Households Secretariat:
Co-ordination between the FCO and Royal Households, especially on overseas visits by the Royal Family. Royal Visits Committee.

Old Admiralty Building,
Whitehall
LONDON SW1A 2PA
Superintending Deputy Under Secretary: Peter Collecott
Head of Division and Vice Marshal of the Diplomatic Corps: Kathryn F Colvin
Deputy Head of Division and Assistant Marshal of the Diplomatic Corps: Bill Henderson LVO

Public Diplomacy Department (Formerly Information Department)

Strategic guidance on public diplomacy to Foreign and Commonwealth Office Commands and Posts overseas. Management of public diplomacy resources services including: the London Correspondents' Service; sponsored visits by journalists; press, TV and radio material; publications about Britain; the FCO website; the FCO Information Centre; FCO Open Days and Policy on Expositions. Administration of the Grants in Aid to the BBC World Service. Responsibility for the Wilton Park Executive Agency.

King Charles Street,
LONDON SW1A 2AH
Enquiries: 020 7270 5926
GTN 270 5926
Superintending Director: David Reddaway CMG MBE
Head of Department: John Buck
Deputy Heads of Department: Carole Sweeney, Caroline Matthews

Purchasing Directorate

Advice and guidance to FCO departments and posts overseas on best practice in the purchase of goods and services; sponsorship and selling into wider markets; operational environmental issues.

Old Admiralty Building,
Whitehall
LONDON SW1A 2PA
Enquiries: 020 7008 0924
GTN 7008 0924
Superintending Director: Simon Gass CMG
Head of Purchasing Directorate: Michael Gower
Deputy Head of Purchasing Directorate: Charles Sime

Quality & Efficiency Unit

Better Quality Services review programme, Business Audit, Efficiency Techniques and Targets, Benchmarking, Internal Market, Civil Service Reform, Service First, Liaison with and training for Management Officers.

Old Admiralty Building
LONDON SW1A 2PA
Enquiries: 020 7008 1057
GTN: 7008 1057
Superintending Director: Simon Gass CMG
Head of Unit: Karen Jackson
Head of Business Audit: Chris Green
Head of Value for Money Section: Anne Jarrett
Head of Management Officer Section: Diana Lees

Records and Historical Department

Open government, data protection, freedom of information; records custody, access and release; registry policy and training; treaty information and publication; historical advice; publication of Documents on British Policy Overseas.

Old Admiralty Building
LONDON SW1A 2PA
Hanslope Park
MILTON KEYNES MK19 7BH
Enquiries: 020 7008 1129
GTN 7008 1129
Superintending Director: Peter Collecott
Head: Heather Yasamee
Deputy Head and Chief Historian: Gill Bennett

Research Analysts

Contributes to the formulation of overseas policy through the provision of assessments and advice based on specialist experience.

King Charles Street,
Whitehall,
LONDON SW1A 2AH
Enquiries: 020 7270 5942
GTN 270 5942
Deputy Under Secretary: Peter Westmacott CMG LVO
Head of Research Analysts: Adam Noble
Heads of Research Groups: Lillian Wong (African Research Group), Patrick Holdich (Americas Research Group)
Laurence Broyd (Central European & Eastern Adriatic Research Group)
Janet Gunn (Eastern Research Group)
Babu Rahman (Global Issues Research Group)
Greg Shapland (Middle East & North Africa Research Group)
Peter Clark (Northern Asia/Pacific Research Group)
Andrew Hall (South & South East Asia Research Group)
Ted Hallett (Western & Southern European Research Group)

Resource Accounting Department

Preparation of Appropriation and Resource Accounts. Payment of salaries, travel accounts and invoices. Debtor control, maintenance and development of Fixed Asset Register and

Management Accounts. Funding of FCO posts. FMAS, Dynamics and other financial training.

Old Admiralty Building,
LONDON SW1A 2PA
Enquiries: 020 7008 1063
GTN 7008 1063

Hanslope Park,
MILTON KEYNES MK19 7BH
Enquiries: 01908 515531
GTN 3905 5531
Superintending Director: Simon Gass CMG
Head of Department and Chief Accountant: Mike Brown

Resource Budgeting Department
Resource planning, budgeting and allocation, expenditure monitoring and performance measurement, fees and charging.

Old Admiralty Building,
LONDON SW1A 2PA
Enquiries: 020 7008 1085
GTN: 7008 1085
Superintending Director: Simon Gass CMG
Head of Department: Martin Williamson
Deputy Heads of Department: Ian Robinson, Asif Ahmad

Science and Technology Unit
Management of S&T work overseas by embassies.

King Charles Street
LONDON SW1A 2AH
Enquiries: 020 7008 4113
GTN: 7008 4113
Superintending Director: Nicola Brewer
Head of Unit: Robert Barnett

Security Policy Department
NATO, and EU security and defence policy issues; the foreign policy implications of British defence policy as regards Transatlantic and European defence, including nuclear weapons issues; nuclear and conventional arms control and disarmament; missile defence issues; UN disarmament fora; armaments policy and defence equipment procurement including collaborative projects; conflict prevention; UK defence attaches.

Downing Street East,
LONDON SW1A 2AH
Enquiries: 020 7270 2459
GTN 270 2459
Superintending Director: William Ehrman CMG
Head of Department: Adam Thomson
Deputy Heads of Department: James Sharp, Robert Deane

Security Strategy Unit
Formulation of FCO security policy and co-ordination of physical, technical and personnel counter measures, and security education training.

Old Admiralty Building,
LONDON SW1A 2PA
Enquiries: 020 7008 1153
GTN 7008 1153

Superintending Director: Peter Collecott
Head of Unit: Judith Macgregor LVO
Deputy Head of Unit: Michael Balmer

South Asian Department
Relations with India, Pakistan, Bangladesh, Sri Lanka, Afghanistan, Nepal, Bhutan, the Maldives.

Whitehall,
LONDON SW1A 2AL
Enquiries: 020 7270 2388
GTN 270 2388
Superintending Director: Rosalind Marsden
Head of Department: Stephen Evans OBE
Deputy Head of Department: Iain Lindsay

South East Asian Department
Political and economic relations with Brunei, Burma, Cambodia, East Timor, Indonesia, Laos, Malaysia, Philippines, Singapore, Thailand and Vietnam; ASEAN and ASEM.

FCO,
Whitehall,
LONDON SW1A 2AH
Enquiries: 020 7270 2442
GTN 270 2442
Superintending Director: Rosalind Marsden
Head of Department: Robert Gordon CMG OBE
Deputy Head of Department: Richard Powell

Southern European Department
Political and bilateral relations with Cyprus, Malta and Turkey. UK policy towards the UN-sponsored discussions on the future of Cyprus. External relations and some aspects of internal administration of Gibraltar.

King Charles Street,
LONDON SW1A 2AH
Enquiries: 020 7270 2975
GTN 270 2975
Superintending Director: John Macgregor CVO
Head of Department: Geoff Gillham
Deputy Head of Department (Eastern Mediterranean): Deborah Bronnert
Deputy Head of Department (Gibraltar): Simon Martin

United Nations Department
Policy towards the United Nations, particularly the Security Council, General Assembly and ECOSOC; United Nations peace-keeping operations; sanctions; conflict prevention; International humanitarian law (including Geneva Conventions); Red Cross/Crescent issues; International Criminal Tribunals for former Yugoslavia and Rwanda; International Criminal Court; war crimes; humanitarian mine action; migration/refugee policy; general aspects of policy towards the UN specialised agencies.

King Charles Street,
LONDON SW1A 2AH
Enquiries: 020 7270 3583/3581
GTN 270 3583/3581
Superintending Director: Nicola Brewer
Head of Department: Stephen Pattison

War Crimes Co-ordinator: John Tucknott
Deputy Head of Department: Jan Thompson

Whitehall Liaison Department
General co-ordination duties and responsibility for
liaison with the Cabinet Office and other
Government Departments.

Downing Street West,
LONDON SW1A 2AH
Enquiries: 020 7270 2350
GTN 270 2350

Vauxhall Cross,
85 Albert Embankment,
LONDON SE1 7TP
Superintending Deputy Under Secretary: Stephen J
L Wright CMG
Head of Department: Matthew Kidd
Deputy Head of Department: Paul Fox

Wilton Park
Wilton Park conferences usually last up to three
and a half days, examine current international
issues, especially EU issues, security policy,
European and Atlantic relations; Russia, the CIS
and Central Europe; areas of conflict in the
developing world and global economic policies.
Conference participants are experts on the
conference topic drawn from different professions
and from all over the world. Wiston House is also
available for conferences organised by other
institutions.

Wiston Park,
Wiston House,
STEYNING,
West Sussex BN44 3DZ
Telephone: 01903 817772
Chief Executive: Colin Jennings

Lists of British Representatives in Commonwealth and Foreign Countries and in the Republic of Ireland

British Missions Overseas (addresses and contact Numbers of Missions and Consulates etc.)

PART II. Embassies, High Commissions, Deputy High Commissions and Consular Posts.

AFGHANISTAN

Kabul
British Embassy (Post currently vacant)

ALBANIA

Tirana
British Embassy
Rruga Skenderbeg 12
Tirana
Telephone: (00) (355) (42) 34973/4/5
Facsimile: (00) (355) (42) 47697
Office Hours (GMT): Mon - Thur: 06 30 - 15 00
Fri: 06 30 - 12 30
Ambassador: Dr David Landsman, OBE
Deputy Head of Mission and Consul: Mr G Scott
First Secretary (Political): Mr L Whitehead
Defence Attaché (Resides at Tirana): Lieutenant
Colonel P G Cox
Assistant Defence Attaché: Major B Davie
*Third Secretary Management Officer and Vice
Consul:* Mr D Brierley
Third Secretary (Political): Mr T Brown
Third Secretary (Immigration): Mr H Ryan
Attaché: Mrs L Towner-Evans

ALGERIA

Algiers
British Embassy
6 Avenue Souidani Boudjemaa,
BP08 Alger-Gare 16000, Algiers
Telephone: (00) (213) (21) 23 00 68
Facsimile: (00) (213) (21) 23 00 67 and 23 07 51
                 23 01 83 Chancery
Airtech: (00) (213) (21) 23 00 69
Office Hours (GMT): Sun, Wed, Thur: 07 15 -
13 30
Mon, Tue: 07 15 - 11 30 and 12 00 - 16 00,
Ambassador: Mr R J S Edis, CMG
Deputy Head of Mission: Mr J L Hartley
Defence Attaché (Resides in London): Commander
D M Evans, RN
Second Secretary (Management): (vacant)
General Registry: Miss M Charge

ANDORRA

British Embassy
Ambassador (resides at Madrid): Mr Peter J Torry
Consul-General (resides at Barcelona): Mr
Richard Thomson

e-mail: bcon@cyberbcn.com
N.B Consular and Commercial Enquiries should be
addressed to Barcelona
British Honorary Consulate
Casa Jacint Pons, 3/2
La Massana
Principality of Andorra
Telephone: (00) (376) 839 840
Facsimile: (00) (376) 839 840
e-mail: britconand@mypic.ad
Honorary Consul: Mr Hugh Garner

ANGOLA

Luanda
British Embassy
Rua Diogo Cao, 4
Caixa Postal 1244, Luanda
Telephone: (00) (244) (2) 334582, 334583,
392991, 387681
Facsimile: (00) (244) (2) 333331 (U/C)
Satellite fax: 00 871 144 5140 (Airtech)
e-mail: postmaster.luanda@fco.gov.uk
Office hours (GMT): Mon & Fri 07 00 - 13 00
Tue-Thur 07 00 - 11 30 and 13 00 - 16 00
Ambassador: Miss C M T Elmes, CMG
(Mr J Thompson, MBE w.e.f. February 2002)
Consul and Deputy Head of Mission:
Mr L Banks, OBE
Counsellor (Political): Mr S C E Holt, OBE
Defence Attaché: Lieutenant Colonel
A A Gilbert, MBE BA
Defence Attaché Assistant: Staff Sergeant T Stead
Second Secretary (Political): Mr J Astill-Brown
Second Secretary (Commercial): Mr S Graham
Third Secretary (Management) and Vice-Consul:
Ms L Sayle
Registrar: Ms K D H Sowerby

ANTIGUA & BARBUDA

St. John's
British High Commission
P.O. Box 483, Price Waterhouse Centre, 11,
Old Parham Road, St. John's Antigua
Telephone: (00) (1) (268) 462 0008/9, 463 0010
Facsimile: (00) (1) (268) 562 2124
Airtech: (00) (1) (268) 462 2806
Office Hours (GMT): Mon-Thurs: 12 00 - 16 30
and 17 30 - 20 00
Fri: 12 00 - 16 30 (only)
**High Commissioner:* Mr J White

Resident Acting High Commissioner: Mrs S
Murphy
*Deputy High Commissioner: Mr M J E Mayhew
*Defence Adviser: Captain Steve C Ramm, RN
*Counsellor (Regional Affairs): Mr N J L Martin
*First Secretary (Chancery): Mr Graham Honey
*Second Secretary (Chancery): Mr P Marshall
*Second Secretary (Management/Consular): Mr G
I Brammer
*Second Secretary (Chancery/Information): Mr N
Pyle, MBE
*Third Secretary (Consular/Immigration): Mr S
Minshull
*Resides at Bridgetown

ARGENTINA

Buenos Aires
British Embassy
Dr. Luis Agote 2412/52, 1425 Capital Federal,
Buenos Aires
Telephone: (00) (54) (11) 4576 2222 Switchboard
4803 7799 Direct Extension Access
Facsimile: (00) (54) (11) 4803 1731 General
4806 5713 Commercial
4807 3202 Press & Public
Diplomacy
4801 4766 Political/
Economic
Section
4807 3157 Defence
Section
Office Hours (GMT): Mon-Thurs: 12 45 - 17 00
and 18 00 - 21 30 (Mar-Dec)
Fri:12 45 - 18 00
Mon-Fri: 12 45 - 18 30 (Jan- Feb)
Ambassador (Ext 2202): Sir Robin Christopher
KBE, CMG
Minister and Deputy Head of Mission (Ext 2204):
Mr Steve Williams
Counsellor: (Ext. 2209): Mr Nick J G Beer
Defence, Naval and Military Attaché (Ext 2218):
Colonel Peter A Reynolds, RM
Air Attaché (Ext 2218): Group Captain Tim P
Brewer, OBE, RAF
*First Secretary (Head of Political/Economic
Section) (Ext 2205):* Mr Hugh S M Elliott
First Secretary (Commercial) (Ext 2251): Ms
Helen H Deas
First Secretary (Political) (Ext 2312): Mrs Emily
Fisher
*Cultural Attaché (British Council Director)
(Tel: 4311 9814 Ext 140):* Mr Paul Dick
First Secretary (Ext 2251): Mr Mike Cavanagh
*Consul and First Secretary (Management) (Ext
2255):* Miss Christine E McEwen
*First Secretary (Technical Works Officer) (Ext
2291):* Mr David Holmes
Second Secretary (Political) (Ext 2207): Ms Freya
Jackson
Second Secretary (Political) (Ext 2275): Mr Thom
Reilly
Second Secretary (Commercial) (Ext 2268): Ms
Paula Walsh
Second Secretary (Technical) (Ext 2215): Mr Stuart
Moss

*Vice-Consul and Second Secretary (Management)
(Ext 2294):* Miss Caroline M C Whitehorn
*Assistant Cultural Attaché (Deputy Director British
Council) (Tel: 4311 9814 Ext 142):* Mr David
Alderdice
Third Secretary (Political) (Ext 2210): Mr
Matthew Withers
Third Secretary (Commercial) (Ext 2292): Mrs
Wendy De Luca

Mendoza
Honorary Consulate
Emilio Civit 778,
Mendoza
Telephone: (00) (54) (261) 4238529/4238514
Facsimile: (00) (54) (261) 4238565
Office Hours: Mon-Fri 08 30 – 13 00 and 17 00 –
20 30
Honorary Consul: Mr Carlos Alberto Pulenta

Córdoba
Honorary Consulate
Chacabuco 716,
Córdoba
Telephone: (00) (54) (351) 4208293
Facsimile: (00) (54) (351) 4208201/4208259
Office Hours: Mon-Fri 09 00 – 13 00 and 16.30 –
20 30
Honorary Consul: Mr Fulvio Pagani

Santa Fe
Honorary Consulate
Av Pte J D Perón 8101,
Rosario
Telephone/Fax: (00) (54) (341) 4590206
Office Hours: Mon-Fri 09 00 – 13 00 and 14 30 –
17 30
Honorary Consul: Mr Carlos Gollan

ARMENIA

Yerevan
British Embassy
28 Charents Street, Yerevan
Telephone: (00) 3741 151841, 3741 151842
Facsimile: (00) 3741 151807 (Unclassified)
(00) 3741 151064 (Airtech)
(00) 3749 402184 (Duty Officer Mobile)
e-mail: hma@arminco.com (HMA)
dhm@arminco.com (DHM)
movc@arminco.com (MO/VC)
infdpt@arminco.com (Information Department)
dfid@arminco.com (DFID)
britemb@arminco.com
(Commercial/General/Other Enquiries)
Office Hours (GMT) 05 00 - 09 00 and 10 00 -
13 30
Ambassador: Mr T A Jones
Deputy Head of Mission: Mr D M Lingwood
Third Secretary (Management and Vice Consul):
Ms S L Bee, MBE
Defence Attaché (resides at Tbilisi): Wing
Commander A W Kerr, RAF
TMO's (reside at Ankara): Mr C Fox/Mr D
Kingdom
Attaché: Mr J D Greenwood

AUSTRALIA

Canberra

British High Commission
Commonwealth Avenue, Yarralumla,
Canberra, ACT 2600
Telephone: (00) (61) (2) 6270 6666
Facsimile: (00) (61) (2) 6273 3236 General
                  6273 4360 Economic
                  6270 6653 Chancery
e-mail: bhc.canberra@ukemb.gov.au
Consular Section:
Level 10, S A P House,
Canberra Centre, Canberra, ACT 2601
Telephone: (00) (61) (2) 1902 941 555
Passports/Entry Clearances: 0394 145 517
Facsimile: (00) (61) (2) 1902 941 600
e-mail: bhc.consular@ukemb.gov.au
Office Hours (GMT): Apr-Oct 22 45 - 02 30 and
03 30 - 07 00,
Nov-Mar 21 45 - 01 30 and 02 30 - 06 00
High Commissioner: Sir Alastair Goodlad, KCMG
Deputy High Commissioner: Mr Robert Court
Counsellor (Multilateral): Mr Andrew Dean
Defence and Naval Adviser and Head BDLS:
Commodore J Graham Wiltshire, RN
Military and Air Adviser: Group Captain Nick C
Rusling, RAF
First Secretary (Political): Mrs Jean Harrod
First Secretary (External Affairs): Mr Jeff Harrod
First Secretary (Management): Mr Alan Gee
*First Secretary (Defence/Research) Head of the
British Defence Research and Supply Staff:* Dr
Graham Stott
First Secretary (Defence Equipment Cooperation):
Mr Roger Matthews
First Secretary (Information/Economic): Mr Rod
Bunten
First Secretary: Mr Struan Macdonald
First Secretary: Dr Robert Vickery
First Secretary (Technical Management): Mr Rod
Bronson
First Secretary (Technical Security): Mr Mark
Lewington
Second Secretary (TWO): Mr Brien Hooker
Second Secretary (Consular): Mr Stan Blake
Third Secretary (Political): Mr Simon Horner
Third Secretary (External Affairs): Mr Danny
Woodier
Third Secretary (Passports): Mr Graham Hart

Adelaide

British Consulate
Level 22, 25 Grenfell Street,
Adelaide SA 5000
Telephone: (00) (61) (8) 8212 7280
Facsimile: (00) (61) (8) 8212 7282
Airtech: (00) (61) (8) 8212 7283
e-mail: bcadel@camtech.net.au
Consul: Mr V S Warrington

Brisbane

British Consulate-General
Level 26, Waterfront Place,
1 Eagle Street, Brisbane, Queensland, 4000

Telephone: (00) (61) (7) 3223 3200 General/
                  Consular
            3223 3206/7 Commercial
                  Section
Facsimile: (00) (61) (7) 3236 2576
e-mail: BRITISHCONSULATE@bigpond.com
(All information, visa and routine passport work is
centralised in Canberra).
Office Hours (GMT): 23 00 - 07 00
Consul-General: Mr S J Hiscock
Deputy Consul General: Ms C A Saunders
Vice Consul/Management Officer: Mrs M M
Hunt, MBE

Melbourne

British Consulate-General 17th Floor,
90 Collins Street, Melbourne, Victoria 3000
Telephone: (00) (61) (03) (9650) 3699 Commercial
                  4155 Consular
Facsimile: (00) (61) (03) (9650) 2990
Office Hours (GMT): Apr-Oct 23 00 - 07 30
Nov-Mar 22 00 - 06 30
Consul-General: Mr P M Innes
Deputy Consul-General: Mr R F Terry
Vice-Consul: Mr P J Mudie

Perth

British Consulate-General
Level 26, Allendale Square,
77 St. George's Terrace,
Perth, Western Australia 6000
Telephone: (00) (61) (8) 9221 4422 Commercial
                  5400 Consular and
                  General
Facsimile: (00) (61) (8) 9221 2344 Consular
                  1944 Management
                  1586 Commercial
                  9421 1959 Airtech
e-mail:
BCGCOMMERCIAL_PERTH@bigpond.com
Issue of all information, visas/Ecs, and standard
passports centralised at Canberra
Office Hours (GMT): 01 00-05 00, 06 00-09 00
(Public counter 01 00-07 00)
Consul-General: Mr H Dunnachie
Deputy Consul-General: Mr P P Hagger
Vice-Consul: Mr R J Andrews

Sydney

British Consulate-General and
Directorate of Trade and Investment Promotion
Level 16, The Gateway,
1 Macquarie Place, Sydney NSW, 2000
Telephone: (00) (61) (2) 9247 7521 (8 lines)
Facsimile: (00) (61) (2) 9233 1826 Commercial
                  9251 6201 Consular,
                  Management,
e-mail: bcg-syd2@enternet.com.au (Commercial)
bcg-syd@enternet.com.au (Press and Public
Affairs)
Offices Hours (GMT): Apr-Oct 23 00 - 02 30 and
03 30 - 07 00
Nov-Mar 22 00 - 01 30 and 02 30 - 06 00
Consul-General: Mr P Beckingham
Director of Trade & Investment Promotion: Mr F J
Cochrane-Dyet

Deputy Consul General: Mr John Atkinson
Vice-Consul (Commercial): Mrs A Ross McDowell
Management Officer: Mrs Heather Halliwell
Consular/Admin Officer: Mr Les Tod
Press and Public Affairs Manager: Mr R Swift

Tasmania
British Honorary Consulate
1a Brisbane St
Hobart TAS 7000
Telephone: (00) (61) (3) 6230 3400
Facsimile: (00) (61) (3) 6231 1139
e-mail: djmotors@onaustralia.com.au
Office Hours (GMT): Apr - Oct: 23 00 - 07 30
Nov - Mar: 22 00 - 06 30
Honorary Consul: Mr Michael Johns

AUSTRIA

Vienna
British Embassy
Jaurèsgasse 12, 1030 Vienna
Telephone: (00) (43) (1) 716 130
Facsimile: (00) (43) (1) 71613 2999 Chancery
71613 6900 Commercial
71613 2900 Management
Airtech: (00) (43) (1) 71613 2310
e-mail: britem@netway.at

Consular Section
Jaurèsgasse 10, 1030 Vienna
Telephone: (00) (43) (1) 71613 5151 or 00 43 1
71613 followed by individual extension number
Facsimile: (00) (43) (1) 71613 5900
(All mail should be addressed to the British
Embassy)

Office Hours (GMT): Winter: Mon - Fri   08 00 -
12 00 and 13 00 - 16 00
Summer: Mon - Fri   07 00 - 11 00 and 12 00 -
15 00
Ambassador: (2202) Mr Antony Ford, CMG
*Counsellor, Consul-General, Dep. Head of
Mission:* (2204) Dr Piers Baker
Counsellor (Chancery): (2211) Mr George B J P
Busby, OBE
Counsellor (Labour) (resides at Bonn): Miss
ElaineTrewartha
Defence Attaché: (2216) Lieutenant Colonel Julian
A Bourne
First Secretary (Management) and Consul: (2261)
Mr Hamilton D Marcelin
First Secretary (2213): Mr James Hall
Second Secretary (2219): Mr Michael B Deane
Second Secretary (Technical Works): (2264) Mr
Carl B Gray
Second Secretary (EU Affairs): (2343) Miss
Rebecca Hall
Second Secretary (Chancery): (2220) Mr Steve A
Hunt
Second Secretary (Chancery): (2224) Mr Mark
Wardle
Second Secretary: (2256) Mr Chris Humphrey
Second Secretary: (2210) Mr Ian Purvis
Attaché and Vice-Consul: (5330) Mr Stuart Adam
Third Secretary (Commercial/Information): (6248)
Mrs Anne L Hudman

Third Secretary (Management): (2260) Mr Andy
W Partridge
Vice-Consul: (5332) Miss Paula Hoppe
**Vienna United Kingdom Mission to The United
Nations in Vienna, see part II**
**Vienna United Kingdom Delegation to the
Organisation for Security and Cooperation in
Europe (OSCE), see part II**

Bregenz
British Consulate
Bundesstrasse 110
A-6923 Lauterach/Bregenz
Telephone: (00) (43) (5574) 78586
Facsimile: (00) (43) (5574) 70928
Office Hours (GMT): Winter   08 00 - 11 00
Summer 07 00 - 10 00
Honorary Consul: Dipl-Ing P Senger-Weiss

Graz
British Consulate
Schmiedgasse 12, A-8010 Graz
Telephone: (00) (43) (316) 8216 1621
Facsimile: (00) (43) (316) 8216 1645
Office Hours (GMT): Mon –Thurs 08 00 - 11 00
and 13 30 15 00 and Fri 08 00 - 11 00
Honorary Consul: Mr K D Bruhl, OBE
Honorary Vice-Consul: Ms Eva Bruhl
Secretary: Ms Alexandra Macher

Innsbruck
British Consulate
Kaiserjagerstrasse 1/Top B9
A-6020 Innsbruck
Telephone: (00) (43) (512) 588320
Facsimile: (00) (43) (512) 5799738
Office Hours (GMT): Winter 08 00 - 11 00,
Summer 07 00 - 10 00
Honorary Consul: Ing Hellmut Buchroithner
Honorary Vice-Consul: Dr Ivo Rungg
Secretary: Ms Claudia Loidl

Salzburg
British Consulate
Alter Markt 4, A-5020 Salzburg
Telephone: (00) (43) (662) 848133
Facsimile: (00) (43) (662) 845563
Office Hours (GMT): Winter 08 00 - 11 00,
Summer 07 00 - 10 00
Honorary Consul: Mr M M Kaindl
Honorary Pro-Consul: Mrs Helga Danmayr

AZERBAIJAN

Baku
British Embassy
2 Izmir Street, Baku 370065
Telephone: (00) (99 412) 975188/89/90,924813
Facsimile: (00) (99 412) 922739, 972474
(Commercial Section)
Airtech: (00) (99 412) 975893
e-mail: office@britemb.baku.az
office@ukemb.baku.az (Commercial Section)
Website: www.britishembassy.az
Office Hours (GMT): Summer: Mon - Fri: 04 00 -
1200

Winter: Mon - Fri: 05 00 - 13 00
Ambassador: Mr Andrew Tucker
Deputy Head of Mission: Ms Sylvia Parnell
Defence Attaché (resides at Tbilisi): Wing
Commander Andrew W Kerr, RAF
Cultural Attaché (British Council): Ms Margaret S
Jack
First Secretary (Political): Mr Julian Coulter
Second Secretary (Commercial): Miss Doris Davis
Second Secretary (Political): Miss Fem M Horine
Vice-Consul: Miss Christine L Richardson
Third Secretary (Management): Miss Carol Wright
Third Secretary (Political): Mr Simon B Price
Attaché: Miss Amanda Jones

BAHAMAS, THE

Nassau
British High Commission
Ansbacher House (3rd Floor),
East Street, P.O. Box N7516, Nassau
Telephone: (00) (1) (242) 325 7471
Facsimile: (00) (1) (242) 323 3871
Airtech: (00) (1) (242) 325 7474
Office Hours (GMT): 13 30 - 18 00, 19 00 - 21 30
High Commissioner: Mr Peter Heigl
Deputy High Commissioner: Mr Dave Wells
Defence Adviser (resides at Kingston): Colonel
Rob A Hyde-Bales
First Secretary (resides at Kingston): Mr Malcolm
Bragg
Commercial/Information Officer: Mrs Helen Wells
Second Secretary (resides at Kingston): Mr Keith
Wiggins

BAHRAIN

Bahrain
British Embassy
21 Government Avenue, Manama 306,
P.O. Box 114, Bahrain
Telephone: (973) 534404
Telegrams: PRODROME, BAHRAIN
Facsimile: (00) (973) 531273 Chancery,
                               Information
                    536109 Commercial
                    533307 Consular,
                               Management
                    531472 Visa section
                    727473 TWO Juffair
e-mail: britemb@batelco.com.bh
Website: www.ukembassy.gov.bh
Office Hours (GMT): Sat - Wed 04 30 - 11 30
Ambassador and Consul-General: Mr P Ford
*First Secretary (Commercial), Consul and Deputy
Head of Mission:* Dr R T O Wilson
Defence Attaché: Commander M Dodds, RN
First Secretary (Political): Mr P V Kennedy
Second Secretary (Commercial): Ms I Mulvaney
Airline Liaison Officer: Mr R Britton
Third Secretary (Chancery/Information): Ms T
Clayton
Third Secretary (Consular/Management): Mr G
Fisher
Third Secretary (ECO): Mr J Carney

BANGLADESH

Dhaka
British High Commission
United Nations Road, Baridhara Dhaka
Postal address: P.O. Box 6079, Dhaka-1212
Telephone: (00) (880) (2) 8822705 (5 lines)
followed by individual extension number
8821273 DHC Direct line
Facsimile: (00) (880) (2) 8826181 High
                               Commissioner's
                               Office
                    8823437 Management/
                               Chancery
                    8823666 Immigration
                    8822819 Consular
e-mail: ukcomsec@bol-online.com (Commercial
Section)
Dhaka.Commercial@fco.gov.uk (Commercial
Section)
Dhaka.Consular@fco.gov.uk (Consular)
Dhaka.Immigration@fco.gov.uk (Immigration)
Dhaka.Press@fco.gov.uk (Press and Public Affairs)
Website: www.ukinbangladesh.org
Office Hours (GMT): Sun to Thurs 02 15 – 09 15
High Commissioner (2201): Dr D Carter, CVO
*Deputy High Commissioner & Commercial
Counsellor (2203):* Mr S E Turner
Defence Adviser (resides in New Delhi): Brigadier
S M A Lee, OBE
First Secretary (Medical Officer): Dr A Reekie, OBE
*First Secretary (Senior Management Officer)
(2230):* Mr J B Greenlee
First Secretary (Immigration/Consular) (2300): Mr
G M Johnson
*First Secretary (Drug Liaison) (resides in New
Delhi):* Mr P C Free
*Second Secretary (Commercial/Press & Public
Affairs) (2209):* Mr K Sharpless
Second Secretary (Commercial) (2313): Mr A
McAllister
Second Secretary (Political) (2210): Mr G Clough
Second Secretary (Management) (2231): Mrs S
Oulmi
Second Secretary (Airline Liaison Officer) (2212):
Mr I Angell
Second Secretary (Immigration) (2301): Ms M
Joshi
Second Secretary (Immigration) (2302): Mr A
Loxton
Third Secretary (Vice Consul) (2303): Mr D
Crooks
Registrar (2217): Mr S Mitchell

Dhaka
Department for International Development (DFID)
(B)
Address and Telephone as for British High
Commission
Facsimile: (00) (880) (2) 882 3474
Head of DFID Bangladesh: Mr P Ackroyd
Economics Adviser: Mr R Islam
Economics Adviser: Mr B Sundstrom
Economics Adviser: Mr P Walters
Enterprise Development Adviser: Mr F Matsaert
Governance Adviser: Mr C Murgatroyd

Governance Adviser: Ms I Wilson
Social Development Adviser: Mr R Montgomery
Social Development Adviser: Ms L Payne
Health Adviser: Mr F Atherton
Education Adviser: Ms T Kelly
Education Assistant Adviser: Ms L Banham
Engineering Adviser: Mr P Swann
Fisheries Adviser: Mr T Robertson
Natural Resources Adviser: Mr D Brown
First Secretary (Multi-Sector): Mr A Fernie
Estate Manager: Mr G Bond
First Secretary (Management Unit): Mr P Troy
Health Sector Manager: Mr J Leigh
Health Sector Manager: Mr A Mercer
Programme Officer: Mr Y Bewick
Deputy Programme Manager: Mr J Reid
Governance Sector Manager: Ms S Nicoll
Governance Accessible Justice: Ms B Parkes
Deputy Programme Manager: Mr L Docherty
Deputy Programme Manager: Mr T Cushnan
Engineering Sector Manager: Mr C Benham
Engineering Sector Manager: Mr R Dyer
Fisheries Sector Manager: Mr D King
Natural Resources Sector Manager: Ms L Stubblefield
Programme Officer: Ms P Barrett
Deputy Programme Manager: Ms L Reid
Workshop Manager: Mr F Ward

BARBADOS

Bridgetown
British High Commission
Lower Collymore Rock (P.O. Box 676),
Bridgetown
Telephone: (00) (1) (246) 430 7800
Facsimile: (00) (1) (246) 430 7851 Chancery
                430 7860 Management/
                             Consular
                430 7826 Commercial/
                             Information
e-mail: britishhc@sunbeach.net
Office Hours (GMT): 12 00 – 16 30 and 17 00- 20 00 Monday to Thursday
12 00 – 16 00 Friday
High Commissioner: Mr J White
Also High Commissioner (Non Resident)
To Antigua and Barbuda, Commonwealth of Dominica, GrenadaSt Kitts and Nevis, St Lucia and St Vincent and the Grenadines.
Deputy High Commissioner: Mr M J E Mayhew
Defence Adviser: Captain S C Ramm, RN
Counsellor (Regional Affairs): Mr N J L Martin
First Secretary (Regional Affairs): Mr V J Auster
First Secretary (Chancery): P Curwen
Second Secretary (Management/Consular): Mr G I Brammer
Second Secretary (Chancery/Information): Mr N Pyle
Second Secretary (Chancery): Mr P Marshall
Second Secretary (Technical Works) (Resides Washington): Mr I Sweeney
Third Secretary (Management/ Consular): Mrs C Fallon
Third Secretary: Mr T White
Third Secretary (Consular): Mr S Minshull

Third Secretary: Miss V A Stock
Head of Commercial Section: Mr H S Howell, MBE
Overseas Territories Advisers
First Secretary (Financial Services Adviser): Mr R M Gallagher, OBE
First Secretary (Legal Adviser): Ms S J Dickson

Department for International Development Caribbean
Lower Collymore Rock
(P.O. Box 167), St Michael
Telephone: (00) (1) (246) 430 7900
Facsimile: (00) (1) (246) 430 7959
Office Hours (GMT): 12 00 – 20 00
Head of DFID (C): Mr D Curran
Senior Natural Resources Adviser: Mr R Beales
Engineer Adviser: Mr G Biffa
Programme Manager: Mr R Smith
Economist: Mr J Piper
Economic Adviser: Mr A Hall
Deputy Programme Manager: Ms K English
Office Manager: Ms J Armstrong
Deputy Programme Manager: Mrs G Whitley
Senior Education Adviser: Mr R Cunningham
Regional Police Adviser: Mr P Matthias
Senior Social Development Adviser: Mr J Harrison
Senior Governance Adviser: Mr W Baker
Social Development Adviser: Ms D Newman
Deputy Programme Manager: Ms N Thompson
Senior Social Development Adviser: Ms A Keeling
Enterprise Development Adviser: Ms S Barlow
Natural Resources Adviser: Mr G Chaplin
Governance Adviser: Ms K Higgins
Programme Officer: Ms E Hamer
Programme Officer: Mr R Bateson
Programme Officer: Ms L Wade
Economist: Mr M Mulraine

BELARUS

Minsk (SP)
British Embassy
37 Karl Marx Street, 220030 Minsk, Belarus
Telephone: (00) (375) (172) 105920 (Switchboard)
292310 (Visa and Consular – Recorded Information)
Facsimile: (00) (375) (172) 292306 (General)
                            292311 (Visa Section)
Airtech: 292315
e-mail: pia@bepost.belpak.minsk.by (Information only)
postmaster@minsk.mail.fco.gov.uk (General)
Office Hours (GMT): Summer: Mon-Thurs 06 00 - 10 00 and 11 00 - 14 30; Fri 06 00 - 12 00
Winter: Mon-Thurs 07 00 - 11 00 and 12 00 - 15 30; Fri 07 00 - 13 00
Ambassador and Consul General: Mr Iain C Kelly
Deputy Head of Mission: Mr Martin Fenner
Defence Attaché (resides at Moscow): Captain Simon R Lister, RN
Assistant Defence Attaché (resides at Moscow): Lieutenant Commander P E 'Beach' Seakins, RN
Second Secretary (Technical Works) (resides in Vienna): Mr Carl Gray
Second Secretary (Technical. Management.) (resides in Warsaw): Mr Jim Dunn

Third Secretary (Immigration) and Vice Consul:
Mr Julian Pearson
Attaché: Mr Steve Haines

BELGIUM

Brussels
British Embassy
Rue D'Arlon 85,
B-1040 Brussels
Telephone: (00) (32) (2) 287 6211
Facsimile: (00) (32) (2) 287 6355 Political
        6270 Consular
        6240 Commercial
        6360 Press and Public
        Affairs
e-mail: firstname.surname@fco.gov.uk
Website: www.british-embassy.be
Ambassador: Mr G Hewitt, CMG
Deputy Head of Mission, Consul-General and Counsellor
(Commercial and Economic): Mr J S Smith
Counsellor (Political): Mr C P Burrows
Defence Attaché: Group Captain J D Bullen, OBE, RAF
Cultural Counsellor (British Council): Mr M Rose
First Secretary (Political): Mr J McManus
First Secretary (Political): Mr J L Baxendale
First Secretary (Political): Miss J W Bird
First Secretary (Labour Attaché) (Hague): Mr P E D Drummond
First Secretary (Commercial): Mr D J Currie
First Secretary (Technical): Mr I Willsher
Second Secretary (EU/Economic): Ms S Cullum
Second Secretary (PPA/Political): Ms L Joyce
Second Secretary (Consul): Miss C F Armstrong
Second Secretary (Technical): Mr R Bruton
Second Secretary (Technical): Mr S Willliams
Third Secretary (Political): Mr M O'Reilly

Brussels United Kingdom Delegation to NATO, see part II
Brussels United Kingdom Delegation to the WEU, see part II
Brussels Office of the United Kingdom Permanent Representative to the European Union, see part II

Brussels
British Embassy
Joint Management Office
Rue d'Arlon 85, 1040 Brussels
Telephone: (00) (32) (2) 287 6211
Facsimile: (00) (32) (2) 287 6320
Counsellor: Mr P Newall
First Secretary: Ms J Sweid
Second Secretary: Mr D L Walker
Third Secretary: Miss G Adams

Antwerp
British Consulate-General
C/o Immobilien Hugo Ceusters
Frankrijklei 31 33
B-2000 Antwerp
Telephone: (00) (32) (3) 213 2125
Facsimile: (00) (32) (3) 213 2991
Office Hours: Wednesdays 14 30 – 16 30
Thursdays 10 00 – 12 30

Honorary Consul-General: Baron P Buysse, CBE
Pro-Consul: Mrs A M Marinus

Liège
British Honorary-Consulate
Quai de Maestricht 14, 4000 Liège
Telephone: (00) (32) (4) 232 9797
Facsimile: (00) (32) (4) 223 1109
Office Hours: Mon-Fri: 8.00 - 12.00
Honorary Consul: Marie-Dominique Laurence Paule Simonet

BELIZE

Belmopan (SP)
British High Commission
P. O. Box 91 Belmopan, Belize or B.F.P.O 12
Telephone: (00) (501) (8) 22146/7
Facsimile: (00) (501) (8) 22761
Airtech: (00) (501) (8) 23694
e-mail: brithicom@btl.net
High Commissioner: Mr Philip J Priestley, CBE
Deputy High Commissioner: Mr Martin Fidler
Defence Adviser (resides in Kingston): Colonel Rob A Hyde-Bales
Second Secretary (resides in Miami): Mr Brendan Foreman
Second Secretary (Consular/Management): Mr Carl Mackerras
Third Secretary (Development): (Vacant)

BENIN

Cotonou
British Embassy (all staff resident in Nigeria)
Ambassador: Mr Philip Thomas, CMG
Counsellor: Mr D Wyatt
Consul: Mrs J Finnamore-Crorkin
Second Secretary (Commercial): Ms S Pickering
Vice-Consul: Mr T Sanmoogan

BOLIVIA

La Paz (SP)
British Embassy
Avenida Arce No.2732
Casilla 697
Telephone: (00) (591) (2) 433424 (connects to 9 lines)
Facsimile: (00) (591) (2) 431073
Airtech: (00) (591) (2) 432301
Duty Officer: (00) (591) (12) 92311
e-mail: (Embassy): ppa@mail.megalink.com
(DFID): dfid@zuper.net
Office Hours (GMT): Mon - Thur 12 30 - 16 30 and 17 30 - 21 00 Fri   12 30 - 17 30
Ambassador: Mr W B Sinton, OBE
Deputy Head of Mission and HM Consul: Mr Philip Hogarth
Development Attaché (Head of Development Cooperation-DFID): Ms Rosalind Eyben
Defence Attaché (resides in Santiago): Colonel R M J Rollo-Walker, OBE
First Secretary: Mr Reginald Low, MBE
Development Attaché (Rural Livelihoods, Health-DFID): Ms Elizabeth Ditchburn
Development Attaché (Health-DFID): Dr Jason Lane

Cultural Attaché (Director of British Council): Mr Eric Lawrie
Third Secretary (Management/Consular/Visa): Mrs Deborah Aliaga
Third Secretary (Technical Management) (resides in Brasil): Mr Richard Wildman
Commercial Officer: Mr Eduardo Suarez

BOSNIA AND HERZEGOVINA

Sarajevo
British Embassy
8,Tina Ujevica, Sarajevo, Bosnia and Herzegovina
Telephone: (00 387 33) 444 429 Chancery; Management
204 781/2/3 Commercial, KHF; Consular/Visa
Facsimile: (00 387 33) 666 131 Chancery;
                                    Management
                    204 780 Commercial; KHF;
                                    Consular/Visa
Airtech: 663 492
e-mail:
PoliticalEnquiries@sarajevo.mail.fco.gov.uk
CommercialEnquiries@sarajevo.mail.fco.gov.uk
KHFEnquiries@sarajevo.mail.fco.gov.uk
ConsularEnquiries@sarajevo.mail.fco.gov.uk
VisaEnquiries@sarajevo.mail.fco.gov.uk
britemb@bih.net.ba
Office Hours (GMT): Mon-Fri 07 30 – 1200 and 13 00 - 16 00
Ambassador: Mr Ian Cliff, OBE
Deputy Head of Mission: Mr Daniel Fearn
First Secretary (Commercial): Mr Tim Hanson
First Secretary (Chancery): Mr Alistair Sommerlad
First Secretary (British Council Director): Ms C Newton
Second Secretary (Management and Consul): Mr Doug Winter
Second Secretary (KHF): Mr Alan Holmes
Second Secretary (Political/PPA): Ms Fiona McIlwham
Second Secretary (Political): Mr Richard Gould
Third Secretary (Chancery): Ms Michelle Morgan
Vice-Consul: Mr Mark Patterson

Banja Luka
British Embassy Office
8 Simeuna Dzaka, Banja Luka,
Bosnia and Herzegovina
Tel/Fax: (00 387 51) 212 395/216 842
Mobile: (00 387 66) 512 698
e-mail: beo-bl@inecco.net
Head of Office: Mr Roy Wilson

BOTSWANA

Gaborone
British High Commission
Private Bag 0023, Gaborone
Telephone: (00) (267) 3 52841/2/3
Facsimile: (00) (267) 3 56105
Airtech: (00) (267) 3 52650
e-mail: bhc@botsnet.bw
Office Hours (GMT): Mon - Thur: 06 00 - 10 30 and 11 30 - 14 30
Fri: 06 00 - 11 00
High Commissioner: Mr D B Merry, CMG

Deputy High Commissioner: Mr J L Smith
Defence Adviser (resides at Harare): Colonel J S Field, CBE
Second Secretary (Development/Regional Affairs): Mr J L Riley
Third Secretary (Consular and Management): Mr A K Bedforth

BRAZIL

Brasilia
British Embassy
Setor de Embaixadas Sul, Quadra 801, Conjunto K, CEP 70.408-900, Brasilia DF or Avenida das Nacões,
Caixa Postal 07-0586, 70359 Brasilia -DF
Telephone: (00) (55) (61) 225 2710
Facsimile: (00) (55) (61) 225 1777
Airtech: (00) (55) (61) 225 2710 ext 2343
e-mail: britemb@terra.com.br
Website: www.reinounido.org.br
Office Hours (GMT)   Mon - Thurs: 11 30 - 20 30 (UK Summer)
Fri: 11 30 - 15 30
Mon - Thurs: 10 30 - 19 30 (UK Winter)
Fri: 10 30 - 14 30
Ambassador: Mr Roger B Bone, CMG
Deputy Head of Mission: Mr Andrew K Soper
Defence, Military and Air Attaché: Colonel J Michael Bowles, MBE
Naval Attaché: Captain Stephen J Timms, OBE, RN
First Secretary (Economic & Commercial): Mr Nicholas D Low
First Secretary (Management) and Consul: Mr Stephen M Weinrabe
First Secretary: Mr Francis A Dick
First Secretary (Technical Co-operation): Mr Stewart S Mills
Second Secretary: Miss Lisa Whanstall
Second Secretary: Miss Harriet L Mathews
Third Secretary (Technical Management): Mr Richard H Wildman
Third Secretary (Management) and Vice-Consul: Miss Kate L Goulden

Belém – PA
British Consulate
Av. Governador Malcher, 815 Ed Palladium Center Conj. 410/411,
Belém – Para,
CEP 66.035-900,
Caixa Postal 98
Telephone: (00) (55) (91) 222 5074, 223 0990
Facsimile: (00) (55) (91) 212 0274
Honorary Consul: Dr A M dos Santos

Manáus - AM
British Consulate
Swedish Match da Amazonia S.A
Rua Poraque 240
Distrito Industrial
Manaus – Am
CEP 69075 –180
Telephone: (00) (55) (92) 613 1819
Facsimile: (00) (55) (92) 613 1420
Honorary Consul: Mr V J Brown

Rio de Janeiro – RJ
British Consulate-General
Praia do Flamengo, 284/2 andar,
Rio de Janeiro - RJ, CEP 22210-030
Telephone: (00) (55) (21) 555 9600 (Switchboard)
                                  9640 (Consular
                                           Section)
Facsimile: (00) (55) (21) 555 9672 (Management)
                                  9604 (Chancery)
                                  9670 (Commercial)
                                  9671 (Consular)
Airtech: (00) (55) (21) 555 9608
e-mail: britconrio@openlink.com.br (General)
consular.section@riodejaneiro.mail.fco.gov.uk
(Consular Section)
Office Hours (GMT): Mon - Fri: March -
November: 11 30 - 20 00
December - February: 10 00 - 19 00
Consul-General: Mr Geoffrey S Cowling
Deputy Consul-General and Consul (Commercial):
Mr Michael John Holloway
Vice-Consul (Commercial): Mr Gery Juleff
Vice-Consul (Management): Mr Stuart Smith
Vice-Consul (Consular/Immigration): Mr Andrew J
Snook
Pro-Consul: Mrs Sara Pereira

Belo Horizonte - MG
British Consulate
Rua dos Inconfidentes, 1075, Sala 1302
Belo Horizonte – MG – 30140 120
Savassi
Telephone: (00) (31) 3261 2072
Facsimile: (00) (31) 3261 0226
e-mail: britcon.bhe@terra.com.br
Honorary Consul: Mr Roger A Gough, MBE
Commercial Officer: Mr Rogerio Pacheco, MBE

Fortaleza - CE
British Consulate
c/o Grupo Edson Queiroz, Praca da Imprensa s/n,
Aldeota, Fortaleza - CE, CEP 60135-900
Telephone: (00) (55) (85) 466 8580/8582
Facsimile: (00) (55) (85) 261-8763
e-mail: annette@edsonqueiroz.com.br
Honorary Consul: Mrs Annette T Reeves de Castro

Recife - PE
Av. Conselheiro Aguiar, 2941/3°,
Boa Viagem,
Recife-PE, CEP 51020-020
Telephone: (00) (55) (81) 3465-0230
Facsimile: (00) (55) (81) 3465-0247
e-mail: recife@britishconsulate-org.br
Honorary Consul: Mr Alan E Fiore

Salvador - BA
British Consulate
Av. Estados Unidos, No 18-B
8 Andar-Comercio, Ed-Estados Unidos
CEP 40010 - 020, Salvador - BA
Telephone: (00) (55) (71) 243-7399
Facsimile: (00) (55) (71) 242-7293/243-7856
e-mail: adcos@allways.com.br
Honorary Consul: Mr Nigel Lee

São Paulo - SP
British Consulate-General
Centro Brasileiro Britanico
Rua Ferreira de Araujo, 2nd Floor
Pinheiros
05428-002-São Paulo-SP
Brazil
Telephone: (00) (55) (11) 3094 2700
Facsimile: (00) (55) (11) 3094 2717 (Commercial)
                                  3094 2750 (Management)
Airtech: (00) (55) (11) 3816 4887
e-mail: consulad@uol.com.br
Website: www.Gra.bretahanha.org.br
Office Hours (GMT): Mon - Thurs: 11 30 - 19 45,
Fri 11 30 - 19 30 (UK Summer)
Mon - Thurs: 10 30 - 18 45, Fri 10 30 - 18 30 (UK
Winter)
*Consul-General & Director of Trade & Investment
Brazil:* Mr Bernard Everett, CVO
*Deputy Consul-General and Deputy Director of
Trade & Investment:* Mr Patrick Ashworth
Vice-Consul (Consular/Management): Mr David
Paginton
Vice-Consul (Commercial): Mr Tim Dearden
Vice-Consul (Commercial): Ms Gale Jenkinson
Vice-Consul (Customs): Mr David Sterling
Pro-Consul (Consular/Management): Ms Lisa Evely

Curitiba - PR
British Trade Office and British Consulate
Rusa Presidente Faria, 51, 2 andar,
CJ.705 - Curitiba, PR CEP 80020-290
Telephone: (00) (55) (41) 322-1202
Facsimile: (00) (55) (41) 322-3537
e-mail: consuladobritanico@mais.sul.com.br
Commercial Officer and Honorary Consul: Mr
Peter ter Poorten

Porto Alegre - RS
British Consulate
Edificio Montreal, Rua Itapeva,
110 Conjunto 505, Passo D'Areia
91350-080 Porto Alegre - RS
Telephone: (00) (55) (51) 341-0720
Facsimile: (00) (55) (51) 341-0720
Honorary Consul: Mr Geoffrey Powell

Porto Alegre - RS
British Commercial Office
Rua Antenor Lemos 57 Cj 403,
Bairro Menino Deus, 90850-100,
Porto Alegre -RS
Telephone: (00) (55) (51) 232 141
Facsimile: (00) (55) (51) 231 6094
e-mail: britconpoa@portoweb.con.br
Commercial Officer: Mrs Denise Pellin

Rio Grande - RS
British Consulate
Wilson Sons, Rua Riachuelo, 201 terreo,
CEP 96200-390, Rio Grande - RS
Porto Alegre - RS
Telephone: (00) (55) (53) 233-7700
Facsimile: (00) (55) (53) 233-7701
(00) (55) (53) 231 1530
e-mail: rjg@wilson.com.br
Honorary Consul: Mr Richard Grantham

Santos - SP
British Consulate
Rua Tuiuti 58, 2 andar, Caixa Postal 204,
11101-220-220, Santos
Telephone: (00) (55) (13) 3211 2300, Direct: (55)
(13) 3219 4659
Mobile: (55) (13) 9972 1622
Facsimile: (00) (55) (13) 3210 3840
              (55) (13) 3219 5250
e-mail: daw@wilson.com.br
Honorary Consul: Mr David A Walton

BRUNEI

Bandar Seri Begawan
British High Commission
PO Box 2197
Bandar Seri Begawan 8674
Telephone: (00) (673) (2) 222231/223121 Chancery
                                            & Commercial
                        226001 Management &
                                            Consular
Facsimile: (00) (673) (2) 234315
Airtech: (00) (673) (2) 226002
e-mail: brithc@brunet.bn
Office Hours (GMT): Mon to Thurs 00 30 - 04 45
and 06 00 - 09 00
Fri 00 30 - 04 30
High Commissioner: Mr Andrew J F Caie
Deputy High Commissioner: Mr Edward Bousfield
Defence Adviser: Captain P H Jones, OBE, RN
First Secretary (Defence Cooperation): Mr Colin
Britteon
Second Secretary (Chancery/Information): Miss
Sue Elliott, MBE
Third Secretary (Commercial/Economic): Mr Brian
Price
Third Secretary (Management/Consular): Mr
Simon Hart
Attaché: Mrs Val Porter
Attaché: Miss Sian Bloxham

BULGARIA

Sofia
British Embassy
9 Moskovska Street, Sofia
Telephone: (00) (359) (2) 980-12-20
            (00) (359) (2) 963-06-67 Consular/Visa
Out of Hours: (00) (359) (2) 981-77-65
Facsimile: (00) (359) (2) 980-12-29
980-12 28 (Airtech)
981-77-53 Consular/Visa
983-33-07 KHF
963-06-64 Chancery
Airtech: 980-12-28
e-mail: britembsof@mbox.cit.bg
Website: www.british-embassy.bg
Office Hours (GMT): Mon to Thurs 06 30 - 15 30,
Fri 06 30 - 11 00 (Summer time, one hour earlier
GMT)
Ambassador: Mr Ian Soutar
First Secretary and Deputy Head of Mission: Mr
Tim Colley
Defence Attaché: Colonel Ryszard Z A Ciaglinski
First Secretary (Political): Mr John Davies

Cultural Attaché (British Council Director): Mr
Kevin Lewis
First Secretary (Commercial): Mr Dennis Leith
Assistant Defence Attaché: Lieutenant Commander
Mark R N Warlow, RN
Second Secretary (Management): Mr Tony
Williams
*Assistant Cultural Attaché (British Council Deputy
Director):* Mr David Kirwan
Second Secretary (Political/Information): Mrs
Christine Winterburn
Second Secretary (DLO): Mr Lee Williams
Second Secretary Consul & Immigration: Ms
Hilary Arthur
Attaché (Immigration): Mr Mark Griffith
Attaché (Immigration): Mr Gary McCall
Attaché (Security): Mr David Williams
Chaplain (resides at Bucharest): Rev. Steve
Hughes
Head of Know How Fund: Mrs Toni Grancharova

Varna
British Consulate
40, Graf Ignatiev Street,
PO Box 229
Varna
Telephone: (00) (359) (52) 6655 555
Facsimile: (00) (359) (52) 6655 755
e-mail: bozhilov@unimasters.bg
Honorary Consul: Mr N Bozhilov

BURKINA

Ouagadougou
British Embassy (all staff reside at Abidjan)
Ambassador: Mr J F Gordon, CMG
*First Secretary (Commercial), Consul and Deputy
Head of Mission:* Mr M J K Rickerd, MVO
Second Secretary (Political/Information): Ms K
Miller, MBE
Second Secretary (Management) and Vice-Consul:
Mr D Summers
Second Secretary (Commercial/Political): Mr C
Frean
*Third Secretary & Vice- Consul (Passports &
Visas):* Mr M McGuinness
Third Secretary (Chancery): Ms N McBratney

British Honorary Consulate
Hotel Yibi
10 BP 13593
Ouagadougou
Burkina Faso
Telephone: (00) (226) 30 73 23
Facsimile: (00) (226) 30 59 00
e-mail: ypi@cenatrin.bf
Honorary Consul: Mr A R Turner

BURMA (UNION OF MYANMAR)

Rangoon
Rangoon (Yangon)
British Embassy
80 Strand Road (P.O. Box 638), Rangoon
Telephone: (00) (95) (1) 295300, 295309, 285929,
281702, 281700, (out of hours: 295309)
Facsimile: (00) (95) (1) 289566

Airtech: (00) (95) (1) 295306
Office Hours (GMT): 01 30 - 10 00
Except Wed 01 30 - 06 30
Ambassador: Dr John Jenkins, LVO
Deputy Head of Mission and HM Consul: Mr
Francis J Marshall
*Cultural Attaché, British Council Director
(Tel: 256290 ext:312):* Mr Graham Millington
Second Secretary (Political): Miss Victoria Billing
Second Secretary (Management) and Vice-Consul:
Miss Karen Williams, MBE
Third Secretary (Political): Mr Alastair Totty
Attaché: Miss Helen Larmouth

BURUNDI

Bujumbura
British Embassy (all staff resident in Kigali)
Ambassador: Mrs S E Hogwood, MBE
Deputy Head of Mission: Ms J A Curry-Jones
Defence Attaché (resides at Kampala): Lieutenant
Colonel C E Thom, OBE

CAMBODIA

Phnom Penh
British Embassy
29 Street 75, Phnom Penh
Telephone: (00) (855 23) 427124, 428295
Facsimile: (00) (855 23) 427125
e-mail: BRITEMB@bigpond.com.kh
Consular@phnompenh.mail.fco.gov.uk
Office Hours (GMT): Mon, Tues, Thurs, Fri: 01 00 -
10 00   Wed: 01 00 - 06 00
Ambassador: Mr S J Bridges
Second Secretary and Deputy Head of Mission: Mr
I Felton

CAMEROON

Yaoundé
British High Commission
Avenue Winston Churchill,
BP 547, Yaoundé
Telephone: (00) (237) 22 05 45, 22 07 96
Facsimile: (00) (237) 22 01 48
Airtech: (00) (237) 22 91 55
e-mail: BHC@yaounde.mail.fco.gov.uk
BHC.yaounde@camnet.cm
Office Hours (GMT): Mon: 06 30 - 13 30
Tue - Fri: 06 30 – 13 00
High Commissioner: Mr Peter Boon
Deputy High Commissioner: Mr David Williams
Second Secretary: Mrs Pam Tarif
Vice-Consul (Consular/Management): Mrs Marion
Guthrie

Douala
British Consulate
Standard Chartered Bank Cameroon SA,
Boulevard de la Liberté
BP 1784, Douala, Cameroon
Telephone: (00) (237) 42 21 77, 42 81 45
Facsimile: (00) (237) 42 88 96
Office Hours (GMT): Mon: 06 30 - 13 30
Tues-Fri: 06 30 – 13 00
Commercial Officer: Mrs Genevieve Faure

CANADA

Ottawa
British High Commission
80 Elgin Street, Ottawa, Ontario K1P 5K7
Telephone: (00) (1) (613) 237 1530
Voicemail & Direct Lines: (00) (1) (613) 237 1542 -
(key in extension shown by name)
Facsimile: (00) (1) (613) 237 7980
                        232 0738 Management
                        232 2533 Visa
                        237 5211 Economic
                        237 6537 Passport
                        567 8045 Political
e-mail: BHC@fco.gov.uk
management@fco.gov.uk
information@fco.gov.uk
chancery@fco.gov.uk
consular@fco.gov.uk
trade-econ@fco.gov.uk
Website: www.britain-in-canada.org
Office Hours (GMT): 13 00 - 21 00
High Commissioner: Sir A Burns KCMG
Deputy High Commissioner (343) Mr R J
Codrington
Counsellor (Trade/Economic) (324): Mr N R
Chrimes
Counsellor (380): Mr R A Foulsham
*Counsellor (Cultural Affairs)
(British Council Director) (318):* Mr P Chenery
Defence and Military Adviser (369): Brigadier C J
R Day
Naval and Air Adviser (384): Captain D M Booth
DSC RN
*First Secretary (Head of Political/Information
Section) (274):* Mr C O'Connor
First Secretary (355): Mrs L Cooper
First Secretary (Management) (326): Mr J P M
Farrand
*First Secretary (Head of Media & Public Affairs)
(262):* Mr D Belgrove
First Secretary (214): Mr B Pearson
Second Secretary (Economic) (247): Mr A Richmond
Second Secretary (Trade) (282): Mr M Dolan
Assistant Naval Adviser B.D.L.S. (234): Sqn Ldr
Chris McKiernan
Second Secretary (Consular) (320): Mr R J Fielder
Third Secretary (Political) (228): Mr A Campbell
Third Secretary (Economic) (331): Mrs E Mamet

Montreal
British Consulate-General
Suite 4200, 1000 De La Gauchetiere West,
Montreal, Quebec
Canada
H3B 4W5
Telephone: (00) (1) (514) 866-5863
Direct Line - see individual officers
Facsimile: (00) (1) (514) 866-0202
Airtech: (00) (1) (514) 866 4867
Office Hours (GMT): 14 00 - 22 00
Consul-General (233): Mr Marcus L Hope, OBE
Deputy Consul-General (230): Mr Philip Hagger
Consul (Commercial) (225): Mrs Debbie J Fern

Montreal United Kingdom Representative on the Council of the International Civil Aviation Organisation, see part II

Toronto
British Consulate-General
British Trade & Investment Office
777 Bay Street, Suite 2800, College Park,
Toronto, Ontario M5G 2G2
Telephone: (00) (1) 416 593-1290
Facsimile: (00) (1) 416 593-1229
Airtech: (00) (1) 416 593-1425
e-mail: britcon2@gta.igs.net
Office Hours (GMT): 12 30 - 21 00
Consul-General: Mr Peter Agar
Deputy Consul-General (2236): Mr Stanley Calder
Consul (Inward Investment) (2234): Mr John Williams
Consul (Commercial) (2231): Ms Sheila Towe
Vice-Consul/Management Officer (2227): Miss Jo Bowyer

Vancouver
British Consulate-General
1111 Melville Street, Suite 800,
Vancouver, British Colombia, V6E 4V6
Telephone: (00) (1) (604) 683-4421
Direct Lines - see individual officers
Facsimile: (00) (1) (604) 681-0693
Airtech: (00) (1) (604) 683-7768
Office Hours (GMT): 16 30 - 00 30
Consul-General (1-2205): Mr Ian Kydd
Deputy Consul-General (1-2208): Mr David Roberts

Calgary
British Trade Office
Suite 1500, Bow Valley Square IV
250-6th Avenue S.W
Calgary, Alberta T2P 3H7
Telephone: (00) (1) (403) 705-1755
Facsimile: (00) (1) (403) 264-1262
Office Hours (GMT): 15 30 – 23 30
Director: Mr Clark Grue
Trade Assistant: Ms Tara Meinhardt

Halifax/Dartmouth
British Consulate
1, Canal Street, P.O. Box 605,
Dartmouth, Nova Scotia B2Y 3Y9
Telephone: (00) (1) (902) 461-1381
Facsimile: (00) (1) (902) 465-2578
Honorary Consul: Mr A A Smithers

St. John's
British Consulate
113 Topsail Road, St. John's,
Newfoundland A1E 2A9
Telephone: (00) (1) (709) 579 2002
Facsimile: (00) (1) (709) 579 0475
Honorary Consul: Mr F D Smith

Winnipeg
British Consulate
229, Athlone Drive, Winnipeg,
Manitoba, R3J 3L6
Telephone: (00) (1) (204) 896 1380
Facsimile: (00) (1) (204) 269 3025
Honorary Consul: Mr R M Hill

Quebec City
British Consulate
Le Complexe St-Amable
700 - 1150 Claire-Fontaine, Quebec City
Quebec, G1R 5G4
Telephone: (00) (1) (418) 521 3000
Facsimile: (00) (1) (418) 521 3099
Honorary Consul: Mr R Drouin

CAPE VERDE

Praia
British Embassy (all staff resident in Dakar)
Ambassador: Mr E A Burner
First Secretary and Deputy Head of Mission: Mr P T D O'Brien, MBE
Education Attaché and British Council Director: Mr S McNulty
Second Secretary (Political/Press and Public Affairs): Mr S Bond
Third Secretary (Management) and Vice-Consul: Ms A J Lavocat

Cape Verde
British Consulate
Shell Cabo Verde, Sarl, Av Amilcar Cabral CP4,
Sao Vincente
Telephone: (00) (238) 32 66 25/26/27
Facsimile: (00) (238) 32 66 29
e-mail: antonio.a.canuto@scv.sims.com
Consul (resides at Dakar): Mr P T D O'Brien, MBE
Vice-Consul (resides at Dakar): Ms A J Lavocat
Honorary Consul: Mr A Canuto

CENTRAL AFRICAN REPUBLIC

Bangui
British Embassy (all staff reside at Yaoundé)
Ambassador and Consul-General: Mr Peter Boon
First Secretary and Consul: Mr David Williams

CHAD

Ndjamena
British Embassy (all staff reside at Yaoundé)
Ambassador: Mr Peter Boon
First Secretary and Consul: Mr David Williams
Ndjamena
British Consulate
BP1060
Ndjamena
Tel/Fax: (00) (235) 52 39 70
Mobile: (00) (235) 841 11 02
e-mail: econsit@hotmail.com
Honorary Consul: Mrs Ermanna Delacroix

CHILE

Santiago
British Embassy
Av. El Bosque 0125, Casilla 72-D
or Casilla 16552, Santiago
Telephone: (00) (56) (2) 370 4100
Facsimile: (00) (56) (2) 370 4180 Commercial
                                    4170 Consulate
                                    4160 Management
                                    335 5988 Information

4140 Chancery
235 7375 British Council
e-mail: chancery@santiago.mail.fco.gov.uk
commercial@santiago.mail.fco.gov.uk
consulate@santiago.mail.fco.gov.uk
defence@santiago.mail.fco.gov.uk
Web page: www.britemb.cl
Office Hours (GMT): (October - March) Mon-
Thurs: 12 00 - 20 30
(October - March) Fri: 12.00 - 16 00
(March - October) 14 00 - 18.30
Ambassador: Mr G Faulkner
*Counsellor, Consul-General and Deputy Head of
Mission:* Mr P Whiteway (Ext 4112)
Counsellor: Mr N M Jacobsen (Ext 4123)
Defence Attaché: Colonel R M J Rollo-Walker
(Ext 4120)
First Secretary (Commercial): Mr P Taylor
(Ext 4174)
Cultural Attaché (British Council Director): Mr J
Knagg
Second Secretary and Consul: Miss D E Gordon, MBE
(Ext 4138)
Second Secretary (Commercial): Mr S Wadvani
(Ext 4175)
Second Secretary: Miss E Wade (Ext 4114)

Valparaíso
British Consulate
Blanco 1199 Piso 5
Casilla 68 – V
Valparaíso, Chile
Tel/fax: (00) (56) (32) 213063
e-mail: hardy@entelchile.net
Honorary Consul: Mr Iain Hardy

Punta Arenas
British Consulate
Roca 924, Casilla 327, Punta Arenas
Tel/fax: (00) (56) (61) 227221
Honorary Consul: Mr J C Rees

CHINA

Beijing
British Embassy
11 Guang Hua Lu, Jian Guo Men Wai,
Beijing 100600
Telephone: (00) (86) (10) 6532 1961 (plus
extension if known)
6532 6895 (plus extension if known)
Facsimile: (00) (86) (10) 6532 1937
6532 0901 (Development Section)
e-mail: Commercial Section:
commercialmail@peking.mail.fco.gov.uk
Commercial Library:
library@peking.mail.fco.gov.uk
Science and Technology:
bescitec@peking.mail.fco.gov.uk
Development Section:
dfid@peking.mail.fco.gov.uk
Office Hours (GMT): 03 00 - 04 00 and 05 30 -
09 00

Consular & Visa Section
21st Floor
Kerry Centre

1, Guang Hua Lu
Beijing 100600
Telephone: (00) (86) (10) 8529 6600, 6075, 6084
(office hours)
(00) (86) (10) 6532 1961, 6750
(out of hours):
(00) (86) (10) 8529 6600
(24 hour recorded information service)
Facsimile: (00) (86) (10) 8529 6081 (Consular)
(00) (86) (10) 8529 6080 (Visa)
Telegrams: RTI:PEVIS ROU:PV CIR:PVA
e-mail: consularmail@peking.mail.fco.gov.uk
visamail@peking.mail.fco.gov.uk
Office Hours (GMT): 00 30 – 04 00 and 05 00 –
08 30

Cultural and Education Section
4th Floor Landmark Building, Tower 1,
8 North Dongsanhuan Road, Chaoyang District,
Beijing 100004
Telephone: (00) (86) (10) 6590 6903
Facsimile: (00) (86) (10) 6590 0977
e-mail: enquiry@britishcouncil.org.cn
Ambassador: Sir A C Galsworthy, KCMG (Mr C O
Hum, CMG w.e.f March 2002)
*Minister, Consul-General and Deputy Head of
Mission:* Mr N J Cox
Counsellor (Political/Economic): Ms C Nettleton
Counsellor (Commercial): Mr C Haswell
*Counsellor (Cultural) (British Council Director)
(ext 219):* Mr M O'Sullivan
Counsellor (Public Affairs): Mr N P Westgarth
Defence, Military and Air Attaché: Brigadier J G
Kerr, OBE,QGM
Naval Attaché: Captain A A Ainslie, RN
First Secretary (Political): Mr D Ellis
First Secretary (Political): Ms T Redshaw
First Secretary (Political): Mr M Pettigrew
First Secretary (Commercial): Mr S Buckley
First Secretary (Commercial): Mr M Mielniczek
First Secretary (Commercial): Mr K Brown
*First Secretary (Commercial/Science and
Technology):* Mr P Wusterman
*First Secretary (Cultural and Scientific) (British
Council):* Mr K R Davies
First Secretary (Education) (British Council): Mr
A G Slaven
*First Secretary (Cultural) (British Council) (ext
227):* Mr D Knox
*First Secretary (Assistant Director) (British
Council):* Ms M Day
First Secretary (Cultural): Mr P Clementson
First Secretary (Bilateral): Mr I Richards
First Secretary (Economic): Ms S A McLean
First Secretary (Economic): Ms R Cohen
First Secretary (Management): Mr P Robinson
First Secretary (Consul): (Vacant)
First Secretary (Development): Ms F McConnon
First Secretary (Development): Ms J Haycock
First Secretary (Development): Ms S Milner
First Secretary (Development): Ms P de Waal
First Secretary (Development): Ms C Martin
First Secretary (Development): Ms J Popkins
First Secretary (Technical Management): Mr P Kelly
First Secretary (Nurse): Ms J Senior
Second Secretary (Economic): Ms S Peters

Second Secretary (Political): Mr W D Morgan
Second Secretary (Commercial): Mr B Ladd
Second Secretary (Commercial): Mr P J Ambrose
Second Secretary (Commercial): Mrs T Evans
Second Secretary (Commercial): Miss J Haworth
Second Secretary (Press and Public Affairs): Mr B Fender
Second Secretary (Cultural) (British Council) (ext 232): Ms V Grant
Second Secretary (Cultural -Scientific) (British Council)(ext 228): Mrs L Watkins
Second Secretary (Cultural) (British Council): Mr A Sheard
Second Secretary (Cultural) (British Council): Mr S Forbes
Second Secretary (Immigration): Mr G S Flett
Second Secretary (Immigration-Airport Liaison): Mr R Montgomery
Second Secretary (Management): Mr T O'Connell
Second Secretary (Management): Mr M Page
Second Secretary (Technical Management): Mr R Parker
Second Secretary (Development): Mrs V Malloo
Third Secretary (Vice-Consul): Mr J Murphy
Third Secretary (Immigration): Mr I Howell
Third Secretary (Immigration): Mr D Scott
Third Secretary (Immigration): Mrs G Lowson
Third Secretary (Immigration): Mr G Stein
Third Secretary (Immigration): Mrs S Stilgoe
Third Secretary (Immigration): Mr C Glen
Third Secretary (Immigration): Mrs L Heseltine
Third Secretary (Immigration): Mr S Thomas
Third Secretary (Immigration): Ms W Shepherd
Third Secretary (Technical Works): Mr G Caldwell
Third Secretary (Visits): Mrs E Evans

Shanghai
British Consulate-General
Suite 301, Shanghai Centre
1376 Nan Jing Xi Lu,
Shanghai 200040
Telephone: (00) (86) (21) 6279 7650
Facsimile: (00) (86) (21) 6279 7651 (General)
                        6279 7388 (Commercial)
e-mail: britishconsulate@shanghai.mail.fco.gov.uk
firstname.lastname@shanghai.mail.fco.gov.uk
Website: www.britishconsulate.sh.cn
Office Hours (GMT): 01 00 - 09 30

Visa Section
Suite 751, Shanghai Centre
1376 Nan Jing Xi Lu
Shanghai 200040
Telephone: (00) (86) (21) 6279 8130
Facsimile: (00) (86) (21) 6279 8254
e-mail: visa@shanghai.mail.fco.gov.uk
Office Hours (GMT): 00 00 (Midnight) - 08 30

British Council
1 Floor Pidemco Tower
318 Fu Zhou Lu
Shanghai 200001
Telephone: (00) (86) (21) 6391 2626
Facsimile: (00) (86) (21) 6391 2121
e-mail: bc.shanghai@britishcouncil.org.cn
firstname.lastname@britishcouncil.org.cn
Website: www.britishcouncil.org.cn

Office Hours (GMT): 00 30 - 09 00
Consul-General: Mr Paul Sizeland
Deputy Consul-General: Mr Steve Codd
Consul (Commercial): Mr Barry Nicholson
Consul (Commercial): Mr Bryan Scarborough
Consul (Economic/Press & Public Affairs): Mr John Edwards
Consul (Commercial): Mr Douglas Barrett
Consul (Management): Mr Duncan Hill
Consul (Cultural and Education): Ms Joanna Burke
Consul (Education): Ms Jane Henry
Consul (Education): Mr Richard Everitt
Consul (Entry Clearance Manager): Mrs Suzanne Ivins
Vice-Consul (Visa): Miss Sue Harsent
Vice-Consul (Visa): Mr John Neil
Pro Consul (Consular): Miss Amanda Cooper

Guangzhou
British Consulate-General
2nd Floor Guangdong International Hotel
(Visa/Consular/Management Sections)
7th Floor Guangdong International Hotel
(Commercial/Political/Economic Sections)
339 Huanshi Dong Lu
Guangzhou 510098
Telephone: (00) (86) (20) 8335 1354 General
                  (00) (86) (20) 8333 6520 Commercial
                                    8333 6623 Management/
                                                  Consular and
                                                  Visa
                                    8333 1316 British Council
Facsimile: (00) (86) (20) 8331 2799 Management/
                                                  Consular
                                    8333 6485 Commercial
                                    8332 7509 Visa
                                    8335 1321 British Council
e-mail: guangbcg@gitic.com.cn (Consulate)
bc.guangzhou@britishcouncil.org.cn (British Council)
Office Hours (GMT): Mon-Fri: 01 00 - 04 30 & 05 30 - 09 00
Consul General: Mr S Lillie
Deputy Consul General: Mr J Wilkins
Consul (Political/Economic): Mr N Whittingham
Consul (Commercial): Mr R J Shead (Mr H Spicer w.e.f Feb 2002)
Consul (Consular/Management): Mr G Nicholls
Consul (Visas): Miss S Stowe
Consul (Cultural and Education): Mr J Gilbert
Consul (Education): Mr S Healy
Vice-Consul (Visa): Miss J Carey
Vice-Consul (Visa): Mr J Kennedy
Vice-Consul (Visa): Mr T Symon
Vice-Consul (Visa): Mr D Jones
Vice-Consul: (Commercial): (Vacant)
Attaché: Miss J Blacklock

Chongqing
British Consulate-General
Suite 2801, Metropolitan Tower,
68 Zourong Road
Chongqing
40010 People's Republic of China
Telephone: (00) (86) (23) 6381 0321
Facsimile: (00) (86) (23) 6381 0322

Airtech: (00) (86) (23) 6381 0320
e-mail: bcgchq@public.cta.cq.cn
Office Hours (GMT): Mon - Fri 01 00 - 04 00 and
05 00 - 09 00
Consul General: Miss Carma Elliot
Consul: Mr Scott Strain

Hong Kong Special Administrative Region
British Consulate General
No. 1 Supreme Court Road, Central, Hong Kong,
(PO Box 528)
Telephone: (00) (852) 2901 3000
Facsimile: (00) (852) 2901 3066 Commercial
3007 Management
3008 Press and Public
Affairs
3204 Consular
3347 Visa
3420 Fiscal & Drugs
Liaison Office
3143 BC Passport
3195 Passport
3295 Airport Liaison
Office
e-mail: political@brisitshconsulate.org.hk Political
and Economic
commercial@britishconsulate.org.hk Commercial
management@britishconsulate.org.hk Management
press@britishconsulate.org.hk Press and Public
Affairs
consular@britishconsulate.org.hk Consular
visa@britishconsulate.org.hk Visa
passport@britshconsulate.org.hk Passport
Website: www.britishconsulate.org.hk
Office Hours (GMT): Mon - Fri: 00 30 - 09 15
Consul-General: Sir James Hodge, KCVO, CMG
Deputy Head of Mission and Director of Trade: Mr
Greg Dorey, CVO
Deputy Consul-General (Political/Economic): Ms
Barbara Ellington, OBE
*Deputy Consul-General (Security and Regional
Affairs):* Mr Malcolm Davies
Consul (Management): Mr Michael Hannant
Consul (Trade Commissioner): Miss Jean Sharpe, OBE
Consul (Trade Commissioner, Projects): Mr Nick
Khosla
Consul: Mr Bill Ridout
Fiscal & Drugs Liaison Officer: Mr Ken Newhouse
Consul (Press and Public Affairs): Mr Trevor Adams
Consul (Passports): Mr John Geoghegan
Airline Liaison Officer: Mrs Sandra Tilley
Consul (Political/Economic): Mr Tim Summers
Consul (Political/Economic): Miss Jane Elliott
Vice-Consul (Management): Mr Mark Forrester
Vice-Consul (Assistant Trade Commissioner): Mr
Malcolm Whatley
Vice-Consul (Technical Management): Mr Andrew
Friis
Vice-Consul (IT Management): Mr Paul Francis
Vice-Consul (Security Management): Mr Mike
Sanders
Vice Consul (Political/Economic): Mr Warren Pain
Vice-Consul (Economic/Finance): Ms Kirsty Paton
Vice-Consul (Political/Economic): Ms Sophie Gregg
Vice-Consul (Political/Economic): Mr Michael Blake

Vice-Consul (Security and Regional Affairs): Mrs
Deborah Forrester
Vice Consul (Visas): Mr Colin Green
Vice-Consul (Passports): Mrs Clarice Whiteside
Vice-Consul (Consular): Mr L B T Jackson
*Vice-Consul (Executive Assistant to the Consul
General):* Miss Gill Remmington

Invest - UK Regional Office
British Consulate General,
No 1 Supreme Court Road,
Central, Hong Kong, (PO Box 528)
Telephone: (00) (852) 2901 3266, 3367
Facsimile: (00) (852) 2901 3155
e-mail: investukasia@fco.gov.uk
Website: www.investukasia.org
Regional *Director:* Mr J Rutherford

FCO Procurement Group Hong Kong
2/F, 3 Supreme Court Road, Central, Hong Kong
Telephone: (00) (852) 2901 3488
Facsimile: (00) (852) 2901 3477
e-mail salesgphk@hongkong.mail.fco.gov.uk
Office Hours (GMT): Mon-Fri 00 15 - 09 30
General Manager: Mr C J Davis

Macau
British Consulate General
No. 1 Supreme Court Rd, Central, Hong Kong
PO Box 528
Telephone: (00) (852) 2901 3000
Facsimile: (00) (852) 2901 3066
Consul General (Resides at Hong Kong): Sir
James Hodge, KCVO, CMG
Deputy Consul-General (Resides at Hong Kong):
Ms B M Ellington, OBE
Consul (Resides at Hong Kong): Mr P A Robinson
*Vice-Consul (Commercial) (Resides at Hong
Kong):* Mr M G Whatley
Vice Consul (Resides at Hong Kong): Mr L B T
Jackson
Honorary Consul/General Manager: Mr Edward J
Machin
Est. Cheok Van R/C 13
Ed. hao Yuen
House Number 13
Coloane, Macau
Telephone: (00) (853) 882797
Facsimile: (00) (853) 850083

COLOMBIA

Bogotá
British Embassy
Edificio ING Barings
Carrera 9 No 76 - 49 Piso 9
Bogotá
Telephone: (00) (57) (1) 317 6690, 6310, 6321
Facsimile: (00) (57) (1) 317 6265 Management
Section
317 6523 Commercial
Section
317 6298 Political Section
317 6401 Visa/Consular
Section
Faxlok: 317 6534
e-mail: britain@cable.net.co

Office Hours (GMT): Mon-Thurs: 13 30 - 17 30
and 18 30 - 2130   Fri: 13 30 - 1830
Ambassador: Mr Tom Duggin
Deputy Head of Mission: Mr Russell Thomson
Counsellor: Mr Robert Church
*Counsellor (Cultural: British Council Director)
(Tel: 618 0118 ext 146):* Mr Joe Docherty
Defence Attaché: Colonel Robert J Griffiths, MBE
First Secretary: Mr Ray Tyler
First Secretary: Mr David Wright
First Secretary: Mr David Miller
First Secretary (Commercial): Mr Mel Cumming
First Secretary: Mr Stephen Reynolds
First Secretary (Management): Mr David Gardner
Second Secretary: Mr Robert Tinline
Second Secretary: Miss Moira Allen
Second Secretary (Immigration/Consular): Mr
Chris Wigginton
Second Secretary: Mr Andy Bonsey
Second Secretary: Mr Nigel Thomas
Second Secretary: Mr Hank Cole
Second Secretary: Mr Mark Sprawson
*Second Secretary (Education: British Council)
(Tel: 618 0175/218 7518):* Mr John Bryant MBE
*Second Secretary (Cultural: British Council)
(Tel: 618 0118):* Mr Richard Shackleton
Third Secretary (Management): Ms Jan Nicol
Third Secretary (Management): Miss Cindy Parker
Third Secretary (Immigration): Mrs Anesha Bayley
Third Secretary (Immigration): Miss Dawn Farr
Third Secretary: Mr David Brough

Cali
British Consulate
Calle 25 No 1N - 65 (Air Mail Box 1326)
Cali
Telephone/Facsimile: (00) (57) (2) 896 1235
e-mail: Britaincali@uniweb.net.co
Honorary-Consul: (Vacant)
Honorary Vice-Consul: Mr Peter Laurence
Consular Assistant: Ms Helen de Frappier

Medellín
British Consulate
Calle 49 No 46A Sur - 103, (Air Mail Box 3372)
Envigado, Medellín
Telephone: (00) (57) (4) 331 8625
Facsimile: (00) (57) (4) 331 0046
e-mail: Embajadabr@geo.net.co
Honorary-Consul: Mr Fernando Osorio
Consular Assistant: Ms Maria Mercedes Botero

COMOROS

Moroni
British Embassy (all staff resident in Madagascar)
Ambassador: Mr C F Mochan
Deputy Head of Mission: Ms R M Owens

Moroni
British Consulate - vacant

CONGO (THE DEMOCRATIC REPUBLIC OF)

Kinshasa
British Embassy
83 Avenue du Roi Baudouin,

Kinshasa
Telephone: (00) (243) 88 46102 (fax after 1330z)
Duty Officer: (00) (243) 88 46101
(00) (243) 88 01738 (fax after 1330z) DHM: (00)
(243) 88 44923
e-mail: ambrit@ic.cd
Office Hours (GMT): Mon -Thur 06 30 - 13 30;
Fri 06 30 - 13 00
Ambassador: Mr Jim Atkinson
Consul and Deputy Head of Mission: Mr Ken Price
Third Secretary (Consular/Management): Ms
Bernadette Wheeler
Defence Attaché: Lieutenant Colonel C Tim B
Brown

CONGO (THE REPUBLIC OF)

Brazzaville
British Embassy (all staff reside in Kinshasa)
Ambassador: Mr Jim Atkinson
Consul and *Deputy Head of Mission:* Mr Ken Price
Brazzaville
Ets LISA (à côté de DHL)
Avenue Fosch, Brazzaville
Telephone: (00) (242) 44904
(761) 480259 (satellite)
Facsimile: (00) (242) 838543
e-mail: yorick@congonet.cg
Honorary Consul: Mr Dominique Picard

COSTA RICA (SP)

San José
British Embassy
Apartado 815, Edificio Centro Colon,
(11th Floor), San José 1007
Telephone: (00) (506) 258 2025
Facsimile: (00) (506) 233 9938
e-mail: britemb@sol.racsa.co.cr
Office Hours (GMT) Mon-Thurs 14 00 - 22 00
Fri 14 00 - 19 00
Ambassador and Consul-General: Mr P J Spiceley,
MBE (Ms G S Butler w.e.f February 2002)
*First Secretary (Commercial) and Director of
Trade Promotion:* Mr C J Edge
Third Secretary, Vice-Consul and DHM: Mrs H
Johnson
Second Secretary (Resides in Panama City): Mr A
J Davenport

COTE D'IVOIRE

Abidjan
British Embassy
3rd Floor, Immeuble "Les Harmonies",
Angle Boulevard Carde et Avenue Dr Jamot,
Plateau, Abidjan
Postal Address: 01 BP 2581, Abidjan 01
Telephone: (00) (225) 20226850, 20226851,
20221092, 20226852, 20218209
Visa Section: (00) (225) 20217032
Facsimile: (00) (225) 20223221 Chancery
                         20220092 Commercial
                         20220438 Visa Section
Airtech: (00) (225) 20217036
e-mail: britemb.a@aviso.co
Website www.britaincdi.com

Office Hours (GMT): Mon - Thur 08 30 - 13 00
and 13 30 - 16 00   Fri 08 30 - 13 30
Ambassador: Mr J F Gordon, CMG
*First Secretary (Commercial), Consul and Deputy
Head of Mission:* Mr M J K Rickerd, MVO
Defence Attaché (resides Accra): Lieutenant
Colonel S K E Clarke, OBE
Second Secretary (Political/ Information): Ms K
Miller, MBE
Second Secretary (Management): Mr D Summers
Second Secretary (Commercial/Political): Mr C
Frean
Third Secretary Vice-Consul (Visas & Passports):
Mr M McGuinness
Third Secretary (Chancery): Ms N McBratney

**Abidjan   UK Representation at the African
Development Bank see part II**

CROATIA

Zagreb
British Embassy
Vlaska 121/III Floor, PO Box 454, 10001 Zagreb
Telephone: (00) (385) (1) 455 5310 (Switchboard)
615 6621/6623/6624/6625 (Visa & Consular)
Facsimile: (00) (385) (1) 455 1685
                          615 6628/6629 (Visa&
                                  Consular)
                          466 4379 (Political
                                  Section)
                          455 6304 (Commercial)
                          466 4090 (Development
                                  Section)
e-mail: british-embassy@zg.tel.hr
commercial.section@zg.tel.hr
Office Hours (GMT): Summer: 06 30 - 15 00
Mon-Thur
06 30 - 12 00 Fri
Winter: 07 30 - 16 00 Mon-Thur
07 30 - 13 00 Fri
Ambassador: Mr N R Jarrold
Deputy Head of Mission: Mr D J R Austin, OBE
Defence Attaché: Lieutenant Colonel R M Thornely
First Secretary (Commercial): Mr G Kirby
First Secretary (Political): Mr C M C Reeve
Second Secretary (Immigration): Ms F Maxton
Second Secretary (Development): Mr R A O Jones
Second Secretary (Management): Ms P J Clarke
Third Secretary (Political/PPA): Ms F Sinclair
Third Secretary (Vice-Consul): Mr R N Rose
Third Secretary (Immigration): Mr M J Davies
Third Secretary (Immigration): Ms J Duxbury
Assistant Defence Attaché: Sergeant S Marshall

Split
British Consulate
Obala Hrvatskog Narodnog Preporoda 10/III,
21000 Split
Telephone: (00) (385) (21) 341 464
Facsimile: (00) (385) (21) 362 905
e-mail: british-consulat-st@st.tel.hr
Office Hours (GMT): Summer: 06 30 - 13 30
Mon-Thur
06 30 - 11 00 Fri
July, August 05 30 - 12 30 Mon-Fri
Winter: 07 30 - 14 30 Mon-Thur

07 30 - 12 00 Fri
Honorary Consul: Captain A Roje
Pro Consul: Mrs S Kalebota

Dubrovnik
British Consulate
Atlas, Pile 1, 20000 Dubrovnik
Telephone/Facsimile: (00) (385) (20) 412 916
Office Hours (GMT): Summer: 08 00 - 11 00 Mon,
Tue, Thur & Fri
Winter: 09 00 - 12 00 Mon, Tue, Thur & Fri
Honorary Consul: Mrs S Marojica, MBE

CUBA

Havana
British Embassy
Calle 34 No. 702/4 entre 7ma Avenida y 17,
Miramar, Havana
Telephone: (00) (53) (7) 24-1771 Switchboard
Facsimile: (00) (53) (7) 24-8104 Consular/
                                  Management
                          24-9214 Commercial/
                                  Information
e-mail: embrit@ceniai.inf.cu (Embassy)
britcoun@ip.etecsa.cu (British Council)
Office Hours (GMT): Summer: 12 00 - 19 30
Winter: 13 00 - 20 30
Ambassador: Mr P Hare, LVO
First Secretary and Deputy Head of Mission: Mr J
D W Saville
Defence Attaché (resides at Caracas): Captain E F
Searle, RN
First Secretary (Commercial/Economic): Mr N D
Sutcliffe
First Secretary (Management) and Consul: Mr B
H Garside
*First Secretary (Science/Culture, British Council
Director):* Mr M White
First Secretary (resides at Kingston): Mr M Bragg
Second Secretary (Political/Information): Ms K G
L M Ward
Second Secretary (resides at Kingston): Mr K
Wiggins
Second Secretary (resides at Mexico City): Mr P
Haley
Attaché (Chief Security Officer): Mr J P Vowles, MBE
Third Secretary (Commercial/Immigration): Ms A
Carrick
Third Secretary (Aid/Political): Ms N Terrett
Attaché: Miss P A Langridge
Attaché: Ms K Robinson
Attaché (Works): Mr D Snooks

CYPRUS

Nicosia
British High Commission
Alexander Pallis Street (PO Box 21978), 1587
Nicosia or BFPO 567
Telephone: (00) (357) (2)
Facsimile: (00) (357) (2) 861125 Information
                          861315 Chancery
                          861175 Management
                          861200 Consular:
                          861150 Commercial
Airtech: 861287

e-mail: infobhc@cylink.com.cy
Office Hours (GMT): Mon - Fri 05 30 - 12 00
(Except Tue) Tue 05 30 - 11 00 and 12 00 - 15 30
High Commissioner: Mr Lyn Parker
Counsellor and Deputy High Commissioner: Mr Philip Barton, OBE
Defence Adviser: Colonel James Anderson
Counsellor (Political): Mr Paul Ritchie, OBE
First Secretary (Consular): Mr Gifford Harrison (tel; 861360)
First Secretary (Commercial): Mr Lawson Ross (tel; 861340)
First Secretary (Chancery): Mr Mick Bispham (tel; 861250)
First Secretary (Chancery): Mr Charlie Beckford (tel; 861220)
First Secretary (Management): Mr Roger Davies (tel; 861350)
Second Secretary (Chancery): Ms Bethan West (tel; 861251)
Second Secretary (Political): Mr Peter Boxer (tel; 861230)
Second Secretary (Chancery): Mr Emrys Tippett (tel, 861252)
Second Secretary (Chancery): Mr Troy Arnold (tel: 861231)
Second Secretary (Chancery/Information): Mr Jonathan Allen (tel; 862380)
Second Secretary (Political/Military): Ms Siân Jones
Second Secretary (resides in Tel Aviv): Mr Simon Gudgeon
Attaché (Consular): Mr Tony Boyce (tel; 861362)
Attaché (Consular): Ms Rosaleen Wotton (tel, 861362)
Attaché (Consular): Mr Ian Swann (tel; 861361)
Attaché (Consular): Mrs Jackie Brown (tel; 861364)
Attaché (Chancery): Mr Ian Hirchfield (tel; 861331)

Zygi
British East Mediterranean Relay Station
PO Box 4912, Limassol
Telephone: (00) (357) (4) 332511, 332341
Facsimile: (00) (357) (4) 332595, 332180
Office Hours (GMT): Mon - Fri 05 50 - 12 40
First Secretary (Management) (Resides in Nicosia): Mr Roger Davies

CZECH REPUBLIC

Prague
British Embassy
Chancery, Consular/Visa, Economic/Know How Fund
Information and Management Section, Defence Attaché
Thunovska 14,
118 00 Prague 1
Telephone: (00) (420) (2) 5753 0278 (5 lines)
Facsimile: (00) (420) (2) 5753 0285
e-mail: info@britain.cz
Airtech: (00) (420) (2) 5753 0275

Commercial Section
Palac Myslbek
Na Prikope 21
117 19 Prague 1
Telephone: (00) (420) (2) 2224 0021/2/3

Facsimile: (00) (420) (2) 2224 3625
e-mail: commerce@prague.mail.fco.gov.uk

British Council
Narodni 10,
125 01 Prague 1
Telephone: (00) (420) (2) 2491 2179/83
Facsimile: (00) (420) (2) 2491 3839
Telex: 122097 (a/b BCCZ C)
e-mail: forename.surname@britcoun.cz
Office Hours (GMT): end Oct - end Mar 07 30 - 16 00
Ambassador: Ms Anne Pringle
Counsellor and Deputy Head of Mission: Mr Denis Keefe
Defence Attaché: Colonel David A Wynne Davies
Cultural Attaché (British Council Director): Mr Paul Doherty
First Secretary (Commercial): Mr Martin Day
First Secretary (EU/Economic): Mrs Judith Gardiner
First Secreatry (Management/Consul): Mr Dick Coleman
First Secretary (Political/External): Mr Paul Coggles
British Council Assistant Director: Ms Elizabeth White
Assistant Defence Attaché: Squadron Leader Simon C Buckingham RAF
Second Secretary (Political/Press & Public Affairs): Mr Giles Portman
Second Secretary (Commercial): Mrs Karen Rae
Second Secretary (Commercial): Miss Harriet Fear
Second Secretary (resides at Vienna): Mr David Hollingbury
Second Secretary (resides at Vienna): Mr Ian Purvis
Third Secretary and Vice-Consul: Mr Nick Burns
Third Secretary (Commercial): Miss Kate Batty-Smith
Third Secretary (Political): Mr Karl Tluczek
Third Secretary (Political/EU): Mr Alan Caughey
Third Secretary (Management): Miss Tina Deaney

DENMARK

Copenhagen
British Embassy
Kastelsvej 36/38/40, DK-2100 Copenhagen Ø
Telephone: (00) (45) 35 44 52 00
Facsimile: (00) (45) 35 44 52 93 Information
Section
52 14 Political Section
52 46 Commercial
Department
52 53 Consular
52 59 Management
e-mail: www.brit-emb@post6.tele.dk
Office Hours (GMT): end Mar - end Oct 07 00 - 15 00 and end Oct - end Mar 08 00 - 16 00

Consular/Visa Section:
Consular: end Mar - end Oct 07 00 - 10 30 and 11 30 - 13 00
end Oct - end Mar 08 00 - 11 30 and 12 30 - 14 00
Visa: end Mar - end Oct 07 00 - 10 00
end Oct - end Mar 08 00 - 11 00
Commercial: end Mar - end Oct 06 30 - 10 30 and 11 30 - 14 30
end Oct - end Mar 07 30 - 11 30 and 12 30 - 15 30

British Council (Cultural Section)
Director: Dr Michael Sorensen-Jones
Gammel Mønt 12. 3. 1117 Copenhagen K
Telephone: (00) (45) 33 36 94 00
(Tel. Hours: 09 00 - 12 00, 13 00 - 15 30)
Educational Enquiries:
Telephone: (00) (45) 33 36 94 04
(Tel. Hours: 12 30 - 15 30)
e-mail: british.council@britishcouncil.dk
Ambassador: Mr P S Astley, LVO
Counsellor and Deputy Head of Mission: Mr P B Yaghmourian
Counsellor: Mr I I McMahon
Defence Attaché: Commander R P B Ayers RN
First Secretary (Commercial): Mr F J Martin
First Secretary (Political): Mr Peter Cook
First Secretary (Management) & Consul: Mr J T Fraser
Second Secretary (Political): Mr A Mace
Second Secretary (Political): Miss G G Sharp
Second Secretary (Technical/Management): Mr A Jones
Third Secretary (Political): Mr A Fehintola
Attaché (AMO/Vice-Consul): Miss B Pitts, MVO
Vice-Consul: Mrs J T Christoffersen
Vice-Consul: Mrs S Oxfeldt Jensen

Aabenraa
British Consulate
Turistchef
Turistbureauet
H.P. Hansens Gade 5
6200 Aabenraa
Telephone: (00) (45) 74 62 35 00
Facsimile: (00) (45) 74 63 07 44
Office Hours (GMT): 06 30 - 14 30
Honorary Consul: Mr W Klinker (Danish)

Aalborg
British Consulate
Hasserisvej 112
Postboks 23
9100 Aalborg
Telephone: 98 11 34 99
Facsimile: 98 11 56 99
Office Hours (GMT): 05 30 - 13 30
Honorary Consul: Mr J Bladt (Danish)

Aarhus
British Consulate
Skolegade 19B, 8100 Aarhus C
Telephone: 87 30 77 77
Facsimile: 87 30 77 07
Office Hours (GMT): 06 30 - 14 30
Honorary Consul: Mr C R Herluf (Danish)

Esbjerg
British Consulate
Kanalen 1, 6700 Esbjerg
Telephone: 79 11 19 00
Facsimile: 79 11 19 01
Office Hours (GMT): 06 30 - 14 00
Honorary Consul: Mr G Kragelund (Danish)

Fredericia
British Consulate
Vesthavnen, 7000 Fredericia

Telephone: 75 92 20 00
Facsimile: 76 20 29 80
Office Hours (GMT): 06 00 - 14 30
Honorary Consul: Mr M Rahbek Hansen (Danish)

Herning
British Consulate
Nr. Lindvej 35, 7400 Herning
Telephone: 97 22 02 88
Facsimile: 97 21 44 10
Office Hours (GMT): 06 30 - 14 30
Honorary Consul: Mr N C Jensen (Danish)

Odense
British Consulate
Albani Torv 4, Postboks 308
5100 Odense C
Telephone: 66 14 47 14
Facsimile: 66 14 61 30
Office Hours (GMT): 06 00 - 14 00
Honorary Consul: Mr F Niegel, MBE (Danish)

Rønne (Bornholm) - closed

Tórshavn (Faroe Islands)
British Consulate
Niels Finsensgøta 5,
P O Box 154
FR-110 Tórshavn,
Faroe Islands
Telephone: 298 35 99 77
Facsimile: 298 35 99 80
Office Hours (GMT): 09 00 - 17 00
Honorary Consul: Mr Tummas H Dam

DJIBOUTI
British Embassy (All staff resident at Addis Ababa)
Ambassador: Mr M A Wickstead
First Secretary (Management and Consul): Miss A Marriott, MBE
Second Secretary: Mr D J Williams

British Consulate
PO Box 169, Rue de Djibouti
Djibouti
Telephone (00) (253) (3) 35007
Facsimile: (00) (253) (3) 52543
e-mail: martinet@intnet.dj
Honorary Consul (Resident in Djibouti): Mr A Martinet

DOMINICA

Roseau
British High Commission
Lower Collymore Rock (PO Box 676),
Bridgetown, Barbados
Telephone: (00) (1) (246) 430 7800
Facsimile: (00) (1) (246) 430 7851 Chancery
(246) 430 7860 Management/Consular
(246) 430 7826 Commercial/Information
e-mail: britishhc@sunbeach.net
Office Hours (GMT) 12 00 – 16 30 and 17 30 – 20 00
High Commissioner: Mr J White
Deputy High Commissioner: Mr M J E Mayhew
Defence Adviser: Captain S C Ramm, RN
Counsellor (Regional Affairs): Mr N J L Martin

First Secretary (Chancery): Mr P Curwen
Second Secretary (Management/Consular): Mr G
I Brammer
High Commissioner's Special Representative: Mr
R C Morris
**Second Secretary:* Mr P Marshall
Third Secretary (Consular/Immigration): Ms S J
Verma
*Resides at Bridgetown **Resides at Kingston

Roseau
British Consulate
Office of the Honorary British Consul
c/o Courts (Dominica) Ltd
PO Box 2269, Roseau
Commonwealth of Dominica
Telephone: Office: (1 767) 448 7655
Facsimile: (1 767) 448 7817
Honorary Consul: Mr P Fletcher

DOMINICAN REPUBLIC

Santo Domingo
British Embassy
Ave 27 de Febrero No 233,
Edificio Corominas Pepin,
Santo Domingo, Dominican Republic
Telephone: (00) (1) (809) 472 7111
472 7905 (Commercial)
472 7373/7671 (Consular)
Facsimile: (00) (1) (809) 472 7190 (Chancery/
                                        Commerial)
                    472 7574 (Consular/
                                        Management)
Airtech: (00) (1) (809) 472 7475
e-mail: brit.emb.sadom@codetel.net.do
david.ward@sadom.mail.fco.gov.uk
sarah.hildersley@sadom.mail.fco.gov.uk
Office Hours (GMT): Mon-Thurs 12 30 - 21 00
Fri 12 30 - 17:30
Ambassador: Mr David Ward
Deputy Head of Mission: Ms Sarah Hildersley

Puerto Plata
British Consulate
Calle Beller No.51,
Puerto Plata, R.D.
Telephone: (00) (1) (809) 586-4244, 586-8464
Facsimile: (00) (1) (809) 586-3096
Honorary Consul: Mrs Cindy Salem

EAST TIMOR

Dili
British Mission
Bantai Kelapa (Avenida de Portugal)
Dili, East Timor
Telephone: (00) (61) 417 841 046 (British
                                        Representative)
                    408 010 991 (Deputy
                                        Representative)
Facsimile: (00) (670) 390 312 652
Airtech: (00) (870) 600 132 620
e-mail: dili.fco@gtnet.gov.uk
By Post: Bag via Jakarta or PO Box 358, Darwin,
NT 0801, Australia

Office Hours (GMT): Mon-Fri 23 30 - 03 30 and
04 30 - 08 45
British Representative: Jane Penfold
Deputy British Representative: Jo Pendered

ECUADOR

Quito (SP)
British Embassy
Citiplaza Building,
Naciones Unidas Ave and República de El
Salvador 14th Floor
(Consular Section 12th Floor)
Telephone: (00) (593) (2) 970 800 / 970 801
Facsimile: (00) (593) (2) 970 807 Consular
                        970 809 Commercial
                        970 810 Management
                        970 811 Chancery
P.O. Box: 17 – 17 - 830
e-mail: britembq@interactive.net.ec
Office Hours (GMT): Mon – Thur 13 30 - 17 30
and 18 30 - 22 00
Fri 13 30 - 18 30
Ambassador: Mr Ian Gerken, LVO
Consul and Deputy Head of Mission: Mr Patrick
Mullee
Cultural Attaché (British Council): Mr John Knagg
Defence Attaché (resides at Caracas): Captain
Edward F Searle, RN
Second Secretary (TC/Chancery): Mr Robin J
Shackell
Second Secretary: Mr Brian Corbett
Third Secretary (Management): Mr Martin G
Webber
Third Secretary (Vice-Consul): Miss Clare Spencer
Vice-Consul: Mr Uwe Roepke

Guayaquil
British Consulate
c/o Agripac
General Córdova 623 y Padre Solano,
PO Box 09-10-8598, Guayaquil
Telephone: (00) (593) (4) 560400, ext 318
Facsimile: (00) (593) (4) 562641
e-mail: carmstro@agripac.com.ec or
rtorres@agripac.com.ec
Office Hours (GMT): 14 30 - 18 00 and 20 00 -
23 00
Honorary Consul: Mr Colin R Armstrong, OBE
Honarary Vice Consul: Mrs Rocio Torres

Guayaquil
British Embassy - Trade Office
Torres del Norte Building,
Torre A, 5th Floor, Office 503
Kennedy Norte, Av. Miguel H. Alcivar,
Manzana 506,
Telephone: (00) (593) (4) 687112
Facsimile: (00) (593) (4) 687113
e-mail: britembg@interactive.net.ec
Office Hours (GMT): Mon-Thur: 13 30 - 17 30
and 18 30 - 22 00
Fri: 13 30 - 18 30

Galápagos
British Consulate
c/o Etica Office, Barrio Estrada,

Puerto Ayora, Isla Santa Cruz, Galápagos
Telephone: (00) (593) (5) 526157 / 526159
Facsimile: (00) (593) (5) 526591
Office Hours (GMT): 13 00 - 17 00 and 19 00 - 23 00
Honorary Consul: Mr David Balfour

EGYPT

Cairo
British Embassy
7, Ahmed Ragheb Street, Garden City, Cairo
Telephone: (00) (20) (2) 794 0850, 794 0852/8
Facsimile: 796 1458 Political,
      794 3065 Consular & Information
      794 0859 Commercial
      796 3222 Management
      795 1235 Visa
Airtech: 794 0850 (ext. 215)
e-mail: britemb@idsc.gov.eg
Website: www.britishembassy.org.eg
Office Hours (GMT): Sun-Wed: 05 30 - 12 30
Thur: 05 30 - 12 00
Ambassador: Mr John Sawers, CMG
Counsellor and Deputy of Mission: Mr Michael Gifford
Defence and Military Attaché: Colonel Peter E Dennison, OBE
Cultural Counsellor (British Council Director): Dr John Grote, OBE
Counsellor (Regional Affairs): Mr Graham J Ley
Naval and Air Attaché: Commander John A Barltrop, RN
First Secretary (Commercial): Mr Steven Wheeler
First Secretary & Head of Political & Economic Section: Mrs Jacqueline L Perkins
First Secretary (Cultural) & British Council Deputy Director: Mrs Ruth Addison
First Secretary and Consul: Mr Gordon Brown
First Secretary (Cultural): Mr Paul Morris
First Secretary (Regional Affairs): Mr Kareem Chaudhry
First Secretary (Technical Works Officer): Mr Ronald Clarke
First Secretary (Management): Mr Shaun Flaherty
Second Secretary (Aid): Mr Colin D Clark
Second Secretary (Commercial): Miss Jacqueline H Mullen
Second Secretary (Technical Management): Mr Simon Lochmuller
Second Secretary (Immigration): Mr James Marshall
Second Secretary (Cultural): Miss Samantha Harvey
Third Secretary (Political): Ms Caroline E Alcock
Third Secretary (Commercial): Ms Sheridan Grice
Deputy Management Officer: Ms Sarah Spencer
Attaché and Vice-Consul: Miss Helen L Collins
Attaché and Vice-Consul: Miss Stephanie Webb
Attaché and Vice-Consul: Mr Andrew Ziardis
Attaché: Mr Robert McCallum
Attaché: Mr Michael Whyte
Attaché: Mr Keith Squibb
Attaché: Mr Roger Clark
Attaché: Mrs Susan K Turunc
Attaché: Ms Sharon White
Attaché: Mr Colin Murray
Attaché: Mrs Ruth Whelan
Attaché: Ms Rebecca Jones

Alexandria (SP)
British Consulate-General
3 Mina Street, Kafr Abdou, Roushdi,
Ramley Alexandria, 21529
Telephone: (00) (20) (3) 5467001, 5467002
Facsimile: (00) (20) (3) 5467177
Office Hours (GMT): Sun - Wed: 05 30 - 12 30
Thur: 05 30 - 12 00
Consul-General: Mr Mark Stevens
First Secretary (Cultural Affairs and Director British Council): Ms Amanda Burrell

Suez
British Consulate
HS Supply Co.
9 El-Galaa Street, Suez
Telephone: (00) (20) (62) 334102 (Consulate & Office), 320727 (Home)
Telex: 66112 DRHSS UN
Facsimile: (00) (20) (62) 320729
Honorary Consul: Dr Hussein Samir

Luxor
British Honorary Consular Agent
Gaddis Hotel
Khaled Ibn El Walid St.
Luxor
Telephone: (00) (20) (95) 382838 (Consulate & Office), 374814 (Home)
Facsimile: (00) (20) (95) 380814, 382837
Mobile: 012 2327612, 012 3517441
Honorary Consular Agent: Mr Ehab Gaddis

EL SALVADOR

San Salvador
British Embassy
Edificio Inter-Inversiones, Paseo General Escalón
4828, PO Box 1591, San Salvador
Telephone: (00) (503) 263 6527, 263 6529, 263 6520
Facsimile: (00) (503) 263 6516
e-mail: britemb@sal.gbm.net
Office Hours (GMT): Mon-Thur 14 00 - 19 00,
20 00 - 22 30   Fri 14 00 - 19 00
Ambassador and Consul-General: Mr Patrick Morgan
Deputy Head of Mission and Vice-Consul: Mr Keith Allen
First Secretary (Commercial) and Director Of Trade Promotion for Central America (resides at San Jose): Mr Christopher J Edge
Defence Attaché (resides at Guatemala City): Colonel I C D Blair-Pilling OBE
DLO (resides at Panama City): Andy Davenport

EQUATORIAL GUINEA

Malabo
British Embassy (all staff reside at Yaounde)
Ambassador and *Consul-General:* Mr Peter Boon
First Secretary and Consul: Mr David Williams

ERITREA

Asmara
British Embassy (All staff resident at Addis Ababa)
Emperor Yohannes Avenue

House no 24
PO Box 5584 Asmara, Eritrea
Telephone: (00) (291) 1 12 01 45
Facsimile: (00) (291) 1 12 01 04
e-mail: alembca@gemel.com.er
Office Hours (GMT):11 00 - 3.30 and 4 30 - 7 30
Ambasssador: Mr M Wickstead
Defence Attaché (Resident in Nairobi): Colonel R J
Barnes
First Secretary: (Management and Consul): Miss
A M Marriott, MBE
Second Secretary: Mr D J Williams
Honorary Consul: (Resident in Asmara): Mr T
Thodensen

ESTONIA (SP)

Tallinn
British Embassy
Wismari 6
Tallinn 10136
Estonia
Telephone: (00) (372) 667 4700
Facsimile: (00) (372) 667 4755 (Political/HMA/
                                   DHM)
               667 4724 (Commercial/DFID
                          Programme Office)
               667 4756 (Management/
                          Defence)
               667 4725 (Consular/Visa)
e-mail: information@britishembassy.ee
Website: www.britishembassy.ee
Office Hours (GMT): Summer 06 00 - 14 00,
Winter 07 00 - 15 00
Ambassador: Mrs Sarah Squire
Deputy Head of Mission: Miss Ceinwen Jones
Defence Attaché (resides at Helsinki): Lieutenant
Colonel Patrick W Clarke
*First Secretary (British Council Director) (resides
at Riga):* Mr Ian Stewart
First Secretary (Political): Mr Pablo Miller
*Second Secretary (Technical Management)
(resides at Helsinki):* Mr Paul Jackson, MBE
Third Secretary (Management) and Consul: Mr
John Devine
Third Secretary (Politcal): Mr Richard Dewell
Third Secretary (Regional Affairs): Mr Simon Shaw
Commercial and Press Officer: Mrs Neve Hobemägi
Vice-Consul and ECO: Mr Lionel Khoo
Attaché and Archivist: Mr Alex Stalker-Booth

ETHIOPIA

Addis Ababa
British Embassy
Fikre Mariam Abatechan Street, Addis Ababa
Postal address: Post Office Box 858
Telephone: (00) (251) 1 612354
Facsimile: (00) (251) 1 610588
1 614154 Consular and Visa Section
e-mail: b.emb4@telecom.net.et
Office Hours (GMT): Mon-Thurs 05 00 - 13 30
Fri 05 00 - 10 00
Consular /Visa Section Public Opening Hours:
Mon-Fri 05 30 - 09 00
Ambassador: Mr Myles Wickstead

First Secretary and Deputy Head of Mission: Ms
Di Skingle
Defence Attaché (Resides at Nairobi): Colonel R J
Barnes
First Secretary (Management) and Consul: Miss
Allison M Marriott, MBE
Second Secretary (Aid): Dr Nick Taylor
British Military Liaison Officer: Lieutenant
Colonel Charles Comyn
Cultural Attaché (British Council Director): Ms
Rosemary Arnott, OBE
Assistant Cultural Attaché (British Council): Mr
Simon Winetroube
Second Secretary (Political): Mr David J Williams
Second Secretary (Political/Information): Miss
Laura Williams
Attaché and Vice-Consul: Mr Ian Crammen

FIJI ISLANDS

Suva
British High Commission
Victoria House
47 Gladstone Road
Suva
Fiji Islands (PO Box 1355)
Telephone: (00) (679) 311033
Facsimile: (00) (679) 301406
Airtech: (00) (679) 305035
e-mail: Public Affairs: ukinfo@bhc.org.fj
Commercial Office: uktrade@bhc.org.fj
Consular & Management Sections:
ukconsular@bhc.org.fj
e-mail for individual officers – insert:
firstname.surname + @suva.mail.fco.gov.uk
Website: http://www.ukinthepacific.bhc.org.fj
Office Hours (GMT): Sun -Wed 20 15 - 01 00 and
02 00 - 05 00
Thurs 20 15 - 01 00
*High Commissioner, also Pitcairn Alternate
Representative for the South Pacific Commission;
non-resident High Commissioner to Nauru, Kiribati
and Tuvalu:*Mr Michael A Price, LVO (Ext 120)
*Deputy High Commissioner; also non-resident
Ambassador to Micronesia, Marshall Islands and
Palau; Deputy High Commissioner to Nauru,
Kiribati and Tuvalu:* Mr Christopher Haslam
(ext 122)
Defence Adviser (resides at Wellington): Colonel A
A Peebles
*Second Secretary (Political, Press & Public
Affairs) Deputy Head of Mission and Consul to
Micronesia, Marshall Islands and Palau:* Mr
Malcolm Russell (ext110)
*Third Secretary (Management/Consular/
Immigration):* Miss Angela Morgan (Ext 105)

**Department for International Development,
Pacific**
Vanua House,
Victoria Parade (Private Mail Bag)
Suva
Fiji Islands
Telephone: (00) (679) 301 744
Facsimile: (00) (679) 301 218

e-mail for individual officers - insert first initial-
surname + @dfid.gov.uk (eg j-
creighton@dfid.gov.uk)
Head DFID Pacific: Ms J Creighton
Deputy Head: DFID Pacific: Mr J Medhurst
Regional Educational Adviser: Mr I Collingwood
Governance Fund Manager: Mr L Chan

FINLAND

Helsinki
British Embassy
Itainen Puistotie 17, 00140
Helsinki
Telephone: (00) (358) (9) 2286 5100
Telefax: Political Section (00) (358) (9) 2286 5284
All other Sections (00) (358) (9) 2286 5262,5272
e-mail: info@ukembassy.fi
Office Hours (GMT): Sep-Apr: 07 00 - 15 00
Apr-Aug: 06 30 - 14 00
Ambassador: Ms Alyson Bailes, CMG
Counsellor and Deputy Head of Mission: Mr R A
Cambridge
Counsellor (Political): Mr T I Priest
Defence Attaché: Lieutenant Colonel P W Clarke
First Secretary (Political/EU): Mr D Borland
First Secretary (Commercial): Mr M Towsey
*First Secretary (Inward Investment) (Resident in
Stockholm):* Mr M Cronin
First Secretary (Management and Consul): Mr J P
G Woodrow
Second Secretary (Commercial): Mr S Rebecchi
Second Secretary (Political/Information): Miss V
Harrison
Second Secretary (Management/Technical): Mr P
M Jackson, MBE
*Third Secretary/Vice-Consul/ Assistant Mangement
Officer:* Mr S M Anderson
Attaché: Miss S Burden
Chaplain: Rev. R Moreton

Jyväskylä
British Consulate
Valmet Corporation, Corporate Head Office
Rautpohjankatu, PO Box 587
40101 Jyväskylä
Telephone: (00) (358) (204) 82150
Telefax: (00) (358) (204) 826526
Honorary Consul: Mr H Siztanen (Finnish)

Kotka
British Consulate
Port Authority of Kotka, Laivurinkatu 7,
48100 Kotka
Telephone: (00) (358) (5) 234 4281
Telefax: (00) (358) (5) 218 1375
Honorary Consul: Mr L I Arminen (Finnish)

Kuopio
British Consulate
Kolari, Heikinheimo,Palsola and Reinikainen, Oy
Kauppakatu 39 A
70100 Kuopio
Telephone: (00) (358) (17) 265 7777
Telefax: (00) (358) (17) 261 1085
Honorary Consul: Mr H A Palsola (Finnish)

Åland Islands
British Consulate
Köpmansgatan 12
22100 Mariehamn, Aland Islands
Telephone: (00) (358) (18) 13591,47720
Telefax: (00) (358) (18) 13196
Honorary Consul: Mr B H Olofsson (Finnish)

Oulu
British Consulate
Stora Enso Fine Paper Oy
PO Box 196, 90101 Oulu
Telephone: (00) (358) (204) 63373
Telefax: (00) (358) (204) 633649
Honorary Consul: Mr J Vanhainen (Finnish)

Pori
British Consulate
United Sawmills Ltd, PO Box 66, Antinkatu 2,
28101 Pori
Telephone: (00) (358) (204) 164002, 164000
Telefax: (00) (358) (204) 16132
Honorary Consul: Mr K J Anttilainen (Finnish)

Tampere
British Consulate
Pirkanmaan Työvoima-ja
Elinkeinokeskus
Kauppakatu 4
PO Box 467
33101 Tampere
Telephone: (00) (358) (3) 256 5701
Telefax: (00) (358) (3) 256 5739
Honorary Consul: Mrs R K Varpe (Finnish)

Turku
British Consulate
Turun Kauppakamari, Puolalankatu 1,
20100 Turku
Telephone: (00) (358) (2) 274 3410
Telefax: (00) (358) (2) 274 3440
Honorary Consul: Mr Jari Lahteenmaki (Finnish)

Vaasa
British Consulate
Kotipizza Oy
Hovioikeudenpuistikko 11,
65100 Vaasa
Telephone: (00) (358) (6) 2822 000
Telefax: (00) (358) (6) 2822 055
Honorary Consul: Mr R Grönblom (Finnish)

FRANCE

Paris
British Embassy
35 rue du Faubourg St. Honoré, 75383
Paris Cedex 08
Telephone: (00) (331) 44 51 31 00
Facsimile: (00) (331) 44 51 34 83 Ambassadors
Office/Chancery
32 88 Management
34 01 Commercial
32 34 Press and Public
Affairs
34 85 Political/
Economic

34 40 Defence/
Technology
31 27 Consular
31 28 Visa
Telephone: (00) (331) 49 55 73 00 British Council
Facsimile: (00) (331) 47 05 77 02 British Council
Website: http://www.amb-grandebretagne.fr
Office Hours (GMT): Summer 08 30 - 12 00 and
13 30 - 17 00
Winter 09 30 - 13 00 and 14 30 - 18 00
Ambassador: Sir John Eaton Holmes, KBE, CVO, CMG
Minister: Mr Stephen F Howarth
Defence/Air Attaché: Air Commodore Chris J
Blencowe, RAF
Naval Attaché: Captain Allan A S Adair, RN
Military Attaché: Brigadier Roy E Ratazzi, CBE
Counsellor (Political): Mr Simon J Fraser
Counsellor: Mr Nigel A R Backhouse
Counsellor (Finance and Economic): Mr David
Frost
Counsellor (Trade, Promotion and Investment): Mr
Stephen E Bradley
Counsellor (Management): Mr Ian R Whitehead
Counsellor (Cultural) (British Council Director):
Mr John Tod
Counsellor (Technology): Mr Rupert Huxter
First Secretary and Consul-General: Mr Stuart
Gregson
First Secretary (Political): Mr Richard D Spearman
First Secretary (Political/Internal): Mr Angus
Lapsley
First Secretary (Political): Mr Paul Arkwright
First Secretary (Political): Mr Stuart Gibby
First Secretary (Economic): Mr David I Bendor
First Secretary (Commercial): Mr Philip Shaw
First Secretary (Economic): Ms Joanna Kuenssberg
First Secretary (International Finance): Mr
Christopher D Steele
*Cultural Attaché (British Council Deputy
Director):* Mr Roger Budd
First Secretary (Agriculture): Mr David C Barnes
First Secretary (Science and Technology): Mr
Andrew P Holt
First Secretary (PPA): Mr Richard de R Morgan
First Secretary/Defence Equipment: Mr Mark Bason
First Secretary /Defence Procurement: Mr Robin C
B Little
First Secretary (Management): Mr Peter Duffy
First Secretary and Consul: Mr Michael R Foord
Assistant Air Attaché: Wing Commander Graham I
August, RAF
First Secretary (Labour and Social Affairs): Ms
Helen Pilkington
First Secretary (Management): Mr Brian Farnham
Second Secretary (Political): Mr Peter Hill
Second Secretary (Political): Miss Alexandra
Martens
Second Secretary (Commercial): Mr John
Greengrass, MBE
Second Secretary (Technology): Mr Alistair W J Kerr
Second Secretary (Technical Management Officer):
Mr Alexander Bennett
Second Secretary (Labour and Social Affairs): Ms
Claire Etches
Second Secretary (PPA): Mrs Phillipa Thompson
Second Secretary: Mr Joe F Griffin

Private Secretary: Mr Nicolas Hailey
Third Secretary (Management): Mr Mark D Korad
Third Secretary (Passports): Mrs Gillian Roberts
Visits Officer: Mrs Bridget O'Kelly / Mrs Marina
Pettigrew
Third Secretary (Commercial): Mrs Sarah J Morris

**Paris   British Consulate General (see entry
under Paris below)**

**Paris   United Kingdom Delegation to OECD,
see part II**

**Paris United Kingdom Delegation to UNESCO,
see part II**

**Strasbourg   United Kingdom Delegation to
Council of Europe, see part II**

Biarritz
British Consulate
"Askenian"
7 Boulevard Tauzin
64200 Biarritz
Telephone: (00) (335) 59 24 21 40
Facsimile: (00) (335) 59 22 33 27
Honorary Consul: Mr Robert Hope, MBE

Bordeaux
British Consulate-General
353 Boulevard du President Wilson,
33073 Bordeaux Cedex
Telephone: (00) (335) 57 22 21 10
Facsimile: (00) (335) 56 08 33 12
e-mail: gb@bordeaux.mail.fco.gov.uk
Office Hours (GMT): Summer: 07 00 - 10 30 and
12 00 - 15 30
Winter: 08 00 - 11 30 and 13 00 - 16 30
Consul-General: Mr James Rawlinson
Consul (Commercial): Mr Alastair Roberts, MBE
Vice-Consul: Mr Paul Dixon

Toulouse
Hon British Consul
Victoria Center
20 Chemin de Laporte
31300 Toulouse
Telephone: (00) (335) 61 15 02 02
Facsimile: (00) (335) 61 15 08 92
Honorary Consul: Mr Roger Virnuls, MBE

Lille
British Consulate-General
11 Square Dutilleul, 59800 Lille
Telephone: (00) (33) 3 20 12 82 72
Facsimile: (00) (33) 3 20 54 88 16
Airtech: (00) (33) 3 20 54 46 15
Office Hours (GMT): Summer 07 30 - 10 30 and
12 00 - 15 00
Winter 08 30 - 11 30 and 13 00 - 16 00
Consul-General: Miss Monica Harper
Vice-Consul (Commercial): Mr David Hinchliffe
Vice-Consul (Commercial): Mr John Gleave
Vice-Consul: Mrs Carol Vorobieff, MBE

Amiens
c/o Ecole Superieure de Commerce
18 Place Saint Michel, 80000 Amiens
Telephone: (00) (33) 3 22 72 08 48

Facsimile: (00) (33) 3 22 82 23 01
Office Hours (GMT): Summer 06 30 - 10 30 and
12 00 - 16 00
Winter 07 30 - 11 30 and 13 00 - 17 00
Honorary British Consul: Mr Roger Davis

Boulogne-sur-Mer
British Consulate
c/o Cabinet Barron et Brun, 28 rue Saint Jean
62200 Boulogne-sur-Mer
Telephone: (00) (33) 3 21 87 16 80
Facsimile: (00) (33) 3 21 91 30 30
Office Hours (GMT): Summer 06 00 - 10 00 and
12 00 - 16 00
Winter 07 00 - 11 00 and 13 00 - 17 00
Honorary Consul: Mr Gerard Barron, MBE

Calais
British Consulate
c/o P&O Stena Line, 20 rue du Havre,
62100 Calais
Telephone: (00) (33) 3 21 96 33 76
Facsimile: (00) (33) 3 21 19 43 69
Office Hours (GMT): Summer 06 30 - 16 00
Winter 07 30 - 17 00
Honorary Consul: Mr Jean-Michael Inglis, MBE

Dunkirk
British Consulate
c/o Lemaire Freres & Fils
Chaussee des Darses
Mole 1 - Batiment M _
Quai Freycinet 3
59376 Dunkerque
Telephone: (00) (33) 3 28 66 11 98
Facsimile: (00) (33) 3 28 59 09 99
Office Hours (GMT): Summer 06 30-10 00 and
1200-1600
Winter 07 30-11 00 and 1300-1700
Honorary Consul: Mr Christopher R Baker, MBE

Lyon
British Consulate-General
24 rue Childebert, 69002 Lyon
Telephone: (00) 4 72 77 81 70
Facsimile: (00) 4 72 77 81 79
Airtech: (00) 4 78 38 27 77
Office Hours (GMT): Summer 07 00 - 10 30 and
12 00 - 15 30
Winter 08 00 - 11 30 and 13 00 - 16 30
Consul-General: Mr Jonathon Noakes
Consul (Commercial): Mr Graham B Romaine
Vice-consul (Commercial): Mrs Françoise Holl
Vice-consul: Mrs Jeannie Labaye

Marseille (SP)
British Consulate-General
24 Avenue de Prado, 13006 Marseilles
Telephone: (00) (33) (4) 91 15 72 10
Facsimile: (00) (33) (4) 91 37 47 06
Airtech: (00) (33) (4) 91 57 16 38
Office Hours (GMT): Summer 07 00 - 10 30 and
12 00 - 15 30
Winter 08 00 - 11 30 and 13 00 - 16 30
Consul-General (also for Monaco): Mr Ian Davies
Consul (Commercial): Mr Jo J Patanchon, MBE
Vice-Consul: Mrs Donna Faure

Nice
British Consulate
"Le Palace",Entrée A, 8 Rue Alphonse Karr,
06000 Nice
Telephone: (00) (33) (4) 93 82 32 04
Facsimile: (00) (33) (4) 93 82 48 24
Honorary Consul: Ms Simone J Paissoni

Perpignan
British Consulate
Honorary British Consul: (Vacant)

Montpellier (HC)
British Consulate-General
271 Le Capitole Bat A, 64 Rue Alcyone,
34000 Montpellier
Telephone/Facsimile: (00) (33) (4) 67 15 52 07
Honorary British Consul: Mr Norman J Paget

Paris
British Consulate-General
18bis rue d'Anjou 75008 Paris
(All mail should be sent to the British Embassy,
Paris)
Telephone: (00) (331) 44 51 31 00
Facsimile: (00) (331) 44 51 31 27
          (00) (331) 44 51 31 28 (Visas)
Office Hours (GMT): 07 30 - 11 00 and 12 30 - 16
00 (Summer)
08 30 - 12 00 and 13 30 - 17 00 (Winter)
Consul-General: Mr Stuart W Gregson
Consul: Mr Michael R Foord
Vice Consul: Mr Steven J Donnelly, MBE
Vice Consul (Passport Officer): Mrs Gillian Roberts
Vice Consul (Immigration): Mr Bill Hadley
Vice Consul (Immigration): Mr Christopher H
Thornett
Vice Consul (Immigration): Mr Frederick Cracknell
Vice Consul: Mr Simon M Taylor
Vice Consul: Mr Mark Pettigrew

Cherbourg
British Consulate
P&O European Ferries, Gare Maritime
Transmanche,
BP 46
50652 Cherbourg Cedex
Telephone: 02 33 88 65 60
Facsimile: 02 33 88 67 07
Honorary Consul: Mr Gerard R Caron, MBE

French Guiana (Cayenne)
16 avenue Président Monnerville, BP 211
97324 Cayenne
Telephone: (00) (594) 311034
Facsimile: (00) (594) 304094
Honorary Consul: Mr Joseph G Nouh-Chaia, MBE

French Polynesia (Papeete)
British Consulate
Propriété Boubée, Route Pinae Tane,
Pirae - Tahiti
BP 1064 Papeete, 98114 Tahiti
Telephone: (00) (689) 424355 Home
419841 Office
Facsimile: 412700
Honorary Consul: Mr Robert J Withers

Nantes
British Consulate
16 Boulevard Guist'Hau
BP 22026
44020 Nantes
Telephone: 02 51 72 72 60
Facsimile: 02 40 47 36 92
Office Hours (GMT): 07 00 - 10 15 and 12 00 -
15 00
Honorary Consul: Mrs Angela M Stokes

St Malo-Dinard
British Consulate – 'La Hulotte'
8 bd des Marechaux
35800 Dinard
Telephone: 02 99 46 26 64
Facsimile: 02 99 16 09 26
Honorary Consul: Mr Ronald Frankel, MBE

Le Havre
British Consulate
c/o P&O European Ferries
Terminal de la Citadelle – B.P. 439
76057 Le Havre Cedex
Telephone: 02 35 19 78 88
Facsimile: 02 35 19 78 98
Honorary Consul: Mme Nadine H Corbel

Lorient
British Consulate
c/o Plastimo
15 Rue Ingénieur Verrière
56325 Lorient Cedex
Telephone: (00) (2) 97 87 36 20
Facsimile: (00) (2) 97 87 36 49
Honorary Consul: Mr Anthony M Le Saffre

Saumur
Chateau de Chaintre
49400 Dampiers Sur Loire
Telephone: (00) 2 41 52 90 54
Facsimile: (00) 2 41 52 99 92
Consular Agent: Mr Khrisna C Leister

Martinique (Fort de France)
British Consulate
Route du Phare, 97200 Fort de France,
Martinique FWI
Telephone: (00) (596) 618892
Facsimile: (00) (596) 613389
Honorary Consul: Mme Alison J Ernoult

Guadeloupe
British Consulate
23 Rue Sadi Carnot
197110 Pointe-à-Pitre
Telephone: (00) (590) 825757
Facsimile: (00) (590) 828933
Honorary Consul: Mr David A Wood

La Réunion
British Consulate
Honorary Consul: (Vacant)
New Caledonia
British Consulate
BP 362, 98845 Noumea Cedex,
Nouvelle Caledonie
Telephone: (00) (687) 282153

Facsimile: (00) (687) 285144
Honorary Consul: Mrs Hilary Shekleton

Tours
British Consulate
7 Route des Rosiers
37510 Savonnieres
Telephone/Facsimile: 02 47 43 50 58
Honorary Consul: Mr Brian J Cordery, OBE

GABON

Libreville
British Embassy (except where shown all staff
reside at Yaoundé)
Ambassador and Consul-General: Mr Peter Boon
First Secretary and Consul: Mr David Williams
Defence Attaché (resides at Kinshasa): Lieutenant
Colonel C Tim B Brown

British Consulate
c/o Brossette, BP 486,
Libreville
Telephone: (00) (241) 76 22 00/74 20 41
Facsimile: (00) (241) 76 57 89
Mobile: (00) (241) 75 86 36
Honorary Consul: Mr David Harwood, MBE

GAMBIA, THE

Banjul
British High Commission
48 Atlantic Road, Fajara (PO Box 507), Banjul
Telephone: (00) (220) 495133, 495134
Facsimile: (00) (220) 496134
Airtech: (00) (220) 494505
e-mail: bhcbanjul@gamtel.gm
Office Hours (GMT): Mon-Thurs 08 00 - 15 00
and Fri 08 00 - 13 00
High Commissioner: Mr J Perrott
Deputy High Commissioner: Mr B Joshi
Third Secretary (Management/Consular): Mr C
Barratt
Third Secretary (Immigration): Mr S Percival

DFID Office
c/o Britsh High Commission
Banjul
Telephone: (00) (220) 497537
Facsimile: (00) (220) 494127
e-mail: mmdfid@qanet.gm
Head of DFID Office: Mrs M Morrison

GEORGIA

Tbilisi
British Embassy
Sheraton Metechi Palace Hotel,
380003 Tbilisi
Telephone: (00) (995 32) 955497, 998447, 988796
Facsimile: (00) (995 32) 001065
Airtech: (00) (995 32) 775030
e-mail: british.embassy@caucasus.net
Office Hours (GMT): Mon-Fri 04 00 - 12 00
Ambassador: Ms D Barnes-Jones
Deputy Head of Mission: Mr D S McLaren
Defence Attaché: Wing Commander A W Kerr, RAF
First Secretary (Cultural): Mrs J Bakowski

Second Secretary (Political): Mr B Critchley
Second Secretary (Technical Management) (based in Ankara): Mr C Fox
Third Secretary (Management/Vice Consul): Mr P W Ford
Attaché (Immigration): Ms K Moss
Defence Assistant: Staff Sergeant T Storer

GERMANY

Berlin
British Embassy
Wilhelmstrasse 70
10117 Berlin
Telephone: (00) (49) (30) 20457-0
Facsimile: (00) (49) (30) 20457-571 (Ambassador)
20457-572 (DHM's Office)
20457-573 (Political)
20457-574 (Media)
20457-594 (Public Relations)
20457-575 (EU & Economics)
20457-576 (Labour & Social Affairs & Environment)
20457-577 (Commercial)
20457-578 (Management)
20457-579 (Consular)
20457-581 (Defence)
20457-582 (Defence Supply)
Website: http://www.britischebotschaft.de
Office Hours (GMT): 08 00 - 12 00 and 13 00 - 16 30

British Embassy Bonn Office
Argelanderstrasse 108a
53115 Bonn
Telephone: (00) (49) (228) 9167-0
Facsimile: (00) (49) (228) 9167 241 (Management/ General)
163 (Agriculture/ Economic)
264 (Research/ Technology)
277 (Fiscal Liaison)
Office Hours (GMT): 08 00 – 12 00 and 13 00 – 16 30
Ambassador: Sir Paul Lever, KCMG (101)
Deputy Head of Mission and Head of Political & Public Affairs: Mr Jeremy Cresswell (151)
Counsellor (Global Issues): Mr Martin Clements (451)
Counsellor (Research & Technology): Mr J Farrel (Resides Munich)
Defence & Military Attaché: Brigadier Brian Isbell (401)
Counsellor and Head of Defence Supply Section: Mr Trevor Strong (421)
Counsellor and Head of EU and Economic Section: Mr Leigh Turner (301)
Counsellor (Labour): Miss Elaine Trewartha (310)

First Secretary (Economic): Mr Mike Bolton (321)
First Secretary (Political External): Mr Nat Dawbarn (221)
First Secretary (Environment): Ms Catrione Garrett (341)
First Secretary (Research And Technology): Ms Helen Hughes-McKay (Bonn Office)
First Secretary (Political/External): Mr Nigel Ingram (222)
First Secretary (Technical Management): Mr Bob Jones (521)
First Secretary and Head of Media: Mr Alp Mehmet, MVO (251)
Air Attaché: Group Captain J P Moloney, RAF (405)
First Secretary (Fiscal Liaison Officer): Mr Steve Muchall (241)
First Secretary (Political Internal): Mr Hugh Powell (211)
First Secretary (Political External): Ms Patricia Ramsey (223)
First Secretary and Head of Commercial Section: Mr Dominic Schroeder (451)
First Secretary (European Union): Ms Susannah Simon (331)
First Secretary (Head of Public Relations): Ms Susan Speller (253)
First Secretary (Agriculture): Mr Gareth Steel (Bonn Office)
First Secretary and Head of Management: Mr Ramsey Tonkin (501)
Naval Attaché: Captain Dickon Wilkinson, RN (403)
Second Secretary (Technical Management): Mr Peter Bishop (522)
Assistant Defence Attaché: Major Nigel Dunkley, MBE (407)
Second Secretary (European Union): Mrs Sophie Goodrick (332)
Second Secretary (Defence Supply): Mr Terry Hughes (423)
Second Secretary (Political Internal): Mr Andrew Massey (212)
Second Secretary (Bilateral Relations): Mr Paul Parish (224)
Second Secretary (Fiscal Liaison Officer): Mr Steve Pope (Bonn Office)
Second Secretary (Estate Management): Miss Helen Roscoe (531)
Second Secretary (PS/Ambassador): Mr Jonathan Walters (102)
Third Secretary (Consular/Management): Mrs Trudi Curry (541)
Third Secretary (Management): Mr Les Jones (551)

Leipzig
British Trade Office
Gohliser Str 7
0-04105 Leipzig
Telephone: (00) (49) 0341 564 9672, 564 9674
Facsimile: (00) (49) 0341 564 9673
Commercial Officer: Frau K Rath
Commercial Assistant: Frau Pia Mann

Düsseldorf
British Consulate-General
Yorckstrasse 19, 40476 Düsseldorf

(Mail from United Kingdom only can be sent to Box 2002, BFPO 105)
Telephone: (00) (49) (211) 9448-0 (Switchboard) + (see officers individual extensions below)
Direct Lines: 9448 234 Passport Section
9448 260 Visa Section:
9448 222 Commercial Section
9448 245 Press and Public Affairs
Facsimile: (00) (49) (211) 48 63 59 Commercial & Investment Sections
48 81 90 Press, Passport, Consular and Management
48 86 03 Visa Section
Airtech: 94 48 242
e-mail:
Consular.Section@duesseldorf.mail.fco.gov.uk (Passport Section)
Visa.Section@duesseldorf.mail.fco.gov.uk (Visa Section)
Commercial.Section@duesseldorf.mail.fco.gov.uk (Commercial Section)
Website: www.british-consulate-general.de
www.british-passports.de (for British nationals resident in Germany)
www.british-visas.de
www.britische-handelsfoerderung.de (trade and investment promotion in Germany)
Office Hours (GMT): Winter: Mon-Thurs 07 30 - 11 30 and 12 30 - 16 00
Fri 07 30 - 11 30 and 12 30 - 15 30
Summer: Mon-Thurs 06 30 - 10 30 and 11 30 - 15 00
Fri 06 30 - 10 30 and 11 30 - 14 30
Consul-General and Director of Trade and Investment in Germany (201): Mr W Boyd McCleary
Deputy Consul-General and Deputy Director for Trade and Investment in Germany (202): Mr Richard D Folland
Consul (Commercial/Investment) (203): Mr John G Hall
Consul (Management) (231): Mr John K Hague
Consul (Commercial/CCU) (206): Mr Ralph Morton
Consul (Consular/Immigration) (260): Ms Creena M Lavery
Vice-Consul (Commercial) (208): Mr Ed Noble
Vice-Consul (Immigration) (264): Mr Tony R Salter
Vice-Consul (Consular/ Passports) (226): Miss Natalie L Hearn
Vice-Consul (Immigration) (267): Mr Sean M Rooney
Vice-Consul (Consular) (255): Mr David Kelly
Pro-Consul (Passports) (234): Mr Howard J Bevan
Commercial Officer (209): Ms Annette Klerks
Commercial Officer (213): Mr Peter Foster
Commercial Publicity (243): Mr Hans Kleyenstüber
Inward Investment (205): Mr Christian Fehling
Press and Public Affairs (223): Mrs Laura Heidgen

Frankfurt
British Consulate-General
Triton Haus
Bockenheimer Landstrasse 42,

60323 Frankfurt-am-Main
Telephone: (00) (49) (69) 1700020
Facsimile: (00) (49) (69) 729553
Office Hours (GMT): Winter: 07 30 - 12 00 and 13 00 - 16 00
Summer: 06 30 - 11 00 and 12 00 – 15 00
Consul-General: Mr W N C Paterson
Consul (Financial): Mr J A A Arrowsmith
Consul (Consular/Management): Mrs C A Schumann
Vice-Consul: Mr C Shepherd
Commercial Officer: Herr R Schneider
Commercial Officer: Frau S Schnurbusch
Press and Public Affairs Officer: Dr W Dobler
Attaché: Mr A Dean
Attaché: Mr D Connelly
(Visa and Passport work is centralised in Dusseldorf.)

Hamburg
British Consulate-General
Harvestehuder Weg 8a, 20148 Hamburg
Telephone: (00) (49) (40) 448 0320
Facsimile: (00) (49) (40) 410 7259
Airtech: (00) (49) (40) 448 032 31
Office Hours (GMT): Summer: 06 30 - 10 30 and 11 30 - 15 00
Winter: 07 30 - 11 30 and 12 30 - 16 00
Consul-General: Mr Douglas McAdam
Consul: Mr Anthony J Hackett
Vice-Consul (Consular): Mrs Mary Sanderson
Commercial Officer: Herr Thomas Siems
Commercial Officer: Mr John Holway
Commercial Officer: Herr Bernd Klein
Press & Public Affairs Officer: Ms Jo Dawes
(Visa and Passport work is centralised in Dusseldorf.)

Bremen
British Consulate
Herrlichkeiten 6, Postfach 10 38 60, 28199 Bremen
Telephone: (00) (49) (421) 590708
Facsimile: (00) (49) (421) 5907109
Office Hours (GMT): Summer: 06 30 - 10 30 and 12 30 - 13 30
Winter: 07 30 - 11 30 and 13 30 - 14 30
Honorary Consul: Herr H-C Enge

Hanover
British Consulate
Hannover Ruchversicherungs AG
Karl-Wiechart-Allee 50
30625 Hannover
Telephone: (00) (511) 3883808
Facsimile: (00) (511) 5604690
Office Hours (GMT): 06 30 - 10 00 and 10 30 - 12 00
Honorary Consul: Herr W Zeller

Kiel
British Consulate
United Canal Agency GmbH
Schleuse, Maklerstrasse 11-14, 24159 Kiel
Telephone: (00) (49) 431 331971
Facsimile: (00) (49) 431 3053746
Telex: 299829 (a/b UBCK D)
Office (GMT): 06 30 - 11 00 and 12 00 - 15 00
Honorary Consul: Herr J Petersen

Munich
British Consulate-General
Bürkleinstrasse 10,
D - 80538 München
(Mail from United Kingdom only should be addressed:
British Consulate-General, Munich,
PO Box 2010, BFPO 105)
Telephone (00) (49) (89) 211090
Facsimile   21109 166 Consul-General
            21109 166 Press &Public Affairs
            21109 166 Research & Technology
                  Section
            21109 155 Commercial Section
            21109 155 Investment Section
            21109 144 Management Section
            21109 144 Consular Section
Office Hours (GMT): Winter: 07 30 - 11 00 and
12 00 - 16 00
Summer: 06 30 - 10 00 and 11 00 – 15 00
Consul-General/Counsellor R&T: Mr J Farrel
Consul: Mr G Deane
Consul Commercial: Mr H Taylor
Consul (Consular/Management): Mrs M Timsit
Vice-Consul (Consular): Mrs C Ruhstorfer
Press & Public Affairs Officer: Mrs B I Dammert
Vice-Consul (Commercial): Mr C Pattinson
Commercial Officer: Mr R Schemien
Inward Investment Officer: (Vacant)
Research & Technology Officer: Ms M Kistenfeger
(Visa and Passport work is centralised in
Dusseldorf.)

Nuremburg
British Consulate
M Schmitt & Sohn Gmbh &Co
Hadermuhle 9-15
D - 90402 Nuremburg
Telephone: (00) (49) (911) 2404-303
Facsimile: (00) (49) (911) 2404-111
Honorary Consul: Dr J Schmitt

Stuttgart
British Consulate-General
Breite Strasse 2, 70173
Telephone: (00) (49) (711) 16 26 9-0
Facsimile: (00) (49) (711) 16 26 9-30
Office Hours (GMT): As Frankfurt
Consul-General: Mr W N C Paterson
Commercial Officer/Pro-Consul: Herr W R Seidler
Commercial Officer: Frau A Seidler
Pro-Consul: Mrs M Braun

GHANA

Accra
British High Commission
Osu Link, off Gamel Abdul Nasser Avenue
(PO Box 296), Accra
Telephone: (00) (233) (21) 7010650, 221665
(24 hours)
7010721 Immigration Section
Facsimile: (00) (233) (21) 7010655
                      783552 Chancery
                      221715 Immigration
                            Section
Airtech: (00) (233) (21) 242936

e-mail: High.Commission@fco.gov.uk
Office Hours (GMT): 07 45 - 14 45
Immigration Section Public Hours 07 45 - 10 45
Consular Section Public Hours 07 30 - 13 30
High Commissioner: Mr Rod Pullen
Deputy High Commissioner: Mr Craig Murray
Defence Adviser: Lieutenant Colonel Steen K E
Clarke, OBE
First Secretary (Development): Mr Tony Gardner
First Secretary (Commercial): Mr Kevin Lynch
First Secretary (Political/External): Mr David
Keegan
Second Secretary (Immigration/Consular): Mrs
Caroline Cross
Second Secretary (Development): Mr Desmond
Woode
*Second Secretary (Political, Press and Public
Affairs):* Mr Gregory Quinn
Second Secretary (Management): Mr Seif Usher
Second Secretary (Airline Liason Officer): Mr
Derek McDougal Swanson
Second Secretary (Immigration): Ms Debra Poulier
Second Secretary: Mr Andrew Eelbeck
Third Secretary (Commercial): Mrs Carol Turvill
Third Secretary (Chancery): Mr Jonathan Saunders
Third Secretary (Immigration): Mr Jim Beach
Third Secretary (Immigration): Mr Brendan Gill
Third Secretary (Immigration): Mr Alan Green
Third Secretary (Immigration): Mr Althea Ramsey
Third Secretary (Immigration): Mrs Tracey Singh
Third Secretary (Immigration): Mr Stuart Turvill
Third Secretary (Immigration): Mr Simon Winter

GREECE

Athens
British Embassy
1 Ploutarcou Street, 106 75 Athens
Telephone: (00) (30) (1) 727 2600
Night (RSO): (00) (30) (1) 723 7727
                        724 1331
Facsimile: (00) (30) (1) 727 2734 Political &
                                  Commercial
                                  Section
                            2720 Consular
                                  Section
                            2876 Management
                                  Section
                            2723 Chancery
                            2743 Press and Public
                                  Affairs
                            2725 Residence
Airech: (00) (30) (1) 722 7122
e-mail: britania@hol.gr
Website: http://www.british-embassy.gr
Office Hours (GMT): 06 00 - 13 00
Ambassador: Mr David C A Madden, CMG
*Counsellor, Consul-General and Deputy Head of
Mission:* Mr Peter J Millett
Counsellor: Mr Nicholas J Foster
Defence, Naval and Air Attaché: Commodore John
L Milnes, RN
Military Attaché: Lieutenant Colonel S W L
Strickland, OBE
Counsellor (Cultural): Mr Chris Hickey

First Secretary (Economic): Mr David S Gordon-MacLeod
First Secretary (Political, Press and Public Affairs): Mrs Francesca J G Flessati
First Secretary (External): Mr Krishna Shanmuganathan
First Secretary (Defence Supply): Mr John Bewley
First Secretary (Management): Mr Michael D Morley
First Secretary (Commercial): Mr Graeme G Thomas
First Secretary and Consul: Mr David J Holder
First Secretary (Cultural Affairs): Mr Christopher Gibson
Second Secretary and Vice-Consul: Mr Simon Batty
Second Secretary (Political/Information): Ms Emma C Mills
Second Secretary: Mr Paul Weldon
Third Secretary (Economic): Miss Margaret M Belof
Third Secretary (Management): Mr Nigel S Chadwick
Third Secretary and Vice-Consul: Miss Christine Waterhouse

Corfu
British Consulate
2 Alexandras Avenue, 491 00 Corfu
Telephone: (00) (30) (661) 30055
Facsimile: (00) (30) (661) 37995
Consul: Mr Anthony (Tony) Arnold

Heraklion (Crete)
British Consulate
16 Papa-Alexandrou Street
712 02 Heraklion
Telephone: (00) (30) (81) 224012
Facsimile: (00) (30) (81) 243935
e-mail: crete@british-consulate.gr
Consul: Mrs Marion R Tzanaki, MBE

Kos
British Vice-Consulate
8, Annetas Laoumtzi Street,
853 00 Kos
Telephone: (00) (30) (242) 21549
Facsimile: (00) (30) (242) 25948
Honorary Vice-Consul: Mr Konstantinos Kourounis

Patras
British Vice-Consulate
Votsi 2
262 21 Patras
Telephone: (00) (30) (61) 277329
Facsimile: (00) (30) (61) 225334
Honorary Vice-Consul: Mrs Marie Jeanne Morphy-Karatza, MBE

Rhodes
British Consulate
Pavlou Mela 3
PO Box 47
851 00 Rhodes
Telephone: (00) (30) (241) 27247 or 22005
Facsimile: (00) (30) (241) 22615
e-mail: rhodes@british-consulate.gr
Honorary Consul: Mr Dimitrios E Demetriades, MBE

Thessaloniki
British Consulate
8th Floor, 8 Venizelou Street,
Eleftheria Square, PO Box 10332
541 10 Thessaloniki
Telephone: (00) (30) (31) 278006 or 269984
e-mail: salonika@british-consulate.gr
Honorary Consul: Mr George K Doucas, MBE

Thessaloniki
British Embassy Commercial Liaison Office
c/o The British Council
9 Ethnikis Amynis Street, PO Box 50007
540 13 Thessaloniki
Telephone: (00) (30) (31) 267114, 266711
Facsimile: (00) (30) (31) 267114, 282498
e-mail: sarah.edwards@britcoun.gr
Head of British Embassy Commercial Liaison Office: Mrs Sarah Edwards-Economidi

Syros
British Vice-Consulate
8 Akti Petrou Ralli,
Hermoupolis
841 00 Syros
Telephone: (00) (30) (281) 82232 or 88922
Facsimile: (00) (30) (281) 83293
Honorary Vice-Consul: Mrs Virginia Parissi-Thermou

Zakynthos
British Vice-Consulate
5 Foskolos Street
291 00 Zakynthos
Telephone: (00) (30) (695) 22906 or 48030
Facsimile: (00) (30) (695) 23769
Honorary Vice-Consul: Mrs Evridiki (Vicky) Vitsou-Kotsoni

GRENADA

St George's
British High Commission
14 Church Street, St George's, Grenada
Telephone: (00) (1) (473) 440 3536, 440 3222
Facsimile: (00) (1) (473) 440 4939
e-mail: bhcgrenada@caribsurf.com
Office Hours (GMT): Mon - Thurs: 12 00 - 17 00 and 17 30 - 20 00   Fri: 12 00 - 17 00
* *High Commissioner:* Mr J White
Resident Acting High Commissioner: Mr D R Miller
* *Deputy High Commissioner:* Mr M J E Mayhew
* *Defence Adviser:* Captain S C Ramm, RN
* *Counsellor (Regional Affairs):* Mr N J L Martin
* *First Secretary (Chancery):* Mr P Curwen
* *Second Secretary (Management/Consular):* Mr G I Brammer
* *Second Secretary (Chancery/Information):* Mr N J Pyle, MBE
** *Second Secretary (Technical Works):* Mr M Jones
* *Second Secretary (Chancery):* Mr P Marshall
* *Third Secretary:* Mr A W White
* *Third Secretary (Consular/Immigration):* Mr S Minshull
*Resides at Bridgetown
**Resides at Mexico City

GUATEMALA

Guatemala City
British Embassy
Avenida La Reforma 16-00, Zona 10,
Edificio Torre Internacional, Nivel 11
Telephone: (00) (502) 367 5425 to 29
Facsimile: (00) (502) 367 5430
e-mail: embassy@terra.com.gt
Office Hours (GMT): Mon-Thurs 14 30 - 18 30
and 19 30 - 23 00   Fri 14 30 - 18 30
Ambassador: Mr Richard D Lavers
*First Secretary, Consul and Deputy Head of
Mission:* Ms Caitlin Jones
Defence Attaché: Colonel I C D Blair-Pilling, OBE
*First Secretary (Commercial and Director of Trade
Promotion for Central America, resides at San
José):* Mr Colin J Edge
Second Secretary (Management and Consular): Mr
David MacDougall
Assistant Defence Attache: Flt Sgt Glenn Walker
Third Secretary (Acccounts and Registry): Mr Tony
Mesarowicz

GUINEA

Conakry
British Embassy (except where shown all staff
resident in Dakar)
Ambassador: Mr E A Burner
Defence Attaché (resides in Freetown): Lieutenant
Colonel J J P Poraj-Wilczynski
First Secretary and Deputy Head of Mission: Mr P
T D O'Brien, MBE
*Second Secretary (Political/Press and Public
Affairs):* Mr S Bond
Third Secretary (Management) and Vice-Consul:
Ms A J Lavocat

Conakry
British Consulate
BP 834 Conakry, Republic of Guinea
Telephone: (00) (224) 45 58 07 / 45 60 20 (Office)
(224) 45 29 59 (Home)
Facsimile: (00) (224) 45 60 20
Satellite Phone: 00 874 762 471260
Satellite Fax: 00 874 762 471262
e-mail: britcon.vat@eti.net.gn
Consul (resides at Dakar): Mr P T D O'Brien, MBE
Vice-Consul (resides at Dakar): Ms A J Lavocat
Consul: Mrs V A Treitlein, MBE

GUINEA-BISSAU

Bissau
British Embassy (all staff resident in Dakar)
Ambassador (non-resident): Mr E A Burner
First Secretary and Deputy Head of Mission: Mr P
T D O'Brien, MBE
*Second Secretary (Political/Press and Public
Affairs):* Mr S Bond
Third Secretary (Management) and Vice-Consul:
Ms A J Lavocat

Bissau
British Consulate
Mavegro Int., CP100, Bissau

Telephone: (00) (245) 20 12 24/20 12 16 (Office)
(00) (245) 20 16 07 (Home)
Facsimile: (00) (245) 20 12 65
Satellite Phone: 00 871 7624 76380
Satellite Fax: 00 871 7624 76382
Consul (resides at Dakar): Mr P T D O'Brien, MBE
Vice-Consul (resides at Dakar): Ms A J Lavocat
Honorary Consul: Mr J Van Maanen

GUYANA

Georgetown
British High Commission
44 Main Street, (PO Box 10849), Georgetown
Telephone: (00) (592) (22)65881/2/3/4
Facsimile: 53555 Development/Commercial/
Management
50671 Consular and Immigration
37321 Chancery
68818 (Airtech)
e-mail:
firstname.surname@georgetown.mail.fco.gov.uk
Office Hours (GMT): 11 30 - 18 30
High Commissioner: Mr E C Glover, MVO
Deputy High Commissioner: Mr S Crossman
Defence Adviser (resides at Bridgetown): Captain
S C Ramm, RN
Second Secretary (Management): Ms A M Fairley
Second Secretary (Development): Mr J C Brady
Second Secretary (Chancery) (resides at Caracas):
Mr D Stewart
Third Secretary (Immigration / Consular): Mr A J
McFarlin
*Third Secretary (Technical Management)
(resides at Bridgetown):* Mr A W White

HAITI

Port-au-Prince
British Embassy
Ambassador (resides Santo Domingo): Mr David
Ward
*Second Secretary and Consul (resides Santo
Domingo):* Ms Sarah Hildersley

Port-au Prince
British Consulate
Hotel Montana (PO Box 1302), Port-au-Prince
Telephone: (00) (509) 257 3969
Facsimile: (00) (509) 257 4048
Office Hours (GMT): 13 00 - 18 00
Vice-Consul: (Vacant)

HOLY SEE

British Embassy
91 Via dei Condotti, I-00187, Rome
Telephone: (00) (39) (06) 699 23561
Facsimile: (00) (39) (06) 6994 0684
Office Hours (GMT): Oct-Mar   08 00 - 12 00 and
13 00 - 16 00
Apr-June and Sep 07 00 - 11 00 and 12 00-15 00
Jul-Aug 06 00 - 12 00
Ambassador: Mr M E Pellew, CVO
First Secretary and Deputy Head of Mission: Mr D
A Dewberry

HONDURAS

Tegucigalpa
British Embassy
Edificio Financiero BANEXPO
3er Piso
Boulevard San Juan Bosco
Colonia Payaqui
PO Box 290, Tegucigalpa
Telephone: (00) (504) 232 0612, 232 5144
Facsimile: (00) (504) 232 5480
Airtech: (00) (504) 232 0612 - Ext. 2025
Office Hours (GMT): Mon-Thurs 14 00 - 19 00
and 20 00 - 22 30 and Fri 14 00 - 19 00
Ambassador and Consul-General: Mr David Osborne
Second Secretary and Deputy Head of Mission: Mr
Neal Carlin
Defence Attaché (resides at Guatemala City):
Colonel Ian C D Blair-Pilling, OBE
*First Secretary (Commercial) and Director of
Trade Promotion for Central America (resides at
San José):* Mr Christopher Edge
Second Secretary (resides at Panama City): Mr
Andrew Davenport

San Pedro Sula
British Consulate
Sermares, Barrio Suyapa,
PO Box 4512
San Pedro Sula
Telephone: (00) (504) 557 2046
Facsimile: (00) (504) 552 9764
Office Hours (GMT): 13 30 - 17 00 (Mon-Fri)
Honorary Consul: Mr F P Barber, OBE

HUNGARY

Budapest
British Embassy
Harmincad Utca 6, Budapest 1051
Telephone: (00) (36) (1) 266 2888
Facsimile: (00) (36) (1) 266 0907 Management/
PPA/KHF
Sections
429 6360 Consular/Visa/
Commercial
Sections
429 6301 Political Section
Airtech: (00) (36) (1) 429 6299
e-mail: info@britemb.hu.
Website: http://www.britishembassy.hu
Office Hours (GMT): Summer 07 00 - 15 00,
Winter 08 00 - 16 00
Ambassador: Mr Nigel Thorpe, CVO
Counsellor and Deputy Head of Mission: Mr
Gordon Reid
Counsellor: Dr Dudley Ankerson
Defence Attaché: Colonel S Jonathan B Frere,
MBE BA RLC
Cultural Attaché (British Council Director): Dr
John Richards
First Secretary (Commercial): Miss Debbie
Goldthorpe, LVO
First Secretary (Political/Economic): Mr Robert
Dear
First Secretary (Management/Consul): Mr Bernard
Halliwell, MBE

First Secretary (Political): Mr Ian Anderson
First Secretary (Cultural): Mr John Mitchell
First Secretary (Cultural): Mr Peter Brown
Assistant Defence Attaché: Squadron Leader Alan
Fisher, RAF
Second Secretary (Know How Fund/Political): Mr
Jason Moore
Second Secretary (Commercial): Mr Colin Parish
Second Secretary (Political): Mr Stephen Burdes
Second Secretary (Political): Miss Katy Ransome
Second Secretary (Technical Management): Mr
John Walker
Second Secretary (Technical Management): Mr
Terry Wiltshire
Second Secretary (Airline Liaison): Mr Robin
Humphris
Second Secretary: Mr Andy Hewett
Second Secretary: Mr Jason Clarke
Third Secretary (Management): Mr Richard Homer
Third Secretary (Press and Public Diplomacy):
Miss Joanne Penfold
Attaché and Vice-Consul: Mr Brian Simpson

Pécs
British Consulate
Megye Utca. 21
Pécs 7621
Tel/Fax: (00) (36) (72) 210 091
Office Hours (GMT) 08 00- 11 00 Monday to
Friday
Honorary Consul: Dr Zsolt Páva

ICELAND

Reykjavik
British Embassy
Laufasvegur 31, 101 Reykjavik
Postal Address: PO Box 460, 121 Reykjavik
Telephone: (00) (354) 550 5100
Facsimile: (00) (354) 550 5105
Airtech: (00) (354) 550 5104
e-mail: britemb@centrum.is
Office Hours (GMT): Mon-Thurs 08 30 - 16 00,
Fri 08 30 - 15 30
Ambassador and Consul-General: Mr John Culver,
LVO
Deputy Head of Mission and Consul: Mr Peter
Evans
Commercial Officer: Mrs Elsa Einarsdottir
*First Secretary Inward Investment (resides in
Stockholm):* Mr Martin Cronin

Akureyri
British Vice-Consulate
Central Hospital (Fjordungssjukrahusid a
Akureyri)
v/Eyrarlandsveg PO Box 380
IS-602 Akureyri
Telephone: (00) (463) 0102
Facsimile: (00) (462) 4621
Office Hours (GMT): 09 00 - 12 00 and 13 00 -
17 00
Honorary Vice-Consul: Mr Halldor Jonsson

INDIA

New Delhi
British High Commission
Chanakyapuri, New Delhi 110021
Telephone: (00) (91) (11) 687 2161
Facsimile: (00) (91) (11) 687 2882 Management
Dept
687 0068 Political Dept
687 0062 Economic &
Commercial
Dept
687 0065 Press & Public
Affairs
687 0060 Visa Dept
611 4603 Defence Dept
Airtech: 611 4601
e-mail: postmaster.NewDelhi@fco.gov.uk
Office Hours (GMT): Mon-Fri: 03 30 - 07 30 and
08 30 - 11 30
High Commissioner: Sir Rob Young, KCMG
Minister and Deputy High Commissioner: Mr Tom
Macan
Defence and Military Adviser: Brigadier Mervyn
Lee, OBE
Counsellor (Political): Mr Dominic Martin
Counsellor (Economic and Commercial): Mr John
Dennis
Counsellor: Mr Kevin Sloane
Counsellor (Management): Mr Norman King,
LVO, OBE
Air and Naval Adviser: Group Captain Nick B
Spiller
First Secretary (Medical Officer): Dr John Llewellyn
First Secretary (Press & Public Affairs): Mr Gerry
McCrudden, MBE
First Secretary (Commercial): Mr Peter Stephenson
First Secretary (Economic): Mr John Burton
First Secretary (Political): Mr David Quarrey
First Secretary (Political/Military): Mr Nigel Dakin
First Secretary (Internal): Mr Peter Holland
First Secretary (Science & Technology): Mr Simon
Hosking
First Secretary (Environment & Trade Policy): Dr
David McMahon
First Secretary (Immigration/Consular): Mr Chris
Dix
First Secretary (Estate Manager): Mr John
McLean, OBE
First Secretary (Procurement): Mr Phil George, TD
First Secretary (Management): Mr Richard Sharp
First Secretary (ALO Regional Manager): Ms
Janet Battersby
First Secretary (Defence Supplies): Mr James
Catchpole
First Secretary (Technical Management): Mr Barry
Vargas
First Secretary (Drug Liaison Officer): (Vacant)
First Secretary (Technical Works): Mr Ian Jack
First Secretary (Consular): Mrs Angela Slater
First Secretary (Matron): (Vacant)
Assistant Defence Adviser: Lieutenant Commander
Ian A Jackson
Second Secretary (Technical Management): Mr
Terence Watson
Second Secretary (Immigration): Mr Tom Burke

Second Secretary (Immigration): Mr Steve Burns
Second Secretary (Commercial): Mr David Slater
Second Secretary (Commercial): Mr Neil Brigden
Second Secretary (Political): Mr Jonathan Sinclair
Second Secretary (Management): Mr Christopher
Stacey
Second Secretary (Airline Liaison Officer): Mr
David Westgate
Third Secretary (Economic & Commercial): Mr
Danny Wells
Third Secretary (Commercial): Mr Alistair Elder
Third Secretary (Political): Mr Eric Taylor
Third Secretary (Political): Mr John Bradshaw
Third Secretary (Political): Mr Simon Williams
Third Secretary (Consular): Ms Claire Lawley
Attaché (Pensions Liaison Officer): Ms Helen Ibbott

New Delhi
DFID (Department For International Development) India
B-28 Tara Crescent
Qutab Institutional Area
New Delhi 110 016
Telephone: (00) (91) (11) 6529123
Facsimile: (00) (91) (11) 6529296
Minister (Development) & Head, DFIDI: Mr
Robert Graham-Harrison
Deputy Head DFIDI: Mr Rick Woodham
First Secretary (Economic): Mr John Burton
First Secretary (Environment): Dr Yusaf Samiullah
First Secretary (Social Development): Dr D J Pain
First Secretary (Development): Mr Peter Rose
First Secretary (Governance): Mr Roderick Evans
First Secretary (Governance): Ms Paula Hayes
First Secretary (Development): Ms S Taylor
First Secretary (Development): Mr Peter Zoller
First Secretary (Economic): Mr Shan Mitra
First Secretary (Education): Mr Marshal Elliott
First Secretary (Education): Ms Felicity Townsend
First Secretary (Social Development): Mr A De Haan
First Secretary (Management): Mr Niall Coffey
First Secretary (Contracts/Procurement): Mr Will
Starbuck
First Secretary (Health): Mr Desmond Whyms
First Secretary (Health): Mr Tim Martineau
First Secretary (Engineering): Mr Peter Davies
First Secretary (Power Policy): Mr Geoff Hayton
First Secretary (Water & Sanitation): Mr Nigel
Kirby
First Secretary (Forestry): Mr Kevin Crockford
First Secretary (Rural Livelihoods): Mr Simon
Croxton
First Secretary (Engineering and Finance): Mr
Simon Kenny
Second Secretary (Development): Mrs Linda
Campbell
Second Secretary (Development): Mrs Kate
Alexander
Second Secretary (Development): Ms Anna Walters
Second Secretary (Development): Mr Steve Burton
Second Secretary (Development): Mr Ian Alexander

British Council Division
17 Kasturba Gandhi Marg, New Delhi 110001
Telephone: (00) (91) (11) 3711401
Facsimile: (00) (91) (11) 3710717

e-mail: delhi.enquiry@in.britishcouncil.org
Minister (Cultural Affairs): Mr Edmund Marsden
Counsellor (Human Resource Development): Dr
Morna Nance
First Secretary (Resources Management): Ms
Grace Conacher
First Secretary (Education Promotion): Mr John
Nance
First Secretary (Educational Services): Mr Nick
Humphries
First Secretary (Law and Governance): Mr Sital
Dhillon

Mumbai (Bombay)

Office of the British Deputy High Commissioner
Maker Chambers IV, 222 Jamnalal Bajaj Road,
(PO Box 11714) Nariman Point, Mumbai 400 021
Telephone: (00) (91) (22) 283 0517, 283 2330,
283 3602
Facsimile: (00) (91) (22) 202 7940
e-mail: postmaster@bombay.mail.fco.gov.uk
Office Hours (GMT): 02 30 - 07 30 and 08 30 -
10 30
Deputy High Commissioner: Mr Howard
Parkinson, cvo
First Secretary (Commercial): Mr Merrick Lowes
First Secretary (British Council Director): Mr Paul
Smith
First Secretary (Consular/Management): Mr David
Allan
Second Secretary (Drug Liaison Officer): Mr Chris
Noon
Second Secretary (Commercial): Mr Steve
Firstbrook
Second Secretary (Immigration): Mr Charles Molloy
Second Secretary (Immigration): Mr Nick Enescott
Second Secretary (Airline Liaison Officer): Mr
Simon Rose
Attaché (Consular): Mr Ian Reakes

Goa

British Consular Office
302 Manguirish Building
3rd Floor, 18 June Road
Opp. Gulf Supermarket
Panaji 403001, Goa
Telephone: (00) (91) (832) 228571
Facsimile: (00) (91) (832) 232828
e-mail: bcagoa@goatelecom.com
British Consular Assistant: Mrs Shilpa Caldeira

Kolkata (Calcutta)

Office of the British Deputy High Commissioner
1A Ho Chi Minh Sarani, Kolkata, 700 071
Telephone: (00) (91) (33) 288 5172/3/4/5/6
5172 after office hours
Facsimile: (00) (91) (33) 288 3435
Airtech: 5010
e-mail: postmaster@calcutta.mail.fco.gov.uk
Office Hours (GMT): 03 30 - 07 30 and 08 30 - 11
30
Deputy High Commissioner: Dr John Mitchiner
First Secretary (British Council Director): Mr
David Evans
Second Secretary (Commercial): Mr Harvey Bell
Third Secretary (Consular): Mr Bernie Andrews
Chennai (Madras)

Office of the British Deputy High Commissioner in Southern India

24 Anderson Road, Chennai 600 006
Telephone: (00) (91) (44) 8273136, 8273137,
8257422, 8257433
Facsimile: (00) (91) (44) 8269004 Commercial
8203790 Management/
PPA
8275130 Visa
e-mail: bdhcchen@vsnl.com
Office Hours (GMT): 03 00-07 30 and 08 00-10 30
Deputy High Commissioner: Mr Michael Herridge
First Secretary (British Council Division): Ms
Eunice Crook
Second Secretary (Commercial): Mr Doug Williams
Second Secretary (Immigration): Mr Geoff Wood
Third Secretary (Management/Consular): Mr
Stephen Bailey

Bangalore

British Trade Office
7/4, Thapar Niketan
Brunton Road
Bangalore 560 025
Telephone: (00) (91) (80) 5586687, 5588661/3
Facsimile: (00) (91) (80) 5586690
e-mail: bto.bangalore@fco.gov.uk
Second Secretary: Mr Kelvin E Green

Ahmedabad

British Trade Office
907, Shitiratna
Near Pachwati Circle
Ellisbridge
Ahmedabad 380 006
Telephone: (00) (91) (79) 6467138
Facsimile: (00) (91) (79) 6403537
e-mail: btoabad@icenet.net
Commercial Information Officer: Milind Godbole

Hyderabad

British Trade Office
H-3-6-322, Chamber 104
1st Floor, Mahavir House
Basheerbagh
Hyderabad 300 029
Telephone: (00) (91) (40) 6669147/8
Facsimile: (00) (91) (40) 6669149
e-mail: btohyd@hd2.dot.net.in
Senior Trade Promotion Adviser: M C Srinagesh

INDONESIA

Jakarta

British Embassy
Jalan M H Thamrin 75, Jakarta 10310
Telephone: (00) (62) (21) 315 6264 (Switchboard)
314 4229 (Auto attendant - see individual
extension numbers)
Facsimile: (00) (62) (21) 314 1824 Development
315 4061 Commercial
390 7493 Management
392 6263 Chancery/
Economic
390 2726 Defence
Office Hours (GMT): Mon - Thur 00 45 - 09 00
and Fri 00 45 - 05 45

British Consulate General
Deutsche Bank Building, (19th Floor)
J1 Imam Bonjol 80
Jakarta 10310
Telephone: (00) (62) (21) 390 7484 - 87
Facsimile: (00) (62) (21) 316 0858
Office Hours (GMT): Mon - Thur 00 45 - 09 00
and Fri 00 45 - 05 45
Ambassador (4201): Mr Richard Gozney, CMG
*Deputy Head of Mission and Consul-General
(4203):* Mr Andy Sparkes
Counsellor (Commercial/Development) (4232): Mr
Anthony Godson
Counsellor (Political) (4205): Mr John Fisher
Defence Attaché (4215): Colonel Alan J Roberts
First Secretary (Political/Economic) (4245): Mr
Hamish St. Clair Daniel, MBE
First Secretary (Commercial) (4239): Mr Mark
Walmsley
First Secretary (Management) (4263): Mr Mike
Tomkins
First Secretary (Development) (4252): Mr Gordon
Saggers
DFID – Governance Adviser (4295): Mr Ben
Dickinson
DFID – Social Development Adviser (4260): Ms
Elizabeth Carriere
DFID – Forestry Adviser (4220): Mr Yvan Biot
Second Secretary (Consular): Mr Alan Marshall
Second Secretary (Political) (4208): Mr Simon
Tonge
Second Secretary (Political/Economic) (4284): Mr
Alex Martin
Third Secretary (Political) (4241): Miss Naomi
Kyriacopoulos
Third Secretary (Immigration): Mr John Mellor
Third Secretary and Vice-Consul: Mr Alasdair
Hamilton
Third Secretary (Commercial) (4236): Mr Bikash
Dawahoo
Third Secretary (Management/Press) (4267): Miss
Mary Gilbert
Third Secretary (Estate) (4266): Mr Asif Choudhury

Medan
British Consulate
Jl Kap. Pattimura 459
PO Box 1286,
Medan 20153
Telephone: (00) (62) (61) 821 0559
Facsimile: (00) (62) (61) 821 0991
Office Hours (GMT): Mon-Fri 01 00 - 05 00
Honorary Consul: Mr Pat Baskett

Surabaya
British Consulate
Hong Kong Bank, Hyatt Bumi Modern,
Skyline Building 3rd Floor JL Basuki Rachmat
106-128
Surabaya, 60271, Jawa Timur
Telephone: (00) (62) (31) 5326381, 5326375
Facsimile: (00) (62) (31) 5326380
Office Hours (GMT): 01 30 - 09 00
Honorary Consul: Mr Simon Williams

Bali
British Consulate
Jalan Mertasari No. 2,
Sanur
Denpasar 80227
Bali
Telephone: 0361 270 601
Facsimile: 0361 270 572
Office Hours (GMT): 01 30 - 09 00
Honorary Consul: Mr Mark Wilson

IRAN

Tehran
British Embassy
143 Ferdowsi Avenue, Tehran 11344
(PO Box No 11365-4474)
Telephone: (00) (98) (21) 6705011/19 (8 lines)
Facsimile: (00) (98) (21) 6708021 Commercial
6700720 Visa
6710761 Management/
Consular
Office Hours (GMT): Sun – Thurs 04 00 - 11 00
Ambassador: Mr Nick W Browne, CMG
*First Secretary (Chancery) and Deputy Head of
Mission:* Mr Neil Crompton
First Secretary (Commercial): Mr Eric Jenkinson
*First Secretary (Education/British Council
Director):* Mr Michael Sargent, OBE
First Secretary (Management) and Consul: Mr
Paul Seaby
Second Secretary (Public Diplomacy): Mr Nick Cox
Second Secretary (Commercial): Mr Steve Smith
Second Secretary (Political): Mr Simon Shercliff
Second Secretary (Immigration): Mr Gavin Baptie
Third Secretary (Management) and Vice-Consul:
Mr Doug Tunn
Third Secretary (Immigration): Ms Barbara Moser-
Andon
Third Secretary (Immigration): Ms Marie Hilley
Third Secretary (Immigration): Mr Paul Kingford
Third Secretary (Immigration): Mr Martin Waspe

IRELAND

Dublin
British Embassy
29 Merrion Road, Ballsbridge, Dublin 4
Telephone: (00 3531) (1) 205 3700 Commercial
3757 Commercial
3792 Defence
3822 Passports/Visa
3700 Passports/Visa
3742 Information
Facsimile: (00 3531) (1) 205 3885 Management
3880 Commercial
3870 Chancery
3890 Consular/
Passport/Visa
3893 Information
3870 Airtech
e-mail: bembassy@internet-ireland.ie
bembassy.trade1@internet-ireland.ie (Commercial
Section)
Office Hours (GMT): Mon - Thur 09 00 - 12 45
and 14 00 - 17 15

Fri 09 00 - 12 45 and 14 00 - 17 00
Ambassador: Sir Ivor Roberts, CMG
Counsellor and Deputy Head of Mission: Mr John Rankin
Defence Attaché: Colonel Paul Cummings
Counsellor (Commercial): Mr Martin McIntosh
First Secretary (EU/Economic): Ms Sarah Tiffin
First Secretary (Political): Mr Ashley Ray
First Secretary (Management): Mr David Spires
Second Secretary (Press & Public Affairs): Mr Andrew Pike
Second Secretary (Commercial): Mr Steve Richards
Second Secretary (Agriculture/EU): Mr Tom Hoskin
Second Secretary (Management): Mr Robbie Robinson
Third Secretary (Management): Ms Gillian Edwards
Third Secretary (Chancery): Ms Sharon Brant
Third Secretary (Passports/Visas): Mr Tim Freeman
Attaché: Ms Margaret Rixon
Attaché (Defence): Mr Chris Ruhle

ISRAEL

Tel Aviv
British Embassy
192 Hayarkon Street, Tel Aviv 63405
Telephone: (00) (972) (3) 7251222
Facsimile: (00) (972) (3) 524 3313 Commercial
                          527 1572 Chancery
                          527 8574 Management
                          510 1167 Consular
Office Hours (GMT): Mon - Thur 06 00 - 14 00
Fri 06 00 - 11 30 (Sept-Mar)
Mon - Thur 07 00 - 15 00
Fri 07 00 - 12 30 (April-Aug)
Ambassador: Mr Sherard Cowper-Coles, CMG LVO (tel 7251245)
Counsellor, Consul-General and Deputy Head of Mission: Mr Peter L Carter (7251246)
Counsellor: Mr Nick Marden (7251261)
Defence and Military Attaché: Colonel Tom M Fitzalan Howard, OBE (7251256)
Naval and Air Attaché: Wing Commander Stephen Cummings RAF (7251257)
Cultural Attaché (British Council Director): Mr David Elliott
First Secretary (Commercial): Mr Ian Morrison (7251231)
First Secretary (Chancery): Ms Menna Rawlings (7251248)
First Secretary (Management): Mr John Fielder (7251260)
Second Secretary and Consul: Mr Peter McGregor (7251222)
Second Secretary (Chancery): Mr Tim Smart (7251266)
Second Secretary (Technical Management): Mr Simon Gudgeon (7251265)
Assistant Cultural Attaché (British Council): Mr Keith Lawrence
Third Secretary and Vice-Consul: Mr Paul T Stokes (7251222)
Third Secretary (Chancery): Mr Mark Kelly (7252219)

Tel Aviv
British Consulate-General
Migdalor Building (6th Floor)
1 Ben Yehuda Street, Tel Aviv 63801
Telephone: (00) (972) (3) 7251222
Facsimile: (00) (972) (3) 5101167
Office Hours (GMT): Mon - Thur 05 30 - 13 00
Fri 05 30 - 11 30 (Sept to Mar)
Mon - Thur 06 30 - 14 30
Fri 06 30 - 12 00 (Apr to Aug)
Consul-General: Mr Peter Carter
Consul: Mr Peter McGregor
Vice-Consul: Mr Paul T Stokes

Eilat
British Consulate
c/o Aqua Sport
Coral Beach
P.O. Box 300
Eilat 88102
Telephone: (00) (972) (7) 6326287
Honorary Consul: Mrs Dafna Budden

ITALY

Rome
British Embassy
Via XX Settembre 80a, 00187 Roma
Telephone: (00) (39) 06 4220 0001
06 478141 British Council
Facsimile: (00) (39) 06 487   3324 Information
                        06 4220 2333 Chancery
                        06 4890 4285 E&C Dept
                                 4201 1507
                        06 4220 2335 Management
                        06 4220 2334 Consular
                        06 4220 2283 Defence
Airtech: 06 4220 2257
Website: www.UKinItalia.it
Office Hours (GMT): Sept-July: Mon-Fri 08 00 - 16 00
Aug: Mon-Fri 08 00 - 14 00
Ambassador: Sir John Shepherd, KCVO, CMG
Deputy Head of Mission and Minister: Mrs Alison Mariot Leslie
Defence and Military Attaché: Brigadier Allan L Mallinson
Naval Attaché: Captain Angus H Sinclair, RN
Air Attaché: Group Captain D H White
Counsellor (Political): Mr Adrian M Fulcher
Counsellor (Economic & Commercial): Mr Martin A Hatfull
Counsellor (British Council Director): Mr Richard H Alford, OBE
First Secretary (Political, Press & Public Affairs): Mr Andrew Jackson
First Secretary (Economic): Mr Robert D R Vaughn-Fenn
First Secretary (Management): Mr Peter J Phelan, OBE
First Secretary (Agriculture & Environment): Mr James P Howie
First Secretary (Social /Science &Technology Affairs): Mr Robert L Embleton
First Secretary (Consul): Mr Alan J Mayland
First Secretary (Political): Mr Adrian Gamble

First Secretary (Political): Mrs Patricia Fiona Bottomley
First Secretary (Political): Mr Nicholas D Hopton
Second Secretary (Management): Mr David P Goodall
Second Secretary (Energy/Commercial): Mr John R Thurlow
Second Secretary: Mr Graham J Dempsey
Second Secretary: Mr Simon Grunwell
Third Secretary: Mr Alexander E Madisons
Third Secretary (Political): Miss Emma C Lockwood, MVO
Third Secretary (Vice-Consul): Miss Deborah M Williams
Vice-Consul: Mrs Angela T Sweeney, MBE

Rome United Kingdom Representation to the United Nations Food and Agriculture Agencies in Rome, see part II

Florence
British Consulate
Lungarno Corsini 2,
50123 Florence
Telephone: (00) (39) 055 284133 (including Airtech)
(00) (39) 055 289556 (Commercial)
Facsimile: (00) (39) 055 219112
e-mail: bcflocom@tin.it
Office Hours (GMT): Apr-Oct 07 00 - 11 00 and 12 00 - 15 00
Nov-Mar 08 00 - 12 00 and 13 00 - 16 00
Consul (also Consul-General for the Republic of San Marino): Mr Ralph Griffiths, OBE
Vice-Consul: Ms Jane H de C Ireland, MBE
Pro-Consul: Ms Diane Johnson

Milan (SP)
British Consulate-General
Via San Paolo 7, 20121 Milan
Telephone: (00) (39) 02 723001
Facsimile: (00) (39) 02 72020153 Commercial
                86465081 Consular and Management
                8692405 Information
(Visa and Passport work is centralized in Rome)
Office Hours (GMT): Apr – Oct 07 00 - 11 00 and 12 00 - 15 00
Nov – Mar 08 00 - 12 00 and 13 00 - 16 00
Director General for British Trade Development in Italy and Consul-General: Mr R Northern, MBE
Deputy Consul-General and Consul (Commercial): Mr B Doyle
Consul (Consular/Management): Mr A Reuter
Consul (Commercial/Press/PR): Mr I Shand, LVO
Consul (Inward Investment): Ms F Corby
Vice-Consul: Mrs E Crosley
Pro-Consul: Mrs J Billingsley

Genoa
British Consulate
c/o Coeclerici Armatori S.p.A
Via di Francia, 28 16149 Genoa
Telephone: (00) (39) 010 416828
Facsimile (00) (39) 010 416958
Office Hours (GMT): Apr-Oct: Mon - Thur 07 30 – 10 30

Nov-Mar: Mon - Thur 08 30 – 11 30
Honorary Consul: Mr G A Edmonds

Turin
British Consulate
The British Council, Via Saluzzo, 60 10125 Turin
Telephone: (00) (39) 011 6509202
Facsimile: (00) (39) 011 6695982
e-mail: bcturin@yahoo.com
Office Hours (GMT): Apr - Oct Mon & Thur: 07 00 - 10 00 Nov - Mar Mon & Thur: 08 00 - 11 00
Honorary Consul: Mr T R Priesack

Venice
British Consulate
Accademia, Dorsoduro, 1051,
30123 Venice
Telephone: (00) (39) 041 5227207
Facsimile: (00) (39) 041 5222617
e-mail: britconvenice@tin.it
Office Hours (GMT): Apr - Oct Mon - Fri 08 00 - 11 00
Nov - Mar Mon - Fri 09 00 - 12 00
Honorary Consul: Mr I N Coward
Pro-Consul: Mrs M Santin

Trieste
British Consulate
Via Dante Alighieri, 7
34122 Trieste
Telephone: (00) (39) 040 3478303
Facsimile: (00) (39) 040 3478311
Office Hours (GMT): Apr - Oct Tue 08 00 - 10 00 and Fri 12 30 - 14 30
Nov - Mar Tue 09 00 - 11 00 and Fri 13 30 - 15 30
Honorary Consul: Prof. J Dodds

Cagliari
British Consulate
Viale Colombo,160 Quartu S.E.
09045 Cagliari
Telephone: (00) (39) 070 813412
Facsimile: (00) (39) 070 862293
Honorary Consul: Mr A Graham, MBE

Naples
British Consulate
Via dei Mille 40, 80121 Naples
UK Postal Address: Consulate, BFPO 8 London
Telephone: (00) (39) (081) 423 8911
Facsimile: (00) (39) (081) 422 434
422 419 (Commercial Section)
e-mail: info.naples@fco.gov.uk
Office Hours (GMT): Summer: 07 00 - 13 00
Winter: 08 00 - 12 00 and 13 00 - 16 00
Consul: Mr Michael Burgoyne, MBE
Commercial Officer: Mr Giuseppe Saraceno
Political &Public Diplomacy: Mr Gerardo Kaiser
Vice Consul: Mr Brian McKeever

Bari
British Consulate
David H Gavan and Sons Shipping SrL,
Via Dalmazia 127, 70121 Bari
Telephone: (00) (39) (080) 554 3668
Facsimile: (00) (39) (080) 554 2977
e-mail: davidhg@tin.it
Honorary Consul: Mr David Gavan

Catania
British Consulate
Via G Verdi 53,
95129 Catania
Telephone: (00) (39) 095 715 1864
Facsimile: (00) (39) 095 715 1503
e-mail: british@tau.it
Honorary Consul: Mr Richard Brown

Brindisi
British Consulate
Temporarily Closed – Refer To Naples
Honorary Consul: (Vacant)

Palermo
British Consulate
S Tagliavia & Co, Via Cavour 117,
90133 Palermo
Telephone: (00) (39) 091 326412
Facsimile: (00) (39) 091 584240
e-mail: luigi@tagliavia.it
Honorary Consul: Mr Luigi Tagliavia

JAMAICA

Kingston
British High Commission
PO Box 575, Trafalgar Road, Kingston 10
Telephone: (00) (1) (876) 926 9050
Telegrams: UKREPKIN JA
Facsimile: (00) (1) (876) 929 7869 (Management/
Commercial)
926 6932 (Chancery)
960 3287 (Immigration/
Consular)
Airtech: (00) (1) (876) 929 5019
e-mail: bhckingston@cw.com or
bhckingston@infochan.com
bhcjamaica@cw.com (Chancery) or
bhcjamaica@mail.infochan.com (Chancery)
Office Hours (GMT): Mon - Thu: 13 00 - 18 00
and 19 00 - 21 30 Fri: 13 00 - 18 00
High Commissioner: Mr Anthony F Smith
Deputy High Commissioner: Mr Phil Sinkinson
Defence Adviser: Colonel Rob A Hyde-Bales
First Secretary (Management): Mr Roger Patten
First Secretary (Chancery): Mr Malcolm Bragg
Second Secretary (Chancery): Mr Keith A Wiggins
Second Secretary (Chancery): Mr Stewart Lister
Second Secretary (Chancery): Mr Tony Ridout
Second Secretary (Chancery): Mr Gavin Tench
Second Secretary (Development): Mr Graham
Glover
Second Secretary (Immigration/Consular): Mr
Mike Goodwin
*Third Secretary (Chancery/Press and Public
Affairs):* Ms Mags Fenner
Third Secretary (Commercial): Mr Stewart Gorman
Third Secretary (Immigration): Mr Ed Fuller
Third Secretary (Immigration): Miss Tina Harrup

Montego Bay
Telephone/Facsimile: (00) (1) (876) 912 6859/9117
(Home)
(00) (1) (876) 954 6394/5 (Office Hours)
Honorary Consul: Mr John Terry

JAPAN

Tokyo
British Embassy
No 1 Ichiban-cho, Chiyoda-ku, Tokyo 102-8381
Telephone: (00) (81) (3) 5211-1100
Facsimile: (00) (81) (3) 5275-3164 All Sections
except those listed below
5211-1111 Ambassador's
Office
5211-1345 Minister's
Office
5211-1270 Energy Section
3265-5580 Commercial
Section
5275-0346 Consular &
Visa Section
5211-1254 Defence
Section
5211-1121 Financial
Section
5211-1344 Political
Section
3230-0624 Press & Public
Affairs
3230-4800 Science &
Technology
Section
Airtech: 5211-1266
Office Hours (GMT): 00.00 - 03.30 and 05.00 -
08.30
email:
General Enquiries embassy.tokyo@fco.gov.uk
Consular and Visa Section
c&vsection.tokyo@fco.gov.uk
Commercial Section commercial-
section.tokyo@fco.gov.uk
Defence Section defence.tokyo@fco.gov.uk
Energy Section energy.tokyo@fco.gov.uk
Inward Investment Section
investukjapan.tokyo@fco.gov.uk
Management Section
management.tokyo@fco.gov.uk
Political Section political.tokyo@fco.gov.uk
Press and Public Affairs Section
ppas.tokyo@fco.gov.uk
Trade Policy Section trade-
policy.tokyo@fco.gov.uk
Science and technology Section
science.tokyo@fco.gov.uk
Embassy Website: www.uknow.or.jp
Ambassador: Sir Stephen J Gomersall, KCMG
Minister: Mr Stuart Jack, CVO
Defence Attache: Captain Jim A Boyd, RN
Counsellor (Political): Mr Colin Roberts
Counsellor (Political Affairs): Mr Patrick W Sprunt
Counsellor (Commercial): Mr Peter Bateman
Counsellor (Trade and Investment): Mr Tim C
Morris
Counsellor (Management) & Consul General: Mr
Robin R Hoggard
*Counsellor (Cultural and Director, British Council)
(Tel: 3235 8041 ext 8290):* Mr Terry Toney
Counsellor (Energy): Mr Bob Rayner
Counsellor (Science & Technology): Dr Mike G
Norton

Counsellor (Financial): Mr Peter Green
First Secretary (Political): Mr Chris Trott
First Secretary (Press and Public Affairs): Mrs Sue Kinoshita
First Secretary (Commercial): Mrs Karen Stanton
First Secretary (Commercial): Mr Matthew J Rous
First Secretary (Inward Investment): Mr Richard C B Jones
First Secretary (Deputy Director, British Council) (Tel: 3235 8041): Mr Mike Winter
First Secretary (Science & Technology): Mr Chris Stuart
First Secretary (Commercial): Mr Denis Healy
First Secretary (Science & Technology): Mr Brian Ferrar
First Secretary (Trade Policy): Mr Tom Goodwin
First Secretary (Technical Works): Mr John Warrener
First Secretary (Management): Mr Steve James
Second Secretary (Political): Ms Mara Myers
Second Secretary (Political): Mr Simon N Brown
Second Secretary (Financial): Mr Nick Bridge
Second Secretary (Political): Mr Jonathan H S Thomson
Second Secretary (Commercial): Ms Penny Miller
Second Secretary (Commercial): Ms Marie-Claire Joyce
Second Secretary & Consul: Mr Alan Sutton
Second Secretary (Trade Policy): Dr John Murton
Second Secretary (Technical Management): Mr Hugh Smith
Third Secretary (Management): Mr Shaun Clarke
Third Secretary & Vice Consul: Mrs Katherine Hickey
Third Secretary & Vice Consul: Mr Iain Ferguson
Third Secretary (PS to Ambassador): Mr Gary Leslie
Third Secretary (Political): Ms Lisanne Heaslip
Third Secretary (Press and Public Affairs): Ms Clare Allbless

British Consulate General
No 1 Ichibancho, Chiyoda-ku, Tokyo 102-8381
Telephone: (00) (81) (3) 5211-1100
Facsimile: (00) (81) (3) 5275-0346
Office Hours (GMT): 00 00 – 03 30 and 05 00 – 08 30
Consul General: Mr Robin R Hoggard
Consul: Mr Alan Sutton
Vice-Consul: Mr Iain Ferguson
Vice-Consul: Mrs Katherine Hickey

British Council
2 Kagurazaka 1-chome Shinjuku-ku Tokyo 162-0825
Telephone: (00) (81) (3) 3235 8031
Facsimile: (00) (81) (3) 3235 8040
e-mail: bctokyo@britishcouncil.or.jp
Website: www.uknow.or.jp
Office Hours (GMT): Monday-Friday 0000 - 0800
Director: Mr Terry Toney
Assistant Director: Mr Mike Winter

Sapporo
British Consulate
c/o Sapporo Nissan Motor Co Ltd
17-1-23 O-dori Nishi Chuo-ku
Sapporo-shi, Hokkaido 060-0042
Telephone: (00) (81) (11) 613 1123

Facsimile: (00) (81) (11) 613 4210
Office Hours (GMT): 0000-0820
Honorary Consul: Mr Y Kaneko

Osaka
British Consulate-General
Seiko Osaka Building, 19F, 3-5-1 Bakuro-machi, Chuo-ku, Osaka 541-0059
Telephone: (00) (81) (6) 6281 1616
Facsimile: (00) (81) (6) 6281 1731
e-mail: bcgosaka@gol.com
Consul-General & Director of Trade Promotion: Mr R Cummins
Deputy Consul General and Consul, Inward Investment: Mr D Smith
Consul (Commercial): Mr D Chapman
Consul: Ms D Lloyd

Nagoya
British Consulate
Nishiki Park Building 17F
2-4-3 Nishiki, Naka-ku
Nagoya 460-0003, Japan
Telephone: (00) (81) (52) 223 5031
Facsimile: (00) (81) (52) 223 5035
Consul: Mr S Wooten

Fukuoka
Honorary British Consulate
c/o The Nishi-Nippon Bank Ltd,
1-3-6 Hakata-Ekimae,
Hakata-ku, Fukuoka City
Telephone: (00) (81) (92) 476-2154
Facsimile: (00) (81) (92) 476-2619
Office Hours (GMT): Mon - to Fri 03 00 - 07 00
Honorary Consul: Mr S Koga

British Trade Promotion Office
Hakata Riverain 11F
3-1 Shimokawabatamachi
Hakata-ku
Fukuoka 817-0027
Telephone: (00) (81) (92) 262 0405
Facsimile: (00) (81) (92) 262 0374
Office Hours (GMT): Mon - to Fri 03 00 - 07 00
Head of British Trade Promotion Office: Mr R Cowin
Commercial and Inward Investment Assistant: Mr K Fujii

Hiroshima
British Consulate
c/o Hiroshima Bank Ltd, 3-8,
1-Chome Kamiyacho,
Naka-ku, Hiroshima
Telephone: (00) (81) (82) 247 5151
Facsimile: (00) (81) (82) 240-5759
Honorary Consul: Mr O Hashiguchi

JERUSALEM

Jerusalem
British Consulate-General
19 Nashashibi Street, Sheikh Jarrah Quarter,
PO Box 19690 East Jerusalem, 97200
Telephone: (00) (972) (2) 541 4100 (Chancery, Commercial, Information, Management and Visa)
(2) 671 7724 (Consular)

(2) 532 8459/540 0451
(Development)
(2) 626 4392 (British
Council)
Facsimile: (00) (972) (2) 532 5629 (Chancery)
(2) 532 2368 (Management,
Visa and
Commercial)
(2) 672 9820 (Consular)
(2) 628 3021 (British
Council)
e-mail: britain@palnet.com
Website: http://www.britishconsulate.org
Office Hours (GMT): Sept - Mar: Mon – Thurs
05 30 – 13 30 and Fri 05 30 – 11 30
Apr - Sept: Mon – Thurs 06 30 – 14 30 and Fri
06 30 – 12 30
Consul-General: Mr Geoffrey Adams
Deputy Consul General: Mrs Valerie Brownridge,
MVO (541 4108)
Consul (Political): Mr James Arroyo (541 4103)
Consul (Political): Mr Gerard Russell (5414108)
Consul (Development): Mr Chris Metcalf (532 8459)
Vice-Consul (Management): Mrs Angela
MacKenzie (541 4130)
Vice-Consul (Consular/Immigration): Ms Dawn
Naughton (541 4129)
Vice-Consul (Political): Mrs Sarah Clarke (541
4115)
Vice-Consul (Political): Mr Jayd Davies (541
4119)
Vice-Consul (Political): Ms Rachel Blanche (541
4133)
Vice-Consul (Development): Mr Peter Cardy (540
0451)
Attaché: Miss J McGregor (541 4112)
Attaché: Miss Jane Farrer (541 4105)
Cultural Attaché (British Council Director): Mr
David Martin (626 4392)
*Assistant Cultural Attaché (British Council Deputy
Director):* Mr D Codling (626 4392)

West Jerusalem:
British Consulate-General
Tower House,
Kikar Remez, Jerusalem 93541
Telephone: (00) (972) (2) 6717724
Facsimile: (00) (972) (2) 6729820
e-mail: britain2@palnet.com
Office Hours (GMT): Sept - Mar: Mon - Fri 07 00 -
10 00
Apr - Sept: Mon - Fri 08 00 - 11 00

Gaza:
British Information and Services Office
1st Floor, Al-Riyad Tower,
Jerusalem Street,
Al-Rimal South, Gaza
Telephone: (00 972 0) 8 283 7704/14/24
Facsimile: (00 972 0) 8 283 7734
e-mail: bisogaza@palnet.com
Office Hours (GMT) Sept - Mar: Sun – Wed 05 30 –
13 30, Thurs 05 30 – 11 30
Apr - Sept: Sun – Wed 06 30 – 14 30, Thurs 06 30 –
11 30

JORDAN

Amman
British Embassy
(PO Box 87) Abdoun, Amman
Telephone: (00) (962) (6) 5923100
Facsimile: (00) (962) (6) 5923759
Telex: 22209 (a/b 22209 PRODRUM JO)
e-mail: becommercial@nets.com.jo (commercial)
Website: www.britain.org.jo (Information)
Office Hours (GMT): Sun - Mon 06 00 - 13 30
Tue - Thur 06 00 - 13 00
Ambassador: Mr E G M Chaplin, OBE
*Counsellor, Consul-General and Deputy Head of
Mission:* Mr M D Aron
Counsellor: Mr D F Middleton
Defence, Naval and Military Attaché: Colonel C R
Romberg
Air Attaché: Wing Commander S J Orwell, RAF
First Secretary (Chancery): Mr T R B Hurd
Consul and First Secretary (Management): Mr R
K Dixon
Second Secretary (Commercial): Mrs D A Dixon
*Second Secretary
(Political/Economic/Development):* Ms J Chappell
Second Secretary (Political): Mr N H L Watson
Third Secretary (Political): Mr A J Wells
Third Secretary: Mr L Fennell
Vice-Consul: Mrs N Humphreys
Assistant Management Officer: Ms J Evans
Accountant: Mrs S El Ouassi

KAZAKHSTAN

Almaty
British Embassy
U1 Furmanova 173, Almaty,
Republic of Kazakhstan
Telephone: (00) (73272) 506191, 506192, 506229
Facsimile: (00) (73272) 506260
Opening hours (GMT): winter 0300-10 00
summer Monday to Friday 0200-1030
e-mail: british-embassy@kaznet.kz

Visa/Consular Section
158 Panfilova Street, Almaty
Telephone: (00) (73272) 508280
Facsimile: (00) (73272) 507432
e-mail: visa-british-embassy@nursat.kz
Opening Hours: Mon-Fri 08.30 – 11.00
Ambassador: Mr R G Lewington
Defence Attaché: Lieutenant Colonel G J Sheeley,
AFC
Cultural Attaché (British Council Director): Mr J
Kennedy (Designate)
Deputy Head of Mission: Mr A Dinsley
Second Secretary (Commercial): Ms J Stevens
Third Secretary and Vice-Consul: Mr P Edwards
Third Secretary (Political/Aid): Mr M Waller
Management Officer: Mr S M Brown
Defence Assistant: Mr M Headley

KENYA

Nairobi
British High Commission
Upper Hill Road, Nairobi, PO Box 30465, Nairobi

Commercial Department: PO Box 30133, Nairobi
Consular Department: PO Box 48543, Nairobi
Telephone: (00) (254) (2) 714699 (15 Lines)
Facsimile: (00) (254) (2) 719942 Consular
       714760 Chancery
       719082 Commercial
       719664 UK Permanent
           Mission to UNEP
           and UNCHS
           HABITAT
       719486 Management
       719112 DFID EA
       719110 Visa
Airtech: 719107 Chancery
e-mail: consular@nairobi.mail.fco.gov.uk
(Consular)
visa@nairobi.mail.fco.gov.uk   (Visa)
commercial@nairobi.mail.fco.gov.uk
(Commercial)
information@nairobi.mail.fco.gov.uk   (Press &
Public Affairs)
management@nairobi.mail.fco.gov.uk
(Management)
Office Hours (GMT): Mon - Thur 07 45 - 12 30
and 13 30 - 16 30 Fri 07 45- 13 00
High Commissioner: Mr E Clay, CMG
Deputy High Commissioner: Mr C P D Harvey
Counsellor: Mr I P Simmons
Defence Adviser: Colonel J R Barnes
First Secretary (Commercial): Mr J Chandler
First Secretary (Political): Mr H Evans
First Secretary (Management): Mrs S Gregory
First Secretary (United Nations): Mr J P T Bell
First Secretary (Consular): Mr D C Levoir
First Secretary (Development): Mr D Bell
First Secretary: Mr M Denton
Second Secretary (Political/Economic): Mr J A St J
Fisher
Second Secretary (Political/Economic): Mr T
Fletcher
Second Secretary (Immigration/ECM): Miss J
Montgomery-Ribbon
Second Secretary (Chancery): Miss J D Miles, MBE
Second Secretary (Commercial): Mr C D R Smart
Second Secretary (Development): Mr A Reid
Second Secretary (Works): Mr D J Gillies
Second Secretary: Mr T Bilimoria
Second Secretary (Management): Mr S Burns
Second Secretary: Mr K Knight
Third Secretary: Mr T Oxley
Third Secretary (Information/Press): Mr R J Drabble
Third Secretary (Communications): Mr J Mortimer
Third Secretary (Communications): Mr S M Grinling
Third Secretary (Management/Accounts): Mr R
Mardlin
Third Secretary (Immigration): Mr S Groves
Third Secretary (Immigration): Mr J Lambert
Third Secretary (Immigration): Mr M C Gregory

**Department for International Development
Eastern Africa**
c/o British High Commission
Upper Hill Rd
PO Box 30465, Nairobi
Telephone: (00) (254) (2) 717609 (5 lines)
Facsimile: (00) (254) (2) 719112

Office Hours (GMT): Mon – Thur: 07 45 - 12 30
and 13 30 - 16 30 Fri: 07 45 - 13 00
Head of Development Division: (Vacant)
First Secretary/Senior Education Adviser: Mr A
Penny
First Secretary/Senior Natural Resources Adviser:
Mr M C Leach
*First Secretary/Development/Head of DFIDEA
Kenya:* Mr D Bell
First Secretary/Senior Engineering Adviser: Mr J
A Smallwood
First Secretary/Senior Economist: Mr N Dyer
Second Secretary Personnel/Office Manager: Mr G
Dixon
Second Secretary/Development: Mr A Reid
Second Secretary/Health & Population Adviser:
Ms M C Donagh
*Second Secretary/Senior Social Development
Adviser:* Dr R Hogg
Second Secretary/Economic Assistant: Ms S Ahmed
Second Secretary/Governance Adviser: Ms K de
Jong
Third Secretary/ IT Manager: Mr A Galbraith
Senior Programme Officer, Kenya: Ms T
Bebbington, MBE
Assistant Office Manager: Ms N Gateru
Assistant Engineering Adviser: Mr L Simon
Regional IT Systems Supervisor: Mr I Rivers
IT Systems Manager, Kenya: Mr J Nyoike
Enterprise Development Adviser: Ms C Masinde
Health and Population Adviser: Mr J Lane
Education Co-ordinator: Mr C Kirkcaldy
Small Grants Scheme Co-ordinator: Ms S Harley
Urban Poverty Programme Co-ordinator: Ms W
Taylor
Training Liaison Officer: Ms A Dearing
Special Projects: Mrs S Unsworth

**Nairobi United Kingdom for Human
Settlements (Habitat), see part II**

**Nairobi United Nations Environment
Programme, see part II**

Mombasa
Honorary British Consular Representative
Cotts House (First Floor)
Moi Avenue
PO Box 85593, Mombasa
Telephone: (00) (254) (11) 313609
Facsimile: (00) (254) (11) 312416
e-mail: seaforth@africaonline.co.ke
Honorary British Consular Representative: Mr J W
L Knight
*Assistant British Honorary Consular
Representative:* Mr J Attenborough

**Assistant Honorary Consular Representative in
Mombasa**
c/o Mission to Seamen,
Mogadishu Road,
PO Box 80424, Mombasa
Telephone: (00) (254) (11) 230027/8, 316502/3,
316486, 316285
Facsimile: (00) (254) (11) 230001

KIRIBATI

Tarawa
British High Commission
PO Box 5
Bairiki
Tarawa, Kiribati
Telephone: (00) (686) 22501
Facsimile: (00) (686) 22505
e-mail: ukrep@tksl.net.ki
Britainkiribati@tskl.net.ki
Office Hours (GMT): Sun-Wed 20 15 – 01 00 and
02 00 – 05 00, Thur 20 15 – 01 00
High Commissioner: Mr Michael A Price, LVO
Resident Deputy High Commissioner: Mr Vernon
Scarborough
*Deputy High Commissioner and First Secretary
(Consular):* Mr Christopher Haslam
* Resides at Suva

KOREA (NORTH)

Pyongyang
British Embassy
Munsu Dong District
Pyongyang
Democratic People's Republic of Korea
Telephone: (00) (850) (2) 381 7980/4 (five lines)
Facsimile: (00) (850) (2) 381 7985
*Chargé d'Affaires and Consul-General (resides at
Seoul):* Dr J E (Jim) Hoare
Management Officer and Consul: Mr Jim Warren

KOREA (SOUTH)

Seoul
British Embassy
4, Chung-Dong, Chung-Ku, Seoul
100-120
Republic of Korea
Telephone: (00) (82) (2) 3210 5500
Facsimile: (00) (82) (2) 725 1738
    722 7270 (Airtech)
    736 6241 Commercial
        Section
    3210 5653 Consular
        Section
    3210 5528 Defence
        Section
    733 8368 Defence
        Supplies
    738 2797 Economic
        Section and
        Science/Technol
        ogy/Environment
        Section
    735 7473 Political Section
    720 4928 Press and Public
        Affairs Section
    736 3174 Residence
e-mail: bembassy@britain.or.kr
postmaster.seoul@fco.gov.uk
Website: www.britain.or.kr
Office Hours (GMT): Mon - Fri 00 01 - 08 30
Ambassador: (5510/5511): Mr Charles Humfrey, CMG

Deputy Head of Mission and Consul General:
(5517): Mr Derek Marsh, CVO
Counsellor (and Chargé d'Affaires a.i. Pyongyang):
Dr Jim Hoare
Counsellor (Regional Affairs): (5535): Mr Colin
Partridge
Counsellor and British Council Director: (3702
0600 ext 0677): Mr Mark Baumfield
Defence and Military Attaché: (5524): Brigadier
John C L King, MBE
Naval and Air Attaché: (5525): Captain Paul
Robinson, MBE, RN
First Secretary (Defence Supplies) (5520): Mr
David Bullas
*First Secretary (Science/Technology/Environment)
(5590):* Dr Jim Thomson
First Secretary (Political) (5530): Dr Antony Stokes
First Secretary (Commercial): (5620): Mr David
Brown
First Secretary (Management and Consul) (5655):
Mr Mike Hentley
*First Secretary (Education/British Council Deputy
Director):* Mr Brendan Barker
Second Secretary (Political/Public Affairs) (5560):
Mr Adrian Chapman
Second Secretary (Investment) (5610): Mr
Jonathan Dart
Second Secretary (Political) (5531): Mr Chris Gotch
Second Secretary (Economic) (5600): Mr Guy
Harrison
Second Secretary (Commercial) (5621): Mr Jeremy
Hill
Assistant Cultural Attaché (British Council): Mr
Fred O'Hanlon
*Second Secretary (Technical Works Office) (resides
at Tokyo):* Mr John Warrener
*Second Secretary (Management/Consular)
(5560/5656):* Mr Phil Wyithe
Third Secretary (Regional Affairs) (5536): Mr
Andy Brown
*Third Secretary (Technical Management Officer)
(resides Tokyo):* Mr Hugh Smith
Attaché (language training): Mr Phil Ellis
Attaché (language training): Mr Chris Sims

Pusan
Honorary Consul's Office
12th Floor
Yuchang Building, 25-2,
Chungang-Dong, 4 -Ga
Chung-Gu,
Pusan, 600-014
PO Box No 75
Telephone: (00) (82) (051) 463 0041 and 463 4630
Facsimile: (00) (82) (051) 462 5933
Honorary Consul: Mr S E Wang, CBE
Honorary Vice-Consul: Mr H Guack

KUWAIT

British Embassy
Arabian Gulf Street
Postal Address: PO Box 2, Safat, 13001 Kuwait,
Commercial Section Address: PO Box 300, Safat,
13003, Kuwait
Telephone: (00) (965) 240 3334/5/6

Facsimile: 240 7395 Commercial
242 6799 Chancery/Defence
242 5778 Consular/Visa
240 7633 Management
e-mail: general@britishembassy-kuwait.org
Office Hours (GMT): Sat - Wed: 04 30 - 11 30
Ambassador: Mr Richard Muir, CMG
Counsellor and Deputy Head of Mission: Mr Brian Stewart
Defence Attaché: Colonel The Honourable Alastair Campbell
First Secretary (Political): Mr Alexander Creswell
First Secretary (Management) and Consul: Mr John Francis
First Secretary (Commercial): Mr Bernard Wilson
First Secretary (Defence Supply): Mr Keith Harper
First Secretary (British Council): Mr John Gildea
Second Secretary (Political/Press & Public Affairs): Mr Mark Ellam
Third Secretary (Commercial): Mr Yemi Odanye
Vice-Consul and Third Secretary (Management): Mr Neil Frape
Third Secretary: Mr Kurt Sutherland
Third Secretary: Mr Bernard Ley

KYRGYZSTAN

Bishkek
British Embassy
Ambassador (resides at Almaty): Mr R G Lewington
Defence Attaché (resides at Almaty): Lieutenant Colonel G J Sheeley, AFC
Cultural Attaché (resides at Almaty): Ms L Cowcher
Deputy Head of Mission (resides at Almaty): Mr A Dinsley
Second Secretary (Commercial) (resides at Almaty): Ms J Stevens
Third Secretary (Political/Aid) (resides at Almaty): Mr M Waller
Third Secretary and Vice-Consul (resides at Almaty): Mr P Edwards

British Consulate
Tacis Banking Project Office
195A Abdimumonova St
Bishkek
Republic of Kyrgyzstan
Telephone: (00) (7 3312) 660869
Facsimile: (00) (7 3312) 660869
Honorary Consul: Mr L Johnson

LAOS

Vientiane
British Embassy
(All staff reside at Bangkok)
PO Box 6626, Vientiane, Las, PDR
Telephone: (00) (856) (21) 413606
Facsimile: (00) (856) (21) 413607
Ambassador: Mr L B Smith, CMG
Counsellor: Mr P R Sizeland
Counsellor (Commercial): Mr M Greenstreet
First Secretary (Political): Dr N A D Stokes
First Secretary (Management): Mr R H Tonkin
First Secretary and Consul: Mr B P Kelly
First Secretary: Mr P J W Hardman
First Secretary: Mr G Atkinson

Second Secretary: Mr N Clayton
Second Secretary (Technical Works): Mr A Gillott
Second Secretary (Immigration): Mr S Blake

British Trade Office
(All Staff reside at Bangkok)
Office Hours (GMT): Mon - Fri 01 00 - 05 00 and 06 00 - 09 30
Head of British Trade Office: Mr M R Eyre

LATVIA

Riga (SP)
British Embassy
5 J. Alunana Street, Riga,
Latvia, LV 1010
Telephone: (00) (371) 7 338126, 7 338127, 7 338128, 7 338129, 7 338130
Facsimile: (00) (371) 7 338132
Chancery/Commercial/Information
338154 Management/Consular
Airtech: (00) (371) 7 338140
e-mail: british.embassy@apollo.lv
Website: www.britain.lv
Office Hours (GMT): 07 00 - 11 00 and 12 00 - 15 00
Ambassador: Mr Stephen Nash, CMG
(Mr HAP Tesoriere w.e.f. March 2002)
Deputy Head of Mission and Consul: Mr Nick Carter
Defence Attaché: Lieutenant Colonel Andrew S Tuggey
First Secretary (British Council Director): Mr Ian Stewart
First Secretary (resides in Vilnius): Mr Martin Thursfield
Second Secretary (Commercial): Mrs Jean Quinn
Second Secretary (British Council, Deputy Director): Ms Catherine Stead
Third Secretary: Ms Sarah Murrell
Third Secretary/Vice-Consul and Management Officer: Mr Gordon Horne
Third Secretary (resides in Helsinki): Mr Paul Jackson
Attaché: Mr Garth Robinson
Attaché: FS Joe Stansfield
Technical Works Officer: Mr Andrew Moore

LEBANON

Beirut
British Embassy
Chancery: 8th Street, Rabieh
Telephone: (00) (961) (4) 417007-405070-403640,
Facsimile: (00) (961) (4) 402032
Aitech: (00) (961) (4) 403025
e-mail: britemb@cyberia.net.lb

Commercial, Visa, Consular, Management Section:
Autostrade Jal El Dib, Coolrite Building
Telephone: (00) (961) (4) 715 900-03
Facsimile: (00) (961) (4) 715 904 for Commercial/Management Section
(00) (961) (4) 715 906 for Consular/Visa Section
PO Box: 60180 Jal El Dib - Beirut – Lebanon
Office Hours (GMT): Mon: 04 30 - 12 00,
Tue-Fri: 04 30 - 11 30
Ambassador: Mr Richard Kinchen

Deputy Head of Mission: Mr Adrian Bedford
Defence Attaché: Lieutenant Colonel Desmond J A
Bergin, OBE
*First Secretary (Education Culture) (British
Council Director):* Mr Kenneth Churchill, MBE
Second Secretary (Commercial): Ms Wendy Freeman
Second Secretary (Chancery) (resides in Nicosia):
Mr John Houston
Second Secretary (Management): Mrs Patricia
Fletcher
Vice-Consul: Mr Melvyn James Buglass
Third Secretary (Chancery): Ms Alison Keeling
Attaché: Mrs Sandra Farish
Honorary Consul (Mount Lebanon): Mr William
Zard, MBE

Tripoli
British Consulate
Daar Al Ain, Tripoli
Telephone: (00) (961) (6) 621320
Honorary Consul: Mr Anwar Arida, MBE

LESOTHO

Maseru
British High Commission
PO Box Ms 521 Maseru 100
Telephone: (+) (266) 313961
Facsimile: (+) (266) 310120
Airtech: (+) (266) 310387
e-mail: hcmaseru@lesoff.co.za
www.bhc.org.ls
Individual Officers e-mail =
Firstname.Surname@maseru.mail.fco.gov.uk
Office Hours (GMT): Mon - Thur 06 00 - 11.00
and 11 45 - 14 30; Fri 06 00-11.00
High Commissioner: Miss Kaye Oliver, OBE, CMG
*Deputy High Commissioner and Development
Secretary:* Mr Matthew Forbes
Defence Adviser (Resides at Pretoria): Brigadier M
R Raworth
e-mail: Mike.Raworth@pretoria.mail.fco.gov.uk
Third Secretary (Consular/Management): Mr
Andrew Osborn

LIBERIA

Monrovia
British Embassy
(All staff resident at Abidjan)
Ambassador: Mr J F Gordon, CMG
Second Secretary (Political/ Information): Ms K
Miller, MBE
Second Secretary (Management): Mr D Summers
Second Secretary (Commercial/Political): Mr C
Frean
*Third Secretary (Visa and Passports) and Vice
Consul:* Mr M McGuinness
Third Secretary (Chancery): Ms N McBratney

Office of the Honorary British Consul
UMARCO (Liberia) Corp.
UN Drive, Bushrod Island
PO Box 10-1196
Monrovia, Liberia
Telephone: (00) (231) 22 60 56
Facsimile: (00) (231) 22 60 61

Office Hours: 08 00 - 16 00 Mon – Fri
Honorary British Consul: Mr E R Chalkley

LIBYA

Tripoli
British Embassy
PO Box 4206,
Tripoli, Libya
Telephone: (00) (218) (21) 334 3630/1 (Chancery)
335 1084 (Consular/Visa/Management)
Facsimile: (00) (218) (21) 334 3634 (Chancery)
335 1425 (Consular/
Visa/
Management)
Office Hours (GMT): Sun - Thur: 07 00 - 14 00
Ambassador: Mr Richard Dalton, CMG
Deputy Head of Mission and Consul General: Dr
Noel J Guckian, OBE
First Secretary (Management & Immigration): Mr
John W C Heffer
First Secretary (Commercial): Mr G P Glover
*First Secretary (Education & British Council
Director):* Mr Tony D Jones
Second Secretary (Political): Ms Bridget Brind
Second Secretary (Commercial): Ms Jacqueline
Lawson-Smith
Third Secretary (Management) and Vice Consul:
Mr Steve Auld
Third Secretary (Immigration): Mr Jim Davidson
Third Secretary (Immigration): Mr Gordon Summers
Attaché: Ms Lesley Brewer
Attaché: Ms Jill Mundy

LIECHTENSTEIN

Vaduz
Ambassador (resides at Berne): Mr B Eastwood, CMG
Consul-General (resides at Berne): Mr D G Roberts

LITHUANIA

Vilnius
British Embassy
2 Antakalnio, 2055 Vilnius
Telephone: (00) (370) 2 22 20 70, 2 22 70 71
Direct lines:(00) (370) 2 66 10 23 Ambassador
(00) (370) 2 66 10 17 Deputy Head of
Mission
(00) (370) 2 66 10 13 First Secretary
(Political)
(00) (370) 2 66 10 21 Third Secretary
(Political/Econo
mic/Public
Affairs
(00) (370) 2 66 10 15 Commercial
Section
(00) (370) 2 66 10 19 Press/Public
Affairs Section
(00) (370) 98 37 097 Duty Officer contact number
Facsimile: (00) (370) 2 72 75 79
Airtech: (00) (370) 2 66 10 20
Website www.britain.lt
Office Hours (GMT): Mon - Thur 0630 - 1000 and
1100 - 1500
Fridays 0630 - 1000 and 1100 - 1400
Ambassador: Mr Jeremy Hill

Deputy Head of Mission and Consul: Mr Stephen Tarry
Defence Attaché: Lieutenant Colonel Peter R P Swanson, MBE
First Secretary (Political): Mr Martin Thursfield
First Secretary (British Council) (Resides at Riga): Mr Ian Stewart
Second Secretary (British Council) (Resides at Riga): Ms C Stead
Third Secretary (Political): Mr David Buckley
Third Secretary (Political/Economic/Public Affairs): Mr Nicholas Collier
Third Secretary (Management) and Vice-Consul: Mr Ryan Griffin
Assistant Defence Attaché: CPO(W) Paul Hutton
Attaché: Miss Judith Hitchings
MOD Attaché to Lithuanian Ministry of Defence: Mr Graham Roberts

LUXEMBOURG

Luxembourg
British Embassy
14 Boulevard Roosevelt, L-2450 Luxembourg
Telephone: (00) (352) 22 98 64/65/66
Facsimile: (00) (352) 22 98 67 (Office)
(00) (352) 22 98 68 (Residence)
Airtech: (00) (352) 22 98 64 (Ext. 2231)
e-mail: britemb@pt.lu
Web Page: webplaza.pt.lu/public/britemb
Office Hours (GMT): Summer 07 00 - 11 00 and 12 00 - 15 00
Winter 08 00 - 12 00 and 13 00 - 16 00
Ambassador and Consul-General: Mr Gordon Wetherell
Counsellor (Commercial) (resides at Brussels): Mr Stephen Smith
First Secretary, Consul and Deputy Head of Mission: Mr David Herbert
Defence Attaché (Resides at Brussels): Group Captain Jeff D Bullen, OBE, RAF
Cultural Attaché (British Council Director) (resides at Brussels): Mr Martin Rose
First Secretary (Labour) (resides at The Hague): Mr Peter Drummond
First Secretary (Commercial) (resides at Brussels): Mr Jim Curry
Third Secretary (Management) and Vice-Consul: Mr Adam Perks

MACEDONIA

Skopje
British Embassy
Dimitrija Chupovski 26
4th Floor
Skopje 9100
Telephone: (00) (389) (2) 116 772, 109 941
Facsimile: (00) (389) (2) 117 555
e-mail: beskopje@mt.net.mk
Office Hours (GMT): Summer:- Mon-Thurs: 06 00 - 14 30; Fri till: 11 00
Winter:- Mon-Thurs: 07 00 - 15 30; Fri till: 12 00
Ambassador: Mr C G Edgar
Deputy Head of Mission: Mr R W Potter
Defence Attaché: Colonel M I V Dore

First Secretary (KHF): Mrs R Mustard
Second Secretary (Management/Consular/Chancery): Mr R Rimmer
Second Secretary (Political): Mrs H Bridge
Third Secretary (Management/Consular): Mr J Mitchell

Bitola
Honorary British Consulate
Dobrovoje Radosavljevic No.3
Telephone:(00) (389) (47) 360 32 (Work)
(00) (389) (47) 254 945 (Home)
(00) (389) (47) 228 765 (British /Macedonian Friendship Association)
Facsimile: (00) (389) (47) 222 080
Honorary Consul: Mrs Lijala Spirovska

MADAGASCAR

Antananarivo
British Embassy
Lot II 164 Ter,
Alarobia – Amboniloha, BP 167,
Antananarivo 101
Telephone: (00) (261) (20) 22 49378/79/80
Facsimile: (00) (261) (20) 22 49381
e-mail: ukembant@simicro.mg
Office Hours (GMT): Mon-Wed: 04 30 - 09 00 and 09 30 - 13 00
Thur-Fri: 04 30 - 10 00
Ambassador: Mr C F Mochan
Deputy Head of Mission: Ms R M Owens
Defence Attaché (resides at London): Lieutenant Colonel G M Thomas, MBE
Commercial Officer: Mr Tsiry Wilkinson

Toamasina
British Consulate
Seal Tamatave
Telephone: (00) (261) (20) 5332548/5332569
Facsimile: (00) (261) (20) 5333937
e-mail: sealtmm@bow.dts.mg
Honorary Consul: Mr M Gonthier

MALAWI

Lilongwe
British High Commission
PO Box 30042, Lilongwe 3
Telephone: (00) (265) 772-400,683,701,182,027,123,550
Facsimile: (00) (265) 772-657
Airtech: (00) (265) 772-153
e-mail: bhc@wiss.co.mw
Office Hours (GMT): Mon - Thur 05 30 - 10 00 and 1130 - 14 30
Fri 05 30 - 10 30
High Commissioner: Mr Norman Ling
First Secretary (Development): Mr Michael Wood
Defence Adviser (resides at Harare): Colonel John S Field, CBE
First Secretary (Natural Resources): Dr Harry Potter
First Secretary (Health and Population): Ms Jean-Marion Aitken
First Secretary (Education): Mr Keith Gristock
First Secretary (Governance): Ms Sheelagh Stewart
First Secretary (Infrastructure): Mr Jim Craigie

First Secretary (Infrastructure): Mr Joe Mumar
First Secretary (Economics): Mr Karl Livingstone
First Secretary (Social Development): (Vacant)
First Secretary (Regional Medical Adviser): Dr
Howard Friend
Second Secretary (Management/Consular): Mrs
Julie Bell
Second Secretary (Political/Press & Public Affairs):
Mr Michael Nevin
Second Secretary (Development): Ms Trudi Crabb
Third Secretary (Consular/Commercial): Mr Shaun
Earl

MALAYSIA

Kuala Lumpur
British High Commission
185 Jalan Ampang, 50450 Kuala Lumpur,
or PO Box 11030, 50732 Kuala Lumpur
Telephone: (00) (60) (3) 21482122
          21482354 Commercial
          Section
          21487122 Consular
          Section
Voicemail numbers: See individual officers
Facsimile: (00) (60) (3) 21447766 Management
          21421054 Political
          21480880 Commercial
          21449692 Consular
Airtech: (00) (60) (3) 21487348
e-mail: political.kualalumpur@fco.gov.uk
(Political)
press.kualalumpur@fco.gov.uk (Press and Public
Affairs)
programmes.kualalumpur@fco.gov.uk
(Scholarship)
trade.kualalumpur@fco.gov.uk (Commercial)
defence.kualalumpur@fco.gov.uk (Defence)
consular.kualalumpur@fco.gov.uk (Consular)
webmaster.kualalumpur@fco.gov.uk (IT)
Website: www.britain.org.my
Office Hours (GMT): Mon - Fri 24 00 - 04 30 and
05 15 - 08 30
High Commissioner (PA: 224): Mr Bruce E
Cleghorn
Deputy High Commissioner (238; PA: 244): Mr
Mark Canning
Counsellor (Commercial) (PA: 307): Mr Michael
Horne, OBE
Counsellor (Political) (PA: 222): Mr Andrew Barber
Defence Adviser (PA: 206): Colonel Roger J Little
First Secretary (Political) (202; PA: 203): Mr John
Marshall
First Secretary (Defence Supply) (PA: 206): Mr
Rob Lingham
First Secretary (Commercial) (232): Mr Steven
Green
First Secretary (Management) (258): Mrs Di Hansen
First Secretary (resides at Bangkok): Mr John Hector
Assistant Defence Adviser (228): Lieutenant
Commander Michael P O'Riordan RN
Second Secretary (Economic) (245): Mr Jeremy
Pilmore-Bedford
Second Secretary (Political): Miss Clare Bond
Second Secretary (Management): Mr Ian Attwood

Second Secretary (Immigration Attaché) (327):
Mrs Karen Kyle
*Second Secretary (Political/Press & Public Affairs)
(209):* Mrs Nicola Bowling
Second Secretary (Commercial) (210): Mr Neil
Floyd
Second Secretary (Consular) (204): Ms Julie
Johnson
Third Secretary (Commercial) (223): Mrs Marion
Guthrie
Third Secretary (Management) (254): Miss
Margaret Gallacher

Johor
Office of the Honorary British Representative
Lucas Automotive Sdn Bhd, PLO 17,
Senai Industrial Estate,
KB 105, 81400 Senai, Johor, Malaysia
Telephone: (00) (60) (7) 2249055
Facsimile: (00) (60) (7) 5994301
e-mail: john.w.bradbury@trw.com
Honorary British Representative: Mr John
Bradbury, MBE

Kota Kinabalu (Sabah)
Office of the Honorary British Representative
c/o Pekah Sdn Bhd
WDT No 46
88862 Kota Kinabalu
Sabah, Malaysia
Telephone: (00) (60) (88) 253333
Facsimile: (00) (60) (88) 267666
e-mail: pmole@pc.jaring.my
Honorary British Representative: Mr Peter Mole

Kuching (Sarawak)
Office of the Honorary British Representative
1st and 2nd Floors
183 C/D/E Fortune Land Business Centre
Jalan Rock
Kuching, Sarawak, East Malaysia
Tel/Fax: (00) (60) (82) 250950
e-mail: valm@pc.jaring.my
Honorary British Representative: Mrs Valerie
Mashman

Miri (Sarawak)
Office of the Honorary British Representative
NJV Sarawak Shell Berhad,
98100 Lutong, Miri
Sarawak, East Malaysia
Telephone: (00) (60) (85) 475865/452736
Facsimile: (00) (60) (85) 653877
e-mail: sroddy@pc.jaring.my
Honorary British Representative: Mr Simon Roddy

Penang
Office of the Honorary British Representative
c/o Plantation Agencies Sdn Bhd,
PO Box 706,
10790 Penang, Malaysia
Telephone: (00) (60) (4) 2625333
Facsimile: (00) (60) (4) 2622018
e-mail: pasb@mailworld.net
Honorary British Representative: Mr John West, MBE

MALDIVES

Malé
British High Commission
(All staff resident in Colombo except where
otherwise stated)
High Commissioner: Ms L Duffield
Deputy High Commissioner: Mr M H P Hill
Defence Adviser: Lieutenant Colonel M H De W
Weldon
Cultural Attaché (British Council Director): Ms S
M Maingay
First Secretary (Economic and Commercial): Mr A
Madeley
Second Secretary (Management): Mr R Morris
Second Secretary (Chancery): Miss A Kemp
Second Secretary (Immigration/Consular): Mr J
Kenny
Second Secretary (Immigration): Mr R P Tate
Second Secretary (resides at Mumbai): Mr C Noon
Second Secretary (Development): Mr M Dawson
Deputy Cultural Attaché (British Council): Ms J
Morgan
Third Secretary (Management): Mr E Groves
Attaché (Immigration): Mr A Dick
Attaché (Immigration): Mr M Redden
Attaché (Immigration/Consular): Mr D Love

MALI

Bamako
British Embassy
Ambassador: Mr G N Loten

Bamako
British Consulate
BP 2069
Bamako
Tel/Fax (Office): (00) (223) 23 34 12
Telephone (Home): (00) (223) 21 25 30
Satellite Phone: 00 874 762 471265
Satellite Fax: 00 874 762 471267
e-mail: britcon@spider.toolnet.org
Consul (resides at Dakar): Mr P T D O'Brien, MBE
Vice-Consul (resides at Dakar): Ms A J Lavocat
Consul: Mrs V G Diallo

MALTA

Valletta
British High Commission
PO Box 506, 7 St Anne Street, Floriana,
Malta GC
Telephone: (00) (356) 233134-7
Facsimile: (00) (356) 242001 Consular/
                                   Management
                        233184 Chancery
                        251684 Consular & Visa
                                   Section
e-mail: bhc@vol.net.mt (Information Section)
bhccomm@vol.net.mt (Commercial Section)
Website: www.Britain.com.mt
Office Hours (GMT): Winter: Mon - Thur 07 00 -
15 45; Fri 07 00 - 12 15
Summer: Mon - Fri 05 30 - 11 30
(Individual e-mail: First name.Last
name@Valletta.mail.fco.gov.uk

High Commissioner: Mr Howard Pearce, CVO
*Deputy High Commissioner and First Secretary
(Commercial/Economic):* Mr Philip Tissot
First Secretary (Political): Mr Nigel Eager
Second Secretary (Management/Consular): Ms
Jenny Fenton
Third Secretary (Political/Information/Cultural):
Mr Iain Willis
Third Secretary (Consular/Immigration): Mr Neil
Porter

MARSHALL ISLANDS

Majuro
British Embassy
Ambassador (resides at Suva): Mr Christopher
Haslam

MAURITANIA

Nouakchott
British Embassy
(All staff resident in Rabat)
Ambassador: Mr Anthony M Layden
Counsellor and Deputy Head of Mission: Mr J L
Buchanan, LVO
Defence Attaché: Lieutenant Colonel G D Duthoit
Third Secretary (Political/Information): Ms H
Cross

Nouakchott
B9, 2069 Nouakchott
Telephone: (00) (222) 2 51 756
Facsimile: (00) (222) 2 92 053
Honorary Consul: Mrs N Abeiderrahmane, MBE

MAURITIUS

Port Louis
British High Commission
Les Cascades Building, Edith Cavell Street,
Port Louis, PO Box 1063
Telephone: (00) (230) 211 1361
Facsimile: (00) (230) 211 1369
e-mail: bhc@intnet.mu
bhc@intnet.mu (Consular and Immigration Section)

Commercial Section:
Les Cascades Building,
Edith Cavell Street, Port Louis, PO Box 1063
Telephone: (00) (230) 208 9850
Facsimile: (00) (230) 211 1369

Consular and Immigration Section:
Les Cascades Building
Edith Cavell St
Port Louis, PO Box 1063
Telephone: (00) (230) 211 1361
Facsimile: (00) (230) 212 8470
e-mail: bhc@intnet.mu
Office Hours (GMT): Mon - Thur 03 45 - 11 45
Fri 03 45 - 09 30
High Commissioner: Mr David Snoxell
*Deputy High Commissioner and
First Secretary (Commercial):* Mr John Taylor
Defence Adviser (resides at Nairobi): Colonel J
Ralph Barnes
British Council Director: Mrs Shoba Ponnappa, OBE

Second Secretary (Chancery): Mr Chris Tunnicliffe
Third Secretary (Immigration/Consular): Mr Tony Ward
Third Secretary (Management): Miss Debbie Pow
Third Secretary (Immigration): Miss Jane Atkinson

MEXICO

Mexico City

British Embassy
Rio Lerma 71, Col Cuauhtémoc,
06500 Mexico City
Telephone: (00) (52) (5) 242 8500
Facsimile: (00) (52) (5) 242 8517
e-mail: infogen@mail.embajadabritanica.com.mx
Website: www.embajadabritanica.com.mx
Office Hours (GMT): Mon - Fri 14 30 - 21 30
(Winter) Mon - Fri 15 30 - 22 30 (Summer)
Ambassador: Mr A C Thorpe, CMG
Deputy Head of Mission, Minister-Counsellor and Consul-General: Mr I Hughes
Counsellor (Cultural) (British Council Director) (263 1900 ext. 1992): Mr A Curry
Defence Attaché (resides at Guatemala City): Colonel I C D Blair-Pilling, OBE
First Secretary (Political and Economic): Mr J Thornton
First Secretary (Cultural) (British Council): Mr S Milner
First Secretary (Commercial): Mr M A G Kent
First Secretary (Political/Information/Press & Public Affairs): Ms Y Cherrie
First Secretary (Management): Ms L E Brettle
Second Secretary and Consul: Ms V Lucien
Second Secretary (Commercial): Mr D Lelliott
Second Secretary (Commercial): Mr A J F Ford
Second Secretary (Visits): Mrs I L Page
Second Secretary (Works) (Resides at Miami): Mr M H Jones
Third Secretary (Management): Mr A S Page

Mexico City

British Consulate
Embassy, Consular Section
Rio Usumacinta 30, Col Cuauhtémoc,
06500, Mexico DF
Telephone: As for Embassy
Facsimile: (00) (52) (5) 242 8523
e-mail: consular.section@mail.fco.gov.uk
Consul: Mr V Lucien
Vice-Consul: Ms J E Grant

Acapulco

Honorary British Consulate
Centro Internacional Acapulco
Casa Consular
Costera Miguel Aleman,
39851, Acapulco, Guerrero
Telephone: (00) (52) (7) 484 1735
Facsimile: (00) (52) (7) 449 4266
Honorary Consul: Mrs L E Bajos

Ciudad Juárez

Honorary British Consulate
Calle Fresno 185, Campestre Juárez,
32460 Ciudad Juárez, Chihuahua
Telephone: (00) (52) (16) 175 791/175088

Facsimile: (00) (52) (16) 187 351
Honorary Consul: Mr C R Maingot

Guadalajara

Honorary British Consulate
Paseo del Eden No 2449-4
Prolongacion Colinas de San Javier
45110 Guadalajara, Jalisco
Telephone: (00) (52) (3) 343 2296
Facsimile: (00) (52) (3) 640 1514 (ask for tone)
Honorary Consul: Mr S Cohen, MBE

Mérida (Closed)

Please note that the Honorary Consulate in Mérida, Yucatán has been permanently closed. Yucatán will now be covered from the Honorary Consulate in Cancun. A Consular Agent in Mérida has been appointed to assist the Honorary Consul in Cancun (see Cancun entry for details).

Monterrey

British Consulate
Ave. Ricardo Margain Zozaya 240
Colonia Valle del Campestre
C P 66225
San Pedro Garza Garcia
Nuevo Leon
Telephone: (00) (52) (8) 356 5359
Facsimile: (00) (52) (8) 356 5379
Consul: Mr Karl Burrows
Commercial Officer: Mr Horacio Licon

Monterrey

Honorary British Consulate
Tucan No. 365-A
Col. Country El Tesoro
64850 Monterrey
Nuevo Leon
Telephone: (00) (52) (8) 478 6659
Facsimile: (00) (52) (8) 478 6659 (ask for tone)
Honorary Vice-Consul: Mr C Morris

Tampico (Closed)

Oaxaca

Hotel Posada del Parque
Flamboyant No. 306
La Crucesita, Zocalo
70989 Huatulco, Oaxaca
Telephone: (00) (52) (958) 70219
Facsimile (00) (52) (958) 71425
Consular Correspondent: Mr W Wilczek

Veracruz

Honorary British Consulate
Independencia No 1349-1
Zona Centro (PO Box 724), 91700 Veracruz,
Telephone: (00) (52) (29) 311285
Facsimile: (00) (52) (29) 311285, (ask for tone)
Honorary Consul: Mr L Carbajal

Tijuana

Honorary British Consulate
Blvd Salinas No 1500, Fracc Aviación Tijuana,
22420 Tijuana, BCN
Telephone: (00) (52) (66) 865 320/817 323
Facsimile: (00) (52) (66) 818 402
Honorary Consul: Mr E M Baloyan

Cancun
Honorary British Consulate
The Royal Sands
Blvd Kulkukan,Km 13.5
Zona Hotelera
77500 Cancun, Quintana Roo
Telephone: (00) (52) (98) 810100
Facsimile: (00) (52) (98) 488229
Honorary Consul: Mr M Carney

Consular Agent in Mérida:
El Castallano Hotel,
Mérida
Telephone: (00) (52) (99) 26 27 55
Facsimile: (00) (52) (99) 26 66 29
Mobile: 044 99 700 359
Chief Financial Officer for Royal Resorts: Mr
Joaquin Castillo

MICRONESIA

Pohnpei
British Embassy
Ambassador (resides at Suva): Mr Christopher
Haslam

MOLDOVA

Chisinau
British Embassy
Ambassador (resides at Bucharest): Mr R Ralph,
CVO, CMG
Defence Attaché (resides at Bucharest): Colonel A
T Bruce, MBE

MONACO (HC)

British Consulate
33 Boulevard Princesse Charlotte,
BP 265, MC 98005 Monaco CEDEX
Telephone: (00) (377) 93 50 99 66
Facsimile: (00) (377) 97 70 72 00
Consul-General (resides at Marseille): Mr I Davies
Honorary British Consul: Mr E J F Blair

MONGOLIA

Ulaanbaatar
British Embassy
30 Enkh Taivny Gudamzh (PO Box 703),
Ulaanbaatar 13, Mongolia
Telephone: (00) (976) (11) 458133
Facsimile: (00) (976) (11) 458036
e-mail: britemb@magicnet.mn Registry/Chancery
britemb1@magicnet.mn Visa/Consular
Office Hours (GMT): Winter 01 00 - 05 00 and
06 00 - 09 00
Summer 02 00 - 06 00 and 07 00 - 10 00
Ambassador and Consul-General: Mr P T Rouse, MBE
*Second Secretary, Consul and Deputy Head of
Mission:* Mr S Brier
Defence Attaché (resides at Peking): Brigadier J G
Kerr, OBE, QGM

MOROCCO

Rabat
British Embassy
17 Boulevard de la Tour Hassan (BP 45), Rabat
Telephone: (00) (212) (37) 72 96 96
Facsimile: (00) (212) (37) 70 45 31 (Management/
Consular)
26 08 39 (Chancery)
e-mail: britemb.@mtds.com
Office Hours (GMT): Winter: Mon - Thurs 08 00 -
16 30; Fri 08 00 - 13 00
Summer: Mon - Thurs 08 00 - 14 00
Fri 08 00 - 13 00
Ambassador: Mr Anthony M Layden
Deputy Head of Mission: Mr Rupert Joy
Defence Attaché: Lieutenant Colonel Graham D
Duthoit
Cultural Attaché (British Council Director): Mr G
McCulloch, MBE
First Secretary and Consul: Miss E A Dow
Second Secretary (Political/Information): Ms H
Cross
Second Secretary (Commercial/Economic): Miss K
Hall
Second Secretary: Mr M Vertigen
*Assistant Cultural Attaché (British Council Asst
Director):* Mr J Shackleton
Vice Consul: Mrs A M Teeuwissen

Tangier
British Consulate
41 Boulevard Mohamed V, (BP 2122) Tangier
Telephone: (00) (212) (39) 94 15 57, 94 18 78
Facsimile: (00) (212) (39) 94 22 84
e-mail: uktanger@mtds.com
Office Hours (GMT): Winter: Monday to Thursday
08 00 - 16 30
Summer: Monday to Thursday 08 00 - 14 00;
Friday 08 00 - 13 00
Consul: Miss S L Sweet, MBE

Casablanca
British Consulate-General
43 Boulevard d'Anfa
(BP 13.762)
Casablanca 01
Telephone: (00) (212) 22 22 17 41, 22 22 31 85,
22 20 33 16, 22 20 33 19, 22 20 33 76, 22 29 58 96
22 22 16 53 Answer-phone out of hours & Duty
Officer
Facsimile: (00) (212) 22 26 57 79
Visa Section Fax: (00) (212) 22 20 74 34
Airtech: (00) (212) 22 29 88 21
e-mail: british.consulate@casanet.net.ma
Office Hours (GMT): Winter: Mon – Thur 08 00 -
16 30; Fri 08 00 - 13 00
Summer: Mon - Thur 08 00 - 14 00; Fri 08 00 -
13 00
*Consul-General and Director, British Trade
Promotion:* Mr Alan Michael
Consul (Commercial): Mr Gordon MacLeod
Vice-Consul (Commercial): Mr Driss Amal
Vice-Consul/Management Officer: Mr Ian Fox
Vice-Consul (Immigration): Mrs Karen Rogers
Vice-Consul (Immigration): Mr Danny De Silva

Agadir
British Consulate
Complet Tours
Immeuble Oumlil
No. 26 3rd Floor
Avenue Hassan II
Agadir, Morocco
Telephone: (00) (212) 48 823401,823402
Facsimile: (00) (212) 48 823403
Honorary Consul: Ms Lesley Sanchez

Marrakech
British Consulate
55 Boulevard Zerktouni, Residence Taib,
Marrakech
Telephone: (00) (212) (44) 435095
Facsimile: (00) (212) (44) 439217
Honorary Consul: Mr Mohamed Zkhiri

MOZAMBIQUE

Maputo
British High Commission
Av Vladimir I Lenine 310, Caixa Postal 55,
Maputo
Telephone: (00) (2581) 420111/2/5/6/7
Facsimile: (00) (2581) 421666
Airtech: (00) (2581) 429194
e-mail: bhc@virconn.com
Office Hours (GMT): Mon - Thur 06 00 - 10 30-
12 00 - 15 00; Fri 06 00 - 11 00
High Commissioner: Mr Bob Dewar
Deputy High Commissioner and Consul: Mr Peter
Butcher
Defence Adviser (resides at Harare): Colonel John
Field, CBE
First Secretary (British Council Director): Mr
Simon Ingram-Hill
Second Secretary (Management/Consular): Mr
John Gibson
Third Secretary (Commercial): Mr David Harries OBE
*Third Secretary (Vice-Consul/Press and Public
Affairs):* Mr Andrew Bowes

**Department for International Development
(DFID) Mozambique**
Head of Office: Mr Eamon Cassidy
First Secretary (Rural Livelihoods): Ms Julia
Compton
First Secretary (Health and Education): Dr Allison
Beattie
First Secretary (Economic): Dr Nick Highton
First Secretary (Social Development): Mr Robin
Milton
First Secretary (Governance Adviser): Ms Caroline
Rickatson
Second Secretary (Deputy Programme Adviser):
Mr Tom Jamieson
Second Secretary (Management): Mr John Hawkes

Beira
British Honorary Consulate
Rua Paiva Couceiro 175,
Beira CP 1401
Telephone: (00) (258) 3 311 763
Facsimile: (00) (258) 3 312 318
Honorary Consul: Mr Colin Cronin

NAMIBIA

Windhoek
British High Commission
116 Robert Mugabe Avenue,
Windhoek
Postal Address: PO Box 22202,
Telephone: (00) (264) (61) 274800
Facsimile: (00) (264) (61) 228895
Airtech: (00) (264) (61) 239004
e-mail: bhc@mweb.com.na
Consular@windhoek.mail.fco.gov.uk
Visa@windhoek.mail.fco.gov.uk
Commercial@windhoek.mail.fco.gov.uk
Opening Hours: (April - September GMT+2)
Mon-Thurs 06 00 – 11 00; 12 00 – 15 00
Fri 06 00 – 10 00
(September - April GMT+1) Mon-Thurs 07 00 –
12 00; 13 00 – 16 00 Fri 07 00 – 11 00
High Commissioner: Mr Brian Donaldson
(Mr AT MacDermott w.e.f. April 2002)
Deputy Head of Mission: Mr Neal Hammond
Defence Adviser (Resides at Pretoria): Wing
Commander T A (Tony) Harper, RAF
Third Secretary: Mr Jim Couzens
Attaché: Ms Margaret Horsley

British Council
1–5 Peter Muller Street
Windhoek West
Windhoek
Postal Address: PO Box 13392
Telephone: (00) (264) (61) 226776
Facsimile: (00) (264) (61) 227530
e-mail: general.enquiries@bc-namibia.bcouncil.org
Website: www.britcoun.org/namibia
Opening Hours: same as British High Commission
Director: Ms P. Mahlalela

**Department for International Development
(DFID) Field Office**
11th Floor
Sanlam Centre
Independence Avenue
Windhoek
Postal Address: 20689
Telephone: (00) (264) (61) 256294/5; 256251/17
Facsimile: (00) (264) (61) 256296
Opening Hours: same as British High Commision
*Head of DFID Field Office/Programme
Administrator:* Ms Rachel Malone
e-mail: r-malone@dfid.gov.uk

NAURU

Nauru
British High Commission
(All staff resident at Suva)
High Commissioner: Mr Michael A Price, LVO
*Deputy High Commissioner and First Secretary
(Consular):* Mr Christopher Haslam

NEPAL

Kathmandu
British Embassy
Lainchaur Kathmandu (PO Box 106)

Telephone: (00) (977) (1) 410583, 411281, 411590, 414588
Facsimile: (00) (977) (1) 411789, 416723
e-mail: britemb@wlink.com.np
Office Hours (GMT): Mon - Thur: 02 30 - 06 45 and 07 45 - 11 15; Fri: 02 30 - 06 45 and 07 45 - 09 30
Ambassador: Mr R P Nash, LVO
First Secretary and Deputy Head of Mission: Mr A Mitchell
Defence Attaché: Colonel M Dowdle
First Secretary (Development) (Head of DFID Nepal): Ms S Wardell
First Secretary (Cultural) (British Council Director): Ms B Wickham
Assistant Defence Attaché: Lieutenant Colonel B D Spencer
First Secretary (Resident in New Delhi): Mr P Free
Head of Management: Mr B A Davison
Third Secretary (Chancery): Mr J Goddard
Vice-Consul: Ms J Ferguson
Second Secretary, HM Consul/ECM, (Head, Consular & Immigration Services): Mr J C Chick
Attaché: Ms R Howes
Attaché: Ms A Garrity
Political Attaché and Information Officer: Mr D B Thapa
Commercial Attaché: Mr P G Karmacharya

Department For International Development, Nepal (DFIDN)
Telephone: (00) (977) (1) 542980/542981
Facsimile: (00) (977) (1) 542979
First Secretary (Head of DFID Nepal): Ms S Wardell
First Secretary (Deputy Head of DFID Nepal): Mr A Harper
First Secretary (Government and Institution Adviser): Mr S Sharpels
First Secretary (Economic Adviser): Mr C Jackson
First Secretary (Rural Livelihoods Adviser): Mr S Bickersteth
First Secretary (Health Adviser): Dr M O'Dwyer
First Secretary (Engineering Adviser): Mr M Harvay
First Secretary (Social Development Adviser): Ms F Winter
First Secretary (Senior Education Adviser): Mr K Lillis
Second Secretary (Head of Finance): Mr M McGill
Deputy Programme Manager: Mrs S McGill
Third Secretary (Change Facilitator): Mr J Black
Third Secretary (Change Facilitator): Ms V Malloo

British Council
Lainchaur, PO Box 640,
Kathmandu
Telephone: (00) (977) (1) 410798, 413003
Facsimile: (00) (977) (1) 410545
Office Hours: Mon - Thurs: 08 00 - 17 00 (Office)
Fri: 08 00 - 13 00 (Office)
Winter: Mon - Fri: 10 00 - 18 00 (Library)
Director (British Council and Cultural Attaché): Ms B Wickham
Assistant Director (British Council): Mr C Early

NETHERLANDS

The Hague
British Embassy
Lange Voorhout 10, 2514 ED, The Hague
Telephone: (00) (31) (70) 427 0427
Facsimile: (00) (31) (70) 427 0345 General
                          0346 Commercial
                                 Section
                          0347 Ambassador's
                                 Office, DHM
                                 and Political
                                 Section
Website: www.britain.nl
Office Hours (GMT): Mon - Fri 08 00 - 16 30
Ambassador: Mr C R Budd, CMG
Deputy Head of Mission/Consul-General: Mr T C Holmes
Counsellor (Commercial and Economic): Ms C Bradley
Counsellor: Mr W L Jackson-Houlston, OBE
Defence and Naval Attaché: Captain N A M Butler, RN
Military and Air Attaché: Lieutenant Colonel S J A Lloyd, MBE
First Secretary and Head of Political Section: Mrs J Longbottom
First Secretary (Chemical Weapons): Mr G D Cole
First Secretary (Labour): Mr P E Drummond
First Secretary (Press & Public Affairs): Mr W Evans
First Secretary (Commercial): Mr A J Hennessy
First Secretary (Management): Mr M K Oliver
Second Secretary (Labour): Mr A Kirk
Second Secretary (Chemical Weapons): Mr J P Murphy
Second Secretary (Economic): Mrs C Lufkin
Second Secretary (Political): Ms J Cooper
Second Secretary (Political): Miss J Hollywood
Attaché: Mr K Ditcham
Attaché: Mr P Harris
Attaché: Mr G Bertie
Attaché: Mr M T Bonfield
Attaché: Mr A Obee

Amsterdam (SP)
British Consulate-General
Koningslaan 44,
(PO Box 75488, 1070 AL Amsterdam)
Telephone: (00) (31) (20) 676 43 43 (6 lines) for extensions see individual officers
Facsimile: (00) (31) (20) 676 10 69
                          675 83 81 Consular
                                 Section
Airtech: (00) (31) (20) 676 4343 (Option 1, 2252#)
Telex: 15117 (a/b UKAMS NL)
e-mail: PassportEnquiries.amsterdam@fco.gov.uk
VisaEnquiries.amsterdam@fco.gov.uk
Office Hours (GMT): Mon-Fri 08 00 - 16 00
Consul-General (resides at The Hague): Mr Timothy Holmes
Consul (2209): Mr Peter Barklamb
Vice-Consul (Management) (2210): Ms Vanessa Jennison
Vice-Consul (Consular) (2222): Mr Malcolm Mason, MBE
Vice-Consul (Immigration) (2216): Mr Barry Wilde

Willemstad (Curacao)
British Consulate
Jan Sofat 38
(PO Box 3803)
Curacao
Netherlands Antilles
Telephone: (00) (599) (9) 747 3322
Facsimile: (00) (599) (9) 747 3330
e-mail: Owers@curinfo.an
Office Hours (GMT): 12 00 - 16 00
Honorary Consul (see address above): Mr Antony
Owers

Philipsburg (St Maarten)
(Netherlands Antilles)
British Vice-Consulate
(Temporarily closed)

NEW ZEALAND

Wellington
British High Commission
44 Hill Street, Wellington 1
Mailing Address: British High Commission,
PO Box 1812, Wellington
Telephone: (00) (64) (4) 472 6049
Facsimile: (00) (64) (4) 473 4982 Economic/Trade
                                        Policy Section
                          471 1974 Consular
                          495 0831 Chancery
                          495 0809 Management
Airtech: 495 0836
e-mail: bhc.wel@xtra.co.nz
Website: www.britain.org.nz
Office Hours (GMT): 20 45 - 05 00
High Commissioner (Ext 874): Mr R T Fell, CVO
Deputy High Commissioner (Ext 859): Mr M Bourke
Defence Adviser (Ext. 875): Colonel A A Peebles
First Secretary (Economic/Trade Policy) (Ext 842):
Ms R L Foxwell
*First Secretary (Political/Press/Public Affairs) (Ext
861):* Mrs K S Wolstenholme
First Secretary (British Council Director) (Ext 853):
Mr P N Atkins
First Secretary (Political/External) (Ext 881): Mr
R J Dean
*First Secretary (Senior Technical Management
Officer) (resides at Canberra):* Mr R Bronson
Second Secretary (Management) (Ext 871): Miss A
Bouch
Second Secretary (Political) (Ext 862): Mr J D
Wolstenholme
Second Secretary (Consular) (Ext 899): Mr W S
Robertson

Auckland
British Consulate-General
Level 17 NZI House, 151 Queen Street, Auckland 1
Mailing Address: British Consulate-General,
Private Bag 92014, Auckland 1
Telephone: (00) (64) (9) 303 2973
Facsimile: (00) (64) (9) 303 1836
e-mail: postmaster@auckland.mail.fco.gov.uk
Website: www.brittrade.org.nz
Office Hours (GMT): 20 45 - 05 00
Consular, Visa and Passport work is centralised in
Wellington

Consul-General and Director of Trade Promotion:
Mr T N Byrne
Deputy Consul-General: Mr W G D Johnson, MBE
Trade Promotion Manager: Mrs F Griffith
Trade Promotion Manager: Mrs B Harris
Trade Promotion Manager: Mr G Mitchell
Pro-Consul (Management): Ms D Clay

Christchurch
British Trade Office and Consulate
PO Box 13292, Christchurch 8031
Telephone: (00) (64) (03) 337 9933
Facsimile: (00) (64) (03) 337 9938
Office Hours (GMT): 21 00 - 05 00
Trade Representative and Honorary Consul: Mr I
D Howell, OBE

Office of the Honorary British Consul
Muri Beach
PO Box 104
Rarotonga
Cook Islands
Telephone: (00) (682) 26 662
Facsimile: (00) (682) 28 662
e-mail: mckegg@oyster.net.ck
Honorary British Consul: Mr N McKegg, OBE

NICARAGUA

Managua
British Embassy
Plaza Churchill, Reparto "Los Robles",
Managua, Apartado A-169
Telephone: (00) (505) (2) 780014, 780887, 674050
Facsimile: (00) (505) (2) 784085
Airtech: (00) (505) (2) 678271
e-mail: britemb@ibw.com.ni
Office Hours (GMT): 13 30 - 20 30
Consular 15 00 - 18 00
Ambassador and Consul-General: Mr Hal Wiles
*Second Secretary, Vice Consul and Deputy Head of
Mission:* Mr Gary Scroby
*First Secretary (Commercial) and Director of
Trade Promotion, Central America (resides at San
José):* Mr Christopher Edge
Defence Attaché (resides at Guatemala City):
Colonel Ian Blair-Pilling, OBE
Second Secretary (resides at Panama City): Mr
Andrew Davenport

**Department for International Development,
Central American Regional Office**
Casa 17A, Reparto 'Los Robles'
Managua
Telephone: (00) (505) (0) 88 38769
Head of DFID (CARO) and Development Adviser:
Ms Georgia Taylor
Regional Health Adviser: Miss Luana Reale

NIGER

Niamey
British Embassy
(All staff resident in Abidjan)
Ambassador and Consul-General: Mr J F Gordon,
CMG

First Secretary (Commercial) & Consul: Mr M J K Rickerd, MVO
Second Secretary (Political/Information): Ms K Miller, MBE
Second Secretary (Commercial/Political): Mr C Frean
Third Secretary, (Visas/Passports) and Vice-Consul: Mr M McGuinness
Third Secretary (Management) and Vice Consul: Mr D Summers

British Consulate
BP11926, Niamey, Niger
Telephone: (00) (227) 72 46 76 or 75 24 59
Facsimile: (00) (227) 74 46 76
Honorary Consul: Mr B Niandou

NIGERIA

Abuja
British High Commission
Shehu Shangari Way (North),
Maitama, Abuja
Telephone: (00) (234) (9) 413 2010, 2011, 2796, 2880, 2883, 2887, 9817 (Chancery And Defence Sections)
Facsimile: (00) (234) (9) 413 3552 (Chancery and Defence Sections)
Airtech: (00) (234) (9) 413 2010
e-mail: Chancery@abujx.mail.fco.gov.uk
Defence@abujx.mail.fco.gov.uk
Commercial@abuja.mail.fco.gov.uk
Consular@abuja.mail.fco.gov.uk
Management@abuja.mail.fco.gov.uk
VisaEnquiries@abuja.mail.fco.gov.uk
Office Hours (GMT): 07 00 - 14 00

Commercial, Management, Consular and Visa Sections:
Dangote House, Aguyi Ironsi Street,
Maitama, Abuja
Telephone: (00) (234) (9) 413 4559-4564, 0899,.0900, 3885-7, 3889
Facsimile: (00) (234) (9) 413 4565 (Visa Section)
(00) (234) (9) 413 3888 (Management, Commercial and Consular Sections)

Development Section
Telephone/Facsimile: (00) (234) (9) 413 0715
e-mail: wendyjphillips@compuserve.com

British Council
Telephone: (00) (234) (9) 413 0901
Facsimile: (00) (234) (9) 413 0902
e-mail: Abuja@bc-abuja.bcouncil.org
High Commissioner
(also Ambassador non –resident to the Republic of Benin): Mr Philip Thomas, CMG
Deputy High Commissioner: Mr Charles Bird
Defence Adviser: Colonel John R Lemon
Counsellor (Developmental): Mr Paul Spray
Counsellor (Cultural): Mr Simon Kay
First Secretary (Political): Mr Ian Baharie
First Secretary (Political): Mr Nigel Bowie
First Secretary (Management): Mr Rob D Elliott
First Secretary (Development): Mrs Wendy Phillips

First Secretary (Cultural and Aid): Mr David Roberts
Second Secretary (Economic): Mrs Karen Bell
Second Secretary (Political): Mr Arthur Snell
Second Secretary (Political): Mr Colin Wells
Second Secretary (Immigration): Mr Simon Rose
Third Secretary (Political): Mr John Hamilton
Attaché (Management) & Vice Consul: Mr Kevin Newman
Attaché (Management): Mr Keith Rowlands
Attaché (Immigration): Mrs Lynn Taylor
Attaché (Immigration): Mr Neil Collyer
Attaché (Immigration): Mr Kingsley Magee

Lagos
Chancery Building
British Deputy High Commission
11 Walter Carrington Crescent
Victoria Island
(Private Mail Bag 12136)
Telephone: (00) (234) (1) 2619531, 2619537, 2619541, 2619543, 2619566, 2619588, 2619592, 2619598
Facsimile: (00) (234) (1) 2614021
Office Hours (GMT): 0700 – 1400

Consular and Visa Sections
11 Walter Carrington Crescent
Victoria Island
Telephone: (00) (234) (1) 2625930-7
Facsimile: (00) (234) (1) 2625940 Consular
(00) (234) (1) 2625941 Visa
Office Hours (GMT): 0630 – 1330
Deputy High Commissioner: Mr D Wyatt
Deputy Head of Mission and First Secretary (Management): Mr C W Crorkin
First Secretary (Political): Mr N J Carrick
First Secretary (Commercial): Mr I M Birks
First Secretary (Immigation): Mr R Gemmell
First Secretary (Medical): (Vacant)
First Secretary (Technical Management): Mr A Bagnall
Second Secretary (Political): Mr C Tennant
Second Secretary (Political/Press): Mr J D Sharp
Second Secretary (Management): Mr A J Kirkpatrick
Second Secretary (Commercial): Ms S E Pickering
Second Secretary (Consular): Mrs J Finnamore-Crorkin
Second Secretary (Immigration): Mr K Simpson
Second Secretary (Immigration): Mr K Chaplin
Second Secretary (Immigration): Mr A McCann
Second Secretary (Nurse): Mrs Y Gibney
Second Secretary (Technical Management): Mr J M Lawrie
Third Secretary (Political): Mr D M Paterson
Third Secretary (Management): Mr G R Williams
Third Secretary (Management): Mr K Curran
Third Secretary (Management): Mr P A Smith
Third Secretary (Consular): Mr T Sanmoogan

Kano
2 Tsauna Close
Off Amadu Bello Way
PO Box 11872
Kano
Telephone: (00) (234) (64) 631 686
Facsimile: (00) (234) (64) 632 590

e-mail: bhc.kan@skannet.com
Honorary Consul: Mr Harold Blackburne, OBE

Kaduna
British Commercial/Liaison Office
3 Independence Way, Kaduna
Telephone: (00) (234) (62) 233380/1
Facsimile: (00) (234) (62) 237267
e-mail: bhc.kad@skannet.com
Port Harcourt
British Commercial/Liaison Office
Plot 300, Olu Obasanjo Road, Port Harcourt,
Rivers State
Telephone: (00) (234) (84) 237173, 335104
Facsimile: (00) (234) (84) 237172

Ibadan
British Liaison Office
Rotimi Williams Avenue, Bodija, Ibadan
Telephone: (00) (234) (22) 810 4953
Lagos
British Council Division (Lagos and Enugu)
11 Kingsway Road, Ikoyi, Lagos
Telephone: (00) (234) (1) 2692193, 2690646
Facsimile: (00) (234) (1) 2690646, 2692193
Telex: 22071 (a/b 22071 BRICO NG)
Office Hours (GMT): 06 30 - 13 30
Counsellor (Cultural and Aid): Ms C Stephens
First Secretary (Cultural and Aid): Mr N Townson
First Secretary (Aid/Management): Mr A Campbell
First Secretary (Book Aid): Ms K Sanders

British Council Division (Enugu, Ibadan, Kaduna and Kanu)
Teachers House, Ogui Road, Enugu
Telephone: (00) (234) (42) 255577, 255677, 258456
Facsimile: (00) (234) (42) 250158
53 Magazine Road, PMB 5314, Jericho, Ibadan
Telephone: (00) (234) (22) 2410299, 2410678
Facsimile: (00) (234) (22) 2410796
Yakubu Gwan Way, Kaduna
Telephone: (00) (234) (62) 236033-5
Facsimile: (00) (234) (62) 236330
10 Emir's Place Road, Kano
Telephone: (00) (234) (64) 646652, 643489
Director's Direct Line: (00) (234) (64) 643861
Facsimile: (00) (234) (64) 632500
First Secretary (Cultural and Aid, Kano): Mr P
Morison

NORWAY

Oslo
British Embassy
Thomas Heftyesgate 8, 0244 Oslo
Telephone: (00) (47) 23 13 27 00
Facsimile: (00) (47) 23 13 27 41 Management
27 89 Chancery
27 38 Consular/Visa
Section
27 05 Economic/
Commercial
Section
27 27 Information
Section
Office Hours (GMT): Summer 06 30 - 14 00,
Winter 07 30 - 15 00

Ambassador (2701): Sir R N Dales, KCVO, CMG
*Counsellor, Consul-General, Deputy Head of
Mission (2707):* Mr D G Blunt, CVO
Counsellor (2716): Mr A J G Insall, LVO
Defence and Naval Attaché (2711): Commander D
L Stanesby, RN
Military and Air Attaché (2715): Lieutenant
Colonel J A Poole-Warren
*First Secretary (Economic and Commercial)
(2752):* Dr L Bristow-Smith
First Secretary (Management/Consul) (2751): Mr
I J Stevens, LVO
*Second Secretary (Economic and Commercial)
(2759):* Mr S J Cartwright
Second Secretary (Information) (2718): Mr C Davies
Second Secretary (2719): Mr M R Syrett
Second Secretary (Chancery) (2708): Ms J Wright
Vice Consul: Mr M Scales

Bergen
British Consulate
PO Box 7255, 5020 Bergen
VISITING ADDRESS:
Carl Konowsgate 34, 5161 Laksevåg
Telephone: (00) (47) 55 94 47 05
Telefax: (00) (47) 55 34 34 28
Honorary Consul: Mr R C Hestness (Norwegian)

Harstad
British Consulate
PO Box 322, 9483 Harstad
VISITING ADDRESS:
Sjøgata 7, 9405 Harstad
Telephone: (00) (47) 77 06 46 31
Facsimile: (00) (47) 77 06 77 45
Honorary Consul: Mr T O Jacobsen (Norwegian)

Kristiansand (S)
British Consulate
Post Box 8207, Vågsbygd, 4676 Kristiansand (S)
VISITING ADDRESS:
Lumberveien 49, 4621 Kristiansand (S)
Telephone: (00) (47) 38 01 94 50
Facsimile: (00) (47) 38 01 91 01
Honorary Consul: Mr T Wiese-Hansen (Norwegian)

Kristiansund (N)
British Consulate
Post Box 148, 6501 Kristiansund N
VISITING ADDRESS:
Vågeveien 7, 6509 Kristiansund N
Telephone: (00) (47) 71 67 53 33
Telefax: (00) (47) 71 67 53 52
Honorary Consul: Mr J Loennechen, MBE
(Norwegian)

Stavanger
British Consulate
PO Box 28, 4001 Stavanger
VISITING ADDRESS:
Prinsensgate, 12 4008 Stavanger
Telephone: (00) (47) 51 53 83 00
Facsimile: (00) (47) 51 53 83 01
Honorary Consul: Mr T Falck, Jnr (Norwegian)

Tromsø
British Consulate

c/o Mack's Ølbryggeri, 9291, Tromsø
VISITING ADDRESS:
c/o Mack's Ølbryggeri, Storgaten 5-13, 9291
Tromsø
Telephone: (00) (47) 77 62 45 00
Facsimile: (00) (47) 77 65 86 77
Honorary Consul: Mr H Bredrup (Norwegian)

Trondheim
British Consulate
Post Box 2521, 7413 Trondheim
VISITING ADDRESS:
Beddingen 8, 7037, Trondheim
Telephone: (00) (47) 73 60 02 00
Facsimile: (00) (47) 73 60 02 50
Honorary Consul: Mrs B Kjeldsberg (Norwegian)

Ålesund
British Consulate
Post Box 1301, 6001 Ålesund
VISITING ADDRESS:
Farstadgården, St Olav's Plass, 6001 Ålesund
Telephone: (00) (47) 70 12 44 60
Facsimile: (00) (47) 70 12 85 30
Honorary Consul: Mr S A Farstad (Norwegian)

OMAN

Muscat
British Embassy
PO Box 300, Muscat, Postal Code 113,
Sultanate of Oman
Telephone: (00) (968) 693077
                693086 (Commercial)
                693112 (Commercial)
                693094 (Defence)
Facsimile: (00) (968) 693087 (General)
                693179 (Chancery)
                693088 (Commercial)
                693091 (Consular)
                693089 (Defence)
e-mail: becomu@omantel.net.om
Office Hours (GMT): Sat - Wed 03 30 - 10 30
Ambassador: Sir Ivan Callan, KCVO, CMG (Mr J
Stuart Laing w.e.f.April 2002)
Counsellor and *Deputy Head of Mission:* Mr A J N
Tansley
Defence and Military Attaché: Brigadier Mike
Smith, CBE, MC
Naval and Air Attaché: Wing Commander Graham
R Warburton, RAF
First Secretary (Political): Mr Craig Drysdale
First Secretary (Commercial): Mr Malcolm Ives
First Secretary (Management) and Consul: Mr M
G Snell
Second Secretary (Chancery/Information): Mr
Nicholas K Latta
Third Secretary (Commercial): Mrs Fiona M S
Perkins
British Vice-Consul: Mrs Susan Ives
BERS Liaison Officer: Mrs Cynthia A Smith

PAKISTAN

Islamabad
British High Commission
Diplomatic Enclave, Ramna 5,

PO Box 1122, Islamabad
Telephone: (00) (92) (51) 2206071/5, 2822131/5,
Direct Lines: (00) (92) (51) 2822996 High
                                                    Commissioner
                                        2823436 Deputy Head
                                                    of Mission
                                        2206067 Chancery
                                        2206056 Counsellor
                                                    (Political)
                                        2820917 Visa
                                                    Settlement
                                                    Section
                                        2820934 Visa Visits
                                                    Section
                                        2821079 Health &
                                                    Population
                                                    Office
                                        2828456 Clinic
Facsimile: (00) (92) (51)   2825299 Chancery
                                        2823439 General
                                        2826217 Commercial
                                        2206069 Visa Tel.
                                                    Corres. Unit
                                        2824728 Visa
                                                    Settlement
                                                    Section
                                        2279355 Head of Visa
                                                    Section
                                        2279356 Consular
                                        2279351
                                                    Accommodation/TWG
                                        2277159 Clinic
                                        2823017 Health &
                                                    Population
                                                    Office
Telegrams: Prodrome, Islamabad
e-mail: bhctrade@isb.comsats.net.pk (Commercial
Section)
bhcmedia@isb.comsats.net.pk (Media and Public
Affairs)
Office Hours (GMT): Mon - Thu: 03 00 - 11 00;
Fri: 03 00 - 07 00

Immigration/Consular Sections:
Office Hours (GMT): Mon-Fri: 02 30 - 09 30
High Commissioner: Mr Hilary Synnott, CMG
Deputy High Commissioner: Mr Michael F Smith
Counsellor (Immigration/Management): Mr Ian D
Marsh
Counsellor (Political): Mrs Claire Smith
Counsellor (Regional Affairs): Mr Michael J
Crawford
Defence and Military Adviser: Brigadier Edward J
Torrens-Spence
Naval and Air Adviser: Captain Andrew T Welsh, RN
First Secretary (Political): Mr Nicholas Cannon
First Secretary (Political): Mr WilliamBlanchard
First Secretary (Head of Visa Section): Mr Colin
Mulcahy
First Secretary (Visa): Mrs Debbie Benyon
First Secretary (Management): Mr Nicholas A
Starkey
First Secretary (Works): Mr Geoffrey C Mallery
First Secretary (Technical Manager): Mr Peter
Mawston
First Secretary (Development): Mr Gareth Aicken

First Secretary (Commercial): Mr Murray Pakes
First Secretary (Drugs): Mr Paul Barrett
First Secretary (Social Development Adviser):
Miss Kirsty Mason
First Secretary (Consultant Programme Manager):
Dr Ann Freckleton
First Secretary (Health & Population Adviser): Mr
Chris Allison
First Secretary (Education Adviser): Dr. Hazel Bines
SAP Co-ordinator: Ms Juliette Seibold
First Secretary (Governance Adviser): Ms Jackie
Charlton
Second Secretary (Political): Ms Rebecca Ann Sagar
Second Secretary (Political/External): Mr Richard
J Joynson-Squire
Second Secretary (Political): Miss Grace Cassy
Second Secretary (Political): Mr Brendan Hughes
Second Secretary (Political): Mr Adrian Scott
Second Secretary (Management:) Ms Sally Biskin
Second Secretary (Estates Manager): Mr David
Walters
Second Secretary (Commercial): Miss Sheila J
Bramley
Second Secretary (Drugs): Mr Roy Affleck
Second Secretary (Development): Mr Angus Miller
Second Secretary (Humanitarian Adviser): Mr
Adrian Ouvry
Second Secretary (Visa): Ms Carol Doughty
Second Secretary (Visa): Mrs Diane Drew
Second Secretary (Visa): Mr Mike Crozier
Second Secretary (Visa): Miss Jenny Lock
Second Secretary (Visa): Mr Peter Brown
Second Secretary (Works): Mr John Denoon
Second Secretary (Nurse): Mrs Elizabeth McManus
Second Secretary (Visa/Consular): Miss Linda Smith
Second Secretary (Consular): Mr Mark Kettle
Second Secretary (Air Liaison Officer): Mr Paul
Van Denbulcke
Third Secretary (Media & Public Affairs): Ms
Rachel Jamieson
Third Secretary (Management): Miss Eram Qureshi
Third Secretary (Management): Mrs Yvonne C
Haseldine
Third Secretary (Asst. Estate Manager): Mr Donal
Michael Ahern

Lahore
Office of the British Honorary Correspondent
2nd Floor, Syed Babar Ali Foundation Building,
308 Upper Mall, Lahore
Telephone: (00) (92) (042) 5753414-6, 5710597
(042) 5753420 (Direct Line)
Facsimile: (00) (92) (042) 5710598
UAN: (042) 111-234 -234
Honorary Consul: Mr Fakir S Aijazuddin, OBE

**British High Commission Visa and Consular
Office**
PO Box 2172
Avari Plaza
87 Shahrah-e-Quaid-e-Azam
Lahore 54000
Pakistan
Telephone: (00) (92) (42) 6307575
Facsimile: 6307857
Airtech: 6307858

Website: www.britainonline.org.pk
Opening times (GMT) 0230-1030 Mon-Thursday
0230-0830 Friday
ECM & Head of Post: Mr Myron Reid
Second Secretary (MO/VC): Mr Stephen Rapp
Third Secretary (ECO): Mr Ian Marson
Third Secretary (ECO): Mrs Clare Bloomfield
Third Secretary (ECO): Mrs Sally Allbeury
Third Secretary (ECO): Mr Derek Jones
Third Secretary (ECO): Mr Les Tant
Third Secretary (ECO): Mr Michael Murtagh

The British Trade International office continues to
run as a separate entity from dedicated offices in
the British Council Building

British Trade Office
65 Mozang Road, PO Box 1679, Lahore
Telephone: (00) (92) (042) 6316589-90
Facsimile: (00) (92) (042) 6316591
Office Hours (GMT): Mon - Thurs 03 30 - 11 30
Fri: 03 30 - 07 30
Director (Resides at Islamabad): Miss Sheila J
Bramley
Lahore Trade Promotion Adviser: Mr Imran
Masood Chaudhry

Karachi
British Deputy High Commission
Shahrah-e-Iran, Clifton, Karachi 75600
Telephone: (Landline): (92) (21) 5872431-6,
5874300, 5863534
     (51) 5862389 (Commercial)
     (51) 5874316 (DLO)
Facsimile: (92) (21) 5874014 General
     5862316 Chancery
     5874328 Visa
e-mail: bdhc@crestarnet.net
Office Hours (GMT): Mon – Thu 0330 - 1100
Fri 0330 - 0730
Deputy High Commissioner: Mr David D Pearey
Deputy Head of Mission: Mr Richard W Hyde, MBE
First Secretary (Management): Mr Mick J
Mitchell, MVO
Second Secretary: Mr Barry S Watson
Second Secretary (Visa): Ms Amanda Ivemy
Third Secretary (Visa): Mr Simon Regan
Third Secretary (Visa): Ms Collette Goddard
Third Secretary (Visa): Mr Dave Temperley
Third Secretary (Visa): Mr Lesley Nicol
Third Secretary (Visa): Mr Valentine Madojemu
Third Secretary (Visa): Mr David Greenfield
Third Secretary (Commercial/Aid): Mr Mustaq A
Birader
Third Secretary (Consular): Mr Stephen B Smart
Security Officer: Mr Brian Davison

PALAU

Koror
British Embassy
Ambassador (resides at Suva): Mr Christopher
Haslam

PANAMA

Panama City
British Embassy
Swiss Tower, Calle 53
(Apartado 889) Zona 1,
Panama City, Republic of Panama
Telephone: (00) (507) 269 0866 (5 lines)
Facsimile: (00) (507) 223 0730
Airtech: (00) (507) 264 6846
e-mail: britemb@cwp.net.pa
Office Hours (GMT): Mon - Thurs 12 30 - 18 00
and 19 00 - 21 30 Fri 12 30 - 17 30
Ambassador and Consul-General: Mr R H G Davies
(Mr J I Malcolm OSE w.e.f. March 2002)
Deputy Head of Mission and Second Secretary: Mr
A Newlands
Second Secretary: Mr A Davenport
Defence Attaché (resides at Caracas): Captain E
Searle, RN
*First Secretary (Commercial) and Director of
Trade Promotion for Central America (resides at
San José):* Mr C J Edge
Second Secretary (Technical) (resides at Caracas):
Mr A Linnell
Second Secretary (Technical) (resides at Caracas):
Mr K Gibbs

PAPUA NEW GUINEA

Port Moresby (SP)
British High Commission
PO Box 212, Waigani NCD 131,
Papua New Guinea
Telephone: (00) (675) 3251643, 3251645,
3251659, 3251677
Facsimile: (00) (675) 3253547
Airtech: (00) (675) 3253953
e-mail: bhcpng@datec.com.pg
Office Hours (GMT): 22 00 - 06 00
High Commissioner (ext 1207/9): Mr Simon Scadden
Deputy High Commissioner (ext.1208): Mr
Christopher Thompson
Defence Adviser (resides at Canberra): Group
Captain Nick C Rusling, RAF

PARAGUAY

Asunción
British Embassy
Avda. Boggiani 5848
C/R I6 Boquerón
Asunción
Telephone: (00) (595) (21) 612611
Facsimile: (00) (595) (21) 605007
Airtech: (00) (595) (21) 612611 ext. 2131
e-mail: brembasu@rieder.net.py
Office Hours (GMT): 12 00 - 19 00
Ambassador and Consul-General: Mr A J J Cantor
First Secretary and Deputy Head of Mission: Mr N
R Martin
Defence Attaché (resides at Buenos Aires): Group
Captain T P Brewer, OBE, RAF
Commercial Officer: Mr J Cano
Deputy Commercial Officer: Ms D Diaz de Espada
Aid/Information Officer: Mrs S Melamed
Management Officer/Accountant: Ms J Spalding

PERU

Lima
British Embassy
Edificio El Pacifico Washington (Piso 12),
Plaza Washington, Avenida Arequipa
(PO Box No 854), Lima 100
Telephone: (00) (51) (1) 433-4738 4839, 4932,
5032, 5137 Chancery
433-1233, 1890, 8923, 8916 Consular/Visa
Facsimile: (00) (51) (1) 433-2222 Chancery
433-4735 Management/Press and Public Affairs
330-5101 Commercial
433-8922 Consular,Visa
Airtech: (00) (51) (1) 332-5710
e-mail: britemb@terra.com.pe (General.)
britcom@terra.com.pe (Commercial)
Office Hours (GMT):
Summer (Dec - Apr approx): Mon, Thurs, Fri 13
00 - 18 30; Tues and Wed 13 00 - 21 15
Winter (Apr - Nov approx): Mon-Thurs 13 00 -
21 15;   Fri 13 00 - 18 15
Ambassador: Mr Roger Dudley Hart, CMG
Deputy Head of Mission: Mr John Patrick
Girdlestone
Defence Attaché (Resides at Bogota): Colonel
Robert J Griffiths, MBE
*Cultural Attaché (British Council Director) (Tel:
221 7552):* Ms Gail Liesching
First Secretary: Mr James Phillips
First Secretary (Commercial): Mr Douglas James
Kerr
First Secretary (Development): Mr Mark Lewis
First Secretary (Health Sector): Mr David Lewis
First Secretary (Management) and HM Consul: Mr
Neil W Storey
Second Secretary (Works) (resides at Brasilia): Mr
David Holmes
Second Secretary: Mr David James Grey
Third Secretary (Chancery): Mr Graeme Bannatyne
*Third Secretary (Management) (resides at
Brasilia):* Mr Richard Wildman
Third Secretary (Immigration) and Vice-Consul:
Mr Scott Simpson
British Vice-Consul: Mrs Maureen Anne
Chesterton MBE

Arequipa
British Consulate
Tacna y Arica 145, Arequipa
Telephone: (00) (51) (54) 241 340
Facsimile: (00) (51) (54) 236 125
Office Hours (GMT): Mon - Fri 13 30 - 17 30 and
20 00 - 23 30
Honorary Consul: Mr J R G Roberts, MBE

Cusco
British Consulate
Av. Pardo 895
PO Box 606, Cusco
Telephone: (00) (51) (84) 22-6671/23-9974
Facsimile: (00) (51) (84) 23-6706
Office Hours (GMT): 16 00 - 17 00
Honorary Consul: Mr B Walker

Iquitos
British Consulate
Putumayo 182a,
Iquitos
Telephone: (00) (51) (94) 22 2732
Facsimile: (00) (51) (94) 22 3607
Office Hours (GMT): 16 00 – 1700
Honorary Consul: Mr P Duffy

Piura
British Consulate
Huancavelica 223, Piura
Telephone: (00) (51) (74) 333 300/326 233
Facsimile: (00) (51) (74) 327 009
Office Hours (GMT): 14 00 - 18 00/ 21 00 -23 59
Honorary Consul: Mr H E Stewart

Trujillo
British Consulate
Jesus de Nazareth No 312, Trujillo
Telephone: (00) (51) (44) 23 55 48
Facsimile: (00) (51) (44) 25 58 18
Office Hours (GMT): 14 00 - 22 00
Honorary Consul: Mr W Barber

PHILIPPINES

Manila
British Embassy
15th-17th Floors LV Locsin Building,
6752 Ayala Avenue cor Makati Avenue,
1226 Makati, (PO Box 2927 MCPO)
Telephone: (00) (63) (2) 816 7116 Switchboard
816 7271/2, 816 7348/9 Visa & Consular Sections
Facsimile: (00) (63) (2) 813 7755 Chancery
819 7206 Management
815 4809 Information
810 2745 Visa
840 1361 Consular
815 6233 Commercial
Airtech: 894 3367
Telex: 63282 (a/b 63282 PRODME PN)
e-mail: Information Section: uk@info.com.ph
Commercial Section: uktrade@info.com.ph
Office Hours (GMT): Mon – Thurs: 00 00 - 08 30,
Fri 00 00 - 06 00
Consular/Visa Office Hours: 00 00 - 05 00
Ambassador: Mr A S Collins, CMG (Mr P S Dimond
w.e.f. March 2002)
Deputy Head of Mission: Mr D Campbell
Defence Attaché: Colonel M K Stretch
First Secretary (Commercial): Mr E Staunton
*First Secretary (Cultural) (British Council
Director) (914 1011 ext 20):* Ms G Westaway
HM Consul: Mr I C Sargeant
Second Secretary (Management): Mr G K Hodgson
Second Secretary (Commercial): Mr G Wain
Second Secretary (Political): Mr N D Jagoe
Second Secretary (Immigration): Mr S R Ladva
Third Secretary (Immigration): Mr M Delaney
Third Secretary (Immigration): Mrs A Trott-
Charpentier
Third Secretary (Immigration): Mrs K Wain
Third Secretary (Immigration): Miss E Gola
Third Secretary (Political): Mr D Painter
Third Secretary: Mr G Walker
Attaché: Mrs C L Rickward

Attaché: Mrs S Edghill
Attaché: Mr J Hopkins
Attaché: CPO D Finch

**Manila UK Representation at the Asian
Development Bank, see part II**

Cebu
British Consulate
Villa Terrace, Greenhills Road,
Casuntingan, Mandaue City, Cebu
Telephone: (00) (63) (32) 3460 525
Facsimile: (00) (63) (32) 3460 269
e-mail: moke@gsilink.com
Honorary Consul: Mrs M P Jackson

POLAND

Warsaw
British Embassy
Aleje Roz No 1, 00-556 Warsaw
Telephone: (00) (48) (22) 628 1001-5, 625 6262
Facsimiles: (00) (48) (22) 621 7161
622 7659 (Management)
622 7698 (Chancery)
e-mail: britemb@it.com.pl

Commercial, Visa and Consular Sections:
Warsaw Corporate Centre, 2nd Floor,
Emilii Plater 28, 00-688 Warsaw
Telephone: (00) (48) (22) 625
3030/3032/3099/3163/3248/3293
Facsimile: (00) (48) (22) 625 3472
e-mail: ukembwcc@it.com.pl (Commercial)
Consular&Visa@Warsaw.mail.fco.gov.uk
Office Hours (GMT): Summer 06 30 - 14 30
Winter 07 30 - 15 30
Ambassador: The Honorable Michael Pakenham, CMG
Counsellor and Deputy Head of Mission: Mr
Robin Barnett
Counsellor: Mr Peter Harris
Director of Trade Promotion/Consul-General: Mr
Michael Davenport, MBE
Counsellor (Cultural): Mr Jerry Eyres
Defence and Air Attaché: Group Captain Tim J
Williams, AFC, RAF
Naval and Military Attaché: Lieutenant Colonel
Ian F Watts
First Secretary (Political): Mr Dominic Meiklejohn
First Secretary (Management): Mr Paul Chatt
First Secretary (Commercial): Mr Wavell Magor, MBE
First Secretary (Commercial): Mr Howard Lattin-
Rawstrone
First Secretary (Education): Mr Robin Rickard
Second Secretary (Political): Miss Anne Jackson
Second Secretary (Consul/Commercial): Mr Niall
Cullens
Second Secretary (KHF): Mr Gilbert Hyde
Second Secretary (Political): Mr Simon Thomas
Second Secretary (DLO): Mr George Rakowski
Third Secretary: Mr Jim Dunn
Third Secretary (Political): Miss Sara Hunt
Third Secretary (Information): Ms Alicia Clyde
Attaché and Vice-Consul: Mr Simon Atkinson
Attaché: Mr Scott Melling
Attaché: Miss Nicola Grant

Katowice
British Consulate
ul PCK 10, 40-057 Katowice
Telephone: (00) (48) (32) 206 9801
Facsimile: (00) (48) (32) 205 4646
e-mail: honcon@silesia.top.pl
Office Hours (GMT): Winter: 08 00 - 16 00
Honorary Consul: Mr Alan Stretton

Poznan
British Consulate
ul Wroclawska 6, 61-837 Poznan
Telephone: (00) (48) (61) 851 72 90 Hotel Poznan
– Telephone: (00) (48) (61) 833 19 61
Facsimile: (00) (48) (61) 853 29 19
e-mail: ukcons@protea.pl
dyr.hpoz@orbis.pl
Office Hours (GMT): Winter: 08 00 - 14 00
Honorary Consul: Mr Wlodzimierz Walkowiak

Gdansk

British Consulate
ul Grunwaldzka 102, 80-224 Gdansk
Telephone: (00) (48) (58) 341 4365
Facsimile: (00) (48) (58) 344 1608
e-mail: consul@abcc.com.pl
Office Hours (GMT): Winter: 08 00 - 15 00
Honorary Consul: Mr Andrzej Kanthak

Szczecin
British Consulate
ul. Starego Wiarusa 32
71-206 Szczecin
Telephone: (00) (48) (91) 487 0302
Facsimile: (00) (48) (91) 487 3697
e-mail: gacszz@fnet.com.pl
Office Hours (GMT): Winter: 07 00 - 15 00
Honorary Consul: Mr Ryszard Karger

Wroclaw
British Consulate
ul. Olawska 2, 50-123 Wroclaw
Telephone/Facsimile: (00) (48) (71) 344 8961
e-mail: consulate@kmc.com.pl
Office Hours (GMT): Winter: 08 00 - 14 00
Honorary Consul: Mr Marek Grzegorzewicz

Kraków
British Consulate
ul. Sw.Anny 9
31-008 Kraków
Telephone: (00) (48) (12) 421 7030
Facsimile: (00) (48) (12) 422 4264
e-mail: ukconsul@bci.krakow.pl
Office Hours (GMT): Winter: 08 00 - 15 00
Honorary Consul: Mr Kazimierz Karasinski

PORTUGAL

Lisbon
British Embassy
Rua de São Bernardo 33, 1249-082 Lisboa
Telephone: (00) (351) (21) 392 4000
Facsimile: 4178 Chancery
　　　　　4184 Defence
　　　　　4185 Information
　　　　　4186 Commercial
　　　　　4187 Management

　　　　　4188 Consular
e-mail: Chancery@Lisbon.mail.fco.gov.uk
Commercial@Lisbon.mail.fco.gov.uk
Consular@Lisbon.mail.fco.gov.uk
Management@Lisbon.mail.fco.gov.uk
Political2@Lisbon.mail.fco.gov.uk
PPA@Lisbon.mail.fco.gov.uk
Website: www.uk-embassy.pt
Office Hours (GMT): Summer 08 00 - 12 00 and
13 30 - 16 30
Winter　09 00 - 13 00 and 14 30 - 17 30
Ambassador: Dame M G D Evans, CMG, DBE
Deputy Head of Mission: Mr R M Publicover
Counsellor (Political): Mr K D Evetts, OBE
Defence Attaché: Commander A J Bull, RN
Counsellor (Cultural) (British Council Director):
Mr R Ness
First Secretary (Head of Political Section): Miss F
Patterson
First Secretary (Cultural): Mrs R Woodward-Carrick
First Secretary (Commercial): Mr M Turner
First Secretary and Consul: Mr J Blakemore
Second Secretary (Political/EU): Mr C Keller
Second Secretary (Commercial): Mr M Stead
Second Secretary (Management): Mr I Haywood
Second Secretary: Mr M Cox
Third Secretary (Press & Public Affairs): Mrs S
Tyler-Haywood
Third Secretary and Vice-Consul: Mr S Askham
Attaché (PA to Ambassador): Miss A Marshall

Oporto
British Consulate
Avenida da Boavista 3072,
4100-120 Oporto
Telephone: (00) (351) (22) 618 4789
Facsimile: (00) (351) (22) 610 0438
e-mail: All.oporto@fco.gov.uk
Consul: Mr Louis Taylor
Pro-Consul: Mrs Z M N Gomes

Portimão
British Consulate
Largo Francisco A Mauricio 7-10,
8500 Portimão
Telephone: (00) (351) (282) 417 800/4
Facsimile: (00) (351) (282) 417 806
e-mail: portimao.lisbon@fco.gov.uk
Honorary Consul: Mr R Nuttall

Funchal (Madeira)
Honorary British Consulate
Avenida de Zarco 2, CP 417,
9000 - 956 Funchal, Madeira
Telephone: (00) (351) (291) 221 221
Facsimile: (00) (351) (291) 233 789
e-mail: brit.confunchal@mail.eunet.pt
Honorary Consul: Mr C H Gedge

Ribeira Grande (Azores)
Honorary British Consulate
Quinta do Bom Jesus, Rua das Almas,
23, Pico da Pedra,
9600 Ribeira Grande, São Miguel,
Azores
Telephone: (00) (351) (296) 498 115
Facsimile: (00) (351) (296) 498 330

Honorary Consul: Mr J A de Vaz Carreiro
Consul (resides at Hong Kong): Mr M J Lowes

QATAR

Doha
British Embassy
PO Box 3, Doha, Qatar
Telephone: (00) (974) 4421991
Facsimile: (00) (974) 4438692
Telegrams: PRODOME DOHA
e-mail: Defence Section defatdoh@qatar.net.qa
Commercial Section bembcomm@qatar.net.qa
Office Hours (GMT): Sat & Wed 04 30 - 11 30

Visa Section:
Ground Floor, AKC Building,
Al Saad Street
Telephone: (00) (974) 4364189
Facsimile: (00) (974) 4364139
Commercial Section:
8th Floor, Toyota Towers
Telephone: (00) (974) 4353543
Facsimile: (00) (974) 4356131
Ambassador: Mr David A Wright, OBE
First Secretary (Commercial) and Deputy Head of Mission: Mr Mike Purves
Defence Attaché: Wing Commander Phil K Keating, RAF
Second Secretary (Commercial): Mr Peter Harrington
Second Secretary (Defence Sales): Mr Steve May
Second Secretary (Chancery/Information): Mr Brian G Forsyth
Second Secretary (Management) and Vice-Consul: Mrs Sarah V Davidson
Third Secretary (Immigration): Mrs Sarah Taylor
Third Secretary (Commercial): Mrs Marie Forsyth
Generalist (Registry): Mr Andy Dallas
Military Assistant to Defence Attaché: Sgt Pete Mould

British Council
PO Box 2992, Doha
Telephone: (00) (974) 4426185
Facsimile: (00) (974) 4423315

ROMANIA

Bucharest
British Embassy
24 Strada Jules Michelet, 70154 Bucharest
Telephone: (00) (40) (1) 312 0303
Facsimile: (00) (40) (1) 312 0229 Embassy
9652 Consular
9742 Commercial
Airtech: (00) (40) (1) 312 0307
Office Hours (GMT): Apr - Oct: Mon - Thurs: 05 30 - 14 00; Fri 05 30 - 10 30
Nov - Mar: Mon - Thurs: 06 30 - 15 00; Fri 06 30 - 11 30
Ambassador: Mr Richard Ralph, CVO CMG
Counsellor & Deputy Head of Mission: Mr Andrew Pearce
Defence Attaché: Colonel Andrew T Bruce, MBE
Assistant Defence Attaché: W.O. Ian Fraser
Cultural Attaché (British Council Director): Ms Helen Meixner, CMG

First Secretary (Political): Mr Jonathan K M Mitchell
First Secretary (Economic): Miss Susan Laffey
First Secretary (Commercial): Mr Richard J Cork
First Secretary: Mr Michael White
Assistant Defence Attaché: Squadron Leader Keith A Marshall, RAF
Second Secretary (Management): Mr David P Gething
Second Secretary and Consul: Mr James Cameron
Second Secretary (Political/Information): Mr Anthony Kay
Second Secretary (KHF): Mrs Tanya S Collingridge
Second Secretary (Works) (resides at Vienna): Mr Carl B J Gray
Third Secretary (Management): Mr Andrew Collingridge
Third Secretary (Commercial): Mr Jeremy Hodges
Vice-Consul: Mr Gerard Healy
Vice-Consul: Mr Alec Hafele
Attaché (resides at Budapest): Mr John Walker
Attaché (Works): Mr George Manson
Chaplain: The Revd Steve Hughes

RUSSIA

Moscow
British Embassy
Smolenskaya Naberezhnaya 10,
Moscow 121099
Telephone: (00) (7) (095) 956 7200 (Main Switchboard)
Direct Dial: 956 + 4 figure extension
Facsimile: (00) (7) (095) 956 7201 General
7440 Visa Section
7430 Press and Public Affairs
7389 7254, 7443 Management
7442 Building Services Section
7264 Defence
7446 Surgery
Airtech: (00) (7) (095) 956 7398 Embassy
7464 Commercial
e-mail: britembppas@glas.apc.org
Cultural Department/The British Council
Library for Foreign Literature, Nikoloyamskaya 1, Moscow 109189
Telephone: (00) (7) (095) 234 0201(Switchboard)
Facsimile: (00) (7) (095) 975 2561
(095) 234 0206/07
Office Hours (GMT): Winter   06 00 - 10 00 and 11 00 -14 00 (GMT)
Summer 05 00 - 09 00 and 10 00 - 13 00 (GMT)
Ambassador: Sir Roderic Lyne, KBE, CMG
Minister and Deputy Head of Mission: Mr D J Gowan
Defence and Air Attaché: Air Commodore J C Jarron, RAF
Counsellor (Political): Mr A C Crombie
Counsellor (British Council Director): Mr A Greer
Counsellor (Economic, Commercial and Science): Mr S J M Smith
Counsellor (Political Affairs): Dr J A Brewer

Counsellor (Management) and Consul-General:
Mr P A McDermott, MVO
Counsellor (Post Security): Mr N Trapé
*Cultural Attaché (British Council Deputy
Director):* Mrs S Wallace-Shaddad
Naval Attaché: Captain S R Lister, RN
Military Attaché: Colonel M H Auchinleck
First Secretary (Political): Ms S Hyland
First Secretary (Political): Mr C Lonsdale
First Secretary (Political): Mr J M O'Callaghan
First Secretary (Political): Mr J Aves
First Secretary (Commercial): Mr J Dauris
First Secretary (Economic): Mr T Drew
First Secretary (Development): Mr M F Harris
First Secretary (Press and Public Affairs): Mr R
Turner
First Secretary (British Council): Dr E Bell
First Secretary (Consular/Immigration): Mr J F
Thompson
First Secretary (Regional Medical Adviser): (Vacant)
*First Secretary (Fiscal, Drugs & Crime Liaison
Officer):* Mr R K Gray
First Secretary (Technical Management): Mr K
Reynolds
First Secretary (Technical Management): Mr S
Huckle
First Secretary (Management): Mr M Walley
First Secretary (Science and Technology): Mr S
Evans
First Secretary (Building Services): Mr D Evans
First Secretary (British Council): Mr T Walsh
Assistant Naval Attaché: Lieutenant Commander B
Seakins, RN
Assistant Military Attaché: Major P J F Daniell
Assistant Air Attaché: Squadron Leader M
Cunningham, RAF
Second Secretary (Economic): Mr R Crowder
Second Secretary (Economic): Miss R C A Edwards
Second Secretary (Political): Ms R Low
Second Secretary (Political): Mr M D Clayton
Second Secretary (Technical Management): Mr S
Tetlow
Second Secretary (Technical Management): Mr S
Forrester
Second Secretary (Technical Management): Mr M
Thompson
Second Secretary (Commercial): Mrs C Cottrell
Second Secretary (Commercial): Mr S Boyden
Second Secretary (Immigration): Mr M Bates
Second Secretary (Immigration): Mrs H Reynolds
Second Secretary (Immigration): Mrs C J Hall
Second Secretary (Development): Mr G Ward
Second Secretary (Development): Mr R Watt
Second Secretary (British Council): Mr T Hubbard
Second Secretary (British Council): Mr S
Winetroube
Head of Defence Secretariat: Flight Lieutenant R
Corbould, RAF
Third Secretary (Press and Public Affairs): Mr D
Arkley
Third Secretary (Management): Miss L Stephens
Third Secretary (Development): (Vacant)
Third Secretary (Visits): Miss I Kerrison
Third Secretary (Political Affairs): Mrs S Murray
Attaché Vice-Consul: Mr N Snee
Attaché (Visas): Mr D Jones

Attaché (Visas): Ms S Manley
Attaché (Visas): Mrs M Helmer
Attaché (Visas): Mr J Akers
Attaché (Visas): Mr T Van der Eyken
Attaché (Visas): Mr G Jones
Attaché (Visas): Mrs J Tranter
Attaché (Visas): Mrs J Bayliss
Attaché (Visas): Mr D Herbert
Attaché (Technical Management): Mr J Clark
Attaché (Chief Security Officer): Mr R Dalton

St Petersburg
British Consulate General
PL Proletarskoy Diktatury 5, Smolninskiy Raion
193124 St Petersburg
Telephone: (00) (7) (812) 320 32 00 Switchboard
320 32 39 Visa Reception
Facsimile: (00) (7) (812) 320 32 11 General
320 32 22 Commercial
Section
320 32 33 Visa Section
320 32 44 Chancery
(Airtech)
e-mail: bcgspb@peterlink.ru
dfid@peterlink.ru (Development Section)
management@stpetersburg.mail.fco.gov.uk
commercial@stpetersburg.mail.fco.gov.uk
consular@stpetersburg.mail.fco.gov.uk
information@stpetersburg.mail.fco.gov.uk
visa@stpetersburg.mail.fco.gov.uk
Consul-General: Ms B L Hay, CMG, MBE
Deputy Head of Mission/Consul (Commercial): Mr
P O'Connor
Consul (Cultural) (British Council Director): Mrs
S Boardman
Consul (Consular/Management): Mr T M Waite
Vice-Consul (Immigration): Mr P M Marsh
Vice-Consul (Immigration): Mr J A Hudson
Attaché: Mr R A Heseltine

British Council
Fontank Reki Nab 46
St Petersburg Tel: (00) (7) (812) 325 6074
Facsimile: (00) (7) (812) 325 6073

Yekaterinburg
British Consulate-General
15a Gogol Street,
620075, Yekaterinburg,
Russian Federation
Telephone: (00) (7) (3432) 564 931
569 201 Visa Section
Facsimile: (00) (7) (3432) 592 901
Airtech: (00) (7) (3432) 777 068
e-mail: brit@sky.ru   (General
Enquiries/Commercial Department)
britvisa@sky.ru (Visa Enquiries/Know How Fund)
Website: www.britain.sky.ru
Consul General: Mrs L Cross
Vice Consul: Mr S R Rapp

Novorossiysk
British Consulate
3a Fabrichnaya Street,
Novorossiysk, PO Box 85
Novorossiysk 353923
Telephone: (00) (7) (8617) 618100

Facsimile: (00) (7) (8617) 618291
e-mail: ecr@laroute.net
Honorary Consul: Mr E C Rumens

Vladivostok
British Consulate
5 Svetlanskaya Street, Vladivostok
Telephone: (00) (7) (4232) 411312
Facsimile: (00) (7) (4232) 410643
e-mail: tiger@ints.vtc.ru
Honorary Consul: Mr A M Fox

RWANDA

Kigali
British Embassy
Parcelle No 1131
Boulevard de l'Umuganda
Kaciryu Sud
BP 576 Kigali
Rwanda
Telephone: (00) (250) 85771, 85773, 84098, 86072
Facsimile: (00) (250) 82044
e-mail: britemb@rwanda1.com
Office Hours (GMT): Mon - Thurs 06 00 - 10.00
and 11 00 - 15 00
Fri 06 00 - 10.00
Ambassador: Mrs S E Hogwood, MBE
Deputy Head of Mission: Mr P Lawrence
Defence Attaché (resides at Kampala): Lieutenant
Colonel C E Thom, OBE
Third Secretary: Mr T Fisher

**Department for International Development
Programme Office (Rwanda)**
BP 576 Kigali, Rwanda
Telephone: (00) (250) 85771, 85773, 84098, 86072
Facsimile: (00) (250) 510588
e-mail: @dfid.gov.uk
Office Hours (GMT): Mon-Thurs 06 00-10 00 and
11 00-15 00   Friday 0600- 10:00
First Secretary Developmental/Head of Office: Mr
Giles Bolton
First Secretary/Education Adviser: Dr Mark Poston
First Secretary/Social Development Adviser: Mr
Gerard Howe
First Secretary/Governanace Adviser: Mr Rupert
Bladon

ST KITTS AND NEVIS

Basseterre
British High Commission
PO Box 483, Price Waterhouse Centre, 11
Old Parham Rd,
St John's, Antigua
Telephone: (00) (1) (268) 462 0008/9, 463 0010
Facsimile: (00) (1) (268) 462 2806
Office Hours (GMT): 12 00 - 16 30 (Open to the
Public) and 17 30 - 20 00
* *High Commissioner:* Mr J White
Resident Acting High Commissioner: Mrs S Murphy
Deputy High Commissioner: Mr M J E Mayhew
* *Defence Adviser:* Captain S C Ramm, RN
* *Counsellor (Regional Affairs):* Mr N J L Martin
** *First Secretary:* Mr M Bragg

* *Second Secretary (Management/Consular):* Mr G
I Brammer
* *Second Secretary (Chancery/Information):* Mr R
C Morris
** *Second Secretary:* Mr A A Tenger
* *Third Secretary:* Mr A L Mott
* *Third Secretary (Consular/Immigration):* Ms S J
Verma
*Resides at Bridgetown **Resides at Kingston

British Consulate
Office of the Honorary British Consul
PO Box 559, Basseterre
St Kitts
Telephone: (00) (1 869) 466 5620
466 8888 Home
Facsimile: (00) (1 869) 466 8889
Honorary Consul: Mr P Allcorn

ST LUCIA

Castries
British High Commission
NIS Waterfront Building, 2nd Floor (PO Box 227),
Castries, Saint Lucia
Telephone: (00) (1) (758) 45 22484/5
Facsimile: (00) (1) (758) 45 31543
e-mail: postmaster@castries.mail.fco.gov.uk
britishhc@candw.lc
Airtech: (00) (1) (758) 45 22486
Office Hours (GMT): Mon- Thurs 12 00 - 16 30
and 17 00 - 20 00   Fri 12 00 - 17 00
* *High Commissioner:* Mr J White
Resident Acting High Commissioner: Mr Douglas
Rice
* *Deputy High Commissioner:* Mr M J E Mayhew
* *Defence Adviser:* Captain S C Ramm, RN
* *Counsellor (Regional Affairs):* Mr N J L Martin
* *First Secretary (Chancery):* Mr G Honey
* *Second Secretary (Management/Consular):* Mr G
I Brammer
* *Second Secretary (Chancery/Information):* Mr N
J Pyle, MBE
* *Second Secretary (Chancery):* Mr P Marshall
** *Second Secretary (Technical Works):* Mr M Jones
* *Third Secretary:* Mr A W White
* *Third Secretary (Consular/Immigration):* Mr S
Minshull
*Resides at Bridgetown **Resides at Mexico City

ST VINCENT

Kingstown
British High Commission
Granby Street (PO Box 132),
Kingstown, St Vincent
Telephone: (00) (1) (784) 457 1701
Facsimile: (00) (1) (784) 456 2750
Office Hours (GMT): 12 30 - 20 00
* *High Commissioner:* Mr J White
Resident Acting High Commissioner: Mr B
Robertson
* *Deputy High Commissioner:* Mr M J E Mayhew
* *Defence Adviser:* Captain S C Ramm, RN
* *Counsellor (Regional Affairs):* Mr N J L Martin
* *First Secretary (Chancery):* Mr P Curwen

* *Second Secretary (Management/Consular):* Mr G I Brammer
* *Second Secretary (Chancery/Information):* Mr R J Morris
* *Second Secretary (Chancery):* Mr P Marshall
* *Third Secretary:* Mr A L Mott
Third Secretary: Miss S J Verma
*Resides at Bridgetown

SAMOA

Apia
British High Commission (all staff resident in Wellington)
Telephone: (00) (64) (4) 472 6049
Facsimile: (00) (64) (4) 473 4982
High Commissioner: Mr R T Fell, CVO
Deputy High Commissioner: Mr M Bourke
First Secretary (External): Mr R Dean
First Secretary (Economic/Trade Policy): Ms R L Foxwell
First Secretary (Political/Press and Public Affairs): Mrs K S Wolstenholme
Second Secretary (Political): Mr J D Wolstenholme
Second Secretary (Consular): Mr W S Robertson

Office of the Honorary British Consul
c/o Kruse Enari and Barlow, 2nd Floor, NPF Building
Beach Rd, Central Apia
PO Box 2029, Apia
Telephone: (00) (685) 21895
Facsimile: (00) (685) 21407
e-mail: barlow@samoa.ws
Honorary British Consul: Mr R M Barlow, MBE

SAN MARINO

San Marino
British Embassy
Via XX Settembre 80/A
00187 Rome
Ambassador (resides at Rome): Sir John Shepherd, KCVO, CMG

British Consulate-General
Lungarno Corsini 2,
50123 Florence
Telephone: (00) (39) 055 284133 (including Airtech)
(00) (39) 055 289556 (Commercial)
Facsimile: (00) (39) 055 219112
e-mail: bcflocom@tin.it
Office Hours (GMT): Apr-Oct 07 00 - 11 00 and 12 00 - 15 00
Nov-Mar 08 00 - 12 00 and 13 00 - 16 00
Consul-General:
(Resides at Florence) Mr Ralph Griffiths, OBE

SÃO TOMÉ AND PRINCIPE

São Tomé
British Embassy
(All staff resident in Luanda)
Ambassador: Ms C Elmes, CMG
Consul: Mr F J Martin
First Secretary: Mr D G Cox
Second Secretary (Aid): Mr E Rich

São Tomé
British Consulate
Residencial Avenida,
Avienda Da Independencia
CP 257, Sao Tomé
Telephone: (00) (239) (12) 21026/7, 22505 (Home)
Facsimile: (00) (239) (12) 21372
Honorary Consul: Mr J Gomes

SAUDI ARABIA

Riyadh
British Embassy
PO Box 94351, Riyadh 11693
Telephone: (00) (966) (1) 488 0077
Facsimile: (00) (966) (1) 488 2373, 488 0623
Management,
488 1209 Consular
Voicemail Numbers: see individual officers
e-mail: Officers firstname.surname followed by
@riyadh.mail.fco.gov.uk
Office Hours (GMT): Sat - Wed 05 00 - 12 00
Ambassador: Sir Derek Plumbly, KCMG
Counsellor, Deputy Head of Mission and Consul General (2204): Mr Simon McDonald
Counsellor (Commercial) (2240): Mr Philip Parham
Cultural Attaché (British Council Director): Dr David Burton, OBE
Defence and Military Attaché (2230): Brigadier John D Deverell
Naval Attaché (2233): Commander Rupert R D'E Head, RN
Air Attaché (2234): Wing Commander John A Bartram, RAF
First Secretary (2217): Mr Nic Coombs
First Secretary (Economic) (2242): Mr Nick Abbott
First Secretary (Commercial) (2206): Mr Mike Nithavrianakis
First Secretary (Management) (2264): Mr Colin Lane
First Secretary and Consul (2271): Mr Ian Wilson
Second Secretary (Information) (2211): Mrs Cecille El Beleidi
Second Secretary (Commercial) (2243): Mr Frank Drayton
Second Secretary (Political) (2208): Mr Nicholas Harrocks
Second Secretary (Political) (2330): Mr Simon Walters
Second Secretary (2265): Mr Simon Page
Third Secretary and Vice-Consul (2272): Mrs Janice Banks
Third Secretary and Vice-Consul (2277): Mrs Andrea McGlone
Third Secretary (Management) (2261): Mr Steve Mitchell
Third Secretary (2220): Mr Sanjay Shah

Jedda
British Consulate-General
PO Box 393, Jedda 21411
Telephone: (00) (966) (2) 622-5550, 5557, 5558
Facsimile: (00) (966) (2) 622-6249
Airtech: (00) (966) (2) 622-5551
e-mail: Officers first name . surname followed by
@Jeddah.mail.fco.gov.uk

Office Hours (GMT): Sat-Wed 05 00 - 12 00
Consul-General: Mr Andrew Henderson
*Consul (Commercial) and Deputy Head of
Mission:* Mr Roger Church
Consul (Commercial): Mr Gareth O'Brien
Vice-Consul: Mr Ian Hodges
Vice-Consul (Immigration): Miss Morven
Williamson
Vice Consul (Management): Mr John Barclay

Al Khobar
British Trade Office
PO Box 1868,
Al Khobar 31952
Telephone: (00) (966) (3) 882 5300
Facsimile: (00) (966) (3) 882 5384
e-mail: btokhobar@hotmail.com
officers firstname.surname followed by
@ALKHOBAR.mail.fco.gov.uk
Office Hours (GMT): Sat –Wed: 05 00 - 12 00
Head of British Trade Office: Mr R M S Sykes
Second Secretary (Commercial): Mr R F Jackson
*Third Secretary (Commercial/Management) and
Vice-Consul:* Mr S Thiruchelvam
Pro-Consul: Mr A Abdalla
(Visa and Passport work for Eastern Province is the
responsibility of Riyadh)

SENEGAL

Dakar
British Embassy
20 Rue du Docteur Guillet
(Boite Postale 6025), Dakar
Telephone: (00) (221) 823 7392, 823 9971
Facsimile: (00) (221) 823 2766
e-mail: britemb@telecomplus.sn /
Comaid@telecomplus.sn
British Council e-mail: Bcdakar@enda.sn /
bcdakar@sonatel.senet
Office Hours (GMT): Mon - Thurs 08 00 - 16 30,
Fri 08 00 - 12 30
Ambassador: Mr E A Burner
*First Secretary and Deputy Head of Mission and
Consul:* Mr P T D O'Brien, MBE
Defence Attaché (Resides at Rabat): Lieutenant
Colonel G D Duthoit
Education Attaché and British Council Director:
Mr S McNulty
Third Secretary (Management) and Vice-Consul:
Ms A J Lavocat
*Second Secretary (Political/Press and Public
Affairs):* Mr S Bond
Attaché: Ms J Downing

SEYCHELLES

Victoria
British High Commission
3rd Floor,
Oliaji Trade Centre,
PO Box 161, Victoria, Mahé
Telephone: (00) (248) 225225, 225356
Facsimile: (00) (248) 225127
e-mail: bhcsey@seychelles.net
Office Hours (GMT): Mon - Thurs 04 00 - 12 00
Fri 04 00 – 11 00

High Commissioner: Mr J W Yapp (Mr F A
Wilson, MBE w.e.f. Apr 2002)
Deputy High Commissioner: Ms J Currie
Defence Adviser (Resides in Nairobi): Colonel J R
Barnes
British Council Director (Resides in Port Louis):
Mrs S Ponnappa, OBE

SIERRA LEONE

Freetown
British High Commission
Spur Road, Freetown
Telephone: (00) (232) (22) 232961, 232362,
232563-5
Facsimile: (00) (232) (22) 228169, 232070
Airtech: (00) (232) (22) 231824
e-mail: bhc@sierratel.sl
Office Hours (GMT): Mon-Thurs 08 00 - 16 30
Fri 08 00 - 13 00
High Commissioner: Mr David Alan Jones
Deputy High Commissioner: Ms Andrea Reidy
Defence Adviser: Lieutenant Colonel Joe J P Poraj-
Wilczynski
First Secretary (Political): Mr Jamie Miller
First Secretary (Development): Mr Ian Stuart
Second Secretary (PPA): Mr Derek Smith
Third Secretary (Management): Ms Alison Baker-
Mavin, BEM
Third Secretary (Immigration/Consular): Mr Greg
Gibson
Third Secretary (Development): Mrs Nancy Stuart
Attaché: Miss Tracey Coleman
Attaché: Staff Sergeant Pete King
Cultural Attaché (British Council Director): Mr
Rajiv Bendre
Deputy Director (British Council): Ms Honor
Flanaghan

SINGAPORE

Singapore
British High Commission
Tanglin Road, Singapore 247919
Commercial Section: Tanglin PO Box 19,
Singapore 247919
Telephone: (00) (65) 4739333 (General)
                                  4740461 (Commercial)
                                  4748466 (Visa/Consular)
Facsimile: (00) (65) 4741958 (Chancery)
                                  4759706 (Management)
                                  4752320 (Commercial)
                                  4740468 (Consular)
e-mail: brithc@pacific.net.sg/firecrest
Website: www.britain.org.sg
Office Hours (GMT): Mon - Fri 00 30 - 05 00 and
06 00 - 09 00
High Commissioner: Sir Stephen Brown, KCVO
*Counsellor (Economic/Commercial) and Deputy
High Commissioner:* Mr Paul D Madden
Defence Adviser: Group Captain Martin D
Stringer, RAF
Head of Chancery: Mr Clive Alderton
*Cultural and Educational Adviser (British Council
Director) (Tel: 470 7101):* Mr Les Dangerfield
Deputy Cultural and Educational Adviser

(Director, English Language Centre) (Tel: 470 7103): Mrs Barbara Hewitt
First Secretary (Management/Consular): Mrs Jacqueline Bersin
First Secretary (Political): Mr William Brandon
First Secretary (Commercial): Mrs Rosemary P Clarke, MBE
First Secretary (Technical): Mr Richard M Hardy
First Secretary (Estate): Mr John McClean
Assistant Defence Adviser: Commander P S Doyne-Ditmas, MBE, RN
Assistant Cultural and Educational Adviser (British Council Assistant Director): Mr David Tupper
Second Secretary (Commercial): Miss Adele J Taylor
Second Secretary (Commercial): Mr Roger Whitehead
Second Secretary (Commercial): Mr Matthew E Oakley
Second Secretary (Economic/Commercial): Mr Martin Reynolds
Second Secretary (Defence): Mr Julian Williams
Second Secretary (Technical): Mr Nick Folker
Third Secretary (Political): Mr Dudley Crossland
Third Secretary (Consular): Mr Paul Worster
Third Secretary (Management): Mrs Jacqueline Fay
Third Secretary (Commercial): Mrs Niki Wright
Assistant Attaché: Mr Kunle Ogunbanjo
Assistant Attaché: Miss Heidi Reilly
Assistant Attaché: Mrs Stephanie Keep
Commercial Officer: Mrs Valsa Panicker
Commercial Officer: Mr Teo Chong Kee
Press Public Affairs: Ms Elisabeth Brodthagen
Accountant: Mr Alan Yeong
Estate Manager: Mr Terlok Singh
Systems Administrator: Miss Serene Cheong

SLOVAKIA

Bratislava
British Embassy
Panska 16, 811 01 Bratislava
Telephone: (00) (421) (2) 5441 9632/9633/0005/3673
5441 0007 (out of hours)
5441 9240/7623 or 5443 0970 Visa Section
Facsimile: (00) (421) (2) 5441 0002 General
    0001 Management/ Consular
    0003 KHF
    0004 Defence Section
    7639 Commercial Section
    5443 0969 Visa Section
e-mail: bebra@internet.sk
Website: www.britemb.sk
Ambassador: Mr R Todd
Deputy Head of Mission: Mr J R Setterfield
Defence Attaché: Lieutenant Colonel N S Southward, OBE
Second Secretary (Commercial): Mr S Digby
Second Secretary (KHF): Mr A Anstead
Second Secretary (Political): Mr G S Pollard
Second Secretary (Management) & HM Consul: Miss S Perry

Assistant Defence Attaché: Squadron Leader G Clarke, RAF
Vice Consul/Third Secretary (Management): Mrs C F Slaymaker
Third Secretary (Immigration): Mr G J Winter
Third Secretary (Immigration): Ms E Ryan
Cultural Attaché (British Council Director): Mr J A D McGrath

SLOVENIA

Ljubljana (SP)
British Embassy
4th Floor Trg Republike 3,
1000 Ljubljana
Telephone: (00) (386) (1) 200 3910 Main Reception
    200 3940 Commercial Section
Facsimile: (00) (386) (1) 425 0174 Chancery
    425 9080 Commercial Section
e-mail: info@british-embassy.si
postmaster.ljubljana@fco.gov.uk
Website: www.british-embassy.si
Ambassador (ext 3921): Mr H Mortimer, LVO
Deputy Head of Mission (Commercial) (ext 3922): Mr J Bedingfield
Defence Attaché (3950): Lieutenant Colonel A R Manton
Second Secretary and HM Consul (ext 3914): Mr S Hall
Third Secretary (Political) (3928): Mr N Abbott
Cultural Attaché (Director, British Council): Mr S Green

SOLOMON ISLANDS

Honiara
British High Commission
Telekom House, Mendana Avenue,
Honiara, Solomon Islands
Postal Address: PO Box 676
Telephone: (00) (677) 21705, 21706
Facsimile: (00) (677) 21549
e-mail: bhc@welkam.solomon.com.sb
Office Hours (GMT): Mon - Fri 21 00 - 01 00 and 02 00 - 05 00
High Commissioner: Mr B P Baldwin
Deputy High Commissioner: Mr D S Jones

SOMALIA

Mogadishu
British Embassy
Waddada Xasan Geedd Abtoow 7/8
(PO Box 1036), Mogadishu
Telephone: (00) (252) (1) 20288/9, 21472/3
Telex: 3617 (a/b PRODROME SM)
Staff temporarily withdrawn from post

SOUTH AFRICA

Cape Town
British High Commission
91 Parliament Street,
Cape Town 8001
Telephone: (00) (27) (21) 461 7220

Facsimile: (00) (27) (21) 461 0017
e-mail: britain@icon.co.za
bhcppa@iafrica.com   - Press and Public Affairs
Section
Office Hours (GMT): Mon -Thurs: 06 30 - 15 15
Fri: 06 30 - 10 30

Pretoria
British High Commission
255 Hill Street, Arcadia 0002
Telephone: (00) (27) (12) 483 1200
Facsimile: (00) (27) (12) 483 1302
e-mail: bhc@icon.co.za
Website: http://www.britain.org.za
Office Hours (GMT): Mon-Thurs: 06 00 - 15 00
Fri: 06 00 - 10 30
(* Staff based in Cape Town)
* *High Commissioner:* Ms Ann Grant
Counsellor and Deputy High Commissioner: Mr S
L Gass, CMG, CVO
Counsellor (Political): Mr D J Woods
Defence and Military Adviser: Brigadier M R
Raworth
Air and Naval Adviser: Wing Commander T A
Harper, RAF
* *First Secretary (Political):* Mr A Turner
First Secretary: Mr M Frost, OBE
First Secretary: Mr N Fisher
First Secretary (Management): Mr R Calder
First Secretary (Technical Works): Mr P J Sullivan,
MBE
First Secretary: Mr A Millar
First Secretary (PPA): Mr N Sheppard
First Secretary (Technical Management): Mr M A
Elvins
Second Secretary: Mr D Thomas
Second Secretary (Management): Mr M P Kay
Second Secretary (Technical Management): Mr P
Cullen
Second Secretary (Technical Management): Mr N
Roper
Second Secretary: Mr R Watters
* *Second Secretary:* Mr J Barbour
Second Secretary: Mr J Plank
* *Second Secretary:* Miss D Sheard
Second Secretary: Miss S Campbell

Consular Section
Liberty Life Place, Block B
256 Glyn Street, Hatfield 0083
Postal Address: P O Box 13611
and P O Box 13612,
Hatfield, 0028, Pretoria
Telephone: (00) (27) (12) 4831 402 Visas
                              4831 401 Passports
Facsimile: (00) (27) (12) 4831 433 Visas
                              4831 444 Passports
e-mail: Passport.enquiries@Precg.mail.fco.gov.uk
Visa.enquiries@Precg.mail.fco.gov.uk
Office Hours (GMT): Mon-Thurs: 06 00-14 00
Fri: 06 00-12 30
(* Based at High Commission, Pretoria)
* *Consul General:* Mr S L Gass, CMG, CVO
Consul: Mr R Thain
Second Secretary (Immigration/ECM): Mr R T Jones
Second Secretary (ALO): Mr T Moloney

Third Secretary (Consular): Ms J A Sibbons
Third Secretary (Immigration): Mr M L Gee
Third Secretary (Immigration): Miss S Dolan
Third Secretary (Immigration): Miss M Coleman
Third Secretary (Immigration): Mr M Wardle
Third Secretary (Immigration): Mrs P Garnham

Pretoria
Department for International Development:
Southern Africa
Suite 208, Infotech Building,
1090 Arcadia Street,
Hatfield 0083, Pretoria, Gauteng
Telephone: (00) (27) (12) 342 3360
Facsimile: (00) (27) (12) 342 3429
Counsellor (Head of Office): Mr S Sharpe
First Secretary (Senior Education Adviser): Ms B
Payne
*First Secretary (Senior Natural Resources
Adviser):* Ms P Chalinder
First Secretary (Senior Governance Adviser): Mrs
A Newsum
*First Secretary (Regional Sustainable Livlihoods
Adviser):* Mr A T Barrett
*First Secretary (Programme Manager BLSN and
Deputy Head of Division):* Dr J C Barrett
First Secretary (Economic Adviser): Mr P Barbour
First Secretary (Social Development Adviser):
Miss B Dillon
First Secretary (Enterprise Development Adviser):
Mr H Scott
*First Secretary (Senior Health and Population
Adviser):* Dr D Tracey
First Secretary (Environmental Adviser): Mr D Brew
First Secretary (Engineering Adviser): Mr M Harvey
First Secretary (Reproductive Health Adviser): Mrs
A De Cleene
First Secretary (Regional Forestry Adviser): Mr T
Foy
*Second Secretary (Senior Economist Assistant:
BLSN/SADC):* Mr P Ladd
*Second Secretary Deputy Programme Manager
RSA (Governance):* Mr D Fidler
Second Secretary (Programme Manager – BLSN):
Mr A Moir
Deputy Programme Manager: RSA (SL): Mr R
Taylor
Second Secretary Programme Manager (RSA): Ms
E Back
Second Secretary (IT Manager): Mr A Bromley
Second Secretary (Finance and Contracts Officer):
Mr D Collingwood
Third Secretary (Programme Officer - BLNS): Ms
P Hoffman
Programme Officer (Governance and Economics):
Mr F Anton (Temporary)
Programme Officer (Health): Ms D Webster
(Temporary)

Cape Town
British Consulate General
Postal address: PO Box 500,
Cape Town, 8000
Callers: 15th Floor, Southern Life Centre,
8 Riebeeck Street, Cape Town, 8001
Telephone: (00) (27) (21) 405 2400

422 7741 Commercial
Section
Facsimile: (00) (27) (21) 425 1427
425 3660 Commercial
Section
Airtech: (00) (27) (21) 425 1423
Office Hours (NOT PUBLIC HOURS) (GMT):
Mon-Thurs: 06 00 - 10 30 and 11 15 - 14 30
Fri: 06 00 - 11 30
Consul-General (228): Mr Peter D Broom
Vice-Consul (Commercial) (220): Ms Janet Usher
Vice-Consul (Management/Consular) (221): Mrs
Sarah L Young
Vice-Consul (232): Mr Iain D Bain
Vice-Consul (213): Mrs Lisa Woolley

East London
British Consulate
c/o Price Waterhouse Coopers & Lybrand, Suite 7,
Norvia House, 34 Western Avenue,
Vincent 5247
Postal Address:
P O Box 19537, Tecoma,
East London 5214
Telephone: (00) (27) (43) 726 9380
Facsimile: (00) (27) (43) 726 9390
Honorary Consul: Mr John L Fletcher

Port Elizabeth
British Consulate
5th Floor 1st Bowring House
66 Ring Road, Greenacres
Port Elizabeth, 6045
Postal Address: PO Box 35098
Newton Park
Port Elizabeth, 6055
Telephone: (00) (27) (41) 363 8841
Facsimile: (00) (27) (41) 363 8842
Telex: 242326
Telegraphic Address: Britain, Port Elizabeth
Office Hours (GMT): 07 00 - 10 30
Honorary Consul: Mr Harry Marston

Johannesburg
British Consulate-General
Callers - Dunkeld Corner, 275 Jan Smuts Avenue,
Dunkeld West, 2196
Postal Address:
P O Box 1082, Parklands 2121, Johannesburg
Telephone: (00) (27) (11) 325 2330 Commercial
Services
Facsimile: (00) (27) (11) 325 2131
Public Information Line:
Telephone: (00) (27) (11) 325 2330
Facsimile: (00) (27) (11) 325 2132
Management:
Telephone: (00) (27) (11) 325 2330
Facsimile: (00) (27) (11) 325 2132
Office Hours: Mon- Thurs 06 00 - 14.30 Fri 06 00 -
11.30
Consul General and Director of Trade Promotion:
Mr N McInnes
*Deputy Consul-General and Head of Southern
Africa Regional Commercial Hub:* Ms J M Leon
Vice-Consul (Commercial): Mrs H McKenzie
Vice-Consul (Commercial): Ms L S Hill
Vice-Consul (Management): Mr R A Sylvester

British Council
8th Floor, 76 Juta St
Braamfontein
PO Box 30637
Braamfontein 2017
Telephone: (00) (27) (11) 403 3316
Facsimile: (00) (27) (11) 339 3715
Cultural Attaché (British Council Director): Mr C
Gobby

Durban
British Consulate
Suite 1901, 19th Floor, The Marine,
22 Gardiner Street, Durban 4001
Postal Address: P O Box 1404,
Durban, 4000
Telephone: (00) (27) (31) 305 3041
Facsimile: (00) (27) (31) 307 4661
Office Hours (GMT): Mon-Thurs: 06 00 - 15 00
Fri: 06 00 - 11 30
Consul: Mr D Pearce
Vice-Consul: Mrs J M Smith
Vice-Consul (Commercial): Mr W G Tyler
Vice-Consul (Management): Mrs J Busch

SPAIN

Madrid
British Embassy
Calle de Fernando el Santo 16,
28010 Madrid
Telephone: (00) (34) 91 700 82 00
Facsimile: (00) (34) 91 700 83 09 Chancery
83 07 Defence
83 29 EU/Economic
83 11 Commercial
82 72 Information
82 10 Management
Office Hours (GMT): Winter 07 00-15 30
Summer Mon - Thurs 06 30-13 00 Fri 06 30-12 30
Ambassador: Mr Peter J Torry
Deputy Head of Mission: Mr Edward A Oakden
*Counsellor (Commercial) and Director of Trade
Promotion:* Mr John Hawkins
Counsellor: Ms Rosie Sharpe
Defence and Naval Attaché: Captain Anthony
Croke, RN
Military and Air Attaché: Group Captain Gavin C
Daffarn, RAF
*Counsellor (Cultural Affairs) (British Council
Director):* Mr Peter Sandiford
First Secretary (Head of Public Affairs & Press):
Mr Jon Davies
First Secretary and Consul-General: Mr Jeffrey
Thomas
First Secretary (Management): Mr Michael H F Legg
First Secretary (Press Officer): (vacant)
First Secretary (Agriculture): Mr Anthony J Bastian
First Secretary (Political/Economic): Mr Anthony
J Ball
First Secretary (Labour): Mr Giles Dickson
First Secretary (Cultural Affairs): (vacant)
First Secretary (Political/Economic): Mr
Christopher Sainty
*First Secretary (Cultural Affairs) (British Council
Deputy Director):* Ms Christine Melia

British Council: Ms Margaret Douglas
Second Secretary: Mr David Sykes
Second Secretary: Mr Michael Keogh
Second Secretary: Mr Mark Cox
Second Secretary (Management): Ms Karen Roskilly
Second Secretary (Commercial): Mr David J Chun
Second Secretary (Commercial): Mr Trevor Cayless
Second Secretary (Political/Economic): Ms Priya Guha
Second Secretary: Mr Keith Ager
Senior Economic Officer: Mr William Murray
Third Secretary (Press Attaché): Ms Caroline Sprod
Third Secretary/Vice-Consul: Mr Steve Morgan
Attaché: Mr Paul Oliver
Attaché: Mr Benedict Lyons

Madrid
British Consulate-General
Centro Colon Marques
de la Ensenada 16,
28004 Madrid
Telephone: (00) (34) 91 308 52 01
Facsimile: (00) (34) 91 308 08 82
Office hours (GMT): Winter: 06 30-13 30
Summer: 06 30-12 30
Consul-General: Mr J Thomas
Vice-Consul: Mr S Morgan
Vice-Consul: Mr D Wickham

Alicante
British Consulate
Plaza Calvo Sotelo 1-2,
Apartado De Correos 564,
03001 Alicante
Telephone: (00) (34) 96 521 60 22
Facsimile: (00) (34) 96 514 05 28
e-mail: alicanteconsulate@ukinspain.com
Office Hours (GMT): Winter: 06 00-13 30
Summer: 06 00-12 30
Consul: Mr Michael Mcloughlin
Vice-Consul: Mr Amos A Santolaya Diaz, MBE
Vice-Consul: Mr George Outhwaite
Honorary Vice-Consul (resides at Benidorm): Mr John A Seth-Smith (e-mail: jass@ctv.es)

Andorra
Tel/Fax: (00) (34) 376 83 98 40
e-mail: britcoand@mypic.ad
Honorary Consul: Mr Hugh Garner

Las Palmas (Canary Islands)
British Consulate
Edificio Cataluña,
Calle Luis Morote 6-3
35007 – Las Palmas de Gran Canaria
(Postal address: PO Box 2020, 35080 - Las Palmas de Gran Canaria)
Telephone: (00) (34) 928 262 508
Facsimile: (00) (34) 928 267 774
e-mail: laspalmasconsulate@ukinspain.com
firstname.surname@fco.gov.uk
Office Hours (GMT): Winter: 08 00-15 30
Summer: 07 00-14 30
Consul: Mr Peter J Nevitt
Vice-Consul: Mrs Anita J Pavillard
Commercial Officer: Mrs Montse Clemente

Málaga
British Consulate
Edificio EUROCOM
C/Mauricio Moro Pareto, 2, 2
29006 Málaga
Telephone: (00) (34) (95) 235 2300
Facsimile: (00) (34) (95) 235 9211
e-mail: postmaster@malaga.mail.fco.gov.uk
Office Hours (GMT): Winter: 07 00-14 30
Summer: 06 00-12 30
Consul: Mr Bruce McIntyre, MBE
Vice-Consul: Mr Patrick Boyce
Vice-Consul: Ms Rosslyn D Crotty
Commercial Officer (Tel/Fax: (00) (34) 95 4187032): Mr Joseph Cooper
Commercial Officer (Tel/Fax: (00) (34) 95 4915874): Ms Caroline Gray

Santa Cruz de Tenerife
British Consulate
(Canary Islands)
Plaza Weyler 8-1,
Santa Cruz de Tenerife 38003
Telephone: (00) (34) 922 28 68 63, 28 66 53
Facsimile: (00) (34) 922 28 99 03
e-mail: tenerifeconsulate@ukinspain.com
Office Hours (GMT): Winter: 08 30-14 00
Summer: 08 00-13 30
Consul: Mr Keith Hazell
Vice-Consul: Mrs Helen Diaz de Arcaya Keating

Vigo
British Consulate
Plaza de Compostela 23-6 I
(Aptdo 49), 36201 Vigo
Telephone: (00) (34) 986 43 71 33
Facsimile: (00) (34) 986 43 71 33
e-mail: vigoconsulate@ukinspain.com
Office Hours (GMT): 07 00-12 00
Honorary Consul: Mr John M Cogolludo

Barcelona
British Consulate-General
Edificio Torre de Barcelona,
Avenida Diagonal
477-13o, 08036 Barcelona
Telephone: (00) (34) 933 666 200 (6 lines)
Facsimile: (00) (34) 933 666 221
e-mail: barcelonaconsulate@ukinspain.com
Website: www.ukinspain.com
Office Hours GMT: 07 00-16 00 April – June, September and October
08 00-17 00 November to March
06 30-12 30 July to August
Consul-General (also Consul-General for Co-Principality of Andorra): Mr Richard Thomson
Consul (Commercial): Mr David N Broomfield
Director, The British Council: Mr Andrew Mackay
Vice-Consul: (Vacant)
Vice-Consul (Commercial): Mr John H V Hankin
Commercial Officer: Miss Eva Prada
Pro-Consul: Ms Joan W Millet

Bilbao
British Consulate-General
Alameda de Urquijo 2-8, 48008 Bilbao

Telephone: (00) (34) 94 415 76 00, 415 77 11, 415 77 22
Facsimile: (00) (34) 94 416 76 32
Airtech: (00) (34) 94 416 47 51
e-mail bcgbilbo@readysoft.es
Office Hours (GMT): 07 00 - 16 00 (Apr - Jun, Sept & Oct)
08 00 - 17 00 (Nov - Mar)
06 30 - 12 30 (Jul - Aug)
Consul-General: Mr Ian Lewis
Vice-Consul: Mr Derek Doyle, MBE
Pro-Consul: Mrs Flora Dorronsoro
Commercial Officer: Mr Angel Beti

Santander
British Consulate
Paseo de Pereda 27, 39004 Santander
Telephone: (00) (34) 942 22 00 00
Facsimile: (00) (34) 942 22 29 41
e-mail: mpineiro@nexo.es
Office Hours (GMT): 07 00 - 11 00 and 13 30 - 16 00 (April to mid June, mid Sept to Oct)
08 00 - 12 00 and 14 30 - 17 30 (Nov- March)
06 00 - 12 30 (Mid Jun to mid Sept)
Honorary Consul: Mr Modesto Pineiro, MBE

Palma
British Consulate
Balearic Islands
Plaza Mayor 3D,
07002 Palma de Mallorca,
Balearic Islands, Spain
Telephone: (00) (34) 971 712445, 712085, 716048,718501,712696
Facsimile: (00) (34) 971 717520
e-mail: consulate@palma.mail.fco.gov.uk
Office Hours (GMT): Nov-March: 07 00 - 14 30
Apr-Jun & Sep-Oct: 06 00 - 13 30
Jul-Aug: 06 00 - 12 30
Consul: Mr Alan J Smith
Vice-Consul: Mr Esteban Mas Portell

Ibiza
British Vice-Consulate
Avenida Isidoro Macabich
45-1, Apartado 307,
07800 Ibiza
Telephone: (00) (34) 971 301818, 303816, 301058
Facsimile: (00) (34) 971 30 19 72
e-mail: ibizacons@worldonline.es
Office Hours (GMT): Nov-March: 07 00 - 14 30
Apr-Jun & Sep-Oct: 06 00 - 13 30
Jul-Aug: 06 00 - 12 30
Vice-Consul: Mrs Helen Watson, MBE
Pro-Consul: Miss Raquel de la Osa

Menorca
British Vice-Consulate
St Casa Nova, Cami de Biniatap 30,
07720 Es Castell, Menorca
Telephone: (00) (34) 971 36 33 73
Facsimile: (00) (34) 971 35 46 90
e-mail: deborah@infotelecom.es
Honorary *Vice-Consul:* Mrs Deborah Hellyer

SRI LANKA

Colombo
British High Commission
190 Galle Road, Kollupitiya
(PO Box 1433),
Colombo 3
Telephone: (00) (94) (1) 437336/43
Facsimile: (00) (94) (1) 430308,
                                      335803 Consular/Visa
e-mail: bhc@eureka.lk
Office Hours (GMT): Mon - Thurs: 02 00 - 11 00;
Fri: 02 30 - 07 30
Visa Hours (GMT): Mon - Thurs: 02 00 - 05 30;
Fri: 02 30 - 04 30
British Council: 49 Alfred House Gardens
(PO Box 753), Colombo 3
Telephone: (00) (94) (1) 581171/2, 587078, 580301,502487, 582449
Facsimile: (00) (94) (1) 587079
e-mail: enquiries@britishcouncil.lk
High Commissioner (also High Commissioner to the Republic of Maldives): Ms Linda Duffield
Deputy High Commissioner: Mr M H P Hill
Defence Adviser: Lieutenant Colonel M H De W Weldon
Cultural Attaché (British Council Director): Ms S M Maingay
First Secretary (Commercial and Economic): Mr A Madeley
Second Secretary (Management): Mr R Morris
Second Secretary (Chancery): Miss A Kemp
Second Secretary (Immigration/Consular): Mr J Kenny
Second Secretary (Immigration): Mr R Goodall
Second Secretary (resides at Mumbai): Mr C Noon
Second Secretary (Development): Miss P Thorpe
Deputy Cultural Attaché: (British Council) Ms J Morgan
Third Secretary (Management): Mrs R Brett
Attaché (Immigration): Mr S Gordon
Attaché (Immigration/Consular): Mr M Redden
Attaché (Immigration/Consular): Mrs C Botha
Attaché: Mrs S Grimes
Attaché: Ms D White
Attaché: Mr P Nalden
Attaché: Staff Sergeant N Pusey
Attaché: Mr F Denn

SUDAN

Khartoum
British Embassy
Off Sharia Al Baladia, Khartoum East
(PO Box No 801)
Telephone: (00) (249) (11) 777105
Facsimile: (00) (249) (11) 776457
775562 (Consular/Visa)
Airtech: 775492
e-mail: british@sudanmail.net
Office Hours (GMT): Sun - Thur: 04 30 - 11 30
Visa Office Hours (GMT): Sun - Thur: 04 30 - 11 30
Ambassador: Mr Richard Makepeace
DHM/Consul General: Mr Lawrence Pickup
First Secretary (British Council): Mr Paul Doubleday

Second Secretary (Management/Commercial): Mr Malcolm Collard
Second Secretary (Aid): Mr Graham Wicks
Second Secretary (Political/Information): Mr Alastair King-Smith
Third Secretary and Vice-Consul: Miss Tiiu Morris
Third Secretary Entry Clearance Officer: Mr Jonathan Knight

SURINAM

Paramaribo
British Embassy
* *Ambassador:* Mr E C Glover, MVO
* *Second Secretary (Commercial), Consul and Deputy Head of Mission:* Mr S Crossman
Defence Attaché (Resides at Bridgetown): Captain S C Ramm, RN
* *Second Secretary (Management):* Ms A M Fairley
* *Third Secretary (Immigration/Consular):* Mr A J McFarlin
* Resides at Georgetown

Paramaribo
British Consulate
c/o VSH United Buildings, Van't Hogerhuysstraat, 9-11
PO Box 1860, Paramaribo, Surinam
Telephone: (00) (597) 402558,402870
Facsimile: (00) (597) 403515,403824
e-mail: united@sr.net
Office Hours (GMT): Mon - Fri: 11 00 - 20 15
Honorary Consul: Mr J J Healy, Jr

SWAZILAND

Mbabane (SP)
British High Commission
Callers: 2nd Floor, Lilunga House,
Gilfillan Street
Mbabane
Postal: Private Bag, Mbabane
Telephone: (00) (268) 404 2581/2/3
Facsimile: (00) (268) 404 2585
e-mail: bhc@realnet.co.sz
Office Hours (GMT): Mon - Thur: 06 00 - 11 00 and 12 00 - 14 45   Fri: 06 00 - 11 00
High Commissioner: Mr D G Reader
Deputy High Commissioner: Mrs C M McNeill
Defence Adviser (resides at Pretoria): Brigadier M R Raworth
Attaché: Ms L M Chatfield

Department for International Development
Telephone: (00) 268 404 9731/2/3
Facsimile: (00) 268 404 9734
British Council
Lilunga House, Gilfillan Street
Private Bag, Mbabane
Telephone: (00) (268) 404 2918/3101/4605
Facsimile: (00) (268) 404 2641
e-mail: general.enquiries@bc-swaziland.bcouncil.org
Office Hours (GMT): Mon - Fri: 07 00 - 14 30
Sat: 07 00 - 10 30
Director (Resides at Maseru): Mr P Feeney

SWEDEN

Stockholm
British Embassy
Skarpögatan 6-8, Box 27819,
115 93 Stockholm
Telephone: (00) (46) (8) 671 3000 Direct Dial - use extensions below in brackets
Facsimile: (00) (46) (8) 662 9989 Management
671 3104 Chancery/Defence
671 3077 Commercial
661 9766 Consular/Visa
671 3100 Information
Airtech: 671 3137
Office Hours (GMT): Winter: 08 00 -16 00
Summer 06 30 -14 30
Ambassador: (3102) Mr John Grant, CMG
Counsellor, Consul-General/Deputy Head of Mission (3110): (Vacant)
Counsellor (Economic and Commercial) (3050): Mr Peter Mathers, LVO
Counsellor (3112): Mr Andrew Stafford
Defence Attaché (3105): Wing Commander Phil M Leadbetter, MVO, MIMgt, RAF
Cultural Attaché (British Council Director) (3082): Mr Jim Potts
First Secretary (Political) (3119): Miss Alison Blackburne
First Secretary (Political) (3111): Mr Andrew Brear
First Secretary (Political) (3006): Mr David Dunn
First Secretary (Inward Investment) (3067): Mr Martin Cronin
First Secretary (Management and Consul) (3070): Mr Peter Langham
First Secretary (Commercial) (3053): Mr Ian Cormack
Second Secretary (Political/Information) (3108): Mrs Emma Sundbland
Second Secretary (Political/Economic) (3115): Mr Steve Frost
Third Secretary (Political) (3191): Mr Rupert Potter
Vice-Consul (3023): Ms Karen Farley
Vice-Consul (3022): Mr Henry Hodge
Honorary Chaplain: The V Rev. David Ratcliff

Gothenburg
British Consulate-General
Södra Hamngatan 23,
S 41114 Göthenburg
Telephone: (00) (46) (31) 339 3300
Facsimile: (00) (46) (31) 339 3302
Consul-General: Mr Chris P Greenwood
Consul (Commercial/Consular): Mr Alan J White, OBE

Malmö
British Consulate
Hyregatan 8,
211 21 Malmö
Telephone: (00) (46) (40) 611 55 25
Facsimile: (00) (46) (40) 611 55 25
Honorary Consul: Mr Anders Wixell (Swedish)

Sundsvall
British Consulate
SCA Graphic
Sundsvall AB,

Ostrand Pulp Mill,
861 81 Timra
Telephone: (00) (46) (60) 16 40 00
Facsimile: (00) (46) (60) 57 49 90
Honorary Consul: Mr Ola Hildingsson (Swedish)

SWITZERLAND

Berne
British Embassy
Thunstrasse 50, 3005 Berne
Telephone: (00) (41) (31) 359 7700
Facsimile: (00) (41) (31) 359 7701 General
Facsimile: (00) (41) (31) 359 7769 Political and
Information Section
Internet Address: http://www.british-embassy-berne-ch
Office Hours (GMT): 07 30 - 11 30 and 12 30 - 16 00
Ambassador: Mr B Eastwood, CMG*
Counsellor and Deputy Head of Mission, Director of Trade Promotions (also Consul-General for the Principality of Liechtenstein): Mr D G Roberts
Counsellor (Science and Technology) (resident at Bonn): Ms H Hughes-McKay
Counsellor: Mr H W G Patterson
Defence Attaché: Lieutenant Colonel E J Gould
First Secretary (Political): Dr S Harkin
First Secretary (Commercial): Miss A J Pring
First Secretary (Management) and Consul: Mr A Bates, MVO
Third Secretary (Political): Mr I Paterson
Vice Consul (Commercial): Mr B Haessig
Vice Consul (Commercial): Mrs S Valdettaro
Vice Consul (Commercial): Mr H Kuepfer
* Also Ambassador to the Principality of Liechtenstein

Geneva
British Consulate General
37-39 Rue de Vermont (6th Floor),
1211 Geneva 20
Telephone: (00) (41) (22) 918 24 00
Facsimile: (00) (41) (22) 918 23 22
Telex: 414195 (a/b 414195 UKGV CH)
Office Hours (GMT): Summer: 06 30 - 10 30 and 12 00 - 15 00
Winter: 07 30 - 11 30 and 13 00 - 16 00
HM Consul General: Mr I A Crees
HM Consul: Mrs V H Rowe
British Vice-Consul: Mrs L H Aviram
Vice-Consul (Commercial): Mrs E C Baha
Pro-Consul: Ms J Murray

Geneva
Joint Management Unit
37-39 Rue de Vermont, 1211 Geneva 20
Telephone: (00) (41) (22) 918 23 00
Facsimile: (00) (41) (22) 918 23 10
Telex: 414195 (a/b 414195 UKGV CH
Office Hours (GMT): Summer: 07 00 - 11 00 and 12 30 - 16 00 Winter: 08 00 - 12 00 and 13 30 - 17 00
First Secretary, Joint Management Officer: Mr I A Crees
Deputy Management Officer: Mr R W Harmer
Assistant Management Officer: Mrs L H Aviram

Montreux/Vevey
British Consulate
13 chemin de l'Aubousset,
1806 St Légier, Vaud
Telephone and Facsimile: (00) (41) (21) 943 3263
Honorary Consul: Mrs S Darra, MBE

Valais
British Vice-Consulate
Rue des Fontaines,
CH 3974 Mollens - Valais
Telephone: (00) (41) (27) 480 32 10
457 51 11 (Radio Pager)
Facsimile: (00) (41) (27) 480 32 11
Honorary Vice Consul: Mr A Bushnell

Geneva United Kingdom Mission to United Nations, see part II

Geneva United Kingdom Permanent Representation to the Conference on Disarmament, see part II

Zurich
British Vice-Consulate
Minervastrasse 117
CH- 8032 Zurich
Telephone: (00) 01 383 65 60
Facsimile: (00) 01 383 65 61
Honorary Consul: Mr A L T McCammon

Lugano
British Vice-Consulate
Via Sorengo 22,Third Floor
PO Box 184
6903 Lugano
Telephone: (00) (41) (91) 950 0606
Facsimile: (00) (41) (91) 950 0609
Office Hours (GMT): 10 00 - 12 00
Honorary Consul: Mr J Takield OBE

Basel
British Vice-Consulate
Innovation Centre
Gewerbestrasse 14
CH4123
Allschwill
Tel/fax: (00) (41) (61) 483 0977
Mobile: (00) (41) 763 789 987
Honorary Consul: Dr A Chalmers

SYRIA

Damascus
British Embassy
Kotob Building,
11 Mohammad Kurd Ali Street,
Malki, PO Box 37, Damascus
Telephone: (00) (963) (11) 373 9241/2/3/7
Facsimile: (00) (963) (11) 373 1600
Office Hours (GMT): Sun - Wed 06 00 - 13 15;
Thur 06 00 - 12 00
Ambassador: Mr H G Hogger
Counsellor and Deputy Head of Mission: Mr S H Innes
Defence Attaché: Colonel R C J Martin, OBE
British Council Director: Dr P Brazier
First Secretary (Political): Dr D M Haines

First Secretary (Management) and Consul: Mr T A Walford
Second Secretary (Commercial): Mr J A Chadwick
Vice-Consul (Immigration): Mr J S Walker
Third Secretary (Political/Information): Mr M R Bell
Third Secretary (Economic): Miss E J Robertson

Aleppo
British Consulate
PO Box 199
Telephone: (00) (963) (21) 267 2200, 2336771 (Office),
267 5033 (Home)
Facsimile: (00) (963) (21) 267 7640
Office Hours (GMT): 06 00 - 09 00
Honorary Consul: Mr Alexander Akras

British Trade Office
P O Box 5547
Aleppo
Telephone: (00) (963) (21) 268 0502/3
Facsimile: (00) (963) (21) 268 0501
Senior Commercial Officer: Mr Z Abu Baker

TAIWAN
See Annex for details.

TAJIKISTAN

Dushanbe
c/o British Embassy Tashkent
All staff resident in Tashkent/Moscow
Ambassador: Mr Christopher J Ingham
Deputy Head of Mission: Ms Karen Moran
Defence Attaché (resides at Almaty): Lieutenant Colonel Graham J Sheeley, AFC
Third Secretary (Political/PPA): Mr Chris Hirst
Third Secretary (Vice Consul/MO/ECO): Mr Dave J Muir
Attaché: Ms Jackie Bates
British Council Director: Mr Michael A Moore, MBE

TANZANIA

Dar es Salaam
British High Commission
Social Security House, Samora Avenue
PO Box 9200
Dar es Salaam
Telephone: (00) (255) (22) 2117659-64, 2113501, 2112953
Facsimile: (00) (255) (22) 2112952 Chancery
2116703 Management
2113586 Consular
2123948 Commercial
e-mail: bhc.dar@dar.mail.fco.gov.uk
Office Hours (GMT): Mon-Fri 04 30 - 12 00
High Commissioner: Mr R Clarke
Deputy High Commissioner: Mr S Banks
Defence Adviser (resides at Nairobi): Colonel J R Barnes
British Council Director: Mr T Cowin
Second Secretary (Commercial/Consular): Mr M Rash
Second Secretary (Management): Ms H M Feather
Second Secretary (Political/Press and Public affairs): Ms S Hussey

Third Secretary (Consular/Immigration): Ms P Smith
Third Secretary (Immigration): Mr D Mills

Department for International Development Eastern Africa (Tanzania)
c/o British High Commission
Social Security House, Samora Avenue
(PO Box 9200)
Dar es Salaam
Telephone: (00) (255) (22) 2117659-64, 2113501, 2112953
Facsimile: (00) (255) (22) 2112951
Office Hours (GMT): Mon-Fri 04 30 - 12 00
Head of DFIDEA (T): Ms C Sergeant
Second Secretary/Senior Programme Officer: Miss L M Saunderson
Second Secretary/Senior Programme Officer: Mr J Carpy
Third Secretary/Programme Officer: Mr J Orton
Renewable Natural Resources Adviser: Mr J Salmon
Economic Adviser: Ms F Shera
Social Development Adviser: Ms A Albee
Health & Population Adviser: Mr P Smithson
Education Adviser: Mr J Baxter
Engineering Adviser: Mr G Macdonald
Enterprise Development Adviser: Miss M Owusu-Gyamfi
Governance Adviser: Mr P Van Heesewijk
Governance and Civil Society - APO: Mr S Kossof
Management Supervisor: Ms M Negri

THAILAND

Bangkok
British Embassy
Wireless Road, Bangkok, 10330
Telephone: (00) (66) (2) 253-0191-9
Facsimile: (00) (66) (2) 254 9578 Chancery
(66) (2) 255 8619 Commercial/
Press and Public
Affairs
(66) (2) 255 9278 Management
(66) (2) 255 6051 Consular
(66) (2) 254 9579 Immigration
Airtech: (66) (2) 254 4720
Office Hours (GMT): Mon-Thurs: 0100 - 0500 and 0545 - 0930
Fri: 0100 - 0600 (Duty Staff until 0930)
Extn
Ambassador: Mr L B Smith   301
Counsellor and Deputy Head of Mission: Mr P B West   266
Counsellor (Commercial): Mr D Wyatt   319
Defence Attaché: Colonel A R E Singer, OBE   222
Counsellor and Permanent Representative to ESCAP: Dr P Haggie   288
First Secretary (Political): Mr T Carter   224
Consul & First Secretary (Management): Mr D J Fisher   208/239
First Secretary: Mr J Hector   232
First Secretary: Mr D Kilby   226
Second Secretary (Political): Mr M R Findlay   230
Second Secretary (Commercial): Mr K Cunningham   294
Second Secretary (Technical): Mr K Griggs   267

Second Secretary (Immigration): Mrs J Lacey-Smith   245
Second Secretary (Airline Liaison Officer): Miss D Broderick   362
Second Secretary (Technical Works Officer): Mr G Ward   212
Third Secretary (Technical): Mr P Haigh   369
Third Secretary (Management): Mrs C L Shaw 317
Third Secretary (Commercial): Mr M Woodham 350
Third Secretary (Economic/Development): Mr A J Shaw   291
Third Secretary and Vice-Consul: Ms F Lavender 229
Third Secretary (Immigration): Mrs G Lewis   363
Third Secretary (Immigration): Mrs D Tok   352
Third Secretary (Immigration): Mr N Faulkner 529

Department for International Development (DFID SEA)
C/O British Embassy
Wireless Road, Bangkok, 10330
Telephone: (00) (66) (2) 253 0191-9
Facsimile: (00) (66) (2) 253 7124
Extn
Head of Division: Mr M Mallalieu   250
Senior Engineering Adviser: Mr M McCarthy   233
Senior Education Adviser: Mr S Passingham   295
Senior Governance Adviser: Mr P Owen   532
Senior Economic Adviser: Mr P Balacs   227
Senior Social Development Adviser: Mr R Edwards 272
Social Development Adviser: Mr A Burke   214
Health and Population Adviser: Dr D Ghandhi
Economist: Mr O Bargawi   247
Senior Natural Resources and Environment Adviser: Mr S Bland   261
Programme Manager: Dr C Athayde   202
Programme Manager: Mr J McAlpine   204
Programme Officer: Ms D Avery
Programme Officer: Mr J Black   280
Deputy Programme Manager: Mrs K Parsons

Chiang Mai
British Consulate
British Council Offices,
198 Bumrungraj Rd
Muang, Chiang Mai, 5000
Telephone: (00) (66) (53) 242103, 248706
Facsimile: (00) (66) (53) 244781
Office Hours (GMT): Mon – Thur: 01 00 - 05 00
and 05 45 - 09 45
Fri: 01 00 - 06 30
Honorary Consul: Mr S Waller

TOGO

Lomé
British Embassy
(All staff resident in Accra)
Ambassador and Consul-General: Dr Rod Pullen
Counsellor and Deputy Head of Mission: Mr Craig Murray
Defence Attaché: Lieutenant Colonel Steen K E Clarke, OBE
First Secretary (Development): Mr Tony Gardner

First Secretary (Commercial): Mr Kevin Lynch
First Secretary (Political/External): Mr David Keegan
Second Secretary and Vice-Consul: Mrs Caroline Cross
Second Secretary (Development): Mr Desmond Woode
Second Secretary (Political, Press and Public Affairs): Mr Gregory Quinn
Second Secretary (Management): Mr Seif Usher
Second Secretary (Airline Liaison Officer): Mr Derek McDougal Swanson
Second Secretary (Immigration): Ms Debra Poulier
Second Secretary: Mr Andrew Eelbeck
Third Secretary (Commercial): Mrs Carol Turvill
Third Secretary (Chancery): Mr Jonathan Saunders
Third Secretary (Immigration): Mr Jim Beach
Third Secretary (Immigration): Mr Brendan Gill
Third Secretary (Immigration): Mr Alan Green
Third Secretary (Immigration): Mr Althea Ramsey
Third Secretary (Immigration): Mrs Tracey Singh
Third Secretary (Immigration): Mr Stuart Turvill
Third Secretary (Immigration): Mr Simon Winter

Lomé
British Consulate
British School of Lomé, BP 20050, Lomé
Telephone: (00) (228) 264606
Facsimile: (00) (228) 264989
e-mail: "For Mrs Jeni Sayer, British Consulate"
Admin@bsl.tg
Office Hours (GMT): Mon - Fri: 09 00 - 11 00
Honorary Consul: Mrs J A Sayer

British Commercial Office
Concession OTAM, Zone Portuaire,
Port de Peche, BP 9224, Lomé-Port, Lomé, Togo
Telephone: (00) (228) 271141, 275054
Facsimile: (00) (228) 274207
Mobile: 042180
e-mail: tom@netcom.tg
Commercial Officer: Captain R A M Jones

TONGA

Nuku'alofa
British High Commission
PO Box 56, Nuku'alofa, Tonga
Telephone: (00) (676) 24285/24395
Facsimile: (00) (676) 24109
Airech: (00) (676) 23922
e-mail: britcomt@kalianet.to
Office Hours (GMT): Sun - Wed: 19 15 - 23 30
and 00 30 - 03 45
Thurs: 19 15 - 00 15
High Commissioner and Consul for American Samoa: Mr Paul Nessling
Management Officer: Mrs Terrie Connelly
Defence Adviser (resides at Wellington): Colonel A A Peebles

TRINIDAD AND TOBAGO

Port of Spain
British High Commission
19 St Claire Avenue, St Clair
Port of Spain, Trinidad

Telephone: (00) (1) (868) 622 2748, 622 8960/1/2, 622 9895/6
Facsimile: (00) (1) (868) 622 4555 Management
　　　　　　　　　　 622 9087 Commercial
　　　　　　　　　　 628 3064 Consular
　　　　　　　　　　 628 8715 Chancery
　　　　　　　　　　 628 9380 HC/DHC
Airtech: (00) (1) (868) 622 4533
e-mail: csbhc@opus.co.h
Office Hours (GMT): Mon - Thurs: 11 30 - 16 00
and 17 00 - 20 00
Fri: 11 30 - 16 30
High Commissioner: Mr P G Harborne
Deputy High Commissioner: Mr P Bromley
Defence Adviser (Resides at Bridgetown): Captain
S C Ramm, RN
*Counsellor (Regional Affairs) (Resides at
Bridgetown):* Mr N J L Martin
Second Secretary (Management/Consular): Mrs S
Nicholas
Second Secretary (Commercial/Consular): Mr B
Nicholas
Third Secretary (Chancery/Information): Mr C
Hilton
Second Secretary (resides at Caracas): Mr D
Stewart

TUNISIA

Tunis
British Embassy
5 Place de la Victoire, Tunis 1000
Telephone: (00) (216) 1 341 444
Facsimile: (00) (216) 1 354 877
Airtech: (00) (216) 1 350 707
e-mail: british.emb@planet.tn
Consular and Visa Sections: 141-143 Avenue de la
Liberté, Tunis 1002
Telephone: (00) (216) 1 793 322 Visa
(216) 1 846 184 Consular
Facsimile: (216) 1 792 644
e-mail: uk.visa@planet.tn
Office Hours (GMT): Mon - Friday 07 00 - 11 00
and 12 00 - 15 00
July/August (GMT): Mon - Friday 06 30 - 13 30
Ambassador and Consul-General: Mr Robin A
Kealy, CMG
Deputy Head of Mission: Ms Janet C Hancock
Defence Attaché (resides in London): Commander
R Woods, RN
Cultural Attaché (British Council Director): Mr
John Whitehead
*Second Secretary (Commercial/Press & Public
Affairs):* Mr Brian J Conley
Second Secretary (Management): Miss Joanna J
Lowis
*Second Secretary (Entry Clearance Manager and
Consul):* Mr John P R Jeffrey
Vice-Consul: Mrs Val Zaoui, MBE
Third Secretary (Immigration): Mr Gary E Benham
Third Secretary (Immigration): Mr Chris Daltrey
Attaché: Mr Robert F McGlennan
Attaché: Mrs Lorraine H McColl
Honorary Chaplain: (Vacant)

Sfax
Honorary British Consulate
55 Rue Habib Maazoun, 3000,
Sfax, Tunisia
Telephone: (00) (216) (4) 223 971
Facsimile: (00) (216) (4) 299 278
Honorary Consul: Mr M Sellami

TURKEY

Ankara
British Embassy
Sehit Ersan Caddesi 46/A
Cankaya, Ankara
Telephone: (00) (90) (312) 455 3344
455 + extension number
Facsimile: (00) (90) (312) 455 3351
Commercial/Economic
　　　　　　　　　　 455 3353 Consular/Visa
　　　　　　　　　　 455 3386 Clinic
　　　　　　　　　　 455 3226 Defence
　　　　　　　　　　 455 3259 Drugs
　　　　　　　　　　 455 3356 Information
　　　　　　　　　　 455 3352 Management
　　　　　　　　　　 455 3350 Political
　　　　　　　　　　 455 3320 HMA
Airtech: 468 6770
e-mail: britembank@fco.gov.uk (check Firecrest
for individuals)
Website: www.britishembassy.org.tr

British Council
Esat Caddesi 41
Kucukesat, Ankara 06660
Telephone: (00) (90) (312) 424 1644
Facsimile: (00) (90) (312) 427 6182
Office Hours (GMT): Summer 05 45 - 10 00 and
11 15 - 14 30
July, August 05 45 - 10 00 and 11 15 - 14 30 (Mon -
Thurs)
05 45 - 10 00 (Fri)
Winter 06 45 - 11 00 and 12 15 - 15 30
Extn
Ambassador: Mr Peter J Westmacott, CMQ, LVO 3201
Counsellor and Deputy Head of Mission: Mr
David J Fitton 3203
Defence and Military Attaché: Brigadier Kim O
Winfield 3221
*Counsellor (British Council Director, Cultural
Affairs):* Dr Ray Thomas, OBE
Naval & Air Attaché: Commander Steve M Pegg, RN
3223
*Counsellor (Head of Economic/Commercial
Section):* Mr Chris Innes-Hopkins 3241
First Secretary (Head of Political Section): Dr
Laurence Bristow 3205
First Secretary (Political): Mr David Craig 3207
First Secretary (Political/Military): Dr Liane
Saunders 3210
First Secretary (Management) and Consul: Mr
Dominic Clissold 3261
*First Secretary (British Council and Cultural
Affairs):* Mr Michael Thornton
*First Secretary (British Council and Cultural
Affairs):* Mrs Joanne Speakman

First Secretary (Defence Equipment): Mr Chris
Comper 3225
First Secretary (Drugs): Mr David Parker 3360
First Secretary (Technical Management): Mr
David Kingdom 3214
Second Secretary (Economic): Mr Rafe P G
Courage 3244
Second Secretary (Political/Information): Dr
Sangeeta Ahuja 3209
Second Secretary (Drugs): Mr Warren Spivey 3380
Second Secretary (Technical Management): Mr
Chris Fox 3218
Third Secretary (Political): Ms Lynne F Allan 3219
Third Secretary (Management): Mr Richard
Whiteley 3262
Vice-Consul: Mrs Trudie Pak 3257

Antalya
British Vice-Consulate
Fevzi Çakmak Cad
1314 Sokak No.6/8
Antalya
Telephone: (00) (90) (242) 244 5313
Facsimile: (00) (90) (242) 243 2095
e-mail: britconant@celik.net.tr
Vice Consul: Mrs Jane Baz

Bodrum
British Consulate
Kibris Sehitleri Caddesi
Konacik Mevkii No 401/B
Bodrum
Telephone: (00) (90) (252) 317 0093-94
Facsimile: (00) (90) (252) 317 0095
e-mail: britconbod2@superonline.com
Honorary Consul: Mrs Fatma Nese Coskunsu

Izmir
British Consulate
1442 Sokak No 49
Alsancak
PK 300 Izmir
Telephone: (00) (90) (232) 463 5151
Facsimile: (00) (90) (232) 465 0858
e-mail: postmaster@izmir.mail.fco.gov.uk (check
Firecrest for individuals)
Consul: Mr Willie Buttigieg

Marmaris
British Consulate
c/o Yesil Marmaris Tourism & Yacht Management
Inc.
Barbaros Caddesi 11, Marina
P O Box 8, 48700 Marmaris
Telephone: (00) (90) (252) 412 6486
Facsimile: (00) (90) (252) 412 5077
e-mail: brithonmar@superonline.com
Honorary Consul: Mr Adnan Dogan Tugay

Mersin
British Vice-Consulate
Cakmak Caddesi, 124 Sokak
Mahmut Tece Is Merkezi, A Blok, Kat 4/4
Mersin
Telephone: (00) (90) (324) 232 1248, 237 8687
Facsimile: (00) (90) (324) 232 2991
Honorary Vice-Consul: Mr Andre Nofal

Istanbul
British Consulate-General
Mesrutiyet Caddesi No 34,
Tepebasi, Beyoglu,
PK 33 Istanbul 80072
Telephone: (00) (90) (212) 293 7540, 293 7545/9
Facsimile: 245 4989

Visa Section:
Telephone: (00) (90) (212) 252 6436/40
Facsimile: 252 6441 Visa
                     245 6354 Consular
                     252 8682 British
                             Council
e-mail: brcgist@verisoft.com.tr
comsec@escortnet.com.tr
Office Hours (GMT): Summer: 05 30 - 11 00 and
11 45 - 13 45 Winter: 06 30 - 11 00 and 11 45 - 14 45
Consul-General and Director of Trade Promotion:
Mr Roger Short
Deputy Consul-General: Mr Jim Begbie
*Consul (British Council Director and Cultural
Affairs):* Ms Sue Barnes
Consul (Management): Mr David Morton
Consul (Political Affairs): Mr Owen Traylor
Consul: Mr Paul Free
Consul: Mr Kevin Grist
Consul: Mr Andy Kellaway
Consul (Immigration): Ms Kim Charman
Consul (Immigration): Ms Janice Mills
Consul (Project Liaison Officer): Mr John Collier
Vice-Consul (Technical Works Officer): Mr Gavin
Thomas
Vice-Consul: Mr Shane Campbell, MBE
Vice-Consul (British Council and Cultural Affairs):
Mr Barry Breary
Vice-Consul (Commercial): Mr Richard di
Salvatore, MBE
Vice-Consul (Commercial): Mrs Lynne Smith
Vice-Consul: Mr Tom Revington
Vice-Consul (Information): Mrs Najma Bouakaze-
Khan
Vice-Consul (Management): Mr Les Rowlands
Vice-Consul (Immigration): Mr Hector Hughes
Vice-Consul (Immigration): Mrs Alison Jones-Early
Vice-Consul (Immigration): Mr Charlie Cosker
Vice-Consul (Immigration): Mr Paul Hardy
Vice-Consul (Immigration): Mr Steve McBride
Vice-Consul (Immigration): Mr Eddie Scanlon
Vice-Consul (Immigration): Ms Jenni Williams
Vice-Consul: Ms Carole Jarvie

Bursa
British Honorary Consulate
Ressam Sefik Bursali Sokak,
Basak Caddesi No.
Zemin Kat, 16010 Bursa
Telephone: (00) (90) (224) 221 25 34
Facsimile: (00) (90) (224) 221 88 01
Home Telephone: (00) (90) (224) 221 29 84
Honorary Consul: Mr E Kagitcibasi

TURKMENISTAN

Ashgabat
British Embassy
3rd Floor, Office Building

Four Points Ak Altin Hotel,
Ashgabat, Turkmenistan
Telephone: (00) (993) (12) 363462, 363463,
363464, 363466, 363498, 363474
Facsimile: (00) (993) (12) 363465
Airtech: (00) (993) (12) 363463 x292
e-mail: beasb@online.tm (General)
beasbtrade@online.tm (Commercial)
beasbppa@online.tm (Press & Public Affairs)
Website: www.britishembassytm.org.uk
Office Hours (GMT): Mon - Fri: 04 00 - 08 00 and
09 00 - 12 30
Ambassador: Mr Fraser A Wilson, MBE
Deputy Head of Mission: Mr Clive J McGill
Defence Attaché (resides at Moscow): Colonel M
H Auchinleck
Cultural Attaché (Resides at Tashkent): Mr
Michael A Moore, MBE
Assistant Defence Attaché (resides at Moscow):
Major Peter J F Daniell
Third Secretary (Chancery): Mr Justin D Tait
Third Secretary (Management) and Vice-Consul:
Ms Jane E Rowlands

TUVALU

Funafuti
British High Commission
(All staff resident at Suva)
High Commissioner: Mr Michael A Price, LVO
*Deputy High Commissioner and First Secretary
(Consular):* Mr Christopher Haslam

UGANDA

Kampala
British High Commission
10/12 Parliament Avenue,
PO Box 7070, Kampala
Telephone: (00) (256) (78) 312000 (Main
  Switchboard)
  312278 (Consular /Visa
  Section
  Enquiries)
  312261
  (Communications)
Facsimile: (00) (256) (78) 312282
  312281 (Consular /Visa
  Section)
  312267 (Chancery)
Airtech: (00) (256) (78) 312210
e-mail: bhcinfo@starcom.co.ug. (Press and Public
Affairs Section)
bhccomm@starcom.co.ug (Commercial Section)
firstname.lastname@kampala.mail.fco.gov.uk
Office Hours (GMT): Mon to Thurs: 05 30 - 10 00
and 11 00 - 14 00   Fri: 05 30 - 10 00

British Council
Ground Floor, Rwenzori Courts
Plot 2 Nakasero Road
PO Box 7070
Kampala
Telephone: (00) (256) (41) 234 725/234
730/7/9/234 748
Facsimile: (00) (256) (41) 254 853

e-mail: firstname.lastname@bc-
kampala.swiftuganda.com
High Commissioner: Mr Tom Phillips, CMG
Deputy High Commissioner: Mr Chris Skilton
Defence Adviser: Lieutenant Colonel Charles E
Thom, OBE
First Secretary (Regional Affairs): Mr Justin
Hustwitt
First Secretary (British Council Director): Ms Sue
Beaumont
First Secretary (Management): Mr Brian Cope, MVO
Second Secretary (Commercial/Consular): Ms
Helen Rawlins
Second Secretary (British Council): Ms Kate
Ewart-Biggs
Second Secretary (Economic): Miss Joanne Cetti
*Second Secretary (Political/Press and Public
Affairs):* Mr Ewan Ormiston
Third Secretary (Management): Mr Matt Proctor

**Department for International Development
Eastern Africa (Uganda)**
3rd Floor Rwenzori Courts
Plot 2 Nakasero Road
P O Box 7070, Kampala
Telephone: (00) (256) (41) 348727/9 & 348730/7
Facsimile: (00) (256) (41) 348732, 348735
e-mail: initial-surname@dfid.gov.uk
Head of Office: Mr Mike Hammond
Education Adviser: Mr Michael Ward
Renewable Natural Resources Adviser: Dr Alwyn
Chilver
Health & Population Adviser: Ms Ros Cooper
Assistant Health Adviser: Ms Angela Spilsbury
Engineering Adviser: Mr Philip Barlow
Social Development Adviser: Ms Bella Bird
Governance Adviser: Mr Tim Williams
Economic Adviser: Mr Paul Mullard
Enterprise Development Adviser: Mr Anthony Way
Emergencies Adviser: Mr Graham Carrington
Deputy Programme Manager: Miss Alison Batt
Deputy Programme Manager: Miss Sarah Metcalf
Programme Officer: Miss Sandra Grant
Governance & Civil Society Coordinator: Mr
Jeremy Armon
Assistant Health & Population Field Manager: Mr
James Thornberry

UKRAINE

Kiev
British Embassy
01025 Kiev Desyatinna 9
Telephone: (00) (380) (44) 462 0011, 462 0012,
462 0014
Facsimile: (00) (380) (44) 462 0013
e-mail: ukembinf@sovam.com

Consular/Visa Section:
01021 Kiev, 6 Mazepy Street (Formerly -
Sichnevoho,
Povstannya 6)
Telephone: (00) (380) (44) 290 7317,290 2919,
Facsimile: (00) (380) (44) 290 7947
Office Hours (GMT): Mon – Thurs 06 00 – 14 15
Fri 06 00 – 14 00

British Council:
040704 Kiev
4/12, Hruhoria Skovorody
Telephone: (00) (380) (44) 490 5600
Facsimile: (00) (380) (44) 490 5605
Ambassador: Mr R H Smith, CMG
Consul-General and Deputy Head of Mission: Mr
D Maclaren
Defence Attaché: Captain R E Drewett, MBE, RN
First Secretary (Political): Miss F F MacCallum
First Secretary (Commercial): Mr R C C Cook
First Secretary (Management/Consular): Mr R B
Smith
First Secretary (British Council Director): Ms L
Biglou
Second Secretary (Chancery/Information): Miss N
A Davison
Second Secretary (Development): Mr S Clark
Second Secretary (Immigration): Mrs E Allen
*Second Secretary (Deputy Director, British
Council):* Mr S Williams
*Second Secretary (Assistant Director, British
Council):* Mr I Law
Assistant Defence Attaché: Major S I Mehers
Third Secretary (Political): Mr D E Hunter
Third Secretary (Management): Mrs S Garnham
Third Secretary (Immigration/Vice-Consul): Miss
N Rennie
Third Secretary (Immigration): Mr A M Lake
Third Secretary (Immigration): Miss J Connor
Assistant Defence Attaché: Staff Sergeant P Durkin

UNITED ARAB EMIRATES

Abu Dhabi
British Embassy
PO Box 248, Abu Dhabi,
United Arab Emirates
Telephone: (00) (971) (2) 6326600 (7 lines),
                           6321364 (Night Service).
                           6321660 (Commercial)
Facsimile: (00) (971) (2) 6318138 (Chancery)
                           6341744 (Commercial)
                           6345968 (Consular/
                               Management)
                           6342676 (Visa Section)
e-mail: chancery@abudhabi.mail.fco.gov.uk
Website: www.britain-uae.org
Office Hours (GMT): Sat - Wed 03 30 - 10 30
Ambassador: Mr Patrick M Nixon, CMG, OBE
Counsellor and Deputy Head of Mission: Mr
Alistair W McKenzie, MBE
First Secretary (Political): Mr Andrew Neil
Defence Attaché: Colonel Anthony V Malkin
*Counsellor (Cultural Affairs) (British Council
Director):* Mr Robert L T Sykes
First Secretary (Commercial): Mr John E Gardner
First Secretary, Defence Sales: Mr Navin Patel, MBE
Second Secretary (Management/Consul/ECM): Mr
Stephen A J Davies
*Second Secretary (Chancery/Press and Public
Affairs):* Mr Jason R Smith
Second Secretary (Commercial): Mr Rahat Siddiqi
Third Secretary and Vice-Consul: Mr Amias S
Moores

Third Secretary (Chancery/Consular): Mr Andrew
J Miller
Third Secretary (ECO): Mrs Anne V Hammond

Dubai
British Embassy
PO Box 65, Dubai, United Arab Emirates
Telephone: (00) (971) (4) 3971070
3971893 Commercial Section
Facsimile: (00) (971) (4) 3971095 Commercial
                               Section
                           3971620 Chancery
                           3972153 Management/
                               Consular
                           3977539 Visa
Office Hours (GMT): Sat - Wed 03 30 - 10 30
Consul-General and Counsellor: Mr Simon Collis
*First Secretary (Commercial) Consul and Deputy
Head of Mission:* Mr Ted Cole, OBE
First Secretary (Political): Mr David Spencer, MBE
Royal Navy Liaison Officer: Commander Steve
Bennett, RN
Customs Liaison Officer: Mr Chris Hardwick
Cultural Attaché (British Council Director): Mr
Tim Gore
First Secretary (Management/Consul/ECM): Mr
Anthony Mills
Airline Liaison Officer: Mr Steve Hart
Second Secretary (Commercial): Mr Lee Jennings
Second Secretary (Technical): Mr Robert Fletcher
Second Secretary (Press and Public Affairs): Mr
Jon Yarrow
Second Secretary (Economic): Miss Blaise Metreweli
Third Secretary (Political): Mr Alex Bannerman
Third Secretary (Commercial/Information): Mr
Darren Forbes-Batey
Third Secretary (Immigration): Mr Neale Jones
Third Secretary (Immigration): Mrs Joan Fontaine-
Harvey
Third Secretary (Immigration) and Vice-Consul:
Mrs Suzanne Bastin

UNITED STATES

Washington
British Embassy
3100 Massachusetts Avenue,
NW, Washington DC 20008
Telephone: (00) (1) (202) 588 6500 Embassy
Facsimile: (00) (1) (202) 588 7870 Chancery
                               7866 Management
                               7901 Trade
                               7850 Consular
Office Hours (GMT): Winter: 14 00 - 22 30
Summer: 13 00 - 21 30
Ambassador: Sir Christopher Meyer, KCMG
Minister: Mr A R Brenton
Minister (Economic): Mr S J Pickford
*Defence Attaché and Head of British Defence
Staff:* Air Vice-Marshal J H Thompson, CB, RAF
Minister (Defence Material): Mr S French
Naval Attaché and Commander British Naval Staff:
Commodore N H L Harris, MBE, RN
*Military Attaché and Commander British Army
Staff:* Brigadier J J Keeling

Air Attaché and Commander British Air Force Staff: Air Commodore G D Simpson, CBE, AFC, RAF
Counsellor (Political and Public Affairs): Mr R Peirce
Counsellor (Political/Military/Europe): Mr P O Gooderham
Counsellor (Trade & Transport): Mr N J Westcott
Counsellor: Mr I F McCredie, OBE
Counsellor (Management) and Consul-General: Mr W D Townend
Counsellor (External Affairs): Mr S Wood
Counsellor (Science Technology, Environment and Energy): Mr C Whaley
Counsellor: Mr J V Silcock
Counsellor: Mr J King
Counsellor (NIB): Dr P Smyth
Counsellor (DST): Mr C Pell
Counsellor (Defence Equipment): Mr S S McCarthy
Counsellor (Head of NSD): Mr D Dearden
Counsellor (Economic): Ms S J Owen
Cultural Attaché (British Council Director) (Tel: 588 7843): Mr D Blagbrough
Attaché (Defence Equipment - Sea/Air): Mr T Whitemore
Attaché (Defence Equipment - Land): Mr J Platt
Attaché (Defence Equipment - Legal): Mr G Jones
Attaché (Defence Equipment - Commercial): Mr M Newman
First Secretary (Political): Mr M J Rycroft
First Secretary (Chancery): Mr R N P Macaire
First Secretary (Chancery): Mr C Newns
First Secretary (Chancery): Ms A Blake
First Secretary (Agricultural): Mr J Hughes
First Secretary (Science and Technology): Mr C Pook
First Secretary (Economic): Mr D Finch
First Secretary (Trade Policy): Mr A J Phillipson
First Secretary (Transport): Mr S Knight
First Secretary (Press and Public Affairs): Mr P Reid
First Secretary (Politico/Military): Mr M A O'Neill
First Secretary: Mr N MacGinness
First Secretary (Political): Mr S Hill
First Secretary (Latin America/OAS/Caribbean): Mr J Gimblett
First Secretary (Management): Mr P Newman
First Secretary (Technical Manager): Mr K Edwards
First Secretary (Scottish Affairs): Ms S Stewart
First Secretary (Technical Manager): Mr S Drew
First Secretary (Defence Equipment): Mr C Cook
First Secretary (Trade Policy): Mr S E Towler
First Secretary: Mr R Seddon
First Secretary (Trade Promotion): Mr A Attryde
First Secretary: Mr S Rowton
First Secretary (NIB): Mr N Houston
Assistant Naval Attaché: Captian Eric Fraser, RN
Head of BDILS (NA): Colonel M Hill
Assistant Military Attaché: Colonel T L S Weeks, OBE
Assistant Air Attaché: Group Captain B T Dingle, RAF
First Secretary (Defence Trade): Mr T Johnson
First Secretary (Defence Supply - Land and Sea Systems): Mr A Nisbet
First Secretary (Technical Works Officer): Mr J Miles
First Secretary (Consul): Mrs C Priestley
Second Secretary (PS to Ambassador): Mr J Casson
Second Secretary (Management): Mr J Burran
Second Secretary (Transport): Mr C Sutcliffe
Second Secretary (Chancery): Mr P Jones

Second Secretary (Chancery/External): Miss R J Laycock
Second Secretary (Education): Ms J A Scott
Second Secretary: Mr I Allan
Third Secretary (Vice-Consul): Ms E Marsh
Head of Defence Administration: Mr P Jones

Washington United Kingdom Delegation to the International Monetary Fund and International Bank for Reconstruction and Development, see part II

Washington United Kingdom Representation at the Inter-American Development Bank, see part II

Atlanta
British Consulate-General
Suite 3400, Georgia Pacific Center
133 Peachtree Street NE,
Atlanta, GA 30303
Telephone: (00) (1) (404) 954 7700
Facsimile: (00) (1) (404) 954 7702
Voicemail Numbers: see individual officers
Office Hours (GMT): 13.00 - 23.00
e-mail - officers first name.surname followed by @fco.gov.uk
Consul-General (Ext 7716): Mr Michael Bates, OBE
Deputy Consul-General and Consul (Trade) (Ext 7720): Mr Steve Collier, MVO, RVM
Vice-Consul (Management/Consular) (Ext 7313): Ms Linda Nassar
Vice-Consul (Trade) (Ext 7725): Mr J Mel Pinson
Vice-Consul (Trade) (Ext 7722): Ms Mary Storch
Vice-Consul (Investment) (Ext 7730): Mr Glen Whitley
Vice-Consul (Investment) (Ext 7731): Mr Ian Stewart
Vice Consul (Press and Public Affairs) (Ext 7706): Ms Jo Le Good

Miami
British Consulate
Suite 2800, Brickell Bay Office Tower,
1001, Brickell Bay Drive, Miami
Florida 33131
Telephone: (00) (1) (305) 374 1522
Facsimile: (00) (1) (305) 374 8196
Consul: Mr R G Bayliss OBE, MVO
Vice-Consul (Commercial): Mrs B George-Hoerber
Vice-Consul (Commercial): Mr J Wright
Vice-Consul (Customs): Mr B Foreman
Vice-Consul (OTRCIS): Mr L Covington

Nashville
British Consulate
c/o Nashville Area Chamber of Commerce
211 Commerce Street
Nashville, TN 37201
Telephone: (00) (1) 615 743 3061
Facsimile: (00) (1) 615 256 6982
e-mail: jbutler@nashvillechamber.com
Honorary Consul: Mr J Butler

Orlando
British Vice-Consulate
Suite 2110, SunTrust Center,
200 South Orange Avenue,
Orlando, Fl 32801

Telephone: (00) (1) 407 426 7855 Consular
Facsimile: (00) (1) 407 426 9343
Pager No: 407 981 5588
Vice-Consul: Mr H Hunter

Charlotte

British Consulate
NC0748
Two First Union Center
301 South Tryon Street, 7th Floor
Charlotte, NC 28288-0748
Telephone: (00) (1) 704 383 4359
Facsimile: (00) (1) 704 383 6545
e-mail: mteden@carolina.rr.com
Honorary Consul: Mr M Teden, OBE

Boston

British Consulate-General
25th Floor, Federal Reserve Plaza,
600 Atlantic Avenue,
Boston MA 02210
Telephone: (00) (1) (617) 2489555
Facsimile: (00) (1) (617) 2489578 Group 3
e-mail: British.Consulate@boston.mail.fco.gov.uk
Postmaster@boston.mail.fco.gov.uk
Officers first name.last name followed by
@boston.mail.fco.gov.uk
Consul-General (0102): Mr G D Fergusson
Deputy Consul-General (0115): Mr M G Plant
Vice-Consul (Trade) (0103): Ms M Meyer
Vice-Consul (Trade) (0100): Mr J Shipala
Vice-Consul (Press & Public Affairs) (0113): Mrs
T Evans
Vice-Consul (Management) (0110): Mrs K M Tunsley
Vice-Consul (Investment) (0107): Ms A Sloan
*Vice-Consul (US-wide Life Sciences & Healthcare)
(0111):* Ms A Lin

Chicago

British Consulate-General
13th Floor, The Wrigley Building,
400 N Michigan Avenue, Chicago,
Illinois 60611
Telephone: (00) (1) (312) 970 3800
Facsimile: (00) (1) (312) 970 3852
970 3854 Consular and Visa Sections only
Airtech: (00) (1) (312) 970 3818
Office Hours (GMT): 13 30 - 22 00
HM Consul-General: Mr Robert Culshaw, MVO
Deputy Consul-General: Mr Michael Murray
HM Consul - Trade & Consular: Mr James Halley
Consul - Investment: Mr Ian Gavin Head of
Politics, Press & Public Affairs: Ms Caroline
Cracraft, MBE
Head of Management: Mr Chris Shaw
Trade Officer: Mr Robert Blackburn
Trade Officer: Mrs Reet Robinson
Trade Officer: Mr Fred Levitan
Trade Officer: Mr Richard Knox
Trade Officer: Mr Brian Shapiro
Investment Officer: Mr Kevin Wilson
Investment Officer: Mr Jonathan Wood
Entry Clearance Manager/British Vice-Consul:
Mrs Janet Bershers, MBE

Minneapolis

British Consulate
2600 U.S Bancorp Centre,
800 Nicollet Mall
Minneapolis, MN 55402-7035
Telephone: (00) (1) (612) 338 2525
Facsimile: (00) (1) (612) 339 2386
Office Hours (GMT): 14 30 - 23 00
Honorary Consul: Mr W R McGrann

Kansas City

British Consulate
12109 Aberdeen Road,
Shawnee Mission, KS 66209
Telephone: (00) (1) (913) 469 9786
Facsimile: (00) (1) (913) 469 8597
e-mail: britconkswmo@hotmail.com
Office Hours (GMT): 14 30 - 23 15
Honorary Consul: Mr J Scott Brown

St Louis

British Consulate
2323 Manor Grove Drive
#8, Chesterfield, Missouri 63017
Telephone: (00) (1) (636) 227 1334
Honorary Consul: Mr V W Lammert

Houston

British Consulate-General
Suite 1900, Wells Fargo Plaza,
1000 Louisiana, Houston, Texas 77002
Telephone: (00) (1) (713) 659 6270
659 6275 Commercial Department
Facsimile: (00) (1) (713) 659 7094
Office Hours (GMT): 15 00 - 23 00
Consul-General: Mr I R Murray
Deputy Consul-General and Consul (Commercial):
Mr P Williams
Vice-Consul (Commercial): Mr K Rost
Vice-Consul (Commercial, oil and gas): Mr M
Somers
Vice-Consul (Information): Ms H Mann
Consul (Investment): Mr D Goodwin
Vice-Consul (Investment): Mr B Medd-Sygrove
Vice-Consul (Consular): Miss L Kelly
Management Officer: Ms A Medlin

Denver

British Consulate
Suite 1030, World Trade Center
1675 Broadway
Denver,
Colorado 80202
Telephone: (00) (1) (303) 592 5200 (General)
5205 (Consul–direct)
5212 (Trade
Assistant–
direct)
Facsimile: (00) (1) (303) 592 5209
e-mail: John.Maguire@britcondenver.com
info@britcondenver.com
Office Hours (GMT): 16 00 - 24 00
Consul (Commercial): Mr John Maguire
Commercial Assistant: Ms Vicky Lea

Dallas
British Consulate
2911 Turtle Creek Blvd.,
Suite 940, Dallas TX75219
Telephone: (00) (1) (214) 521 4090
Facsimile: (00) (1) (214) 521 4807
e-mail: bc@airmail.net.
Office Hours (GMT): 15 00 - 23 00
Consul (Commercial): Mr P L Martinez
Vice-Consul (Commercial): Mrs B Schnaufer

New Orleans
British Consulate
10th Floor, 321 St Charles Avenue,
New Orleans, Louisiana, 70130
Telephone: (00) (1) (504) 524 4180
Office Hours (GMT): Sat & Wed 04 30 - 11 30
Honorary Consul: Mr J J Coleman Jr
Consular Assistant: Ms W Roberts

Los Angeles
British Consulate-General
11766 Wilshire Boulevard, Suite 400,
Los Angeles, California 90025-6538
Telephone: (00) (1) (310) 477 3322 (for officers
direct numbers see below)
Facsimile: (00) (1) (310) 575 1450
                          575 1451 Airtech
                          477 2693 Visas only
e-mail: trade.losangeles@fco.gov.uk
invest.losangeles@fco.gov.uk
pppa.losangeles@fco.gov.uk
visas.losangeles@fco.gov.uk
firstname.lastname@fco.gov.uk
Website: www.BritainUSA.com
Office Hours (GMT): 16 30 - 01 00
Consul-General (310 481 2950): Mr Paul Dimond
*Deputy Consul-General & Consul (Trade) (310
996 3036):* Mr Alan Cobden
Consul (Investment) (310 996 3021): Ms Lorraine
Johnson
*Consul (Consular/Entry Clearance) (310 481
2919):* Mr Paul Stevens
*Vice-Consul (Press, Political & Public Affairs)
(310 996 3028):* Mr Angus Mackay
Vice-Consul (Management) (310 996 3020): Mrs
Nancy Bridi
Vice-Consul (Trade) (310 996 3030): Mr Carl Gipson
Vice-Consul (Investment) (310 996 3024): Mr
Kevin Aisbitt
Vice-Consul (Trade) (310 996 3031): Ms Patrice
Brayer
Director (British Film Office) (310 481 2933): Ms
Susan Finlayson-Sitch
*Vice-Consul (Consular/Entry Clearance) (310 481
2903):* Ms Anne Morton
Vice-Consul (Entry Clearance) (310 481 2912):
Ms Francesca Dooley
Vice-Consul (Entry Clearance) (310 481 2915): Mr
Des Brewer

Phoenix
British Consulate
15249 North 59th Avenue
Glendale, Arizona 85306-6000
Telephone: (00) (1) (602) 978 7200
Facsimile: (00) (1) (602) 978 9663

Office Hours (GMT): 16 30 - 01 00
Honorary Consul: Dr Roy Herberger

British Trade and Investment Office
3800 North Central, Suite 1500,
Phoenix, Arizona 85012
Telephone: (00) (1) (602) 280 8189
Facsimile: (00) (1) (602) 280 1378
e-mail: BTIOPhoenix@aol.com
Office Hours (GMT): 15 00 - 23 30
Director: Mr Hank Marshall

Salt Lake City
British Consulate
Eagle Gate Tower, Suite 2100,
60 East South Temple,
Salt Lake City, Utah 84111
Telephone: (00) (1) (801) 297 6922
Facsimile: (00) (1) (801) 297 6940
Office Hours (GMT): 16 00 - 01 00
Honorary Consul: Mr G Frank Joklik

San Diego
British Consulate
7825 Fay Ave, Suite 200
La Jolla, California 92037
Telephone: (00) (1) (858) 459 8231
Facsimile: (00) (1) (858) 459 9250
Office hours (GMT): 15.00-01 00
Honorary Consul: Mr William Black

New York
British Consulate-General
(incorporating British Trade and Investment
Offices)
845 Third Avenue, New York, N.Y. 10022
Telephone: (00) (1) (212) 745 0495 Trade
0300 Investment
Facsimile: (00) (1) (212) 745 0456 Trade and
                                    Investment
                          754 3062 Consular/Visa
Airtech: (00) (1) (212) 745 0296
*Consul General and Director-General of
Trade and Investment:* Mr Thomas G Harris, CMG
Deputy Consul-General and Director of Trade: Mr
Mike Cohen
*Deputy Consul-General and Director of
Investment:* Mr Howard R Drake
Deputy Consul-General and Director BIS: Mr
Duncan J R Taylor
Head of Joint Management Office: Ms Madeleine
Campbell
Consul (Investment): Mr Ian Gibbons
Consul (Press and Public Affairs): Ms Sara G Everett
*Consul (Press and Public Affairs, Northern
Ireland):* Mr Paul Johnston
Consul (Trade): Mr Clive V Thompson
Consul (Trade): Mr Colin Brazier
*Consul and Director of Entry Clearance Issuing
Posts:* Mr Patrick Owens
Vice-Consul: Mrs Jacqueline Cerdan
Vice-Consul (Political): Dr Ray Raymond, MBE
Vice-Consul (Trade): Mr Charles Picarelli
Vice-Consul (Trade): Mr Robert F Lomnicki
Vice-Consul (Trade): Mr Robert Cassidy
Vice-Consul (Trade): Mr Michael Formosa
Vice-Consul (Trade): Ms Christina Lynton

Vice-Consul (Investment): Ms Kerry Appleton
Vice-Consul (Investment): Mr Ian Baines
Vice-Consul (National Market Research Co-ordinator): Mrs Francine J Conran
Vice-Consul (Fairs and Promotions): Ms Annie Wildey
Vice-Consul (Commercial Publicity): Mr Dominic Varle

New York (SP)
British Information Services
845 Third Avenue, New York, NY 10022
Telephone: (00) (1) (212) 745 0200
Public Inquiries: (00) (1) (212) 745 0277
Facsimile: (00) (1) (212) 745 0359
e-mail: public.enquiries@newyork.mail.fco.gov.uk
Office Hours (GMT): Summer: 13 00 - 21 30
Winter: 14 00 - 22 30
Counsellor (Political &Public Affairs) and Head of BIS (resides at Washington): Mr Robert N Pearce
Director of BIS and Deputy Consul General: Mr Duncan J R Taylor
Deputy Director, BIS and Consul (Press & Public Affairs): Ms Sara G Everett
Consul (Press & Public Affairs) (Northern Ireland): Mr Paul Johnston
Vice-Consul (Political): Dr Ray Raymond
Vice-Consul (Press & Public Affairs): Mrs Leslie Slocum
Vice-Consul (Press & Public Affairs): Mr Ray Donoghue
Head of Internet Division: Mr Ashok Khosla
Visits Officer (for all British Government Offices in New York): Ms Louise Redmond

Joint Management Office (SP)
One Dag Hammarskjold Plaza,
27th Floor, 885 Second Avenue,
New York, NY 10017
Telephone: (00) (1) (212) 745 9222
Facsimile: (00) (1) (212) 745 9292
Postal Address: PO Box 5238 NY 10150-5238
Office Hours (GMT): Summer: 13 00 - 21 30
Winter: 14 00 - 22 30
Head of Joint Management Office: Ms Madeleine Campbell
First Secretary (Management): Mr Andrew T Dimbleby
Second Secretary (Technical Management): Mr Mel Bell
Deputy IT Coordinator (North America): (Vacant)
Accountant: Ms Hayley Kirkham

New York   United Kingdom Mission to United Nations, see part II

Philadelphia
British Consulate
33rd Floor, 1818 Market St
Philadelphia, PA 19103
Telephone: (00) (1) (215) 557 7665
Facsimile: (00) (1) (215) 557 6608
Honorary Consul: Mr O St C Franklin

Pittsburgh
British Consulate
Buchanan Ingersoll

301 Grant Street
One Oxford Center, 20th Floor
Pittsburgh, PA 15219-1410
Telephone: (00) (1) (412) 562 8872
Facsimile: (00) (1) (412) 391 0910
Honorary Consul: Mr W Newlin

Puerto Rico
British Consulate
Banktrust Plaza
Suite 807
255 Ponce de Leon Avenue
San Juan, Puerto Rico 00917
Telephone: (00) (1) (787) 758 9828
Facsimile: (00) (1) (787) 758 9809
e-mail: btopr1@coqui.net
Vice Consul: Mrs Patricia T Martinez

Pacific Islands
(American Samoa)
British Consulate (US Territories South of the Equator)
Consul (resides at Nuku'alofa): Mr Paul Nessling

San Francisco
British Consulate-General
Suite 850, 1 Sansome Street,
San Francisco, California 94104
Telephone: (00) (1) (415) 617 1300
Facsimile: (00) (1) (415) 434 2018 Group 3
Website: www.britainusa.com/sf
Office Hours (GMT): 16 30 - 01 00
Consul-General: Mr D R Thomas
Deputy Consul-General and Consul (Commercial): Mr G G Simpson
Consul (Investment): Mr J Lindfield, MBE
Vice-Consul (Information): Ms E Stevenson
Vice-Consul (Commercial): Mr B Frieder
Vice-Consul (Commercial): Mrs A Eisler
Vice-Consul (Investment): Mr M Corson
Vice-Consul (Management/Consular): Mrs K S Thomas
Vice-Consul (Commercial): (Vacant)
Vice-Consul (Commercial): Ms M S Katari

Anchorage (Alaska)
British Consulate
College of Arts and Sciences
University of Alaska Anchorage
3211 Providence Drive
Anchorage, AK 99508
Telephone: (00) (1) (907) 786 4848
Facsimile: (00) (1) (907) 786 4647
e-mail: afdh1@uaa.alaska.edu
Honorary Consul: Dr Diddy R M Hitchins

Portland (Oregon)
British Consulate
1300 SW Fifth Avenue
Suite 2300
Portland, OR 97201
Telephone (Direct Line): (00) (1) (503) 778 5337
227 5669 Consulate
Facsimile: (00) (1) (503) 778 5299
e-mail: iainlevie@dwt.com
Honorary Consul: Mr I Levie

San Jose (California)
British Consulate
1139 Karlstad Drive
Sunnyvale
San Jose, CA 94089
Telephone: (00) (1) (408) 747 7140 x1200 or
x1400 (Assistant)
Facsimile: (00) (1) (408) 747 7198
e-mail: belder@genus.com
Honorary Consul: Dr W R Elder

Pittsburgh
British Consulate
Buchanan Ingersoll
301 Grant Street
One Oxford Centre, 20th Floor
Pittsburgh PA 15219 –1410
Telephone: (00) (1) (412) 562 8800
Facsimile: (00) (1) (412) 5629316
Honorary Consul: Mr W R Newlin

Seattle
British Consulate
900 Fourth Avenue,
Suite 3001,Seattle, WA 98164
Telephone: (00) (1) (206) 622 9255
Facsimile: (00) (1) (206) 622 4728
Office Hours (GMT): 16 30 - 01 30
Consul (Commercial) (4178): Mr D Broom
Vice-Consul (Commercial) (4183): Mr R Alvarez
Vice-Consul (Commercial) (4183): Mr D Baron

Nashville (Tennessee)
British Consulate
PO Box 50135
6107 Robin Hill Rd
Nashville Tennessee 37205
Telephone: (00) (1) (615) 356 8049
Facsimile: (00) (1) (615) 354 0879
e-mail: Jbutle69@mail.idt.net
Honorary Consul: Mr J Butler

UPPER VOLTA   SEE BURKINA FASO

URUGUAY

Montevideo (SP)
British Embassy
Calle Marco Bruto 1073, 11300 Montevideo, PO
Box 16024
Telephone: (00) (598) (2) 622 3630, 622 3650
Facsimile: (00) (598) (2) 622 7815
Office Hours (GMT): Mid Mar - Mid Dec: 12 00 -
16 00 and 17 00 - 20 15
Mid Dec - Mid Mar: 11 00 - 17 00
e-mail: officers first name.surname@
MONTEVIDEO.mail.fco.gov.uk
Embassy e-mail: bemonte@internet.com.uy
For officers residing in Buenos Aires refer to e-
mail addresses in Argentina.
Ambassador: Mr John Everard
*Deputy Head of Mission, First Secretary and
Consul:* Mr Redmond Norton
Defence Attaché (resides at Buenos Aires): Group
Captain T P Brewer, OBE, RAF
First Secretary (resides at Buenos Aires): Mr
Michael Cavanagh

Second Secretary (Management) and Vice-Consul:
Mr Gerald S Evans
Second Secretary (TMO) (resides at Buenos Aires):
Mr Stuart Moss

UZBEKISTAN

Tashkent
British Embassy
Ul. Gulyamova 67, Tashkent 700000, Uzbekistan
Telephone: (00) (99871)
1206451,1206288,1207852,1207853,1207854
Facsimile: (00) (99871) 1206549 (General)
1206430 (Consular/Visa)
e-mail: brit@emb.uz
Office Hours (GMT)
Winter: 04 00-07 30 and 08 30-12 00 (GMT + 5
hours)
Summer: 05 00-08 30 and 09 30-13 00 (GMT + 4
hours)
Ambassador: Mr Christopher J Ingham
Deputy Head of Mission: Ms Karen Moran
Defence Attaché (resides at Almaty): Lieutenant
Colonel Graham J Sheeley, AFC
Third Secretary (Political/PPA): Mr Chris Hirst
Third Secretary (Vice Consul/MO/ECO): Mr Dave
J Muir
Attaché/ECO: Ms Jackie Bates
British Council Director: Mr Neville McBain
(Designate)

VANUATU

Vila
British High Commission
KPMG House, Rue Pasteur, Port Vila, Vanuatu
PO Box 567, Port Vila, Vanuatu
Telephone: (00) (678) 23100 (3 lines)
25550 (1 line) DFID (Pacific) Vila
Facsimile: (00) (678) 27153 (Airtech) .
23651 (General)
25280 DFID (Pacific) Vila
e-mail: bhcvila@vanuatu.com.vu
n-duggin@dfid.gov.uk
dfidpacific@vanuatu.com.vu
firstname.surname@vila.mail.fco.gov.uk
Office Hours (GMT): Mon, Tue, Thu & Fri: 20 30
- 00.45 and 02 00 - 05 30
Wed: 20 30 - 00 45
High Commissioner: Mr Michael T Hill
Deputy High Commissioner: Mr Chris J Poll
DFID Programme Support Officer: Mr Nick Duggin

VENEZUELA

Caracas
British Embassy
Edificio Torre Las Mercedes (Piso 3), Avenida La
Estancia, Chuao, Caracas 1061
Postal Address: Embajada Britanica, Apartado
1246,Caracas 1010-A
Telephone: (00) (58) (21) (2) 993 41 11, 993 42 24
03 39 Commercial Section
02 64 Management Section
Facsimile: (00) (58) (21) (2) 993 99 89
Commercial, Information, Management
03 15 Chancery

Airtech: (00) (58) (21) (2) 993 0376
e-mail: britishembassy@internet.ve
Website: www.britain.org.ve
Office Hours (GMT): Mon-Thur: 1200 - 1630 and
17 30 - 20 30
Fri: 12 00 -17 30
Consular Section Hours (GMT): Mon-Fri 1230-1600
Ambassador: Mr E J Hughes
Deputy Head of Mission: Mrs S J le Jeune
d'Allegeershecque
Defence Attaché: Captain E F Searle RN
Cultural Attaché (British Council Director)
(Tel: 952 9965/9757): Mr J C Greenwood
First Secretary: Mr A Buckingham
First Secretary (Commercial): Mr S J Seaman MBE
Second Secretary (Management) and Consul: Mrs
S I Campbell
Second Secretary (Political): Mr A Tate
Second Secretary: Mr R A Williams
Second Secretary (Technical): Mr A Linnell
Second Secretary (Commercial): Mr C J Campbell
Third Secretary (Management/Consular): Mrs J M
De Larrabure
Third Secretary (Technical): Mr K Gibbs
Attaché: Mr D P Morgan
Attaché: Mrs J P Micallef
Attaché: Mrs S V Diaz

Maracaibo
British Consulate
Avenida 2G, #67-49, Sector La Lago,
Urbanizacion Virginia (diagonal al Club Creole)
Telephone: (00) (58) (2) (61)
915589/921355/925557
Facsimile: (00) (58) (2) (61) 913487
Office Hours (GMT): 12 00 - 16 30
Honorary Consul: (Vacant)

Margarita
British Consulate
Av. Principal No B-14, (Callejón) Urb. Playas del
Angel
Pampatar, Distrito Maneiro, Island of Margarita
Telephone/Facsimile: (00) (58) (2) (95) 262 46 65/
0149951267
e-mail: dw@enlared.net
Honorary Consul: Mr D M Weller

Mérida
British Consulate
Avenida Las Americas
Edificio Don Chabelo, Apto PH-4,
(Freate a la Urb.Humboldt), Merida 5101
Telephone: (00) (58) (2) (74) 266 20 22
Facsimile: (00) (58) (2) (74) 266 33 69
Honorary Consul: Dr R G Kirby

Valencia
Agropecuaria Flora C.A
Calle 143, No 100-227
Callejon La Cieba, Urbanizacion La Cieba
Valencia, Estado Carabobo, Venezuela
Telephone: (00) (58) (2) 41 82 38 401
Facsimile: (00) (58) (2) 41 82 34 742
e-mail: agroflora@compuserve.com
Office Hours: Mon, Wed, Fri 09 00 - 11 30
Honorary Consul: Mr D Martin

San Cristobal
British Consulate
Anglo Venezuelan Engineering & Controls
CA AVECO Britania House
Av. Rotaria, Esq.Av Parque Exposición,
La Concordia, San Cristobal
Telephone: (00) (58) (2) 76 471644/460434
Facsimile: (00) (58) (2) 76 470544
Honorary Consul: Mr R Burnison

VIETNAM

Hanoi
British Embassy
Central Building, 31 Hai Ba Trung
Telephone: (00) (84) (4) 8252510, 8267560-5,
8267558-9
Facsimile: (00) (84) (4) 8265762 Chancery/
Commercial
8252349 Consular/
Management
e-mail: behanoi@fpt.vn
Website: www.uk-vietnam.org
Office Hours (GMT): Mon-Fri 01 30 - 10 00

British Council:
40 Cat Linh Street, Hanoi
Telephone: (00) (84) (4) 8436780/2
Facsimile: (00) (84) (4) 8434962
Office Hours (GMT): Mon - Fri 01 30 - 05 00 and
07 00 - 10 00
Ambassador: Mr W Morris
Deputy Head of Mission and Consul: Mr M
McLachlan
British Council Director and Cultural Attaché
(114): Mr D Cordingley
British Council Assistant Director and Cultural
Attaché (107): Ms K Owen
British Council Deputy Director and Cultural
Attaché (112): Mr P Zetter
Defence Attaché (resides at Kuala Lumpur):
Colonel R J Little
First Secretary (Development): Mr A Johnson
First Secretary (Development): Mr S Ray
First Secretary (Development): Ms L Cameron
Second Secretary (Chancery, Press and
Information): Mr J Dunn
Second Secretary (Management): Mr T D C Fisher
Second Secretary (Commercial): Mr R Lally
Third Secretary, Vice Consul & Development: Ms
E M Henry
Attaché: Mr A Painter
Attaché: Ms S Allen
Attaché: Ms A-M Meconi

Ho Chi Minh City (SP)
British Consulate General
25 Le Duan,
District 1, Ho Chi Minh City,Vietnam
Telephone: (00) (84) (8) 8298433
Facsimile: (00) (84) (8) 8295257 (Visa/Consular)
8221971 (Commercial/Information)
e-mail: bcghcmc@hcm.vnn.vn
Office Hours (GMT): Mon - Fri 01 30 – 0500 and
0630 – 1000

British Council:
25 Le Duan,
District 1, Ho Chi Minh City, Vietnam
Telephone: (00) (84) (8) 8232862 (Main Office)
8256403 (Teaching Centre)
Facsimile: (00) (84) (8) 8232861 (Main Office)
8222105 (Teaching Centre)
e-mail: bchcmc@britishcouncil.org.vn
Office Hours (GMT): Mon-Fri: 01 30 - 05 00, 06
30 - 10 00
Consul-General: Mr A C Stephens
Second Secretary (Commercial): Mr C Gracey
*British Council Director and Cultural Consul (Tel:
825 6402):* Mr J Spence
Management Officer: Ms C Rimmer

YEMEN

Sanaa
British Embassy
129 Haddah Road, Sanaa
Postal address: PO Box 1287
Telephone: (00) (967) (1) 264081/82/83/84
Facsimile: (00) (967) (1) 263059
Office Hours (GMT): Sat - Wed: 04 30 - 11 30
Ambassador and Consul General: Ms Frances Guy
Deputy Head of Mission and Consul: Mr M H
Lamport
Defence Attaché (resides at Riyadh): Brigadier J D
Deverell
British Council Director: Mr A T N Chadwick
Second Secreteary (Political/Aid/Information):
(Vacant)
Second Secretary (Management) and HM Consul:
Mr R Hunter
Second Secretary (Political/Aid): Mr C R Heatly
Third Secretary (Immigration): Mr G Sykes
Third Secretary/Vice Consul: Ms J Crabtree

Aden
British Consulate-General
20 Miswat Road
Postal address: P O Box 6304, Khormaksar, Aden
Telephone: (00) (967) (2) 232712-4
Facsimile: (00) (967) (2) 231256
Office Hours (GMT): Sat - Wed: 04 30 - 11 30
Vice-Consul (Commercial): Mr M Rajamanar

Hodeidah
British Consulate
Sanaa Road, KM7,
P O Box 3337, Hodeidah
Telephone: (00) (967) (3) 238130/131, 238958
Facsimile: (00) (967) (3) 211533
238269
Office Hours (GMT): Mon - Wed: 08 00 - 13 00
Honorary Consul: Mr Abdul Gabbar Thabet

YUGOSLAVIA

Belgrade
British Embassy
Resavska 46, 11000 Belgrade
Telephone: (00) (381) (11) 645 055, 3060 900,
3615 660
Facsimile: (00) (381) (11) 659 651
3061 089 (Chancery)

3061 072 (Consular/
Visa)
3061 059 (Commercial)
642 293 (Information)
Airtech: 3061 020
e-mail: britemb@eunet.yu
ukembcom@eunet.yu (Commercial)
ukembbg@eunet.yu (Information)
Website: britemb.org.yu
Office Hours (GMT): Mon - Thur: 07 00 - 15 30;
Fri: 07 00 - 12 00
Ambassador: Mr C G Crawford, CMG
Deputy Head of Mission: Ms S H Price
Counsellor: The Hon. A L C Monckton
Defence Attaché: Colonel W Nowosylski-
Schlepowron
First Secretary (Political): Mr D A Slinn
First Secretary (Commercial): Mr D Webb
First Secretary (Development): Ms J Creighton
Second Secretary (Management and Consul): Ms
A M Fowle
Second Secretary (Chancery): Mr T M Tomlinson
Second Secretary (Economic): Mr J A Dancer
Attaché: Mr I G Storey, MBE

Podgorica - Montenegro
British Consulate
National Library "Radosav Ljumovic"
Njegoseva 22
81000 Podgorica
Telephone: (00) (381) (812) 44 495
Facsimile: (00) (381) (812) 44 543 Management
Section
Office hours (GMT): Mon, Wed & Friday: 07 45 -
15 00
Tue and Thur: 10 45 - 18 00
Honorary Consul: Mr D Vugdelic

Pristina - Kosovo
British Office
Xhemajl Nr 37
Dragodan
Pristina
Telephone: (00) 381 38 549 559
Satellite fax: (00) 870 761 841 167
Office Hours (GMT): Mon – Thur: 07 30 - 16 00
Fri: 07 30 - 16 30
Head of Office: Mr D A Slinn, OBE
Deputy Head of Office: Ms S Crombie
Second Secretary (Political): Mr A R H Thomson
Management Officer: Ms E Mills, MBE

ZAMBIA

Lusaka
British High Commission
5210 Independence Avenue
P.O.Box 50050
15101 Ridgeway, Lusaka
Telephone: (00) (260) (1) 251133
Facsimile: (00) (260) (1) 253798 Management/
Press and Public Affairs/Development)
251923 Commercial
252842 Visa/Consular
e-mail: brithc@zamnet.zm
Office Hours (GMT): Mon - Thur: 06 00 - 11 00
and 12 00 - 14 30

Fri: 06 00 - 11 00
High Commissioner: Mr T N Young
Deputy High Commissioner: Mr P W D Nessling
Counsellor (Regional Affairs): Mr Michael Wood
Head of DFID Zambia: Ms Helen Mealins
Defence Adviser (Resides in London): Lieutenant
Colonel G M Thomas, MBE
Second Secretary (Management): Mrs C Cullen
Second Secretary (Political/Press/Public Affairs):
Mr Ian Mason
Deputy Head of DIFD Zambia: Mr Steve Graham
Second Secretary: Mr Alex Holey
Second Secretary (Consular/Commercial/ECM):
Mrs Lyn Shaw
Third Secretary (Immigration): Mr O Everitt

ZIMBABWE

Harare
British High Commission
Corner House, 7th Floor
Samora Machel Avenue/Leopold Takawira Street
(PO Box 4490), Harare
Telephone: (00) (263) (4) 772990,774700
Facsimile: (00) (263) (4) 774617
Airtech: (00) (263) (4) 774703
e-mail: british.info@fco.gov.uk (Press & Public
Affairs)
british.management@fco.gov.uk (Management
Section)
british.passports@fco.gov.uk (Consular/Visa Section)
british.trade.harare@fco.gov.uk (Commercial
Section)
Website: www.britainzw.org
Office Hours (GMT): 06 00 - 10 30 and 11 30 -
14 30 (Mon-Thu), 06 00 - 12 00 (Fri)
High Commissioner: Mr J B Donnelly, CMG
Deputy High Commissioner: Ms D Corner
Counsellor: Mr A Stones
Defence Adviser: Colonel J S Field, CBE
*First Secretary (Medical Officer) (resides in
Lilongwe):* Dr H Friend
First Secretary (Commercial): Mr D Seddon
First Secretary (Management): Mr R D Hazlewood
Second Secretary (Political): Mr R S Lindsay
Second Secretary (Consular/Immigration): Mr J
Liddell
Third Secretary (Management): Mrs S C Howard
Third Secretary (Political/Press & Public Affairs):
Mrs T Wicke
Third Secretary (Consular/Immigration): Mr W N
Pagett
Assistant to Defence Adviser: WO. D A Hardinges

Department for International Development:
Central Africa (Regional Office)
Corner House, 6th Floor, Samora Machel
Avenue/Leopold Takawira Street
PO Box 1030 Harare
Telephone: (00) (263) (4) 774719-28
Facsimile: (00) (263) (4) 775695
Office Hours (GMT): 06 00 – 14 30 (Mon-Fri)
Head of DFID Central Africa: Mr J Winter
Regional Health & Population Adviser: Dr C
Presern
Regional Social Development Adviser: Mr E Hanley

Regional Natural Resources Adviser: Mr J Hansell,
OBE
Regional Education Adviser: Mr T Allsop
Regional Engineering Adviser: Mr J Hyde
Regional Private Sector Adviser: Mr D Spence
Regional Environmental Adviser: (Vacant)
Zimbabwe & Regional Programme Manager: Mrs
G Wright
Economic Adviser: Ms V Plater
Governance Adviser (saic): Mr L Mukubvu
Assistant Health Adviser: Ms M Temin
Assistant Private Sector Adviser: Ms A Harper
Deputy Programme Manager: Mr S Sabey

**See also DFIDCA country programme offices
Lilongwe, Lusaka and Maputo.**
e-mail: initial-surname@dfid.gov.uk (eg: J-
Winter@dfid.gov.uk)

PART II: MISSIONS AND DELEGATIONS

UNITED KINGDOM MISSION TO THE UNITED NATIONS

New York
One Dag Hammarskjold Plaza, 28th Floor,
885 Second Avenue, New York, N.Y. 10017
Telephone: (00) (1) (212) 745 9250
Facsimile: (00) (1) (212) 745 9316
Airtech: (00) (1) (212) 745 9272
Postal address: PO Box 5238 New York, NY 10150-5238
e-mail: UK@UN.INT
Office Hours (GMT): Summer 13 00 - 22 00
Winter 14 00 - 2300
United Kingdom Permanent Representative to the United Nations and United Kingdom Representative on the Security Council (with personal rank of Ambassador): Sir Jeremy Greenstock, KCMG
Deputy Permanent Representative to the United Nations (with personal rank of Ambassador): Mr Stewart Eldon, CMG, OBE
Counsellor and Head of Chancery: Mr Alistair Harrison, CVO
Counsellor (Economic, Social and Humanitarian Affairs): Mr Mark Runacres
Counsellor (Political): Mr Eugene Curley, OBE
Counsellor (Legal Adviser): Mr Iain MacLeod
Counsellor (ACABQ): Mr Nick Thorne
Counsellor (Finance): Dr Richard Moon
Military Adviser to UK Permanent Representative: Colonel Nicholas Seymour
Deputy Military Adviser: Mr Peter Hunter
First Secretary (Chancery): Ms Anna Clunes
First Secretary (Chancery): Mr Dominic Fortescue
First Secretary (Chancery/Press): Ms Catherine Mackenzie
First Secretary (Economic): Ms Sarah MacIntosh
First Secretary (Chancery): Mr Mike Anderson
First Secretary (Social Development Adviser): Ms Pat Holden
First Secretary (Chancery): Miss Vanessa Howe-Jones
First Secretary (Human Rights): Mr Jolyon Welsh
First Secretary (Finance): Mr Bill Longhurst
First Secretary (Environment): Ms Alice Walpole
First Secretary (Chancery): Mr Carne Ross
First Secretary (Management): Ms Madeleine Campbell
First Secretary (Management): Mr Andrew Dimbleby
First Secretary (Humanitarian Affairs): Mr Tom Kelly
Assistant Legal Adviser: Ms Alice Burnett
Second Secretary (Chancery): Ms Charlotte Cutler
Second Secretary (Chancery): Ms Rosemary Davis
Second Secretary (Management): Mr Melvin Bell
Second Secretary (Chancery): Ms Sarah Broughton
Second Secretary (Finance): Mr David Turnbull
Second Secretary (Chancery): Miss Tina Falzarano
Second Secretary (Chancery): Miss Kathy Mackay
Second Secretary (Chancery): Mr Gerard McGurk, MBE

Second Secretary (Social Affairs): Mr Matthew Johnson
Third Secretary (Economic): Ms Beverley Simpson
Third Secretary (Library): Mr Andrew Davidson

New York Joint Management Office, British Government Offices, see part I

UNITED KINGDOM MISSION TO THE OFFICE OF THE UNITED NATIONS AND OTHER INTERNATIONAL ORGANISATIONS AT GENEVA

Geneva
37-39 rue de Vermont, 1211 Geneva 20
Telephone: (00) (41) (22) 918 23 00
Facsimile: (00) (41) (22) 918 23 33 Main No
                        24 35 Chancery
                        24 44 Spec Agencies
                        23 77 WTO/
                               Economic
                        23 10 Joint
                               Management
                               Unit
Telex: 414195 (a/b 414195 UKGV CH)
Office Hours (GMT): Summer: 07 00 - 11 00 and 12 30 - 16 00
Winter: 08 00 - 12 00 and 13 30 - 17 00
United Kingdom Permanent Representative (holds personal rank of Ambassador): Mr S W J Fuller, CMG
Minister and Deputy Permanent Representative: Mr N M McMillan, CMG
Counsellor (UN Affairs): Mr T A Willasey-Wilsey
First Secretary (Head of Chancery, Human Rights): Mr K Lyne
First Secretary (UN, Press Officer): Mrs S E March
First Secretary (Legal Adviser): Mrs S McCrory
First Secretary (Specialised Agencies): Mr G M Warrington
First Secretary (WTO): Mr A G Sims
First Secretary (Humanitarian): Mrs J Caley
First Secretary (Management): Mr I A Crees
First Secretary (UNCTAD, ECE): Mrs E Fuller
First Secretary (Economic Affairs): Mr J C G Cooper
Second Secretary (WTO): Mr E J M Brown, MBE
Second Secretary (WTO): Miss J Lomas
Second Secretary (Specialised Agencies): Mr J M Bradley
Second Secretary (ECE, UNCTAD): Mr C J R Moore
Second Secretary (Humanitarian, Human Rights): Mr P Bentall
Second Secretary (Management): Mr R W Harmer
Second Secretary (Political): Mr A Wurr

UNITED KINGDOM DELEGATION TO THE UNITED NATIONS EDUCATIONAL, SCIENTIFIC AND CULTURAL ORGANISATION (UNESCO)

Paris
1 Rue Miollis
75732 Paris
Cedex 15
Telephone: (00) (331) 45 68 27 84
Facsimile: (00) (331) 47 83 27 77
United Kingdom Permanent Delegate (holds
personal rank of Ambassador): Mr D L Stanton
United Kingdom Deputy Permanent Delegate: Ms
C Atkinson
Third Secretary: Mrs H J Izon

UNITED KINGDOM MISSION TO THE UNITED NATIONS IN VIENNA

Vienna
Jaurèsgasse 12, 1030 Vienna
Telephone: (00) (43) (1) 716 130 or (43) (1) 71613
+ extension
Facsimile: (00) (43) (1) 71613 4900
e-mail: ukmisv@netway.at
Office Hours (GMT): Winter: Mon - Fri 08 00 -
12 00 and 13 30 - 16 30
Summer: Mon - Fri 07 00 - 11 00 and 12 30 - 15 30
United Kingdom Permanent Representative (with
personal rank of Ambassador): (4237) Mr P Jenkins
First Secretary and United Kingdom Deputy
Permanent Representative: (4234) Mr Mark Etherton
First Secretary (IAEA): (4240) Miss Alison Giles
First Secretary (IAEA): (4232) Mrs Carol Cliff
First Secretary (CTBTO): (4296) Ms Tracey Roberts
First Secretary (CTBTO): (4328) Dr J A Davies
Second Secretary (UN/UNIDO): (4297) Mr David
Lusher
Third Secretary (IAEA/UN): (4239) Mr Barry Wynne

Joint Management
First Secretary (Management): (2261) Mr
Hamilton Marcelin
Third Secretary (Management): (2260) Mr Andy
Partridge

UNITED KINGDOM PERMANENT REPRESENTATION TO THE CONFERENCE ON DISARMAMENT

Geneva
37-39 rue de Vermont, 1211 Geneva 20
Telephone: (00) (41) (22) 918 23 00
Facsimile: (00) (41) (22) 918 23 44
Telex: 414195 (a/b 414195 UKGV CH)
Office Hours (GMT): Summer: 07 00 - 11 00 and
12 30 - 16 00,
Winter: 08 00 - 12 00 and 13 30 - 17 00
United Kingdom Permanent Representative: (holds
personal rank of Ambassador): Mr D S Broucher
Deputy Permanent Representative: Mr I Donaldson
First Secretary (Legal Adviser): Mrs S McCrory
Second Secretary: Mr J Wattam
Second Secretary: Mr A Wurr

UNITED KINGDOM DELEGATION TO THE ORGANISATION FOR SECURITY AND COOPERATION IN EUROPE (OSCE) IN VIENNA

Vienna
Jaurèsgasse 12, 1030 Vienna
Telephone: (00) (43) (1) 716130
71613 + extension (for direct lines and voicemail)
Facsimile: (00) (43) (1) 71613 3900
Telegraphic address: UKDEL Vienna
e-mail: ukdel@netway.at
Office Hours (GMT): Summer: Mon-Fri 0700-1600
Winter: Mon - Fri 08 00 - 17 00
Head of Delegation (Personal rank of Ambassador)
(PA 3302): Mr John R de Fonblanque, CMG
Counsellor and Deputy Head of Delegation (PA
3304): Mr Ian A M Bond
Counsellor (Arms control) (PA 3318): Mr Andrew
Brentnall
Military Adviser (PA 3318): Colonel George A Young
First Secretary (Political) (3319): Ms Kate Knight-
Sands
First Secretary (Political) (3318): Mr Eric Penton-
Voak
First Secretary (Arms Control) (PA 3336): Mr
Henry Bradley
Second Secretary (Political) (3306): Dr Liz J Kane
Second Secretary (Political) (3307): Mr David
Townsend
Third Secretary (3320): Mr Grant Pritchard
Joint Management Office
First Secretary (Management) (2261): Mr
Hamilton Marcelin
Third Secretary (Management) (2260): Mr Andy
Partridge

UNITED KINGDOM DELEGATION TO THE NORTH ATLANTIC TREATY ORGANISATION

Brussels
OTAN/NATO, Autoroute Bruxelles - Zavbentem,
Evere
1110 Brussels
Telephone: (00) (32) (2) 707 7211
Facsimile: (00) (32) (2) 707 7596
e-mail: ukdelnato@csi.com
United Kingdom Permanent Representative on
the North Atlantic Council (holds personal rank
of Ambassador): Dr Emyr Jones Parry, CMG
Minister, United Kingdom Deputy Permanent
Representative: Mr B E Cleghorn
United Kingdom Military Representative:
Lieutenant General Sir Michael Willcocks, KCB
Deputy United Kingdom Military Representative:
Air Commodore N J Day, CBE, RAF
Counsellor (Political): Mr D Powell
Counsellor (Defence): Mr J Colston
Counsellor (Budget and Infrastructure): Mr R Preston
First Secretary (Political): Mr P Moody
First Secretary (European Defence): Mr P V Devine
First Secretary (Defence Equipment): Mr J Mattiussi
First Secretary (Nuclear Cooperation): Mr J
Dickinson
Staff Officer Plans & Policy: Captain I K Goddard, RN

First Secretary (Defence Plans and Policy): Mr G Muir
Staff Officer Operations: Wing Commander A Flint, RAF
Staff Officer (Operations/Plans): Lieutenant Colonel G A Gelder, RM
First Secretary (Infrastructure and Military Budget): Mr S Tessier
Staff Officer Intelligence: Lieutenant Colonel W J Heminsley, OBE
Staff Officer (Resources and Arms Control): Wing Commander K L O'Dea, RAF
First Secretary (Infrastructure and Military Budgets): Mr D Smith
First Secretary (Information/Management): Mr D Morley
Second Secretary (Political): Mr J E L Paver
Second Secretary (Operations and Exercises): Mr R Ladd-Jones
Second Secretary (Defence): Mr C M Hodge
Second Secretary: Mr L Cameron
Attaché (Political): Mr E Manley
Attaché (Defence): Mrs S Cronin
Attaché (Defence): Mr D J Harris
Attaché (Budget and Infrastructure): Mrs M Harte
Staff Officer (CIS): Lieutenant Colonel M S Reid
Staff Officer (Cooperation): Lieutenant Colonel C J A Witton

UNITED KINGDOM DELEGATION TO THE WESTERN EUROPEAN UNION

Brussels
c/o UK Permanent Representation to the EU,
Avenue d'Auderghem 10
1040 Bruxelles
Telephone: (00) (32) (2) 287 8346
Facsimile: (00) (32) (2) 287 8396
United Kingdom Permanent Representative - (holds personal rank of Ambassador): Mr David Richmond
Military Delegate: Lieutenant General Sir Michael Willcocks, KCB
Deputy Permanent Representative - First Secretary (Pol/Mil Affairs): Jennifer Anderson
Deputy Military Delegate: Colonel Hamish Fletcher
First Secretary (Defence): Mr Sandy Johnston
Third Secretary (WEAG/WEAO): Mr David Harris
Assistant Military Delegate: Wing Commander (rtd) Barry Horton, RAF
Assistant Military Delegate: Sergeant Chris Vear

UNITED KINGDOM DELEGATION TO THE ORGANISATION FOR ECONOMIC CO-OPERATION AND DEVELOPMENT

Paris
19 Rue de Franqueville, 75116 Paris
Telephone: (00) (331) 45 24 98 28
Facsimile: (00) (331) 45 24 98 37
Office Hours (GMT): Nov-Mar 08 30 - 17 00,
Apr-Oct 07 30 - 16 00
United Kingdom Permanent Representative (holds personal rank of Ambassador): Mr Christopher D Crabbie, CMG
Deputy United Kingdom Permanent Representative

and Counsellor (Economic and Financial): Mr David Moran
Counsellor (Management): Mr Ian Whitehead
First Secretary (Energy & Environment): Mr A Shaun Cleary
First Secretary (Economic): Mr Martyn K Roper
First Secretary (Trade & Investment): Mr Jonathan Knott
First Secretary (Employment, Education & Social Affairs,
Science & Technology, Public Management): Ms Jo Newstead

OFFICE OF THE UNITED KINGDOM PERMANENT REPRESENTATIVE TO THE EUROPEAN UNION

Brussels
Ave d'Auderghem 10, 1040 Brussels
Telephone: (00) (32) (2) 287 8211
Facsimile: (00) (32) (2) 287 8398 (2 lines)
Telex: 24312 (a/b 24312 UKEC BR B)
e-mail: ukrep@fco.gov.uk
Website: http://ukrep.fco.gov.uk
United Kingdom Permanent Representative (holds personal rank of Ambassador): Sir Nigel Sheinwald, KCMG
Deputy UK Permanent Representative: Mr W Stow
Interim Political Security Committee Representative: Mr D Richmond
Counsellor (Political & Institutional): Mr G Paxman
Counsellor (Agriculture): Ms K Williams
Counsellor (External Relations): Mr D Chilcott
Counsellor (JHA): Mr N Baird
Counsellor (Industry): Mr A Vinall
Counsellor (Economics and Finance): Mr N Ilett
Counsellor (Social Affairs, Environment, Regional Policy): Mr S Morgan
Counsellor (Legal Adviser): Ms S Brooks
Counsellor (Development): Mr A Wood
First Secretary (External Relations): Mr R Drummond
First Secretary (External Relations): Mr K O'Flaherty
First Secretary (External Relations): Mr A J H Cowell
First Secretary (Trade Policy): Mr T Smith
First Secretary (Institutions): Mr P Wilson
First Secretary (Commercial): Ms J Martin
First Secretary (Transport): Mr D Tripp
First Secretary (Research and Telecoms): Mr N Leake
First Secretary (Energy): Mr I Holt
First Secretary (Industry and Competition): Mr J Fiennes
First Secretary (Internal Market): Mr S Gill
First Secretary (Consumer Affairs and Industry): Ms B Schwarz
First Secretary (Economics and Finance): Mr S James
First Secretary (Press and Information): Mr D Pruce
First Secretary (Budget): Mrs F Jones
First Secretary (JHA): Ms S Langrish
First Secretary (Legal): Mr P McKell
First Secretary (Justice and Home Affairs): Mr A Jones
First Secretary (Justice and Home Affairs): Mr N Bradley
First Secretary (Customs and Finance): Ms L Clare

First Secretary (Agriculture): Dr K Riggs
First Secretary (Fisheries): Dr D Bates
First Secretary: Mr C Hay
First Secretary (Agriculture and Food): Mr R Norton
First Secretary: Ms C Wilson
First Secretary (Political): Mr S McGregor
First Secretary (Social Affairs): Mr A Dalgleish
First Secretary (Environment): Mr M Nesbit
First Secretary (Social Affairs): Mr J Kittmer
First Secretary (Regional Policy): Ms A Rose
First Secretary (Management): Mr P May
Second Secretary (EU Staffing): Mr M Hancock
Second Secretary (Institutions): Mr S Furssedonn
Second Secretary (Agriculture and Forestry): Mr S Stannard
Second Secretary (Agriculture): Mr K Morrison
Second Secretary (JHA): Ms E Gibbons
Second Secretary (Industry): Ms K L Siddall
Second Secretary (Developing Countries): Ms H Corbett
Second Secretary (Transport): Mr S Johnston
Second Secretary (Budget): Ms L Ryan
Second Secretary (Trade Policy): Ms L Boyles
Second Secretary (External Relations): Ms C Van der Walt
Second Secretary (Health): Ms L Stewart
Second Secretary (Management): Mr D Harrison
Third Secretary (External Relations): Mrs R Pearson
Third Secretary (External Relations): Ms K Hill

Strasbourg
(Office only open when the EUROPEAN PARLIAMENT is in session in Strasbourg)
Offices 561/562 IPE 1 Building, Strasbourg
Telephone: (00) (333) 88 17 68 15
Facsimile: (00) (333) 88 35 41 30
First Secretary (Institutions): Mr P Wilson
Second Secretary (Institutions): Mr S Furssedonn

Brussels Joint Management Office for the four Missions, see part I

UNITED KINGDOM DELEGATION TO THE COUNCIL OF EUROPE

Strasbourg
18 rue Gottfried, 67000-Strasbourg
Telephone: (00) (333) (88) 35 00 78
Facsimile: (00) (333) (88) 36 74 39
United Kingdom Permanent Representative to Council of Europe (holds personal rank of Ambassador): Mr A Carter, CMG
Deputy United Kingdom Permanent Representative: Mr M M Hall
Second Secretary: Mr T F Robins
Third Secretary (Chancery/Management): Mr J A Webster

UNITED KINGDOM DELEGATION TO THE INTERNATIONAL MONETARY FUND AND INTERNATIONAL BANK FOR RECONSTRUCTION AND DEVELOPMENT

Washington
Room 11-120, International Monetary Fund, 700 19th Street, NW, Washington, DC 20431

Telephone: (00) (1) (202) 623 4562
Facsimile: (00) (1) (202) 623 4965
United Kingdom Executive Director of the International Monetary Fund and World Bank: - e-mail: spickford@imf.org *Mr S Pickford*
Alternate Executive Director of the World Bank:- e-mail: mwickstead@imf.org *Mr M Wickstead*
Alternate Executive Director of the International Monetary Fund: - e-mail: scollins@imf.org *Mr S Collins*
Assistant (IMF/IBRD): - e-mail: dmerotto@imf.org *Mr D Merotto*
Assistant (IMF/IBRD): - e-mail: dtaylor@imf.org *Mr D Taylor*
Assistant (IMF/IBRD): - e-mail: bkelmanson@imf.org *Mr B Kelmanson*
Assistant (IMF/IBRD): - e-mail: rburgess@imf.org *Mr R Burgess*
Assistant (IMF/IBRD): - e-mail: mwalsh@imf.org *Mr M Walsh*
Assistant (IMF/IBRD): - e-mail: hhagan@imf.org *Mr H Hagan*

UNITED NATIONS CENTRE FOR HUMAN SETTLEMENTS (HABITAT)

Nairobi
United Kingdom Permanent Representative to the United Nations Centre for Human Settlements (Habitat): Mr E Clay, CMG
Alternate Permanent Representative: Mr A V G Tucker
Deputy United Kingdom Permanent Representative: Mr J P T Bell

UNITED NATIONS ENVIRONMENT PROGRAMME

Nairobi
United Kingdom Permanent Representative to the United Nations Environment Programme: Mr E Clay, CMG
Alternate Permanent Representative: Mr A V G Tucker
Deputy United Kingdom Permanent Representative: Mr J P T Bell

UNITED KINGDOM REPRESENTATION AT THE AFRICAN DEVELOPMENT BANK

Abidjan
Rue Joseph Anoma, Abidjan
Postal Address: 01 BP 1387, Abidjan 01
Telephone: (00) 20 40 23, 20 43 43
Telex numbers: 22203/2202/27717/23263
Executive *Director:* Mr M Bauer (German)
Alternate Executive Director: Mr W Bronkhurst (Dutch)
Assistant to the Executive Director: Mr P R Williams (British)

UNITED KINGDOM REPRESENTATION AT THE ASIAN DEVELOPMENT BANK

Manila
6 ADB Avenue, Mandaluyong Metro-Manila, Philippines

Postal address: PO Box 789, 1099 Manila, Philippines
Telephone: (00) (63) (2) 632 6079, 632 4444
Facsimile: (00) (63) (2) 636 2056
Executive Director e-mail: uhenrich@adb.org Mr
Uwe Henrich (German)
Alternate Director e-mail: fblack@adb.org Mr
Frank Black (British)
Director's Adviser e-mail: mheinz@adb.org Mr
Marcus Heinz (Austrian)

UNITED KINGDOM REPRESENTATION AT THE INTER-AMERICAN DEVELOPMENT BANK

Washington
1300 New York Avenue, N W Washington, DC
20577
Telephone: (00) (1) (202) 623
1059/1058/1773/1179
Facsimile: (00) (1) (202) 623 3610
Cable address: Intambanc, Washington, DC
Telex numbers: 64141, 44240
Executive *Director:* Mr Y Veda (Japanese)
Alternate Executive Director: Mr M Power
(British)
Senior Counsellor: Mr Kurosawa (Japanese)
Counsellor: Ms Ivandic (Croatia)

UNITED KINGDOM REPRESENTATION TO THE UNITED NATIONS AGENCIES FOR FOOD AND AGRICULTURE IN ROME

Rome
Viale Aventino, 36/1. 00153 Roma
Telephone: (00) (39) 06 578 1535, 574 4438
Facsimile: (00) (39) 06 572 85010
United Kingdom Permanent Representative: Mr
Anthony Beattie
Deputy Permanent Representative: Mr Mike Ellis
First Secretary: Mr Julian Hamilton-Peach
First Secretary: Mr Peter Reid

UNITED KINGDOM REPRESENTATIVE ON THE COUNCIL OF THE INTERNATIONAL CIVIL AVIATION ORGANISATION

Montreal
Suite 1415, 999 University Sreet,
Montreal, Quebec
Canada
H3C 5J9
Telephone: (00) (514) 954 8302/3
Direct Line – see individual officers
Facsimile: (00) (514) 954 8001
Airtech: (00) (1) (514) 866 4867 (Located in
British Consulate-General Offices)
Office Hours (GMT) 14 00 – 22 00
United Kingdom Representative: Mr Douglas S
Evans (00) (1) (514) 954 8326
Deputy United Kingdom Representative: Mr
Richard W Allison (00) (1) (514) 954 8327

ORGANISATION FOR THE PROHIBITION OF CHEMICAL WEAPONS

The Hague
United Kingdom Permanent Representative: Mr C
R Budd, CMG
First Secretary: Mr D G Cole
First Secretary: Mr M E Rack

GOVERNORS AND COMMANDERS-IN-CHIEF ETC. OF THE UK OVERSEAS TERRITORIES

Anguilla
Government House, Anguilla Telephone: Office:
Governor/EA: (00) (1) (264) 497 2621/2622
Deputy Governor: (00) (1) (264) 497 3312/3313
Staff Officer: (00) (1) (264) 497 3315
Residence: (00) (1) (264) 497 2292 (Tel/Fax)
Facsimile: (00) (1) (264) 497 3314 (Unclassified)
(00) (1) (264) 497 3151 (Airtech)
e-mail: govthse@anguillanet.com
Office Hours (GMT): 12 00 – 16 00, 17 00 20 00
Governor: Mr Peter Johnstone
Deputy Governor: Mr Roger Cousins, OBE
Staff Officer: Mr Dave Bicker
Defence Adviser (resides at Bridgetown): Captain
Steve C Ramm, RN
Executive Assistant to the Governor: Miss Sarah Reid

Bermuda
Government House, Hamilton
Telephone: (00) (1) (441) 292 3600
Deputy Governor's Office: (00) (1) (441) 292 2587
Calls from UK:
(00) (1) (441) 292 3600 Government House
                         2587 Deputy Governor's Office
Facsimile: (00) (1) (441) 295 3823
e-mail Address: depgov@ibl.bm
Office Hours (GMT): Summer: 11 45 - 16 00 and
17 15 - 20 00
Winter: 12 45 - 17 00 and 18 15 - 21 00
Governor: Mr J T Masefield, CMG (Sir John
Vereker w.e.f Feb 02)
Deputy Governor: Mr T Gurney
Registrar: Mr P O'Brien

British Antarctic Territory
Foreign and Commonwealth Office,
Overseas Territories Department
Telephone: 020 7270 2742
Commissioner: Mr C J B White (non-resident)
Administrator: Dr M G Richardson (non-resident)

British Indian Ocean Territory
Foreign and Commonwealth Office,
Overseas Territories Department
Telephone: 020 7270 2890
Commissioner: Mr C J B White (non-resident)
Deputy Commissioner: Mr W A Dickson (non-resident)
Administrator: Ms L M Savill (non-resident)
Diego Garcia, c/o BFPO Ships
(Telex 938 6903 (a/b RNLO DG)
Commissioner's Representative: Commander S
Jackson, RN JP

British Virgin Islands (SP)
Government House, Road Town,
Tortola,
British Virgin Islands
Telephone: (00) (1) (284) 494 2345/494 2370/494
3520 Office
494 2721/494 3400 Residence
Facsimile: (00) (1) (284) 494 5790 Office
494 8871 Residence
Airtech: (00) (1) (284) 494 5582
e-mail: bvigovernor@bvigovernment.org
Website: http://www.bvigovernment.org
Office Hours (GMT): 12 30 - 20 30
Governor: Mr F J Savage, CMG, LVO, OBE
*Second Secretary and Private Secretary (External
Affairs):* Mr M B Kirk
Defence Adviser (resides at Bridgetown): Captain
S C Ramm, RN
Personal Assistant: Ms C Kerry

Office of the Deputy Governor
Government Administration Building
Road Town, Tortola
Telephone: (00) (1) (284) 468 0346
Facsimile: (00) (1) (284) 494 6481
Deputy Governor: Mr E Georges, OBE
Royal Virgin Island Police Force
Telephone: (00) (1) (284) 494 3822 (24 hrs)
Immigration Department
Telephone: (00) (1) (284) 494 3471

Cayman Islands (SP)
Government Administration Building,
George Town, Grand Cayman,
Cayman Islands
Telephone: (00) (1) (345) 949 7900 Switchboard
                                5776 PA direct
                                0980 Staff Officer
Facsimile: (00) (1) (345) 945 4131 Government
                                Office
Airtech: 949 6556
                      945 5537 Social
                                Secretary
e-mail: staffoff@candw.ky
Office Hours (GMT): 13 30-17 30 and 19 00 - 22 00
Governor: Mr Peter J Smith, CBE
Chief Secretary: Mr James M Ryan, MBE, JP
Deputy Chief Secretary: Mr Donnie Ebanks, MBE
Defence Adviser (Resides at Kingston): Colonel
Rob A Hyde-Bales
*Second Secretary and Staff Officer to the
Governor:* Mr Kevin L Mowbray
Secretary to the Governor: Mrs Fiona Mowbray

Government Information Services
Telephone: (00) (1) (345) 949 8092
Facsimile: (00) (1) (345) 949 5936/946 0664

Immigration Department
Telephone: (00) (1) (345) 949 8344
Enquiries within the UK: Cayman Islands
Government Office,
6 Arlington Street, London SW1A 1RE
Telephone: 020 7491 7772
Facsimile: 020 7491 7944
Representative: Mrs Jennifer P Dilbert

Falkland Islands
Government House, Stanley,
Falkland Islands
Telephone: (00) (500) 27433 Office
22210 Residence
Facsimile: (00) (500) 27434
e-mail: gov.house@horizon.co.fk
Office Hours (GMT): Winter: 11 00-15 15 and
16 30 - 19 30
Summer: 12 00-16 15 and 17 30-20 30
Governor: Mr Donald A Lamont
First Secretary: Mr Russ T Jarvis

South Georgia and the South Sandwich Islands
Government House, Stanley
Falkland Islands
Telephone: (00) (500) 27433 Office
22210 Residence
Facsimile: (00) (500) 27434
e-mail: gov.house@horizon.co.fk
OfficeHours (GMT): Winter 11 00 - 15 15 and
16 30 - 19 30
Summer 12 00 - 16 15 and 17 30 - 20 30
Commissioner (Resides in Falkland Islands): Mr
Donald A Lamont
Assistant Commissioner and Director of Fisheries:
Mr Russ T Jarvis

Gibraltar
Office of the Governor
The Convent, Main Street
Gibraltar
Telephone: (00) (350) 45440 (Switchboard)
                      47828 (PA to the Governor)
Facsimile: (00) (350) 47823 (Unclassified)
                      47830 (Airtech)
e-mail: convent@gibnet.gi
Office Hours (GMT) 08 00 - 16 15 (Winter); 07 30 -
13 30 (Summer)
Governor and Commander-in-Chief: Mr David R
C Durie, CMG
Deputy Governor: Mr Paul A Speller
Assistant Deputy Governor: Mr Ian F Powell, OBE
Second Secretary (Convent Liaison Officer): Mr
Lawrence J Weldon, MVO
Second Secretary (EU Affairs): Ms Alison F
MacMillan
Third Secretary (Political): Mr Timothy J Freeman
Third Secretary (Management Officer): Ms Lauren
Johnstone

Consular/Visa inquiries:
Civil Status and Registration Office
Telephone: (00) (350) 51727/59839/59840
Facsimile: (00) (350) 42706

Commercial inquiries:
Department of Trade and Industry:
Telephone: (00) (350) 52052
Facsimile: (00) (350) 71406

Montserrat
Lancaster House
Olveston
Telephone: (00) (1) (664) 491 2688/9 Office
6124 Governor's Residence
Facsimile: (00) (1) (664) 491 8867

Airtech: 4553
e-mail: govoff@candw.ag
monmedia@candw.ag Information section
Office Hours (GMT): 12 00 - 16 00 and 17 00 -
20 00
Governor: Mr A J Longrigg, CMG
First Secretary and Head of Governor's Office: Mr
D F Graham
Personal Assistant to the Governor: Miss D Baker
Defence Adviser (resides at Bridgetown): Captain
S C Ramm, RN
Third Secretary and Staff Officer: Mr G J Patton

Pitcairn Henderson Ducie and Oeno Islands
British High Commission,
Wellington, New Zealand
Governor: Mr R T Fell, CVO
(non-resident)
Pitcairn Islands Administration, Private Box
105696
Auckland, New Zealand
Commissioner: Mr L Salt (non resident)
Telephone: (00) (9) (64) 366 0186
e-mail: pitcairn@iconz.co.nz
Website: http://www.government.pn

St Helena
Governor's Office
The Castle, Jamestown
St Helena Island,
South Atlantic Ocean
Telephone: (00) (290) 2555 Office
                                    4444 Residence
Facsimile: (00) (290) 2598 Office
                                    4418 Residence
Airtech: 2476
e-mail: OCS@helanta.sh
joany@sainthelena.gov.sh
Office Hours (GMT): 08 30 – 12 30 and 13 00 –
16 00 (Mon – Fri)
Governor and Commander-in Chief: Mr David J
Hollamby
Chief Secretary's Office
The Castle, Jamestown
St Helena Island, South Atlantic Island
Telephone: (00) (290) 4552 Residence
                                    2525 Office
Facsimile: (00) (290) 2598 Office
e-mail: OCS@helanta.sh
sandrab@sainthelena.gov.sh
Office Hours (GMT): 08 30 – 12 30 and 13 00 –
16 00 (Mon – Fri)
Chief Secretary: Mr John Styles

Ascension Island (Dependency of St Helena)
The Administrator's Office, Georgetown
Ascension Island,
South Atlantic Ocean, ASCN IZZ
Telephone: (00) 247 6311 Office
4525 Home
Facsimile: (00) 247 6152
Airtech: (00) 247 6892
e-mail: administrator@atlantis.co.ac
Website: http://www.ascension-island.gov.ac
Office Hours (GMT): 08 30 - 12 30 and 13 30 -
16 30 (Mon-Fri)

*Governor and Commander-in-Chief (Resides in St
Helena):* Mr David J Hollamby
Administrator: Mr Geoffrey Fairhurst

Tristan da Cunha (Dependency of St Helena)
The Administrator's Office
Edinburgh of the Seven Seas
Tristan da Cunha, South Atlantic Ocean
e-mail: hmg@cunha.demon.co.uk
Office Hours (GMT): 08 30 - 12 30 and 13 00 -
16 30 (Mon-Fri)
*Governor and Commander-in-Chief (Resides in St
Helena):* Mr D J Hollamby
Administrator: Mr B P Baldwin

Turks and Caicos Islands
Waterloo, Government House,
Grand Turk, Turks and Caicos Islands
Telephone: (00) (1) (649) 946 2309
Facsimile: (00) (1) (649) 946 2903
Airtech: (00) (1) (649) 946 2766
e-mail: govhouse@tciway.tc
Governor: Mr M T Jones
Second Secretary and Assistant to Governor: Mr D
V E Vickers
Personal Assistant: Mrs J White
Chief Secretary's Office
Government Secretariat, Grand Turk
Telephone: (00) (1) (649) 946 2702
Facsimile: (00) (1) (649) 946 2886
Chief Secretary: Mrs C Astwood, MBE
Defence Adviser (resides at Kingston): Colonel R
A Hyde-Bales
Office Hours (GMT): Winter: 13 00-17 30 and
19 00 - 21 30 (Mon-Thu),
13 00-17 30 and 19 00-21 00 (Fri)
Summer: 12 00-16 30 and 18 00-20 30 (Mon-Thu),
12 00-16 30 and 18 00-20 00 (Fri)

PART IV SMALL POSTS

SOVEREIGN
Abidjan
Algiers
Almaty
Antananarivo
Ashgabat
Asuncion
Baku
Banjul
Belmopan
Bratislava
Castries
Dakar
Freetown
Gaborone
Georgetown (Guyana)
Guatemala City
Holy See (Vatican)
Honiara
Kigali
Kingstown, St Vincent
Kinshasa
La Paz
Luxembourg
Ljubljana
Managua
Maseru
Mbabane
Minsk
Montevideo
Nassau
Nuku'alofa
Panama City
Phnom Penh
Port Moresby
Port of Spain
Quito
Rangoon
Reykjavik
Riga
St George's (Grenada)
San José
Santo Domingo
San Salvador
Skopje
Strasbourg
Suva
Tallinn
Tashkent
Tbilisi
Tegucigalpa
Tirana
Ulaanbaatar
Victoria
Vila
Vilnius
Windhoek
Yerevan

SUBORDINATE
Al Khobar
Alexandria
Amsterdam
Atlanta
Auckland
Barcelona
Bilbao
Bordeaux
Boston
Brisbane
Cape Town
Casablanca
Chiang Mai
Chicago
Dallas
Durban
Frankfurt
Guangzhou (Canton)
Hamburg
Ho Chi Minh City
Houston
Kolkata (Calcutta)
Kuching
Lille
Los Angeles
Lyon
Marseille
Melbourne
Miami
Milan
Montreal
Munich
Naples
Oporto
Palma
Perth
San Francisco
Seattle
Stuttgart
Sydney
Toronto
Vancouver
Yekaterinburg
Zurich

OVERSEAS TERRITORY
Anguilla
Georgetown, Ascension Island
Gibraltar
Grand Cayman, Cayman Islands
Grand Turk, Turks and Caicos Islands
Hamilton, Bermuda
Plymouth, Montserrat
Stanley, Falkland Islands
Jamestown, St Helena
Tortola, British Virgin Islands
Tristan Da Cunha

ANNEX: NON GOVERNMENTAL TRADE OFFICES

TAIWAN

Her Majesty's Government do not recognise Taiwan as a sovereign state and consequently have no diplomatic relations with it. However, there are non- governmental trade and cultural offices at the following addresses:

Taipei
British Trade and Cultural Office
8-10th Floor Fu Key Building
99 Jen Ai Road, Section 2,Taipei 100
Telephone: (00) (886) (2) 2322 4242
Airtech: (00) (886) (2) 2322 3265
Facsimile: (00) (886) (2) 2394 8673(Commercial)
                            2397 3559 (Inward
                                Investment)
                            2393 1985 (Visa Handling
                                Unit)
                            2397 3609 (Management)
Internet Website: www.btco.org.tw
Office Hours (GMT): 01 00 - 04 30 and 05 30 - 09 00
Director General: Mr David Coates (ext 709)
Deputy Director General: Mr Jeremy Larner (ext 701)
Head of Commercial Section: Ms Pam Balkin (ext 706)
Head of Inward Investment Section: Mr Bob Manning (ext 766)
Head of Political and Economic Section: Ms Kate White (ext 755)
Head of Management Section: Mr Peter Karmy (ext 702)
Science and Technology Officer: Mr Andrew Garth (ext 746)
Head of Visa Handling Unit: Ms Andrea Massingham (ext 740)
Press and Public Affairs Officer: Ms Emma Lee (ext 715)

Education and Cultural Section
British Trade and Cultural Office
7th Floor Fu Key Building
99 Jen Ai Road, Section 2,Taipei 100
Telephone: (00) (886) (2) 2396 2238
Facsimile: (00) (886) (2) 2341 5749
e-mail: inquiries@britcoun.org.tw
Website: www.britishcouncil.org.tw
Director, Educational and Cultural Operations (British Council Director, Taipei): Mr Geoffrey Evans (ext 729)

Kaohsiung
British Trade and Cultural Office
3F Bao Chen Enterprise Building
6 Min Chuan 2nd Road,Kaohsiung
Telephone: (00) (886) (7) 337 7350
Facsimile: (00) (886) (7) 526 4144
e-mail: btcokh@seed.net.tw
Deputy Commercial Officer: Ms Anne Lai

Education and Cultural Section
13F-6 New Century Building
56 Min Sheng First Road

Kaohsiung
Telephone: (00) (886) (7) 229 0817
Facsimile: (00) (886) (7) 229 0827
e-mail: inquiries@britcoun.org.tw
www.britishcouncil.org.tw.
Branch Manager: Ms Fay Chen

Guide to places and countries
Embassies, High Commissions, Deputy High Commissions and Consular Posts – Part 1

Note: There is no HMG representation in Bhutan.
It is therefore omitted from the List.

Aabenraa, Denmark
Aalborg, Denmark
Aarhus, Denmark
Abidjan, Côte d'Ivoire
Abuja, Nigeria
Abu Dhabi, United Arab
    Emirates
Acapulco, Mexico
Accra, Ghana
Addis Ababa, Ethiopia
Adelaide, Australia
Aden, Yemen
Agadir, Morocco
Ahmedabad, India
Akureyri, Iceland
Aleppo, Syria
Ålesund, Norway
Alexandria, Egypt
Algiers, Algeria
Alicante, Spain
Al Khobar, Saudi Arabia
Almaty, Kazakhstan
Amiens, France
Amman, Jordan
Amsterdam, Netherlands
Anchorage, United States
Anguilla, See Part III
Ankara, Turkey
Antalya, Turkey
Antananarivo, Madagascar
Antwerp, Belgium
Apia, Samoa
Arequipa, Peru
Ascension Island,
See Part III
Ashgabat, Turkmenistan
Asmara, Eritrea
Asunción, Paraguay
Athens, Greece
Atlanta, United States
Auckland, New Zealand
Bahrain, Bahrain
Baku, Azerbaijan
Bali, Indonesia
Bamako, Mali
Bandar Seri Begawan,
    Brunei
Bangalore, India
Bangkok, Thailand
Banja Luka, Bosnia and
    Herzegovina
Banjul, The Gambia
Barcelona, Spain
Bari, Italy
Basel, Switzerland
Basseterre, St Kitts and Nevis
Beijing, China
Beira, Mozambique
Beirut, Lebanon

Belém, Brazil
Belgrade, Yugoslavia
Belmopan, Belize
Belo Horizonte, Brazil
Bergen, Norway
Berlin, Germany
Berne, Switzerland
Biarritz, France
Bilbao, Spain
Bishkek, Kyrgyzstan
Bissau, Guinea Bissau
Bitola, Macedonia
Bodrum, Turkey
Bogotá, Colombia
Bonn, Germany
Bordeaux, France
Boston, United States
Boulogne-sur-Mer, France
Brasilia, Brazil
Bratislava, Slovakia
Brazzaville, Congo
Bregenz, Austria
Bremen, Germany
Bridgetown, Barbados
Brindisi, Italy
Brisbane, Australia
Brussels, Belgium
Bucharest, Romania
Budapest, Hungary
Buenos Aires, Argentina
Bursa, Turkey
Cagliari, Italy
Cairo, Egypt
Calais, France
Calgary, Canada
Cali, Colombia
Canberra, Australia
Cancun, Mexico
Cape Town, South Africa
Caracas, Venezuela
Casablanca, Morocco
Castries, St Lucia
Catania, Italy
Cayenne, French Guiana
Cebu, Philippines
Charlotte, United States
Chennai (Madras), India
Cherbourg, France
Chiang Mai, Thailand
Chicago, United States
Chisinau, Moldova
Chongqing, China
Christchurch, New Zealand
Ciudad Juárez, Mexico
Colombo, Sri Lanka
Conakry, Guinea
Copenhagen, Denmark
Córdoba, Argentina
Corfu, Greece

Cotonou, Benin
Cuenca, Ecuador
Curitiba, Brazil
Cusco, Peru
Dakar, Senegal
Dallas, United States
Damascus, Syria
Dar es Salaam, Tanzania
Denver, United States
Dili, East Timor
Dhaka, Bangladesh
Djibouti, Djibouti
Doha, Qatar
Douala, Cameroon
Dubai, United Arab Emirates
Dublin, Irish Republic
Dubrovnik, Croatia
Dunkirk, France
Dushanbe, Tajikistan
Durban, South Africa
Düsseldorf, Germany
East London, South Africa
Eilat, Israel
Esbjerg, Denmark
Florence, Italy
Fort de France
    (Martinique)
Fortaleza, Brazil
Frankfurt, Germany
Fredericia, Denmark
Freetown, Sierra Leone
Fukuoka, Japan
Funchal (Madeira), Portugal
Gaborone, Botswana
Galápagos, Ecuador
Gävle, Sweden
Gdansk, Poland
Geneva, Switzerland
Genoa, Italy
Georgetown, Guyana
Gothenburg, Sweden
Graz, Austria
Guadalajara, Mexico
Guadeloupe, France
Guangzhou, China
Guatemala City, Guatemala
Guayaquil, Ecuador
Halifax, Canada
Hamburg, Germany
Hanoi, Vietnam
Hanover, Germany
Harare, Zimbabwe
Harstad, Norway
Havana, Cuba
Havre (Le), France
Helsinki, Finland
Heraklion, Crete (Greece)
Herning, Denmark
Hiroshima, Japan

Ho Chi Minh City, Vietnam
Hobart, Australia
Hong Kong, China
Honiara, Solomon Islands
Houston, United States
Hyderabad, India
Ibadan, Nigeria
Ibiza, Spain
Innsbruck, Austria
Iquitos, Peru
Islamabad, Pakistan
Istanbul, Turkey
Izmir, Turkey
Jakarta, Indonesia
Jedda, Saudi Arabia
Jerusalem, Jerusalem
Johannesburg, South Africa
Johor, Malaysia
Jyväskylä, Finland
Kabul, Afghanistan
Kaduna, Nigeria
Kampala, Uganda
Kano, Nigeria
Kansas City, United States
Karachi, Pakistan
Kathmandu, Nepal
Katowice, Poland
Khartoum, Sudan
Kiel, Germany
Kiev, Ukraine
Kigali, Rwanda
Kingston, Jamaica
Kingstown, St Vincent and the
   Grenadines
Kinshasa, Democratic Republic
   of Congo
Kolkata (Calcutta), India
Kos, Greece
Kota Kinabalu, Malaysia
Kotka, Finland
Kraków, Poland
Kristiansand, Norway
Kristiansund, Norway
Kuala Lumpur, Malaysia
Kuching, Malaysia
Kuopio, Finland
Kuwait, Kuwait
Lagos, Nigeria
Lahore, Pakistan
La Paz, Bolivia
Las Palmas, Spain (Grand
   Canary)
Le Havre, France
Leipzig, Germany
Libreville, Gabon
Liège, Belgium
Lille, France
Lilongwe, Malawi
Lima, Peru
Lisbon Portugal
Ljubljana, Slovenia
Lomé, Togo
Lorient, France
Los Angeles, United States
Luanda, Angola
Lugano, Switzerland

Lusaka, Zambia
Luxembourg, Luxembourg
Luxor, Egypt
Lyon, France
Macau, China
Madrid, Spain
Málaga, Spain
Malé, Maldives
Malmö, Sweden
Managua, Nicaragua
Manáus, Brazil
Manila, Philippines
Maputo, Mozambique
Macaibo, Venezuela
Margarita, Venezuela
Mariehamn, Finland
Marmaris, Turkey
Marrakech, Morocco
Marseille, France
Martinique, France
Maseru, Lesotho
Mbabane, Swaziland
Medan, Indonesia
Medellin, Colombia
Melbourne, Australia
Mendoza, Argentina
Menorca, Spain
Mérida, Mexico
Mérida, Venezuela
Mersin, Turkey
Minneapolis, United States
Mexico City, Mexico
Miami, United States
Milan, Italy
Minsk, Belarus
Miri, Malaysia
Mogadishu, Somalia
Mombasa, Kenya
Monaco, Monaco
Monrovia, Liberia
Montego Bay, Jamaica
Monterrey, Mexico
Montevideo, Uruguay
Montpellier, France
Montreal, Canada
Montreux, Switzerland
Moroni, Comoros
Moscow, Russian Federation
Mumbai (Bombay), India
Munich, Germany
Muri Beach, Cook Islands
Muscat, Oman
Nagoya, Japan
Nairobi, Kenya
Nantes, France
Naples, Italy
Nashville, United States
Nassau, Bahamas
Ndjamena, Chad
New Caledonia, France
New Delhi, India
New Orleans, United States
New York, United States
Niamey, Niger
Nice, France
Nicosia, Cyprus

Norfolk, United States
Nouakchott, Mauritania
Novorossiysk, Russia
Nuku'alofa, Tonga
Nuremburg, Germany
Oaxaca, Mexico
Odense, Denmark
Oporto, Portugal
Orlando, United States
Osaka, Japan
Oslo, Norway
Ottawa, Canada
Ouagadougou, Burkina Faso
Oulu, Finland
Palermo, Italy
Palma, Spain
Panama City, Panama
Papeete, France (French
   Polynesia)
Paramaribo, Surinam
Paris, France
Patras, Greece
Pécs, Hungary
Perpignan, France
Perth, Australia
Philadelphia, United States
Phoenix, United States
Phnom Penh, Cambodia
Penang, Malaysia
Pittsburgh, United States
Piura, Peru
Plymouth, Montserrat
Podgorica - Montenegro,
   Yugoslavia
Pointe- à-Pitre, France
   (Guadeloupe)
Pori, Finland
Ponta Delgada, Portugal
   (Azores)
Port-au-Prince, Haiti
Port Elizabeth, South Africa
Port Harcourt, Nigeria
Portimão, Portugal
Portland (Oregon), United
   States
Port Louis, Mauritius
Port Moresby, Papua New
   Guinea
Port of Spain, Trinidad and
   Tobago
Porto Alegre, Brazil
Poznan, Poland
Prague, Czech Republic
Praia, Cape Verde
Pretoria, South Africa
Pristina - Kosovo, Yugoslavia
Puerto Plata, Dominican
   Republic
Puerto Rico, United States
Punta Arenas, Chile
Pusan, Korea (Republic of)
Pyongyang, Korea (Democratic
   Republic of)
Quebec City, Canada
Quito, Ecuador
Rabat, Morocco

Rangoon, Burma (Union of
  Myanmar)
Recife, Brazil
Réunion, France
Reykjavik, Iceland
Rhodes, Greece
Riga, Latvia
Rio de Janeiro, Brazil
Rio Grande (do Sul), Brazil
Riyadh, Saudi Arabia
Rome, Italy
Roseau, Dominica
St George's, Grenada
St John's, Antigua and Barbuda
St John's, Canada
St Louis, United States
St Malo-Dinard, France
St Petersburg, Russian
  Federation
Salonika, Greece
Salt Lake City, United States
Salvador, Brazil
Salzburg, Austria
Sanaa, Yemen
San Cristobal, Venezuela
San Diego, United States
San Francisco, United States
San Jose (California), United
  States
San José, Costa Rica
San Pedro Sula, Honduras
San Salvador, El Salvador
Santa Cruz de Tenerife, Spain
  (Canary Islands)
Santa Fe, Argentina
Santander, Spain
Santiago, Chile
Santo Domingo, Dominican
  Republic
Santos, Brazil
São Tomé, São Tomé and
  Principe
São Paulo, Brazil
Sapporo, Japan
Sarajevo, Bosnia and
  Herzegovina
Saumur, France
Seattle, United States
Seoul, Korea (Republic of)
Sfax, Tunisia
Shanghai, China
Singapore, Singapore
Skopje, Macedonia
Sofia, Bulgaria
Split, Croatia
Stavanger, Norway
Stockholm, Sweden
Stuttgart, Germany
Suez, Egypt
Sundsvall, Sweden
Surabaya, Indonesia
Suva, Fiji
Sydney, Australia
Syros, Greece
Szczecin, Poland
Taipei, Taiwan (China)

Tallinn, Estonia
Tampere (Tammerfors),
  Finland
Tangier, Morocco
Tarawa, Kiribati (Republic of)
Tashkent, Uzbekistan
Tasmania, Australia
Tbilisi, Georgia
Tegucigalpa, Honduras
Tehran, Iran
Tel Aviv, Israel
The Hague, Netherlands
Tijuana, Mexico
Tirana, Albania
Toamasina, Madagascar
Tokyo, Japan
Toronto, Canada
Tørshavn, Denmark (Faroes)
Tortola, British Virgin Islands
Toulouse, France
Tours, France
Trieste, Italy
Tripoli, Lebanon
Tripoli, Libya
Tromso, Norway
Trondheim, Norway
Trujillo, Peru
Tunis, Tunisia
Turin, Italy
Turku, Finland
Ulaanbaatar, Mongolia
Vaasa (Vasa), Finland
Varna, Bulgaria
Vaduz, Liechtenstein
Valais, Switzerland
Valencia, Venezuela
Valletta, Malta
Valparaíso, Chile
Vancouver, Canada
Venice, Italy
Veracruz, Mexico
Victoria, Seychelles
Vienna, Austria
Vientiane, Laos
Vigo, Spain
Vila, Vanuatu
Vilnius, Lithuania
Vladivostok, Russia
Warsaw, Poland
Washington, United States
Wellington, New Zealand
Willemstad, Netherlands
  Antilles
Windhoek, Namibia
Winnipeg, Canada
Wroclaw, Poland
Yaoundé, Cameroon
Yekaterinburg, Russian
  Federation
Yerevan, Armenia
Zagreb, Croatia
Zakynthos, Greece
Zurich, Switzerland

Chronological Lists from 1981 onwards
of Secretaries of State,
Ministers of State,
Permanent Under-Secretaries of State,
British Ambassadors etc.,
High Commissioners,
Permanent Representatives
to International Organizations and
Governors and Commanders-in-chief
of Dependent territories

*Reference should be made to the Foreign Office and
Commonwealth Relations Office Lists of 1965, to the
Colonial Office List of 1966 and to the Diplomatic Service
List 2001 and earlier Lists for previous lists of officers
holding these appointments.*

Part III: Chronological Lists

The Foreign and Commonwealth Office was formed in October 1968 by the merger of the former Foreign Office and the Commonwealth Office

SECRETARIES OF STATE FOR FOREIGN AND COMMONWEALTH AFFAIRS 1981-2001

1982   Apr5 The Rt Hon. Francis Pym, MC, MP (later Lord Pym)

1983   June11 The Rt Hon. Sir Geoffrey Howe, PC, QC, MP (later Baron Howe of Aberavon)

1989   July25 The Rt Hon. John Major, MP

1989   Oct26 The Rt Hon. Douglas Hurd, CBE, MP (later Baron Hurd of Westwell)

1995   July6 The Rt Hon. Malcolm Rifkind, QC, MP

1997   May2 The Rt Hon. Robin Cook, MP

2001   June8 The Rt Hon. Jack Straw, PC, MP

MINISTERS OF STATE FOR FOREIGN AND COMMONWEALTH AFFAIRS 1981-2001

1981   Sept14 The Rt Hon. Humphrey Atkins, MP• (later the Rt Hon. Sir Humphrey Atkins, MP)

1981   Sept14 Richard Luce (later the Rt Hon. Sir Richard Luce, MP)

1982   April5 The Lord Belstead

1982   April5 Cranley Onslow, MP

1983   June14 Malcolm Rifkind, MP

1983   June14 The Rt Hon. Baroness Young

1983   June14 Richard Luce (later the Rt Hon. Sir Richard Luce, MP)

1983   June14 The Rt Hon. Timothy Raison, MP

1984   Sept11 Timothy Renton, MP (later the Rt Hon, Baron Renton)

1986   Jan13 Mrs Lynda Chalker, MP (later the Rt Hon. Baroness Chalker)

1986   Sept8 Christopher Patten, MP (later the Rt Hon. Christopher Patten)

1987   June16 The Lord Glenarthur

1987   June16 David Mellor, QC, MP (later the Rt Hon. David Mellor)

1988   July16 The Rt Hon. William Waldegrave, MP (later Baron Waldegrave)

1989   July25 The Hon. Francis Maude, MP (later the Rt Hon. Francis Maude MP)

1989   July25 The Lord Brabazon

1989   July25 The Hon. Timothy Sainsbury, MP (later the Rt.Hon Timothy Sainsbury)

1990   July23 Tristan Garel-Jones, MP (later the Rt Hon. Tristan Garel-Jones, MP)

1990   July23 The Rt Hon. The Earl of Caithness

1990   July23 The Hon. Mark Lennox-Boyd, MP (later the Hon. Sir Mark Lennox-Boyd)

1990   Nov1 The Hon. Douglas Hogg, QC, MP (later the Rt Hon. Douglas Hogg, QC, MP)

1992   The Rt Hon. Alastair Goodlad, MP

1994   July20, David Davis MP (later the Rt Hon. David Davis MP)

1995   July5, The Rt Hon. Sir Nicholas Bonsor(Bt), MP

1995   July5, The Rt Hon. Jeremy Hanley, MP (later the Rt.Hon Sir Jeremy Hanley)

1997   May5, Derek Fatchett, MP (later the Rt Hon. Derek Fatchett, MP)

1997   May5, Tony Lloyd, MP

1997   May5, Doug Henderson, MP

1998   July28, Ms Joyce Quin, MP (later the Rt Hon. Joyce Quin, MP)

1999   May17, Geoff Hoon, MP

1999   July29, Peter Hain, MP

1999   July29, John Battle, MP

1999   July29, Baroness Scotland, MP

1999   Oct12, Keith Vaz, MP

2001   Jan25, Brian Wilson, MP

2001   June11, Peter Hain, MP

2001   June11, Baroness Symons

2001   June11, Ben Bradshaw, MP

2001   June11, Denis MacShane, MP

2001   June11, Baroness Amos

•Lord Privy Seal

PERMANENT UNDER-SECRETARIES OF STATE FOR FOREIGN AND COMMONWEALTH AFFAIRS AND HEAD OF HM DIPLOMATIC SERVICE 1975-2002

1975   November22, Sir Michael Palliser KCMG (later GCMG) (later The Rt Hon)

1982   April8, Sir Antony (Arthur) Acland, KCMG KCVO (later KG GCMG GCVO)

1986   June23, Sir Patrick (Richard Henry) Wright, GCMG (later Baron Wright of Richmond)

1991   June28, Sir David (Howe) Gillmore, KCMG (later Baron Gillmore)(Dec'd 20th March 1999)

1994   Aug1, Sir (Arthur) John Coles, KCMG (later GCMG)

1997   Nov13, Sir John (Olav) Kerr, GCMG

2002   Jan, Sir Michael (Hastings) Jay, KCMG

CHRONOLOGICAL LIST OF BRITISH REPRESENTATIVES ABROAD INCLUDING COMMONWEALTH COUNTRIES 1981-2001

Afghanistan
1981   John Donald Garner, Chargé d'Affaires a.i. Feb20
1984   Charles David Stephen Drace-Francis, Chargé d'Affaires a.i. July18
1987   Ian Warren Mackley, Chargé d'Affaires a.i. Jan8
       Staff temporarily withdrawn from post February 1989
1994   Sir Nicholas Barrington, amb. ex. and plen. Feb22

Albania
1992   Sir Patrick (Stanislaus) Fairweather, amb. ex. and plen. July20
1996   Harcourt Andrew Pretorius Tesoriere, amb.ex. and plen. Jan21
1998   Stephen Nash amb. ex. and plen. May15
1999   Dr Peter January amb. ex. and plen. March1
2001   Dr David Maurice Landsman OBE, amb. ex. and plen. July16

Algeria
1981   Benjamin Leckie Strachan, amb. ex. and plen. May17
1984   Alan (later SirA) Gordon Munro, amb. ex. and plen. Jan21
1987   Patrick Howard Caines Eyers amb. ex. and plen. April12
1990   Christopher Charles Richard Battiscombe amb. ex. and plen. March6
1994   Christopher Donald Crabbie amb. ex. and plen Aug2
1996   Peter James Marshall, amb. ex. and plen Jan6
1997   (Jean) Francois Gordon, amb. ex. and plen. Nov4
1999   William Baldie Sinton OBE, amb. ex. and plen. July16
2001   Richard John Smale Edis, amb. ex. and plen. Sept15

Andorra
1994   Anthony David Brighty amb. ex. and plen. Aug25
1998   Peter Torry amb. ex. and plen. Sep2

Angola (Republic of)
1981   Francis Kennedy, amb. ex. and plen. June10
1983   Marrack Irvine Goulding, amb. ex. and plen. June29
1985   Patrick Stanislaus Fairweather, amb. ex. and plen. Oct2
1987   Michael John Carlisle Glaze, amb. ex. and plen. Nov18
1990   John Gerrard Flynn, amb. ex. and plen. May9
1993   Anthony Richard Thomas, amb. ex. and plen. April8
1995   Roger Dudley Hart, amb. ex. and plen. July24
1998   Caroline Elmes, amb. ex. and plen. Sept14
2002   John Thompson, amb. ex. and plen. Feb

Antigua and Barbuda
HIGH COMMISSIONERS
1981   James Stanley Arthur. Nov1
1982   Viscount (John William) Dunrossil. Sept25
1983   Giles (later SirG) (Lionel) Bullard. Aug6
1986   Kevin Francis Xavier Burns. Oct19
1991   Emrys Thomas Davies. Feb15
1994   Richard Thomas. Oct7
1998   Gordon Meldrum Baker Aug3
2001   (Charles) John (Branford) White. Aug11

The Argentine Republic
Diplomatic and Consular relations with the Argentine Republic were broken off with effect from 2 April 1982. Consular Relations were resumed on 19 October 1989 and Diplomatic Relations on 15th February 1990.

1989   Alan Charles Hunt Consul General. Oct19
1989   Alan Charles Hunt Chargé d'Affaires a.i. and Consul General. Feb15
1990   The Hon Humphrey (John Hamilton) Maud, amb. ex. and plen. July15
1993   Sir Peter Hall, amb. ex. and plen. Sept8
1997   William Marsden, amb. ex. and plen. July27
2000   (Duncan) Robin Carmichael Christopher, amb. ex. and plen. Nov17

Armenia
1992   Sir Brian (James) (Proetel) Fall, amb. ex. and plen. July15
1995   David Ivimey Miller, amb. ex. and plen. July31
1997   John Edward Mitchiner, amb. ex. and plen. April1
1999   Timothy Aidan Jones, amb. ex. and plen. Nov13

Australia
HIGH COMMISSIONERS
1984   Sir John (Henry Gladstone) Leahy. Oct13
1988   (Arthur) John (later SirJ) Coles. March22
1991   Brian (later SirB) (Leon) Barder. April11
1994   Roger John Carrick. July27
1997   Alexander Claud Stuart Allan. Nov16
1999   Sir Alastair Goodlad KCMG. May25.

Austria (Republic of)
1982   Michael O'Donel Bjarne Alexander, amb. ex. and plen. Jan25
1986   Robert James O'Neill, amb. ex. and plen. Sept2
1989   Brian Lee Crowe, amb. ex. and plen. May31
1992   Terence Courtney Wood, amb. ex. and plen. April30
1996   Anthony (later Sir A)St John Howard Figgis, amb. ex. and plen. Sept29
2000   Antony Ford, amb. ex. and plen. Sept1

Azerbaijan
1992   Sir Brian (James) (Proetel) Fall, amb. ex. and plen. July14
1993   Thomas Nesbitt Young, amb. ex. and plen. Sept1
1997   Roger Thomas, amb. ex. and plen. July1
2000   Andrew Victor Gunn Tucker, amb. ex. and plen. Nov1

Bahamas

HIGH COMMISSIONERS
1981   Achilles Symeon Papadopoulos. May2
1983   Peter William Heap. May23
1986   Colin Garth Mays. Oct16
1991   Michael John Gore. July16
1992   Brian Attewell. Sept16
1996   Peter Michael Heppell Young. May1
1999   Peter Richard Heigl. July15

Bahrain

1981   David Gordon Crawford, amb. ex. and plen.
       Aug9
1981   (William) Roger Tomkys, amb. ex. and
       plen. Dec7
1984   Francis Sidney Edward Trew, amb. ex. and
       plen. Dec5
1988   John Alan Shepherd, amb. ex. and plen.
       April4
1992   Hugh James Oliver Redvers Tunnell, amb.
       ex. and plen. Feb16
1996   David Ian Lewty, amb. ex. and plen. Jan13
1999   Peter Ford, amb. ex. and plen. April18

Bangladesh (People's Republic of)

HIGH COMMISSIONERS
1981   Frank (later SirF) Mills. Oct23
1983   Terence George (later SirT) Streeton. Dec20
1989   Colin (later SirC) (Henry) Imray. Oct21
1993   Peter James Fowler. Sept21
1996   David Critchlow Walker. Sept15
2000   David Carter. Jan19

Barbados

HIGH COMMISSIONERS
1982   Viscount (John William) Dunrossil. Sept25
1983   Giles (later SirG) (Lionel) Bullard. Aug6
1986   Kevin Francis Xavier Burns. Oct19
1991   Emrys Thomas Davies. Jan13
1994   Richard Thomas. Oct7
1998   Gordon Meldrum Baker. Mar8
2001   (Charles) John (Branford) White. Aug11

Belarus

1992   Sir Brian (James) (Proetel) Fall, amb. ex.
       and plen. July27
1993   John Vivian Everard, amb. ex. and plen.
       Oct12
1996   Jessica Mary Pearce, amb. ex. and plen.
       Jan22
1999   Iain Kelly, amb. ex. and plen. April6

Belgium

1982   John (later SirJ) Edward Jackson, amb. ex.
       and plen. April30
1985   Peter (later SirP) (Charles) Petrie, amb. ex.
       and plen. July7
1989   Robert James O'Neill, amb. ex. and plen.
       May10
1992   Sir John (Walter) (David) Gray, amb. ex.
       and plen. June18
1996   David Hugh Colvin, amb. ex. and plen.
       Oct6
2001   Gavin Wallace Hewitt, amb. ex. and plen.
       Feb2

Belize

HIGH COMMISSIONERS
1981   Francis Sidney Edward Trew. Sept21
1984   John Michael Crosby. Oct19
1987   Peter Alexander Bremner Thomson. Nov10
1991   David Patrick Robert Mackilligin. Feb13
1995   Gordon Meldrum Baker. March30
1998   Timothy James David. April15
2001   Philip John Priestley. July16

Republic of Benin

1983   William Erskine Hamilton Whyte, amb. ex.
       and plen. Aug18
1986   Martin (later SirM) (Kenneth) Ewans, amb.
       ex. and plen. Aug8
1988   Brian (later sir B) Leon Barder, amb. ex.
       and plen. Sept23
1991   (Alastair) Christopher (later Sir C)(Donald
       Summerhayes) MacRae, amb. ex. and plen.
       June17
1994   (John) Thorold Masefield, amb. ex. and
       plen. May14
1997   Graham (later Sir G) Stuart Burton, amb.
       ex. and plen. May2
2001   Philip Lloyd Thomas, amb. ex. and plen.
       March5

Bolivia

1981   Stanley Frederick St Clare Duncan, amb.
       ex. and plen. Sept15
1985   Alan White, amb. ex. and plen. March9
1987   Colum John Sharkey, amb. ex. and plen.
       Aug19
1989   Michael Francis Daly, amb. ex. and plen.
       June4
1991   Richard Michael Jackson, amb. ex. and
       plen. May15
1995   David Frederick Charles Ridgway, amb. ex.
       and plen. June1
1998   Graham Leslie Minter, amb. ex. and plen.
       Aug15
2001   William Baldie Sinton, amb. ex. and plen.
       Oct15

Bosnia and Herzegovina

1994   Robert William Barnett, amb. ex. and plen.
       April26
1995   Bryan Hopkinson, amb. ex. and plen.
       March30

When Yugoslavia broke up "The Republic of
Bosnia and Herzegovina" emerged as a new
country. At Dayton in 1995 it was agreed that the
country should be renamed "Bosnia and
Herzegovina". This took effect in 1996

1996   Charles Graham Crawford, amb. ex. and
       plen. July2
1998   Graham Stewart Hand, amb. ex. and plen.
       July25
2001   Ian Cameron Cliff, amb. ex. and plen. Oct

Botswana

HIGH COMMISSIONERS
1981   Wilfred Jones. Sept3
1986   Peter Albert Raftery. Feb21
1989   Brian Smith. Feb18
1991   John Coates Edwards. Nov19

1994 David Colin Baskcomb Beaumont. Dec19
1998 John Wilde. May17
2001 David Byron Merry. Aug18

Brazil
1981 George William (later SirW) Harding, amb. ex. and plen. March9
1984 John Burns Ure, amb. ex. and plen. Feb26
1987 Michael John Newington amb. ex. and plen. Dec15
1992 Peter William (later Sir P) Heap, amb. ex. and plen. Aug4
1995 Donald Keith Haskell, amb. ex. and plen. May15.
1999 Roger Bridgland Bone, amb. ex. and plen. May20.

Brunei
HIGH COMMISSIONERS
1983 (Robert) Francis Cornish. Aug5
1986 Roger Westbrook. Sept8
1991 Adrian John Sindall. April9
1994 Ivan (later Sir I)Roy Callan. July7
1998 Stuart Laing. July27
2002 Andrew John Forbes Caie. Jan

Bulgaria (Republic of)
1983 John Michael Owen Snodgrass, amb. ex. and plen. Sept6
1986 John Harold Fawcett, amb. ex. and plen. Aug30
1989 Richard Thomas, amb. ex. and plen. May5
1994 Roger Guy Short, amb. ex. and plen. Sept29
1998 Richard Stagg, amb. ex. and plen. July 8
2001 (Samuel) Ian Soutar, amb. ex. and plen. Dec

Burkina Faso (formerly Upper Volta)
(Country re-named on 3August 1984)
1983 John Michael Wilson, amb. ex. and plen. July12
1988 Veronica Evelyn Sutherland, amb. ex. and plen. Jan26
1990 Margaret Irene Rothwell, amb. ex. and plen. Dec17
1997 Haydon Boyd Warren-Gash, amb. ex. and plen. Oct7
2001 Jean Francois Gordon, amb. ex. and plen. June7

Burma (Union of Myanmar)
1982 Nicholas Maed Fenn, amb. ex. and plen. Oct20
1986 Martin Robert Morland, amb. ex. and plen. Oct19
1990 Julian Dana Nimmo Hartland-Swann, amb. ex. and plen. May5
1995 Robert Anthony Eagleson Gordon, amb. ex. and plen. Sept6
1999 John Jenkins, amb. ex. and plen. April26

Republic of Burundi
1984 Nicholas Peter Bayne, amb. ex. and plen. Feb7
1985 Patrick Howard Caines Eyers, amb. ex. and plen. Sept23
1987 Robert Linklater Burke Cormack, amb. ex. and plen. June11
1994 Edward Clay, amb. ex. and plen. Sept19

1995 Kaye Wight Oliver, amb. ex. and plen. Dec11
1998 Graeme Neil Loten. amb. ex. and plen. May11
2001 Susan Elizabeth Hogwood. amb. ex. and plen. July26

Cambodia
1994 Paul Reddicliffe, amb. ex. and plen. June24
1997 Christopher George Edgar, amb. ex. and plen. July29
2000 Stephen John Bridges, amb. ex. and plen. Dec17

Republic of Cameroon
Ambassadors
1981 Bryan Sparrow, amb. ex. and plen. Aug4
1984 Michael John Carlisle Glaze, amb. ex. and plen. July7
1987 Martin Reith, amb. ex. and plen. Oct15
1991 William Ernest Quantrill, amb. ex. and plen. April16
1995 Nicholas Melvyn McCarthy, amb. ex. and plen. April11

In 1995 Cameroon joined the Commonwealth.

High Commissioners
1998 George Peter Richard Boon. Feb8

Canada
HIGH COMMISSIONERS
1981 The Lord Moran. June15
1984 Sir Derek (Malcolm) Day. Aug1
1987 Sir Alan (Bedford) Urwick. Dec4
1989 Brian James Proetel Fall. Oct5
1992 Nicholas (later SirN) (Peter) Bayne. April7
1996 Anthony (later SirA) Michael Goodenough. Mar6
2000 Sir Robert (Andrew) Burns. July7

Cape Verde (Republic of)
1982 (Peter) Laurence O'Keeffe, amb. ex. and plen. Sept15
1986 John Esmond Campbell Macrae, amb. ex. and plen. June17
1990 Roger Campbell Beetham, amb. ex. and plen. Oct18
1993 Alan Edwin Furness, amb. ex. and plen. Oct13
1997 David Raymond Snoxell, amb. ex. and plen. April 26
2000 Edward Alan Burner, amb. ex. and plen. Aug10

Central African Republic
1982 Bryan Sparrow, amb. ex. and plen. Jan28
1985 Michael John Carlisle Glaze, amb. ex. and plen. Feb9
1987 (vacant)
1988 Martin Reith, amb. ex. and plen. July2
1991 William Ernest Quantrill, amb. ex. and plen.
1998 George Peter Richard Boon, amb. ex. and plen. Feb8

Chad (Republic of)
1982 (Alistair) Christopher (Donald Summerhayes) MacRae, amb. ex. and plen. Feb2

1985   Michael Francis Daly, amb. ex. and plen.
        March20
1987   Maeve Geraldine Fort, amb. ex. and plen.
        March7
1990   Charlotte Susanna Rycroft, amb. ex. and
        plen. March19
1991   William Ernest Quantrill, amb. ex. and plen.
        June
1994   John Thorold Masefield, amb. ex. and plen.
        May14
1995   Nicholas Melvyn McCarthy, amb. ex. and
        plen. April11
1998   George Peter Richard Boon, amb. ex. and
        plen. Feb8

Chile
1982   John Kyrle Hickman, amb. ex. and plen.
        June13
1987   Alan White, amb. ex. and plen. July31
1990   Richard Alvin Neilson, amb. ex. and plen.
        Aug31
1993   Frank Basil Wheeler, amb. ex. and plen.
        Oct27
1997   Madelaine (later Dame M) Glynne Dervel
        Evans, amb. ex. and plen. June8
2000   Leo Gregory Faulkner, amb. ex. and plen.
        April1

China (People's Republic of)
1984   Sir Richard (Mark) Evans, amb. ex. and
        plen. Jan19
1988   Alan (later SirA) (Ewen) Donald, amb. ex.
        and plen. May14
1991   Sir Robin (John Taylor) McLaren, amb. ex.
        and plen. June5
1994   Sir Leonard (Vincent) Appleyard, amb. ex.
        and plen. Sept8
1997   Anthony (later Sir A) Charles Galsworthy,
        amb. ex. and plen. May21
2002   Christopher Owen Hum, amb. ex. and plen.
        March

Colombia
1982   John (later SirJ) Adam Robson, amb. ex.
        and plen. May29
1987   Richard Alvin Neilson, amb. ex. and plen.
        Feb5
1990   Keith (later Sir K) Elliott Hedley Morris,
        amb. ex. and plen. Sept26
1994   (Arthur) Leycester (later Sir Leycester)
        (Scott) Coltman, amb. ex. and plen. Nov1
1998   Jeremy Walter Thorp, amb. ex. and plen.
        May,31
2001   Thomas Joseph Duggin, amb. ex. and plen.
        Aug16

Comoros (Federal Islamic Republic of)
1984   James Nicholas Allan, amb. ex. and plen.
        June7
1986   Richard Borman Crowson, amb. ex. and
        plen. Aug29
1989   Michael Edward Howell, amb. ex. and plen.
        Sept27
1991   Dennis Oltrieve Amy, amb. ex. and plen.
        May14
1992   Peter John Smith, amb. ex. and plen. Oct20

1996   Robert Scott Dewar, amb. ex. and plen.
        April14
1999   Charlie Mochan, amb. ex. and plen. March30

Democratic Republic of The Congo
1983   Nicholas Peter Bayne, amb. ex. and plen.
        Nov23
1985   Patrick Howard Caines Eyers, amb. ex. and
        plen. Feb24
1987   Robert Linklater Burke Cormack, amb. ex.
        and plen. June11
1991   Roger Westbrook, amb. ex. and plen. July30
1996   Marcus Laurence Hulbert Hope, amb. ex.
        and plen. Jan21
1998   Doug Scrafton CMG, amb. ex. and plen.
        June15
2000   James Oswald Atkinson, amb. ex. and plen.
        May3

Costa Rica
1983   Peter Wayne Summerscale, amb. ex. and
        plen. Jan24
1986   Michael Francis Daly, amb. ex. and plen.
        June6
1989   William Marsden, amb. ex. and plen.
        April14
1992   Mary Louise Croll, amb. ex. and plen. July5
1995   Richard Michael Jackson, amb. ex. and
        plen. Sept1
1997   Alan Stanley Green, amb. ex. and plen.
        Sept10
1999   Peter Joseph Spiceley, amb. ex. and plen.
        Jan5
2002   Georgina Susan Butler, amb. ex. and plen.
        Feb

Côte d'Ivoire (Ivory Coast)
1983   John Michael Wilson, amb. ex. and plen.
        Feb2
1987   Veronica (later Dame V) Evelyn Sutherland,
        amb. ex. and plen. June27
1990   Margaret Irene Rothwell, amb. ex. and plen.
        Dec17
1997   Haydon Boyd Warren-Gash, amb. ex. and
        plen. Oct7
2001   Jean Francois Gordon, amb. ex. and plen.
        June7

Croatia
1992   Bryan Sparrow, amb. ex. and plen. July23
1994   Gavin Wallace Hewitt, amb. ex. and plen.
        June16
1997   Colin Andrew Munro, amb. ex. and plen.
        Aug8
2000   Nicholas Jarrold, amb. ex. and plen. Nov10

Cuba
1981   David Churchill Thomas, amb. ex. and plen.
        March16
1984   (Patrick) Robin (later Sir R) Fearn, amb. ex.
        and plen. Feb29
1986   Andrew Eustace Palmer, amb. ex. and plen.
        July15
1989   (Anthony) David Brighty, amb. ex. and
        plen. Jan22
1991   (Arthur) Leycester (later Sir Leycester)
        (Scott) Coltman, amb. ex. and plen. March3

1994 Philip Alexander McLean, amb. ex. and
plen. Nov25
1998 David Frederick Charles Ridgway, amb. ex.
and plen. July27
2001 Paul Webster Hare, amb. ex. and plen.
July11

Cyprus (Republic of)
HIGH COMMISSIONERS
1982 (William) John (Antony) Wilberforce.
May10
1988 The Hon. Humphrey Maud. Sept7
1990 David (later Sir, David) John Michael Dain.
July4
1994 David Christopher Andrew Madden. May14
1999 Edward Clay. March12
2001 Lyn Parker. Sept

Czech Republic
1985 Stephen Jeremy Barrett, amb. ex. and plen.
March8
1988 (Peter) Laurence O'Keeffe, amb. ex. and
plen. Nov1
1991 (Anthony) David Brighty, amb. ex. and
plen. July21
1994 Sir Michael (St Edmund) Burton, amb. ex.
and plen. Sept19
1997 David Stuart Broucher, amb. ex. and plen.
Oct1
2001 Anne Fyfe Pringle, amb. ex. and plen. Nov

Denmark
1983 James Mellon, amb. ex. and plen. May7
1986 Peter William Unwin, amb. ex. and plen.
July9
1989 Nigel Christopher Ransome Williams, amb.
ex. and plen. Jan4
1993 Hugh James Arbuthnott, amb. ex. and plen.
June6
1996 Andrew Philip Foley Bache, amb. ex. and
plen. Nov8
1999 Philip Astley, amb. ex. and plen. June4

Djibouti
1985 David Everard Tatham, amb. ex. and plen.
Jan14
1988 Mark Anthony Marshall, amb. ex. and plen.
Jan18
1993 (Robert) Douglas Gordon, amb. ex. and
plen. March20
1994 Duncan Robin Carmichael Christopher,
amb. ex. and plen. April1
1997 Gordon Geoffrey Wetherell, amb. ex. and
plen. Sept11
2000 Myles Antony Wickstead, amb. ex. and
plen. Nov9

Dominica
HIGH COMMISSIONERS
1982 Viscount (John William) Dunrossil. Sept25
1983 Giles (later SirG) (Lionel) Bullard. Aug6
1986 Kevin Francis Xavier Burns. Oct19
1991 Emmrys Thomas Davies. Feb20
1994 Richard Thomas. Oct7
1998 Gordon Meldrum Baker. March8
2001 (Charles) John (Branford) White. Aug11

Dominican Republic
1983 Roy George Marlow, amb. ex. and plen.
July1
1985 Michael John Newington, amb. ex. and
plen. July7
1988 Giles Eden FitzHerbert, amb. ex. and plen.
May11
1993 John Gerrard Flynn, amb. ex. and plen.
April4
1995 Dick Thomson, amb. ex. and plen. Sept.15
1998 David Gordon Ward, amb. ex. and plen.
Sept18

East Timor
BRITISH REPRESENTATIVES
New British Mission (Dili) was formally opened in
January 2000
2000 Dominic James Robert Jermey, Brit. Rep.
Jan5
2000 Jane Elizabeth Mary Penfold, Brit. Rep.
Nov21

Ecuador
1981 Adrian Clarence Buon, amb. ex. and plen.
April16
1985 Michael William Atkinson, amb. ex. and
plen. June28
1989 Frank Basil Wheeler, amb. ex. and plen.
Aug18
1993 Richard Douglas Lavers, amb. ex. and
plen.Nov18.
1997 John William Forbes-Meyler, amb. ex. and
plen. June27
2000 Ian Gerken, amb. ex. and plen. Feb4.

Egypt (Arab Republic of) (formerly the United Arab Republic)
1985 Sir Alan (Bedford) Urwick, amb. ex. and
plen. Feb15
1987 (William) James (later SirJ) Adams, amb.
ex. and plen. Dec14
1992 Christopher William Long, amb. ex. and
plen. April26
1995 David Elliott Spiby Blatherwick, amb. ex.
and plen. April25
1999 Graham (later SirG) Boyce, amb. ex. and
plen. Feb10
2001 (Robert) John Sawers, amb. ex. and plen.
Sept

El Salvador
1982 Colum John Sharkey, amb. ex. and plen.
Feb11
1984 Bryan Oliver White, amb. ex. and plen.
Dec5
1987 David Joy, amb. ex. and plen. Sept8
1989 Peter John Streams, amb. ex. and plen.
Sept13
1991 Michael Henry Connor, amb. ex. and plen.
Nov25
1995 Ian Gerken, amb. ex. and plen. July1
1999 Patrick Morgan, amb. ex. and plen. July5

Republic of Equatorial Guinea
1982 Bryan Sparrow, amb. ex. and plen. Feb11
1985 Michael John Carlisle Glaze, amb. ex. and
plen. April25

1987   Martin Reith, amb. ex. and plen. Nov26
1991   William Ernest Quantrill, amb. ex. and plen.
1998   George Peter Richard Boon, amb. ex. and plen. Feb8

Eritrea (Republic of)
1994   Duncan Robin Carmichael Christopher, amb. ex. and plen. April29
1997   Gordon Geoffrey Wetherell, amb. ex. and plen. Sept11
2000   Myles Antony Wickstead, amb. ex. and plen. Nov9

Estonia (Republic of)
1991   Brian Buik Low, amb. ex. and plen. Oct8
1994   Charles Richard Lucien de Chassiron, amb ex. and plen. Oct15
1997   Timothy James Craddock, amb. ex. and plen. Sept20
2000   Sarah Squire, amb. ex. and plen. Sept6

Ethiopia
1982   Brian Leon Barder, amb. ex. and plen. Sept21
1986   Harold (later Sir H) Berners Walker, amb. ex. and plen. April29
1990   Michael John Carlisle Glaze, amb. ex. and plen. March21
1994   Duncan Robin Carmichael Christopher, amb. ex. and plen. April18
1997   Gordon Geoffrey Wetherell, amb. ex. and plen. Sept11
2000   Myles Antony Wickstead, amb. ex. and plen. Nov9

Fiji
HIGH COMMISSIONERS
1982   Roger Arnold Rowlandson Barltrop. July30
AMBASSADORS
†1988 Roger Arnold Rowlandson Barltrop, amb. ex. and plen. March1
1989   (Alexander Basil) Peter Smart, amb. ex. and plen. Aug19
1992   Timothy James David, amb. ex. and plen. March14

†From 1March 1988, the British High Commission became the British Embassy

1995   Michael John Peart, amb. ex. and plen. April14.
1997   Michael Alan Charles Dibben, amb. ex. and plen. Dec3
2000   Michael Anthony Price, amb. ex. and plen. Oct16

Finland
1983   Alan Brooke Turner, amb. ex. and plen. Jan25
1986   (Hubert Anthony) Justin Staples, amb. ex. and plen. Feb25
1989   (George) Neil Smith. Nov21
1995   David Allan Burns, amb. ex. and plen. March9.
1997   Gavin Wallace Hewitt, amb. ex. and plen. Sept15
2001   Alyson Judith Kirtley Bailes, amb. ex. and plen. Jan5

France
1982   Sir (Major) John (Emsley) Fretwell, amb. ex. and plen. March4
1987   Sir Ewen Alastair John Fergusson, amb. ex. and plen. June22
1993   Sir Christopher (Leslie) George Mallaby, amb. ex. and plen. Jan29
1996   Sir Michael Hastings Jay, amb. ex. and plen. July10
2001   Sir John Eaton Holmes, amb. ex. and plen. Oct16

Gabon (Republic of)
1982   Alan Hartley Grey, amb. ex. and plen. April25
1985   Ronald Henry Thomas Bates amb. ex. and plen. Feb18
1986   Mark Aubrey Goodfellow, amb. ex. and plen. Feb3
1990   Philip John Priestley, amb. ex. and plen. Nov22
1994   William Ernest Quantrill, amb. ex. and plen. Aug12
1995   Nicholas Melvyn McCarthy, amb. ex. and plen. April11.
1998   George Peter Richard Boon, amb. ex. and plen. Feb8

The Gambia
HIGH COMMISSIONERS
1981   David Francis Battye Le Breton. Oct24
1984   John Donald Garner. Nov6
1988   Alec Ibbott. Feb20
1990   Alan John Pover. Oct12
1994   Michael John Hardie. Jan7
1995   John Wilde. Feb13
1998   Tony Millson. March13
2000   John Gayford Perrott. April1

Georgia
1992   Sir Brian (James) (Proetel) Fall, amb. ex. and plen. June22
1995   Stephen Thomas Nash, amb. ex. and plen. Oct15
1998   Richard Thomas Jenkins, amb. ex. and plen. Jan27
2001   Deborah Elizabeth Vavasseur Barnes Jones, amb. ex. and plen. Apr6

Germany (Federal Republic of)
1981   Sir John (Lang) Taylor, amb. ex. and plen. March17
1984   Sir Julian (Leonard) Bullard, amb. ex. and plen. Sept1
1988   Sir Christopher (Leslie George) Mallaby, amb. ex. and plen. March20
1993   Nigel Hugh Robert Allen Broomfield, amb. ex. and plen. Jan17
1997   Sir Christopher Meyer, amb. ex. and plen. March5
1997   Sir Paul Lever, amb. ex. and plen. Dec31

German Democratic Republic
1981   Peter Malcolm Maxey, amb. ex. and plen. Aug19
1984   Timothy John Everard, amb. ex. and plen. Aug21

1988 Nigel Hugh Robert Allen Broomfield, amb. ex. and plen. May10
1990 Patrick Howard Eyers, amb. ex. and plen. Jan26

On 3 October 1990 the German Democratic Republic ceased to exist.

Ghana
HIGH COMMISSIONERS
1983 Kevin Francis Xavier Burns. May30
1986 Arthur Hope Wyatt. Oct24
1989 Anthony Michael Goodenough. Oct16
1992 David Critchlow Walker. June14
1996 Ian Warren Mackley. July21
2000 Roderick Allen Pullen. Oct11

Greece
1982 Peregrine (later SirP) (Alexander) Rhodes, amb. ex. and plen. May28
1985 Sir Jeremy (Cashel) Thomas, amb. ex. and plen. June6
1989 Sir (Henry) David (Alastair Capel) Miers, amb. ex. and plen. May24
1993 (Richard) Oliver Miles, amb. ex. and plen. July19
1996 Michael (later Sir M) John Llewellyn Smith, amb. ex. and plen. April4
1998 David Madden CMG, amb. ex. and plen. Dec,8

Grenada
HIGH COMMISSIONERS
1982 Viscount (John William) Dunrossil. Sept25
1983 Giles (later SirG) (Lionel) Bullard. Aug6
1986 Kevin Francis Xavier Burns. Oct19
1991 Emrys Thomas Davies. Feb5
1994 Richard Thomas. Oct7
1998 Gordon Meldrum Baker. March8
2001 (Charles) John (Branford) White. Aug11

Guatemala
1987 Bernard Jonathan Everett, amb. ex. and plen. June25
1991 Justin Patrick Pearse Nason, amb. ex. and plen. March22
1995 Peter Marcus Newton, amb. ex. and plen. March28
1998 Andrew John Forbes Caie, amb. ex. and plen. July21
2001 Richard Douglas Lavers, amb. ex. and plen. Oct

Guinea (Republic of)
1982 (Peter) Laurence O'Keeffe, amb. ex. and plen. Sept15
1986 John Esmond Campbell Macrae, amb. ex. and plen. May6
1990 Roger Campbell Beetham, amb. ex. and plen. Nov29
1994 Alan Edwin Furness, amb. ex. and plen. April21
1997 David Raymond Snoxell, amb. ex. and plen. April4
2000 Edward Alan Burner, amb. ex. and plen. Aug10

Guinea Bissau
1982 (Peter) Laurence O'Keeffe, amb. ex. and plen. Sept15
1986 John Esmond Campbell Macrae, amb. ex. and plen. May30
1990 Roger Campbell Beetham, amb. ex. and plen. April12
1994 Alan Edwin Furness, amb. ex. and plen. Jan18
1997 David Raymond Snoxell, amb. ex. and plen. April4
2000 Edward Alan Burner, amb. ex. and plen. Aug10

Guyana
HIGH COMMISSIONERS
1982 (William) Kenneth Slatcher. Aug28
1985 John Dudley Massingham. April6
1987 David Purvis Small, July16
1990 (Robert) Douglas Gordon, Oct24
1993 David John Johnson, March22
1998 Edward Glover, Nov19

Haiti
1982 Barry Granger Smallman, amb. ex. and plen. Jan8
1984 (Harold) Martin (Smith) Reid, amb. ex. and plen. March9
1987 Alan Jeffrey Payne, amb. ex. and plen. Oct15
1989 Derek Francis Milton, amb. ex. and plen. June29
1995 Anthony Richard Thomas, amb. ex and plen. Oct15
1998 David Gordon Ward, amb. ex. and plen. Sept18

Holy See
1982 Sir Mark (Evelyn) Heath, amb. ex. and plen. March4
1985 David Neil Lane, amb. ex. and plen. May16
1988 John Kenneth Elliott Broadley, amb. ex. and plen. May18
1991 Andrew Eustace Palmer, amb. ex. and plen. Aug21
1995 Maureen Elizabeth MacGlashan, amb. ex. and plen. May27.
1998 Mark Edward Pellew, amb. ex. and plen. Jan1

Honduras
1981 Colum John Sharkey, amb. ex. and plen. June13
1984 Bryan Oliver White, amb. ex. and plen. Nov20
1987 David Joy, amb. ex. and plen. July17
1989 Peter John Streams, amb. ex. and plen. July30
1992 Patrick Morgan, amb. ex. and plen. Jan30
1995 Peter Rodney Holmes, amb. ex. and plen. Aug3
1998 David Allan Osborne, amb. ex. and plen. July31

Hungary (Republic of)
1983 Peter William Unwin, amb. ex. and plen. July5

1986   Leonard Vincent Appleyard, amb. ex. and
       plen. July30
1989   John (later SirJ) Allan Birch, amb. ex. and
       plen. Aug21
1995   Christopher William Long, amb. ex. and
       plen. June2.
1998   Nigel James Thorpe, amb. ex. and plen. Apr17

Iceland (Republic of)
1981   William Roger McQuillan, amb. ex. and
       plen. March26
1983   Richard Thomas, amb. ex. and plen. April30
1986   Mark Fenger Chapman, amb. ex. and plen.
       Oct8
1989   Richard (later SirR) (Radford) Best, amb.
       ex. and plen. March15
1991   Patrick Francis Wogan, amb. ex. and plen.
       Sept16
1993   Michael Stuart Hone, amb. ex. and plen.
       June21
1996   James Rae McCulloch, amb. ex. and plen.
       May12
2001   John Howard Culver, amb. ex. and plen.
       Jan15

India
HIGH COMMISSIONERS
1982   Robert (later SirR) Lucian Wade-Gery.
       July31
1986   Sir (Arthur) David (Saunders) Goodall.
       April2
1991   Sir Nicholas (Maxted) Fenn. Nov13
1996   The Hon. David (Alwyn) Gore-Booth. Mar9
1999   Sir (John) Rob(ertson) Young. Jan18

Indonesia
1981   Robert Brash, amb. ex. and plen. June17
1984   Alan Ewen Donald, amb. ex. and plen.
       May16
1988   (William) Kelvin (Kennedy) White, amb.
       ex. and plen. March9
1990   Roger John Carrick, amb. ex. and plen.
       Aug3
1994   Graham Stuart Burton, amb. ex. and plen.
       Aug18
1997   (Duncan) Robin Carmichael Christopher,
       amb. ex. and plen. April13
2000   (Richard) Hugh Turton Gozney, amb. ex.
       and plen. Aug16

Iran
1988   Gordon Andrew Pirie, Chargé d'Affaires a.i.
       Dec4
1989   Nicholas Walker Browne, Chargé d'Affaires
       a.i. Feb1
1990   David Norman Reddaway, Chargé
       d'Affaires a.i. Oct28
1993   Jeffrey Russell James, Chargé d'Affaires a.i.
       Aug16
1997   Nicholas Walker Browne, Chargé d'Affaires
       a.i. Nov13
1999   Nicholas Walker Browne, amb. ex. and
       plen. May

Iraq
1982   John (later SirJ) (Campbell) Moberly, amb.
       ex. and plen. Oct29

1985   Terence Josph Clark, amb. ex. and plen.
       March18
1990   Harold (later SirH) Berners Walker amb. ex.
       and plen. Feb9
1991   Embassy Staff Withdrawn.

Diplomatic relations with Iraq were broken off
with effect from 6 February 1991.

Ireland
1983   Alan (later SirA) (Clowes) Goodison, amb.
       ex. and plen. June17
1986   Nicholas (later SirN) Maxted Fenn, amb.
       ex. and plen. Dec7
1991   David Elliott Spiby Blatherwick, amb. ex.
       and plen. Sept10
1995   Veronica (later Dame V) Evelyn Sutherland,
       amb. ex. and plen. March29
1999   Ivor (later Sir I) Anthony Roberts, amb. ex.
       and plen. Feb20

Israel
1981   Patrick Hamilton Moberly, amb. ex. and
       plen. July15
1984   (Clifford) William Squire, amb. ex. and
       plen. Sept11
1988   Mark Elliott, amb. ex. and plen. June19
1992   Robert Andrew Burns, amb. ex. and plen.
       July12
1995   David Geoffrey Manning, amb. ex. and
       plen. Nov11
1998   Francis Cornish, amb. ex. and plen. Sept7
2001   Sherard Louis Cowper-Coles, amb. ex. and
       plen. Sept16

Italy
1983   The Lord Bridges, amb. ex. and plen.
       March1
1987   Sir Derek (Morison David) Thomas amb.
       ex. and plen. Dec3
1989   Sir Stephen (Loftus) Egerton, amb. ex. and
       plen. Nov14
1992   Sir Patrick (Stanislaus) Fairweather, amb.
       ex. and plen. July5
1996   Thomas Leigh Richardson, amb. ex. and
       plen. July10
2000   John (later Sir J) Alan Shepherd, amb. ex.
       and plen. July26

Ivory Coast see Côte d'Ivoire

Jamaica
HIGH COMMISSIONERS
1982   Barry Granger Smallman. Jan8
1984   (Harold) Martin (Smith) Reid. March9
1987   Alan Jeffrey Payne. June23
1989   Derek Francis Milton. April13
1995   Anthony Richard Thomas. Oct1
1999   Anthony Smith. March29

Japan
1984   Sir (Charles) Sydney (Rycroft) Giffard,
       amb. ex. and plen. March1
1986   Sir John (Stainton) Whitehead, amb. ex. and
       plen. Nov12
1992   Sir John (Dixon) (Ikl) Boyd, amb. ex. and
       plen. July7
1995   David John Wright, amb. ex. and plen. Jan1

1999   Stephen John Gomersall, amb. ex. and plen. May28

Jordan
1984   (Arthur) John Coles, amb. ex. and plen. Nov4
1988   Anthony Reeve, amb. ex. and plen. Feb3
1991   Patrick Howard Caines Eyers, amb. ex. and plen. April27
1993   Peter Robert Mossom Hinchcliffe, amb. ex. and plen. Oct19
1997   Christopher Charles Battiscombe, amb. ex. and plen. April14
2000   Edward Graham Mellish Chaplin, amb. ex. and plen. May16

Kazakhstan
1992   Sir Brian (James) (Proetel) Fall, amb. ex. and plen. Sept14
1993   Noël Stephen Andrew Jones, amb. ex. and plen. Oct26
1996   Douglas Baxter McAdam, amb. ex. and plen. March7
1999   Richard George Lewington. Feb7

Kenya
HIGH COMMISSIONERS
1982   Sir (Walter) Leonard Allinson. Sept20
1986   John (later SirJ) (Rodney) Johnson, June15
1990   (William) Roger (later SirR) Tomkys, Oct19
1992   Sir Kieran Prendergast, Oct19
1995   Simon Nicholas Peter Hemans. April14
1997   Jeffrey Russell James, July7
2001   Edward Clay. Dec16

Kiribati (Republic of)
HIGH COMMISSIONERS
1983   Charles Thompson. Sept26
1990   Derek Leslie White. Jan17
1993   Frank McDermott. April14
1994   Timothy James David. Sept1
1995   Michael John Peart. April14
1997   Michael Alan Charles Dibben. Dec3
2000   Michael Anthony Price. Oct16

Korea (Democratic People's Republic of)
New British Embassy (Pyongyang) was formally opened in July 2001

2001   Dr James Edward Hoare, Chargé d'Affaires Feb

Korea (Republic of)
1983   (John) Nicholas (Teague) Spreckley, amb. ex. and plen. May4
1986   Lawrence John Middleton, amb. ex. and plen. Oct7
1990   David John Wright, amb. ex. and plen. April9
1994   Thomas George Harris, amb. ex. and plen. March19
1997   Sir Stephen David Reid Brown, amb. ex. and plen. April4
2000   Charles Thomas William Humfrey CMG, amb. ex. and plen. July1

Kuwait
1982   (Michael) Ramsay Melhuish, amb. ex. and plen. Sept5
1985   Sir Peter (James Scott) Moon, amb. ex. and plen. Feb17
1987   Peter Robert Mossom Hinchcliffe, amb. ex. and plen. May30
1990   Michael (later SirM) Charles Swift Weston amb. ex. and plen. March18
1992   William Hugh Fullerton, amb. ex. and plen. Aug3
1996   Graham Hugh Boyce, amb. ex. and plen. March17
1998   Richard Muir CMG, amb. ex. and plen. Dec14

Kyrgyzstan
1992   Sir Brian (James) (Proetel) Fall, amb. ex. and plen. Oct26
1994   Noël Stephen Andrew Jones, amb. ex. and plen. Feb2
1996   Douglas Baxter McAdam, amb. ex. and plen. March7
1999   Richard George Lewington. Feb7

Laos
1982   (William) Bernard (Josph) Dobbs, amb. ex. and plen. March22
1985   (Hubert Anthony) Justin Staples. April25
1986   Derek Tonkin, amb. ex. and plen. June4
1990   (Michael) Ramsey Melhuish, amb. ex. and plen. Jan24
1992   (Charles) Christian (Wilfrid) Adams, amb. ex. and plen. March14
1997   Sir James William Hodge, amb. ex. and plen. Sept6
2000   Lloyd Barnaby Smith, amb. ex. and plen. March1

Latvia
1992   Richard Christopher Samuel, amb. ex. and plen. Feb2
1993   Richard Peter Ralph, amb. ex. and plen. Aug8
1996   Nicholas Robert Jarrold, amb. ex. and plen. Feb1
1999   Stephen Thomas Nash CMG, amb. ex. and plen. July16
2002   (Harcourt) Andrew (Pretorius) Tesoriere, amb. ex. and plen. March.

Lebanon
1981   David (later SirD) Arthur Roberts, amb. ex. and plen. May17
1983   Henry David (later SirD) Alastair Capel Miers, amb. ex. and plen. Nov11
1985   John (later Sir,J)Walton David Gray, amb. ex. and plen. Nov28
1988   Allan John Ramsay, amb. ex. and plen. June16
1990   David Everard Tatham, amb. ex. and plen. April28
1992   Maeve (later Dame M) Geraldine Fort, amb. ex. and plen. July31
1996   David Ross MacLennan amb. ex. and plen. Oct9
2000   Richard Kinchen amb. ex. and plen. Dec16

Lesotho (Kingdom of)

Liberia (Republic of)

Libya

Liechtenstein

Lithuania

Luxembourg

Macedonia (Former Yugoslav Republic of)

Madagascar (Republic of)

Malawi

Malaysia

†Maldives (Republic of)

†From 9July 1982 the British Embassy became a
High Commission

Mali (Republic of)

Malta

1995 Graham Robertson Archer. Jan3
1999 Howard John Pearce. June14

Marshall Islands (Republic of)

1992 Derek Leslie White, amb. ex. and plen. July22
1996 Vernon Marcus Scarborough, amb. ex. and plen. July23
2000 Christopher Haslam, amb. ex. and plen. Jan15

Mauritania (Islamic Republic of)

1982 (Peter) Laurence O'Keeffe, amb. ex. and plen. Oct5
1986 John Esmond Campbell Macrae, amb. ex. and plen. April24
1993 Sir Allan (John) Ramsey, amb. ex. and plen. April26
1996 William Hugh Fullerton, amb. ex. and plen. April17
1999 Anthony Layden, amb. ex. and plen. March16

Mauritius

HIGH COMMISSIONERS
1981 James Nicholas Allan. Jan19
1985 Richard Borman Crowson. Dec11
1989 Michael Edward Howell. Aug12
1993 John Clive Harrison. May5
1997 James Daly. May30
2000 David Snoxell. Sept

Mexico

1981 Crispin (later SirC) (Charles Cervantes) Tickell, amb. ex. and plen. Aug21
1983 Cynlais (later SirC) (Morgan) James, amb. ex. and plen. Nov7
1986 John (later SirJ) Albert Leigh Morgan, amb. ex. and plen. May21
1989 Michael (later SirM) Keith Orlebar Simpson-Orlebar, amb. ex. and plen. July27
1992 Sir Roger (Blaise) (Ramsay) Hervey, amb. ex. and plen. March2
1994 Adrian John Beamish, amb. ex. and plen. Oct2
1998 Adrian Charles Thorpe CMG, amb. ex. and plen. Oct30

Micronesia (Federated States of)

1992 Derek Leslie White, amb. ex. and plen. July22
1996 Vernon Marcus Scarborough, amb. ex. and plen. July23
2000 Christopher Haslam, amb. ex. and plen. Jan15

Moldova (Republic of)

1992 Sir Brian (James) (Proetel) Fall, Aug28
1995 Sir Andrew (Marley) Wood. July12
1999 Richard Peter Ralph. Aug27

Mongolian People's Republic

1982 James Rupert Paterson, amb. ex. and plen. April1
1984 Allan Geoffrey Roy Butler, amb. ex. and plen. Oct11
1987 Guy William Pulbrook Hart, amb. ex. and plen. March19

1989 David Keith Sprague, amb. ex. and plen. April20
1991 Anthony Bernard Nicholas Morey, amb. ex. and plen. May29
1994 Ian Christopher Sloane, amb. ex. and plen. Jan18
1997 John Clive Durham, amb. ex. and plen. March1
1999 Kay Coombs, amb. ex. and plen. July30
2001 Philip Terence Rouse, amb. ex. and plen. Dec15

Morocco

1982 (Sydney) John (Guy) Cambridge, amb. ex. and plen. Dec1
1985 Ronald Archer Campbell Byatt, amb. ex. and plen. Jan28
1987 John William Richmond Shakespeare amb. ex. and plen. Nov15
1990 John Esmond Campbell Macrae, amb. ex. and plen. June12
1992 Sir Allan (John) Ramsey, amb. ex. and plen. Dec21
1996 William Hugh Fullerton, amb. ex. and plen. April17
1999 Anthony Layden, amb. ex. and plen. March16

Mozambique (Republic of)

1984 Eric Victor Vines, amb. ex. and plen. Feb6
1986 James Nicholas Allan, amb. ex. and plen. Feb21
1989 Maeve (later Dame M) Geraldine Fort, amb. ex. and plen. Sept10
1992 Richard John Smale Edis, amb. ex. and plen. Aug10
1996 Bernard Jonathan Everett, amb. ex. and plen. Jan1
2000 Robert Scott Dewar, amb. ex. and plen. Aug4

Namibia

HIGH COMMISSIONERS
1990 Francis Neville Richards. June4
1992 Henry George Hogger. Oct3
1996 Glyn Davies. Feb1
1999 Brian Donaldson. Jan17
2002 Alasdair Tormod MacDermott, April

Nauru

HIGH COMMISSIONERS
1982 Roger Arnold Rowlandson Barltrop. July30
1990 (Alexander Basil) Peter Smart. March15
1995 Michael John Peart. April14
1997 Michael Alan Charles Dibben. Dec3
2000 Michael Anthony Price. Oct16

Nepal

1983 Anthony (later SirA) Gerald Hurrell, amb. ex. and plen. Nov2
1987 Richard Eagleson Gordon Burges Watson, amb. ex. and plen. March1
1990 Timothy John Burr George, amb. ex. and plen. Oct16
1995 Lloyd Barnay Smith, amb. ex. and plen. Dec9
1999 Ronald Nash, amb. ex. and plen. March26

Netherlands
1981   Philip (later SirP) (Robert Aked) Mansfield, amb. ex. and plen. March14
1984   John (later SirJ) William Denys Margetson, amb. ex. and plen. Nov30
1988   Michael Romilly Heald Jenkins, amb. ex. and plen. Jan23
1993   Sir (Henry) David (Alastair) Miers, amb. ex. and plen. July1
1996   Dame Rosemary Jane Spencer, 1999, amb. ex. and plen. Nov15
2001   Colin Richard Budd, amb. ex. and plen. Apr4

New Zealand
HIGH COMMISSIONERS
1984   Terence Daniel O'Leary. July24
1987   Ronald Archer Campbell Byatt. Dec15
1990   David Joseph Moss. Sept27
1994   Robert Alston. Aug1
1998   Martin Williams OBE. Apr15
2001   Richard Taylor Fell. Dec

Nicaragua
1983   Peter Wayne Summerscale, amb. ex. and plen. Jan24
1986   Michael Francis Daly, amb. ex. and plen. July14
1989   William Marsden, amb. ex. and plen. April19
1991   Roger Hugh Brown, amb. ex. and plen. Dec3
1992   John Howard Culver, amb. ex. and plen. Nov25
1997   Roy Paul Osborne, amb. ex. and plen. July15
2000   Harry Wiles, amb. ex. and plen. Sept

Niger (Republic of)
1983   John Michael Willson, amb. ex. and plen. Feb2
1987   Veronica (later Dame V) Evelyn Sutherland, amb. ex. and plen. Oct16
1990   Margaret Irene Rothwell, amb. ex. and plen. July10
1997   Haydon Boyd Warren-Gash, amb. ex. and plen. Oct7
2001   Jean Francois Gordon, amb. ex. and plen. June7

Nigeria (Federal Republic of)
HIGH COMMISSIONERS
1983   William Erskine Hamilton Whyte. Aug18
1986   Sir Martin (Kenneth) Ewans. Feb28
1988   Brian (later Sir, B)Leon Barder. July27
1991   (Alistair) Christopher (Donald) Summerhaves) MacRea. March7
1994   (John) Thorold Masefield. May14
1997   Graham (later Sir G)Stuart Burton. May2
2001   Philip Lloyd Thomas. March5

Norway
1981   Gillian (later DameG) (Gerda) Brown, amb. ex. and plen. Jan12
1983   William (later SirW) Bentley, amb. ex. and plen. Sept18
1987   John Adam (later SirJ) Robson, amb. ex. and plen. March9

1990   David John Edward Ratford, amb. ex. and plen. May7
1994   Mark Elliott CMG, amb. ex. and plen. June4
1998   Richard (later SirR) Dales CMG, amb. ex. and plen. July3

Oman
1981   Duncan Slater, amb. ex. and plen. Dec20
1986   Robert John Alston, amb. ex. and plen. June3
1990   Terence Joseph (later SirT) Clark, amb. ex. and plen. Jan29
1994   Richard John Sutherland Muir, amb. ex. and plen. June5
1999   Sir Ivan Callan amb. ex. and plen. Feb15
2002   (John) Stuart Laing, amb. ex. and plen. Apr

†Pakistan
AMBASSADORS
1984   Richard Alwyne Fyjis-Walker, amb. ex. and plen. Oct12
1987   Nicolas John (later SirN) Barrington, amb. ex. and plen. July20

HIGH COMMISSIONERS
†1989 Nicholas (later SirN) John Barrington. Oct1
1994   Sir (Alastair) Christopher (Donald) (Summerhayes) MacRae, May31
1997   David (later Sir, D) John Michael Dain, May5
2000   Hilary Nicholas Hugh Synnott. Oct15

†From 30January 1972, the British High Commission became the British Embassy, then from 1October 1989 it reverted to the British High Commission

Palau (Republic of)
1996   Vernon Marcus Scarborough, amb. ex. and plen. July23
2000   Christopher Haslam, amb. ex. and plen. Jan15

Panama (Republic of)
1981   Stanley Stephenson, amb. ex. and plen. Feb2
1983   Terence Harry Steggle, amb. ex. and plen. May18
1986   Margaret Bryan, amb. ex. and plen. April9
1990   John Grant MacDonald, amb. ex. and plen. Jan6
1992   Thomas Herbert Malcomson, amb. ex. and plen. Jan31
1996   William Baldie Sinton, OBE (1999); amb. ex. and plen. Jan19
1999   Robert Harold Davies, amb. ex. and plen. Mar15
2002   James Ian Malcolm, amb. ex. and plen. March.

Papua New Guinea
HIGH COMMISSIONERS
1982   Arthur John Collins. Jan18
1986   Michael Edward Howell. Jan27
1989   (Edward) John Sharland. June11
1991   John Westgarth Guy. July12
1994   Brian Buik Low. Dec12
1997   Charles Drace-Francis. Dec16
2000   Simon Mansfield Scaddan. March1

Paraguay
1984   Bernard Coleman, amb. ex. and plen. Jan19

1986   John Grant MacDonald, amb. ex. and plen.
       May3
1989   Terence Harry Steggle, amb. ex. and plen.
       May31
1991   Michael Alan Charles Dibben, amb. ex. and
       plen. March2
1995   Graham John Campbell Pirnie, amb. ex. and
       plen. Aug31
1998   Andrew Neil George, amb. ex. and plen.
       Oct15
2001   Anthony John James Cantor, amb. ex. and
       plen. Nov

Peru
1983   John William Richmond Shakespeare, amb.
       ex. and plen. Oct30
1987   Adrian John Beamish, amb. ex. and plen.
       Dec16
1990   (Donald) Keith Haskell, amb. ex. and plen.
       Feb11
1995   John Illman, amb. ex. and plen. May5
1999   Roger Hart, amb. ex. and plen. June4

Philippines
1981   Michael Hugh Morgan, amb. ex. and plen.
       April9
1985   Robin John Taylor McLaren, amb. ex. and
       plen. May15
1987   Keith Gordon MacInnes, amb. ex. and plen.
       April27
1992   Alan Everard Montgomery, amb. ex. and
       plen. July11
1995   Adrian Charles Thorpe, amb. ex. and plen.
       July8
1998   Alan Stanley Collins CMG, amb. ex. and plen.
       Dec31
2002   Paul Stephen Dimond, amb. ex. and plen.
       March

Poland (Republic of)
1981   Cynlais Morgan James, amb. ex. and plen.
       May19
1983   John Albert Leigh Morgan, amb. ex. and
       plen. May16
1986   Brian (later Sir B)Leon Barder, amb. ex.
       and plen. May27
1988   Stephen (later Sir S) Jeremy Barrett, amb.
       ex. and plen. Aug20
1991   Michael John Llewellyn Smith, amb. ex.
       and plen. Sept20
1996   Christoper Owen Hum, amb. ex. and plen.
       May6
1998   John Macgregor, amb. ex. and plen. Sept7
2001   The Hon Michael (Aidan) Pakenham, amb.
       ex. and plen. Jan5

Portugal
1981   Hugh (later Sir H) (Campbell) Byatt, amb.
       ex. and plen. May30
1986   Michael Keith Orlebar Simpson-Orlebar,
       amb. ex. and plen. March15
1989   Hugh James Arbuthnott, amb. ex. and plen.
       Aug23
1993   John Stephen (later Sir S) Wall, amb. ex.
       and plen. May31
1995   Roger Westbrook, amb. ex. and plen. July24

1999   John (later Sir John) Holmes, amb. ex. and
       plen. June14
2001   Dame (Madelaine) Glynne Dervel Evans,
       amb. ex. and plen. Sept16

Qatar
1981   Stephen Peter Day, amb. ex. and plen. Sept17
1984   Julian Fortay Walker, amb. ex. and plen.
       Oct10
1987   Patrick Michael Nixon, amb. ex. and plen.
       June11
1990   Graham Hugh Boyce, amb. ex. and plen.
       Feb27
1993   Patrick Francis Michael Wogan, amb. ex.
       and plen. Oct23
1997   David Alan Wright OBE, amb. ex. and plen.
       June4

Romania
1983   Philip McKearney, amb. ex. and plen. Oct19
1986   Hugh James Arbuthnott, amb. ex. and plen.
       Nov14
1989   Michael William Atkinson, amb. ex. and
       plen. Sept4
1992   Andrew Philip Foley Bache, amb. ex. and
       plen. April15
1996   Christopher Donald Crabbie, amb. ex. and
       plen. June30
1999   Richard Peter Ralph, amb. ex. and plen.
       Aug27

Russian Federation
1992   Sir Brian (James) (Proetel) Fall, amb. ex.
       and plen. June3
1995   Sir Andrew (Marley) Wood, amb. ex. and
       plen. July12
2000   Sir Roderic Michael Lyne, amb. ex. and
       plen. Jan14

Rwanda (Republic of)
1984   Nicholas Peter Bayne, amb. ex. and plen.
       Feb7
1985   Patrick Howard Caines Eyers, amb. ex. and
       plen. Aug20
1987   Robert Linklater Burke Cormack, amb. ex.
       and plen. June11
1991   Roger Westbrook, amb. ex. and plen. July30
1994   Edward Clay, amb. ex. and plen. Jan10
1995   Kaye Wight Oliver, amb. ex. and plen.
       Dec11
1998   Graeme Neil Loten, amb. ex. and plen. May11
2001   Susan Elizabeth Hogwood. amb. ex. and
       plen. July26

Saint Kitts and Nevis
HIGH COMMISSIONERS
1983   Giles (later SirG) (Lionel) Bullard. Sept19
1986   Kevin Francis Xavier Burns. Oct19
1991   Emrys Thomas Davies. Feb13
1994   Richard Thomas. Oct7
1998   Gordon Meldrum Baker. March8
2001   (Charles) John (Branford) White. Aug11

St Lucia
HIGH COMMISSIONERS
1982   Viscount (John William) Dunrossil. Sept25
1983   Giles (later SirG) (Lionel) Bullard. Aug6
1986   Kevin Francis Xavier Burns. Oct19

1991   Emrys Thomas Davies. Feb13
1994   Richard Thomas. Oct7
1998   Gordon Meldrum Baker. March8
2001   (Charles) John (Branford) White. Aug11

St Vincent and the Grenadines
HIGH COMMISSIONERS
1982   Viscount (John William) Dunrossil. Sept25
1983   Giles (later SirG) (Lionel) Bullard. Aug6
1986   Kevin Francis Xavier Burns. Oct19
1991   Emrys Thomas Davies. Feb11
1994   Richard Thomas. Oct7
1998   Gordon Meldrum Baker. March8
2001   (Charles) John (Branford) White. Aug11

Samoa
HIGH COMMISSIONERS
1984   Terence Daniel O'Leary. July24
1987   Ronald Archer Campbell Byatt. Dec15
1991   David Joseph Moss. Aug6
1994   Robert Alston. Aug1
1998   Martin Williams. Apr15
2001   Richard Taylor Fell. Dec

São Tomé and Principe
1981   Francis Kennedy, amb. ex. and plen. Nov20
1983   Marrack Irvine Goulding, amb. ex. and
        plen. Oct24
1986   Patrick Staislaus Fairweather, amb. ex. and
        plen. June9
1988   Michael John Carlisle Glaze, amb. ex. and
        plen. March25
1990   John Gerrard Flynn, amb. ex. and plen.
        May22
1993   Anthony Richard Thomas, amb. ex. and
        plen. April27
1996   Roger Dudley Hart, amb. ex. and plen.
        Sept18
1999   Caroline Elmes, amb. ex. and plen. Sept14

Saudi Arabia
1984   Sir Patrick (Richard Henry) Wright, amb.
        ex. and plen. Sept4
1986   Stephen (later Sir S) (Loftus) Egerton, amb.
        ex. and plen. April20
1989   Alan Gordon (later Sir A) Munro, amb. ex.
        and plen. Aug16
1993   The Hon. David (Alwyn) Gore-Booth, amb.
        ex. and plen. April4
1996   Andrew (later Sir A) Fleming Green, amb.
        ex. and plen. March27
2000   Derek (later Sir D) John Plumbly, amb. ex.
        and plen. June15

Senegal (Republic of)
1982   (Peter) Laurence O'Keeffe, amb. ex. and
        plen. Sept15
1985   John Esmond Campbell Macrae, amb. ex.
        and plen. Dec18
1990   Roger Campbell Beetham, amb. ex. and
        plen. July7
1993   Alan Edwin Furness, amb. ex. and plen.
        Aug24
1997   David Raymond Snoxell, amb. ex. and plen.
        April4
2000   Edward Alan Burner, amb. ex. and plen.
        Aug10

Seychelles
HIGH COMMISSIONERS
1983   Colin Garth Mays. Oct1
1986   (Alexander Basil) Peter Smart. Sept30
1989   Guy William Pulbrook Hart. June22
1992   Edward John Sharland. Jan24
1995   Peter Alexander Bremner Thomson. Feb17
1997   John William Yapp. Nov1
2002   Fraser Andrew Wilson. April

Sierra Leone
HIGH COMMISSIONERS
1981   Terence Daniel O'Leary. May11
1984   Richard Dennis Clift. Sept7
1986   Derek William Partridge. June6
1991   David Keith Sprague. May30
1993   Ian McCluney. Sept23
1997   Peter Alfred Penfold. March10
2000   David Alan Jones. May4

Singapore (Republic of)
HIGH COMMISSIONERS
1982   Sir Peter (James Scott) Moon. June14
1985   Sir (William Erskine) Hamilton Whyte.
        March16
1987   Michael Edmund Pike. (later SirM) July13
1991   Gordon Aldridge Duggan. Jan12
1997   Alan Charles Hunt. Aug8
2001   Sir Stephen David Reid Brown. March1

Slovakia (Republic of)
1993   David Brighty, amb. ex. and plen.
1994   Michael Charles Bates, amb. ex. and plen.
        July1
1995   Peter Gale Harborne, amb. ex. and plen.
        Feb20
1998   David Edward Lyscom, amb. ex. and plen.
        Oct15
2001   Damian Roderic Todd, amb. ex. and plen.
        Nov16

Slovenia (Republic of)
1992   Gordon Mackenzie Johnston, amb. ex. and
        plen. Aug25
1997   David Andrew Lloyd, amb. ex. and plen.
        Feb21
2001   Hugh Roger Mortimer, amb. ex. and plen.
        Jan1

Solomon Islands
HIGH COMMISSIONERS
1982   George Norman Stansfield. June15
1986   John Bramble Noss. March17
1988   (David) Junor Young. Oct10
1991   Raymond Francis Jones. May12
1995   Brian Norman Connelly. Dec31
1998   Alan Waters. Sept1.
2001   Brian Paul Baldwin. May16

Somali Democratic Republic
1983   William Hugh Fullerton, amb. ex. and plen.
        Sept26
1987   Jeremy Richard Lovering Grosvenor
        Varcoe, amb. ex. and plen. Feb15
1989   Ian McCluney, amb. ex. and plen. July9

South Africa (Republic of)
HIGH COMMISSIONERS
1994 Sir Anthony Reeve. June1
1996 Maeve (later Dame Maeve) Geraldine Fort. Nov11
2000 Ann Grant. Oct1

AMBASSADORS
†1982 Ewen Alastair John Fergusson, amb. ex. and plen. April29
†1984 Patrick (later SirP) Hamilton Moberly, amb. ex. and plen. Oct8
†1987 Robin (later SirR) William Renwick, amb. ex. and plen. July24
†1991 Anthony (later SirA) Reeve, amb. ex. and plen. July1

†From 10 May 1961, the British High Commission became the British Embassy, then from 1June 1994 it reverted to the British High Commission.

Soviet Union now see Russian Federation
1982 Sir Iain (Johnstone Macbeth) Sutherland, amb. ex. and plen. Sept16
1985 Sir Bryan (George) Cartledge, amb. ex. and plen. July18
1988 Sir Rodric (Quentin) Braithwaite, amb. ex. and plen. Sept20

Spain
1984 Lord Nicholas (Charles) Gordon Lennox, amb. ex. and plen. July2
1989 (Patrick) Robin (later SirR) Fearn, amb. ex. and plen. Nov23
1994 Anthony David Brighty, amb. ex. and plen. Sept1
1998 Peter Torry, amb. ex. and plen. Sept2

Republic of Sri Lanka (Ceylon)
HIGH COMMISSIONERS
1984 John Antony Benedict Stewart. Nov11
1987 David Arthur Stuart Gladstone. June29
1991 Edward John Field. Nov22
1996 David Everard Tatham. Mar21
1999 Linda Duffield, Jan18

Sudan (Republic of)
1984 Sir Alexander (John Dickson) Stirling, amb. ex. and plen. Sept1
1986 John Lewis Beaven, amb. ex. and plen. Dec3
1990 Allan John Ramsay, amb. ex. and plen. June23
1991 Peter John Streams, amb. ex. and plen. Nov29
1995 Alan Fletcher Goulty, amb. ex. and plen. March23
1999 Richard Edward Makepeace, amb. ex. and plen. July13

Surinam (Republic of)
1982 (William) Kenneth Slatcher. Aug28
1985 John Dudley Massingham, amb. ex. and plen. July3
1987 David Purvis Small, amb. ex. and plen. July16
1991 (Robert) Douglas Gordon, amb. ex. and plen. April27

1993 David John Johnson, amb. ex. and plen. Feb19
1998 Edward Glover, Nov19

Swaziland
HIGH COMMISSIONERS
1983 Martin Reith. July29
1987 John Gerrard Flynn. May26
1990 Brian Watkins. May20
1993 Richard Hugh Turton Gozney. Aug8
1996 John Frederick Boble. Feb29
1999 Neil Kenneth Hook, Oct4
2001 David (George) Reader, Sept

Sweden
1984 Sir Richard (Edmund Clement Fownes) Parsons, amb. ex. and plen. July26
1987 Sir John (Burns) Ure, amb. ex. and plen. Dec7
1991 Robert Linklater Burke Cormack, amb. ex. and plen. June17
1995 Roger Bridgland Bone, amb. ex. and plen. Sept1
1999 John Douglas Kelso Grant CMG, amb. ex. and plen. April6

Switzerland
1982 John Ernest Powell-Jones, amb. ex. and plen. May24
1985 John Rowland Rich, amb. ex. and plen. May2
1988 Christopher William Long, amb. ex. and plen. July25
1992 David Beattie, amb. ex. and plen. May5
1997 Christopher Hulse, amb. ex. and plen. April
2001 Basil Stephen Talbot Eastwood, amb. ex. and plen. Aug15

Syria
The Syrian Republic severed Diplomatic and Consular Relations with the United Kingdom on 6June 1967 until 28May 1973

1982 The Hon. Ivor (Thomas Mark) Lucas, amb. ex. and plen. Jan27
1984 (William) Roger Tomkys, amb. ex. and plen. Nov13

Diplomatic and Consular relations with the Syrian Arab Republic were broken off with effect from 31October 1986. They were resumed on 28November 1990

1991 Andrew (later Sir, A)Fleming Green, amb. ex. and plen. Feb17
1994 Adrian John Sindall, amb. ex. and plen. May28
1996 Basil Stephen Talbot Eastwood, amb. ex. and plen. Sept30
2000 Henry George Hogger, amb. ex. and plen. June12

Tajikistan (the Republic of)
1994 Alexander Paul A'Court Bergne, amb. ex. and plen. Jan27
1995 Barbara Logan Hay, amb. ex. and plen. May15

1999   Christopher Ingham, amb. ex. and plen.
       Feb3

Tanzania (United Republic of)
HIGH COMMISSIONERS
Diplomatic Relations were broken off with
Tanzania from 15December 1965 to 4July 1968

1982   John Anthony Sankey. June23
1986   Colin (later SirC) Henry Imray. Jan6
1989   (John) Thorold Masefield. July22
1992   Roger Westbrook. Sept30
1995   Alan Everard Montgomery. July15
1998   Bruce Harry Dinwiddy. April22
2001   Richard Ian Clarke. Aug2

Thailand
1981   (Herbert Anthony) Justine Staples, amb. ex.
       and plen. April24
1986   Derek Tonkin, amb. ex. and plen. Feb18
1989   (Michael) Ramsay Melhuish amb. ex. and
       plen. Nov7
1992   Charles Christian Wilfrid Adams, amb. ex.
       and plen. March14
1996   James (later Sir, J) William Hodge, amb. ex.
       and plen. Sept6
2000   Lloyd Barnaby Smith, amb. ex. and plen.
       March1

Togo
1983   Kevin Francis Xavier Burns, amb. ex. and
       plen. May30
1986   Arthur Hope Wyatt, amb. ex. and plen.
       Oct24
1989   Anthony Michael Goodenough, amb. ex.
       and plen. Dec5
1992   David Crithlow Walker, amb. ex. and plen.
       June16
1996   Ian Warren Mackley CMG, amb. ex. and plen.
       Jul7
2000   Roderick Allen Pullen, amb. ex. and plen.
       Oct 11

Tonga
HIGH COMMISSIONERS
1984   Gerald Francis Joseph Rance. Jan4
1987   Andrew Paul Fabian. March7
1990   William Lawson Cordiner. April3
1994   Andrew James Morris. Nov8
1998   Brian Connelly. Aug20
2002   Paul William Downs Nessling. Jan14

Trinidad and Tobago
HIGH COMMISSIONERS
1985   Martin (later SirM) Seymour Berthoud.
       April11
1991   Brian Smith. Nov11
1996   Leo Gregory Faulkner. July3
1999   Richard Gale Harborne. July15

Tunisia (Republic of)
1981   Alexander (later SirA) (John Dickson)
       Stirling, amb. ex. and plen. Jan27
1984   (William) James Adams, amb. ex. and plen.
       Aug21
1987   Stephen Peter Day, amb. ex. and plen.
       Dec17

1992   Michael Logan Tait, amb. ex. and plen.
       July9
1995   Richard John Smale Edis, amb. ex. and
       plen. Dec4
1999   Ivor Rawlinson, amb. ex. and plen. Feb15
2002   Robin Andrew Kealy, ex. and plen. Jan15

Turkey
1983   (Robert) Mark (later SirM) Russell, amb.
       ex. and plen. Feb28
1986   Timothy (later SirT) Lewis Achilles Daunt,
       amb. ex. and plen. Nov1
1992   Peter John Goulden, amb. ex. and plen.
       Oct23
1995   Sir (Walter) Kieran Prendergast, amb. ex.
       and plen. March23
1997   David Brian Carleton Logan, amb. ex. and
       plen. March28
2002   Peter (John) Westmacott, amb. ex. and plen.
       Jan

Turkmenistan
1993   Sir Brian (James) (Procter) Fall, amb. ex.
       and plen. Jan31
1995   Neil Kenneth Hook, amb. ex. and plen.
       Sept15
1998   Fraser Wilson MBE, amb. ex. and plen. July6

Tuvalu
HIGH COMMISSIONERS
1982   Roger Arnold Rowlandson Barltrop. July30
1989   (Alexander Basil) Peter Smart. Nov29
1995   Michael John Peart. April14
1997   Michael Alan Charles Dibben. Dec3
2000   Michael Anthony Price. Oct16

Uganda
HIGH COMMISSIONERS
Diplomatic Relations were broken off on 28July
1976 until 21April 1979
1983   Colin McLean. Sept14
1986   Derek (later SirD) (Maxwell) March.
       June29
1989   Charles Augustine Kaye Cullimore. Dec21
1993   Edward Clay. Oct1
1997   Michael Edgar Cook. April10
2000   Tom Richard Vaughan Phillips. May15

Ukraine
1992   David Arthur Stewart Gladstone, Chargé
       d'Affaires. Jan17
1992   Simon Nicholas Peter Hemans, amb. ex.
       and plen. June4
1995   Roy Stephen Reeve, amb. ex. and plen.
       June5
1998   Roland Smith, amb. ex. and plen. Nov3

United Arab Emirates
1981   Harold (later Sir H) Berners Walker, amb.
       ex. and plen. May18
1986   Michael Logan Tait, amb. ex. and plen.
       April27
1990   Graham Stuart Burton, amb. ex. and plen.
       Feb6
1994   Anthony Davis Harris, amb. ex. and plen.
       June25
1998   Patrick Michael Nixon, amb. ex. and plen.
       Nov1

United States
1982   Sir (John) Oliver Wright. Sept2
1986   Sir Antony (Arthur) Acland, amb. ex. and
       plen. Aug28
1991   Sir Robin (William) Renwick, amb. ex. and
       plen. Aug20
1995   Sir John Olav Kerr, amb. ex. and plen.
       Aug15
1997   Sir Christopher Meyer, amb. ex. and plen.
       Oct31

Upper Volta (Republic of) (now see Burkina Faso)
1983   John Michael Willson, amb. ex. and plen.
       July12

Uruguay (Oriental Republic of)
1983   Charles William Wallace, amb. ex. and plen.
       Oct12
1986   Eric Victor Vines, amb. ex. and plen.
       March14
1989   Colum John Sharkey, amb. ex. and plen.
       July14
1991   Donald Alexander Lamont, amb. ex. and
       plen. July14
1994   Robert Andrew Michie Hendrie, amb. ex.
       and plen. Sept1
1998   Andrew Murray, amb. ex. and plen. May23
2001   John Vivian Everard. ex. and plen. Aug

Uzbekistan
1992   Sir Brian (James) (Proetel) Fall; amb. ex.
       and plen. Oct21
1993   Alexander Paul A'Court Bergne; amb. ex.
       and plen. Oct29
1995   Barbara Logan Hay, amb. ex. and plen.
       May15
1999   Christopher Ingham, amb. ex. and plen.
       Feb3

Vanuatu (Republic of) (formerly New Hebrides)
HIGH COMMISSIONERS
1982   Richard Bostock Dorman. April25
1985   Malcolm Lars Creek. Aug27
1988   John Thompson. March25
1992   Thomas Joseph Duggin. Jan15
1997   Malcolm Geoffrey Hilson.
2000   Michael Thomas Hill. Nov16

Vatican City (see Holy See)

Venezuela
1982   Hugh (Michael) Carless, amb. ex. and plen.
       June26
1985   Michael John Newington, amb. ex. and
       plen. April28
1988   Giles Eden FitzHerbert, amb. ex. and plen.
       Jan18
1993   John Gerrard Flynn, amb. ex. and plen.
       April4
1997   Richard Denys Wilkinson, amb. ex. and
       plen. May2
2000   Dr Edgar John Hughes, amb. ex. and plen.
       July22

South Vietnam (Republic of)
(Vietnam was formally unified in July 1976)

Vietnam (Socialist Republic of)
1982   Michael Edmund Pike, amb. ex. and plen.
       Dec17
1985   Richard Gilbert Tallboys, amb. ex. and plen.
       June12
1987   Emrys Thomas Davies, amb. ex. and plen.
       May27
1990   Peter Keegan Williams, amb. ex. and plen.
       Oct27
1997   David William Fall, amb. ex. and plen. Apr25
2000   Warwick Morris, amb. ex. and plen. June16

Yemen (Republic of)
1984   David Everard Tatham, amb. ex. and plen.
       Sept19
1987   Mark Anthony Marshall, amb. ex. and plen.
       Nov23
1993   (Robert) Douglas Gordon, amb. ex. and
       plen. March20
1995   Douglas Scrafton amb. ex. and plen.
       March4
1997   Victor Joseph Henderson CMG, amb. ex. and
       plen. Oct19
2001   Frances Mary Guy, amb. ex. and plen. Mar9

Yemen, People's Democratic Republic of (formerly South Yemen, The People's Republic of)
1983   Peter Keegan Williams, amb. ex. and plen.
       Feb23
1986   Arthur Stirling-Maxwell Marshall, amb. ex.
       and plen. Jan4
1989   (Robert) Douglas Gordon, amb. ex. and
       plen. Jan29

The People's Democratic Republic of Yemen and
the Yemen Arab Republic merged on 22May 1990
to become the Republic of Yemen

Yugoslavia (Federal Republic of)
1996   Ivor (later Sir I) Antony Roberts, amb. ex.
       and plen. May6
1997   Joseph Brian Donnelly, amb. ex. and plen.
       Nov17

Diplomatic Relations with The Federal Republic of
Yugoslavia were broken off with effect from 26
March 1999 and were restored on 17 November
2000.

2000   David Maurice Landsman, OBE, Chargé
       d'Affaires Nov17
2001   Charles Graham Crawford, CMG, Chargé
       d'Affaires Jan12

Zambia (Republic of)
HIGH COMMISSIONERS
1984   (William) Kelvin (Kennedy) White. Sept10
1988   John Michael Wilson. Jan21
1990   Peter Robert Mossom Hinchcliffe. May19
1994   Patrick Michael Nixon. Feb1
1998   Thomas Nesbitt Young. Jan3

Zimbabwe (Republic of) (formerly Southern Rhodesia)
HIGH COMMISSIONERS
1983   Martin Kenneth Ewans. April9
1985   (Michael) Ramsay Melhuish. Feb20
1989   (Walter) Kieran (later SirK) Prendergast.
       Aug10

1992   Richard Nigel Dales. Sept21
1995   Martin John Williams. Nov28
1998   Peter Longworth. Apr7
2001   Joseph Brian Donnelly. June30

CHRONOLOGICAL LIST OF BRITISH REPRESENTATIVES TO INTERNATIONAL ORGANISATIONS 1981-2000

UNITED KINGDOM MISSION TO THE UNITED NATIONS

New York

1982   Sir John (Adam) Thomson, Perm. Rep. and Rep. on the Security Council with personal rank of amb. Aug17
1987   Sir Crispin (Charles Cervantes) Tickell, Perm. Rep. and Rep. on the Security Council with personal rank of amb. May29
1990   Sir David (Hugh Alexander) Hannay Perm. Rep. and Rep. on the Security Council with personal rank of amb. Sept7
1995   Sir (Philip) John Weston, Perm. Rep. and Rep. on the Security Council with personal rank of amb. July15
1998   Sir Jeremy (Quentin) Greenstock, Perm. Rep. and Rep. on the Security Council with personal rank of amb. Aug8

UNITED KINGDOM MISSON TO THE OFFICE OF THE UNITED NATIONS AND OTHER INTERNATIONAL ORGANISATIONS AT GENEVA

1983   Dame Anne (Marion) Warburton, Perm. Rep. with personal rank of amb. May16
1985   John Anthony Sankey, Perm. Rep. with personal rank of amb. Dec17
1990   Martin Robert Morland, Perm. Rep. with personal rank of amb. July13
1993   Nigel Christopher Ransome Williams, Perm. Rep. with personal rank of amb. Sept15
1997   Roderic Michael Lyne, Perm. Rep. with personal rank of amb. May1
2000   Simon William Fuller, Perm. Rep. with personal rank of amb. Jan16

UNITED KINGDOM DELEGATION TO THE CONFERENCE ON DISARMAMENT
(formerly the UK Delegation to the Conference of the 18-Nation Committee on Disarmament)
Geneva

1982   (Ronald) Ian (Talbot) Cromartie, Leader of Del. with personal rank of amb. Oct1
1987   Tessa Audrey Hilda Solesby, Leader of Del. with personal rank of amb. Oct10
1992   Sir Michael (Charles) (Swift) Weston, Leader of Del. with personal rank of amb. April6
1997   (Samuel) Ian Soutar, Leader of Del. with personal rank of amb. Aug8
2001   David (Stuart) Broucher, Leader of Del. with personal rank of amb. Oct1

UNITED KINGDOM DELEGATION TO THE NORTH ATLANTIC TREATY ORGANISATION

Brussels

1982   Sir John (Alexander Noble) Graham, Perm. Rep. on the North Atlantic Council with personal rank of amb. Feb15
1986   Michael (later SirM) (O'Donel Bjarne) Alexander, Perm. Rep. on the North Atlantic Council with personal rank of amb. Aug30
1992   Sir (Philip) John Weston, Perm. Rep. on the North Atlantic Council with personal rank of amb. Jan25
1995   Peter John Goulden, Perm. Rep. on the North Atlantic Council with personal rank of amb. April1
2000   David (later SirD) Geoffrey Manning, Perm. Rep. on the North Atlantic Council with personal rank of amb. Dec
2001   Dr Emyr Jones Parry, Perm. Rep. on the North Atlantic Council with personal rank of amb. Sept16

UNITED KINGDOM DELEGATION TO THE WESTERN EUROPEAN COUNCIL

Brussels

1993   Sir (Philip) John Weston, Perm. Rep. on the Permanent Council of the Western European Union with personal rank of amb. Jan1

UNITED KINGDOM DELEGATION TO THE ORGANISATION FOR ECONOMIC CO-OPERATION AND DEVELOPMENT

Paris

1982   Kenneth James Uffen, Perm. Rep. with personal rank of amb. May2
1985   Nicholas Peter Bayne, Perm. Rep. with personal rank of amb. Oct1
1988   John Walton David Gray, Perm. Rep. with personal rank of amb. July11
1992   Keith Gordon MacInnes, Perm. Rep. with the personal rank of amb. July1
1995   Peter William Medlicott Vereker, Perm. Rep. with the personal rank of amb. Sept1
1999   Christopher Crabbie Perm. Rep. with the personal rank of amb. June11

OFFICE OF THE UNITED KINGDOM PERMANENT REPRESENTATIVE TO THE EUROPEAN UNION (formerly UK Delegation to the European Communities)

Brussels

1985   David (later SirD) (Hugh Alexander) Hannay, Perm. Rep. with personal rank of amb. Oct14
1990   John (later SirJ) Olav Kerr, Perm. Rep. with personal rank of amb. Sept2
1995   John (later Sir, S) Stephen Wall, Perm. Rep. with personal rank of amb. Aug15
2000   Nigel (later Sir N) Elton Sheinwald, Perm. Rep. with personal rank of amb. Aug31

UNITED KINGDOM DELEGATION TO THE COUNCIL OF EUROPE

Strasbourg
1983 Christopher Duncan Lush, Perm. Rep. with personal rank of amb. Jan6
1986 Colin McLean, Perm. Rep. with personal rank of amb. Aug6
1990 Noël Hedley Marshall, Perm. Rep. with personal rank of amb. Sept6
1993 Roger Campbell Beetham, Perm. Rep. with personal rank of amb. Aug1
1997 Andrew Carter, Perm. Rep. with personal rank of amb. Aug1

UNITED KINGDOM MISSION TO THE INTERNATIONAL ATOMIC ENERGY AGENCY, THE UNITED NATIONS INDUSTRIAL DEVELOPMENT ORGANISATION AND THE UNITED NATIONS (VIENNA) (formerly UK Mission to the IAEA and to UN Organisations at Vienna)

Vienna
1981 (Ronald) Ian (Talbot) Cromartie, Perm. Rep. with personal rank of amb. July1
1982 Michael Joseph Wilmshurst, Perm. Rep. with personal rank of amb. Aug16
1987 Gerald Edmund Clark, Perm. Rep. with personal rank of amb. June3
1992 Christopher Hulse, Perm. Rep. with personal rank of amb. Nov26
1997 John Patrick George Freeman, Perm. Rep. with personal rank of amb. May2
2001 Peter Redmond Jenkins, Perm. Rep. with personal rank of amb. Aug9

UNITED KINGDOM DELEGATION TO THE CONFERENCE ON SECURITY AND COOPERATION IN EUROPE (CSCE) IN VIENNA

Vienna
1989 (John) Michael Edes, Perm. Rep. with personal rank of amb. March6
1990 Paul Lever, Head of Del. with personal rank of amb. May7
1992 Terence Courtney Wood, Head of Del. with personal rank of amb. April4
1993 Simon William John Fuller, Head of Del. with personal rank of amb. Sept1
1999 John Robert de Fonblanque, Head of Del. with personal rank of amb. June16

BRITISH MISSION TO THE SUPREME NATIONAL COUNCIL OF CAMBODIA
Phnom Penh
1991 David Allan Burns, British Rep. with personal rank of amb. Nov11

CHRONOLOGICAL LIST OF GOVERNORS AND COMMANDERS-IN-CHIEF ETC. OF OVERSEAS TERRITORIES 1980-2000 (MEMBERS HM DIPLOMATIC SERVICE ONLY)

Anguilla
1982 Charles Henry Godden

1985 Alistair Turner Baillie
1990 Brian George John Canty
1992 Alan William Shave
1995 Alan Norman Hoole
1997 Robert Malcolm Harris
2000 Peter Johnstone

Bermuda
1982 Sir Richard (Neil) Posnett
1984 Viscount Dunrossil
1988 Major General Sir Desmond Langley
1992 The Rt Hon The Lord Waddington
1997 Thorold Masefield
2002 Sir John Vereker

British Indian Ocean Territory
1983 William Nigel Wenban-Smith
1986 William Marsden
1988 Richard John Smale Edis
1991 Thomas George Harris
1994 David Ross MacLennan
1996 Bruce Dinwiddy
1999 John White

British Virgin Islands
1987 John Mark Ambrose Herdman
1992 Peter Alfred Penfold
1995 David Patrick Robert Mackilligin
1998 Francis Joseph Savage

Cayman Islands
1992 Michael Edward John Gore
1995 John Wynne Owen
1999 Peter Smith

Falkland Islands/British Antarctic Islands
1986 Gordon Wesley Jewkes
1989 William Hugh Fullerton
1993 David Edward Tatham
1996 Richard Peter Ralph
1999 Donald Lamont

Gibraltar
1992 Sir Hugo White
1997 The Rt Hon Sir Richard Luce
2000 David Robert Campbell Durie

Hong Kong
1983 Sir Edward Youde
1987 Sir David Wilson
1992 The Rt Hon. Christopher Patten

Montserrat
1985 Arthur Christopher Watson
1987 Christopher John Turner
1990 David Pendleton Taylor
1993 Francis Joseph Savage
1997 Anthony John Abbott
2001 Anthony James Longrigg

Pitcairn, Henderson, Ducie and Oeno Islands
1981 Sir Richard James Stration
1985 Terrence Daniel O'Leary
1988 Robert Archer Campbell Byatt
1991 David Joseph Moss
1994 Robert John Alston
1998 Martin Williams
2001 Richard Taylor Fell

St Helena (incl. Ascension and Tristan da Cunha)
1982   John Dudley Massingham
1989   Robert Frederick Stimson
1991   Alan Norman Hoole
1995   David Leslie Smallman
1999   David James Hollamby

Turks and Caicos Islands
1982   Christopher John Turner
1987   Michael John Bradley
1993   Martin Bourke
1996   John Philip Kelly
2000   Mervyn Thomas Jones

**Biographical Notes and
List of Staff**

ABBREVIATIONS

m	married
ptnr	partner
d	daughter
s	son
Diss	Dissolved
Dec'd	Deceased
AUSS	Assistant Under Secretary of State
BOTB	British Overseas Trade Board
CDA	Career Development Attachment
CDE	Conference on Confidence and Security- Building Measures and Disarmament in Europe
CENTO	Central Treaty Organisations
CFE	Negotiations on Conventional Armed Forces in Europe
CO	Cabinet Office
COI	Central Office of Information
CRO	Commonwealth Relations Office
CSBM	Negotiations on Confidence-and-Security Building Measures
CSC	Civil Service Commission
CSCE	Conference on Security and Co-operation in Europe
CSD	Civil Service Department
CSO	Chief Security Officer
CSSB	Civil Service Selection Board
DfID	Department for International Development
DHC	Deputy High Commissioner
DoE	Department of Environment
DETR	Department for Environment, Transport and the Regions
DoI	Department of Industry
DoT	Department of Trade
DS	Diplomatic Service
DSAO	Diplomatic Service Administration Office
DSS	Department of Social Security
DTI	Department of Trade and Industry
DUSS	Deputy Under Secretary of State
ECGD	Export Credits Guarantee Department
ECSC	European Coal and Steel Community
ENA	Ecole Nationale d'Administration (Paris)
FCO	Foreign and Commonwealth Office
FO	Foreign Office
HCS	Home Civil Service
HMOCS	Her Majesty's Overseas Civil Service
HO	Home Office
IISS	International Institute for Strategic Studies
JSDC	Joint Services Defence College
MBFR	Mutual Reduction of Forces and Armaments (Vienna)
MECAS	Middle East Centre for Arab Studies
MoD	Ministry of Defence
MPBW	Ministry of Public Buildings and Works
MPNI	Ministry of Pensions and National Insurance
MPO	Management and Personnel Office
NATO	North Atlantic Treaty Organisation
OEEC	Organisation for European Economic Co-operation
OMCS	Office of the Minister for the Civil Service
POMEF	Political Office Middle East Forces
PRO	Principal Research Officer
RCDS	Royal College of Defence Studies
SEATO	South East Asia Treaty Organisation
SO	Security Officer
SOAS	School of Oriental and African Studies
SOWC	Senior Officers War Course
SRO	Senior Research Officer
SUPL	Special Unpaid Leave
UN	United Nations
UNHCR	United Nations High Commission for Refugees
WO	War Office

Part IV: Biographical List

Statement concerning the present appointments and some other particulars of the careers of established members of Her Majesty's Diplomatic Service.

A

Abbott, David; FCO since August 1994; born 6.6.64; FCO 1983; Singapore 1985; Africa/ME Floater 1989; Kaduna 1991; Abuja 1993; Band B3; m 1990 Nor Hayati Binte Ibrahim (1d 1992; 1s 1993).

Abbott, Neil Middleton; Third Secretary Ljubljana since 1999; born 21.6.65; FCO 1987; Riyadh 1990; FCO 1994; Third Secretary (Chancery/Consular) Abu Dhabi 1996; Band B3; m 1990 Janet Probyn (1s 1992, 1d 1995).

Abbott, Nicholas Robert John; First Secretary (Economic) Riyadh since September 2000; born 25.4.63; FCO 1985; Language Training 1986; Third Secretary (Chancery/Inf) Riyadh 1988; Brussels-Stagiare 1991; Third Secretary (Econ) Paris 1992; Second Secretary (Commercial) Doha 1995; FCO 1998; m 1989 Marcelle Ghislaine Julienne Delvaux (2d 1995, 1996).

Abbott-Watt, Thorhilda Mary Vivia; FCO/Home Office Joint Entry Clearance Unit since April 1999; FCO 1974; SUPL 1977; FCO 1978; Latin America Floater 1979; Paris 1981; UKREP Brussels 1984; Second Secretary FCO 1986; Second Secretary Bonn 1988; First Secretary FCO 1991; First Secretary (Commercial/Know How Fund) Kiev 1995.

Abel, Martin Jeremy; First Secretary (Management/Consul) Istanbul since December 2001; born 30.4.51; MPBW 1969; FCO 1971; Paris 1974; Madras 1976; FCO 1978; Luxembourg 1979; Peking 1982; FCO 1984; Istanbul 1988; Wellington 1993; FCO 1997; m(1) 1974 Lynne Diane Bailey (1d 1978; 1s 1980); (diss); (2) 1992 Nilufer Fasiha Kantarci (1d 1984).

Abrahams, David William; Second Secretary FCO since August 1983; born 14.7.53; FCO 1974; Geneva 1978; Brussels 1981; Band C4; m 1978 Susan Joy Denise Gibson (3d 1987, 1988, 1990).

Ackerman, Erica Alexandra (née Smith); Second Secretary (Commercial) Manila since November 2001; born 9.4.63; FCO 1983; Caracas 1985; SUPL 1989; FCO 1995; Third Secretary (Aid/Commercial) Manila 1998; SUPL 1998; Band C4; m 1989 Robert Joseph Ackerman (dec'd 1992) (1s 1999).

Adam, Stuart William; Vienna since June 2000; born 20.3.71; FCO 1990; Bonn 1992; Peking 1995; Band B3; m, Lesley Elizabeth (1d 2000).

Adams, Brian David, OBE (1992); Counsellor/ Manager (Head of JMO) New York since November 1998; born 17.12.41; CRO 1958; Nairobi 1963; Delhi 1966; Dar es Salaam 1970; FCO 1974; Third later Second Secretary (Aid) Jakarta 1977; Second later First Secretary (Human Rights) UKMIS Geneva 1981; Overseas Inspectorate 1986; Dhaka 1989; First Secretary later Counsellor FCO 1993; m 1963 Beryl Pauline Laming (2s 1966, 1971).

Adams, Catherine Elizabeth; Assistant Legal Adviser FCO since February 2000; born 29.11.65; Assistant Legal Adviser FCO 1994; First Secretary (Legal) UKREP Brussels 1997 Band D7.

Adams, Geoffrey Doyne; Consul-General Jerusalem since May 2001; born 11.6.57; FCO 1979; Language Training 1980; Third, later Second Secretary Jedda 1982; First Secretary ENA Paris 1985; FCO 1986; Private Secretary to the PUS 1987; First Secretary (Head of Political Section) Pretoria/Cape Town 1991; FCO 1994; On loan to Cabinet Office (European Secretariat) 1996; Counsellor and DHM Cairo 1998; m 1999 Mary Emma Baxter.

Adams, Gillian; JMO Brussels since June 1998; born 10.6.65; MOD 1982; FCO 1984; Nicosia 1986; Africa/Middle East Floater 1989; FCO 1993; Language Training 1997; Band B3.

Adams, Trevor Malcolm; First Secretary (Press & Public Affairs) Hong Kong since April 1998; born 16.4.51; FCO 1971; Paris 1973; Middle East Floater 1976; Bucharest 1977; JAO New York 1979; FCO 1982; Vientiane 1984; Rangoon 1985; HM Consul Casablanca 1988; FCO 1993; m 1979 Linda Jane Burgess (1d 1985).

Adamson, Donald Snaith; FCO since January 2000; born 3.4.49; Ministry of Social Security 1967; FCO 1968; Khartoum 1971; Brussels (EC) 1972; Wellington 1975; Dacca 1978; loan to ODA 1981; FCO 1983; Cape Town 1985; FCO 1988; Second Secretary (Consular) Islamabad 1992; Second Secretary FCO 1993; Abuja 1996; m 1970 June Alice Manson Hall (1s 1973; 1d 1977).

Adamson, Joanne; On Secondment to UNWRA since January 1999; born 9.7.67; FCO 1989; Language Training Cairo June 1991; Third later Second Secretary (Chancery/Comm) Jerusalem 1992.

Addiscott, Emily Margaret (née Dallas); SUPL since April 1997; born 27.5.72; FCO 1991; SUPL 1994; Kiev 1996; Band A2; m 1993 Fraser John Addiscott (2d 1997, 1999).

Addiscott, Fraser John; SUPL since January 2001; born 4.9.71; FCO 1990; Vice Consul Helsinki 1994; Third Secretary (Management) Kiev 1996; Third Secretary (Political) Singapore 1997; Band C4; m 1993 Emily Margaret Dallas (2d 1997, 1999).

Ager, Keith; FCO since July 1991; born 25.6.48; FO 1965; Bonn 1975; FCO 1977; Lilongwe 1979; FCO 1982; Montevideo 1982; FCO 1985; Rome 1988; Band C4; m 1969 Ann Simmons (2d 1974, 1978).

Ager, Martyn Eric; FCO since August 1993; born 17.6.55; FCO 1972; Moscow 1982; FCO 1985; Amman 1990; Band C4; m 1981 Kathryn Margaret Pierson (2s 1984, 1992, 1d 1986; twins, 1s, 1d 1994).

Agnew, Gail Eileen; Second Secretary FCO since November 1988; born 21.1.48; FCO 1966; Lisbon 1970; Peking 1973; Bonn 1974; Vientiane 1977; FCO 1980; Nicosia 1982; Budapest 1985.

Ahmad, Asif Anwar; Deputy Head of Resource Budgeting Department since January 2000; born 21.1.56; DTI Business Link 1996; First Secretary FCO 1999; m(1) (diss 1991); m(2) 1993 Zubeda Khamboo (1d 1975; 3s 1980, 1982, 1984).

Albright, John Rowland; First Secretary (Commercial) Singapore since March 1996; born 14.7.44; DHSS 1962; DSAO 1966; Havana 1968; Brussels (EC) 1969; Moscow 1972; FCO 1973; Nairobi 1976; Muscat 1979; FCO 1981; Second Secretary (Comm) Manila 1985; First Secretary (Comm/Aid) Colombo 1989; First Secretary FCO 1993; m(1) 1969 Gillian Susan Long (1d 1972; 1s 1974); m(2) 1993 Maria Alma Samaniego.

Alcock, Caroline; Third Secretary Bahrain since August 1996; FCO 1993; born 8.12.70; Full time language training 1993; Band B3 m1996 Amr Waguih.

Alcock, Michael Leslie, MBE (1986); FCO since April 1999; born 7.8.50; Ministry of Labour 1967; DSAO (later FCO) 1968; Bangkok 1971; Port of Spain 1975; Tehran 1977; FCO 1979; Second Secretary (Chancery) and Vice-Consul Addis Ababa 1984; Second later First Secretary (Comm/Econ) New Delhi 1987; First Secretary FCO 1991; First Secretary (Aid/Commercial) Kathmandu 1994; m 1971 Barbara Ann Couch (2s 1972, 1976).

Alderton, Clive; Head of Chancery Singapore since September 1998; born 9.5.67; FCO 1986; Vice-Consul Warsaw 1988; Third Secretary

(External Relations) UKREP Brussels 1990; Second later First Secretary FCO 1993; m 1990 Catriona Mitchell Canning (1d 1998; 1s 2000).

Aldridge, Terence John; FCO since February 2000; born 11.9.56; FCO 1980; Darwin 1982; FCO 1984; Tel Aviv 1987; FCO 1988; Rome 1997; Band C4; m 1988 Janet Lorna Shore (1d 1991, 1s 1994).

Alessandri, Madeleine Kay (née Hateley); FCO since June 2000; born 6.3.65; FCO 1988; Second Secretary (Chancery/Inf) Vienna 1990; Second later First Secretary FCO 1993; Consul (Economic) Frankfurt 1996; Language training 1999; Band D6; m 1990 Enrico Alessandri; (1d 1993 1s 1998).

Aliaga, Deborah Joy; Third Secretary (Man/VC/ECO) La Paz since September 1997; born 8.7.60; FCO 1979; Bonn 1980; La Paz 1983; Resigned 1986; Reinstated FCO 1987; Band B3; m 1989 Kenny Aliaga (1d 1996; 1s 2000).

Allan, Duncan Brierton; FCO since August 1996; born 22.11.61; FCO 1989; Moscow 1992; Principal Research Officer; m 1994 Joanne Clare Youde.

Allan, Jane Alison (née Higgs); SUPL since June 1998; born 9.3.63; HCS 1981; FCO 1981; Washington 1984; FCO 1987; SUPL 1989; Peking 1990; SUPL 1991; FCO 1996; Band A2; m 1987 Ian Allan.

Allan, Justine Rachel Anne; Floater duties since July 1999; born 15.7.69; FCO 1990; Cape Town/Pretoria 1992; Band B3.

Allan, Keith Rennie; FCO since August 2000; born 25.8.68; MOD 1986; FCO 1988; Gaborone 1990; Floater Duties 1993; FCO 1996; Deputy Head of Mission Tashkent 1997; Band C5; m 1996 Martha Harriette Medendorp (1s 2000).

Allan, Lynne Fleming; Ankara since July 1998; born 22.10.68; FCO 1989; Moscow 1993; FCO 1995; Band B3; m 1999 Marat Ucer (1s 2001).

Allan, Moira; Second Secretary Bogotá since March 2000; born 27.5.61; FCO 1983; Prague 1985; FCO 1987; Mexico City 1989; Santiago 1993; FCO 1996; Band C4.

Allan, Nicholas Edward; Third Secretary (Political) Brussels since July 1996; born 3.8.65; FCO 1990; UKREP Brussels 1993; Africa/ Middle East Floater Duties 1994.

Allan, Richard Joseph; FCO since April 1995; born 3.10.48; FO (later FCO) 1966; Berlin 1970; Kathmandu 1973; FCO 1977; Milan 1980; FCO 1982; Canberra 1984; Colombo 1987; Islamabad 1990; Band B3; m(1) 1972 Jeanette Marshall (1s 1974); (2) 1985 Margaret Janette Smylie.

Allbless, Clare Brickley; Third Secretary (PPA) Tokyo since October 2000; born 4.5.71; FCO 1997; Band B3; m, Dan Lindfield.

Allen, Jonathan Guy; Nicosia since August 1999; born 5.3.74; FCO 1997; Band C4.

Allen, Keith; San Salvador since June 2000; born 5.9.72; FCO 1992; New Delhi 1996; FTLT 2000; Band B3.

Allen, Mark John Spurgeon; Counsellor FCO since February 1994; born 3.7.50; Third Secretary FCO 1973; Language Student MECAS 1974; Third later Second Secretary Abu Dhabi 1975; Second Secretary FCO 1977; Second later First Secretary Cairo 1978; FCO 1981; First Secretary (Econ) Belgrade 1982; First Secretary FCO 1986; Counsellor FCO 1990; m 1976 Margaret Mary Watson (1s 1978, 1d 1980).

Allen, Rory James Colclough; First Secretary FCO since December 1992; born 5.9.48; FCO 1972; Second Secretary Jakarta 1974; First Secretary FCO 1978; Language Training Hong Kong 1981; Bangkok 1982; First Secretary FCO 1985; First Secretary (Political) Rome 1991; Band D6; m 1982 Hazel Rose Dawe (1s 1983).

Allen, Ruth Alexandra; FCO since September 2000; born 31.8.76; Band C4.

Allen, Sylvia Ann; Hanoi since December 1999; born 8.8.60; FCO 1984; La Paz 1986; Tunis 1990; Floater duties 1995; Band A2.

Allhusen, Elnor Lucy Clare; FCO since September 2001; born 10.12.72; Band C4.

Allison, Diana Margaret Jane; FCO since July 1990; born 27.7.46; FCO 1971; Moscow 1973; FCO 1974; Jakarta 1978; Madrid 1980; Kuala Lumpur 1983; FCO 1986; SUPL 1989; Band A2.

Alloway, Terence Michael; FCO since October 1998; born 18.5.59; FCO 1980; Budapest 1982; Tel Aviv 1983; FCO 1986; SE Asia Floater 1987; FCO 1988; Kuwait 1992; FCO 1994; Full-time Language Training 1994; Third later Second Secretary (Chancery) UKDIS Geneva 1995; Band D6; m 1991 Christine Ann Carr.

Ambrose, Philip John; Full time language training since November 2001, born 3.11 59, FCO 1978, UKREP Brussels 1980, Jedda 1983, Riyadh 1986, South East Asia Floater 1987, Buenos Aires 1990, Tehran 1991, FCO 1992, Deputy Head of Mission and Consul Kinshasa additionally Second Secretary and Consul Brazzaville (non resident) 1995. Second Secretary (Commercial) Beijing July 1997.

Amin, Jacqueline Harris; FCO since October 1989; born 2.6.62; FCO 1984; Port Stanley 1985; Luanda 1986; Band A2; m 1989 Paul John Harms.

Amos, Rex; FCO since November 1999; born 24.9.72; Band B3; m 1999 Jacqueline Palin.

Anderson, Annabel Mary; Paris Embassy since December 1998; born 15.7.50; FCO 1995; Band A2; m 1974.

Anderson, Henry Ian; First Secretary Budapest since September 1997; born 20.8.52; HO 1974; Dhaka 1983; Second Secretary FCO 1987; Vice-Consul Munich 1989; Second Secretary FCO 1994; Band C5; m 1976 Janice Irene Leeman (1s 1984; 1d 1987).

Anderson, Jennifer Elizabeth; Second later First Secretary FCO since August 1997; born 16.11.68; m 1997 Stephen Ashworth.

Anderson, John; FCO since September 1998; born 25.8.49; FCO 1966; Abu Dhabi 1970; Peking 1974; Lagos 1975; FCO 1978; HM Consul Istanbul 1982; Second later First Secretary (Comm) Paris 1987; First Secretary FCO 1991; First Secretary (Management) Harare 1995; m 1970 Jacqueline Thorburn (2d 1981; 1990; 1s 1983).

Anderson, Lorraine Michelle; FCO since May 1994; born 29.12.63; FCO 1989; Damascus 1992; Band A2; m (1) 1988 Lawrence Malcolm Reginald Simpson (diss 1994), (2) 1999 Neil Barrowman (1s 2000).

Anderson, Michael James; First Secretary (Political) UKMIS New York since July 2000; born 3.4.61; FCO 1984; Language training 1986; Second Secretary (Scientific/Econ) Moscow 1988; First Secretary FCO 1989; First Secretary UKDIS Geneva 1992; FCO 1997; T/D Doha 2000; Band D6; m 1987 Julie Ann Dickens (2s 1992, 1994, 1d 1996).

Anderson, Philip Brian; Nicosia since April 1999; born 18.7.73; HCS 1993; FCO 1997; Band A2; m 1997 Jennie Linda Willis (1s 1996).

Anderson, Steven Martin; Third Secretary (Management/VC) Helsinki since December 2000; born 29.12.70; FCO Home Civil Service 1991; Dubai 1997; Moscow 1998; Band B3; ptnr, Eevamaija Sofia Laitinen.

Andrews, Francesca Therese; FCO since July 1989; born 23.2.54; FCO 1973; Cape Town/Pretoria 1975; Moscow 1978; FCO 1980; UKDEL Brussels 1982; FCO 1985; Port of Spain 1986; Band A2.

Andrews, Moira Fraser TD (1992); Legal Counsellor FCO since June 2000; born 22.3.59; Department of Trade and Industry 1995; Assistant Legal Adviser FCO 1998; m 1985 Ian Andrews (1s 1989; 1s and 1d 1992).

Andrews, Paul Philip; FCO since June 1998 born 24.9.68; FCO 1988; Hong Kong 1993; Seoul 1996. Band B3.

Andrews, Timothy John; First Secretary FCO since September 1997; born 1.8.55; FCO 1976; Dacca 1979; Stuttgart 1982; Bonn 1984; FCO 1987; Second Secretary (Chancery/Inf) Lusaka 1990; Deputy Head of Mission Port Louis 1994; m 1987 Carolyn Mary Moffat (1d 1989, 1s 1991).

Angell, Ben Thomas; FCO since September 2000; born 27.12.76; Band C4.

Angell, Neil Christopher; Third Secretary (Political) Lima since April 1999; born 31.10.66; FCO 1989; Bangkok 1991; Moscow 1991; T/D Bangkok 1994; FCO 1995; Band B3; m 1995 Suntraree Charoenwattana (1s 1997).

Angrave, Gillian Linda; FCO since October 1994; born 16.4.45; FCO 1976; Manila 1976; Lima 1980; Guatemala City 1981; Santiago 1982; FCO 1985; Mexico City 1987; Budapest 1991; Band B3.

Ankerson, Dr Dudley Charles; Counsellor Budapest since July 1998; born 4.9.48; Second Secretary FCO 1976; Second Secretary Buenos Aires 1978; First Secretary FCO 1981; First Secretary Mexico City 1985; First Secretary FCO 1988; First Secretary FCO on secondment to the Private Sector 1991; FCO 1991; Counsellor Madrid 1993; FCO 1997; m 1973 Silvia Ernestina Galicia (1d 1985, 1s 1986).

Ansell, Carolyn; FCO since April 1991; born 28.12.63; FCO 1984; Warsaw 1989; Band A2.

Anstead, Alan Roger Hugh; Bratislava since August 2000; born 6.2.62; FCO 1980; Moscow 1983; Monrovia 1985; Hamburg 1989; FCO 1991; On loan to the DTI 1993; Deputy Head of Mission Riga 1996; Band C4; m 1986 Paula Marita Nikkanen (1s 1991).

Anthony, Helen Louise; FCO since June 1988; born 6.12.67; Band A2.

Anthony, Ian Nicholas; First Secretary FCO since April 1997; born 18.1.60; FCO 1985; Second later First Secretary Lisbon 1988. First Secretary FCO 1990; First Secretary (Political) Brasilia 1993; Band D6.

Anthony-Rigsby, Lisa; FTLT since March 2000; born 1.4.65; FCO 1998; Band A2.

Arbon, Helen Marie; FCO since April 1999; born 21.4.70; FCO 1988; Jakarta 1991; World-wide Floater 1995; SUPL 1998; T/D Montevideo 1998; SUPL 1999; Band B3; m 1998 Adolfo Pando Molina.

Archer, Marie-Louise; DHM Managua since September 1996; born 27.10.61; FCO 1984; Resigned 1986; Reinstated 1987; FCO 1987; Third Secretary (Immigration) Karachi 1991; Third Secretary FCO 1995; Language Training 1996; Band B3.

Archer, Nicholas Stewart, MVO (2001); Counsellor FCO since March 2001; born 24.12.60; FCO 1983; Third later Second Secretary (Chancery) Amman 1986; Second later First Secretary FCO 1989; PS/Minister of State 1992. Full-time Language Training 1995; First Secretary (Commercial) Oslo 1995; on loan to St James' Palace 1997; m 1999 Erica Margaret Power.

Arkley, David Ballantine; Third Secretary (PPA) Moscow since October 2000; FCO 1986; born 10.10.66; FCO 1986; Moscow 1988; Floater Duties 1990; MO/Vice Consul São Paulo 1992; FCO 1995; Third Secretary (PPA) Washington 1997; Band B3; m 1992 Melissa Lea Buchanan.

Arkwright, Paul Thomas; First Secretary (Chancery) Paris since June 1998; born 2.3.62; FCO 1986; Second Secretary (Chancery) BMG Berlin 1988; First Secretary FCO 1991; First Secretary (Chancery) UKMIS New York 1993;

Attachment to Quai d'Orsay 1997; m 1997 Patricia Anne Holland (1d 1999).

Armour, Nicholas Hilary Stuart; Head of North America Department FCO since November 2000; born 12.6.51; Third Secretary FCO 1974; Language Student MECAS 1975 and FCO 1976; Third later Second Secretary Beirut 1977; First Secretary FCO 1980; Head of Chancery Athens 1984; First Secretary FCO 1989; Counsellor and Deputy Head of Mission Muscat 1991; Counsellor on loan to the DTI 1994; Consul General/Counsellor Dubai 1997; m 1982 Georgina Elizabeth Fortescue (2d 1985, 1987).

Armstrong, Catherine Fraser; HM Consul Brussels since September 2000; born 16.7.53; FCO 1971; Paris 1974; Gaborone 1977; FCO 1980; Manila 1985; Athens 1989; FCO 1990; Full-time Language Training 1994; Second Secretary (Consular/Management) Caracas 1995; Second Secretary FCO 1997; m 1981 Clive Paul Ranson; diss 1986.

Arnold, Troy Zachary Moncur; Second Secretary (Economic) Nicosia since October 2000; born 19.12.72; Second Secretary FCO 1997; Language training 1999; Band C4.

Aron, Michael Douglas; Deputy Head of Mission Amman since August 1999; born 22.3.59; FCO 1984; Conference Support Officer UKMIS New York 1985; on Secondment to European Commission 1986; Second later First Secretary FCO 1986; First Secretary Brasilia 1988; First Secretary FCO 1991; First Secretary (Political) UKMIS New York 1993; First Secretary later Counsellor FCO 1996; m 1986 Rachel Ann Golding Barker (2d 1986, 1996, 2s 1990, 1994).

Aron, Peter James; Counsellor FCO since December 2000; born 27.2.46; FO (later FCO) 1965; Bonn 1968; Second later First Secretary FCO 1971; First Secretary (Chancery) Singapore 1984; First Secretary (Chancery) Washington 1986; First Secretary FCO 1990; Counsellor (Regional Affairs) Seoul 1997; m 1968 Penelope Joan Sebley (2d 1969, 1971; 2s 1976, 1988).

Aron, Dr Rachel Ann Golding (née Barker); SUPL (Amman) since August 1999; born 18.7.51; First Secretary FCO 1984; Head of Chancery Brasilia 1988; SUPL 1990; First Secretary FCO 1992; First Secretary (Political) UKMIS New York 1993; SUPL 1996; Counsellor on loan to RAS as CSSB Chairman 1997; m 1986 Michael Douglas Aaron (2d 1986, 1996, 2s 1990, 1994).

Arroyo, James Jos Maria; Consul (Political) Jerusalem since January 1999; born 25.3.67; FCO 1990; Full-time Language Training 1991; Full-time Language Training Cairo 1992; Second Secretary (Political) Amman 1993; Cairo 1996; Band D6; m 1992 Kerry Ann Louise Ford.

Arthur, Hilary Jane; Second Secretary (Development) Lusaka since April 1998; born 28.1.61; FCO 1984; Karachi 1987; Vice-Consul

(Consular) Düsseldorf 1991; Frankfurt 1993; T/D Islamabad 1994; FCO 1995; Band C4.

Arthur, Michael Anthony, CMG (1992); Minister Washington since June 1999; born 28.8.50; FCO 1972; New York 1972; FCO 1973; Second Secretary UKREP Brussels 1974; Second Secretary Kinshasa 1976; Second later First Secretary FCO 1978; PS to Lord Privy Seal 1980; PS to Minister of State 1982; First Secretary (Chancery) Bonn 1984; Counsellor FCO 1988; Counsellor (Political) Paris 1993; Director (Resources) and Chief Inspector 1997; m 1974 Plaxy Gillian Beatrice Corke (2d 1978, 1980; 2s 1982, 1985).

Ash, Elizabeth; On secondment to Buckingham Palace since July 1996; born 31.7.52; FCO 1975; New Delhi 1976; UKMIS Geneva 1978; Peking 1980; FCO 1982; Kingston 1983; FCO 1987; East Berlin 1988; FCO 1990; Band B3.

Ashcroft, Andrew Richard; FCO since 1999; born 28.5.61; FCO 1980; Muscat 1982; Tel Aviv 1987; (Second Secretary 1989); FCO 1991; First Secretary Harare 1996.

Ashdown, Julie Anne; Second Secretary (Aid) Quito since June 1996; born 31.8.57; FCO 1976; Amman 1978; Asunción 1982; Brasilia 1983; FCO 1985; Belgrade 1990; Second Secretary FCO 1993.

Ashford, Leslie David; T/D Abu Dhabi since June 2000; born 7.9.50; Royal Air Force 1967-1996; FCO 1996; T/D Khartoum 2000; Band B3; m 1971 Francetta Xavier Marie (1d 1973, 1s 1979).

Ashton, John; Counsellor FCO since May 1998; born 7.11.56; FCO 1978; Language Student Hong Kong 1980; Third later Second Secretary Peking 1981; FCO 1984; First Secretary on loan to Cabinet Office 1986; Rome 1988; First Secretary later Counsellor Deputy Political Adviser Hong Kong 1993; On Secondment as Visiting Fellow, Green College Oxford 1997; m 1983 Kao Fengning (1s 1986).

Ashworth, Patrick; Deputy Consul-General and Deputy Director of Trade Promotion São Paulo since January 2001; born 2.11.50; FCO 1968; Dar es Salaam 1971; Castries 1975; Moscow 1978; FCO 1980; Valletta 1983; Vice Consul (Commercial) São Paulo 1987; Second Secretary (UNCED) Brasilia 1992; Second Secretary FCO 1992; First Secretary (Press and Public Affairs) The Hague 1995; Band D6; m 1973 Pauline Mary Harrison (1d 1982, 1s 1986).

Askham, Denise Ann; SUPL since January 1999; born 15.10.64; FCO 1983; Bonn 1985; UKDEL CSCE Vienna 1988; Washington 1988; Berne 1991; FCO 1995; SUPL 1995; FCO 1998; Band B3; (1d 1997, 1s 2000).

Askham, Stephen David; Lisbon since October 2000; born 20.5.60; RAF 1976-1984; FCO 1984; Bonn 1991; FCO 1994; Bahrain 1999; FTLT 2000; Band B3; m 1998 Denise Ann Vaughan (1d 1997, 1s 2000).

Aspden, Susan Elizabeth; on loan to the DTI since October 1996; born 20.1.57; FCO 1980; Rabat 1981; Jakarta 1983; Havana 1987; FCO 1989; Band B3.

Aspery, Kevin; Hong Kong since September 1999; born 5.4.52; Army 1968-92; Havana 1993; Moscow (MNEB) 1997; Colombo 1998; m Penelope Jane (1d 1973, 2s 1975, 1977).

Asquith, Hon Dominic Anthony Gerard; Minister and Deputy Head of Mission Buenos Aires since August 1997; born 7.2.57; FCO 1983; Second Secretary and Head of Interests Section Damascus 1986; First Secretary (Chancery) Muscat 1987; First Secretary FCO 1989; PS/Minister of State 1990; Washington 1992; m 1988 Louise Cotton (2d 1989, 1990; 2s 1992, 1994).

Astbury, Nicholas Paul; First Secretary FCO since April 1999; born 13.8.71; FCO 1994; Second Secretary (Chancery) Colombo 1995; m 1995 Elayna Joanne Gutteridge (1s 1999).

Astle, Marilia Silva; FCO since April 1998; born 14.4.68; FCO 1991; Vice-Consul later Press & Public Affairs Lisbon 1994; Band C4; m2000 Jonathan Jones.

Astley, Philip Sinton, LVO (1979); HM Ambassador Copenhagen since August 1999; born 18.8.43; British Council 1965-73; First Secretary FCO 1973; First Secretary Copenhagen 1976; First Secretary and Head of Chancery East Berlin 1980; First Secretary FCO 1982; Counsellor, Home Inspectorate 1984; Head of Management Review Staff 1985; Counsellor (Econ/Comm/Aid) and Consul-General Islamabad 1986; Deputy Head of Mission Copenhagen 1990; Counsellor FCO 1994; AUSS (Protocol) and Vice Marshal of the Diplomatic Corps 1996; m 1966 Susanne Poulsen (2d 1969, 1972).

Astill-Brown, Jeremy; Second Secretary (Political/ Development) Luanda since September 1999; born 14.3.67; FCO 1987; Kampala 1990; Addis Ababa 1993; FCO 1997; Band B3; m 1991 Marie-Louise (Marisa) Alegria Gunner.

Atkinson, Christine; Deputy Permanent Delegate UKDEL UNESCO Paris since June 2001; born 5.7.57; British Museum 1979; COI 1986; FCO 1990; APS/Minister of State 1996; PS/PUSS DFID 1997.

Atkinson, James Oswald; HM Ambassador to the Democratic Republic of Congo and non-resident Ambassador to the Republic of Congo (Brazzaville) since May 2000; born 20.10.44; Board of Trade 1964; DSA 1966; Commonwealth Office (later FCO) 1967; Nicosia 1969; Gabarone 1972; Second Secretary (Comm) Damascus 1976; FCO 1980; First Secretary (Comm) Athens 1984; First Secretary (Chancery/Inf) Jakarta 1988; First Secretary FCO 1990; Deputy Head of Mission Kampala 1993; FCO 1997; m 1980 Annemiek van Werkum (1d 1981).

Atkinson, Jane; Port Louis since June 1999; born 20.7.60; MOD 1978-87; FCO 1987; Quito 1988; Floater Duties 1992; FCO 1996; Band B3.

Atkinson, Kim Louise (née Kemp); Warsaw since September 1999; born 4.4.74; FCO 1992; Islamabad 1996; Band A2; m 1999 Simon Manington Atkinson.

Atkinson, Simon Manington; ECO/Vice-Consul Warsaw since March 2000; born 11.5.71; FCO 1989; Oslo 1992; FCO 1995; Pro-Consul Islamabad 1995; Band B3; m 1999 Kim Kemp.

Attryde, Alan Robert James; First Secretary (Commercial) since July 2000; born 21.8.47; Ministry of Labour 1966; DSAO 1967; FCO 1968; Middle East Floater 1970; Washington 1971; Jakarta 1974; FCO 1978; Cairo 1980; on loan to DTI 1985 (Second Secretary 1985); Consul (Comm) Shanghai 1987; Second Secretary (Man/Cons) Caracas 1990; Full-time Language Training 1992; First Secretary (Comm) Al Khbar June 1993; FCO since October 1997; T/D as First Secretary (Management) Washington 1999; Band C5; m 1992 Ana Maria Diaz Molina.

Attwood, Ian; Kuala Lumpur since March 2000; born 14.4.62; FCO 1983; Hong Kong 1991; FCO 1992; Bangkok 1993; FCO 1996; Band C4; m 1987 Tina Louise (1d 1989; 1s 1991).

Augustine-Aina, Felicity; Islamabad since March 2000; born 10.7.56; MAFF; FCO 1989; Lagos 1991; FCO 1994; Dublin 1998; SUPL 1999; Band B3; m 1992 Henry Abayomi Aina.

Auld, Steven James; Third Secretary (Management) and Vice Consul Tripoli since January 2001; born 9.7.71; FCO 1990; Moscow 1993; Nuku'alofa 1995; FCO 1996; Band B3; m2001 Andrea Baity.

Aust, Anthony Ivall CMG (1995); Legal Counsellor FCO since September 1991; born 9.3.42; Solicitor 1967; Assistant Legal Adviser Commonwealth Office 1967; Assistant Legal Adviser FCO 1968; Legal Adviser Berlin (BMG) 1976; FCO 1979 (Legal Counsellor 1984); Counsellor (Legal Adviser) UKMIS New York 1988; Band D6; m(1) 1969 Jacqueline Antoinette Thérèse Paris (diss 1986) (2d 1974, 1980); (2) 1988 Kirsten Kaarre Jensen.

Austen, Richard James, MBE (1996); Deputy High Commissioner Port Louis since September 2001; born 25.5.55; Inland Revenue 1972-77 (SUPL 1974-77); FCO 1981; Dar es Salaam 1983; Third Secretary (Cons) Ottawa 1987. Second Secretary FCO 1990; Deputy High Commissioner Banjul 1993; First Secretary FCO 1996.

Austin, David John Robert; OBE (1999); Deputy Head of Mission, Zagreb since August 1999; born 7.10.63; FCO 1986; Third, later Second Secretary Dhaka 1989; FCO 1992; Second, later First Secretary (Political/Information) Belgrade 1993; On Secondment to ICFY/OHR as Political Adviser to Carl Bildt 1995; FCO 1997; m 1990 Emma Jane Carey (1d 1995, 1s 1997).

Austin, Rebecca-Jane Victoria (née Hall); SUPL since March 1996; born 27.2.68; FCO 1990; Port Louis 1993. FCO 1994; Band B3; m 1994 J Mark Austin (1d 1996).

Austin, Vanessa Anne; Nairobi since July 2000; born 4.8.71 FCO 1994; Cairo 1996; Band A2.

Avery, Raymond Rember; First Secretary (Management) Oslo since September 1994; born 31.1.46; DSAO 1965; Port of Spain 1968; since September 1994; Colombo 1972; FCO 1975; Amman 1978; Helsinki 1980; FCO 1982; Second Secretary (Comm) Kuala Lumpur 1987; Second Secretary FCO 1991; m 1967 Christine Ruth Floate (1s 1968; 1d 1971).

Axworthy, Michael George Andrew; SUPL since July 2000; born 26.9.62; FCO 1986; Third later Second Secretary Valletta 1988; Second Secretary FCO 1991; Second Secretary (Political/Military)Bonn 1993; Second Secretary (Economic)Bonn 1996; First Secretary FCO 1998; m 1996 Sally Hinds (1d 1999).

Axworthy, Sally Jane; SUPL since June 2000; born 1.9.64; FCO 1986; Language Training 1988; Third Secretary Moscow 1989; Second Secretary Kiev 1989; First Secretary FCO 1993; First Secretary Bonn 1994; FCO 1998; m 1996 Michael G A Axworthy.(1d 1999).

Ayre, Andrew; Third Secretary Tel Aviv since May 1998; born 30.4.66; FCO 1986; Warsaw 1988; Rio de Janeiro 1990; FCO 1991; Nicosia 1994; Band B3; SUPL 1997; m 1990 Bettina Mooseberger.

Ayres, Robert Charles; Second later First Secretary FCO since February 1990; born 12.12.41; CRO 1958; Seconded to Department of Technical Co-operation 1961; CRO 1963; DSAO 1965; Tripoli 1967; Lahore 1969; Islamabad 1971; FCO 1972; Brussels (NATO) 1975; Second Secretary FCO 1978; Second Secretary (Admin) Brussels (JAO) 1985; m 1978 Elizabeth Anne Kirkland (1d 1979).

B

Babbage, Ann Michelle; FCO since May 1995; born 18.5.72; Band A2.

Bach, Alison Helen (née Clews); Reykjavik since January 2000; born 4.11.65; ODA 1987; FCO 1990; Manila 1992; FCO 1994; T/D Sarajevo 1996; SUPL 1996; Bonn 1997; Band A2; m 1997 Anthony Gordon James Bach (1s 1998).

Backhouse, Nigel Antony Richard, MVO (1986); Counsellor Paris since April 1998; born 19.1.56; FCO 1982; Second Secretary Kabul 1984; Second later First Secretary Kathmandu 1985; FCO 1986; First Secretary (Chancery) Madrid 1989; 1992; FCO 1992; m (1) 1979 Kathleen Helen Gordon (diss 1988) (2s 1983, 1985); (2) 1996 Sharon Lindsay Rathbone (1d 1998).

Bagnall, Andrew William; Second Secretary Nairobi since June 1994; born 28.2.48; GPO 1964-70; FCO 1970; Pretoria 1982; Second Secretary

FCO 1985; Attaché Caracas 1987; m 1981
Margaret Christine Bromwich (1s 1981; 1d 1985).

Baharie, Ian Walter; First Secretary (Political)
Abuja since March 1999; born 3.5.61; FCO 1982;
Language Student SOAS 1983; Third later Second
Secretary (Chancery) Cairo 1985; Second later
First Secretary FCO 1987; First Secretary Abu
Dhabi 1991; First Secretary FCO 1994; Consul
Jerusalem 1996; Band D6; m 1991 Bonaventura
Agatha Jasperina Buhre (3d 1991, 1998, 2001).

Bailes, Alyson Judith Kirtley, CMG (2001); HM
Ambassador Helsinki since January 2001; born
6.4.49; Third Secretary FCO 1969; Budapest 1970;
Second Secretary Brussels (NATO) 1974; Second
later First Secretary FCO 1976 on loan to MOD
1979; First Secretary (Chancery) Bonn 1981; First
Secretary FCO 1984; Language Training 1986;
Counsellor Head of Chancery and Consul-General
Peking 1987; Deputy Head of Mission and
Consul-General Oslo 1990; Counsellor FCO 1994;
SUPL 1996; Language Training 2000.

Bailey, Ian Peter; FCO since December 1998;
born 21.8.57; DTI 1985; FCO 1987; Language
Training 1988; Third Secretary (Pol) Muscat 1990;
Second Secretary (Commercial) Seoul 1995; Band
C5; m 1990 Teresa Weronika Maria Frosztega (1s
1998).

Bailey, Michael; Third Secretary FCO since
January 1991; born 24.2.41; FO 1965; Singapore
1967; FCO 1969; Khartoum 1971; FCO 1973;
StHelena 1974; FCO 1976; Muscat 1977; FCO
1980; Peking 1981; FCO 1983; Rangoon 1984;
FCO 1986; Third Secretary Rome 1988; Band C4;
m 1967 Wendy Nichol Pocklington (2s 1969,
1970).

Bailey, Rosemarie Anne (née Edwards); FCO
since December 1997; born 20.4.59; FCO 1979;
Tokyo 1983; FCO 1986; SUPL 1988; Vice-Consul
Singapore 1992; Band C4; SUPL 1996; m 1982
Mark Adrian Stephen Bailey (1s 1996).

Bailey, Stephen; Madras since January 2000; born
13.4.53; FCO 1971; Mexico City 1975; Gaborone
1977; Sana'a 1981; FCO 1983; Wellington 1987;
Budapest 1990; FCO 1995; Band B3; m 1975
Carol Joan Sterritt (1d 1980).

Baines, Paul Vincent; FCO since November 1996;
born 22.7.47; Inland Revenue 1966; Registrar
General's Office 1966; DSAO (later FCO) 1967;
Zomba 1997; Blantyre 1971; Algiers 1973;
Warsaw 1976; FCO 1978; Lusaka 1981; FCO
1984; Second Secretary (Admin) Riyadh 1988;
Consul Tokyo 1992; m 1969 Edith Lauraine
Baxter Price.

Baird, Nicholas Graham Faraday; Counsellor
(Justice/Home Affairs) UKREP Brussels since
December 1998; born 15.5.62; FCO 1983; Third
later Second Secretary Kuwait 1986; Second later
First Secretary (Econ/Finance) UKREP Brussels
1989; First Secretary FCO (Private Secretary to
the Parliamentary Under Secretary of State) 1993;
Counsellor and Deputy Head of Mission Muscat

1997; m 1985 Caroline Jane Ivett (1s 1989, 2d
1990, 1992).

Baker-Mavin, Alison Bertha (née Baker); bem
(1991); SUPL since March 2001; born 9.5.62;
FCO 1989; Algiers 1991; Banjul 1995; Third
Secretary Management/Commercial Freetown
1998; Band B3; m 1997 G J Mavin.

Baker, Catherine Margaret; FCO since January
1998; born 11.9.68; FCO 1991; Third
Secretary(Chancery/Information) Tel Aviv 1994;
Band B3.

Baker, Denise; Belgrade since April 1994;
27.9.67; FCO 1987; Brussels 1991; Band A2.

Baker, Francis Raymond, OBE (1997); Private
Secretary to the Minister of State since July 1998;
born 27.1.61; FCO 1981; Panama City 1983; Third
later Second Secretary Buenos Aires 1986; Second
Secretary FCO 1991; First Secretary
(Political/Military) Ankara 1993; First Secretary
on secondment to State Department Washington
1996; First Secretary FCO 1997; m 1983 Maria
Pilar Fernandez (1d 1989; 1s 1991).

Baker, Nigel Marcus; On loan to St James's
Palace since June 2000; born 9.9.66; Third
Secretary FCO 1989; Third later Second Secretary
(Econ) Prague 1992; Second Secretary later DHM
Bratislava 1993; Resigned 1995; Reinstated 1998;
First Secretary FCO 1998; m 1997 Alexandra
Cechova.

Baker, Piers Howard Burton; Deputy Head of
Mission Vienna since January 2001; born 23.7.56;
Second Secretary FCO 1983; First Secretary
(Chancery Brussels 1985; First Secretary FCO
1988; First Secretary UKREP Brussels 1993; First
Secretary FCO 1996; m 1979 Maria Eugenia
Vilaincour (1s 1984).

Baker, Rodney Kelvin Mornington; Third
Secretary Madrid since October 1989; born
24.3.49; FO (later FCO) 1966; Warsaw 1974; FCO
1975; Athens 1977; Ankara 1978; FCO 1981;
Third Secretary Tokyo 1984; FCO 1986; Band C4;
m 1971; Christine Mary Holt (2d 1979, 1983).

Baker, Russell Nicholas John; First Secretary
(Commercial) Dublin since June 1996; born
6.10.53; FCO 1977; Language Training 1979;
Prague 1979; Bonn 1982 (Private Secretary to
HMA) 1982; Second Secretary FCO 1986; APS to
the Minister of State 1987. Second Secretary
(Pol/Info/Comm) Lima 1990. First Secretary FCO
1994; m 1996 Silvia Chavez Montoya.

Baldwin, Brian Paul; High Commissioner Honiara
since May 2001; born 7.12.44; Ministry of
Transport 1964; Board of Trade 1965; FCO 1967;
Johannesburg 1970; Belgrade 1973; FCO 1976;
Vice-Consul (Pol) Johannesburg 1979; Second
later First Secretary FCO 1983; First Secretary
(Comm) Muscat 1988; Deputy Head of Mission
Port Moresby 1993; Tristan da Cunha
Administrator 1998; m. Elizabeth Mary Evans (3s
1969, 1970, 1973; 1d 1971).

Baldwin, Peter Graham; FCO since April 1998; born 28.8.43; Paymaster General's Office 1962; CRO 1963; Lusaka 1964; Calcutta 1967; Vienna 1971; Second Secretary Brussels (UKREP) 1973; FCO 1977; Algiers 1981; Second Secretary FCO 1983; Second Secretary (Immigration/Consular) Colombo 1987; Second Secretary (Consular) Jakarta 1991; Second Secretary (Immigration) Islamabad 1995; m 1968 Patricia Joyce Carter (2d 1970, 1972; 1s 1980).

Bale, Caroline Margaret; FCO since June 1991; born 25.7.57; FCO 1980; UKMIS Geneva 1981; Moscow 1983; Port Stanley 1986; Sofia 1987; Gaborone 1989; Band A2.

Balfour, Alison Hannah; FCO since July 1999; born 13.5.61; Scottish Office 1980-87; FCO 1987; Mexico City 1989; Nicosia 1992; Rome 1995; Band B3.

Ball, Anthony James; First Secretary (Political) Madrid since July 1999; born 18.12.68; FCO 1989; Full-time Language Training 1991; FCO 1993; Second Secretary (Economic) Kuwait 1994; FCO 1996; Band D6; m 1995 Celia Garcia-Marugan Mino.

Ballett, Sarah Elizabeth; FCO since August 2000; born 31.10.71, FCO 1990; Washington 1994; SUPL 1997; Washington 1997; Band B3.

Balmer, Michael Anthony; FCO since September 2000; born 21.7.51; MOD (Navy) 1969; FCO 1971; UKMIS Geneva 1973; Moscow 1975; LA Floater 1977; Jedda 1979; Second Secretary (Comm) Warsaw 1981; Second later First Secretary FCO 1984; Language Training 1987; First Secretary (Comm) Athens 1988; First Secretary FCO 1992; Deputy Consul-General Düsseldorf and Deputy Director-General for Trade and Investment Promotion in Germany 1996; Band D7; m 1982 Helen Charmian Burgoine (2d 1984, 1987).

Bamber, Jonathan James; Third Secretary (Commercial) Maputo since August 2001; born 24.9.65; FCO 1994; ECO later Vice-Consul Bangkok 1997; FTLT 2000; Band B3; m2001 Sarah Louise Cooke.

Bamber, Sarah Ann; Second Secretary FCO since March 2001; born 6.1.74; FCO 1996; Second Secretary UKMIS New York 1998; Band C4.

Bamford, Victoria Jane; SUPL since February 2001; born 23.12.67; FCO 1989; Moscow 1992; FCO 1995; Nicosia 1996; FCO 1999; Band B3.

Banham, Michael Kent; First Secretary (Management) Cairo since May 1998; born 20.9.44; FO 1963; Rawalpindi 1967; Quito 1970; FCO 1974; Tripoli 1976; Nairobi 1980; FCO 1983; Second Secretary (Comm) Bombay 1987; Second Secretary (Management/Consular) Lima 1990; First Secretary (Management) Riyadh 1994; m (1)1965 Christine Scott (1s 1969; 1d 1971) (diss); (2) 1995 Marie Louise Smith.

Banks, Alison Elizabeth; FCO since April 2000; born 10.1.70; FCO 1992; Canberra 1994; Peking 1998; Band B3.

Banks, Jacinta Mary Catharine (née Cookson); FCO since August 2000; born 25.11.57; FCO 1977; Paris 1980; Bombay 1983; FCO 1987; Nicosia 1990; Damascus 1994; Islamabad 1996; Band B3; m 1982 Jamie Paul Banks (1d 1992).

Banks, Jamie Paul; Deputy Head, Asia Pacific, Invest UK since March 2001; born 9.6.57; FCO 1977; UKDEL OECD Paris 1980; Bombay 1983; FCO 1987; Nicosia 1990; Second Secretary (Commercial) Damascus 1994; Second Secretary (Development) Islamabad 1996; FCO 2000; Band C5; m 1982 Jacinta Mary Catharine Cookson (1d 1992).

Banks, Larry, OBE; Consul and Deputy Head of Mission Luanda since August 2000; born 15.6.42; FO 1961; New York 1963; Lagos 1966; Aden 1968; MECAS 1969; MECAS (Admin Officer) 1971; Muscat 1973; FCO 1975; Second Secretary (Comm) Tripoli 1977; Second Secretary (Admin) and Vice-Consul Sana'a 1980; Second later First Secretary FCO 1984; First Secretary and Consul Kuwait 1988; First Secretary and Consul (Comm) Hamburg 1992; Deputy Head of Mission Beirut 1996; m 1969 Elizabeth Ann Collins (1d 1970; 2s 1971, 1976).

Banks, Simon John; Deputy High Commissioner Dar es Salaam since August 1999; born 5.4.66; FCO 1988; Language Training 1990; Third later Second Secretary (Economic) Warsaw 1990; On Secondment to DGIA EC Commission Brussels 1993; First Secretary FCO 1996; m 1989 The Hon Rowena Joynson-Hicks. (3s 1994, 1996, 1999).

Bannatyne, William Graeme; Lima since May 2000; Born 5.3.67; FCO 1988; Canberra 1990; FCO 1993; Sofia 1993; FCO 1995; FTLT 2000; Band B3; m 1990 Caterina Prestigiacomo (1d 1995).

Banner, Nick; First Secretary FCO since June 2000; born 28.2.74; FCO 1999; Band D6; m 1999 Emma Reisz.

Bannerman, Alexander Campbell; Dubai since May 1998; born 29.9.67; FCO 1988; Nicosia 1993; FCO 1995; Band B3; m 1998 Fiona Vari MacKillop.

Bannister, Irene Marshall; SUPL since August 1993; born 14.3.67; FCO 1988; Lusaka 1990; Band A2.

Baptie, Gavin William; Second Secretary (Immigration) Tehran since November 2000; born 7.11.70; Home Office 1993; FCO 1998; Band C4; m2000 Caroline Jane Houston.

Barber, Andrew John; Counsellor (Political) Kuala Lumpur since July 1998. born 19.2.59; FCO 1981; Second Secretary Jakarta 1985; Second Secretary FCO 1987; First Secretary Addis Ababa 1990; On loan to the Cabinet Office 1994; m 1990 Caroline Jane Hart (2d 1991, 1993).

Barber, Caroline Jane; SUPL since May 1993; born 5.8.56; FCO 1978; UKMIS Geneva 1980; Jakarta 1983; FCO 1985; Full-time language training 1990 Second Secretary (Chancery/Info) Addis Ababa 1990; m 1990 Andrew John Barber (2d 1991, 1993).

Barclay, John Hamish; Jedda since June 2000; born 11.9.64; Royal Air Force 1983-1992; Department of Transport 1993-1995; FCO 1995; Abu Dhabi; Band A2.

Barclay, Karl Phillip; Counsellor FCO since October 1999; born 28.5.48; Army 1967-86; First Secretary FCO 1986; First Secretary Hong Kong 1989; First Secretary FCO 1992; Counsellor Buenos Aires 1996; m(1)1974 Gillian Davies (Diss)(2s 1976, 1983; 1d 1979), (2)1998 Andrea Carey Smith.

Barclay, Philip Jeremy; FCO since January 1999; born 14.10.67; Band C4; m 1996 Emma Robinson.

Barker, Caroline Susan; FCO since July 1999 SUPL 1997; born 15.9.69; 1992; Full-time Language Training 1993; Second Secretary (KHF) Bratislava 1994; Second Secretary FCO 1995.

Barker, Philip John; Berlin since December 1998; born 18.11.70; FCO 1989; m 1998 Elizabeth Margaret Jean Hindle.

Barker, Rowland Gifford Palgrave; FCO since September 2000; born 6.6.75; Band C4.

Barklamb, Peter Richard; Consul (Head of Post) Amsterdam since November 1998; born 18.7.51; FCO 1970; Delhi 1973; Islamabad 1975; Geneva 1976; Brussels 1978; FCO 1981; Warsaw 1984; Second Secretary (Chancery/Inf) Accra 1985; Second Secretary (Comm/Aid) Bridgetown 1989; Second Secretary (Commercial) Riyadh 1991; FCO 1994; Band C5; m 1974 Jane Bosworth (2d 1979, 1981; 1s 1984).

Barlow, Andrew Watson; FCO since October 1987; born 23.12.54; UKAEA 1977; FCO 1978; UKAEA 1981; PS to Chairman 1983/4; Band D6.

Barlow, Jacqueline; Third Secretary (Commercial) Kuwait since September 1997; born 21.7.47; FCO 1969; Berne 1969; Baghdad 1971; Islamabad 1972; Moscow 1973; Phnom Penh and Hanoi 1975; FCO 1976; Moscow 1977; Floater duties 1980; FCO 1984; Tokyo 1987; FCO 1990; Vice-Consul Shanghai 1994.

Barlow, Richard David; FCO since September 2000; born 17.1.75; Band C4; ptnr, Silvia Claudia Da Graça.

Barnard, Michael Trevelyan; FCO since October 1995; born 15.12.61; FCO 1986; Dar es Salaam 1989; Bratislava 1993; Band B3; m 1993 Tracy Dawn Clifford.

Barnes, Catherine Eleanor; Human Rights Officer Jakarta since January 1998; born 12.6.68; FCO 1995; Band B3.

Barnes, Nicholas John; FCO since September 2000; born 25.11.72; Band D6.

Barnes, Stewart George; First Secretary FCO since February 1991; born 8.7.48; FCO 1967; Tel Aviv 1973; SUPL 1980; Second Secretary FCO 1980; Second later First Secretary Vienna 1987; Band C5; m 1975 Jennifer Mary Windebank (1s 1977; 1d 1979).

Barnes Jones, Deborah Elizabeth Vavasseur (née Barnes); HM Ambassador Tbilisi since April 2001; born 6.10.56; FCO 1980; Moscow 1983; First Secretary on loan to Cabinet Office 1985; Resigned 1986; Reinstated 1988; First Secretary (Chancery) Tel Aviv 1988; First Secretary FCO 1992; Deputy Head of Mission Montevideo 1996; m 1986 Frederick Richard Jones (2d (twins) 1991).

Barnsley, Pamela Margaret; SUPL since November 1999; born 2.6.57; FCO 1982; Second Secretary (Chancery) Brasilia 1983; First Secretary (Comm/Econ) Peking 1987; Trade Commissioner BTC Hong Kong 1989; SUPL 1990; First Secretary FCO 1995; Band D6; m 1986 Perry Neil Keller (1d 1999).

Barnett, Robert William; Counsellor (Review of FCO Science and Technology) since September 1999; born 25.5.54; FCO 1977; Language Training SOAS 1979; Language Student, Kamakura 1980; Tokyo 1981; Second later First Secretary FCO 1983; First Secretary (Economic) Bonn 1988; Seconded to State Economics Ministry Dresden 1992; First Secretary FCO 1993; HM Ambassador Sarajevo 1994; Counsellor (Science Technology and Environment) Bonn 1995; m 1979 Caroline Sara Weale (2s 1982, 1984).

Barnett, Robin Anthony; Deputy Head of Mission Warsaw since July 1998; born 8.3.58; FCO 1980; Third later Second Secretary Warsaw 1982; Second later First Secretary FCO 1985; First Secretary UKDEL Vienna 1990; First Secretary UKMIS New York 1991; First Secretary FCO 1996; m(1)1989 Debra Marianne Bunt)(diss 1999)(1 step s1987, 1s 1990), (2) Tesca Maria Osman (1 step d 1990 1 step s 1990).

Barr, Christopher; Second Secretary FCO since September 1997; born 23.7.57; FCO 1975; Dublin 1979; FCO 1983; Sana'a 1988; FCO 1992; Third later Second Secretary (Political) Kuwait; Band C4; m 1982 Bronwyn Patricia Morrison (2s 1983, 1988; 1d 1984).

Barr, Richard Barclay; Second Secretary (Press & Public Affairs) since July 1997; Full Time Language Training January 1997; born 3.5.55; FCO 1975; Freetown 1977; FCO 1980; Prague 1981; Düsseldorf 1983; Accra 1988; FCO 1992 (Second Secretary 1994); m 1977 Jane Anne Greengrass (1s 1978).

Barras, Ian Alexander; FCO since March 1998; born 27.4.50; FCO 1976; Geneva 1979; Peking 1981; Douala 1984; FCO 1986; Athens 1989; FCO 1990; Washington 1991; Third Secretary (Information/Visits) Islamabad 1994; Band B3.

Barratt, Colin Ernest; Third Secretary (Management/Vice-Consul) Banjul since June 1999; born 2.3.62; FCO 1995. Band B3

Barrett, Douglas Wilson; Second Secretary (Commercial) Shanghai since February 2001; born 28.1.56; HCS 1976; FCO 1978; UKREP Brussels 1980; Havana 1983; Latin America Floater 1986; Islamabad 1988; T/D Manila 1992; T/D UKDEL Geneva 1993; FCO 1993; Second Secretary Management Officer/HM Consul Bombay 1996; m2000 Gayle Viegas.

Barrett, Janet Ceclyn; FCO since May 2000; born 19.12.67; HCS 1988; FCO 1994; UKMIS Geneva 1997; Band A2.

Barrett, Jill Mary; Assistant Legal Adviser FCO since 1997; born 6.7.58; Assistant Legal Adviser FCO 1989; First Secretary (Legal) UKMis New York 1994.

Barrett, Richard Martin Donne, OBE (1993); Counsellor FCO since October 1998; born 14.6.49; MOD 1975-81; First Secretary FCO 1982; First Secretary Ankara 1983; First Secretary FCO 1986; First Secretary UKMIS New York 1988; First Secretary later Counsellor FCO 1992; Counsellor Amman 1997; m 1973 Irene Hogg (1d 1976; 2s 1980, 1981).

Barrie, Patrica Ann (née Gallagher); FCO since October 1998; born 17.4.65; FCO 1988; Athens 1991; Montevideo 1993; Band A2; m 1993 Alexander Barrie (1d 1995; 1s 1998).

Barron, Elaine Marie; FCO since June 1993; Luxembourg 1991; born 30.1.63; FCO 1984; Istanbul 1988; Phnom Penh 1992; Band B3.

Barros, Lesley Susan; Riyadh since August 2000; born 2.5.60; FCO 1980; Brussels 1981; Havana 1982; Brasilia 1984; FCO 1987; Paris 1990; Tokyo 1993; Gibraltar 1996; Band B3; m 1989 José Barros Filho (2d 1991, 1994).

Barrow, Christine Louise; Lagos since May 1996; born 7.9.71; FCO 1991; Band B3; m 1998 David P J Hills.

Barrow, Sarah Jane (née Green); on loan to DTI since March 1995; born 8.6.64; FCO 1982; UKDEL OECD Paris 1985; San José 1988; FCO 1991; Band B3; m 1989; Diego Leonardo Barrow Clevas (1s 1991).

Barrow, Timothy Earle, LVO (1994); First Secretary UKREP Brussels since June 1996; born 15.2.64; FCO 1986; Language Training 1988; Second Secretary (Chancery) Moscow 1990; First Secretary FCO 1993.

Barrs, Neville Stuart; FCO since March 1987; born 20.5.55; FCO 1971; Nairobi 1978; FCO 1980; Dubai 1983; Band C4; m(1) 1978 Alison Cambers; m(2) 1983 Susan Rosemary Walker (1s 1985; 1d 1987).

Barson, Jacqueline Anne, MBE (1995); Olympic Attaché Sydney since September 1999; born 26.5.59; FCO 1979; Prague 1981; Belgrade 1982; Abu Dhabi 1982; Brunei 1985; UKMIS Geneva 1986; FCO since 1990; Copenhagen 1992; Brussels 1992; Athens 1993; Ottawa 1994; Band C5.

Barter, Craig Alan Roger; FCO since July 2001; born 24.7.69; HCS 1990; FCO 1996; Tehran 1999; Band A2; m2000 Lilis Purhaniah

Barton, Helen Mary; SUPL since October 1999; born 5.12.65; FCO 1991; Second Secretary (Political) The Hague 1996; m 1996 Alastair Matthew Wright.

Barton, Philip Robert, OBE (1997); Deputy High Commissioner Nicosia since July 2000; born 18.8.63; FCO 1986; Third later Second Secretary Caracas 1987. First Secretary on loan to the Cabinet Office 1991; First Secretary FCO 1993; First Secretary (Political) New Delhi 1994; On loan at No. 10 as Private Secretary to the Prime Minister January 1997; m (1) 1995 Sabine Friederike Schnittger (diss) (2) 1999 Amanda Joy Bowen.

Bassnett, Stephen Andrew, MBE (1983); First Secretary FCO since July 1999; born 24.1.49; Army 1967-86; FCO 1986; First Secretary (Chancery) Cairo 1991; First Secretary FCO 1993; First Secretary (Political) Bahrain 1997; Band D6; m 1980 Judith Christine Anne Whitty.

Bastin, Suzanne Sarah (née Baxter); Dubai since September 2000; born 3.7.69; Home Office 1989; Bombay 1994; Home Office 1994; Peking 1996; FCO 2000; Band B3; m 1998 David Richard Bastin.

Bastyan, Vivienne Elizabeth (née Stearns); Bonn later Berlin since March 1999; born 2.10.61; FCO 1991; Warsaw 1992; FCO 1993; Moscow 1996; SUPL 1998; Band A2; m 1995 Anthony James Bastyan (1d 1998).

Bateman, Peter; Counsellor (Commercial) Tokyo since March 1998; born 23.12.55; FCO 1984; Language Training Tokyo 1986; Second later First Secretary Tokyo 1987; First Secretary (FCO) 1991; First Secretary (Commercial) Berlin 1993; FCO 1997; m1985 Andrea Subercaseaux-Peters (2s 1987, 1990; 1d 1992).

Bates, Anthony Michael; MVO (1994); First Secretary (Management) and Consul Berne since August 2001; born 12.11.58; FCO 1978; Islamabad 1980; Wellington 1982; FCO 1987; Language Training 1990; Private Secretary Bonn 1990; Cayman Islands 1993; Second Secretary FCO 1996; Band C5; m 1985 Colette Ann Stewart (2d 1988,1992).

Bates, Michael Charles; OBE (1994); Consul-General Atlanta since April 2001; born 9.4.48; DSAO later FCO 1966; Delhi 1971; Third Secretary Moscow 1974; Second Secretary FCO 1977; Second, later First Secretary Singapore 1979; First Secretary (Inf/Chancery) Brussels 1983; On loan to No.10 Downing Street 1987; First Secretary FCO 1990; First Secretary Riga 1991; Chargé d'Affaires later HM Ambassador

Bratislava 1993; First Secretary FCO 1995; Deputy High Commissioner Bombay 1996; m 1971 Janice Kwan Foh Yin (1d 1977; 1s 1978).

Bates, Nicholas Hilary; Counsellor FCO since August 2001; born 5.2.49; Third later Second Secretary FCO 1973; Language Student 1976; FCO 1977; First Secretary UKMIS Geneva 1979; FCO 1983; Cairo 1984; First Secretary FCO 1988; First Secretary (Chancery) Muscat 1989; First Secretary FCO 1993; Counsellor (Regional Affairs) Kingston 1996; FCO 1997; Counsellor (Regional Affairs) Kampala 1998; m 1971 Rosemary Jane Seaton (3d 1973, 1975, 1976).

Batson, Philip David; Second later First Secretary FCO since October 1997; born 26.6.68; FCO 1987; Bombay 1991 Third Secretary Paris 1995.

Battson, Andrew John; SUPL since December 2000; born 8.5.66; FCO 1984; Bombay 1991; Bonn 1995; Port of Spain 1997; Band C4; m 1993 Andrea Jaun.

Batty, Simon Robert; Second Secretary Athens since September 2000; born 30.9.62; FCO 1982; New Delhi 1985; FCO 1989; Cairo 1990; Second Secretary FCO 1993; Second Secretary Bogotá 1997; Band C4; m 1991 Sharon Morris.(1d 1996, 1s 1998).

Batty-Smith, Katharine Amelia Louise; Prague since December 1999; born 19.8.64; FCO 1984; Budapest 1986; Brasilia 1988; Floater Duties 1992; On loan to the DTI 1994; Vice Consul Sana'a 1997; Band B3.

Bavinton, Sharon Jayne (née Vince); FCO since January 1999; born 17.12.58; FCO 1979; UKMIS New York 1981; FCO 1983; Canberra 1984; FCO 1987; Abu Dhabi 1989; FCO 1993; Overseas Inspectorate 1995; Band A2; Band B3; m 1982 Russell Alexander Bavinton (diss 1992).

Baxendale, James Lloyd; First Secretary (Political) Brussels since January 1999; born 23.2.67; FCO 1991; Language Training 1993; Language Training Cairo 1994; Second Secretary FCO 1995; First Secretary (Political) Amman 1997; Band D6; m 1996 Valerie Nathalie Bouchet (1s 2001).

Baxter, Alison Jane; Canberra since July 1993; born 15.5.67; FCO 1990; Islamabad 1992; Band B3.

Baxter Amade, Vicki Louise; FCO since September 2000; born 18.3.63; FCO 1982; T/D Luxembourg 1983; Lisbon 1984; Maputo 1987; FCO 1990; Khartoum 1993; Canberra 1996; Band B3; m 1990 Amade Chababe Amade (diss 2000) (1s 1992).

Baylis, Robin Grenville; OBE (1996) MVO (1981); Consul (Commercial) Miami since November 1996; born 9.11.41; Passport Office 1959; CRO 1963; Lagos 1963; Bonn 1967; FCO 1970; Detroit 1973; Canberra 1975; Second Secretary FCO 1978; Colombo 1981; Second Secretary (Comm) Washington 1983; First Secretary Port Stanley 1987; First Secretary FCO 1990; First Secretary

Antigua 1993; m(1) 1963 Camellia Elizabeth Idris-Jones (diss 1986); (2d 1964, 1966); (2) 1987 Kathleen Dawn Willetts.

Bayliss, Jill Elizabeth (née Hooper); Moscow since May 1998; born 3.8.68; FCO 1989; Colombo 1995; Band B3; m 1994 (Buster) IHW Bayliss.

Beach, Louise Eleanor, (née Horwood) FCO since July 1995; born 27.3.68; FCO 1989; Nicosia 1993; Second Secretary (Political) The Hague 1996; Band A2; m 1998 Charles Beach.

Beal, Gordon Kenneth; FCO since September 1988; born 21.10.53; MAFF 1978; FCO 1980; Port of Spain 1981; Paris 1983; Kuwait 1986; Band A2.

Beale, Gideon David; First Secretary FCO since May 1999; born 9.7.62; FCO 1986; Third Secretary/Vice Consul Athens 1990; Second Secretary FCO 1994; First Secretary (Political) Lagos later Abuja 1995; Band D6.

Beats, Lesley; FCO since July 1998; born 1.4.65; FCO 1988; Prague 1989; UKREP Brussels 1991; Phnom Penh 1994; UKREP Brussels 1996; Band B3.

Beattie, Phoebe; Brussels Embassy since April 1998; born 25.11.59; FCO 1984; Bangkok 1985; Stanley 1988; Floater Duties 1989; FCO 1993; Jakarta 1994; Band B3.

Beaumont, David Colin Baskcomb; High Commissioner Gaborone since November 1994; born 16.8.42; CRO 1961; Nairobi 1965; Bahrain 1967; Second Secretary 1969; FCO 1970; Second Secretary (Comm) Accra 1974; First Secretary FCO 1977; First Secretary (Aid) Kathmandu 1981; First Secretary and Head of Chancery Addis Ababa 1983; First Secretary later Counsellor FCO 1986; m 1965 Barbara Morris (1d 1970; 2s 1972, 1973).

Beaven, Keith Andrew; First Secretary FCO since August 1997; born 7.1.61; FCO 1983; Third later Second Secretary (Chancery) Mexico City 1986; First Secretary FCO 1988; First Secretary (Political) Pretoria 1993; Band D6; m 1986 Jane Marion Wells; (1s 1996, 1d 1999).

Beckett, Alison Joan; Second Secretary (Political) Bucharest since March 1999; born 1.7.61; FCO 1989; Third Secretary (Management/Cons) Kiev 1992; UKDEL OECD Paris 1996; Band C4.

Beckford, Charles Francis Houghton; First Secretary (Political) Nicosia since October 1999; born 4.11.63; FCO 1991; First Secretary (Political) Islamabad 1993; First Secretary FCO 1995; Band D6; m 1993 Clare Elizabeth Stourton (twin s 1997; 1d 1999).

Beckingham, Peter; Consulate-General Sydney since August 1999; born 16.3.49; BOTB 1974; Director BIS New York 1979; First Secretary FCO 1983; First Secretary (Commercial) Stockholm 1988; First Secretary, later Head of Political Section Canberra 1992; Director Joint Export

Promotion Directorate (FCO/DTI) 1996; m 1975 Jill Mary Trotman (2d 1980, 1982).

Bedford, Adrian Frederick; First Secretary and Deputy Head of Mission Beirut since December 1999; born 30.10.56; Land Registry 1975; FCO 1976; Islamabad 1978; Hanoi 1981; Johannesburg 1982; FCO 1985; Bogotá 1988; Second later First Secretary FCO 1992; Tehran 1996; Band D6; m 1995 Alexandra Pamela Cole.

Bedforth, Andrew Kenneth; Lagos since May 1995; born 18.2.71; Band B3; m 1994 Samantha Louise Stevens.

Bedingfield, Julian Peter; Deputy Head of Mission, Ljubljana since December 1999; born 23.7.45; FO 1964; language training 1968; Scientific Attaché Moscow 1969; FCO 1971; Düsseldorf 1971; Bonn 1973; Second Secretary (Comm) Dacca 1975; Ulaanbaatar 1977; FCO 1978; Second Secretary (Admin) and Consul Berne1982; Second Secretary (Chancery/Inf) Rabat 1986; Second later First Secretary FCO 1992; First Secretary UKDEL NATO Brussels 1994; First Secretary and DHM Ljubljana 1999; m 1975 Margery Mary Jones Davies (2d 1979, 1984; 1s 1982).

Bee, Stephanie Louise, MBE; Third Secrtary and Vice-Consul Yerevan since June 2001; born 27.1.67; FCO 1986; UKDEL Brussels 1988; Warsaw 1988; Moscow 1992; FCO 1995; Hong Kong 1998; Band B3.

Beer, Nicholas James Gilbert; Counsellor (Regional Affairs) Buenos Aires since June 1999; born 6.12.47; Second Secretary FCO 1976; Nairobi 1977; FCO 1979; First Secretary Madrid 1982; First Secretary FCO 1986; First Secretary later Counsellor (Political) The Hague 1992; FCO 1996; m 1975 Diana Eva Brooke (diss 1996) (1d 1977, 1s 1980).

Beeson, Richard John; FCO since July 2001; born 7.6.54; FCO 1973; East Berlin 1975; Damascus 1976; FCO 1977; UKREP Brussels 1978; Peking 1980; FCO 1983; Tripoli 1984; FCO 1986; Singapore 1988; Third Secretary (Management) and Vice Consul Hamburg 1991; Second Secretary FCO 1994; Full-time Language Training 1996; m(1) 1978 Kim Margaret Cotter; (2) 1989 Elizabeth Ann Allin.

Begbie, James Alexander; Deputy Consul Istanbul since May 1999; born 10.12.53; FCO 1973; Bahrain 1975; Middle East Floater 1979; FCO 1980; Tunis 1983; Shanghai 1986 Third later Second Secretary (Comm) Muscat 1989; FCO 1993; Band B3; m 1980 Janice Isobel Mills (1s 1984; 1d 1985).

Begbie, Janice Isobel (née Mills); Istanbul since October 1999; born 18.4.51; FCO 1971; Lusaka 1973; FCO 1975; Middle East Floater 1977; FCO 1980; SUPL 1983; Muscat 1989; SUPL 1993; FCO 1994(Second Secretary 1996); SUPL 1999; m 1980 James Alexander Begbie (1s 1984; 1d 1985).

Belcher, Patrick Fred; Hong Kong since December 1998; born 25.8.48; Royal Air Force 1965-90; LCD 1990-92; Prague 1992; Moscow 1994 World-wide Floater Duties 1996; Band B3; m 1971 Ann Carr (1s 1977).

Belgrove, David Raymond; Ottawa since April 1998; born 18.1.62; FCO 1982; Prague 1984; Kuwait 1986; FCO 1991; Third Secretary (Consular/Economic) Calcutta 1994 m1985 Mette Ofstad (2d 1986, 1989). Band C4;

Belfitt, Sandra Jane; Brasilia since August 1997; born 14.3.65; HM Customs and Excise 1986-93; FCO 1996; Band A2; m 1984 Andrew Belfitt (1d 1990, 1s 1993).

Bellham, Richard Anthony; FCO since 1998; born 26.1.50; HM Forces 1968-1974; FCO 1976; Bangkok 1986; FCO 1989; Tokyo 1995; Band C5; m 1987 Chidphan Jaiprasat (1d 1989).

Bell, Alan Douglas; Phnom Penh since March 2001; born 26.5.72; FCO 1995; Madrid 1997; Band A2.

Bell, Anne-Marie; Lima since November 1998; born 12.2.68; FCO 1993; Seoul 1996; Band A2.

Bell, Harvey Spencer; Second Secretary (Consular/Management) Calcutta since January 1999; born 7.7.45; Royal Navy 1960-72; FCO 1972; Bonn 1975; Peking 1977; Wellington 1980; FCO 1982; Mogadishu 1985; Milan 1988, FCO 1991; DTI 1993; Lagos 1995; m 1978 Wendy Lydia Frances Ellis.

Bell, Jeremy Paul Turnbull; First Secretary (United Nations) Nairobi since July 1998; born 4.1.52; FCO 1974; The Hague 1976; Bahrain 1981; Hanoi 1982; FCO 1985; Tokyo 1988; Third Secretary (Management/Cons) Gaborone 1992; Second Secretary FCO 1996; Band C5; m(1) 1978 Jane Dorron Lee (diss 1981) (2) 1991 Setsuko Yamamoto (1d 1995).

Bell, Julie Dawn (née Raines); Second Secretary (Management/Consular) Lilongwe since March 2001; born 12.11.66; FCO 1989; Language Training 1990; Moscow 1991; Budapest 1994; Belgrade 1995; Second Secretary FCO 1997; m 1991 Andrew Michael Bell (2d 1993, 1997).

Bell, Karen Ann (née Norris); Second Secretary (Commercial) Abuja since August 1999; born 22.4.66; FCO 1983; Strasbourg 1986; New Delhi 1988; FCO 1991; Ottawa 1996; Band C4; m 1987 Adrian Bell (2s 1993, 1996).

Bell, Kay Beverley; UKMIS New York since July 1993; born 11.6.57; FCO 1984; Bonn 1986; Floater Duties 1989; Band A2.

Bell, Laura (née Page); FCO since April 2000; born 6.9.69; FCO 1995; Algiers 1997; Bridgetown 1998; SUPL 1999; Band A2; m 1999 Ian McDonald Bell.

Bell, Mark Robert; Full Time Language Training Cairo since June 1999; born 4.5.71; FCO 1997; Band B3.

Bell, Melvin; UKMIS New York since November 1999; born 14.5.65; FCO 1984; Madrid 1987; FCO 1990; Third Secretary Mexico City 1993; FCO 1997; Band C4; m 1997 Maria Louisa Toxtle de Bautista.

Bell, Samantha Jane; Athens since April 1999; born 1.10.71; FCO 1997; Band A2.

Bellass, David Livingston; FCO since September 2000; born 6.11.74; Band C4.

Bellerby, Julie; FCO since September 1985; born 26.11.60; Band A1; m 1986 Andrew Patrick Myers.

Belof, Margaret Mary; Third Secretary (Economic) Athens since December 1998; born 6.9.61; FCO 1990; Third Secretary Bucharest 1994; Band B3.

Bendor, David Ian; First Secretary (Financial & Economic) Paris since March 1999; born 14.3.66; FCO Economic Advisers 1991-1996; T/D Paris 1993; On secondment to IMF (European Division) 1996-1998; Band D6.

Benjamin, Jon; FCO since May 2000; born 19.1.63; ODA 1986; FCO 1986; Third later Second Secretary Jakarta 1988; First Secretary FCO 1992; Private Secretary to Minister of State 1993; Full Time Language Training 1995; Ankara 1996; SUPL 1999; Band D7.

Bennett, Alexander; Paris since January 1998; born 4.11.67; FCO 1987; Band C4; m 1997 Deborah Karen Stirzaker.

Bennett, Brian Maurice; Deputy Head of Mission Tunis since May 1997; born 1.4.48; FCO 1971; Prague 1973; Helsinki 1977; Second Secretary FCO 1979; Second Secretary (Comm/Aid) Bridgetown 1983; Second later First Secretary UKDEL MBFR Vienna 1986; First Secretary (Chancery/Inf) The Hague 1988; First Secretary FCO 1992; m 1969 Lynne Skipsey (3s 1974, 1978, 1991).

Bennett, Frederick Michael; Peking since November 1997; born 7.12.49; Royal Military Police 1967-1992; Prague 1992; Floater Duties 1994; FCO 1997; Band B3; m 1978 Lynne Louise Jane Russell (2d 1979, 1980).

Bennett, Marylyn; Second Secretary (Chancery) Lilongwe since November 1996; born 16.12.48; New Delhi 1972; Monrovia 1974; FCO 1977; South America Floater 1979; FCO 1982; Floater duties 1983; Panama City 1986; Second Secretary FCO 1988; Deputy Head of Mission Asunción 1993.

Bennett, Stephen Paul; FCO since October 1997; born 28.10.62; FCO 1982; Nairobi 1986; FCO 1990; SUPL 1993; FCO 1994; Moscow 1995; Band A2; m 1990 Stephanie Cattermole (1 step d 1986, 1s 1991).

Bennett-Dixon, Vanessa May (née Bennett); Paris since July 2001; born 12.1.57; FCO 1975; Nairobi 1978; Havana 1981; Kuwait 1982; Montserrat 1988; Stanley 1992; Hanoi 1994; Luanda 1996; Band A2; m 1987 Ronald William Dixon.

Bensberg, Jacqueline Margaret (née Campbell); Third Secretary (Political) Brussels since November 1998; born 6.6.63; FCO 1983; Accra 1994; Cape Town/Pretoria 1985; UKDEL CSCE 1987; Third Secretary UKDEL CFE 1989; FCO 1990; Accra 1994; FCO 1997; Band B3; m 1991 Mark Bensberg (1d 1999).

Bensberg, Mark; Second Secretary (Political/Press & Public Affairs) Brussels since October 1997; born 19.7.62; FCO 1980; Paris 1982; Africa/ME Floater 1985; Vice-Consul Vienna 1988; FCO 1991; Accra 1994; m 1991 Jacqueline Margaret Campbell (1d 1999).

Berg, Geoffrey, MVO (1976); Deputy Consul General and Director of Trade New York since April 1997; born 5.7.45; CRO 1963; DSA 1965; LA Floater Duties 1968; Bucharest 1970; Second Secretary 1970; FCO 1971; Second later First Secretary (Inf) Helsinki 1975; FCO 1979; First Secretary (Comm) Madrid 1984; First Secretary FCO 1988; Counsellor on loan to the DTI 1990; Deputy Head of Mission Mexico City July 1993; m 1970 Sheila Maxine Brown (1s 1975).

Berman, Paul Richard; On loan to Attorney General's Chambers (LSLO) since September 2000; born 23.11.64; called to the Bar, Gray's Inn 1990; Assistant later Senior Assistant Legal Adviser FCO 1991; Seconded to International Committee of the Red Cross Geneva 1996; FCO 1998.

Berry, Susanna Gisela; SUPL since September 1997; born 6.9.62; FCO 1986; Second Secretary UKDEL Vienna 1989; Second Secretary (Economic) Vienna 1990; Full-time Language Training FCO 1992; Full-time Language Training Cairo 1993. FCO 1994; Band D6; m 1996 Paul Adams (1s 1999).

Bersin, Jacqueline; First Secretary (Management/ Consular) Singapore since November 1999; born 13.8.58; FCO 1977; SUPL 1978; Islamabad 1979; SUPL 1980; FCO 1981; Rome 1982; Warsaw 1983; FCO 1985; Port Louis 1988; Montserrat 1993; Second Secretary FCO May 1995; Band C5; m 1990 Alan Maurice Bersin.

Bertie, Julie Karina (née Finnigan); SUPL since October 1999; born 8.6.71; FCO 1990; Nairobi 1996; Band A2; m 1995 Stewart Valentine Bertie. (2d 1998, 2000).

Bertie, Stewart Valentine; Paris since October 1999; born 19.2.66; FCO 1986; UKMIS Geneva 1992; FCO 1995; SUPL 1996; Band A2; m 1995 Julie Karina Finnigan. (2d 1998, 2000).

Best, Christopher Davey; Second later First Secretary FCO since August 1989; born 3.8.47; Army 1966-69; FCO 1969; Muscat 1971; Jedda 1973; FCO 1974; Sana'a 1975; FCO 1976; Hong Kong 1981; Second Secretary Lagos 1986; Band C5; m 1971 Mary Elizabeth Cannon (4d 1977, 1979, 1981, 1982).

Best, Eleanor Marion; Copenhagen since May 2000; born 28.4.63; MOD 1986-1989; FCO 1996; Brussels Embassy 1997; Band A2.

Bethel, Samantha Claire Risby; Pro Consul Düsseldorf since July 1997; born 25.2.70; FCO 1990; Jakarta 1993; Band A2.

Betterton, Judith Anne; Amman since December 1998; born 2.8.57; FCO 1983; Warsaw 1984; Lilongwe 1987; Bogotá 1989; Canberra 1991; FCO May 1994; Band B3.

Bevan, Howard James; Pro Consul Düsseldorf since August 2000; born 19.11.54; Royal Signals 1970-1992; FCO 1995; UKREP Brussels 1997; Band A2; m 1973 Christine (1d 1975, 1s 1986).

Bevan, James David; FCO since July 1998; born 13.7.59; FCO 1982; Kinshasa 1984; Second later First Secretary UKDEL Brussels 1986; First Secretary FCO 1990; First Secretary Paris 1993; First Secretary (Political) Washington 1994; m 1984 Alison Janet Purdie (3d 1986, 1989, 1998).

Bevan, Terence Richard; First Secretary FCO since May 1992; born 10.4.54; FCO 1970; Bonn 1977; FCO 1980; Second later First Secretary Oslo 1988; Band C5; m 1978 Gillian Margaret Francis (2d 1981, 1984).

Bewley, Sarah Margaret; Second Secretary FCO since May 1999; born 5.8.73; FCO 1995; Kuala Lumpur 1997; Band C4.

Beynon, Debra Jane; Second Secretary (Immigration/Consular) Dhaka since July 1995; born 22.7.62; Dept of Transport 1978; Dept of Employment 1979; FCO 1983; BMG Berlin 1985; Kingstown 1988; Dhaka 1989; FCO 1993; m 1985 Paul Ogwyn Beynon.

Bibby, Sue Wendy; FCO since August 1994; born 12.1.67; MOD 1986; Band A2.

Bicker, David Alan; Anguilla since November 1998; born 25.10.48; Army 1966-88; UKDEL Brussels 1989; Cairo 1991; FCO 1994; Tirana 1996; Band B3; m 1974 Molly Patricia (1d 1976; 2s 1978, 1983).

Bickers, Esmé Lillian; FCO since June 2000; born 18.12.54; FCO 1988; Ottawa 1989; FCO 1992; The Hague 1997; Band A2.

Biggerstaff, Sarah Jane; FCO since April 2000; born 4.11.70; Budapest 1998; FCO 1977; Band A2.

Bielby, Richard Stephen; FTLT since November 1999; born 18.9.65; FCO (HCS) 1989; FCO 1991; Islamabad 1993; FCO 1997; Band B3.

Bilimoria, Tehemton Pirosha; Second Secretary Nairobi since August 2000; born 21.1.46; HM Forces 1964-70; PO 1970-76; FCO 1979; Washington 1984; FCO 1987; Paris 1992; Band C5; m 1980 Tayariez Dastoor (1d 1984; 1s 1986).

Billing, Victoria Elizabeth; Rangoon since June 1999; born 31.5.75; FCO 1997; SOAS University of London 1998; Band C4.

Billinger, Claire Louise; Vienna since August 1998; born 15.6.72; FCO 1990; Hong Kong 1995; FCO 1996; Band A2.

Binfield, Marella Jane; Warsaw since August 1996; born 12.1.69; FCO 1995; Band A2.

Binnie, Serena Clare; FCO since October 1990; born 4.9.63; FCO 1986; Montevideo 1989; Band C4.

Binns, Angela Jane; New Delhi since December 1993; born 25.6.69; MOD 1988-1990; FCO 1990; Band A2.

Birch, Ann Elizabeth (née Ridge); FCO since January 2000; born 23.10.62; FCO 1990; New Delhi 1992; FCO 1995; Hanoi 1997; Band B3; m 1996 Paul David Birch.

Bird, Charles Philip Glover; First Secretary (Political) Athens since September 1995; born 8.10.54; Second Secretary FCO 1986; Language Training 1987; Language Training Cairo 1988; Second Secretary (Chancery) Abu Dhabi 1989; Second Secretary Belgrade 1992; Second later First Secretary FCO 1993; m 1975 Clare St.John (2s 1978, 1980; 1d 1982).

Bird, Christabel Helen; Second later First Secretary FCO since May 1993; born 18.11.53; Tehran 1978; FCO 1979; Caracas 1980; FCO 1982; Second Secretary UKMIS Geneva 1989. Consul Geneva 1990; Band C5.

Bird, Juliette Winsome; First Secretary (Political) Brussels since April 2001; born 4.10.63; FCO 1990; New Delhi 1992; Second later First Secretary FCO 1994; Band D6.

Birks, Ian Martin; Second Secretary (Commercial) New Delhi since August 1997; born 3.6.52; FCO 1971; Canberra 1973; Belgrade 1976; Georgetown 1978; New York 1981; FCO 1984; Islamabad 1988; Second Secretary (Aid) Lagos 1992; Second Secretary FCO 1994; m(1) 1976 Sheridan Elizabeth Grice (diss 1997) (2d 1987, 1991); (2) Anny Bhatti 1997 (1d 1999).

Bish, Michael William; Second Secretary FCO since January 1992; born 3.12.42; CRO 1964; DSAO 1965; Rawalpindi 1966; Bonn 1970; FCO 1972; JAO Brussels 1976; Wellington 1979; Second Secretary FCO 1982; Second Secretary (Comm) Johannesburg 1987; m 1966 Patricia June Bedingfield.

Bishop, Peter George; Bonn since December 1998; born 23.11.55; Home Civil Service 1984; Band B3; m 1983 Fiona Christine Buchanan.(2s 1988,1992).

Biskin, Sally-Ann (née Peters); Second Secretary (Management) Islamabad since June 2001; born 8.2.65; FCO 1983; Brussels 1985; Harare 1988; Maputo 1989; Lagos 1989; Istanbul 1990; FCO 1993; SUPL 1994; FCO 1994; SUPL 1997 FCO 1998; Band C4; m 1991 Cneyt Cem Biskin (diss) (2d 1992, 1994).

Black, Peter John William; First Secretary FCO since January 2000. born 19.12.46; Army 1965-73; Second Secretary FCO 1973; Language Student MECAS 1975 and FCO 1976; Kuwait 1977; First Secretary (Inf) Amman 1980; First Secretary FCO 1983; First Secretary (Chancery) Dhaka 1987; FCO 1990; Deputy Head of Mission Skopje 1996; Band D6; m 1976 Fiona Rosaline Procter (2s 1981, 1982; 3d 1986, twins 1988).

Blackburn, Derek; Second later First Secretary FCO since August 1982; born 6.12.44; GPO 1961; FO (later FCO) 1968; Beirut 1969; FCO 1972; Islamabad 1973; FCO 1974; Washington 1979; Band C4; m 1967 Dorothy Margaret Fawcett (1s 1968; 1d 1972).

Blackburne, Alison; First Secretary (Political) Stockholm since April 2000; born 20.6.64; FCO 1987; Third later First Secretary (Chancery) Warsaw 1989; First Secretary FCO 1992; First Secretary UKMIS New York 1996; Band D6.

Blacker, Catherine Louise; T/D Islamabad since April 2000; born 15.9.68; FCO 1989; UKDEL Brussels 1991; FCO 1997; Band B3.

Blackwell, Christopher Robert; Second Secretary FCO since May 1984; born 11.8.58; FCO 1975; UKMIS Geneva 1978; FCO 1981; Aden 1983; Band C4; m 1982 Catherine Rose Gallagher (1d 1987; 1s 1989).

Bladen, John; Second Secretary FCO since February 1987; born 8.7.44; FCO 1971; Bangkok 1973; FCO 1975; Accra 1976; FCO 1979; Kingston 1980; FCO 1983; Second Secretary Harare 1984; m 1969 Nina Shaw (1d 1972).

Blair, Camilla Frances Mary; First Secretary FCO since November 1994; born 23.11.65; FCO 1988; Full-time Language Training 1990; Third later Second Secretary Prague 1991; m2000 Colin Roberts.

Blair, Katherine; Tokyo since December 1998; born 11.2.69; FCO 1988; Tokyo 1989; Colombo 1992; Peking 1993; Full Time Language Training 1997; Band B3.

Blake, Michael David; FCO since April 1984 (Second Secretary 1988) (First Secretary 1991); born 19.1.55; FCO 1971; HCS 1976; FCO 1978; Washington 1979; FCO 1981; Ottawa 1981; m 1978 Audrey Layfield (1s 1983).

Blake, Michael John Warwick; Consul (Political/Economic) Hong Kong since December 2000; born 5.3.75; FCO 1997; Full time language training Peking 1999; Band C4.

Blake, Stanley Clement; Second Secretary (Consular/Immigration) Accra since October 1993; born 14.7.44; FO 1964; UK Delegation NATO Paris and Brussels 1966; Amman 1969; FCO 1970; Moscow 1974; Paris 1975; FCO 1978; Tunis 1981 (Second Secretary 1984); Second Secretary (Admin) and Consul Muscat 1984; Second Secretary FCO 1988; Second Secretary (Management) Addis Ababa 1991; Second

Secretary FCO 1992; m(1) 1967 Marion Lesley Jelly (diss 1972) (1s 1968); (2) 1977 Lindsay Jane Townsend (1s 1981).

Blakemore, John Laurence; First Secretary and Consul, Lisbon since December 2000; born 21.1.44; RAF 1961-69; FCO 1969; Mexico City 1972; Caracas 1975; FCO 1978; on loan to DOE 1979; Second Secretary Buenos Aires 1981; Second Secretary (Commercial) Madrid 1982; Second later First Secretary FCO 1986; First Secretary (Commercial) Milan 1990; Consul Palma 1994; m 1967 Joan Eileen Black (2s 1972, 1974).

Blanchard, William Hume James, OBE (1997); MVO (1993); First Secretary (Chancery) Islamabad since December 1998; born 8.1.67; FCO 1988; Second Secretary (Information) Budapest 1992; Second Secretary FCO 1995; SUPL 1997; Band D6; m 1998 Meriel Beattie (1s 2000).

Blanche, Rachel Mignonne Bridget; Vice-Consul (Political) Jerusalem since June 2000; born 17.1.74; FCO 1997; Band B3; m2000 Stuart Duncan.

Blogg, David John; Second Secretary FCO since August 1998; born 8.9.48; FCO 1971; East Berlin 1973; Khartoum 1974; Dacca 1977; FCO 1979; Calcutta 1981; Baghdad 1982; Jedda 1983; Athens 1986; Second Secretary Tripoli 1989; Second Secretary FCO 1991; Second Secretary (Management/Consular) Sana'a 1993; Second Secretary Ulaanbaatar 1994; Second Secretary FCO 1995; Second Secretary Lima 1996; Consul (Management) St Petersburg 1997; m 1973 Susan Robinia Meloy.

Bloomfield, Keith George; FCO since October 1998; born 2.6.47; HCS 1969-80; UKREP Brussels 1980; First Secretary FCO 1985; Head of Chancery Cairo 1987; Counsellor, Consul-General and Deputy Head of Mission Algiers 1990; Counsellor (Political/Management) Rome 1994; Minister and Deputy Head of Mission Rome 1996; m 1976 Geneviève Paule (3d 1979, 1982, 1985).

Blows, Glyn Christopher; FCO since April 1999; born 27.8.70; FCO 1990; Nicosia 1995; Band A2.

Bloxham, Siân Landis; Bandar Seri Begawan since July 2000; born 11.11.64; HCS 1990; FCO 1996; St Petersburg 1998; Band A2.

Blunt, David Graeme, CVO (2001); Deputy Head of Mission and Consul General Oslo since July 1997; born 19.1.53; FCO 1978; Second later First Secretary Vienna 1979; First Secretary (External Affairs) Peking 1983; FCO 1987; First Secretary (Chancery) Canberra 1989; Counsellor FCO 1994; m 1975 Geirid Bakkeli (3s 1982, 1984, 1990).

Blyth, Fraser Alexander; born 7.6.69; FCO 1990; Sofia 1994; Peking 1996; Band B3; m 1994 Deborah Robertson.

Boam, Rachel Christine (née Wickens); PA/Ambassador Berlin since May 2000; born 5.11.68; FCO 1988; UKMIS New York 1991; PA/DHM Athens 1995; FCO 1998; SUPL 1999;

language training 1999; Band A2; m 1993 Jason Daniel Boam (1s 1999).

Boardman, Clarence Ronald; Deputy High Commissioner Bandar Seri Begawan since July 1995; born 11.12.48; DSAO/FCO 1965; Algiers 1970; Ottawa 1972; Warsaw 1974; FCO 1977; MECAS 1978; Aden 1979; Riyadh 1982; Second Secretary FCO 1986; Consul (Comm) Vancouver 1989; m 1973 Marion Lynn Fraser (1s 1991).

Boardman, Sarah Christine; Floater Duties since June 1996; born 17.8.67; FCO 1990; Third Secretary (UN) UKMIS Geneva 1993; Band D6.

Boffa, Sandra Jean (née Isaac); Vienna since November 1999; born 22.8.67; Ministry of Agriculture 1984-1990; FCO 1990; Tokyo 1995; FCO 1998; Band A2; m 1992 Anthony Paul Vincent Boffa (1d 1993, 2s 1994, 1998).

Bolton, Ada Winefride; Copenhagen since March 1997; born 26.12.44; Jakarta 1973; Rangoon 1978; FCO 1980; Sana'a 1988; Lagos 1989; UKDEL Brussels 1992; FCO 1996; Band A2.

Bond, Clare Elizabeth; Second Secretary (Political) Kuala Lumpur since August 1999; born 17.1.75; FCO 1997; Band C4.

Bond, Ian Andrew Minton; Counsellor UKDel OSCE Vienna since June 2000; born 19.4.62; FCO 1984; Third later Second Secretary (Political) UKDEL NATO Brussels 1987; First Secretary FCO 1990; First Secretary (Political) Moscow 1993; First secretary FCO 1996; m 1987 Kathryn Joan Ingamells (1d 1989, 1s 1993).

Bond, Simon; Dakar since March 2000; born 23.4.65; Port of Spain 1993; Home Office 1988-89; FCO 1989; Kampala 1997; FCO 1999; Band C4.

Bone, Roger Bridgland, CMG (1996); HM Ambassador Brasilia since September 1999; born 29.7.44; Third Secretary UKMIS New York 1966; FCO 1967; Stockholm 1968; Third later Second Secretary FCO 1970; First Secretary Moscow 1973; First Secretary FCO 1975; First Secretary UKREP Brussels 1978; Asst Private Secretary to the Secretary of State 1982; Harvard University (Center for International Affairs) 1984; Counsellor and later Head of Chancery Washington 1985; Counsellor FCO 1989; AUSS FCO 1991; HM Ambassador Stockholm 1995; m 1970 Lena Marianne Bergman (1s 1977; 1d 1980).

Bonnici, Gail Margaret; SUPL since December 1997; born 11.12.60; FCO 1984; Madrid 1985; LA Floater 1988; Valletta 1989; FCO 1991; Riyadh 1992; Buenos Aires 1996; Band A2; m 1990 Martin Mario Bonnici. (1s 1991).

Bonsey, Jennifer Elaine; Bucharest since January 2001; born 23.12.46; MOD 1964; FCO 1981; Paris 1982; Tunis 1985; UKREP Brussels 1988; FCO 1989; Singapore 1997; Band B3.

Booker, Jacqueline Alice; FCO since June 1997; born 19.1.62; FCO 1982; Athens 1984; Hanoi 1987; LA Floater 1988; FCO 1992; Dar es Salaam 1995; Band B3.

Boon, George Peter Richard; High Commissioner Yaoundé since January 1998; born 2.11.42; CRO 1963; Bombay 1966; Brussels 1969; Second Secretary 1970; Vienna 1971; Seconded to Department of Trade 1974; FCO 1975; The Hague 1978; First Secretary (Inf) BMG Berlin 1981; First Secretary FCO 1986; First Secretary (Political) Dhaka 1990; First Secretary FCO 1994; m 1971 Marie Paule Calicis (1s 1976).

Booth, Mark James; Hong Kong since November 1998; born 13.3.72; FCO 1991; UKMIS Geneva 1995; Band A2.

Booth, Susan Jane; (née Corcoran) FCO since March 1996; born 3.8.68; FCO 1986; UNGA UKMIS New York 1988; Cape Town/Pretoria 1989; Warsaw 1991; Rabat 1993; Band B3; m 1991 Rodney James Booth.

Borland, David; First Secretary (EU) Helsinki since January 2000; born 20.6.60; Second Secretary FCO 1991; T/D Second Secretary (Political) Maputo 1993; Second Secretary (Political) Caracas 1994; First Secretary (Political/Economic) Mexico City 1995; on loan to DTI; Band D6.

Borley, Salud Maria Victoria; FCO since August 1998; born 6.5.70; FCO 1989; Caracas 1992; Floater Duties 1996; Band B3.

Bossley, Edward; FCO since November 1999; born 22.9.71; FCO 1991; UKMIS New York 1994; Islamabad 1997; Band B3; m 1994 Stefany Elizabeth Rocque (1d 1997).

Bossley, Stefany Elizabeth (née Rocque); FCO since April 1999; born 28.7.66; FCO 1989; World-wide Floater Duties 1992; UKMIS New York 1994; Islamabad 1997; Band B3; m 1994 Edward Bossley (1d 1997).

Boswell, Clive Timothy; UKREP Brussels since July 1998; born 29.8.70; FCO 1996; Band A2.

Botha, Caroline Jane; Attaché (Immig/Cons) Colombo since August 2000; born 01.04.70; FCO 1996; Bratislava 1997; Band B3; m 1993 Peter Botha (1d 1994 1s 1998).

Bottomley, Patricia Fiona; First Secretary (Political) Rome since September 2000; born 29.3.59; FCO 1983 (Second Secretary 1985); Second Secretary and Vice-Consul Havana 1986; First Secretary (Chancery) Mexico City 1988; First Secretary FCO 1991; Brussels 1994; FCO 1998; Band D6; m 1997 Arno Baecker (1s 1999).

Bouakaze-Khan, Najma (née Khan); Istanbul since December 1999; born 11.6.67; FCO 1987; Addis Ababa 1989; UKDEL NATO Brussels 1993; FCO 1996; Full Time Language Training 1999; Band B3; m 1992 Didier Bouakaze-Khan (2s 1996, 1999).

Bourke, Martin; Deputy High Commissioner Wellington since May 2000; born 12.3.47; Third Secretary FCO 1970; Brussels 1971; Second Secretary Singapore 1974; Second later First Secretary FCO 1975; First Secretary Lagos 1978; FCO 1980; on loan to DOT 1980; Consul (Comm)

Johannesburg 1984; First Secretary FCO 1988; Governor Turks and Caicos Islands 1993; m 1973 Anne Marie Marguerite Hottelet (4s 1974, 1977, 1979, 1983).

Bousfield, Edward; Deputy High Commissioner Bandar Seri Begawan since May 1998; born 9.10.42; FO 1959; Moscow 1964; UK Mission Geneva 1965; Rabat 1968; FCO 1970; MECAS 1973; Kuwait 1974; Abu Dhabi 1976; Paris 1978; Second Secretary FCO 1981; Second Secretary (Aid/Comm) Suva 1984; Second Secretary (Management) Lusaka 1987; First Secretary FCO 1990; First Secretary (Development) Lilongwe 1993; m(1) 1975 Madeleine Jean Dart (1s 1979); m(2) 1986 Wan Noor Siha Wan Din.

Bowden, Christopher John; Maputo since June 2001; born 6.7.59; FCO 1977; Copenhagen 1979; Karachi 1982; Bucharest 1983; Paris 1985; FCO 1988; Calcutta 1991; Istanbul 1994; FCO 1998; Band C4; m 1983 Jane Susan Manville (1d 1986).

Bowden, James Nicholas Geoffrey; First Secretary (Economic) Riyadh since April 1999; born 27.5.60; Royal Green Jackets 1979-86; Second Secretary FCO 1986; Language Training 1988; Language Training Cairo 1989; Deputy, later Acting Consul-General Aden 1990; Second later First Secretary (Chancery) Khartoum 1991; First Secretary FCO 1994; Washington June 1996; m(1) 1985 Alison Hulme (diss) (1s 1993 1d 1995); m(2) 1999 Sarah Peaslee.

Bowe, Michael Henry; Second Secretary (Consular) Sarajevo since March 1997; born 8.3.46; FCO 1971; Lagos 1974; New Delhi 1978; FCO 1981; Second Secretary (Comm) Lilongwe 1982; Second Secretary (Comm) Gaborone 1986; Second Secretary FCO 1990; Second Secretary (Management) and Consul Maputo 1993; m(1) 1970 Anne Frances Ballard (diss 1985) (1d 1976, 1s 1979); m(2) 1985 Sandra Jean Brown Lassale.

Bowes, Andrew Martin; Third Secretary (Vice Consul/ Press and Public Affairs Maputo since July 1999; FCO 1997.

Bowes, Jacqueline; FCO since October 1990; born 28.2.60; Inland Revenue 1976-90, Band A2.

Bowie, Nigel John Graydon; First Secretary (Political) Abuja since January 1999; born 31.5.51; FCO 1975; Seoul 1977; Paris 1981; Athens 1983; Second Secretary FCO 1985; Second Secretary (Comm/Econ) Oslo 1988; First Secretary (Comm) Athens 1992; FCO 1997; m 1977 Mildred Alice Sansom (2s 1979, 1984; 1d 1982).

Bowling, Nicola Carron (née Jackson); Second Secretary Kuala Lumpur since April 1998; born 1.12.67; FCO 1991; Third Secretary (Aid/ Commercial) Maputo 1994; Band C4; m 1996 David John Robinson Bowling (1s 2000).

Bowman, Victoria Jane (née Robinson); SUPL since September 1999; born 12.6.66; FCO 1988; Third later Second Secretary Rangoon; First Secretary FCO 1993;); First Secretary

(Information/Press) UKREP Brussels; m 1991 Mark Andrew Bowman

Bowskill, Robert Colin; Tel Aviv since May 1998; born 21.9.43; Army 1959-77; Police 1977-84; Prague 1984; Lusaka 1987; Warsaw 1989; New Delhi 1991; Bucharest 1995; Band C4; m 1966 Jean Spencer (2s 1967, 1968).

Bowyer, Aileen Jane (née Gemmell); SUPL since January 1994; born 10.9.62; FCO 1983; Belgrade 1985; SUPL 1987; Kaduna 1990; FCO 1990; Band A2; m 1987 Anthony Harvey Bowyer (1d 1992).

Bowyer, Anthony Harvey; FCO since January 2001; born 21.11.62; FCO 1982; Belgrade 1984; Kaduna 1987; FCO 1990; Harare 1994; Band B3; m 1987 Aileen Jane Gemmell (1d 1992).

Bowyer, Joanne Louise; Toronto since June 2001; born 30.3.68; FCO 1989; Bogotá 1991; Abuja 1994; FCO 1998; Band B3.

Boxer, Peter John; Second Secretary (Political) Nicosia since September 1997; born 24.7.71; FCO 1995; Band C4.

Boyd, Andrew Jonathan Corrie, OBE (1992); Counsellor FCO since June 1999; born 5.5.50; Royal Navy 1968-80; FCO 1980; First Secretary (Econ) Accra 1981; FCO 1984; First Secretary (Chancery) Mexico City 1988; First Secretary FCO 1991; Counsellor Islamabad 1996; m 1979 Ginette Anne Vischer (2s 1985, 1987, 1d 1991).

Boyden, Simon Denis, Second Secretary (Commercial) Moscow since March 1999; born 24.2.68; FCO 1997; Band C4; m 1998 Geraldine Gallagher.

Boyles, Elizabeth; Second Secretary (Trade Policy) UKREP Brussels since August 2000; born 28.8.67; FCO 1990; Third Secretary (Political) Brussels 1994; UKMIS New York 1996; DHM San Salvador 1997; Band C4; m 1997 Patrick Dens.

Bradbury, Jonathan Edward; Dublin since August 2000; born 16.12.67; HCS 1989-1995; Nairobi 1997; Band A2; m 1994 Rebecca Clare Sebborn. (2s 1998, 2000).

Bradford, Peter; Riyadh since September 1999; born 30.1.54; Royal Navy 1971-94; FCO 1994; Paris 1996; Band A2; m 1976 Rosemary Ann Slater (2s 1977, 1983; 1d 1979).

Bradley, Guy; FCO since April 1987; born 3.2.62; FCO 1981; New Delhi 1983; Band C5; m 1987 Andrea Stannard. (1s 1993, 1d 1994).

Bradley, Henry Alexander Jarvie; First Secretary UKDEL OSCE Vienna since May 2000; born 23.7.52; HM Customs and Excise 1969; FCO 1971; EC Brussels 1975; Budapest 1978; Bahrain 1979; FCO 1982; Munich 1984; Third Secretary (AO/Vice-Consul) Maseru 1987; Second Secretary FCO 1992; Deputy High Commissioner Banjul 1996; Band C5; m 1979 Gabriella Maria Schwery.

Bradley, Joseph Maxwell; Second Secretary UKMIS Geneva since November 1998; Third

Secretary (Information) Berlin 1995; born 14.2.60; FCO 1978; East Berlin 1981; Resigned 1983 (Reinstated 1986); Lusaka 1987; UKDEL Vienna 1990; FCO 1993; Full-time Language Training 1995; m 1987 Melanie Rose (2d 1988, 1992, 1s 1990).

Bradley, Stephen Edward; Counsellor and Director of Trade Paris since June 1999; born 4.4.58; FCO 1981; Language Training 1982; Second later First Secretary Tokyo 1983; SUPL 1987; Deputy Political Adviser Hong Kong 1988; SUPL 1993; FCO 1995; m 1982 Elizabeth Gomersall (1s 1985).

Bradley, Susan Pauline; Pretoria since February 1999; born 16.5.62; FCO 1987; FCO 1996; Band A2.

Bradley, Timothy Gawin, OBE (1991); First Secretary FCO since May 1999; born 3.6.59; FCO 1983; Language Training 1984; Second later First Secretary (Chancery) Kuwait 1986; First Secretary FCO 1989; Belgrade 1996; Band D6; m 1990 Kathleen Scanlon (3s 1993, 1995, 1997).

Bradshaw, John Vincent; New Delhi since November 2000; born 19.8.64; FCO 1999; Band B3; m 1994 Doris Jungling (2s 1994, 1996).

Bradshaw, Philip James; FCO since June 1993; born 11.6.70; FCO 1988; SUPL 1990; Band A2.

Braidford, Lindsey; FCO since February 1988; born 20.4.47; Jedda 1975; Belize 1976; The Hague 1979; Rangoon 1982; Pretoria/Cape Town 1984; Band B3.

Braithwaite, Angela; Moscow since May 1992; born 13.11.1970; FCO 1989; Band A2.

Braithwaite, Julian Nicholas; Prime Minister's Speech Co-ordinator since June 2000; born 25.7.68; Second Secretary FCO 1994; seconded to ICFY Zagreb 1995; Second later First Secretary (Chancery) Belgrade 1996; on loan to No10 Press Office 1998; seconded to SHAPE 1999; m 1999 Biljana Njagulj (1d 2000).

Bramley, Sheila Jane; Second Secretary (Commercial) Islamabad since October 1998; born 25.10.63; FCO 1982; Tokyo 1984; Sofia 1987; SE Asia/FE Floater 1989; FCO 1991; Kuala Lumpur 1994; Canberra 1995.

Brammer, Geoffrey Ian; Second Secretary (Management)Bridgetown since July 1998; born 9.6.65. FCO 1985; Kaduna 1987; Nassau 1990; Tehran 1991; FCO 1992; Deputy Head of Mission Ashgabat 1995; Band B3; m 1991 Shelley Diane Chalmers.

Brandon, William Roland; First Secretary (Political) Singapore since April 2001; born 7.6.64; FCO 1993; First Secretary (Economic) Vienna 1996; First Secretary FCO 1999; Band D6; m 1991 Polly Jennifer Nyiri (3d (twins) 1996, 1998).

Brannigan, Virginia (née Reynolds); SUPL since July 1999; born 16.1.62; FCO 1985; San José

1986; Madrid 1990; FCO 1998. Band A2; m 1992 Stuart Patrick Brannigan.

Brant, Astrid Lorita Sophia; Tunis since December 1992; born 27.2.53; DHSS 1980-91; FCO 1991; Band A2.

Brant, Sharon Linda (née Acheson); Third Secretary (Chancery) Dublin since July 2001; born 15.2.73; FCO 1992; Kuala Lumpur 1995; Kingston 1997; Band B3; m 1996 Andrew Brant.

Braun, David Alan; FCO since February 2000; born 27.2.71; FCO 1991; Madrid 1998; Band B3; m 1998 Susan Jane Robottom.

Brazier, Colin Nigel; Consul (Commercial) New York since September 2000; born 31.10.53; FCO 1973; Warsaw 1976; Singapore 1977; Accra 1980; FCO 1982; Dhaka 1985; Third Secretary (Comm) later Second Secretary (Development) Kingston 1989; Second Secretary FCO 1992; Deputy High Commissioner Georgetown 1997; m 1975 Jane Anne Pearson (1d 1979, 1s 1983).

Brear, Andrew James; First Secretary (Political) Stockholm since March 2000; born 28.1.60; Army 1979-90; Second later First Secretary FCO 1991; First Secretary (Inf) Santiago 1994; First Secretary FCO 1997; Band D6; m 1986 Jane Susan Matthews (1d 1991, 1s 1993).

Breeze, Christopher Mark; First Secretary (Political) Ankara since December 1997; born 13.8.63; FCO 1985; Second Secretary (Chancery) Nicosia 1988; Second later First Secretary FCO 1991; First Secretary (Trade Policy) New Delhi 1994; Band D6; m 1990 Janet Suzanne Champion (2d 1995, 1998).

Brennan, Anthony Bradford; Second Secretary (Economic/KHF) Prague since August 1996; born 6.2.66; FCO 1994.

Brenton, Anthony Russell, CMG (2001); Minister, Washington since January 2001; born 1.1.50; FCO 1975; MECAS 1977; First Secretary Cairo 1978; FCO 1981; Presidency Liaison Officer Brussels (Embassy) 1982; FCO 1982; First Secretary (Energy) UKREP Brussels 1985; on loan to European Commission 1986; Counsellor FCO 1989; CDA Harvard University 1992; Full-time Language Training 1993; Counsellor (Economic/Aid/Scientific) Moscow 1994; Director FCO 1998; m(1) 1971 Susan Mary Blacker (diss 1978); (2) 1982 Susan Mary Penrose (1s 1984; 2d 1987, 1988).

Brenton, Jonathan Andrew; First Secretary (Economic) Moscow since March 1999; born 24.12.65; FCO 1994; Moscow 1996; Band D6.

Brett, David Lawrence; First Secretary FCO since April 1996; born 20.9.52; FCO 1978; Tehran 1980; Chicago 1983; FCO 1986; Second Secretary (Chancery) Kingston 1989; Consul-General Alexandria 1992; m 1984 Carol Sue Lane (2s 1986, 1991, 1d 1988).

Brett, Rebecca Louise (née Fenwick); Colombo since September 2000; born 27.11.64; FCO 1984;

Washington 1987; The Hague 1990; SUPL 1992; FCO 1994; Band B3; Abu Dhabi 1996; m 1987 Paul Brett (2d 1992; 1996, 1s 1994).

Brett, Russell Michael; FCO since January 1999; born 14.9.69; FCO 1989; Athens 1995; Band B3; m 1999 Simone Walsh (1d 2000).

Brett Rooks, Bedelia, LVO; FCO since August 2001; born 9.12.46; FCO 1969; 1993; On loan to SEATO Bangkok 1972; Copenhagen 1975; Rome 1976; Second Secretary FCO 1978; Second Secretary Accra 1983. UKREP Brussels 1986; First Secretary FCO 1987; First Secretary (Inf) BMG Berlin 1989; First Secretary FCO 1993; First Secretary Brussels 1996.

Brettle, Lynda Elizabeth; Mexico City since July 2000; born 2.10.62; FCO 1980; Tokyo 1983; FCO 1985; SE Asia Floater 1987; Islamabad 1988; SUPL 1992; FCO 1993; Second Secretary (Management) and Consul Caracas 1997; Band C5; m 1994 Michael Anthony Cockman (1d 1994).

Brewer, Dr Jonathan Andrew; Counsellor (Political Affairs) Moscow since August 1998; born 20.3.55; FCO 1983; Second later First Secretary Luanda 1986; First Secretary FCO 1988; First Secretary (Chancery) Mexico City 1991; Counsellor FCO 1995; m(1) 1978 Tessa Alexandra Swiney (diss. 1990). (2) 1993 Angela Margarita Sosa Teran.

Brewer, Lesley Ann; Tripoli since March 2000; born 29.7.57; FCO 1995; Prague 1997; Band A2.

Brewer, Nicola Mary; Counsellor New Delhi since June 1998; born 14.11.57; FCO 1983; Second Secretary (Chancery) Mexico City 1984; First Secretary FCO 1987; First Secretary (Economic) Paris 1991; SUPL 1994; Counsellor FCO 1995; m 1991 Geoffrey Charles Gillham (1d 1993, 1s 1994).

Bridge, Heather Susan (née Brown); Second Secretary Skopje since April 2000; born 19.4.62; FCO 1985; Band C4; m 1986 Christopher Martin Gibbons Bridge (2d 1990, 1992).

Bridge, Karen Maria; (née Chadbourne); Riyadh since January 1999; born 3.9.70; FCO 1990; UKREP Brussels 1993; FCO 1995; UKREP Brussels 1996; FCO 1997; SUPL 1998; FCO 1998; Band A2; m 1992 Peter Charles Benson Bridge.

Bridge, Richard Philip; Counsellor FCO since July 2001; born 24.3.59; FCO 1984; Second Secretary (Inf) Warsaw 1986; FCO 1988; First Secretary (Chancery) Moscow 1989; FCO 1993; Counsellor New Delhi 1998; m 1994 Philippa Anne Leslie-Jones (2s 1995, 1997).

Bridges, Stephen John; HM Ambassador Phnom Penh since December 2000; born 19.6.60; FCO 1980; Africa/ME Floater 1983; Luanda 1984; Third later Second Secretary (Comm) Seoul 1987; Second later First Secretary FCO 1992; First Secretary Kuala Lumpur 1996; m 1990 Yoon Kyung Mi.

Bridgwood, Alistair Charles Jeudwine; FCO since September 2001; born 12.5.73; Band C4; m2001 Rachel Beale.

Brier, Lucy Jane; (née Richardson); SUPL since December 2000; born 18.3.69; FCO 1995; Kuala Lumpur 1997; Band A2; m 1996 Simon Richard Brier.

Brier, Simon Richard; Kuala Lumpur since June 1997; born 15.9.67; FCO 1987; Prague 1989; SE Asia/Far East Floater Duties 1991; FCO 1994; m 1996 Lucy Jane Richardson.

Brierley, David Anthony; Kuwait since March 1996; born 14.10.47; Royal Marines 1965; Budapest 1987; Madrid 1989; FCO 1991; Band B3; m 1993 Denise Mary Jones (1s 1998).

Brigden, Neil Stephen; Second Secretary (Commercial) New Delhi since October 2000; born 7.8.68; Colombo 1989; Bucharest 1992; Sana'a 1995; FCO 1996; Band C4.

Brigenshaw, David Victor; First Secretary FCO since April 1998; born 1.6.56; FCO 1973; Nairobi 1976; FCO 1981; Kuala Lumpur 1983; Third Secretary (Comm) Quito 1986; Second Secretary FCO 1990; m 1977 Yvonne Lesley Bush.

Briggs, Geoffrey; Second Secretary FCO since July 1997; born 20.2.64; FCO 1988, Third Secretary (Econ/Aid) Cairo 1990; Second Secretary FCO 1992; Tirana 1995; Band C4.

Bright, Colin Charles; FCO since April 1998; born 2.1.48; Second Secretary FCO 1975; First Secretary Bonn 1977; FCO 1979; on loan to Cabinet Office 1983; Consul BTDO New York 1985; Counsellor and Head of Chancery Berne 1989; Consul-General Frankfurt 1993; m(1) 1978 Helen-Anne Michie (diss 1990); (2) 1990 Jane Elizabeth Gurney Pease (1s 1992, 1d 1995).

Brimfield, Valerie; Bucharest since November 1997; born 27.7.49; FCO 1979; Tunis 1980; Tehran 1983; New Delhi 1985; Dhaka 1989; Ottawa 1992; FCO 1995; Tokyo 1996; Band B3.

Brind, Kevin James; Second Secretary FCO since April 1998; born 5.10.59; FCO 1977; Bonn 1980; Khartoum 1982; Moscow 1986; FCO 1987; Canberra 1990; Third Secretary (Development) Kathmandu 1993; Second Secretary, Deputy Head of Mission Ulaanbaatar 1997; m 1983 Jane Louise Burns.

Brinkley, Robert Edward; Head of (FCO/Home Office) Joint Entry Clearance Unit since March 2000; born 21.1.54; FCO 1977; Third Secretary UKDEL Comprehensive Test Ban, Geneva 1978; Language Training 1978; Second Secretary Moscow 1979; First Secretary FCO 1982; First Secretary (Pol/Mil) Bonn 1988; First Secretary later Counsellor FCO 1992; Counsellor (Political) Moscow 1996; m 1982 Frances Mary Webster (3s 1982, 1984, 1989).

Bristow, Dr Laurence Stanley Charles; Ankara since June 1999; born 23.11.63; FCO 1990; Full-time Language Training 1991; Second Secretary

(Chancery Inf) Bucharest 1992; First Secretary FCO 1995; Private Secretary to Minister of State 1996; Full Time Language Training 1998; m 1988 Fiona McCallum.

Britt, Alan Arthur; FCO since October 1985; born 17.4.44; CRO 1961; Calcutta 1965; Washington 1968; Bogotá 1971; FCO 1972; Port of Spain 1975; Second Secretary FCO 1978; Manila 1982; m 1965 Mary Lilian Draper (1s 1965; 1d 1966).

Britton, Catherine Mary; FCO since July 1988; First Secretary 1989; born 13.4.61; FCO 1983; Dar es Salaam 1985; m 1986 Rhodri James Lewis Britton.

Bromley, Peter Richard Ober; Deputy High Commissioner Port of Spain since January 2000; born 14.10.47; FCO 1966; Kuala Lumpur 1970; Dacca 1973; Georgetown 1976; on loan to DoT 1980; Oslo 1982; Second Secretary (Comm) Dubai 1984; Second Secretary FCO 1987; Second later First Secretary (Dev) Lilongwe 1989; Deputy High Commissioner Maseru 1993; First Secretary FCO 1995; Band D6; m 1978 Yasmin Amna Majeed (2s 1981, 1984).

Bronnert, Deborah Jane; FCO since October 1999; born 31.1.67; DOE 1989; Royal Commission on Environmental Pollution 1990; UKREP Brussels 1991; DOE 1993; FCO 1994; on secondment to European Commission (Kinnock Cabinet) 1995; Band D7.

Bronson, Rodney Charles; Canberra since October 1999; born 9.8.46; FCO 1971; Brussels 1974; FCO 1977; Moscow 1977; Copenhagen 1980; Cairo 1984; Second Secretary FCO 1988; Second Secretary Singapore 1991; m 1968 Margaret Ann Williams (2d 1972, 1974).

Brook, John Edwin; FCO since November 1997; born 21.3.45; FO 1964; Moscow 1967; Latin America Floater 1970; Calcutta 1972; Second Secretary FCO 1975; Second Secretary (Comm) Moscow 1978; Second later First Secretary Berne 1981; First Secretary (Comm) East Berlin 1984; First Secretary on attachment to JSDC 1988; First Secretary FCO 1989; Full-time Language Training 1993; Consul-General Stuttgart 1993; m 1981 Moira Elizabeth Lands (1d 1983, 1s 1986).

Brook, Simon Douglas; FCO since February 1989; born 5.2.61; FCO 1982; Geneva 1986; Band B3; m 1995 Lesley June Holmwood.

Brooke, Sandra Jane; SUPL since May 1994; born 21.8.63; FCO 1985; Algiers 1987; FCO 1989; Bahrain 1991; Band A2; m 1991 Jean-Marc Jefferson. (1s 1993).

Brookes, Carter, MBE (1990); FCO since December 1992; born 13.12.46; FCO 1971; Saigon 1973; FCO 1974; St Helena 1976; FCO 1978; Singapore 1980; FCO 1983; Moscow 1986; New Delhi 1989; Beirut 1991; Band B3; m 1971 Margaret Jean Stewart (3s 1974, 1976, 1977).

Brookes, Diana Lorriane, Legal Counsellor FCO since December 1999; born 19.4.64; Solicitor

1989; Assistant Legal Adviser FCO 1989; First Secretary (Legal) UKREP Brussels 1995; FCO 1998; m 1990 Gerard Blais (1d 1999).

Brookes, Maurice John; Third Secretary (Immigration/Visa) Harare since August 1997; born 14.6.49; FCO 1968; Accra 1971; Aden 1972; Nairobi 1974; Karachi 1976; FCO 1978; Tehran 1981; FCO 1982; Kampala 1982; FCO 1985; Paris 1986; Warsaw 1989; FCO 1989; Abidjan 1993; Band B3.

Brooking, Karen (née Moore); FCO since November 1995; born 15.7.64; FCO 1987; Peking 1990; FCO 1992; SUPL 1994; Band A2.

Brooking, Stephen John Allan; First Secretary FCO since June 2001; born 13.3.64; FCO 1986; Second Secretary (Econ) Peking 1989; Second Secretary FCO 1992; First Secretary (Political) Sarajevo 1994; FCO 1995; First Secretary (ESCAP) Bangkok 1998; Band D6.

Brooks, Helen Katherine; First Secretary FCO since September 1999; born 21.6.67; FCO 1991; on loan to the Hong Kong Government 1994; Hong Kong 1997; SUPL 1998; Principal Research Officer.

Brooks, Shelagh Margaret Jane; UKREP Brussels since October 1998; FCO 1979; On loan to Hong Kong Government 1987; Legal Counsellor; FCO 1991.

Brooks, Stuart Armitage, CMG (2001), OBE (1991); Counsellor FCO since October 1997; born 15.5.48; Third Secretary FCO 1970; Vice-Consul (Dev) Rio de Janeiro 1972; Second Secretary on loan to HCS 1974; Second later First Secretary Lisbon 1975; FCO 1978; Moscow 1979; First Secretary FCO 1982; Stockholm 1987; First Secretary FCO 1991; Counsellor Vienna 1993; m 1975 Mary-Margaret Elliott (2d 1977, 1980).

Broom, David Charles; Second Secretary (Commercial) Kuala Lumpur since May 1996; born 17.9.54; FCO 1973; Islamabad 1975; FCO 1976; UKREP Brussels 1977; Baghdad 1981; Home Civil Service 1982; FCO 1983; Rome 1986; FCO 1989; Paris 1989; Second Secretary FCO 1993; m 1976 Diana Josephine Hewer (1s 1978; 1d 1989).

Broom, Peter David; Consul-General Cape Town since July 2000; born 7.8.53; FCO 1970; Oslo 1974; Jedda 1977; Islamabad 1979; FCO 1981; Mbabane 1984; New Delhi 1987; Second Secretary FCO 1989; Consul (Commercial) Brisbane 1991; First Secretary (Commercial), Consul and DHM Yaoundé 1997; Band C5; m 1976 Vivienne Louise Pyatt (5d 1979, 1981, 1985, 1988, 1994).

Broomfield, David Norman; Consul Commercial Barcelona since July 1998; born 21.5.54; FCO 1973; Banjul 1975; LA Floater 1978; Prague 1980; FCO 1983; Tripoli 1986; Second Secretary (Chancery/Inf) Lusaka 1987; Vice-Consul Naples 1991; First Secretary FCO 1995.

Brosnan, Sheryl (née Landman); Abidjan since October 2000; born 5.12.71; FCO 1991; Bangkok 1993; Istanbul 1997; m 1994 Mark Paul Brosnan (2s 1998, 2000).

Broucher, David Stuart; UK Permanent Representative to the Conference on Disarmament in Geneva since October 2001; born 5.10.44; FO 1966; Berlin 1968; Second Secretary on loan to Cabinet Office 1972; First Secretary 1973; First Secretary Prague 1975; FCO 1978; First Secretary (ECOFIN) UKREP Brussels 1983; Counsellor (Comm/Aid) Jakarta 1985; Counsellor (Econ) Bonn 1989; Counsellor later AUSS FCO 1994; HM Ambassador Prague 1997; m 1971 Marion M Blackwell (1s 1972).

Broughton, Sarah; Second Secretary (Economic/Social) UKMIS New York since December 1999; born 12.8.66; FCO 1984; Ottawa 1987; Lilongwe 1990; Floater 1992; FCO 1995; Full time language training 1999; Band C4.

Brown, Alexander Mark; Ashgabat since December 1997; born 21.7.64; DHSS 1986; FCO 1988; Lagos 1991; FCO 1992; Full-time Language Training 1993; Hamburg 1994; Band B3; m 1997 A Gehrke.

Brown, Alexander Nicholas Seaton; FCO since September 2000; born 31.7.72; Band C4.

Brown, Andrew Paul; Third Secretary Seoul since May 1998; born 12.10.68; FCO 1987; UKMIS New York 1991; FCO 1994; Band B3; m 1998 Joanna Beresford.

Brown, Christine Audrey Frances; Attaché (Aid) Dhaka since May 1991; born 22.6.51; FCO 1970; New Delhi 1971; Lagos 1973; Bucharest 1975; Kuala Lumpur 1977; FCO 1981; Floater Duties 1982; FCO 1985; Johannesburg 1988; Band B3.

Brown, Deirdre Rebecca (née Herdman); FCO since October 1998; born 19.7.66; FCO 1986; Dhaka 1988; FCO 1992; Third Secretary (Political/Economic) Bangkok 1995; Band C4; m 1991 Stephen William Brown (1d 1992, 1s 1994).

Brown, Donald Leslie, CBE (1997); Deputy Consul-General and Counsellor (Management); New York since January 1994; born 30.6.40; FO 1957; Dakar 1961; FO 1962; Vice-Consul Moscow 1965; Vancouver 1968; Second Secretary (Comm) Kampala 1969; FCO 1973; Second Secretary (Commercial) Moscow 1974; Ottawa 1977; First Secretary and Consul (Comm) Edmonton 1978; FCO 1982; First Secretary later Counsellor (Admin) and Consul-General Tokyo 1984; Counsellor (Comm) Moscow 1988; Counsellor FCO 1992; m 1962 Pamela Patricia Wright (1d 1963; 1s 1969).

Brown, Edward James Murch, MBE (1991); Second Secretary UKMIS Geneva since April 1996; born 27.8.59; FCO 1978; Bonn 1980; Prague 1983; Rabat 1985; FCO 1987; Düsseldorf 1992; FCO 1995; m 1980 Hannah Jane Gibbons.

Brown, Gordon William; First Secretary and HM Consul Cairo since May 2001; born 17.10.54; Inland Revenue 1975; FCO 1976; Guatemala City 1979; The Hague 1981; SE Asia Floater 1983; Kampala 1985; FCO 1988; Second Secretary (Man and Consul) Havana 1991; Second Secretary (Management) and HM Consul Muscat 1995; British Trade International 1998; m 1985 Rosalind Patricia Harwood (2s 1992, 1993).

Brown, Herbert George, MBE (1981); FCO since February 2001; born 2.1.43; FO 1964; Rawalpindi 1966; Kuala Lumpur 1969; FCO 1973; Barcelona 1975; Maseru 1978; FCO 1981; Second Secretary and Vice-Consul Baghdad 1982; on loan to DTI 1985; First Secretary (Comm) Rio de Janeiro 1988; First Secretary FCO 1990; HM Consul later HM Consul-General Cape Town 1996; m 1975 Susan Atkin (1d 1977).

Brown, John Mark; Damascus since March 1999; born 15.5.43; RAF 1962-1984; Islamabad 1990; Belgrade 1993; Moscow 1996; Band B3; m 1965 Carole Elizabeth Thompson (2d 1966, 1970).

Brown, Linda; Moscow since January 1996; born 24.12.55; FCO 1974; Bonn 1977; FCO 1980; Budapest 1980; Oslo 1982; FCO 1985; Rome 1992 Band B3.

Brown, Richard Anthony; FCO since January 1996; born 29.10.72; Band B3.

Brown, Simon Nicholas; Second Secretary Tokyo since October 2000; born 19.7.73; FCO 1997; Full time language training 1998; Full time language training Kamakura 1999; Band C4.

Brown, Sir Stephen (David Reid); KCVO (1999); High Commissioner Singapore since March 2001; born 26.12.45; HM Forces 1964-76; FCO 1976; First Secretary Nicosia 1977; First Secretary (Comm) Paris 1980; FCO 1985; Temporary Duty DTI 1989; Consul-General Melbourne 1989; Counsellor (Commercial) Peking 1994; HM Ambassador Seoul 1997; Pre Post Training FCO 2000; m 1966 Pamela Gaunt (1s 1965; 1d 1969).

Brown, Stephen Leonard; Riyadh since July 1999; FCO 1998; born 7.3.56; Army 1974-96. Band A2; m 1978 Gaynor Ruth (2d 1974 ,1982).

Brown, Stephen Michael; Third Secretary (Management) Almaty since February 2000; born 9.6.63; Household Cavalry 1980-1995; FCO 1997; Mostar 1997; Amman 1998; Band B3.

Brown, Stuart James; Kiev since August 2001; born 29.4.75; FCO 1994; Band B3; ptnr, Fiona Brougham.

Brownbill, Timothy Patrick; On loan to the DTI since September 2000; born 6.2.60; FCO 1979; Lagos 1982; Madrid 1986; FCO 1989; Resigned March 1990; Reinstated July 1990; FCO 1990; Language Training 1992; Deputy Head of Mission Vilnius 1992; Second Secretary 1994; Second Secretary (Commercial) Havana 1996.

Browne, Dr Carolyn; Counsellor FCO since September 1999; born 19.10.58; FCO 1985;

Language Training 1987; Second later First Secretary Moscow 1988; FCO 1991; First Secretary UKMIS New York 1993; FCO 1997.

Browne, Nicholas Walker; CMG (1999); H M Ambassador Tehran since May 1999; born 17.12.47; Third Secretary FCO 1969; Tehran 1971. Second later First Secretary FCO 1975; on loan to Cabinet Office 1976; First Secretary and Head of Chancery Salisbury 1980; First Secretary FCO 1981; First Secretary (Environment) UKREP Brussels 1984; Chargé d'Affaires Tehran 1989; Counsellor FCO 1989; Counsellor (Press and Public Affairs) Washington and Head of BIS New York 1990; Counsellor FCO 1994; Chargé d'Affaires Tehran November 1997 m1969 Diana Marise Aldwinckle (2s 1970, 1980; 2d 1972, 1976).

Brownhut, Naomi Judith; SUPL since May 1995; born 7.6.69; HM Customs and Excise 1988; FCO 1990; Prague 1993; Band A2.

Brownridge, Valerie (née Ewan); Deputy Consul General Jerusalem since October 1999; born 10.12.56; FCO 1979; ENA Paris 1980; Third Secretary Paris 1981; Third Secretary Lagos 1986; Second Secretary FCO 1988; Second Secretary Berlin 1991; First secretary FCO 1994; Band D6; m 1999 John L. F. Brownridge.

Broyd, Laurence Paul; FCO since February 1999; born 12.11.60; FCO 1990; First Secretary (Economic) Moscow 1995; Principal Research Officer; m 1990 Catherine Mary Carslake (1s 1994, 1d 1998).

Bruce, Dawn Susan; Cairo since March 1989; born 18.12.61; FCO 1981; Muscat 1983; Peking 1986; Band B3.

Brummell, Paul; First Secretary (Political and information) Rome since November 1995; born 28.8.65; FCO 1987; Third later Second Secretary (Chancery) Islamabad 1989; First Secretary FCO 1993; Full-time Language Training 1994.

Brunton, Janice Louise; Colombo since January 1996; born 19.6.71; FCO 1991; Moscow 1993; Band A2.

Bruton, Robert James; Brussels since August 1999; born 1.1.57; FCO 1980; Band C4.

Bryant, John Edward; First Secretary FCO since 2000; born 4.1.51; FCO 1970; Canberra 1972; Kingston 1975; FCO 1977; Bahrain 1978; Cairo 1979; FCO 1983; Nairobi 1986; FCO 1990; Dubai 1994; m 1972 Joyce Anne Barrie (1d 1975; 2s 1985, 1988).

Bryant, Richard John; FCO since June 1998; born 22.9.53; DTI 1973; Dept of Energy 1973; DOT 1975; DTI 1982; FCO 1984; Dhaka 1986; UKREP Brussels 1990; Brunei 1993; Temporary Duty Islamabad 1997 Floater duties 1997; Band B3; m 1986 Rosalyn Louise Morris. (diss 1991) (1s 1991)

Bryden, Lara-Jean; Floater Duties since June 1997; born 15.10.71; FCO 1996; Employment Service 1991-1996; Band A2.

Bryson, Alan Robert; Bangkok since October 1998; born 12.3.70; FCO 1991; Riyadh 1995; Band A2.

Bryson-Richardson, Mark Edward; FTLT since October 2000; born 30.10.76; FCO 1999; Band C4

Bubbear, Alan Keith; Second Secretary (Commercial) Helsinki since July 1996; born 14.9.64; FCO 1983; Moscow 1985; SUPL 1988; Johannesburg 1990; FCO 1992; (Second Secretary 1994); m 1988 Thérésa Bernice Allen (3d twins 1992, 1995).

Bubbear, Thérésa Bernice (née Allen); Second Secretary (Political) Helsinki since July 1996; born 14.12.62; FCO 1985; Moscow 1987; Johannesburg 1990; FCO 1992; (Second Secretary 1993); m 1988 Alan Keith Bubbear (3d twins 1992, 1995).

Buchanan, Sara Louise (née Allen); FCO since March 2000; born 31.7.69; FCO 1991; Full Time Language Training 1994; Vice Consul Stockholm 1994; Full Time Language Training 1997; Third Secretary (Political/Press) Tel Aviv 1997; Band B3; m 1995 Hamish Malcolm Robert Buchanan (1s 1998).

Buck, John Stephen; FCO since July 2000; born 10.10.53; FCO 1980; Second Secretary Sofia 1982; First Secretary FCO 1984; Head of Chancery Lisbon 1988; First Secretary FCO 1992; Counsellor on loan to the Cabinet Office 1994; Counsellor and Deputy Head of Mission Nicosia 1996; m 1980 Jean Claire Webb (1d 1985, 1s 1989).

Buckley, Stephen; First Secretary (Commercial) Peking since July 2000; born 18.6.53; Export Credit Guarantee Department 1972; FCO 1972; Amman 1975; Canberra 1978; FCO 1980; Dakar 1983; Third later Second Secretary (Comm) Seoul 1987; Second later First Secretary FCO 1992; First Secretary (Commercial) Kuala Lumpur 1996; m 1974 Barbara Frances Yelcich.

Bucknell, Bruce James; FCO since July 1999; born 15.4.62; FCO 1985; Third Secretary Amman 1988; Secondment to EBRD 1992; FCO 1992; HM Consul Milan 1995; Band C4; m 1993 Henrietta Dorrington-Ward (2s 1994, 1996)

Budd, Colin Richard, CMG (1991); HM Ambassador The Hague since April 2001; born 31.8.45; Third Secretary FCO 1967; (Assistant Private Secretary to Minister without Portfolio 1968-1969); Third later Second Secretary Warsaw 1969; Second later First Secretary (Chancery) Islamabad 1972; First Secretary FCO 1976; Head of Chancery The Hague 1980; Assistant Private Secretary to the Secretary of State 1984; Counsellor 1986; on loan to the Cabinet Office 1987; Counsellor and Head of Chancery Bonn 1989; On loan to the European Commission as Chef de Cabinet to Sir Leon Brittan 1993; On loan to the Cabinet Office 1996; FCO 1997 (DUS EU and Economic); m 1971 Agnes Antonia Maria Smit (1d 1979; 1s 1986).

Budden, Alexander James; Third Secretary (Development) Zagreb since September 1998; born 18.4.68; FCO 1991; Kathmandu 1994; Band B3; m 1995 Diane Margaret Scott (1d 2000).

Budden, Philip Marcus; First Secretary FCO since July 1999; born 12.9.65; Second Secretary FCO 1993; Vienna 1995; m 1992 Deborah Allen Tripp (1d 1997).

Buglass, Melvyn James; Vice-Consul Beirut since 1998; born 25.9.46; Army 1966-89; Rome 1989 UKDEL NATO Brussels 1992; DSLC 1995; Band B3; m 1973 Sandra Anne Whitehouse (1d 1974; 1s 1975).

Bull, Carol Elizabeth (née Gardener); FCO since February 1993; born 10.8.66; FCO 1988; Athens 1990; Band A2; m 1999 Keith Leslie Bull.

Bull, David Thomas John; On loan to the DTI since June 2000; born 20.2.61; FCO 1982; Rio de Janeiro 1983; Lusaka 1986; FCO 1990; Band C4; Third Secretary (Consular/Passports) Kingston 1994; Second Secretary (Management) Kathmandu 1997; m 1989 Aisling Maccobb (1d 1989).

Bulmer, Sandra Kay (née Ferguson); FCO since June 1998; born 11.11.67; FCO 1986; Vienna 1989; FCO 1991; Ottawa 1995; Band A2; m 1995 Ian Bulmer (1s 1998).

Bundy, Rosalind (née Johnson); Moscow since July 1999; born 25.1.45; FCO 1977; Paris 1977; Tripoli 1980; FCO 1983; Bonn 1985; FCO 1987; Algiers 1993, Ottawa 1995. Band B3; m 1984 David Alan Bundy.

Bunten, Roderick Alexander James; First Secretary (Information) Canberra since August 1997; born 24.11.59; FCO 1984; SOAS 1985; Language Training 1986; On Secondment to Hong Kong Government as Assistant Political Adviser 1987; SUPL 1990; Second Secretary FCO 1991.

Burch, Andrew David; on loan to DTI since October 1999; born 18.3.57; Department of the Environment 1972; FCO 1976; Nicosia 1980; New Delhi 1982; FCO 1986; Nairobi 1989; Budapest 1994; British Trade International 1998; Band C4; m 1982 Sarah Miranda Hodgson Clarke (2s 1989, 1991; 1d 1995).

Burch, Stella Jane; FCO since September 2000; born 30.5.76; Band C4.

Burdekin, Elizabeth Mary; FCO since September 1972; born 16.10.54; Band A2.

Burdes, Stephen Edward; Second Secretary (Political) Budapest since August 2000; born 17.12.71; FCO 1996; Band C4.

Burgin, Allan Lewis; FCO since November 1995; born 22.3.48; Royal Navy 1968-1990; Moscow 1990; Paris 1991; Belgrade 1994; Band B3; m 1970 Susan Hewison (2s 1978; 1982).

Burke, Alison Jane (née Wickham); New Delhi since March 1999; born 25.7.65; FCO 1983; Prague 1988; Canberra 1990; SUPL 1991; Bucharest 1992; SUPL 1995; FCO 1998; SUPL

1998; Band A2; m 1991 Thomas John Burke (1d 1995, 1s 1996).

Burke, Thomas John; Second Secretary (Immigration) New Delhi since July 1998; born 12.12.50; Treasury 1968; FCO 1974; Brasilia 1976; FCO 1979; Harare 1979; Islamabad 1983; FCO 1984; Canberra 1987; Vice-Consul Düsseldorf 1991; Vice-Consul Bucharest 1992; (Second Secretary 1996); m 1991 Alison Jane Wickham (1d 1995, 1s 1996).

Burke-Wood, Alison Carmen (née Ferry); Canberra since September 1997; born 7.6.66; FCO 1996; Band A2; m 1997 Joseph Burke-Wood.

Burlison, Sharon (née Clarke); Cape Town since May 1999; born 22.7.70; FCO 1993; Harare 1996; Band A2; m 1998 Andrew Burlison.

Burner, Edward Alan; HM Ambassador Dakar since August 2000; born 26.9.44; Commonwealth Office (later FCO) 1967; Sofia 1970; Bonn 1972; Second Secretary 1973; Second Secretary (Comm) Bridgetown 1974; Second later First Secretary FCO 1979; Assistant Private Secretary to Minister for Overseas Development 1979; FCO 1981; First Secretary, Head of Chancery and Consul Sofia 1984; On loan to ODA 1987; FCO 1990; Counsellor (Comm) Lagos 1992; Consul-General Munich 1995; FCO 1999; m 1969 Jane Georgine Du Port (2d 1970, 1972; 1s 1977).

Burnett, Alice Margaret; First Secretary (Legal) UKMIS New York since July 2000; born 17.10.68; Senior Assistant Legal Adviser; called to the Bar, Middle Temple 1991; FCO since 1994; Band D6.

Burnhams, Robin Edward; FCO since January 1997; born 10.12.42; CSC 1960; FCO 1967; Buenos Aires 1970; Moscow 1973; FCO 1974; Kingston 1978; Mbabane 1982; Second Secretary FCO 1984; Second Secretary (Admin) and Consul Caracas 1987; Second Secretary FCO 1990; Second Secretary (Aid) Dar es Salaam since August 1992; T/D Bosnia Conference, Lancaster House 1996; m 1978 Hilda Charlotte Patricia Phibbs (1d 1985).

Burns, Lynda Edwards; FCO since March 1999; born 19.7.75; Band B3.

Burns, Nicholas John; Third Secretary and Vice-Consul Prague since September 2000, born 20.3.62; FCO 1980; The Hague 1983; Kuala Lumpur 1984; Hanoi 1988; FCO 1989; Third Secretary (Management) Riyadh 1992; FCO 1995; Band B3.

Burns, Sir (Robert) Andrew KCMG (1997), CMG (1992); British High Commissioner Ottawa since July 2000; born 21.7.43; Third Secretary FO 1965; SOAS 1966; Third later Second Secretary Delhi 1967; Second later First Secretary FCO 1971; First Secretary and Head of Chancery Bucharest 1976; FCO 1978; Private Secretary to Permanent Under-Secretary of State 1979; CDA Harvard University 1982; Counsellor (Information) Washington and Head of British Information Services New York 1983; Counsellor FCO 1986; AUSS (Asia/Far

East) FCO 1990; HM Ambassador Tel Aviv 1992; DUSS (Non-Europe, Trade and Investment Promotion) 1995; Consul-General Hong Kong and Macau 1997; m 1973 Sarah Cadogan (1 step d 1968; 2s 1975, 1977).

Burns, Sarah Elizabeth; SUPL since September 1998; born 20.4.66; FCO 1988; Third later Second Secretary (Chancery) Vienna 1991; Second Secretary FCO 1995; Band C4.

Burns, Sean Gilbert Peter, MBE (2001); Second Secretary (Management) Nairobi since September 2000; born 19.2.61; FCO 1978; Dar es Salaam 1983; Antigua 1987; FCO 1991; Dhaka 1993; Third Secretary (Management) and Vice Consul Dakar 1997; m 1983 Marina Higgins; (1d 1989, 1s 1991).

Burran, John Eric; Washington since February 2001; born 18.5.63; FCO 1982; Bucharest 1987; LA/Caribbean Floater 1989; Islamabad 1992; FCO 1995; On Loan To DCMS 1998; Band C4.

Burrell, Demelza Fiona; World Wide Floater Duties since 2000; born 9.12.70; FCO 1994; Madrid 1996; FCO 1999; Band A2.

Burrett, Louise Victoria; SUPL since May 2000; born 16.8.61; FCO 1978; Bridgetown 1981; Dublin 1984; Bombay 1987; FCO 1990; SUPL 1993; on loan to the DTI 1995; SUPL since January 1997; Second Secretary (Management) Tripoli 1999; Band C4.

Burrows, Christopher Parker; First Secretary (Political) Brussels since April 1998; born 12.9.58; FCO 1980; East Berlin 1982; Africa/Middle East Floater 1985; Bonn 1987 (Second Secretary 1988); Second Secretary FCO 1989; First Secretary (Political/External) Athens 1993; First Secretary FCO 1996; m 1988 Betty Cordi; (2d, 1987, 1990, 1s 1992).

Burrows, Karl; Consul Monterrey since July 2000; born 8.5.68; FCO 1988; Floater Duties 1990; Tegucigalpa 1992; FCO 1993; Panama City 1996; Band C4; m 1991 Jane Marie O'Mahoney.

Burt, Nicola Jayne; Stockholm since July 2001; born 6.2.67; FCO 1986; Moscow 1989; FCO 1992; Tel Aviv 1993; FCO 1996; Kuala Lumpur 1997; FCO 2000; Band A2.

Burton, John Francis; Moscow since November 1997; Army 1963-87; New Delhi 1989; Prague 1989; Pretoria/Cape Town 1991; Peking 1994; Band B3; m 1971 Christine (2d 1973, 1974).

Burton, Simon David; FCO since July 1998; born 11.04.73. Band A2.

Busby, George Benedict Joseph Pascal, OBE (1996); Counsellor Vienna since January 2000; born 18.4.60; FCO 1987; Second later First Secretary (Chancery) Bonn 1989; First Secretary FCO 1991; First Secretary (Belgrade) 1992; First Secretary FCO 1996; m 1988 Helen Frances Hurll (3d 1989, 1994, 2000, 1s 1991).

Busk, Lieutenant Colonel Walter, Patrick Anthony; Queen's Messenger since 1989; born 20.9.39 HM Forces 1961-89.

Busvine, Nicholas John Lewis, OBE (1995); First Secretary FCO since January 1995; born 13.5.60; FCO 1982; Third later Second Secretary Kuala Lumpur 1985; FCO 1988; First Secretary Maputo 1991; m 1991 Sarah Ann Forgan (diss 1996) (2) 1997 Madeleine Ann Lewis (1d 1999).

Butcher, Peter Roderick; Maputo since March 2000; born 6.8.47; FCO 1974; Second Secretary Lima 1979; Second Secretary (Comm) Bombay 1983; First Secretary FCO 1987; Deputy High Commissioner Maseru 1990; First Secretary FCO 1994; On secondment to DfID 1997; Band D6.

Bute, Paul Kenrick; First Secretary FCO since July 1999; born 18.5.73; FCO 1994; full-time Language Training 1995; Third later Second Secretary (Chancery) New Delhi 1996.

Butler, Christopher Giles Moffat; Second Secretary Berne since January 1995; born 13.3.40; HM Forces 1960-77; FCO 1977; Durban 1979; Johannesburg 1980; FCO 1982 (Second Secretary 1985); m 1973 Sandra Ann Barnes (1s 1974; 1d 1978).

Butler, Georgina Susan; HM Ambassador San José since February 2002; Born 30.11.45; FCO 1968; Paris 1969; resigned on marriage 1970; re-employed on contract FCO 1971; reinstated in service 1972; SUPL 1975 (New York and UKREP Brussels); seconded to European Commission, Brussels 1982; FCO 1985; resigned 1987 (New Delhi/UKREP Brussels/Washington); re-employed FCO 1999; m 1970 Stephen John Leadbetter Wright (diss 2000) (1d 1977; 1s 1979).

Butler, Penelope Margaret; FCO since May 1972; born 14.2.52; Band A2.

Butler, Sally-Anne; SUPL since June 1996; born 30.3.69; FCO 1988; Stanley 1990; Istanbul 1993; Band A2; m 1991 Jonathan Jeffers Butler.

Butt, Simon John; Head of Eastern Department since April 2001; born 5.4.58; FCO 1979; Third later Second Secretary Moscow 1982; Second Secretary Rangoon 1984; Second Secretary FCO 1986; First Secretary (External Relations) UKREP Brussels 1990; First Secretary FCO 1994; Deputy Head of Mission Kiev 1997.

Butt, Stephen; First Secretary Athens since August 2001; born 7.5.63; FCO 1981; Cairo 1986; Athens 1991; Third Secretary FCO 1992; Second Secretary (Chancery) Islamabad 1997; FCO 2000; Band C5.

Butterfield, Sarah Jane; FCO since March 1992; born 1.7.72; Band A2.

Butterworth, Pamela Cynthia Anne, MBE (1987); FCO since December 1988; (Second Secretary 1995); born 24.4.43; FO 1964; Geneva 1964; Hong Kong 1967; FCO 1969; Peking 1971; FCO 1973; New York 1976; FCO 1978; Washington 1986; Band C4.

Bye, Adam William, On loan to the Cabinet Office since September 2000; born 6.11.72; Customs & Excise 1994; FCO 1996; Second Secretary on Attachment to the European Commission 1997; FCO 1998; First Secretary FCO 1999.

Byford, Rebecca; (née Mills) Washington since November 1999; born 30.8.69; FCO 1991; Athens 1995; FCO 1996; Band A2; m 1999 David Byford

Byrd, Margaret (née Allen); Lagos since October 1998; born 19.6.61; FCO 1987; Nairobi 1990; SUPL 1993; Washington 1994; Band B3; m 1993 Roger Anthony Byrd.

Byrde, Petronella Leonie Diana; First Secretary (Consul) Cairo since February 1998; born 20.10.48; DSAO (later FCO) 1967; Gaborone 1971; Dacca 1974; FCO 1977; Second Secretary 1979; Tokyo 1981; First Secretary (Comm) Colombo 1986; First Secretary FCO 1990; First Secretary (Aid/Economic) Kampala 1994.

Byrne, Terence Niall; Consul-General and Director of Trade Promotion Auckland since April 1999; born 28.4.42; MHLG 1964; MAFF 1971; First Secretary (Agriculture), The Hague 1978; First Secretary FCO 1982; Head of Chancery Quito 1986; Counsellor and Deputy High Commissioner Lusaka 1990; Director of Trade Promotion Canberra 1993; Deputy High Commissioner Kuala Lumpur 1994; m(1) 1966 Andrea Dennison (diss 1977) (1s 1968, 1d 1969); (2) 1981 Susan Haddow Neill (2d 1985, 1987).

Byroo, Jacqueline Sandra; Kampala since July 2001; born 30.4.63; FCO 1982; FCO 1989; UKREP Brussels 1987; UKREP Vienna 1991; Copenhagen 1993; Kingston 1999; Band A2.

C

Caie, Andrew John Forbes; High Commissioner Bandar Seri Begawan since January 2002; born 25.7.47; FCO 1969; SRO (DS Gr. 7) 1972; Second Secretary Manila 1976; PRO(DS Gr. 5) FCO 1980 (First Secretary 1983); First Secretary, Head of Chancery and Consul Bogotá 1984; First Secretary later Counsellor FCO 1988; Deputy Head of Mission Islamabad 1993; on loan to the CSSB 1996; FCO 1997; HM Ambassador Guatemala City 1998; m 1976 Kathie-Anne Williams (1s 1979; 1d 1987).

Cairaschi, Lucien Marius; FCO since October 1985; born 11.2.65; HCS 1984; Band A2.

Cairns, Alison Marie; Tehran since November 2000; born 3.12.72; FCO 1994; Tallinn 1996; Band A2.

Cairns, David Seldon; Private Secretary to Baroness Amos since August 2001; born 17.4.69; FCO 1993; Second Secretary Tokyo 1995; FCO 1999; Private Secretary to Baroness Scotland 2000; m 1996 Sharon Anouk Aeberhard (1d 2000).

Cairns, Donald Hunter; British Trade International since June 1998; Counsellor UKMIS New York since August 1992; born 29.10.46; Post Office 1967; FCO 1969; Anguilla 1972; Montevideo

1974; Abu Dhabi 1977; FCO 1980; Second Secretary (Comm) Bogotá 1982; Second Secretary (Admin) and HM Consul Caracas 1984; First Secretary (Comm) Canberra 1988; Deputy Consul General (Comm) Melbourne 1990; First Secretary FCO 1992; Counsellor UKMIS New York 1992; m 1972 Judy Francis Woods (1s 1977).

Cairns, Gina Stephanie (née Tart), MVO (1992); SUPL since January 2000; born 21.9.65; FCO 1984; Bridgetown 1986; Bonn 1990; FCO 1993; Vice-Consul Amsterdam 1997; Band C4; m 1987 William John Cairns (1s 1995, 1d 1998).

Cairns, Julie Margaret; FCO since September 1997; born 13.3.59; FCO 1977; Bonn 1979; Africa/ME Floater 1982; JAO Brussels 1984; FCO 1986; Gaborone 1990; Second Secretary (Finance) UKMIS New York 1993.

Calder, Robert; First Secretary (Management) Pretoria since May 1999; born 27.10.41; CRO 1960; Karachi 1963; Warsaw 1966; Kampala 1968; FCO 1971; Kampala 1972; FCO 1974; Frankfurt 1974; Second Secretary Vientiane 1977; Accra 1978; BMG Berlin 1980; First Secretary FCO 1983; Deputy Consul General and First Secretary (Comm) Düsseldorf 1986. First Secretary FCO 1991; Islamabad 1993; Cleveland 1997; m 1966 Janet Rosemary Allen (Diss. 1993) (2d 1967, 1978, 2s 1968, 1976).

Calder, Stanley Shearer; Deputy Consul-General Toronto since May 2001; born 7.2.44; Immigration Service 1965; Islamabad 1972; Second Secretary Lima 1975; FCO 1980; Deputy High Commissioner Belmopan 1982; First Secretary Peking 1986; First Secretary FCO 1990; First Secretary (Commercial) Caracas 1994; First Secretary (Commercial) Paris 1996; m 1967 Isobel Masson Leith (1s 1968; 1d 1970).

Caldwell, Christine Bernadette; ECO Vienna since May 1999; born 31.7.56; HCS 1973-77; FCO 1977; Warsaw 1979; Ankara 1979; Tripoli 1983; FCO 1984; SUPL 1986; Band B3; Vice-Consul Johannesburg 1991; FCO 1993; SUPL 1995; m 1982 Clive David Wright (2d 1986, 1989).

Caley, Joanne; First Secretary (Chancery) UKMIS Geneva since April 1999; born 13.8.65; FCO 1991; Second Secretary Maputo 1993; FCO 1996; m 1991 Peter David Morgan (2s 1996, 1998).

Callan, Sir Ivan Roy, KCVO (1998), CMG (1990); HM Ambassador Muscat since February 1999; born 6.4.42; Second Secretary FCO 1969; MECAS 1970; Second Secretary (Chancery) later First Secretary (Information) Beirut 1972; First Secretary FCO 1975; First Secretary Ottawa 1980; Counsellor, Consul-General and Head of Chancery Baghdad 1983; Consul-General Jerusalem 1987; Counsellor FCO 1990; High Commissioner Bandar Seri Begawan 1994; m(1) 1965 Hilary Margaret West (née Flashman) (1d 1971); (2) 1987 Mary Catherine Helena Williams (2 step s, 1 step d).

Callow, Judith Elizabeth; Athens since May 2001; born 27.12.48; FCO 1970; Tananarive 1971; UK

Mission Geneva 1973; Belgrade 1974; Abidjan 1975; UKREP Brussels 1977; Dakar 1979; Madrid 1983; Paris 1985; UKDEL Brussels 1987; Ottawa 1990; FCO 1993; Stockholm 1996; Band B3.

Callun, Rosemary (née Beckmann); FCO since February 1987; born 17.1.54; FCO 1975; Cairo 1976; Bangkok 1978; Prague 1979; Pretoria 1981; Accra 1983; Port Stanley 1985; Harare 1986; Band B3.

Calvert, Andrew Paul; Floater Duties since June 1999; born 17.1.69; HCS Cadre of the FCO 1989; FCO 1992; Bonn 1994; Band B3; m 1994 Julie Louis (1d 1995).

Cambridge, Roger Alan, MVO (1985); Deputy Head of Mission Helsinki since February 1999; born 12.9.52; FCO 1972; Africa Floater 1975; Stockholm 1977; Dar es Salaam 1979; Second Secretary (Chancery/Inf) Port of Spain 1983; Second later First Secretary FCO 1986; Consul (Commercial) BTIO New York 1990; First Secretary UKMIS New York 1993; FCO 1996.

Cameron, James; Second Secretary and Consul Bucharest since January 2001; born 21.4.50; Army 1966-90; FCO 1990; Peking 1990; Bucharest 1991; FCO 1993; Taipei 1994; Band C4; m 1977 Angela Jane Arnold (2d 1977, 1979).

Cameron, Lee; Second Secretary UKDEL NATO Brussels since October 2000; born 1.9.76; FCO 1999; Band C4.

Campbell, Amanda Joan; Floater duties since June 2000; born 24.1.69; FCO 1990; full-time language training 1999; Band B3.

Campbell, Christopher John; Second Secretary (Commercial) Caracas since April 1999; born 12.4.63; FCO 1982; Khartoum 1985; Dhaka 1988; Jakarta 1992; FCO 1995; Band C4; m 1989 Sharon Isabel Hale.

Campbell, David Ian; Deputy Head of Mission Manila since March 2000; born 9.7.58; FCO 1981; Budapest 1984; Third later Second Secretary Georgetown 1985; Second Secretary FCO 1988; First Secretary (Humanitarian) UKMIS Geneva 1989; First Secretary (Political) Belgrade 1994; First Secretary FCO since September 1994.

Campbell, Robert Pius; Counsellor (ESCAP) Bangkok since August 2001; born 19.10.57; FCO 1980; Second Secretary Nairobi 1984; FCO 1985; First Secretary (Economic) Belgrade 1986; First Secretary FCO 1990; First Secretary (Political) Helsinki 1992; First Secretary (Political) Skopje 1994; First Secretary FCO 1997; m(1) 1985 Amanda Jane Guy (diss 1992) (1s 1989) (2) m1992 Ailsa Irene Robinson (1s 1999).

Campbell, Sharon Isabel (née Hale); SMO/Consul Caracas since May 2000; born 12.2.62; FCO 1983; Warsaw 1985; FCO 1986; Dhaka 1988; Jakarta 1992; FCO 1995; (Second Secretary 1996); Caracas 1999; SUPL 1999; m 1989 Christopher John Campbell.

Campbell, Susan Margaret; Pretoria since January 2000; born 28.7.64; FCO 1984; Harare 1986; FCO 1990; Brasilia 1991; Floater Duties 1993; FCO 1995; Band B3.

Campbell-Birkett, Frances Mary (née Campbell); SUPL since March 1995; born 3.4.62 HCS 1981; FCO 1982; Budapest 1984; FCO 1985; Jakarta 1987; FCO 1990; Band A2; m 1992 Christopher Michael Fraser Birkett (1s 1994).

Canning, Mark; FCO since December 1998; born 15.12.54; FCO 1974; Freetown 1976; FCO 1978; SUPL 1978; FCO 1981; Georgetown 1982; Chicago 1986; First Secretary FCO 1988; First Secretary (Commercial) Jakarta 1994; m 1988 Leslie Marie Johnson.

Cannon, Nicholas; First Secretary (Chancery) Islamabad since June 2000; born 29.5.58; FCO 1988; Second Secretary Paris 1990; Second Secretary FCO 1992; Second Secretary (Political/Commercial) Nicosia 1994; FTLT 2000; Band D6; m 1982 Alice Cheung (2s, 1992,1993).

Cantor, Anthony John James; HM Ambassador Asunción since November 2001; born 1.2.46; DSAO 1965; Rangoon 1968; Language Training Sheffield University 1971; Tokyo 1972; Second Secretary (Consular) Accra and Vice Consul Lomé 1977; Second Secretary FCO 1980; Consul (Commercial) Osaka 1983; Deputy Head of Mission Hanoi 1990; On loan to Invest in Britain Bureau DTI 1992; First Secretary (Commercial) Tokyo 1994; Consul (Commercial) later Deputy Consul-General Osaka 1995; T/D Hanover 2000; m 1968 Patricia Elizabeth Naughton (2d 1969, 1972, 1s 1980).

Canvin, Alan Robert; Bucharest since March 1988; Second Secretary 1992; born 23.12.46; FCO 1965; Jedda (later Riyadh) 1984; m 1981 Susan Paviour (1 step d 1963; 1 step s 1966).

Capelin, Melanie Jane; PA/DHC Bridgetown since June 2000; born 19.12.65; FCO 1998; Band A2.

Capes, Mark Andrew; First Secretary FCO since July 1999; born 19.2.54; FCO 1971; UKREP Brussels 1974; Lisbon 1975; Zagreb 1978; FCO 1980; Lagos 1982; Vienna 1986; Second Secretary FCO 1989; Deputy Chief Secretary Providenciales Turks and Caicos Islands 1991; First Secretary (Economic) Wellington 1994; m 1980 Tamara Rossmanith (2d 1985, 1988).

Carbine, Michael Julian; SUPL since March 2000; born 16.1.56; FCO 1975; Budapest 1977; Khartoum 1979; FCO 1982; Budapest 1983; Second Secretary FCO 1986; Second Secretary (Visas) Düsseldorf 1990; Sofia 1995; On Secondment to ICL 1998; Band C5; m 1975 Marian Parkinson (1s 1975).

Carew-Hunt, Robert Anthony; Second Secretary FCO since September 1988; born 11.10.49; FO (later FCO) 1968; Bonn 1972; FCO 1975; Cairo 1975; FCO 1979; Second Secretary Bandar Seri Begawan 1986; Band C4.

Carey, Colin Paul; FCO since August 1990 (Second Secretary 1994); born 21.9.57; FCO 1974; Bonn 1988; m 1981 Janet Coleman (1d 1984, 2s 1986 1990).

Carey, Joanne Claire; Guangzhou since September 2000; born 6.2.72; FCO 1991; Islamabad 1995; T/D Peking 1999; Vienna 2000; Band B3.

Carlin, Neal Daniel; Second Secretary and Deputy Head of Mission Tegucigalpa since August 2000; born 22.3.71; FCO 1990; UKMIS Geneva 1994; Vice-Consul Khartoum 1996; FTLT 2000; Band B3.

Carnall, Philippa Jane, MBE (1986); FCO since August 2000; born 31.7.57; FCO 1980; Beirut 1983; Damascus 1984; FCO 1986; Hanoi 1988; Washington 1991; FCO 1993; Cairo 1997; Band B3.

Carney, Jonathan Patrick; Bahrain since October 1999; born 23.2.68; DHSS 1986; FCO 1989; Islamabad 1992; Riyadh 1995; Band B3; m 1996 Rhonda Ann Fitzgerald (2d 1997, 1999).

Carr, Corrine (née Cannard); SUPL since July 1999; born 28.2.70; FCO 1991; Berne 1994; FCO 1996; Band A2; m 1996 Darren Andrew Carr.

Carr, Peter Douglas; Second Secretary (Consular) Jakarta since March 1997; born 2.5.47; DSAO (later FCO) 1967; Kaduna 1969; FCO 1970; Delhi 1971; Bogotá 1974; FCO 1978; Kuwait 1981; FCO 1984; JAO New York 1985; Second Secretary FCO 1988; m 1972 Cynthia Jane Begley (1s 1975; 2d 1977, 1983).

Carr-Alloway, Christine Anne (née Carr); FCO since October 1998; born 13.2.60; FCO 1978; Paris 1980; UKREP Brussels 1983; FCO 1986; Kuwait 1992; FCO 1994; Full-time language training 1994; Third later Second Secretary UKMIS Geneva 1995; Band C4; m 1991 Terry Alloway.

Carrick, Aileen Margaret; Floater Duties since June 1995; born 21.2.69; FCO 1989; Rome 1992; Band B3.

Carrick, Nicholas John; First Secretary Lagos since June 1999; born 1.2.67; FCO 1990; Second Secretary (Political) Berlin 1993; FCO 1995; Band D6.

Carrick, Robert Thomas; Jerusalem since October 2001; born 5.5.64; FCO 1987; Damascus 1994; FCO 1997; SUPL 2000; Band B3; m 1997 Rachel Woodward.

Carroll, Heidi Amanda; FCO since September 2000; born 9.5.68; FCO 1988; Brussels 1992; FCO 1995; Floater duties 1998; Band B3.

Carson, Christine; Seoul since September 1998; born 18.5.65; FCO 1990; JLG Hong Kong 1992; Lima 1995; Band A2.

Carter, Andrew, CMG (1995); UK Permanent Representative with Personal rank of Ambassador, to the Council of Europe at Strasbourg; born 4.12.43; FCO 1971; Second Secretary Warsaw 1972; First Secretary 1974; Bonn 1975; FCO 1978; on Loan to MOD 1981; FCO 1983; Counsellor, CDA Chatham House 1984; Counsellor and Head of Chancery UKDEL NATO Brussels 1986; Deputy Governor Gibraltar 1990; Minister Moscow 1995; Ambassador Moscow 1997; m(1) 1973 Anne Caroline Morgan (diss 1986) (1d 1978); (2) 1988 Catherine Mary Tyler (1d 1989, 1s 1993).

Carter, Dr David, CVO (1995); High Commissioner Dhaka since January 2000; born 4.5.45; FCO 1970, (Research Cadre); Second Secretary Accra 1971; FCO/Cabinet Office 1975; First Secretary 1977; First Secretary and Head of Chancery Manila 1980; FCO 1983; Deputy High Commissioner and Head of Chancery Lusaka 1986; Counsellor FCO 1990; Deputy Head of Mission, later Deputy High Commissioner (1994) Cape Town/Pretoria 1992; Minister and Deputy High Commissioner New Delhi 1996; m 1968 Susan Victoria Wright (1d 1975, 1s 1978).

Carter, Dennis Sidney; First Secretary FCO since April 1999; born 12.6.47; Commonwealth Office 1964; DSAO (later FCO) 1966; Bogotá 1969; Moscow 1973; FCO 1974; Bonn 1978; Washington 1982; Harare 1984; Second Secretary FCO 1987; Second Secretary (Aid) Addis Ababa 1991; Second Secretary (Comm/Man/Vice Consul) Montevideo 1995; First Secretary (Management Officer) T/D Madrid 1998; m 1968 Catherine Rose (2s 1969, 1975).

Carter, Hannah Katharine; FCO since November 1998; born 20.8.74.

Carter, Kevin Robert; T/D Amsterdam and Brussels since January 2000; born 26.8.55; OPCS 1972-76; Dar es Salaam (LE) 1979-82; FCO 1983; Warsaw 1984; Third Secretary (Cons) Valletta 1987; FCO 1989; Peking 1992 (Second Secretary 1994); Full-time Language Training 1994; Vice-Consul (Commercial) Düsseldorf 1995; Band C4; m 1976 Sandra Ann McHugh (2d 1985, 1986).

Carter, Nicholas Paul; Deputy Head of Mission Riga since December 1999; born 13.3.46; Commonwealth Office (later FCO) 1966; Belgrade 1970; Bombay 1972; Prague 1976; on loan to Midland Bank (International) 1980; FCO 1981; Second Secretary Bonn 1983; First Secretary (Comm) Kuala Lumpur 1986; First Secretary FCO 1990; Consul General Ho Chi Minh City 1994; Attached to the Department for International Development 1997; Band D6; m(1)1970 (2s 1971, 1978; 1d 1974) m(2) 1994 Andrea Helen Abrahams.

Carter, Peter Leslie; Counsellor, Consul-General and Deputy Head of Mission Tel Aviv since May 2001; born 19.11.56; FCO 1984; Second later First Secretary (Chancery) New Delhi 1986; First Secretary FCO 1989; Principal Administrator, CFSP Unit, EU Council Secretariat, Brussels 1994 (on secondment); Counsellor FCO 1998; m 1985 Rachelle Hays (1d 1991).

Carter, Thomas Henry; First Secretary (Head of Political Section) Bangkok since October 1999; born 22.11.53; FCO 1976; ENA Paris 1978; Paris 1979; Vice-Consul later Second Secretary (Chancery) Bogotá 1983; Second Secretary FCO 1987; T/D Paris 1990; First Secretary (Environment) Bonn 1990; FCO 1995; Full Time Language Training 1999; m 1997 Carolyn Jayne Davidson (2s 1998, 1999).

Cartmell, Glyn Richard; Kampala since May 1998; born 23.2.69; British Army 1985-92 and 1996; Royal Air Force 1997; FCO 1996; Kiev 1997; FCO 1997; Band A2; ptnr, Vanessa Cathy Thom (1s 1992).

Carwithen, Paul Ivor; Second Secretary FCO since January 1999; born 18.2.64; FCO 1993; Copenhagen 1996; Band C4; m 1992 Ann Davies (2s 1994, 1996).

Cartwright, Peter John; On Secondment to Business Link Shropshire, DTI, since March 1999; born 23.3.55; FCO 1975; On loan to Masirah 1978; Athens 1979; Paris 1982; Kabul 1984; FCO 1986; UKDEL NATO 1990; Banjul 1992; FCO 1996; Band B3; m 1984 Pamela Jane Edwards (2s 1988, 1992, 1d 1986).

Cartwright, Stephen Mark; Oslo since March 2000; born 23.8.64; FCO 1985; East Berlin 1987; Bombay 1988; FCO 1993; Third Secretary (Aid) Gaborone 1996; Band C4; m 1988 Nicola Bjorg Joyce (1s 1991).

Carty, Helen Elizabeth (née Measures); Floater Duties since June 2001; born 23.6.66; FCO 1992; Johannesburg 1994; Bonn 1998; Jedda 2000; Band B3; m 1994 Daniel Lee Carty.

Cary, Anthony Joyce; CMG (1997); SUPL since September 1999; born 1.7.51; FCO 1973; Third Secretary BMG Berlin 1975; Second later First Secretary FCO 1978; Harkness Fellow at Stanford Business School 1980; FCO 1982; PS to the Minister of State 1984; First Secretary and Head of Chancery Kuala Lumpur 1986; On loan to the EC Commission 1989; Counsellor FCO 1993; Counsellor Washington 1997; m 1975 Clare Louise Katharine Elworthy (3s 1978, 1980, 1983, 1d 1985).

Casey, Claudia; Third later Second Secretary (Political/Information) Addis Ababa since June 1998; born 5.10.67; FCO 1996.

Casey, Kevin Anthony Michael; Second Secretary (Consular/Immigration) Dhaka since August 1997; born 18.11.41; FO 1959; New York (UKMIS) 1963; Baghdad 1966; Bonn 1967; FCO 1970; Addis Ababa 1973; FCO 1977; Islamabad 1979; Freetown 1981; Georgetown 1984; Second Secretary FCO 1986; Second Secretary (Cons) Canberra 1989; Second Secretary (Immigration) New Delhi 1994; m(1) 1963 Denise Patricia Byrne (3d 1964, 1967, 1970); (2)1989 Mrs Linda Roberts.

Casey, Nigel Philip, MVO (1995); FCO since December 1998; born 29.5.69; FCO 1991; Vice-Consul (Political/Aid/Information) Johannesburg 1993; Second later First Secretary Washington 1996.

Casey, Sheila Mary; Dhaka since July 1997; born 21.7.42; FCO 1971; Tehran 1972; FCO 1974; Lusaka 1976; FCO 1978; Nicosia 1979; FCO 1982; Prague 1984; UKREP Brussels 1986; FCO 1988; UKREP Brussels 1992; New Delhi 1993; Copenhagen 1994; Band B3.

Cassidy, Sarah Jayne (née Gardner); FCO since January 1998; born 27.12.68; FCO 1986; Bangkok 1989; Lilongwe 1992; SUPL 1996; Band B3; m 1995 Eamon Martin Cassidy.

Cassy, Grace Aldren; Second Secretary Islamabad since September 2000; born 4.8.76; FCO 1998; Band C4.

Castillo, Oscar Luis; Floater duties since October 1999; born 5.8.69; FCO 1990; Islamabad 1993; FCO 1995; Band A2.

Caton, Michael Malusi; SUPL since 1999; born 18.5.64; DHSS 1986-89; FCO 1989; Third Secretary (Chancery) Canberra 1992; Third Secretary (Chancery) Durban 1995; Band B3; m 1991 Ann Margaret Elliott.

Caton, Dr Valerie; Counsellor (Financial & Economic) Paris since 1997; born 12.5.52; FCO 1980; Second later First Secretary (EC Affairs) Brussels 1982; First Secretary FCO 1984; First Secretary (Chancery) Paris 1988; Counsellor and Consul-General Stockholm 1993; m 1987 David Mark Harrison (1d 1992, 1s 1994).

Caulfield, Tracy Ann; FCO since February 1998; born 10.3.70; FCO 1988; UKMIS Vienna 1990; FCO 1993; Wellington 1994; Band B3.

Caughey, Alan Marsh; Third Secretary (Political/EU) Prague since February 2001; born 17.11.71; FCO 1990, UKMIS Geneva 1994; Bombay 1997; Band B3.

Cavagan, John Raymond; FCO since May 2001; born 9.10.66; FCO 1990; Bogotá 1993; Band B3.

Cayless, Trevor Martin; Second Secretary (Commercial) Madrid since August 2001; born 18.5.66; DHSS 1985; FCO 1986; Third Secretary (Aid) Lusaka 1990; Full-time Language Training 1993; Frankfurt 1994; Second Secretary FCO 1997; m 1989 Rosemary Anne Whiting (1s 1996, 1d 1999).

Cazalet, Piers William Alexander; Second Secretary (Political/Information) Nicosia since September 1995; born 20.10.66; FCO 1991; Language Training 1994; m Alyana Sharafutdinova (1s 1990, 1d 1995).

Cetti, Joanne Martine; Second Secretary (Economic) Kampala since January 2000; born 18.1.72; Second Secretary FCO 1997; Band C4.

Chadwick, Janine Linda (née Laurence); Khartoum since November 1999; born 9.4.54; FCO 1983; Brasilia 1987; UKMIS Vienna 1991;

Reykjavik 1994; FCO 1997; Band A2; m 1985 Peter Guy Chadwick.

Chadwick, John Anthony; Second Secretary (Commercial) Damascus since February 2000; born 16.12.52; FCO 1971; Malta 1973; Manila 1976; FCO 1980; Islamabad 1983; São Paulo 1988; FCO 1992; (Second Secretary 1994); Second Secretary (Commercial) Riyadh 1996; Band C4; m 1976 Jane Saliba (3d 1979, 1983, 1986; 1s 1981).

Chadwick, Nigel Spencer; Athens since September 1999; born 17.9.52; FCO 1971; Berne 1973; Buenos Aires 1977; Dacca 1980; Lima 1981; FCO 1984; Bombay 1988; FCO 1992; Banjul 1996; Band B3.

Chalmers, Kathleen Corbett; SUPL since September 1997; born 19.8.59; Brasilia 1981; FCO 1982; Hanoi 1983; FCO 1986; Rome 1987; SUPL 1990; FCO 1991; Hong Kong 1994; Band A2.

Chalmers, Nicholas John Pender; First Secretary Pristina since July 2000; born 4.5.71; FCO 1993; Second Secretary (Political) Islamabad 1995; FCO 1998; Band D6.

Chamberlain, Valerie Ann (née Crocombe); SUPL since June 2001; born 16.7.62; FCO 1980; Washington 1984; Gibraltar 1987; Prague 1989; FCO 1991; Bombay 1998; Band B3; m 1997 Martin Chamberlain.

Chambers, Dr David Ian; First Secretary FCO since April 1998; born 4.12.47; Principal Research Officer; FCO 1987; First Secretary and Consul Macao BTC Hong Kong 1994; Band D6; m(1) 1978 Merilyn Figueroa (diss 1990); (2) 1991 Tharinee Plobyon.

Chambers, David Michael Anthony; Deputy High Commissioner Victoria since February 1999; born 12.11.61; Inland Revenue 1986; FCO 1993; Lagos 1995; Band B3; m 1990 Tracey Robinson (1s 1994, 1d 1999).

Chandler, Julian; First Secretary (Commercial) Nairobi since December 1998; born 7.7.50; DSAO (later FCO) 1967; Istanbul 1971; Singapore 1976; Kuala Lumpur 1977; FCO 1979; Port Stanley 1982; Assistant Trade Commissioner Hong Kong 1984; First Secretary FCO 1989; Deputy High Commissioner Mbabane 1992; m 1988 Caroline Louise Parkinson (1d 1980, 3s 1982, 1992, 1994).

Chandler, Steven; T/D Belgrade since January 2000; born 27.1.71; FCO 1994, Ottawa 1994; SUPL 1999; Band B3; m 1996 Jenny Wieslander (1s 1997).

Chandler, Steven Clive; Third later Second Secretary FCO since October 1998; born 16.3.68; DHSS 1986; FCO 1987; BMG Berlin 1989; Dhaka 1992; Istanbul 1995; Sarajevo 1997; Band C4.

Chaplin, Edward Graham Mellish, OBE (1988); HM Ambassador Amman since May 2000; born 21.2.51; FCO 1973; MECAS 1974; Third

Secretary Muscat 1975; Second Secretary Brussels 1977; ENA Paris 1978; Private Secretary to Lord President of the Council 1979; First Secretary FCO 1981; First Secretary and Head of Chancery Tehran 1985; First Secretary FCO 1987; Counsellor FCO on secondment to Price Waterhouse Management Consultants 1990; Deputy Permanent Representative and Head of Chancery, UKMIS Geneva 1992; Counsellor FCO 1996; m 1983 Nicola Helen Fisher (2d 1984, 1989; 1s 1987).

Chapman, Adrian Paul; Second Secretary (Political/Public Affairs) Seoul since June 2001; born 14.8.69; FCO 1988; UKREP Brussels 1990; Islamabad 1993; FCO 1996; On loan to the DTI 1998; Band C4; m 1999 Fiona Witty (1d 2000).

Chapman, Colin; FCO since September 2000; born 12.1.58; Army 1974-79; FCO 1980; Bonn 1986; FCO 1988; Third Secretary Rome 1991; Second Secretary Ankara 1997; m 1983 Katherine Anne French (1d 1987).

Chapman, Frederick John; FCO since November 1997; born 15.10.44; GPO 1961; FCO 1968; Singapore 1969; Bahrain 1972; FCO 1972; Helsinki 1973; FCO 1975; Nairobi 1979; FCO 1982; Addis Ababa 1983; FCO 1986; Third Secretary Brasilia 1990; FCO 1994; Attaché Vienna 1995; m(1) 1967 Mary Patricia Clarke (diss. 1988) (1d 1968, 1s 1973); (2) Maria Schuh (née Hedl).

Chapman, Yvonne Kay; UKMIS Geneva since November 1999; born; 28.9.62; DETR 1987; FCO 1998; Band A2; (1s 1991).

Chappell, Julie Louise Jo; Second Secretary (Political/Economic) Amman since November 2000; born 2.4.78; FCO 1999; FTLT 2000; Band C4.

Chapple, Katherine Margaret; FCO since October 1990; born 19.9.64; Home Civil Service 1988; Band A2.

Charlton, Alan, CMG (1996); Director South East Europe, FCO since January 2001; born 21.6.52; FCO 1978; Language Training 1979; Second later First Secretary Amman 1981; First Secretary FCO 1984; First Secretary (Deputy Political Adviser) BMG Berlin 1986; On loan to the Cabinet Office 1991; Counsellor FCO 1993; Counsellor (Political) and then Minister and Deputy Head of Mission Bonn 1996; Minister and Deputy Head of Mission Berlin 1999; m 1974 Judith Angela Carryer (2s 1979, 1985; 1d 1981).

Chase, Robert John; Consul-General Milan since July 1996; born 13.3.43; FO 1965; Third later Second Secretary Rangoon 1966; FCO 1969; First Secretary (Inf) Rio de Janeiro 1972; FCO 1976; on secondment to ICI Ltd 1980; First Secretary FCO 1982; Counsellor (Comm) Moscow 1985; Counsellor FCO 1988; Consul-General Chicago 1993; m 1966 Gillian Ann Shelton (1d 1968; 1s 1969).

Chassels, Lilias Penman Morton; FCO since May 1993; born 8.5.66; FCO 1988; Addis Ababa 1991; Band A2.

Chatfield, Louise Mary; Mbabane since January 1999; born 28.4.71; FCO 1997; Band A2.

Chatt, Paul Anthony; First Secretary (Management) Warsaw since January 2000; born 7.4.56; FCO 1975; Ottawa 1977; East Berlin 1979; Khartoum 1981; FCO 1984; Third (later Second) Secretary (Aid/Comm) Banjul 1987; Second Secretary (Man/Cons) Berne 1990; Second later First Secretary FCO 1995; Band C5; m(1) 1979 Delyth Hudson (diss. 1988); (2) 1990 Tracie Cavell Heatherington (2d 1992, 1993).

Chatterton-Dickson, Robert Maurice French; First Secretary FCO since September 2000; born 1.2.62; FCO 1990; Second Secretary (Chancery/Information) Manila 1991; First Secretary FCO 1994; First secretary (Press, later PS/HMA) Washington 1997; m 1995 Teresa Bargielska Albor (2d 1996, 1997, 1 step d 1982, 1 step s 1984).

Chaudhry, Kareem Arthur; First Secretary (Regional Affairs) Cairo since May 2001; born 3.3.70; FCO 1994; Dubai 1996; Second Secretary FCO 1999; Band D6; m 1993 Nicola Lauraine Kelly (2s 1994, 1998).

Cherrie, Yvonne Elizabeth; Second later First Secretary (Pol/PPA) Mexico City since July 1997; born 31.3.62; FCO 1980; UKREP Brussels 1982; Sana'a 1985; Bahrain 1988; FCO 1989; on secondment to the Birmingham Chamber of Commerce 1991; Third Secretary (Comm) Berlin 1993; Band C4; m 1996 William Theodore von Minden.

Chesman, Rebecca; Second Secretary (Commercial) Peking since November 1997; born 31.10.72; FCO 1994; Full Time Language Training (Mandarin) 1995; Band C4.

Chick, John Charles; Second Secretary (HM Consul/ECM) Kathmandu since September 2000; born 22.10.47; FCO 1971; Baghdad 1973; FCO 1975; Amman 1976; FCO 1979; Darwin 1980; FCO 1984; Hanoi 1985; FCO 1988; Third Secretary (Man) and Vice Consul Quito 1990; Third Secretary (Comm/Chan/P&PA) Dhaka 1995; Second Secretary FCO 1999; m(1) 1971 Denese Irene Smalley; (diss) (2) 1989 Tran Thi Thuy Duong (1s 1989; 1d 1994).

Chilcott, Dominick John; Counsellor UKREP Brussels since July 1998; born 17.11.59; Royal Navy 1978-79; FCO 1982; Language Training 1984; Third later Second Secretary Ankara 1984; First Secretary FCO 1988; First Secretary Lisbon 1993; First Secretary FCO 1996; m 1983 Jane Elizabeth Bromage (1d 1986, 3s 1988, 1991, 1995).

Childs, Marie-Louise; Quito since January 1995; born 23.3.66; FCO 1989; Vice Consul Bangkok 1991; Band B3; m 1997 Mr S O'Sullivan.

Chown, Christopher James; Paris since March 1993; born 5.3.67 FCO 1988; Band C4; (1s 1994).

Chrimes, Neil Roy; Counsellor (Trade/Economic) Ottawa since July 2001; born 10.6.54; MAFF 1975; Harkness Fellow MIT 1977; MAFF 1979; FCO Economic Adviser 1981; IMF Research Dept, 1987; FCO Senior Economic Adviser 1989; Deputy Permanent Representative UKDel OECD Paris 1994; Jakarta 1998; Head of African Department (Southern) 1999; m 1982, Anne (Henny) Barnes (1s 1988, 1d 1990).

Christie, Iain Robert; SUPL since October 2000; born 7.12.65; called to the Bar (Inner Temple) 1989; Assistant Legal Adviser FCO 1992; Senior Assistant Legal Adviser FCO 1995; FCO 1992; Bridgetown 1998; m Katherine Ann Gillam (2d 1996, 1997).

Christie, Katherine Ann (née Gillam) SUPL since November 1997; born 25.1.69 Band B3; FCO 1992; m 1995 Iain Robert Christie. (2d 1996,1998).

Christopher, Sir Duncan Robin Carmichael, KBE (2000), CMG (1997); HM Ambassador Buenos Aires since November 2000; born 13.10.44; FCO 1970; Second later First Secretary New Delhi 1972; First Secretary FCO 1976; Head of Chancery Lusaka 1980; First Secretary FCO 1983; On loan to Cabinet Office 1985; Counsellor (Comm) Madrid 1987; Counsellor FCO 1991; HM Ambassador Addis Ababa 1994; HM Ambassador Jakarta 1997; m 1980 Merril Stevenson (2d 1989, 1991).

Chubbs, Sylvia Sharon; Budapest since March 2001; born 9.5.58; FCO 1984; Paris 1986; Colombo 1989; Moscow 1993; UKREP Brussels 1995; FCO 1998; Band A2.

Chugg, Daniel Patrick; Vice-Consul (Political) Hong Kong since August 2001; born 26.1.73; FCO 1998; Language Training FCO 1999; Language Training Hong Kong 2000; Band C4; m 1999 Alison Fiona Cubie.

Chun, David John; Second Secretary (Commercial) Madrid since August 1999; born 4.4.64; FCO 1985; Lagos 1987; Moscow 1992; FCO 1996; Band C4; m 1987 Grace Fotheringham (1d 1994).

Chun, Grace (née Fotheringham); SUPL since August 1999; born 24.7.66; FCO 1985; Lagos 1987; Moscow 1992; FCO 1996; Band B3; m 1987 David John Chun (1d 1994).

Church, Alistair John Bentley; SUPL since July 2000; born 23.8.63; FCO 1992; Kiev 1995; Second Secretary FCO 1998; Band C4; m 1990 Michelina Patrizia Forgione (1d 1997).

Church, Bettina Frances; SUPL since June 1997; born 30.4.63; FCO 1983; Gaborone 1984; UKMIS Geneva 1987; SUPL 1990; UKMIS New York 1991; FCO 1992; Band B3; m 1990 Julian Andrew Church (1s 1995).

Church, Roger Gilbert; Jedda since March 2000; born 1.6.46; FO 1965; Abu Dhabi 1968; Bonn

1970; East Berlin 1973; Lusaka 1974; FCO 1976; Madras 1979; Colombo 1980; Quito 1982; Second Secretary (Comm) Madras 1983; Second Secretary FCO 1988; Deputy High Commissioner Nassau 1990; Deputy Head of Mission Lima 1994; FCO 1998; Band C5; m 1972 Kathleen Wilson Dryburgh (2s 1974, 1977).

Clare, Debbie Marie; FCO since June 2000; born 21.3.69; FCO 1987; resigned 1990; reinstated 1994; FCO 1994; Berne 1996; Dar es Salaam 1997; Bonn 1998; Lusaka 1999; Band B3.

Claridge, Susan Elisabeth; FCO since November 1998; born 10.5.60; FCO 1984; UKREP Brussels 1987; UKDIS Geneva 1990; FCO 1993; Bonn 1995; Band B3.

Clark, Angela; Dubai since May 1999; born 22.11.67; FCO 1997; Kuala Lumpur 1998; SUPL 2000; Band A2; m 1998 Christopher Neil Walker (2s 1996, 1999).

Clark, Catherine Elizabeth (née Ferguson); SUPL since May 2000; born 12.6.59; FCO 1979; Singapore 1981; Istanbul 1985; FE/SEA Floater 1988; UKDEL NATO Brussels 1991; Band C4; m 1990 Eldred Richard Wraighte Clark (2d 1994, 1996).

Clark, Christopher George; Floater Duties since February 1999; born 15.4.70; FCO 1990; T/D Mostar 1994; Santiago 1995; Band B3.

Clark, Hilary Mary; FCO since April 1985; born 10.4.62; FCO 1980; UKREP Brussels 1982; Bonn 1983; Band B3.

Clark, James Frame; Head of Conference and Visits Group since August 1999; born 12.3.63; FCO 1988; Second Secretary 1989; full time language training Cairo 1990; FCO 1990; Second Secretary (External Relations) UKREP Brussels 1991; Second later First Secretary FCO 1993; on loan to German Foreign Ministry 1997; First Secretary (EU) Bonn 1998; m 1990 Michele Taylor (diss 1998).

Clark, Janet E; FCO since April 1998; born 18.7.67; Band A2.

Clark, Katherine Margaret (née Storey); FCO since June 1985; born 18.3.50; FCO 1971; Muscat 1972; Budapest 1974; FCO 1975; Peking 1977; UKMIS New York 1978; Rio de Janeiro 1982; Band B3; m 1987 Richard William Clark.

Clark, Kenneth; FCO since August 1997; born 18.8.49; Post Office Savings Department 1966; DSAO 1967; Kuwait 1971; Moscow 1974; Rio de Janeiro 1975; FCO 1978; New York 1981; Jedda 1983; Second Secretary FCO 1986; Second Secretary (Comm) Gabarone 1989; Second Secretary (Management) and Consul Lima 1994; m 1970 Agnes Pearson Elder (3s 1971, 1974, 1978).

Clark, Michael; FCO since September 1996; born 21.9.59; FCO 1979; Georgetown 1983; Stockholm 1986; Kuwait 1988; Montreal 1992; Band D6; m 1983 Jacqueline Anne Wilkins (2s 1985, 1987).

Clark, Paul Nicholas; T/D Bratislava since July 2000; born 26.1.69; FCO 1988; Vienna 1992; UKDEL NATO Brussels 1993; Dhaka 1996; Band B3; m 1991 Katherine Walsh (1s 1991).

Clark, Peter; FCO since February 2001; born 18.4.54; FCO 1982; Principal Research Officer; First Secretary (Chancery) Peking 1988; First Secretary FCO 1992; First Secretary Canberra 1996; m 1977 Alison Padgett (1d 1982; 1s 1984).

Clark, Peter; Tehran since January 2000; born 26.3.47; Royal Air Force 1962-87; FCO 1987; Nairobi 1991; FCO 1995; Band B3 (2s 1974, 1977).

Clark, Sandra Jean; Vice-Consul Düsseldorf since January 1989; born 3.12.67; FCO 1985; UKDEL NATO Brussels 1987; Band B3; m 1990 Mark Stephen Parnell.

Clark, Teresa Melanie; FCO since November 1990; born 29.5.70; Band A2.

Clarke, Julie Linda; Brasilia since April 1999; born 13.1.64; FCO 1988; Moscow 1990; UKMIS New York 1993; Band A2.

Clarke, Pauline Joyce; Zagreb since April 1999; born 8.10.67; FCO 1987; Dhaka 1989; Floater Duties 1993; FCO 1996; Band B3.

Clarke, Peter Michael; FCO since January 1998; born 23.8.63; FCO 1988; Language Training 1990; Full-time Language Training Taiwan 1991 Second Secretary Peking. (Science/Technology) 1993;

Clarke, Richard Ian; High Commissioner Dar es Salaam since August 2001; born 7.9.55; FCO 1977; Caracas 1978; Second later First Secretary FCO 1983; First Secretary Washington 1987; First Secretary later Counsellor FCO 1991; Deputy Head of Mission Dublin 1996; FCO 1998; m 1978 Ann Menzies (1s 1984), (diss) m1993 Sheenagh Marie O'Connor (2s 1995 1997)

Clarke, Roger Colin; Cairo since April 2000; born 1.10.52; Armed Forces 1969-92; FCO 1992; Moscow 1993; New Delhi 1996; C4; m(1) 1971 Linda (2s 1973)(diss 1998), (2) Maria Louise Wesstrom.

Clarke, Roger Stephen Graver, LVO (1991); Deputy Observer later Deputy High Commissioner Windhoek since March 1989; born 8.5.55; FCO 1977; Third Secretary Kinshasa 1978; Second Secretary Paris 1980; First Secretary FCO 1984; on loan to DTI 1986.

Clarke, Rosemary Protase, MBE (1992); First Secretary (Commercial) Singapore since July 2000; born 13.2.50; FCO 1977; Port Louis 1978; FCO 1982; Manila 1984; Bahrain 1988; Second Secretary FCO 1991; Second Secretary (Immigration) Dhaka 1992; Band C5; m 1982 Daniel Sinassamy (1s 1984; 1d 1987).

Clarke, Sarah (née Hutson); Vice-Consul (Political) Jerusalem since August 1998; born 28.1.61; FCO 1983; Accra 1985; Ankara 1988;

FCO 1991; Islamabad 1993; FCO 1996; Band B3; m 1993 Richard Henry Clarke.

Clarke, Shaun Jerome; Third Secretary (Management) Tokyo since July 2001; born 7.11.67 (Home Civil Service 1989-1993); FCO 1993; Amman 1996; Valletta 1999; Band B3; m 1996 Karen Angela Evans.

Clasen, Peter; FCO since September 1998; born 2.12.74; Band C4.

Clay, Edward CMG (1994); High Commissioner Nairobi since December 2001; born 21.7.45; Third Secretary FO (later FCO) 1968; Nairobi 1970; Second later First Secretary (Chancery) Sofia 1973; FCO 1975; First Secretary (Comm) Budapest 1979; First Secretary FCO 1982; Counsellor and Head of Chancery Nicosia 1985; Counsellor FCO 1989; High Commissioner Kampala 1993 additionally HM Ambassador Burundi and Rwanda 1994; FCO 1997; High Commissioner Nicosia 1999; m 1969 Anne Stroud (3d 1972, 1974, 1978).

Clay, Pamela; (née Kendall); SUPL since April 2001; born 26.11.62; FCO 1986; Moscow 1989; FCO 1990; Copenhagen 1992; FCO 1995; Helsinki 1997; The Hague 1998; Band A2; m 1998 Andrew Garry Clay (1d 2000).

Clayden, Dr Timothy, OBE (2000); Counsellor (Political) Islamabad since October 2001; born 28.3.60; Second later First Secretary FCO 1989; First Secretary (Info) Warsaw 1991; FCO 1994; Lagos 1995; First Secretary FCO 1999; m 1984 Katharine Susan Jackson.

Clayton, Mark Darrell, Third Secretary (Political) Moscow since August 1998; born 12.6.73; FCO 1997; Band C4.

Cleary, Anthony Shaun; First Secretary (Energy) Paris (OECD) since September 1998; born 27.10.65; Third later Second later First Secretary (Chancery) Pretoria/Cape Town 1990; FCO 1988; First Secretary FCO 1994.

Cleaver, Helen Louise; FCO since June 2001; Born 11.12.68; FCO 1989; Brussels 1996; FCO 1999; Stockholm 2000; Band A2.

Clegg, Laura Margaret; SUPL since June 2000; born 29.3.65; FCO 1989; Vice Consul Bucharest 1994; Deputy Head of Mission Antananarivo 1997; Band C4.

Clegg, Leslie David; MVO (1985); Deputy Head Consular Division since March 2000; born 12.10.49; FO (later FCO) 1967; Banjul (formerly Bathurst) 1971; Wellington 1974; FCO 1977; New Delhi 1980; Second Secretary Lisbon 1984; First Secretary FCO 1988; First Secretary (Comm) Madrid 1992; First Secretary (Management) Nairobi 1996; FCO 2000; m 1970 Louise Elizabeth Straughan (3d 1973, 1976, 1984).

Cleghorn, Bruce Elliot; High Commissioner Kuala Lumpur since November 2001; born 19.11.46; Second Secretary FCO 1974; Second Secretary UKDEL CSCE Geneva 1974; Second Secretary FCO 1975; First Secretary (NATO)

Brussels 1976; First Secretary New Delhi 1980; First Secretary FCO 1983; Counsellor UKDEL CSCE Vienna 1987; Deputy Head of Delegation UKDEL CFE Vienna 1989; Counsellor and Deputy High Commissioner Kuala Lumpur 1992; Head of Non Proliferation Dept FCO 1995; Minister and Deputy Permanent Representative, UKDEL NATO Brussels 1997; m 1976 Sally Ann Robinson (3s 1978, 1981, 1986).

Cleland, Deborah Julia (née Caldow); Second Secretary FCO since February 1999; born 8.9.67; FCO 1987; Accra 1990; FCO 1992; Oslo 1994; Band C4; m 1993 James Cleland.

Clements, Martin Hugh; First Secretary Bonn since July 1998; born 26.7.61; FCO 1983; Second Secretary (Chancery) Tehran 1986; FCO 1987; First Secretary (IAEA) UKMIS Vienna 1990; First Secretary FCO 1994.

Clements, Michael Colin; SUPL since September 1992; born 24.8.49; FCO 1974; Second later First Secretary Athens 1976, on loan to the Cabinet Office 1980; FCO 1982; First Secretary and Head of Chancery Singapore 1985; First Secretary FCO 1989; Counsellor and Deputy High Commissioner Nicosia 1990; m 1972 Julia Mary Roebuck.

Clemitson, Lynne Dawn; FCO since July 1991; born 4.5.61; FCO 1979; Washington 1982; Dhaka 1985; Wellington 1988; Band B3; m 1983 Malcolm John Clemitson.

Clephane, James Cavin Alexander, OBE (1996); SUPL since November 1999; born 3.2.54; Second later First Secretary Bandor Seri Begawan 1991; FCO 1973; Budapest 1976, Seoul 1977; Jakarta 1980; FCO 1983; Third later Second Secretary Muscat 1986; First Secretary (Defence Co-operation) Bandar Seri Begawan 1995; On loan to the MOD 1998; Band D6; m 1974 Mary Buchanan Dorman.

Clews, Anthony Edward; Moscow since October 1996; Floater Duties 1988; born 31.5.38; RAF 1955-78; Lusaka 1978; Havana 1979; Damascus 1980; Ankara 1982; Rome 1983; Kampala 1986; Budapest 1991; Rome 1994 Band C4.

Cliff, Ian Cameron, OBE (1991); HM Ambassador Sarajevo since October 2001; born 11.9.52; FCO 1979; Language Training 1980; Second later First Secretary Khartoum 1982; First Secretary FCO 1985; First Secretary (Chancery) UKMIS New York 1990; Counsellor on loan to the DTI 1993; Deputy Head of Mission Vienna 1996; m 1988 Caroline Mary Redman (1s 1989, 1d 1993).

Clissold, Sean Dominic; First Secretary (Management) and Consul Ankara since November 2000; born 6.4.58; FCO 1975; UKMIS Geneva 1978; Rabat 1981; Ankara 1983; Lagos 1987; FCO 1990; Third Secretary (Commercial) Istanbul 1993; Second Secretary (Consular) Warsaw 1997; Band C5; m 1986 Belgin Savaci.

Clough, Graham Ronald; Second Secretary (Political) Dhaka since November 1998; born

13.5.55; FCO 1995; Band B3; m 1995 Harvinder Kaur Sabharwal.

Cloughton, Stephen Paul; FCO since June 2000; born 4.11.65; FCO 1986; Bangkok 1991; FCO 1994; Skopje 1996; Band B3; m 1997 Karen Dowen.

Clunes, Anna Louise; First Secretary (Chancery) UKMIS New York since February 2000; born 12.3.73; FCO 1994; Full-time Language Training 1996; Second Secretary (KHF) Warsaw 1996; Band D6.

Clydesdale, William Reginald; FCO since January 1997; born 12.8.43; MOD 1960; FCO 1980; Lagos 1985; Third Secretary Sofia 1987; FCO 1990; Washington 1994; Band C4; m 1969 Noreen Foister (2s 1973, 1976).

Coates, David; Director-General Of Trade Taipei since April 1999; born 13.11.47; Second later First Secretary FCO 1974; Language Student Hong Kong 1977; First Secretary (Comm) Peking 1978; FCO 1981; First Secretary UKMIS Geneva 1986; Counsellor Peking 1989; Counsellor FCO 1993; m 1974 Joanna Kay Weil (2d 1976, 1978).

Coates, Sally Ann (née Mawby); Accra since October 1998; born 29.7.60; FCO 1979; Washington 1984; FCO 1987; Tortola 1988; Georgetown 1992; FCO 1992; Mbabane 1993; Beirut 1996; Band A2; m 1995 Alan Roger Coates.

Cobden, Alan; HM Deputy Consul-General and Consul (Commercial) Los Angeles since September 1998; born 15.7.54; FCO 1970; Canberra 1975; Tehran 1977; Africa Floater 1978; Bombay 1980; FCO 1983; Third later Second Secretary Sofia 1986; Second Secretary (Agriculture/Environment) Dublin 1989; Second Secretary FCO 1994; m 1982 Karen Anne Fawn (1s 1985, 1d 1987).

Cochrane-Dyet, Fergus John; Deputy Consul-General and Director of Trade and Investment Promotion Sydney since September 1998; born 16.1.65; FCO 1987; Third later Second Secretary (Political) Lagos 1990; Second Secretary (Political) Abuja 1993; First Secretary FCO 1994; Head of BIS Tripoli 1996; First Secretary (Commercial) Jakarta 1998; m 1987 Susan Emma Aram (3s 1990, 1991, 1996).

Cockel, Susan Jane; FCO since 1996; born 9.3.66; FCO 1989; Language Training 1990; Full-time Language Training Peking 1991; Third Secretary (Commercial) Peking 1992; On loan to China-Britain Trade Group 1995; T/D Moscow 1996.

Codd, Steven; Deputy Consul-General Shanghai since December 2000; born 19.5.61; FCO 1981; Baghdad 1982; FCO 1985; Beirut 1986; FCO 1988; Hanoi 1990; Lusaka 1993; Second Secretary FCO 1996; First Secretary (Management) Kuala Lumpur 1997; Band C5; m 1993 Ruth Brown Mulligan.

Codrington, Richard John; Deputy High Commissioner Ottawa since May 1999; born

18.12.53; MOD 1975; FCO 1978; Second Secretary (later First Secretary) Dar es Salaam 1980; FCO 1983; New Delhi 1985; First Secretary FCO 1989; on loan to SG Warburg & Co Ltd 1992; Counsellor on loan at the Department of National Heritage 1994; Counsellor (Trade Promotion and Investment) Paris 1995; m 1985 Julia Elizabeth Nolan (Twin s 1991).

Cogger, Darren Barry; Third Secretary (Management) Kiev since December 1997; born 20.5.63; FCO 1984; Athens 1988; Belgrade 1991; New Delhi 1993; FCO 1996; Band B3; m 1986 Johanna Lesley Payne (1d 1989).

Coggles, Paul James; First Secretary (Political) Prague since September 2000; born 24.6.66; FCO 1989; Third Secretary (Chancery) Sofia 1992. Third Secretary FCO 1995; Full Time language Training 1996; Second Secretary (Political) Prague 1997; Band C5.

Coglin, Gillian Joanna; SUPL since April 2000; born 9.8.67; FCO 1989; Bucharest 1991; Bombay 1994; Second Secretary FCO 1997; Band C4.

Colby, Sheila Joan, MBE (2001); Mexico City since July 1998; born 7.5.56; FCO 1979; Lima 1980; FCO 1983; Floater Duties 1984; FCO 1988; Kuala Lumpur 1990; Madrid 1993; FCO 1996; Band B3.

Cole, Alexandra Pamela; FTLT since February 2000; born 2.6.70; FCO 1990; Tehran 1996; Band B3; m 1995 Adrian Frederick Bedford.

Cole, Norman Edward, OBE (1985); First Secretary (Commercial) Riyadh since August 1995; born 24.4.43; Crown Estate Office 1962; DSAO (later FCO) 1967; Karachi 1969 (Second Secretary 1972); (Vice-Consul 1972); Ottawa 1973; on loan to DOT 1977; Second Secretary FCO 1980; First Secretary (Comm) Lusaka 1981; First Secretary FCO 1984; First Secretary (Management) Rome 1987; First Secretary FCO 1992; m 1966 Loretta Scott (2s 1970, 1972; 1d 1975).

Coleman, Julie; Colombo since June 2001; born 13.3.67; Department of Employment 1989-1995; FCO 1995; Addis Ababa 1997; Band A2.

Coleman, Richard Alan; First Secretary (Management/Consul) Prague since July 2000; born 1.2.45; CRO later FCO 1963; Dacca 1968; FCO 1971; Salisbury 1972; FCO 1972; Freetown 1973; Tehran 1975; FCO 1979; Vientiane 1982; Kingston 1985; Second Secretary FCO 1988; Second Secretary (Consular) Peking 1991; Bridgetown 1995; Karachi 1999; FCO 1999; m(1) 1968 Susan Robertson (diss 1973) (1s 1969), (2) 1973 Celia Frances Burnett (1d 1986).

Coleman, Sandra Marie (née Duffy); Washington since June 1997; born 21.11.60; FCO 1984; Algiers 1985; Jerusalem 1987; Turks and Caicos Islands 1991; Dakar 1993; SUPL 1996; Band A2; m 1995 Scott Stanley Coleman.

Coleman, Tracey; Freetown since March 1999; born 23.1.71; FCO 1990; Ottawa 1992; World-wide Floater Duties 1995; Band A2.

Collard, James Malcolm John; MO Khartoum since August 1999; born 30.7.43; DSAO 1965; Belgrade 1968; Colombo 1971; East Berlin 1975; FCO 1976; Dacca 1979; Zurich 1981; FCO 1985; Rome 1989; Second Secretary (Management) Islamabad 1992; Band C4; m 1971 Margaret Mary Melver (1d 1980; 1s 1982).

Collard, Timothy Michael; First Secretary (Hong Kong) Peking since August 1995; born 21.3.60; FCO 1986; Language Training SOAS 1987; Language Training Hong Kong 1988; Second Secretary (Science and Tech) Peking 1989; First Secretary FCO 1993; m 1985 Patricia Polzer (2s 1987, 1989).

Collecott, Peter Salmon; Director Resources, FCO since June 1999; born 8.10.50; Second Secretary FCO 1977; MECAS 1978; (First Secretary 1979); First Secretary (political) Khartoum 1980; First Secretary (Economic/Commercial/Agricultural) Canberra 1982; FCO 1986; Counsellor (Head of Chancery, later DHM) Jakarta 1989; Counsellor (EU and Economic) Bonn 1994; FCO 1998; m 1992 Judith Patricia Pead.

Colley, Timothy John; Deputy Head of Mission Sofia since July 2000; born 13.3.65; FCO 1989, (Second Secretary 1991); Full-time Language Training 1991; Second Secretary (Political) Islamabad 1992; First Secretary FCO 1995; Full time language training 1999; Band D6; m 1993 Janet Mary Rodemark (1s 1997, 1d 1999).

Collier, Geoffrey Thomas Grey; FCO since May 2000; born 27.4.68; FCO 1990; Belgrade 1993; Dakar 1997; m 1999 Müge Elif Törüner.

Collier, Nicholas Gavin; Third Secretary (Political/Economic) Vilnius since May 1998; Born 10.2.69; FCO 1996; Band C4; m 1999 Simona Gatti.

Collier, Stephen John, MVO (1991), RVM (1979); Deputy Consul General and Consul (Commercial) Atlanta since October 1999; born 11.1.52; DTI 1968; FCO 1969; Bonn 1972; Aden 1975; Lilongwe 1976; Lagos 1979; FCO 1983; Amman 1985; Second Secretary Windhoek 1989; Second Secretary FCO 1992; First Secretary (Commercial) Lima 1996; m 1987 Erica Mary Cholwill Wilson.

Collingridge, Andrew; Third Secretary (Management) since June 1998; born 2.11.62; FCO 1985; Lagos 1990; FCO 1994; Band C4; m 1993 Tanya Suzanne Parsons (1d 1998).

Collingridge, Tanya Suzanne (née Parsons); Second Secretary (Political/Information) Bucharest since June 1998; born 4.2.65; FCO 1984; Warsaw 1987; UKDEL Vienna 1989; Lagos 1991; FCO 1994; Full time Language Training 1997; Band C4; m 1993 Andrew Collingridge (1d 1998).

Collings, Barry Anthony; First Secretary FCO since September 1996; born 14.6.50; RAF 1968-69; FCO 1970; Holy See 1974; Beirut 1975; Berlin 1976; Budapest 1980; Second Secretary 1981; FCO 1983; Islamabad 1985; FCO 1988; First Secretary (Bilateral Relations) Bonn 1991;

Consul Munich 1993; Band C5; m 1973 Shirley Gibson (1s 1980; 1d 1984).

Collins, Alan Stanley; CMG; HM Ambassador Manila since December 1998; born 1.4.48; Ministry of Defence 1970; Private Secretary to Vice Chief of the Air Staff 1973-1975; FCO 1981; First Secretary and Head of Chancery Addis Ababa 1986; Counsellor (Commercial) and Deputy Head of Mission Manila 1990; Counsellor FCO 1993; Director of BTCO Taipei 1995; m 1971 Ann Dorothy Roberts (1d 1985, 2s 1988, 1995).

Collins, Helen Laura; Cairo since May 1998; born 15.11.70; FCO 1990; Washington 1994; Band A2.

Collins, James Robert; FCO since January 1993; born 9.11.63; FCO 1986; Strasbourg 1988; Moscow 1990; Band A2; m 1987 Sheila Marie Barry.

Collis, Simon Paul; Consul General Dubai since March 2000; born 23.2.56; FCO 1978; Language Training 1979; Third later Second Secretary Bahrain 1981; First Secretary FCO 1984; UKMIS New York 1986; FCO 1987; First Secretary and Head of Chancery Tunis 1988; FCO 1990; First Secretary (Political) New Delhi 1991; First Secretary FCO 1994; Counsellor and Deputy Head of Mission Amman 1996; secondment to BP Amoco 1999.

Collyer, Neil Patrick; Abuja since August 2000; born 28.5.66; ODA 1985-89; FCO 1991; Pretoria 1996; Lagos 1999; Band B3; m 1997 Sara-Louise Hall.

Collyer, Sara-Louise (née Hall); Abuja since August 2000; born 28.10.73; FCO 1992; SUPL 1996; Pretoria 1997; Lagos 1999; Band A2; m 1997 Neil Patrick Collyer.

Collyer, Nicholas Edwin; Second Secretary (Commercial/Consular) Port of Spain since August 1995; born 15.9.52; Forestry Commission 1969; FCO 1971; Moscow 1974; Colombo 1975; Budapest 1979; FCO 1981; UKMIS Geneva 1983; FCO 1986; New Delhi 1987; Second Secretary FCO 1989; Second Secretary (Comm) Seoul 1992; m 1973 Kathryn Dobson (2s 1978, 1983).

Colvin, Kathryn Frances; Vice Marshal of the Diplomatic Corps since August 1999; born 11.9.45; FO (later FCO) since July 1968; Principal Research Officer 1980; m 1971 Brian Trevor Colvin.

Conley, Brian John; Second Secretary (Commercial/Information) Tunis since April 1999; born 10.4.67; FCO 1986; Lusaka 1989; Third Secretary (Management) and Vice Consul Auckland 1993; FCO 1994.

Connolly, Patrick Anthony, OBE (2001); SMO Peking since October 1998; born 15.2.45; CO 1964; FO 1966; Salisbury 1967; Pretoria 1969; Islamabad 1970; FCO 1973; Vienna 1976; Baghdad 1979; Second Secretary (Aid) New Delhi 1981; FCO 1984; Second Secretary and Vice-Consul Dubai 1986; First Secretary (Commercial)

Tel Aviv 1990; FCO 1995; m 1967 Teresa
Bernadette Crinion (twin s 1969; 1s 1973).

Connolly, Peter Terence; Second Secretary
(Political) Lisbon since November 1996; born
2.5.65; FCO 1988; Third Secretary Managua 1990;
UKREP Brussels 1993; Second Secretary FCO
1994.

Connor, Michael Leslie; First Secretary
(Commercial) Prague since September 1995; born
15.11.49; FCO 1971; UKDEL Vienna 1975;
Moscow 1975; Tehran 1977; FCO 1980; (APS to
Minister of State 1982); Second Secretary Bonn
1983; Second later First Secretary (Comm) Abu
Dhabi 1987; First Secretary FCO 1991; m 1973
Linda Helen Woolnough (1d 1984).

Conroy, Anne Elizabeth, MVO (1991); FCO since
October 2001; born 30.8.63; FCO 1985; Third
later Second Secretary (Chancery) Manila 1988;
Second later First Secretary FCO 1992; Full-time
Language Training 1995; First Secretary (Political)
Budapest 1996.

Contractor, Robert; FCO since 1997; born
17.5.68; FCO 1989; Floater Duties 1992; FCO
1993; Warsaw 1995; Band C4.

Conway, Benjamin Simon; FCO since September
2001; born 19.9.78; Band C4.

Cook, Michael Edgar, CMG (2000); High
Commissioner Kampala since March 1997; born
13.5.41; DSA 1966; Oslo 1967; FCO 1970; First
Secretary and Head of Chancery Accra 1973; First
Secretary (Comm) Stockholm 1977; Resigned
September 1980; Reinstated August 1981; First
Secretary and Head of Chancery Port of Spain
1981; Deputy High Commissioner, Counsellor and
Head of Chancery Dar es Salaam 1984;
Counsellor FCO 1987; HM Consul-General
Istanbul 1992; m(1) 1970 Astrid Edel Wiborg (1d
1971; 1s 1974), (2) 1983 Annebritt Maria Aslund.

Cook, Peter Duncan Gifford; Second later First
Secretary (Chancery) Copenhagen since June
1997; born 15.8.63; FCO 1982; Georgetown 1985;
Doha 1989; Third later Second Secretary FCO
1992; Second Secretary (Political/Information)
Bridgetown 1995; m 1993 Maureen Nanette
Sharp; (2s, 1995, 1996)

Cook, Roger Charles Colbourne; First Secretary
(Commercial/KHF) Kiev since August 1998; born
27.3.42; FO 1960; Stockholm 1963; Bonn 1967;
FCO 1969; Moscow 1971; FCO 1972; Second
Secretary (Comm) Lagos 1976; Moscow 1979;
Second Secretary (Cons) Dar es Salaam 1981; on
loan to DTI 1984; First Secretary FCO 1986; First
Secretary (Tech) Paris 1988; First Secretary (FCO)
1990; First Secretary (Econ/Comm) Kiev 1993;
First Secretary Moscow 1995; First Secretary
Algiers 1996; m 1963 Anne May Fountaine (2s
1963, 1966; 1d 1970).

Cooke, Ann; Hong Kong since March 2000; born
26.2.66; DoT 1982; CAA 1989; FCO 1992;
UKMIS New York 1996; Band A2; m 1986 Lloyd
Norman Cooke (1d 1990).

Coombs, Kay; HM Ambassador Ulaanbaatar since
July 1999; born 8.7.45; DSAO later FCO 1967;
Bonn 1971; Latin America Floater 1973; Second
Secretary (Consul) Zagreb 1976; FCO 1979;
Second Secretary (Aid/Inf) La Paz 1982; First
Secretary (Inf) Rome 1987; First Secretary FCO
1991; Peking 1995.

Coombs, Nicholas Geoffrey; First Secretary
(Political) Riyadh since June 2000; born 14.12.61;
FCO 1984; Language Training 1985; Second
Secretary (Chancery) Riyadh 1987; Second later
First Secretary FCO 1989; First Secretary Amman
1993; First Secretary FCO 1997; Band D6; m
1990 Julie Elizabeth Hardman (2d 1996, 1998).

Cooper, Amanda Jane; Shanghai since October
1999; born 2.3.60; HSE 1987-95; FCO 1995;
Vilnius 1996; Band A2.

Cooper, Andrew George Tyndale; Counsellor
FCO since May 1999; born 13.12.53; FCO 1983;
First Secretary Canberra 1984; FCO 1987; First
Secretary (UN/Press) UKMIS Geneva 1988; First
Secretary later Counsellor FCO 1992; Stockholm
1995; m 1981 Donna Mary Elizabeth Milford (2s
1988, 1996).

Cooper, Derek John William; Second Secretary
(Political) Riyadh since July 2001; born 7.1.68;
FCO 1986; Islamabad 1989; FCO 1992; Zagreb
1994; FCO 1998; Band C4; m 1998 Sanja Vilus.

Cooper, Jonathan Charles Gerard; First Secretary
(Economic Affairs) UKMIS Geneva since July
1999; born 9.2.66; FCO 1996; Band D6; m2000
Taryn Victoria Cosgrove.

Cooper, Julie Maria (née Ingham); Pretoria since
January 1999; born 3.1.65; FCO 1984; Harare
1986; SUPL 1990; Dhaka 1991; SUPL 1994; FCO
1997; Cape Town 1997; Gaborone 1997; Band A2;
m 1987 Eric Robert Cooper (diss 1994) (2s 1989,
1990).

Cooper, Rachel Elizabeth; FCO since May 1999;
born 3.11.65; FCO 1989; Vice-Consul Copenhagen
1992; Deputy Head of Mission Bratislava 1995.

Cooper, Robert Francis; CMG(1997), MVO (1975);
Head of Overseas Defence Section, Cabinet
Office, since December 1999; born 28.8.47; Third
Secretary FCO 1970; Sheffield University 1971;
Tokyo 1972; Second Secretary 1973; First
Secretary 1976); FCO 1977; Seconded to Bank of
England 1982; First Secretary (External Trade)
UKREP Brussels 1984. Counsellor FCO 1987
Counsellor (Political) Bonn 1993; Minister Bonn
1996; Director FCO 1998.

Cope, Brian Roger, MVO (2000); Kampala since
January 2000; born 1.3.59; Inland Revenue 1975;
FCO 1976; Paris 1979; Bucharest 1982; Islamabad
1984; FCO 1988; Third Secretary Colombo 1991;
Second Secretary (Management) Accra 1995;
Band C5; m 1982 Heather Margaret Frensham (1d
1990, 1s 1993).

Cope, John Charles; Second Secretary
(Management/Consular) Prague since February

1995; born 10.8.46; FO 1964; Paris 1968; Moscow 1971; Delhi 1972; Karachi 1974; FCO 1976; Dakar 1978; Warsaw 1981; FCO 1982; Hanoi 1985; FCO 1987; Second Secretary (Admin/Cons) Kathmandu 1988; Second Secretary FCO 1991.

Copland, Joanne Catherine; SUPL since August 2000; born 2.9.71; FCO 1990; Washington 1993; Peking 1996; On Loan to The Cabinet Office 1999; Band B3.

Copleston, John de Carteret; Counsellor FCO since September 2000; born 26.1.52; FCO 1971; Paris 1975; Third later Second Secretary FCO 1978; Second later First Secretary Islamabad 1980; First Secretary FCO 1983; First Secretary (Chancery) Jakarta 1987; First Secretary FCO 1990; Counsellor Abuja later Lagos 1993; Counsellor FCO 1995; Counsellor (Multilateral) Canberra 1997; m 1987 Jane Marie Francesca Wilcox (4d 1988, 1991, 1993, 1997).

Copley, Caroline Helen (née Hall); SUPL since June 2001; born 19.1.65; FCO 1987; Third later Second Secretary (Chancery) Oslo 1990; Floater Duties 1991; FCO 1992 (First Secretary 1994); First Secretary (Political) Paris 1997; SUPL 1999; First Secretary (Political) Paris 2000; Band D6; m 1996 John Richard Copley (1d 1999).

Coppin, Nicholas James; First Secretary FCO since November 1999; born 27.3.71; FCO 1992; Second Secretary (Pol/PPA) Bucharest 1995; First Secretary Skopje 1999.

Corbett, Hannah Kathleen Taylor; Second Secretary (External) UKREP Brussels since June 1999; born 4.8.74; FCO 1997; Band C4.

Cordery, Andrew David; Counsellor FCO since June 1999; born 2.5.47; Second Secretary FCO 1974; Nairobi 1975; First Secretary UKMIS New York 1977; FCO 1981; First Secretary (Econ) Lusaka 1984; First Secretary BM Berlin 1988; First Secretary later Counsellor FCO 1991; Counsellor Oslo 1995; m 1970 Marilyn Jean Smith (2d 1975, 1977).

Cork, Richard John; First Secretary (Commercial) Bucharest since August 1998; born 14.11.42; FO 1960; Kathmandu 1964; Bonn 1968; FCO 1971; Manila 1974; FCO 1976; Ottawa 1977; Vice-Consul (Admin) Karachi 1980; Second later First Secretary (Comm) Bahrain 1984; First Secretary FCO 1988; First Secretary (Comm) Manila 1990; First Secretary (Management/Consular) Stockholm 1994; m(1) 1964 Joan Dorothy Seabourne (1d 1969); (2) 1976 Annabelle Alvestir y Empleo (1d 1978; 2 step d 1969, 1974).

Cormack, Ian Ronald; First Secretary (Commercial) Stockholm since September 1998; born 20.11.56; FCO 1975; Nairobi 1978; Havana 1980; Latin America Floater 1982; Africa/Middle East Floater 1984; FCO 1986; Shanghai 1988; Third Secretary Stockholm 1991; FCO 1995.

Corner, Diane Louise; Deputy Head of Mission Harare since February 2001; born 29.9.59; FCO 1982; Second Secretary (Chancery) Kuala Lumpur

1985; Second Secretary FCO 1989; SUPL 1989; First Secretary FCO 1989; On loan to the Cabinet Office 1991; Deputy Head of Mission and First Secretary (Pol) Berlin 1994; FCO 1998; NATO College Rome 2000; m 1986 Peter Timothy Stocker (3d 1989, 1991, 1994).

Corrans, Paula Anne; Sao Paulo since November 1998; born 4.2.70; FCO 1995; UKREP Brussels 1997; Band A2.

Correa, Clive Joel; On loan to British Trade International since October 2000; born 5.11.64; FCO 1988; Transferred to Diplomatic Service 1989; Rangoon 1991; Full-time Language Training 1995; Budapest 1996; FCO 1998; Band C4; m 1990 Andrea Parker (2d 1993, 1996).

Corrigan, Rosalind Mary; Third Secretary (Chancery) Buenos Aires since May 1994; born 7.12.66; FCO 1991; UKMIS New York 1993; Band B3.

Cottrell, Cathy; Second Secretary (Commercial) Moscow since January 1999; born 3.4.63; FCO 1991; Band C4; m 1984 Simon John (2d 1990, 1992).

Coulson, Andrew John, LVO (1984), Counsellor FCO since March 1998; born 17.12.50; FCO 1973; Tel Aviv 1976; Tehran 1978; Second later First Secretary FCO 1980; First Secretary (Inf.) Amman 1983; FCO 1986; First Secretary (Chancery) Harare 1989; First Secretary FCO 1991; First Secretary (Political) Muscat 1995; m 1978 Merope Jane Wilkinson (1d 1982, 1s 1986).

Coulson, Graham; Kingston since August 1999; born 11.10.46; Army 1962-86; Vienna 1988; New Delhi 1989; Sofia 1992; Floater Duties 1996; Band B3; m 1971 Maureen Joyce Howard (diss 1994) (1s 1971, 1d 1974).

Coulter, Anthony Julian; First Secretary (Chancery) Baku since January 1999; born 1.11.61; FCO 1984; Second Secretary (Chancery) Ankara 1987. Second Secretary FCO 1990. First Secretary (Political) Amman 1994; FCO 1998; Band D6; m 1997 Munire Gulay Kilic (1d 2000).

Courage, Rafe Philip Graham; Second Secretary (Economic/Commercial) Ankara since November 1998; born 20.10.63; FCO 1986; Third Secretary Brussels 1989; Third Secretary Islamabad 1991; Second Secretary FCO 1995; Full time language training 1997; m 1988 Theresa Jayne Pile (4d 1990; 1992; 1996, 1997).

Court, Robert Vernon; Deputy High Commissioner Canberra since April 2001; born 28.1.58; FCO 1981; concurrently Third Secretary and Vice-Consul Chad; Second Secretary Bangkok 1984; First Secretary FCO 1986; Private Secretary to the Minister of State 1988; First Secretary (Political) UKDEL NATO Brussels 1990; First Secretary (Press/Information) UKREP Brussels 1993; on loan to Rio Tinto plc 1996; SUPL 1997; m 1983 Rebecca Ophelia Sholl (3s 1986, 1988. 1990, 1d 1993).

Couzens, James McGeorge Dale; Third Secretary Windhoek since January 2001; born 19.2.67; FCO 1990; Bridgetown 1995; Third Secretary Tunis 1997; Band B3; m 1993 Susan Ann Phillips (1d 1994, 1s 1996).

Covington, Susan Elsie (née Perin); SUPL since 2000; born 4.11.52; FCO 1987; UKDEL Vienna 1989; FCO 1991; UKDEL Brussels 1996; Band A2; m 1993 Colin Covington.

Cowan, Anthony Evelyn Comrie; Counsellor FCO since May 2000; born 28.3.53; Third Secretary FCO 1975; Language Student Cambridge 1977; Language Student Hong Kong 1978; Second later First Secretary Peking 1980; First Secretary FCO 1982; First Secretary (Chancery) Brussels 1987; First Secretary FCO 1991; Consul (Political and Economic) Hong Kong 1996.

Coward, Ruth Valerie; The Hague since June 1996; born 18.9.60; FCO 1985; New Delhi 1988; Mexico City 1991; Band B3; m2000 Barry Willis.

Cowell, (Andrew) (John) Hamish; FCO since September 1999; born 31.1.65; FCO 1987; UKMIS New York 1988; Douala 1989; Third later Second Secretary Colombo 1989; First Secretary (Chancery) and Deputy Head of Mission, Tehran 1992; First Secretary FCO 1994; Head of Political, Economic and Aid Sections Cairo 1996.

Cowell, Anita Ann; Jakarta since March 2000; born 7.5.74; FCO 1993; Band A2.

Cowling, Geoffrey Stanley; Consul-General Rio de Janeiro since September 1999; born 20.9.45; Board of Trade 1964; Colonial Office later Commonwealth Office (later FCO) 1966; Vice-Consul and Third Secretary Kabul 1970; Vice-Consul and Third Secretary Port Moresby 1974; Second Secretary (Tech Asst) Lima 1976; FCO 1979 (First Secretary 1982); First Secretary (Econ) Copenhagen 1982; Joint Service Defence College 1987; First Secretary FCO 1988; Deputy Consul General São Paulo 1991; on Loan to Rover International 1995; FCO 1996; m 1970 Irene Joyce Taylor (1s 1971; 2d 1975, 1980).

Cowper-Coles, Sherard Louis, CMG (1997), LVO (1991); HM Ambassador Tel Aviv since September 2001; born 8.1.55; FCO 1977; Language Student MECAS 1978; Third later Second Secretary Cairo 1980; First Secretary FCO 1983; Private Secretary to the Permanent Under-Secretary 1985; First Secretary (Chancery) Washington 1987; First Secretary FCO 1991; on secondment to the International Institute of Strategic Studies 1993; Counsellor FCO 1994; Counsellor (Political) Paris 1997; Private Secretary to the Secretary of State for Foreign and Commonwealth Affairs 1999; m 1982 Bridget Mary Elliot (4s 1982, 1984, 1987, 1990; 1d 1986).

Cox, David George; First Secretary FCO since April 2000; born 7.12.61; FCO 1984; Third later Second Secretary (Chancery) Canberra 1986; Second later First Secretary (Econ) Islamabad

1989; FCO 1992; First Secretary (Political) Luanda 1995; Band D6.

Cox, David Thomas; On loan to the DTI since December 1998; born 27.4.44; FO (later FCO) 1967; Berlin 1970; FCO 1972; Prague 1974; Munich 1976; FCO 1979; Lusaka 1982; Second Secretary (Commercial) Budapest 1986; First Secretary FCO 1990; Copenhagen 1993; m 1975 Claudia Zeillinger (1s 1981, 1d 1989).

Cox, Jeffrey William; FCO since December 1997; born 26.10.43; Second Secretary FCO 1973; First Secretary Vienna 1975; First Secretary FCO 1978; First Secretary Madrid (CSCE Delegation) 1980; Pretoria 1981; First Secretary FCO 1985; First Secretary BMG Berlin 1988; First Secretary, later Counsellor FCO 1990; Consul Munich 1994; m 1969 Elizabeth Louise Bendle (3d 1971, 1973, 1978).

Cox, Jolyon Nicholas; Second Secretary FCO since September 2001; born 21.9.61; FCO 1979; Bonn 1983; Sana'a 1985; FCO 1988; Second Secretary (Bilateral Relations) Bonn 1993; Second Secretary FCO 1998; Second Secretary (Political) Tehran 2000; Band C4; m 1986 Francesca Ann Hindson. (1s 1993).

Cox, Julie Ann, MVO (1996); New Delhi since January 2001; born 10.7.62; FCO 1986; Peking 1988; Jerusalem 1990; Warsaw 1993; FCO 1996; Band B3.

Cox, Nigel John; Minister, Peking, since January 2000; born 23.4.54; FCO 1975; Language Student Cambridge 1976; Language Student Hong Kong 1977; Second Secretary Peking 1978; Second later First Secretary FCO 1981; ENA Paris 1984; First Secretary Paris 1985; First Secretary FCO 1990; Counsellor Peking 1992; Counsellor FCO 1996; m 1992 Olivia Jane Paget.

Cox, Olivia Jane (née Paget); SUPL since December 1999; born 31.7.57; FCO 1978; Mexico City 1980; FCO 1982; Third Secretary (Chancery) Paris 1987; FCO 1990; (Second Secretary 1991); SUPL 1992; FCO 1996; Band C4; m 1992 Nigel John Cox.

Cox, Richard James; Third Secretary (Management) Hanoi since August 1997; born 7.8.67; FCO 1991; Addis Ababa 1993; Band B3.

Crabbie, Christopher Donald, CMG (1995); UK Representative for the Organisation for Economic Co-operation and Development Paris since October 1999; born 17.1.46; Second Secretary FCO 1973; First Secretary Nairobi 1975; Washington 1979; FCO 1983; Counsellor on loan to HM Treasury 1985; Counsellor FCO 1987; Counsellor (Financial and European Community) Paris 1990; HM Ambassador Algiers 1994; HM Ambassador Bucharest 1996; m 1992 Frances Patricia Bogan.

Crabtree, Joanne Elizabeth; Sana'a since December 1999; born 26.9.68; FCO 1988; Mexico City 1990; Dubai 1993; Band B3.

Craddock, Timothy James; On loan to DFID since October 2000; born 27.6.56; FCO 1979; Vice-Consul (Information), Istanbul 1981; Second Secretary Ankara 1982; First Secretary FCO 1985; First Secretary UKDEL Paris 1990; First Secretary FCO 1995; HM Ambassador Tallinn 1997.

Craig, David Hamilton; First Secretary (Political) Ankara since August 2001; born 5.12.61; FCO 1989; Language Training 1990; Second Secretary (Chancery) Nicosia 1991; Second later First Secretary FCO 1993; Full-time Language Training 1994; Full-time Language Training Cairo 1995; Consul Jedda 1996; First Secretary FCO 1999; Band D6; m 1994 Hala el-Kara (2s 1995, 1997; 1d 1999).

Craig, Deborah Louise (née Tyson); Islamabad since February 2000; born 1.1.72; FCO 1990; Nicosia 1995; FCO 1998; Band A2; m 1995 Ian Douglas Craig (1d 1999; 1s 2000).

Craig, John Jenkinson; Second Secretary FCO since September 1979; born 8.1.49; FCO 1972; Third Secretary Rome 1978; Band C4; m 1965 Glenys Menai Edmunds (2d 1977, 1984; 2s 1979, 1981).

Craig, Lesley, MBE (1995); Tel Aviv since June 2000; born 13.5.67; FCO 1988; T/D Islamabad 1990; Vice-Consul Kathmandu 1991; Third Secretary (Chancery) Kampala 1994; FCO 1997; Band B3.

Craig, Robyn Jean; Addis Ababa since August 1996; born 9.3.65; FCO 1984; Moscow 1986; Oslo 1987; Rabat 1990; FCO 1993; Band B3.

Cramman, Ian Pallister; Addis Ababa since November 2000; born 11.3.70; FCO 1989; Khartoum 1992; Full-time Language Training 1994; Düsseldorf 1995; Band B3; m 1997 Ding Yu.

Craven, Stella Susan; Wellington since July 2001; born 24.3.50; WRAF 1967-71; FCO 1972; Suva 1973; FCO 1975; Khartoum 1976; FCO 1977; Resigned 1978; Reinstated 1979; FCO 1979; Islamabad 1981; FCO 1984; Harare 1986; FCO 1989; Band B3.

Crawford, Charles Graham, CMG; Chargé d'Affaires Belgrade since January 2001; born 22.5.54; FCO 1979; Second later First Secretary (Information) Belgrade 1981; First Secretary FCO 1984; First Secretary Cape Town/Pretoria 1987; First Secretary FCO 1991; Counsellor Moscow 1993; HM Ambassador Sarajevo 1996; Harvard University 1998; Director South East Europe 1999; m 1990 Helen Margaret Walsh (2s 1991, 1993; 1d 1999).

Crawford, Fabiola Magdalena; Riyadh since April 1996; born 1.4.66; FCO 1987; UKDEL Vienna 1988; Damascus 1991; FCO 1994; Band B3.

Crawford, Marilyn Elisabeth; FCO since July 1995; born 16.8.47; FCO 1975; UKDEL NATO Brussels 1977; Antigua 1980; FCO 1982; UKDEL Brussels 1988; FCO 1991; Paris 1994; Band A2.

Crawford, Michael James; Counsellor Islamabad since June 1999; born 3.2.54; FCO 1981; Second later First Secretary Cairo 1983; First Secretary Sana'a 1985; First Secretary Riyadh 1986; First Secretary FCO 1990; First Secretary (Political) Warsaw 1992; FCO 1995; m 1984 Georgia Anne Moylan (twins, 1s 1d 1986, 1s 1989).

Crees, Ian Alec; HM Consul General and Joint Management Officer Geneva since March 1999; born 31.1.43; Air Ministry 1960; Passport Office 1961; CRO 1963; Nairobi 1963; Nicosia 1966; FCO 1968; Rawalpindi (later Islamabad) 1971; Vice Consul, Strasbourg 1975; FCO 1978; Second Secretary (Political/Aid) Kinshasa 1980 (also accredited to Congo-Brazzaville, Rwanda and Burundi); Second Secretary (Comm) Seoul 1984 (First Secretary 1988); First Secretary FCO 1989; First Secretary (Comm/DHM) Bombay 1993; FCO, Conference Department (European Council) 1998; T/D Islamabad 1998; m 1963 Betty Winifred Kelder (1d 1965; 1s 1967).

Cresswell, Jeremy Michael, CVO (1996); Deputy Head of Mission and Head of Political and Public Affairs Berlin since June 2001; born 1.10.49; FCO 1972; Third later Second Secretary Brussels 1973; Second Secretary Kuala Lumpur 1977; First Secretary FCO 1978; Private Secretary to Parliamentary Under-Secretary, then Minister of State 1981-82; Deputy Political Adviser BMG Berlin 1982; First Secretary FCO 1986; Counsellor and Head of Chancery UKDEL Brussels 1990; Full-time Language Training 1994; Deputy Head of Mission Prague 1995; Counsellor FCO 1998; m 1974 Ursula Petra Forwick (1d 1978; 1s 1985).

Creswell, Alexander John Peter; First Secretary (Political) Kuwait since July 2001; born 27.7.65; FCO 1993; Second Secretary (Political) Pretoria 1995; Second Secretary FCO 1998; Band D6; m 1995 Katharine Louise Reid.

Critchley, Benjamin Hugh Sutherland; Second Secretary (Political) T/D Tbilisi since September 2000; born 23.8.73; FCO 1997; Second Secretary (Economic) Vienna 1999; Band C4.

Critoph, Tracey Marjorie; Bombay since December 1998; born 26.8.64; FCO 1988; Jakarta 1990; Port Louis 1994; FCO 1997; Band A2; m 1997 M J E Fleurot.

Crockard, Gavin; Floater duties since August 1998; born 11.2.68; FCO 1989; Bombay 1991; Pretoria 1995; FCO 1996; Band B3.

Crocker, Helen; Madrid since September 2000; born 24.10.67; FCO 1999; Band A2.

Crocker, John Michael; on loan to Shell since May 1997; born 27.6.63; FCO 1988; Second Secretary 1989; Full-time Language Training Cairo 1991; Second Secretary (Chancery) Riyadh 1992; First Secretary FCO 1995.

Crockett, Patricia Anne; Nicosia since November 1993; born 19.11.48; Tokyo 1974; Copenhagen

1977; FCO 1980; Port Louis 1981; FCO 1983; Lusaka 1985; Peking 1989; FCO 1991; Band B3.

Crombie, Anthony Campbell, OBE (1997); Counsellor (Political) Moscow since September 1999; born 18.10.56; COI 1980; FCO 1985; later First Secretary Havana 1987; First Secretary FCO 1990; Deputy Head of Mission Belgrade 1994; SUPL 1997; m 1982 Jane Nicholls Talbot; (diss 1987).

Crompton, Angela Louise; Maputo since August 2001; born 4.5.64; FCO 1988; Oslo 1991; T/D Islamabad 1994; Brasilia 1995; FCO 1999; Band A2.

Crompton, Richard Anthony Neil; Deputy Head of Mission Tehran since May 1999; born 25.09.64; FCO 1995; Senior Research Officer, First Secretary FCO 1997; FTLT 1998; m 1996 Rosa Zaragoza (1d 2000).

Cronin, Martin Eugene; First Secretary Stockholm since September 1999; born 22.1.65; DoE 1987; FCO 1988; Vice-Consul/AMO Sana'a 1990; FCO 1993; Second Secretary (Political/Economic/ Development) Amman 1994; Band D6.

Cronin, Susan Mary (née Hartland); UKDEL NATO Brussels since August 1999; born 16.4.64; FCO 1983; Washington 1986; Riyadh 1988; FCO 1991; Vice-Consul Singapore 1995; Band B3; m 1985 Neil Cronin. (Diss 1994) (1s 1993)

Crooke, Alastair Warren; Counsellor FCO since March 1995; born 30.6.49; FCO 1974; Third later Second Secretary (Comm) Dublin 1975; First Secretary (Pol/Press) Pretoria 1978; First Secretary FCO 1981; Islamabad 1985; First Secretary FCO 1988; Counsellor Brasilia 1991; Counsellor Bogotá 1993; m 1976 Carole Cecilia Flaxman (1s 1979; twin s 1981).

Crooks, Colin James, LVO (1999); First Secretary FCO since June 1999; born 18.2.69; FCO 1992; Full-time Language Training (Korean) in London 1993 and Seoul 1994; Seoul 1995; m 1996 Kim Young-Kee (1s 1997).

Crooks, Daryl; ECO later Vice-Consul Dhaka since December 1998; born 27.5.68; FCO 1991; Transferred to Diplomatic Service 1999; Band B3; m 1999 Dina R Napao (1d 2000).

Crorkin, Colin Wynn, MBE (1993); First Secretary (Management) later Deputy Head of Mission Lagos since 1997; born 31.1.57; FCO 1975; Rome 1977; Beirut 1980; UKREP Brussels 1983; FCO 1984; Kinshasa 1987; Second Secretary BTIO New York 1992; Second later First Secretary FCO 1993; m(1) 1978 Gillian Smith (diss 1991), (2) 1991 Joanne Lynn Finnamore (1s 1985; 1d 1998).

Cross, Caroline Janice, MBE (1991); Second Secretary (Immigration/Consular) Accra since June 2001; born 30.9.64; FCO 1984; Warsaw 1986; Floater Duties 1989; Third Secretary (Chancery/Information) Kampala 1991; Third later Second Secretary FCO 1994; SUPL 1999; Band C4; m 1998 M Higgins.

Cross, Harriet Victoria Saltonstall; Second Secretary (Political) Rabat since October 1998; Born 25.9.74; FCO 1997; Band C4; m 1999 Lieutenant Philip Saltonstall RN.

Cross, Linda Mary (née Guild); Third Secretary (Political) UKMIS New York since December 1994; born 15.3.56; FCO 1978; Rabat 1978; Prague 1981; Quito 1983; Paris 1985; FCO 1988; Vienna 1991; m 1989 Michael John Cross.

Cross, Margaret Christine; SUPL since April 1992; born 13.1.62; FCO 1980; Dhaka 1985; Frankfurt 1989 (Second Secretary 1991); FCO 1991.

Cross, Shelley; SUPL since June 1996; born 19.11.59; FCO 1980; Bonn 1982; Floater Duties 1985; FCO 1989; Third Secretary (Commercial) Paris 1993; m 1990 Robert Simon George Parker (1d 1992).

Crossland, Dudley Stewart; Third Secretary (Political) Singapore since January 2001; born 2.5.63; FCO 1987; Berne 1989; UKREP Brussels 1990; FCO 1993; New Delhi 1995; Band B3; m 1993 Jennifer Patricia Brown (diss 2000).

Crossland, Jennifer Patricia (née Brown); SUPL since August 2001; born 28.8.64; FCO 1988; UKREP Brussels 1990; FCO 1993; SUPL 1995; New Delhi 1996; Bangkok 1998; Band A2; m 1993 Dudley Stewart Crossland (diss 2000).

Crossman, Steven Nigel; Deputy High Commissioner Georgetown since April 2001; born 16.11.55; FCO 1975; Muscat 1977; Washington 1978; New Delhi 1984; FCO 1987; Third Secretary (Aid) Dar es Salaam 1990; Hanoi 1995; Deputy High Commissioner Freetown 1999; m 1988 Le Hoang Lan.

Crosthwaite, Maureen; FCO since November 1990; born 4.5.43; FCO 1987; Vienna 1988; Band A2.

Croucher, Lance Hans Frederick, MBE (2000); Second Secretary (Consular/Management) Dar es Salaam since August 1996; born 17.3.40; RAF 1956-83; FCO 1983; Karachi 1985; Pretoria 1988; Third later Second Secretary FCO 1991; Second Secretary (Immigration/Consular) Colombo 1994; m(1) 1965 (1d 1966; 1s 1967), (2) 1981 Hildegard Faller (2d 1986, 1987).

Crowder, Richard Lawrence Robert; Second Secretary (Economic) Moscow since October 1999; born 14.11.73; FCO 1996; full time language training (Russian) 1998; Band C4; m2000 Hilary Jane Louise Scott.

Crowther, Diane Elaine; FCO since November 1981; born 5.9.64; Band A2.

Crowther, Kathryn Valerie Bryden; SUPL since September 1996; born 14.2.47; FCO 1987; Rabat 1989; FCO 1992; Gibraltar 1992; Band A2.

Cruickshank, Diane (née Robinson); New Delhi since January 1998; born 15.7.60; FCO 1981; Bogotá 1982; Jakarta 1985; FCO 1988; Lusaka

1990; SUPL 1992; Band B3; Tehran 1994; m 1994 Douglas Graham Cruickshank.

Cullen, Carol Dulceta (née Fisher); Lusaka since April 1999; born 12.11.56; DoE 1975; FCO 1977; Paris 1979; Dublin 1982; FCO 1985; Nairobi 1988; SUPL 1992; FCO 1993; Bridgetown 1996; Band C4; m 1979 Thomas Cullen (1d 1984, 1s 1988).

Cullens, Niall James David; Second Secretary Consul (Commercial) Warsaw since July 2000; born 28.2.65; FCO 1986; BMG Berlin 1988; LA/Caribbean Floater 1990; FCO 1993; Rome 1996; Band C4; m 1998 Caroline Anne Stramik.

Culligan, Phillip David; Deputy High Commissioner Nassau since September 1997; born 27.2.61; FCO 1981; Tripoli 1982; Pretoria/Cape Town 1983; Düsseldorf 1986; FCO 1989 (Second Secretary 1992); Budapest 1993; m (1) 1982 Carole Anne Rouse (diss); (2) 1997 Elizabeth June Huggins (1d 1999).

Culshaw, Robert Nicholas, MVO (1979); Consul General Chicago since June 1999; born 22.12.52; Third Secretary FCO 1974; Language Student MECAS 1975 and FCO 1976; Third Secretary Muscat 1977; Second Secretary Khartoum 1979; First Secretary Rome 1980; FCO (APS to the Secretary of State) 1984; First Secretary and Head of Chancery later Counsellor, Consul General and Deputy Head of Mission Athens 1989; Counsellor and Head of News FCO 1993; Minister-Counsellor (Trade and Transport) Washington 1995; m 1977 Elaine Ritchie Clegg (1s 1992).

Culver, John Howard, LVO (2000); HM Ambassador Reykjavik since January 2001; born 17.7.47; Board of Trade 1967; FO later FCO 1968; Latin America Floater 1971; FCO 1973; Third Secretary Moscow 1974; Second Secretary La Paz 1977; Second later First Secretary FCO 1980; First Secretary (Comm) Rome 1983; Head of Chancery Dhaka 1987; First Secretary FCO 1990; HM Ambassador and Consul General, Managua 1992; Consul General Naples 1997; T/D Rome 2000; Band D7; m 1973 Margaret Ann Davis (1d 1974; 2s 1978, 1981).

Cumming, Melvyn Robert Wilson; First Secretary (Commercial) Bogotá since June 1999; born 17.3.42; FO 1959; Africa Floater 1963; Abu Dhabi 1965; FCO 1968; Seoul 1972; Lagos 1975; Vice-Consul Naples 1978; Second later First Secretary FCO 1983; First Secretary (Comm) Madrid 1987; First Secretary FCO 1992; First Secretary (Comm) Stockholm 1996; m 1971 Pamela Jean Huckle (1d 1975; 1s 1976).

Cummins, John, MBE (1983); First Secretary FCO since November 1995; born 7.9.46; FO (later FCO) 1964; Budapest 1969; Luxembourg 1971; Tunis 1973; FCO 1976; (Second Secretary 1978); Consul and Second Secretary (Admin) Santiago 1980; First Secretary Libreville 1985; First Secretary FCO 1988; Full-time Language Training 1991; First Secretary (Commercial) Prague 1992; m 1969 Gillian Anne Biss (2s 1970, 1972).

Cunningham, Kevin Francis; Second Secretary (Commercial) Bangkok since June 1999; born 8.3.63; Civil Aviation Authority /National Air Traffic Services 1982; Royal Navy 1987; FCO 1992; Gaborone 1995; Band C4; m 1993 Alison Hilary Kathleen Leeland. (2d 1995, 1999).

Cunningham, Raymond Peter, MBE (2001); Islamabad since January 2000; born 21.1.45; Army 1963-1989; FCO 1989; T/D Helsinki 1989; Warsaw 1990; Floater Duties 1992; FCO 1994; Floater Duties 1997; Band B3.

Cupac, Dawn (née Womersley); Vienna since May 2000; born 2.2.64; FCO 1992; Belgrade 1995; Vienna 1999; SUPL 2000; Band A2; m 1997 Dkordje Cupac.

Curle, Moira Rosemary; FCO since November 1997; born 8.10.68; FCO 1986; Belgrade 1990; Bombay 1994; Band B3; m 1995 Ivor MacNamara.

Curley, Eugene Gerard, OBE (1991); Counsellor UKMIS New York since September 2000; born 30.9.55; FCO 1981; Second later First Secretary Mexico City 1984; First Secretary FCO 1986; First Secretary later Counsellor Paris 1993; Counsellor FCO 1998; m 1982 Joanne England (diss 1991); (2) 1993 Jane Margaret Crosland (1d 1996; 1s 2000).

Curley, Jane Margaret (née Crosland); Second Secretary FCO since February 1998; born 24.11.61; FCO 1989; Second Secretary (Political) Copenhagen 1992; SUPL 1993; Band C4; m 1993 Eugene Gerard Curley (1d 1996; 1s 2000).

Curotto, Francine Elene; FCO since November 1999; born 29.8.63; FCO 1990; Copenhagen 1993; FCO 1995; Havana 1997; Band B3.

Curran, David; First Secretary FCO since November 2000; born 8.6.60; FCO 1987; Second later First Secretary Manila 1989; First Secretary (Chancery), UKMIS New York 1992; First Secretary FCO 1994; First Secretary (Political) Lusaka 1997; Band D6; m 1989 Lesley Jane Thomas.

Curran, Lynn Marie, MBE (1997); FCO since October 1994; born 19.4.66; FCO 1984; Athens 1986; Kinshasa 1989; UKDEL Brussels 1992; Band B3.

Currie, David James; First Secretary Commercial Brussels since June 1998; born 21.10.46; CRO (later FCO) 1963; Peking 1969; Helsinki 1971; FCO 1972; Hanoi 1975; Brussels 1976; Manila 1978; Second Secretary FCO 1982; Second Secretary (Comm) Algiers 1986; Assistant Trade Commissioner, later Trade Commissioner (China Trade) BTC Hong Kong 1989; First Secretary FCO 1993; m(1) 1968 Valerie Kirk (1s 1970) (diss 1975); (2) 1977 Joyce Rosalie Deacon; (1 step s 1970, 1 foster s 1970).

Currie, Jacqueline Ann; Deputy High Commissioner Victoria since January 2001; born 8.2.67; FCO 1987; Baghdad 1989; FCO 1991; LA

Floater 1992; Atlanta 1994; Kigali 1998; Gibraltar 2000; Band C4.

Curry, Trudy Gay (née Hibbs); Third Secretary (Consular/Management) Berlin since June 2001; born 9.12.57; FCO 1975; SUPL 1980; Canberra 1981; Brussels 1984; SUPL 1987; FCO 1992; Accra 1994; Doha 1997; Band B3; m(1) 1980 Peter Ian Webb (diss 1983); (2) 1983 Peter Lester Curry (1d 1987; 1s 1990).

Curtis, Penelope Ann; Madrid since November 1996; born 24.6.68; FCO 1990; Mexico City 1992; Band B3.

Cuthbertson, Deborah Ann; Islamabad since November 2000; born 7.4.72; FCO 1991; Band C4.

Cutler, Charlotte Margaret; Second Secretary (Chancery) UKMIS New York since February 2001; born 16.10.72; FCO 1998; Band C4.

Cuxford, Stephanie Anne; FCO since August 1982; born 20.7.65; Band A1.

Cvetkovic, Joanne Davida (née Sayer); FCO since January 2000; born 13.11.66; FCO 1986; Hong Kong 1991; Belgrade 1995; Copenhagen 1998; Band B3; m 1997 Dejan Cvetkovic (1s 1999).

D

Dacey, Alan Treharne; born 10.4.70; FCO since November 1998. FCO 1988; UKDEL NATO Brussels 1991; Africa/Middle East Floater Duties 1994; Band B3; m 1999 Salome Maritz.

Dakin, Nigel John; First Secretary New Delhi since August 1999; born 28.2.64; FCO 1996; Band D6; m 1987 Amanda Louise Johnson (1d 1995).

Dales, Sir Richard Nigel, KCVO (2001), CMG; HM Ambassador Oslo since October 1998; born 26.8.42; FO 1964; Third Secretary Yaoundé 1965; FO (later FCO) 1968; Second Secretary 1969; Copenhagen 1970; First Secretary 1972; FCO 1973; Assistant Private Secretary to the Secretary of State, FCO 1974; First Secretary Head of Chancery and Consul Sofia 1977; FCO 1981; Counsellor and Head of Chancery Copenhagen 1982; DHC, Counsellor and Head of Chancery Harare 1986; Counsellor FCO 1989; On attachment to the CSSB Recruitment and Assessment Services Agency 1991; High Commissioner Harare 1992; Director (Africa and the Commonwealth) FCO 1995; m 1966 Elizabeth Margaret Martin (1s 1973, 1d 1976).

Daley Goldsmith, Robyn Jean; FCO since May 2001; born 08.08.69; FCO 1990; World-wide Floater Duties 1993; Third Secretary Bombay 1995; Third later Second Secretary Belmopan 1998; Grade C4; m 1995 Simon Geoffrey Goldsmith.

Dallas, Andrew James; Doha since February 1999; born 15.1.71; FCO 1990; Dublin 1995; Band A2; m 2001 Sarah Gordon.

Dallas, Ian Michael; First Secretary Dublin since January 1997; born 13.12.42; Board of Trade

1961; Commonwealth Office 1966; Peking 1969; Lagos 1971; Accra 1973; FCO 1975; Chicago 1978; Second Secretary FCO 1982; Second Secretary (Admin) Lusaka 1985; FCO 1988; Vice-Consul (Comm) Karachi 1989; First Secretary (Comm/Aid) Colombo 1993; m 1968 Angela Margaret Moore (1s 1971; 1d 1976).

Dalton, Andreina; Third Secretary (Management) Budapest since December 1997 born 12.7.66; FCO 1986; Paris 1988; Warsaw 1991; FCO 1992; Islamabad 1994; Band B3.

Dalton, Raymond Glyn; Moscow since April 1999; born 25.4.45; Royal Air Force 1960-85; MOD Police 1985-88; Warsaw 1988; Pretoria/Cape Town 1990; Santiago 1992; Sofia 1996; Band C4; m 1964 Mary.

Dalton, Richard John, CMG (1996); Ambassador, Tripoli, since December 1999; born 10.10.48; Third Secretary FCO 1970; MECAS 1971; Second Secretary Amman 1973; Second later First Secretary UKMIS New York 1975; FCO 1979; First Secretary Head of Chancery and Consul Muscat 1983; First Secretary FCO 1987; Counsellor on loan to MAFF 1988; Counsellor on CDA at Chatham House 1991; Counsellor FCO 1992; Consul-General Jerusalem 1993; Counsellor FCO 1998; m 1972 Elisabeth Keays (2s 1978, 1982; 2d 1973, 1979).

Daltrey, Christopher; Secondment to China - Britain trade Group since October 1997; born 21.9.68; FCO 1988; Rome 1990; FCO 1992; Third Secretary BTC Hong Kong 1993; m 1991 Kim Rowena Newson (1s 1992, 2d 1993, 1995).

Daltrey, Kim Rowena; SUPL since April 1992; born 5.5.63; FCO 1986; Berne 1988; FCO 1989; Rome 1990; Band A2; m 1991 Christopher Daltrey (1s 1992; 2d 1993, 1995).

Damper, Carol Ann; FCO since February 2000; born 17.12.44; FCO 1975; Mogadishu 1975; Bonn 1977; Belmopan 1979; FCO 1982; Vienna 1984; FCO 1987; Athens 1988; Bucharest 1991; FCO 1993; Sofia 1997; Band B3.

Dancer, James Anthony; Second Secretary (Political) Belgrade since August 2001; born 19.4.75; FCO 1999; Band C4.

Daniel, Hamish St Clair, MBE (1992); First Secretary (Political/Economic) Jakarta since April 1997; born 22.8.53; FCO 1973; Algiers 1975; Prague 1977; Lisbon 1978; Islamabad 1980; FCO 1982; San Francisco 1985; Second Secretary (Chancery/Aid) Khartoum 1989; Second Secretary FCO 1992; Deputy Head of Mission and HM Consul Sana'a 1994; m 1975 Susan Mary Ann Brent (1d 1981; 1s 1985).

Daniels, Malcolm; FCO since September 1986; born 4.9.48; FCO 1965; Singapore 1980; Helsinki 1984; Band C5; m 1976 Jeannette Susan (2s 1977, 1980).

Daniels, Mark Ian; FCO since January 1994; born 30.8.65; FCO 1982; New Delhi 1985; Washington 1989; Band B3; m 1989 Suzanne Jayne Woodworth.

Darby, Jane; FTLT since June 2001; born 1.4.53; FCO 1984; Bonn 1990; HM Treasury 1994; Cabinet Office 1995; FCO 1996; m 1984 Michael Reece (1s 1986; 1d 1988).

Darby, Jonathan; FCO since February 1999; born 28.12.69; Band D6.

Dare, Gillian Angela; FCO since March 1999; born 7.7.48; Band D6.

Darke, John Martin Jamie; First Secretary FCO since June 1999; born 2.5.53; FCO 1975; MECAS 1977; FCO 1979; MBA London Business School 1981, Management Consultant, HAY-MSL 1983; First Secretary FCO 1985; First Secretary (Chancery) Cairo 1988; First Secretary FCO 1991; First Secretary (Political) Dubai 1996; Band D6; m 1980 Diana Taylor (1d 1989, 1s 1991).

Darker, Aidan; Bahrain since February 1999; born 8.10.62; Royal Air Force 1983-1995; FCO 1995; Hong Kong 1996; m 1989 Angela Darker (1s 1999).

Darker, Angela; SUPL since February 1999; born 12.2.68; Royal Air Force 1986-1990; FCO 1995; Hong Kong 1996; m 1989 Aidan Darker (1s 1999).

Darroch, Nigel Kim, CMG; Counsellor FCO since July 1998; born 30.4.54; FCO 1976; Third later Second and later First Secretary Tokyo 1980; FCO 1985; (Private Secretary to Minister of State January 1987); First Secretary (Econ) Rome 1989; First Secretary later Counsellor FCO 1993; Counsellor (External Relations) UKREP Brussels 1997; m 1978 Vanessa Claire Jackson (1s 1983; 1d 1986).

Dart, Jonathan, MVO; Second Secretary (Inward Investment/Financial Services) Seoul since August 1999; born 14.7.64; FCO 1988; Third Secretary (Science and Technology) Bonn 1991; Third Secretary Pretoria 1994; Full time language training 1998; Band B3; m1990 Claire Emma Juffs (2s 1992, 1994; 1d 1998).

Dauris, James Edward; First Secretary (Commercial) Moscow since January 1999; born 15.1.66; FCO 1995; Band D6; m 1995 Helen Parker.

Davenport, Michael Hayward, MBE (1994); Consul-General and Director of Trade Promotion Warsaw since March 2000; born 25.9.61; FCO 1988; Warsaw 1990; FCO 1993; First Secretary (Political) Moscow 1996; m 1992 Lavinia Sophia Elisabeth Braun (1s 1994, 1d 1996).

Davey, Denise; FCO since October 1996; born 8.5.69; HCS 1987; FCO 1989; Dubai 1990; FCO 1994; Mexico City 1994; Guatemala City 1995; Band B3.

Davey, Simon James MBE (1985); FCO since June 1999; born 1.2.47; Army 1965-68, FCO 1969; Latin America Floater 1972; Havana 1973; Second Secretary (Aid/Comm) Kathmandu 1976; Second later First Secretary FCO 1980; Consul Durban 1983; First Secretary (Comm) Prague 1988; First

Secretary FCO 1992; First Secretary (Commercial) Bogotá 1995; m 1992 Marcela Eva Dzurikova.

David, Timothy James; High Commissioner Belmopan since April 1998. born 3.6.47; FCO 1974; Second later First Secretary Dar es Salaam 1977; FCO 1980; loan to ODA 1983; First Secretary UKMIS Geneva 1985; First Secretary later Counsellor FCO 1988; HM Ambassador Suva 1992. Deputy High Commissioner Harare 1996; m 1996 Rosemary Kunzel.

Davidson, Barry Alexander; Vice Consul Kathmandu since November 1997; born 1.8.64; HCS 1985; UKMIS Geneva 1988; Freetown 1990; FCO 1994; Band B3; m 1985 Elizabeth Helen Oxley (1s 1992; 2d 1994, 1999).

Davidson, Brian John; FTLT since April 2001; born 28.4.64; FCO 1985; Language Training 1986; Third later Second Secretary (Chancery/Inf) Peking 1988; First Secretary On loan to the Cabinet Office 1992; First Secretary FCO 1994; First Secretary (Political) Canberra 1996.

Davidson, Carolyn Jayne; SUPL since January 2000; born 18.4.64; FCO 1986; Language Training FCO 1987; Language Training Kamakura 1988; Tokyo 1989; European Commission 1993; Bonn 1993; Second later First Secretary FCO 1995; Band D6; m 1997 Thomas Henry Carter (2s 1998, 1999).

Davidson, James Gerard; Tripoli since March 2000; born 20.5.67; MOD 1985; FCO 1988; Budapest 1989; Lagos 1991; FCO 1994; Jerusalem 1997; Band B3.

Davidson, Raymond John Bruce, MBE (1995); Islamabad since August 1999; born 24.12.62; FCO 1995; Paris 1997; Band A2 m1988 Shivaun Anne (2s 1991, 1994).

Davidson, Sarah Victoria (née Fox); Doha since January 2000; born 8.10.65; FCO 1985; Warsaw 1987; Hamilton 1989; Budapest 1992; FCO 1994; SUPL 1999; Band B3; m 1997 Fraser Reid Davidson (1s 1999).

Davidson, Susan; SUPL since August 2001; born 13.12.57; FCO 1987; Tokyo 1990; FCO 1992; Bangkok 1996; FCO 1998; Band A2.

Davies, Bethany Louise (née Rowland); SUPL since August 2001; born 11.12.68; FCO 1988; Mexico City 1991; FCO 1993; Band A2; m 1997 Peter George Davies.

Davies, Caroline Elizabeth; World Wide Floater Duties since October 2000; born 4.6.63; RAF 1983-88; FCO HCS 1991-99; Kuwait 1998; Band B3.

Davies, David Gerald; First Secretary FCO since February 1995; born 1.10.40; Ministry of Works 1959; MPNI 1960; DSAO 1966; Brussels (NATO) 1969; Second Secretary (Inf/Admin) Madras 1972; Freetown 1975; FCO 1978; First Secretary (Admin) Athens 1981; First Secretary (Admin) Addis Ababa 1986; First Secretary FCO 1988;

Deputy High Commissioner Lilongwe 1991; m 1969 Pamela Arlotte (2s 1974, 1978).

Davies, Deborah Ann (née Kidd); Seoul since December 2000; born 23.9.70; FCO 1992; Islamabad 1996; FCO 1999; Band A2.

Davies, Elved Richard Malcolm; Deputy Consul-General Hong Kong since April 2000; born 19.1.51; Army 1972-75; Third later Second Secretary FCO 1975; Language Student 1977; Second later First Secretary Jakarta 1977; FCO 1980; Athens 1984; FCO 1985; First Secretary (Chancery) Nairobi 1989; FCO 1991; First Secretary later Counsellor Oslo 1991; Counsellor FCO 1995; m 1976 Elizabeth Angela Osborne (1d 1981; 1s 1984).

Davies, Gerald Howard; Consul Brussels since October 1995; born 24.4.48; FCO 1968; Paris 1971; Karachi 1973; Ibadan 1977; FCO 1978; Warsaw 1981; FCO 1984; Melbourne 1986; FCO 1988; Consul and Second Secretary (Man) Muscat 1990; m 1972 Yvonne Arnold (2d 1984, 1988).

Davies, Griselda Christian Macbeth (née Todd); SUPL since October 1999; born 20.2.59; Budapest 1981; FCO 1982; Buenos Aires 1983; FCO 1985; Damascus 1987; FCO 1988; SUPL 1989; FCO 1990; Riga and Vilnius 1993; FCO 1997; Band A2; m 1989 John Howard Davies.

Davies, Ian; Consul-General Marseille since March 1997; born 1.8.56; FCO 1976; Moscow 1978; SUPL 1980; FCO 1983; Paris 1985; Third later Second Secretary Moscow 1988; Second Secretary FCO 1990; Second Secretary (Comm/Con) and Deputy Head of Mission La Paz 1993; m 1979 Purificacion Bautista Hervias (2d 1985, 1988).

Davies, Jennifer Ann Tudor; Second Secretary FCO since February 1995; born 2.3.50; FCO 1969; Khartoum 1972; Valletta 1974; Singapore 1977; FCO 1979; Buenos Aires 1980; FCO 1982; New Delhi 1984; FCO 1987; Hong Kong 1992; Band C4.

Davies, John Howard; First Secretary (Political) Sofia since October 1999; born 31.1.57; FCO 1980; Riyadh 1983; Second later First Secretary FCO 1985; First Secretary and Head of Interests Section Damascus 1987; First Secretary FCO 1990; First Secretary (Political) Riga and Vilnius 1993; First Secretary FCO 1997; Band D6; m 1989 Griselda Christian Macbeth Todd.

Davies, Jonathan Mark; Counsellor, Madrid since November 2000; born 1.12.67; FCO 1990; Language Training Cairo 1992; Second Secretary (Political/Information) Kuwait 1993; on loan to the Cabinet Office 1996.

Davies, Maureen Kerr Stewart (née Paisley); UKREP Brussels since August 1994; born 12.6.53; FCO 1984; Washington 1987; Kathmandu 1990; Band A2; m 1988 Maxim Philip Davies.

Davies, Nicola Claire (née Dixon); Third Secretary FCO since July 1996; born 10.7.68;

FCO 1990; Third Secretary (Political) Singapore 1993; Band C4; m 1996 Jonathan Mark Davies.

Davies, Nicola Jane, Gibraltar since September 1996; born 18.8.65; RAF 1983-1991; FCO 1995; Band B3; m 1999 Henry T Gill.

Davies, Patrick James; Private Secretary FCO since August 2000; born 8.5.68; FCO 1993; full-time language training 1994; Second Secretary (Political/Press) Rabat 1995; First Secretary FCO 1999.

Davies, Paul Ronald; First Secretary FCO since May 2000; born 30.3.53; FCO 1970; Africa Floater 1974; Dacca 1976; FCO 1979; Tripoli 1982; Kingston 1984; Third Secretary (Commercial) Peking 1988; Second Secretary FCO 1990; Second Secretary (Political/Commercial/ Information) Lima 1993; Consul (Commercial/ Economic/ Press and Public Affairs) Shanghai 1996; Deputy Consul General Shanghai 1997; m 1976 Fiona Avril Canning (1d 1979; 1s 1981).

Davies, Peter Brian; Counsellor FCO since October 1999; born 30.12.54; Third Secretary FCO 1977; Language Training Hong Kong 1980; Second Secretary FCO 1981; Second later First Secretary Rome 1983; First Secretary FCO 1987; First Secretary and Consul Peking 1988; First Secretary FCO 1992; Counsellor (Political) Jakarta 1996; m 1981 Charlotte Helena Allman Hall (1d 1984; 1s 1986).

Davies, Robert Harold Glyn; HM Ambassador Panama City since April 1999; born 23.3.42; FO 1963; Havana 1964; FO 1964; Third later Second Secretary (Inf) Mexico City 1968; Second Secretary FCO 1972 (First Secretary 1974); Consul (Comm) Zagreb 1980; T/D Guatemala City 1983; First Secretary on loan to Cabinet Office 1983; First Secretary (Comm), Consul and Head of Chancery Luanda 1986; First Secretary FCO 1989; High Commissioner Windhoek 1996; m 1968 Maria del Carmen Diaz (1s 1970).

Davies, Roger James; First Secretary (Management) Nicosia since June 2001; born 23.9.47; HCS 1965; FO (later FCO) 1967; Moscow 1970; Kampala 1971; Islamabad 1973; Kathmandu 1974; FCO 1978; Baghdad 1981; Vice-Consul (Comm) Johannesburg 1985; Second Secretary FCO 1987; Second Secretary (Management/Consular) Doha 1991; Deputy Consul-General Melbourne 1994; FCO 1998; m, (1) 1974 Catherine Yvonne Moorby (diss 1990) (1s 1982); 1d 1984) (2) 1990 Jean Heather Thérésa Austin.

Davies, Tracy Denise (née Chagnot); SUPL since March 2001; FCO 1986; Vancouver 1987; Rome 1988; Paris 1988; FCO 1990; SUPL 1991; FCO 1992; Bangkok 1993; SUPL 1997; FCO 1999; Band B3; m 1990 Mark John Henry Davies (1s 1991; 1d 1994).

Davis, Andrew Cornwall; Santiago since February 1999; born 29.4.68; FCO 1995; HCS 1995-97; ECMM Sarajevo 1997; FCO 1998; Band A2.

Davis, Ashley James; FCO since July 1991; born 23.2.59; FCO 1986; Islamabad 1987; Band B3; m 1998 Roberta Scott (1d 2000).

Davis, Carole May; FCO since August 1994; born 26.3.59; Band A2.

Davis, Doris; Second Secretary (Commercial) Baku since October 1999; born 26.1.47; DSAO 1967; Baghdad 1968; Sofia 1970; FCO 1971; Kuala Lumpur 1972; Peking 1973; Washington 1975; FCO 1978; Cairo 1980; Cape Town/Pretoria 1984; FCO 1988; Washington 1992; Third Secretary (Man) Rangoon 1995; Band C4.

Davis, Kevin Roy, SUPL since July 1997; born 2.1.65; FCO 1981; Washington 1989; Band C4; FCO 1991; m 1991 Karen Roberts (1s 1994).

Davis, Rosemary; Second Secretary (Chancery) UKMIS New York since August 2001; born 28.1.63; FCO 1987; Language Training 1988; Language Training Cairo 1989; FCO 1990; UKREP Brussels 1991; Third Secretary (Chancery) Damascus 1994; FCO 1998; Band D6.

Davis, Stephen Alexander James; Management Officer Abu Dhabi since May 2001; born 24.9.65; FCO 1983; Mexico City 1986; Warsaw 1990; FCO 1993; Third Secretary (Commercial) Accra 1997; m 1986 Maureen Patricia Oates.

Davison, Andrew James; Third Secretary New Delhi since January 2000; born 11.8.70; FCO 1992; Kiev 1997; Band B3; m 1997 Lana Jane Sawa.

Davison, Brian William Edward; Karachi since February 1999; born 6.6.45; Royal Marines 1961; MOD Police 1985; HM Prison Service 1986; Lusaka 1988; Cairo 1992; Lagos 1995; Band B3; m 1966 Sandra June Thompson (2s 1970, 1971).

Davison, John Paul; First Secretary later Counsellor FCO since April 1989; born 25.6.50; FCO 1974; MECAS 1975; Abu Dhabi 1977; Resigned 1978; Reappointed 1985; First Secretary Dubai 1986; m 1978 Elizabeth Jane Clark (2d 1981, 1986; 1s 1983).

Davison, Nicole April; Third Secretary FCO since January 1996; born 6.8.68; FCO 1988; Pretoria/Cape Town 1990; Dhaka 1991; Band B3.

Dawbarn, John Nathaniel Yelverton; First Secretary (Political) Berlin since June 1998; born 3.5.65; FCO 1987; Language Training 1990; Third later Second Secretary (Chancery/Inf) Belgrade 1990; Second Secretary FCO 1993; (First Secretary 1994); First Secretary T/D (Political/Information) Belgrade 1995; FCO 1996; m 1989 Katherine Sarah Urry.

Dawber, Mary Welsh (née Campbell); SUPL since April 1997; born 4.4.56; FCO 1996; Band A2; m 1975 Philip Dawber (1d 1976).

Dawber, Philip; Ankara since May 2000; born 1.4.54; Armed Forces 1971-1994; FCO 1995; Band A2; m 1995 Mary Welsh Campbell (1d 1976).

Day, Mark Christopher; Lusaka since January 1999; born 1.5.63; FCO 1994; Hong Kong 1996; Band A2.

Day, Martin Charles; First Secretary (Commercial) Prague since March 2000; born 4.11.65; FCO 1989; Language Training Cairo 1991; Second Secretary (Chancery) Cairo 1992; First Secretary FCO 1995; Band D6.

Day, Rosamund; SUPL since 1999; born 27.6.64; FCO 1983; Bonn 1985; Suva 1987; Africa/ME Floater 1989; FCO 1991; Second Secretary (Management) Colombo 1996; Band C5; m 1993 Nicholas John Pyle (1s 1995; 1d 1999).

Dean, Andrew John; Counsellor (Multilateral) Canberra since September 2000; born 6.2.55; FCO 1982; Second Secretary (UNIDO/UN) UKMIS Vienna 1984; Second later First Secretary FCO 1986; First Secretary (Chancery) Hanoi 1990; First Secretary FCO 1992; São Paulo 1997; First Secretary FCO 1999; m 1989 Nicola Moreton. (1s 1993).

Dean, Robert John; First Secretary (External) Wellington since November 1999; born 21.5.59; MOD 1977; FCO 1978; Second Secretary Copenhagen 1987; Second later First Secretary FCO 1992; On secondment to MOD 1994; FCO 1995; Band C5; m 1981 Julie Margaret Stott (2d 1986, 1988).

Deane, Geoffrey; HM Consul Munich since July 2001; born 19.2.50; FCO 1976; Nairobi 1980; Second Secretary FCO 1984; First Secretary (Chancery) East Berlin 1988; FCO 1991; First Secretary FCO 1997; Band D6; m. Karen Aileen Wallace (4d 1980, 1983, 1986, 1994).

Deane, Michael Boyd; Second Secretary (Economic) Vienna since January 2001; born 1.8.72; Second Secretary FCO 1999; Band C4.

Deane, Robert Edward; FCO since 1998; born 28.9.62; HM Treasury 1985; Bonn 1994; Band D6; m 1993 Corinna Osmann (1s 1998).

Deaney, Tina Marie; Prague since January 1999; born 18.4.72; FCO 1991; Islamabad 1995; Band A2.

Dear, Robert Edward; First Secretary (Political/Economic) Budapest since October 2000; born 19.2.55; FCO 1986; First Secretary 1987; First Secretary FCO 1992; Deputy Head of Mission Havana 1994; m 1982 Caroline Margaret Reuss.

Dearden, Christopher Robert; Vice-Consul Warsaw since January 1997; born 7.12.59; FCO 1978; Wellington 1981; Ankara 1984; LA/Caribbean Floater 1987; FCO 1989; Athens 1993.

Dearden, Janine Elaine (née Lawrence); SUPL since June 2001; born 18.10.60; FCO 1982; Rome 1983; Nairobi 1985; SUPL 1988; FCO 1989; SUPL 1990; FCO 1998; Band A2; m 1985 Timothy John Dearden (2s 1987, 1989).

de Chassiron, Charles Richard Lucien, CVO (2000); Consul General Milan since August 1997; born 27.4.48; FCO 1971; Third Secretary Stockholm 1972; First Secretary Maputo 1975; FCO 1978; First Secretary (Comm) Brasilia 1982; First Secretary later Counsellor FCO 1985; Counsellor (Comm/Econ) Rome 1989; HM Ambassador Tallinn 1994; m 1974 Britt-Marie Sonja Medhammar (1d 1975; 1s 1976).

De Csillery, Patricia Katrina; FTLT since March 2001; born 30.4.69; FCO 1993; Second Secretary (Political) UKMIS New York 1996; Second Secretary 1998; Band C4; m 1993 Michael de Csillery (1d 2000).

De Gier, Helen Majorie; Peking since April 1998; born 19.2.59; HCS 1976-84; FCO 1984; Freetown 1986; Band A2; FCO 1989; m 1992 Joseph Eugene O'Carroll.

Dee, Pauline (née Thompson); SUPL since September 2000; born 11.10.63; FCO 1987; Bridgetown 1989; FCO 1992; Peking 1993; Grand Turk 1996; Sarajevo 1998; Band A2; m 1998 Stewart Dee (1d 1999).

Dee, Stewart; Third Secretary (Political) Gibraltar since November 2000; born 12.8.69; FCO 1988; Bonn 1990; FCO 1993; SUPL 1996; Vice Consul Sarajevo 1998; Band B3; m(1) 1991 Claire Duggan (diss 1996); m(2) 1998 Pauline Thompson (1d 1999).

Deffee, Robert Edward Delves, MBE (1980); Kuala Lumpur since July 1997; born 10.10.41; FO 1960; Sofia 1962; Phnom Penh 1963; Rome 1965; Lusaka 1966; Vice-Consul Managua 1969; FCO 1970; Khartoum 1974; Dubai 1976; FCO 1980; Second Secretary (Admin) Jedda 1984; FCO 1986; Second Secretary (Cons) Mexico City 1989; Second Secretary FCO since September 1993; m 1969 Mireya Mayorga Delgado (1d 1972; 2s 1974, 1978).

De Fonblanque, John Robert MBE (1993), Head of UK Delegation to OSCE Vienna since August 1999; born 20.12.43; Third Secretary FCO since 1968; Jakarta 1969; Second later First Secretary UKDEL Brussels EEC 1972; on loan to HM Treasury 1977; FCO 1980; Counsellor FCO 1983; Counsellor on loan to the Cabinet Office 1983; Head of Chancery New Delhi 1986; Head of Chancery UKREP Brussels 1988; AUSS International Organisations 1994; AUSS Director Europe 1998; m 1984 Margaret Prest (1s 1985).

Delaney, Michael; Colombo since March 1995; born 14.12.67; FCO 1988; Ankara 1989; Lagos 1990; Abuja 1992; Band B3; m 1990 Zeliha Doganavsargil.

De Larrabure, Jacqueline Mary (née Elliot); Caracas since July; born 25.1.64; Lima 1986; LA Floater 1989; San José 1991; FCO 1996; Band B3; m 1991 Jos Larrabure Muro (1d 1991).

de Mauny, Alix Claire Evelyne; FCO since September 2001; born 23.12.73; Band C4.

Dempster, Sharon Louise; Paris since February 1991; born 13.2.69; FCO 1989; Band A2.

Deneiffe, Paul Michael; Madrid since November 1995; born 21.6.63; FCO 1982 Cairo 1987; FCO 1989; Band C4.

Dening-Smitherman, Major Peter Clemens Henri; Queen's Messenger since 1990; born 12.7.47 HM Forces 1967-90.

Dennis, Catherine Teresa; UKDEL Vienna since August 1999; born 20.5.70; FCO 1998; Band A2.

Dennis, John David; Counsellor (Economic and Commercial) New Delhi since July 2001; born 6.8.59; FCO 1981; Hong Kong 1983; Peking 1985; Second later First Secretary FCO 1987; First Secretary Kuala Lumpur 1992; on secondment to Standard Chartered Bank 1997; Counsellor, on loan to the DTI 1998; m 1989 Jillian Margaret Kemp. (2s 1994, 1999).

Denny, Ross Patrick; São Paulo since June 1998; born 13.9.55; RN 1972-79; FCO 1979; Santiago 1980; Doha 1983; Warsaw 1985; FCO 1988; Second Secretary (Political) The Hague 1992; FCO 1997; m(1) 1977 Barbara Harvard (diss 1996) (1d 1979; 1s 1981); (2) 2000 Claudenise De Lima.

Dent, Alastair Ross Moller; Second Secretary (Management) Manila since November 1997; born 7.2.54; DHSS 1972; FCO 1974; UKREP Brussels 1976; Moscow 1979; FCO 1981; LA Floater 1984; Mexico City 1986; FCO 1989; (Second Secretary 1991); Second Secretary (Commercial/Information) Gaborone 1993; Deputy High Commissioner Gaborone 1996; m(1) 1977 (diss 1983); m(2) 1985 Ligia Esperanza Zeledon Castillo (2s 1988, 1996).

Dent, Shannon Elizabeth; Dubai since April 1985; born 29.3.58; FCO 1979; Lusaka 1979; Peking 1981; Athens 1982; Band A2.

Denwood, Judith Elizabeth; Second Secretary FCO since April 2000; born 21.10.65; FCO 1986; Bridgetown 1988; FCO 1991; Third Secretary FCO 1993; T/D New Delhi, Accra, Damascus 1995; Third Secretary (Management) and Vice Consul Bahrain 1997; Band C4.

De Pauw, Amanda Jane (née Rutter); Ottawa since June 2000; born 20.3.64; HM Land Registry 1984; FCO 1988; UKREP Brussels 1989; Yaoundé 1993; FCO 1996; Band A2; m 1993 Luc Paul Solange Marie de Pauw (1d,1998).

De Ramos, Nicola Anne (née Smyth); Mexico City since July 1999; born 11.8.65; FCO 1988; Bucharest 1989; Quito 1992; Havana 1996. Band A2; m 1994 Bryan Dubal Ramos Montero (2d 1995, 1997).

de Ridder, Kathryn Louise Carmel (née Peacock); Tel Aviv since July 1998; born 16.7.60; FCO 1984; New Delhi 1985; UKREP Brussels 1988; FCO 1991; SUPL 1992; Lagos 1994; SUPL 1997; Band B3; m 1992 Wouter de Ridder (1d 1993).

Desloges, Christina Anne (née Sanders); Stanley since August 2000; born 30.11.63; FCO 1984; Lagos 1987; FCO 1991; Harare 1992; Bandar Seri Begawan 1996; Band A2; m 1989 Daniel Albert Joseph Desloges (1d 1990, 1s 1997).

De Sousa, Louise Amanda (née Clark); First Secretary FCO since February 1997; born 23.7.68; FCO 1991; Second Secretary(Political/Information/Aid) Brasilia 1993; m 1994 Allan Rivail de Sousa (1s 1998).

de Valencia, Michelle (née Lawler); Second Secretary FCO since July 1999; born 8.6.64; FCO 1987; Bogotá 1990; Third Secretary (Commercial) Stockholm 1993; Third Secretary (Chancery) Stockholm 1997; Band C4; m 1993 Jairo Alberto Valencia Diaz (1d 1996; 1s 1998).

De Vere Lane, Graham Vaughan, MBE (1991); FCO since July 1993; born 5.5.45; FCO 1968; Singapore 1969; FCO 1971; Lusaka 1973; FCO 1975; Darwin 1976; FCO 1978; Amman 1979; FCO 1983; Khartoum 1984; FCO 1987; Moscow 1988 Pretoria 1990; Band C4; m 1964 Janet Pine (1s 1964; 2d 1967, 1979)

Devine, John Joseph; Third Secretary (Management) and Consul Tallinn since February 2000; born 3.7.70; FCO 1991; Floater Duties 1994; New Delhi 1996; Band B3.

Devine, Paul Grahame; FCO since May 1995; born 19.1.51; DHSS 1973; FCO 1981; Bonn 1983; Riyadh 1985; Suva 1988; Düsseldorf 1992; Band B3; m 1993 Losana Lewamoqe Di Lo Tuisawau.

Devlin, Francis Patrick; Second Secretary Pretoria since April 1996; born 29.7.41; GPO 1957; FO 1965; Singapore 1967; FCO 1968; Lagos 1969; FCO 1970; Cairo 1974; FCO 1978; Amman 1980; Madrid 1984; Second secretary FCO 1987; Second Secretary Caracas 1991; Second Secretary FCO 1994; m 1966 Dorothy Daley.

Dew, John Anthony; Head of Latin America and Caribbean Department FCO since January 2000; born 3.5.52; FCO 1973; Third Secretary Caracas 1975; Second later First Secretary FCO 1979; First Secretary OECD Paris 1983; First Secretary FCO 1987; Counsellor and Deputy Head of Mission Dublin 1992; Minister Madrid 1996; m 1975 Marion Bewley Kirkwood (3d 1977, 1980, 1984).

de Waal, James Francis, FCO since February 1998; born 18.12.68; FCO 1990; UKMIS New York 1992; Full-time Language Training 1994; Second Secretary (Political/Information) Berlin 1994.

Dewar, Robert Scott; High Commissioner Maputo since August 2000; born 10.6.49; FCO 1973; Third later Second Secretary Colombo 1974; First Secretary FCO 1978; First Secretary (Comm) Head of Chancery and Consul Luanda 1981; First Secretary FCO 1984; First Secretary and Head of Chancery Dakar 1988; Deputy Head of Mission Harare 1992; HM Ambassador Antananarivo 1996; FTLT 2000; m 1979 Jennifer Mary Ward (1d 1988).

Dewberry, David Albert; Deputy Head of Mission Holy See since October 1996; born 27.9.41; CRO 1958; Karachi 1963; Kingston 1966; Warsaw 1970; Brussels 1971; Second Secretary (Aid) Dacca 1972; FCO 1974; Second Secretary Mexico City 1977; First Secretary (Consul/Admin) Buenos Aires 1980; First Secretary FCO 1982; Head of Chancery Dar es Salaam 1987; First Secretary FCO 1991; Full-Time Language Training 1995; m 1974 Catherine Mary Stabback (3s 1976, 1977, 1981; 1d 1979).

Diaz, Alison Jean; OSCE Vienna since April 1999; born 24.2.68; FCO 1991; Belgrade 1993; Lima 1995; Band A2; m 1998 Juan Carlos Diaz (2s 1998, 2001).

Diaz, Sharon Vanessa (née Gordon); Caracas since August 1999; born 28.9.69.FCO 1998. Band A2; m 1998 Tirso Diaz Garcia.

Dibble, Hilary Anne (née Light); FCO since June 1998; born 17.7.51; FCO 1973; Moscow 1974; FCO 1975; Rome 1976; Kingston 1980; Islamabad 1983; FCO 1987; Moscow 1990; Third later Second Secretary (Consular) Canberra 1993; m 1980 Geoffrey Walter Dibble.

Dick, Colin John; Second Secretary (Economic) Singapore since 2001; born 22.6.70; FCO 1990; World Wide Floater Duties 1994; Third later Second Secretary FCO 1996; Band C4; m2001 Elaine Hargreaves.

Dick, Paula Jayne; Cairo since July 1998; born 20.6.69; FCO 1988; Amman 1990; Belmopan 1994; Band B3.

Dickerson, Nigel Paul; Deputy High Commissioner and Second Secretary (Aid) Windhoek since September 1995; born 25.4.59; FCO 1978; Bonn 1981; Warsaw 1984; FCO 1987 (Second Secretary 1990); Second Secretary (Management) and Consul Santiago 1992; m 1984 Marianne Gaye Tatchell (2d 1992, 1994, 1s 1995).

Dickins, Nicholas William; UKMIS New York since May 1997; born 15.11.56; FCO 1985; Tel Aviv 1991; FCO 1994; Band C4; m 1991 Marina Papaspyrou.

Dickinson, Woodman Mark Lowes, OBE (2000); HM Ambassador Skopje since April 1997; born 16.1.55; FCO 1976; Second Secretary Ankara 1979; First Secretary FCO 1983; First Secretary (Pol/Inf) Dublin 1987; First Secretary FCO 1991; First Secretary on loan to the Bank of England 1994; Full-time Language Training 1996; m(1) 1986 Francesca Infanti (diss 1991); (2) 1995 Christina Houlder.

Dickson, Susan Jane; Senior Assistant Legal Adviser FCO since 2000; born 30.7.64; Admitted as Solicitor 1990; Assistant later Senior Assistant Legal Adviser FCO 1990; First Secretary (Legal) UKMIS New York 1997.

Dickson, William Andrew; FCO since August 1998; born 17.12.50; FCO 1969; SUPL to attend University 1970; FCO 1974; Cairo 1976; Nairobi

HOSPITAL FOR TROPICAL DISEASES
TRAVEL CLINIC

Appointments Tel: 020 7388 9600
Healthline: 09061 337733 (50p/min)

WHAT IS DIARRHOEA?

Diarrhoea when travelling abroad is caused by bacteria, viruses or parasites. Up to 50% of travellers suffer from it.

Results in 4–5 loose or watery stools per day for 2–4 days, and maybe abdominal cramps, nausea, vomiting, bloating, fever and lethargy.

DIARRHOEA PREVENTION INVOLVES:

- CARE WITH FOOD/WATER
- GOOD HYGIENE PRACTICES
- TREATING DEHYDRATION

HOW DO YOU CATCH IT?

From eating food or drinking water that is unclean and contaminated.
Often flies have infected the food or cooks haven't been hygienic when preparing meals.

RISKY COUNTRIES

HIGH RISK ....Latin America
Africa
Middle East
Asia

MEDIUM RISK ....Southern Europe
Some Caribbean islands

LOW RISK ....Northern Europe
Australia
New Zealand
USA
Some Caribbean islands

There are no vaccines against travellers' diarrhoea and preventative antibiotics should only be used in special circumstances.

Prevention means eating and drinking uncontaminated food and water, and practising good hygiene.

▲ FOOD

Contaminated food may look, smell and taste normal.

DON'Ts

- Do not eat salads.
- Do not eat raw vegetables.
- Do not eat raw or undercooked meat.
- Do not eat undercooked eggs.
- Do not eat raw fish or any shellfish.
- Do not eat food exposed to flies.
- Do not buy food from street vendors.

DOs

- Do eat well cooked, freshly prepared, piping hot food.
- Do peel all fruit yourself.
- Avoid unpasteurised milk (unless boiled first) and milk products, eg. cheese and ice cream.
- Avoid reheated food.

Remember cook it, peel it, or leave it!

▲ HYGIENE

Ensure that you, and all members of your group, wash their hands after using the toilet and before preparing or eating food.

Anyone who has diarrhoea should not prepare food for the rest of the group.

▲ WATER

- Use clean water for drinking, brushing teeth, washing cutlery and crockery, washing hands, and washing fruit and vegetables.
- Avoid tap water.

  Avoid ice cubes.

- Drink hot tea and coffee (made from water that has been boiled) and canned drinks.
- Sealed bottled mineral water is usually clean but in some countries even this cannot be trusted.

Clean the water by:—

Bringing it to boiling point (boil for 5 minutes at high altitude). Boiling is the most effective way of treating water but may not always be convenient.

or   treat with iodine drops/tablets. Follow the makers' instructions carefully, if the water isn't clear you will need more drops or tablets.

or   treat with chlorine tablets (such as Puritabs®).

Water filter systems usually contain iodine. They are useful for short trips and for emergencies but may be inconvenient for longer trips as filters need changing regularly (and more often with dirty water).

TREATMENT

▲ ORAL REHYDRATION SOLUTIONS

Most cases of travellers' diarrhoea are self-limiting. The greatest danger is dehydration which if untreated, can kill. An adult can loose 2–4 litres with severe diarrhoea.

Rehydrate by drinking an oral rehydration solution.

You can use commercially prepared sachets/tablets such as Dioralyte® or by mixing a teaspoon of sugar and a pinch of salt to a glass of clean water. The water must not be more salty than tears.

An oral rehydration spoon is useful if you have table salt and granulated sugar.

Whether using Dioralyte® or mixing your own sugar and salt, drink one glass after every motion for adults and one glass hourly to replace normal losses.

Continue to eat as normal (food shortens the illness and lessens fluid loss). Avoid dairy products because for some people, they aggravate the diarrhoea.

▲ ANTIDIARRHOEAL DRUGS

ANTIDIARRHOEAL drugs stop the diarrhoea by reducing the body's natural response, which is to flush out the infection.

They should be used when it is impossible to use a toilet, such as a long bus journey.

They should not be used if there is blood in the diarrhoea, or when feverish.

Children under 10 years of age should not be given antidiarrhoeal tablets.

Commonly used preparations are Imodium® (loperamide), Lomotil® (diphenoxylate) and Arret® (loperamide).

Inactivated charcoal is ineffective.

Antibiotic use in travellers' diarrhoea

Antibiotics must be specifically prescribed for the treatment of travellers' diarrhoea.

Only certain bacterial infections will improve on treatment with antibiotics.

The antibiotic Ciprofloxacin, has been found to significantly reduce severity and length of diarrhoea.

If you have been prescribed Ciprofloxacin for self-treatment of diarrhoea.

- Take it only for diarrhoea.
- Take a single 500mg tablet.
- Take the dose as soon after the first symptoms as possible.
- If the symptoms do not improve within 12 hours further doses are unlikely to have any benefit.

If any of the problems listed in the section **WHEN TO GET A DOCTOR** occurs do not use/continue the antibiotics.

WHEN TO GET A DOCTOR

- IF YOU HAVE A TEMPERATURE (FEVER).
- IF THERE IS BLOOD IN THE DIARRHOEA.
- IF THE AFFECTED PERSON IS CONFUSED.
- IF THE DIARRHOEA DOESN'T STOP AFTER 72 HOURS (24 for infants, children and the elderly).

1980; Second Secretary FCO 1982; Second Secretary (Comm) Budapest 1982; Second later First Secretary FCO 1986; First Secretary (IAEA) Vienna 1989; First Secretary (Information) Hong Kong 1994; Band D6; m 1981 Gillian Ann Hague.

Digby, Simon; Consul and Second Secretary (Commercial) Bratislava since May 1999; born 4.8.55; Crown Agents 1977; FCO 1980; Tehran 1982; LA Floater 1986; FCO 1987; Third Secretary (Admin/Cons) Mbabane 1989; FCO 1991; Luanda 1997.

Dillan, Rachel Elizabeth; Amman since September 1985; born 22.8.63; FCO 1983; Band A2.

Dimbleby, Andrew Timothy; Second Secretary (Commercial) Manila since October 1996; born 20.5.59; FCO 1979; Accra 1981; FCO 1985; Pretoria 1986; Third Secretary (Commercial/Information/Chancery) Dubai 1989; Second Secretary (Management/Consular) Jedda 1994; Band C4; m 1981 Susan Margaret Joy Irvine (1s 1988, 2d 1991, 1996).

Dimond, Paul Stephen; HM Ambassador Manila since March 2002; born 30.12.44; FO 1963; DSA 1965; Language Training Tokyo 1966; Osaka 1968; Consul (Comm) 1970; Second Secretary Tokyo 1972; On loan to DTI 1973; Second Secretary FCO 1975; First Secretary (Econ) Stockholm 1977; First Secretary FCO 1980; First Secretary (Comm) Tokyo 1981; First Secretary FCO 1986; on secondment to Smiths Industries plc 1988; Counsellor (Comm) Tokyo 1989; Deputy Head of Mission The Hague 1994; Consul-General Los Angeles 1997; m 1965 Carolyn Susan Davis-Mees (2s 1968, 1970).

Dinsdale, Ian McLean Taylor; Second Secretary (Consular) Wellington since August 1997; born 20.10.49; FCO 1969; Nairobi 1972; Colombo 1976; Second Secretary FCO 1979; Second Secretary Santo Domingo 1982; Maseru 1985; Second Secretary Riyadh 1986; Second Secretary FCO 1989; Second Secretary Islamabad 1993; m 1975 Elizabeth Ann Montaut.

Dinsley, Andrew; Deputy Head of Mission Almaty since August 2000; born 22.8.66; FCO 1990; Kiev 1992; FCO 1996; Band C4; m 2000 Larissa Kolomiyets (1s 1986).

Dinwiddy, Bruce Harry; FCO since August 2001; born 1.2.46; Second Secretary FCO 1973; First Secretary UKDEL MBFR Vienna 1975; FCO 1977; First Secretary and Head of Chancery Cairo 1981; First Secretary FCO 1983; Counsellor on loan to the Cabinet Office 1986; FCO 1988; Counsellor Bonn 1989; Deputy High Commissioner Ottawa 1992; High Commissioner Tanzania 1998; m 1974 Emma Victoria Llewellyn (1d 1976; 1s 1979).

Dix, Christopher John; First Secretary (Visa/Consular) New Delhi since 1999; born 30.9.64; FCO 1983; UKMIS Geneva 1985; Dhaka 1988; Second Secretary FCO 1993; Language Training 1995; Second Secretary (Commercial)

Madrid 1995; Band C5; m 1988 Julia Milward (1d 1991; 1s 1994).

Dixon, Debra Audrey (née Churchill); Lusaka since November 1993; born 6.4.58; FCO 1978; Washington 1980; Sana'a 1983; FCO 1986; Düsseldorf 1989; SUPL 1992; Band C4; m 1978 Russell Kenneth Dixon (2d 1985, 1992, 1s 1990).

Dixon, Hazel; Maputo since May 2001; born 19.8.49; HM Forces 1967-77; Ankara 1989; Peking 1992; Moscow 1999; Band B3.

Dixon, Russell Kenneth; First Secretary (Management) Amman since July 2000; born 24.1.58; MOD 1976; FCO 1978; Washington 1980; Sana'a 1983; FCO 1985; Düsseldorf 1989; SUPL 1993; Second Secretary (Political/Information) Lusaka 1993; Band C5; m 1978 Debra Audrey Churchill (2d 1985; 1992, 1s 1990).

Dobson, Sharon Gail; Third Secretary UKDEL NATO since April 1997; born 4.1.68; FCO 1991; Third Secretary (Chancery) Dakar 1995; Band B3.

Docherty, Claire Elizabeth; SUPL since June 2000; born 30.7.68; FCO 1992; Santiago 1995; Havana 1999; Band A2.

Doherty, Emer Maria; T/D Paris since December 1996; born 10.1.69; FCO 1990; Full-time Language Training 1993; UKMIS Geneva 1993; Band C4.

Doherty, Felicity Mary (née Tebboth); Second Secretary FCO since April 1988; born 24.10.52; FCO 1970; Bonn 1975; SUPL 1976; Moscow 1979; FCO 1981; Second Secretary 1983; Second Secretary (Comm) Lisbon 1986; m 1977 Francis Doherty (diss) (2d 1982, 1984).

Doherty, Francis Anthony; First Secretary FCO since August 1996; born 4.7.41; FO 1960; Brazzaville 1963; Kuching 1965; Saigon 1966; DSAO (later FCO) 1967; Colombo 1970; Peking 1973; Assistant Private Secretary to the PUSS/Minister of State FCO 1976; Second Secretary Hamilton 1979; Second Secretary (Aid) Dar es Salaam 1981; First Secretary (Information) Rome 1983; First Secretary (Information) Milan 1984; First Secretary FCO 1986; First Secretary (Management) Mexico City 1990; Deputy Head of Mission The Holy See 1993; m 1964 Noreen Mary Cairns (3s 1971, 1972, 1976).

Doidge, Mary Ellen; FCO since April 1995; born 21.1.46; Bonn 1971; FCO 1974; Warsaw 1975; Tokyo 1977; FCO 1980; Floater duties 1982; Moscow 1983; FCO 1985; Brussels (UKDEL NATO) 1988; on loan to Home Office 1991; Band B3.

Doig, Michael David; Second Secretary (Press & Public Affairs) Cape Town since March 1998; born 28.5.54; FCO 1973; Tokyo 1975; Karachi 1979; Vienna 1982; Kaduna 1983; FCO 1987; Third Secretary (Comm/Econ) Ottawa 1990; FCO 1993; m 1983 Mary Walker McKinnie (diss 2000) (1d 1985).

Dolan, Sharon Beverley; ECO Pretoria since September 1999; born 28.11.66; MAFF 1991; FCO 1993; Peking 1994; MO/VC Guangzhou 1998; Band B3.

Donaldson, Brian; High Commissioner Windhoek since January 1999; born 6.4.46; Ministry of Aviation 1963; DSAO later FCO 1965; Algiers 1968; La Paz 1971; FCO 1974; Lagos 1975; Luxembourg 1979; Second Secretary FCO 1982; APS to the Minister of State 1983; Second later First Secretary (Aid/Comm) Port Louis 1985; First Secretary (Comm) Head of Chancery and Consul Yaoundé 1989; FCO 1992; First Secretary (Immigration/Consular) Dhaka 1992; FCO 1996; m 1969 Elizabeth Claire Sumner (3s 1971, 1973, 1979).

Donaldson, Ian Martin; First Secretary UKDEL Geneva since July 1999; born 21.7.66; FCO 1988; Third later Second Secretary (Political) Jakarta 1991; FCO 1995; m 1990 Elspeth Jane Chovil Maguire (2d 1996, 1997).

Donegan, Susan Peta (née McAllister); SUPL since March 1997; born 28.5.67; FCO 1985; Paris 1987; LA Floater Duties 1990; Caracas 1992; SUPL 1993; Accra 1994; Band B3; m 1993 James Edward Donegan.

Donnelly, Joseph Brian, CMG; High Commissioner Harare since June 2001; born 24.4.45; Second Secretary FCO 1973; First Secretary (ECOSOC) UKMIS New York 1975; First Secretary and Head of Chancery Singapore 1979; First Secretary FCO 1982; Counsellor on loan to Cabinet Office 1985; Counsellor and Consul-General Athens 1988; RCDS course 1991; Counsellor FCO 1992; Minister and Deputy Permanent Representative UKDEL NATO Brussels 1995; HM Ambassador Belgrade 1997; m (1)1966 Susanne Gibb (diss 1994) (1d 1970) (2) 1997 Julia Mary Newsome.

Donnelly, Matthew; FCO since November 1999; born 21.11.61; FCO 1981; Algiers 1985; Nassau 1988; FCO 1990; Lagos 1992; Third Secretary (Commercial) Buenos Aires 1996; Band C4; m(1) 1982 Lesley-Ann Jones (diss 1988), (2) 1988 Tracy May Basnett (1s 1989).

Donnelly, Tracy May (née Basnett); SUPL since May 1995; born 26.3.62; FCO 1982; Berne 1983; Algiers 1985; SUPL 1988; T/D Lagos 1994; Band A2; m 1988 Matthew Donnelly (1s 1989).

Dorey, Gregory John; Deputy Consul General/Trade Counsellor Hong Kong since June 2000; born 1.5.56; MOD 1977; on loan at UKDEL NATO 1982; MOD 1984; First Secretary FCO 1986; First Secretary (Chancery) Budapest 1989; First Secretary and PS/Minister of State FCO 1992; Counsellor (Economic)and later Deputy High Commissioner Islamabad 1996; m 1981 Alison Patricia Taylor (1d 1990, 2s 1988, 1994).

Dorrian, Claire Hicks (née Jones); Kampala since August 1999; born 15.7.68; HCS 1987; DS 1989; Stanley 1992; Riyadh 1995; Band B3; m 1992 Stuart Forsyth Dorrian (1s 1996).

Douglas, Janet Elizabeth; First Secretary (Political) Stockholm since April 1996; born 6.1.60; FCO 1985; Language Training 1987; Second later First Secretary (Chancery/Inf) Ankara 1988; First Secretary FCO 1991; First Secretary on Loan to the ODA 1993.

Douglas, Paul Leslie; SUPL since June 1999; born 5.11.58; Army 1975-1988; Hanoi 1998; Band A2; m 1993 Tina Marie Field.

Douglas-Hiley, Mark Charles Piers Quentin; Third Secretary (Consular/Management) Kinshasa since November 2001; born 6.11.54; Dept of Employment 1972; DHSS 1973; FCO 1974; Castries 1977; FCO 1979; UKMIS Geneva 1980; FCO 1983; Lagos 1987; JMO New York 1991; FCO 1994; FCO 1997; Sofia 1998; FCO 2000; Band B3.

Douse, Sarah Louise (neé Ansell); FCO March 1998; born 8.4.70; FCO 1990; Rome 1992; Bonn 1995; Band B3; m2001 Carl Anthony Douse .

Doust, Claire Heather (née Barlow); Third Secretary (Management) Islamabad since June 1998; born 7.3.72; FCO 1991; UKDEL NATO Brussels 1995; Band B3; m 1998 Stephen Terence Doust.

Doust, Stephen Terence; Islamabad since June 1998; born 4.12.72; FCO 1992; UKDEL NATO Brussels 1995; Band A2; m 1998 Claire Heather Barlow.

Douthwaite, Ann Mary, MBE (1991); Canberra since May 1996; born 25.4.40; Düsseldorf 1961; Warsaw 1962; Paris 1963; Moscow 1965; Beirut 1966; FCO 1969; New York (UKMIS) 1970; Muscat 1973; Manila 1976; FCO 1978; Tokyo 1984; Algiers 1987; Jakarta 1991; Band B3.

Dove, John Henry; FCO since October 1997; born 10.3.65; HM Customs & Excise 1989; FCO 1990; Full-time Language Training 1991; Deputy Head of Mission Tallinn 1992; Moscow 1993; Second Secretary Tashkent 1996.

Dow, Elizabeth Anne; Consul Rabat since January 1999; born 9.3.58; FCO 1976; New Delhi 1978; Brasilia 1982; FCO 1984; New York (CG) 1988; Vice Consul/MO Jerusalem 1991; FCO 1995.

Downer, James Robert Stephen; FCO since September 1998; born 9.7.68; FCO 1992; Full-time Language Training 1993; Full-time Language Training Cairo 1994; Sana'a 1995; Band D6; m 1998 Nicola Marguerite Neary.

Downing, Joanna Watson; Attaché Dakar since February 1998; born 17.12.71; FCO 1995; Bosnia 1997; Band A2.

Dowse, Timothy Michael; Counsellor on loan to HM Treasury since October 1998; born 18.12.55; FCO 1978; Manila 1980; Second later First Secretary Tel Aviv 1982; First Secretary FCO 1986; Washington 1992; Counsellor, Cabinet Office 1997; m 1989 Vivien Frances Life (2ds 1991, 1994).

Dowsett, Moira, SUPL since May 1999; born 6.11.61; FCO 1988; Brussels 1991; FCO 1993; Band A2; m. Dominic O'Donnell (2s 1998, 2000).

Drace-Francis, Charles David Stephen, CMG (1987); High Commissioner Port Moresby since November 1997; born 15.3.43; Third Secretary FO 1965; Tehran 1967; Second later First Secretary FCO 1971; Assistant Political Adviser Hong Kong 1974; First Secretary UKREP Brussels 1978; FCO 1980; Counsellor attached to All Souls Oxford 1983; Counsellor and Chargé d'Affaires a.i. Kabul 1984; Counsellor (Commercial) Lisbon 1987; On loan to British Aerospace 1991; Counsellor FCO 1994; m 1967 Griselda Hyacinthe Waldegrave (2s 1969, 1971; 1d 1979).

Drabble, Rufus John; Nairobi since June 1998; born 12.2.70; Band B3; FCO since 1995; m 1997 Stella Elizabeth Waldron.

Drake, David Allen; Consul (Commercial) New York since July 1996; born 1.9.47; RAF 1967-75; FCO 1977; Lagos 1979; Kuwait 1982 (Second Secretary 1984); Second later First Secretary FCO 1985; First Secretary (Civil Aviation) Bonn 1989; First Secretary (Commercial) Singapore 1991; m 1972 Anne Veronica Paice.

Drake, Howard Ronald; Deputy Consul General New York since September 1997; born 13.8.56; FCO 1975; LA Floater 1979; Los Angeles 1981; Second Secretary 1982; Second Secretary FCO 1983; Second Secretary (Chancery/Inf) Santiago 1985; First Secretary FCO 1988; First Secretary (Political/Co-ordination) Singapore 1992; First Secretary FCO 1995; m 1988 Gill Summerfield (1s 1992; 1d 1994).

Drayton, Frank Anthony; FCO British Trade International since April 1997; born 10.12.54; FCO 1974; Islamabad 1976; Cape Town 1979; Munich 1982; FCO 1985; Prague 1989; Vice-Consul Doha 1990; FCO 1994; Band B3; m1988 Fidelma Bernadette Tuohy.

Drew, Simon Richard; Second Secretary FCO since May 1997; born 7.5.65; FCO 1981; Pretoria/Cape Town 1989; FCO 1992; Ankara 1993; m 1991 Katharine Chappell (1d 1995).

Drew, Thomas; First Secretary (Economic) Moscow since November 2000; born 26.9.70; FCO 1995; Second Secretary Moscow 1998.

Drew, Timothy James; Riyadh since September 2000; born 2.4.65; FCO 1994; UKMIS Geneva 1996; FCO 1999; Band B3; m 1991 Claire Melanie (1d 1998).

Dring, Sarah Anne Maxwell; FCO since March 2000; born 23.11.48; FCO 1974; Sofia 1975; Nicosia 1977; FCO 1979; South East Asia Floater 1983; Algiers 1985; FCO 1987 (Second Secretary 1989); Johannesburg 1991; FCO 1995; First Secretary (Management) Kampala 1997.

Drummond, Roderick Ian; First Secretary (External) UKREP Brussels since September 1998; born 7.9.62; FCO 1985; SOAS Language Training 1986; University of Jordan 1987; Second Secretary (Political/Economic) Algiers 1988; First Secretary FCO 1992; Deputy Consul-General (Trade/Investment) Johannesburg 1996; m 1985 Carolyn Elizabeth Elliott (1s 1986, 2d 1988, 1990).

Drury, Alan Hyslop; FCO since July 1998 1994; born 21.2.52; FCO 1970; Budapest 1973; Dacca 1975; LA Floater 1977; FCO 1980; Second Secretary (Comm) Muscat 1983; Second later First Secretary FCO 1987; Resident Representative St.Georges 1989; Consul (Commercial) Barcelona 1994; m 1980 Joan Lamb (1d 1984; 1s 1986).

Drysdale, Craig Morrison; First Secretary (Political) Muscat since April 2001; born 22.3.56; FCO 1981; Full-time Language Training 1994; Full-time Language Training Cairo 1995; First Secretary FCO 1996; Band C5; m 1988 Clare Elizabeth (2d 1993, 1996).

Drysdale, Heather; Third Secretary KHF Warsaw since June 1997; born 2.6.56; FCO 1977; NATO Brussels 1977; Tokyo 1980; FCO 1983; Reykjavik 1984; Floater duties 1987; FCO 1987; Valletta 1993; Band B3.

Dryden, Paul James; Ashgabat since June 1999; born 15.6.69; FCO 1990; Berlin 1992; Ottawa 1993; Hamilton 1996; Band B3.

Duckett, Keith Dyson; T/D Harare since April 2000; born 11.4.58; FCO 1977; Kuala Lumpur 1979; Maputo 1983; Brasilia 1985; FCO 1986; Jakarta 1989, Third Secretary (Man) Paris 1993; Second Secretary (Management) Damascus 1995; TD Peking 1998; Ulaanbaatar 1998; Band C4; m 1989 Diane Puckridge (1d 1990; 1s 1991).

Duddy, Fiona Lindsay; Stockholm since December 1994; born 30.8.72; FCO 1991; Band A2.

Duff, Janet Nancy; FCO since October 1997; born 3.12.67; FCO 1990; Language Training FCO 1991; Chiang Mai 1992; Vice-Consul Bangkok 1993; Addis Ababa 1996; Band D6.

Duff, Morwenna Marion Finlayson; SUPL since July 1993; born 6.10.65; HCS 1988; FCO 1989; Jakarta 1990; Band A2.

Duffield, Linda Joy; High Commissioner Colombo since May 1999; born 18.4.53; DHSS 1976; ENA Paris 1986; First Secretary FCO 1987; First Secretary (Comm) Moscow 1989; First Secretary later Counsellor FCO 1992; Deputy High Commissioner Ottawa 1995;

Duffin, David Robert; FCO since 1996; born 4.11.53; FCO 1972; New Delhi 1979; FCO 1981; Singapore 1987; FCO 1990; Berlin 1995; Band C5; m (1) 1980 Angela Thicke (diss 1984); (2) Carole Susan Matthews (diss 1996).

Duffy, Peter John; First Secretary (Management) Paris since April 2001; born 20.6.50; Ministry of Aviation (later Ministry of Technology) 1966; FCO 1967; Addis Ababa 1971; Maseru 1974; Khartoum 1977; FCO 1978; Yaoundé 1982;

Johannesburg 1985; Attaché later Second
Secretary Budapest 1989; Second Secretary FCO
1991; Second Secretary Amsterdam 1994; Second
later First Secretary (Management) Kingston 1995;
m 1971 Juliet Heather Woodward (1s 1972).

Duggin, Thomas Joseph; Ambassador Bogotá
since August 2001; born 15.9.47; Commonwealth
Office (later FCO) 1967; Oslo 1969; Bucharest
1973; Assistant Private Secretary to the PUSS,
FCO 1977; Second Secretary Bangkok 1979; First
Secretary FCO 1982; First Secretary (Comm),
Consul and Head of Chancery La Paz 1985; First
Secretary and Head of Chancery Mexico City
1989; High Commissioner Vila 1992; Counsellor
FCO 1995; m(1) 1968(diss 1983) (2s 1973, 1975);
(2)1983 (diss 1996) (3) 1999, Janette Mortimer
(née David).

Dun, Peter John; On Commercial Secondment
since August 2000; born 6.7.47; FCO 1970; Third
later Second Secretary Kuala Lumpur 1972;
Second later First Secretary FCO 1976; First
Secretary (External Relations) UKREP Brussels
1980; First Secretary UKMIS New York 1983;
FCO 1987; Counsellor on secondment to RCDS
1989; Counsellor (Economic) Islamabad 1990;
Foreign Policy Adviser to External Affairs
Commissioner, EC Brussels 1993; Counsellor
FCO 1996; m 1983 Cheng-Kiak Pang (2s 1987,
1989).

Duncan, Colin; Floater duties since September
1998; born 3.3.70; DSS 1988; FCO 1989; UKREP
Brussels 1992; Sofia 1995; Band B3.

Duncan, John Stewart; OBE (1993) On loan at
SACEUR since August 1998; born 17.4.58; FCO
1980; Paris 1982; Khartoum 1985; Second
Secretary FCO 1988; on loan to the ODA as APS
to Minister of State 1991; NATO Defence College
Rome 1992; Chargé d'Affaires Tirana 1992;
UKDEL WEU/NATO Brussels 1993; First
Secretary FCO 1996; m 1984 Anne Marie Jacq (1d
1990, 1s 1994).

Duncan, Reginald Arthur; Stanley since May
2000; born 23.8.45; HM forces 1963-1993; Band
B3; FCO 1995; Ankara 1997; m 1967 Cecily
Coleman (2d 1971, 1974).

Duncan-Smith, Louise-Marie Veronica; Sanaa
since August 2000; born 16.12.62; FCO 1984;
Ottawa 1986; Banjul 1989; FCO 1989; Victoria
1992; Berne 1996; SUPL 1999; Berne 1999;
SUPL 2000; Band A2; m 1986 Brian David Smith.

Dunlop, Alexander James Macfarlane; UKDel
OSCE Vienna since March 2000; born 14.6.48;
FCO 1968; Ottawa 1971; Vientiane 1974; Sana'a
1980; Vienna 1983; FCO 1986; Second later First
Secretary (Chancery/Info) Lilongwe 1989; First
Secretary FCO 1994; First Secretary (Consular)
Nairobi 1996; Band C5; m 1978 Ortrud Wittlinger.

Dunn, Andrew Patrick Rymer; FCO since
September 2000; born 14.9.69; Band C4; m 1995
Caroline Nicola Cann (1s 1998).

Dunn, David Hedley; T/D Stockholm since
October 2000; born 21.9.68; FCO 1989; Oslo
1992; LA/Caribbean Floater Duties 1995; On
secondment to UNEP Nairobi as Second Secretary
Environment 1998; Band C4.

Dunn, James Michael; Warsaw since June 1999;
born 7.1.59; FCO 1980; Washington 1984; FCO
1986; Paris 1990; Band C4; Third Secretary Lagos
June 1993 m.1993 B C Boyle.

Dunn, Jonathan Michael; Second Secretary
(Chancery) Hanoi since October 2000; born
7.3.75; FCO 1997; SOAS University of London
1998; Full Time Language Training Hanoi 1999;
Band C4.

Dunn, Michael George; FCO since November
2000; born 8.11.48; FO (later FCO) 1966; New
York 1971; Lima 1974; FCO 1976; Copenhagen
1980; Harare 1983; Caracas 1986; FCO 1989;
Quito 1992; Bogotá 1997; m 1983 Mercedes
Josefina Fuguet-Sanchez (3ds 1987,1990, 1998).

Dunnachie, (Doreen) Carole (née Cleaver); Abu
Dhabi since April 1997; born 20.12.46; FCO 1973;
Kinshasa 1974; FCO 1976; Helsinki 1977; Suva
1980; The Hague 1982; FCO 1984; SUPL 1986;
FCO 1989; SUPL 1992; Canberra 1994; SUPL
1996; Band B3; m 1986 Hugh Dunnachie.

Dunnachie, Hugh MBE (1987); Consul-General
Perth since March 2000; born 7.12.44; MOD
(Navy) 1961-75; DSAO 1965; Singapore (Political
Adviser's Office) 1967; Warsaw 1972; Vice-
Consul Cairo 1973; Second Secretary FCO 1976;
Second Secretary (Commercial) The Hague 1980;
Consul and Head of British Interests Tripoli 1984;
First Secretary FCO 1989; Deputy Consul-General
Melbourne 1992; First Secretary
(Economic/Agriculture) Canberra 1994; Deputy
Head of Post and HM Consul Dubai 1996; m(1)
1963 Elizabeth Mosman Baxter (diss 1986) (3d
1964, 1971, 1980; 1s 1965); (2) 1986 (Doreen)
Carole Cleaver.

Dunne, John Richard; FCO since January 2001;
born 4.10.67; FCO 1992; Third later Second
Secretary UKMIS New York 1996; Band C4; m
1997 Naomi Anita Scott.

Duranko, Elizabeth Jean; (née Paris); SUPL since
August 2000; born 23.1.69; FCO 1993; Geneva
1996; SUPL 1998; Pretoria 1999; Band C4; m
1997 John Eric Duranko (1d 1998).

Dutch, Alastair Keith; Second later First Secretary
FCO since January 1980; born 4.5.52; FCO 1971;
Ankara 1974; Moscow 1977; Bombay 1978; m
1974 Lesley Joan Carol Hearsum (2s 1975, 1983).

Duxbury, Julie Annette; Third Secretary
(Immigration) Zagreb since August 2000; born
5.2.70; FCO 1988; UKDEL NATO Brussels 1990;
FCO 1993; Full-time Language Training 1995;
Vice Consul Athens 1996; Dubai 1998; Band B3.

Dwyer, Michael John; HM Consul/ECM, and later
First Secretary Director of US ECIPs, New York
since February 1995; born 29.12.55; DOE 1972-

74; FCO 1974; Ottawa 1977; Belmopan 1979; Islamabad 1982; FCO 1986; Vice-Consul (Man/Comm/Con) Toronto 1990; Second Secretary (Commercial) Toronto 1991; m 1982 Karen Leolin Meighan (2s 1983, 1985, 1d 1989).

Dyson, John Alva, MVO (1995); T/D Asmara since August 2001; born 15.4.49; DSAO (later FCO) 1966; Port of Spain 1970; Geneva 1973; Yaoundé 1976; FCO 1978; Nuku'alofa 1982; FCO 1985; Second Secretary (Comm) Jedda 1987; Vice-Consul (Management Officer) Cape Town 1991; First Secretary FCO 1996; m 1971 Deirdre Anne George (2s 1974, 1981).

E

Ead, Mark; FCO since December 1997; born 20.4.76; Band A2; m2001 Victoria Swan.

Eager, Helen Christine (née Gillings), BEM (1991); SUPL since May 1998; born 10.6.65; FCO 1985; SUPL 1986; FCO 1988; Baghdad 1988; FCO 1990; Bangkok 1993; FCO 1997; Band A2.

Eager, Nigel Dominic; First Secretary (Political) Valletta since September 1998; born 9.5.62; FCO 1981; Dublin 1986; Third Secretary/Vice-Consul Baghdad 1988; FCO 1990; Band C5; m (1) 1987 Helen Christine Gillings (diss 1993), (2) 1998 Catherine Thomas.

Eakin, Christopher Howard; SUPL since July 2000; born 1.12.64; FCO 1984; East Berlin 1985; Paris 1987; FCO 1990; Vienna 1993; Grand Cayman 1996; Band C4.

Ealand, Jane Elizabeth; FCO since November 1991; born 10.8.67; FCO 1986; New Delhi 1988; FCO 1990; Paris 1990; Band A2.

Eames, Nigel Anthony; Second later First Secretary FCO since April 1979; born 19.10.42; FO 1962; UKDEL NATO Paris 1963; UKDIS Geneva 1966; FCO 1969; Warsaw 1973; FCO 1974; Paris 1976; m 1966 Jean Morgan Fletcher (2d 1975, 1981).

Earl, Jane Ann (née Kerr); SUPL since February 2001; born 15.6.68; FCO 1989; Luanda 1991; Islamabad 1995; SUPL 1998; Brussels Embassy 2000; Band B3; m 1991 Shaun Earl (1d 1997).

Earl, Shaun; Third Secretary UKDEL Brussels since December 1998; born 4.1.70; FCO 1989; Luanda 1991; Band B3; m 1991 Jane Ann Kerr (1d 1997).

Easson, Hilary; Vienna since September 2000; born 10.1.68; FCO 1987; Kuwait 1990; Algiers 1991; FCO 1994; Bogotá 1995; FCO 1999; Band A2.

Easter, Christine Marie; FCO since July 1994; born 22.11.44; FCO 1975; Cape Town 1975; FCO 1979; Luxembourg 1982; Anguilla 1985; Rangoon 1987; Budapest 1989; Washington 1991; Band B3.

Easton, Suzanne Katharine Mary; SUPL since September 1999; born 9.9.63; FCO 1990; Buenos Aires 1992; Third Secretary (Chancery) New Delhi 1995; Band B3; m (1) 1986 Thomas Ross

Yuill (dec'd 1993) (1d 1986) (2) 1997 John Andrew Easton. (1s 1998).

Eastwood, Basil Stephen Talbot; CMG (1999); HM Ambassador Berne additionally HM Ambassador (non-resident) Liechtenstein since August 2001; born 4.3.44; Third Secretary FO 1966; MECAS 1967; Jedda 1968; Third later Second Secretary Colombo 1969; Second later First Secretary Cairo 1972; on loan to Cabinet Office 1976; FCO 1978; Bonn 1980; Counsellor and Head of Chancery Khartoum 1984; Counsellor (Econ/Comm) Athens 1987; Counsellor FCO 1991; HM Ambassador Damascus 1996; m 1970 Alison Faith Hutchings (4d 1972, 1973, 1977, 1979).

Eastwood, Helen; SUPL since April 1996; born 10.12 63; FCO 1989; Dubai 1992; Band A2; m 1990 David Allan Eastwood, (1d 1996).

Eatwell, Jonathan David; SUPL since July 2001; born 8.11.67; FCO 1986; Lusaka 1988; FCO 1992; Dhaka 1995; FCO 1998; Jakarta 1998; Band B3; m 1991 Lisa Ann Brecknell (1d 1997).

Ebeling, Adrian Stanley Arthur; FCO since November 2000; born 20.1.48; FCO 1984; Paris 1989; FCO 1992; Pretoria 1998; Band C4; m 1979 Laura Phipps (1s 1987).

Edgar, Christopher George; HM Ambassador Skopje since September 2001; born 21.4.60; FCO 1981; Moscow 1983; Lagos 1986; FCO 1988; resigned 1992; reinstated 1995; First Secretary FCO 1995; HM Ambassador Phonm Penh 1997; FTLT 2001; m 1994 Yelena Nagornichnykh (2d 1994, 1998).

Edge, Christopher James; First Secretary (Commercial) San José and Director of Trade Promotion in Central America since July 1999; born 30.8.53; FCO 1972; Kabul 1975; East Berlin 1977; Rome 1980; Kaduna 1981; FCO 1984; Beirut 1985; Third Secretary (Commercial) Mexico City 1987; Deputy Head of Mission Tegucigalpa 1988; Second, later First Secretary (Commercial) Madrid 1992; FCO 1996.

Edghill, Susan Christine (née Cranwell); Manilla since September 1998; born 14.7.58; FCO 1990; Paris 1993; Port Louis 1996; Band A2; m 1996 Samuel Carlisle Edghill.

Edis, Rachel Pauline; FCO since September 2001; born 24.11.76 Band C4.

Edis, Richard John Smale, CMG (1994); HM Ambassador Algiers since September 2001; born 1.9.43; Third Secretary FO 1966; Third later Second Secretary Nairobi 1968; Second later First Secretary Lisbon 1971; FCO 1974; First Secretary (ECOSOC) New York 1977; FCO 1981; Counsellor on secondment to NIO 1982; Deputy Leader UKDIS Geneva 1984; Counsellor FCO and Commissioner British Indian Ocean Territory 1988; CDA at Cambridge University 1991; HM Ambassador Maputo 1992; HM Ambassador Tunis 1995; On loan to MOD as Senior Director (Civ) RCDS 1999; m 1971 Genevieve Nanette Suzanne Cerisoles (3s 1971, 1972, 1975).

Edusei, Charmaine (née Howe); FCO since 1997; born 17.9.59; FCO 1988; UKDEL NATO Brussels 1991; FCO 1993; Valletta 1994; Band B3; m 1989 Isaac Edusei (1d 1993).

Edwards, Carole Lilian (née Hellier); FCO since June 1992; born 7.7.45; FCO 1973; Freetown 1973; Washington 1975; Prague 1978; Belgrade 1978; FCO 1979; Beirut 1980; Ottawa 1982; Moscow 1985; FCO 1986; Washington 1989; Band B3.

Edwards, David Vaughan; Tehran since May 2001; born 27.9.43; RAF 1961-89; Budapest 1989; Islamabad 1990; Kingston 1994; Moscow 1996; Riyadh 1998; Band B3; m 1967 Patricia Ann (2d 1968, 1969; 1s 1972).

Edwards, Gillian Rose; Dublin since January 2000; born 7.2.64; FCO 1983; Resigned 1987; Reinstated 1988; FCO 1988; World wide floater duties 1991; St Petersburg 1993; FCO 1994; Vice-Consul New York 1996; Band B3; m 1995 David Jonathan Mead.

Edwards, Keith Nigel; Second Secretary FCO since April 1995; born 9.5.53; FCO 1969; Warsaw 1977; Athens 1978; FCO 1981; Hong Kong 1985; FCO 1988; Second Secretary Madrid 1992; m 1975 Wendy Ann Carrington (2d 1980, 1982).

Edwards, Mannetta Beverley (née Leigh); FCO since July 1994; born 14.2.59; FCO 1979; Kuwait 1982; FCO 1986; UKDEL NATO Brussels 1991; Band C4; m 1980 Christopher James Edwards (2s 1981, 1986).

Edwards, Paul Martin; Third Secretary Management and Vice- Consul Almaty since September 1998; born 11.11.66; FCO 1996; Band B3; m 1990 Jane Baker (1d 1993).

Edwards, Rose Catherine Amy; Second Secretary (Economic) Moscow since February 2001; born 10.11.73; FCO 1998; FTLT 1999; Band C4.

Eelbeck, Andrew; Accra since July 1997; born 2.3.59; FCO 1979; Islamabad 1980; FCO 1982; Singapore 1982; FCO 1986; Third Secretary Prague 1988; Third Secretary Pretoria 1992; FCO 1995; Band C4; m 1994 Miss F Botes; (1s 1995).

Ehrman, William Geoffrey, CMG (1998); Director (International Security) since September 2000; born 28.8.50; Third Secretary FCO 1973; Language Student Hong Kong 1975; Third later Second Secretary Peking 1976; First Secretary (ECOSOC) UKMIS New York 1979; First Secretary Peking 1983; FCO 1985; on Secondment at Hong Kong as Political Adviser to the Governor 1989; Counsellor FCO 1993; Principal Private Secretary to the Secretary of State for Foreign and Commonwealth Affairs 1995; on secondment to Unilever 1997; HM Ambassador Luxembourg 1998; m 1977 Penelope Anne Le Patourel (1s 1981; 3d 1977, 1979, 1986).

El Beleidi, Cecille Maude (née Greaves); Second Secretary (Chancery) Riyadh since March 2000; born 22.11.62; FCO 1982; Kuwait 1985; FCO 1986; Kathmandu 1989; Vice Consul Casablanca 1992; APS/Baroness Symons FCO 1995; Second Secretary (Chancery) Riyadh 1999; SUPL 1999; Band C4; m 1987 Magdi El Beleidi (1d 1999).

Elder, Alistair Alexander; Third Secretary (Commercial) New Delhi since July 2001; born 14.5.71; FCO 1989; UKREP Brussels 1992; FCO 1994; Vice Consul Tel Aviv 1997; m. Charlotte Dawson (2d 1992,1995).

Elder, Peter Edward; FCO since December 1997; born 14.3.68; FCO 1989; Brussels 1992; FCO 1994; New Delhi 1994; Band B3; m 1994 Rosalind Anita Hall (1d 1997).

Elder, Rosalind Anita (née Hall); FCO since December 1997; born 19.7.65; FCO 1990; UKREP Brussels 1992; New Delhi 1994; Band A2; m 1994 Peter Edward Elder (1d 1997).

Eldon, Stewart Graham, CMG (1999); OBE (1991); Deputy Permanent Representative (with the personal rank of Ambassador) UKMIS New York since September 1998; born 18.9.53; UK Mission New York 1976; FCO 1976; Third later Second Secretary Bonn 1978; First Secretary FCO 1982; Private Secretary to Minister of State 1983; First Secretary (Chancery) UKMIS New York 1986; First Secretary FCO 1990; Counsellor on loan to the Cabinet Office 1991; Fellow, Center for International Affairs, Harvard University 1993; Counsellor (Political) UKDEL NATO/WEU Brussels 1994; Director (Conferences) FCO 1997; m 1978 Christine Mary Mason (1d 1982; 1s 1985).

Elliot, Caroline Margaret (Carma); Consul General Chongqing since March 2000; born 24.8.64; FCO 1987; Peking 1989; Brussels 1991; EC Presidency Liaison Officer Bonn, Paris and Madrid 1995-1996; Second Secretary later First Secretary FCO 1996; Band D6.

Elliot, Christopher Lowther; Second Secretary FCO since March 1997; born 26.12.54; DNS 1974; DOE 1975; FCO 1975; Cairo 1979; Bridgetown 1982; FCO 1986; Islamabad 1990; Muscat 1993; m 1975 Julie Lorraine Inman (1s adopted 1975; 1d 1982).

Elliot, Hugh Stephen Murray; Buenos Aires since May 1999; born 21.8.65; FCO 1989; Third later Second Secretary (Chancery) Madrid 1991; FCO 1996; m 1989 Toni Martin-Elena. (1s 1993, 1d 1995).

Elliot, Jonathan Andrew; Full time Language Training Tokyo since August 1994; born 3.9.66; FCO 1991; Full-time Language Training 1993; Band D6.

Elliott, Jane Susan; Consul Hong Kong since April 2000; born 16.6.55; FCO 1980; Hong Kong 1991; FCO 1997; Band D6.

Elliott, Robert David; First Secretary (Management) Abuja since November 2000; born 25.11.60; FCO 1980; Prague 1981; Peking 1982; Language Training 1983; Abu Dhabi 1984; Port Louis 1988; FCO 1993; HM Consul Jerusalem

Biographical List

1997; Band C5; m 1998 Victoria Louise Holloway. (1s 1988; 1d 2000).

Elliott, Stuart; Athens since October 1999; born 15.4.75; HCS 1994; FCO 1997; Athens 1999; Band A2; m 1999 Margaret Redmond.

Elliott, Susan Jayne, MBE (1991); Second Secretary (Chancery) Bandar Seri Begawan since January 1999; born 13.6.61; FCO 1978; SUPL 1980; Rome 1982; SUPL 1982; Cairo 1984; FCO 1985; Band B3; Beirut 1988; Bombay 1992; FCO 1992; m 1980 John Anthony Tucknott (diss 1992).

Elliott, William; Second Secretary (Political) Warsaw since October 1995; born 16.3.68; Second Secretary FCO 1993; Language Training 1994.

Ellis, Alexander Wykeham; First Secretary (Economic) UKREP Brussels since June 1996; born 5.6.67; FCO 1990. Third later Second Secretary (Political/Economic) Lisbon 1992; m 1996 Maria Teresa Adegas.

Ellis, Amanda Jane; Quito since July 1999; born 7.12.60; FCO 1987; Brussels 1989; FCO 1991; Jakarta 1995; Band A2.

Ellis, Ann; FCO since September 1990; born 19.11.47; Band A2.

Ellis, Hugo; FCO since January 1999; born 13.9.66; FCO 1988; Riyadh 1992; UKDEL Strasbourg 1995; Band B3.

Ellis, John Arthur; Second Secretary FCO since September 1996; born 27.3.52; DHSS 1969-71; FCO 1971; Wellington 1974; Khartoum 1976; Dar es Salaam 1979; FCO 1981; Islamabad 1982; Seoul 1986; Second Secretary FCO 1989; Second Secretary (Commercial/Aid) Cairo 1993; m 1974 Law Kwai Chun (1s 1980, 1d 1983).

Ellis, Philip Donald; First Secretary FCO since October 1997; born 9.5.57; FCO 1978; Brussels (NATO) 1981; Peking 1984; FCO 1987; New Delhi 1990; Vice Consul São Paulo 1995; m 1981 Gail Teresa Drayton. (1s 1997).

Ellis, Richard Anthony; FCO since September 2000; born 2.2.77; Band C4.

Ellwood, Dr Sheelagh Margaret; FCO since October 1998; born 21.2.49; FCO 1988; Assistant Deputy Governor, Gibraltar 1995; Senior Principal Research Officer 1998.

Elmes, Caroline Myfanwy Tonge, CMG (2001); HM Ambassador Luanda since November 1998; born 20.9.48; Second Secretary FCO 1975; Language Student 1977; First Secretary Prague 1978; First Secretary FCO 1981; First Secretary (Econ) Rome 1985; Deputy High Commissioner and Head of Chancery Colombo 1989; Deputy Head of Mission Prague 1992; Counsellor FCO 1995; full time language training 1998.

El Ouassi, Sabine; Amman since September 1999; born 29.1.64; HCS 1990-1993; FCO 1994; Band A2; Riyadh 1995; m 1988 Mohamed El Ouassi (1s 1994).

El Roubi, Julie Anne (née Mooney); Abu Dhabi since December 2000; born 21.4.71; UKDEL NATO Brussels 1991; Khartoum 1995; Lagos 1998; Band A2; m(1) 1992 Prince Felix Lewis (diss) (1d 1992); (2) 1999 Murtada Saad El Roubi (1s 2000).

Elvins, Christine Patricia (née Pettit); SUPL since February 1999; born 4.6.60; FCO 1979; Bonn 1983; Pretoria 1986; FCO 1987; SUPL 1988; FCO 1993; Band C4; m 1988 Martyn Andrew Elvins.

Elvins, Martyn Andrew; Pretoria since February 1999; born 13.2.58; FCO 1984; Warsaw 1988; Band C4; m 1988 Christine P Pettit.

Elvy, Simon David; Second Secretary (Political) Stockholm since June 1996; born 8.12.61; FCO 1983; Baghdad 1985; Stockholm 1989; FCO 1992; Band B3; m 1985 Lesley Jane (1s 1991).

Embleton, Robert Leitch; First Secretary (Social /Science) Rome since August 1998; born 9.10.42; FO 1960; Leopoldville 1964; Bonn 1968; StVincent 1969; FCO 1973; Stuttgart 1976; Prague 1979; Second Secretary FCO 1980; Second later First Secretary (Chancery) Washington 1984; Consul (Commercial) Düsseldorf 1989; First Secretary FCO 1993; m 1970 Ursula Biebricher (1d 1975).

Emery, Peter Michael; Tokyo since February 2000; born 25.11.72; FCO 1997; Helsinki 1999. Band A2.

Emery, Simon Richard; FCO since June 1985; born 22.8.57; FCO 1981; OECD Paris 1982; Band A2; m 1981 Dorothy Seery.

Enescott, Nicholas John; Second Secretary FCO since January 1995; born 6.12.51; FCO 1972; Cape Town 1975; Ankara 1977; Tripoli 1980; FCO 1983; Hanoi 1986; Third Secretary (Comm) and Vice-Consul Dakar 1989; Second Secretary (Management) Lilongwe 1991.

Engdahl, Denise Jean (née Sanders); Stockholm since March 2000; born 19.9.60; FCO 1982; Wellington 1983; Colombo 1986; Mbabane 1989; FCO 1993; SUPL 1995; Kingston 1996; Band B3; m 1989; Geran Magnus Engdahl (1s 1991, 1d 1994).

England, Barrie, LVO (2000); First Secretary FCO since July 1997; born 22.5.42; Commonwealth Office 1966; MECAS 1968; Kuwait 1970; Athens 1972; FCO 1975; (Second Secretary 1977); Colombo 1977; FCO 1981; Second later First Secretary (Chancery/Inf) Berne 1984; FCO 1989; Tunis 1994 m1967 Betty Anne Loible (1d 1969; 1s 1972).

Estlin, Jennifer Frances (née Haxton); MBE (1999); Montserrat since January 1996; born 21.4.44; FCO 1992; Sana'a 1993; Band A2; m 1995 Boyd Estlin (1s 1970).

Esling, Paul Francis; Lagos since August 2000; born 16.11.73; FCO 1996; Harare 1998; Band B3; m 1997 Lindsey Jane Esling (1s 2000).

Etherington, Richard David Ernest; FCO since September 1999; born 29.11.73; Band C4.

Etherton, Mark Roy; Deputy Permanent Representative UKMIS Vienna since April 1999; born 17.3.58; FCO 1983; Second Secretary (Chancery) Paris 1988; First Secretary (Political/Economic) Warsaw 1991; First Secretary on loan to Cabinet Office 1994; FCO 1996; m 1991 Suzanne Margaret Miskin (2d 1994, 1996).

Evans, Alison Joan; FCO since July 1990; born 30.10.63; FCO 1982; Caracas 1984; African/ME Floater 1988; Band B3.

Evans, Carol Jeanette (née Kendall); SUPL since July 1997; born 10.4.59; FCO 1982; UKDEL Vienna 1984; Warsaw 1987; FCO 1988; Band B3; m 1991 Keith Dennis Evans.

Evans, Claire Elizabeth; First Secretary FCO since June 2000; born 2.11.61; FCO 1987; Jakarta 1989; Third Secretary (Commercial) Islamabad 1992; Second Secretary FCO 1996; Band C5.

Evans, Claire Margaret (née Bolland); Second Secretary FCO since April 1994; born 13.1.70; Band C4; m 1996 David Howard Evans (2d 1997, 1999).

Evans, Elizabeth Ann (née McNab); Third Secretary (Visits, Press and Public Affairs) Peking since November 1999; born 26.7.61; FCO 1998; Band B3; m 1987 Laurance Bolton Evans (1s 1989).

Evans, David Hugh; First Secretary (Political) Nairobi since May 2001; born 27.3.59; FCO 1985; Islamabad 1988; FCO 1989; First Secretary (Political) Washington 1995 (on loan to the US State Department); on secondment to the CBI as Senior Policy Adviser 1999; Band D6; m 1988 Nirmala Vinodhini Chrysostom (2d 1996, 2001).

Evans, Gayle Evelyn Louise (née Sperring); SUPL since April 1997; born 1.9.62; FCO 1983; Accra 1984; Moscow 1986; FCO 1987; Floater Duties 1990; SUPL 1991; UKMIS New York 1992; FCO 1996; Band B3; m 1991 Julian Ascott Evans (2d 1997, 1999).

Evans, Gerald Stanley; Deputy Head of Mission Asunción since November 1996; born 26.10.51; FCO 1971; Havana 1973; Bonn 1974; Jedda 1977; FCO 1977; Third Secretary and Vice Consul Dubai 1979; FCO 1983; Third Secretary (Commercial) Bogotá 1986; Third Secretary (Management) Athens 1990; Second Secretary FCO 1994; m 1991 Graciela Elisa Casetta.

Evans, Gillian; Rabat since September 2000; born 1.9.59; FCO 1981; BMG Berlin 1982; Kinshasa 1984; Africa/Asia/ME Floater 1988; Zagreb 1992; Damascus 1996; Band A2.

Evans, Jennifer Mary (née Lewis); SUPL since May 1997; born 3.3.59; FCO 1978; Far East Floater 1981; SUPL 1983; Vienna 1984; SUPL 1985; Dhaka 1989; Second Secretary FCO 1993; m 1982 Wayne Evans (3d 1985, 1988, 1994; 1s 1997).

Evans, Julian Ascott; First Secretary FCO since February 1996; born 5.7.57; FCO 1978; Language Training 1980; Moscow 1982; Zurich 1985; Second Secretary FCO 1987; Second later First Secretary UKMIS New York 1991; m 1991 Gayle Evelyn Louise Sperring (2d 1997, 1999).

Evans, Karen-Lane (née Williams); SUPL since February 1998; born 9.4.63; FCO 1989; Second Secretary (Chancery) The Hague 1992; Second Secretary FCO 1996; Band C4; m 1998 Paul Lawson Evans.

Evans, Laurance Bolton; First Secretary and HMC Peking since April 1999; born 30.3.43; FO 1962; Saigon 1964; Washington 1968; FCO 1970; Brussels (JAO) 1974; Paris 1976; FCO 1979; Vienna 1982; Second Secretary (Dev) Amman 1984; Second Secretary (Cons) Dar es Salaam 1988; Second Secretary FCO 1992; Manila 1995; m(1) 1963 Heather Duxbury (dec'd 1986) (2s 1965, 1968); (2) 1987 Elizabeth Ann McNab (1s 1989).

Evans, Dame Madelaine Glynne Dervel, DBE (2000), CMG (1992); HM Ambassador Lisbon since September 2001; born 23.8.44; Second Secretary FCO 1971; Buenos Aires 1972; First Secretary FCO 1975; Private Secretary to PUSS 1976; on loan to UN Secretariat New York 1978; First Secretary UKMIS New York 1979; First Secretary later Counsellor FCO 1982; Counsellor and Head of Chancery Brussels 1987; Counsellor FCO 1990-1996; (IISS) 1996; HM Ambassador Santiago 1997; Attachment to ACAD/IND as Detached National Expert 2000.

Evans, Paul Lawson; Counsellor on secondment to HM Customs and Excise since October 1999; born 26.5.55; Royal Navy 1973-80; FCO 1983; UKMIS Vienna 1986; First Secretary FCO 1988; First Secretary later Counsellor Washington 1992; Counsellor FCO 1994; Counsellor Vienna 1997; m 1998 KarenLane-Williams.

Evans, Peter Dering; Third later Second Secretary FCO since February 1993; born 9.4.57; FCO 1976; Dacca 1978; FCO 1980; Barcelona 1985; San Salvador 1988; Third Secretary (Management/Accounts) Caracas 1990; m 1985 Susan Elizabeth Parker (2s 1987, 1989).

Evans, Rosemary Isabel (née Collier); FO (later FCO) since December 1966 (Second Secretary 1973); (First Secretary 1997); born 4.8.44; m 1972 Ronald Evans.

Evans, Stephen Nicholas, OBE (1994) Counsellor FCO since March 1997; born 29.6.50; Third Secretary FCO 1974; Language Student SOAS 1975; Second Secretary FCO 1976; Head of Chancery and Consul Hanoi 1978; FCO 1980; Language Training Bangkok 1982; First Secretary Bangkok 1983; First Secretary FCO 1986; First Secretary (Political) Ankara 1990; Counsellor (Economic/Commercial/Aid) Islamabad 1993; Secondment to United Nations Special Mission to Afghanistan 1996; m 1975 Sharon Ann Holdcroft (2d 1981, 1984; 1s 1986).

Evans, Stephen Paul; FCO since January 2000;
born 28.10.57; HM Forces (Army) 1975; Police
Constable 1997; Band B3; m 1986 Julie Spackman
(1s 1988, 1d 1990).

Evans, Stephen Shane; FCO since July 2001; born
7.12.54; FCO 1992; Second Secretary Zagreb
1998; Band C4; m 1995 Susan Jane (1s 1987).

Evans, Wayne; First Secretary (Political) The
Hague since July 2000; born 29.8.53; FCO 1971;
Paris 1974; Maseru 1977; FCO 1979; Baghdad
1981; Vienna 1984; FCO 1987; Second Secretary
(Aid) Dhaka 1989; Second later First Secretary
FCO 1993; Deputy Head of Mission and Consul
(Commercial) Jedda 1996; Band C5; m 1982
Jennifer Mary Lewis (3d 1985, 1988, 1994; 1s
1997).

Evans, William John Eldred; Second Secretary
FCO since June 1999; born 13.4.71; FCO 1994;
Language training 1996; on loan to OHR Sarajevo
1997; Second Secretary (Political/Military)
Sarajevo 1998; Band C4.

Everard, John Vivian; HM Ambassador
Montevideo since August 2001; born 24.11.56;
FCO 1979; Third later Second Secretary Peking
1981; Second Secretary Vienna 1983; Resigned
1984. Reinstated 1987; Second later First
Secretary 1987; First Secretary (Commercial)
Santiago 1990; HM Ambassador Minsk 1993; T/D
OSCE Vienna 1995; Counsellor FCO 1996;
Counsellor Peking 1998; m 1990 Heather Ann
Starkey.

Everard, Thomas James; Tehran since June 2001;
born 11.8.75; FCO 1998; Band A2.

Everett, Bernard Jonathan; cvo (1999); Consul
General São Paulo and Director of Trade
Promotion for Brazil since September 2000; born
17.9.43; FO 1966; Third later Second Secretary
Lisbon 1967; Second later First Secretary FCO
1971; Consul (Pol) Luanda 1975; First Secretary
FCO 1975; First Secretary and Head of Chancery
Lusaka 1978; Consul (Comm) Rio de Janeiro
1980; First Secretary FCO 1983; Counsellor on
loan to DTI 1984; HM Ambassador Guatemala
City 1987; Consul General Houston 1991; High
Commissioner Maputo 1996; m 1970 Maria
Olinda Goncalves de Albuquerque (1d 1974; 2s
1980, 1981; 1d 1976, dec'd 1979).

Everett, Sara Gillian; Deputy Director BIS New
York since January 1996; born 6.7.55; FCO 1979;
ENA Paris 1981; Caracas 1983; Second Secretary
(Econ) UKREP Brussels 1986; Second Secretary
(Econ) Brussels (Embassy) 1987; First Secretary
FCO 1991; m 1989 Christopher Ian Montague
Jones (1s 1994).

Everitt, Oliver Hunter; Vienna since September
1995; born 28.12.71; FCO 1992; Band A2.

Everson, Clare Elizabeth; SUPL since November
1999; born 20.12.59; FCO 1981; Karachi 1983;
SE Asia Floater 1988; FCO 1990; Deputy High
Commissioner Vila 1994; Band D6.

Evetts, Keith Derek, obe (1989); Counsellor
Lisbon since September 1998; born 20.5.48; Third
Secretary FCO 1973; Language Student 1974;
Second Secretary Warsaw 1975; Language Student
FCO 1976; First Secretary Maputo 1977; FCO
1980; UKMIS New York 1983; Kingston 1986;
First Secretary (Chancery) Lisbon 1988; First
Secretary later Counsellor FCO 1991; Counsellor
Brussels 1995; Counsellor FCO 1998; m(1) 1971
Bridget Elizabeth Peachey (diss 1988) (2s 1981,
1982); (2) 1988 Lesley Ann Myers (1s 1989, 2d
1990, 1996).

Ewart, Fiona Margaret; Now see under Morrison.

Ewen, Janice Susan Genevieve; FCO since May
1991; born 23.8.44; FCO 1970; Rome 1973;
Budapest 1976; FCO 1978; Madrid 1979; FCO
1981; Moscow 1986; FCO 1988; JMO Brussels
1989; Band B3.

F

Fairhurst, Geoffrey; Administrator Ascension
Islands since July 1999; born 27.10.42; DSAO
1965; Nairobi 1967; Peking 1970; FCO and Malta
1971; Havana 1971; Milan 1973; FCO 1976;
Second Secretary (Aid/Admin) later
(Admin/Consular) Bridgetown 1979; FCO 1983;
Second later First Secretary (Admin) and Consul
Doha 1985; First Secretary Kaduna 1989; First
Secretary FCO 1994; Dhaka 1996; m 1971 Wendy
Metcalfe (3d 1973, 1976, 1978).

Fairley, Averil Margaret; Second Secretary
(Management) Georgetown since March 2001;
born 18.6.67; FCO 1986; East Berlin 1988; Hanoi
1990; European Council Unit Edinburgh 1992;
Bombay 1993; FCO 1997; Band C4.

Fairweather, Maria Louise (née Latta); FCO
since March 1996; born 25.5.67; MOD 1986; FCO
1988; Berne 1989; FCO 1992; Peking 1993; T/D
Kiev 1995; Band B3; m 1993 Robert John
Fairweather.

Fairweather, Robert John; FCO since July 1996;
born 26.2.67; HMCE 1987-96; Band B3; m 1993
Maria Louise.

Falconer, Lynne Marie; Lisbon since August
2000; born 27.9.67; HM Forces 1986-1995; FCO
1995; Helsinki 1997; Band A2.

Fall, David William; HM Ambassador Hanoi since
April 1997; born 10.3.48; Third Secretary FCO
1971; Language Student Bangkok 1973; First
Secretary Bangkok 1976; On loan to Cabinet
Office 1977; FCO 1979; First Secretary
(Chancery) Pretoria/Cape Town 1981; First
Secretary later Counsellor FCO 1985; Deputy
Head of Mission and Counsellor (Commercial)
Bangkok 1990; Deputy High Commissioner
Canberra 1993; m 1973 Margaret Gwendolyn
Richards (3s 1976, 1977, 1980).

Fallon, Helen Clare; ECO/VC Bridgetown since
November 1998; born 13.6.68; FCO 1987; Lagos
1990; FCO 1994; Band B3; m 1990 Michael
Thomas Fallon. Diss 1998. (2s 1991,1992)

Falzarano, Assuntina; Second Secretary (Chancery) UKMIS New York since December 2000; born 10.8.73; FCO 1998; Band C4.

Farish, Sandra Mary (née Olley); Beirut since June 2000; born 7.6.71; FCO 1995; Copenhagen 1996; Band B3; m 1996 Joseph Farish.

Farnham, Brian George; Paris since April 2000; born 16.4.52; FCO 1968; Paris 1974; FCO 1977; Baghdad 1978; FCO 1980; Tokyo 1981; FCO 1984; Hong Kong 1988; Second Secretary FCO 1991; Singapore 1995; FCO 1998; Band C5; m 1982 Emiko Ishida (2d 1985, 1990).

Farnsworth, Lee; La Paz since May 1999; born 28.1.71; FCO 1998; Band A2.

Farr, Charles Blanford; First Secretary FCO since February 1995; born 15.7.59; Second Secretary FCO 1985; Second Secretary Pretoria 1987; Second Secretary FCO 1990; First Secretary (Chancery) Amman 1992; Band D6.

Farr, Dawn Margaret; Seoul since December 1996; born 5.7.70; FCO 1989; Nicosia 1992; Mostar 1995; Band A2.

Farrand, John Percival Morey; First Secretary (Management) Ottawa since November 1997.born 4.6.54; HM Customs and Excise 1971; FCO 1972; Tokyo 1974; Mexico City 1977; Kuala Lumpur 1981; FCO 1985; San Francisco 1988; FCO 1990; Second Secretary FCO 1991; Deputy High Commissioner Nassau 1994; Band C5; m 1979 Sharon Anne Eddie (3d 1980, 1982, 1987).

Farrant, David Cornelius; Second later First Secretary FCO since January 1987; born 5.7.53; FCO 1972; UKMIS Geneva 1976; Moscow 1978; FCO 1980; Athens 1984; Band C5; m 1976 Anne Laing (2s 1982, 1987).

Farrare, Jane; Jerusalem since September 2000; born 5.2.72; FCO 1999; Band A2.

Farrell, Sarah; Taipei since April 2000; born 27.6.69; FCO 1991; Lisbon 1995; Istanbul Floater 1998; FCO 1999; Taipei 1999; SUPL 1999; Band A2.

Farrent, Susan Jennifer; Dhaka since September 2000; born 17.1.48; FCO 1986; Monrovia 1987; Port Moresby 1991; Port of Spain 1992; FCO 1995; Bangkok 1996; Band B3.

Farrey, Sonia Louise; FCO since September 2001; born 21.1.77; Band C4.

Farrington, Angela (née Hunt); FCO since April 1985; born 28.9.62; Band A2; m 1987 Danny Farrington.

Farrington, Ian Francis; First Secretary FCO since December 1995; born 21.8.63; FCO 1986; Third later Second Secretary (Econ) Athens 1989. Second later First Secretary FCO 1991; First Secretary Lagos 1993; Band D6.

Farrow, Stephen Alan; Dar es Salaam since August 1997; born 23.7.56; Armed Forces 1972-

1996; FCO 1996; Band A2; m 1979 Linda Alexis Jeffrey (1s 1979, 1d 1981).

Faulkner, Leo Gregory; Ambassador to Republic of Chile since April 2000; born 21.9.43; FCO 1968; Second later First Secretary Lima 1972; First Secretary Lagos 1976; FCO 1979; First Secretary and Head of Chancery Madrid 1982; Counsellor on loan to DTI 1984; Counsellor (Comm) The Hague 1986; Minister, Consul-General and Deputy Head of Mission Buenos Aires 1990; Counsellor FCO 1993; High Commissioner Port of Spain since May 1996; Counsellor FCO 1999; m,1970 Fiona Hardie Birkett (3rd 1973, 1975, 1978).

Faulkner, Nicholas Anthony; Bonn since July 1994; born 19.5.72; FCO 1991; Band A2.

Faulkner, Richard John; FCO since August 1998; born 20.2.48; FCO 1969; Seoul 1972; Dubai 1975; FCO 1979; Islamabad 1983; Rome 1986; Second Secretary FCO 1989; Second Secretary Washington 1993; m 1973 Francoise Marie Christine Armande Trine (1d 1979).

Fawcett, Christine Anne; Second Secretary FCO since October 1993; born 17.8.50; FCO 1968; Dar es Salaam 1971; Lima 1973; Havana 1976; Freetown 1977; FCO 1979; SEA Floater 1982; Belgrade 1983; FCO 1986 (Second Secretary 1989) Second Secretary (Management/Consular) Port of Spain 1991.

Fay, Jacqueline Ann (née Builder); Third Secretary (Management/Consular) Bratislava since March 1995; born 22.9.61; FCO 1980; Dhaka 1983; Peking 1985; Vice-Consul New York 1987; SUPL 1991; FCO 1991; Band B3; m 1987 Kevin Michael Fay (1s 1990, 1d 1994).

Fean, Vincent; on loan to the DTI (sub-Saharan Africa, South Asia) since July 1999; born 20.11.52; FCO 1975; MECAS 1977; Third Secretary Baghdad 1978; Gaborone 1979; Second later First Secretary Damascus 1979; FCO 1982; First Secretary UKREP Brussels 1985; First Secretary FCO 1990; Counsellor Paris 1992; FCO 1996; m 1978 Anne Marie Stewart (2d 1979, 1981; 1s 1983).

Fear, Harriet; Third Secretary (Commercial) Prague since November 1997; born 11.8.68; Department of Employment 1986; FCO 1987; Dakar 1989; Africa/Middle East Floater 1992; Temporary Duty Phnom Penh 1994; FCO 1994; Band B3.

Fearis, Timothy Rupert; FCO since July 1989; born 5.2.58; FCO 1979; Accra 1982; FCO 1984; Attaché Islamabad 1987; Band B3.

Fearn, Thomas Daniel; Deputy Head of Mission Sarajevo since January 2001; born 16.9.62; FCO 1991; Second Secretary (Political) Budapest 1992; First Secretary FCO 1996; Band D6.

Feasey, Susan Catherine; Floater duties since October 1998; born 8.5.64; FCO 1983; UKMIS Vienna 1985; Dakar 1988; FCO 1990; Riga 1992; FCO 1993; Band B3.

Feather, Helen Mary; Second Secretary (Management) Dar es Salaam since February 2000; born 2.1.63; FCO 1982; Moscow, 1985; Gaborone 1988; Latin American Caribbean Floater October 1990; Third Secretary UKDEL WEU Brussels 1993; Third Secretary FCO 1994; DTI 1996; Third Secretary (Immigration) Dar es Salaam 1999; Band B3; m 1999 L. Ross Field.

Featherstone, Simon Mark; Counsellor FCO since September 1998; born 24.7.58; FCO 1980; Language Training Hong Kong 1982; Second Secretary (Chancery) Peking 1984; First Secretary FCO 1987; On loan to Cabinet Office 1988; First Secretary (Environment) UKRep Brussels 1990; HM Consul-General Shanghai 1994; Political and Economic Counsellor Peking 1996; m 1981 Gail Teresa Salisbury (2d 1985, 1992; 1s 1988).

Fehintola, Adebowale Bamidele; Copenhagen since May 2000; born 14.11.67; FCO 1987; Copenhagen 1989; Sana'a 1992; Gaborone 1993; Band B3.

Feliks, Michael Edward Joseph; SUPL since December 1997; born 3.9.64; FCO 1990; Full-time Language Training 1992; Full-time Language Training Peking 1993; First Secretary FCO 1994; First Secretary (Economic) BTC Hong Kong 1995; Band D6; m 1993 Valerie Jane Brown.

Fell, Richard Taylor, cvo (1996); British High Commissioner Wellington since December 2001; Also, British High Commissioner(Non resident) Samoa, Governor, (Non resident) of the Pitcairn, Henderson, Ducie and Oeno Islands; born 11.11.48; FCO 1971; Third Secretary Ottawa 1972; Second Secretary Saigon 1974; Vientiane 1975; Second later First Secretary FCO 1975; Chargé d'Affaires a.i. Hanoi 1979; Brussels (NATO) 1979; First Secretary and Head of Chancery Kuala Lumpur 1983; First Secretary FCO 1986; On secondment to Industry 1988; Counsellor (Comm/Econ) Ottawa 1989; Counsellor and Deputy Head of Mission Bangkok 1993; Counsellor FCO 1997; Consul-General Toronto (T/D) 2000; m 1981 Claire Peta Gates (3s 1983, 1987, 1990).

Fell, William Varley; Counsellor FCO since May 1992; born 4.3.48; FCO 1971; Third later Second Secretary (UNEDO/IAEA) Vienna 1973; Second later First Secretary (Econ/Comm) Havana 1976; FCO 1978; Warsaw 1979; First Secretary FCO 1982; Counsellor Athens 1988; m 1970 Jill Pauline Warren (1s 1974; 1s, 1d (twins) 1976).

Felton, Ian; Deputy Head of Mission Phnom Penh since May 2000; born 16.5.66; FCO 1986; Brussels 1987; Floater Duties 1990; FCO 1993; (ECOSOC) UKMIS New York 1995-1999; Band C4.

Fenn, Robert Dominic Russell; First Secretary UKMIS New York since August 1992; born 28.1.62; FCO 1983; Third Secretary (Chancery) The Hague 1985; Second Secretary (Chancery) Lagos 1988; First Secretary FCO 1990.

Fennell, Leigh; Amman since March 2000; born 13.12.60; FCO 1982; Darwin 1986; FCO 1988; Third Secretary Accra 1993; FCO 1997; Band C4.

Fenner, Margaret Patricia Jean (née Watson); Kingston since November 1999; born 29.1.66; Wellington 1986; Warsaw 1988; FCO 1988; Lagos 1990; Tehran 1993; Helsinki 1994; FCO 1995; Band B3; m 1989 Martin David Fenner (diss 1994) (1s 1990).

Fenning, Camilla Jane Vance (née Packman); FCO since October 1990 (Second Secretary 1991, First Secretary 1994); born 29.4.64; FCO 1985; Language Training 1986; Tokyo 1987; m 1988 Richard John Fenning. (1s 1993, 1d 1995).

Fenton, Jennifer Muriel; Second Secretary (Management) Valletta since December 1999; born 30.12.57; HCS 1976; FCO 1977; Beirut 1980; Floater duties 1982; Singapore 1984; SUPL 1986; FCO 1987; New Delhi 1989; Mbabane 1993; Second Secretary FCO 1996; (1d 1986).

Ferguson, Christine Julia; FCO since March 1998; born 5.10.57; FCO 1982; Language Training 1983; Second Secretary Cairo 1985; Second later First Secretary FCO 1987; First Secretary UKDIS Geneva 1990; m 1990 Michael (later Sir Michael) Charles Swift Weston (1s 1993, 1d 1996).

Ferguson, Iain; Vice-Consul Tokyo since April 1999; born 18.2.70; FCO 1990; Lagos 1995; Band B3; m 1994 Helen Jane Lennie.

Ferguson, Jean McCauley; ECO/Vice-Consul Kathmandu since July 1999; born 8.10.55; Department of Employment 1985; Inland Revenue 1988; FCO 1998; Band B3; (1d 1975)

Fergusson, George Duncan; Consul-General Boston since August 1999; born 30.9.55; NIO 1978 (Private Secretary to NIO Minister of State 1982-83) First Secretary Dublin 1988; Transferred to Diplomatic Service 1990; First Secretary FCO 1991; First Secretary (Political/Information) Seoul 1993; First Secretary FCO 1996; Counsellor FCO 1997; m 1981 Margaret Wookey (3d 1982, 1986, 1991; 1s 1984).

Ferrand, Simon Piers; on loan to DTI since September 1999; born 5.3.68; FCO 1989; Kinshasa 1991; Paris 1996; FCO 1999; Band B3; m 1995 Bettina Barbara Paustian (1s 1998).

Fewster, Miles Nicholas, mbe (1991); Second Secretary FCO since August 1999; born 26.8.62; FCO 1982; Khartoum 1985; Riyadh 1989; FCO 1992; Second Secretary (Political) Nairobi 1996; Band C4; m 1986 Alexandria Fusco (3d 1992, 1993,1998).

Fidler, Martin Alfred; Deputy High Commissioner Belmopan since November 1999; born 10.12.53; DHSS 1972; FCO 1974; Belmopan 1977; Africa/ME Floater 1980; Havana 1981; Third Secretary UKMIS New York 1984; FCO 1987; Nuku'alofa 1989; Gibraltar 1992; FCO 1996; Band C4; m 1981 Nicky Williams (2s 1982, 1985).

Field, Robert; Second Secretary FCO since November 1995; born 4.1.53; FCO 1971; Karachi 1975; Far East Floater 1979; Second Secretary (Comm) Harare 1982. Second Secretary FCO 1987; Second Secretary (Management) Addis Ababa 1992.

Fielder, John; HM Consul Tel Aviv since July 1994; born 27.6.47; CO (later Commonwealth Office) 1966; HM Forces 1967-73; FCO 1974; Accra 1976; Nassau 1977; Prague 1980; SE Asia/FE Floater 1982; FCO 1987; Second Secretary (Management Consular) Maputo 1990.

Fielder, Richard John; Second Secretary Ottawa since July 1997; born 28.3.52; FCO 1971; Tokyo 1974; FCO 1975; Stockholm 1978; Khartoum 1981; FCO 1982; Dhaka 1985; Chicago 1988; Freetown 1990; FCO 1995; m 1988 Samantha Louise Monton (3d 1988,1993, 1996, 1s 1990).

Fiksen, Michael James; born 27.2.67; FCO 1986; Rome 1989; FCO 1992; Cairo 1994; FCO 1997; Riyadh 1998; Band B3; m 1993 Louise Elizabeth French.

Finch, Peter Leonard; FCO since November 1997; born 1.1.58; FCO 1975; UKMIS Geneva 1978; Tel Aviv 1981; New Delhi 1983; FCO 1986; Tokyo 1991; Manila 1994; Band C4; m 1979 Mitsue Uchida (1d 1990).

Findlay, Matthew Ross; Second Secretary (Political) Bangkok since July 1999; born 2.5.68; FCO 1996; Full-time Language Training Bangkok 1998; Band C4.

Fines, Barry John; New Delhi since March 1991; born 13.9.69; FCO 1988; Band A2; m 1997 Monika Graf.

Finlay, Norah Ferguson Watson; Islamabad since November 1995; born 13.4.70; FCO 1989; Singapore 1992; Band A2.

Finnamore-Crorkin, Joanne Lynn; Lagos since December 1997; born 22.9.63; FCO 1982; Moscow 1984; Colombo 1985; Floater Duties 1989, SUPL 1992; Consulate-General New York 1992; FCO 1994 (Second Secretary 1996); m 1991 Colin Wynn Crorkin (1d 1998).

Finnerty, Kevin John; First Secretary and Consul Washington since August 1997; born 1.2.49; FCO 1967; Kuwait 1970; Warsaw 1974; FCO 1976; Full-time Language Training 1978; FCO 1979; Mogadishu 1983; FCO 1985; Chicago 1985; Second Secretary FCO 1989; Full-time Language Training 1993; Düsseldorf 1993; m(1) 1970 Sandra Tidy (diss 1982); (2) 1982 Norma Collins.

Firstbrook, Steven Paul; Second Secretary (Commercial) Mumbai since November 2000; born 22.2.70; FCO 1989; Helsinki 1992; World-wide Floater Duties 1994; FCO 1996; Band C4.

Firth, Catherine Alison Jane, (née Readdie); Second Secretary (Political) Mexico City since June 2001; born 17.6.66; FCO 1990; Third Secretary (Chancery) Warsaw 1992; FCO 1994; Vice Consul Caracas 1995; FCO 1998; FTLT 2001; Band C5; m 1994 Andrew Charleson Firth.

Fish, Rosemary; SUPL since November 1992; born 28.8.49; Ankara 1974; Honiara 1976; Bogotá 1978; FCO 1979; Far East Floater 1980; FCO 1982; on loan to DTI 1984; Rio de Janeiro 1986; FCO 1988; m 1987 Anthony John Stafford (1s 1991, 1d 1993).

Fisher, Deborah Joan; FCO since July 1997; born 4.3.62; FCO 1985; Second Secretary (Chancery) Dar es Salaam 1988; First Secretary FCO 1991; SUPL 1996; m 1992 William James Lodge.

Fisher, Deryck John; First Secretary (Management) Bangkok since May 2000; born 26.7.46; Inland Revenue 1961; Department of Technical Co-operation/ODA 1964; FCO 1973; Kinshasa 1975; Islamabad 1978; Second Secretary FCO 1980; Second Secretary (Consular) Accra 1983; First Secretary (Admin/Consul) Copenhagen 1987; First Secretary FCO 1991; First Secretary (Management) Dhaka 1996; Band D6; m 1973 Lynda Elizabeth Robinson (2d 1974, 1975; 3s 1976, 1979, 1983).

Fisher Emily Caroline Gay (née Shapland); First Secretary (Political) Buenos Aires since September 2000; born 5.5.72; FCO 1997; Lusaka 1998; Band D6; m 1998 Roland Barnabas Fisher.

Fisher, Gary John; Third Secretary (MO/VC) Bahrain since March 2000; born 27.12.69; FCO 1989; Peking 1992; Third Secretary Düsseldorf 1996; Band B3; m 1992 Claire Louise White (1s 1998).

Fisher, John; Counsellor (Political) Jakarta since October 1999; born 3.8.48; Third later Second Secretary FCO 1974; Language student SOAS 1975 and Bursar 1976; Second Secretary (Inf) Ankara 1976; First Secretary FCO 1979; UKMIS Vienna (IAEA) 1982; First Secretary FCO 1986; Counsellor Santiago 1993; Counsellor FCO 1997; m 1970 Lynette Joyce Corinne Growcott (1d 1978, 1s 1980).

Fisher, Julian Alexander St.John; Second Secretary (Political/Economic) Nairobi since November 2000; born 12.2.70; FCO 1998; Band C4; m 1998 Alex Gillian Wood.

Fisher, Kate; SUPL since January 1996; born 12.11.70; FCO 1991; Lusaka 1993; Band A2.

Fisher, Miles Lyndon; SUPL since March 1999; born 28.11.61; FCO 1981; Vienna 1995.

Fisher, Simon John; SUPL since May 2000; born 8.6.59; FCO 1983; Athens 1985; Language Training Kamakura 1989; Tokyo 1990; Osaka 1992; Second later First Secretary FCO 1996; Deputy Head of Mission and Consul-General Hanoi 1999; Band D6.

Fisher, Steven Mark; FCO since August 1998; born 7.2.65; FCO 1993; Second Secretary (Economic/Commercial) Singapore 1995; Band D6; m 1990 Linda Westwood (3s 1993, 1995, 1997).

Fisher, Thérésa Ellen; Manila since May 1987; born 5.6.60; FCO 1977; UKMIS Geneva 1982; Belgrade 1984; Band A2; m 1985 Ali Gecim.

Fisher, Timothy Dirk Colomb; Third later Second Secretary (Aid) Jakarta since August 1991; born 23.8.47; FCO 1975; Moscow 1976; FCO 1977; Port Moresby 1978; Nairobi 1981; FCO 1985; Colombo 1987; m 1992 Patricia-Jane Van Der Vooren (1d 1993, 1s 1994).

Fishman, Jason; Peking since November 1997; 5.10.69; FCO; 1990; Berlin 1994; Band A2.

Fishwick, Nicholas Bernard Frank; First Secretary FCO since September 1997; born 23.2.58; FCO 1983; Language Training 1986; First Secretary (Inf) Lagos 1988; First Secretary FCO 1991; Consul (Political Affairs) Istanbul 1994; Band D6; m 1987 Susan Thérésa Rouane Mendel (2s 1987, 1995, 1d 1989).

Fitch, Diana May (née Francis); FCO since August 1998; born 26.12.53; FCO 1975; Dar es Salaam 1976; Tortola 1977; FCO 1981; SE Asia Floater 1984; Singapore 1986; FCO 1988; Second Secretary Honiara 1995; m Geoffrey William Fitch. (1s 1988, 1d 1993).

Fitchett, Robert Duncan; FCO since September 1998; born 10.6.61; FCO 1983; Dakar 1984; Second Secretary (Chancery) Bonn 1988; First Secretary FCO 1990; First Secretary on loan to the Cabinet Office 1993; Paris 1994; m 1985 Adèle Thérèse Hajjar (1s 1987, 2d 1988, 1993).

Fitton, David John; Deputy Head of Mission Ankara since January 2001; born 10.1.55; FCO 1980; Language Training Kamakura 1982; Second later First Secretary (Econ) Tokyo 1983; FCO 1986; First Secretary (Chancery) New Delhi 1990; First Secretary FCO 1994; Head of Chancery Tokyo 1996; m 1989 Hisae Iijima (1d 1996, 1s 1999).

Fitton-Brown, Edmund Walter; First Secretary (Political) Kuwait since June 1998; born 5.10.62; FCO 1984; Third later Second Secretary Helsinki 1987; Second Secretary FCO 1989 (First Secretary 1991). Language Training Cairo 1991. First Secretary FCO 1992; First Secretary (Political) Cairo 1993; First Secretary FCO 1996; Band D6; m 1995 Julie Ann Herring. (1d 1996; 1s 1998).

FitzGerald, Jillian; (née Lane) FCO since September 1998; born 29.1.69; FCO 1989; Bonn 1992; Islamabad 1995; SUPL 1997; Band B3; m 1998 Paul Edward Fitzgerald (1s 1997).

Fitzgerald-Prono, Antonia; (née Fitzgerald)FCO since September 1999; born 13.6.71; FCO 1990; Brasilia 1991; UKDel WEU Brussels 1995; Paris 1996; SUPL 1999; m 1999 Raphael Jacques Gerard Prono (1s, 1999).

Flaherty, Shaun David; First Secretary (Management) Cairo since June 2001; born 29.1.66; FCO 1984; Washington 1987; Ankara 1990; Lagos 1992; FCO 1996; Band C5.

Flear, Timothy Charles Fitzranulf, MVO (1989); FCO since May 2000; born 22.1.58; FCO 1980;

Third Secretary (Comm/Inf) Dubai 1982; resigned and reinstated 1985; FCO 1985; Third later Second Secretary Kuala Lumpur 1987; Second Secretary FCO 1991 (APS/Minister of State 1993); First Secretary (Economic)later First Secretary (Investment) subsequently First Secretary (Political) Seoul 1996; ptnr, Christopher Curtain.

Fleming De Luca, Wendy Alexandra; Third Secretary (Commercial) Buenos Aires since May 1999; born 11.5.70; FCO 1991; Jakarta 1995; Band B3; m 1995 Dino De Luca.

Flessati, Francesca Josephine Giovanna; First Secretary (Political) Athens since April 1999; born 27.10.58; FCO 1990; Language Training 1991; Third Secretary (Aid) Moscow 1992; FCO 1996; m 1985 Nicholas John Foster.

Fletcher, Elaine Karen; Rabat since February 1996; born 5.1.63; FCO 1984; Budapest 1987; East Berlin 1988; Suva 1989; Floater Duties 1992; FCO 1993; Band A2.

Fletcher, Patricia Anne (née Jones); FCO since February 2000; born 12.5.70; FCO 1989, Bonn 1991; FCO 1993; Brasilia 1994; SUPL 1999; Band B3; m 1993; Richard Fletcher (1s 1996).

Fletcher, Patricia May; Second Secretary (Management) Beirut since January 2000; born 8.9.42; FCO 1983; BMG Berlin 1984; Tortola 1986; FCO 1988; UKDEL Brussels 1990; FCO 1991; Munich 1994; Tel Aviv 1997; Band C4; m 1974 Herbert Fletcher (dec'd 1986) (1s 1978).

Fletcher, Thomas Stuart Francis; FCO since September 1997; born 27.3.75; Band C4.

Flint, David Leonard; Liaison Officer Gibraltar since April 2001; born 21.10.56; FCO 1975; Budapest 1979; Jedda 1980; FCO 1984; Athens 1986; Lagos 1990; Second Secretary FCO 1994; Deputy High Commissioner Gaborone 1997; m 1984 Mary Anne Elizabeth Goodale (3s twins 1986, 1988).

Flint, John David; Antigua since May 2001; born 5.11.69; FCO 1996; Third Secretary (Political/PPA) Tallinn 1998; Band B3; m 1998 Sally Brazier.

Flisher, Nigel Frederick; Second Secretary (Immigration) Moscow since May 1996; born 20.4.53; FCO 1971; Singapore 1974; Vientiane 1978; Colombo 1979; FCO 1982; Islamabad 1984; Third Secretary (Passports/Visas) Dublin 1988; FCO 1991; (Second Secretary 1994); m 1977 Valerie Tay Kim Heok (1d 1978; 1s 1980).

Floyd, Linda Vivienne (née Colvin); SUPL since August 2000; born 17.3.65; FCO 1987; New Delhi 1989; SUPL 1991; Georgetown 1994; SUPL 1997; FCO 1999; Band A2; m 1990 Neil Floyd (1d 1991, 2s 1993, 1995).

Floyd, Neil; FCO since July 1997; born 20.5.67; FCO 1987; New Delhi 1989; Warsaw 1991; Georgetown 1993; Band C4; m 1990 Linda Vivienne Colvin; (1d 1991, 2s 1993, 1995).

Foakes, Joanne Sarah; Legal Counsellor since 1997; born 9.3.57; called to the Bar, Inner Temple 1979; FCO 1984; Deputy Principal Crown Counsel Hong Kong 1991; Assistant Legal Adviser FCO 1994; SUPL 1995.

Foley, Victoria Beth Louise; FCO since December 1986; born 23.6.60; FCO 1978; Budapest 1982; Paris 1984; Band A2.

Folker, Nicholas Mark; Singapore since October 2000; born 20.5.67; FCO 1989; Band C4; m 1998 Laura Elizabeth Samm (1d 2000).

Folland, Richard Dudley; Deputy Consul General Düsseldorf since August 2000; born 10.3.61; FCO 1981; Moscow 1983; Third Secretary (Coms/Information)Gaborone 1985; FCO 1988; Second Secretary (Political/Inf) Stockholm 1991; First Secretary FCO 1996; On secondment to British Aerospace 1998; m 1985 Gwen Alison Evans (2s 1989, 1993).

Folliss, Tarquin Simon Archer; Counsellor Copenhagen since September 2001; born 23.10.57; HM Forces 1981-86; Second Secretary FCO 1986; Second later First Secretary (Chancery) Jakarta 1989; First Secretary FCO 1992; First Secretary Bucharest 1995; First Secretary FCO 1998; Band D6; m 1991 Anne Mary Segar (1d 1996, 2s 1998, 1999).

Fontaine-Harvey, Joan; Dubai since May 2000; born 3.10.67; FCO 1990; Band B3; m 1999 Christopher Antonio Harvey.

Foord, Michael Robert; HM Consul Paris since July 1997; born 24.1.42; FO 1966; Dar es Salaam 1968; Sofia 1972; Kuwait 1974; FCO 1975; Jedda 1977; Athens 1979; Tegucigalpa 1982; Second Secretary FCO 1984; Second Secretary (Dev) Colombo 1988; Second Secretary (Consular) New Delhi 1993; m 1968 Christine Edwards (1s 1972; 1d 1974).

Foote, Daniel Edward; Pretoria since October 1997; born 11.2.46; Royal Navy 1965-90; Moscow 1991; Lagos 1992; Abuja 1994; FCO 1996; Band A2; m 1967 Carol Elizabeth Combe. (2d 1970, 1971).

Forbes, Lachlan Pelly Ferrar; FCO since January 2001; born 24.4.70; Second Secretary FCO 1996; Second Secretary (Political) Nairobi 1998; Band C4; m 1999 Melanie Fiona Knights (1s 2000; 1s, 1d (twins) 2001).

Forbes, Matthew Keith; Deputy High Commissioner Maseru since July 1999; born 19.4.66; FCO 1987; Peking 1989; Colombo 1990; FCO 1995; Band C4; m 1988 Lydia Mary Bagg (2s 1989, 1991, 1d 1994).

Forbes, Melanie Fiona (née Knights); FCO since May 2001; born 3.3.64; FCO 1996; Second Secretary (Political) Nairobi 1999; Band C4; m 1999 Lachlan Pelly Ferrar Forbes (1s 2000; 1s, 1d (twins) 2001).

Forbes Batey, Darren Francis; Third Secretary (Management) Dublin since August 1996; born 9.1.66; FCO 1984; Rabat 1987; Kampala 1990;

FCO 1993; Band B3; m 1993 Sarah Frances Trevelyan.

Ford, Andrew James Ford, MVO (1995); Second Secretary (Commercial) Mexico City since February 2000; born 21.6.64; FCO 1987; Third Secretary (Chancery/Information/Consular) Georgetown 1990; Third Secretary (Political) Pretoria/Cape Town 1993; Second Secretary FCO 1996; m 1994 Claudeli Edna Dos Santos Silva (2 step d 1985, 1987).

Ford, Antony, CMG (1997); HM Ambassador Vienna since September 2000; born 1.10.44; Commonwealth Office 1967; Third later Second Secretary Bonn 1968; Kuala Lumpur 1971; First Secretary FCO 1973; First Secretary (Comm) Washington 1977; First Secretary FCO 1981; Counsellor East Berlin 1984; Counsellor FCO 1987; Consul-General San Francisco 1990; Attached to RAS as CSSB Chairman 1994; Minister Berlin 1996; on secondment to Andersen Consulting 1999; m 1970 Linda Gordon Joy (1d 1970; 1s 1976).

Ford, Kerry May; SUPL since March 2001; born 4.5.67; Home Office 1990-1993; FCO 1994; T/D Hanoi 1996; T/D The Hague 1996; Hong Kong 1997; FCO 2000; Band A2.

Ford, Peter William; HM Ambassador Bahrain since April 1999; born 27.6.47; Third Secretary FCO 1970; MECAS 1971; Beirut 1973; Second later First Secretary Cairo 1974; First Secretary FCO 1977; ENA Paris 1980; First Secretary Paris 1981; First Secretary FCO 1985; Counsellor (Comm) Riyadh 1987; University of Harvard 1990; Counsellor Singapore 1991; Counsellor FCO 1994; m(1) 1975 (diss 1991) Aurora Raquel Garcia Mingo; (2) 1992 Alganesh Haile Beyene.

Forrester, Mark Adrian; Second Secretary (Management) Hong Kong since November 1999; born 29.6.59; FCO 1978; UKMIS Geneva 1980; Santiago 1983; Third Secretary FCO 1986; Dhaka 1989; Third Secretary (Management/Consular) Nuku'alofa 1992; Second Secretary FCO 1995; m 1982 Deborah Cannell (1d 1987, 1s 1990).

Forrester, Sally Joanne (née Watmough); SUPL since August 1997; born 22.5.64; FCO 1984; Belgrade 1987; FCO 1989; Buenos Aires 1990; FCO 1992; Vienna 1994; Band A2; m 1993 Guy Hamilton Forrester (1d 1995; 1s 1998).

Forrester, Stuart Russell; Moscow since October 2000; born 10.2.62; FCO 1983; Washington 1990; FCO 1994; Band C4; m 1990 Deborah Channon.

Forryan, Anne May; SUPL since November 1999; born 3.8.66; FCO 1990; Düsseldorf 1993; Vice-Consul Madrid 1996; SUPL 1997; Madrid 1997; Band B3; m 1996 Joaquin Rodriguez-Toubes Muniz.

Forsyth, Brian Gilbert; Doha since August 1999; born 27.2.65; FCO 1984; Bucharest 1987; Dhaka 1989; FCO 1992; Third Secretary Cairo 1996; Band B3; m 1987 Marie Boyle (1s 1989, 1d 1992).

Forsyth, Marie (née Boyle); SUPL since January 2000; born 26.4.66; FCO 1984; Mexico City 1986; SUPL 1987; Dhaka 1990; FCO 1993; Cairo 1996; Band B3; m 1987 Brian Gilbert Forsyth (1s 1989, 1d 1992).

Fortescue, Dominic James Lewis; First Secretary UKMIS New York since July 2000; born 9.10.66; FCO 1991; Second Secretary (Political) Pretoria 1993; Cape Town 1995; Second later First Secretary FCO 1996; Band D6; m 1990 Miriam Cathleen Rolls (1s 2001).

Fossaluzza Lydia; Buenos Aires since September 1999; born 12.3.64; FCO 1996; Band A2.

Foster, Hazel; FCO since May 1998; born 10.4.69; FCO 1989; Ankara 1991; World Wide Floater duties 1996; Band A2.

Foster, John Michael; FCO since 1997; born 7.5.55; FCO 1989; New Delhi 1991; Third Secretary Tel Aviv 1994; Band B3; m 1986 Julie Bearfoot.

Foster, Julie Maria (née Bearfoot); Second Secretary FCO since July 1998; born 19.12.59; FCO 1978; UKDEL NATO Brussels 1981; Doha 1983; FCO 1987; Third Secretary New Delhi 1991; Tel Aviv 1994; on loan to the DTI 1997; Band C4; m 1986 John Michael Foster.

Foster, Nicholas John; Counsellor Athens since September 1998; born 3.9.57; Second Secretary FCO 1984; Second later First Secretary (Chancery) Nicosia 1986; First Secretary FCO 1989; First Secretary (Chancery) Moscow 1992; First Secretary FCO 1995; m 1985 Francesca Josephine Giovanna Flessati.

Foster, Sarah Louise; Tokyo since January 2000; born 4.11.73; FCO 1992; UKMIS later UKDEL Vienna 1995; Band B3.

Foster, Victoria Evelyn; FCO since January 1997; born 28.12.72; FCO 1990; UKMIS Geneva 1994. Band A2.

Foulcer, Monique Antoinette (née Twigg); FCO since December 2000; born 22.7.64; DTI 1985; FCO 1987; Kinshasa 1989; Third Secretary (Chancery) UKDIS Geneva 1992; FCO 1995; SUPL 1997; Second Secretary (Political) Paris Embassy 1998; SUPL 1999; Band C5; m 1995 Kevin Andrew Foulcer.

Foulds, Sarah Ann; SUPL since September 1998; born 10.8.57; FCO 1979; PRO (Band D6) 1987; First Secretary FCO 1992; First Secretary UKMIS Geneva 1995; m(1) 1981 (diss 1995) (1d 1985; 1s 1988); m(2) 1999 Peter van Wulfften Palthe (3 step d).

Foulsham, Richard Andrew; Counsellor Ottawa since February 2001; born 24.9.50; Second Secretary FCO 1982; First Secretary Badar Seri Begawan 1984; First Secretary (Chancery) Lagos 1986; First Secretary FCO 1990; Counsellor (Political) Rome 1995; Counsellor FCO 1999; m 1982 Deirdre Elizabeth Strathairn (1d 1984; 1s 1986).

Fowle, Angela Mary (née Hatcher); Belgrade since January 2000; born 25.4.44; FO 1964; Bangkok 1966; Moscow 1968; Athens 1969; FCO 1972; Santiago 1974; FCO 1976; UKMIS Geneva 1980; FCO 1983; Düsseldorf 1986; FCO 1989, SUPL 1990; SUPL 1993; FCO 1995; Belgrade 1998; First Secretary (Management) Madrid 1999; Band B3; m 1978 Leslie Thomas Fowle (1s 1983).

Fowler, Joanna; Madrid since February 1999; born 12.4.43; FCO 1976; Tehran 1977; Rangoon 1979; FCO 1982; Belgrade 1983; Abu Dhabi 1985; FCO 1989; Islamabad 1994; Band B3.

Fowler, Rosalind Mary Elizabeth; First Secretary FCO since July 1994; born 27.9.65; FCO 1987; Language Training 1988; Language Training Hong Kong 1989; Second Secretary (Inf) Hong Kong 1990; Language Training 1993; Band D6.

Fox, Christopher Roderick Henry; Ankara since July 2000; born 19.9.70; FCO 1991; Band C4.

Fox, Ian David; secondment to London Chamber of Commerce since March 1995; born 2.6.66; FCO 1987; Peking 1988; Floater Duties 1991; FCO 1993; Band B3; m 1993 Alison Elizabeth Margaret Bain.

Fox, John Frederick; FCO since September 2000; born 9.4.75; FCO 1997; Brussels 1999; SUPL 1999; Band C4.

Fox, Michael Roger; FCO since October 1997; born 9.7.58; FCO 1988; Consul Geneva 1993; Band C4; m 1993 Charlotte Jane Gray.

Fox, Paul Leonard; FCO since April 1999; born 24.7.62; FCO 1987; New Delhi 1990; Baku 1994; Bangkok 1996; Band D6; m 1991 Vicki Ann Rathbun (2d 1997, 1998).

Foxwell, Rachael Louise; First Secretary (Economic/Commercial) Wellington since June 1999; born 29.10.59; FCO 1982; Africa/Middle East Floater 1984; Harare 1985; Third later Second Secretary Hanoi 1988; Second Secretary FCO 1991; Tunis 1992; (1d 1991).

Francis, Catherine Joan; Jakarta since December 1997; born 1.4.50; FCO 1972; Brussels 1972; Kuala Lumpur 1976; Bonn 1980; FCO 1980; Helsinki 1985; FCO 1987; Riyadh 1989; FCO 1991; Sofia 1993; Band B3; m 1991 John Treharne Francis.

Francis, John Alexander; HM Consul Kuwait since September 1999; born 14.12.42; FO 1962; Athens 1964; Beirut 1964; Stockholm 1965; Seoul 1968; Malta 1971; Paris 1972; FCO 1972; Dacca 1975; Prague 1979; Kaduna 1981; Second Secretary FCO 1983; Consul Bangkok 1988; First Secretary (Management) Ankara 1992; First Secretary (Management/Consular) Seoul 1996; m 1981 Grace Engelen.

Francis, Julie Mary; FCO since August 1990; born 21.2.50; FCO 1976; Kabul 1976; FCO 1978; Sofia 1979; UKDEL NATO Brussels 1981; FCO 1984; Kathmandu 1987; Band A2.

Franklin, Elizabeth Fay (née Bolton); SUPL since March 1995; born 25.11.60; FCO 1981; Khartoum 1985; Valletta 1988; Dhaka 1992 Band B3; m 1994 John William Franklin.

Franklin, Joanna Mary Clare; SUPL since November 2000; born 12.8.60; FCO 1978; Peking 1981; FCO 1982; Cairo 1986; Yaoundé 1989; FCO 1990; Beirut 1994; FCO 1997; Canberra 1998; Band C4; m 1988 Habib Elie Gouel.

Franklin, Sarah Louise; FCO since April 2001; born 2.4.66; FCO 1985; UKMIS Geneva 1989; FCO 1991; Warsaw 1997; Band B3.

Franklin-Brown, Alexander; FCO since February 1991; born 30.3.72; Band A2.

Fransella, Cortland Lucas; Counsellor FCO since September 1995; born 9.9.48; Third Secretary FCO 1970; Language Student Hong Kong 1971; Assistant Trade Commissioner Hong Kong 1973; Second later First Secretary FCO 1975; Kuala Lumpur 1980; Santiago 1982; FCO 1986; Counsellor (Political) Rome 1991; m 1977 Laura Ruth Propper (2s 1979, 1981).

Frape, Neil Jeremy; Kuwait since July 2000; born 16.11.63; FCO 1984; Addis Ababa 1986; Paris 1990; FCO 1992; Full-time Language Training 1995; Vice-Consul (Press and Public Affairs) Istanbul 1996; Band B3; m 1987 Christine Mary Allen (1d 1989, 1s 1992).

Frary, Helen Elizabeth; Third Secretary (UN) UKMIS Geneva since July 1995; born 23.2.69; FCO 1988; New Delhi 1991; Band B3.

Fraser, James Terence; First Secretary (Management) and HM Consul Copenhagen since December 1997; born 12.4.49; GPO 1966; FCO 1967; Nicosia 1971; Johannesburg 1972; Prague 1974; Africa Floater 1975; FCO 1978; Vice-Consul (Information) Düsseldorf 1981; Language training 1983; Commercial Attaché Baghdad 1984; FCO 1988; Deputy Head of Political and Information Section, later Head of Consular Section Ottawa 1993; m 1988 Nada Babic (1s 1992, 1d 1995).

Fraser, Shelley; FCO since February 1991; born 21.3.70; Band A2.

Fraser, Simon James; SUPL since March 1997; born 3.6.58; FCO 1979; Third later Second Secretary Baghdad 1982; Second Secretary (Chancery). Damascus 1984; First Secretary FCO since 1986 (Private Secretary to Minister of State) 1989; First Secretary (Economic) Paris 1994; Counsellor on secondment to the EU Commission 1996.

Fraser Darling, Richard Ogilby Leslie, OBE(2001); First Secretary later Counsellor; FCO since August 1988; born 2.3.49; Third Secretary FCO 1971; Language Student Helsinki 1973, Third later Second Secretary Helsinki 1974; First Secretary FCO 1978; Washington 1984; m 1991 Nicola Kirkup.

Frean, Christopher William; Third Secretary (Commercial/Political) Abidjan since April 1999; born 31.7.64; HCS 1988; FCO 1990; Abidjan 1992; Karachi 1995; FCO 1997; Band B3; m 1994 Aya Esperance Gbakatchetche (2d 1995, 1996).

Freel, Philip John; Third Secretary (Management) since December 1995; born 24.12.55; FCO 1974; Paris 1976; Mogadishu 1979; Lisbon 1980; Addis Ababa 1983; FCO 1985; on loan to CAD Hanslope Park 1986; Lagos 1987; Rome 1991; FCO 1992; m 1977 Joan Winifred Hill (1d 1979; 1s 1986).

Freeman, John Michael Giles; Second later First Secretary FCO since August 1978; born 18.11.49; FCO 1971; Rome 1975; Band C5; m 1986 Anne Sarah Holliday (2d 1988, 1990).

Freeman, Judith Louise; UKMIS Geneva since January 2000; born 24.3.61; FCO 1984; Berne 1985; East Berlin 1989; Floater Duties 1991; FCO 1994; Luxembourg 1996; T/D Berlin 1999; Band A2.

Freeman, Timothy John; Third Secretary (Passports/Visas) Dublin since March 2001; born 24.4.65; FCO 1989; Paris 1992; Honiara since April 1996; Third Secretary (Aid/Chancery) Gibraltar 1997; Band B3.

Freeman, Wendy Paula; Second Secretary (Commercial) Beirut since April 2001; born 9.3.61; FCO 1980; Bonn 1982; Africa/ME Floater 1985; Abidjan 1988; FCO 1992; Kingston 1997; SUPL 1999; Band C4.

Freeman, William Henry; First Secretary FCO since January 1985; born 16.12.42; CRO 1961; New Delhi 1964; FO 1966; Saigon 1967; Kota Kinabalu 1969; Paris 1970; Copenhagen 1971; Second Secretary (Comm/Inf) Bombay 1974; FCO 1978; First Secretary Tunis 1980; Marseilles 1981; First Secretary (Inf/Chancery) UKDEL NATO Brussels 1983; m 1970 Veronica Vivien Ratnam (1s 1972).

French, Roger; Counsellor (Management) Washington since January 1997; born 3.6.47; FCO 1965; Havana 1970; Madrid 1971; San Juan 1973; FCO 1977; Second later First Secretary (Chancery), Washington 1980; First Secretary (Comm) Muscat 1985; Deputy Head North America Dept FCO 1988; Deputy Consul-General Milan 1992; m 1969 Angela Joyce Cooper (1d 1974, 1s 1980).

Friel, Nicola; Floater Duties since November 1998; born 8.3.70; FCO 1989; Washington 1992; Moscow 1995; Band B3.

Friis, Andrew Stuart; Hong Kong since October 1997; born 4.4.60; Metropolitan Police 1981; FCO 1982; Kuwait 1986; Band C4; FCO 1988; m 1989 Maria Carina Lumatan Reyes (1s 1991, 1d 1994).

Friston, Paula Jane; Algiers since July 1999; born 27.1.69; FCO 1992; Washington 1996; Band A2.

Frizzel, Squadron Leader John, Stewart; Queen's Messenger since 1989; born 12.7.46 HM Forces 1966-89.

Frost, David George Hamilton; Counsellor (EU/Economic) Paris since April 2001; born 21.2.65; FCO 1987; Third Secretary Nicosia 1989; resigned 1990; reinstated 1992; First Secretary UKREP Brussels 1993; First Secretary UKMIS New York 1996; FCO 1998; m 1993 Jacqueline Elizabeth Dias. (1d 1998).

Frost, Michael Reginald, OBE (2001); First Secretary (Political) Pretoria since June 2000; born 2.12.52; FCO 1971; Prague 1974; Dar es Salaam 1976; Peking 1979; FCO 1982; Washington 1984; Consul (Political/Inf) Cape Town 1986; First Secretary (Aid/Comm) Kampala 1991; First Secretary FCO 1994; First Secretary (Political) Lagos 1996; Band D6; m 1973 Marie Thérésa McAllen.

Frost, Simon Jaye; FCO since March 1996; born 24.5.70; FCO 1990; World-wide Floater Duties 1993; T/D Mostar 1995; Band B3.

Frost, Steven Alan; Stockholm since February 1999; born 21.9.64; FCO 1987; Islamabad 1992; FCO 1996; Band C4; m 1993 Angela Elaine Morrissey.

Fry, Graham Holbrook; FCO since September 2001; born 20.12.49; FCO 1972; Third later Second Secretary Tokyo 1974; First Secretary on loan to DoI 1979; FCO 1981; First Secretary Paris 1983; FCO 1987; Counsellor (Chancery) Tokyo 1989; Counsellor FCO 1993; AUSS (Northern Asia and the Pacific) 1995; High Commissioner Kuala Lumpur 1998; m(1) 1977 Meiko Iida (diss); (2) 1994 Toyoko Ando.

Fuguet Debarr, Margaret (née Debarr); FCO since March 1993; born 2.1.48; Inland Revenue 1964; FCO 1967; UKDEL Brussels EC 1970; FCO 1972; Copenhagen 1974; FCO 1977; Harare 1982; FCO 1985; Dublin 1990; Band B3; m 1976 Juan Inocencio Fuguet Sanchez (1s 1977).

Fulcher, Michael Adrian; Counsellor Rome since October 1999; born 15.10.58; FCO 1982; Second later First Secretary Athens 1985; First Secretary FCO 1989; First Secretary (Political) Sofia 1993; First Secretary FCO 1996; m 1983 Helen Parkinson (1s 1987; 1d 1988).

Full, Ian Francis; Suva since January 1994; born 16.8.54; FCO 1972; Paris 1975; San José 1978; Jedda 1981; FCO 1986; Islamabad 1989; Band B3.

Fuller, Eleanor Mary (née Breedon); First Secretary UKMIS Geneva since January 2000; born 31.12.53; FCO 1975, ENA course, Paris 1977, Paris 1978, Resigned 1980; Reinstated 1981, FCO 1981; on loan to the ODA 1983; SUPL 1986; Second later First Secretary FCO 1990; SUPL 1993; UNRWA Vienna 1994-1996; First Secretary UKDEL Vienna 1998; m 1984 Simon William John Fuller (3s 1986, 1988, 1991).

Fuller, Martin John; FO (later FCO) since May 1965; born 26.1.41; Principal Research Officer; Senior Principal Research Officer in 1990.

Fuller, Rebecca Margaret; MBE (1998) UKDEL Brussels since October 1998; born 25.1.59; FCO 1995; Sarajevo 1996; Band A2; m 1996 Peter Richard Miller.

Fuller, Simon William John, CMG (1994); Permanent Representative UKMIS Geneva since January 2000; born 27.11.43; Third Secretary FCO 1968; Second Secretary Singapore 1969; Kinshasa 1971; First Secretary seconded to Cabinet Office 1973; FCO 1976; First Secretary UKMIS New York 1977; First Secretary FCO 1980; Counsellor, Deputy Head of Personnel Operations Department, FCO 1984; Counsellor, Head of Chancery and Consul-General, Tel Aviv 1986; Counsellor FCO 1990; Permanent Representative UKDEL CSCE, Vienna 1993; m 1984 Eleanor Mary Breedon (3s 1986, 1988, 1991).

Fulton, Craig John; FCO since April 1996; born 30.10.67; FCO 1987; Singapore 1990; Islamabad 1992; Band B3; m 1992 Claire Elizabeth Evans.

Fussey, Lorraine Helen; SUPL since October 2000; born 30.1.67; FCO 1989; Bombay 1991; Tel Aviv 1995; FCO 1998; Band C4; m 1996 Alastair Walton Totty (1s 1997).

G

Gallacher, Ian Charles; FCO since March 1993; born 2.5.63; FCO 1983; Paris 1988; Peking 1990; Band B3; m 1987 Diane Warren.

Gallacher, Margaret; Anguilla since December 1997; born 5.12.63; MOD 1986-1996; FCO 1996; Band A2.

Gallagher, Francis Xavier, OBE (1986); Deputy Head of Mission Copenhagen since August 1995; born 28.3.46. Third Secretary FCO 1971; MECAS 1972; Second Secretary March 1972; Second Secretary Beirut 1974; Second later First Secretary FCO 1975; Copenhagen 1979; First Secretary and Head of Chancery Beirut 1984; First Secretary FCO 1987; Counsellor, Head of Chancery Khartoum 1989; Counsellor and Deputy Head of Mission Kuwait 1992; m 1981 Marie-France Martine Guiller.

Gallagher, Tracy Anne; First Secretary FCO since September 1998; born 22.1.58; FCO 1981; Language Training 1982; Third later Second Secretary (Comm) later First Secretary (Econ) Moscow 1983; First Secretary FCO 1988; First Secretary (Chancery) Dublin 1991; SUPL 1994; m 1986 Ian Robert Whitting (2d 1990, 1994).

Galsworthy, Sir Anthony Charles, KCMG (1999); HM Ambassador Peking from December 1997 to February 2002; born 20.12.44; Third Secretary FO 1966; Hong Kong 1967; Third later Second Secretary and Consul Peking 1970; Second later First Secretary FCO 1972; First Secretary (Econ) Rome 1977; First Secretary later Counsellor Peking 1981; Counsellor and Head of Hong Kong Department, FCO 1984; Principal Private Secretary to the Secretary of State 1986; Chatham House 1988; British Senior Representative JLG Hong Kong 1989; On loan to the Cabinet Office 1993; DUSS (Intelligence/Defence) FCO 1995; m 1970 Jan Dawson-Grove (1s 1974; 1d 1975).

Galvez, Elizabeth Ann (née Sketchley); On secondment since January 2001; born 24.12.51; FCO 1970; SUPL to attend University 1970; FCO 1973; Helsinki 1974; UKMIS Geneva 1977; FCO 1981; Second Secretary Tegucigalpa 1981; Second Secretary FCO 1985; SUPL 1987; FCO 1988; First Secretary UKDEL Vienna 1989; First Secretary FCO 1994; Full Time Language Training 1997; Deputy Head of Mission Bucharest 1997; m 1985 Roberto Arturo Galvez Montes (1d 1987).

Gamble, Adrian Mark; First Secretary (Political) Rome since July 1998; born 30.3.61; FCO 1991; Second Secretary (EC Affairs) Brussels 1993; First Secretary FCO 1995; Band D6; m 1990 Jane Brison (2s 1991, 1993, 1d 1995).

Ganderton, Jennifer Louise; SUPL since September 1999; born 15.6.70; Inland Revenue 1988; MOD 1988; FCO 1989; Stockholm 1992; World-wide Floater 1995; Band B3.

Ganney, Sharon Ann (née Feeney); Vice-Consul St Petersburg since November 1998; born 11.10.70; FCO 1989; Warsaw 1992; Hamilton 1994; FCO 1996; T/D Doha 1997; Band B3; m 1998 Mark William Ganney.

Garden, Alyson Margaret; FCO since September 1999; born 21.3.69; FCO 1988; Canberra 1991; FCO 1994; Warsaw 1996; Band B3.

Gardener, Carol Elizabeth; FCO since February 1993; born 10.8.66; FCO 1988; Athens 1990; Band A2.

Gardiner, Judith Margaret (née Farnworth); Second Secretary (Chancery/Press and Public Affairs) Kiev since March 1996; born 25.4.66; FCO 1991; Senior Research Officer 1992; m 1994 Christopher Gardiner.

Gardner, David Martin; First Secretary (Management) Bogotá since February 2001; born 11.11.60; FCO 1978; Mexico City 1981; Tegucigalpa 1984; FCO 1988; Third Secretary (Chancery) Warsaw 1991; Vice-Consul Paris 1993; Second Secretary (Commercial) Mexico City 1996; Band C5; m 1983 Ana Luisa Dominguez Ortiz (1s 1992, 1d 1994).

Gardner, John Ewart; First Secretary (Commercial) Abu Dhabi since November 2000; born 28.2.53; FCO 1971; Abu Dhabi 1974; Kinshasa 1978; Wellington 1981; FCO 1984; Lagos 1986; Los Angeles 1989; FCO 1992; (Second Secretary 1994); Deputy Head of Mission and Consul La Paz 1996; Band C5; m 1975 Alexandra Marie Donald.

Gardner, Julie Ann (née Taylor); SUPL since June 1999; born 15.2.67; FCO 1988; Peking 1990; Buenos Aires 1993; Karachi 1997; Band A2; m 1997 Stuart William Gardner (1d 1999).

Gardner, Stuart William; Brussels since August 2001; born 10.3.70; FCO 1989; Buenos Aires 1993; Karachi 1999; Band B3; m 1997 Julie Taylor.

Garn, Carl Raymond; FCO since September 2000; born 17.10.56; Cabinet Office 1977; CSD 1979; FCO 1981; Dacca 1982; SEA Floater 1985; Vice-Consul Istanbul 1986; FCO 1990; Deputy Head of Mission Tallinn 1993; Tortola 1996; Band C4; m 1987 Lisa Elaine Walter (1d 1995, 1s 1997).

Garner-Winship, Stephen Peter; First Secretary FCO since September 1994; born 26.10.56; FCO 1989; Consul Rio de Janeiro 1991; First Secretary (Political) Lisbon 1993; Band D6; m 1978 Mary Carmel (1s 1979, 1d 1982).

Garnham, Penelope Jane (née White) Dubai since October 1996; born 13.7.71; FCO 1989; Kingston 1992; Band B3; m 1993 Glen Joseph Garnham.

Garnham, Sandra Jayne (née Hibbert); Islamabad since April 1998; born 15.9.68; FCO 1989; Rome 1992; FCO 1996; Band B3; m 1992 Clive Julian Marcus Westbrook Garnham.

Garrett, Charles Edmund; First Secretary Berne since July 1997; born 16.4.63; FCO 1987; Language Training 1988; Language Training Hong Kong 1989; Second Secretary Nicosia 1990; Second Secretary UKREP JLG Hong Kong 1991; First Secretary FCO 1993; m 1991 Véronique Frances Edmonde Barnes (2d 1992, 1993, 3s 1995, 1999, 2000).

Garrett, Martin MVO (1996); Second Secretary FCO since June 1997; born 21.2.54; FCO 1974; Governor's Office Honiara 1976; Paris 1979; BERS Masirah 1981; Tripoli 1982; FCO 1984; Stockholm 1990. Second Secretary (Commercial/Aid) Hanoi 1994; Bangkok 1996.

Garrity, Alison; Kathmandu since January 2001; born 19.10.71; FCO 1999; Band A2.

Garside, Bernhard Herbert; Second later First Secretary (Management) and HM Consul Havana since April 1999; born 21.1.62; FCO 1983; Masirah 1986; Dubai 1987; Lagos 1990; FCO 1994; Band C5; m 1989 Jennifer Susan Yard; (2d 1992, 1998; 1s 1996).

Garth, Andrew John; Taipei since October 1999; born 28.9.69; FCO 1988; Warsaw 1990; South/South East Asia Floater Duties 1992; on loan to the DTI 1998; FCO 1996; Band B3.

Garvey, Kevin Andrew; First Secretary (Deputy Head of Mission) and HM Consul Guatemala City since December 2001; born 10.8.60; FCO 1978; Bangkok 1981; Hanoi 1985; Latin America Floater 1986; FCO 1988; Phnom Penh 1992; Second Secretary Turks and Caicos Islands 1993; FCO 1996; on loan to British Trade International 1999.

Gaskin, Rupert John Addison; Second Secretary FCO since May 2001; born 19.6.74; FCO 1997; Second Secretary (Political) Cairo 1999; Band C4.

Gass, Simon Lawrance, CMG (1998); CVO (1999); Deputy High Commissioner Pretoria since October 1998; born 2.11.56; FCO 1977; Lagos 1979; Second later First Secretary Athens 1984; First Secretary FCO 1987; APS to the Secretary of State

1990; Rome 1993; FCO 1995; m 1980 Marianne Enid Stott (2s 1986, 1989; 1d 1995).

Gates, Helen Deborah; T/D Johannesburg since July 2001; born 31.1.67; FCO 1990; Third Secretary (Political) Berlin 1993; World-wide Floater Duties 1996; FCO 1997; Second Secretary UKDIS Geneva 1999.

Gatward, William Henry Richard; FCO since 1999; born 1.3.73; Band C4; ptnr, Lynne Morrice.

Gault, Jean Jos MBE (1999); FCO since January 1995; born 15.10.45; FCO 1970; Madrid 1971; Warsaw 1974; Rome 1975; FCO 1977; Caracas 1980; Paris 1983; The Hague 1986; FCO 1988; Copenhagen 1992; Band B3.

Gay, Andrew Michael; First Secretary FCO since March 1998; born 4.3.70; Band D6.

Gebicka, Anna Maria Teresa; FCO since November 1999; born 27.1.64; FCO 1990; Tokyo 1992; Caracas 1995; T/D Stanley 1999; Band B3.

Gecim, Thérésa Ellen; SUPL since July 1993; born 5.6.60; FCO 1977; UKMIS Geneva 1982; Belgrade 1984; Manila 1987; FCO 1990; Band B3; m 1985 Ali Gecim (1d 1993 1s 1995).

Geddes, Jonathan Paul; FCO since June 2001; born 3.9.65; FCO 1985; Rome 1987; Madras 1990; FCO 1994; Dhaka 1998; Band C5; m 1996 Susan Jane Fleming.

Geddes, Susan Jane (née Fleming); SUPL since June 2000; born 2.8.64; FCO 1984; UKREP Brussels 1985; Nassau 1988; FCO 1990; Dhaka 1998; Band B3; m 1996 Jonathan Paul Geddes.

Gedny, Philippa; SUPL since August 2000; born 9.8.59; FCO 1977; Bonn 1979; Montevideo 1982; Antigua 1985; FCO 1987; APS to the PUS 1988; Lisbon 1992; Dubai 1995; FCO 1998; Band C4; (1d 1999).

Gee, Alan Francis; First Secretary (Management) Canberra since October 2000; born 2.12.43; FO 1960; Tokyo 1967; Blantyre 1970; Nicosia 1973; FCO 1975; JAO Brussels 1978; Lagos 1981; Second Secretary FCO 1984; Second Secretary (Admin) Sofia 1988; Second later First Secretary FCO 1992; First Secretary (Management) Brasilia 1997; m 1970 Wendy Rugman (1s 1973).

Gee, Mark Leonard; Pretoria since April 1999; born 27.6.70; FCO 1991; Moscow 1995; Band B3; (1d 2000).

Gemmell, Roderick; First Secretary (Consular/Immigration) later Director of Entry Clearance Lagos since March 1998; born 19.8.50; POSB 1966; DSAO (later FCO) 1967; Bahrain 1971; Washington 1972; The Hague 1975; FCO 1979; Mbabane 1982; Stockholm 1984; Second Secretary (Comm/Econ) Ankara 1987; Second Secretary FCO 1991; First Secretary (Management) Kampala 1994; m 1975 Janet Bruce Mitchell (1d 1981).

George, Andrew Neil; HM Ambassador Asunción since October 1998; born 9.10.52; Third Secretary

FCO 1974; Third later Second Secretary Bangkok 1976; Second later First Secretary FCO 1980; First Secretary Canberra 1984; First Secretary and Head of Chancery Bangkok 1988; First Secretary FCO 1992; m 1977 Watanalak Chaovieng (1d 1979; 1s 1982).

George, Christopher Stephen; First Secretary (Commercial/Economic) Havana since June 2001; born 8.5.62; Home Office 1982; FCO 1991; Band D6; m 1993 Susan Vince (1s 1999).

Gerken, Ian, LVO (1992); HM Ambassador Quito since January 2000; born 1.12.43; FO 1962; Budapest 1965; Buenos Aires 1966; FCO 1968; Vice-Consul Caracas 1971; FCO 1975; Second Secretary 1978; Second later First Secretary Lima 1979; First Secretary FCO 1985; Deputy High Commissioner and Head of Chancery Valletta 1988; Counsellor FCO 1992; HM Ambassador San Salvador 1995; m 1976 Susana Drucker (1 step d, 2s 1980, 1982).

German, Robert Charles; First Secretary FCO since November 1999; born 17.1.58; FCO 1978; Masirah 1985; FCO 1986; Third Secretary Kuala Lumpur 1990; Third Secretary FCO 1993; Second Secretary Tel Aviv 1997; m 1982 Penelope Jane Cooper (2s 1986, 1989, 1d 1996).

Gething, David Philip, MBE (1991); Second Secretary (Management) Bucharest since June 1999; born 2.3.46; FO 1965; Cairo 1968; Brussels (NATO) 1970; Moscow 1972; La Paz 1973; Tegucigalpa 1974; Budapest 1975; FCO 1977; Caracas 1979; Manila 1982; FCO 1985; Second Secretary Mogadishu 1990; Second Secretary (Management/Consular) Dubai 1991; HM Consul Havana 1994; m 1993 Ulla Kristina Lindholm.

Gibb, Fionna; Third Secretary (KHF) Kiev since October 1995; born 10.11.63; Vice-Consul Berlin 1993; FCO 1990; Band B3.

Gibbins, Ian Paul; Second Secretary Brussels since November 1995; born 27.6.47; GPO 1963; FCO 1969; Washington 1975; FCO 1977; Brussels 1981; Third Secretary Prague 1984; Second Secretary Bonn 1990; Second Secretary FCO 1992; m 1975 Rose Elizabeth Devlin (2s 1978, 1980; 1d 1983).

Gibbs, Andrew Patrick Somerset, OBE (1992); Counsellor FCO since October 1998; born 8.12.51; Third later Second Secretary FCO 1977; Vice-Consul, later Consul (Econ) Rio de Janeiro 1979; First Secretary FCO 1981; Language Training 1983; First Secretary Moscow 1984; First Secretary FCO 1985; First Secretary (Inf) Pretoria 1987; First Secretary FCO 1989; SUPL 1991; First Secretary FCO 1993; Counsellor Lisbon 1994; m 1981 Roselind Cecilia Robey (2d 1982, 1986; 2s 1983, 1990).

Gibbs, Kristian Mark; Caracas since March 2000; born 12.5.74; FCO 1997; Band C4.

Gibbs, Timothy; FCO since September 1981; born 20.10.48; FO (later FCO) 1967; Beirut 1974; FCO

1976; Paris 1978; Band C4; m 1978 Catherine MacDougall.

Gibson, John Stuart; Second Secretary (Consular/Management) Kathmandu since September 1994; born 15.3.48; Commonwealth Office 1967; FCO 1969; Moscow 1970; Bonn 1972; Berne 1974; Helsinki 1975; FCO 1977; Cairo 1979; Riyadh 1983; Düsseldorf 1984; Dhaka 1987; Second Secretary FCO 1991; m 1972 Grete Sandberg (2d 1975, 1977).

Gibson, Louise Anne; Helsinki since January 1997; born 20.4.40; Ankara 1962; Cairo 1965; FO 1966; Berlin 1968; Washington 1970; FCO 1972; Peking 1976; FCO 1978; Nairobi 1979; FCO 1982; Islamabad 1988; FCO 1990; Prague 1993; Band B3.

Gibson, Pamela Ann (née O'Hanlon) MBE (2000); FCO since April 1996; born 27.9.56; FCO 1975; Geneva (UKMIS) 1978; Kuwait 1981; FCO 1983; Copenhagen 1984; SUPL 1987; FCO 1990; Nairobi 1995; Band A2; m 1987 Graeme Robert Gibson (dec'd 1996).

Gibson, Robert Winnington; FCO since October 1999; born 7.2.56; FCO 1978; Jedda 1981; Second Secretary UKREP Brussels 1984; Second Secretary (Chancery/Inf) Port of Spain 1986; Second later First Secretary FCO 1989; First Secretary (Political) UKDEL OECD Paris 1995.

Gifford, Michael John; Deputy Head of Mission Cairo since January 2001; born 2.4.61; FCO 1981; Language Training 1982; Third Secretary (Comm); Abu Dhabi 1983; Second Secretary (Chancery) Oslo 1988; On loan to European Commission Brussels 1990; Second later First Secretary FCO 1991; First Secretary (Econ) Riyadh 1993; First Secretary FCO 1996; m 1986 Patricia Anne Owen (1d 1989, 1s 1991).

Gilbert, Juliet; UKMIS New York since September 1999; born 20.2.69; FCO 1998; Band A2.

Gilbert, Mary Jean; Jakarta since January 1999; born 17.1.52; New Zealand Army 1979-1994; FCO 1995; Band B3.

Gildea, John Joseph; FCO since April 1983; born 25.5.41; FO 1958; Bucharest 1963; Rio de Janeiro 1964; FO (later FCO) 1966; New York (UKMIS) 1969; Dar es Salaam 1972; Cape Town/Pretoria 1973; FCO 1976; Islamabad 1980; Band B3; m 1968 Marilyn Brenda Carruthers (3d 1971, 1973, 1980; 1s 1978).

Giles, Alison Mary; First Secretary (IAEA) UKMIS Vienna since August 1998; born 15.9.64; FCO 1988; Third later Second Secretary Pretoria 1990; Second Secretary FCO 1993; Band D6.

Gill, Anne Frances; Tehran since March 1999; born 6.7.63; FCO 1988; East Berlin 1989; FCO 1990; UKREP Brussels 1992; Rangoon 1995; Band B3.

Gillett, Sarah, MVO (1986); First Secretary (Political) Brasilia since December 1996; born 21.7.56; FCO 1976; SUPL 1978; FCO 1982; Washington 1984; Third later Second Secretary

Paris 1987; Second Secretary on secondment to ODA 1990; Vice Consul Los Angeles 1992; First Secretary FCO 1994.

Gillham, Geoffrey Charles; Head of Southern European Department FCO since April 2001; born 1.6.54; FCO 1981; Second Secretary Caracas 1983; On loan to the Cabinet Office 1986; FCO 1988; First Secretary (Chancery) Madrid 1989; First Secretary (Economic) UKDEL OECD Paris 1991; First Secretary later Counsellor FCO 1995; Counsellor New Delhi 1998; m 1991 Dr Nicola Mary Brewer; (1d 1993, 1s 1994).

Gillon, Angela May; FO (later FCO) since September 1964; born 27.9.41; Principal Research Officer; Senior Principal Research Officer in 1990; m 1966 Raanan Gillon (1d 1977).

Gilmore, Julie Louise; FCO since September 1986; born 10.12.63; FCO 1981; Bridgetown 1984; Band B3; m 1983 Brian Gilmore.

Gimblett, Jonathan James; First Secretary (Political) Washington since August 1998; born 3.3.65; FCO 1988; Third later Second Secretary OECD Paris 1989; Chargé d'Affaires Tirana 1993; First Secretary FCO 1993; m 1987 Elizabeth Marie Bauer.

Gingell, Colin John; Tehran since April 1999; born 5.3.45; Royal Marines 1966-88; Warsaw 1988; Madrid 1989; Bonn 1992; Kiev 1993; Khartoum 1995; Band C4; m 1964 Sandra Hall.

Girdlestone, John Patrick; Deputy Head of Mission Lima since January 1998; born 26.9.46; FO 1964; Khartoum 1968; Mexico City 1971; Cairo 1974; FCO 1976; MECAS 1978; Doha 1979; Madrid 1983; Second Secretary and Consul Al Khbar 1986; Second Secretary FCO 1991; Chairman, Diplomatic Service Trade Union Side 1991; First Secretary (Commercial) Abu Dhabi 1994; m 1975 Djihan Labib Nakhla (1d 1976).

Glackin, Clare Siobhan; FCO since September 1999; born 13.12.70; Band C4.

Gladwin, Rob William; Third Secretary (Science and Technology) OECD Paris since January 1998; born 21.3.64; Home Office 1987; FCO 1989; UKMIS Geneva 1992; Third Secretary Tehran 1996; Band B3; m 1992 Edwige Denis Danielle Foltte (1s 1998).

Glass, Colin; MBE, Deputy High Commissioner Freetown since June 1995; born 6.2.55; FCO 1973; Paris 1975; Luanda 1977; Warsaw 1978; Luanda 1981; Stockholm 1985; FCO 1988; Vice Consul Bahrain 1991; m 1981 Ruth Kathleen Elizabeth Pearce (1s 1986, 1d 1989).

Glover, Edward Charles, MVO (1976); High Commissioner Georgetown and Ambassador Paramaribo since December 1998; born 4.3.43; Board of Trade 1962; FO 1966; Postgraduate University Research 1968-69; Third Secretary Canberra 1971; Second Secretary Washington 1973; Second later First Secretary FCO 1978; First Secretary FCO (Seconded Guinness Peat) 1980;

First Secretary FCO 1983; BMG Berlin 1985; First Secretary, later Counsellor FCO 1989; Brussels 1994; m 1971 Audrey Frances (née Lush) (2d 1973, 1976; 2s 1980, 1983).

Glover, Graham Dingwall; On loan to DfID (Guyana) since October 1998; born 14.8.68; FCO 1988; Peking 1989; FCO 1992; Warsaw 1993; Band B3; m 1992 Joanne Whittle.

Glover, Joanne (née Whittle); SUPL since January 1999; born 20.4.67; FCO 1986; Peking 1989; FCO 1992; Warsaw 1993; FCO 1996; Kingston; Band B3; m 1992 Graham Dingwall Glover.

Glynn, Christopher Barry; Deputy Consul-General Sydney since August 2001; born 23.12.49; FO (later FCO) 1967; Bonn 1971; Abidjan 1973; FCO 1975; Alexandria 1978; FCO 1982; Canning House 1983; Vice-Consul (Comm) São Paulo 1985; Second Secretary (Comm) later First Secretary Consul Lisbon 1988; First Secretary FCO 1992; First Secretary (Commercial) Manila 1994; Deputy Consul General and Deputy Director of Trade Promotion São Paulo 1997; m 1988 Dr Wilma Sarino Ballat.

Glynn, Vanessa Jane; First Secretary UKREP Brussels since July 1996; born 5.8.60; FCO 1983; SUPL 1985; Second Secretary FCO 1987; Second Secretary (E Trade) UKREP Brussels 1988; First Secretary 1990; SUPL 1990; m 1984 Colin Thomas Imrie (1d 1985).

Goddard, Colette (née Boyd); Karachi since September 2000; born 9.5.65; FCO 1995; Singapore 1997; Band B3; m 1997 Paul Anthony Goddard (1s 1995).

Goddard, Jonathan; Third Secretary (Chancery) Kathmandu since March 2000; born 21.12.66; Home Office 1994; FCO 1997; Band B3; m 1996 Hayley Morgan (2s 1998, 2000).

Godfrey, Ian David; Third Secretary Islamabad since November 1993; born 2.10.60; FCO 1980; Washington 1987; FCO 1989; m 1994 C Hochreiter (1s 1994).

Godson, Anthony; Counsellor Jakarta since October 1998; born 1.2.48; FCO 1966; Bucharest 1970; Third Secretary Jakarta 1972; Private Secretary to the High Commissioner Canberra 1976; FCO 1979; Second Secretary 1980; Second later First Secretary UKMIS New York 1983; First Secretary FCO 1988; Deputy Head of Mission Bucharest 1990; First Secretary UKMIS Geneva 1991; m 1977 Marian Jane Margaret Hurst.

Goksin, Jill Elaine (née Cooke); Addis Ababa since August 1997; born 15.9.58; FCO 1982; Belgrade 1983; FCO 1986; Gaborone 1987; FCO 1989; Istanbul 1989; Colombo 1992; FCO 1996; Band A2; m 1994 Cenk Bulent Goksin (2d 1996, 1997).

Gola, Elizabeth Ann; ECO Manila since October 2000; born 4.7.61; FCO 1996; Havana 1998; Band B3.

Golding, Terence Michael; Second Secretary Singapore since April 1996; born 26.7.49; FCO 1969; Washington 1973; Berne 1975; São Paulo 1978; FCO 1981; Budapest 1986; Kaduna 1988; FCO 1990 later Second Secretary 1992; m 1978 Irene Elizabeth Blackett.

Goldsmith, Simon Geoffrey; Third Secretary (On secondment to DfID) Belmopan since March 1998; born 23.1.69; FCO 1990; Paris 1992; Bombay 1994; Band B3; m 1995 Robyn Jean Daley.

Goldthorpe, Debra Kay; LVO (1999); First Secretary (Commercial) Budapest since November 2000; born 30.1.58; FCO 1977; Africa Floater 1981; New York 1982; Second Secretary FCO 1985; Language Training 1989; Second Secretary Budapest 1989; First Secretary FCO 1993; HM Consul Durban 1996; Band D6; m,1989 Roger William Lamping.

Golland, Roger James Adam; OBE (1993); Counsellor FCO since January 2001; born 8.5.55; FCO 1978; Third later Second Secretary Ankara 1979; FCO 1982; Language Training 1983; First Secretary Budapest 1984; FCO 1986; First Secretary Buenos Aires 1989; First Secretary FCO 1992; Counsellor (Political) Brussels 1998; m 1978 Jane Lynnette Brandrick (2s 1985, 1987).

Gomersall, Sir Stephen John, KCMG (2000); CMG (1997); HM Ambassador Tokyo since July 1999; born 17.1.48; FCO 1970; Language Student Sheffield and Tokyo 1971; Third later First Secretary Tokyo 1972; FCO 1977; Private Secretary to Lord Privy Seal 1979; First Secretary Washington 1982; Counsellor (Econ) Tokyo 1986; Counsellor FCO 1990; Minister UKMIS New York 1994; m 1975 Lydia Veronica Parry (2s 1978, 1980; 1d 1982).

Goodall, Clare; New Delhi since June 2001; born 8.5.61; FCO 1982; Lima 1983; FCO 1986; Islamabad 1988; SUPL 1991; Paris 1991; SUPL 1993; Belgrade 1998; SUPL 1999; FCO 2000; Band A2; m 1987 David Spires (1s 1986, 1d 1990).

Goodall, David Paul; Second Secretary (Management) Rome since May 1998; born 16.4.57; FCO 1976; Wellington 1978; Seoul 1981; SEA Floater 1985; FCO 1987; Third Secretary (Commercial) Accra 1990; (Second Secretary 1994); Second Secretary FCO 1994; m 1996 Diane Bainbridge.

Goodall, Diane (née Bainbridge); Rome since December 1998; born 7.10.58; FCO 1985; Ankara 1987; Accra 1991; FCO 1995; Band B3; m 1996 David Paul Goodall.

Gooderham, Peter Olaf; Counsellor (Political) Washington since June 1999; born 29.7.54; FCO 1983; Second later First Secretary (Chancery) UKDEL NATO Brussels 1985; First Secretary FCO 1987; First Secretary (Econ) Riyadh 1990; First Secretary FCO 1993; UKMIS New York 1996; m 1985 Carol Anne Ward.

Gooding, Mark; FTLT (Peking) since September 2001; born 17.12.74; FCO 1999; SUPL 2000; Band C4.

Goodman, James Henry Adam; Second Secretary FCO since November 1999; born 31.12.65; FCO 1993; Full-time Language Training 1995; Full-time Language Training Cairo 1996; Second Secretary (Political) Riyadh 1997; Band C4; m 1992 Andrea Dawn Wells (3s 1994, 1996, 1998).

Goodman, Sean Adrian; FCO since December 1990; born 19.3.64; FCO 1983; Riyadh 1989; Band B3; m 1991 Sara Ashley Palmer (1d 1998)

Goodrick, Clair Isabella; Zagreb since March 1999; born 16.9.71; FCO 1993; Pretoria 1996; Band A2.

Goodrick, Sophie Louise; on secondment to Berlin since July 2000; born 28.2.70; FCO 1997; FTLT 2000; Band C4

Goodwin, Andrew John; DHM and Consul Ulaanbaatar since April 1998; born 22.3.59; FCO 1978; Hong Kong 1980; Dhaka 1982; Africa/ME Floater 1984; Aden 1987; Lagos 1992; FCO 1993 (Second Secretary 1995); m 1997 (Carol) Louise Mottershead.

Goodwin, David Howard; T/D Deputy Project Director Expo 2000 Hanover since May 2000; born 16.8.46; FO (later FCO) 1964; Budapest 1969; Kinshasa 1970; Montevideo 1973; FCO 1975; Moscow 1978; San Francisco 1980; FCO 1983; Second Secretary (Imm) New Delhi 1987; Second later First Secretary FCO 1990; First Secretary Commercial The Hague 1996; Band C5; m 1968 Dorothea Thompson (2d 1970, 1976).

Goodwin, Michael Roy; Second Secretary (Immigration/Consular) Kingston since January 2001; born 17.3.60; FCO 1981; Victoria 1983; FCO 1987; Dublin 1987; Third Secretary (Aid) Banjul 1990; FCO 1992; Ottawa 1995; Band C4; m 1983 Kerry Linda Graney (2d 1986, 1992).

Goodworth, Adrian Francis Norton; SUPL since January 2001; born 6.7.53; FCO 1982; Third Secretary Seoul 1984; Third later Second Secretary UKREP Brussels 1988; FCO 1990; Second Secretary (Commercial) Jakarta 1992; First Secretary (Commercial) Caracas 1996; m,(1) 1981 Caroline Ruth Steele (diss 1985), (2) 1987 Valerie Ann Chipcase (diss) (1s 1990, 1d 1992), (3) 1996 Susanti Djuhana (1s 1997).

Gordon, Claire Sandra; Lima since July 1999; born 19.11.76; FCO 1998.

Gordon, Diane Eily MBE; Santiago since February 1999; born 26.8.43; Lagos 1965; Ankara 1968; FCO 1970; Buenos Aires 1971; FCO 1974; Madrid 1978; FCO 1983; Bridgetown 1985. Bogotá 1989; (Second Secretary 1992); Second Secretary FCO 1994.

Gordon, Jean Francois, CMG (1999); HM Ambassador Abidjan and HM Ambassador non-resident to Liberia, Niger and Burkina Faso since June 2001; born 16.4.53; FCO 1979; Second, later First Secretary Luanda 1981; First Secretary

UKDIS Geneva 1983; First Secretary FCO 1988; First Secretary (Political) Nairobi 1990; First Secretary FCO 1992; HM Ambassador Algiers 1996; seconded to Royal College of Defence Studies 2000; mElaine Margaret Daniel (2d 1984, 1988).

Gordon, Robert Anthony Eagleson, OBE (1983), CMG (1999); Counsellor FCO since June 1999; born 9.2.52; FCO 1973; Language Student 1974; Third later Second Secretary Warsaw 1975; Second later First Secretary (Head of Chancery) Santiago 1978; First Secretary FCO 1983; First Secretary (Econ) UKDEL OECD Paris 1987; Deputy Head of Mission Warsaw 1992; HM Ambassador Rangoon 1995; m 1978 Pamela Jane Taylor (2d 1980, 1981; 2s 1985, 1988).

Gordon-MacLeod, David Scott; First Secretary (Economic)Athens since July 1998; born 4.5.48; ODA 1973; Mbabane 1978; Second, later First Secretary FCO 1983; First Secretary and Head of Chancery Maputo 1987; First Secretary FCO 1991; Full-time Language Training 1994; DHM Bogotá 1994; m 1988 Adrienne Felicia Maria Atkins (2d 1989, 1992, 2s 1994, 1996).

Gotch, Chris; Second Secretary (Political) Seoul since September 1997; born 28.11.69; FCO 1996.

Gould, Clive Anthony; First Secretary Washington since May 1999; born 28.6.44; GPO 1960; FO 1968; Attaché Brussels 1970; FCO 1972; Vienna 1973; Third Secretary FCO 1976; Budapest 1979; Third Secretary FCO 1982; Hong Kong 1983; Second Secretary FCO 1986; Second Secretary Berlin 1990; FCO 1993; m 1969 Barbara Sheila Austin (1s 1972).

Gould, David Christopher; FCO then FCO Services since November 1990; born 31.12.55; FCO 1976; Washington 1982; FCO 1985; on loan to Cabinet Office 1987; Band C5; m 1977 Susan Kensett (2d 1975, 1980).

Gould, John Richard William; Second Secretary Sarajevo since February 2000; born 28.11.73; FCO 1997; Band C4.

Gould, Matthew Steven MBE (1998); FCO since October 1997; born 20.8.71; FCO 1993; Manila 1994; Band D6.

Gould, St John Byrhtnoth; First Secretary (Political) Washington since July 2000; born 12.8.68; FCO 1995; Band C5; m 1993 Siân Elizabeth Edwards.

Gould, Tina Louise; FCO since January 1991; born 7.6.70; Band A2.

Goulden, Katherine Lucy; Brasilia since January 1998; born 20.6.67; FCO 1991; Third Secretary (Aid/Chancery) Port Louis 1994; Band B3.

Goulty, Alan Fletcher, CMG (1998); Director, Middle East since June 2000; born 2.7.47; Third Secretary FCO 1968; MECAS 1969; Third later Second Secretary Beirut 1971; Khartoum 1972; Second later First Secretary FCO 1975; On loan to the Cabinet Office 1977; Washington 1981; First Secretary later Counsellor FCO 1985; Deputy

Head of Mission Cairo 1990; HM Ambassador Khartoum 1995; m(1) 1968 Jennifer Wendy Ellison (1s 1970); (2) 1983 Lillian Craig Harris.

Gowan, David John; Minister and Deputy Head of Mission Moscow since November 2000; born 11.2.49; Ministry of Defence 1970; HCS 1973; Second Secretary FCO 1975; Second later First Secretary (Comm) Moscow 1977; First Secretary FCO 1981; Head of Chancery and Consul Brasilia 1985; on loan to the Cabinet Office 1988; FCO 1989; Counsellor On loan to the Cabinet Office 1990; Counsellor (Commercial and Know How Fund) Moscow 1992; Counsellor and Deputy Head of Mission Helsinki 1995; Counsellor FCO 1999; On loan at St Antony's College Oxford 1999; FTLT 2000; m 1975 Marna Irene Williams (2s 1978, 1982).

Gowen-Smith, Stephen Donald; FCO since August 2000; born 10.12.59; FCO 1984; Vice-Consul Geneva 1997; Band C4; m 1981 Janet Elizabeth (1s 1987, 1d 1991).

Gozney, Richard Hugh Turton, CMG (1993); HM Ambassador Jakarta since August 2000; born 21.7.51; FCO 1973; Third Secretary Jakarta 1974; Second later First Secretary Buenos Aires 1978; First Secretary FCO 1981; Head of Chancery Madrid 1984; APS later PPS to Secretary of State FCO 1989; High Commissioner Mbabane 1993; Counsellor FCO 1996; On loan to Cabinet Office (Chief of Assessment Staff) 1998; m 1982 Diana Edwina Baird (2s 1987, 1990).

Gracey, Colin; Consul (Commercial) Ho Chi Minh City since December 1999; born 25.3.47; FCO 1965; Anguilla 1969; Lima 1971; Bombay 1974; FCO 1976; La Paz 1979; FCO 1983; UKMIS Geneva 1986; Islamabad 1989; FCO 1992; Third later Second Secretary (Commercial) Caracas 1996; Band C4; m 1972 Mercedes Ines Rosenthal (1d 1973, 1s 1977).

Graham, Alison Forbes; FCO since January 1994; born 24.8.59; FCO 1980; East Berlin 1982; FCO 1984; Ottawa 1987; Paris 1990; Band A2.

Graham, David Frank; First Secretary (Head of Governor's Office) Montserrat since July 2000; born 27.6.59; FCO 1978; Munich (Vice Consul Commercial) 1982; LA Floater 1985; Warsaw (Third, later Second Secretary Economic) 1987; FCO 1991; Berlin (Second Secretary Commercial) 1992; Seoul (First Secretary Commercial) 1997; m 1990 Anne Marie D'Souza.

Graham, Iain George; FCO since June 2001; born 1.3.70; FCO 1989; Cairo 1991; Anguilla 1995; Islamabad 1998; Band B3.

Graham, Steven; Second Secretary (Commercial) Luanda since May 2001; born 8.7.68; FCO 1989; Islamabad 1993; Full Time language Training 1996; Vice-Consul (Commercial) Rio de Janeiro 1996; Band B3; m(1) 1991 Pauline Lannie (diss 1995), (2) 2000 Luisa Maria Satiago.

Grainger, David Quentin; Kampala since September 1996; born 2.2.69; FCO 1990; Lusaka 1992; Band B3.

Grainger, John Andrew; Legal Counsellor UKMIS New York since August 1997; born 27.8.57; called to the Bar (Lincoln's Inn) 1981; Assistant Legal Adviser FCO 1984; First Secretary (Legal Adviser) BMG (later BM) Berlin 1989; Assistant Legal Adviser FCO 1991; Legal Counsellor FCO 1994; m 1998 Katherine Veronica Bregou.

Grainger, Susan Carol; Dublin since April 1997; born 17.6.67; FCO 1987; UKMIS New York 1989; Montserrat 1992; FCO 1996; Band A2; m 1991 Angus James Robert Steele.

Grant, Ann; High Commissioner Cape Town since October 2000; born 13.8.48; FCI 1971; Calcutta 1973; FCO 1975; on loan to the Department of Energy 1976; First Secretary FCO 1979; Head of Chancery and Consul Maputo 1981; FCO 1984; First Secretary (Energy) UKREP Brussels 1987; resigned 1989; Communications Director OXFAM 1989-91; reinstated FCO 1991; Counsellor (ECOSOC) UKMIS New York 1992, Counsellor FCO 1996; Director FCO 1999.

Grant, John Douglas Kelso, CMG (1999); HM Ambassador Stockholm since August 1999; born 17.10.54; FCO 1976; Stockholm 1977; Language Training 1980; Moscow 1982; FCO 1984; Resigned 1985; Reinstated 1986; First Secretary FCO 1986; First Secretary (Press) UKREP Brussels 1989; First Secretary On loan to the Cabinet Office 1993; UKREP Brussels 1994; Principle Private Secretary to the Secretary of State for Foreign and Commonwealth Affairs 1997; m 1983 Anna Lindvall (1d 1987).

Gray, Douglas Macdonald; Counsellor FCO since September 1997; born 13.3.54; FCO 1975; Far East Floater 1978; Istanbul 1980; Second Secretary Yaoundé 1983; Second Secretary FCO 1986; First Secretary (Comm) Seoul 1989; Deputy Head of Mission and Consul Quito 1994; m 1980 Alison Ann Hunter (1d 1985).

Gray, John Charles Rodger; SUPL; born 12.3.53; Third Secretary FCO 1974; Language training 1975; Third later Second Secretary Warsaw 1976; FCO 1979; First Secretary FCO 1981. First Secretary UKDEL OECD Paris 1983; On loan to Cabinet Office 1987; First Secretary FCO 1989; Deputy Head of Mission Jakarta 1993; on secondment to Harvard University 1996; Washington 1997; m 1988 Anne-Marie Lucienne Suzanne de Dax d'Axat (3s 1995, 1997, 2000).

Gray, Trudi Elisabeth Mary; Bogotá since July 2001; born 19.7.47; FCO 1978; Buenos Aires 1979; Prague 1982; Port Stanley 1984; Nassau 1985; Lima 1988; Lisbon 1992; FCO 1995; Seoul 1997; Band A2.

Greany, John Terence; FCO since November 1981; born 30.3.42; FO 1961; Singapore 1965; FCO 1967; Rawalpindi 1968; FCO 1970; Nairobi

1975; FCO 1978; Darwin 1979; Band C4; m 1973 Maria Ann Cushen (2s 1975, 1978).

Greatrex, Avril; Second Secretary FCO since February 1995; born 17.4.47; DSAO (later FCO) 1967; Kuwait 1971; Lagos 1973; Latin America Floater 1976; FCO 1979; Second Secretary (Management) and Vice Consul Buenos Aires 1991.

Green, Alan Stanley, OBE (1987), MVO (1975); First Secretary, later Deputy Head of Mission, later HM Ambassador San José since October 1991. born 28.8.41; HO 1960; DSAO 1966; Washington 1967; Amman 1970; Lahore 1971; Second Secretary Mexico City 1972; Second Secretary FCO 1978; on loan to DOT 1979; First Secretary and Consul (Comm) Tel Aviv/Jerusalem 1982; First Secretary FCO 1987; on loan to Rank Xerox 1987; First Secretary FCO 1989; First Secretary, Director of Trade Promotion in Central America, San Jos, 1991; m 1969 Suzanne Mary Holl (1s 1971; 1d 1976), (diss) (2) 1995 Maria Cecilia Padilla.

Green, Andrew Philip; Third later Second Secretary FCO since August 1992; born 12.5.58; FCO 1975; Moscow 1982; FCO 1984; Third Secretary Tokyo 1989; m 1982 Susan Mary Merry.

Green, Colin Harvey; Hong Kong since March 2001; born 22.5.69; FCO 1989; UKMIS New York 1992; Abidjan 1995; Band B3; m 1997.

Green, Frances Moira; Valletta since July 1997; born 29.4.48; Washington 1975; Georgetown 1977; The Hague 1981; FCO 1984; Maseru 1987; FCO 1991; UKREP Brussels 1993; Band A2.

Green, Helen; FCO since March 1996; born 5.9.71; FCO 1990; Madrid 1992; Band A2.

Green, John Edward; World-wide Floater Duties since May 1994; born 15.2.65; FCO 1983; Tehran 1991; Band B3; m 1994 Caroline Ann Hockings (1s, 1d (twins) 1999).

Green, Keith William; First Secretary Sarajevo since April 1998; born 14.2.64; FCO 1990; Second Secretary (Chancery) Buenos Aires 1992; Second Secretary FCO 1995; Band D6.

Green, Kelvin Edward; born 19.1.63; Second Secretary Bangalore since January 2001; Inland Revenue 1981; FCO 1982; Washington 1984; Kampala 1987; Lilongwe 1990; FCO 1993; Second Secretary (Comm/Cons) Dar es Salaam 1997; Band C4; m 1984 Gillian Mary Lewis (2d 1991, 1993).

Green, Muriel Ruth (née Bailey); On loan to The Cabinet Office since February 1999; born 13.6.49; WRAF 1971-75; FCO 1975; Mexico City 1976; Islamabad 1982; FCO 1984; SUPL 1992; FCO 1993; Band A2; m 1981 William Charles Green (1s 1984).

Green, Noël Frank; First Secretary FCO since June 1996; born 8.1.49; FCO 1968; Jedda 1971; Brussels (Embassy) 1974; Private Secretary to the Ambassador, UKDEL NATO Brussels 1975; FCO 1977; Second Secretary 1977; Second Secretary

(Comm) Lagos 1981; Second Secretary (Admin) Moscow 1985; First Secretary FCO 1987; First Secretary (Management/Consular) Stockholm 1990; First Secretary (Commercial) Kuala Lumpur 1995; m 1984 Kerstin Anita Maria Höijer.

Green, Richard Charles Benedict, (1983); First Secretary FCO since November 1990; born 2.5.49; FCO 1971; Kuwait 1975; FCO 1977; Ankara 1978; FCO 1979; Second Secretary Beirut 1980; Second Secretary FCO 1982; Second Secretary (Chancery) Pretoria 1985; Second later First Secretary (Chancery) Bangkok 1988; Band C5.

Green, Steven John; First Secretary (Commercial) Kuala Lumpur since August 2000; born 17.5.55; HM Customs and Excise 1972-74; FCO 1974; Peking 1976; Stockholm 1978; SUPL (Exeter University) 1980; FCO 1983; Third Secretary Lilongwe 1985; Third Secretary UKDIS Geneva 1989; Second Secretary FCO 1992; Full-time Language Training 1995; Second Secretary (Commercial) Paris 1996; m 1978 Ulla Marianne Nilsson (1s 1980; Twin d 1986).

Greene, Bernadette Theresa; T/D Port of Spain since April 2001; born 17.4.66; FCO 1988; UKDEL Geneva 1991; Maseru 1994; T/D Bosnia 1996; FCO 1997; on loan to DTI 2000; Band B3.

Greengrass, John Kenneth; MBE (1999); Second Secretary (Commercial) Paris since June 2000; born 19.7.53; Ministry of Housing and Local Government 1970; FCO 1971; UKREP Brussels 1975; Washington 1978; Islamabad 1981; FCO 1983; Lagos 1986; Second Secretary Kuala Lumpur 1989; Second Secretary (FCO)1993; Second Secretary (Consular) New Delhi 1996; Band C4; m 1975 Marian Cecilia Williams (3d 1981, 1983, 1986).

Greenland, Samuel John; Second Secretary (Political) Kiev since January 1999; born 28.5.74; FCO 1997; Band C4.

Greenlee, James Barry; First Secretary (Management) Dhaka since March 2000; born 21.12.45; FO (later FCO) 1963; Vienna 1969; Tokyo 1971; FCO 1974; Calcutta 1979; Second Secretary (Admin) and Consul Budapest 1983; Second Secretary (Comm) Lagos 1986; Second Secretary FCO 1989; First Secretary (Management) and Consul Seoul 1993; First Secretary (Management) Warsaw 1996; Band D6; m 1971 Amanda Jane Todd (2d 1979, 1981).

Greenslade, Natalie Samantha Juliet; FCO since March 2000; born 28.6.72; FCO 1993; Tokyo 1994; Floater duties 1998; Band B3.

Greensmith, Lynn (née Baxter); UKDEL Geneva since December 1996; born 24.1.72; FCO 1995; Band A2; m 1997 David John Greensmith.

Greenstock, Andrew John; Second Secretary (DFID/Public Diplomacy) Tehran since July 2001; born 26.10.72; Second Secretary FCO 1998; FTLT 2000; Band C4; m 1999 Katherine Emma Gardner.

Greenstock, Sir Jeremy (Quentin), KCMG (1998); CMG(1991), United Kingdom Permanent

Representative to the United Nations at New York and the United Kingdom Permanent Representative on the Security Council since July 1998; born 27.7.43; Second Secretary FCO 1969; MECAS 1970; Second later First Secretary Dubai 1972; First Secretary (Private Secretary to the Ambassador) Washington 1974; FCO 1978; Counsellor (Comm) Jedda (later Riyadh) 1983; Head of Chancery Paris 1987; Deputy Political Director and AUSS (Western and Southern Europe) FCO 1990; Minister (Political) Washington 1994; DUS (Middle East/Eastern Europe) 1995.DUS (Political Director 1996); m 1969 Anne Ashford Hodges (2d 1970, 1975; 1s 1973).

Greenwood, Christopher Paul; Consul General Göthenburg since September 1999; born 22.4.53; FCO 1973; Islamabad 1975; Moscow 1977; Manila 1980; FCO 1982; APS to Secretary of State 1982; Los Angeles 1985; Third later Second Secretary Budapest 1988; (Second Secretary 1989); Second Secretary FCO 1992; Full-time Language Training 1994; Second later First Secretary (Comm) Berne 1995; m 1976 Dorothy Gwendolyn Margaret Hughes (1s 1983; 1d 1988).

Greenwood, Jeremy David; Attaché Yerevan since August 2000; born 1.10.70; FCO 1991; UKMIS New York 1995; Band A2.

Greenwood, Rachael; Full-time Language Training Tokyo since August 1995; born 4.3.68; FCO 1993; Language Training 1994; Band B3.

Gregg, Sophie Catherine; Consul (Political/Economic) Hong Kong October 2000; born 17.4.72; FCO 1998; full time language training 1999; Band C4.

Gregson, Stuart Willens; Consul General Paris since April 2000; born 26.4.50; FO (later FCO) 1966; Cairo 1971; Yaoundé 1973; Islamabad 1976; FCO 1978; Gaborone 1982; Vice-Consul Johannesburg 1983; Second Secretary FCO 1987; (First Secretary 1989); First Secretary (Information) Rome 1991; First Secretary FCO 1996; FTLT 2000; Band D6; m 1976 Anne-Christine Wasser (1d 1976; 1s 1979).

Greig, Rosalind Philippa; FCO since October 1996; born 16.4.66; FCO 1989; Third Secretary Bangkok 1992; SUPL 1995; T/D Moscow 1996; m 1997.Band B3.

Grennan, Gemma Brigid Anne, ; FCO since September 1986; born 4.7.43; FO 1962; Vientiane 1967; Singapore 1969; Brussels 1971; Special leave 1973; Addis Ababa 1974; FCO 1977; Islamabad 1981; FCO 1983; Ottawa 1984; Band C4; m 1973 Christopher Roy Heaven (1s 1981).

Grice, Sheridan Elizabeth; Third Secretary (Commercial) Cairo since June 1999; born 14.7.54; FCO 1973; Canberra 1974; SUPL 1976; Belgrade 1976; Georgetown 1978; UKMIS New York 1981; FCO 1984; SUPL 1987; Islamabad 1988; Lagos 1992; Third Secretary FCO 1994; SUPL 1997; (2d 1987).

Griffin, Joseph Francis; Second Secretary Paris since May 1999; born 14.3.73; FCO 1996; Band C4.

Griffin, Ryan John; Vilnius since July 1999; born 9.4.72; FCO 1991; Rome 1994; Band A2.

Griffiths; Major David Allison; Queen's Messenger since 1990; born 28.7.43; HM Forces 1966-90.

Griffiths, Glyn Justyn; FCO since December 1998; born 11.7.61; FCO 1980; Darwin 1990; FCO 1993; Bonn 1996; Band C4; m 1989 Susan Caroline Dover (1s 1995, 1d 1998).

Griffiths, Nicholas Mark; First Secretary UKDEL OECD since June 1996; born 20.11.58; FCO 1985; Moscow 1988; FCO 1990.

Griffiths, Trudy Maureen; UKDEL NATO Brussels since July 1999; born 10.9.70; FCO 1991; Warsaw 1993; Lusaka 1996; Band A2.

Griggs, Kenneth John; Bangkok since April 1999; born 2.9.61; FCO 1984; Washington 1985; FCO 1988; Athens 1989; FCO 1992; BTC Hong Kong 1993; FCO 1996; Band C4; m 1986 Leisa Jayne (3d 1988, 1991, 1992).

Grime, Ann Kathleen (née Jenkins); Budapest since December 1998; born 18.6.51; FCO 1975; Muscat 1976; FCO 1978; Moscow 1979; UKREP Brussels 1981; Resigned 1983; Reinstated 1988; Bucharest 1988; Islamabad 1989; FCO 1990; Luxembourg 1990; Colombo 1993; FCO 1997; Band B3; m 1983 Stephen Howard Grime.

Grimes, Eleanor Claire; First Secretary FCO since September 1997; born 22.8.63; Band D6; m 1998 Major Sean Robert Armstrong (1d 1999).

Grimes, Rachel Claire; FCO since November 1995; born 16.1.72; Band B3.

Grimes, Susan (née Metcalfe); Colombo since February 1998; born 2.10.65; DHSS 1984; FCO 1987; Copenhagen 1990; FCO 1993; Nairobi 1994; Band A2; m 1989 Jason Richard Grimes (1d 1993, twin s 1996).

Grinling, Scott MacKenzie; Third Secretary FCO since January 1998; born 29.10.49; FCO 1991; m 1974 Anita Fitzhugh.

Gristock, Frances Lorraine (née Alexander); SUPL since September 1998; born 21.7.59; FCO 1981; SE Asia Floater 1983; FCO 1985; Third Secretary Quito 1986; FCO 1990; SUPL 1991. Second Secretary (Comm/Consular) Victoria 1992; m 1986 Keith Gristock (1s 1994).

Grover-Minto, Helen Katherine (née Grover); Harare since April 1999; born 18.4.65; FCO 1986; Addis Ababa 1988; FCO 1991; Lagos later Abuja later Lagos 1992; FCO 1995; Band B3; m 1991 John Minto.

Groves, Eliot Sion; New York since October 2000; born 17.7.69; FCO 1988; UKMIS New York 1994; Colombo 1997; Band B3; m 1996 Christine Ann Reynolds.

Growcott, Michael William; FCO since March 1998; born 15.11.48; FCO 1968; Kampala 1972; Peking 1974; Pretoria 1975; FCO 1978; Assistant to Governor Port Stanley 1979; Second Secretary (Inf/Aid/Econ) Kuala Lumpur 1982; Second Secretary FCO 1986; Chairman Diplomatic Service Whitley Council Trade Union Side 1987; First Secretary (Management) Brussels 1990; Resident Acting High Commissioner Castries 1994 m1971 Avril Heather Kemp (2d 1972, 1976; 1s 1974).

Guckian, Lorna Ruth (née Warren); SUPL since July 1994; born 18.6.63; FCO 1983; Port Stanley 1986; Düsseldorf 1987; Africa/ME Floater 1989; FCO 1990; Kuwait 1991; FCO 1992; Band B3; m 1990 Dr Noël Joseph Guckian (2d 1992, 1994; 1s 1997).

Guckian, Dr Noël Joseph, OBE (2001); DHM Tripoli since December 1999; Head of British Interests Section Tripoli September 1998; Chargé d'Affaires July 1999; born 6.3.55; FCO 1980; Consul (Comm) Jedda 1984; Second Secretary FCO 1987; Paris 1988; Second later First Secretary FCO 1988; Deputy Head of Mission Muscat 1994; FCO 1997; m 1990 Lorna Ruth Warren (2d 1992, 1994; 1s 1997).

Gudgeon, Jonathan Roy; FCO since May 1995; born 9.5.64; GPO 1980-1984; FCO 1984; Moscow 1988; Vienna 1992; Band C5; m 1988 Lisa Anne Forte (2s 1992, 1993).

Gudgeon, Simon Peter; Tel Aviv since July 1999; born 8.2.66; FCO 1982; Lagos 1987; Moscow 1992; FCO 1996; Band C4; m 1994 C J Stewart (1s 1999).

Guha, Priya Victoria; Second Secretary (EU) Madrid since September 1999; born 21.9.73; FCO 1996; Band C4.

Gunn, (née Podolier), Janet Frederica; FCO since June 1997; born 4.10.48; FCO 1970; SUPL 1976; FCO 1978; Moscow 1984; FCO 1985; DHM Sofia 1994; Senior Principal Research Officer; m 1975 Ian Gunn (diss 1979) (1s 1976).

Gunnett, Martin John; Second Secretary Peking since August 1995; born 1.4.50; FO 1967; Darwin 1976; FCO 1978; Belgrade 1987; Second Secretary Prague 1990; Second Secretary FCO 1994; m 1973 Linda Leah (1d 1979, 1s 1981).

Gurney, Tim; Deputy Governor Bermuda since September 1998; born 28.4.55; FCO 1973; Istanbul 1976; Karachi 1979; Montreal 1982; Second Secretary FCO 1985; Second Secretary (Chancery/Inf) Accra 1989; Deputy Director and Consul (Information) BIS New York 1991; First Secretary FCO 1996; m 1976 Denise Elizabeth Harker (1d 1984; 1s 1986).

Guthrie, Marion (née Whalley); Yaoundé since June 1999; born 4.3.69; FCO 1988; Paris 1990; Islamabad 1992; Belgrade 1994; FCO 1996; Band B3; m 1998 Robin Guthrie.

Guy, Frances Mary; HM Ambassador Sana'a since March 2001; born 1.2.59; FCO 1985; Language Training 1987; Second Secretary (Chancery) Khartoum 1988; First Secretary FCO 1991; First Secretary and Head of Political Section Bangkok 1995; Deputy Head of Mission Addis Ababa 1997; m 1989 Guy Charles Maurice Raybaudo (2d 1991, 1996, 1s 1993).

Guy, John Westgarth, OBE (1986); Consul General St Petersburg since January 1996; born 17.7.41; CRO 1960; Karachi 1961; Calcutta 1964; New York (CG) 1968; FCO 1970; Moscow 1972; Jakarta 1974; Second Secretary 1975; Vice-Consul (Inf) São Paulo 1975; FCO 1977; On loan to the DOT 1979; First Secretary Yaoundé 1981; First Secretary, Head of Chancery and Consul Maputo 1984; First Secretary FCO 1987; High Commissioner Port Moresby 1991; Counsellor Royal College of Defence Studies 1995; m 1961 Sylvia Kathleen Stokes (1s 1962; 1d 1964).

Guymont, Sarah Jean (née Crouch); Washington since August 1997; born 8.8.52; FCO 1975; Islamabad 1976; FCO 1977; Moscow 1978; resigned 1980; reinstated FCO 1982; Africa/ME Floater 1983; FCO 1987; Dar es Salaam 1989; SUPL Cairo 1992; Cairo 1993; SUPL 1996; Band B3; m 1991 Frederick James Guymont.

Gwynn, Diana Caroline (née Hamblyn); SUPL since February 1997; born 15.8.64; DOE 1986-89; FCO 1989; Third Secretary (Political/ Information) Nairobi 1992; SUPL 1995; Third later Second Secretary FCO 1996; m 1988 Robert Charles Patrick Gwynn (1d 1995; 1s 1997).

Gwynn, Robert Charles Patrick, First Secretary FCO since May 1995; born 17.3.63; Dept. of Employment 1986-88; FCO 1988; Second Secretary (Chancery/Inf) Nairobi 1992; m 1988 Diana Caroline Hamblyn (1d 1995 1s 1997).

H

Hackett, Anthony John; HM Consul Hamburg since July 2001; born 19.12.55; FCO 1975; Muscat 1977; FCO 1981; Karachi 1981; FCO 1985; Manila 1988; Oslo 1992; FCO 1996; On loan to the DTI 1999; m 1983 Nilofer Akbar (1d 1986).

Haddock, Michael Kenneth; First Secretary (Information) Moscow since November 1997; born 25.9.50; FCO 1973; UKDEL Geneva 1978; Moscow 1981; Kuwait 1983; Second Secretary Damascus 1986; Second Secretary (Commercial) Prague 1988; First Secretary (Commercial) Abu Dhabi 1991; First Secretary FCO 1995; m 1972 Irene Doughty (1d 1979, 1s 1984).

Hadley, William Gerard; Vice Consul Paris since March 1998; born 6.11.70; Customs and Excise 1989; MOD 1990; FCO 1991; UKRep Brussels 1994; FCO 1996; Full time language training 1997; Band B3; m 1996 Jacqueline Lillian Smart.

Hafele, Alec Graham; Bucharest since 1999; born 10.5.50; FCO 1995; Band B3; m 1976 Brigitte Ann.

Hagart, Peter Richard; Consul (Commercial) Auckland since May 1994; born 11.7.48; Department of Agriculture and Fisheries for Scotland 1966; FCO 1969; Bucharest 1972; Quito 1974; Bonn 1975; FCO 1977; FE Floater 1980; Hanoi 1982; Second Secretary (Admin) and Vice-Consul Brasilia 1983; Second Secretary FCO 1986; Second later First Secretary (Comm) Bombay 1990; Consul and Deputy Head of Mission Rangoon 1992.

Hagger, Philip Paul; Second Secretary (Commercial) Perth since January 1997; born 5.9.50; FCO 1970; Singapore 1973; FCO 1974; Washington 1975; Nicosia 1978; Casablanca 1981; Lagos 1982; Second Secretary FCO 1987; Second Secretary (Comm) Riyadh 1989; Second Secretary (Consul) Caracas 1992; Second Secretary The Hague 1994; Second Secretary FCO 1995; m(1) 1971 Janet Mary Milnes (dec'd 1975) (1s 1972); (2) 1976 Julie Elizabeth Eastaugh (diss 1988, 1d 1977) (3) 1990 Linda Mary Parmegiani; (2s 1993, 1996).

Haggie, Paul; Counsellor (ESCAP) Bangkok since July 1998; born 30.8.49; Third Secretary FCO 1974; Second later First Secretary Bangkok 1976; FCO 1980; First Secretary (Econ) Islamabad 1982; First Secretary FCO 1986; First Secretary (Chancery) Pretoria 1989; First Secretary FCO 1993; Counsellor on loan to the Cabinet Office 1994; Counsellor FCO 1995; m 1979 Deborah Frazer (1s 1984, 1d 1986).

Hague, John Keir; First Secretary FCO since December 1995; born 26.3.47; CO (later FCO) 1966; Dakar 1970; Kuala Lumpur 1973; Munich 1975; Moscow 1977; FCO 1979; Houston 1983; Second Secretary Islamabad 1985; Second Secretary FCO 1989; Second Secretary (Comm) Seoul 1992; m 1969 Julie Anne Knight (2d 1972, 1975).

Haigh, Trevor Denton; Lusaka since February 1997; born 7.8.44; FCO 1982; Hong Kong 1985; FCO 1988; Moscow 1990; FCO 1993; m 1977 Freda Mary Porritt.

Haig-Thomas, Hugo Alistair Christian; Second Secretary (Economic) Berlin since November 1996; 21.5.47; FCO 1974; MECAS 1975; Language Training Amman 1976; Sana'a 1977; Vice-Consul Düsseldorf 1980; FCO 1982; Second Secretary on loan to ODA 1982; Second Secretary (Deputy Economic Adviser) BMG Berlin 1986; Second Secretary (Chancery) Copenhagen 1989; Second Secretary (Press and Information) Bonn 1992.

Hailey, Nicolas James; Seconded to Ecole Nationale D'Administration Paris since September 1999; born 27.1.75; FCO 1997. Band C4.

Haines, Dr David Michael; First Secretary (Political) Damascus since September 2000; born 6.4.63; FCO 1989; Full-time Language Training 1991; Full-time Language Training Cairo 1992; First Secretary (Political) Tunis 1993; Consul (Political) Jerusalem 1994; First Secretary FCO 1996; Band D6; m 1993 Susan Caroline Goodman (1d 1994, 1s 1996).

Haines, Stephen Andrew; Minsk since August 1999; born 12.6.64; FCO 1997; Band A2.

Haley, Anthony Peter; Mexico City since April 1997; born 14.3.59; RAF 1979; FCO 1988; New Delhi 1991; Third Secretary FCO 1994; m 1979 Elaine Cuthbertson (3s 1979, 1982, 1985).

Hall, Andrew Rotely, OBE (1994); FCO since January 1995; born 3.5.50; FCO 1980; First Secretary New Delhi 1984; First Secretary FCO 1987; Deputy Head of Mission and Consul Kathmandu 1991; Senior Principal Research Officer (1996); m 1973 Kathleen Dorothy Wright (2d 1973, 1978).

Hall, Brian John; T/D Belgrade since August 2001; born 29.6.40; RAF 1958-67/71-87; Sofia 1989; UKMIS New York 1991; UKMIS Geneva 1993; Cairo 1996; Band B3; m 1963 Lilian May (3d 1966, 1968, 1970).

Hall, Caroline Jane (née Oakley) Second Secretary (Immigration) Moscow since October 1998; born 16.9.64; FCO 1984; Santiago 1987; Floater Duties 1990; SUPL 1992; Karachi 1993; FCO 1996. Band C4; m 1992 James William Hall .

Hall, Harriet; FCO since September 1999; born 24.12.69; FCO 1992; Full-time Language Training FCO 1994; full-time Language Training Peking 1995; Second Secretary (Political) Peking 1996.

Hall, James William, QGM (1974); Moscow since October 1998; born 20.9.49; Royal Marines 1966-89; Bucharest 1990; Karachi 1992; SUPL 1996; Band D6; m 1992 Caroline Jane Oakley.

Hall, James William David; First Secretary Vienna since May 1999; born 1.3.65; FCO 1987; Third later Second Secretary (Economic) Lusaka 1989; Second Secretary (Commercial) New Delhi 1991; Second Secretary FCO 1994.

Hall, John George; Consul (Commercial) Düsseldorf since October 1998; born 7.8.51; FCO 1971; Pretoria/Cape Town 1976; The Hague 1979; Nairobi 1982; FCO 1986; Second Secretary (Aid) Dar es Salaam 1989; Second Secretary FCO 1993; First Secretary Hamburg 1996; m(1) 1974 Alison Margaret Eden (2s 1976, 1979); (2) 1990 Margaret Elizabeth Bell (1d 1991).

Hall, Margaret Ann; FCO since December 1991; born 1.4.48; FCO 1975; PRO; on CDA at SOAS 1991 m1974 Govind Anant Walawalkar.

Hall, Martin Vivian; Second later First Secretary FCO since February 1991; born 10.11.50; FCO 1970; Singapore 1972; FCO 1974; Paris 1975; FCO 1977; Second Secretary (Chancery) Lagos 1989; Second Secretary (Commercial) Baghdad 1990; Band C5; m 1972 Mary Rawkins (2s 1976, 1980; 1d 1987).

Hall, Mary Eleanor (née Ford); Gibraltar since July 2000; born 26.9.53; FCO 1978; Aden 1979; UKMIS Geneva 1980; Paris 1983; Ankara 1985;

Warsaw 1988; Belgrade 1990; Lagos 1992; FCO 1995; Cape Town 1997; Band B3; m 1983 Peter Henry Hall.

Hall, Michael Morden; Deputy UK Permanent Representative to the Council of Europe, Strasbourg since September 1998; born 26.3.42; Central Office of Information 1969-73; FCO 1973; British Election Commission Rhodesia 1979-80; First Secretary (Chancery/Information) The Hague 1984; First Secretary FCO 1988; Consul (Commercial) Frankfurt 1991; First Secretary FCO 1996; (1s 1974, 1d 1977).

Hall, Rebecca; Second Secretary (Political)(EU) Vienna since June 1999; born 29.9.72; FCO 1994; FCO 1996; UKREP Brussels 1997; m2000 Robert Page.

Hall, Russell David; Santiago since August 2000; born 12.3.64; FCO 1984; Sofia 1996; Band A2; m 1985 Karen Hipkiss (1s 1985, 2d 1988, 1993).

Hall, Simon David; FCO since September 2000; born 20.3.76; Band C4.

Hall, Simon Lee; Second Secretary FCO since May 2000; born 29.4.63; FCO 1982; Rome 1984; Hanoi 1986; Africa/Middle East Floater 1987; FCO 1990; Seconded to the DTI 1991; Ottawa 1993; Kingston 1996; Band B3.

Hall, Simon Philip; Consul/Management Officer Ljubljana since September 1999; born 29.5.70; FCO 1988; Singapore 1990; FCO 1994; Tunis 1995; Band B3; m 1991 Deborah Jane Hudson (1d 1994, 1s 2000).

Hall, Thomas Mark; FCO since December 1985; born 15.9.47; HM Inspector of Taxes 1964; Commonwealth Office (later FCO) 1967; Tokyo 1970; FCO 1973; Milan 1979; Algiers 1981; Athens 1984; Band B3.

Hallett, Edward Charles; Senior Principal Research Officer FCO since 1995; born 15.7.47; FCO 1971; Bonn 1972; FCO 1975; PRO (Band D6) 1979; Dublin 1984; FCO 1985; on loan to NIO 1988; FCO 1990; Dublin T/D 1996, 1997, 1998; m 1972 Audrey Marie Tobin.

Halley, James Henry; Consul/Management Officer and later Consul (Commercial) Chicago since August 1995; born 27.5.53; FCO 1970; The Hague 1973; San José 1976; Vienna 1978; FCO 1980; Third later Second Secretary Seoul 1983; Second Secretary (Consular/Admin) Sana'a 1987; Second Secretary FCO 1989; Consul (Information) Milan 1991; m 1972 Patricia Catherine Bennett (1d 1977; 1s 1983).

Hall Hall, Alexandra Mary; SUPL since July 2001; born 1.2.64; FCO 1986. Full-time Language Training Bangkok 1989; (Second Secretary 1989); First Secretary FCO 1993; On loan to the Cabinet Office 1995; Washington 1999.

Halling, Kathleen (née Stevens); FCO since October 1992; born 22.9.39; FCO 1984; Brussels 1991; Band A2; m 1961 (2s 1964, 1970, 1d 1967).

Halliwell, Bernard, MBE (1981); First Secretary (Management/Consul) Budapest since November 1999; born 31.1.45; FO 1963; Salisbury 1967; Bahrain Residency 1969; Muscat 1970; FCO 1974; Ulaanbaatar, Geneva and Beirut 1973-74; Addis Ababa 1975; FCO 1975; Hong Kong 1977; Peking 1978; Second Secretary (Chancery/Inf) later (Admin/Cons) Bridgetown 1981; Second Secretary FCO 1985; First Secretary (Management) Bangkok 1988; First Secretary (Trade Promotion) Washington 1992; FCO 1996; Language Training 1999; m 1981 Vanessa Diane Brierley (3s 1984, 1986, 1989).

Hallsworth, Valerie; FCO since November 1988; born 9.11.48; Band A2; m 1999 Yousif Rahhal.

Hallworth, Lisa; Istanbul since May 2000; born 29.6.65; FCO 1987; Madrid 1989; UKMIS Geneva 1991; FCO 1994; Band A2.

Halpin, Michael Christopher; Floater Duties since November 2000; born 4.9.75; FCO 1999; Band A2.

Hamblett, Christine; Tel Aviv since February 1995; born 8.12.60; FCO 1990; Rome 1992; Band A2.

Hamill, Brian William; Third Secretary (Commercial) Berlin since July 1996; born 8.1.63; FCO 1981; Masirah 1983; Manila 1983; Budapest 1988; FCO 1989; Paris 1992; m 1987 Katrina Lacson Puentevella (1d 1991); Band B3.

Hamilton, Alasdair Alexander; Jakarta since June 1999; born 13.4.71; FCO 1990; Kuala Lumpur 1993; Port Moresby 1997; Freetown 1998; Band B3; m 1998 Erie Alu (1s 1999).

Hamilton, Charles Allan; Deputy Consul General Montreal since May 1997; born 5.12.48; DSAO 1968; Vice-Consul Düsseldorf 1970; Third Secretary Prague 1973; Vice-Consul Phnom Penh 1974; Third later Second Secretary Cairo 1975; FCO 1979; Second Secretary Addis Ababa 1981; DHC and Head of Chancery Port Louis 1984; FCO 1988; Deputy Head of Mission Yaoundé 1992; m Mary Indiana Lazare.

Hamilton, Jacqueline Ann (née Hopkins); Oslo since March 1997; born 10.6.43; Kampala 1983; Amman 1986; SUPL 1989; FCO 1992; Brussels 1994; Band A2; m 1967 William Hamilton (1s 1968; 1d 1971).

Hamilton, John; Third Secretary (Political) Abuja since October 1998; born 28.9.68; FCO 1988; UKDEL NATO Brussels 1990; Windhoek 1993; FCO 1996; Band B3; m 1998 Maxine Jones (1d 1999).

Hamilton, Josephine Anne Temple, MBE (1989); FCO since February 1996; born 15.6.45; FCO 1972; Georgetown 1974; FCO 1976; Ankara 1978; FCO 1982; Kingston 1986; FCO 1989; Rome 1993; Band A2.

Hamilton, Roger Patrick; Counsellor FCO since June 2000; born 27.5.48; FCO 1971; Second Secretary 1976; First Secretary Jakarta 1978; First Secretary Tokyo 1982; FCO 1983; on loan to the Hong Kong Government 1984; FCO 1986; First

Secretary (Chancery) Copenhagen 1989;
Counsellor; FCO 1993; Counsellor Santiago 1997;
m 1976 Linda Anne Watson.

Hampson, Fiona Patricia; SUPL since June 1997;
born 13.12.67; FCO 1987; Santiago 1992; Band
A2; (1s 1996).

Hancock, Janet Catherine; Deputy Head of
Mission Tunis since July 2000; born 5.1.49; FCO
1970; SRO 1975; PRO 1983; First Secretary FCO
1995; FTLT 2000; Band D7; m 1973 Roger A
Hancock (diss 1980).

Hancock, Michael John; Second Secretary
Chancery, UKREP Brussels since July 1998; born
21.10.62; FCO 1982; Bonn 1984; Belgrade 1987;
Islamabad 1989; FCO 1991; Vice Consul Rome
1995; Deputy Head of Mission Tbilisi 1995; Band
C4; m(1) 1983 Elizabeth Alison Ormrod (diss
1999) (2s 1989, 1991, 1d 1987), (2) 1999 Rusudan
Gachechiladze (2s 1992; 2001).

Hancock, Nicola Jane; FCO since September
1995; FCO 1989; Rome 1992; born 30.7.66; Band
B3; m 1993 Mark Westwood.

Hancon, John Anthony; FCO since July 1991;
born 5.1.48; GPO 1965; FCO 1969; Kuala
Lumpur 1971; FCO 1973; Paris 1976; FCO 1978;
Sofia 1982; FCO 1984; Nicosia 1988; Band C4; m
1970 Anne Lesley Hawke (1d 1975; 1s 1980).

Hand, Graham Stewart; Ambassador Bosnia
Herzegovina since July 1998; born 3.11.48; HM
Forces 1967-80; FCO 1980; Second later First
Secretary Dakar 1982; First Secretary FCO 1984;
Language Training 1987; First Secretary and Head
of Chancery, Helsinki 1987; Counsellor FCO
1992; Deputy High Commissioner Lagos 1994; on
loan to the Royal College of Defence Studies
1997; m 1973 Anne Mary Seton Campbell (1s
1979; 1d 1984).

Hand, Jessica Mary (née Pearce); First Secretary
FCO since March 1999; born 1.9.57; FCO 1985;
Second Secretary (Chancery) Dakar 1987; First
Secretary FCO 1990; full-time Language Training
1994; HM Ambassador Minsk 1996; m 1999
Robert Wayne Hand.

Handley, Timothy Sean; FCO since October 1994;
born 8.2.51; HCS 1969; FCO 1971; Abu Dhabi
1973; Stockholm 1976; Warsaw 1979; FCO 1981;
Georgetown 1985; FCO 1986; Düsseldorf 1988;
Tel Aviv 1991; Band B3; m 1985 Julie Anne
Russell (1s 1986, 1d 1989).

Handyside, Nancy Patricia; UKREP Brussels
since May 1999; born 27.8.51; Islamabad 1984;
Kampala 1988; Khartoum 1991; Sana'a 1995;
Bucharest 1998; Band A2.

Hannah, Craig John; born 2.6.63; FCO since
November 1999; Department of Employment
1980; FCO 1983; Accra 1984; Sofia 1987; FCO
1990; Kuala Lumpur 1994; Vienna 1998; Band B3.

Hannah, Jane Patricia; LA/Caribbean Floater
Duties since March 1995; born 23.9.70; FCO
1989; Athens 1991; Band A2.

Hannant, Michael Thomas Moss; Senior
Management Officer Hong Kong since February
1998; born 21.11.42; CRO 1963; Dar es Salaam
1964; Karachi 1968; FCO 1972; Second Secretary
(Admin/Chancery) Johannesburg 1974; Second
Secretary (Comm) Tripoli 1980; First Secretary
FCO 1982; First Secretary (Comm) The Hague
1986; First Secretary FCO 1991; Consul
(Commercial) Zurich 1994; m 1966 Penelope
Rosann Butcher (1d 1969; 1s 1971).

Hans, Ravinder; Buenos Aires since November
1997; born 17.3.73; FCO 1996; Band A2.

Hansen, Caroline (née Thearle); SUPL since
October 1999; born 17.2.66; FCO 1984;
Copenhagen 1987; SUPL 1990; Bangkok 1992;
SUPL 1995; Dhaka 1996; Band B3; m 1989 Jakob
Hansen.

Hansen, Diane (née Davies); First Secretary
(Management) Kuala Lumpur since July 2000;
born 23.7.45; FCO 1974; Lagos 1974; Athens
1977; FCO 1980; Copenhagen 1987; Port
Moresby 1991; FCO 1993; Wellington 1996;
FTLT 1999; Band C5; m 1988 Jan B Hansen.

Hanson, Timothy Myles; First Secretary
(Commercial) Sarajevo since June 2001; born
27.6.65; FCO 1984; Third Secretary (Chancery)
Muscat 1987; Third Secretary (Aid) New Delhi
1991; Second Secretary FCO 1994; Second
Secretary (Commercial) Kuala Lumpur 1997.

Harborne, Peter Gale; British High Commissioner
Port of Spain since 1999; born 29.6.45; DHSS
1966; FCO 1972; Ottawa 1974; Mexico City
1975; Resigned 1979; Reinstated 1981; First
Secretary FCO 1981; First Secretary and Head of
Chancery Helsinki 1983; Counsellor and Head of
Chancery Budapest 1988; FCO Overseas
Inspectorate 1991-94; HM Ambassador Bratislava
1995-98; m 1976 Tessa Elizabeth Henri (2s 1980,
1981).

Hardie, Alison; Yaoundé since May 2000; born
31.3.65; FCO 1988; Washington 1990; FCO 1992;
Canberra 1994; FCO 1997; Floater duties 1998;
Band A2.

Hardman, Peter James William; T/D Shanghai
since February 2000; born 28.10.56; FCO 1974;
SE Asia Floater 1978; Bombay 1979; Perth 1983;
Bangkok 1986; Second Secretary on loan to ODA
1988; Language Training 1990; Second Secretary
Sofia 1991; First Secretary (Commercial) Bangkok
1996; Band C5; m 1982 Joelle Helene Schneider
(1d 1984).

Hardy, Richard Martin; Singapore since July
2001; born 7.10.50; FCO 1967; Brussels 1976;
FCO 1978; Buenos Aires 1979; FCO 1982;
Bridgetown 1986; Second Secretary FCO 1989;
Paris 1993; FCO 1997; Band C5; m (1) 1975
Amanda Smith (diss 1981), (2) 1982 Astrid Posse
(diss 1996), m (3) 2001 Alison Jane Fossey.

Hare, Paul Webster; LVO (1985); HM Ambassador
Havana since July 2001; born 20.7.51; FCO 1978;
Second Secretary/PS to HMA UKREP Brussels

1979; First Secretary Lisbon 1981 (Head of Chancery 1983); FCO 1985; Consul (Investment) and Deputy Director Investment USA BTIO New York 1988; Deputy Head of Mission and later Counsellor (Commercial/Economic) Caracas 1994; Counsellor FCO 1997; m 1978 Lynda Carol Henderson (3d 1979, 1982, 1994, 3s 1984, 1988, 1991).

Hargreaves, Elaine; FCO since July 1998; born 29.10.71; FCO 1991; Harare 1995; Band B3.

Hargreaves, Roger John; First Secretary FCO since September 1999; born 8.12.50; FCO 1968; Hong Kong 1973; FCO 1975; Sana'a 1976; FCO 1977; Second Secretary Hong Kong 1985; Second later First Secretary FCO 1990; First Secretary (Political) Wellington 1996; Band C5; mAndrea Margaret Kent (1s 1989, 1d 1992).

Harkin, Simon David; FTLT since November 2000; born 4.10.58; FCO 1989; UKMIS New York 1990; FCO 1991; Second Secretary (Political) Harare 1992; First Secretary FCO 1996.

Harland, Jeremy; Washington since September 1999; born 8.4.63; FCO 1983; Moscow 1988; FCO 1992; Bridgetown 1992; FCO 1996; Band C4.

Harle, Roger William; FCO since August 1988; born 4.2.59; FCO 1982; Darwin 1986; Band C4.

Harmer, Roger William; Geneva (Joint Management Office) since July 1998; born 5.1.53; FCO 1972; Bucharest 1974; La Paz 1976; Maseru 1978; FCO 1980; Third Secretary Muscat 1983; Ottawa 1986; FCO 1989; Riga 1992; Second Secretary FCO 1993; m 1976 Cristobalina López Munoz (1d 1977).

Harper, Maurice Bertrand; HM Consul Bucharest since October 1996; born 3.12.46; FCO 1974; Bangkok 1976; East Berlin 1980; FCO 1981; Bombay 1984; Port Louis 1988; Second Secretary FCO 1993; m(1) 1977 Susan Hayward (1s 1979); m(2) 1986 Veera Printer (1d 1987).

Harper, Monica Celia; Consul General Lille since September 1998; born 18.8.44; FCO 1967; SEATO (Bangkok) 1969; ENA Paris 1972; BMG Berlin 1974; Second Secretary Bonn 1977; FCO 1979; Second Secretary Mexico City 1982; First Secretary UKDEL NATO Brussels 1984; First Secretary FCO 1989; Deputy Head of Mission Luxembourg 1994.

Harries, David George, MBE (1990), OBE (1998); Third Secretary (Commercial/Development) Maputo since February 1998; born 10.3.60; FCO 1980; BGWRS Darwin 1982; FCO 1984; Islamabad 1986; FCO 1988; Beirut 1988; FCO 1991; Third Secretary (Consular/Management) Freetown 1993; Band B3; m 1993 Carol Chammas.

Harrington, Clare Elizabeth; FCO since August 1980; born 30.8.61; Band A2.

Harrington, Peter; Madras since August 1997; born 29.9.62; FCO 1981; Baghdad 1984;

Stockholm 1988; Georgetown 1990; FCO 1994; On loan to DTI 1995; Band C4; m(1) 1984 Angela Elizabeth Dent (diss), (2) m1993 Veronica Ann Clementson (1s 1993,1d 1995).

Harris, Alistair James; FCO since December 2000; born 12.9.73; FCO 1997; Banja Luka on secondment to MOD 1998; Second Secretary (Regional Affairs) Budapest 1999; Band C4.

Harris, Graham Peter, OBE (2001), MBE (1985); Pretoria since October 1997; born 15.10.41; Army 1958-88; Nairobi 1989; Warsaw 1992; Maputo 1994; Band B3; m 1965 Tessa E Sharp (1s 1965; 1d 1967).

Harris, Joan; FCO since July 1995; born 27.12.49; FCO 1975; Dakar 1976; Budapest 1978; Oslo 1981; FCO 1983; Paris 1987; FCO 1990; Third Secretary (Science and Tech) Moscow 1992; Band B3.

Harris, Karina Lynn; World Wide Floater Duties since July 2001; born 28.2.62; FCO 1983; Cairo 1984; Tokyo 1988; FCO 1990; UKMIS Vienna 1993; Rabat 1997; T/D Jerusalem 2000; Band A2.

Harris, Kay; Islamabad since 1998; born 25.11.72; FCO 1992; Band B3.

Harris, Martin Fergus; On loan to DfID as First Secretary (KHF), Moscow, since November 1999; born 17.5.69; FCO 1991; (CFE) UKDEL Vienna 1992; FCO 1997; Full Time Language Training 1998; m 1993 Linda Margaret Maclachlan (1d 2001).

Harris, Peter Harold Charles; Counsellor Warsaw since May 1998; born 25.1.50; FCO 1981; Second later First Secretary (Social and Agriculture) Lisbon 1981; FCO 1984; First Secretary Moscow 1985; FCO 1988; First Secretary Santiago 1990; FCO 1993; m 1976 Maria Judith Ocazionez (4s 1980, 1982, 1984, 1993).

Harris, Thomas George, CMG (1995); Consul-General New York and Director-General Trade & Investment USA since June 1999; born 6.2.45; BOT 1966; Third Secretary Tokyo 1969; DOT 1971; Cabinet Office 1976; DTI 1979; Counsellor (Commercial) Washington 1983; Counsellor and Head of Chancery Lagos 1988; Deputy High Commissioner 1990; Counsellor FCO and Commissioner British Indian Ocean Territories 1991; HM Ambassador Seoul 1994; m 1967 Mei-Ling (3s 1969, 1970, 1984).

Harrison, Anthony Gifford; First Secretary (Consular) Nicosia since February 1998; born 21.2.43; Ministry of Defence (Air) 1964; FCO 1967; Helsinki 1969; Kathmandu 1971; Dacca 1974; Nicosia 1976; FCO 1979; Second Secretary (Admin/Cons) Colombo 1982; Second Secretary and Consul Oslo 1987; Second Secretary FCO 1992; First Secretary (Immigration) Moscow 1995; m 1970 (1) Marianne Versteeg (2s 1971, 1973); (2)1985 Azniv Salakian; (3)2001 Elena Dobrorodnaya.

Harrison, Anthony Julian; Second Secretary FCO since May 1981; born 19.3.53; FCO 1975; Pretoria 1978; Band C4; m 1978 Sharon Readman (1d 1986, 1s 1990).

Harrison, Caroline Margaret; First Secretary FCO since August 1999; born 8.9.66; FCO 1989; First Secretary Helsinki 1997; Band C5.

Harrison, Charles Dale; Second Secretary (Management) UKREP Brussels since July 1998; born 23.2.55; MOD 1971; FCO 1976; Accra 1978; Mbabane 1982; FCO 1985; Rome 1988; Islamabad 1991; Band C4; FCO 1994; m 1978 Lorraine Josie Richards (1d 1987, 1s 1990).

Harrison, Guy Andrew; Second Secretary (Economic) Seoul since September 1998; born 30.5.64; FCO 1986; Language Training and later Third Secretary (Political) Seoul 1987; Munich 1992; Hanoi 1993; FCO 1995; Band C4; m 1996 Ann Van Dyck (1d 1999).

Harrison, Mark Simon; Abidjan since May 2000; born 8.7.68; FCO 1989; Montevideo 1991; SUPL 1992; Jedda 1994; Nairobi 1996; Band C4; m 1992 Roxane Miller (1s 2000).

Harrison, Paula Leslie; FCO since September 2000; born 5.9.78; Band C4.

Harrison, Stephen Thomas, MBE (2001); Consul General Ekaterinburg since February 1998; born 14.8.64; FCO 1986; Language Training SOAS 1987; Language Training Cairo 1988; Third Secretary (Chancery) Bahrain 1989; Full-time Language Training (Russian) 1993; Moscow 1994; Band C5; m 1995 Philippa Capper (1d 1993, 1s 1998).

Harrison, Victoria Jane; Second Secretary (Political) Helsinki since August 2000; born 31.10.74; FCO 1997; Full-time Language Training 1999; Band C4.

Harrison, William Alistair, CVO (1996); Counsellor and Head of Chancery UKMIS New York since February 2000; born 14.11.54; FCO 1977; Third later Second Secretary Warsaw 1979; Second later First Secretary FCO 1982; Private Secretary to the Parliamentary Under Secretary 1984; First Secretary UKMIS New York 1987; First Secretary FCO 1992; Deputy Head of Mission Warsaw 1995; on loan to European Commission as Foreign Policy Adviser 1998; m(1) 1981 Thérésa Mary Morrison (diss 1991), (2) 1996 Sarah Judith Wood (1d 1999).

Harrocks, Nicholas James Laurent; Second Secretary (Political) Riyadh since May 1999; born 16.4.73; FCO September 1996; (Economic Relations Department); Full-time Language Training 1998.

Harrod, Christine Margaret; FCO since December 1984; born 27.12.49; FCO 1967; Paris 1972; Caracas 1975; FCO 1978; Manila 1981; Band B3; m 1984 David Stanley Martin.

Harrod, Jean (née Geary); First Secretary (Political) Canberra since October 2000; born 28.4.54; FCO 1972; Geneva (CSCE) 1973; East Berlin 1975; Port Louis 1977; Peking 1980; SUPL 1983; FCO 1986; Third later Second Secretary (Chancery) UKREP Brussels 1992; Second Secretary and Consul Jakarta 1994; FCO 1997; m 1974 Jeffrey Harrod.

Harrod, Jeffrey; First Secretary (External Affairs) Canberra since October 2000; born 1.4.54; FCO 1970; Geneva (CSCE) 1973; East Berlin 1975; Port Louis 1977; Vice-Consul (Commercial) and later Second Secretary Peking 1980; Consul (Commercial) Shanghai 1984; Second later First Secretary FCO 1986; First Secretary (Commercial) UKREP Brussels 1990; First Secretary (Political/Economic) Jakarta 1994; m 1974 Jean Geary.

Harrower, Hazel; Tehran since July 1997; born 18.12.64; FCO 1985; Bucharest 1988; Seoul 1989; FCO 1994; Band B3.

Harrup, Christine Mary; Kingston since December 2000; born 18.4.49; FCO 1974; Baghdad 1974; Lagos 1977; FCO 1978; Dublin 1981; FCO 1985; Addis Ababa 1987; Colombo 1992; Budapest 1994; Kiev 1999; Band B3.

Harsent, Susan Elizabeth; Shanghai since April 1998; born 16.6.49; FCO 1970; Bonn 1972; FCO 1975; Suva 1976; FCO 1978; Tel Aviv 1982; FCO 1984; UKREP Brussels 1989; Band B3.

Harston, Stewart Ian; FCO since January 1994; born 3.11.63; Singapore 1990; Band C4; m(1) 1990 Marianne Stallard (diss) (2) 1994 BG Carvello (2s 1995, 1998).

Hart, Graham Donald; New Delhi since March 1994; born 25.10.46; FCO 1975; Tokyo 1977; Monrovia 1982; FCO 1985; JMO New York 1988; FCO 1992; Band B3.

Hart, Jeremy Michael; Second Secretary FCO since November 1990; born 24.2.57; FCO 1975; Paris 1978; FCO 1980; Second Secretary FCO 1986; Second Secretary (Vice-Consul) Athens 1986; Band C4; m (1) 1979 Alison Jane Morrell (diss 1993) (1d 1984); (2) 1995 Penelope Helen Margaret Smyth. (1d 1996).

Hart, Roger Dudley, CMG (1998); HM Ambassador Lima since September 1999; born 29.12.43; Third Secretary FO 1965; Third later Second Secretary Berlin 1967; Bahrain 1970; Second later First Secretary FCO 1972; First Secretary (Aid) Nairobi 1975; First Secretary Lisbon 1978; First Secretary FCO 1983; CDA at RCDS 1985; Consul-General Rio de Janeiro 1986; Deputy Head of Mission Mexico City 1990; Counsellor FCO 1993; HM Ambassador Luanda 1995; m 1968 Maria de los Angeles de Santiago Jimnez (2s 1969, 1970).

Hart, Simon Charles; Bandar Seri Begawan since June 2000; born 13.12.57; FCO 1975; Brussels 1978; Tehran 1981; LA Floater 1983; Bogotá 1985; FCO 1989; Third Secretary Panama City 1993; Brasilia 1997; Band B3; m 1987 Amparo Meza (2s 1993, 1995, 1d 1996).

Harte, Josephine Moira (née Campbell); Brussels since February 2000; born 17.11.67; FCO 1988; Prague 1990; FCO 1992; Full-time Language Training 1994; Vice Consul Berlin 1995; SUPL 1999; Band B3; m 1996 Derek Thomas Harte.

Hartley, James Leslie; Deputy Head of Mission Algiers since November 1999; born 18.8.49; St Helena 1975; FCO 1977; Lusaka 1978; FCO 1980; LA Floater 1983; Khartoum 1985; Second Secretary and Head of Chancery Ulaanbaatar 1989; Second Secretary FCO 1992; Deputy Head of Mission Phnom Penh 1994; First Secretary and Consul Kuwait 1997; Band C5; m 1984 Ann Lesley Oakley.

Harvey, Christopher Paul Duncan; Deputy Head Commissioner Nairobi since April 2000; born 21.7.56; FCO 1986 (Second Secretary 1986); Second Secretary Suva 1988; First Secretary (Chancery) Brussels 1990; First Secretary FCO 1995; UK Special Representative for Peace in Sierra Leone 1999; m 1989 Anasaini Vesinawa Kamakorewa (1 step d 1987; 1 step s 1988).

Harvey, David; Second Secretary (WTO) UKMIS Geneva since January 1997; born 10.11.57; FCO 1977; Dublin 1980; Kinshasa 1982; East Berlin 1986; FCO 1988; Guatemala City 1992; m 1983 Bernadette Louise McMahon (1s 1987, 1d 1990).

Harvey, Lindsay; Grand Cayman since February 1997; born 31.3.59; FCO 1984; Tehran 1986; Budapest 1987; Bridgetown 1988; FCO 1993; SUPL 1993; Band B3.

Haslam, Christopher Peter de Landre; Deputy High Commissioner Suva and HM Ambassador (non resident) to Micronesia, Palau and Marshall Islands since January 2000; born 22.3.43; Admiralty and Ministry of Defence (Navy) 1960; DSAO 1966; Jakarta 1969; Sofia 1973; FCO 1974; Canberra 1978; Lagos 1981; Second Secretary FCO 1986; First Secretary (Comm) Copenhagen 1989; First Secretary FCO 1993; First Secretary (Commercial) Colombo 1996; Band D6; m 1969 Lana Whitley (2s 1971, 1973).

Haslem, Michelle; Second Secretary Kuala Lumpur since September 2001; born 18.2.74; FCO 1999; Band C4.

Haswell, Charles Chetwynd Douglas; On loan to British Invisibles since June 1998; born 18.2.56; FCO 1979; Language Training Hong Kong 1981; Peking 1982; Third later Second Secretary (Chancery) Ottawa 1986; Second later First Secretary FCO 1989; First Secretary (Political) UKDEL Vienna 1994; First Secretary FCO 1996; m 1991 Sarah Caroline Folkes (1s 1994, 1d 1995).

Hatfull, Martin Alan; Counsellor (Economic and Commercial) Rome since July 1998; born 7.6.57; FCO 1980; Language Training 1982; Second, later First Secretary Tokyo 1983; First Secretary FCO 1987; First Secretary UKREP Brussels 1991; First Secretary later Counsellor FCO 1995; m 1980 Phyllis Morshead (2s 1984, 1987).

Haveron, Monica; Tel Aviv since November 2001; born 29.6.67; FCO 1987; Nicosia 1990; FCO 1993; Valletta 1995; FCO 1998; World Wide Floater 2000; Band A2.

Hawkes, Julie Anne (née Carr); SUPL since November 1996; born 5.7.64; FCO 1990; Budapest 1992; FCO 1996; Band A2; m 1996 Edward Clifford Hawkes.

Hawkins, Carl McArthur; First Secretary Singapore since July 1998; born 25.9.50; FCO 1967; HCS 1974; FCO 1977; Third Secretary Bangkok 1989; Second Secretary FCO 1992; m 1987 Yuko Shibuya (1d 1988).

Hawkins, John Mark; Counsellor (Commercial) Madrid and Director of Trade and Investment Promotion for Spain since March 2000; born 30.4.60; FCO 1982; Third later Second Secretary (Chancery) Pretoria/Cape Town 1984; First Secretary FCO 1989; First Secretary (Commercial) New Delhi 1993; First Secretary later Counsellor FCO 1997; m 1991 Rosemarie Anne Kleynhans (2s 1993, 1996).

Hay, Barbara Logan, CMG (1998), MBE (1991); Consul General St Petersburg since August 2000; born 20.1.53; FCO 1971; Language Student 1974; Moscow 1975; Johannesburg 1978; Second Secretary FCO 1980; Vice-Consul (Comm) Montreal 1985; First Secretary (Info) Moscow 1988; HM Consul General St Petersburg 1991; First Secretary FCO 1992; Language Training 1994; HM Ambassador Tashkent and non-resident Dushanbe 1995; Language Training 1999.

Hay, Charles John, MVO (1996); First Secretary (Econ/Finance) UKREP Brussels since November 1999; born 22.9.65; HM Forces (Army) 1987-93; FCO 1993; Second Secretary (Pol/Info) Prague 1995; First Secretary FCO 1998; Band D6; m 1992 Caroline Jane Windsor (diss 1997).

Hay, James Stewart; Belgrade since February 1997; born 2.2.43; Army 1962-84; Moscow 1989; Ankara 1992; UKMIS New York 1994; Band B3; m 1992 Carol Elizabeth Gomme.

Hay-Campbell, (Thomas) Ian, LVO (1994); FTLT since May 2001; born 19.5.45; BBC 1972-84; First Secretary FCO 1984; First Secretary Head of Chancery and Consul Kinshasa 1987; First Secretary FCO 1990; full-time Language Training 1993; First Secretary (Press and Public Affairs Unit) Moscow 1994; Deputy High Commissioner Harare 1998; m 1970 Margaret Lorraine Hoadley (4s 1973, 1974, 1977, 1979).

Haydon, Joanna Mary; FCO since October 1999; born 14.3.69; FCO 1992; Full Time Language Training in Bangkok 1995; Vice Consul Bangkok 1995; Band B3; m 1998 Peter L Spoor.

Hayes, Julie Patricia; SUPL since August 2001; born 22.7.59; FCO 1988; Hanoi 1991; FCO 1993; Harare 1996; FCO 1999; Band B3.

Haywood, Ian; Lisbon since February 1998; born 2.10.59; FCO 1978; Kampala 1981; Düsseldorf

1985; FCO 1989; Peking 1994; Full Time
Language Training 1997; m(1) 1984 Angela Jane
Kennedy (diss 1988); (2) 1991 June Sandra Tyler.

Haywood, Nigel Robert; Counsellor OSCE
Vienna since April 1996; born 17.3.55; Army
1977-80; FCO 1983; Second later First Secretary
Budapest 1985; First Secretary FCO 1989; Deputy
Consul-General Johannesburg 1992; m 1979 Mary
Louise Smith (3s 1984, 1985, 1991).

Hazlewood, Roger Derek; First Secretary
(Management) Harare since January 2001; born
10.1.50; FCO 1968; Georgetown 1971; Bonn
1975; Paris 1977; FCO 1980; Cairo 1983; UKREP
Brussels 1987; FCO 1990; (Second Secretary 1991);
full-time Language Training 1993; Second Secretary
(Commercial) Warsaw 1994; Second Secretary
(Management) Dhaka 1997; m 1971 Yvonne Helen
Betty Johnston McPhee (3s 1973, 1976, 1978).

Head, Ian; FCO since April 1993; born 21.10.46;
Home Civil Service 1987; Bonn 1990; Band C4;
m 1992 S. Bigonesse-Caron.

Healy, Denis Terence; First Secretary
(Commercial) Tokyo since August 2000; born
18.11.43; FO 1963; DSAO 1965; Belgrade 1967;
FCO 1970; Port of Spain 1974; Second Secretary
1975; Vice-Consul Douala 1976; FCO 1979; Second
Secretary (Chancery/Aid) Bridgetown 1983; First
Secretary (Comm) UKREP Brussels 1985; First
Secretary FCO 1990; First Secretary (Commercial)
Ankara 1991; First Secretary FCO 1996.

Healy, Dora Claire Sarah; First Secretary
(Political) Nairobi since September 1995; born
30.8.52; FCO 1982; Language Training 1986;
Second (later First) Secretary (Chancery/Inf)
Addis Ababa 1987; Principal Research Officer;
FCO 1991; m 1983 Nicholas Guttmann (2d 1976,
1983, 1s 1985).

Healy, Martin Frederick; FCO since October
2000; born 21.10.55; FCO 1972; Moscow 1978;
FCO 1979; Third Secretary Pretoria 1984; FCO
1987; Hong Kong 1990; Second Secretary FCO
1993; Second Secretary Nairobi 1997; m 1977
Jane Catherine Stacey (2d 1981, 1983).

Hearn, Natalie Louise; ECO/VC Düsseldorf since
September 1998; born 13.7.72; FCO 1992; Peking
1995; Band B3.

Heaslip, Lisanne Marie; Tokyo since September
2000; born 16.1.69; FCO 1988; Belgrade 1998;
FCO 1999; Band B3.

Heath, Gillian Carol; Suva since April 2001; born
21.8.45; FCO 1969; Islamabad 1970; Kampala
1971; San Salvador 1973; Panama 1973; Kuala
Lumpur 1975; Brunei 1976; FCO 1978; Havana
1980; Dar es Salaam 1981; Singapore 1984;
Washington 1988; FCO 1989; Algiers 1990; FCO
1994; Cairo 1996; T/D Canberra 2000; Band B3.

Heatly, Charles Robert; Second Secretary
(Political/ Economic) Amman since June 1997;
born 7.8.70; FCO 1993; Full Time Language
Training Cairo 1995.

Hebden, Ian Mark; Washington since January
2001; born 25.3.60; Royal Navy 1976-1987; FCO
1987; Bonn 1990; Harare 1992; FCO 1996;
UKREP Brussels 1997; Band A2.

Heffer, John William Charles; First Secretary
(Management) Tripoli since June 2000; born
31.7.52; FCO 1971; Kampala 1973; FCO 1974;
Victoria (Seychelles) 1975; Bogotá 1977; Peking
1980; FCO 1981; Warsaw 1983; FCO 1984;
Valletta 1988; Pretoria 1991; FCO 1994 (Second
Secretary 1995); Band C4; m 1975 Lynne Ida
Brown (2s 1977, 1980).

Hefford, Brian; FCO since October 1997; born
10.8.48; FCO 1969; Karachi 1972; Paris 1976;
FCO 1979; Islamabad 1983; FCO 1986; Colombo
1989; Second Secretary Bangkok 1994; m 1971
Susan Mary Gorman (1s 1975 (dec'd 1991)).

Heigl, Peter Richard; High Commissioner Nassau
since July 1999; born 21.2.43; Ministry of Power
1963; Ministry of Technology 1968; DTI 1971; on
secondment to FCO as Second Secretary (Comm)
Kuala Lumpur 1974; Accra 1975; First Secretary
FCO 1981; First Secretary (Comm) Riyadh later
Consul (Comm) Jedda 1984; First Secretary FCO
1989; First Secretary, Consul-General and Deputy
Head of Mission Khartoum, 1991; Language
Training 1994; First Secretary, Deputy Head of
Mission Kathmandu 1994; m 1965 Sally Lupton
(3s 1971, 1973, 1977 1d 1982).

Helke, Jill Beynon (née Barker-Harland); SUPL
since April 1999; born 10.4.56; FCO 1978;
Language Training Hong Kong 1981; Peking
1983; Second Secretary UKMIS New York 1986;
First Secretary FCO 1990; SUPL 1990; UKMIS
New York 1992; SUPL 1993; (UN) UKMIS
Geneva 1993; m 1987 Heinz Michael Rudolf
Juergen Helke (1s 1988, 1d 1990).

Hellen, Gary David; Nicosia since May 1999;
born 24.6.70; FCO 1990; ECMIS Zagreb 1992;
FCO 1993; Dhaka 1995; Band A2.

Helmer, Victoria Jane; Second Secretary Amman
since October 2001; born 19.10.75; FCO 1998;
FTLT 1999; FTLT (Cairo) 2000; Band C4.

Hemmings, Kathryn Louise; born 20.8.70; SUPL
since November 1999; FCO 1991; UKMIS New
York 1993; FCO 1996; Nairobi 1999; Band A2.

Hemingway, Janette (née Hunt); Abidjan since
February 1997; born 17.8.59; FCO 1984; UKDEL
Vienna 1986; FCO 1990; Dhaka 1993; Band B3;
m 1988 William Piers Hemingway.

Hemingway, William Piers; SUPL since May
1999; born 10.11.60; Kuala Lumpur 1981; Luanda
1985; Vienna 1987; FCO 1979; Dhaka 1993;
Abidjan 1997; Band B3; m 1988 Janette Hunt.

Henderson, Andrew David Forbes; Consul-
General Jedda since April 2000; born 12.7.52;
FCO 1971; Latin America Floater 1975; Rio de
Janeiro 1977; Second Secretary (Chancery) Oslo
1980; APS/Minister of State FCO 1985; Consul,
New York (CG) 1987; First Secretary Washington

1988; Consul and Deputy Head of Mission Luanda 1992; Cairo 1994; Head of Parliamentary Relations Department FCO 1998; m 1987 Julia Margaret King (2d 1988, 1990).

Henderson, Christopher George; Third Secretary FCO since 1999; born 23.4.66; Metropolitan Police Office (Civil Staff) 1987; FCO 1990; Lilongwe 1993; FCO 1996; Jedda 1997; Bridgetown 1997; Amman 1997; St. Petersburg 1997; Madras 1997; BTCO Taipei 1997; Kinshasa 1998; Banjul 1998; Accra 1998; Bahrain 1998; Lagos 1998; Naples 1999; Pristina 1999; Band B3.

Henderson, Lesley; SUPL since October 2000; born 21.11.67; FCO 1987; Paris 1989; FCO 1991; Turks and Caicos Islands 1993; FCO 1996; Floater duties 1998; Band A2.

Henderson, Matthew Magnus Murray; First Secretary FCO since March 1996; born 19.7.60; Second Secretary FCO 1986; Second later First Secretary BTC Hong Kong 1988; First Secretary FCO 1990; First Secretary (External/Press) Peking 1992; Band D6.

Henderson, William Robert, LVO (1988); First Secretary FCO since February 1996; born 7.11.47; DSAO later FCO 1965; Moscow 1970; Sana'a 1971; Lima 1972; Rio de Janeiro 1973; FCO 1976; MECAS 1977; Dubai 1978 (Second Secretary 1980); FCO 1983; First Secretary (Inf) Madrid 1985; First Secretary FCO 1989; Deputy Head of Mission Abu Dhabi 1992; m 1969 Carol Mary Smith (1d 1973; 1s 1976).

Hendry, Carol Anne Walls; on loan to DTI since December 1999; born 7.12.66; FCO 1985; UKREP Brussels 1987; Tokyo 1990; World Wide Floater Duties 1993; FCO 1995; Band B3.

Hendry, Ian Duncan, CMG (1996); Deputy Legal Adviser FCO since October 1999; born 2.4.48; Assistant Legal Adviser FCO 1971; First Secretary (Legal Adviser) BMG Berlin 1982; Assistant Legal Adviser, later Legal Counsellor; FCO 1986; Counsellor (Legal Adviser) UKREP Brussels 1991; Legal Counsellor FCO 1995; m(1)1973 Elizabeth Anne Southall (1d 1975; 1s 1977); (2) 1991 Sally Annabel Hill.

Hennessy, Alexandra Mary (née Wintour); T/D The Hague since may 2000; born 25.3.66; Office of Fair Trading 1985; FCO 1987; UKMIS New York 1988; Vienna 1991; FCO 1995; SUPL 1996; Band A2; m 1993 Anthony John Hennessy (1d 1996).

Hennessy, Anthony John; First Secretary (Commercial) The Hague since June 2000; born 1.2.55; FCO 1980; Singapore 1981; FCO 1985; Second Secretary (Commercial) Riyadh 1987; Second Secretary (UN/UNIDO) UKMIS Vienna 1991; First Secretary FCO 1995; Band C5; m 1993 Alexandra Mary Wintour (1d 1996).

Henry, Elaine Monica; FCO since April 2001; born 11.9.69; FCO 1989; New Delhi 1993; Maputo 1997; FCO 1999; T/D La Paz 2000; Band B3; (1d 1991).

Hentley, Michael Joseph; First Secretary and Consul Seoul since May 1999; born 13.7.46; CRO 1964; DSAO 1965; Benghazi 1969; Moscow 1972; Lagos 1973; Kaduna 1976; FCO 1978; Second Secretary (Comm) Port of Spain 1982; Second Secretary FCO 1985; First Secretary (COCOM) Paris 1987; Deputy Head of Mission Dakar 1992; First Secretary FCO 1995; m 1969 Janice Paterson (1s 1971; 2d 1973, 1979).

Herbert, David; Deputy Head of Mission Luxembourg since June 1998; born 13.7.47; CO 1966; Algiers 1969; Baghdad 1970; Tananarive 1971; FCO 1974; Second Secretary Luxembourg 1977; Second Secretary (Comm) Prague 1981; First Secretary FCO 1985; Consul (Comm) Montreal 1988; First Secretary (Pol/Econ) Abuja 1993; First Secretary FCO 1995; m 1970 Maureen Violet Edmundson (2d 1976, 1978).

Herd, Theresa Ann; Deputy Head of Mission Kinshasa since August 1999; born 24.10.54; FCO 1972; Resigned 1974; Reinstated 1980; Lilongwe 1981; FCO 1984; Pretoria 1986; Cape Town 1987; LA/Caribbean Floater 1989; FCO 1991; Full-time Language Training 1994; Luanda 1995; Second Secretary FCO 1996; Full-time Language Training 1999; Band C4.

Herridge, Michael Eric James; Deputy High Commissioner Madras since February 1999; born 23.9.46; DSAO 1966; FCO 1968; Düsseldorf 1969; Prague 1969; Nairobi 1972; FCO 1975; Lagos 1979; Second later First Secretary UKMIS New York 1982; First Secretary FCO 1986; First Secretary (Management) Madrid 1990; FCO 1995; m 1968 Margaret Elizabeth Bramble (1d 1971).

Herring, Julie Ann; SUPL since August 1994; born 10.4.65; FCO 1984; Helsinki 1987; FCO 1989; SUPL 1993; Cairo 1994; Band B3.

Heseltine, Lavinia Pauline; Peking since May 2000; FCO 1974; Brussels 1975; Moscow 1979; Canberra 1981; Khartoum 1984; Lagos 1988; Dhaka 1992; SUPL 1995; FCO 1998; Band B3; m 1990 Barry Heseltine.

Heseltine, Robert Andrew; St Petersburg since February 2000; born 18.11.73; MAFF 1996-97; FCO 1997; Band A2.

Hetherington, Martin Duncan; FCO since December 1998; born 22.2.74; DETR 1997.

Hewer, Susan Jane; Floater Duties since April 2001; born 18.9.61; FCO 1980; Washington 1982; FCO 1985; New Delhi 1985; UKDEL Strasbourg 1989; Kuwait 1991; FCO 1995; UKMIS New York 1997; Band B3.

Hewitt, Gavin Wallace, CMG (1995); HM Ambassador Brussels since February 2001; born 19.10.44; Ministry of Transport 1967; On secondment as Third later Second Secretary from Ministry of Transport (later Department of the Environment) to Brussels (EEC) 1970; FCO 1972; First Secretary Canberra 1973; First Secretary FCO 1978; First Secretary and Head of Chancery Belgrade 1981; Counsellor attached to BBC (for

Review of External Services) 1984; Counsellor on loan to the HCS 1984; Deputy Permanent Representative (Head of Chancery) UKMIS Geneva 1987; Counsellor FCO 1992; HM Ambassador Zagreb 1994; HM Ambassador Helsinki 1997; m 1973 Heather Mary Clayton (2d 1975; 1979 2s 1977, 1982).

Hewitt, Norman; FCO since January 1989; born 12.9.46; FCO 1981; Washington 1985; Band C4; m 1968 Catherine Georgina Sahadeo (1s 1975; 2d 1970, 1983).

Hewitt, Simon; SUPL since January 1999; born 31.5.70; FCO 1989; UKREP Brussels 1995; Band A2; m 1992 Jacqueline Mary McQueen.

Heyn, Andrew Richard; First Secretary (Political) Lisbon since February 1996; born 14.1.62; DTI 1985-89; Second Secretary FCO 1989; Second Secretary (Chancery) Caracas 1991; First Secretary FCO 1994; m 1988 Jane Carmel (1d 1994).

Hickey, Patricia Helen; FCO since September 1997; born 2.2.55; FCO 1975; Bangkok 1977; FCO 1979; Canberra 1981; FCO 1984; New York 1986; Berlin 1988; FCO 1991; Hong Kong 1995; Band C4.

Hicking, Nicola Jane (née Boyles); Montevideo since 1999; born 28.7.63; FCO 1983; Brasilia 1985; Lagos 1987; FCO 1988; Band A2; m 1992 Robert Hicking (2s 1994, 1996).

Hicks, Colin Michael; Islamabad since January 2001; born 4.3.74; MAFF 1993-1996; FCO 1996; Dublin 1997; Band B3; m 1998 (1s 1999).

Hickson, Philip John; FCO since November 1997; born 21.3.65; FCO 1984; Kingston 1986; Floater Duties 1990; Tehran 1993; New Delhi 1996; Band B3; m 1992 Amanda Ruth Woolham (2s 1993, 1995).

Higgins, Gillian (née Newbury); FCO since 2000; born 23.3.63; FCO 1987; Budapest 1989; FCO 1991; Grand Cayman 1995; Band A2; m 1995 Russell Mark Higgins. (1d 1997)

Higgins, Robert Geoffrey; FCO since November 1985; (Second Secretary 1989); born 23.3.48; FCO 1968; The Hague 1971; Phnom Penh 1974; Caribbean Floater 1975; Dacca 1977; FCO 1978; Far East Floater 1980; Bridgetown 1982.

Higginbottom, Sandra Patricia (née Wright); Lagos since October 2000; born 3.3.65; Brussels 1986; FCO 1984; Dhaka 1989; FCO 1992; Tunis 1997; Band B3; m (1) 1989 Robert Freeman Walker (diss); (2) 1997 Andrew Higginbottom (1s 1996).

Higham, Andrew Bolton; FCO since July 1997; born 28.10.59; FCO 1982; Singapore 1986; FCO 1988; Government Secretary Hong Kong 1993; Band C4; m 1989 Veronica Jane Nazareth (1d 1990, 1s 1993).

Hildersley, Sarah Jane; Deputy Head of Mission, Santo Domingo since October 1998; born 30.5.68; FCO 1987; UKDEL NATO Brussels 1988; FCO

1989; Third Secretary (Management) JMO Brussels 1990; Floater Duties 1991; FCO 1994; Band C4; (1s 1996).

Hill, Charles Edward; First Secretary FCO since September 2000; born 31.3.63; FCO 1990; Third Secretary Chancery Doha 1993; DHM Almaty 1997; Band C5; m 1996 Suzanne Victoria Stock.

Hill, Duncan N; MO/Consul Shanghai since September 2000; born 8.12.68; FCO 1989; Berlin 1991; Full-time Language Training 1994; Rio de Janeiro 1995; FCO 1997; Band C4; m 1992 Lisa Pegram.

Hill, Jeremy John Leonard; Second Secretary (Commercial) Seoul since November 1998; born 3.5.57; FCO 1975; SOAS 1978; Tokyo 1979; Jakarta 1982; FCO 1986; Harare (1990); (Second Secretary 1994); Second Secretary FCO 1994; Sana'a 1996; m 1985 Roossnadia Peni Hestiani Roesno (1s 1990, 1d 1992).

Hill, Kristina Maria; Third Secretary (External Relations) UKREP Brussels since June 2000; born 10.4.72; FCO 1999; Band B3.

Hill, Lauren Sarah; Johannesburg since May 1999; born 14.2.73; FCO 1992; Conference Officer UKREP Brussels 1995; world-wide Floater Duties 1997; Band B3.

Hill, Martin Henry Paul; Deputy High Commissioner Colombo since November 1998; born 17.5.61; Ministry of Agriculture, Fisheries and Food 1983; Privy Council Office 1985; MAFF 1986; Bonn 1993; FCO 1996; Band D6; m, Kim Lydyard (3d 1992, 1993, 1996).

Hill, Michael Thomas; High Commissioner, Vila since November 2000; born 2.1.45; FO 1963; UKMIS New York 1966; Vientiane 1969; Kaduna 1970; FCO 1974; T/D Sana'a 1975; Second Secretary, DHM and Vice-Consul Ulaanbaatar 1978; Second Secretary (Cons/Immig/Aid) Port of Spain 1981; Second later First Secretary FCO 1985; Assistant to Deputy Governor, Gibraltar 1988; First Secretary (Aid) Nairobi 1993; First Secretary FCO 1997; m 1977 Elizabeth Louise Carden (3s 1981, 1988, 1990; 1d 1983).

Hill, Peter Jeremy Oldham; HM Ambassador Vilnius since November 2001; born 17.4.54; FCO 1982; First Secretary (Legal Adviser) Bonn 1987; on loan to the Law Officers' Department 1991; Legal Counsellor UKREP Brussels 1995; Counsellor FCO 1999; m 1981 Katharine Hearn (1d 1987, 1s 1989).

Hill, Sarah; First Secretary FCO since August 2000; born 18.9.72; FCO 1995; Third Secretary (Aid) Belgrade 1996; Second Secretary (Political) Buenos Aires 1997; Band C4.

Hill, Simon Robert; SUPL since October 2000; born 18.3.67; FCO 1994; Brussels 1996; FCO 1999; Band B3; m 1998 Carina Megia Abarca.

Hill, Steven John; First Secretary (Political) Washington since August 2001; born 7.4.62; FCO 1984; Second Secretary (UNIDO/UN) UKMIS

Vienna 1988; Second later First Secretary FCO 1990; First Secretary UKMIS New York 1996; First Secretary FCO 1999; Band D6; m 1998 Geraldine Steele (2d 1995, 2001; 1s 1998).

Hill, Suzanne Victoria (née Stock); Second Secretary FCO since August 2000; born 1.12.65; Home Office 1988-91; FCO 1991; T/D Accra 1993; Doha 1994; Third Secretary (Political/Aid) Almaty 1997; SUPL 1999; Band C4; m 1996 Charles Edward Hill.

Hilley, Marie Thérésa (née Donnelly); Tehran since May 2001; born 21.5.61; FCO 1996; Kathmandu 1997; Band A2.

Hillman, John; First Secretary FCO since January 1997; born 30.5.48; FO (later FCO) 1967; Dhaka 1971; Budapest 1974; Calcutta 1975; Second Secretary (Comm) Dublin 1979; Second Secretary FCO 1983; First Secretary and Consul Cairo 1988; Deputy Consul-General Sydney 1991; m 1978 Pushp Kanta Sahney (1d 1981).

Hilson, Marian Joan; SUPL since May 1997; born 5.2.44; FCO 1988; New Delhi 1990; FCO 1993; Band B3; m 1965 Malcolm Geoffrey Hilson (2s 1966, 1968).

Hilton, Christopher Charles Donald; Third Secretary (Chancery) Port of Spain since July 1999; born 7.11.69; FCO 1988; Budapest 1991; World-wide Floater Duties 1994; FCO 1997; Band B3.

Hilton, Margaret; FCO since September 1995; born 9.8.53; FCO 1990; Strasbourg 1993; Band A2.

Hilton, Michael Anthony; First Secretary (Comm) Tehran since December 1992; born 7.3.50; Department of Employment 1973; FCO 1973; Manchester Business School 1975; Frankfurt 1977; FCO 1979; Second Secretary Ulaanbaatar 1981; Second later First Secretary FCO 1983; First Secretary (Dev/Comm) Kathmandu 1987; Hanoi 1990; m 1976 Janet Elizabeth Tyler.

Himmer, Melanie (née Read-Ward); SUPL since December 1997; born 16.5.68; FCO 1989; Warsaw 1991; Tashkent 1994; Band B3; m 1993 Alan Keith Himmer.

Hinchley, Carol Ruth; Second Secretary (Chancery) Wellington since August 1994; born 9.4.59; FCO 1981; Gaborone 1983; Stockholm 1987; Second Secretary FCO 1991.

Hinchon, David Alan; FCO since March 2000; born 15.4.67; Band B3; ptnr, Anna Taylor (2s 1997, 1999).

Hines, Trevor John; British Trade International (London) since October 2000; born 10.11.60; FCO 1979; Floater 1982; Third Secretary (Consular) Jedda 1984; Riyadh 1985; FCO 1987; Third Secretary (Man/Cons) Belmopan 1990; Second Secretary (Commercial) Mexico 1995; Secondment to Industry May 2000; Band C4; m 1985 Sandra Bradley (1s 1992, 1d 1994).

Hirst, Harold Christopher; Tashkent since August 2000; born 26.12.66; DHSS 1984; FCO 1984; Maseru 1987; Peking 1991; FCO 1994; Hong Kong 1995; Band B3.

Hiscock, Stephen John; Consul-General Brisbane since January 1997; born 16.6.46; Inland Revenue 1963; FO 1965; Kuala Lumpur 1968; Lusaka 1972; FCO 1976; Second Secretary 1977; Islamabad 1978; First Secretary (Comm/Inf) Seoul 1982; First Secretary FCO 1986; Deputy High Commissioner Georgetown 1988; First Secretary FCO 1993; m(1) (diss 1982) (2s 1967, 1971); (2) 1983 Denise Mary Forster (1d 1986, 2s 1989, 1991).

Hitchens, Timothy Mark, On secondment to Buckingham Palace since January 1999; born 7.5.62; FCO 1983; Language Training Tokyo 1985; Second Secretary Tokyo 1986; Second later First Secretary FCO 1989; (Private Secretary to the Minister of State 1991); First Secretary (Political/Info) Islamabad 1994; FCO 1997; m 1985 Sara Kubra Husain (1d 1991, 1s 1993).

Ho, David Tat Lun; UKDEL NATO Brussels since November 1999; born 5.5.61; Home Civil Service 1989-1998; FCO 1998; Band A2.

Hoar, Gareth Keith; Consul (Economic) Guangzhou since October 1999; born 23.6.65; FCO 1984; Peking 1986; Santiago 1989; Washington 1991; FCO 1994; Language training Guangzhou 1998; m2000 Rebecca Xie.

Hoare, James Edward; Chargé d'Affaires and Consul-General Pyongyang since February 2001; born 16.4.43; Research Analysts FCO 1969; Principal Research Officer 1975; Head of Chancery/Consul Seoul 1981; FCO 1985; Head of Chancery/Consul-General Peking 1988; seconded to International Institute of Strategic Studies 1992; Senior Principal Research Officer FCO 1993; Research Counsellor 1998; m(1) 1965 Jane Maureen Fletcher (diss) (2s 1968, 1972); (2)1978 Susan Pares (1d 1978).

Hobart, Edward Andrew Beauchamp; First Secretary FCO since May 1998; born 30.11.71; FCO 1993; Third later Second Secretary Havana 1995; Band D6; m 1999 Suzanna Louise Massey.

Hobbs, Jeremy Alexander, Principal Research Officer FCO since September 1999; born 8.2.61; SRO; FCO 1991; Second Secretary (Political/Technical Co-operation) Bogotá 1995; Band D6; m 1983 Ana Maria Erndira (1s 1990, 1d 1994).

Hodge, Sir James William, KCVO (1996), CMG (1996); Consul-General Hong Kong since July 2000; born 24.12.43; Third Secretary Commonwealth Office 1966; Tokyo 1967; Second Secretary (Inf) Tokyo 1970; First Secretary FCO 1972; First Secretary (Dev) later (Chancery) Lagos 1975; FCO 1978; First Secretary (Econ) Tokyo 1981 later Counsellor (Commercial); Counsellor and Head of Chancery Copenhagen 1986; Counsellor FCO 1990; On loan at RCDS 1994;

Minister, Deputy Head of Mission and HM Consul-General Peking 1995; HM Ambassador Bangkok 1996; m 1970 Frances Margaret Coyne (3d 1973, 1975, 1979).

Hodges, Ian Foyle; Vice-Consul Jedda since April 2001; born 30.10.67; FCO 1987; Budapest 1989; Paris 1990; FCO 1994; Third Secretary (Consul) Karachi 1994; Third Secretary FCO 1994; Third Secretary (Management) and Vice-Consul Tehran 1997; m 1991 Patricia Paule Andre Seguin (1s 1992,1d 1993).

Hodges, Jeremy Andrew; Full time language training since May 1998; born 16.7.67; FCO 1988; Floater Duties 1990; Peking 1992; Karachi 1994; m 1992 Adele Bushnell.

Hodgetts, Susan Jacqueline; Second Secretary FCO since January 1995; born 7.11.48; DSAO (later FCO) 1967; Lagos 1970; Warsaw 1973; Montevideo 1975; FCO 1978; Bridgetown 1981; FCO 1985; Vice-Consul Bucharest 1990; Second Secretary (Consular/Immigration) Algiers 1993; Band C5.

Hodgson, Allen Richard; Second Secretary (Regional Affairs) Cairo since September 1998; born 8.2.60; FCO 1977; UKMIS Geneva 1991; FCO 1995; Band C4; m 1989 Sally Maureen Cole-Hamilton (1d 1993, 1s 1997).

Hodgson, George Kenneth; Second Secretary Nicosia since April 1997; born 15.2.49; FCO 1969; Lagos 1971; Belgrade 1974; Berlin CG 1975; Reykjavik 1976; Karachi 1977; FCO 1979; DHSS 1980-84; FCO 1984; Colombo 1985; Luxembourg 1989; Second Secretary FCO 1992; Ulaanbaatar 1995; m 1971 Jill Taylor (1s 1975; 2d 1978, 1980).

Hogarth, Philip; Deputy Head of Mission/Consul La Paz since March 2000; born 10.5.55; FCO 1976; Damascus 1978; Accra 1982; FCO 1984; Tokyo 1988; Paris 1991; Second Secretary FCO 1995; Band C4; m 1978 Monique Marie Therese Morand.

Hoggard, Robin Richard; Counsellor (Management/Con) Tokyo since November 1998; born 26.11.56; FCO 1982; Language Training SOAS 1983; Kamakura 1984; Second First Secretary (Comm) Tokyo 1985; (later First Secretary (Econ)); First Secretary FCO 1989. On loan to DTI 1991; First Secretary (Political) UKDEL NATO Brussels/UKDEL WEU 1994 m1988 Tonoko Komuro (1s 1995).

Hogger, Henry George; HM Ambassador Damascus since June 2000; born 9.11.48; Third Secretary FCO 1969; MECAS 1971; Aden 1972; Second Secretary Caracas 1972; Second later First Secretary Kuwait 1975; FCO 1978; First Secretary, Head of Chancery and Consul Abu Dhabi 1982; FCO 1986; Counsellor and Head of Chancery Amman 1989; High Commissioner Windhoek 1992; Counsellor FCO 1996; m 1972 Fiona Jane McNabb (2d 1979, 1982; 2s 1984).

Hogwood, Jonathan Felix; Second Secretary British Trade International since June 1998; born 24.7.52; FCO 1971; Warsaw 1974; Islamabad 1975; Luanda 1978; FCO 1981; Dhaka 1986; Tokyo 1989; FCO 1992; SUPL 1995; Second Secretary (Commercial) Nairobi 1996; m 1978 Susan Elizabeth Farmer.

Hogwood, Susan Elizabeth (née Farmer), MBE (1981); HM Ambassador Kigali since July 2001; born 27.5.52; FCO 1971; Islamabad 1974; SUPL 1978; Second Secretary FCO 1982; Second Secretary (Aid) Dhaka 1986; Second later First Secretary (Consular) Tokyo 1989; First Secretary FCO 1992; First Secretary (Humanitarian) Nairobi 1994; FCO 1998; m 1978 Jonathan Felix Hogwood.

Holder, Donald John; HM Consul Athens since October 2000; born 16.8.50; FCO 1976; Bonn 1978; Islamabad 1981; FCO 1984; Auckland 1985; BMG Berlin 1987; FCO 1988. Second Secretary (Commercial) Bahrain 1990; Language Training 1994; Second Secretary(Info/Visits) Warsaw 1995; Consul (Immigration/Passports) Düsseldorf 1996.

Holdich, Patrick Godfrey Hungerford; First Secretary (Chancery) Ottawa since December 1992; born 19.9.56; Senior Research Officer; Principal Research Officer 1990; FCO 1985; m 1987 Ailsa Elizabeth Beaton; (diss 1992).

Holifield, Martin; FCO since March 2001; born 8.9.61; FCO 1979; Islamabad 1986; FCO 1989; Kuwait 1991; FCO 1995; Luanda 1997; Band B3; m (1) 1985 Morag Catherine Fraser (diss 1995); (2) 1996 Anna Maria Sandelin (1s 1998).

Hollamby, David James; Governor St. Helena, Ascension Island and Tristan da Cunha since June 1999; born 19.5.45; CO 1961; DSAO 1964; Beirut 1967; Latin America Floater 1970; Asunción 1972; Second Secretary FCO 1975; Vice-Consul (Comm) BTDO New York 1978; Consul (Comm) Dallas 1983; First Secretary FCO 1986; First Secretary Rome 1990; First Secretary FCO 1994; m 1971 Maria Helena Guzman (2 step s 1961, 1964).

Holland, Denise Ann; on loan to DTI since July 2000; born 13.4.63; FCO 1986; Washington 1989; JLG Hong Kong 1991; FCO 1994; British Trade International 1997; Band C4; m2000 Anthony James Dudgeon.

Holland, Henry Robert Cumber; First Secretary FCO since September 1997; born 25.11.57; FCO 1984; Second Secretary (Chancery) Nairobi 1986; First Secretary FCO 1989; First Secretary (Political/Information) Canberra 1993; m 1983 Anne Elizabeth Wardle (2s 1987, 1990, 1d 1988).

Holland, Patricia Anne (Tricia); SUPL since February 2001; born 2.4.64; FCO 1986; Third Secretary (Chancery) Prague 1988; Second later First Secretary FCO 1989; First Secretary (Finance) UKMIS New York 1993; SUPL 1997; First Secretary (EU Affairs) Paris 1998; m 1997 Paul Thomas Arkwright (1d 1999).

Holland, Stephen Peter; First Secretary (Internal) New Delhi since December 2000; born 31.8.65; FCO 1999; Band D6; m Judith Kent.

Holland, Tracey Joanne; SUPL since March 1996; born 16.7.66; FCO 1990; Language Training 1991; Full-time Language Training Tokyo 1992; FCO 1993; Band B3.

Hollas, Robert Richmond Maxwell; Second Secretary (Management) The Hague since March 1996; born 9.4.41; CRO 1959; Salisbury 1962; DSAO 1965; Prague 1966; Kinshasa 1967; Cairo 1970; FCO 1974; Rome 1977; Second Secretary (Admin) The Hague 1980; Second Secretary FCO 1984; m 1962 Virginia Christine Watson (3s 1965, 1968, 1974).

Hollis, Anthonia; FCO since October 1994; born 2.1.66; FCO 1987; Bonn 1992; Band A2.

Hollis, Ian Malcolm; Lisbon since July 1997; born 16.12.70; FCO 1989; Bonn 1994; Band A2; m 1997.

Holloway, Michael John; Deputy Consul General Rio de Janeiro since April 1998; born 14.1.57; FCO 1976; Dubai 1978; Bucharest 1979; Africa/Middle East Floater 1981; Mexico City 1983; FCO 1984; Barcelona 1988; FCO 1991; Second Secretary (Political/Information/Aid) Mexico City 1994.

Hollywood, Jane Christina Emma; Second Secretary (Political) The Hague since September 1998; born 7.3.66; FCO 1991; Band C4.

Holmes, Alan Thomas; Second Secretary Sarajevo since October 2000; born 25.9.53; FCO 1977; UKDEL NATO Brussels 1980; FCO 1982; Bridgetown 1986; Cairo 1989; FCO 1992; Full time Language Training 1996; Moscow 1997; FCO 1998; Band C4; m 1980 Helen Hook.

Holmes, Helen (née Hook); Second Secretary FCO since December 1998; born 26.5.51; Department of Employment and Productivity 1969; FCO 1969; Bangkok 1973; Lagos 1975; FCO 1976; SUPL 1980; FCO 1982; Bridgetown 1986; Cairo 1989; FCO 1992; Moscow 1998; m 1980 Alan Thomas Holmes.

Holmes, John Dominic; Full Time Language Training since January 1999; born 18.8.59; Inland Revenue 1977; FCO 1978; Paris 1984; FCO 1987; Warsaw 1989; The Hague 1991; FCO 1994; Band B3.

Holmes, Sir John Eaton KBE (1999), CVO (1998), CMG (1997); HM Ambassador Paris since October 2001; born 29.4.51; Third Secretary FCO 1973; Language training 1975; Third Secretary Moscow 1976; Second later First Secretary FCO 1978; First Secretary (Econ) Paris 1984; First Secretary FCO 1987; Counsellor 1989; on Secondment to the De La Rue Company 1989; Counsellor and Head of Chancery (later Counsellor (Econ/Comm) New Delhi 1991; Head of European Union Department (External) FCO 1995; Private Secretary to the Prime Minister for Overseas Affairs 1996; Principal Private Secretary to the Prime Minister 1997; HM Ambassador Lisbon 1999; m 1976 Margaret Penelope Morris (3d 1981, 1982, 1985).

Holmes, Michael, MVO (1991); Auckland since June 2001; born 3.4.54; FCO 1973; Belmopan 1975; Rio de Janeiro 1978; Baghdad 1981; FCO 1985; Third Secretary Harare 1988; Second Secretary (Cons/Comm) Melbourne 1992; Second Secretary later Consul (Comm) Casablanca 1994; FCO 1998; m 1980 Jennifer Margaret Lesley Pike (1d 1982; 1s 1985).

Holmes, Paul Barry; FCO since 1997; born 15.11.54; FCO 1972; Warsaw 1978; Bonn 1980; FCO 1982; Third Secretary Accra 1986; Addis Ababa 1990; FCO 1993; Hong Kong 1995; FCO 1997; Band C5; m (1) 1975 Elaine Down (diss) (2S 1981, 1983), (2) 1988 Sarah Penelope Briggs (1d 1989, 1s 1991).

Holmes, Timothy Charles; Deputy Head of Mission and Consul General The Hague since October 1997; born 26.4.51; Third Secretary FCO 1974; Language training SOAS 1975; Language training Tokyo 1976; Second later First Secretary Tokyo 1977; on loan to DOT 1981; First Secretary FCO 1983; First Secretary (Chancery) Islamabad 1986; First Secretary FCO 1990; Deputy Head of Mission and Counsellor (Commercial/Economic) Seoul 1994; m 1973 Anna-Carin Magnusson (1s 1977, 1d 1988).

Holt, Denise Mary (née Mills); Director (Personnel Command) FCO since September 1999; born 1.10.49; Research Analyst FCO 1970; First Secretary (Political) Dublin 1984; SUPL 1987; FCO 1988; SUPL 1990; First Secretary (Political) Brasilia 1991; FCO 1993; SUPL 1994; Counsellor and Deputy Head of Mission Dublin 1998; m 1987 David Holt (1s 1987).

Holt, Sean Christopher Eric; OBE (1999); Counsellor Freetown since November 2001; born 18.12.49; Army 1968-78; FCO 1978; Second Secretary Havana 1979; First Secretary FCO 1980; Athens 1982; First Secretary FCO 1984; First Secretary (Chancery) Khartoum 1987; First Secretary FCO 1990; First Secretary (Political) Accra 1991; First Secretary FCO 1994; Counsellor Bogotá 1995; Counsellor Luanda 1999; m (1) 1973 Jennifer Patricia Trevaskis (diss 1987) (1s 1974; 1d 1976); (2) 1987 Joyce Amanda Anderson (diss 1994); (3) 1999 Johanna Antonia Maria Rutten.

Holtum, Roger Adrian; Third Secretary Lilongwe since August 1993; born 2.10.51; FCO 1972; Port of Spain 1975; Tel Aviv 1978; FCO 1981; Dhaka 1983; Helsinki 1986; FCO 1989; Third Secretary (Aid/Commercial) Kampala 1991; Band B3; m 1983 Nina Lange (1d 1984, 1s 1986).

Holyer, John Albert; Second Secretary FCO since February 1993; born 26.4.41; RAF 1958-70; FCO 1971; Freetown 1974; Budapest 1978; Lisbon 1980; FCO 1983; Bombay 1986; Third Secretary (Consular) Ottawa 1990; m (1) 1964 Morag Reid (diss) (2d 1968, 1969) (2) 1996 Milka Ivanova.

Homer, Richard David; Budapest since January 2001; born 24.12.72; FCO 1992; Stockholm 1995; FCO 1997; Washington 1997; Band B3.

Hood, Laura Elizabeth, FCO since November 1989; born 27.4.63; FCO 1983, Bucharest 1985; Port of Spain 1987; Band A2.

Hook, David; Skopje since January 2000; born 26.5.51; FCO 1971; Kuala Lumpur 1973; La Paz 1975; Amman 1976; FCO 1977; Tripoli 1980; Stockholm 1983; FCO 1985; Third Secretary (Admin) and Vice-Consul Kabul 1988; New Delhi 1989; Vice-Consul Houston 1991; FCO 1994; Band C4; m 1973 (1) Jannette Marie Sharp (diss 1980); (2) 1984 Anna-Karin Bengttson; (1 s 1988 (dec'd), 1s 1995).

Hook, Neil Kenneth, MVO (1983); High Commissioner Mbabane since October 1999; born 24.4.45; FCO 1968; Moscow 1971; FCO 1972; Language training Sheffield University 1974; Tokyo 1975; Second Secretary (Aid) Dhaka 1980; First Secretary FCO 1984; On loan to DTI 1986; First Secretary (Commercial) Tokyo 1987; First Secretary FCO 1992; HM Ambassador Ashgabat 1995; m 1973 Pauline Ann Hamilton (1d 1975; 1s 1977).

Hope, Marcus Laurence Hulbert; OBE,Consul General Montreal since July 1998; born 2.2.42; Third Secretary CRO 1965; MECAS 1966; Second Secretary (Inf) Tripoli 1968; FCO 1970; First Secretary Dubai 1974; First Secretary (Comm) Bonn 1976; FCO 1980; Counsellor NDC Rome 1984; Counsellor Beirut 1984; Counsellor FCO 1985; Head of Chancery Berne 1985; Counsellor (Comm) Jakarta later Deputy Head of Mission 1989; Counsellor FCO 1992; HM Ambassador Kinshasa additionally HM Ambassador to the Republic of Congo (non-resident) 1996; m 1980 Uta Maria Luise Müller-Unverfehrt (1s 1985).

Hopkins, Kathleen Elizabeth; Paris since December 1999; FCO 1994; Vienna 1996; language training 1999; Band A2.

Hopkinson, Celia Lois; FCO since September 1995; born 9.10.59; FCO 1979; UKMIS New York 1982; Sofia 1984; Paris 1986; FCO 1988; Lusaka 1992; Band B3.

Hopkinson, Moira Elizabeth; FCO since April 1994; born 28.8.59; FCO 1980; Copenhagen 1982; Peking 1985; Islamabad 1986; FCO 1990; Beirut 1992; Band B3.

Hopper, Colin David; FCO since March 1982; born 31.10.53; FCO 1971; Paris 1979; Band C4; m 1979 Lesley Greaves.

Hopton, Nicholas Dunster; First Secretary (Political) Rome since October 2000; born 8.10.65; FCO 1989; Second Secretary (Political/Information) Rabat 1991; First Secretary FCO 1995; m 1993 Maria Alejandra Echenique.

Horine, Fern Marion; Second Secretary (Political) Baku since August 2000; born 28.7.69; FCO 1987;

UKDEL Vienna 1990; FCO 1995; On loan to the DTI 1998; Band C4.

Horne, Gordon; FCO since September 1994; born 5.12.66; FCO 1986; Riyadh 1988; UKMIS New York 1992; Band B3; m 1989 Susan Lisa Berry.

Horne, Michael John, OBE (1996); Counsellor (Commercial) Kuala Lumpur since June 2000; born 29.5.44; FO 1961; Bucharest 1965; Bangkok 1967; Accra 1971; FCO 1975; Second Secretary (Comm) Kuala Lumpur 1978; Second later First Secretary Libreville 1981; on loan to No 10 Downing Street 1985; Consul (Inf) and Deputy Director, later Director BIS New York 1987; FCO 1992; on loan to World War II Commemorations Team, MOD 1994; Counsellor on loan to the Cabinet Office (Office of Deputy Prime Minister) 1995; Consul-General Perth 1997; m 1965 Deborah Elaine Hopkinson (1s 1966; 1d 1971).

Horner, Katharine Sarah Julia; First Secretary Political (Internal) Moscow since July 1997; born 15.8.52; FCO 1980; Moscow 1985; Senior Research Officer FCO 1987; PRO 1996.

Horner, Simon; Canberra since May 1998; born 10.12.69; DHSS 1987; FCO 1988; Nassau 1991; Floater Duties 1993; FCO 1995; Band B3; m 1995 Katherine Jean Gallager.

Horton-Jones, Sarah Caroline; Second Secretary FCO since July 1998; born 13.10.68; Lord Chancellor's Department 1991-93; FCO 1993.

Hosie, Angela June (née Binns); SUPL since July 1999; born 25.6.69; MOD 1988-1990; FCO 1990; New Delhi 1994; Accra 1997; Band C4; m 1993 Colin Hosie (1s 1995).

Hosker, Colin; FCO since January 1983; born 24.1.42; FO 1964; Delhi 1965; FO 1967; Baghdad 1968; FCO 1969; Peking 1970; FCO 1972; St Helena 1974; FCO 1976; Tripoli 1976; FCO 1979; Havana 1980; Band C4; m 1973 Joan Lavinia Martin (1s 1977; 1d 1979).

Hosking, Simon Paul; First Secretary (Science and Technology) New Delhi since January 2001; born 15.6.71; FCO 1993; Second Secretary Santiago 1997; First Secretary FCO 1999; Band D6; m 1995 Allison Jane Christou. (2d 1998,1999).

House, Gregory Stewart; Floater Duties since May 1999; born 3.6.68; FCO 1988; Lilongwe 1991; Lagos 1995; Band B3.

Houston, Sharon (Sher) Linda; Islamabad since July 1998; born 14.06.68; FCO 1989; Bridgetown 1991; UKREP Brussels 1995; Band B3; m 1993 Steve Giovanni Campbell (diss 1997); (1s 1996).

Howard, Alayne Anne (née Whitehouse); First Secretary FCOS since April 2000; born 4.6.63; FCO 1982; New Delhi 1985; Third Secretary (Consular) Bridgetown 1989; SUPL 1992; Second Secretary FCO 1993; Second Secretary (Immigration) Islamabad 1996; FCO 1997; Band C5; m 1984 Paul Howard (2s 1987, 1988).

Howard, (Charles Andrew) Paul, Second Secretary FCOS since November 1999; born 23.9.60; FCO 1983; New Delhi 1985; Third Secretary Bridgetown 1989; FCO 1992; Third Secretary (Consular) Islamabad 1996; FCO 1997; Band C4; m 1984 Alayne Anne Whitehouse (2s 1987, 1988).

Howard, Sarah Catherine (nee Sullivan); Harare since December 1998; born 5.11.68; FCO 1987; Kingston 1989; Tehran 1993; FCO 1995; Band B3; m 1989 Simon James Howard.

Howarth, Stephen Frederick; Minister Paris since November 1997; born 25.2.47; FCO 1966; Vice Consul Rabat 1971; Third later Second Secretary Washington 1975; Second later First Secretary FCO 1980; Seconded ENA Paris 1982; First Secretary FCO 1984; Deputy Head of Mission Dakar 1984; First Secretary FCO 1988; Counsellor and Deputy Head of PUSD 1990; Head of Consular Department later Division 1992; m 1966 Jennifer Mary Chrissop (2d 1966, 1970; 1s 1974).

Howden, Yvonne Catherine Helen; Prague since April 2000; born 6.3.73; FCO 1997; Luanda 1998; FCO 1999; Band A2.

Howe-Jones, Vanessa Jane; T/D UKREP Brussels since November 2000; born 23.6.65; FCO 1991; Full-time Language Training 1992; Second Secretary (KHF) Budapest 1993; First Secretary FCO 1996.

Howel, Iwan Gruffydd; Peking since June 1999; born 5.1.68; FCO 1988; Washington 1991; Brasilia 1994; Band B3.

Howells, Julie (née Satchell); SUPL since July 2001; born 3.6.64; FCO 1982; UKDEL Nato Brussels 1986; Seoul 1991; Dar es Salaam 1996; Band B3; m 1991 David Howells.

Howitt, Derrick; Istanbul since May 1999; born 14.2.43; Royal Navy 1958-83; Moscow 1983; Paris 1985; Singapore 1988; Colombo 1991; Floater 1995; Band B3; m 1966 Averil E Rose (1d 1968; 1s 1972).

Howlett, David John; FCO since June 1982; born 17.1.55; Principal Research Officer; m 1979 Bridget Mary de Boer.

Howlett, Keith Raymond; FCO since 1998; born 29.3.50; FCO 1968; Moscow 1980; FCO 1982; Tokyo 1986; Second Secretary FCO 1989; Second Secretary Caracas 1994; m 1984 Claudine Cecile Odette Stedman.(diss 1998) (2) 1998 Natasha Mota Hurtado (1step d 1996)

Huckle, Alan Edden; Counsellor, Head of OSCE/Council of Europe Department FCO since August 1998; born 15.6.48; Civil Service Department 1971; on loan to Northern Ireland Office 1974; Civil Service Department 1975; on loan to Northern Ireland Office 1978; First Secretary FCO 1980; Executive Director British Information Services, New York 1983; Head of Chancery Manila 1987; First Secretary FCO 1990; Counsellor and Deputy Head of Delegation UKDEL CSCE Vienna 1992; Head of Dependent Territories Regional Secretariat Bridgetown 1996; m 1973 Helen Myra Gibson (1s 1981; 1d 1985).

Huckle, Steven Allan; First Secretary Moscow since August 2000; born 24.10.64; FCO 1981; UKREP Brussels 1989; FCO 1992; Sofia 1994; FCO 1997; Band C5; m 1987 Alison Elaine Porter (1s 1990, 1d 1991).

Hudman, Anne (née Lister); Third Secretary (Commercial) Vienna Embassy since February 1999; born 1.9.62; FCO 1987; Helsinki 1989; FCO 1992; Bonn 1993; St Petersburg 1996; Band B3; m 1991 Roger Grenville Hudman.

Hudson, James Alexander; St Petersburg since December 2000; born 14.1.72; FCO 1994; Havana 1996; FCO 1998; Tirana 1999; T/D Budapest 2000; T/D Skopje 2000; Band B3; m 1996 Sally Barrett (diss 1997) (1d 1995).

Hudson, Julie Marie; Gaborone since August 1988; born 25.5.65; FCO 1984; Riyadh 1986; Band A2.

Huggins, Elaine Anne; Lisbon since July 1998; born 4.5.59; WRAC 1978-82; MOD 1983-86; FCO 1997; Band A2; m Michael James Huggins.

Huggins, Elizabeth June; SUPL since May 1998; born 25.6.70; DSS 1987; FCO 1989; Copenhagen 1992; FCO 1993; Budapest 1995; Band A2; m 1997 Phillip David Culligan (1d 1999).

Hughes, Beverley Elizabeth (née Lewis); SUPL since January 1998; born 22.7.66; HCS 1985; FCO 1985; Karachi 1987; Africa/ME Floater Duties 1991; FCO 1994; m Peter John Hughes 1997; Band B3.

Hughes, Brendan Christopher; Second Secretary (Political) Islamabad since October 1999; born 31.10.71; FCO 1996; Band C4.

Hughes, Edgar John; HM Ambassador Caracas since May 2000; born 27.7.47; FCO 1973; On secondment to Cabinet Office 1979; First Secretary CSCE Madrid 1981; FCO 1982; First Secretary and Head of Chancery Santiago 1983; First Secretary (Inf) Washington 1985; First Secretary later Counsellor FCO 1989; Deputy Head of Mission Oslo 1993; Change Manager, FCO 1997; On secondment to BAe Systems 1999; m 1982 Lynne Evans (2s 1984, 1988).

Hughes, Ian Noël; Deputy Head of Mission Mexico City since July 2000; born 5.12.51; FCO 1971; Latin America Floater 1974; Kabul 1976; Warsaw 1980; FCO 1982; Second Secretary and Vice-Consul Tegucigalpa 1985; First Secretary (Pol) Berne 1988; First Secretary FCO 1993; First Secretary (Press/Information) New Delhi 1993; First Secretary FCO 1997; m 1978 Teresa June Tinguely (2s 1979, 1981; 1d 1984).

Hughes, Peter John; Acting High Commissioner Castries since January 1998; born 14.9.53; FCO 1976; Islamabad 1978; Rome 1980; Warsaw 1983; FCO 1985 (Second Secretary 1987); Vice-Consul (Comm) Sydney 1989; Second later First Secretary FCO 1994; m(1) 1978 Jacqueline

Alexander (diss 1987), (2) Beverley Elizabeth Lewis 1997.

Hulands, Michael Robert; FCO since February 2000; born 29.11.53; FCO 1970; Singapore 1976; Tel Aviv 1978; FCO 1981; Third Secretary Bangkok 1983; Addis Ababa 1986; FCO 1990; Second Secretary Bonn 1995; FCO 1998; North American IT Advisor Washington 1999; m 1979 Normah Binti Maznun (2d 1981, 1986).

Hulbert, Neil Peter; Berlin since January 1997; born 21.6.63; FCO 1995; Band A2.

Hum, Christopher Owen, CMG (1996); HM Ambassador Beijing w.e.f. March 2002; born 27.1.46; FO 1967; Hong Kong 1968; Peking 1971; Second later First Secretary/Private Secretary to Permanent Representative UKREP Brussels 1973; FCO 1975; First Secretary Peking 1979; First Secretary (Chancery) Paris 1981; First Secretary FCO 1983; Counsellor and Deputy Head of Falkland Islands Department FCO 1985; Counsellor FCO 1986; Counsellor and Head of Chancery UKMIS New York 1989; AUSS (Northern Asia and the Pacific) FCO 1992; HM Ambassador Warsaw 1996; Chief Clerk 1998; m 1970 Julia Mary Park (1d 1974; 1s 1976).

Humfrey, Charles Thomas William, CMG (1999); HM Ambassador Seoul since August 2000; born 1.12.47; Third Secretary FCO 1969; Language student Sheffield University 1970; Tokyo 1971 (Second Secretary 1972, First Secretary 1976); FCO 1976; Private Secretary to Minister of State 1979; UKMIS New York 1981; First Secretary FCO 1985; Counsellor Ankara 1988; Tokyo 1990; Counsellor FCO 1994; Minister Tokyo 1995; m 1971 Enid Wyn Thomas (2s 1975, 1983; 1d 1977).

Humphreys, Lucy Ann Marie; Peking since June 2001; born 17.6.72; FCO 1993; T/D CHOGM Auckland 1995; T/D UKREP Brussels 1996; UKMIS New York 1996; T/D Brussels Embassy 1998; T/D Helsinki 1998; SUPL 1999; FCO 2000; Band A2.

Humphreys, Nita (née Saha); FCO since December 1998; born 23.12.69; FCO 1990; SUPL 1998; Band B3; m 1997 Phillip David Humphreys (1d 1998).

Humphries, Eric Henri Edward; Dhaka since March 1995; 1992; born 11.10.59; FCO 1978; Islamabad 1982; Nairobi 1984; Victoria 1987; FCO 1990; Zagreb 1992; FCO 1993; Band B3; m 1982 Sara Dorothy Watts (1d 1984).

Hunt, Peter Lawrence, CMG (2001); Consul General Istanbul since February 1997; born 10.6.45; FO 1962; DSAO 1965; Africa Floater duties 1967; Brussels 1969; Managua 1970; FCO 1973; Second Secretary (Comm) Caracas 1978; First Secretary FCO 1982; Head of Chancery Montevideo 1987; FCO 1990; Deputy Head of Mission Santiago 1993; m 1971 Anne Langhorne Carson (2d 1972, 1977; 2s 1974, 1984).

Hunt, Sara Jennifer; Third Secretary (Political) Warsaw since October 1999; born 29.10.67; FCO

1987; Bonn 1990; Full-time Language Training 1993; Latin America/Caribbean Floater 1993; FCO 1995; Band B3.

Hunt, Stephen Anthony; Second Secretary (Political) Vienna since January 1999; born 3.9.57; MOD 1977; FCO 1978; Lisbon 1981; Prague 1984; Gaborone 1986; Moscow 1988; FCO 1990; La Paz 1994; Full time language training 1997; Band C4; m 1984 Eileen Crossan (2s 1994, 1s 1996).

Hunt, Stephen Paul; First Secretary FCO Services since 1998; born 13.1.61; FCO 1993; Brussels 1994; FCO 1997.

Hunter, David Eric; Third Secretary (Political) Kiev since May 1998; born 8.12.71; FCO 1989; Band B3; m2000 Peta Leigh Brennan.

Hunter, Paulette Elaine; Nairobi since August 2001; born 17.10.65; FCO 1985; Lagos 1987; Peking 1990; Bridgetown 1993; T/D Islamabad 1997; FCO 1997; Band B3.

Hunter, Robert; Second Secretary (Management) and Consul Sana'a since September 2000; born 10.8.47; HM Forces 1964-70; Merchant Navy 1973-74; FCO 1974; Darwin 1975; Beirut 1976; Peking 1977; FCO 1979; Lilongwe 1980; Jedda 1981; FCO 1984; Pretoria 1985; FCO 1988; Vice-Consul (Consular/Management) Suva 1989; Full Time Language Training 1994; Deputy Head of Mission Antananarivo 1995; Second Secretary FCO 1997; FTLT 2000; Band C5; m 1981 Carol Mary Chorley.

Hunter, Sally; Karachi since January 1985; born 10.12.65; FCO 1985; Band A2.

Hunter, Wendy; FCO since September 1987; born 9.11.67; Band B3.

Huntington, Janet Elizabeth (née Bull); First Secretary FCO since July 2001; born 22.9.63; FCO 1986; Third later Second Secretary (Chancery) Managua 1988; Second Secretary (Chancery) Lisbon 1990; Second later First Secretary FCO 1993; First Secretary (Political) Caracas 1995; First Secretary (Trade Policy) New Delhi 1997; Band D6; m 1995 Daniel Peter Huntington(2d 1997, 1999).

Hurd, Thomas Robert Benedict; First Secretary Amman since April 1998; born 22.9.64; FCO 1992; Language Training 1994; First Secretary (Political) Warsaw 1995; Band C4; m 1994 Katherine Siân Aubrey (2s 1996, 1998; 1d 1997).

Hustwitt, Justin John; First Secretary (Regional Affairs) Kampala since April 2001; born 8.9.67; FCO 1991; Full-time Language Training 1992; Language Training Cairo 1993; Second Secretary (Political) Cairo 1994; Second Secretary (Commercial) Riyadh 1995; First Secretary FCO 1997; Band D6.

Hutchison, Jacqueline Margaret (née Wigzell); Third later Second Secretary FCO since July 1997; born 12.5.65; FCO 1987; Third Secretary (Comm) Berlin 1990; Third Secretary Port of Spain 1993;

Band C4; m 1993 Ian James Hutchison (1s 1995; 2d 2000).

Hyde, Richard Damian; Vice Consul Paris since March 1995; born 18.9.69; FCO 1989; Hamilton 1991; Band B3; m 1994 Jacqueline Pearl Sadio.

Hyde, Richard Wingfield, MBE (1981); First Secretary/Deputy Head of Mission Karachi since March 1999. born 29.3.42; Board of Trade 1965; FCO 1968; Vienna 1971; Rangoon 1974; Brussels (EC) 1976; FCO 1980; West Africa Floater 1983; Second Secretary Antananarivo 1984; Second Secretary (Admin) and Vice Consul Yaoundé 1988; First Secretary/Principal Welfare Officer FCO 1992; Dakar 1995; m 1985 Ana Julie Rasoanaivo.

Hyland, Mark; Sarajevo since October 2000; FCO 1990; born 3.7.69; HCS 1986; UKDEL NATO Brussels 1993; T/D UKMIS New York 1995; Belgrade 1996; SUPL 1999; Band A2; m 1992 Deborah Jane Tomlinson.

Hyland, Susan Margaret; Private Secretary to the Permanent Under Secretary since June 2001; born 30.10.64; Second Secretary FCO 1990; Second Secretary (Political) Oslo 1992; UKMIS New York 1992; Second Secretary UKDEL OECD 1993; ENA Paris 1994; First Secretary FCO 1996; First Secretary (Political) Moscow 2000; Band D7.

Hyne, Sarah Jean; UKMIS New York since August 2001; born 20.4.74; FCO 1999; PA to Deputy Heads of Economic Policy 1999; Band A2.

I

Ingamells, John Mawgan; SUPL since December 1999; born 8.6.61; FCO 1984; Language Training Seoul 1985; Third Secretary (Chancery) Seoul 1987; Third Secretary (Comm) later Second Secretary (Inf) Buenos Aires 1990; Second later First Secretary FCO 1994; on secondment to Fidelity Investments 1999; m 1990 Nicola Jane Dobb (2s 1991, 1993).

Ingham, Christopher John; HM Ambassador Tashkent since June 1999; born 4.6.44; FCO 1968; Moscow 1972; Calcutta 1974; Kuwait 1975; Second Secretary 1976; FCO 1977; First Secretary and Deputy Permanent Representative UKMIS Vienna 1981; First Secretary FCO 1985; First Secretary (Comm) Mexico City 1987; First Secretary FCO 1989; Counsellor and Deputy Head of Mission Bucharest 1991; Counsellor (Economic/EU) Madrid 1995; m 1968 Jacqueline Anne Clarke (1s 1971; 2d 1973, 1985).

Ingle, Alan Richmond, CMG (2000); Head of Delegation JMO Brussels since April 1996; born 16.10.39; Board of Trade 1957; Accra (Trade Commission Service) 1961; FO 1965; Kingston 1966; Christchurch 1970; FCO 1974; Second Secretary (Comm) Singapore 1977; Second later First Secretary FCO 1981; Consul (Inf) BIS New York 1983; First Secretary FCO 1988, Counsellor (Management) Lagos 1993; m,1963 Gillian Marsha Hall (1d 1965; 1s 1968).

Inglehearn, Catherine Mary; Third Secretary Ljubljiana since April 1996; born 15.5.65; FCO 1990; Rome 1992; Band B3.

Ingold, Andrew Henrik; FCO since September 1994; born 30.7.53; Customs and Excise 1972; FCO 1973; Valletta 1975; Monrovia 1978; Paris 1982; FCO 1984; Bombay 1987; Vice Consul Abu Dhabi 1990; Band B3.

Ingram, Rachel Victoria; World Wide Floater Duties since December 1998; born 25.4.69; FCO 1994; Berne 1996; Band C4.

Inkster, Nigel Norman; Counsellor FCO since January 1998; born 11.4.52; Third Secretary FCO 1975; Language Student1/Third Secretary Kuala Lumpur 1976; Third later Second Secretary FCO 1976; Second later First Secretary Bangkok 1979; FCO 1982; First Secretary and Consul Peking 1983; Buenos Aires 1985; First Secretary FCO 1989; Counsellor Athens 1992; Counsellor BTC Hong Kong 1994; m 1977 Leong Chui Fun (1d 1980; 1s 1981).

Innes, Stuart Harcourt; Deputy Head of Mission Damascus since May 1999; born 30.10.55; FCO 1980; Doha 1983; Second Secretary Cairo 1986; First Secretary FCO 1989; Deputy Permanent Representative UKMIS New York 1993; m 1983 Susan Jane Wood (1s 1987; 1d 1989).

Innes-Hopkins, Christopher Randolph; First Secretary (Commercial) Ankara since June 2001; born 26.11.53; FCO 1976; Georgetown 1979; Paris 1982; Second Secretary FCO 1985; Second Secretary Tunis 1988; Deputy Consul General Jerusalem 1993; on secondment to the European Union 1997; First Secretary FCO 1999; m 1983 Soraya Nizamodin Dookie (1s 1986, 1d 1993).

Insall, Anthony John Godwin LVO (1986); Counsellor Oslo since April 1999; born 27.6.49; FCO 1973; Third later Second Secretary (Inf) Lagos 1975; Second later First Secretary FCO 1977; Language Training Hong Kong 1982; First Secretary FCO 1983; First and Consul Peking 1985; First Secretary FCO 1988; Counsellor Kuala Lumpur 1992; Counsellor FCO 1995; m 1979 Leonie Bridget Meryon (3s 1980, 1982, 1984).

Insall, Christopher Wharton; FCO since October 1984; born 31.12.45; FCO 1966; Jedda 1970; FCO 1971; Paris 1981; Band B3; m 1982 Lynn Melrose Irvine.

Ives, Malcolm Albert; First Secretary (Commercial) Accra since November 1997; born 10.3.47; MPNI 1964; FO (later FCO) 1966; Dacca 1969; FCO 1971; Sana'a 1973; Addis Ababa 1974; Warsaw 1976; FCO 1978; São Paulo 1981; Jakarta 1985; Second Secretary (Dev) Amman 1987; Second Secretary FCO 1991; on loan to the DTI 1992; Second Secretary (Commercial) Riyadh 1994; m 1973 Susan Robertson (3s 1969, 1974, 1976).

Ives, Susan; SUPL since October 1997; born 8.2.44; FCO 1992; Riyadh 1994, Band A2, FCO 1997; m 1973 Malcolm Albert Ives (3s 1969, 1974, 1976).

Ivey, Peter Robert; First Secretary (Commercial) Zagreb since February 1996; born 25.5.58; FCO 1982; Bahrain 1983; Language Training 1987; Second Secretary (Inf/Chancery) Helsinki 1988; On loan to the London Chamber of Commerce 1992; On loan to the DTI 1993; Full-time Language Training 1995; Band C5; m Sally Helen Elizabeth Hill (1998) (2s 1998, 2000).

Ivey, Sally Helen Elizabeth (née Hill); SUPL since September 1998; born 25.10.65; FCO 1987; New Delhi 1988; FCO 1990; World-wide Floater 1992; Full-time Language Training 1995; Zagreb 1996; Band A2; m Peter Robert Ivey (2s 1998, 2000).

Ivins, Suzanne Gillian (née Parker); Second Secretary (Immigration) Shanghai since December 2000; born 5.2.65; FCO 1983; Tokyo 1985; FCO 1988; Third Secretary (Consular) Ottawa 1992; Third Secretary Ho Chi Minh City 1996; Band C4; m 1988 James Browell Ivins (1d 1994).

Ivory, Jason; New Delhi since July 2000; born 4.8.70; Madrid 1991; Bombay 1994; FCO 1998; Band B3; m 1992 Susannah Ruth Knowles (1s 1994, 1d 1995).

Izzard, Richard Brian George; FTLT since April 2000; born 4.1.69; Metropolitan Police 1987; FCO 1988; Sofia 1990; Accra 1992; World Wide Floater Duties 1993; FCO 1997; Luanda 2000; Band B3.

J

Jack, Stuart Duncan Macdonald, cvo (1994); Minister Tokyo since April 1999; born 8.6.49; FCO 1972; Third later Second later First Secretary Tokyo 1974; FCO 1979; First Secretary and Press Attaché Moscow 1981; First Secretary FCO 1984; Bank of England 1984; First Secretary (Econ) Tokyo 1985; Counsellor FCO 1989; HM Consul-General St Petersburg 1992; FCO 1996; m 1977 Mariko Nobechi (2d 1980, 1982, 1s 1986).

Jackson, Andrew Michael; Second Secretary FCO since July 1991; born 6.11.58; FCO 1984; Third Secretary (Chancery) Bonn 1987; Band C4; m 1987 Susan Elizabeth Welsh (2d 1989,1992).

Jackson, Anna Elizabeth; Second Secretary (EU) Warsaw since May 2001; born 8.6.78; FCO 1999; Band C4.

Jackson, Elizabeth Anne (née Irwin); SUPL First Secretary FCO since February 1992; born 8.8.55; FCO 1977; Moscow 1980; Second later First Secretary UKDEL NATO Brussels 1982; First Secretary FCO 1985; First Secretary FCO 1986; m 1981 Richard Charles Edward Jackson (2s 1986, 1988, 1d 1990).

Jackson, Freya; Second Secretary Buenos Aires since June 2000; born 10.4.74; FCO 1997; Support Officer UKMIS New York 1999; FTLT 2000; Band C4.

Jackson, Helen; SUPL since September 1999; born 27.1.62; FCO 1981; Stockholm 1983; Port of Spain 1986; Moscow 1990; Bridgetown 1993; FCO 1998; Band A2; (1d 1998).

Jackson, John, obe (1998); First Secretary FCO since July 1981; born 20.7.42; FO (later FCO) 1965; Tokyo 1970; FCO 1974; Attachment to Hong Kong Government 1978; Band C5; m 1966 Ann Marie Phelan (1s 1968; 2d 1970, 1976).

Jackson, Lee Barry Thomas; Vice Consul (Consular) Hong Kong since January 2000; born 2.7.65; FCO since July 1996; Full Time Language Training Hong Kong 1997; Band B3; m 1995 Vanda Morais-Jackson (diss 1999).

Jackson, Linda Margaret; On loan to the Cabinet Office since September 2000; born 21.12.46; FO 1965; Prague 1968; Santiago 1969; Moscow 1972; FCO 1973; UKDEL Vienna 1976; Peking 1978; FCO 1979; Paris 1981; FCO 1984; Brussels 1986; FCO 1989; Band B3.

Jackson, Paul Michael, mbe (2000); Helsinki since July 1999; born 5.4.63; HCS 1982; FCO 1983; Islamabad 1985; FCO 1987; Washington 1991; FCO 1994; Belgrade 1997; Band C4; m 1984 Cheryl Barrington (1d 1986, 1s 1988).

Jackson, Robert Frederick; Assistant Trade Commissioner BTC Hong Kong since June 1995; born 8.2.57; FCO 1975; Prague 1978; Bandar Seri Begawan 1979; Gaborone 1981; Sana'a 1987; FCO 1990; Band C4; m(1) 1977 Rosalind Barbara Sackett; (diss) (2d 1983, 1986) m(2) 1995 Maria Mouskovias.

Jackson-Houlston, William Lester, obe (1994); Counsellor The Hague since August 1999; born 6.10.52; FCO 1979; Second Secretary UKREP Brussels 1980; Second later First Secretary FCO 1981; BIS Buenos Aires 1982; FCO 1986; First Secretary Belgrade 1990; First Secretary FCO 1993; m 1985 Susana Olivia Fitzpatrick (twins, 1s and 1d 1989).

Jacobs, Kenneth Robert; First Secretary FCO since January 1999; born 10.1.46; GPO 1963; FCO 1969; Warsaw 1970; UKDEL NATO Brussels 1972; FCO 1975; Addis Ababa 1977; FCO 1980; Nicosia 1980; FCO 1983; Second Secretary Canberra 1986; FCO 1989; Second Secretary Buenos Aires 1991; FCO 1995; Second Secretary Lagos 1995; m 1967 Jacqueline Diane Leeks (1d 1969; 1s 1972).

Jacobs, Lisa Claire; Peking since November 1995; born 21.3.65; FCO 1986; Moscow 1988; Riyadh 1990; FCO 1993; Band B3.

Jacobsen, Neil Marius; First Secretary (Regional Affairs) Santiago since May 2000; born 16.6.57; Second Secretary FCO 1984; Second later First Secretary (Econ) Athens 1986; First Secretary FCO 1989; First Secretary (Political) Madrid 1992; First Secretary FCO 1996; Band D6; m 1982 Susan Clark (1d 1984; 2s 1988, 1990).

Jacobson, Charles Eugene; On loan to Oldham Chamber of Commerce since October 1999; born 17.9.64; FCO 1988; Third Secretary (Chancery) Tel Aviv 1991; FCO 1995; Manila 1995; Band B3; m 1993 Sarah Madeline Henry (1s 1997; 1d 1999).

James, Jeffrey Russell, KBE (2001), CMG (1994); High Commissioner Nairobi from July 1997 to December 2001; born 13.8.44; Third Secretary Commonwealth Office (later FCO) 1967; Tehran 1969; Third later Second Secretary Kabul 1970; First Secretary FCO 1973; BMG Berlin 1978; FCO 1982; Counsellor on loan to Cabinet Office 1984; Counsellor and Head of Chancery Pretoria/Cape Town 1986; Counsellor (Econ/Comm) New Delhi 1988; Head of European Council Unit (In Edinburgh) 1992; Chargé d'Affaires Tehran 1993; m 1965 Carol Mary Longden (2d 1965, 1969).

James, Neill; Manila since January 1998; born 6.7.71; FCO 1991; Dhaka 1994; Band A2; m 1997 Rangsiya Promsrisuk (1 step s 1990, 1s 1999).

James, Nia Llewelyn (née Hughes); FCO since November 1997; born 26.4.74; Band B3; m 1999 Christopher John James.

James, Nicola Patricia; FCO since September 1993; born 29.9.60; FCO 1980; Peking 1983; Kuala Lumpur 1985; Bandar Seri Begawan 1988; Band B3.

James, Stephen Anthony; Second Secretary (Management) Tokyo since April 1996; born 1.9.51; Customs and Excise 1968; FCO 1971; Saigon 1973; Peking 1975; Warsaw 1976; Manila 1977; Berne 1981; FCO 1984; Islamabad 1987; Third Secretary (Aid/Comm) Mbabane 1990; Second Secretary FCO 1994; m 1979 Nikki Jean Smith (2d 1980, 1982; 1s 1984).

Jamieson, Rachel Janet; Islamabad since November 1999; born 31.5.68; FCO 1993; Full-time Language Training 1995; Bucharest 1996; Band B3.

January, Dr Peter; Head of OSCE/CoE Department FCO since July 2001; born 13.1.52; FCO 1983; First Secretary (Comm) Budapest 1985; First Secretary FCO 1988; Consul and Deputy Head of Mission Maputo 1991; First Secretary later Counsellor FCO 1993; HM Ambassador Tirana 1999.

Jardine, Martine; Madrid since July 1993; born 27.9.70; FCO 1990; Band A2.

Jarrett, Anne; First Secretary (Economic) Bucharest since July 1997; born 26.1.60; FCO 1978; Moscow 1981; Africa/ME Floater 1984; UKDEL NATO Brussels 1986; Second Secretary (FCO) 1989; Second Secretary (Political) Peking 1993; Full Time Language Training 1997.

Jarrett, Caroline Julia Rachel; FCO since September 1999; born 7.9.76; Band C4.

Jarrold, Nicholas Robert; HM Ambassador Zagreb since August 2000; born 2.3.46; Third Secretary FCO 1968; Third later Second Secretary The Hague 1969; Dakar 1972; First Secretary FCO 1975; Nairobi 1979 (Head of Chancery 1983); FCO 1983; Counsellor and Deputy Head of Mission Havana 1989; CDA at St Antony's College Oxford University 1991; Counsellor

(Commercial/Economic) Brussels 1992; HM Ambassador Riga 1996; m 1972 Anne Catherine Whitworth (2s 1976, 1979).

Jarvie, Carole Marina; ECO Istanbul since June 2000; born 26.9.54; FCO 1984; The Hague 1986; Canberra 1989; UKDEL Brussels 1992; FCO 1998; Band B3.

Jarvis, Russell Thomas; Deputy Head of Mission Stanley since January 1997; born 27.9.47; Commonwealth Office (later FCO) 1964; Sofia 1969; EC Brussels 1972; Sana'a 1972; Islamabad 1973; FCO 1975; Dar es Salaam 1978 (Second Secretary 1979); Vice-Consul (Comm) BTDO New York 1982; First Secretary FCO 1986; First Secretary (Management) BTC Hong Kong 1990; First Secretary FCO 1994; m 1969 Joan Ann Wyard (2s 1971, 1986; 1d 1973).

Jay, Sir Michael Hastings, KCMG (1997), CMG (1992); Permanent Under Secretary of State and Head of the Diplomatic Service since January 2002; born 19.6.46; ODM 1969; UKDEL IMF/IBRD Washington 1973; ODM 1975; First Secretary (Dev) New Delhi 1978; First Secretary FCO 1981; Private Secretary to Permanent Under Secretary of State FCO 1982; Counsellor on loan to Cabinet Office 1985; Counsellor (Fin/Comm) Paris 1987; AUSS (European Community) FCO 1990; HM Ambassador Paris 1996; m 1975 Sylvia Mylroie.

Jebb, Christopher Quayle Gladwyn; Second Secretary FCO since March 1996; born 2.10.50; FCO 1970; Caribbean Floater 1973; Vientiane 1975; Düsseldorf 1978; FCO 1980; Tristan da Cunha 1982; Istanbul 1984; FCO 1987; Second Secretary (Head of Chancery) Asunción 1988; Second Secretary (Commercial/Information) Kingston 1991; Mexico City 1992; m 1975 Maria Aida Hoyos (1d 1979; 1s 1981).

Jeenes, Kelley Elizabeth, Nairobi since August 1995; born 23.2.71; FCO 1992; Band A2.

Jeffrey, Frieda King (née Rolland); Bridgetown since April 2000; born 17.10.63; FCO 1988; UKRep Brussels 1990; Manila 1993; FCO 1996; Uganda 1997; Band A2; m 1997 Bruce Jeffrey.

Jeffrey, John Peacock Reid; Second Secretary FCO since February 1996; born 4.4.53; FCO 1971; Jakarta 1974; Singapore 1975; Africa Floater 1977; FCO 1980; Mexico City 1982; Bucharest 1986; Second Secretary FCO 1988; Second Secretary (Commercial/ Consular/Management) Montevideo 1992; m 1980 Arlene Elizabeth Watson (1s 1991).

Jeffreys, Stella Ann; FCO since December 1999; born 16.11.62; FCO 1990; Dar es Salaam 1992; Hannoi 1996; Band A2.

Jenkins, John, LVO (1989); HM Ambassador Rangoon since April 1999; born 26.1.55; Second Secretary FCO 1980; Second later First Secretary Abu Dhabi 1983; First Secretary FCO 1986; First Secretary and Head of Chancery Kuala Lumpur 1989; First Secretary FCO 1992; Deputy Head of

Mission Kuwait 1995; SOAS University of
London 1998; m 1982 Nancy Caroline Pomfret.

Jenkins, Owen John; FCO since January 1998;
born 21.8.69; FCO 1991; Full-time Language
Training 1993 Third/Second Secretary
(Political/Information) Ankara 1994; m 1998
Catherine Margaret Baker.

Jenkins, Paul David; Yaoundé since May 2000;
born 22.6.51; FCO 1968; Bonn 1972; FCO 1974;
Prague 1974; Monrovia 1976; Kaduna 1978; FCO
1981; Nairobi 1984; Gaborone 1986; Second
Secretary FCO 1990; Second Secretary
(Commercial) Lagos 1992; First Secretary
(Commercial) Islamabad 1996; m(1)1972 Jennifer
Whitmarsh (diss) (2s 1976, 1979) (2) 1987 Elaine
Vera Walsh (née Avery).

Jenkins, Peter Redmond; UK Permanent
Representative Vienna with Personal rank of
Ambassador since August 2001; born 2.3.50; FCO
1973; Third later Second Secretary
(UNIDO/IAEA) Vienna 1975; First Secretary FCO
1978; First Secretary and PS to HM Ambassador
Washington 1982; First Secretary FCO 1984; First
Secretary (Econ) Paris 1987; Minister/Counsellor,
Consul-General and Deputy Head of Mission
Brasilia 1992; Minister and Deputy Permanent
Representative UKMIS Geneva 1996; m 1990
Angelina Chee-Hong Yang (1d 1992, 1s 1994).

Jenkinson, Eric; First Secretary Tehran since
August 1999; born 13.3.50; FO 1967; EC Brussels
1971; Islamabad 1973; Second Secretary (Comm)
Jedda 1978; Second Secretary FCO 1982; First
Secretary (Econ) Bonn 1986; Consul and Deputy
Head of Mission Bahrain 1992; First Secretary, FCO
1995; m 1973 Kathleen Forster (2s 1980, 1981).

Jenkinson, Gale Louise; São Paulo since March
2000; born 24.11.63; FCO 1984; Islamabad 1986;
Ottawa 1989; FCO 1992; Third Secretary
(Management) and Vice Consul Doha 1996; Band
C4; m 1990 Tony Takashi Baba (1d 1992).

Jennings, Katharine Mary; Second Secretary FCO
since January 1998; born 20.9.65; FCO 1990;
Full-time Language Training FCO 1992. Full-time
Language Training Peking 1993; Second Secretary
(Political) Peking 1994; Band C4; m 1994
Anthony Donald Thomas Pincham (2d 1998,
2000).

Jennings, Kay (née Henderson); Nicosia since
October 2001; born 27.2.72; FCO 1993; Band A2;
m2000 Richard Llewellyn Jennings.

Jennison, Vanessa Sandford; Vice-Consul
Amsterdam since April 2000; born 25.2.64; FCO
1988; Third Secretary UKMIS Geneva 1990; FCO
1993; Vice-Consul Paris 1995; SUPL 1998; m
1989 Geoffrey John Peck (2s 1993, 1997).

Jermey, Dominic James Robert, OBE (2001); FCO
since October 2000; born 26.4.67; FCO 1993; FTLT
1994; Second Secretary (Political/Information)
Islamabad 1995; First Secretary Afghanistan 1998;
T/D Skopje 1999; T/D Dili 2000; Band D6.

Joad, Kate Louise; Second Secretary FCO since
July 1999; born 18.3.69; FCO 1990; Tokyo 1992;
Floater Duties 1996; T/D Pretoria 1999; Band C4.

de Jeune d'Allegeershecque, Susan Jane (née
Miller); Deputy Head of Mission Caracas since
September 1999; born 29.4.63; FCO 1985;
UKREP Brussels 1987 (Second Secretary 1989);
FCO 1990; Second Secretary
(Economic/Information) Singapore 1992; First
Secretary FCO 1995; m 1991 Stephane Herv
Marie le Jeune d'Allegeershecque (2s 1993, 1995).

Johns, Allison Marie; Damascus since August
2000; born 20.11.66; FCO 1988; Washington
1991; Bonn 1993; FCO 1997; Band A2.

Johnsen, Emma Louise (née Williams); SUPL
since September 1998; born 23.2.66; FCO 1990;
UKMIS Geneva 1993; FCO 1996; Band B3; m
1992 Per-Arne Johnsen.

Johnson, Alison Jane (née Sindon); FCO since
March 1999; born 16.11.63; FCO 1983; Mexico
City 1985; Asunción 1988; FCO 1991; Sofia 1995;
SUPL 1997; Band B3; m 1997 Clive Andrew
Johnson.

Johnson, Christine; Dakar since August 2001;
born 12.4.73; FCO 1997; Budapest 1998; FTLT
2001; Band A2.

Johnson, George Michael; Dhaka since April
1999; born 10.1.43; Post Office 1960; FO 1961;
Kinshasa 1965; Moscow 1967; Paris 1968; FCO
1971; Lagos 1973; Sofia 1976; FCO 1979 (Second
Secretary 1980); Vice-Consul (Comm) Toronto
1984; First Secretary (Admin) Brasilia 1988; First
Secretary FCO 1994; Harare 1995; m 1971 Anne
Marion Little (diss) (1s 1971); (2) m1992 Cecilia
Da Conceicao Dos Santos Rodrigues.

Johnson, Helen (née Matthews); SUPL since
September 2000; born 27.3.62; FCO 1981; Dhaka
1984; Moscow 1985; Tunis 1985; Berne 1988;
FCO 1991; Islamabad 1994; San José 1998; Band
B3; m(1) 1987 R B L Marzouk (diss 1999) (1s
1994), (2) 2000 Ridha Ben Larbi.

Johnson, Julie Michelle; Second Secretary
(Consular) Kuala Lumpur since September 2000;
born 12.11.63; FCO 1983; Port Stanley 1985; FCO
1986; Vienna 1987; Hong Kong 1990; FCO May
1991; Bombay 1993; FCO 1993; Third Secretary
(Management) and Vice-Consul Guatemala City
1996; Band C4.

Johnson, Katrina; SUPL since June 2001; born
10.3.66; FCO 1985; Paris 1987; FCO 1990; SUPL
1992; Third Secretary (Institutions) UKREP
Brussels 1993; On loan to the ODA/DFID 1996;
SUPL 1998; Second Secretary (Economic/Trade
Policy) New Delhi 1999; Band D6; m 1994
Richard Adam Noble (2s 1996 1998).

Johnson, Matthew Alfred; on loan to No 10
Downing Street since July 1999; born 11.6.70;
FCO 1988; Cape Town/Pretoria 1990; FCO 1993;
Osaka 1994; FCO 1996; Band C5; m 1993 Heidi
Suzanne Burton (1s 1997; 1d 1999).

Johnson, Sandra Lissenden; FCO since July 1999; born 13.2.43; FCO 1970; Washington 1971; Resigned 1973; Reinstated 1982; UKDEL CSCE Madrid 1982; Moscow 1983; Rangoon 1984; FCO 1987; Helsinki 1992; Nairobi 1995; Seconded to the Cabinet Office 1998-1999; Band B3.

Johnson, Simon William; Third Secretary (Visits) Peking since July 1996; born 26.5.64; FCO 1983; Budapest 1987; Istanbul 1989; FCO 1993.

Johnson, Stuart James; Second Secretary (Pol/Mil) Banja Luka on secondment to MOD since November 2000; born 8.5.72; Second Secretary FCO 1998; Band C4.

Johnson, Tamsin Jane; Addis Ababa since February 1991; born 15.1.70; FCO 1989; Band A2.

Johnson, Walter George Devon, MBE (1982); Deputy Consul-General Auckland since July 1998; born 28.6.44; FO 1963; Mexico City 1965; Sofia 1968; FCO 1969; Wellington 1970; Bogotá 1973; FCO 1975; UKDEL NATO Brussels 1978; Caracas 1981; Second Secretary, Bursar, Wiston House 1983; Second Secretary (Comm) Abidjan 1987; Second later First Secretary (Management) JMO New York 1990; First Secretary FCO 1995; m 1989 Margaret Murray-Lee (2d 1969, 1972).

Johnston, Elizabeth Ann (née Barker); SUPL since October 1987; born 2.12.57; FCO 1978; Belgrade 1980; FCO 1982; Pretoria/Cape Town 1983; FCO 1986; Band A2; m 1987 Paul Neville Johnston.

Johnston, Paul Charles; FCO since May 1999; born 29.5.68; MOD 1990-93; FCO 1993; PS/Lord Owen (International Conference on Former Yugoslavia) 1994; Second Secretary (PS/HMA) Paris 1995; Second Secretary (Political)Paris 1997.

Johnstone, James; Hong Kong since July 1998; born 16.3.44; Army 1962-88; New York 1988; Peking 1991; UKMIS Geneva 1992; T/D Moscow 1995; Moscow 1996; Band B3; m(1) 1967 Patricia Anne Strong (1d 1968, 2s 1969, 1974) (diss 1983); (2) 1986 Rachel Baliti (1s 1991).

Johnstone, Lauren Clair (née Blagburn); Gibraltar since July 1997; born 21.7.70; FCO 1989; SUPL 1992; Scottish Office 1992; FCO 1993; Band B3; m 1992 Andrew Johnstone (Diss 1999).

Johnstone, Peter; Governor Anguilla since January 2000; born 30.7.44; FO 1962; Berne 1965; Benin City 1966; Budapest 1968; Maseru 1969; FCO 1973; Second Secretary 1975; Second Secretary (Chancery) Dacca 1977; First Secretary (local rank) Dublin 1979; First Secretary FCO 1983; First Secretary (Comm) Harare 1986; Consul-General Edmonton 1989; First Secretary FCO 1991; Counsellor (Commercial/Development) Jakarta 1995; m 1969 Diane Claxton (1s 1971; 1d 1977).

Jones, Alison; World Wide Floater since 1999; born 19.12.72; DSS 1995; FCO 1998; Band A2.

Jones, Amanda Louise; Baku since January 2001; born 16.3.69. FCO 1997; Kigali 1998; Band A2.

Jones, Andrew; FCO since August 2000; born 2.3.67; FCO 1988; Hong Kong 1997; Band C4; m 1989 Lisa Roberts (1d 1993, 2s 1997, 2000).

Jones, Andrew Martin; Copenhagen since March 2000; born 14.12.59; FCO 1980; Darwin 1981; FCO 1984; Singapore 1986; FCO 1989; Third Secretary Amman 1993; FCO 1997; Band C4; m 1985 Amanda Wainer (1s 1988, 1d 1990).

Jones, Annabel Nicole (née Russ) FCO since November 1994; born 26.10.60; FCO 1981; Floater duties 1983; Washington 1986; FCO 1988; (Second Secretary 1990); SUPL 1994; m 1989 Gareth Richard Jones.

Jones, Barrie Samuel, LVO (1985); Deputy High Commissioner Lusaka since July 1993; born 10.8.40; Crown Agents 1959; CRO 1962; Calcutta 1962; CRO later Commonwealth Office 1964; Karachi 1967; Rio de Janeiro 1970; Second Secretary 1970; Vice-Consul (Comm) Los Angeles 1971; FCO 1976; First Secretary and Head of Chancery Mbabane 1979; FCO 1984; Consul-General Brisbane 1988; m 1962 Pamela Anne Trowman (2s 1965, 1973; 1d 1968).

Jones, Caitlin Olga; Guatemala City since August 1999; born 3.6.67; FCO 1990; Nicosia 1993; UKDEL Brussels 1996; Band C4.

Jones, Catherine Helen Courtier MBE (1999); SUPL since August 2000; born 13.9.56; FCO 1976; Moscow 1979; Latin America Floater 1982; Bogotá 1984 (Second Secretary 1985); Second Secretary FCO 1989; Deputy Head of Mission Tirana 1997.

Jones, Ceinwen Jane; Deputy Head of Mission Tallinn since June 1999; born 2.5.50; FCO 1976; Bangkok 1977; Moscow 1979; UKDIS Geneva 1981; FCO 1984; Banjul 1990; FCO 1992; UKREP Brussels 1995; Band B3.

Jones, David Alan; High Commissioner Freetown since March 2000; born 26.10.53; Lord Chancellor's Department 1970; FCO 1971; Tehran 1975; Islamabad 1978; Second Secretary on loan to MOD 1981; Second Secretary FCO 1983; First Secretary (Comm) Cairo 1986; First Secretary FCO 1989; Full-time Training 1993; Deputy Head of Mission/Consul Luanda 1993; Deputy High Commissioner Dar es Salaam 1996; m (1)1975 Jennifer Anne Wright (diss 1992); (2) 1994 Daphne Patricia Foley.

Jones, David Stephen; Deputy High Commissioner Honiara since June 1998; born 19.9.51; Public Record Office 1970-73; FCO 1976; Port of Spain 1978; Peking 1981; Africa/ME floater 1982; FCO 1984; Brasilia 1988; Tripoli 1991; Second Secretary on loan to the DTI 1994; Second Secretary FCO 1995; m 1973 Jane Martin (diss 1978) (2) Carole Banstead 1997.

Jones, Eric Malcolm; First Secretary FCO since May 1998; born 7.10.45; Passport Office Liverpool 1963; DSAO 1966; Middle East Floater 1969; Düsseldorf 1970; Vice Consul Peking 1973; FCO 1974; Third Secretary (Commercial) Kuwait

1976; Second Secretary FCO 1980; Second Secretary (Aid) later Second Secretary (Chancery) Dhaka 1982; Second Secretary (Comm) later First Secretary (Dev) Lilongwe 1985; First Secretary FCO 1990; First Secretary (Dev) Jakarta 1994; m 1988 Sylvia Margaret Hayhurst (1s 1989).

Jones, Frank; First Secretary (Commercial) Athens since May 2001; born 7.9.48; FO (later FCO) 1967; Kaduna 1970; NATO Brussels 1974; Sana'a 1977; FCO 1978; Ottawa 1982; FCO 1984; Second Secretary (Visas) Paris 1989; Second Secretary (Commercial) Kuala Lumpur 1994; FCO 1997; Band C5; m 1982 Elizabeth Mary Lendrum (1d 1985, 1s 1991).

Jones, Jennifer Ann (née Wright); Second Secretary FCO since January 1990; born 7.8.49; DSAO (later FCO) 1967; Kathmandu 1970; Delhi 1970; Tripoli 1972; Lisbon 1972; Tehran 1975; Islamabad 1978; FCO 1981; Cairo 1986.

Jones, Joan Elizabeth, BEM (1991); Kampala since July 1996; born 6.11.43; FCO 1988; Belmopan 1991; Band A2.

Jones, Leslie Norman; Frankfurt since May 2000; born 26.5.48; Army 1964-88; Cairo 1988; Moscow 1991; Budapest 1993; FCO 1995; language training 1999; Band B3; m 1972 Dorothy Alma Tanner (1s 1977; 1d 1978).

Jones, Llinos Dawn; Santiago since October 1997; born 27.3.68; FCO 1988; Kuwait 1989; Warsaw 1990; UKMIS New York 1992; Bandar Seri Begawan 1993; Band A2.

Jones, Mervyn Thomas; Governor Turks and Caicos Islands since January 2000; born 23.11.42; CRO 1964; Calcutta 1966; Bonn 1967; Language Training RAF North Luffenham 1970; Warsaw 1970; Second Secretary FCO 1973; Second Secretary (Chancery) Oslo 1977; First Secretary (Admin) Bangkok 1981; First Secretary and Head of Chancery Bangkok 1982; JSDC course 1985; Seconded to Commonwealth Secretariat 1985; Consul (Commercial) Los Angeles 1990; FCO 1994; Counsellor (Commercial/Economic) later DHM, Counsellor (Commercial/Economic) and Consul General, Brussels 1996; m 1965 Julia Mary Newcombe (2s 1966, 1969).

Jones, Neale Robert; Dubai since June 1999; born 20.2.63; FCO 1986; Islamabad 1989; Istanbul 1992; Band B3; m(1) 1992 Catherine Ingham (diss 1999) (2s 1993, 1995); (2) 2000 Ebru Jones (1 step d 1996, 1d 2000).

Jones, Peter; Second Secretary (Political) Washington since September 1997; born 23.7.57; FCO 1976; Port Stanley 1979; Madrid 1981; Kathmandu 1984; FCO 1986; Peking 1988; Luxembourg 1992; Third later Second Secretary FCO 1995; m 1979 Elaine Frances Scott.

Jones, Peter Edward; FCO since July 1998; born 28.8.61; FCO 1985; Second later First Secretary UKDEL Vienna 1989; First Secretary FCO 1992; First Secretary (Politico-Military) Bonn 1994; m 1998 Sumita Biswas.

Jones, Phillip Roy; FCO since May 1985; born 18.2.50; FO (later FCO) 1966; Washington 1976; FCO 1979; Attaché Muscat 1982; Band C4; m(1) 1972 Lesley Pamela Goody (diss 1981) (2s 1973, 1978; 1d 1975); m(2) 1982 Karen Patricia Lyle; (1s 1985; 1d 1987).

Jones, Ralph Mahood; World-wide Floater duties since February 1999; born 4.5.69; FCO 1989; Riyadh 1992; T/D New Delhi 1995; Karachi 1996; T/D Kuwait 1997; Band B3.

Jones, Randolph Thomas; Second Secretary (Immigration) Pretoria since June 2000; born 12.9.56; FCO 1976; Islamabad 1978; Colombo 1982; FCO 1985; Peking 1989; Port of Spain 1989; Copenhagen 1993; Second Secretary FCO 1997; Band C4; m 1980 Kathryn Rosemary Smith (2s 1984, 1987).

Jones, Rebecca Louise; Cairo since May 2000; born 18.10.74; FCO 1998; Band A2.

Jones, Richard Alexander Owen; Second Secretary Zagreb since September 2001; born 19.4.71; FCO 1990; World Wide Floater Duties 1993; Third Secretary (Vice-Consul) Tashkent 1997; Band B3; m2000 Madina H Sagindirova.

Jones, Richard Christopher Bentley; First Secretary FCO since June 1992; born 22.3.53; Second Secretary FCO 1978; PS to HM Ambassador Tokyo 1980; First Secretary FCO 1984; First Secretary (Head of Chancery) Suva 1988.

Jones, Richard Hugh Francis; First Secretary FCO since September 1998; born 28.9.62; FCO 1983; Third later Second Secretary Abu Dhabi 1986; Second later First Secretary FCO 1989; First Secretary (External Relations) UKREP Brussels 1994.

Jones, Robert Edward; Second Secretary FCO since October 1994; born 30.5.47; FCO 1966; Singapore 1973; FCO 1974; Belgrade 1978; FCO 1981; Prague 1985; FCO 1988 (Second Secretary 1989); Attaché Budapest 1993; m 1972 Linda Joan Edith Watts (1d 1974, 1s 1977).

Jones, Siân; Second Secretary (Pol/Mil) Nicosia since December 2000; born 8.11.74; FCO 1999; Band C4.

Jones, Timothy Aidan; HM Ambassador Yerevan since November 1999; born 5.9.62; FCO 1984; Language training 1986; T/D UKDEL CSCE Vienna 1987; Second Secretary (Chancery) The Hague 1988; First Secretary FCO 1992; T/D Mostar (EUAM) 1994; Full Time Language Training 1995; Deputy Head of Mission Tehran 1996; m 2001 Christin Marschall.

Jones Parry, Emyr, CMG (1992); Permanent Representative UKDEL NATO Brussels since September 2001; born 21.9.47; FCO 1973; Second later First Secretary (Political) later First Secretary (Economic) Ottawa 1974; FCO 1979; First Secretary (Energy) later First Secretary (Institutions) UKREP Brussels 1982; Counsellor on SUPL-EC Brussels 1987; Counsellor FCO 1989; Deputy Head of Mission Madrid 1993; Deputy Political Director 1996; Director EU 1997; Political Director 1998; m 1971 Lynn Noble (2s 1977, 1979).

Joseph, Nicholas Eli; FCO since September 2000; born 12.1.71; Band C4.

Joshi, Bharat Suresh; Banjul since January 1999; born 23.8.69; FCO 1995; Band B3.

Joy, Rupert Hamilton Neville; Deputy Head of Mission Rabat since January 2000. born 5.9.63; FCO 1990; Full-time Language Training 1991; Full-time Language Training Cairo 1992; Second Secretary (Comm/Econ/Pol) Sana'a 1994; Second later First Secretary (Political) Riyadh 1995; First Secretary FCO 1996; Band D6.

Joyce, Lucy Rebecca; Second Secretary (Political) Brussels since January 2000; born 11.12.69; FCO 1992; Third Secretary (Economic/Management) Sofia 1995; Band C4.

Joyce, Marie-Claire; FCO since November 1995; born 4.5.69; Band B3.

Joynson-Squire, Richard James; Second Secretary (Political/External) Islamabad since December 1999; born 11.9.74; FCO 1996; Full time language training 1998; Band C4; m 1998 Rolla Khadduri.

Judd, Claire (née) Rowswell; FCO since October 1988; born 13.1.55; FCO 1979; Quito 1979; UKREP Brussels 1981; Moscow 1984; FCO 1985; Mexico City 1986; Band B3; m 1996 David Judd.

Judge, Christopher John; FCO since June 2000; born 19.5.64; FCO 1980; Second Secretary Moscow 1996; Band C5; m 1995 Fiona Jane (1s 2000).

Juleff, Andrew John Gerent; Second Secretary (Commercial) Rio de Janeiro since May 2000; born 3.5.60; FCO 1986; Third Secretary (Aid/Comm) Kampala 1989; Vice-Consul CG New York 1991; Second Secretary FCO 1994; Band C4.

Jupp, Sheridan Arlene; Stockholm since January 1993; born 2.1.57; FCO 1990; Band A2.

K

Kahlow, Bonita; Rome since August 1998; born 23.1.66; FCO 1989; Rome 1993; FCO November 1996; Band A2.

Kana-Rupal, Sadhana (née Kana); FCO since January 1995; born 31.5.66; Band A2; m 1996 Animesh Kana.

Kane, Jacqueline; FCO since January 1998; born 25.3.67; FCO 1987; Athens 1990; FCO 1993; New Delhi 1994; Band B3.

Kariuki, James; Second Secretary (Political/Economic) Caracas since July 1995; born 6.5.71; FCO 1993; on secondment to United Nations Special Commission (UNSCOM) Baghdad 1994.

Karmy, Peter John; Head of Management Section Taipei since June 2001; born 1.7.47; FO (later FCO) 1967; Benghazi 1969; San José 1970; Seoul 1973; Kuwait 1976; FCO 1977; Sofia 1980; FCO 1984; Second Secretary (Admin) and Consul Manila 1985; Second Secretary and Consul (later Second Secretary Commercial) Ankara 1989; Second Secretary FCO 1993; Bogotá 1998; m 1977 Eui Jong Han (2ds 1979, 1981).

Kavanagh, Karen Jane (née Williams); Bombay since May 1997; born 28.4.70; FCO 1991; UKDEL NATO Brussels 1994; Band B3; m 1996 Neil Richard Kavanagh.

Kavanagh, Neil Richard; Bombay since May 1997; born 28.3.72; FCO 1992; UKDEL NATO Brussels 1995; Band B3; m 1996 Karen Jane Williams.

Kay, Anthony Paul; Bucharest since April 1999; born 29.6.72; FCO 1992; Hong Kong 1995; Band B3.

Kay, Martin Paul; Pretoria since February 1999; born 21.3.68; FCO 1987; UKMIS New York 1989; Suva 1991; FCO 1994; Band B3.

Kay, Nicholas Peter; First Secretary FCO 2000; born 8.3.58; First Secretary FCO 1994; First Secretary and Deputy Head of Mission Havana 1997; m 1986 Susan Wallace (1s 1987; 2d 1988, 1991).

Kazer, Kathleen; FCO since September 1970; born 1.6.47; Principal Research Officer (Band D6).

Kealy, Robin Andrew, CMG (1991); HM Ambassador and Consul-General Tunis since January 2002; born 7.10.44; Third Secretary FO 1967; MECAS 1968; Tripoli 1970; Second later First Secretary Kuwait 1972; First Secretary FCO 1975; Head of Chancery Port of Spain 1978; Political Adviser Belmopan 1978; First Secretary (Comm) Prague 1982; First Secretary later Counsellor FCO 1986; Counsellor, Consul-General and Deputy Head of Mission Baghdad 1987; Counsellor, Director of Trade Promotion and Investment Paris 1990; Head of AMD FCO 1995; Consul General Jerusalem 1997; m 1987 Annabel Jane Hood (2s 1989, 1992).

Keefe, Denis Edward Peter Paul; DHM Prague since August 1998; born 29.6.58; FCO 1982; Language Training 1984; Second Secretary (Chancery) Prague 1984; First Secretary FCO 1988; First Secretary (Political) Nairobi 1992; First Secretary later Counsellor FCO 1996; m 1983 Catherine Ann Mary Wooding (3d 1985, 1993, 1996; 3s 1987, 1989, 1991).

Keegan, David Barclay; First Secretary (Political) Accra since April 1999; born 4.4.63; FCO 1986; Vice-Consul (Econ) Rio de Janeiro 1989; Second Secretary FCO 1991; Washington 1995; Band D6; m 1987 Susan Amanda Line (1s 1994, 1d 1996).

Keeling, Alison Heather; Third Secretary (Chancery) Beirut since August 1998; born

29.8.72; FCO 1996; UKMIS Geneva 1997; Band B3; ptnr, Reuben Thorpe.

Keen, Gillian; Tokyo since December 1997; born 18.2.61; Home Office 1979; Cabinet Office 1987; FCO 1992; Hanoi 1993; Band A2; m 1987 Raymond Keen.

Keep, Stephanie Marie (née Holmes); Singapore since March 1999; born 28.12.56; FCO 1997; Band A2; m 1999 Richard L. Keep.

Kehoe, Elizabeth Anne (née McEwan); Third Secretary Maseru since July 1995; born 29.4.52; FCO 1972; Suva 1975; EEC Brussels 1977; Budapest 1979; Montserrat 1981; FCO 1985; Anguilla 1986; FCO 1988; m 1991 Anthony Kehoe (1s 1991).

Keith, Deborah Jeanne; FTLT since February 2000; born 1.7.68; FCO 1988; Tokyo 1990; Floater Duties 1993; SUPL 1995; FCO 1996; Band C4; m 1999 Steven Rennie Fern.

Keller, Ciaran Joseph; Second Secretary Lisbon (Political/EU) since October 2000; born 2.2.77; FCO 1998; UKMIS New York 1999; Full Time Language Training (Lisbon) 2000; Band C4.

Kelly, Iain Charles MacDonald; HM Ambassador Minsk since May 1999; born 5.3.49; FCO 1974; Language Training 1975; Moscow 1976; Kuala Lumpur 1979; FCO 1982 (Second Secretary 1984); Istanbul 1986; FCO 1988; Los Angeles 1990; First Secretary (Commercial) Moscow 1992; Consul Amsterdam 1995; m 1981 Linda Clare McGovern (2s 1984, 1988).

Kelly, John Philip, CMG (2000), LVO (1994), MBE (1984); Governor Grand Turks and Caicos Islands since October 1996; born 25.6.41; FO 1959; Leopoldville 1962; Cairo 1965; Bonn 1968; FCO 1970; Canberra 1973; Antwerp 1977; Second Secretary FCO 1978; on loan to DTI 1980; Resident Representative Grenada 1982; First Secretary FCO 1986; Deputy Governor Hamilton 1989; First Secretary FCO 1994; m 1964 Jennifer Anne Buckler (1s 1968).

Kelly, Mark; Third Secretary (Chancery) Tel Aviv since May 2001; born 17.9.71; GCO 1990; Amman 1994; World Wide Floater Duties 1996; Panama 1999; FCO 2000; Band B3.

Kelly, Paul John, MBE (1984); Beijing since March 1999; born 11.3.64; FCO 1982; Pretoria 1987; FCO 1989; Nicosia 1994; FCO 1996; Band C4; m 1993 V L Stone.

Kelly, Peter Joseph; Second later First Secretary; FCO since June 1987; born 16.10.41; HM Forces 1958; FCO 1968; Washington 1971; FCO 1974; Tel Aviv 1975; Ankara 1976; FCO 1978; Bahrain 1981; Third Secretary Copenhagen 1984; Band C5; m 1969 Pamela May King (2s 1972, 1976, 1d 1993).

Kelly, Robert Anthony; Second Secretary FCO since September 2000; born 10.12.59; FCO 1986; Third later Second Secretary Hong Kong 1990; Second Secretary FCO 1994; Second Secretary

and Vice Consul Athens 1996; Band C4; m 1986 Heather Erica Christina Smith (1s 1992, 1d 1993).

Kelly, William Charles; FCO since August 1999; born 5.1.61; FCO 1980; Jedda 1982; Lisbon 1985; Warsaw 1988; FCO 1990; PS/HMA Bonn 1993; Third Secretary (Commercial) Paris 1996; Band C4; m 1983 Carol Ann Villis (4s 1985, 1987, 1990, 1992; 1d 2000).

Kendall, Louise Margaret (née Wood); SUPL since March 2000; born 16.1.63; FCO 1981; Prague 1984; Tel Aviv 1986; FCO 1988; Language Training 1991; Third Secretary (Commercial) Budapest 1992; Vienna 1996; Band B3; m 1988 Philip Gary Kendall (1d 1992).

Kendall, Philip Gary; Vienna since October 1998; born 28.4.65; FCO 1984; Tel Aviv 1986; FCO 1988; Budapest 1992; SUPL 1996; Band A2; m 1988 Louise Margaret Kendall (1d 1992).

Keningale, Jacqueline; SUPL since October 1999; born 18.2.66; FCO 1986; Moscow 1987; SUPL 1990; Jedda 1992; FCO 1994; Damascus 1996; Band B3; m 1990 Paul Bevan Downing.

Kennedy, Alison Cranston; seconded to DfID 1999; born 21.8.62; FCO 1983; Third Secretary (Aid) Khartoum 1987; FCO 1991; Vice-Consul Abidjan 1991; SUPL 1993; Second Secretary FCO 1994; on loan to DfID 1997.

Kennedy, Megan Jordan; FCO since 1996; born 1.4.69; FCO 1989; Moscow 1990; Washington 1993; Band B3.

Kennedy, Paul Vincent; First Secretary (Political) Bahrain since June 1999; born 18.4.57; FCO 1989; Second Secretary (Chancery) Riyadh 1991; FCO 1995; Band D6; m 1984 Najia Ben Salah (1d 1990).

Kennedy, Thomas John; First Secretary FCO since August 1997; born 3.2.57; FCO 1992; Second Secretary (Aid/Information) Buenos Aires 1994; m 1985 Clare Marie Ritchie (1s 2000).

Kenny, John David; Colombo since October 1999; born 7.6.55; FCO 1973; Vienna 1976; Georgetown 1978; E Berlin 1982; FCO 1984; Cairo 1987; Third Secretary Dublin 1991; FCO 1995; Band C4; m 1979 Pamela Bernadette Baptiste (1s 1981; 1d 1985).

Kent, Andrew Magnus; First Secretary FCO since January 2001; born 30.11.65; FCO 1989; Second Secretary (Comm) Tehran 1992; Second Secretary FCO 1995; Consul Jedda 1999; Band D6; m 1991 Sarah Louise Mills (1s 1994).

Kent, Mark Andrew Geoffrey; FTLT since April 2000; born 14.1.66; FCO 1987; Third later Second Secretary (Chancery/Inf) Brasilia 1989; UKREP Brussels 1993; First Secretary FCO 1998; Band D6; m 1991 Martine Delogne (1s 1992, 1d 1995).

Kent, Sarah Louise (née Mills); FCO since April 1996; born 28.1.65; FCO 1983; Prague 1987; FCO 1989; SUPL 1992; Band B3; m 1991 Andrew Magnus Kent.

Kenwrick-Piercy, Theodore Maurice; Counsellor FCO since December 1998; born 16.1.48; Third later Second Secretary FCO 1971; Second later First Secretary (Press) UKREP Brussels 1974; FCO 1977; Nicosia 1982; First Secretary FCO 1986; First Secretary (Chancery) The Hague 1988; First Secretary FCO 1992; Counsellor Athens 1994; m 1976 Elisabeth Kenwrick-Cox (1s 1981; 1d 1983).

Kenyon, Ian Roy; SUPL since February 1993; born 13.6.39; FCO 1974; First Secretary UKDIS Geneva 1976; Bogotá 1979; FCO 1982; Head of Nuclear Energy Department, FCO 1983 Counsellor FCO 1986; Counsellor UKDIS Geneva 1988; m 1962 Griselda Rintoul (1d 1963; 1s 1966).

Keogh, David John; Khartoum since October 1988; born 24.6.56; FCO 1979; Ankara 1980; Abu Dhabi 1981; FCO 1983; Islamabad 1984; FCO 1988; Band B3; m 1987 Carolyn Ann Connolly (diss 1990).

Kernohan, Neil Alexander, MBE (1997); FCO since February 2000; born 20.9.65; FCO 1989; Riyadh 1992; T/D Vice Consul Sana'a 1994; Vice Consul and Third Secretary (Management) BIS Tripoli 1995; Third Secretary (IAEA/UN) UKMIS Vienna 1997; Band B3.

Kerr, Christine; Lilongwe since August 1998; born 7.4.60; FCO 1989; Cape Town/Pretoria 1991; Moscow 1994; FCO 1996; Band A2; m 1991 Andrew Tuck (diss 1996) (1d 1994).

Kerr, Douglas James; First Secretary (Commercial) Lima since April 1999; born 4.11.58; FCO 1980; Bucharest 1982; Kampala 1984; Tel Aviv 1988; FCO 1991.

Kerr, Sir John (Olav), GCMG (2001), KCMG (1991), CMG (1987); Permanent Under Secretary of State and Head of the Diplomatic Service from November 1997 to January 2002; born 22.2.42; Third Secretary FO 1966; Third later Second Secretary Moscow 1967; Second Secretary (Econ) Rawalpindi/Islamabad 1969; First Secretary 1971; FCO 1972; Private Secretary to the PUS 1974; Counsellor and Head of DM Division HM Treasury 1979; PPS to the Chancellor of the Exchequer 1981; Counsellor and Head of Chancery Washington 1984; AUSS (European Community) FCO 1987; UK Permanent Representative with Personal rank of Ambassador to the EC Brussels 1990; HM Ambassador Washington 1995; m,1965 Elizabeth Mary Kalaugher (2s 1967, 1968; 3d 1970, 1976 (twins).

Kerr, Michael John; Second Secretary (Management) Prague since September 1998; born 12.8.49; RAF 1969-73; FCO 1973; Islamabad 1975; FCO 1977; Dakar 1979; FCO 1983; Cairo 1985; Oslo 1989; Second Secretary FCO 1992; Jedda 1995; m 1975 Linda Ruth Campbell; (2s 1982, 1984; 1d 1989).

Kerrison, Irene; Moscow since March 1999; born 9.2.65; FCO 1986; Peking 1988; FCO 1990;

Nassau 1991; FCO 1995; Language Training 1998-99; Band B3.

Kerry, Catherine; Tortola since July 1998; born 31.7.65; FCO 1988; Lagos 1991; Band A2.

Kershaw, Alexander Richard; First Secretary FCO since April 2000; born 15.1.67; FCO 1991; Language Training 1993; Second Secretary FCO 1995; First Secretary (UN) UKMIS Geneva 1997; Band D6; m 1994 Suzanne Michelle Jones (2s 1996,1999).

Kershaw, Roger; FCO since September 2001; born 18.3.58; FCO 1982; Language Training 1983; Second Secretary (Comm) Tehran 1984; First Secretary FCO 1987; First Secretary (Economic) Bonn 1992; First Secretary FCO 1996; Deputy High Commissioner Lagos 2000; m 1983 Annick Marie Jeanne Réné Gourley (2d 1986, 1988; 1s 1993).

Kettle, Mark Brian; Third Secretary (Consular) Islamabad since February 1999; born 22.10.66; FCO 1985; UKMIS Vienna 1990; FCO 1993; Muscat 1995; Band A2; m 1995 Justine Carey.

Khoo, Lionel John; Bandar Seri Begawan since March 1996; born 30.4.68; Northern Ireland Office 1991; FCO 1994; Band A2.

Kidd, John Christopher William; Counsellor (Political) Bonn later Berlin since September 1998; born 4.2.57; FCO 1978; Third later Second Secretary Nicosia 1980; Second Secretary and PS to HM Ambassador Paris 1984; (First Secretary 1985); First Secretary FCO 1986; Deputy Head of Mission Addis Ababa 1990; FCO 1993; Counsellor on secondment to European Commission 1996; m 1995 Carine Celia Ann Maitland (1 step d 1983, 1 step s 1986, Twin d 1996).

Kidner, James Hippisley; First Secretary (Political) Sofia since October 1996; born 26.2.61; FCO 1985; Second Secretary Kuala Lumpur 1987; First Secretary FCO 1990; On attachment to Privy Council Office as PS to Leader of the House of Commons 1992; First Secretary FCO 1993; m 1987 Sally Baillie-Hamilton (2d 1996, 1998).

Kilby, David James; First Secretary (Political) and Deputy Permanent Representative ESCAP, Bangkok since April 2001; born 5.11.66; FCO 2000; Band D6; m 1997 Alison Jean McKenna.

Kilford, Yvonne; World wide floater since April 1997; born 8.1.70; FCO 1988; UKREP Brussels 1993; Band A2.

Kiloh, Eleanor Anne; FCO since September 1999; born 20.4.77; Band C4.

Kilroy, Sarah-Jill Lennard; First Secretary FCO since November 1998; born 19.4.56; FCO 1981; Third Secretary Montevideo 1982; Second Secretary FCO 1983; UKREP Brussels 1983; First Secretary FCO 1985; Budapest 1994; Band D6; m 1987 Mark Kilroy (1s 1989, 1d 1992).

Kilvington, Sally Louise; FCO since July 1995; born 20.2.67; FCO 1989; Santiago 1991; Band A2.

Kinchen, Richard, MVO (1976); HM Ambassador Beirut since December 2000; born 12.2.48; Third Secretary FCO 1970; (temporary secondment to British Commission on Rhodesian Opinion 1972); MECAS 1972; Kuwait 1973; Second Secretary FCO 1974; Second later First Secretary Luxembourg 1975; First Secretary (Econ) Paris 1977; FCO 1980; PS/Parliamentary Under-Secretary of State 1982; First Secretary and Head of Chancery Rabat 1984; Counsellor (Finance) UKMIS New York 1988; Head of Dependent Territories Secretariat Bridgetown 1993; m 1972 Cheryl Vivienne Abayasekera (1s 1976; 3d 1973 (dec'd 1980), 1979, 1982).

King, Albert Norman, OBE, LVO (1983); Counsellor New Delhi since December 1999; born 29.3.43; Customs and Excise 1963; Government Actuary's Department 1963; CRO 1964; DSA 1965; Ibadan 1967; BMG Berlin 1971; Second Secretary (Comm) Singapore 1973; Second Secretary (Comm) Muscat 1976; First Secretary Dacca 1980; First Secretary FCO 1984; First Secretary (Admin) Vienna 1987; First Secretary FCO 1992; First Secretary (Management) Lagos 1994; m 1969 Dympna Mary Farren (1s 1971; 2d 1973, 1979).

King, Alison Jane; FCO since January 1998; born 11.6.66; FCO 1984; UKREP Brussels 1987; Mexico City 1989; Band B3.

King, Julian Beresford, First Secretary (External) UKREP Brussels since August 1998; born 22.8.64; FCO 1985; Third later Second Secretary Paris 1987 (ENA and PS/HMA); EC Presidency Liaison Officer Luxembourg and The Hague 1991; Second later First Secretary FCO 1992; Private Secretary to Permanent Under-Secretary of State FCO 1995; m 1992 Lotte Viwdelov Knudsen.

King, Larry; FCO since March 1998; born 1.7.62; FCO 1982; Amman 1985; Band C4; FCO 1988; m 1988 Elaine Margaret Neeve (1d 1996).

Kingdom, David George; Ankara since August 2000; born 19.8.46; FCO 1986; Third Secretary Brussels 1992; First Secretary FCO 1994; Band C5; m 1968 Janice (2s 1972, 1981).

King-Smith, Alastair; Khartoum since November 1999; born 27.9.74; FCO 1996; Full Time Language Training FCO 1997; Cairo 1998; Band C4.

Kingston, Iain Conger; Second Secretary FCO since 1995; born 30.5.50; DOE (PSA) 1975; FCO 1976; Cairo 1979; Lilongwe 1983; FCO 1985; Houston 1988; Maseru 1991; Band B3; m 1978 Georgia Georgiou (2s 1982, 1983).

Kinoshita, Susan Margaret (née Copnell); First Secretary Press and Public Affairs Tokyo since August 1999; born 28.7.61; FCO 1983; Language Training Tokyo 1985; Tokyo 1986; FCO 1989; SUPL 1991; FCO 1992; SUPL 1993; Osaka 1996;

Band D6; m 1989 Makoto Kinoshita (1d 1991; 1s 1993).

Kirby, Diane (née Tallon); Gibraltar since March 1993; born 25.1.67; FCO 1986; Muscat 1988; Band A2; m 1988 Sean William Kirby.

Kirby, Gordon; First Secretary (Commercial/Economic) Zagreb since April 1999; born 22.2.43; GPO 1960; Ministry of Technology 1968; FCO 1970; Amman 1972; Middle East Centre of Arabic Studies 1975; Vice Consul Beirut 1976; Arabic language training Army School of Languages 1976; Vice Consul Jedda 1977; Serbo-Croatian Language Training 1981; Second Secretary (Comm) Belgrade 1982; FCO 1985; First Secretary/Deputy Head of Mission Sana'a 1989; First Secretary FCO 1994; FCO 1996; m 1972 Kathleen Margaret Dawn (2d 1978, 1982).

Kirk, Andrew Philip; Second Secretary (Development) The Hague since September 1999; born 26.2.54; FCO 1972; Yaoundé 1975; Havana 1979; FCO 1981; Vice Consul Lisbon 1985; Aid Attaché Nairobi 1987; Second Secretary FCO 1991; BTIO New York 1994; FCO 1997; Vice-Consul (Investment) San Francisco 1997; Band C4; m 1978 Cheryl Jeanne Nichols (2d 1983, 1987).

Kirk, Anna Thérèse (née Macey); Counsellor on loan to Civil Service Selection Board as Resident Chair since September 1999; born 1.6.59; FCO 1982; Language Training 1984; Third later Second Secretary Oslo 1984; First Secretary FCO 1988; First Secretary (Political) Paris 1992; First Secretary FCO 1997; m 1989 Matthew John Lushington Kirk (2d 1995, 1998).

Kirk, Malcolm; Staff Officer Tortola since June 2000; born 10.4.59; FCO 1978; Nassau 1980; Dakar 1981; FCO 1984; Havana 1985; FCO 1987; Paris 1990; Deputy Head of Mission Tegucigalpa 1993; FCO 1997; Band C4; m 1982 Linda Patricia Greenwood (1 step s 1980, 1s 1983).

Kirk, Matthew John Lushington; Counsellor FCO since August 1999; born 10.10.60; FCO 1982; Language Training 1984; Third later Second Secretary (Political/Information) Belgrade 1984; Second later First Secretary FCO 1988; ENA Paris 1992; First Secretary (Pol/Mil) Paris 1993; Counsellor FCO 1997; Counsellor on loan to Cabinet Office 1998; m 1989 Anna Thérèse Macey (2d 1995, 1998).

Kirk, Susan Mary; Floater Duties since September 2000; born 28.4.46; FCO 1994; Nairobi 1996; Band A2; m 1969 (1s 1975).

Kirkpatrick, Andrew John; Second Secretary (Management) Lagos since January 1999; born 1.6.63; FCO 1988; Third Secretary (Chancery) Budapest 1990; Third Secretary FCO 1992; Third Secretary (Immigration) Islamabad 1995; Third Secretary FCO 1998; Band C4; m 1992 Sara Elizabeth Pickering.

Kitsell, Corinne Angela; FCO since August 1998; born 18.10.69; FCO 1992; T/D UKMIS New York

1994; T/D Beijing 1995; Vice-Consul Beirut 1996; Band C4.

Knapp, Maria Grace; FCO since September 1999; born 3.4.70; FCO 1989; Madrid 1992; FCO 1995; on loan to HM Customs and Excise at Caracas 1996; Band B3.

Knewstubb, Rosemary Anne (née Urch); Bucharest since January 1999; born 26.10.68; FCO 1992; Ottawa 1995; Band A2; m 1996 Mark Andrew Knewstubb.

Knight, Terence Ronald; First Secretary (Management) Washington since July 1997; born 3.9.51; FCO 1973; Rabat 1976; Lima 1978; Islamabad 1981; FCO 1983; Oslo 1986; Third later Second Secretary (Chancery) Port of Spain 1989; Second Secretary FCO 1993; m 1971 Jane Willcocks (2d 1975, 1980; 2s 1977, 1982).

Knightson, Jean Lesley; SUPL since December 1997; born 22.10.63; FCO 1984; Sofia 1987; FCO 1989; Lagos 1990; FCO 1992; Brussels 1994; Band A2.

Knott, Graeme Jonathan; First Secretary (Trade and Investment) UKDEL OECD Paris since September 2000; born 2.11.66; FCO 1988; Third later Second Secretary (Chancery) Havana 1991; First Secretary FCO 1995; First Secretary Mexico City 1996; FTLT 2000; Band D6.

Knott, Paul Robert; Second Secretary (Commercial) UKREP Brussels since February 2001; born 30.6.70; FCO 1989; Bucharest 1992; Dubai 1993; Full-time Russian language training 1997; Third Secretary (Chancery) Tashkent 1997; Second Secretary (Political) Kiev 2000; Band C4.

Knowlton, Richard Jonathan; Counsellor FCO since February 2000; born 25.3.50; Third later Second Secretary FCO 1973; Language Student FCO and Finland 1977; Second later First Secretary Helsinki 1978; First Secretary FCO 1981; Harare 1984; FCO 1989; First Secretary (Chancery/Econ) Dubai 1991; First Secretary later Counsellor FCO 1995; Counsellor (Regional Affairs) Bridgetown 1997; m 1995 Evelina Ravarino.

Korad, Mark David, Paris (Embassy) since August 1998; born 19.6.69; FCO 1991; Bucharest 1994; Band B3; m 1996 Corina Ioana Mantu.

Kotak, Sheetal Arun; FCO since September 1993; born 27.8.69; FCO 1988; Madrid 1991; Band B3.

Kraus, John Arthur; Second Secretary (Political) Bonn since May 1995; born 7.5.66; FCO 1993; m 1995 Judith Mary Smakman (1s 1996).

Kruger, Gabrielle Lisa; FCO since September 2001; born 22.2.76; Band C4.

Kuenssberg, Joanna Kate; First Secretary (EU Economic) Paris since January 2001; born 6.2.73; FCO 1997; Second Secretary FCO 1997; Attachment, Foreign Ministry, Budapest 1999; Attachment, Quai d'Orsay, Paris 2000; m 1997 Finbarr O'Sullivan.

Kydd, Ian Douglas; Consul General Vancouver since March 1998; born 1.11.47; CO 1966; DSAO (later FCO) 1966; New Delhi 1970; Second Secretary (Radio/TV) BIS New York 1975; FCO 1979; First Secretary on loan to 10 Downing Street 1981; Language Training 1983; First Secretary (Chancery) Lagos 1984; First Secretary (Econ/Comm) Ottawa 1988; First Secretary FCO 1993; Counsellor (Management) Moscow 1995; m 1968 Elizabeth Louise Pontius (1s 1971; 1d 1973).

Kyle, Michael Anthony; Counsellor FCO since February 1998; born 20.7.48; FCO 1970; Third later Second Secretary Saigon 1972; Second later First Secretary FCO 1975; Washington 1978; FCO 1981; First Secretary (Pol/Econ) Accra 1984; First Secretary (Chancery) Dar es Salaam 1988; First Secretary later Counsellor FCO 1991; Counsellor Berlin 1995; m 1976 Wendy Suzanne Sloan (1d 1979; 1s 1981).

Kyles, Raymond William; Deputy Head of News Department FCO since October 2000; born 10.3.56; FCO 1980; UKMIS Geneva 1982; Second Secretary UKREP Brussels 1985; First Secretary FCO 1987; First Secretary (Chancery) Pretoria 1991; First Secretary FCO 1996; Deputy Permanent Representative Paris (OECD) 1998; m 1981 Christine Jane Thompson.

L

Lacey-Smith, Jane Frances; T/D Manila since July 2000; born 20.9.63; FCO 1984; East Berlin 1985; Dublin 1987; Algiers 1990; Vice-Consul/ Management Frankfurt 1997; Bangkok 1999; Band C4; m 1995 Martin Frederick Smith.

Ladd, Michael John; FCO since 1992; born 23.10.54; FCO 1971; Washington 1980; FCO 1983; Baghdad 1986; Vienna 1990; Band C4; m 1979 Christine Jane Tate (1s 1983, 1d 1986).

Ladva, Sharad Raiya; Manila since July 1998; born 12.7.60; FCO 1978; Belmopan 1985; Yaoundé 1989; FCO 1993; T/D Riga 1994; Zagreb 1998; Band B3; m 1988 Ellen Louis Santana (1s 1991).

Laffey, Susan; First Secretary (Political) Bucharest since January 2001; born 9.10.61; FCO 1985; East Berlin 1987; Senior Research Officer (DS Band C4) 1987; Second Secretary (Chancery) Bucharest 1989; FCO 1992; UKDEL OSCE Budapest 1994; Principal Research Analyst FCO 1995; UKDEL OSCE Vienna 1996; FCO 1996; T/D Zagreb 1998; Band D6.

Laing, (John) Stuart; HM Ambassador Muscat since April 2002; Counsellor FCO 1995; born 22.7.48; Third Secretary FCO 1970; MECAS 1971; Third later Second Secretary Jedda 1973; Second later First Secretary UKREP Brussels 1975; FCO 1978; First Secretary and Head of Chancery Cairo 1983; First Secretary FCO 1987; Deputy Head of Mission Prague 1989; Counsellor and Deputy Head of Mission Riyadh 1992; Counsellor FCO 1995; High Commissioner Brunei

1998; m 1972 Sibella Dorman (1s 1974; 2d 1979, 1985).

Laing, Paul James; First Secretary FCO since December 1992; born 1.12.53; HM Customs and Excise 1974-80; FCO 1980; APS to Parliamentary Under Secretary of State 1982; New Delhi 1983; Second later First Secretary FCO 1985; BMG later BEBO Berlin 1990; Band D6; m 1982 Dawn Myerscough (3d 1986, 1988, 1990, 1s 1992).

Laird, Alison Margaret; FCO since September 2000; born 5.12.75; Band C4.

Lake, Robin Duncan; Third Secretary (Immigration) Tehran since January 1998; born 15.12.70; FCO 1989; Berlin 1991; Ottawa 1994; FCO 1997; Band B3.

Lamb, Robin David; On loan at the DTI since May 1999; born 25.11.48; FCO 1971; Language Student MECAS 1974; Research Officer (DS Band C4); FCO 1977; Second Secretary Jedda 1979; Principal Research Officer FCO 1982; First Secretary (Econ) Riyadh 1985; FCO 1988; PRO (Band D6); First Secretary (Head of Political Section) Cairo 1993; FCO 1996; m 1977 Susan Jane Moxon (1d 1982; 1s 1986).

Lambert, Jason Edward; Nairobi since October 1999; born 27.9.71; FCO 1990; Brussels 1994; FCO 1997; Band B3; m 1997 Lucy Anne Edwards.

Lambert, Lucy Anne (née Edwards); Nairobi since July 2000; born 5.5.71; FCO 1993; UKREP Brussels 1995; FCO 1997; SUPL 1999; Band A2; m 1997 Jason Edward Lambert.

Lamont, Donald Alexander; Governor Stanley and Commissioner for South Georgia and Sandwich Islands since May 1999; born 13.1.47; Second later First Secretary FCO 1974; First Secretary (UNIDO/IAEA) Vienna 1977; First Secretary (Commercial) Moscow 1980; First Secretary FCO 1982; Counsellor on Attachment to IISS 1988; Counsellor and Head of Chancery BMG (later BM) Berlin 1988; HM Ambassador Montevideo 1991; Head of Republic of Ireland Department 1994; Chief of Staff, OHR, Sarajevo 1997; m 1981 Lynda Margaret Campbell (1d 1983; 1s 1986).

Lampert, Sarah Jane; SUPL since September 1999; born 8.11.65; FCO 1988; Language Training 1990; Third later Second Secretary (Chancery) Sofia 1991; First Secretary FCO 1995; SUPL 1996; First Secretary FCO 1997; Band D6; m 1993 Andrew William Kenningham (2d 1996, 1998).

Lamport, Martin Henry; Deputy Head of Mission Sana'a since December 1999; born 22.11.52; HM Forces 1972; FCO 1975; SUPL 1976; FCO 1979; Tripoli 1980; Caracas 1983; FCO 1987; Third Secretary (Institutions) UKREP Brussels 1990; Deputy High Commissioner Belopan 1993; FCO 1996; Band C5; m 1990 Catherine Priscilla Maxwell (3d 1992, 1994, 1996).

Lamport, Stephen Mark Jeffrey; SUPL since December 1996; born 27.11.51; UKMIS New York 1974; Third Secretary FCO 1975; Third later Second Secretary Tehran 1975; First Secretary FCO 1980; PS to Minister of State 1981; First Secretary (Chancery) Rome 1984; First Secretary later Counsellor FCO 1988; on loan to the Prince of Wales' Office as Deputy Private Secretary 1993; m 1979 Angela Vivien Paula Hervey (2s 1983, 1985; 1d 1990).

Lancaster, Ian Francis Millar; Counsellor FCO since January 1995; born 23.9.47; Second Secretary FCO 1974; Second later First Secretary and Consul Hanoi 1975; First Secretary FCO 1977; Prague 1978; First Secretary FCO 1981; First Secretary (Chancery) Brussels 1983; First Secretary FCO 1987; First Secretary (Chancery) later Counsellor Ankara 1991; m 1972 Simone Daniel (1d 1978; 1s 1981).

Lance, Andrew Robert; Senior Principal Research Officer FCO since September 1993; born 13.8.43; FO 1962; SUPL 1962; DSAO 1965; Prague 1969; Second Secretary (Chancery) The Hague 1972; FCO 1976; First Secretary (Comm) East Berlin 1977; FCO 1981; transferred to Research Cadre 1990; m 1966 Sandra Rosemarie Jackson (1d 1967).

Landsman, Dr David Maurice, OBE (2000); HM Ambassador Tirana since July 2001; born 23.8.63; FCO 1989; Second Secretary (Economic) Athens 1991; FCO 1994; Deputy Head of Mission Belgrade 1997; FCO 1999; Head of British Embassy Office Banja Luka and concurrently First Secretary (Regional Affairs) Budapest 1999; Chargé d'Affaires Belgrade 2000; m,1990 Catherine Louise Holden (1s 1992).

Lane, Bari Albert; First Secretary (Management) Paris since December 1992; born 6.5.48; Ministry of Technology 1965; FO, DSAO and FCO 1966; Vice-Consul Aden 1970; Warsaw 1973; Bombay 1974; FCO 1975; Second Secretary (Admin) Peking 1978; Vice-Consul (Comm) Sydney 1980; Second later First Secretary FCO 1985; m 1971 Jacqueline Mary Chatt.

Lang, Susan Margaret; Bonn since March 1984; born 30.4.48; Beirut 1970; Brussels 1972; FCO 1978; Dublin 1979; E Berlin 1982; Band B3.

Langham, Elizabeth Jane (née Webb); Second Secretary Stockholm since October 1997; born 4.8.61; FCO 1984; Moscow 1986; Washington 1988; FCO 1991; SUPL 1992; Bahrain 1995; SUPL 1996; m 1989 Peter Andrew Langham (2d 1992, 1994).

Langham, Peter Andrew; Second Secretary Stockholm since April 1998; born 26.9.64; FCO 1983; Moscow 1985; Hamilton 1988; Washington 1990; FCO 1991; Bahrain 1994; m 1989 Elizabeth Jane Webb (2d 1992, 1994).

Langley, Anthony Haydn; First Secretary FCO since April 1997; born 26.3.45; FO (later FCO) 1961; Bonn 1967; Tel Aviv 1970; FCO 1973;

Accra 1973; Moscow 1976; FCO 1978; Helsinki 1981; FCO 1984; Second Secretary Dubai 1987; FCO 1990; Second Secretary Canberra 1994; m 1966 Carole Joy Weaver (3d 1966, 1969, 1973).

Langman, Nicholas John Andrew; First Secretary FCO since September 1998; born 1.11.60; FCO 1983; Second Secretary Montevideo 1986; Second later First Secretary UKMIS New York 1988; First Secretary FCO 1991; Paris 1994; Band D6; m 1992 Sarah Jane Pearcey (2d 1994, 1995).

Langridge, Pauline Anne; Havana since August 2000; born 17.8.63; FCO 1988; Madrid 1990; Guatemala 1993; FCO 1995; Band A2.

Langrish, Sally (née Monk); First Secretary (Legal Adviser) UKREP Brussels since February 2000; born 5.8.68; called to the Bar Middle Temple 1991; Treasury Solicitors Department 1993; Assistant Legal Adviser FCO 1995; Band D6; m 1996 Richard Michael John Langrish.

Lapsley, Angus Charles William; First Secretary (Political/Internal) Paris since April 2001; born 16.3.70; Second Secretary Department of Health 1991; Second Secretary UKREP Brussels 1994; Private Secretary Department of Health 1995; Private Secretary 10 Downing Street 1996; First Secretary Head IGC Unit (EUD(I)) 1999; Band D6; m 1999 Georgina Maria Power.

Larden, Kendra Jane; Peking since April 2000; born 7.3.71; Paris 1993; FCO 1991; Muscat 1996; Band A2.

Larkins, Christopher Paul; FCO since March 2000; born 2.10.63; FCO 1986; Warsaw 1991; FCO 1994; Hong Kong 1996; Band A2; m 1995 Lesley Edith Jean Stuart.

Larmouth, Helen Dorothy; Lilongwe since December 1994; born 22.8.63; FCO 1989; Washington 1992; Band A2.

Larner, Jeremy Francis; Deputy Director General BTCO Taipei since 1999; born 12.11.49; Inland Revenue 1967; FCO 1968; Cairo 1971; Benghazi 1972; Abu Dhabi 1972; Moscow 1975; Seoul 1975; Manila 1976; Monrovia 1977; FCO 1980; Third later Second Secretary (Comm) Tunis 1983; Second Secretary (Comm) Port Louis 1989; Second later First Secretary FCO 1992; Deputy Head of Mission and HM Consul Rangoon 1995; Band D6; m 1975 Sally Dewhurst (2s 1978, 1980).

Lassman, Louise (née Mason); FCO since April 2000; born 30.8.63; FCO 1986; Gibraltar 1993; Hong Kong 1996; Band B3; m 1993 Nigel Abraham Lassman.

Latham, Sarah Jane; Ankara since February 1998; born 24.6.70; FCO 1996; Band A2.

Latta, Nicholas Karim; Second Secretary Muscat since 1998, born 2.9.71; FCO 1995; FTLT 1996; FTLT Cairo 1997; Band C4; m 1997 Susanna Mary Davis (1d 2000).

Latter, Edwin John Scott; First Secretary FCO since August 1997; born 16.2.68; FCO 1991; Vice-Consul Istanbul 1994; Band D6; m 1994 Rosemary Helen Fabre (1d 1996).

Lattin-Rawstrone, Howard; First Secretary (Commercial) Warsaw since August 1999; born 23.3.55; FCO 1975; Buenos Aires 1977; Maputo 1981; Brussels 1982; FCO 1984; Cairo 1988; Second Secretary (Commercial/Aid) Cairo 1991; Second Secretary Lilongwe 1993; FCO 1997; m(1) 1980 Sylvia Christine Waller (diss 1987); (2) 1987 Caroline Sarah Lattin (2 adopted d 1976, 1978; 1s 1987).

Lavender, Fiona Jayne; Bangkok since January 2000; born 12.6.70; FCO 1991; Tokyo 1992; La Paz 1996; Band B3.

Lavers, Richard Douglas; HM Ambassador Guatemala City since October 2001; born 10.5.47; Third Secretary FCO 1969 and Buenos Aires 1970; Second later First Secretary Wellington 1973; FCO 1976; First Secretary (Pol/Econ) Brussels 1981; on secondment to Guinness Mahon 1985; First Secretary FCO 1987; NATO Defence College Rome 1989; Deputy Head of Mission and Consul-General Santiago 1993; HM Ambassador Quito 1993; Counsellor FCO 1997; Head of Research Analysts FCO 1999; m 1986 Brigitte Anne Julia Maria Moers (2s 1988, 1989).

Lavery, Creena Christina Maureen; Consul (Consular/Immigration) Düsseldorf since September 2000; born 17.5.62; FCO 1991; UKDEL NATO Brussels 1993; Presidency Liason Officer Luxembourg 1997; Bonn 1999; Band C4.

Lavery, Derek John; FCO since September 1996; born 1.6.68; FCO 1987; Islamabad 1989; Bonn 1993; Band B3; m 1992 Claire Ruth Haines.

Lavocat, Amanda Joyce (née Thomas); Dakar since August 2000; born 21.12.67; DHSS 1986; FCO 1987; Pretoria 1989; Algiers 1992; FCO 1994; Istanbul 1997; Band B3; m 1993 Frederic Paul Francis Lavocat (1s 1995).

Lawley, Claire Angela; Vice-Consul New Delhi since August 1999; born 14.6.62; FCO 1984; Rome 1985; SUPL 1988; Resigned 1989; Reinstated 1994; FCO 1994; Ottawa 1996; m 1987 David Ghiglieri (diss 1994) (1s 1988); Band B3.

Lawrence, Joanne Louise (née Watson); Islamabad since May 1998; born 30.4.68; FCO 1986; Wellington 1988; SUPL 1992; Stanley 1995; Band B3; m 1991 Martin Lawrence (2d 1993, 1999).

Lawrence, Paul David; Kigali since May 2000; born 10.4.68; FCO 1989; UKMIS New York 1993; world-wide Floater Duties 1997; Band B3.

Lawrie, James Malcolm, MBE (1985); Second Secretary Lagos since November 2000; born 1.6.44; FCO 1970; Jedda 1972; FCO 1973; Islamabad 1975; FCO 1977; Kuwait 1979; FCO 1983; Third Secretary Peking 1984; FCO 1986; Accra 1990; FCO 1993; Cairo 1995; FCO 1998; Band C4; m (1) 1971 Anne Margaret Martin (Diss) (3s 1974, 1977, 1982); m (2) 2000 Sheila Boxer.

Laxton, Rowan James; FCO since October 2000; born 19.02.61; FCO 1993; First Secretary (Chancery) Islamabad 1997; Band D6; M2000 Sonya L. Laxton.

Lay, Christopher James; Washington since March 1996; born 26.6.42; Royal Marines 1961-83; Moscow 1983; BMG Berlin 1984; Baghdad 1987; Kingston 1989; Prague 1993; Band C4; m 1971 Mary (2s 1972, 1973).

Laycock, Rachel Jane; Second Secretary (Chancery) Washington since May 2000; born 20.5.71; FCO 1994; Band C4; m2000 Owen Pengelly.

Layden, Anthony Michael; HM Ambassador Rabat since February 1999; born 27.7.46; Third Secretary FCO 1968; MECAS 1969; Second Secretary Jedda 1971; Second later First Secretary Rome 1973; FCO 1977; First Secretary and Head of Chancery Jedda 1982; First Secretary FCO 1982; Head of Chancery Muscat 1987; Counsellor (Comm/Econ) Copenhagen 1991; Counsellor FCO 1995; m 1969 Josephine Mary McGhee (3s 1973, 1974, 1977; 1d 1982).

Layfield, Jonathan Timothy Whitton; Amman since December 2001; born 9.06.67; FCO 1997; Band B3; m 1997 Rebecca Anne.

Leach, Patricia Kathleen; UKREP Brussels since February 1983; born 15.1.53; DOI 1973-76; FCO 1978; East Berlin 1978; UKMIS New York 1981; Band A2.

Leake, Nicholas Howard; First Secretary (Industry) UKREP Brussels since September 2000; born 15.1.72; FCO 1994; Second Secretary (KHF) Budapest 1996.

LeBlond, Charmaine Mary; FCO since June 1998; born 24.2.43

Leck, George; FCO since July 1991; born 6.4.56; FCO 1979; Ankara 1980; Africa/Middle East Floater 1984; Latin America/Caribbean Floater 1986; Islamabad 1987; Band B3.

Lee, Adrian Jonathan; on loan from Home Office to Peking since May 2000; born 24.10.68; FCO 1989; full-time Language Training Cairo 1991; Riyadh 1992; Full-time Language Training 1996; Third Secretary (Management) and Vice Consul São Paulo 1996; Band C4.

Lee, Julie Yvonne (née Watts); Peking since November 1998; born 22.12.67; FCO 1987; UKMIS New York 1988; Budapest 1991; Banjul 1993; FCO 1994; Band A2.

Lee, Richard John Clifton; Second Secretary FCO since May 1999; born 26.9.51; FCO 1971; Copenhagen 1973; Addis Ababa 1976; Moscow 1979; FCO 1982; Accra 1984; Lusaka 1987; FCO 1989; Second Secretary (Commercial) Kuwait 1992; Jakarta 1994; m 1973 Lesley Eleanor McConnell (1d 1980; 1s 1982).

Lee, Thomas David; Third later Second Secretary FCO since June 1990; born 9.5.63; FCO 1983;

Nicosia 1987; Band C4; m 1995 Louise Janet Helen Birkett.

Lee-Gorton, Victoria (née Lee); FTLT since May 2001; born 5.3.70; FCO 1990; Full-time Language Training 1992; Third Secretary Maputo 1993; Third Secretary EU Presidency Liaison Officer Rome/Dublin/The Hague 1995; Third later Second Secretary FCO 1997; Band C4; m 1992 Christopher John Gorton (1d 2001).

Lees, Andrea Margaret; FCO since June 1989; born 19.7.68; Band A2.

Lees, Diana Jane; Second Secretary FCO since May 1996; born 8.3.44; FCO 1977; New Delhi 1978; Moscow 1981; Bonn 1983; FCO 1985; Valletta 1989; Sana'a 1993.

Legg, Judy; SUPL since September 2000; born 29.4.67; FCO 1991; Full-time Language Training 1992; (Second Secretary 1993); Moscow 1994; First Secretary FCO 1995; Band D6; m 1994 Graham Barry Stanley (1d 1998).

Legg, Michael Henry Frank; First Secretary (Management) Madrid since 1999; born 11.3.43; CRO 1961; DSAO 1965; Beira 1967; Delhi 1968; Belgrade 1972; FCO 1976; on loan to DOT 1978; Second Secretary (Comm) Madras 1980; Consul (Comm) Milan 1984; First Secretary FCO 1989; First Secretary Mexico 1991; First Secretary FCO 1996; Band D6; m 1972 Chantal Violette Gonthier (2s 1976, 1979).

Legg, Rufus Alexander; Second Secretary FCO since October 2000; born 13.3.68; FCO 1990; Third Secretary Port Moresby 1993; Third later Second Secretary and Deputy Head of Mission Tegucigalpa 1997; Band C4.

Leggatt, Alison Elaine; FCO since October 1995; born 6.12.43; FO 1965; Bonn 1967; Frankfurt 1969; Munich 1969; Islamabad 1972; FCO 1973; Bridgetown 1974; FCO 1976; Washington 1977; FCO 1977; Helsinki 1979; FCO 1981; Caracas 1985; FCO 1988; The Hague 1993; Band A2.

Legge, Jeremy John; First Secretary (Political) Paris since August 2001; born 19.5.61; Second Secretary FCO 1985; Second Secretary Lusaka 1987; Second later First Secretary FCO 1989; First Secretary on loan to the Cabinet Office 1989; UKMIS Vienna 1994; First Secretary FCO 1998; Band D6; m 1990 Melanie King; (3s 1991, 1992, 1994).

Leigh, David John; Second later First Secretary FCO since August 1987; born 3.7.48; Post Office 1964; FCO 1969; Lagos 1974; FCO 1975; Third Secretary Tokyo 1978; FCO 1981; Third Secretary Sofia 1984.

Leigh Phippard, Dr Helen Thérèse; FCO since December 1990; born 8.11.64; SRO; m 1990 Anthony David Phippard.

Leister, Helen Grace (née McCarthy); Ottawa since August 2000; born 1.2.64; FCO 1983; Paris 1985; Luxembourg 1988; Paris 1991; Kiev 1994;

FCO 1996; Ottawa 1999; SUPL 2000; Band B3; m 1991 Alan Leister.

Leith, Dennis, RVM (1975); First Secretary (Commercial) Sofia since September 1998; born 10.12.48; FCO 1967; Moscow 1971; Mexico City 1972; Sofia 1975; FCO 1976; Guatemala City 1979; Vienna 1982; Second Secretary FCO 1984; Second Secretary (Comm) Bahrain 1987; on secondment to the London Chamber of Commerce 1991; Consul General Ho Chi Minh City 1992; Second Secretary FCO 1995; m 1971 Barbara Mary Hum (1s 1974; 1d 1979).

Lelliott, David Patrick; Second Secretary (Commercial) Mexico City since June 2000; born 13.9.66; FCO 1993; Third Secretary Doha 1996; Band C4.

Leon, Judith Mary; Deputy Consul-General Johannesburg since June 2001; born 17.7.63; Home Office 1984; FCO 1987; New York 1989; Bangkok 1992; FCO 1994; (Second Secretary 1995); Second Secretary (Commercial) Bombay 1997.

Leslie, Alison Mariot (née Sanderson); Deputy Head of Mission Rome since October 1998; born 25.6.54; FCO 1977; Singapore 1978-1981; Bonn 1982-1986; FCO 1986-1990; Quai d'Orsay Paris 1990-1992; Head of ESED 1992; Scottish Office 1993-1995; Head of Policy Planning Staff FCO 1996; m 1978 Andrew David Leslie (2d 1987, 1990).

Leslie, Thomas Gary; Tokyo since September 1999; born 27.4.69; FCO 1989; Karachi 1991; FCO 1993; Tokyo 1994; Kamakura 1998; Band B3.

Leslie-Jones, Philippa Anne; First Secretary FCO since January 1994; born 19.7.59; FCO 1984; Second Secretary Warsaw 1986; First Secretary FCO 1989; First Secretary (Chancery) Moscow 1991; m 1994 Richard Philip Bridge, (2s 1995; 1997).

Lever, Giles; FTLT since November 2000; born 20.3.68; FCO 1990; Third later Second Secretary (Political) Hanoi 1993; First Secretary FCO 1997.

Lever, Sir Paul, KCMG (1998), CMG (1991); HM Ambassador Bonn from December 1997; Berlin from October 2000; born 31.3.44; Third Secretary FCO 1966; Third later Second Secretary Helsinki 1967; UKDEL NATO Brussels 1971; First Secretary FCO 1973; Assistant Private Secretary to Secretary of State 1978; SUPL with EC Commission Brussels 1981; Head of United Nations Department FCO 1985; Head of Defence, later Security Policy Department 1986; Head of Delegation UKDEL CFE/CSBM Vienna (with personal rank of Ambassador) 1990; AUSS (Defence) FCO 1992; Deputy Secretary, Cabinet Office and Chairman of the Joint Intelligence Committee 1994; DUS (Economic and EU Director) FCO 1996; m 1990 Patricia Anne Ramsey.

Lever, Simon Jeffrey; Peking since May 2000; born 4.1.63; FCO 1983; Doha 1985; SE Asia/FE Floater 1988; Full-time language training FCO 1989; Language Training Hong Kong 1990; Peking 1991; On loan to the DTI 1996; HM Consul Chang Mai 1998; Band C5; m 1993 Krisana Khumnuan.

Levi, Andrew Peter Robert; seconded to Office of the Special Co-ordinator Stability Pact since September 1999; born 4.3.63; FCO 1987; (Second Secretary 1989); Second Secretary (Chancery) Bonn 1990; First Secretary FCO 1993; on Secondment to the EC September 1996; Band D6.

Levey, Joanna Claire; FCO since October 1992; born 22.9.60; FCO 1981; Kuwait 1983; Luanda 1986; FCO 1989; Copenhagen 1990; Band A2 m1997 Robert Edward Levey. (1d 2000).

Levoir, Derek Charles; First Secretary (Consular) Nairobi since September 1999; born 8.8.46; DSAO 1965; Latin America Floater 1969; Rome 1971; FCO 1974; Second Secretary 1976; Asunción 1978; Lisbon 1982; Vice-Consul Naples 1986; FCO 1991; m 1973 Liana Annita Ugo (2d 1975, 1976).

Lewington, Richard George; HM Ambassador Almaty and HM Ambassador (non-resident) Bishkek since July 1999; born 13.4.48; DSAO (later FCO) 1968; Attached to Army School of Languages 1971; Ulaanbaatar 1972; Second Secretary (Chancery/Inf) Lima 1976; FCO 1980; Second Secretary (Comm) Moscow 1982; Second later First Secretary FCO 1983; First Secretary (Comm) Tel Aviv 1986; First Secretary FCO 1990; EU Monitoring Mission Yugoslavia 1991; Deputy High Commissioner Valletta 1995; m 1972 Sylviane Paulette Marie Cholet (1s 1982; 1d 1984).

Lewis, Claire Samantha; New Delhi since March 1998; born 3.6.66; FCO 1990; Madras 1993; Band B3; m2000 Ian David Booth.

Lewis, Ian Roger; Consul General Bilbao since September 1998 born 29.10.43; Ministry of Overseas Development 1964; Commonwealth Office DSAO and FCO 1966; Warsaw 1968; Nicosia 1969; Dacca 1972; FCO 1975; LA Floater 1978; FCO 1979; Paris 1981; Athens 1982; FCO 1984; HM Consul and Second Secretary (Admin) Santiago 1984; Second Secretary FCO 1989; Deputy Head of Mission Tegucigalpa 1992; Second Secretary (Commercial) Bahrain 1994; m 1978 Marina Rosa Diez.

Lewis, Dr John Ewart Thomas; First Secretary FCO since March 1996; born 5.11.55; FCO 1987; First Secretary (Chancery) Bonn 1991; Consul (Economic) Frankfurt 1993; Band D6.

Lewis, Joy Suzanne (née Spalding); FCO since March 1998; born 1.8.60; FCO 1980; Rio de Janeiro 1983; Buenos Aires 1986; FCO 1988; SUPL 1991; Band C4.

Lewis, Marion Rachel (née Douche); SUPL since November 1996; born 19.3.69; FCO 1991; Band

B3; m 1994 Peter Robert Lewis (2s 1997,1999; 1d 2001).

Lewis, Peter Robert; First Secretary FCO since October 1999; born 16.8.68; Second Secretary FCO 1994; Second Secretary Berlin 1997; Band D6; m 1994 Marion Rachel Douche (2s 1997,1999; 1d 2001).

Lewis, Sin; UKDEL NATO Brussels since February 1988; born 23.12.65; FCO 1986; Band A2.

Lewis, Trevor James; Second Secretary (Commercial) Shanghai since April 2000; born 8.10.60; FCO 1979; UKREP Brussels 1982; Accra 1984; FCO 1988; Washington 1991; Third Secretary (Commercial/Information) Dubai 1994; FCO 1997; Band C4; m 1993 Claire Louise Hawthorne.

Ley, Christopher John; Resource Management Officer, Wider Europe Command; born 14.1.46; FO 1964; Sofia 1968; Rawalpindi/Islamabad 1970; Chicago 1973; Ottawa 1974; FCO 1976; Madrid 1980; Bombay 1983; Second Secretary FCO 1984; Second Secretary (Admin) Rome 1989; Second Secretary (Management) Moscow 1994; First Secretary FCO 1998; m 1969 Joan Marie Lager (2s 1971, 1972).

Ley, Graham John; First Secretary (Regional Affairs) Cairo since September 1999; born 31.5.61; FCO 1984; Second Secretary Cairo 1987; Second later First Secretary FCO 1989; First Secretary (Chancery) Nicosia 1994; First Secretary FCO 1998; Band D6; m 1988 Carol Anne Buchan (1d 1991; 1s 1995).

Liddell, James; Harare since October 1998; born 20.6.45; FCO 1970; Buenos Aires 1973; Blantyre 1975; FCO 1977; Seoul 1980; Suva 1984; Second Secretary FCO 1988; Consul (Commercial) Perth 1992; m 1978 Jillian Stella Coventry.

Life, Vivien Frances; Counsellor FCO since April 1999; born 30.5.57; Civil Service Dept. 1979; HM Treasury 1981; FCO 1988; First Secretary Washington 1992; First Secretary FCO 1996; m 1989 Timothy Michael Dowse (2ds 1991, 1994).

Lillie, Stephen; Consul-General Guangzhou since October 1999; born 4.2.66; FCO 1988; Full-time language training 1989; Full-time language training Hong Kong 1990; Second later First Secretary (Economic/Political) Peking 1992; FCO 1996; m 1991 Denise Chit Lo (2s 1997, 1999).

Lillington, Leisa; FCO since April 1995; born 23.1.65; Home Office 1985; FCO 1991; UKDEL Vienna 1992; Band A2.

Linacre, Joanne Tracy; Peking since September 1987; born 22.10.64; DHSS 1981; FCO 1985; Band A2.

Lindfield, John Richard; MBE (1999); Consul (Investment) San Francisco since July 1999; born 12.5.59; DHSS 1978; FCO 1978; Cairo 1981; Floater duties 1984; Karachi 1985; FCO 1989 (Second Secretary 1994); Vice-Consul

(Commercial) Cape Town 1995; m 1985 Judith Christine Brown (2s 1988, 1990).

Lindley, Graham; Kampala since May 2000; born 18.3.46; Royal Navy 1964; HOPD 1982; Bucharest 1988; Prague 1990; Hong Kong 1996; Brussels 1992; Band B3; m 1967 Anita Wood (1s 1969; 1d 1976).

Lindsay, Bridget Clare (née O'Riordan); International Trade Advisor, Business Link Hertfordshire since January 2001; born 13.8.59; FCO 1980; Warsaw 1982; Tokyo 1984; SUPL 1986; Canberra 1987; FCO 1989; SUPL 1991; FCO 1992; T/D Tokyo 1995; SUPL 1995; British Trade International 2000; Band C4; m 1983 Iain Ferrier Lindsay (1s 1991).

Lindsay, Dawn Novelle; On loan to DfID since September 1998; born 6.6.62; FCO 1985; Lagos 1988; FCO 1991; Minsk 1994; Band B3.

Lindsay, Kathryn Hilary (née Buchanan) Dakar since February 1995; born 7.7.70; FCO 1989; UKREP Brussels 1992; Band A2; m 1994 Douglas Tennant Lindsay.

Lindsay, Iain Ferrier; FCO since September 1999; born 9.3.59; FCO 1980; Warsaw 1982; Tokyo 1983; Third later Second Secretary (Political) Canberra 1986; Second Secretary FCO 1989; First Secretary (Political) Tokyo 1994; m 1983 Bridget Clare O'Riordan (1s 1991).

Lindsay, Richard Stephen; Second Secretary Harare since August 1998; born 18 2.69; Second Secretary FCO 1996; m 1997 Xanthe Critchett (1s 1998; 1d 2000).

Ling, Norman Arthur; High Commissioner Lilongwe since September 2001; born 12.8.52; Second Secretary FCO 1978; Second Secretary Tripoli 1980; Second later First Secretary Tehran 1981; First Secretary FCO 1984; Deputy Consul General Johannesburg 1988; full-time Language Training 1992; Deputy Head of Mission Ankara 1993; Counsellor FCO 1997; m 1979 Selma Osman.

Lingwood, Dave Michael; Second Secretary and Deputy Head of Mission Yerevan since August 2000; born 10.5.68; FCO 1989; Cairo 1991; Bonn 1994; FCO 1997; Band C4.

Link, Joan Irene (née Wilmot); LVO (1992); Counsellor FCO since August 1996; born 3.3.53; FCO 1974; Third Secretary Bonn 1975; Third later Second Secretary FCO 1977; Second later First Secretary UKDIS Geneva 1980; First Secretary FCO 1983; First Secretary (Information) Bonn 1990; First Secretary FCO 1994; (2s 1977, 1985).

Linnell, Aidan John; Second Secretary Caracas since December 1998; born 13.4.60; FCO 1982; Canberra 1987; FCO 1989; Third Secretary Bonn 1993; FCO 1996; Band C4; m2000 Zenaida Degadillo.

Lisbey, Lisa Marie (nee Harrison); New Delhi since August 2000; born 23.2.69; Customs and

Excise 1992-1995; FCO 1995; Belmopan 1996; Band A2; m 1999 Nestor Lisbey (1s 2001).

Lintner, Francesca Jane; FCO since March 1995; born 5.4.72; Band A2.

Lion, Stephanie Ann (née Smith); SUPL since August 2000; born 16.2.65; FCO 1986; Madrid 1988; SUPL 1989; FCO 1992; Berne 1994; FCO 1997; Band A2; m 1997 Dominique Lion.

Little, Alison Jane; FCO since August 1997; born 3.4.68; FCO (HCS) 1986; FCO (DS) 1988; Lusaka 1990; FCO 1992; Maseru 1993; Tunis 1994; Band B3.

Little, Jennifer Margaret; FCO since July 1989; born 21.6.47; FCO 1970-72; Senior Research Officer.

Little, Margaret Cambridge; FCO since May 1989; born 5.3.49; FCO 1973; Warsaw 1974; Tehran 1976; Hanoi 1979; Rome 1979; FCO 1982; Colombo 1986; Band B3.

Littlefield, David Leslie; FCO since October 1998; born 22.5.40; Ministry of Housing and Local Government 1958; Customs and Excise 1959; CRO 1961; Dhaka 1962; Kampala 1964; Beirut 1967; Second Secretary (Admin) 1969; Second later First Secretary FCO 1972; National Defence College 1978; Consul (Inf) Sydney 1978; First Secretary and Resident Rep St Lucia 1983; First Secretary FCO 1987; On loan to the DTI 1990; First Secretary (Comm) Nairobi 1993; FCO 1996; Deputy Consul Toronto 1997 m(1) 1961 Georgina MacDonald McKay Provan Allan (diss 1978) (1s 1966); (2) 1978 Marian Peacock Pochin (diss 1981); (3) 1981 Mary Patricia Holman (née Fee).

Livesey, Timothy Peter Nicholas; On Secondment to 10 Downing St (Press Office) since August 2000; born 29.6.59; FCO 1987; Rabat 1988; FCO 1988; Second later First Secretary (Aid) Lagos 1989; FCO 1993; Head of Press and Public Affairs Section Paris Embassy 1996; m 1986 Catherine Eaglestone (3d 1990, 1996, 1999; 2s 1992, 1997).

Livingston, Carolyn B; Abidjan since May 1999; born 4.11.48; FCO 1997; Band B3. (1d 1974).

Livingston, Catherine Mary (née Bramley); Hong Kong since October 1996; born 22.6.56; FCO 1975; Cairo 1977; Resigned 1980; Reinstated 1982; FCO 1982; Rome 1984; Muscat 1986; SUPL 1990; FCO 1991; SUPL 1991; FCO 1995; Band B3; m 1985 Richard Ian Livingston (1s 1990; 1d 1992).

Livingstone, Scott, MBE (1995); First Secretary FCO since January 2000; born 28.11.65; First Secretary (Legal) UKMIS and UKDIS Geneva 1994; First Secretary FCO 1996; First Secretary (Political) Islamabad 1998; Band D6; m 1996 Lorna Jane Pettipher (2d 1998, 2000).

Llewellyn, Huw; Legal Counsellor since 1999; born 21.5.59; Assistant Legal Adviser FCO 1988; m 1990 Fiona Jane Boote (2d 1994, 1995).

Lloyd, Andrew; MBE (1995); Head of Post, Pristina since July 2000; born 22.10.64; FCO 1982; Washington 1984; Kaduna 1987; FCO 1990; (Second Secretary 1992); Second Secretary (Economic) Seoul 1993; Second later First Secretary (Political/Press) UKMIS New York 1995; m 1987 Sandra Leigh Craven (1s 1990).

Lloyd, Diane Elizabeth; Osaka since January 2000; born 27.2.68; FCO 1987; Warsaw 1989; Full-time Language Training FCO 1989; Full-time Language Training Tokyo 1990; Vice-Consul Tokyo 1991; Rabat 1995; T/D Japan 1999; Band B3; m 1994 Souichiroh Saito (née Urushibara).

Lloyd, Susan Jacqueline; Montevideo since November 1998; born 28.2.70; FCO 1989; Harare 1991; Band B3.

Lock, Jennifer Hazel; Second Secretary (Immigration) Islamabad since July 1998; born 9.7.59; FCO 1978; Jakarta 1982; Stockholm 1985; FCO 1988; Tunis 1991; Third Secretary (Management/Consular) Almalty 1994; Band C4.

Lochmuller, Simon; Cairo since June 1998; born 26.7.70; FCO 1986; Bonn 1993; FCO 1996; Band C4; m 1998 Verena Mackenzie (1d 1995).

Lockwood, Emma Constance, MVO (2000); Third Secretary (Political) Rome since December 1999; born 1.1.71; FCO 1996; Language Training 1999; Band B3.

Lodge, Katherine Rosemary; SUPL since August 1994, born 3.8.59; FCO 1984; Language Training Tokyo 1985; Third Secretary Tokyo 1986; FCO 1990; (Second Secretary 1992).

Logan, Sir David Brian Carleton, KCMG (2000); HM Ambassador Ankara since March 1997; born 11.8.43; Third Secretary Istanbul 1965; Third later Second Secretary Ankara 1967; Private Secretary to the Parliamentary Under-Secretary of State 1970; First Secretary 1971; First Secretary UKMIS New York 1973; FCO 1977; Counsellor, Head of Chancery and Consul-General Oslo 1982; Head of Personnel Operations Department 1986; CDA at Oxford University 1988; Minister Moscow 1989; AUS (Central and Eastern Europe) 1992; AUS (Defence Policy) 1994; Minister Washington 1995; m,1967 Judith Margaret Walton Cole (1d 1968; 2s 1970 (dec'd 1988), 1976).

Logan, Jane; T/D Ottawa since February 2000; born 11.10.64; FCO 1984; Pretoria 1986; Port of Spain 1989; FCO 1992; Istanbul 1994; Band A2.

Logan, Marilla Joy Fiona (née Tandy); First Secretary FCO since April 1998; born 12.9.53; FCO 1974; Moscow 1977; FCO 1978; Düsseldorf 1980; FCO 1983; Second Secretary Kuala Lumpur 1992; FCO 1996; m 1986 Allan Robert Logan (1s 1994).

Lomas, Joanne; Second Secretary (WTO) UKMIS Geneva since August 2001; born 7.9.70; FCO 1993; Full Time Language Training 1995; Secondment to UNSCOM Baghdad 1997; Third Secretary (Political/Information) Damascus 1997; Band C4.

Longbottom, Julia Margaret; First Secretary (Political) The Hague since September 1998; born 13.7.63; FCO 1986; Attachment, European Commission 1988; Language training 1988; Second Secretary (Chancery) Tokyo 1990; First Secretary FCO 1994; m 1990 Richard James Sciver (2d 1992, 1993, 1s 1995).

London, David Charles George; First Secretary FCO since June 2000; born 24.1.66; FCO 1994; Second Secretary (Political) Bonn 1996; First Secretary (Political) Buenos Aires 1997; Band D6; m 1996 Monique Day (1s 1998).

Longdon, Catherine Mary; FCO since November 1990; born 15.12.64; Band B3.

Longhurst, William, Jesse; First Secretary (Finance) UKMIS New York since June 2001; born 7.2.67; FCO 1990; Seoul 1992; (Second Secretary) 1992; First Secretary (Commercial) Tokyo 1995; On loan to the DTI 1998; m 1991 Eriko Niimi (2d 1991, 1993).

Longrigg, Anthony James, CMG (1992); Governor Plymouth since May 2001; born 21.4.44; FCO 1972; Second later First Secretary (Pol) Moscow 1975; FCO 1978; First Secretary Head of Chancery Brasilia 1981; First Secretary FCO 1985; Counsellor (Internal) Moscow 1987; Counsellor (Econ/EC) Madrid 1991; Counsellor FCO 1995; Minister Moscow 1997; m 1968 Jane Rosa Cowlin (3d 1970, 1973, 1977).

Lonsdale, Charles John; First Secretary (Political) Moscow since October 1998; born 5.7.65; FCO 1987; Vienna CSCF 1988; FCO 1989; Third later Second Secretary Budapest 1990; On loan to the Cabinet Office 1993 First Secretary FCO 1995; Full time language training in Moscow 1998.

Lorimer, Eamonn Barrington; Valletta since February 1994; born 11.12.64; (Home Civil Service 1985-1988); Washington 1989; FCO 1993; Band A2.

Loten, Graeme Neil; HM Ambassador Bamako, since October 2001; born 10.3.59; FCO 1981; UKDEL NATO Brussels 1983; Khartoum 1986; Second Secretary (Econ/Agric) The Hague 1988; Full-time Language Training 1993; Second Secretary Almaty 1993; FCO 1997.

Lott, Ann Veronica (née Lewis); Second Secretary FCO since November 1996; born 22.11.55; FCO 1978; Algiers 1979; Montevideo 1982; FCO 1984; Latin America Floater 1987; FCO 1988; Canberra 1989; SUPL 1992; m 1989 Justin Karl Lott; (1d 1993).

Louth, Michael; FCO since July 1999; born 21.5.63; FCO 1981; Lagos 1984; East Berlin 1988; FCO 1989; Third Secretary (Management/Comm) Ljubljana 1992; Vienna 1994; Port of Spain 1996; m 1992 Carmen Elena Fuentes (1s 1994, 1d 1998).

Love, Darren Mark; Floater Duties since February 2001; born 26.2.68; FCO 1988; Warsaw 1989; Accra 1991; FCO 1993; Colombo 1997; Band B3.

Love, Stephanie Cynthia; FCO since January 1993; born 24.7.45; Bogotá 1969; Rio de Janeiro 1969; Cairo 1971; Antigua 1971; Manila 1973; UKMIS New York 1975; FCO 1978; Bahrain 1979; FCO 1984, Budapest 1986; Islamabad 1988; FCO 1990; Lisbon 1991; Band B3.

Loveday-Baugh, Christine; FCO since August 2001; born 15.8.59; FCO 1984; Muscat 1986; Kingston 1989; FCO 1991; Rome 1994; UKMIS New York 1999; Band A2; m 1992 C.Anthony Baugh.

Lovett, Simon Joseph, MBE (2000); HM Consul Riyadh since August 1997; born 11.8.57; DHSS 1977; FCO 1981; Bombay 1983; Ottawa 1987; Second Secretary FCO 1990; Second Secretary (Information/Political) Oslo 1993; m 1985 Amita Rani Sarwal (1s 1986).

Low, Nicholas David; Brasilia since November 1999; born 14.12.57; Metropolitan Police 1982-1992; FCO 1993; T/D Rabat 1994; Santiago 1995; Full Time Language Training 1999; Band D6.

Lowen, Barry Robert; FCO since June 2001; born 9.1.64; FCO 1986; Language Training Cairo 1987; Third later Second Secretary (Chancery) Kuwait 1989; First Secretary FCO 1993; First Secretary (Economic) UKMIS New York 1997; Band D7; m 1989 Karin Rhiannon Blizard.

Lowes, Merrick John; First Secretary (Commercial) Mumbai since June 2001; born 14.11.44; RAF 1962-74; FCO 1975; Vienna 1978; Maseru 1981; Vice-Consul Naples 1983; Second Secretary FCO 1986; First Secretary on loan to Office of Fair Trading 1989; First Secretary (Comm) Damascus 1991; Trade Commissioner Hong Kong and Consul Macao 1994; Deputy Consul-General Johannesburg and Head of Southern Africa Regional Commercial Hub 1998; m 1970 (Christine) Wendy Ralley (1s 1975, 1d 1978).

Loweth, Alan Robert; First Secretary FCO since May 1995; born 12.12.52; FCO 1973; Language Student 1977; Copenhagen 1978; FCO 1981; Language Student 1984; Second Secretary Moscow 1985; First Secretary FCO 1988; First Secretary Warsaw 1991; Band D6; m 1986 Linda Susan Parr.

Lowis, Joanna Jill; Second Secretary (Management) Tunis since March 1999; born 2.8.42; Warsaw 1965; Düsseldorf 1966; FCO 1969; Wellington 1972; UKDEL OECD Paris 1974; FCO 1977; Pretoria/Cape Town 1978; FCO 1981; Kathmandu 1984; FCO 1988; Third Secretary (Cons) Ottawa 1989; Second Secretary FCO 1992; Islamabad 1995.

Lownds, Matthew John; First Secretary FCO since February 2000; born 6.8.65; FCO 1987; Dublin 1989; Düsseldorf 1990; Luanda 1992; Second Secretary FCO 1995; Second Secretary (Pol) UKDEL OSCE Vienna 1996; Band D6; m 1996 Rebecca Louise Allen (1s 1997, 1d 1999).

Lucas, Stephen John; FCO since July 2000; born 30.6.62; DTI 1986-1990; FCO 1990; Third Secretary (Press/Information) Paris 1992; HM Consul Mexico City 1996; m 1994 Claudia Bautista Alfonso (1s 1998).

Lucey, Janette Margaret (née Mansley); Canberra since May 1997; born 14.7.64; FCO 1983; New Delhi 1985; Luanda 1989; Suva 1992; Band A2; m 1994 James Courtney Lucey.

Lucien, Valerie Linda; Consul General Mexico City since May 2000; born 12.8.47; FCO 1977; Lagos 1978; UKREP Brussels 1981; Africa/ME Floater 1984; FCO 1987; Third Secretary Kingston 1990; Third Secretary (Cultural/Inf) Valletta 1993; Second Secretary FCO 1996; Second Secretary FCO 1996; Band C4.

Luff, Jonathan James; Second Secretary (Political) Riyadh since September 2001; born 19.4.73; FCO 1998; FTLT 1999; FTLT (Cairo) 2000; Band C4.

Lufkin, Christine Anne (née Wilson), MVO; Second Secretary (Economic) The Hague since November 2000; born 5.1.66; FCO 1988; Washington 1990; Kuwait 1994; Second Secretary FCO 1997; SUPL 2000; m 1996 David Jonathan Peter Lufkin.

Lumsden-Bedingfeld, Ann; Floater Duties since June 1995; born 11.8.62; FCO 1985; East Berlin 1987; FCO 1989; Colombo 1990; FCO 1993; Band A2.

Lungley, Gareth Geoffrey; Second Secretary FCO since June 1999; born 8.1.71; FCO 1994; Full time language training 1996; Second Secretary (Commercial) Tehran 1997; Band C4; mSuzanne Clare Smith (1s 2001).

Lunt, Iain Andrew; FCO since September 2001; born 11.5.77; Band C4.

Lusher, David; Second Secretary (UN/UNIDO) UKMIS Vienna since January 1998; born 27.12.55; DOE 1973; FCO 1975; Belgrade 1977; Seoul 1978; Accra 1982; FCO 1984; Islamabad 1987; Vice-Consul Milan 1991; Second Secretary FCO 1994; m 1978 Soon-Ja Chung (1s 1983).

Lusty, Gregor Malcolm; Third Secretary on loan to the DTI since April 1999; since August 1995; born 12.3.69; FCO 1991; Full-time Language Training 1992; Full-time Language Training Cairo 1993; Third Secretary (Chancery) Amman 1995; T/D Kinshasa 1998.

Luttrell, David Charles; Freetown since August 2001; born 3.6.72; FCO 1999; Band B3.

Lyall, Michael David; Peking since August 1998; born 9.9.43; Royal Navy 1961-1989; Moscow 1991; Warsaw 1992; UKMIS Geneva 1993; Moscow 1996; Band B3; m 1967 Janet Haugh (1s 1969).

Lyall Grant, Mark Justin; Director (Africa) FCO since July 2000; born 29.5.56; FCO 1980; Second Secretary Islamabad 1982; First Secretary FCO 1985; First Secretary (Chancery) Paris 1990; First Secretary FCO 1993; Counsellor on loan to the Cabinet Office 1994; Deputy High Commissioner Pretoria 1996; FCO 1998; m 1986 Sheila Jean Tresise. (1s 1989, 1d 1991).

Lyall Grant, Sheila Jean (née Tresise); FCO since 1999; born 16.12.60; FCO 1980; Islamabad 1982; FCO 1985; Vice-Consul Paris 1990; FCO 1993; SUPL 1997; Band C4; m 1986 Mark Justin Lyall Grant (1s 1989, 1d 1991).

Lycett, Nadine Claire; FCO since July 2000; born 19.4.65; FCO 1984, UKDEL NATO Brussels 1986; FCO 1988; Washington 1992; Ankara 1997; Band A2.

Lygo, Clifford George; FCO since September 1982; born 2.2.51; FCO 1967; Rome 1976; FCO 1979; Khartoum 1980; Band B3; m 1976 Sandra Francida Wilson (2d 1978, 1983).

Lyne, Kevin Douglas; First Secretary (Chancery) UKMIS Geneva since August 1998; born 6.11.61; Research Officer FCO 1988; Senior Research Officer FCO 1989; Second Secretary (Chancery) Santiago 1991; Principal Research Officer FCO 1995; First Secretary FCO 1996; m 1988 Anne Francoise Dabbadie (2d 1989, 1995).

Lyne, Richard John; Deputy Head of Conference and Visits Group FCO since September 2000; born 20.11.48; FCO 1970; Belgrade 1972; Algiers 1974; Damascus 1977; FCO 1980; on loan to DTI 1981; Second Secretary (Comm) New Delhi 1984; Second later First Secretary (Chancery/Inf) Stockholm 1988; First Secretary FCO 1992; Deputy High Commissioner Port of Spain 1996; m 1977 Jennifer Anne Whitworth (1d 1982; 1s 1985).

Lyne, Sir Roderic Michael John, CMG (1992); KBE (1999); HM Ambassador Moscow since January 2000; born 31.3.48; FCO 1970; Attached to Army School of Languages 1971; Moscow 1972; Second Secretary Dakar 1974; FCO 1976; Assistant Private Secretary to Secretary of State 1979; First Secretary UKMIS New York 1982; Chatham House (CDA) 1986; Counsellor (Head of Chancery) Moscow 1987; Counsellor FCO 1990; On loan to No.10 Downing Street as PS/Prime Minister 1993; on loan to British Gas 1996; UK Permanent Representative Geneva 1997; m 1969 Amanda Mary Smith (2s 1971, 1974; 1d 1981).

Lyon, Julian Edmund; Third Secretary and Vice-Consul Yerevan since April 1999; born 20.10.65; FCO 1990; Transferred to Diplomatic Service 1999; Band B3.

Lysaght, Stephen Peter; FCO since 1999; born 17.5.70; FCO 1989; Washington 1992; Moscow 1995; Band B3.

Lyscom, David Edward; HM Ambassador Bratislava since October 1998; born 8.8.51; FCO 1972; Third later Second Secretary Vienna 1973; Second Secretary Ottawa 1977; Second (later First Secretary) FCO 1979; First Secretary 1980; First Secretary Bonn 1984; First Secretary (Economic) Riyadh 1988; First Secretary FCO 1990; Counsellor (Science and Technology) Bonn 1991; Counsellor

FCO 1996; m 1973 Nicole Jane Ward (2d 1983, 1987; 1s 1985).

Lyster-Binns, Benjamin Edward Noël; Second Secretary FCO since 1998; born 19.10.65; FCO 1989; Third Secretary (Chancery/Info) Muscat Lilongwe 1991; Band B3.

M

McAdam, Douglas Baxter; Consul General Hamburg since November 1999; born 25.6.44; FO 1961; Ulaanbaatar 1966; Vice-Consul Luanda 1969; Delhi 1972; FCO 1975; Second Secretary Ulaanbaatar 1978; Vice-Consul (Comm) Rio de Janeiro 1979; Second later First Secretary and Head of Chancery UKDEL Vienna 1983; FCO 1986; First Secretary (Consular/Immigration) Lagos 1990; First Secretary FCO 1994; HM Ambassador Almaty 1996; m 1965 Susan Clare Jarvis (1s 1970; 1d 1975).

McAdam, Susan Clare (née Jarvis); SUPL since February 1996; born 4.10.42; FO 1961; resigned 1965; reinstated 1984; Vienna 1984; FCO 1986; Lagos 1990; Second Secretary FCO 1995; m 1965 Douglas Baxter McAdam (1s 1970; 1d 1975).

Macadie, Jeremy James; Deputy Head of Mission Algiers since October 1997; born 10.7.52; FCO 1972; Dakar 1975; Addis Ababa 1980; FCO 1981; Sana'a 1984; Antananarivo 1986; Band B3; FCO 1991Assistant Private Secretary to Minister of State for Europe 1995; m 1975 Chantal Andrea Jacqueline Copiatti. (1d 1978)

Macaire, Robert Nigel Paul; First Secretary Washington since November 1998; born 19.2.66; MOD 1987-90; FCO 1990; Second Secretary (Know How Fund) Bucharest 1992; FCO 1995; m 1996 Alice MacKenzie (2d 1997, 1999).

McAllister, Andrew Thornton; Second Secretary (Commercial) Dhaka since June 2001; born 30.11.67; FCO 1988; Karachi 1990; Seoul 1993; FCO 1998; Band C4; m 1995 Han Boon AE.

McAllister, Dominic James; Second Secretary (Management) Taipei since March 1998; born 12.2.64; FCO 1990; Full-time Language Training 1992; Full-time Language Training Cairo 1993; Third Secretary (Cypher/Information) Riyadh 1994; m 1993 Hei Yee Chan (2d 1996, 1997).

McAllister, Lesley (née Dorris); Peking since March 2001; born 4.4.72; FCO 1999; Band A2; m2000 Gordon McAllister.

Macan, Thomas Townley; Minister New Delhi since October 1999; born 14.11.46; FCO 1969; Third later Second Secretary Bonn 1971; Second later First Secretary Brasilia 1974; FCO 1978; First Secretary (Press and Inf) Bonn 1981; First Secretary later Counsellor FCO 1986; Counsellor and Deputy Head of Mission Lisbon 1990; HM Ambassador Vilnius 1995; On loan to the BOC Group 1998; m 1976 Janet Ellen Martin (1s 1981; 1d 1984).

McAree, Kevin Thomas; UKDEL Brussels since February 1997; born 27.6.52; FCO 1971; Caracas 1974; FCO 1974; Honiara 1974; Moscow 1977; Georgetown 1979; FCO 1983; Munich 1988; FCO 1989; Istanbul 1993; Band B3; m 1975 Susan Margaret Humphrey.

McAree, Patrick Sean; FCO since March 1991; (Second Secretary 1994); born 30.12.53; FCO 1971; Cairo 1975; Calcutta 1978; FCO 1982; Tehran 1984; Düsseldorf 1988; Band C5; m 1975 Maureen Alexander.

McBride, Christophe Charles Rene; Second Secretary FCO since March 2001; born 20.3.75; FCO 1997; Second Secretary (Political) Abuja 1998; Band C4.

Macartney, Glen Patrick Charles; Second later First Secretary FCO since February 1975; born 24.9.49; Third Secretary FCO 1971; Language Student Sheffield University 1972; Third later Second Secretary Tokyo 1973.

Macaulay, Donald Alistair Robert, MBE (1991); First Secretary New Delhi since March 1993; born 26.6.37; Royal Navy 1958-59; CRO 1963; Freetown 1963; (Second Secretary (Inf) 1964); Bombay 1967; FCO 1970; Lourenco Marques 1973; FCO 1975; Vice-Consul (Cons/Admin) Munich 1976; Second Secretary (Comm) Washington 1981; Second later First Secretary FCO 1985; First Secretary (Comm) Kuwait 1988; FCO 1991; m(1) 1964 Bonnie Robin King (dec'd 1984) (2s 1971, 1973); (2) 1991 Pamela Lesley Wyatt.

McCafferty, Marie Claire; Wellington since May 1998; born 17.5.65; FCO 1988; Bonn 1990; Nairobi 1993; FCO 1996; Band A2.

McCall, Gary; ECO Sofia since October 2000; born 8.2.69; FCO 1987; Bridgetown 1989; Dhaka 1993; Karachi 1997; Band B3; m(1)1990 Patricia Ann Chin; (diss 1993), (2) 1993 Sharon Anne Thomas (diss) (1s 1994); ptnr, Puticha NaNongkai (1d 1998).

MacCallum, Fiona MBE (1997); First Secretary (Political) Kiev since August 2000; born 25.6.62; FCO 1986; Moscow 1989; FCO 1992; Second Secretary Riga 1995; Band C5.

McCallum, Louise Mary; FCO since February 1999; born 26.4.69; FCO 1990; UKDEL Vienna 1992; FCO 1995; Moscow 1996.

McCallum, Robert Campbell; T/D Moscow since January 2001; born 4.11.45; Moscow 1989; UKMIS New York 1991; Kiev 1993; Moscow 1997; T/D Tripoli 2000; Band B3.

McCallum, Ruth Elizabeth; FCO since April 1995; born 12.11.63; FCO 1985; Moscow 1988; FCO 1989; Ankara 1991; Band A2; m 1997 Martin Douglas McCallum.

McCann, Alec; Lisbon since April 1994; born 4.11.70; FCO 1988; Rome 1991; Band A2.

McCann, Gerry; FCO since February 1996; born 24.9.68; FCO 1988; Bangkok 1990; Africa/ ME Floater Duties 1994; Band B3.

McCarthy, Susan Margaret (née Hutton); Tortola since June 1994; born 1.4.59; FCO 1984; Khartoum 1985; Georgetown 1989; Band A2; m 1990 Jonathon Paul McCarthy (1d 1992, 1s 1996).

McCarthy, Tina Ann; FCO since December 1998; born 25.1.66; FCO 1984; Peking 1987; FCO 1988; Dar es Salaam 1990; FCO 1993; Budapest 1995; Band B3.

McCleary, William Boyd; Director General Trade and Investment Promotion and Consul General Düsseldorf since November 2000; born 30.3.49; HCS 1972; First Secretary (Agric later Chancery) Bonn 1975; First Secretary FCO 1981; First Secretary Head of Chancery and Consul Seoul 1985; First Secretary FCO 1988; Counsellor, Deputy Head of Mission and Director of Trade Promotion Ankara 1990; Counsellor (Economic) Ottawa 1993; Head, Estate Strategy Unit, FCO 1997; m(1) 1977 Susan Elizabeth Williams (diss 1999) (2d 1983, 1985); (2) 2000 Jenny Collier.

McCluskie, Matthew William; Warsaw since November 1997; born 6.5.65; FCO 1984; Bonn 1986; Prague 1988; Tunis 1990; FCO 1992; Band B3.

McColl, Lorraine Helen; RVM (1992); Tunis since September 2000; born 20.8.57; FCO 1989; Bonn 1990; Ottawa 1993; Berlin 1996; Band B3; m 1992 Alan McElroy (1d 1996).

McColl, Sally Ann; FCO since February 1990; born 27.11.64; FCO 1983; UKREP Brussels 1987; Band A2.

McColm, Sean; FCO since March 1998; born 10.7.72; FCO 1990; Copenhagen 1994; Dhaka 1997; Band B3.

McCombe, Iain Stewart; FCO since July 1988; born 22.11.69; Band A2.

McConnell, Gillian Anne; FCO since January 1988; born 10.5.68; Band A1.

McCooey, Geraldine Mary; FTLT since October 2000; born 25.5.73; FCO 1996; Second Secretary (Economic) Nicosia 1998; Band C4.

McCormack, Elizabeth (née McKenna); Vienna since February 1999; born 28.06.66; Office of Electricity Regulation 1991; FCO 1996; UKDEL NATO Brussels 1997; Band A2; m 1986 Columbus McCormack (2s 1988, 1996).

McCormick, Stephen; Tokyo since October 1997; born 5.9.67; FCO 1990; Bangkok 1993; Istanbul 1993; Tbilisi 1997; Band B3; m 1996 Sevda Unalan (1d 1999).

McCosh, Andrew David; FCO since November 1999; born 6.1.1972; FCO 1994; Vice Consul (Political) Istanbul 1997; Band C4.

McCoy, Peter Owen David; First Secretary (Commercial) Bombay since December 1996; born 28.4.52; FCO 1971; New Delhi 1974; Kaduna 1977; FCO 1981; Maseru 1984; AO/Vice-Consul/Comm Montreal 1987 (later Second Secretary); Second Secretary FCO 1990; Vice-

Consul (Commercial) Los Angeles 1992; Assistant Trade Commissioner (China Trade) BTC Hong Kong 1993; m 1975 Sally Ann Lord (2d 1976, 1978; 1s 1982).

McCredie, Ian Forbes, OBE (1984); Counsellor Washington since January 1999; born 28.12.50; Third Secretary FCO 1975; Third later Second Secretary (Econ) Lusaka 1976; FCO 1979; First Secretary (Econ/Comm) Tehran 1981; FCO 1983; Copenhagen 1985; First Secretary FCO 1989; Counsellor UKMIS New York 1992; Counsellor FCO 1997; m (1)1976 Katherine Lucy Frank (1s 1981; 1d 1983) (diss 1998), (2) 1998 Katherine Suzanne Heiny (1s 2000).

McCrory, Susan Margaret Thérèse; Assistant Legal Adviser FCO since 1996; born 17.12.64; Legal Adviser MAFF 1992; Solicitor; m 1990 Ignacio de Castro (1s 1998).

McCrudden, Patrick Gerald, MBE (1993); First Secretary (Press and Public Affairs) New Delhi since May 2000; born 22.4.50; FCO 1969; Saigon 1971; Mexico City 1974; Bahrain 1976; FCO 1977; Tristan da Cunha 1980; Brussels 1981; Pretoria 1982; Second Secretary FCO 1985; Second Secretary (Chancery) Bridgetown 1988; First Secretary (Somalia/Humanitarian) and Deputy Permanent Representative UNEP/UNCHS Nairobi 1991; First Secretary FCO 1995; Director BIS and Deputy Consul General New York 1997; Band D6; m 1973 (diss 1989); (1s 1974; 2d 1974, 1976).

McCulloch, Susan Geddes; Kampala since July 1997; born 29.6.70; FCO 1989; Berne 1992; Helsinki 1996; Band B3.

McDermott, Andrew Muir Miller; Second later First Secretary FCO since October 1991; born 24.12.43; Ministry of Transport 1959; MOD (Navy) 1961; FO 1964; Phnom Penh 1965; Pretoria/Cape Town 1969; Dacca 1971; Yaoundé 1974; FCO 1975; MECAS 1977; Kuwait 1978; Second Secretary FCO 1983; Second Secretary (Admin) and Consul Berne 1986; m 1979 Catherine Michelle Brunet.

MacDermott, Alasdair Tormod; High Commissioner Windhoek since April 2002; born 17.9.45; FO (later FCO) 1966; Kabul 1971; FCO 1973; Accra 1973; FCO 1977; Language Training Tokyo 1978; Second Secretary Tokyo 1979; Colombo 1983; First Secretary (Inf) Tokyo 1986; First Secretary FCO 1991; Full-time Language Training 1995; First Secretary (Commercial) Ankara 1995; m(1)1968 Helen Gordon (diss 1992)(2d 1969, 1971),(2) 1994 Gudrun Geiling.

MacDonald, Catriona MacLeod; FCO since November 2000; born 18.4.64; FCO 1988; Belgrade 1990; FCO 1992; Berlin 1993; FCO 1996; Vienna 1997; Band A2.

MacDonald, Michelle; FCO since January 2000; born 18.9.78; Band A2.

McDonald, David Christopher; Washington since June 1990; born 12.5.64; FCO 1984; Band B3.

McDonald, Simon Gerard; Private Secretary to the Secretary of State for Foreign and Commonwealth Affairs since June 2001; born 9.3.61; FCO 1982; Language Student SOAS 1983; Third later Second Secretary Jedda (later Riyadh) 1985; Second Secretary(Economic) Bonn 1988; First Secretary FCO 1990; Private Secretary to Permanent Under-Secretary 1993; First Secretary (Chancery) Washington 1995; Counsellor and Deputy Head of Mission and Consul General Riyadh 1998; m 1989 The Hon. Olivia Mary Wright (2s 1990, 1994; 2d 1992, 1996).

MacDougall, David; Guatemala City since November 1999; born 7.7.73; FCO 1991; Helsinki 1995; Tel Aviv 1997; T/D Kinshasa 1999; Band B3.

McDuff, Nicholas Frederic; Second Secretary FCO since March 1995; born 22.7.50; MOD (Navy) 1967; FCO 1970; Muscat 1972; UKDEL NATO Brussels 1972; BMG Berlin 1975; Karachi 1978; Islamabad 1980; FCO 1982; Athens 1983; UKDEL NATO Brussels 1984; Bandar Seri Begawan 1987; on loan to the DTI 1990; Second Secretary Casablanca 1992; m 1978 Jennifer Mary Cain (3s 1981, 1985, 1986).

McEvoy, Edward James; First Secretary Manila since July 1997; born 6.2.46; CRO later FO 1962; Belgrade 1968; Mbabane 1970; FCO 1972; Aden 1975; Luxembourg 1977; Addis Ababa 1979; on loan to Home Office 1982; Second Secretary (Immig) Dhaka 1985; Second Secretary (Comm) Manila 1989; Vice-Consul (Comm) Cape Town 1990; FCO 1995 m1967 Patricia Gibbs (diss 1991) (1s 1972).

McEwen, Christine Elizabeth; HM Consul and First Secretary (Management) Buenos Aires since April 2001; born 4.10.58; FCO 1978; BMG Berlin 1981; Peking 1984; Bombay 1987; FCO 1990; Rome 1994; Deputy Head of Mission Guatemala City 1997; FCO 2000; Band C5.

McFarlane, David Andrew; FCO since September 1999; born 20.10.77; Band C4.

McFarlane, Jacqueline (née Stewart); Mumbai since January 2002; born 1.11.67; FCO 1986; Manila 1988; FCO 1992; Damascus 1994; Islamabad 1997; SUPL 2001; Band B3; m 1988 Neil Ross McFarlane.

McFarlane, Neil Ross; Mumbai since January 2001; born 26.3.69; FCO 1991; Damascus 1994; Islamabad 1997; Band B3; m 1988 Jacqueline Stewart.

McFarlin, Andrew John; Georgetown since October 1998; born 30.8.70; FCO 1990; Vienna 1993; Floater Duties 1996; Band B3; m 1999 Juanita Adrian.

McGee, Annie (née Brown); CRD since June 1999; born 14.10.68; HCS FCO 1987; FCO 1994; Tunis 1996; Band A2; m 1996 W M V McGee (1s 1999).

McGill, Clive John; Deputy Head Of Mission Ashgabat since April 1999; born 9.10.58; FCO 1978; Belmopan 1982; Stockholm 1985; FCO 1988; Karachi 1991; Baku 1995; Band C4; m(1) 1983 Thelma Garcia; (2) 1988 Angela Raw.

McGinley, Francis John; FTLT since June 2001; born 12.1.49; FCO 1971; NATO Brussels 1974; Nairobi 1977; FCO 1980; Banjul 1982; Second Secretary (Inf) Oslo 1984; Second Secretary FCO 1989; Second Secretary (Comm) Zagreb 1992; First Secretary (Management/Consular/Immigration) Kiev 1995; m 1994 Neriman Kreso.

McGlone, Andrea Lynne; (née Webb); Vice-Consul Riyadh since February 1999; FCO 1990; born 27.3.66; FCO 1985; The Hague 1987; FCO 1990; Harare 1995; Band B3; m 1993 Kevin McGlone (2d 1994, 1997).

McGlone, Jane Mary; UKREP Brussels since September 1988; born 7.12.61; FCO 1987; Band A2.

Macgregor, John Malcolm, cvo (1992); Director Wider Europe since October 2000; born 3.10.46; FCO 1973; Second later First Secretary New Delhi 1975; First Secretary FCO 1979; Private Secretary to Minister of State 1981; Counsellor and Head of Chancery Prague 1986; Counsellor and Head of Chancery Paris 1990; Counsellor FCO 1993; Consul-General Düsseldorf 1995; Ambassador Warsaw 1998; m 1982 Judith Anne Brown (1d 1984; 3s 1986, 1987, 1990).

Macgregor, Judith Anne (née Brown), lvo (1992); Counsellor FCO since March 2001; born 17.6.52; FCO 1976; First Secretary (Chancery/Inf) Belgrade 1978; FCO 1981; SUPL 1986; First Secretary (Political/Inf) Prague 1989; SUPL 1990; First Secretary (Chancery) Paris 1992; SUPL 1993; First Secretary FCO 1993; SUPL 1995; m 1982 John Malcolm Macgregor (1d 1984; 3s 1986, 1987, 1990).

McGregor, Julie; Jerusalem since June 2001; born 23.6.80; FCO 1999; Band A2.

McGregor, Peter; HM Consul Tel Aviv since 1998; born 30.5.50; FCO 1970; Jedda 1972; Lusaka 1976; FCO 1979; Damascus 1982; Port of Spain 1986; New Delhi 1989; Second Secretary FCO 1992; Second Secretary Peking 1994; m(1) 1972 Vanessa Avril Utteridge (dec'd 1989) (1s 1980); (2) 1991 Alexandra Davenport Gillies (1d 1991).

McGregor-Bell, Sharon Ann (née McGregor); Tel Aviv since February 1999; born 23.6.71; FCO 1990; Brussels 1993; FCO 1996; SUPL 1998; Band A2; m 1995 Kevan Watson Bell.

McGuinness, Cheryl Vinetta (née Lynch); Abidjan since June 1994; born 4.11.66; FCO 1988; Peking 1991; Band A2; m 1996 Mark John McGuinness.

McGuinness, Mark Andrew; Abidjan since May 1999; born 25.8.67; FCO 1988; Islamabad 1990; FCO 1992; Doha 1996; Band B3.

McGuinness, Patrick Joseph, obe (1997); First Secretary FCO since September 1999; born

27.4.63; FCO 1985; Language Training 1986; Second Secretary (Chancery) Sana'a 1988; Second Secretary FCO 1991; First Secretary (Political) Abu Dhabi 1994; First Secretary Cairo 1996; Band D6; m 1994 Susannah Imogen Mills.

McGurgan, Kevin; FCO since August 2000; born 31.5.71; FCO 1990; Floater Duties 1992; UKREP Brussels 1994; Sarajevo 1996; Third later Second Secretary (Chancery) UKMIS New York 1997; Band D6; m 1997 Victoria Ann Harrison.

McGurgan, Victoria Ann (née Harrison); FCO since August 2000; born 13.8.71; FCO 1994; UKMIS New York 1997; Band A2; m 1997 Kevin McGurgan.

McGurk, Gerard, MBE (2000); Second Secretary (Chancery) UKMIS New York since August 2000; born 22.12.70; FCO 1988; Athens 1991; Floater Duties 1994; Deputy Head of Mission and Vice Consul Skopje 1996; Band B3; m 1998 Sonja Kurcieva.

McHugh, Susan Mary; Second Secretary FCO since November 1994; born 12.2.44; FCO 1971; on loan to SEATO Bangkok 1974; New Delhi 1977; SUPL 1980; Victoria (Seychelles) 1981, Second Secretary FCO 1983; Second Secretary Nicosia 1994.

Macintosh, Anne; SUPL since October 1997; born 15.4.61; FCO 1980; Rome 1982; Havana 1985; FCO 1988; Third later Second Secretary (Comm) Buenos Aires 1991; m 1993 Gustavo Javier Barreiro (1d 1996).

Macintosh, Kenneth Gilbert; FCO since October 1990; born 29.3.72; Band A2.

MacIntosh, Sarah; First Secretary FCO since July 1997; born 7.8.69; FCO 1991; Third Secretary (AEA/UN) UKMIS Vienna 1994; Second Secretary(Economic/EU) Madrid 1996.

McIntosh, Elaine; FCO since November 1993; born 2.9.68; FCO 1988; Luxembourg 1991 Band A2; m 1990 Angus Lyon McIntosh.

McIntosh, Margaret Claire; World-wide floater since March 1999; born 31.5.63; FCO 1995; UKREP Brussels 1997; Band B3.

McIntosh, Martin Howard, OBE (1994); Counsellor (Commercial) Dublin since April 2001; born 26.12.47; FO (later FCO) 1966; Jakarta 1970; Tokyo 1970; Moscow 1972; Beirut 1973; FCO 1976; Madrid 1979; Second Secretary Bogotá 1982; Second later First Secretary (Comm) Nairobi 1984; First Secretary FCO 1989; First Secretary (Commercial) Buenos Aires 1990; First Secretary (Commercial) Mexico City 1994; on loan to the DTI 1997; m 1970 Erika Wagner (2d 1983, 1985).

McIntyre, Douglas Robert Stuart; First Secretary FCO since December 1995; born 10.5.41; FO 1959; Khartoum 1964; La Paz 1967; Tripoli 1969; Rome 1971; FCO 1974; Second Secretary Mexico City 1977; Vila 1982; First Secretary and Consul Las Palmas 1984; First Secretary FCO 1988; Consul-General Madrid 1991; m(1) 1964 (diss

1968) (1s 1964); (2) 1971 Catherine Campbell Tweed (1d 1974; 1s 1976).

McIver, Damian John; First Secretary (Political) Belgrade since October 1998; born 2.11.61; HM Customs and Excise 1986; FCO 1986; Belgrade 1987; Second Secretary FCO 1991; Second Secretary EC MIS Zagreb 1992; Second Secretary FCO 1993; Language Training 1994; (KHF) Bucharest 1995.

Mackay, Gavin Anderson; MBE (1994); Second Secretary Nicosia since September 1989; born 1.11.49; FCO 1973; Wellington 1975; Suva 1978; Dhaka 1981; FCO 1983; Dubai 1986; (Second Secretary 1988); m 1975 Glenys Pickup (1d 1977; 2s 1980, 1984).

Mackay, Katherine Wendy; Second Secretary UKMIS New York since April 2000; born 6.7.72; FCO 1996; Band C4.

McKee, Tracy Anne; Kigali since December 2000; born 3.6.77; Band A2.

McKell, Paul Leo; Assistant Legal Adviser FCO since May 1997; born 1.9.66; m2001 Elizabeth C Hanlon.

McKelvey, Diane Elizabeth; FCO since July 2001; born 6.7.67; FCO 1989; Third Secretary (Political) Copenhagen 1992; FCO 1994; Second Secretary (Political/Press and Public Affairs) Lusaka 1998.

McKen, Dawn; FCO since January 2000; born 23.7.66; FCO 1995; Second Secretary (Political) Moscow 1996; Band D6.

McKendrick, Ian; Floater Duties since January 1998; born 4.10.70; FCO 1991; BTC Hong Kong 1995; Band B3.

MacKenna, Roderic Hamish; FCO since March 2000; born 15.8.58; Band B3; m 1991 Ayoma Indrani Nethsingha (2d 1992, 1993).

McKenzie, Alistair William, MBE (1980); Counsellor and Deputy Head of Mission Abu Dhabi since July 2001; born 19.2.45; DSAO 1965; Budapest 1967; Singapore 1969; Brasilia 1972; FCO 1975; San Salvador 1978; San José 1980; Commercial Attaché Madrid 1982 (Second Secretary 1983); Second Secretary FCO 1984; Deputy High Commissioner and Head of Chancery Banjul 1986; Consul-General Bilbao 1990; First Secretary (Immigration/Consular) Lagos 1995; British Trade International 1998; m 1968 Margaret Emily Young (2s 1970, 1974).

MacKenzie, Angela Susan (née Wright); SUPL since April 2000; born 17.1.67; FCO 1985; Lilongwe 1989; SUPL 1993; FCO 1995; SUPL 1997; Band B3; m(1) 1988 Mohammed Ouassine (diss 1992), (2) 1997 Graham John MacKenzie.

MacKenzie, Catherine Louise Hay; UKMIS New York since March 2000; born 9.8.66; FCO 1989; Language Training FCO 1991; Language Training Tokyo 1992; Second Secretary 1992; Second Secretary (Chancery) Tokyo 1993; Band D6; m 1992 John Page.

Mackenzie, Dorothy (née Byers); SUPL since January 1999; born 1.3.56; FCO 1974; The Hague 1976; Lusaka 1979; FCO 1982; Ottawa 1985; SUPL 1990; Singapore 1991; FCO 1993; Band C4; m 1978 Robert Mackenzie; (1d 1987).

MacKenzie, Hilary (née Grace); Vice-Consul Helsinki since March 1996; born 1.3.59; FCO 1980; Islamabad 1982; Oslo 1984; Bombay 1987; Amsterdam 1989; FCO 1992; Band B3; m 1989 Ian James McKenzie.

MacKenzie, Ian Johnston; Moscow since March 1998; born 30.8.42; RAF 1958-86; Budapest 1988; Washington 1990; Bonn 1993; World-wide Floater Duties 1996; Band B3; m 1984 Inge Schmitz.

MacKenzie, Josephine Mary (née Gary); SUPL since December 1996; born 7.7.69; FCO 1988; Kuala Lumpur 1990; Pretoria 1994; Band A2; m 1993 Donald McLean MacKenzie.

MacKenzie, Kenneth John Alexander; First Secretary FCO since July 2001; born 9.9.49; FCO 1973; Brussels 1975; Second later First Secretary FCO 1978; Buenos Aires 1981; First Secretary FCO 1982; First Secretary (Econ) Bucharest 1985; First Secretary FCO 1988; First Secretary Vienna 1992; First Secretary FCO 1995; Consul Munich 1997; Band D6; m 1980 Alison Mary Linda Sandford (1d 1983; 1s 1987).

McKenzie, Philip; BTC Hong Kong since October 1996; born 26.4.65; FCO 1986; Lusaka 1987; San José 1991; FCO 1993; Band B3.

Mackenzie, Robert; First Secretary (Commercial) Muscat since July 1998; born 5.3.54; Dept of National Savings 1973; FCO 1974; The Hague 1976; Lusaka 1979; FCO 1982; Ottawa 1985; Second Secretary FCO 1988; Second Secretary (Commercial) Mexico City 1988; Second Secretary (Commercial) Singapore 1990; Second Secretary FCO 1993; m 1978 Dorothy Byers; (1d 1987).

MacKenzie-May, Mary Faith Arbuthnott (née MacKenzie); FCO since July 1984; (Second Secretary 1988); born 22.5.47; FCO 1975; Moscow 1977; FCO 1978; Bahrain 1982; Band C4; m 1989 David Robert May.

McKenzie Smith, Justin James; First Secretary FCO since October 1999; born 4.2.69; FCO 1994; Full-time Language Training 1995; Second Secretary (Political) Moscow 1996.

McKeogh, Fiona (née Sutherland), MBE (1993); UKMIS New York since September 1999; born 17.9.59; FCO 1983; Bonn 1984; Cape Town 1987; UKREP Brussels 1989; FCO 1993; SUPL 1993; FCO 1995; Moscow 1997; Band B3; m 1992 Paul Nicolas McKeogh.

McKeown, Patricia; Banjul since April 1992; born 13.5.69; FCO 1987; UKDIS Geneva 1989; Band A2.

MacKerras, Carl Anthony; Vice Consul Copenhagen since August 1997; born 13.11.69; Land Registry 1988-1990; FCO 1990; St

Petersburg 1995; m 1997 Vera Ermolova (2d 1997, 2000).

McKerrow, Elizabeth Mary (née Foot); FCO since August 1991; born 18.1.67; FCO 1986; Buenos Aires 1990; Band B3; m 1991 Ian Bernard Harry McKerrow.(1s 1998, 1d 2000).

Mackie, Anne Bernadette; UKMIS Geneva since October 1999; born 24.10.59; FCO 1983; Cairo 1985; Lagos 1988; SUPL 1990; FCO 1991; Hong Kong 1995; FCO 1997; Band A2; (1s 1990).

McKie, Margaret Stevenson; UKREP Brussels since May 2001; born 7.8.62; FCO 1988; Prague 1991; Cairo 1993; FCO 1996. Floater 1998; FTLT 2001; Band A2.

McKinlay, Ian Leonard; FCO since June 1997; born 17.9.58; FCO 1978; UKMIS Geneva 1980; Tehran 1983; FCO 1986; Addis Ababa 1989; Dakar 1992; m 1984 Ann Hugoline Cameron (1s 1989; 2d 1991, 1993).

McKnight, Elisabeth Eithne, UKREP Brussels since November 1985; born 2.8.41; FCO 1973; Dacca 1974; FCO 1975; Mbabane 1976; FCO 1978; Grand Turk 1980; UKMIS New York 1983; Band B3.

Mackrell, William Michael; Bonn since June 1992; born 11.8.47; Band B3.

McLachlan, Malcolm Orde; Second later First Secretary (Political) Nairobi since August 1998; born 10.9.63; FCO 1981; Karachi 1984; Guatemala City 1988; FCO 1993; m 1989 Maricruz Mendia Moynes (1d 1995).

The MacLaren of MacLaren, Donald; Consul-General and Deputy Head of Mission Kiev since November 2000; born 22.8.54; FCO 1978; Third later Second later First Secretary BMG Berlin 1980; Language Training 1983; First Secretary and Press Attaché Moscow 1984; First Secretary FCO 1987; Deputy Head of Mission Havana 1991; First Secretary FCO 1994; m 1978 Maida-Jane Aitchison (3s 1980, 1981, 1984; 2d 1987, 1994).

McLaren, Donald Stuart; Deputy Head of Mission Tblisi since June 2001; born 1.8.44; FCO 1971; Jakarta 1973; FCO 1975; St Helena 1976; FCO 1977; Pretoria 1979; FCO 1982; Third Secretary Darwin 1984; FCO 1986; Accra 1988; Third Secretary (Commercial) Kuala Lumpur 1992; Consul Kuching 1995; FCO 1999; Band C4; m 1968 Glenys Catherine Bryant (1d 1971; 2s 1973, 1979).

McLaren, Marilynn; MBE (1993),SUPL since January 1998; born 20.7.47; Scottish Office 1963; FCO 1981; Dacca 1981; Tehran 1985; Lisbon 1987; FCO 1989; Tehran 1990; Washington 1994; Band B3.

McLean, Siân Alexis; First Secretary (Economic) Peking since July 2001; born 12.9.69; FCO 1993; FTLT (Peking) 1996; Consul (Economic) Hong Kong 1997; Band D6.

MacLennan, David Ross; HM Ambassador Beirut since September 1996; born 12.2.45; FO 1963; DSAO 1965; MECAS 1966; Aden 1969; Civil Service College 1972; Second later First Secretary FCO 1972; First Secretary UKDEL OECD Paris 1975; First Secretary Head of Chancery and Consul Abu Dhabi 1979; First Secretary FCO 1982; on secondment to European Commission 1984; Counsellor (Comm) Kuwait 1985; Counsellor and Head of Chancery Nicosia 1989; HM Consul-General Jerusalem 1990; Counsellor FCO 1994; m 1964 Margaret Lytollis (2d 1964, 1966).

MacLeod, Fiona; T/D Belmopan since May 1996; born 19.10.70; FCO 1992; Seoul 1994; Band A2.

MacLeod, Frances Ann; FCO since August 1991; born 4.12.59; FCO 1983; Warsaw 1985; Maputo 1988; Band B3; m 1989 James Robert McDougall.

MacLeod, Gordon Stewart; Consul (Commercial and Information) Casablanca since March 1998; born 15.2.52; FCO 1971; Ankara 1973; Washington 1977; Dacca 1979; FCO 1982; Valletta 1985; Third later Second Secretary New Delhi 1988; Second Secretary FCO 1992; m 1978 Susan Raggatt (2d 1981, 1984).

MacLeod, Iain; Counsellor (Legal Adviser) UKMIS New York since August 2001; born 15.3.62; Assistant Legal Adviser FCO 1987; First Secretary (Assistant Legal Adviser) UKREP Brussels 1991; FCO 1995; on loan to HM Treasury 1997; m 1988 Dr Alison Mary Murchison.

MacLeod, Siân Christina; First Secretary (Political) The Hague since July 1996; born 31.5.62; FCO 1986; Language Training 1987; Second Secretary (Chancery) Moscow 1988; Second later First Secretary FCO 1992; m 1987 Richard Anthony Robinson (2d 1991, 1994, 1s 1998).

McMahon, Brian Patrick; British Trade International since November 1999; born 26.3.46; CRO and DSAO 1963; Prague 1968; Bonn 1969; Kabul 1972; FCO 1975; Islamabad 1978; UKMIS Geneva 1981; Second Secretary FCO 1984; Second Secretary (Immigration/Consular) Colombo 1990; HM Consul Rome 1994; FCO 1999; m 1967 Eileen Conroy (1d 1970; 1s 1975).

McMahon, Dr David John Hugh; First Secretary (Environment and Trade Policy) New Delhi since June 2001; born 4.5.65; FCO 1991; Second Secretary (Political/Inf) Dhaka 1993; FCO 1997; Band D6; m 1994 Kay Taylor Lacey.

McMahon, Ian Irvine; Counsellor Copenhagen since December 1997; born 8.6.55; Army 1973-83; Second Secretary FCO 1983; Second later First Secretary (Chancery) Islamabad 1985; First Secretary FCO 1987; First Secretary (Chancery) New Delhi 1989; First Secretary later Counsellor FCO 1992; m 1979 Anne Elizabeth Baker (1d 1981).

McMahon, Keith David; MBE (1998); FCO since August 1998; born 10.3.68; FCO 1988; Lusaka

1990; SE Asia/Middle East Floater Duties 1993; Deputy Head of Mission Yerevan 1995; Band C4; m2000 Melissa Schwartz.

McManus, John Andrew; First Secretary (Political) Brussels since January 2001; born 20.5.55; FCO 1977; Paris 1980; Algiers 1983; FCO 1985; Language Training FCO 1987 (Second Secretary 1987); Second Secretary Moscow 1988; Second Secretary UKREP Brussels 1992; Second later First Secretary (Information) Berne 1993; FCO 1997; Band D6.

MacMillan, Alison Flora; Second Secretary (EU) Gibraltar since October 1996; born 22.8.61; FCO 1982; Mexico City 1983; Washington 1987; SUPL 1989; FCO 1990; Third Secretary Vice-Consul and Deputy Head of Mission Managua 1993; m 1997 Julian Thomas Lee (1s 1997, 1d 1999).

McMinn, Wendy Lily Alexandra; Canberra since April 2001; born 7.7.71; Ministry of Defence 1991; FCO 1999; Band A2.

McNair, Richard Andrew; FCO since April 1995; born 18.2.59; FCO 1979; Lagos 1980; FCO 1982; Ankara 1984; FCO 1987; Cairo 1991; Band C4; m 1978 Julie Elaine Stephen (1d 1981; 1s 1983).

McNeill, Alasdair Morrell; FCO since February 1999; born 13.11.67; FCO 1988; Istanbul 1992; FCO 1995; Moscow 1997; Band B3; m 1994 Elizabeth Hall (1s 2000).

McNeill, Christine Mary; Deputy High Commissioner Mbabane since January 1999; born 12.3.62; FCO 1979; Cairo 1983; Suva 1987; Second Secretary, FCO 1992; Madras 1995; m 1982 Scott Robertson McNeill (1d 1994; 1s 1998).

Macphail, John Patrick Nicholson; British Trade International FCO since June 1998; born 21.5.48; FCO 1968; Middle East Floater 1971; Moscow 1973; Georgetown 1974; FCO 1976; Budapest 1979; Mexico City 1980; UKDEL NATO Brussels 1983; Second Secretary FCO 1985; Second Secretary (Comm) Lagos 1989; Second Secretary (Comm) Kuala Lumpur 1993; SUPL 1996; m(1) 1981 Joy Chambers (diss 1989) 1d 1983(dec'd 1989); (2) 1992 Carolyn Inness Turner (1s 1998).

McPhail, Dr Alastair David; Second later First Secretary (Political/Military) Ankara since November 1996; born 2.3.61; FCO 1994; Language Training 1995; m 1989 Pamela Joanne Davies (2s 1992, 1994).

McPhail, Pamela Joanne (née Davies); SUPL since September 1996; born 3.12.62; FCO 1990; Third Secretary (Public Affairs) Moscow 1992; FCO 1995; Band B3; m 1989 Alastair David McPhail (2s 1992, 1994).

Macpherson, John Bannerman; Counsellor FCO since November 1996; born 23.6.51; Third later Second Secretary FCO 1975; Language Student MECAS 1977; Second Secretary Khartoum 1979; Second later First Secretary Sana'a 1980; FCO 1983; Language Training 1985; First Secretary Sofia 1987; First Secretary FCO 1990; Counsellor

Cairo 1993; m 1985 Monica Jane Lancashire (2s 1986, 1988; 1d 1992).

Macpherson, Kara Isobel; Second Secretary FCO since September 1998; born 3.8.60; FCO 1981; Islamabad 1983; Prague 1986; Africa/ME Floater 1988; FCO 1992; T/D Khartoum 1994; FCO 1994; T/D UKMIS New York 1996; FCO 1997; Band B3.

MacQueen, Christine Ann; First Secretary later Counsellor FCO 1995; born 24.5.59; FCO 1982; Second Secretary (Econ) Brasilia 1984; Second later First Secretary FCO 1987; New York 1989; First Secretary and UNESCO observer Paris 1990; m 1992 Bruno Pascal Castola (1d 1992, 1s 1994).

McQueen, Jacqueline Mary; SUPL since May 1992; born 27.12.63; Inland Revenue 1980, FCO 1985; Bonn 1986; FCO 1989; Band A2; m 1992 Simon Hewitt.

McQuibban, Peter James; SUPL since September 1995; born 7.11.55; Third later Second Secretary FCO 1981; Second Secretary (Econ) Brasilia 1982; First Secretary FCO 1985; First Secretary (Political) Warsaw 1988; First Secretary FCO 1992; First Secretary on loan to the Cabinet Office 1992; First Secretary on Sabbatical at Copenhagen University since September 1995; Band D6; m(1) 1982 Susan Jennifer Magdalen Hitch (diss 1996), (2) 1996 Annegrette Felter Rasmussen (1d 1996) .

McQuigg, Harold; born 9.6.40; FCO since March 1997; born 9.6.40 Royal Marines 1955-80; Prison Service 1980; Havana 1984; New Delhi 1986; Lagos 1987; Kuala Lumpur 1990; Moscow 1993; Addis Ababa 1995; Band C4; m 1961 Nora Shilliday (3s 1962, 1964, 1968; 1d 1970).

McQuilton, Patricia Bernadette (née Edwards); Nicosia since November 1998; born 15.3.69; Home Civil Service 1988; FCO 1996. Band A2; m 1999 Craig McQuilton.

MacSween, Norman James; Counsellor FCO since October 1998; born 22.1.48; FCO 1970; Third later Second Secretary Nairobi 1972; FCO 1975; language student SOAS 1976 and Shiraz 1977; First Secretary Tehran 1977; FCO 1979; First Secretary (Chancery) Bonn 1983; First Secretary FCO 1987; First Secretary later Counsellor Stockholm 1991; Counsellor Moscow 1995; m 1983 Julia Jane Reid (1s 1988, 1d 1990).

McVey, Andrea; SUPL since August 1997; born 28.1.64; FCO 1988; Paris 1991; Luxembourg 1993; FCO 1996; Band A2.

Madden, David Christopher Andrew, CMG (1996); H M Ambassador Athens since May 1999; born 25.7.46; Third Secretary FCO 1970; Third later Second Secretary BMG Berlin 1972; First Secretary on loan to Cabinet Office 1975; First Secretary Moscow 1978; First Secretary and Head of Chancery Athens 1981; FCO 1984; Counsellor, Head of Chancery and Consul-General Belgrade 1987; Counsellor FCO 1990; High Commissioner Nicosia 1994; m 1970 Penelope Anthea Johnston (1s 1972; 2d 1974, 1975).

Madden, Paul Damien; Deputy High Commissioner and Counsellor (Commercial/Economic) Singapore since November 2000; born 25.4.59; DTI 1980; PS/PUSS 1984; Language Training FCO/Kamakura 1987; First Secretary Tokyo 1988, First Secretary FCO 1992; First Secretary Washington 1996; m 1989 Sarah Pauline Thomas (2s 1991, 1992, 1d 1996).

Maddicott, David Sydney; First Secretary (Head of Pol/Info Section) Ottawa since August 1997; born 27.3.53; First Secretary FCO 1994; Full Time Language Training 1996; on Attachment to the Canadian Government 1996; m 1980 Elizabeth Wynne (4s 1980, 1984, 1990, 1993; 1d 1982).

Maddinson, Paul Francis; First Secretary (Political) Moscow since November 2001; born 16.5.72; FCO 1995; Second Secretary (Political) Nairobi 1996; Second Secretary FCO 1998; FTLT 2000; Band D6; m 1996 Rebecca Anne Jackson (1s 2000).

Madisons, Alexander Emil; Third Secretary Rome since October 1999; born 9.11.62; FCO 1983; Peking 1990; FCO 1997; Belgrade 1994; Band C4.

Madojemu, Valentine Isi; FCO since November 1998; born 27.3.58; Band B3; m 1989 Rita (1s 1992, 1d 1997).

Magor, William Wavell, MBE (2000); First Secretary (Commercial) Warsaw since October 1999; born 11.7.43; CRO later Commonwealth Office 1961; Accra 1966; UKMIS New York 1969; FCO 1971; Algiers 1971; FCO 1973; Caracas 1976; Nassau 1979; FCO 1981; Second Secretary (Admin) (later Admin/Cons) Port of Spain 1983; Second Secretary (Comm) Dubai 1987; Second Secretary FCO 1992; First Secretary (Comm) Tel Aviv 1995; m 1965 Avril Anne Swalwell (1d 1966; 1s 1973).

Maguire, John; HM Consul Denver since January 2000; born 4.6.49; FCO 1968; Moscow 1971; Belmopan 1972; New Delhi 1974; Tokyo 1978; FCO 1982; Alexandria 1985; Consul (Comm) Perth 1988; FCO 1992; Deputy Head of Mission, Consul and First Secretary (Commercial) Doha 1995; FCO 1999; Band C5; m 1978 Mette Lucie Konow Monsen.

Maguire, Natalie (née Rule); Bahrain since June 2001; born 22.5.62; FCO 2000; Band A2; m 1981 Robin Maguire.

Maher, Heather Kirsten Maria; Kiev since November 2000; born 12.1.70; FCO 1988; Bangkok 1990; FCO 1993; Athens 1994; Kuwait 1995; Harare 1999; FCO 1999; Abidjan 2000; Band A2.

Major, Pamela Ann; First Secretary later Counsellor FCO since February 1996; born 4.3.59; FCO 1982; Language Training SOAS 1983; Second Secretary (Chancery) Peking 1986; First Secretary FCO 1988; First Secretary Moscow 1993; m 1992 Robert Leigh Turner (1s 1992, 1d 1994).

Makepeace, Richard Edward; HM Ambassador Khartoum since July 1999; born 24.6.53; FCO 1976; Language Student MECAS 1977; Third later Second Secretary Muscat 1979; Second later First Secretary (Chancery) Prague 1981; FCO 1985; Private Secretary to the Parliamentary Under-Secretary of State 1986; First Secretary UKREP Brussels 1989; Counsellor FCO 1993; Cairo 1995 m1980 Rupmani Catherine Pradhan.

Makin, John; Second Secretary (Commercial) Perth since March 2001; born 13.1.64; DHSS 1984; FCO 1985; Kaduna 1987; Düsseldorf 1990; Floater Duties 1992; FCO 1996; Jakarta 1999; Band C4.

Makriyiannis, Lorraine Elizabeth (née Colhoun); SUPL since May 1999; born 10.6.69; FCO 1991; Sofia 1993; Nicosia 1995; Band A2; m 1995 Michael Makriyiannis.

Malcolm, James Ian; OBE (1995); HM Ambassador Panama City since March 2002; born 29.3.46; MPBW 1964; FO 1966; UKDEL NATO Brussels 1969; Rangoon 1972; FCO 1974; Nairobi 1977; Damascus 1980; Second Secretary (Comm) Luanda 1983; Second Secretary FCO 1985; First Secretary (Pol/Econ) Jakarta 1987; First Secretary FCO 1994; Deputy High Commissioner Kingston 1997; m 1967 Sheila Nicholson Moore (1s 1976; 1d 1980).

Malik, Runa; ECO Dhaka since September 2000; born 23.6.74; FCO 1996.

Malin, Carl Spencer; Vice-Consul Lagos since June 1996; born 7.7.69; FCO 1987; Ottawa 1989; FCO 1992; Floater Duties 1993; FCO 1995; Band B3; m 1995 Kerstin Ruge.

Malin, Keith Ian; Counsellor FCO since November 1999; born 11.12.53; FCO 1976; Third Secretary (Developing Countries) UKREP Brussels 1978; Second later First Secretary FCO 1979; First Secretary on secondment to HCS 1983; First Secretary (UN/Press) UKMIS Geneva 1984; FCO 1986; First Secretary (Chancery/Economic) Sofia 1990; First Secretary later Counsellor FCO 1993; Counsellor Peking 1996; m 1977 Gaynor Dudley Jones (2s 1985, 1992).

Mallery, Geoffrey Charles; Islamabad since 1997; OGD 1968-1988; New Delhi 1988; Bangkok 1992; FCO 1995; Band C5; m 1969 Adriana Elizabeth (2d 1978, 1981).

Mallion, Richard Julian; FCO since July 1999; born 23.12.68; Band A2.

Malone, Philip; First Secretary FCO since May 1999; born 3.12.61; FCO 1981; Buenos Aires 1983; Guatemala City 1986; FCO 1989; Third Secretary (Commercial/Information) Luxembourg 1992; Second Secretary (Chancery) Bandar Seri Begawan 1995; m 1999 Sarah Tan Yee Whey.

Mamet, Emma Kate (née Miller); Third Secretary (Economic) Ottawa since March 1999; born 6.8.70; FCO since 1991; Third Secretary (Chancery) UKMIS Geneva 1994; Port Louis 1995; Band B3; m2000 Anthony Roger Mamet.

Man, Kam Lon; Islamabad since March 2000; born 16.6.72; FCO 1996; Band A2.

Manley, Ernest George; UKDEL NATO Brussels since June 1999; born 15.2.51; FCO 1970; Aden 1973; Milan 1975; East Berlin 1978; FCO 1980; Kuala Lumpur 1983; Consul Milan 1986; FCO 1990; Band C4; m 1973 Mary Catherine Whelan (1s 1975).

Manley, Philip Ernest; FCO since September 1999; born 17.6.44; GPO 1960; FCO 1969; Washington 1971; FCO 1974; Amman 1975; FCO 1976; Attaché Moscow 1978; FCO 1980; Third Secretary Lagos 1981; FCO 1984; Second Secretary Bonn 1987; Second Secretary FCO 1990 (First Secretary 1993); Moscow 1996; Band D6; m 1967 Christine Anne Kellett (1s 1970; 1d 1972).

Manley, Simon John; On secondment to the EU Council Secretariat Brussels since October 1998; born 18.9.67; FCO 1990; on secondment to the European Commission 1993. Second later First Secretary (Political) UKMIS New York 1993; m 1996 Maria Isabel Fernandez-Utges (1d 2000).

Manley, Suzanne Marie Theresa; Moscow since April 2001; born 12.12.64; FCO 1987; La Paz 1990; T/D Havana 1993; Santiago 1994; T/D Buenos Aires 1998; FCO 1998; Band B3.

Manning, Sir David Geoffrey, KCMG (2001), CMG (1992); Foreign Policy Adviser to the Prime Minister since September 2001; born 5.12.49; Third Secretary FCO 1972; Language course 1973; Third later Second Secretary Warsaw 1974; Second later First Secretary New Delhi 1977; FCO 1980; First Secretary Paris 1984; Counsellor on loan to the Cabinet Office 1988; Political Counsellor Moscow 1990; Head of Eastern Department FCO 1993; UK Member of ICFY Contact Group for Bosnia 1994; Head of Policy Planning FCO 1994; HM Ambassador Tel Aviv 1995; Deputy Under-Secretary FCO 1998; Permanent Representative UKDEL NATO Brussels 2000; m 1973 Catherine Parkinson.

Mansfield, Clive; Plymouth since July 1997; born 8.4.54; FCO 1973; Beirut 1975; Bombay 1976; Mexico City 1979; Rome 1981; FCO 1984; Islamabad 1987; FCO 1988; Band B3; m(1) 1980 Gail Denise Purvis (diss 1989), (2) Hilda Margaret Eddie.

Marcelin, Hamilton David; First Secretary (Management) Vienna since June 1997; born 16.11.41; FO 1960; Kuwait 1963; Nairobi 1966; Rio de Janeiro 1967; MECAS 1969; Khartoum 1971; FCO 1974; Second Secretary (Comm) Sydney 1977; First Secretary (Comm) Muscat 1982; FCO 1985; First Secretary (Admin) and Consul Belgrade 1989; First Secretary FCO 1992; m(1) 1966 Mona Druce (diss 1977) (1d 1969), (2) 1977 Pamela Foxall.

March, Shirley Elizabeth; First Secretary (UNPR) UKMIS Geneva since June 2000; born 4.2.61; FCO 1984; Second Secretary (EC Affairs)

Brussels 1988; First Secretary FCO 1990; Band D6; m 1984 Paul Louis March (2s 1990, 1992).

Marchant, Trixie Jane (née Farmer); FCO since February 1991; (Second Secretary 1993); born 1.3.65; FCO 1987; Geneva 1989; Band C4; m 1989 Andrew John Marchant (1s 1998).

Marden, Nicholas; Counsellor Tel Aviv since January 1998; born 2.5.50; Army 1971-74; Third later Second Secretary FCO 1974; Second Secretary Nicosia 1977; First Secretary FCO 1980; Warsaw 1982; FCO 1985; First Secretary Paris 1988; First Secretary FCO 1993; m 1977 Melanie Gaye Glover (2d 1980, 1982).

Mardlin, Robert Andrew; Nairobi since October 1999; born 13.1.65; FCO 1984; Lima 1986; Sofia 1990; Dhaka 1992; FCO 1996; Band B3; m 1988 Amanda Karen Morall.

Marmion, Elisabeth Claire (née Terry); Hong Kong since May 1999; born 9.7.72; FCO 1995; Band A2; m 1999 Nicholas Paul Marmion.

Marren, Marrena Ruby; UKREP Brussels since July 1998; born 15.1.68; FCO 1987; Paris 1989; Prague 1992; Geneva 1994; FCO 1994; Band B3.

Marriott, Allison Mary MBE (1997); First Secretary (Management) Addis Ababa since June 2000; born 31.3.66; FCO 1987; Vice-Consul Amman 1990; Third Secretary UKDEL Brussels 1993; Copenhagen 1996; Second Secretary FCO 1997; Band C5.

Marriott, Anne Stewart Murray (née Corbett); FCO since February 2001; born 29.10.57; FCO 1979; Brasilia 1982; FCO 1984; Abu Dhabi 1985; Bangkok 1988; FCO 1992; Amman 1997; Band B3; m 1988 Paul James Marriott.

Marsden, Ian Thomas; T/D Pristina since August 1999; born 5.10.69; Department of Social Security 1989; FCO 1990; Colombo 1993; FCO 1996; Sarajevo 1997; on loan to the DTI 1998; Band B3.

Marsden, Rosalind Mary; Director Asia-Pacific since December 1999; born 27.10.50; Third Secretary FCO 1974; Language training SOAS 1975; Third, Second and later First Secretary Tokyo 1976; First Secretary FCO 1980; First Secretary (Econ) Bonn 1985; First Secretary FCO 1989; Counsellor on secondment to the National Westminster Bank 1991; Head of Chancery, Tokyo 1993; Counsellor FCO 1996.

Marsh, Elaine (née Skinner); Washington since May 1998; born 6.1.57; FCO 1976; Port of Spain 1978; Bucharest 1982; Valletta 1984; FCO 1987; New Delhi 1989; Third Secretary (Consular) Dar es Salaam 1992; Third Secretary FCO 1994; Band B3; m 1985 Andrew Peter Marsh; (diss 1989) (1s 1988).

Marsh, Ian Dudley; Counsellor (Immigration/ Management/Consular) Islamabad since June 1998; born 17.3.45; FO 1965; Algiers 1967; Benin City 1970; Accra 1971; Kuala Lumpur 1972; FCO 1976; Second Secretary (Aid) Yaoundé 1978; FCO 1980; Vice-Consul (Pol/Inf) Cape Town 1983

(First Secretary 1986); First Secretary FCO 1987; Resident Representative Antigua and St Christopher and Nevis 1990; First Secretary Dhaka 1993; Deputy Head of Mission Sarajevo 1997; m(1) 1969 Susan Mary Walsh (dec'd 1985) (1d 1977); (2) 1991 Margot Anita Gonsalves.

Marshall, Alan John; Second Secretary (Consular) Jakarta since April 2001; born 11.9.52; FCO 1971; Cairo 1973; Lilongwe 1975; Salisbury 1978; Sana'a 1980; FCO 1981; Islamabad 1983; Lisbon 1987; Luanda 1990; Second Secretary FCO 1993; Lisbon 1996; Consul Lisbon 1998; Band C4; (1s 1979; 1d 1986).

Marshall, Angela Rosemary; FTLT since March 2000; born 22.8.60; FCO 1988; Maseru 1991; Kiev 1994; FCO 1997; Band B3.

Marshall, Bernard Alan; Second Secretary (Commercial) T/D Tripoli since July 2001; born 23.3.48; FCO 1968; Bombay 1971; Islamabad 1971; Moscow 1973; Anguilla 1974; Bonn 1976; FCO 1978 (Second Secretary 1979); Vice-Consul (Comm) Melbourne 1982; Second Secretary FCO 1986; First Secretary (Comm) Bucharest 1989; First Secretary FCO 1993; Full-time Language Training 1995; Consul Munich 1995; Sarajevo 1997; First Secretary FCO 1998; T/D Tehran 1999; Band C5.

Marshall, Brian; Second Secretary FCO since April 1985; born 13.12.51; FCO 1971; on loan to HCS 1974; FCO 1977; Second Secretary Muscat 1984; Band C4; m 1973 Susan Joyce Bishop (2d 1976, 1980).

Marshall, Francis James; DHM Rangoon since 1999; born 10.8.46; CRO 1963; Commonwealth Office (later FCO) 1965; Mogadishu 1969; Singapore 1971; FCO 1974; Port Louis 1977; Tripoli 1981; Addis Ababa 1983; FCO 1984; Vice-Consul Toronto 1987; Second Secretary (Management) JMO Brussels 1991; SUPL 1994; m 1971 Clare Wray (1s 1972; 1d 1976).

Marshall, Jonathan Neil; FCO since July 1999; born 26.8.70; FCO 1992; Athens 1994; Band D6; m 1997 Maria Kontou (1s 1999).

Marshall, Michael Gavin; Second later acting First Secretary FCO since December 1998; born 13.9.60; FCO 1980; Moscow 1982; Baghdad 1983; Floater Duties 1988; FCO 1990; Second Secretary (Consul) St.Petersburg 1992; Seoul 1995; m 1993 Amanda Louise O'Connor (1d 1997; 1s 1999).

Marshall, Robert; First Secretary FCO since November 1986; born 21.8.44; First Secretary FCO 1975; First Secretary (Inf) Rome 1977; First Secretary FCO 1980; First Secretary (Chancery) Lagos 1986; Band C5; m (1) 1971 Patricia Daly (decd 1995) (2) 1996 Susan Alexandra Caroline James.

Marshall, Robert John; First Secretary Kuala Lumpur since January 2000; born 19.6.65; FCO 1988; Second Secretary Tokyo 1992; First Secretary FCO 1995; Band D6.

Martens, Alexandra Mary; Second Secretary Paris since May 2000; born 20.10.57; FCO 1978; Johannesburg 1980; FCO 1981; Paris 1987; FCO 1987; Vienna 1989; FCO 1991; Band C4.

Martin, Alexander Benedict Lowry; Second Secretary (Economic) Jakarta since July 1999; born 16.9.70; FCO 1996; Band C4; m 1999 Nicola Barbara Hill.

Martin, Angus; FCO since August 1998; born 27.12.71; FCO 1991; World-wide floater 1995. UKMIS Geneva on temporary duty 1998; Band B3.

Martin, Christopher Nichols; FCO since July 1981; born 4.5.62; Band B3.

Martin, Craig Keith; born 16.11.69; Washington since July 1988. Band B3; m 1998 Natalie Jayne Wren.

Martin, Dominic David William; Counsellor (Political) New Delhi since May 2001; born 25.11.64; FCO 1987. Third later Second Secretary (Chancery) New Delhi 1989; First Secretary FCO 1992; First Secretary (Head of Political and Economic Section) Buenos Aires 1996; FCO 2000; m 1996 Emily Rose Walter (3d 1996, 1998, 2001).

Martin, Emily Rose Ardagh (née Walter); Second Secretary FCO since February 2000; born 18.5.67; FCO 1992; Second Secretary Buenos Aires 1995; Band C4; m 1996 Dominic David William Martin (3d 1996, 1998, 2001).

Martin, Frances Edith Josephine; Second Secretary Montreal since September 1996; born 20.2.48; MOD 1965; FCO 1973; Montevideo 1973; Peking 1976; Tehran 1977; Moscow 1979; FCO 1981; Washington 1987; Athens 1990; FCO 1993.

Martin, Francis James; First Secretary (Commercial) Copenhagen since August 1998; born 3.5.49; DSAO later FCO 1968; Reykjavik 1971; Stuttgart 1973; FCO 1976; Second Secretary 1978; Vice-Consul (Pol/Inf) Cape Town 1979; Second later First Secretary (Institutions) UKREP Brussels 1983; FCO 1988; Deputy High Commissioner Freetown 1988; First Secretary FCO 1991; on loan to DTI 1992; Full-time Language Training 1995; Deputy Head of Mission Luanda 1995; m 1970 Aileen Margaret Shovlin (2s 1973, 1975; 2d 1976, 1978).

Martin, Neil Richard; First Secretary and Deputy Head of Mission Asunción since May 2000; born 14.3.67; FCO 1987; Tunis 1989; Sofia 1991; Ho Chi Minh City 1994; on secondment to China Britain Trade Group 1996; FCO 1997; Band C4.

Martin, Nicholas Jonathan Leigh; Counsellor Regional Affairs Bridgetown since February 2000; born 29.1.48; First Secretary FCO 1979; First Secretary (Chancery) Nairobi 1981; First Secretary FCO 1984; First Secretary (Chancery) Rome 1987; First Secretary FCO 1991; Counsellor

Jakarta 1993; Counsellor FCO 1996; m 1980 Anna Louise Reekie (1s 1983; 2d 1985, 1987).

Martin, Simon Charles; First Secretary (Commercial) Budapest since November 1996; born 15.5.63; FCO 1984; Language Training 1986; Third later Second Secretary and Vice-Consul Rangoon 1987; Second later First Secretary FCO 1990; Full-time Language Training 1995; m 1988 Sharon Margaret Joel (1s 1996; 1d 1998).

Martinez, Paul Lawrence; Consul Dallas since September 1999; born 6.11.53; FCO 1972; Dublin 1975; Paris 1975; Kingston 1977; Chicago 1981; FCO 1984; Second Secretary (Chancery/Inf) Lima 1986; Second Secretary FCO 1990; Second Secretary and HM Consul Mexico City 1993; First Secretary FCO 1996; m 1978 Ann Elizabeth Stokes (2d 1982, 1985).

Maryan-Green, Kerri-Lyn (née Miller); FCO since September 1996; born 11.11.64; FCO 1987; Shanghai 1989; Port Louis 1990; SUPL 1994; Band B3; m 1992 James Richard Maryan-Green. (2d 1993, 1998).

Masefield, (John) Thorold, CMG (1986); Governor Hamilton since May 1997; born 1.10.39; CRO 1962-64; Private Secretary to Permanent Under-Secretary of State 1963; Kuala Lumpur 1964; Second Secretary Warsaw 1966; FO (later FCO) 1967; First Secretary UKDEL Disarmament Conference Geneva 1970; First Secretary FCO 1974; Counsellor and Head of Chancery and Consul-General Islamabad 1979; Counsellor FCO 1982; CDA Harvard 1987; Attached to OMCS (CSSB) 1988; High Commissioner Dar es Salaam 1989; AUS (South and South East Asia) 1992; High Commissioner Lagos 1994; m 1962 Jennifer Mary Trowell (2s 1964,1970; 1d 1966).

Mason, Colette Hazel; MBE (1999); Vice-Consul Maseru since August 1998; born 15.7.65; FCO 1987; Mogadishu 1989; Port of Spain 1991; FCO 1994; Peking 1996; Band B3.

Mason, Edward Charles; Second later First Secretary FCO since October 1995; born 11.5.68; FCO 1990; Third later Second Secretary Oslo 1992.

Mason, Ian David; Second Secretary (Political/Press/Public Affairs) Lusaka since May 2001; born 26.10.67; FCO 1987; Mogadishu 1989; Floater Duties 1991; Phnom Penh 1993; FCO 1994; Third Secretary (Chancery) Buenos Aires 1997; Band C4; m 1992 Judith Caroline Elizabeth Owens (1s 1994, 2d 1996, 1998).

Mason, James Muir Angel; FCO since July 1989; born 13.8.69; Band A2.

Mason, Judith Caroline Elizabeth, (née Owens), SUPL since July 1994; born 11.8.64; FCO 1984; Washington 1986; Warsaw 1988; Floater Duties 1990; Phnom Penh 1993; Band A2; m 1992 Ian David Mason (1s 1994, 2d 1996,1998).

Massam, David Robert; FCO since July 2000; born 2.10.70; Second Secretary FCO 1996;

Second Secretary (IAIE) UKMIS Vienna 1998; Band C4; m 1996 Elisabeth Katharine Jenkinson.(1d 1999).

Massey, Andrew Fraser; Bonn since August 1998; born 24.7.63; FCO 1984; Bangkok 1987; Jedda 1989; FCO 1994; Band C4; m 1996 Patricia Elizabeth Parsons.(1d 1997; 1s 2000).

Massingham, Andrea Sharron; BTCO Taipei since June 1999; born 10.3.71; FCO 1990; SUPL 1992; UKDEL NATO Brussels 1992; FCO 1995; Kathmandu 1995; Band B3.

Masterman, Margaret Alice (née Neal); FCO since June 1988; born 5.6.63; FCO 1984; Warsaw 1985; Band B3; m 1989 Graham Paul Masterman.

Mastin-Lee, Christopher Ernest; Legal Counsellor FCO since April 1995; born 11.8.56; Assistant Legal Counsellor FCO 1990; m 1988 Katherine Louise Heron (2s 1994, 1996; 1d 1998).

Mathers, Peter James LVO (1995); Commercial and Economic Counsellor Stockholm since October 1998; born 2.4.46; HM Forces 1968-71; FCO 1971; SOAS 1972-73; Tehran(Commercial) 1973; Bonn (Chancery) 1976; FCO 1978; Copenhagen (Chancery and Information) 1981; Tehran (Commercial) 1986; FCO 1987; On secondment to UN Offices Vienna 1988; FCO 1991; Deputy High Commissioner Bridgetown 1995; m 1983 Elisabeth Hoeller (1s 1984; 1d 1986).

Mathewson, Iain Arthur Gray; Counsellor FCO since August 1996; born 16.3.52; HM Customs and Excise 1974-77; DHSS 1977-80; FCO 1980; First Secretary UKMIS New York 1981; FCO 1985; Warsaw 1985; First Secretary FCO 1989; Counsellor Prague 1993; m 1983 Jennifer Bloch (1s 1984;1d 1986).

Mattey, Eric; Consul Oporto since September 1995; born 26.3.49; FCO 1968; Bucharest 1971; Rabat 1973; Moscow 1975; FCO 1977; Vienna 1980; Port Louis 1983; Second Secretary FCO 1985; Second later First Secretary (Comm) Kuala Lumpur 1990; m 1970 Janet Walker (1s 1971; 1d 1974).

Matthews, Andrew John; FCO since May 1992; born 28.4.55; FCO 1974; Bonn 1976; Singapore 1979; FCO 1982; Dublin 1982; FCO 1985; Band B3; Colombo 1988; Paris 1992; m (1) 1976 Carole Susan Thomson (diss 1986) (1d 1976; 1s 1978); (2) 1988 Denise Ann Mary Carroll (1d 1992).

Matthews, Harriet Lucy; Second Secretary Brasilia since August 1999; born 22.12.73; FCO 1997; on secondment Brazilian Diplomatic Academy (Instituto Rio Branco) 1999; Band C4.

Matthews, Mark Julian; First Secretary FCO since September 2000; born 24.8.68; FCO 1990; Third Secretary (Defence) UKDEL NATO Brussels 1992; full-time Arabic language training 1996; Second Secretary (Political/Press and Public Affairs) Abu Dhabi 1997; m 1997 Shauna Rudge (1s 1998).

Maxton, Fiona; Zagreb since July 2000; born 19.12.67; FCO 1985; Bonn 1988; Third Secretary (Management) Rabat 1989; Third Secretary FCO 1993; Vice Consul Kiev 1997; Band C4.

Maxwell, Letitia Kelso; FCO since January 1998; born 12.2.42; FCO 1977; Helsinki 1979; Doha 1981; FCO 1984; Copenhagen 1989; FCO 1992; UKDEL NATO Brussels 1995. Band B3.

May, Philip; First Secretary (Management) UKREP Brussels since July 2001; born 12.11.60; Ottawa 1982; Moscow 1985; Islamabad 1986; FCO 1988; Resigned/ reinstated 1990; Tehran 1992; BTC Hong Kong 1994; Second Secretary FCO 1997; DSTUS Chairman 1998; Band C5; m 1985 Susan Ann Checketts; (2d 1989, 1990).

May, Susan Ann (née Checketts); FCO since February 1997; born 18.8.56; FCO 1978; Peking 1980; Ottawa 1982; Moscow 1985; Islamabad 1986; SUPL 1989; Band B3; m 1985 Philip May (2d 1989, 1990).

Mayhew, Michael John Ernest; Deputy Head of Mission Bridgetown since July 1998; born 6.11.46; DSAO (later FCO) 1966; Mexico City 1969; Algiers 1972; Tokyo 1974; FCO 1975; Prague 1978; Second Secretary (Inf) Oslo 1981; Second Secretary FCO 1985; First Secretary (Comm/Dev) Bangkok 1987; First Secretary (Commercial) The Hague 1990; First Secretary FCO 1993; m 1976 Elizabeth Carol Owen (1d 1987).

Mayland, Alan John; Consul Rome since March 1999; born 5.11.46; FO 1965; Warsaw 1968; Cairo 1970; Brussels 1971; Calcutta 1974; Budapest 1975; FCO 1976; Paris 1981; Ottawa 1982; Second Secretary FCO 1986; Second Secretary (Admin) Colombo 1989; Bucharest 1993.

Mayne, Julie Ann; World wide floater duties since January 1999; born 3.4.58; FCO 1989; Caracas 1992; Quito 1996; Band B3.

Mealor, Michelle Louise; Riyadh since September 1991; born 8.4.68; FCO 1988; SUPL 1990; Band A2.

Means, Claire Stewart (née Hunter) UKMIS New York since December 1997; born 2.3.69; FCO 1990; Kuala Lumpur 1993; SUPL 1994; Band A2; m 1994 Thomas E Means.

Mearns, George Ewen; First Secretary (Management) Harare since March 1998; born 18.1.41; FO 1958; Pretoria/Cape Town 1962; Jedda 1964; Stockholm 1966; Bahrain Residency 1969; FCO 1972; Language Student 1974; Moscow 1975; Second Secretary (Admin) Port of Spain 1978; FCO 1981; Second Secretary (Comm) Warsaw 1984; Consul (Comm) Hamburg 1987; Consul (Comm) St Petersburg 1992; First Secretary (Management) and Consul Tehran 1995; m(1) 1961 Elsie Crossley (dec'd 1989) (1d 1966; 1s 1968 (dec'd 1994), (2) 1991 Sylvia Jeanette Mueller (1 step s 1974).

Mearns, Stuart; Paris since July 1995; born 21.11.58; FCO 1982; Khartoum 1985; FCO 1989; Band C4; m 1983 Andrea Chapman; (2s 1993, 1996).

Meath Baker, William John Clovis; First Secretary FCO since October 2000; born 11.5.59; FCO 1985; Second later First Secretary (Chancery and Inf) and Consul Kabul 1988; FCO 1989; First Secretary and Consul Prague 1989; First Secretary FCO 1993; Consul (Political) Istanbul 1997; Band D6; m 1985 Elizabeth Diana Woodham-Smith (4d 1988, 1990, 1992, 1995).

Meconi, Anne-Marie; Hanoi since October 1999; born 14.1.61; transferred from the Scottish Office 1997; FCO 1997; Band A2.

Mee, Jeffery Bryan; Second Secretary FCO since September 1997; born 8.7.56; Passport Office 1975; FCO 1976; Kathmandu 1978; FCO 1980; Khartoum 1982; Peking 1985; Vancouver 1987; FCO 1987; Vice Consul Vienna 1991; Lisbon 1994 (1s 1990, 1d 1993).

Mehmet, Alper, MVO (1990); First Secretary (Information) Bonn since January 1999; born 28.8.48; Immigration Service 1970; Lagos 1979; FCO 1983 (Second Secretary 1986); Bucharest 1986; Second Secretary (Head of Chancery) Reykjavik 1989; FCO 1993; m 1968 Elaine Susan Tarrant (2d 1969, 1971).

Meiklejohn, Dominic Francis; Second later First Secretary (Feb 2000) (EU/Public) Warsaw since June 1993; born 14.11.67; HM Customs and Excise 1989-90; FCO 1990; Full-time Language Training 1993; Band D6; m 1997 Anna Iwona Reichel.

Melbourne, Sean; FCO since January 1998; born 9.12.68; FCO 1988; Maputo 1990; Tashkent 1994; Band B3; m 1997 Elmira Vakkasova.

Melling, Scott Richard; Third Secretary (Management) Warsaw since December 2000; born 10.5.72; FCO 1990; Madrid 1994; FCO 1997; World Wide Floater Duties 1998; FCO 1999; Band B3.

Mellor, John; Jakarta since July 1997; born 9.2.52; Department of National Savings 1968; FCO 1971; Belgrade 1973; Middle East Floater 1975; Dar es Salaam 1977; FCO 1979; Strasbourg 1980; FCO 1982; Washington 1987; Ankara 1990; FCO 1993; Band B3; m 1987 Mary Bridget Ann McGettigan.

Meredith, Richard Evan; First Secretary FCO since August 1998; born 31.1.61; FCO 1983; Third Secretary Bridgetown 1985; Second Secretary Managua 1987; Second later First Secretary FCO 1989; Bonn 1995; Band D6; m 1986 Louisa Jane Oriel (2d 1992, 1995).

Merry, David Byron, CMG (2000); High Commissioner Gaborone since August 2001; born 16.9.45; Ministry of Aviation 1961; CRO (later Commonwealth Office, later FCO) 1965; Bangkok 1969; Second Secretary (Inf) Budapest 1974;

Second later First Secretary FCO 1977; First Secretary (Civil Air Attaché) Bonn 1981; Head of Chancery East Berlin 1985; First Secretary FCO 1989; Deputy Head of Mission Manila 1993; Deputy High Commissioner Karachi 1997; FCO 2000; m 1967 Patricia Ann Ellis (2d 1969, 1972; 1s 1971).

Mesarowicz, Anthony David; Guatemala City since May 1999; born 28.7.70; FCO 1991; Paris 1995; Band A2.

Metcalfe, Caryl Aileen; FCO since January 1987; FCO 1977; Baghdad 1978; Stockholm 1980; FCO 1983; Lilongwe 1985; New Delhi 1988; Band B3; m 1991 Duncan Richard Mackinnon.

Metcalfe, Julian Ross; First Secretary FCO since July 1997; born 24.2.56; Economic Adviser FCO 1983; First Secretary Cairo 1987; First Secretary FCO 1991; Full-time Language Training 1994; Deputy Head of Mission Zagreb 1995; m 1985 Rachel Mai Jones (1d 1997).

Metreweli, Blaise Florence; Second Secretary (Economic) Dubai since September 2000; born 30.7.77; FCO 1999; Band C4.

Meyer, Sir Christopher John Rome, KCMG (1998); CMG (1988); HM Ambassador Washington since October 1997; born 22.2.44; Third Secretary FO 1966; Third later Second Secretary Moscow 1968; Madrid 1970; First Secretary FCO 1973; UKREP Brussels 1978; Counsellor and Head of Chancery Moscow 1982; Counsellor FCO 1984; Harvard University 1988; Minister Washington 1989; Chief Press Secretary to the Prime Minister 1994; Full-time Language Training 1996; HM Ambassador Bonn 1997; m (1)1976 Francoise Elizabeth Hedges(2s 1978, 1984),(2) 1997 Catherine Laylle (2 step s 1985, 1987).

Miah, Faruk; FCO since November 1998; born 18.12.70; FCO 1990; Singapore 1994; Dar es Salaam 1997; Band B3; m 1993 Nilufa Yasmin (1d 1996).

Micallef, Janice Pauline (née Roughley); Caracas since May 2000; born 15.1.66; FCO 1993; New Delhi 1996; SUPL 1999; Band A2; m 1996 Mark Antoine Micallef (1d 1999).

Michael, Alan Rhys; Consul General Casablanca since January 1999; born 2.1.48; FCO 1971; MECAS 1973; Jedda 1975; Jedda/Riyadh 1976; FCO 1978; Second Secretary UKMIS Geneva 1982; First Secretary (Comm) Kuwait 1986; First Secretary FCO 1988; UKREP Brussels 1994; m 1973 Anita Ruth Ford (1s 1973; 1d 1977).

Middel, Julie; on loan to the DTI since November 1996; born 26.4.58; DHSS 1976; FCO 1979; Copenhagen 1982; Floater Duties 1985; Sofia 1986; Brussels 1987; FCO 1990; SUPL 1990; Karachi 1994; FCO 1994; Band B3; m 1988 Wolfgang Middel.

Middlemiss, Matthew MBE (1991); First Secretary (Humanitarian) UKMIS Geneva since July 2001;

born 11.1.62; First Secretary FCO 1998; Band D6; m2001 Phyllida Alison Cheyne.

Middleton, David Farquharson; Counsellor Amman since September 1998; born 21.11.53; FCO 1982; Language Training Kamakura 1984; First Secretary Tokyo 1985; First Secretary FCO 1988; First Secretary Lusaka 1991; First Secretary FCO 1992; Counsellor September 1998; m 1984 Georgina Mary Housman (1s 1987, 2d 1989, 1992).

Miles, Joanne Denise; MBE (1993); Second Secretary (Political) Nairobi since August 1999; born 10.6.57; FCO 1980; Prague 1982; FCO 1984; Bandar Seri Begawan 1986; Guatemala City 1988; San José 1991; FCO 1992; Caracas 1994; FCO 1997; Band C4.

Miles, John; First Secretary Washington since October 2000; born 30.10.46; Nepal 1972; Germany 1974; Home Civil Service 1978; Hong Kong 1980; New Delhi 1984; FCO 1988; Moscow 1995; Band D6; m 1968 Lynda Patricia Frances McNair (1d 1972; 1s 1974).

Millar, Andrew James; First Secretary (Economic/Political) Pretoria since September 2000; born 13.7.65; Office of Gas Supply 1994; FCO E/Advs 1996; FCO 1999; Band D6; m 1996 Catherine Jo Russell Davis.

Millar, Lindsey; The Hague since February 1997; born 18.6.67; Scottish Office 1984-90; FCO 1991; Berlin 1993; Band A2.

Miller, Andrew John; Abu Dhabi since December 1998; born 29.5.66; FCO 1985; Munich 1991; FCO 1995; Band B3; m 1991 Coral Annabel (1d 1997; 1s 1999).

Miller, Anne Virginia; FCO since February 1997; born 16.1.72; FCO 1991; UKDEL NATO Brussels 1995; Band A2.

Miller, David; First Secretary (Chancery) Bogotá since May 2000; born 19.5.66; Second Secretary FCO 1997; Band D6; m 1993 Carmen Delgado.

Miller, David Roland; Resident Acting High Commissioner Grenada since May 1998; born 1.11.52; FCO 1972; Bucharest 1975; Tripoli 1976; Rome 1979; FCO 1982; Kuala Lumpur 1985; Second Secretary FCO 1989; Deputy High Commissioner Vila 1990; Second later First Secretary FCO 1994; m 1976 Gillian Mary Cornthwaite (2s 1980, 1983).

Miller, Jamie Jonathan MBE (1999); First Secretary (Political) Freetown since November 2000; born 1.5.72; FCO 1996; Second Secretary (Chancery) Islamabad 1998; Band D6.

Miller, Julian Peter; FCO since October 1998; FCO 1987; Language Training 1989; Language Training Kamakura 1989; Tokyo 1990; San José 1994; m 1993 Yasuko Yanai (2s 1995, 1998).

Miller, Julie; Buenos Aires since April 1995; born 21.11.70; FCO 1988; Jakarta 1991; FCO 1994; Band B3.

Miller, Nicholas Michael; Hamburg since June 1997; born 10.10.62; FCO 1982; Bangkok 1984; Peking 1987; FCO 1990; Tehran 1993; Full Time Language Training 1996; m 1995 Raquel Evangelina Varela (2d 1994, 1999).

Miller, Pablo; First Secretary Tallinn since September 1997; born 27.2.60; FCO 1990; First Secretary (Political) Abuja later Lagos 1992; First Secretary FCO 1995; Band D6; m 1989 Elke Schmidt (3d 1991; 1994, 1996).

Miller, Penelope Helen; Second Secretary (Commercial) Tokyo since December 1998; born 18.3.70; FCO 1995; Language Training Kamakura 1997; Band C4.

Miller, Peter Charles William; First Secretary (Political) Abuja since December 1992; born 27.8.46; FCO 1964; Madrid 1987; FCO 1989; m(1) 1970 Jennifer O'Toole (diss 1984) (1s 1971; 1d 1973); (2) 1985 Jean Ward (3s 1974, 1976, 1977 1d 1994).

Miller, Shirley; FCO since November 1998; born 6.12.56; FCO 1976; Reykjavik 1981; UKDIS Geneva 1984; Port Stanley 1987; FCO 1988; UKREP Brussels 1992; Helsinki 1995; Band A2; m 1997 Martin Corcoran.

Millett, Peter Joseph; Deputy Head of Mission Athens since August 1997; born 23.1.55; FCO 1974; LA Floater 1976; Caracas 1978; Doha 1981; Second Secretary FCO 1985; First Secretary (Energy) UKREP Brussels 1989; Counsellor FCO 1993; m 1981 June Harnett (3d 1984, 1987, 1991).

Millington, Claire; FCO since January 1999; Band B3.

Mills, Anthony; Second Secretary later First Secretary (Management/HM Consul) Dubai since July 1999; born 29.5.43; Inland Revenue 1966; FCO 1970; Addis Ababa 1973; UKREP Brussels 1975; Prague 1977; Dacca 1979; FCO 1981; Third Secretary (Management) Freetown 1982; Third Secretary later Second Secretary FCO 1986; Second Secretary (Management) Karachi 1990; Second Secretary (Management) Lagos 1995; m 1978 Christine Mary Napp (2s 1979, 1982).

Mills, Anwen Eluned (née Rees); SUPL since April 1999; born 22.7.64; FCO 1991; T/D UKMIS New York 1992; Resigned 1993; Reinstated 1994; Cape Town 1995; Band A2; m 1993 (William) Gary Mills (1s 1997).

Mills, Beverley; Washington since July 1999; born 9.5.69; FCO 1990; Brussels 1995; FCO 1997; Band A2.

Mills, David Paul; T/D Dar es Salaam since January 2000; born 2.10.67; FCO 1987; Cairo 1989; FCO 1992; Addis Ababa 1993; HO 1999; Band B3.

Mills, Emma, MBE (2001); Second Secretary (Political/Information) Athens since March 2001; born 27.2.69; FCO 1988; Baghdad 1990; Peking 1991; Bogotá 1994; FCO 1997; Pristina 1999; Band C4.

Mills, Hilary Clare; FCO since January 1998; born 5.6.46; FCO 1978; Dakar 1978; Rio de Janeiro 1980; Brasilia 1982; Moscow 1984; FCO 1985; Bonn 1987; FCO 1991; Copenhagen 1994; Band C4.

Millson, Tony; Head of Medical and Welfare FCO since June 2001; born 25.11.51; FCO 1970; MECAS 1973; Third Secretary (Comm) Tripoli 1974; Third later Second Secretary (Development) Amman 1976; FCO 1980; Second Secretary BMG Berlin 1983; First Secretary FCO 1986; Head of Chancery Kuwait 1988; First Secretary FCO 1991; HM Ambassador Skopje 1993; Counsellor FCO 1997; High Commissioner Banjul 1998; T/D Abuja 2000.

Milne, Carole Lesley; FCO since August 1999; born 1.10.66; FCO HCS 1989; FCO 1994; Executive Assistant Lusaka 1996; Staff Officer Montserrat 1998; Band B3.

Milne, Hilary Taylor; Moscow since April 1998; born 7.6.65; FCO 1984; Rome 1985; Freetown 1988; FCO 1990; FCO 1991; Windhoek 1994; Band B3.

Milton, Kirstie Jane (née Levitt); FCO since July 1997; born 4.7.69; FCO 1988; Cairo 1991; FCO 1992; The Hague 1995; Band A2; m2000 Jonathan Milton.

Minshall, Heidi Jane; First Secretary FCO since May 1997; born 2.3.67; FCO 1990; Full-time Language Training Cairo 1993; Second Secretary (Political/Information) Abu Dhabi 1995.

Minshull, Simon Peter; Vice-Consul Bridgetown since March 1999; born 21.11.68; FCO 1988; Moscow 1990; Islamabad 1992; FCO 1996; Band B3; m 1991 Hrefna Dis Luthersdottir (2d 1991,1994).

Minter, Graham Leslie, LVO (1983); HM Ambassador La Paz since August 1999; born 4.1.50; FCO 1968; Anguilla 1971; Latin America Floater 1973; Asunción 1975; FCO 1978; First Secretary (Econ) Mexico City 1979; First Secretary FCO 1984; First Secretary (Econ/Agric) Canberra 1990; First Secretary later Counsellor FCO 1994; m 1975 P Anne Scott (1s 1978).

Mistry, Hemlata; FCO since April 1994; born 7.6.62; (FCO Home Civil Service 1988); FCO 1990; Floater Duties 1992; Band B3.

Mirtle, Catherine Grace; Paris since July 1993; born 8.1.69; FCO 1989; Band A2.

Mitchell, Andrew Jonathan; Deputy Head of Mission Kathmandu since May 1999; born 7.3.67; FCO 1991; Second Secretary (Political) Bonn 1993; First Secretary FCO 1996; m 1996 Helen Sarah Anne Magee (2s 1998, 2000).

Mitchell, Carole, RVM (1990); Sarajevo since August 2000; born 7.6.57; Scottish Office 1975; FCO 1987; Reykjavik 1988; The Hague 1991; UKDIS Geneva 1994; FCO 1999; Band A2.

Mitchell, Frederick John, MBE (1991); Third Secretary FCO since June 1993; born 30.5.38; HM Forces 1953-65; FCO 1965; New Delhi 1967; FCO 1968; Benghazi 1969; FCO 1971; Singapore 1973; FCO 1975; Rome 1976; FCO 1979; Sana'a 1979; FCO 1983; Bucharest 1984; Riyadh 1987; Third Secretary Islamabad 1991; Band C4; m 1961 Rosa Leona Vereecke (1d 1962; 1s 1964).

Mitchell, Helen Sarah Anne (née Magee); SUPL (c/o Kathmandu) since May 1999. born 18.10.67; FCO 1990; Second Secretary (EU) Bonn 1993; First Secretary FCO 1997; m 1996 Andrew Jonathan Mitchell. (2s 1998, 2000)

Mitchell, John Steven; Riyadh since June 1999; born 28.11.67; FCO 1985; Tokyo 1988; Stockholm 1990; T/D Riga 1991; FCO 1992; Dhaka 1995.

Mitchell, Jonathan Kenneth Milton; First Secretary Bucharest since June 1998; born 18.12.59; Second Secretary FCO 1987; Second later First Secretary (Info) Amman 1989; First Secretary FCO 1990; First Secretary (Chancery) Harare 1991; First Secretary FCO 1994; Band D6; m 1986 Joyce Ann Henderson (2d 1990, 1993).

Mitchell, Margaret Rose (née Howie); Third Secretary FCO since 1997; born 7.3.66; FCO 1985; Tokyo 1988; Stockholm 1990; FCO 1993; Rome 1994.

Mitchell, Michael James, MVO (1989); First Secretary (Management) Karachi since December 1999; born 7.8.54. HM Customs & Excise 1980; FCO 1985; Third Secretary (Aid) Kampala 1986; Third Secretary (Chancery) Singapore 1989; Full-time Language Training 1993; Deputy Head of Mission Guatemala City 1993; Second Secretary FCO 1997; Band C5; m 1982 Dominique Steggle (1d 1994).

Mitchell, Robert; Second Secretary FCO since September 1983; born 20.10.43; GPO 1967; FCO 1969; Islamabad 1972; Milan 1975; FCO 1978; Second Secretary (Admin) Kabul 1981; m 1981 Janet Frances Booth.

Mitchell, Sheilah Dawn (née Bramley) SUPL since February 1998; born 15.4.59; FCO 1979; UKDEL NATO Brussels 1980; Maputo 1982; Floater duties 1987; FCO 1990; Third Secretary (Management)/Vice Consul Jerusalem 1994; Band B3; m 1994 Alan Stuart Mitchell.

Mitchell, Simon Andrew; FCO since October 1999; born 27.11.64; PSA DoE 1987; The Court Service 1995; Band A2.

Mitchiner, Dr John Edward; Deputy High Commissioner Calcutta since 1999; born 12.9.51; FCO 1980; Third later Second Secretary Istanbul 1982; Second Secretary FCO 1985; Second Secretary (Dev) New Delhi 1987; Second later First Secretary (Political) Berne 1991; First Secretary FCO 1995; HM Ambassador Yerevan 1997; m 1983; Elizabeth Mary Ford.

Mitchison, Pamela Denise; SUPL since December 1997; born 28.12.58; FCO 1978; Far East Floater

1981; Moscow 1982; Paris 1985; Second Secretary FCO 1988; APS Minister of State 1989; First Secretary (Chancery) Washington 1991; First Secretary FCO 1995; SUPL 1996. First Secretary (FCO) 1997; m 1996 Ian Richard Whitehead (1d 1996).

Mititelu, Alexandra Marie; Language Training since September 2001; born 15.9.76; FCO 1999; Band C4.

Mochan, Charles Francis; HM Ambassador Antananarivo since July 1999; born 6.8.48; MOD (Navy) 1966; FCO 1967; Port Elizabeth 1970; Kingston 1972; FCO 1974; Second Secretary 1975; Seoul 1977; FCO 1980; Second later First Secretary (Comm) Helsinki 1981; First Secretary FCO 1984; DHC and Head of Chancery Port Louis 1988; First Secretary FCO 1991; Consul General Casablanca 1995; m 1970 Ilse Sybilla Carleon Cruttwell (1d 1971; 1s 1974).

Monckton, The Honourable Anthony Leopold Colyer; Counsellor Belgrade since March 2001; born 25.9.60; HM Forces 1979-87; Second Secretary FCO 1987; Second later First Secretary UKDEL Geneva 1990; First Secretary FCO 1992; First Secretary (Political) Zagreb 1996; British Embassy Banja Luka Office 1998; First Secretary FCO 1999; Band D6; m 1985 Philippa Susan Wingfield (1s 1988, 1d 1989).

Money, Brian Walter; FCO since September 1999; born 4.1.41; Board of Trade 1960; DSAO (later FCO) 1967; Bonn 1970; Second Secretary BMG Berlin 1971; Kingston 1974; FCO 1978; Second Secretary (Cons/Admin) Dublin 1981; First Secretary (Comm) Jakarta 1984; on loan to MOD 1988; First Secretary (Dev/Comm) Kathmandu 1991; First Secretary FCO 1994; Administrator Tristan da Cunha 1997; Islamabad 1998; m(1)1969 Margaret Askew (1s 1971); (2)1984 Audrey Josephine Pakenham (1d 1985).

Moody, Patrick Thomas Robert; First Secretary (Political) UKDEL NATO Brussels since September 1998; born 17.3.66; FCO 1988; Third later Second Secretary (Pol/Info) Mexico City 1990; First Secretary FCO 1994; m 1996 Atalanta Sturdy (1s 1998, 1d 2000).

Moon, Dorian Lawrence; FCO since March 1993; born 2.1.59; HCS 1985; BEMRS Cyprus 1986; HCS 1989; FCO 1990; Moscow 1992; Band A2; m 1989 Joanne Ashley (1d 1989; 1s 1991).

Moon, Michael Yelland; Second Secretary Bandar Seri Begawan since April 1996; born 19.8.59; FCO 1977; UKREP Brussels 1979; Khartoum 1982; Africa/Middle East Floater 1986; FCO 1990; Third Secretary (Aid/Inf) Mbabane 1993; Consul Brussels 1995.

Moon, Dr Richard John; UKMIS New York since March 1999; born 3.1.59; FCO 1983; Second Secretary Jakarta 1985; First Secretary FCO 1988; First Secretary (Political) Rome 1993; FCO 1997; m 1987 Sandra Sheila Francis Eddis (1s 1990, 1d 1993).

Moon, Sandra Sheila Francis (née Eddis), MVO (1984); SUPL since January 1994; born 11.3.56; FCO 1980; Washington 1982; Jakarta 1984; FCO 1988; Band C4; m 1987 Richard John Moon (1s 1990 1d 1993).

Mooney, Laura; Floater Duties since April 2001; born 30.4.73; FCO 1996; MOD 1989-1996; Wellington 1997; Band B3.

Moonlight, Julie Anne (née Thorpe); SUPL since April 1997; born 12.8.68; FCO 1986; Paris 1989; FCO 1992; Washington 1994; Band A2; m 1991 Philip Lindsay Moonlight.

Moore, Charles Jonathan Rupert; Second Secretary (UN/UNIDO) UKMIS Geneva since August 1998; born 14.4.63; FCO 1982; Harare 1984; Masirah 1987; Gaborone 1987; FCO 1991; Third Secretary (Commercial) Jakarta 1995; Band C4; m 1988 Deborah Mary Ford (1s 1989; 1d 1992).

Moore, David; Madrid since September 1996; born 18.6.59; HO 1977; FCO 1978; Moscow 1980; Wellington 1982; FCO 1986; Vice-Consul Osaka 1990; FCO 1992; (Second Secretary 1994); Full-time Language Training 1996; m (1) 1981 Annette May Gardner (diss) (1d 1982; 1s 1985) (2) 1996 Janice Ann Bell.

Moore, Deborah Mary (née Ford); SUPL since August 1998; born 15.4.63; FCO 1982; Muscat 1985; SUPL 1988; FCO 1991; SUPL 1993;); Jakarta 1995; Band B3; m 1988 Charles Jonathan Rupert Moore (1s 1989; 1d 1992).

Moore, Fiona Charlotte; First Secretary FCO since December 1995; born 15.8.59; FCO 1981; Third later Second Secretary Warsaw 1983; Second later First Secretary FCO 1987; First Secretary (Chancery) Athens 1991; CDA, Imperial College London 1995;

Moore, Geraldine Fiona; FCO since July 1976; born 6.6.54; Band B3.

Moore, Janice Ann (née Bell); Second Secretary Madrid since August 1996; born 6.10.64; FCO 1984; Accountant Nairobi 1986; Vice-Consul Budapest 1989; Resigned 1991; Reinstated (FCO) 1992; Second Secretary 1994; Band C5; m 1996 David Moore.

Moore, Richard Peter; First Secretary FCO since February 1999; born 9.5.63; Second Secretary FCO 1987; Second Secretary Ankara 1990; Consul (Inf) Istanbul 1991; First Secretary FCO 1992; Islamabad 1995; Band D6; m 1985 Margaret Martin (1s 1989, 1d 1992).

Moore, Stephen Lawrence; On loan to DTI since May 1999; born 22.7.68; Paris 1991; FCO 1993; Islamabad 1994; FCO 1997; Band B3; m 1992 Carolyn Andrea. (1d 1998)

Moore, Trevor Charles; First Secretary (CTBT) UKMIS Vienna since April 1997; born 19.1.58; FCO 1980; Belgrade 1982; Vice-Consul New York 1986; Second Secretary Washington 1987; Second later First Secretary FCO 1989; m 1991 Diane Elizabeth Burns (3s 1994, 1997, 1999).

Moores, Amias Steven; Third Secretary and Vice-Consul Abu Dhabi since April 2001; born 31.3.71; FCO 1990; UKMIS Geneva 1994; Abu Dhabi 1997; FCO 1997; Band B3; m2000 Lindsey Cave.

Moorhead, Michelle Anne; FCO since February 2001; born 2.2.70; FCO 1988; Washington 1991; Accra 1995; FCO 1998; SUPL 2000; Band B3; m 1990 Ian William Moorhead (1s 2000).

Moran, David John; Deputy Permanent Representative, Paris UKDEL OSCE since January 2001; born 22.8.59; DTI 1985; ODA 1985; Second Secretary (Programmes Adviser) British Development Division in Eastern Africa, Nairobi 1988; First Secretary ODA/FCO 1991; First Secretary (Know How Fund) Moscow 1993; First Secretary FCO 1996; m 1993 Carol Ann Marquis.

Moran, Karen (née Pinkney); Deputy Head Mission Tashkent since July 2000; born 2.3.65; National Savings Dept 1984; FCO 1984; Washington 1986; Seoul 1989; FCO 1993; Third Secretary (Management) Hong Kong 1996; Band C4; m 1986 Sean Moran.

Moran, Lindy Jane (née Preston); SUPL since July 2000; born 9.10.58; FCO 1981; Caracas 1982; Grand Turk 1986; FCO 1989; Warsaw 1990; Nairobi 1992; Band B3; m 1995 Eamon Andrew Moran.

Moran, Sean; World Wide Floater duties since August 1998; born 6.3.64; Inland Revenue 1984; FCO 1984; Washington 1986; Seoul 1989; FCO 1993; On secondment to DTI 1996; Band B3; m 1986 Karen Pinkney (diss 1995).

Morgan, Angela Merril; Suva since July 2000; born 14.3.68; FCO 1989; Warsaw 1991; FCO 1992; Riga 1993; FCO 1994; New Delhi 1995; FCO 1996; Third Secretary (Political) Suva 1997; SUPL 2000; Band B3; m2001 Sainivalati Tokalau (1d 2000).

Morgan, Deborah Edith; FCO since July 1985; born 31.5.64; Band A1.

Morgan, Mark Scott Thomas, MBE (1997); First Secretary Budapest since July 2001; born 26.4.58; FCO 1976; Geneva 1984; FCO 1986; Second Secretary and Vice-Consul Aden 1988. Second Secretary FCO 1990. Second, later First Secretary Valletta 1994; First Secretary FCO 1998; Band C5; m 1998 Samantha Thompson.

Morgan, Patrick; HM Ambassador San Salvador since September 1999; born 31.1.44; Board of Trade 1963; CRO 1964; FO 1965; Bonn 1967; Kuwait 1969; on loan to DTI 1972; La Paz 1972; FCO 1975; Second Secretary Washington 1979; First Secretary (Chancery/Econ) Jakarta 1983; First Secretary FCO 1987; HM Ambassador Tegucigalpa 1992; Counsellor and Deputy Head of Mission Abu Dhabi 1995; FCO 1998; m 1966 Marlene Collins Beaton (2s 1967, 1968; 2d 1973, 1982).

Morgan, Richard de Riemer; First Secretary (PPA) Paris since September 2000; born 9.5.61; FCO 1984; Language Training Tokyo 1986; Second Secretary (Comm) Tokyo 1987; First Secretary FCO 1991; First Secretary (Political/Aid) Pretoria 1995; m 1987 Susan Carolyn McGaw. (1s 1992, 1d 1994).

Morgan, Steven Leonard; Madrid since October 1999; born 14.1.65; Department of Employment 1983; FCO 1984; Budapest 1986; FCO 1987; Paris 1988; Guatemala City 1990; Mexico City 1993; FCO 1994; Band B3; m 1995 Maria del Carmen Toledo Municio.

Morgan, Stuart John; FCO since December 1990; born 2.12.63; FCO 1983; Khartoum 1988; Band B3; m 1993 Milla Heidi Susan Chapman (1s 2000).

Morgan, William Donovan; Second later First Secretary (Political) Peking since October 2000; born 2.6.71; Second Secretary FCO 1996; Full time language training 1998; Full time language training Peking 1999; Band D6; m 1992 Lucy Bullock (2s 1992, 1995).

Morley, David John; First Secretary (Information) UKDEL NATO Brussels since June 1999; born 23.10.54; MAFF 1972; FCO 1973; UKMIS Geneva 1975; Port Stanley 1978; Kuala Lumpur 1980; FCO 1981; Kaduna 1984; FCO 1988; Second Secretary (Management) Moscow 1991; Second Secretary FCO 1994; Deputy High Commissioner Mbabane 1995; Band C5; m 1978 Jacqueline Ann Wells.

Morley, Ian Robert; Zagreb since October 2000; born 24.7.71; FCO 1992; UKMIS New York 1996; Luanda 1999; Band A2.

Morley, Jacqueline Ann (née Wells), MBE (1991); UKDEL NATO Brussels since February 2000; born 20.7.55; FCO 1973; UKMIS New York 1974; UKMIS Geneva 1975; Port Stanley 1978; SUPL 1980; Kuala Lumpur 1981; FCO 1981; SUPL Kaduna 1984; Kaduna 1987; FCO 1988; Moscow 1991; FCO 1994; SUPL 1995; FCO 1999; SUPL 1999; Band B3; m 1978 David John Morley.

Morley, Michael Donald; First Secretary (Management) Athens since January 1999; born 18.2.53; FCO 1973; Moscow 1975; Kuala Lumpur 1977; Latin America Floater 1981; Beirut 1983; FCO 1984; La Paz 1987 (Second Secretary 1990); Second Secretary (Commercial) Santiago 1991; FCO 1995; m 1983 Carmen Gloria Del Prado (2s 1987, 1989).

Morley, Stuart Richard; First Secretary FCO since April 1999; born 26.1.59; Second Secretary FCO 1988; Second later First Secretary (Chancery/Information) San José 1989; First Secretary (Chancery) Bridgetown 1990; First Secretary FCO 1992; First Secretary (Chemical Weapons) The Hague 1996; Band D6; m 1987 Janet Henry. (3d 1990, 1993 1998; 1s 1996).

Morrell, Susan Mary; Sofia since November 1996; born 7.11.50; FCO 1977; UKMIS New York

1978; Budapest 1981, Khartoum 1982, Islamabad 1985; Moscow 1988; FCO 1992; Band B3.

Morris, Richard Charles; Second Secretary (Political) Bridgetown since November 1996; born 1.11.67; UKMIS New York 1993; Third Secretary (Political) Ottawa 1993; m 1992 Alison Jane Waring; (1d 1996, 1s 1998).

Morris, Richard Peter; Second Secretary (Management) since October 1999; born 8.9.64; FCO 1983; Dhaka 1985; Bucharest 1988; FCO 1991; Full-time Language Training 1995; Vice-Consul Rome 1995; Band C4; m 1990 Diane Jacqueline Harvey.

Morris, Rose Marie June Townson; (née Bennett); FCO since May 1979; born 21.11.45; FCO 1970; Singapore 1971; Beirut 1973; FCO 1976; Lagos 1977; Band B3; m 1980 Jeremy Robin David Morris.

Morris, Sara Joanne; FCO since May 1995; born 19.10.62; FCO 1983; Mexico City 1987; FCO 1991; Floater Duties 1993; Band A2.

Morris, Timothy Colin; Counsellor (Trade and Investment) Tokyo since June 1998; born 17.9.58; FCO 1981; SOAS 1982; Language Student Tokyo 1983; Second Secretary (Comm) Tokyo 1984; First Secretary FCO 1987; on loan to DTI 1989; First Secretary (Head of Political Section) Madrid 1991; First Secretary FCO 1996; m 1996 Patricia Isabel Tena Garcia (2s 1998, 1999).

Morris, Warwick; HM Ambassador Hanoi since June 2000; born 10.8.48; FCO 1969; Paris 1972; Language Student Seoul 1975 (Second Secretary 1977); FCO 1979 (PS to Deputy PUS 1979-80) First Secretary 1982; First Secretary (Comm) Mexico City 1984; First Secretary and Head of Chancery Seoul 1988; First Secretary later Counsellor FCO 1991; New Delhi 1995; Career Development Attachment Royal College of Defence Studies 1999; m 1972 Pamela Jean Mitchell (1s 1976; 2d 1978, 1982).

Morrison, Alan; Ottawa since September 1997; born 4.1.70; FCO 1989; Islamabad 1992; FCO 1995; Band A2; m 1997 Lynne Jean Gregory.

Morrison, Fiona Margaret; Second Secretary FCO since May 2000; born 23.1.67 FCO 1989; Third Secretary (Chancery) UKDEL Brussels 1991; FCO 1994; Third Secretary (Commercial) Oslo 1995; Third Secretary (Chancery/PPA) Kingston 1996; Band B3.

Morrison, Ian Kenneth; First Secretary (Commercial) Tel Aviv since July 1999; born 27.12.54; Inland Revenue 1974; FCO 1977; Budapest 1979; Islamabad 1981; Madrid 1983; FCO 1986; Third Secretary Accra 1988; Band C4; Vice-Consul (Political/Information) Cape Town 1991; FCO 1996; m(1)1978 Gillian Winifred Turk (diss) (1d 1982) (2)1994 Jean MacAlpine Kerr. (2s 1995,1998)

Morrison, Jonathan James Howard; FCO since 1999 Private Secretary to Minister for Europe 2000; born 31.12.67; Third later Second later First Secretary UKRep Brussels 1994; Home Office 1989-91; Band D6; m 1994 Helen Louisa Pope (2d 1996, 1998).

Morrison, Melanie Kathryn (née Girling); Wellington since June 1997; born 18.3.62; FCO 1995; Band A2; m 1997 John Morrison.

Morrison, Thérésa Mary; UKDEL Vienna since January 2000; born 7.1.55; Copenhagen 1976; Warsaw 1978; FCO 1982; resigned 1985; reinstated 1991; Montevideo 1992; FCO 1993; Budapest 1998; FCO 1998; Band A2; m 1981 William Alastair Harrison (diss 1991).

Morrissey, Gillian Lesley (née Worrall); FCO since February 1990; born 2.2.60; FCO 1979; Helsinki 1981; Doha 1984; Bonn 1988; Band C4; m 1984 Patrick John Morissey (1d 1993).

Mortimer, Hugh Roger; LVO (1992); HM Ambassador Ljubljana since January 2001; born 19.9.49; FCO 1973; Rome 1975; Singapore 1978; FCO 1981; Second later First Secretary UKMIS New York 1983; First Secretary FCO 1987; on attachment to the Auswärtiges Amt 1990; First Secretary (Chancery) Berlin 1991; Counsellor FCO 1994; Royal College of Defence Studies (RCDS) 1996; Deputy Head of Mission Ankara 1997; m 1974 Zosia Cecylia Rzepecka (2d 1976, (dec'd 1993) 1980).

Morton, David Stanley Thomas; Consul (Management) Istanbul since August 1998; born 6.12.45; FO 1963; Kinshasa 1967; Cairo 1967; Wellington 1969; UKREP Brussels 1972; FCO 1975; Beirut 1977; Washington 1979; Dacca 1982; Second Secretary FCO 1985; Second Secretary (Commercial) Baghdad 1990; Second Secretary (Comm) Nairobi 1991; Second Secretary FCO 1995; m(1)1972 Judith Anne Amies (diss 1983) (1s 1973); (2)1987 Beverley Anne Sheppard (2s 1988, 1991).

Morton, Ralph Christopher; Consul (Commercial/CCU) Düsseldorf since July 2001; born 13.12.55; FCO 1979; Khartoum 1982; UKDEL NATO Brussels 1984; Third later Second Secretary (Chancery) East Berlin 1987; Second Secretary FCO 1991; Second Secretary (Com/Cons) Kampala 1992; Second Secretary (Commercial) Johannesburg 1995; Second Secretary FCO 1996; Second Secretary (Political) Vienna Embassy 1998.

Moser-Andon, Barbara; Tehran since November 2000; born 4.8.47; FCO 1991; Damascus 1993; FCO 1996; Kathmandu 1997; Band B3.

Moss, Keith Cyril; Consul-General Paris since January 1995; born 11.6.46; FO 1965; Moscow 1968; Tokyo 1969; Budapest 1973; FCO 1974; Paris 1977; Vice-Consul Douala 1981; Second Secretary FCO 1983; Second later First Secretary (Chancery) UKMIS Vienna 1987; First Secretary FCO 1991; m 1969 Lynn Butler (2s 1971, 1975).

Moss, Kylie Joanne; Tbilisi since August 1999; born 22.10.71; FCO 1990; Amman 1993; Band A2.

Moss, Stuart; Second Secretary (Technical) Buenos Aires since March 2001; born 14.6.67; FCO 1987; Washington 1994; FCO 1996; Band C4.

Moss-Norbury, Nicholas Adam; FCO since July 2000; Born 12.5.72; FCO since 1991; Third Secretary Peking 1997; Band C4.

Mott, Alan Lawrence; FCO since August 1991; born 5.10.65; FCO 1984; Washington 1989; Band C4; m 1988 Tina Michaela.

Mowbray, Fiona (née Roberts); Grand Cayman since June 1999; born 8.11.63; FCO 1983; Washington 1984; Addis Ababa 1986; Nassau 1990; Ankara 1991; SUPL 1994; FCO 1996; Band A2; m 1986 Kevin Lewis Mowbray (1s 1993).

Mowbray, Joy Diana (née Smith); SUPL since June 2000; born 1.7.71; FCO 1990; Muscat 1992; Floater duties 1999; Band A2; m 1995 David Jonathan Mowbray.

Mowbray, Kevin Lewis; Grand Cayman since June 2000; born 5.4.59; FCO 1977; UKREP Brussels 1979; ME Floater Africa 1982; FCO 1984; Addis Ababa 1986; Nassau 1990; Second Secretary (Chancery/Consular) Ankara 1991; FCO 1996; SUPL May 1999-May 2000; m 1986 Fiona Roberts (1s 1993).

Muat, David Andrew; Second Secretary FCO since January 1988; born 8.5.42; Post Office 1960; FO 1962; Jakarta 1964; Manila 1964; Buenos Aires 1967; FCO 1970; UKREP Brussels 1974; Paris 1977; FCO 1980 (Second Secretary 1982); Second Secretary (Admin) and Consul East Berlin 1984; m 1988 Susan Jean Grear (2s 1991, 1993).

Muir, David John; Third Secretary (Vice-Consul) Tashkent since December 2000; born 22.5.58; FCO 1995; Floater Duties 1996; Attaché Tashkent 1999; Band B3; m 1999 Deborah Okey.

Muir, Richard John Sutherland CMG (1994); HM Ambassador Kuwait since March 1999; born 25.8.42; FO 1964; MECAS 1965; Second Secretary (Comm) Jedda 1967; Second Secretary (Comm) Tunis 1970; FCO 1973; First Secretary Washington 1975; First Secretary, later Counsellor Riyadh 1981; Counsellor FCO 1985; AUSS (Principal Finance Officer and Chief Inspector) 1991; HM Ambassador Muscat 1994; m 1966 Caroline Simpson (1d 1970, 1s 1972).

Mulcahy, Colin Paul Peter, OBE (2000); First Secretary Consular Islamabad since July 2000; born 21.6.44; CRO 1963; Freetown 1966; DSAO (later FCO) 1968; Attaché (Consular) Bombay 1972; Second Secretary (Chancery) Wellington 1976; Second Secretary FCO 1981; Second Secretary (Comm) Damascus 1984; Vice-Consul later Consul (Comm) Toronto 1985; First Secretary (Management) and Consul Khartoum 1989; Consul Warsaw 1992; First Secretary FCO 1993; First Secretary (Consular/Immigration) New Delhi 1996; m 1969 Josephine Ann Molly Smyth (2s 1973, 1976).

Muldoon, Julie Aileen; Accra since May 1986; born 4.5.61; FCO 1984; Band A2.

Mullee, Patrick; Deputy Head of Mission Quito since August 2000; born 8.10.54; FCO 1974; Prague 1976; Caracas 1977; Africa Floater 1980; Latin America Floater 1983; FCO 1985; Third later Second Secretary San José 1988; Second Secretary (Chancery/Information) Bridgetown 1991; Second later First Secretary FCO 1995; FTLT 2000; Band C5; m 1987 Joanna Louise Johnson (2d 1989, 1994).

Mullender, Andrea; FCO since October 1999; born 16.8.73; Band A2.

Mulvaney, Isabella Maria; FCO since October 1994; born 18.3.68; FCO 1986; UKDEL Brussels 1988; Karachi 1991; Band B3.

Muncie, Heather; SUPL since March 2001; born 19.8.67; FCO 1992; Jakarta 1994; Paris 1998; Band A2.

Mulvein, Helen Jane; Assistant Legal Adviser FCO since April 2000; born 4.12.70.

Mundy, Jill (née Dalgleish); Tripoli since February 2000; born 29.4.42; DTI 1987; FCO 1989; Jerusalem 1992; New Delhi 1997; Band B3; m 1967 Timothy Wingfield Mundy (diss 1992) (2d 1968, 1970).

Munro, Catriona Mairi; FCO since October 1994; born 6.3.65; FCO 1988; Brussels 1991; Band A2.

Munro, Colin Andrew; HM Ambassador Zagreb since August 1997; born 24.10.46; Inland Revenue 1968; Third Secretary FCO 1969; Bonn 1971; Second later First Secretary Kuala Lumpur 1973; FCO 1977; Private Secretary to Minister of State 1979; First Secretary and Head of Chancery Bucharest 1981; First Secretary FCO 1983; Counsellor East Berlin 1987; HM Consul-General Frankfurt 1990; Counsellor FCO 1993; m 1967 Ehrengard Maria Heinrich (2s 1967, 1978).

Murphy, John Matthew; Vice-Consul Beijing since December 1999; born 10.3.70; HCS 1990-1993; Moscow 1995; Band B3.

Murphy, Jonathan Philip; Second Secretary (Chemical Weapons) The Hague since April 2001; born 20.1.77; FCO 1999; Band C4.

Murphy, Sandra; Resident Acting High Commissioner St. John's since October 1999; born 9.4.50; FCO 1968; UKREP Brussels 1972; Resigned 1975; Reinstated 1978; FCO 1978; Harare 1981; Second Secretary FCO 1984; Second Secretary (Aid) Kingston 1987; Second Secretary (Comm) Addis Ababa 1991; Second Secretary (Comm) Caracas 1993; First Secretary FCO 1996.

Murray, Craig John; Deputy High Commissioner Accra since January 1999; born 17.10.58; FCO 1984; Second Secretary (Comm) Lagos 1986; First Secretary FCO 1990; Full-time Language Training 1993; First Secretary (Political/Economic) Warsaw 1994; FCO 1998; m 1984 Fiona Anne.

Murray, Gillian; Vienna since July 1995; born 18.9.69; FCO 1990; Paris 1992; Language Training 1995; Band A2.

Murray, Iain Richard, OBE (1991); Consul-General Houston since January 2001; born 13.8.44; CRO 1963; SUPL at University 1965; Commonwealth Office (later FCO) 1968; Accra 1970; Second Secretary Addis Ababa 1972; Vice-Consul (Comm) Rio de Janeiro 1975; Consul Oporto 1979; First Secretary on loan to No. 10 Downing Street 1983; First Secretary FCO 1985; Chargé d'Affaires San Salvador 1987; First Secretary FCO 1992; Counsellor (Comm/Econ) Kuala Lumpur 1994; Consul General and Director of Trade Promotion in Brazil, São Paulo 1997; m(1)1967 Victoria Crew Gee (1d 1969; 1s 1971); (diss 1983); (2)1993 Norma Agnes Wisden (née Hummel).

Murray, June; Ankara since May 1998; born 9.6.50; FCO 1986; Tegucigalpa 1988; Johannesburg 1990; Moscow 1992; FCO 1995; Band B3.

Murray, Michael Thomas; Deputy Consul General Chicago since September 1999; born 13.10.45; FO DSAO 1964; Prague 1967; Vienna 1971; Vice-Consul (Comm) Frankfurt 1973; Second Secretary (Dev) Khartoum 1977; FCO 1980; First Secretary and Head of Chancery Banjul 1983; First Secretary FCO 1987; First Secretary (Development/Economic) Lusaka 1995; On loan to DfID at Lusaka 1998; Band D6; m 1968 Else Birgitta Margareta Paues (1s 1974; 1d 1981).

Murray, Winston Anthony, Bahrain since May 1994; born 4.7.64; OFT 1985; FCO 1985; Bonn 1991; Band A2; m 1990 Judith Muponda.

Murtagh, Michael Louis; FCO since July 2000; born 12.2.53; RAF Flt Lt 1981-97; Defence Attaché's Office, Moscow 1995-97; Moscow, New Embassy Project 1997-2000; Band B3; m 1988 Diana Morford (2s 1980, 1983).

Murton, John Evan; Full Time Language Training (Tokyo) since October 1998; born 18.3.72; FCO 1997; Band C4.

Musgrave, David William; First Secretary FCO since October 1998; born 12.5.53; FCO 1983; Second later First Secretary Copenhagen 1985; First Secretary FCO 1989; First Secretary (Political/Information) Lagos 1994; First Secretary (Political) Abuja 1995; m 1978 Madeleine Nnomo Assembe (2d 1979, 1991; 1s 1981).

Myers, Sally; Athens since October 1999; born 13.8.68; FCO 1998; Band A2.

Myers, Sharon Theresa; Copenhagen since January 2001; born 19.4.65; FCO 1987; Moscow 1988; Bogotá 1991; FCO 1995; Band B3; m 1993 Manuel Bolano (1s 1996).

N

Nailard, Allison Mary (née Abbott); FCO since August 1999; born 3.7.73; Band A2; m 1999 Michael Nailard.

Nalden, Philip Nigel; Colombo since August 1999; born 30.3.45; Army (CRMP) 1963-88; Moscow 1988; Lagos 1989; Peking 1993; Dhaka 1994; FCO 1997; Belgrade 1998; Band B3; m 1982 Heather McIntosh.

Napthen, Florence Wilson; Addis Ababa since May 1996; born 25.10.61; Crown Office, Edinburgh 1978; FCO 1986; Wellington 1988; FCO 1991; Washington 1993; Band B3; m 1990 Stephen Kenneth Napthen.

Nash, Ronald Peter, LVO (1984), MVO (1983); HM Ambassador Kathmandu since March 1999; born 18.9.46; FCO 1970; Second later First Secretary Moscow 1974; First Secretary UKDEL Vienna 1976; FCO 1979; New Delhi 1983; First Secretary FCO 1986; Counsellor and Head of Chancery Vienna 1988; Deputy High Commissioner Colombo 1992; Counsellor FCO 1996; m 1976 Annie Olsen (3s 1979, 1981, 1983).

Nash, Stephen Thomas, CMG (2000); HM Ambassador Riga since July 1999; born 22.3.42; British Council Baghdad 1965; FO 1967; Third Secretary Caracas 1968; Third later Second Secretary (Chancery) Bogotá 1970; Sabbatical at Oxford University 1972; FCO 1973; SEATO Bangkok 1975; FCO 1977; First Secretary and Deputy Head of Post Guatemala City 1979; Deputy High Commissioner Belmopan 1981; First Secretary FCO 1982; Chargé d'Affaires a.i. and First Secretary Managua 1986; On Secondment to British Aerospace 1989; First Secretary FCO 1992; Chargé d'Affaires Tirana 1993; HM Ambassador Tbilisi 1995; Ambassador Tirana 1998; m (1) 1967 Rose-Marie Bornstrand (diss 1973); (2) 1977 Boonying Permkasikam (1s 1971; 2d 1977, 1985).

Naughton, Dawn Karen; Jerusalem since December 2000; born 22.8.69; FCO 1988; UKDEL Brussels 1990; Maputo 1993; Lagos 1997; Band B3; m 1993 Steven John Horsup (1d 1998; 1s 1999).

Neale, Dawn Teresa; Abuja since April 1998; born 13.8.60; FCO 1996. Band A2; m 1995 John Harry Albert.

Needham, David Brent; UKDEL NATO Brussels since October 1999; born 21.2.51; Royal Marines 1968-91; Moscow 1992; Kingston 1996; Band B3; m,1992 Karen Dawn Ackers. (2s 1993, 1995).

Neely, Maxine Lorna (née Hunter); British Trade International since September 1999; born 9.12.64; FCO 1988; Washington 1989; Bangkok 1992; FCO 1995; Tokyo 1997; Band B3; m2000 Peter Gordon Neely.

Neil, Andrew Alasdair; First Secretary (Political) Abu Dhabi since April 2001; born 11.6.68; FCO 1991; Second Secretary (Political) Nairobi 1994;

Second Secretary FCO 1996; Band D6; m 1998 Amanda Lewis (2s (twins) 2000).

Neil, William John; Vice Consul (Visas) Shanghai since December 1999; born 23.5.67; FCO 1988; T/D Sofia (CSCE Conference) and East Berlin 1989; UKDEL NATO Brussels 1990; UKREP Brussels 1990; Baku 1993; Bombay 1995; Band B3.

Neill, Kenneth Andrew; HM Consul Riyadh since July 2001; born 6.11.44; FO 1961; Tripoli 1967; Moscow 1970; Vientiane 1970; FCO 1974; Hanoi 1977; Karachi 1979; Second Secretary (Chancery/Inf) Lilongwe 1982; Second Secretary FCO 1986; Second later First Secretary Honiara 1988; First Secretary (Comm/Cons) Lusaka 1992; First Secretary FCO 1996; Deputy Head of Mission T/D Yaounde 2000; m 1977 Julie C Brown (2s 1981, 1991; 2d 1987, 1993).

Neilson, James George Lovie; Ankara since November 2000; born 27.7.44; Army 1965-88; Geneva 1988; Moscow 1991; Budapest 1992; Pretoria 1994; Peking 1997; Band B3; m 1967 Lorraine (1d 1968; 1s 1971).

Neilson, Kim; Islamabad since May 1995; born 30.9.71; FCO 1991; Band A2.

Nellthorp, Helen Rosemary; Second Secretary FCO since October 1994; born 10.5.62; FCO 1980; Athens 1984; Floater Duties 1987; Third Secretary (Comm) Washington 1989; Second Secretary (Comm) Prague 1991.

Nelson, Diana June (née Gordon); FCO since September 1997; born 17.6.58; FCO 1981; Paris 1984; Algiers 1987; Second Secretary FCO 1989; SUPL 1991; FCO 1992; SUPL 1995; m 1985 Miles Christopher Nelson (2d 1991, 1993).

Nelson, Emma Sutherland; SUPL since September 1997; born 20.3.71; FCO 1990; Band B3.

Nelson, Matthew Charles; FCO since September 2000; born 19.6.74; Band C4.

Nelson, Philip Raymond; First Secretary later Counsellor FCO since April 1994; born 7.4.50; FCO 1972; Third later Second Secretary (Comm) Budapest 1974; Second later First Secretary Paris 1976; FCO 1979; Rome 1980; First Secretary FCO 1983; First Secretary (Chancery) Manila 1989; First Secretary Budapest 1991; Band D6; m(1)1971 Cynthia Elson (diss 1978); (2)1992 Lyndsay Ann Halper; (2s Twins 1992).

Nessling, Paul William Downs; High Commissioner Nuku' Alofa since January 2002; born 26.9.45; Bahrain 1975 (From DOI); Second Secretary FCO 1979; Lisbon 1981; Warsaw 1982; First Secretary (Aid) Nairobi 1984; FCO 1987; First Secretary (Comm) Harare 1989; First Secretary (Comm) Muscat 1993; First Secretary (Commercial) Sarajevo 1996; FCO 1997; Deputy Head of Mission and First Secretary (Commercial) Lusaka 1998; m 1975 Kathryn Freeman.

Nethersole, Jonathan Sebastian; World Wide Floater Duties since 1998; born 7.11.69; FCO 1988; Pretoria 1990; Sana'a 1993; FCO 1995; Band B3.

Nettleton, Catherine Elizabeth; OBE (1999); Counsellor (Political/Economic) Peking October 2000; born 13.3.60; FCO 1983; Language Training 1984; Peking 1987; Second Secretary 1988; Second Secretary FCO 1989; First Secretary (Political/Economic) Mexico City 1991; First Secretary FCO 1995; Counsellor FCO 1999.

Nevin, Michael Patrick; Second Secretary (Chancery) Lilongwe since December 1999; born 13.1.69; FCO 1993; Osaka 1996. Band B3; m 1997 Sawako (1 step d 1989, 1s 1998).

Newall, Peter; Counsellor, Head of Joint Management Office Brussels since October 1999; born 20.3.47; DSAO (later FCO) 1966; Tehran 1970; Delhi 1972; FCO 1976; Second Secretary (Comm) Belgrade 1979; First Secretary (Comm) Kuwait 1982; FCO 1986; HM Consul Marseilles 1989; First Secretary (Management) UKMIS Geneva 1990; FCO 1995; m 1969 Marina Joy McHugh (2d 1972, 1973; 1s 1976).

Newell, Clive Dare; Counsellor Moscow since October 2001; born 22.12.53; FCO 1976; Third Secretary (Comm) later Second Secretary Tehran 1979; FCO 1980; Second later First Secretary Kabul 1982; FCO 1984; First Secretary Addis Ababa 1986; FCO 1990; First Secretary on secondment to Ministry of Defence 1992; FCO 1993; First Secretary on loan to Cabinet Office 1993; Counsellor (Political) Ankara 1994; Counsellor FCO 1998; m 1997 Gamze Ozen (1s 1999).

Newlands, Andrew; Deputy Head of Mission Panama City since April 2000; born 10.2.68; DHSS 1984; FCO 1988; Bonn 1990; FCO 1992; Manila 1993; T/D Hong Kong 1996; FCO 1997; m 1989 Eileen Mitchell (1s 1993, 1d 1996).

Newman, George William; FCO since March 1983; (Second Secretary 1991); born 16.6.54; FCO 1972; Munich 1976; FCO 1978; Moscow 1981; Band C4; m 1975 Elaine Haron Turner (1s 1983; 1d 1987).

Newman, James Michael; FCO since July 1999; born 31.3.70; Metropolitan Police 1989; FCO 1990; Cairo 1992; Cape Town 1996; Band B3; m2000 Sarah Louise.

Newman, Kevin Paul; Abuja since August 1998; born 31.7.73; Home Office 1994; FCO 1995; Band B3.

Newman, Pauline Agnes; FCO since September 1978; born 7.4.48; FO 1966; Addis Ababa 1969; Sofia 1971; Islamabad 1972; FCO 1973; Tokyo 1975; Band B3.

Newman, Peter James; Deputy Head of Mission Abuja since June 1998; born 29.5.46; FO 1963; Muscat 1968; Bahrain Residency 1970; Tokyo 1971; FCO 1975; Dacca 1978; Second Secretary UKDEL MBFR Vienna 1980; Second Secretary

(Econ) Oslo 1983; First Secretary FCO 1987; Deputy High Commissioner and Head of Chancery Gaborone 1989; First Secretary (Commercial) Nicosia 1992; First Secretary FCO 1996; m 1966 Kathryn Yvonne Alcock (1d 1969; 1s 1972).

Newns, Carl Edwin Francis; First Secretary (Chancery) since March 2000; born 30.6.68; FCO 1989; Second Secretary (Political) The Hague 1992; Private Secretary to Minister of State 1997; Band C4.

Newson, Gavin Erskine Walter; Second Secretary FCO since April 2001; born 20.7.71; FCO 1996; Second Secretary (Financial/Economic) Tokyo 1998; Band C4.

Newton, Alan Peter; FCO since April 1998; born 21.6.46; Inland Revenue 1963; DSAO 1965; Tel Aviv 1969; Accra 1969; San José 1973; Dacca 1976; FCO 1980; Montevideo 1983; Copenhagen 1987; Second Secretary FCO 1989; Second Secretary (Management) Manila 1994; m 1976 Mayra Rosa Antonia Camacho.

Newton, Alastair Dan Barr; on secondment to Lehman Bros as Economic Adviser since March 2000; born 8.1.54; FCO 1985; Second Secretary later First Secretary Kinshasa 1986; First Secretary FCO 1989; First Secretary UKDEL Paris 1992; m 1988 Vivienne Jane Ivanich (2d 1979, 1980).

Nicholas, Barry Stuart; Second Secretary (Commercial) Port of Spain since April 1999; born 1.11.62; FCO 1981; East Berlin 1984; Dubai 1986; Warsaw 1988; FCO 1991; Cairo 1995; m 1989 Susan Jane Parker (1s 1992).

Nicholas, Susan Jane (née Parker); SUPL since January 1999; born 17.9.62; FCO 1981; Warsaw 1984; Bonn 1987; Düsseldorf 1988; Warsaw 1989; (Second Secretary 1991); FCO 1993; SUPL 1995; Cairo 1996; m 1989 Barry Stuart Nicholas (1s 1992).

Nicholas, Suzanne Elizabeth; FCO since March 2000; born 14.8.70; FCO 1995; Second Secretary (Political) Warsaw 1999; Band C4.

Nicholls, Gary Patrick; HM Consul Guangzhou since August 2000; born 4.10.68; FCO 1988; Tokyo 1990; Islamabad 1993; FCO 1998; Band C4; m 1993 Helen Marie Glanfield (Diss 1998) (1s 1994; 1d 1997).

Nichols, John Roland; On secondment to British Invisibles since September 2000; born 13.11.51; Third later Second Secretary FCO 1977; Second later First Secretary Budapest 1979; FCO 1982; First Secretary (Comm) Brasilia 1985; First Secretary FCO 1989; Counsellor and Deputy High Commissioner Dhaka 1993; Consul General Geneva 1995; Deputy Head of Mission and Director of Trade Promotion Berne 1997; m 1983 Angela Suzanne Davies (1s 1987; 1d 1989).

Nichols, Martin Christopher; FCO since August 1994; born 4.5.62; FCO 1981; Tel Aviv 1984; FCO 1987; Darwin 1988; FCO 1990; New Delhi 1991; Band B3; m 1983 Julie Marie Wilkins (2s 1983, 1988; 1d 1992).

Nicholson, Karen Jayne (née Baudains) on loan to the DTI since July 1998; born 29.9.55; FCO 1977; Mexico City 1979; South East Asia Floater Duties 1983; Second Secretary FCO 1985; Second later First Secretary (Commercial) Lisbon 1992; m 1994 David Joseph Nicholson.

Nicolopulo, Evangelo Paul; First Secretary (Political) Copenhagen since June 1995; born 14.1.50; FCO 1969; Lourenco Marques 1972; Saigon 1973; FCO 1974; Kingston 1977; Madrid (CSCE) 1980; Alexandria 1982; Second Secretary FCO 1985; Vice-Consul (Comm) Montreal 1988; First Secretary FCO 1993; m 1981 Kareen Elizabeth Sun.

Nithavrianakis, Elizabeth Rosemary (née Hingston-Jones); T/D Riyadh since June 2001; born 27.6.63; FCO 1983; Peking 1985; Kuala Lumpur 1986; FCO 1990; Moscow 1990; FCO 1992; Band B3; m 1992 Michael Stephen Nithavrianakis (1s 1996, 1d 2000).

Nithavrianakis, Michael Stephen, MVO (2000); First Secretary (Commercial) Riyadh since October 2000; born 30.4.67; FCO 1984; Kuala Lumpur 1987; Moscow 1990; FCO 1992; Second Secretary (Chancery) Accra 1997; Band C5; m,1992 Elizabeth Rosemary Hingston-Jones (1s 1996, 1d 2000).

Nixon, Patrick Michael, CMG (1989), OBE (1984); HM Ambassador Abu Dhabi since November 1998; born 1.8.44; Third Secretary FO 1965; MECAS 1966; Cairo 1968 (Second Secretary 1969); Lima 1970; Second later First Secretary FCO 1973; First Secretary and Head of Chancery Tripoli 1977; Director and Consul (Inf) BIS New York 1980; First Secretary later Counsellor FCO 1983; HM Ambassador and Consul-General Doha 1987; Counsellor FCO 1990; High Commissioner Lusaka 1994; FCO 1997; m 1968 Elizabeth Rose Carlton (4s 1970, 1971, 1975, 1978).

Noakes, Jonathan Arnott; Consul-General Lyon since April 2001; born 4.1.44; FO 1965; Third Secretary Ankara 1966; FO 1967; Second Secretary FCO 1971; First Secretary FCO 1974; First Secretary (Econ) Oslo 1981; First Secretary FCO 1985; Deputy High Commissioner Bridgetown 1991; First Secretary FCO 1995; m 1973 Nicola Jane Macaulay Langley.

Noakes, Stephen Martin, OBE (1993); First Secretary FCO since August 2000; born 6.2.57; Home Civil Service 1979-88; Second Secretary FCO 1988; First Secretary (Chancery) Luanda 1990; First Secretary FCO 1993; First Secretary UKMIS New York 1996; Band D6; m 1989 Hazel Clarke.

Nobes, Paula Louise; Second Secretary FCO since October 1998; born 1.8.69; FCO 1988; Language Training 1990; Third Secretary (Chancery) Belgrade 1991; APS Lord Owen, Peace Conference Geneva 1993; Kiev 1994; Zagreb 1995; Band C4.

Noble, Andrew James, LVO (1995); Deputy Head of Mission Athens since August 2001; born 22.4.60; FCO 1982; Third Secretary (Chancery/Inf) Bucharest 1983; on attachment to Auswärtiges Amt, Bonn 1986; Second Secretary (Chancery) Bonn 1987; First Secretary FCO 1989; First Secretary (Political) and Head of Political Section Pretoria/Cape Town 1994; FCO 1998; m 1992 Helen Natalie Pugh; (2s 1995, 1996).

Noble, Helen Natalie (née Pugh); SUPL since May 1994; born 17.7.66; FCO 1988; On Secondment to the Auswärtiges Amt 1989; Third later Second Secretary Bonn 1990; Second Secretary FCO 1992; Second Secretary on loan to the ODA 1993; m 1992 Andrew James Noble.

Noble, Richard Adam; Head of Research Analysts FCO since June 2001; born 9.6.62; FCO 1987; Third later Second Secretary (Chancery) Moscow 1987; Second later First Secretary FCO 1989; First Secretary The Hague 1993; FCO 1995; First Secretary (Political) New Delhi 1998; m 1994 Katrina Johnson (2s 1996, 1998).

Noble, Robert Antony; FCO since March 1999; born 24.8.66; FCO 1984; Lisbon 1986; Islamabad 1989; FCO 1992; Rio de Janeiro 1995; Band C4; m 1997 Elisabeth Patrice Wilkinson.

Noël, Louisa Veronica; Bangkok since October 1999; born 24.4.62; FCO 1988; Kuala Lumpur 1989; Amman 1993; FCO 1996; Band B3.

Nolan, Julia Elizabeth; SUPL since June 1997; born 2.1.59; FCO 1983; Bangkok 1984; SUPL 1986; New Delhi 1987; Second Secretary FCO 1989; First Secretary FCO 1993; SUPL 1994; First Secretary (Political) Paris 1995; m 1985 Richard John Codrington (Twin s 1991).

Noon, Paul David; FCO since November 1998; born 1.6.68; FCO 1989; Damascus 1991; Bonn 1995; Band C4; m 1990 Karren Lesley Robson (1d 1993, 1s 1998).

Norburn, Jonathan Edward; Second Secretary (Chancery) Bridgetown since March 2001; born 16.8.76; FCO 1999; Band C4.

Norman, Duncan Charles, MBE (2000); FCO since May 2000; born 12.10.71; FCO 1990; Riyadh 1994; Yerevan 1998; m 1997 Kerry Jones (1d 2000).

Norman, Paul Stephen Raymond; First Secretary FCO since May 2000; born 4.5.56; FCO 1992; Consul Hong Kong 1995; Band D6; m 1989 Felicity Shan Abram (1s 1991, 2d 1993, 1998).

Norman, Sarah Caroline; SUPL since September 1994; born 16.12.70; FCO 1990; New Delhi 1991; FCO 1992; Band B3.

Norris, Peter James; FCO since September 2000; born 22.12.55; FCO 1982; First Secretary Lagos 1985; FCO 1988; Deputy Head of Mission and Consul Guatemala City 1990; First Secretary FCO 1993; First Secretary (Political) Jakarta 1997; Band D6; m 1982; Dilvinder Kaur Dhaliwal (2d 1986, 1990, 2s (twins) 1993).

Norsworthy, Sean Francis; FCO since January 1996; born 18.4.68; FCO 1987; Islamabad 1989; Tunis 1992; Band A2.

Northern, Richard James, MBE (1982); Counsellor FCO since August 2000; born 2.11.54; FCO 1976; MECAS 1978; Language Training, FCO 1978; Riyadh 1980; Second later First Secretary (Chancery) Rome 1983; First Secretary FCO 1987; First Secretary (Economic/Commercial) Ottawa 1992; Deputy Consul General and Deputy Director Trade/Investment Toronto 1994; Counsellor (Commercial/Economic) Riyadh 1997; m 1981 Linda Denise Gadd (2s 1983, 1986, 1d 1992).

Norton, Mark Rolffe; Deputy High Commissioner Georgetown since April 2000; born 3.1.55; Customs and Excise 1974; Immigration Service 1983; on secondment to Kaduna 1987; FCO 1992; on secondment to ICFY/Observer Mission to Serbia and Montenegro 1994; Addis Ababa 1995; Copenhagen 1996; Ottawa 1996; m 1995 Gelila Assefa Wedajo (2d 1996, 1998).

Norton, Redmond; Deputy Head Mission Montevideo since October 1999; born 30.4.46; Board of Trade 1962; FCO 1969; Rio de Janeiro 1972; Caracas 1975; Dacca 1977; FCO 1980; Second Secretary (Admin) Tripoli 1984; Second Secretary Quito 1985; Second later First Secretary (Comm) Helsinki 1988; First Secretary FCO 1992; Consul (Commercial) Houston 1994; Band D6; m 1969 Jean McGarrigle (1d 1974; 1s 1979).

Nye, Alison Claire (née Edwards); SUPL since March 2001; born 18.12.64; FCO 1983; SUPL 1985; Vienna 1986, Algiers 1987; Karachi 1990; FCO 1993; Third later Second Secretary (Development) Lilongwe 1997; SUPL 1999; Second Secretary (Development) Lilongwe 2000; Band B3; m 1985 Richard Paul Nye (1s 1999).

Nye, Richard Paul; SUPL since March 2001; born 29.2.64; FCO 1982; Vienna 1984; Algiers 1987; Karachi 1990; FCO 1994; Second Secretary Lilongwe 1997; Band C4; m 1985 Alison Claire Edwards (1s 1999).

O

Oakden, Edward Anthony; DHM and Minister Madrid since January 2000; born 3.11.59; FCO 1981; Third later Second Secretary (Chancery) Baghdad 1984; Second Secretary (Chancery) Khartoum 1985; First Secretary and Private Secretary to HM Ambassador Washington 1988; First Secretary FCO 1992; Private Secretary to Prime Minister (Overseas/Defence) 1995; Counsellor FCO 1997; Counsellor Madrid 1998; m 1989 (diss) (1d 1995).

Oakley, Matthew Edward; MVO (1999); Second Secretary (Commercial) Singapore since June 2000; born 19.7.65; FCO 1983; Athens 1985; Jedda 1988; Riyadh 1990; Third Secretary FCO 1992; Third Secretary (Political) Cape Town 1996; Band C4.

O'Brien, Gareth David; Consul (Commercial) Jedda since December 1998; born 27.7.65; FCO

1982; Copenhagen 1985; Warsaw 1988; Africa/ME Floater 1990; FCO 1991; Belmopan 1995; Band C4; m 1991 Lisa Margaret Donagher (2s 1997, 1999).

O'Brien, Julie Ann Valentine; Kuwait since June 1999; born 20.3.61; FCO 1994; Moscow 1996.

O'Brien, Lisa Margaret (née Donagher); SUPL since June 1997; born 30.10.66; FCO 1984; BMG Berlin 1986; Floater Duties 1989; FCO 1991; Belmopan 1995; Band B3; m 1991 Gareth David O'Brien (2s 1997, 1999).

O'Brien, Patrick Thaddeus Dominic MBE (1995); First Secretary and Deputy Head of Mission Dakar since October 1998; born 3.11.49; Post Office 1966; FCO 1968; Lagos 1971; Georgetown 1975; FCO 1978; JAO Brussels 1982; Abidjan 1984; Second Secretary FCO 1988; Brussels 1993; m 1970 Maureen Mortimer (3d 1970, 1971, 1979; 1s 1973).

O'Callaghan, John Matthew; First Secretary (Political) Moscow since May 1998; born 27.4.66; FCO 1990; Second Secretary (Information) Santiago 1992; Second Secretary FCO 1994; Band D6; m 1996 Sophie Dauchez.(1d 1998)

O'Connell, Philip; FCO since March 2000; born 14.11.66; FCO 1985; Nairobi 1990; FCO 1991; Damascus since July 1997; Band B3; m 1998 Nesrene Masroun.

O'Connell, Terence; Peking since May 2000; born 19.9.58; MOD 1976; FCO 1978; Stockholm 1980; Tripoli 1983; FCO 1984; Santiago 1984; Bombay 1987; FCO 1990; Full-time Language Training 1995; Mexico City 1996; FTLT 2000; Band C4; m 1991 Valerie Anna-Maria Gonsalves.

O'Connor, Christopher Paul; First Secretary (Political) Ottawa since August 1999; born 18.12.68; Third later Second Secretary FCO 1993; Full Time Language Training Cairo 1995; Riyadh 1996.

O'Connor, Lorraine; FCO since November 1994; born 13.2.66; Band A2.

O'Connor, Paul Vincent; Deputy Head of Mission and Consul (Commercial) St. Petersburg since August 1999; born 29.6.56; FCO 1975; Jedda 1977; Washington 1980; Floater Duties 1983; FCO 1985; Istanbul 1987; Second Secretary (Aid/Commercial) Maseru 1991; On loan to the DTI 1995; Language Student 1998; m 1985 Georgina Louise Jayne (2s 1987, 1989, 1d 1991).

O'Connor, Sheila Mary; Third Secretary (Chancery/Development) Kathmandu since January 1997; born 28.12.60; FCO 1982; UKREP Brussels 1983; Yaoundé 1986; Rangoon 1989; Prague 1991; FCO 1993; OSCE Sarajevo 1996.

O'Conor, Fionnuala Katharine; FCO since February 1994; born 10.4.69; Band C4.

O'Donnell, Patricia (née Daubeney); Third Secretary (Press and Public Affairs) Moscow since August 1997; born 22.12.68; FCO 1991; Warsaw 1994; Band C4; m 1993 Simon Tristan O'Donnell.

O'Donnell, Sara Jane (née Sharp); Yaoundé since November 1996; born 24.12.67; FCO 1991; Third Secretary UKDEL WEU Brussels1994; m 1996 Francis Joseph O'Donnell.

Oertle-Hurt, Jane Michelle; Africa/Middle East Floater since April 1994; born 13.9.65; HCS 1987-1989; Rome 1990; Band B3; m 1995 Horst Dietrich Oertle.

O'Flaherty, Kenneth James; First Secretary (external Relations) UKREP Brussels since July 2000; born 4.3.72; FCO 1996; secondment to French Foreign Ministry 1998; Second Secretary (Political) Paris 1999; m 1997 Maria de los Reyes Lopez Garcia (diss 2000) (1d 1998).

O'Flaherty, Stephen John; First Secretary later Counsellor FCO since August 1992; born 15.5.51; Third Secretary FCO 1975; Language Student India 1977; Second Secretary New Delhi 1978; First Secretary FCO 1980; Prague 1981; First Secretary FCO 1984; First Secretary (Chancery) Vienna 1988; m 1975 Sarah Louise Gray (2d 1979, 1987; 1s 1983).

Ogden, Michael Geoffrey; First Secretary on loan to the Cabinet Office since July 1994; born 12.4.48; Second later First Secretary FCO 1977; Pretoria 1980; First Secretary FCO 1981; First Secretary (IAEA) UKMIS Vienna 1986; First Secretary FCO 1990; Band C5; m 1976 Carolyne Bryant (1d 1979; 1s 1980).

Ogg, Fiona; Lagos since August 1999; born 25.7.70; FCO 1989; Warsaw 1992; Paris 1994; FCO 1996; Band B3.

O'Hara, Violet Brown McGregor (née Steele); FCO since 1999; born 22.9.42; FO 1961; Tokyo 1964; Singapore 1964; Kinshasa 1967; FCO 1970; Strasbourg 1971; Jakarta 1975; Hanoi 1978; FCO 1980; Second later First Secretary (Comm) Washington 1985; Consul (Comm) Rio de Janeiro 1990; Consul Dallas 1995; m 1986 Basil Austin Samuel O'Hara (dec'd 2000).

O'Keeffe, Deanna Maureen; FCO since October 1991; born 24.9.61; FCO 1980; Vienna 1989; Band A2.

O'Kelly, Bridget Jane (née Hoare); SUPL since October 2000; born 7.12.67; FCO 1993; Bahrain 1996; SUPL 1997; Third Secretary (Visits) Paris 1999; Band B3; m 1995 Richard Edward Henry O'Kelly (1s 1997).

Oliver, Geoffrey Harold; world-wide Floater Duties since September 1993; born 11.6.48; HM Forces 1965-88; Moscow 1989; Madrid 1991; Band B3.

Oliver, Kaye Wight, CMG (2001), OBE (1994); High Commissioner Maseru since March 1999; born 10.8.43; Customs and Excise 1962; FCO 1965; DSAO (later FCO) 1966; Kuala Lumpur 1970; Second Secretary FCO 1974; Lilongwe 1978; Paris 1981; First Secretary Nairobi 1983; First Secretary Head of Chancery and Consul Yaoundé 1984; First Secretary FCO 1987; First Secretary

Consul and Deputy Head of Mission, later Chargé d'Affaires Kinshasa (also Chargé d'Affaires non-resident to Burundi and Rwanda) 1990; on loan to the ODA 1994; HM Ambassador Kigali (also Ambassador non-resident to Burundi) 1995; Adviser on Burundi to ex-President Nyerere Dar-es-Salaam 1998.

Oliver, Matthew Keith; Second Secretary (Management) Hague since February 1999; born 16.8.51; Blantyre 1973; Washington 1975; Belgrade 1978; FCO 1979; Tehran 1980; Bombay 1980; Warsaw 1983; FCO 1984; Auckland 1986; Istanbul 1989; Second Secretary FCO 1993; Baku 1996; m 1993 Hatice Iker Urgen (dec'd 1999).

Oliver, Paul John; Madrid since July 2000; born 11.2.74; FCO (Hanslope Park) 1996; Band C4.

O'Mahony, Angela Millar (née Lindsay); SUPL since June 2000; born 17.8.66; FCO 1989; Paris 1991; Kampala 1994; Stockholm 1996; FCO 1996; Band B3; m 1994 Daniel Lawrence O'Mahony.

Oman, Magnus Paul; on loan to DTI since November 1999; born 5.8.68; FCO 1989; Doha 1994; Valletta 1991; FCO 1998; Band B3; m 1998 Ms S Broderick.

O'Neill, Douglas Matthew; seconded to Benefits Agency October 1999; born 13.6.69; FCO 1990; Dublin 1994; Floater duties 1998; Band A2.

O'Neill, Michael Angus; First Secretary (Political) Washington since October 1998; born 25.5.65; MOD 1988; Second Secretary, UKDEL NATO/WEU 1991; FCO 1994; m 1991 Claire Bannerman (1d 1994, 3s 1996, 1998, 2001).

Onn, Anthony Wilfred; Belgrade since August 1993; born 16.4.44; Royal Navy 1959-84; Sofia 1987; Bonn 1989; Band B3.

Ord-Smith, Robin Jeremy; Second Secretary (Commercial) Tokyo since January 2001; born 8.10.65; FCO 1989; Bucharest 1991; Third Secretary (Political/Information) 1994; FTLT 2000; m 1995 Tania Jane Vallis.

Ormiston, Ewan Kenneth; Kampala since August 1999; born 27.8.68; FCO 1989; Brussels 1992; Luanda 1995; Third Secretary Lima 1996; Band B3; m 1994 Gillian Keating.

Ormiston, Gillian (née Keating); SUPL since 1999; born 1.6.66; FCO 1988; UKREP Brussels 1991; Luanda 1995; SUPL 1996; Band A2; m 1994 Ewan Kenneth Ormiston.

Ormond, Matthew John; Washington since January 2001; born 23.4.73; FCO 1991; Band C4

O'Rourke, Peter Vincent FCO since April 2000; born 26.9.60; FCO 1980; Maputo 1981; Lisbon 1984; Rabat 1987; FCO 1990; Yaoundé 1993; Third later Second Secretary (Management) Beirut 1997; Band C4; m 1999 Louise Karen.

Orr, Gwendolen; FCO since September 1996; born 16.12.73; FCO 1996; Band C4.

Orr, Iain Campbell; Counsellor Deputy High Commissioner Accra since March 1998; born 6.12.42; Third later Second Secretary FCO 1968; Hong Kong 1969; Second later First Secretary Peking 1972; FCO 1974; Assistant Political Adviser Hong Kong 1978; Dublin 1981; First Secretary FCO 1984; Consul-General Shanghai 1987; Counsellor and Deputy High Commissioner Wellington 1991; FCO 1994; m 1978 Susan Elizabeth Gunter (1d 1983; 1s 1984).

Osborn, Andrew Robert; Third Secretary (Consular/Management) Maseru since August 2001; born 13.2.64; FCO 1982; Lagos 1987; Budapest 1990; Moscow 1992; FCO 1994; Vice Consul Dar-es-Salaam 1997; Band B3; m 1988 Karyn Lindsay Heraty.

Osborn, Karyn Lindsay, (née Heraty); SUPL since July 1997; born 12.2.66; FCO 1986; Lagos 1988; Budapest 1990; Moscow 1992; FCO 1994; Band B3; m 1988 Andrew Robert Osborn.

Osborn, Sally Mary; SUPL since November 1988; born 26.1.57; FCO 1976; Dacca 1978; Amsterdam 1982; Second Secretary FCO 1984; Second

Secretary (Inf/Chancery) Lisbon 1988; m 1988 Neil Gordon Haddock (1s 1990).

Osborne, Christopher Wyndham; Deputy Head of Mission Luanda since March 1998; born 18.6.46; CO 1964; Commonwealth Office (later FCO) 1966; Lusaka 1968; Kampala 1970; Bridgetown 1973; FCO 1976; Second Secretary Dacca 1979; Second Secretary (Comm) Caracas 1982; First Secretary FCO 1986; First Secretary (Inf) BTC Hong Kong 1989; First Secretary FCO 1994, First Secretary T/D BTC Hong Kong; 1996; m 1967 Gillian Mary (3s 1967, 1974, 1979).

Osborne, David Allan; HM Ambassador Tegucigalpa since July 1998; born 31.8.42; CRO 1961; Department of Technical Co-operation 1961; CRO 1963; Accra 1963; DSAO 1966; Guatemala 1968; (Second Secretary 1970); Second Secretary (Inf) Bonn 1973; Second Secretary Valletta 1974; Central London Polytechnic 1977; First Secretary FCO 1978; First Secretary, Head of Chancery and Consul San José also accredited to Nicaragua and El Salvador 1980-84; First Secretary FCO 1984; Deputy Consul General São Paulo 1988; European Union Monitor Yugoslavia 1991; First Secretary FCO 1992; T/D First Secretary (Political) Santiago 1994; First Secretary FCO 1995; Chargé d'Affaires Managua 1997; m 1966 Joan Marion Duck (1s 1970; 2d 1971, 1973).

Osborne, Roy Paul; HM Ambassador Managua since July 1997; born 13.7.51; FCO 1970; Oslo 1972; Islamabad 1974; Vice-Consul Rome 1978; Second Secretary FCO 1981; Second Secretary (Comm/Dev) later First Secretary, Head of Chancery and Consul Yaoundé 1985; First Secretary (Chancery/Inf) Madrid 1989; First Secretary FCO 1993; m 1977 Vivienne Claire Gentry (2d 1983, 1984).

O'Shaughnessy, Jonathan Edward; Islamabad since October 2000; born 7.10.71; FCO 1991; Bonn 1995; Band A2; m 1997.

Ostler, Malcolm Thomas; Bonn since July 1997; born 20.9.66; FCO 1988; Band A2.

Oswald, David; Consul (Commercial/Economic) Shanghai since August 1997; born 15.6.46; FO 1965; Amman 1968; Zomba 1970; Blantyre 1971; Tokyo 1973; FCO 1976; Gaborone 1978; FCO 1982; Jedda 1986; Second Secretary FCO 1990; Second Secretary (Management) Dhaka 1993; m 1972 Jane Avril Bennett Edmunds (2d 1974, 1977).

Oulmi, Sally Teresa (née Cashman); Second Secretary (Management) Dhaka since November 1996; born 4.10.52; FCO 1974; UKREP Brussels 1975; Abidjan 1979; Strasbourg 1983; FCO 1986; Ottawa 1987; Stockholm 1990; FCO 1993; Band C4; m 1976 Hocine (Frank) Oulmi; (2s 1993, 1994).

Owen, Amy Grace; FTLT since October 2000; born 29.8.75; FCO 1999; Band C4.

Owen, Caroline Jane; Jakarta since October 2001; born 29.10.66; FCO 1986; Washington 1990; FCO 1992; Bombay 1994; Dhaka 1998; Band A2.

Owen, Gareth Wynn; Baku since July 1999; born 24.11.69; FCO 1989; Prague 1992; FCO 1993; Warsaw 1994; Lusaka 1996; Band B3.

Owen, Helen Patricia; FCO since August 1987; born 9.4.49; FCO 1974; Sana'a 1974; FCO 1976; Bandar Seri Begawan 1981; Manila 1982; Madrid 1984; Band B3.

Owen, Jane Caroline; Deputy High Commissioner Hanoi since January 2000; born 15.4.63; FCO 1987; Japanese Language Training 1988; Second Secretary (Commercial) Tokyo 1989; First Secretary DTI Exports to Japan Unit 1993; FCO 1996; Deputy Head of Mission Hanoi 1998; SUPL 1999; Band D6; m 1998 David Donnelly.

Owen, Kara Justine (née Palmer); Vice Consul Hong Kong since December 1996; born 27.5.71; FCO 1993; Band C4; m 1995 Craig Sterling Owen.

Owen, Richard Lloyd; Counsellor FCO since January 1998; born 21.4.48; Second Secretary FCO 1975; Language Student 1976; Language Student MECAS 1977; First Secretary Abu Dhabi 1978; Beirut 1980; FCO 1981; San José 1983; BMG Berlin 1986; First Secretary FCO 1988; Counsellor Copenhagen 1993; m 1985 Eva Maria Steller (2d 1986, 1988).

Owens, Patrick Eldred; MBE (1998); HM Consul New York since July 2001; born 20.4.53; FCO 1972; Muscat 1974; Bucharest 1977; Algiers 1979; FCO 1981; Jakarta 1984; Riyadh 1988; (Second Secretary) 1990; Second Secretary FCO 1994; First Secretary (Information) Madrid 1997; m 1978 Merle Quirine de Ceuninck van Capelle (1d 1980, 2s 1982, 1985).

Owens, Ruth Mary; Antananarivo since April 1999; born 28.3.67; FCO 1987; Nairobi 1989; FCO 1992; Moscow 1995; Band B3.

Oxley, Anthony, BEM; Nairobi since July 1999; born 9.9.42; Royal Navy 1961-83; Baghdad 1983; Bucharest 1984; Montevideo 1986; East Berlin 1987; UKMIS New York 1989; Prague 1991; Belgrade 1993; Band C4; m 1964 Wenda Romaine Coper (1s 1966; 1d 1968).

P

Packer, Deborah (née Wilde); Tokyo since August 2000; born 10.5.66; FCO 1985; NEDO 1986; Tokyo 1994; Bridgetown 1997; Band A2; m 1990 Philip Anthony Packer (1s 1995).

Page, Alexander Simon; Third Secretary (Management) Mexico City since December 1999; Dhaka 1989; born 20.10.64; FCO 1987; Warsaw 1989; FCO 1993; Valletta 1996; Band B3; m 1989 Isabella Lynn Marshall (1s 1996).

Page, Andrew John Walter; First Secretary (Chancery) Paris since September 2000; born 17.9.65; FCO 1990; Full-time Language Training 1991; Second Secretary Kiev 1992; First Secretary FCO 1996.

Page, Brian Ronald; Second Secretary (Consular/Immigration) Accra since February 1997; born 5.3.49; FCO 1968; Helsinki 1971; Doha 1973; Cape Town 1976; FCO 1978; Muscat 1979; Singapore 1983; FCO 1986 (Second Secretary 1988); Dubai 1992; m 1973 Susan Frances Vinall (2s 1975, 1979).

Page, Derek Alan; Second Secretary Taipei since November 1994; born 29.9.50; FCO 1975; Pretoria 1977; Bombay 1979; FCO 1981; Frankfurt 1984; Montevideo 1987; FCO 1990; (Second Secretary 1992); m 1972 Inger Merete Ebbesvik (2s 1977, 1981).

Page, Isabella Lynn (née Marshall); Third Secretary (Political/Information) Valletta since May 1996; born 6.1.64; FCO 1981; Kuala Lumpur 1984; Prague 1987; SUPL 1989; Warsaw 1989; Dhaka 1990; FCO 1993; m 1989 Alexander Simon Page (1s 1996).

Page, Martin; Second Secretary (Management) Peking since January 1999; born 16.11.51; MOD 1969; FCO 1970; Beirut 1973; FCO 1976; Lima 1976; Warsaw 1979; FCO 1982; Vila 1983; Dar es Salaam 1987; Second Secretary FCO 1990; Second Secretary (Management) New Delhi 1993; Second Secretary FCO 1997; Band C4; m 1975 Christine Mary Ogilvy (1s 1979; 1d 1984).

Page, Simon David; SUPL since July 1999; born 22.2.67; FCO 1990; Language Training FCO 1991; Language Training Peking 1992. Second Secretary (JLG) Hong Kong 1994; Band D6.

Page, Simon Graham; Second Secretary (Political) Riyadh since February 1998; born 22.11.61; FCO 1979; Kuala Lumpur 1983; Floater Duties 1987; Dublin 1988; FCO 1990; Third Secretary (Chancery) New Delhi 1992; FCO 1996; Band C4;

m 1985 Sharon Ann Murphy (2s 1990, 1995, 1d 2000).

Pagett, Christopher Robert Geoffrey, OBE (1990); Counsellor UKMIS New York since February 1997; born 13.6.52; Third Secretary FCO 1975; Second Secretary Havana 1978; Second later First Secretary (Econ) Lusaka 1979; First Secretary FCO 1984; First Secretary (Chancery) Maputo 1988; First Secretary FCO 1991; m(1)1974 Anne-Marie Roberts; (2)1988 Diane Brown (1s 1993).

Pagett, Ian William; Warsaw since October 1993; born 19.9.69; FCO 1988; Khartoum 1989; FCO 1992; Band A2.

Pagett, Wayne Norman; Third Secretary (Consular/Immigration) Harare since March 2001; born 26.3.67; FCO 1988; New Delhi 1990; Tel Aviv 1994; FCO 1997; Band B3; m 1990 Kay Louise Clements (1d 1994).

Paginton, David Alan; HM Consul Buenos Aires since January 1998; born 1.4.51; Board of Inland Revenue 1968; FCO 1971; Istanbul 1973; UKREP Brussels 1976; Sofia 1979; FCO 1981; São Paulo 1984; Islamabad 1988; FCO 1991; Second Secretary (Commercial) Dar es Salaam 1994; m 1986 Marcia Rosana Antonio (1s 1986, 1d 1987).

Pain, Warren David; Vice-Consul (Political/Economic) Hong Kong since February 2000; born 17.5.71; FCO 1992; Peking 1995; World-wide All-Rounder 1998; m2000 Armine Ghevondyan.

Painter, Anthony Clifford; Paris since August 1996; born 20.3.59; FCO 1994; Band A2; m 1984 Lisa Nelson (1d 1984).

Painting, Julia MBE (1993); First Secretary FCO since December 1998; born 24.4.60; FCO 1981; Prague 1983; Africa/Middle East Floater 1985; South East Asia Floater 1987; FCO 1989; Tallinn 1991; FCO 1992; Milan 1994; HM Consul Naples 1995; Second Secretary FCO 1997.

Pakenham, The Hon Michael (Aidan); HM Ambassador Warsaw since January 2001; born 3.11.43; Third Secretary FO 1966; Third later Second Secretary Warsaw 1967; Second Secretary FCO 1970; Assistant Private Secretary later Private Secretary to the Chancellor of the Duchy of Lancaster 1971; On secondment to Cabinet Office 1972; (First Secretary 1972); UKDEL CSCE Geneva 1974; First Secretary New Delhi 1974; Washington 1978; Counsellor FCO 1983; Counsellor (External Relations) UKREP Brussels 1987; HM Ambassador and Consul-General Luxembourg 1991; Minister Paris 1994; on loan to the Cabinet Office 1997; m 1980 Meta Landreth Doak (2d 1981, 1985).

Pakes, Stuart Murray; Islamabad since August 1998; born 8.5.49; FO 1967; FCO 1968; Aden 1970; Anguilla 1973; Reykjavik 1973; East Berlin 1976; FCO 1977; Madrid 1981; Cairo 1984; FCO 1987 (Second Secretary 1989); Second Secretary (Immig/Cons) Accra 1990; Second Secretary (Commercial) Abu Dhabi 1994; m 1972 Linda Anne Rawlings (2d 1977, 1981; 1s 1984).

Palmer, Andrew David; World Wide Floater duties since February 2000; born 21.1.76; FCO (HCS) 1994; Transferred to Diplomatic Service 2000; Band B3.

Palmer, Sara (née Abbots-Darbyshire); Vice-Consul Geneva since July 1993; born 16.11.64; FCO 1983; UKMIS Geneva 1985; Montevideo 1988; FCO 1991; SUPL Geneva 1991; Band B3; m 1991 Christopher John Palmer.

Palmer, Sidney Hodgson; FCO since February 1999; born 8.6.40; FO 1960; Belgrade 1961; Bangkok 1964; Rangoon 1967; FCO 1971; Baghdad 1974; Assistant to Resident Commissioner Vila 1978; Second Secretary Vila 1980; First Secretary FCO 1983; DHC and Head of Chancery Port Moresby 1986; First Secretary, Head of Chancery and Consul-Luxembourg 1989; Deputy High Commissioner Madras 1994; m (1)1962 Jacqueline Germaine Albiser (diss) (1s 1975); (2) Miss S G Vandersluis.

Pankhurst, Donia Lee; UKMIS Geneva since October 1998; born 27.5.65; House of Commons 1991-97; FCO 1997; Band A2.

Parfitt, Alan Frank, MBE (1997); SUPL since October 1998; born 6.8.66; Senior Research Officer; FCO 1989; UKDEL Vienna 1994.

Parham, Philip John; Counsellor (Commercial) Riyadh since September 2000; born 14.8.60; FCO 1993; (Private Secretary to the Parliamentary Under Secretary of State 1995); First Secretary (Chancery) Washington 1996; m 1985 Kasia Giedroyc (2d 1986, 1994, 5s 1988, 1989, 1990, 1992, 1996).

Parish, Colin; Second Secretary FCO since November 1995; born 27.11.43; Royal Navy 1961-70; FCO 1970; Phnom Penh 1973; Accra 1974; SUPL 1978; FCO 1982; Belgrade 1986; Consul (Commercial) Jedda 1990; m(1) 1966 Carole Grace; (diss. 1978); (2)1978 Fairroligh Janet Lee Syme (2s 1985, 1989).

Parish, Paul Edward; Second Secretary Berlin since August 1999; born 10.8.63; FCO 1983; Vienna 1986; FCO 1989; SUPL 1992; Second Secretary FCO 1995; Second Secretary (Bilateral) Bonn 1998; Band C4.

Parker, Cindy; T/D Third Secretary Tashkent since March 2000; born 1.2.72; FCO 1997; Band B3.

Parker, David John; FCO since November 1989; born 2.6.57; FCO 1978; Mexico City 1987; Band C4; m 1987 Mary Elizabeth Garner.

Parker, Lyn; British High Commissioner Nicosia since September 2001; born 25.11.52; FCO 1978; Second later First Secretary Athens 1980; FCO 1984; Counsellor on loan to the Cabinet Office 1989; Counsellor and Head of Chancery New Delhi 1992; Counsellor (Political) UKREP Brussels 1995; Counsellor FCO 1999; m 1991 Jane Elizabeth Walker; (2d 1993, 1996).

Parker, Nigel Denis; Legal Counsellor FCO since February 2001; born 25.8.61; called to the Bar,

Middle Temple 1985; Assistant Legal Adviser FCO 1988; Legal Adviser Bridgetown 1995; Assistant Legal Adviser FCO 1998.

Parker, Nigel Graham; UKMIS Geneva since April 2000; born 13.9.56; FCO 1982; Kingston 1985; FCO 1988; Budapest 1990; Band C4; m 1983 Paula Northwood (1s 1987, 1d 1991).

Parker, Rod; Peking since June 2000; born 14.11.60; FCO 1996; Band C4; m 1981 Bernadette Corr (2d 1987, 1991).

Parker, Susan Caroline; FCO since June 1993; born 1.7.63; FCO 1985; UKREP Brussels 1987; FCO 1988; Vienna 1990; Band A2.

Parker, Valerie Ann; Jakarta since February 1999; born 21.2.42; FCO 1990; SUPL 1992; FCO 1997; SUPL 1998; Band A2; m 1965 David John Parker (1d 1966, 1s 1968).

Parker-Brennan, Michael; FCO since August 1999; born 30.5.52; Royal Corps of Transport 1967-1992; FCO 1992; Helsinki 1992; Bucharest 1993; Pretoria 1996; Moscow 1997; Band B3; m(1) 1982 Catherine Mary Parker (diss), (2) 1988 Carmen Dorina.

Parkins, David Alan; FCO since August 1997; born 7.5.64; GPO 1980-1984; FCO 1984; Third Secretary Nairobi 1989; FCO 1993; Third Secretary Bucharest 1994; Band C4; m 1991 Diane Reed (2s 1992, 1994).

Parkinson, Guy Paul; Floater duties since July 2000; born 5.6.70; FCO 1989; Budapest 1992; Moscow 1995; Band B3.

Parkinson, Howard, cvo (1998); Deputy High Commissioner Mumbai since January 2001; born 29.3.48; BOT 1967; FCO 1969; LA Floater 1972; Tegucigalpa 1974; Buenos Aires 1975; Second Secretary 1977; Maputo 1978; Second later First Secretary FCO 1981; First Secretary (Comm) Lisbon 1985; First Secretary on loan to British Gas 1989; First Secretary FCO 1991; Consul General and Counsellor (Management) Washington 1994; Counsellor (Commercial) Kuala Lumpur 1997; m 1974 Linda Wood (1d 1979; 1s 1982).

Parmley, Jane Helen (née Buchanan); Lagos since October 1984; born 18.8.63; FCO 1982; Band A2; m 1987 Nigel William Kenneth Parmley.

Parsons, Alexander Colin; Second Secretary FCO since June 2001; born 26.3.73; FCO 1997; Second Secretary (Political) Santiago 1999; Band C4.

Parton, Charles William obe (1995); First Secretary FCO since September 1994; born 23.3.56; FCO 1979; Language Training Hong Kong 1982; Second Secretary FCO 1983; First Secretary (Econ) Peking 1985; First Secretary FCO 1987; First Secretary Joint Liaison Group Hong Kong 1990; Band D6; m 1983 Charmian Constance Denman (1d 1987, 1s 1990).

Partridge, Andrew Warren; Third Secretary Vienna since July 2000; Born 26.4.68; FCO 1986;

Islamabad 1989; Moscow 1992; FCO 1995; SUPL 1997; Band B3; m 1988 Margaret Robertson (1s 1996, 1d 1998).

Partridge, Colin Douglas; Counsellor Seoul since June 2000; born 12.12.55; FCO 1978; Third later Second Secretary (Chancery) New Delhi 1980; Second later First Secretary FCO 1983; Language Training 1986; Head of Chancery and Consul Hanoi 1987; First Secretary FCO 1989; First Secretary Hong Kong 1994; Language Training 1998; m(1)1983 Gita Sahgal (diss 1989); (2)1993 Helena June Beattie; (1d 1996).

Partridge, Diane Freda; T/D Durban since June 2001; born 29.11.44; OECD Paris 1966; Yaoundé 1969; Lagos 1970; Rio de Janeiro 1971; FCO 1972; Antananarivo 1974; FCO 1976; Buenos Aires 1977; FCO 1979; Brasilia 1981; FCO 1985; Third Secretary (Aid) Belmopan 1989; Third Secretary ATTC Taipei 1993; FCO 1995; Second Secretary (Commercial) Luanda 1999; Band C4.

Partridge, Margaret (née Robertson) mbe (1995); SUPL since May 2000; born 3.3.66; FCO 1986; Islamabad 1989; Vice Consul Moscow 1992; FCO 1995; Vice Consul Muscat 1997; Band B3; m 1988 Andrew Warren Partridge (1s 1996, 1d 1998).

Pasquill, Derek James; Vice Consul Abu Dhabi since July 1997; born 11.1.59; HCS 1984; FCO 1986; Kampala 1988; Maseru 1990; FCO 1993.

Patel, Shofiya; Floater duties since March 2000; born 3.2.69; DSS 1988; FCO 1990; Canberra 1992; FCO 1995; Riga 1996; Band B3.

Paterson, Fiona; First Secretary (Political) Lisbon since November 1999; born 6.4.51; FCO 1977; Bogotá 1979; Ottawa 1983; Second Secretary FCO 1987; Second Secretary (Chancery/Info) Bangkok 1989; Second later First Secretary (Info) Paris 1990; First Secretary FCO 1994; Band D6.

Paterson, Ian Robert; Third Secretary (Political) Berne since January 1998; born 22.9.62; FCO Communications 1986; FCO 1996; Band B3; m, Diane (2d 1992, 1997).

Paterson, Lynne Kathryn; FCO since November 1999; born 22.5.63; Band A2.

Paterson, Nicola (née Brydon); SUPL since August 1996; born 11.12.69; MOD 1989; FCO 1990; Nairobi 1992; FCO 1995; Band B3, m1992 Duncan Alexander Paterson.

Paterson, Shona; Chancery Assistant Lagos since August 1997; born 30.8.68; FCO 1986; Band A; m 1991 David Michael Paterson (2d 1993, 1994, 1s 1999).

Paterson, William Neil Carlton; Consul General Stuttgart since August 1997; born 19.10.50; FCO 1978; Sofia 1980; FCO 1981; Düsseldorf 1983; Second Secretary (Comm/Aid) Yaoundé 1986; Second Secretary FCO 1989; Consul (Commercial) Montreal 1992; m 1975 Margaret Christine Schmidt-Feuerheerd (1s 1976; 3d 1978, 1981, 1983).

Patey, William Charters; FCO since December 1998; born 11.7.53; FCO 1975; MECAS 1977; Abu Dhabi 1978; Second Secretary (Comm) Tripoli 1981; First Secretary FCO 1984; First Secretary (Chancery) Canberra 1988; First Secretary later Counsellor FCO 1992; Deputy Head of Mission Riyadh 1995; m 1978 Vanessa Carol Morrell (2s 1987, 1991).

Paton, Kirsty Isobel; Vice-Consul (Political and Economic) Hong Kong since October 2000; born 2.2.77; FCO 1999; Band C4.

Patrick, Andrew Silas; Assistant Private Secretary to Secretary of State since January 1998; born 28.2.66; FCO 1988; Third later Second Secretary (Chancery) Nicosia 1991; First Secretary T/D UKDEL Brussels 1995; FCO 1996; Band D7.

Patten, Roger; First Secretary (Management) Kingston since September 2000; born 24.7.43; CRO 1963; Bombay 1966; Pretoria/Cape Town 1970; Warsaw 1973; FCO 1974; San Juan 1976; FCO 1978; Prague 1980; Düsseldorf 1982; Second Secretary FCO 1987; Nicosia 1989; Second Secretary FCO 1989; Second Secretary (Consular/Visa) Rabat 1991; Second Secretary Addis Ababa 1995; m 1966 Anna Jones (2s 1967, 1970).

Patterson, Ernest Mark; Addis Ababa since September 1996; born 22.2.69; FCO 1989; Vienna 1989; Band A2.

Patterson, Hugh William Grant; Counsellor Berne since April 2000; born 17.10.50; FCO 1979; First Secretary BMG Berlin 1980; First Secretary FCO 1984; First Secretary (Head of Chancery) and Consul Guatemala City 1987; First Secretary FCO 1990; First Secretary later Counsellor Caracas 1992; Counsellor FCO 1995; m 1981 Philippa Anne Colbatch Clark (1d 1986, 1s 1997).

Pattison, Stephen Dexter; Director of Trade Promotion and Consul General Warsaw since February 1997; born 24.12.53; FCO 1981; Nicosia 1983; FCO 1986; First Secretary (Chancery) Washington 1989; FCO 1994; m 1987 Helen Andrea Chaoushis 1987 (1d 1993).

Patton, Geoffrey Joseph Laurence; Plymouth, Montserrat since August 2000; born 26.4.62; MOD 1985-86; FCO 1986; Warsaw 1989; Floater Training 1991; Floater duties since December 1991; Colombo 1994; FCO 1998; T/D Bombay 2000; Band B3.

Paver, James Edward Luke mvo (1994); Second Secretary (Political) UKDEL Brussels since September 1998; born 2.10.63; FCO 1991; Third Secretary(Press/Public Affairs) Moscow 1994; Second Secretary FCO 1997; m 1992 Rebecca Jane Ash; (3d 1993, 1995, 1997).

Paxman, Timothy Giles, lvo (1989); Counsellor (Political) UKREP Brussels since June 1999; born 15.11.51; Department of Environment/Transport 1974; First Secretary UKREP Brussels 1980; FCO 1985; First Secretary Head of Chancery Singapore 1989; Counsellor on loan to the Cabinet Office 1992; Full-time Language Training 1994; Counsellor (Commercial/Economic) Rome 1994; m 1980 Segolene Claude Marie (3d 1982, 1984, 1988).

Peacock, Paula Geraldine (née Hackett); Vice Consul Prague since June 1997; born 1.1.65; FCO 1990; Third Secretary Nairobi 1993; Full-time Language Training 1996; Band B3; m 1997 David Lawrence Peacock.

Peake, Philippa Jane; SUPL since December 2000; born 30.3.64; FCO 1990; Moscow 1993; UKDEL NATO 1996; FCO 1999; Band A2; m 1997 Dominic Alister Stephens.

Pearce, Andrew John; First Secretary (Economic) Pretoria since October 1996; born 7.10.60; FCO 1983; Language Training 1984; Third later Second Secretary Bangkok 1986; First Secretary FCO 1988; First Secretary (Chancery) Tel Aviv 1992; m 1986 Pornpun Pathumvivantana.

Pearce, David Avery; HM Consul Durban since April 2000; born 17.2.52; FCO 1971; UKMIS New York 1973; Rome 1976; FCO 1979; Dhaka 1982; FCO 1986; Paris 1987 (Second Secretary 1987); Second Secretary and Deputy Head of Mission Libreville 1990; Consul Douala 1991; Deputy Head of Mission and Consul General Sana'a and Aden 1996; m(1)1973 Anne Matthews (dec'd 1986) (1d 1980, 1s 1984); (2)1988 Virginia Martin (2d 1991, 1995; 1s 1993).

Pearce, Howard John Stredder, cvo (1993); British High Commissioner Valletta since July 1999; born 13.4.49; FCO 1972; Buenos Aires 1975; First Secretary FCO 1978; First Secretary and Head of Chancery Nairobi 1983; First Secretary later Counsellor FCO 1987; Language Training 1990. Deputy Head of Mission Budapest 1991; on loan at Harvard University 1994; Head of Central European Department 1996.

Pearey, David Dacre; Counsellor (Commercial/Economic) Lagos since October 1995; born 15.7.48; Ankara 1979 (on secondment from MOD); First Secretary FCO 1983; First Secretary & Head of Chancery Kampala 1987; First Secretary later Counsellor FCO 1990; m 1996 Susan Anne Knowles.

Pearey, (Dorothy) Jane, mbe (1980); on secondment to DfID (Harare) since April 1998 born 31.5.45; OECD Paris 1969; Moscow 1972; FCO 1973; Belgrade 1977; FCO 1980; UKMIS New York 1983; Seconded to NATO 1984; Seconded to 21st Century Trust 1988; FCO 1989; (Second Secretary 1991); Second Secretary (Aid) Harare since December 1995.

Pearson, Frances; Buenos Aires since May 1998; born 17.7.54; FCO 1987; Washington 1988; UKREP Brussels 1991; Moscow 1994; FCO 1996; Band A2.

Pearson, John Anthony; FCO since January 2000; born 28.4.68; FCO 1990; Madrid 1992; FCO 1994; Brasilia 1996; Band D6.

Pearson, Julian Christopher; Minsk since September 1998; born 8.7.69; FCO 1990; Third Secretary Prague 1992; Third Secretary Kinshasa 1995; FCO 1998.

Pearson, Nigel John; Islamabad since July 1998; born 4.3.69; FCO 1987; Peking 1992; Band B3.

Pearson, Patricia Ann (née Thomas); Sana'a since August 1998; born 2.6.42; FCO 1969; Beirut 1972; Islamabad 1975; SUPL 1979; FCO 1982; Lilongwe 1988; FCO 1991; Third Secretary (Management) Dhaka 1996; m 1977 Barry Stewart Pearson.

Pearson, Ruth Alexandra (née Stephens); SUPL since March 2000; born 30.1.71; FCO 1993; Full-time Language Training 1995; Budapest 1996; Second Secretary (Political) UKREP Brussels 1999; Band C4; m 1996 Simon Mark Pearson.

Pease, Simon Robert Hellier; DHM and Consul General Tel Aviv since June 1997; born 20.2.52; FCO 1972; Ibadan 1975; SUPL 1978; FCO 1981, (Second Secretary 1982); Second later First Secretary UKDEL CDE Stockholm 1984; First Secretary FCO 1986; First Secretary and Head of Chancery Rabat 1988; First Secretary later Counsellor FCO 1992; m 1975 Catherine Elizabeth Bayley (1d 1981, 1s 1983).

Peate, David James, OBE (1989); Deputy Consul-General Milan since November 1996; born 2.7.44; FO 1964; DSAO 1965; Delhi 1967; Warsaw 1971; Second Secretary Lomé 1972; FCO 1975; Melbourne 1978; FCO 1983; First Secretary Brussels 1984; First Secretary (Comm) East Berlin 1989; First Secretary FCO 1993; m 1971 Siri Jean Jessica Elizabeth Zetter (2d 1973, 1990; 2s 1975, 1986).

Peers, Gary Clive; FCO since June 1997; born 6.12.58; FCO 1985; Third Secretary Bonn 1990; Third Secretary Pretoria 1995; Band C4; m 1979 Pamela Jane Tailby (1d 1981, 2s 1983, 1985).

Peirce, Robert Nigel; Counsellor Washington since October 1999; born 18.3.55; FCO 1977; Language Student Cambridge 1978; Language Student Hong Kong 1979; Second later First Secretary (Chancery) Peking 1980; First Secretary FCO 1983; on loan to Cabinet Office 1985; on Secondment to Hong Kong Government as Deputy Political Adviser 1986; Assistant Private Secretary to the Secretary of State 1988; First Secretary (Chancery) UKMIS New York 1990; Political Adviser Hong Kong 1993; On secondment to the Royal College of Defence Studies 1998; m (1) 1978 Christina Anne Skipworth Davis (1s 1986; 1d 1988), (2) 2000 Robin Lynn Raphael (2 step d 1986, 1990).

Pellew, Mark Edward, CVO (2000); Ambassador The Holy See since January 1998; born 28.8.42; FO 1965-67; Third later Second Secretary Singapore 1967; Second Secretary Saigon 1969; Second later First Secretary FCO 1970; First Secretary (Inf) Rome 1976; First Secretary FCO 1980; Counsellor (Pol) Washington 1983; Counsellor on Secondment to Hambros Bank

1989; Counsellor FCO 1991; m 1965 Jill Thistlethwaite (2s 1966, 1968).

Pemberton, Robert John; FCO since May 1989; born 11.6.63; FCO 1982; Lagos 1985; Band B3; m 1988 Rhonda Karen Leps (1d 1991).

Pendered, Joanne Michelle; Dili since January 2001; born 2.11.65; FCO 1984; Bombay 1987; Santiago 1990; FCO 1992; Third Secretary (Management) Athens 1996; Cape Town 1999; Band B3.

Penfold, Jane Elizabeth Mary (née Govier); First Secretary Dili since November 2000; born 21.3.62; FCO 1984; Language Training 1986; Third Secretary (Comm) Peking 1987; Vice-Consul (Management) Istanbul 1990; Presidency Liaison Officer Luxembourg 1990 (Second Secretary 1991); T/D Bangkok 1991; Second Secretary FCO 1992; Full time Language Training 1994; Second Secretary (Political) Sofia 1995; FCO 1998; m 1997 Nigel John Penfold.

Penfold, Peter Alfred, CMG (1995), OBE (1986); FCO 2000; born 27.2.44; FO 1963; Bonn 1965; Kaduna 1968; Latin America Floater 1970; Canberra 1972; FCO 1972; Second Secretary Addis Ababa 1975; Second Secretary (Inf) Port of Spain 1978; FCO 1981; First Secretary 1983; DHC and Head of Chancery Kampala 1984; First Secretary FCO 1987; Governor British Virgin Islands 1991; Special Adviser on Drugs 1995; High Commissioner Freetown 1997; m(1)1972 Margaret Quigley (diss 1983) (2d 1963, 1974, 2s 1973, 1980); (2) 1992 Celia Delores Koenig.

Pengelly, Rachel Jane (née Laycock); Second Secretary (Chancery/External) Washington since May 2000; born 20.5.71; FCO 1994; Band C4; m2000 Owen Fengelly.

Penrith, Alan Paul; On loan to the DTI since January 1999; born 24.5.58; Inland Revenue 1977; FCO 1978; Mexico City 1980; Yaoundé 1983; FCO 1985; Third later Second Secretary (Political/Information) Ottawa 1988; Assistant to Governor British Virgin Islands 1993; Second, later First Secretary FCO 1996; m,1982 Karen Cooper (2s 1987, 1991).

Penton-Voak, Martin Eric; First Secretary UKDEL Vienna since May 2001; born 9.11.65; Third later Second Secretary FCO 1991; Moscow 1995; First Secretary FCO 1998; Band D6; m 1994 Lucy Katrina Howarth.

Percy, Michael Vivian; Second Secretary British Trade International since August 1998; born 9.8.50; DSAO (later FCO) 1968; Paris 1972; Brasilia 1975; Budapest 1977; FCO 1980; Quito 1983; Warsaw 1987; FCO 1989; (Second Secretary 1991); Deputy Head of Mission Riga 1993; Second Secretary FCO 1994; m 1972 Susan Roslyn Penrose (2d 1974, 1981; 1s 1977).

Perkins, Jacqueline Louise (née Gage); SUPL since July 2001; born 3.10.64; FCO 1989; Second Secretary 1990; Language Training Cairo 1991; Second Secretary (Chancery/Information) Abu

Dhabi 1992; First Secretary FCO 1995; SUPL 1996; First Secretary Cairo 1999; m 1991 Stuart Blair Perkins (1s 1996).

Perks, Adam Cecil; Vice-Consul Luxembourg since July 1998; born 3.5.66; FCO (HCS) 1984; FCO 1987; Kuwait 1988; FCO 1991; Third Secretary (Cons) Ottawa 1991; Third Secretary FCO 1994; m 1990 Nicola Rose Wardle; (2s 1992, 1996; 1d 1998).

Perrin, Geoffrey Gordon; Second later First Secretary FCO since October 1978; born 12.8.49; FCO 1971; Geneva 1975; Band C5; m 1977 Heather Beryl Robson (2s 1979, 1984).

Perrott, John Gayford; High Commissioner Banjul since April 2000; born 5.7.43; CRO 1962; Karachi 1966; Ankara 1970; Calcutta 1972; Second Secretary (Consul/Admin) Calcutta 1974; Second Secretary FCO 1976; Second later First Secretary Kathmandu 1979; Consul (Comm) Istanbul 1984; First Secretary FCO 1988; Chief Secretary St. Helena 1993; FCO 1997; m 1964 Joan Wendy Lewis (1d 1964; 1s 1966).

Perry, Christopher Ian; New Delhi since March 1999; born 27.5.70; FCO 1990; UKREP Brussels 1993; Paris 1995; Band A2; m(1)1992 Charlotte Dawson, (diss 1995); (1d 1992); (2) 1995 Lesa Jayne Elliot (3d 1996, 1997, 1998).

Perry, Geoffrey Colin; First Secretary FCO since August 1996; born 13.1.51; Third Secretary FCO 1973; Language Student Cambridge University 1975; Language Student1/Second Secretary Kuala Lumpur 1976 and Singapore 1977; Second later First Secretary FCO 1977; Trade Commissioner Hong Kong 1981; First Secretary FCO 1986; First Secretary (UN/Press) UKMIS Geneva 1992; Band D6; m 1975 Barbara Elisabeth Gysin (née Kaestlin) (2d 1977, 1979).

Perry, Susan; Vice Consul Shanghai April 1997; born 7.3.44; HCS 1965; FCO 1977; Havana 1979; Tunis 1980; Warsaw 1983; Kathmandu 1986; FCO 1990; Kampala 1993; Band B3.

Perry, Thomas Ian; Jerusalem since May 1998; born 29.3.55; MOD 1972; FCO 1974; UKMIS New York 1976; T/D Dubai 1979; Africa/ME Floater 1979; Jakarta 1981; FCO 1983; The Hague 1986; FCO 1988; T/D Warsaw 1990; T/D Dar es Salaam 1990; Islamabad 1991; FCO 1996; Band B3; m 1982 Jeannie Bell (2s 1992, 1995).

Persighetti, Stephen Victor; Second Secretary (Political/Aid) Cape Town since January 1996; born 31.3.56; FCO 1975; Moscow 1977; Beirut 1978; Tokyo 1981; Floater duties 1983; on loan to ODA 1985; Third Secretary (Aid) Jakarta 1988; Second Secretary FCO 1991; m 1992 Rozany Deen.

Pert, David John; Kiev since March 2001; born 21.1.68; Royal Navy 1987-94; FCO 1994; Third Secretary (Political) Sofia 1996; m 1990 Christine Walsh (2s 1991, 1994).

Petch, Eleanor; FTLT since December 2000; born 26.1.77; FCO 1998; Band C4.

Peters, Mark Crispin; Second Secretary (Chancery) Oslo since August 1996; born 7.6.64; Royal Engineers 1987-94; FCO 1994.

Petherbridge, Richard Sidney; FCO since January 1996; born 23.8.55; DHSS 1975; FCO 1980; Nicosia 1982; Seoul 1985; FCO 1987; Prague 1990; Riyadh 1992; Band A2; m 1982 Pauline Joan Mulvey (1s 1984; 1d 1986).

Pethick, Mark Julian; Deputy Head of Mission Minsk since September 1997; born 3.4.68; FCO 1990; Karachi 1993; Band C4.

Phillips, Alison Jane (née Francis), OBE (1991); First Secretary FCO since September 1990; born 18.4.56; FCO 1974; UKMIS New York 1981; Second Secretary FCO 1982; First Secretary Paris 1986; Band D6; m 1978 Richard Charles Jonathan Phillips, QC.

Phillips, Duncan Keith; FCO since July 1989; born 7.3.69; Band A2.

Phillips, Harjit Kaur (née Jagpal); Moscow since April 1998; born 8.10.68; FCO 1988; Lagos 1991; Abuja 1993; SUPL 1995; Band A2; m 1996 Robin David Phillips.

Phillips, Linda Ann; Washington since November 2000; born 17.1.56; FCO 1995; Accra 1997; Band A2.

Phillips, Patricia Ruth; SUPL since December 2000; born 11.3.62; MAFF 1984; Washington 1992; First Secretary FCO 1997; Band C4.

Phillips, Quentin James Kitson; First Secretary FCO since September 2000; born 20.10.63; FCO 1986; Second Secretary (Info) Budapest 1989; Second later First Secretary FCO 1992; First Secretary (Pol) Moscow 1995; First Secretary FCO 1996; First Secretary (Political) Kiev 1997; Band D6; m 1989 Gillian Lynne Murray; (2d 1993, 1996; 1s 1999).

Phillips, Russell James; Abuja since September 1998; born 24.2.64; FCO 1983; Georgetown 1985; Khartoum 1988; FCO 1991; Bombay 1995; Band C4.

Phillips, Sarah Louise; FCO since February 1995; born 17.12.39; FCO 1969; Delhi 1970; FCO 1971; Vientiane 1972; Washington 1975; FCO 1978; Rabat 1979; Belgrade 1982; FCO 1983; UKMIS Geneva 1985; FCO 1988; Brussels 1991; Band B3.

Phillips, Tom Richard Vaughan CMG; High Commissioner Uganda since May 2000; born 21.6.50; DHSS 1977; FCO 1983; First Secretary Harare 1985; First Secretary FCO 1988; Counsellor Consul-General and Deputy Head of Mission Tel Aviv 1990; Counsellor (External) Washington 1993; Counsellor FCO 1997; m 1986 Anne Renee Marie de la Motte (1s 1987; 2s 1989).

Philpott, Hugh Stanley; First Secretary FCO since August 1999; born 24.1.61; FCO 1980; Oslo 1982; Budapest 1985; Language Training 1987; Third

Secretary (Comm) Baghdad 1988; FCO 1990;
(Second Secretary 1992); Second Secretary
(Pol/Mil) Washington 1993; on loan to DfID 1997;
Band D6; m 1984 Janine Frederica Rule.(1d 1998)

Philpott, Janine Frederica; FCO since January
1998; born 30.1.60; FCO 1980; UKDEL NATO
Brussels 1982; Budapest 1985; FCO 1986;
Baghdad 1988; FCO 1990; Third Secretary (Press)
Washington 1993; Band B3; m 1984 Hugh Stanley
Philpott. (1d 1998)

Pickering, Helen Mary; FCO since June 2001;
born 10.7.64; FCO 1986; Moscow 1988; Algiers
1989; Geneva 1990; FCO 1993; Second Secretary
(EU) Warsaw 1997; Band D6; m 1996 James
Owen.

Pickering, Sara Elizabeth; Second Secretary
(Commercial) Lagos since December 1998; born
22.4.67; FCO 1988; Vice-Consul Budapest 1991;
FCO 1992; Islamabad 1995; Band C4; m 1992
Andrew John Kirkpatrick.

Pickett, Jane Louise (née Houghton) MBE (1994);
FCO since November 1995; born 5.12.64; FCO
1984; Santiago 1987; FCO 1991; Bogotá 1993;
Band C4; m 1998 Peter Derek Pickett.

Pickup, Lawrence; Deputy Head of Mission
Khartoum since May 2000; born 10.9.52; FCO
1976; Dar es Salaam 1980; Dubai 1982; Floater
1986; on loan to the DTI 1989; FCO/DTI 1991;
Consul Warsaw 1993; Deputy Head of Mission
Phnom Penh 1997; Band D6.

Pierce, Anne Nicholson (née Creighton); SUPL
since January 1995; born 20.7.65; ODA 1984-89;
FCO 1989; SUPL 1991; Riyadh 1992; FCO 1993;
Band A2; m 1991 Timothy Karl Pierce (2d 1995,
1999).

Pierce, Karen Elizabeth; First Secretary FCO
since January 1996; born 23.9.59; FCO 1981;
Language Training 1983; Tokyo 1984; FCO 1987;
(Second Secretary 1989); PS to HM Ambassador
Washington 1991; m 1987 Charles Fergusson
Roxburgh.

Pigott, Carsten Orthöfer; Counsellor FCO since
1998; born 31.5.53; FCO 1972; Lagos 1975;
Language Student MECAS 1977 and FCO 1978;
Third Secretary (Comm) Khartoum 1979; Second
Secretary (Comm) Tripoli 1982; Second Secretary
FCO 1984; First Secretary (Chancery) Peking
1987; First Secretary FCO 1991; Deputy Head of
Mission Addis Ababa 1993; First Secretary
(Chancery) New Delhi 1997; m 1976 Susan
Kathlyn Pugh (1d 1981; 1s 1983).

Pike, Andrew Kerry; Second Secretary (Chancery
and Information) Dublin since July 1998; born
6.6.64; Dept of Transport 1982; FCO 1984; Sana'a
1985; Warsaw 1990; FCO 1993; Band C4.

Pilmore-Bedford, Jeremy Patrick; Second
Secretary (Economic) Kuala Lumpur since
September 2001; born 22.8.67; FCO 1990;
Singapore 1993; Full-time Language Training
1995; Third Secretary (Aid) Moscow 1995; FCO

1998; Band C4; m. Amanda Joanne West (1d
1997; 1s 1999).

Pinnock, Stuart Graham; SUPL since September
2000; born 19.5.63; FCO 1981; Paris 1984; Lagos
1986; FCO 1989; (Second Secretary 1997); SUPL
1993; FCO 1995; on loan to the DTI 1998.

Pinsent, Guy Hume; FCO since September 2000;
born 7.3.76; Band C4.

Pinson, David Richard; FCO since September
2000; born 7.5.77; Band C4.

Pinto, Alison Louise (née Johnson); FCO since
October 1997; FCO 1989; Vice-Consul Tokyo
1992; Third Secretary (Chancery) Berlin 1995;
Band D6; m2001 Andrew Pinto.

Pitts, Barbara Anne, MVO (1989); Copenhagen
since October 2000; born 26.1.54; FCO 1975;
Lagos 1975; Moscow 1977; FCO 1979; Nairobi
1981; FCO 1984; Kuala Lumpur 1987; FCO 1990;
New Delhi 1997; Band B3.

Plank, John; Second Secretary (Political) Pretoria
since February 2000; born 3.10.64; FCO 1986;
Band C4; m 1997 Corinne Lambshead.

Plant, Michael Geoffrey; Deputy Consul General
Boston since May 2000; born 12.10.46; Post
Office 1964; DSAO 1966; Moscow 1969; Rabat
1970; Peking 1973; Brussels (JAO) 1975; FCO
1978; Banjul 1980; Los Angeles 1984; Second
Secretary FCO 1987; Second Secretary
(Comm/Con) Al Khbar 1990; First Secretary
(Management) Yerevan, Tbilisi and Ashgabat
1995; FCO 1998; Band C5; m 1971 Hayfa
Theodora Massouh (2d 1972, 1975).

Plater, Stephen James; First Secretary FCO since
February 1995; born 23.1.54; FCO 1976; Second
Secretary Tokyo 1978; Second later First Secretary
FCO 1982; First Secretary and Head of Chancery
UKDEL MBFR Vienna 1987; First Secretary
UKDEL CACN Vienna 1989; First Secretary
(Comm) Tokyo 1990; m 1980 Keiko Kurata (1d
1990).

Platt, David Watson; Third Secretary FCO since
October 1992; born 9.4.54; Inland Revenue 1972;
FCO 1973; Beirut 1977; Brasilia 1980; Sofia
1981; FCO 1983; Dhaka 1985; Third Secretary
(Immig) Bridgetown 1988; Band B3.

Platt, Janet Elizabeth (née Howells); SUPL since
July 2001; born 26.3.61. Brussels (NATO) 1982,
Washington 1985; FCO 1987; Anguilla 1988; FCO
1991; UKREP Brussels 1992; Band A2; m 1988
Philip Charles Platt (2s 1987, 1990, 1d 1997).

Plumb, Michael Barry George; T/D Jakarta since
April 2001; born 16.5.45; DSAO 1965; Kampala
1968; Lahore 1971; FCO 1975; Washington 1977;
Canberra 1979; Baghdad 1982; FCO 1986; Jakarta
1990; FCO 1995; Deputy High Commissioner Port
Moresby 1997; m 1968 Linda Wills Gledhill (1s
1972; 1d 1975).

Plumbly, Sir Derek John, KCMG (2001), CMG
(1991); HM Ambassador Riyadh since September

2000; born 15.5.48; FCO 1972; Reporting Officer New York 1972; FCO 1973; MECAS 1973; Second later First Secretary Jedda 1975; First Secretary Cairo 1977; FCO 1980; First Secretary (Comm) Washington 1984; Counsellor and Head of Chancery Riyadh 1988; Counsellor and Head of Chancery UKMIS New York 1992; AUS, FCO 1996; m 1979 Nadia Youssef Gohar (1d 1983; 2s 1985, 1987).

Pocock, Andrew John; Head of African Department (Southern) FCO since May 2001; born 23.8.55; FCO 1981; Second later First Secretary (Comm) Lagos 1983; First Secretary FCO 1986; First Secretary (Chancery) Washington 1988; First Secretary FCO 1992; Counsellor on loan to the Royal College of Defence Studies 1996; Deputy High Commissioner Canberra 1997; m(1) 1976 Dayalini Pathmanathan (diss), (2)1995 Julie Eyre-Wilson.

Polatajko, Mark Alexander; New Delhi since August 1998; born 16.10.70; FCO 1991; Cairo 1995; Band B3.

Poll, Christopher John; Deputy High Commissioner Vila since November 1997; born 29.6.57; Army 1972-84; FCO 1984; UKREP Brussels 1988; FCO 1991; Canberra 1994; Band C4; m 1988 Gillian Anne Smith (1d 1994; 1s 1998).

Poll, Gillian Anne (née Smith); SUPL since 1994; born 30.4.58; HCS 1976; FCO 1985; Brussels 1987; UKREP Brussels 1990; FCO 1991; Band A2; m 1988 Christopher John Poll (1d 1994; 1s 1998).

Pollard, Guy Sephton; Third later Second Secretary (Political) Bratislava since October 1998; born 3.6.71; FCO 1991; Islamabad 1995; Band C4; ptnr, Catherine Louise Nicol (1d 2000).

Pond, John; UKDEL NATO Brussels since January 1997; born 22.5.52; Armed Forces 1969-92; FCO 1995; Band A2; m 1973 Catherine Herbert (1s 1971).

Ponsonby, Gareth James; FCO since May 2000; born 25.5.70; FCO 1991; Islamabad 1996; Band B3; m 1995 Natalie Lalanie Beverley Yeo (1d 2000).

Poole, Christopher George Robert; T/D Second Secretary (Political) Freetown since March 2000; born 19.4.52; FCO 1970; Algiers 1973; Brasilia 1974; Rio de Janeiro 1976; Freetown 1978; Paris 1981; Kinshasa 1984; FCO 1988; Third later Second Secretary Antananarivo 1991; Vice Consul (Commercial/Information) São Paulo 1995; FCO 1998; Band C5; m 1977 Maria Madalena Gomes Ferreira.

Poole, Christopher James, MBE (1987); First Secretary Commercial Sarajevo since May 1998; born 24.12.46; CRO 1964; FCO 1968; Georgetown 1969; Africa Floater 1969; St Lucia 1971; Bridgetown 1973; FCO 1976; Munich 1979; FCO 1982; Second Secretary Beirut 1985; Second Secretary Luxembourg 1987; EC Monitor Mission,

Former Yugoslavia, 1992; Deputy Head of Mission Zagreb 1993; Deputy Head of Mission, Jerusalem, 1995; First Secretary FCO 1996; m(1) 1973 Lillian Hodgson (diss) (2d 1979, 1980); (2) 1987 Marilyn Kathleen Povey (diss 1996); (3) 1996 Lynne Diana Merrin.

Pooley, Nigel Arthur; On Secondment to OXFAM since September 2000; born 12.11.61; FCO 1991; Third later Second Secretary (Chancery) Vienna 1994; First Secretary FCO 1998; m 1985 Helena Falle (3s 1986, 1991, 1994; 1d 1988).

Porter, Gillian Sarah; UKMis New York since July 2000; born 7.4.66; FCO 1988; Moscow 1991; Manila 1993; Band A2.

Porter, Neil David; Valetta since July 1999; born 14.4.63; FCO 1982; Riyadh 1985; Budapest 1989; FCO 1992; Third Secretary Johannesburg 1996; Band B3; m 1986 Gajetana Dominica Maria de Wit (1s 1988, 1d 1989).

Portman, Giles Matthew; Second Secretary (Political/Information) Prague since April 1998; born 25.5.71; Department of Transport 1994; FCO 1995; Band C4.

Poston, James; FCO since October 1999; born 19.6.45; Third Secretary FCO 1970; concurrently Third Secretary and Vice-Consul HM Embassy to Chad; Second Secretary and Private Secretary to Head of UKDEL EC Brussels 1971; First Secretary Tel Aviv 1973; FCO 1978; First Secretary (Comm) Lagos 1982; FCO 1985; Counsellor and Head of Chancery Pretoria 1988; Counsellor FCO 1992; Consul General Boston 1995 m(1) 1976 Anna Caroline Bos (diss 1980); (2) Rosemary Fullerton (2d 1987, 1988, 1s 1991).

Potter, Richard William; First Secretary Skopje since December 1999; born 22.5.60; FCO 1983; Third later Second Secretary Riyadh 1985; Second Secretary FCO 1988; First Secretary (Inf) Nicosia 1990; First Secretary FCO 1994; First Secretary Sarajevo 1995; FCO 1998; Band D6.

Potter, Rupert James; Third Secretary (Political) Stockholm since April 1999; born 14.11.68; FCO 1992; Amman 1995; Band B3; m 1995 Juliette Wilcox (1s 1998).

Powell, David Herbert; Political Counsellor UKDEL NATO/WEU Brussels since September 1997; born 29.4.52; MOD 1974; FCO 1984; First Secretary Tokyo 1988; First Secretary FCO 1992; Counsellor on loan to Cabinet Office 1995; m 1984 Gillian Mary Croft (1d 1994).

Powell, Hugh Eric; First Secretary Political (Internal) Berlin since April 2000; born 16.2.67; FCO 1991; Second Secretary Paris 1993; First Secretary FCO 1998; FTLT 2000; Band D6; m 1993 Catherine Claire Young (2s 1996, 1997).

Powell, Ian Francis; OBE (1995); First Secretary Gibraltar since September 1998; born 30.12.47; Commonwealth Office (later FCO) 1966; Freetown 1970; Havana 1973; FCO 1975; Stockholm 1978; Dublin 1981; (Second Secretary

1983); Second Secretary FCO 1986; (First Secretary 1988); First Secretary (Management/HM Consul) Kingston 1989; Deputy Head of Mission Sana'a 1994; First Secretary FCO 1995; m 1969 Priscilla Ann Fenton (2d 1974, 1980).

Powell, Leslie; Warsaw since March 1996; born 15.5.66; FCO 1994; Band A2.

Powell, Martin; Second Secretary Singapore since January 1988; born 21.10.46; FCO 1969; Warsaw 1973; FCO 1974; Brussels 1982; FCO 1985; m(1) 1972 Susan Kay Bower (diss); (2) 1982 Patricia Helen Scruby (1s 1987).

Powell, Richard Stephen; FCO since October 1998; born 19.10.59; FCO 1981; Third later Second Secretary Helsinki 1983; First Secretary FCO 1988; First Secretary (Science) Tokyo 1992; CDA Imperial College London 1996.

Power, Anne Maria; FCO since January 1999; born 14.8.65; FCO 1989; UKDEL Strasbourg 1992; Consulate-General Geneva 1993; UKDEL Strasbourg 1993; SUPL 1996; Band C4.

Power, Carmel Angela; Copenhagen since September 2001; born 30.10.63; FCO 1990; Third Secretary (Political) UKDEL Vienna 1992; Vice-Consul (Commercial) Damascus 1995; FCO 1997; Band D6.

Prentice, Christopher Norman Russell; Counsellor FCO since October 1998; born 5.9.54; FCO 1977; Language Student MECAS 1978; Third later Second Secretary Kuwait 1980; First Secretary on loan to Cabinet Office 1983; First Secretary Washington 1985; First Secretary FCO 1989; Deputy Head of Mission Budapest 1994; m 1978 Marie-Josephine (Nina) King (2s 1981, 1988; 2d 1982, 1985).

Preston, James David; On loan to the DTI since September 1999; born 21.4.68; FCO 1987; Helsinki 1994; FCO 1997; Band C4; m 1992 Kim Dickinson (1s 1995).

Preston, Joseph Raymond; on loan to BTI (Institute of Export) since September 1999; born 1.6.61; FCO 1980; Dhaka 1983; Kathmandu 1985; Nicosia 1989; FCO 1993; Third Secretary (Commercial) Islamabad 1995; FCO 1999; Band C4; m 1993 Sandra Elizabeth Cook.

Preston, Sandra Elizabeth (née Cook); FCO since August 1999; born 12.6.64; FCO 1987; Nicosia 1990; FCO 1992; Islamabad 1996; Band A2; m 1993 Joseph Raymond Preston.

Preston, William Edward Johnston; First Secretary Nicosia since January 1996; born 7.7.47; FCO 1965; Ankara 1969; Kinshasa 1972; FCO 1974; Rabat 1976; Oslo 1979; Second Secretary (Admin) Moscow 1983; Second Secretary FCO 1985; Second Secretary (Comm) Port of Spain 1988; First Secretary (Comm) Bucharest 1992; m 1969 Anne Kathleen Smith (1s 1974).

Price, Kenneth George; Second Secretary FCO since September 1998; born 12.4.65; FCO 1983; Bonn 1985; Accra 1988; FCO 1991; Third

Secretary (Political/Aid) Almaty 1994; World Wide floater duties 1997; Band C4.

Price, Michael Anthony, LVO (1991); Ambassador Suva since October 2000, also High Commissioner (non resident)Kiribati, Nauru and Tuvalu; born 13.8.44; Board of Trade 1964; DSAO 1966; Commonwealth Office 1967; New Delhi 1969; Second Secretary (Chancery) Freetown 1972; FCO 1973; Second later First Secretary (Aviation and Defence) Paris 1974; Consul (Comm) Montreal 1979; JSDC Greenwich 1983; First Secretary FCO 1984; Press and Public Affairs First Secretary Washington 1988; Counsellor (Management) and HM Consul General Tokyo 1993; Counsellor on loan to No10 Downing Street 1994; Counsellor (Management) Paris 1995; m 1968 Elizabeth Anne Cook (1d 1972; 1s 1974).

Price, Sarah Helena; Head of British Interests Section Belgrade since October 2000; born 4.6.66; FCO 1990; Second Secretary UKDEL CSCE (Helsinki) 1992; Second Secretary (Economic/KHF) Prague 1993; First Secretary FCO 1996; Secondment to the EU Secretariat of the Finnish Ministry for Foreign Affairs 1999; FTLT 2000; Band D6.

Price, Siân Rhyannon; FCO since January 2000; born 17.2.76; Band B3.

Price, Tristan Robert Julian; SUPL since August 1999; born 24.11.66; Economic Assistant 1993; Economic Adviser 1995; m 1988 Judith Ann Torrance (1d 1996; 1s 1998).

Priest, Timothy Ian; Counsellor (Political) Helsinki since June 1999; born 27.10.47; FCO 1972; Vienna 1975; First Secretary (Chancery) Helsinki 1981; FCO 1985; First Secretary (Chancery/Info) Athens 1989; Counsellor FCO 1993; mTeresa Jean Bagnall (2d 1975, 1980; 2s 1978, 1987).

Priestley, Carol Ann (née Edwards); Second Secretary FCO since May 1993; born 11.11.53; FCO 1974; Paris 1976; Düsseldorf 1979; Kathmandu 1980; FCO 1982; Dhaka 1985; Auckland 1989; m 1976 Lawrence Minton Priestley.

Priestley, Philip John; CBE (1996); High Commissioner Belmopan since July 2001; born 29.8.46; FCO 1969; Third Secretary Sofia 1971; Third later Second Secretary Kinshasa 1973; First Secretary FCO 1976; Head of Chancery Wellington 1979; First Secretary FCO 1984; Counsellor (Comm) Manila 1987; HM Ambassador Libreville 1990; CDA Harvard University 1991; HM Consul-General Geneva 1992; Head, North America Department, FCO, 1996; m 1972 Christine Rainforth (1d 1976; 1s 1978).

Prime, Ashley Walter John; FCO since March 2001; born 6.8.59; FCO 1978; Bonn 1980; Kingston 1983; Peking 1986; FCO 1989; Full-time Language Training 1993; Milan 1993; Rome 1995; Full Time language Training 1996; Deputy Consul

General Guangzhou 1996; On loan to the DTI 1999; Band C4; m 1997 Silvia Ardizzone (1s 1999).

Pring, Alison June; First Secretary (Commercial) Berne since October 1999; born 18.6.61; FCO 1983; SUPL 1983; FCO 1984; Third Secretary Brussels 1986; Third later Second Secretary Caracas 1989; Second Secretary FCO 1991; Full-time Language Training 1995; Second Secretary (DHM/Commercial) St Petersburg 1996; Band C5.

Pring, Mary; FCO since January 1999; born 29.6.60; FCO 1991; Full-time Language Training 1993; Language Training Cairo 1994; Jerusalem 1995; Band B3.

Pringle, Anne Fyfe; HM Ambassador Prague since November 2001; born 13.1.55; FCO 1977; Moscow 1980; San Francisco 1983; Second Secretary UKREP Brussels 1986; Second later First Secretary FCO 1987; First Secretary on secondment to European Political Cooperation Secretariat 1991; First Secretary later Counsellor FCO 1994; FTLT 2001; m 1987 Bleddyn Glynne Leyshon Phillips.

Pringle, Julia Margaret Georgina; Bogotá since December 1998; born 28.3.48; FCO 1966-1971; Metropolitan Police 1971; FCO 1991; SUPL 1993; Band A2; m 1971 Raymond Elliot Pringle (1d 1981).

Pringle, Raymond Elliott; First Secretary (Management) Washington since November 1999; born 28.11.51; Department of Employment 1968-69; FCO 1970; UKREP Brussels 1972; Quito 1975; FCO 1978; Bilbao 1981; Barcelona 1983; Second Secretary (Chancery/Info) Lilongwe 1986; Second later First Secretary FCO 1989; Deputy Consul General and Consul (Commercial) San Francisco 1993; SUPL 1999; m 1971 Julia Margaret Georgina Wright (1d 1981).

Pritchard, Grant; Third Secretary Vienna OSCE since September 2000; born 2.6.70; FCO 1990; Peking 1994; Third Secretary (Management) and Vice Consul Kuwait 1997; m 1996 Rebecca Louise Williams.

Pritchard, Rebecca Louise (née Williams); Berne since January 2000; born 17.8.71; FCO 1989; UKMIS Geneva 1991; Peking 1994; PA/HMA Kuwait 1997; Band A2; m 1996 Grant Pritchard.

Proctor, Jacqueline (née Jones); UKDis Geneva since July 1996; born 3.10.71; FCO 1991; Athens 1993; SUPL 1996; m 1996 Matthew Joel Proctor. Band A2.

Proctor, Matthew Joel; Kampala since December 1999; born 16.7.71; FCO 1991; SUPL 1993; UKMIS Geneva 1996; m 1996 Jaqueline Jones. Band B3.

Prodger, David Wilce; FCO Since February 1999; born 28.9.66; Band D6; m 1993 Tiffany Darwent (2s 1997, 2000).

Proudfoot, David Owen; Sarajevo since May 1998; born 15.4.71; HCS 1991; FCO 1995; Band B3.

Prouten, Matthew David MBE (1996); FTLT since November 2000; born 10.3.69; FCO 1988; Tokyo 1992; FCO 1996; Third Secretary (Political) Vilnius 1997; FCO 2000; Band B3; m 1994 Akino Matsumoto. (1s 1997; 1d 2000).

Pruce, Daniel Robert; First Secretary (Information) UKREP Brussels since September 1999; born 24.7.66; FCO 1990; UKREP Brussels 1993; FCO 1996; Band C4.

Pryce, Andrew William; FCO since November 1997; born 9.2.70; FCO 1988; Washington 1991; FCO 1993; Karachi 1994; Band B3; m 1993 Corienne Marie Madden.

Publicover, Ralph Martin; Deputy Head of Mission Lisbon since January 1999; born 2.5.52; FCO 1976; Language Student MECAS 1977; Second later First Secretary Dubai 1979; First Secretary (Econ) Ottawa 1981; First Secretary on loan to Cabinet Office 1985; FCO 1987; First Secretary (Chancery) Washington 1989; First Secretary FCO 1992; Full-time Language Training 1994; Bucharest 1994; m 1973 Rosemary Sheward (2d 1979, 1988; 1s 1983).

Pugh, David Evan; FCO since July 2000; born 26.4.51; FCO 1982; Pretoria 1983; FCO 1995; Cairo 1988; FCO 1991; Tokyo 1992; FCO 1995; Vienna 1997; Band C5; m(1) 1976 Bethan Jones (diss 1989) (4d 1980, 1982, 1984, 1986), (2) 1992 Sally Anne Jones.

Pullen, Roderick Allen; High Commissioner Accra since October 2000; born 11.4.49; MOD 1975; Second Secretary UKDEL NATO Brussels 1978; MOD 1980; First Secretary UKDEL CSCE Madrid 1981; FCO 1982; DHC Suva 1984; First Secretary FCO 1988; Counsellor (Technology) Paris 1990; Deputy High Commissioner Nairobi 1994; Deputy High Commissioner Lagos 1997; FCO 2000; m 1971 Karen Lesley Sketchley (1d 1975; 2s 1978, 1989, twin sons 1994).

Pullen, Russell Lewis; First Secretary FCO since April 1986; born 10.1.54; Second Secretary FCO 1975; Band C5; m 1979 Gilliam May Wright (1s 1985; 1d 1988).

Purdy, Samantha Louise, MVO (1996); First Secretary FCO since July 1999; born 22.8.71; FCO 1992; Full-time Language Training FCO 1994; Full-time Language Training Bangkok 1995; Second Secretary (Political/Information) Bangkok 1996.

Purves, Michael; First Secretary (Commercial) and Deputy Head of Mission Doha since September 2000; born 3.11.57; FCO 1975; New Delhi 1978; ME Floater 1982; Mogadishu 1983; FCO 1986; Third later Second Secretary (Econ/Aid) Kuala Lumpur 1989; Second Secretary (Management) Colombo 1992; First Secretary FCO 1996; m 1985 Ruth Joan Goodwin (1d 1986, 1s 1990).

Puryer, Stuart John; FCO since July 1996; born 3.6.67; FCO 1987; Copenhagen 1990; Ljubljana 1993; Band C4.

Pyle, Nicholas John; MBE (1999); Second Secretary Bridgetown since February 2000; born 9.12.60; FCO 1981; UKMIS Geneva 1984; Kabul 1986; Jedda 1990; FCO 1992; (Second Secretary 1995); Second Secretary (Immigration) Colombo 1996; Band C4; m 1993 Rosamund Day (1s 1995; 1d 1999).

Pyper, Alan; Berlin since June 2001; born 13.6.62; Department of Social Security 1990-97; FCO 1999; Band A2; m 1995 Patrocinia Haban.

Q

Quarrey, David; First Secretary (Political) New Delhi since September 2000; born 6.1.66; FCO 1994; Second Secretary (Political) Harare 1995.

Quayle, Quinton Mark; International Group Director, Trade Partners UK since October 1999; born 5.6.55; FCO 1977; Language Training 1978; Third Secretary (Chancery) Bangkok 1979 (Second Secretary 1981); FCO 1983 (First Secretary 1984); ENA Paris 1986; First Secretary Paris 1987; First Secretary FCO 1991; First Secretary Secondment to Price Waterhouse 1993; Counsellor FCO 1994; DHM Jakarta 1996; Director British Time International 1999; m 1979 Alison Marshall (2s 1982, 1985).

Quinn, James Gregory; Second Secretary (Pol/PPA) Accra since August 2000; born 16.6.71; Second Secretary FCO 1999; language training 1999; Band C4; m 1995 Wendy Dackombe.

Quinn, Jean Margaret (née Leiper); Second Secretary (Commercial) Riga since February 2000; born 21.3.53; FCO 1975; Abidjan 1978; Brasilia 1982; Second Secretary FCO 1984; SUPL 1990; FCO 1994; Second Secretary (Comm/ECM) Tunis 1996; Band C4; m 1985 Peter Nugent Quinn (1d 1987; 1s 1989).

Quinn, Lorraine; Helsinki since July 2000; born 25.6.66; FCO 1991; Bonn 1993; Gibraltar 1997; Band B3; m(1) 1986 Martin Quinn (diss 2000) (1s 1988); (2) 2000 Stephen Andrew Pettigrew.

R

Raby, Charlotte Jane; Peking since September 1998; born 5.5.72; HCS FCO 1992; FCO 1996; Band A2.

Rack, Martin Elliott; Second Secretary FCO since May 2001; born 30.12.73; FCO 1997; Second Secretary (Political) Hague 1999; Band C4.

Radcliffe, Adam; FCO since October 1996; born 10.6.67; FCO 1988; UKMIS Geneva 1990; Band A2; Istanbul 1993; m 1992 Julie Anne Nichols.

Radcliffe, James Crossley, MVO (1980); Counsellor FCO since October 1998; born 17.3.40; Ministry of Labour 1961; MECAS 1965; Kuwait 1967; Frankfurt 1970; Polytechnic of Central London 1973; FCO 1974; Second Secretary (Comm) Algiers 1977; Consul (Comm) Stuttgart 1981; First Secretary (Chancery) Dublin 1984; First Secretary FCO 1989; Seconded to Inter-Parliamentary Union 1992; First Secretary (Economic) Athens 1995; m 1966 Angela Goldie (2s 1967, 1969).

Rae, Karen (née Hooper); Second Secretary (Commercial) Prague since November 1997; born 28.5.60; FCO 1980; Port Stanley 1983; Berne 1984; Cairo 1987; FCO 1990; Third Secretary (Consular) Islamabad 1993; Language Training 1997; Band C4; m 1984 Thomas Park Rae (1d 1993).

Raine, John Andrew; FCO since June 2000; born 12.7.62; FCO 1984; Language Training 1986; Second Secretary (Inf) Kuwait 1988; First Secretary FCO 1991; First Secretary (Political) Damascus 1994; First Secretary Riyadh 1997; Band D6.

Raine, Sarah Emily; FTLT since April 2001; born 16.7.76; FCO 1999; Band C4.

Rajguru, Harish L; Floater Duties since April 1999; born 23.4.61; HCS cadre of the FCO 1989; FCO 1990; Sofia 1992; Kiev 1994; FCO 1996; Band B3.

Rakestraw, Mark Andrew; Vice Consul Lisbon since August 1997; born 30.11.67; FCO 1988; Athens 1990; FCO 1993; Full Time Language Training 1996; Band C4.

Ralph, Richard Peter, CMG (1997); CVO (1991); HM Ambassador Bucharest since August 1999; born 27.4.46; Third Secretary FCO 1969; Third later Second Secretary Vientiane 1970; Second later First Secretary (Inf) Lisbon 1974; First Secretary FCO 1977; First Secretary and Head of Chancery Harare 1981; First Secretary later Counsellor FCO 1985; Counsellor Washington 1989; HM Ambassador Riga 1993; HM Governor Stanley 1996; m 1970 Margaret Elisabeth Coulthurst (diss 2001) (1s 1970; 1d 1974).

Rampe, Christopher Mark; FCO since June 1999; born 15.1.61; FCO 1988; Second Secretary Accra 1995; Band C4; m 1993 Cecily Jacqueline Newby.

Ramsay, Paul Andrew, MBE (1988); First Secretary (Management) Singapore since January 1997; born 10.10.55; FCO 1975; East Berlin 1977; Istanbul 1979; UKDEL NATO Brussels 1981; Tehran 1984; FCO 1987 (Second Secretary 1990); Second Secretary Madrid 1992; m 1980 Carey-Jane Lambert (1d 1987, 2s 1989, 1993).

Ramscar, Michael Charles; Counsellor FCO since December 2000; born 26.2.48; Second Secretary FCO 1975; Second Secretary (Econ) Lagos 1977; First Secretary (Econ) Brasilia 1979; First Secretary FCO 1982; Madrid 1986; San José 1989; First Secretary FCO 1991; Counsellor Madrid 1997; m 1970 Janis Lemon (2s 1976, 1981).

Ramsden, Sir John (Charles Josslyn), Bt; Head of Central and North West European Department since June 1999; born 19.8.50; FCO 1975; Third later Second Secretary Dakar 1976; First Secretary UKDEL MBFR Vienna 1979; First Secretary Head of Chancery and Consul Hanoi 1980; First

Secretary FCO 1982; on loan to HM Treasury 1988; First Secretary FCO 1988; Counsellor and Deputy Head of Mission East Berlin later British Embassy Berlin Office 1990; Counsellor FCO 1993; Deputy Head of Mission UKMIS Geneva 1996; m 1985 Jane Bevan (2d 1987, 1989).

Ramsey, Patricia Anne; Second later First Secretary (Political) Berlin since September 1998; born 9.1.48; FO 1967; UKDEL EEC Brussels 1969; Rio de Janeiro 1972; FCO 1974; Athens 1980; UKMIS Geneva 1983; FCO 1986; Paris 1987; SUPL 1991; FCO 1992. SUPL 1997. Band C4 m1990 Paul Lever.

Rangarajan, Francis Vijay Narasimhan; FCO since November 1999; born 22.9.69; FCO IGC Unit, EUD(I) 1995; Second later First Secretary UKREP (Trade Policy and Antici) Brussels 1997; Private Secretary to Permanent Under-Secretary of State 1999; m2000 Rosie Francis Cox.

Rankin, John James; Counsellor & Deputy Head of Mission Dublin since September 1999; born 12.3.57; Assistant, later Senior Legal Adviser FCO 1988; Legal Adviser UKMIS and UKDIS Geneva 1991; Legal Counsellor FCO 1995; First Secretary FCO 1996; First Secretary Dublin 1998; m 1987; Lesley Marshall (2d 1989, 1991; 1s 1993).

Ranson, Catherine Fraser (née Armstrong); Athens since February 1989; born 16.7.53; FCO 1971; Paris 1974; Gaborone 1977; FCO 1980; Manila 1985; Band B3; m 1981 Clive Paul Ranson.

Rapp, Stephen Robert; Vice-Consul Lahore since July 2001; born 9.3.52; Home Office 1986; FCO 1986; Accra 1988; Hanoi 1992; FCO 1994; Vice Consul Jedda 1996; Ekaterinburg 1999; Band B3; m 1978 Judy Elizabeth Flewett.

Ratcliffe, Deborah; T/D Islamabad since January 2001; born 6.4.62; FCO 1980; UKMIS Geneva 1982; Harare 1985; Manila 1988; FCO 1991; Vice Consul Hanoi 1995; Third Secretary (Management) Kingston 1997; Band C4.

Ratcliffe, Yvonne; Singapore since August 2000; born 18.6.62; FCO 1988; Athens 1989; Peking 1992; FCO 1994; Prague 1996; T/D Khartoum 1999; Band B3.

Raven, Martin Clark; Counsellor Stockholm since August 1998; born 10.3.54; FCO 1976; Third Secretary Lagos 1978; FCO 1979; Third, later Second Secretary New Delhi 1979; Second later First Secretary FCO 1983; First Secretary UKMIS New York 1988; First Secretary FCO 1993; Counsellor FCO 1996; m 1978 Philippa Michaela Morrice Ruddick (2s 1982, 1984).

Raw, Amanda Jayne; Gibraltar since June 2000; born 22.9.68; FCO 1995; Amman 1997; Band A2.

Rawbone, Jane Lynn; Canberra since April 2000; born 21.3.53; FCO 1976; UKDEL MBFR Vienna 1977; Helsinki 1980; FCO 1982; Mexico City 1984; UKMIS New York 1988; Madrid 1991; FCO 1993; Kuala Lumpur 1996; Band B3.

Rawlins, Helen Catherine; Second Secretary (Consular) Kampala since May 1998; born 31.7.64; FCO 1986; Bonn 1988; Manila 1991; Second Secretary FCO 1994.

Rawlinson, Colin James; Consul-General Bordeaux since January 1998; born 21.2.46; FCO 1967; Reykjavik 1968; Nicosia 1971; Hamburg 1973; Second Secretary FCO 1976; Copenhagen 1979; Second Secretary (Comm) New Delhi 1981; First Secretary FCO 1984; UKMIS New York 1993; FCO 1994; m1966 The Hon Catharine Julia Trend (2d 1967, 1969).

Rawlinson, Ivor Jon, OBE (1988); HM Ambassador Tunis from January 1999 - 2002; born 24.1.42; FO 1964; Warsaw 1966; Bridgetown 1969; Second Secretary FCO 1971; Assistant Private Secretary to Minister of State, FCO 1973; Second Secretary (Econ) Paris 1974; First Secretary FCO 1978; First Secretary (Comm) Mexico City 1980; Consul Florence 1984; First Secretary later Counsellor FCO 1988; Royal College of Defence Studies 1993; Consul General Montreal 1993; m 1976 Catherine Paule Caudal (1s 1980; 2d 1977, 1983).

Rawlinson, Timothy Simeon; First Secretary FCO since May 2000; born 12.1.62; Second Secretary FCO 1988; Second later First Secretary (Inf) Lagos 1991; First Secretary FCO 1993; First Secretary (Political) Stockholm 1996; Band D6; m 1998 Janet Mary Cooper.

Rayner, Robert Alan; Counsellor (Atomic Energy) Tokyo since January 2001; born 14.12.50; FCO 1968; Islamabad 1972; Language Student 1974; Tokyo 1975; DOT 1979; FCO 1981; Second Secretary (Chancery/Inf) and Vice-Consul Lima 1984; FCO 1987; Consul (Comm) Osaka 1989; First Secretary (Press and Public Affairs) Tokyo 1995; First Secretary FCO 1999; m 1984 Dawn Carol Ashton (1d 1991).

Rea, Elizabeth Rose; MBE (1993); FCO since May 1996; born 31.10.54; FCO 1976; Luxembourg 1978; Lima 1981; Washington 1984; FCO 1987; UKREP Brussels 1992; Band B3.

Read, Rachel Frances; FCO since August 1996; born 23.10.65; FCO 1989; Cairo 1991; Sofia 1994; Band A2.

Reader, David George; High Commissioner Mbabane since September 2001; born 1.10.47; CRO, DSAO and FCO 1964; Warsaw 1969; Paris 1972; Bucharest 1974; FCO 1976; Kinshasa 1979; Kathmandu 1982; Second Secretary FCO 1984; Vice-Consul (Comm) Brisbane 1987; First Secretary (Management) and Consul Belgrade 1992; First Secretary FCO 1996; First Secretary Cairo 1998; m 1969 Elaine McKnight (1s 1975; 1d 1980).

Rebecchi, Silvano Marco Raffaele; Second Secretary (Commercial) Helsinki since August 2000; born 14.8.52; Department of Education and Science 1972; FCO 1975; Baghdad 1977; Valletta 1981; Dhaka 1984; FCO 1986; Paris 1990; Amman 1992; Cairo 1992; Second Secretary FCO

1996; FTLT 2000; m 1984 Eileen Zammit (2s 1985, 1987).

Reddaway, David Norman, CMG (1993); MBE (1980); Director, Public Services since April 1999; born 26.4.53; FCO 1975; Language Student SOAS 1976 and Iran 1977; Third later Second Secretary (Commercial) Tehran 1977; Second later First Secretary (Chancery) Tehran 1978; First Secretary (Chancery) Madrid 1980; First Secretary FCO 1985; Private Secretary to Minister of State 1986; First Secretary (Chancery) New Delhi 1988; Chargé d'Affaires a.i. Tehran 1990; (Counsellor 1991); Minister and Deputy Head of Mission Buenos Aires 1993; FCO 1997; m 1981 Roshan Taliyeh Firouz (2s 1983, 1996, 1d 1987).

Redden, Michael James; Colombo since August 1998; born 22.2.70; DHSS 1987; FCO 1990; Khartoum 1994; FCO 1997; Band B3; m 1995 Nicola Jane Elizabeth Sharp. (1d 1997)

Reddicliffe, Paul; OBE, FCO since August 1997; born 17.3.45; FCO 1977; Principal Research Officer (Band D6); First Secretary Canberra 1985; First Secretary FCO 1989; HM Ambassador Phnom Penh 1994; m 1974 Wee Siok Boi (2s 1977, 1979).

Redshaw, Tina Susan; First Secretary (Political) Beijing since July 2000; born 25.1.61; FCO 1999; Band D6.

Reed, Pamela Karen (née Williams); FCO since August 1999; born 10.5.70; HCS 1989; FCO 1994; Brasilia later São Paulo 1997; Band A2; m 1997 Antony Jason Reed.

Reeve, Charles Michael Campbell; First Secretary (Political) Zagreb since April 2001; born 12.7.71; Second Secretary FCO 1997; Second Secretary (Pol/Mil) Banja Luka 1999; Band D6.

Reeve, Richard Robert; Counsellor FCO since June 2000; born 28.7.48; FCO 1971; Third later Second Secretary Singapore 1973; Language student Cambridge University 1975 and Hong Kong 1976; Trade Commissioner Hong Kong 1977; First Secretary FCO 1981; First Secretary Hong Kong 1983; First Secretary FCO 1987; Counsellor Berne 1996; m 1971 Monique Marie-Louise Moggio (2s 1974, 1977).

Reeves, Ceinwen Mary; SUPL since August 2000; born 9.6.57; FCO 1976; SUPL 1976; FCO 1979; Bonn 1982; Lilongwe 1984; Paris 1987; FCO 1989; Vice-Consul Sofia 1993; Second Secretary (Commercial) Peking 1995; m 1990 Peter Clive Wilkinson (diss 1994).

Regan, Michael John; Counsellor FCO since September 1998; born 17.8.55; FCO 1983; Second later First Secretary Kabul 1986; FCO 1988; First Secretary (Chancery/Econ) Dubai 1989; First Secretary FCO 1991; Bangkok 1995; m 1986 Carolyn Gaye Black (2s 1987, 1989).

Rehal, Opinder Kumar; Canberra since April 1992; born 15.9.48; FCO 1979; Bonn 1982; FCO 1985; Islamabad 1989; FCO 1990; Band C4; m

1974 Jagdeep Nandra (1s 1975 (dec'd 1990); 1d 1978).

Reid, Gordon Bryden; Deputy Head of Mission Budapest since July 1998; born 9.5.56; FCO 1980; Second Secretary Budapest 1982; First Secretary FCO 1985; First Secretary (Chancery) Santiago 1988; First Secretary (Chancery) Islamabad 1990; First Secretary FCO 1994; m 1979 Marinella Ferro (2s 1982, 1988; 1d 1984).

Reid, Norma Fraser; Third Secretary (Consular) Nicosia since March 1997; born 19.8.43; Saigon 1968; Rome 1970; Bucharest 1971; FCO 1973; HCS 1975; Latin America Floater 1977; Peking 1979; FCO 1980; Moscow 1983; FCO 1984; Rome 1986; FCO 1988; Bucharest 1993.

Reid, Thomas Samuel; FCO since September 2000; born 28.12.76; Band C4.

Reidy, Andrea Jane; Deputy High Commissioner Freetown since September 2000; born 24.11.58; FCO 1995; Second Secretary (KHF) Bratislava 1997; (1d 1981).

Reilly, Julian; FCO since June 2000; born 3.2.71; FCO 1993; full-time language training 1994; full-time language training Cairo 1995; Second Secretary (Chancery) Khartoum 1996.

Reilly, Michael David; Head of Cultural Relations Department FCO since May 2000; born 1.3.55; FCO 1978; Language Training Seoul 1979; First Secretary FCO 1984; First Secretary UKDEL OECD Paris 1988; First Secretary (Political) and Consul Seoul 1991; First Secretary FCO 1994; Deputy Head of Mission Manila 1996; m 1981 Won-Kyong Kang (1d 1987; 1s 1992).

Reilly, Michael Patrick; FCO since December 1997; born 30.7.66; FCO 1984; Bonn 1987; Bombay 1990; FCO 1991; Third Secretary (Development) Lilongwe 1994; Band C4; m 1991 Andrea Louise Bradley.

Reilly, Patrick; FCO since March 2000; born 3.11.70; FCO 1995; Second Secretary (Political) Cape Town 1997; Band C4.

Reilly, Peter Marius Julian Prowse; Second Secretary FCO since October 1996; born 3.2.71; FCO 1993; Full-time Language Training 1994; Full-time Language Training Cairo 1995; Second Secretary (Chancery) Khartoum 1996.

Reilly, Thomas Saul Anthony; Second Secretary (Political) Buenos Aires since August 2001; born 17.11.70; Second Secretary FCO 1998; Band C4.

Remmington, Gillian Elizabeth; Hong Kong since December 2000; born 26.2.56; FCO 1984; Quito 1985; Berne 1988; World-wide floater duties 1991; FCO 1993; Nicosia 1997; Band B3.

Renfrew, Laura; Abidjan since August 1995; born 16.3.62; FCO 1984; Moscow 1986; FCO 1988; Damascus 1989; FCO 1992; Full-time Language Training 1995; Band B3.

Rennie, Brian William; FCO since December 1989; born 6.2.40; FO 1964; Bangkok 1965; FO (later FCO) 1967; St Helena 1969; FCO 1971; Tehran 1972; FCO 1975; Darwin 1976; FCO 1978; Warsaw 1979; FCO 1981; Attaché Havana 1982; FCO 1985; Rangoon 1986; Band C4; m 1963 Annie Daurge (2s 1964, 1971; 1d 1967).

Rennie, Nadia Jane; Kiev since May 2000; born 30.9.71; FCO 1990; UKDEL NATO Brussels 1994; Band B3.

Reuter, Alan; Consul Milan since February 2000; born 5.7.51; FCO 1970; Bucharest 1972; Kaduna 1974; Frankfurt 1978; Gaborone 1980; FCO 1982; Tel Aviv 1986; Third Secretary (Comm) Kuala Lumpur 1988; Second Secretary FCO 1992; Second Secretary (Consular/Immigration) Lagos 1995; Nairobi 1998; FCO 1999; Band C4; m(1) 1973 Christine Caton; (2) 1982 Brenda Yvonne Mary Neumann (1s 1983; 1d 1985).

Revington, Thomas Mark Bowen; Vice Consul (Political) Istanbul since October 1999; born 19.9.73; FCO 1997; Band C4.

Rey, Rosemary; SUPL since April 1996; born 14.3.55; FCO 1974; Cayman Islands 1976; FCO 1978; Gibraltar 1979; Bogotá 1981; FCO 1986; Bogotá 1988; Caracas 1990; Band B3; m 1983 Alvaro Rey Romero (2s 1991, 1995)

Reynolds, Colin; Assistant Private Secretary to the Minister of State since October 1999; born 3.7.71; FCO 1990; Nicosia 1992; Africa/Middle-East Floater Duties 1995; Second Secretary FCO 1998; Band C4.

Reynolds, Gillian Marjorie; FCO since October 1993; born 16.10.50; FCO 1976; New Delhi 1977; Budapest 1979; Mbabane 1981; FCO 1984; Singapore 1987; Peking 1991; Band B3.

Reynolds, Heather (née Turnbull); FCO since December 1991; born 30.5.54; FCO 1973; Moscow 1975; FCO 1976; Brasilia 1977; Bridgetown 1980; SUPL 1983; Kuala Lumpur 1984; FCO 1986; Prague 1988; SUPL 1990; Band B3; m 1982 Keith James Reynolds (1s, 1990).

Reynolds, Keith James; Moscow since August 1999; born 2.8.44; FCO 1969; Bridgetown 1980; Kuala Lumpur 1982; FCO 1986; Second Secretary Prague 1988; Second Secretary FCO 1990; Second Secretary New Delhi 1993; Second Secretary FCO; Band C5; m 1982 Heather Turnbull (1s 1990).

Reynolds, Leslie Roy; Dublin since May 1997; born 22.9.59; DTI1978; Passport Office 1979; HO 1984; FCO 1984; Wellington 1986; Islamabad 1988; FCO 1992. Band B3; m 1982 Tracey Sapsford.

Reynolds, Martin Alexander Baillie; Second Secretary (Economic/Commercial) Singapore since September 1998; born 5.6.69; FCO 1997; Band C4

Reynolds, Victoria Caroline; FCO since February 2001; born 7.6.69; FCO 1988; Lagos/Abuja 1992; FCO 1994; Mexico City 1996; Tallinn 1997; Band B3.

Rhodes, Ian Peter; Second Secretary FCO since September 1998; born 12.4.60; Second Secretary FCO 1986; Nicosia 1995; Band C4.

Rice, Douglas; Resident Acting High Commissioner Castries since May 2001; born 28.1.46; FO 1964; Jedda 1968; Paris 1970; Sana'a 1972; Sofia 1973; FCO 1974; FTLT 1977; Doha 1978; Düsseldorf 1982; Second Secretary (Consular/Passports) Singapore 1983; Second later First Secretary FCO 1986; First Secretary (Press & Public Affairs) Madrid 1993; FCO 1998; m (1) 1969 Christine Elizabeth Chisholm (1d 1973; 1s 1977); (2) 1995 Allison Denise Hay.

Rice, John Gordon; Deputy Head of Mission Lilongwe since October 1997; born 6.1.46; Home Office 1962; Commonwealth Office DSAO and FCO 1967; Ankara 1969; Paris 1972; FCO 1976; Seoul 1978; Assistant Trade Commissioner (Second Secretary) Hong Kong 1980; FCO 1985; (Parliamentary Clerk); First Secretary (Comm) and Head of Chancery Doha 1988; Deputy High Commissioner Windhoek 1992; First Secretary FCO 1995; m 1972 Gail Marjorie Pearce (2s 1975, 1979; 1d 1976).

Richards, Claire Michelle; FCO since December 2000; born 9.12.72; FCO 1991; Bangkok 1997; Band A2.

Richards, Francis Neville, CMG (1994); CVO (1991); Head of GCHQ Cheltenham since August 1998; born 18.11.45; Army 1967-69; Third Secretary FCO 1969; Moscow 1971; Second later First Secretary UKDEL MBFR Vienna 1973; First Secretary FCO 1976; Counsellor (Comm/Econ) New Delhi 1985; Counsellor FCO 1988; High Commissioner Windhoek 1990; Minister Moscow 1992; AUS (Central and Eastern Europe) FCO 1995; Director (Europe) 1996; DUSS (Defence and Intelligence) 1998; m 1971 Gillian Bruce Nevill (1s 1975; 1d 1977).

Richards, Ian; Consul (Commercial) Shanghai since November 1996; born 7.10.62; FCO 1993; Full Time Language Training 1994; Band C4.

Richards, Miranda Jane; Mexico City since June 1996; born 20.1.69; FCO 1994; Band A2.

Richards, Owen Jeremy; On loan to the DTI since September 2000; born 28.6.66; FCO 1988; Bombay 1991; Third Secretary (ECE/UNCTAD) UKMIS Geneva 1995; Band C4.

Richards, Rodney Elizabeth, MBE (1986); FCO since April 1991; born 27.8.48; FO 1967; Geneva 1970; Phnom Penh 1972; Islamabad 1973; Saigon 1975; FCO 1975; Jakarta 1976; FCO 1978; Nairobi 1983; Kampala 1986; Band A2.

Richards, Steven Thomas; Second Secretary (Commercial) Dublin since July 2000; born 29.1.58; FCO 1978; New Delhi 1980; Beirut 1982; Europe Floater 1985; FCO 1987; Warsaw 1988; FCO 1988; Vice-Consul Moscow 1990; FCO 1993 (Second Secretary 1994); Second Secretary (Management/Consular) Valetta 1996; Band C4; m 1989 Tracey Lee Barnett (1d 1995).

Richardson, Christine Lynn; Baku since June
1998; born 4.10.67; FCO 1987; UKREP Brussels
1989; Floater Duties Africa/Middle East 1992; on
loan to the DTI 1997; Band B3.

Richardson, Michael John; FCO since October
1996; born 16.5.66; FCO 1985; Warsaw 1988;
FCO 1991; Attaché Cairo 1993; Band B3; m 1989
Audrey Zena Fairall (1s 1994).

Richman, Menna Frances; First Secretary Tel
Aviv since September 1998; born 16.9.67; FCO
1989; Third later Second Secretary (Institutions)
UKREP Brussels 1991; Second Secretary
(Econ/Env) Nairobi 1993; FCO 1997; SUPL 1998;
m 1990 Stephen Charles Richman.

Richmond, Alan Thomas; Second Secretary
(Economic) Ottawa since July 1999; born 22.4.55;
Department of Education 1973; FCO 1975;
Maputo 1977; Lima 1981; FCO 1983; Islamabad
1985; Singapore 1988; FCO 1991; Full Time
Language Training 1994; Abidjan 1995; Band C4;
m 1976 Iseabal MacLean Graham (1d 1986).

Richmond, David Frank; Head of Chancery
UKMIS New York since 1996; born 9.7.54; FCO
1976; Language Student MECAS 1977; Third later
Second Secretary Baghdad 1979; Second later
First Secretary FCO 1982; First Secretary
(External Trade) UKREP Brussels 1987; FCO
1991; m1990 Caroline Florence Pascale Gilberte
(1s 1992; 1d 1994).

Rickerd, Martin John Kilburn, MVO (1985);
Deputy Head of Mission Abidjan since August
2000; born 17.8.54; FCO 1972; UKDEL NATO
Brussels 1975; Wellington 1978; Assistant PS to
Parliamentary Under Secretary of State 1980;
Bridgetown 1982; Consul (Inf) Milan 1986; First
Secretary FCO 1991; Head of Chancery Singapore
1995; On Secondment to the Standard Chartered
Bank 1998; FCO 2000; Band D6; m 1976
Charmain Gwendoline Napier (2s 1986, 1988).

Ricketts, Peter Forbes, CMG (1999); Political
Director and Deputy Under-Secretary FCO since
September 2001; born 30.9.52; FCO 1974; New
York 1974; FCO 1975; Third Secretary Singapore
1975; Second Secretary UKDEL NATO Brussels
1978; First Secretary FCO 1982; APS to Secretary
of State 1983; First Secretary (Chancery)
Washington 1986; First Secretary later Counsellor
FCO 1989; Counsellor (EC/Finance) Paris 1994;
Deputy Political Director FCO 1997; Director
International Security FCO 1999; On loan to the
Cabinet Office as Chairman of the Joint
Intelligence Committee 2000; m 1980 Suzanne
Julia Horlington (1s 1982; 1d 1987).

Rickitt, Clare Louise; First Secretary FCO since
August 1996; born 20.9.64; FCO 1991; Full-time
Language Training 1992; Second Secretary
(Economic Trade Policy) Brasilia 1993.

Rickward, Charlotte Lucy; Manila since June
2000; born 12.5.72; FCO 1997; Band A2; m 1994
Jarlath Ambrose.

Ridley, Michelle; UKMIS New York since June
1997; born 22.1.63; DHSS 1986-87; FCO 1987;
Kaduna 1990; Peking 1993; Band A2.

Ridout, Anthony Robert; Second Secretary
(Political) Kingston since June 2001; born 31.3.66;
FCO 1986; New Delhi 1989; Paris 1992; FCO
1995; Second Secretary Cairo 1996; Second
Secretary FCO 1998; Band C4; m 1989 Karen
Marie Hendy (1d 1991).

Ridout, Richard William; FCO since April 1998;
born 19.11.67; FCO 1986; Moscow 1990; FCO
1993; Third Secretary Riyadh 1994; Band B3; m
1992 Sarah Beth Evans (1d 1996).

Ridout, William Anthony Frederick; HM Consul
Hong Kong since July 2001; born 27.4.50; MOD
1970; FCO 1974; Islamabad 1976; Stuttgart 1979;
Bridgetown 1982; FCO 1982; Bombay 1984;
Second Secretary (Comm) East Berlin 1988;
Consul Milan 1990; FCO 1995; DHM Khartoum
1997; First Secretary (Commercial) Tripoli 1999;
m(1) 1971 Muriel Jessica Stewart Benigan (diss);
(2) 1980 Frances Mary Bond (diss); (3) 1996
Louise Victoria Burrett.

Riley, John Lawrence; Third Secretary (Aid)
Gaborone since July 1999; born 13.8.61; FCO
1982; Cairo 1984; FCO 1986; Ankara 1986; Hanoi
1991; FCO 1992; New Delhi 1995; m(1) 1982
Caroline Peacock (diss) m(2) 1990 Ayce Birergin.

Rimmer, Ronald Stanley; Lagos since July 1998;
born 24.2.54; Royal Air Force 1972-1995; FCO
1995; Band C4.

Ringham, Christine Mary; SUPL since February
2000; born 11.12.61; FCO 1988; UKDEL Brussels
1991; Prague 1995; FCO 1998; Band A2; m 1998
Kevin P Ringham.

Ripard, Elizabeth Anne (née Auld); Second
Secretary Abidjan since July 1998; born 27.6.57;
FCO 1976; Madrid 1979; SEA Floater 1982; San
José 1984; FCO 1988; Third Secretary Valletta
1991; Third later Second Secretary FCO 1994;
Language training 1998; m 1992 Nicholas Charles
Ripard (diss).

Ritchie, Joseph Battle; FCO since January 1998;
born 13.7.44; RAF 1961-91. Band A2; m Paula
May (1d 1975,1s 1980).

Ritchie, Paul John; OBE, (1994); Counsellor
Nicosia since July 1999; born 26.3.62; FCO 1983;
Second Secretary (Chancery) Nicosia 1986;
Second later First Secretary FCO 1988; First
Secretary UKMIS New York1991; First Secretary
FCO 1996; m 1991 Jane Risely (1d 1997).

Rixon, Margaret Carol; Dublin since May 1999;
born 16.2.57; FCO 1976; Castries 1978;
Washington 1980; Peking 1982; FCO 1983;
UKMIS Vienna 1984; East Berlin 1987; Kingston
1988; FCO 1991; Band B3.

Road-Night, Susan Catherine; Mexico City since
October 1995; born 13.3.67; FCO 1991; Kiev
1992; Full-time Language Training 1995; Band
A2.

Robbins, Christopher William; Ambassador Lithuania since May 1998; born 16.6.46; First Secretary FCO 1984; First Secretary (Chancery) New Delhi 1987; First Secretary FCO 1990; Counsellor on loan to the DTI 1991; Counsellor(Commercial) The Hague, later also Consul-General Amsterdam 1994;

Roberts, Amanda Claire; FCO since May 2000; born 6.9.67; FCO 1989; Santiago 1996 (Second Secretary 1997); Band C4.

Roberts, Anne Catherine; FCO since November 1997; born 7.5.63; FCO 1985; Bucharest 1988; FCO 1990; Floater Duties 1991; FCO 1993; Athens 1995; Band A2.

Roberts, Catherine Mary; Washington since December 1997; born 5.10.68; FCO 1995; Band A2.

Roberts, Colin; Counsellor (Political) Tokyo since January 2001; born 31.7.59; FCO 1989; Second Secretary (Econ) later First Secretary (Political) Tokyo 1990; First Secretary FCO 1995; First Secretary (Political/Military) Paris 1997; Counsellor FCO 1998; Called to the Bar 1986; m2000 Camilla Frances Mary Blair.

Roberts, David Eric; Vancouver since June 1999; born 15.8.54; Customs and Excise 1971; FCO 1973; Lagos 1977; Doha 1979; FCO 1983; Washington 1986; Helsinki 1989; On Loan to London Chamber of Commerce 1993; HM Consul Jedda 1995; m 1979 Kim Louise Fyleman (3d 1990, 1992, 1993)

Roberts, David George; Deputy Head of Mission, Director of Trade and Investment and Consul General for Switzerland and Liechtenstein at the British Embassy in Berne since August 2000; born 11.4.55; FCO 1976; Third later Second Secretary (Chancery) Jakarta 1977; Second Secretary (Chancery) Havana 1981; First Secretary FCO 1984; First Secretary (Econ) Madrid 1988; First Secretary (Financial/EC) Paris, 1991; FCO 1994; First Secretary FCO 1994; Deputy Head of Mission Santiago 1996; FTLT 2000; m 1985 Rosmarie Rita Kunz (1d 1990, 1s 1992).

Roberts, Gillian (née Phenna); Third Secretary (Passports) Paris Embassy since August 1998; born 3.12.68; FCO 1995; FCO 1986; Cape Town/Pretoria 1988; Buenos Aires 1992; FCO 1995; Band B3; m 1993 Michael John Roberts.

Roberts, Ian; FCO since November 1993; born 26.10.66; FCO 1987; Buenos Aires 1991; Band A2.

Roberts, Sir Ivor Anthony, KCMG (2000), CMG (1995); HM Ambassador Dublin since February 1999; born 24.9.46; Third Secretary FCO 1968; MECAS 1969; FCO 1970; Paris 1970; Second Secretary 1971; Second later First Secretary FCO 1973; First Secretary (Chancery) later First Secretary (Econ/Comm/Agric) Canberra 1978; First Secretary FCO 1982; Counsellor FCO 1986; Minister Madrid 1989; Chargé d'Affaires and HM Consul General later HM Ambassador Belgrade 1994; On loan to St Antony's College, Oxford

1997; m 1974 Elizabeth Bray Bernard Smith (2s 1976, 1979; 1d 1982).

Roberts, Michael John Wyn; Head of Division, Cabinet Office (European Secretariat) since September 1999; born 4.7.60; Second Secretary FCO 1984; Second later First Secretary (Chancery) Athens 1987; First Secretary FCO 1991; First Secretary (Institutions) UKREP Brussels 1995; Band D7; m 1985 Margaret Anne Ozanne (2d 1989, 1991; 1s 1993).

Roberts, Philip John Barclay; Counsellor FCO since June 1999; born 4.12.49; FCO 1973; Third later Second Secretary Islamabad 1977; First Secretary FCO 1980; Head of Chancery and Consul Hanoi 1982; First Secretary Tokyo 1984; First Secretary FCO 1987; First Secretary (Chancery) later Counsellor Lisbon 1991; Counsellor Bogotá 1994; Counsellor FCO 1995; Counsellor Vienna 1997; m 1996 Amparo Jimenez Avilan (1d 1997).

Roberts, Trevor Martin; FCO since October 1995; born 12.7.55; FCO 1974; UKMIS Geneva 1978; Floater duties 1982; Kuwait 1984; Second Secretary FCO 1986; Second Secretary (Commercial) Madrid 1992.

Robertson, Brian; Resident Acting High Commissioner St Vincent and The Grenadines since May 1996; born 24.7.45; FO 1963; Cairo 1967; Washington 1968; Castries 1969; Warsaw 1974; FCO 1976; Gaborone 1979; Second Secretary Maseru 1982; First Secretary and Head of Chancery Asunción 1985; First Secretary FCO 1989; First Secretary (Management and HM Consul) Copenhagen 1991; m 1967 Ellen Roberts.

Robertson, Corin Jean Stella (née Leatherbarrow); Second Secretary (Trade Policy) Tokyo since September 1997; born 15.1.72; FCO 1994; Band C4; Full-time Language Training 1995; m 1996 James Francis Robertson.

Robertson, Emma Jane; Third Secretary (Economic) Damascus since January 2000; born 25.12.71; FCO 1997; Band B3.

Robertson, Henry Macloskie; Second Secretary FCO since January 1987; (First Secretary 1995); born 10.10.41; ECGD 1960; CRO 1961; Zomba 1964; DSAO (later FCO) 1968; Freetown 1970; Tripoli 1972; Vientiane 1974; Kuala Lumpur 1975; FCO 1979; Sana'a 1981; Second Secretary Bridgetown 1985; m 1966 Audrey Lucy Dut (2s 1967, 1970).

Robertson, William Smellie; Third Secretary (Aid/Information) Harare since February 1996; born 5.3.66; FCO 1984; Dublin 1986; Riyadh 1989; On loan to the ODA 1992; Band B3; m 1986 Catherine Elizabeth McGregor (1d 1992; 1s 1995).

Robins, Terence Frederick; Second Secretary (Chancery)Strasbourg since May 1999; born 15.10.66; FCO 1989; Vice-Consul Algiers 1991; Victoria 1995; Band C4; m 1994 Wassila Kerri.

Robinson, David John; FCO since January 1988; born 27.2.45; Army 1962-85; Moscow 1985; Baghdad 1986; Band B3; m 1976 Pauline Reed.

Robinson, Deborah; Tel Aviv since February 1996; born 20.4.58; FCO 1989; Maputo 1990; Algiers 1994; Band A2.

Robinson, Janice Kathleen; Jerusalem since September 1999; born 28.9.56; FCO 1995; Bonn 1997; Band A2.

Robinson, Julia; UKMIS New York since January 2000; born 24.9.50; FCO 1995; The Hague 1996; Band A2.

Robinson, Julie Anne; FCO since September 1995; (née Whitehead); born 2.8.63, FCO 1984; Washington 1985; Bahrain 1988; FCO 1991; SUPL 1993; Band B3.

Robinson, Michael John; Counsellor (Regional Affairs) Budapest since November 2000; born 19.12.46; Third Secretary FCO 1968; Language Student 1969; Third later Second Secretary Moscow 1970; Second later First Secretary (Inf) Madrid 1972; First Secretary FCO 1977; CSCE Madrid 1980; First Secretary and Head of Chancery Madrid 1981; SUPL with OECD Paris 1982; Deputy Head of Delegation, UKDEL UNESCO, Paris 1985; First Secretary FCO 1986 (Counsellor 1990); Deputy Head of Mission and Consul-General Belgrade 1990; Counsellor on CDA at Chatham House 1994; Deputy Governor Gibraltar 1995; FCO 1999; m 1971 Anne Jamieson Scott (2d 1974, 1987; 2s 1977, 1983).

Robinson, Philip Andrew; First Secretary (Management) Beijing since July 2001; born 18.9.51; FCO 1970; Warsaw 1973; Jedda 1974; FCO 1977; Wellington 1978; Islamabad 1980; FCO 1982; Johannesburg 1985; Moscow 1987; (Second Secretary 1988); Second Secretary FCO 1991; HM Consul Hong Kong 1996; Band D6; m 1972 Elizabeth Andrina Mathieson Riding (2d 1976, 1980).

Robinson, Susan Patricia; Gibraltar since July 1995; born 6.11.47; FCO 1979; Paris 1980; Helsinki 1982; Bridgetown 1986; FCO 1989; Band B3.

Robinson, William; Dublin since February 2000; born 26.11.44; RAF Regiment 1962; Islamabad 1987; Moscow 1991; Pretoria 1992; Amman 1996; Band C4; m 1966 Cynthia Margaret Pugh, (2s 1966, 1969).

Robson, Elizabeth Carol; Counsellor (Political) Stockholm since August 1996; born 14.1.55; FCO 1977; Latin America Floater 1981; FCO 1982; Moscow 1984; Second Secretary FCO 1985; Second later First Secretary (Chancery) UKMIS Geneva 1988; Counsellor FCO 1993.

Roche, Claire Louise; Floater Duties since August 1998; born 17.3.72; FCO 1991; Warsaw 1995; Band B3.

Roche, Shaun Martin; Nairobi since April 2001; born 23.1.68; FCO 1992; Band C4; m2001 Rebecca Louise York.

Rock, Gail Denise (née Purvis); SUPL since June 1993; born 26.6.56; FCO 1978; Mexico 1979; Rome 1981; FCO 1984; Islamabad 1987; FCO 1988; Tokyo 1990; Band B3; mDereck Anthony Rock.

Rodemark, Janet Mary; SUPL since July 1999; born 28.5.65; FCO 1988; Islamabad 1992; Second Secretary FCO 1996; Band C4; m 1993 Timothy John Colley (1s 1997, 1d 1999).

Rodgers, Catherine Mary; FCO since November 1996; born 18.4.46; FCO 1965; Resigned 1968; FCO 1990; SUPL 1993; UKMIS New York 1995; Band A2; m 1968 James Patrick Rodgers (2d 1970, 1972 1s 1975).

Roe, Kirstie Gordon; FCO since October 1997. born 25.8.46; WRNS 1965-73; FCO 1974; New Delhi 1976; Hanover 1979; Bonn 1980; FCO 1982; Colombo 1985; Bucharest 1988 (Second Secretary 1991); On secondment to MOD 1992; Full-time Language Training; Temporary duty Belgrade 1997; Deputy Head of Mission Riga 1994.

Rogan, Janet Elizabeth; Deputy Head of Mission Sarajevo since February 1998; born 19.12.62; FCO 1986; Language Training 1988; Language Training Hong Kong 1989; Second later First Secretary (Chancery) Peking 1991; on loan to Cabinet Office 1994; First Secretary FCO 1995.

Rogers, David Alan; Counsellor FCO since December 1996; born 16.5.49; FCO 1971; Copenhagen 1974; Second Secretary 1975; Second later First Secretary FCO 1978; Jakarta 1981; First Secretary Brunei 1983; First Secretary FCO 1985; First Secretary (Chancery) Islamabad 1988; First Secretary FCO 1991; First Secretary (Political) Muscat 1993; First Secretary (Chancery/Economic) Dubai 1995; m 1989 Julie Anne Gardiner (1d 1990; 2s 1992, 1994).

Rogers, Diana Caroline; SUPL since November 2001; born 30.7.74; FCO 1998; World-wide Floater 2000; Band B3.

Rogers, Michael Roy; SUPL since August 2000; born 14.12.48; FCO 1967; Pretoria/Cape Town 1976; Tunis 1973; Bridgetown 1975; FCO 1978; Bahrain 1981; Wellington 1984; Resigned 1989; Reinstated 1990; Second Secretary FCO 1990; Second Secretary (Management) JMO New York 1995; m 1970 Elaine Anne Stewart (2s 1980, 1986).

Roissetter, Frederick Charles; FCO since June 1998; born 9.10.50; Army 1966-77; FCO 1978; Cabinet Office 1979-81; Paris 1982; FCO 1984; Third later Second Secretary Tel Aviv 1989; FCO 1992; Athens 1995; m 1979 Kay Jacqueline (2d 1981, 1984; 1s 1986).

Rolt, Colette; FCO since February 2001; born 10.8.71; FCO 1989; Washington 1997; Band C4.

Ronchetti, Paul Anthony; FCO since September 1982; born 7.4.51; FCO 1969; Washington 1972;

Africa Floater 1975; Port of Spain 1977; Baghdad 1979; Band B3.

Rooney, Kay (née Smith); SUPL since July 1998; born 1.7.68; FCO 1990; Vienna 1993; FCO 1996; Vice-Consul Frankfurt 1996; Band B3; m2000 Michael Rooney.

Rooney, Sean Michael; Düsseldorf since June 2000; born 17.2.72; FCO 1991; UKDEL Vienna 1995; Dhaka 1996; Band B3; m2000 Kay Smith.

Roper, Martyn Keith; First Secretary (Economic) OECD Paris since July 1999; born 8.6.65; FCO 1984; Tehran 1986; Maputo 1988; Vice-Consul Kuwait 1990; Third Secretary (Pol/Aid) Karachi 1993; FCO 1993; Band D6; m 1989 Elisabeth Melanie Harman Watson (1s 1992, 1d 1995).

Roper, Neil Gregson; Second Secretary (Technical Management) Pretoria since August 2000; born 27.11.65; FCO 1987; Madrid 1993; FCO 1995; Band C4.

Roscoe, Helen Margaret; Second Secretary (Management) Berlin since March 2001; born 25.7.67; FCO 1987; Oslo 1989; Lagos 1992; FCO 1995; Band C4.

Rose, Philip Edmond; First Secretary FCO since January 1994; born 12.12.63; FCO 1987; Language Training 1988; Language Training Hong Kong 1989. Second Secretary (Commercial) Peking 1994.

Roskilly, Karen Elizabeth; SUPL since May 1998; born 18.10.65; FCO 1990; Amsterdam 1991; Gibraltar 1994; Band B3; m 1995 Antonio Gonzalez Saugar (1s 2000).

Ross, Barry Thomas; FCO since August 1994; born 22.8.65; FCO 1985; Tokyo 1987; FCO 1990; SUPL 1991; FCO 1993; SUPL 1993; Band B3.

Ross, Carne William; First Secretary FCO since May 1995; born 24.8.66; FCO 1989; Third later Second Secretary (Political) Bonn 1992.

Ross, William Lawson; First Secretary (Commercial) Nicosia since June 2000; born 13.9.53; FCO 1973; UKMIS New York 1975; CG New York 1977; Tunis 1978; Kinshasa 1981; FCO 1984; Nassau 1985; Warsaw 1988; FCO 1991; (Second Secretary 1993); HM Consul and Second Secretary (Comm) Al Khbar 1995; FTLT 2000; Band C5; m 1978 Mary Margaret Delaney (1d 1980; 1s 1982).

Ross, Yolanda Marie; Bucharest since December 1998; born 16.5.69; FCO 1988; Buenos Aires 1993; FCO 1997; FCO 1998. Band A2.

Ross McDowell, Amanda; (née Ross); Vice Consul (Commercial) Sydney since June 1999; born 25.11.62; FCO 1981; 10 Downing St. 1985; Cape Town 1988; Zurich 1991; Second Secretary FCO 1994; Second Secretary (Commercial) Addis Ababa 1997; m 1987 Christopher McDowell (1d 1990; 1s 1992).

Rossiter, Lynne; Floater duties since September 1995; born 10.8.50; FCO 1990; Tel Aviv 1992; Band A2.

Rothery, James Peter; FCO since September 1985; (Second Secretary 1993); born 15.4.51; FCO 1975; Masirah 1977; Washington 1982; Band D6; m 1996 Agnes Maria Smith.

Rous, Matthew James; First Secretary (Commercial) Tokyo since January 1998; born 29.6.64; FCO 1991; Full-time Language Training SOAS 1992; Full-time Language Training Peking 1993; Second later First Secretary (Chancery) Peking 1994; m 1989 Beryl Ann Scott; (2d 1992, 1998; 1s 1994).

Rouse, Philip Terence, MBE (1976); HM Ambassador Ulaanbaatar since December 2001; born 13.10.43; Ministry of Aviation 1960; MOD 1966; FO (later FCO) 1967; Bogotá 1969; Singapore 1973; Saigon 1973; FCO 1975; Bahrain 1979; Asunción 1981; Second Secretary FCO 1985; First Secretary, Resident Representative Castries 1990; First Secretary FCO 1995; Deputy Head of Mission Kampala 1997; m 1968 Janice Eileen Williamson (3s 1971, 1974, 1978).

Rousseau, Jenifer Lesley (née Hill); Paris since December 1986; born 9.7.60; FCO 1983; Kabul 1984; FCO 1986; Band A2; m 1988 Frank Stephane Frederick Rousseau.

Rowbottom, Major Kenneth John; Queen's Messenger since 1988; born 4.3.47; HM Forces 1966-86.

Rowe, David Ian; FCO since November 1992; born 16.6.66; FCO 1985; Addis Ababa 1987; Bucharest 1991; Band C4; m 1993 Nancy Elizabeth Vince.

Rowe, Elizabeth Jane; Floater Duties since January 2001; born 19.1.71; FCO 1997; Sarajevo 1998; Band A2.

Rowe, Victoria Helen (née Goodwin); Vice-Consul Geneva since July 2000; FCO 1995; Band C4; m 1996 Richard David Rowe.

Rowett, Caroline Sarah; FCO since September 1999; born 16.9.58; FCO 1990; Jakarta 1992; Paris 1996; Band C4; m 1992 Joseph Spurgeon.(1d 1998).

Rowland, Keith Irving; Attaché (Management) Abuja since March 2001; born 9.11.46; Royal Navy 1963-88; Islamabad 1988; Moscow 1992; New York 1993; FCO 1996; Band B3; m 1971 Helena Sloan (1s 1972).

Rowlands, Jane Ellen; Third Secretary (Management) and Vice-Consul Ashgabat since August 2001; born 16.3.67; FCO 1987; Mexico City 1989; Seoul 1993; Third Secretary FCO 1997.

Rowlandson, Peter Roderick Saxby; FCO since January 1997; born 22.9.49; FCO 1970; Georgetown 1972; FCO 1976; Brussels 1978; Moscow 1981; FCO 1982; Brussels 1984; Madrid

1985; New Delhi 1988; FCO 1991; Dhaka 1995; Band B3; m(1) 1973 Nancy Lee Townsend (1d 1974); (2) 1989 Jillian Roberts (1s 1990; 1d 1992).

Rowney, Michael Ernest, MBE (1991); First Secretary Security Officer Moscow since June 1998; born 23.6.53; FCO 1972; Warsaw 1975; Kinshasa 1976; Hamilton 1979; Bahrain 1982; FCO 1985; Vice-Consul Monrovia 1988; Lisbon 1991; FCO 1994.

Rowswell, Claire; FCO since October 1988; born 13.1.55; FCO 1979; Quito 1979; UKREP Brussels 1981; Moscow 1984; FCO 1985; Mexico City 1986; Band B3.

Rowton, Alastair Clifford; FCO Since January 1998; born 28.11.46; FCO 1979; Gaborone 1981; FCO 1982; BGWRS Darwin 1984; FCO 1986; Second Secretary Budapest 1994; Band C4; m 1976 Jean Margaret Cowie (2d 1982, 1986).

Royal, Caroline Patricia; Sana'a since June 1998; born 22.1.57; MOD 1973; FCO 1990; Lisbon 1992; FCO 1995; Band A2.

Royle, Catherine Jane; First Secretary (EU/Economic) Dublin since July 1997; born 17.8.63; FCO 1986; Third later Second Secretary (Chancery) Santiago 1988; First Secretary FCO 1991; m 1991 Marcelo Enrique Camprubi Valledor (1s 2000).

Rudge, Peter Alan; Second Secretary (Political) Rome since September 2001; born 5.9.73; Second Secretary FCO 1999; Band C4.

Runacres, Mark Alastair; Counsellor (Economic) UKMIS New York since June 1999; born 19.5.59; FCO 1981; Third later Second Secretary New Delhi 1983; Second later First Secretary FCO 1986; First Secretary (Chancery) Paris 1991; First Secretary FCO 1995; On loan to the DTI 1998; m 1989 Shawn Reid.

Ruse, Lynne Elaine (née Gerrish); FCO since October 1995; born 15.5.58; FCO 1988; Paris 1991; Band A2; m 1996 Howard Michael Ruse.(1d 1998)

Russell, Andrew John; Second later First Secretary later Counsellor FCO since April 1987; born 12.8.48; FO (later FCO) 1967; Bonn 1972; Berlin 1973; FCO 1975; Second Secretary Vienna 1982; m 1972 Marilyn Elizabeth Turp (2d 1974, 1984; 1s 1982).

Russell, Gerard Simon Joseph; Consul (Political) Jerusalem since September 1998; born 11.7.73; FCO 1995; Full Time Language Training (Arabic) 1996; Cairo 1997; Band C4.

Russell, Joan; Kingston since January 2000; born 4.5.43; FCO 1986; UKMIS Vienna 1988; Lima 1992; Madrid 1995; Band B3.

Russell, Malcolm Arthur; Suva since November 1999; born 27.2.54; FCO 1973; Kuala Lumpur 1976; FCO 1980; Frankfurt 1983; Tehran 1985; Third Secretary Nuku'alofa 1988; Peking 1989;

FCO 1992; Band C4; m 1982 Jean Frances Matthews (1d 1987; 1s 1992).

Russell, Neil; SUPL since April 2001; born 18.2.69; FCO 1989; Abu Dhabi 1992; Brasilia 1994; Full time language training 1998; Third Secretary (Information) Warsaw 1998; Band B3; m 1993 Trudie Helen Denby (1d 1995).

Russell, Roger; FCO since June 1999; born 14.5.54; FCO 1970; Brussels 1983; FCO 1986; Canberra 1989; Band C4; m 1983 Teresa Mary McGeough.

Rutherford, John; Regional Director, Invest in Britain Bureau Hong Kong since September 1998; born 2.1.59; FCO 1978; Nairobi 1980; Jedda (later Riyadh) 1983; Second Secretary Warsaw 1990; (Second Secretary 1988); Los Angeles 1994; m 1989 Karen Chapman; (1s 1991).

Rutherford, Karen (née Chapman); SUPL since July 1992; born 19.2.59; FCO 1977; Rome 1979; Floater duties 1982; FCO 1986; Warsaw 1990; Band B3; m 1989 John Rutherford; (1s 1991).

Ryan, Elizabeth Jane Karen; Bratislava since November 1999; born 2.2.61; FCO 1998; m 1993 Chaeil ok-soon (1d 1994); Band B3.

Ryan, Robert Christopher; FCO since January 2001; born 21.2.72; HCS 1991; FCO 1994; New Delhi 1997; Band A2.

Rycroft, Matthew John; First Secretary (Political) Washington since September 1998; born 16.6.68; FCO 1989; Third Secretary UKDIS Geneva 1990; Third later Second Secretary (Chancery) Paris 1991. First Secretary FCO 1995; m 1997 (2d 1998, 2000).

Ryde, John; First Secretary FCO since August 1987; born 26.10.50; Third later Second Secretary FCO 1973; Language Student 1976; MECAS 1977; Second Secretary (Comm) Sana'a 1978; First Secretary Tripoli 1980; FCO 1983; First Secretary (UN/Press) UKMIS Geneva 1986; Band D6; m 1974 Christine May Rydzewska (1s 1979).

Ryder, Martin Frederick John, LVO (1996); First Secretary Management Berlin since February 1997; born 29.5.41; Army 1959-68; Ministry of Defence 1968; FCO 1969; Ankara 1972; Nuku'alofa 1975; UKDEL NATO Brussels 1976; Second Secretary FCO 1979; Language Student 1980; Second Secretary and Consul Ankara 1981; Assistant Trade Commissioner, later Trade Commissioner Hong Kong 1985; First Secretary FCO 1989; First Secretary (Management) Bangkok 1992; First Secretary Energy Washington 1997; m 1973 Susan Mary Longhurst (2s 1978, 1986; 1d 1990).

Ryder, Michael; First Secretary FCO since July 1996; born 13.11.53; FCO 1984; Second later First Secretary BMG Berlin 1986; First Secretary FCO 1988; First Secretary UKREP Brussels 1993.

S

Sadler, Stuart Roger; Karachi since May 2001; born 22.12.70; FCO 1990; Pretoria 1994; Moscow 1998; Band B3.

Sagar, Rebecca Ann; Second Secretary (Political) Islamabad since May 2001; born 9.9.76; FCO 1999; Band C4.

Sage, Kelly Jane; MVO (1996); SUPL since April 2000; born 29.1.68; FCO 1989; The Hague 1992; Third Secretary (Visits/Information) Warsaw 1994; Third Secretary FCO 1996; Band B3.

Sainty, Christopher James; First Secretary (Political/EU) Madrid since March 2000; born 29.3.67; FCO 1989; Language Training FCO 1991; Third later Second Secretary (Chancery) New Delhi 1992; First Secretary FCO 1996; Language Training FCO 1999; Band D6; m 1993 Sarah Helen Norris. (1s 1996, 2d 1998, 2000).

Salkeld, Peter Charles; FCO since May 1993; born 31.8.53; FCO 1969; Bonn 1980; FCO 1983; New Delhi 1989; m 1978 Carol Elizabeth Anne Dent (2s 1985, 1988).

Salt, Richard André; on secondment to Petrofac UK Ltd since May 2000; born 30.7.62; FCO 1980; UKREP Brussels 1983; Algiers 1985; Banjul 1988; FCO 1990; New Delhi 1993; Second Secretary (Commercial) Damascus 1996; Band C4; m 1992 Karen Baden Davies (1s 1995).

Salter, Leigh Audra; Floater duties since September 1998; born 16.3.69; FCO 1988; Wellington 1991; Windhoek 1994; Band B3.

Salvesen, Charles Hugh; FCO since August 2000; born 10.9.55; Second Secretary FCO 1982; First Secretary BMG Berlin 1984; First Secretary Bonn 1985; FCO 1988; Head of Political Section Buenos Aires 1993; Counsellor and Deputy High Commissioner Wellington 1996; m 1983 Emilie Maria Ingenhousz (2s Twins, 1987; 1d 1990 (dec'd 1995)).

Sambrook, Claire; UKREP Brussels since January 1999; born 26.1.66; FCO 1996; Kigali 1997; Band A2.

Sanda, Lorraine (née Rose); SUPL since June 1997; born 18.10.63; FCO 1982; Warsaw 1984; Caracas 1986; FCO 1990; (Second Secretary 1994); m 1987 Manuel Sanda Casal (1s 1998).

Sanderson, Michael John; First Secretary FCO since July 1995; born 21.1.48; FO 1967; Cairo 1972; FCO 1976; UKMIS New York 1979; Second Secretary (Chancery) Oslo 1984; Second Secretary FCO 1988; First Secretary Hong Kong 1993; Band C5; m 1976 Pauline Elizabeth Tippett (1d 1979; 1s 1982).

Sandover, William Geoffrey; First Secretary FCO since July 1996; born 7.4.55; FCO 1979; Third later Second Secretary UKMIS Vienna 1981; First Secretary FCO 1984; First Secretary (Chancery) Dublin 1986; First Secretary FCO 1987; First Secretary (Chancery) Buenos Aires 1992; Band

D6; m(1) 1981 Sharman Winsome Knight (diss 1985) (2) 1992 Beatrice Martin.

Sargeant, Ian Charles; First Secretary and HM Consul Manila since November 1998; born 24.4.52; FCO 1971; Language Student SOAS 1974; Bangkok 1975; LA Floater 1979; FCO 1982; Manila 1986; Deputy Economic Adviser Berlin 1990; Vice Consul (Comm) Düsseldorf 1991; FCO 1995; m 1988 Mari Grace Eddun (diss 1999) (1d 1989).

Sattaur, Christopher; Amman since April 2000; born 25.4.71; FCO 1991; Athens 1996; Band A2.

Saunders, Caroline Ann; Deputy Consul General Brisbane since October 2000; born 28.9.60; FCO 1983; New Delhi 1986; FCO 1988; Third Secretary (Chancery) Kuala Lumpur 1991; Second Secretary FCO 1995; Second Secretary British Trade International 1998; m 1989 Rhodri Christopher Kevin Meredith (1s 1993; 1d 1996).

Saunders, Katharine Angela Margaret; First Secretary FCO since September 1974; born 16.10.38; FO (later FCO) 1963; Second Secretary Peking 1971; First Secretary Hong Kong 1972; Principal Research Officer (Band D6); m 1976 Leonard Michael Peter Kaye.

Saunders, Kirsten Mary Margaret; Bangkok since January 1997; born 8.10.68; FCO 1995; Band A2.

Saunders, Liane; First Secretary (Chancery) Ankara since July 2000; born 24.10.68; FCO 1993; Full-time Language Training FCO 1994; Full-time Language Training Cairo 1995; Second Secretary Kuwait 1996; Band D6; m 1994 Andrew Stewart Smith (1d 1998).

Saunderson, Lesley Margaret; On loan to DfID since June 1998; born 18.11.69; FCO 1991; New Delhi 1993; St Petersburg 1994; Dar es Salaam 1997.

Savage, Francis (Frank) Joseph, CMG (1996), OBE (1989), LVO (1986); Governor of the British Virgin Islands since July 1998; born 8.2.43; Passport Office 1961; FO 1966; Cairo 1967; Washington 1971; Vice-Consul Aden 1973; Second Secretary FCO 1975; Vice-Consul (Comm) later Consul (Comm) Düsseldorf 1978; First Secretary (Management) and HM Consul Peking 1982; First Secretary (Consular) Lagos and HM Consul Republic of Benin (non-resident)1987; First Secretary later Counsellor FCO 1990; Governor Montserrat 1993; Counsellor FCO 1997 (Comprehensive Spending Review Team); m 1966 Veronica Mary McAleenan (2s 1969, 1971).

Savill, Margaret Ann; First Secretary FCO since April 1995; born 6.4.46; FCO 1968; Third Secretary Georgetown 1972; Geneva 1975; Second Secretary Rio de Janeiro 1975; FCO 1980; Second later First Secretary (Inf) Berne 1984; First Secretary FCO 1989; First Secretary (Inf/Man) UKDEL Nato Brussels 1993.

Saville, John Donald William; Deputy Head of Mission Havana since July 2000; born 29.6.60; FCO 1981; Third later Second Secretary Jakarta

1983; FCO 1985; Second later First Secretary (Inf) Warsaw 1988; First Secretary FCO 1991; First Secretary (Political) Vienna 1995; FCO 1998; FTLT 2000; Band D6; m 1992 Fabiola Moreno de Alboran (1d 1993).

Sawers, Robert John, CMG (1996); HM Ambassador Cairo since September 2001; born 26.7.55; FCO 1977; Sana'a 1980; SUPL 1980; Language Training 1981; Second Secretary Damascus 1982; First Secretary FCO 1984 (PS to Minister of State 1986); First Secretary Pretoria/Cape Town 1988; Head of European Union Department (Presidency) 1991; Principal Private Secretary to the Secretary of State for Foreign and Commonwealth Affairs 1993; Career Development Attachment at Harvard 1995; Counsellor (Pol/Mil) Washington 1996; Foreign Affairs Private Secretary to the Prime Minister 1999; m 1981 Avril Helen Shelley Lamb (2s 1983, 1985; 1d 1987).

Say, Sarah Gillian; UKREP Brussels since January 2000; born 2.4.59; FCO 1986; Paris 1988; Washington 1991; Havana 1993; FCO 1994; Mexico City 1996; T/D Helsinki 1999; Band B3.

Sayle, Lorraine Mary; Lilongwe since December 1998; born 22.9.72; FCO 1990; UKDEL NATO Brussels 1994; Lilongwe 1996; SUPL 1998; Band A2; (1s 1998).

Scaddan, Simon Mansfield; British High Commissioner Port Moresby since February 2000; born 22.1.44; FO 1962; Sofia 1966; Zomba 1967; Karachi 1970; Lahore 1971; Karachi 1972; FCO 1974; Durban 1977; Second Secretary Kuala Lumpur 1979; FCO 1982; Aden 1985; First Secretary (Aid) Nairobi 1986; First Secretary Islamabad 1988; First Secretary FCO 1992; Deputy High Commissioner Calcutta 1996; m 1970 Frances Anne Barker (Diss 2001) (1s 1972; 1d 1973); ptnr, Pablo Ganguli.

Scales, Martin Milner; Vice-Consul Oslo since April 2001; born 31.1.65; FCO 1997; Band B3

Scanlon, Edward Joseph; Istanbul since November 1999; born 18.5.70; HCS 1990-1993; FCO 1993; Peking 1995; Band B3.

Scantlebury, Ian Patrick; Second Secretary Lima since August 1997; born 12.9.60; FCO 1978; Georgetown 1981; SEA Floater 1985; Calcutta 1987; FCO 1991; Third Secretary (Commercial) Accra 1994.

Scarborough, Bryan David; Consul (Commercial) Shanghai since May 1999; born 19.1.45; FCO 1973; Warsaw 1975; Douala 1976; Delhi 1979; Freetown 1983; FCO 1985; Lilongwe 1988; Third Secretary (Comm) Jakarta 1991; FCO 1995; m1969 Kathleen Mary Johnston (1s 1980).

Scarborough, Vernon Marcus; Resident Deputy High Commissioner, Tarawa, Kiribati since March 2001; born 11.2.40; Passport Office 1958; CRO 1961; Dacca 1962; CRO 1964; Karachi 1965; Vice-Consul Brussels 1969; Third Secretary Banjul 1971; Second Secretary FCO 1977; Second

Secretary (Comm) Muscat 1980; First Secretary (Admin) Kuala Lumpur 1984; First Secretary FCO 1987; Consul (Commercial) Auckland 1990; Deputy Head of Mission Suva and concurrently HM Ambassador (non-resident) to Palau, Micronesia and the Marshall Islands 1995; T/D Suva 2000; m 1966 Jennifer Bernadette Keane (3d 1970, 1972, 1980).

Scarratt, Claire Rebecca; Stockholm since January 2000; born 7.2.75; HCS 1997; FCO 1999. Band A2.

Schofield, Nigel; Floater duties since March 2000; born 17.4.70; FCO 1990; Bonn 1993; FCO 1993; Lagos 1994; on loan to DTI; Band B3; m 1994 Rebecca Imogen.

Scholes, Elizabeth Marian; First Secretary (Chancery) Tel Aviv since September 1996; born 28.4.66; FCO 1987; Third later Second Secretary (Chancery) Buenos Aires 1990; Second later First Secretary FCO 1993; m 1998 Richard Wrigley.

Schroeder, Dominic Sebastian; First Secretary (Commercial) Berlin since August 1997; born 13.11.65; FCO 1988; Third later Second Secretary Kinshasa 1989; Second Secretary FCO 1992; Second Secretary UKMIS New York 1993; Second later First Secretary FCO 1994; m 1997 Susan Caroline Kerr (1s 2001).

Schroeder, Susan Caroline (née Kerr); on loan to the DTI since December 1996; born 9.4.69; FCO 1988; Prague 1990; Rabat 1992; FCO 1994; Band B3; m 1997 Dominic Sebastian Schroeder (1s 2001).

Schulz, Lynne; SUPL since May 2001; born 16.11.66; HCS 1997; SUPL 1998; FCO 2000; Band A2; m 1994 Sven Schulz (1s 1998).

Schumann, Carol Ann (née Hill); Third Secretary (Finance) Bonn since August 1997; born 18.7.46; FCO 1976; Paris 1977; FCO 1980; Washington 1981; FCO 1987; The Hague 1988; Bonn 1991; SUPL 1996; Band C4; m 1980 Jürgen Klaus Dieter Schumann (2s 1981, 1983).

Scott, Gavin David; On loan to DTI since January 2001; born 26.6.60; FCO 1978; Paris 1981; Beirut 1983; Washington 1985; FCO 1988; Third Secretary (Commercial) Bogotá 1991; Third Secretary FCO 1995; Bridgetown 1995; Band C4; m 1992 Julie Ann Owen.

Scott, George; Tirana since November 1999; born 11.10.56; FCO 1981; E Berlin 1982; Luxembourg 1984; Lagos 1986; FCO 1991; Kigali 1995; Band C4.

Scott, Keith John; on loan to DTI since October 1999; born 19.2.69; FCO 1991; Abuja 1994; Second Secretary FCO 1995; SUPL 1998; Band C4.

Scott, Naomi Anita; SUPL since February 1997; born 25.9.68; FCO 1990; UKMIS Geneva 1995; Band A2; m 1997 John Richard Dunne

Scrafton, Douglas, CMG, FCO since May 2000; born 14.7.49; FCO 1967; UKDEL Brussels 1970; Kampala 1973; Mbabane 1975; FCO 1977; Jedda 1980; Second Secretary Riyadh 1982; Cairo 1984; Second later First Secretary FCO 1985; on loan to Cabinet Office 1987; First Secretary and Head of Chancery Ottawa 1989; First Secretary FCO 1993; HM Ambassador Sana'a 1995; FCO 1997; Ambassador to the Democratic Republic of the Congo 1998; m 1975 Caroline Patricia Collison (1s 1976; 1d 1977).

Scroby, Gary Vance; Deputy Head of Mission Managua since March 1999; born 15.7.69; FCO 1988; UKREP Brussels 1989; Floater Duties 1992; FCO 1994; Band B3; m 1999 Lisa Marie Dowell (1d 2000).

Seaby, Paul Robert; Consul Tehran since April 1999; born 24.5.56; FCO 1975; Warsaw 1978; Masirah 1978; Ottawa 1979; Floater duties 1982; Port Moresby 1984; FCO 1987; Third Secretary (Commercial) Muscat 1991; Lusaka 1994; m 1984 Lynette Margaret Heffernan.

Sealy, Amanda Sarah (née Franklin); FCO since September 1999; born 3.1.59; FCO 1980; Peking 1982; Pretoria/Cape Town 1984; Warsaw 1986; FCO 1988; Windhoek 1991; Jakarta 1995; Band C4; m 1989 Dominic John Sealy (1s 1992; 1d 1995).

Seaman, Michael William; FTLT since August 2001; born 1.11.55; FCO 1975; Jakarta 1977; Bombay 1981; FCO 1984; Second Secretary (Chancery) The Hague 1988; Second Secretary FCO 1992; on loan to MOD 1992; First Secretary FCO 1994; Athens 1999; Band C5; m 1978 Jane Lesley Stockwell (2d 1984, 1987).

Seaman, Stephen James, MBE (1991); First Secretary (Commercial) Caracas since October 2000; born 4.12.55; DOT 1975; Copenhagen 1979; Salisbury 1980; DOT 1980; FCO 1982; Vice Consul Bucharest 1983; FCO 1986; Second Secretary & Deputy Head of Mission Monrovia 1988; Second Secretary (Commercial) Lilongwe 1991; Second Secretary (Management) Nicosia 1993; First Secretary FCO 1997; m 1980 Katherine Ann Barker (dec'd 1996).

Seamer, Helen Maria; SUPL since October 1989; born 25.11.60; FCO 1981; Cairo 1985; SUPL 1988; Amsterdam 1989; Band B3; m(1) 1984 Timothy John Unsworth (diss.); m(2) Raymond Clive Seamer.

Searight, Pauline Mabel; Kuala Lumpur since May 1996; born 27.6.55; FCO 1988; Banjul 1990; Karachi 1993; Band A2; m 1991 Graham Kenneth Denham.

Seaton, Andrew James; Head of China Hong Kong Department FCO since November 2000; born 20.4.54; FCO 1977; Third later Second Secretary Dakar 1979; Trade Commissioner (China) BTC Hong Kong 1981; First Secretary FCO 1987; Trade Counsellor BTC later Deputy Consul-General and Trade Counsellor Hong Kong

1995; m 1983 Helen Elizabeth Pott (3s 1989, 1992, 1995).

Seddon, Christine; FCO since August 1998; FCO 1988; Brasilia 1990; Wellington 1994; Band A2.

Seddon, David William; First Secretary (Commercial) Harare since April 1999; born 30.5.48; FO (later FCO) 1966; Bonn 1970; FCO 1971; Port of Spain 1973; Vila 1977; FCO 1981; Milan 1983; Vice-Consul later Consul (Comm/Admin/Cons) Douala 1987; Second Secretary FCO 1991; Kampala 1995; m 1972 Monica Elisabeth Josefina van Loon (1s 1976).

Seddon, Richard Charles Leslie; First Secretary Washington since April 1999; born 25.9.68; FCO 1992; Second Secretary (Political) New Delhi 1994; First Secretary FCO 1997; Band D6; m 1999 Alice Kim Fugate.

Sedwill, Mark Philip; FCO since December 1999; born 21.10.64; FCO 1989; Language Training 1990; Second Secretary Language Training Cairo 1991. Second Secretary (Political/External) Cairo 1992. First Secretary FCO 1994; First Secretary (Political) Nicosia 1998; m 1999 Sarah-Jane (née Lakeman).

Segar, Christopher Michael John; Counsellor Commercial Peking since May 1997; born 25.11.50; FCO 1973; Language Student MECAS 1974; Third later Second Secretary (Comm) Dubai 1976; First Secretary FCO 1979; First Secretary (Comm) and Head of Chancery Luanda 1984; First Secretary UKDEL Paris 1987; Counsellor Consul-General and Deputy Head of Mission Baghdad 1990 on loan to the MOD 1991; Counsellor Riyadh 1993.

Self, Andrew Paul; Second Secretary FCO since December 1998; born 2.4.64; FCO 1982; Hong Kong 1986; FCO 1988; Third Secretary (Inf) Sana'a since January 1992; Third Secretary FCO 1993; Tehran 1996; Band C4; m(1) 1987 Michele Carmichael Crouch (diss 1995), (2) 1997 Andrea Louise Carter (1s 1998).

Selvadurai, Samuel Dayalan; Second Secretary (KHF) Moscow since August 1995; born 1.10.70; FCO 1993; Full Time Language Training 1994; Band D6; m2000 Louise McCallum.

Senior, Major Michael Roger; Queen's Messenger since 1987; born 15.11.45; HM Forces 1964-87.

Setterfield, (James) Robert; Deputy Head of Mission Bratislava since October 2000; born 6.5.47; DSAO (later FCO) 1967; Bombay 1969; New Delhi 1971; FCO 1973; Second Secretary (Aid/Inf) Rangoon 1976; Assistant Secretary (Political) Vila 1980; Vice-Consul Stuttgart 1980; Vice-Consul (Commercial) Düsseldorf 1982; First Secretary FCO 1985; First Secretary (Chancery) Wellington 1987; FCO 1992; First Secretary Helsinki 1995; FTLT 2000; Band D6; m 1980 Margaret Jean McMahon (1s 1983, 1d 1985).

Seymour, Irene Frances; (née McDonagh) SUPL since September 1995; born 2.12.64; FCO 1984;

San José 1987; FCO 1990; Band A2; m 1991 Peter James Seymour.

Seymour, Peter James; First Secretary FCO since March 2001; born 10.2.62; FCO 1984; Second Secretary (Chancery and Inf) and Vice-Consul San José 1987; Second Secretary FCO 1989; SUPL 1990; First Secretary FCO 1991; Berlin 1995; First Secretary Vienna 1999; Band D6; m 1991 Irene Frances McDonagh.

Shackell, Robin John; Quito since October 1999; born 4.2.63; HCS 1983; FCO 1985; Vienna 1987; T/D Munich 1989; Doha 1990; Management Officer/Vice Consul La Paz 1991; FCO 1995; Band B3; m(1) 1991 Carol Plowman (diss), (2) 1994 Isabel Chavez-Bastos.

Shackleton, Richard David; Third Secretary (Commercial) Bogotá since May 1995; born 26.5.68; FCO 1990; Third Secretary (Political) UKMIS New York 1992; Band B3.

Shaikh, Farida; Third Secretary (Chancery) Singapore since July 1996; born 16.10.65; FCO 1990; Third Secretary (Chancery/Information) Harare 1992.

Shakespeare, Karen Marie; FCO since July 1992; born 25.10.70; Band A2.

Shand, Ian, lvo (2000); Second Secretary (Press/Public Affairs) Milan since June 1999; born 17.1.54; FCO 1973; Accra 1975; Munich 1979; FCO 1982; Bonn 1985; Islamabad 1988; FCO 1991; Language Training 1994; Santiago 1995; m 1975 Lyndsey Elizabeth Hall (2d 1983, 1985).

Shanmuganathan, Krishna; First Secretary (Political) Athens since September 2000; born 14.2.74; FCO 1995; Second Secretary (Political) Pretoria 1998; FCO 2000; Band D6.

Shannon, Keith; First Secretary FCO since July 1999; born 17.9.66; FCO 1988; Third Secretary (Aid/Commercial) Maputo 1991; Second Secretary (Technology) Paris 1995.

Shapcott, William James; SUPL since October 1999 - Counsellor to Dr Javier Solana, EU High Representative for the CFSP, Brussels; born 25.7.61; HM Forces 1983-88; Second Secretary FCO 1988; Second Secretary Bonn 1990; First Secretary FCO 1993; First Secretary Washington 1995 (Counsellor 1999); m 1986 Shelley Mary Harrison (twin s 2001).

Shapland, Anthony Gregory; FCO since July 1992; born 17.12.49; PRO (Band D6); FCO 1979; on loan to the Cabinet Office 1990; m(1) 1973 Margaret Elizabeth Moriarty (diss); m(2) 1982 Leonora Alexandra Hebden (1s 1983).

Sharp, David Stewart; Floater Duties since April 1995; born 19.1.71; FCO 1989; UKMIS New York 1992; Band A2.

Sharp, Gemma Goulding; Second Secretary Political Copenhagen since December 1998; born 7.8.72; Second Secretary FCO 1995; Band C4.

Sharp, James Frederick Bailey; New Delhi since October 2000; born 1.4.72; FCO 1994; SUPL 1998; Band A2; m 1998 Janice Sarah Smail.

Sharp, James Lyall; FCO since September 1998; born 12.4.60; Second Secretary FCO 1987; Language Training Cairo 1988; Second Secretary Cairo 1989; First Secretary FCO 1992; First Secretary UKDEL Vienna 1996; m 1992 Sara Essam el-Gammal.

Sharp, Janice Sarah (née Smail); FCO since March 2001; born 11.8.66; FCO 1987; SUPL 1994; FCO 1995; Second Secretary (Immigration) Tehran 1998; Band C4; m 1998 James Frederick Bailey Sharp.

Sharp, Jonathan Dinsdale; Second Secretary (Political) Lagos since August 2000; born 31.3.67; FCO 1988; Karachi 1990; Paris 1991; LA/Caribbean Floater 1994; FCO 1997; Third Secretary (Political) Tunis 1997; m 1995 Tracey Ennis.

Sharp, Paul John Gibson; Second Secretary FCO since April 1993; born 24.9.48; FCO 1967; New Delhi 1975; FCO 1976; Rome 1978; FCO 1981; Attaché Ankara 1981; FCO 1985; Attaché Moscow 1987; Second Secretary FCO 1989; Second Secretary Pretoria 1990; m(1)1969 Anita Tsang (2s 1972, 1976) (diss 1986), (2) 1996 J Tuckey.

Sharp, Richard; First Secretary Management New Delhi since June 1997; born 8.3.49; FO (later FCO 1967); Karachi 1971; Canberra 1972; Port Moresby 1974; Santiago 1975; Jakarta 1977; FCO 1980; Cairo 1984; Second Secretary (Admin) Moscow 1987; Second Secretary FCO 1990; Second Secretary and Vice-Consul Luanda 1993; m 1974 Patricia Anne Whitby (1s 1979; 1d 1983).

Sharpe, Jean Cynthia; obe (1994); Trade Commissioner Hong Kong since October 1998; born 18.10.47; CO 1964; DSAO 1965; The Hague 1970; Kingston 1973; FCO 1974; Dubai 1974; FCO 1975; Freetown 1978; JAO Brussels 1981; Second Secretary FCO 1984; on loan to DTI 1986; Second Secretary (Comm) Nairobi 1988; First Secretary and Consul Bangkok 1991; First Secretary FCO 1996.

Sharpe, Rosemary Helen; Counsellor Madrid since December 2000; born 11.3.56; Second Secretary FCO 1982; Second Secretary (Inf) New Delhi 1985; First Secretary UKREP Brussels 1987; First Secretary FCO 1988; First Secretary (Economic) Berlin 1991; First Secretary FCO 1996.

Sharpless, Fiona Ure (née McGowan); Dhaka since April 2001; born 23.2.65; FCO 1988; UKREP Brussels 1989; SUPL 1992; Kathmandu 1993; SUPL 1994; Lagos 1998; SUPL 1999; Band B3; m 1990 Kristian Sharpless (1d 1993, 1s 1995).

Sharpless, Kristian; Second Secretary (Commercial/Press and Public Affairs) Dhaka since April 2001; born 17.6.67; Dept of Employment 1985; FCO 1987; Brussels 1989;

Kathmandu 1992; FCO 1995; Lagos 1996; FCO 1999; Band C4; m 1990 Fiona Ure McGowan (1d 1993, 1s 1995).

Shaughnessy, Kevin John; Second Secretary (Commercial) Bahrain since April 1998; born 10.11.64; FCO 1983; Tehran 1986; Kingston 1988; Bonn 1991; Second Secretary FCO 1994; m 1997 Elizabeth Ann Churchill (2d 1998, 2001).

Shaw, Alan John; Prague since October 1999; born 9.6.66; FCO 1987; Washington 1989; Peking 1992; FCO 1995; Bangkok 1998; Band B3; m 1989 Claire Louise Morgan.

Shaw, Andrew William; FCO since February 1997; born 31.3.50; Band A2; m 1981 Ruth Heeps (2s 1984, 1989; 1d 1990).

Shaw, Claire Louise (née Morgan); FCO since May 1995; born 18.6.68; FCO 1987; Washington 1989; FCO 1992; Peking 1993; Band B3; m 1989 Alan John Shaw.

Shaw, Philip; First Secretary (Commercial) Paris since December 1999; born 22.5.45; CRO 1963; DSAO 1965; Khartoum 1966; Language Training 1969; Ulaanbaatar 1970; Nairobi 1973; FCO 1978; seconded to DTI 1980; São Paulo 1982; Brussels 1985; FCO 1990; Lisbon 1991; First Secretary FCO 1997; m (1) 1970 Christine Goodwin (diss) (1d 1974, 1s 1976); (2) 1992 Marthe Vercammen.

Shaw, Samantha; FCO since November 1999 born 31.3.67; Band A2.

Shaw, Sandra Heather; FCO since March 1992; born 7.9.43; Band A2.

Shaw, Sarah Elaine (née Gosling); SUPL since June 1997; born 29.7.69; FCO 1990; Bonn 1992; FCO 1994; Tehran 1994; FCO 1996; Band A2; m 1995 Andrew John Shaw.

Shead, Robert John; Second Secretary Guangzhou since November 1998; born 14.4.50; FCO 1969; Bonn 1973; Seoul 1976; FCO 1977; Paris 1978; Damascus 1982; FCO 1985; Damascus 1986; FCO 1987; Nairobi 1988; Second Secretary Manila 1992; FCO 1997; m(1) 1981 Carol Ann Bostock (diss 1987); (2) 1987 Fayha Sultan (1s 1987).

Shearing, Sally Louise; FCO since August 1995; born 20.4.66; FCO 1985; Budapest 1988; FCO 1990; Sofia 1992; Band A2.

Shearman, Martin James; FCO since May 1999; born 7.2.65; Third later Second Secretary FCO 1989; Language Training 1991; Full-time Language Training Tokyo 1992; Second Secretary (Commercial) Tokyo 1993; First Secretary (Commercial) Tokyo 1994; on loan to the DTI 1996; on loan to the Cabinet Office 1998; NATO Secretariat 1999; m 1996 Miriam Elizabeth Pyburn.

Shearman, Miriam Elizabeth (née Pyburn); SUPL since June 2001; born 11.6.65; FCO 1990; Full-time Language Training 1990; Tokyo 1992; APS/PUS 1996; FCO 1996; T/D UKRep Brussels

2000; FCO 2000; Band D6; m 1996 Martin James Shearman.

Sheikh, Soraya Zia; Brussels since April 2000; born 3.7.72; FCO 1998; Band A2.

Sheinwald, Sir Nigel Elton, KCMG (2001), CMG (1999); Permanent Representative UKREP Brussels since September 2000; born 26.6.53; FCO 1976; Moscow 1978; Second later First Secretary FCO 1979; First Secretary (Chancery) Washington 1983; First Secretary later Counsellor FCO 1987; Counsellor and Head of Chancery UKREP Brussels 1993; Head of News Department FCO 1995; Director FCO (European Union) 1998; m 1980 Julia Dunne (3s 1984, 1985, 1987).

Shelly, Simon Richard; FCO since December 1998; born 5.7.60; HM Customs and Excise 1981-83; FCO 1983; Kabul 1986; Paris 1988; FCO 1991; Ankara 1995; m 1991 Monique Marie Renée Le Roux (1d 1995, 1s 1996).

Shepherd, Sir John Alan, KCVO (2000), CMG (1989); Ambassador Rome since July 2000; born 27.4.43; Third Secretary CRO 1965; MECAS 1966; Second Secretary Amman 1968; Rome 1970; First Secretary FCO 1973; First Secretary (Econ) later Head of Chancery The Hague 1976; First Secretary later Counsellor and Head of Chancery UKRep EC Brussels 1980; Counsellor FCO 1985; HM Ambassador and Consul-General Bahrain 1988; Minister Bonn 1991; Director (Middle East/North Africa) FCO 1996; DUS (Non-Europe, Trade and Investment) 1997; m 1969 Jessica Mary Nichols (1d 1975).

Shepherd, Daniel James Owen; FCO since January 2001; born 5.11.71; FCO 1994; Language Training FCO 1995; Language Training Hanoi 1996; Second Secretary Hanoi 1997; Band D6.

Shepherd, Wendy Elizabeth; Peking since September 2000; born 3.7.71; OFFER 1993; Port of Spain 1997; FCO 1996; Band B3.

Sheppard, David Anthony; Second later First Secretary FCO since November 1995; born 6.7.51; HCS 1968; Hong Kong 1977; FCO 1980; Baghdad 1983; Tel Aviv 1986; FCO 1989 (Second Secretary 1992); Second Secretary Brussels 1993; Band D6; m 1988 Bonita Dorsman.

Sheppard, Jane Louise (née McMullin); Tel Aviv since April 2001; born 19.7.70; FCO 1997; Ottawa 1998; SUPL 2000; Band A2; m 1998 William John Crean.

Sheppard, Nicholas Ugo; First Secretary FCO since October 1998; born 2.6.56; DTI 1973; FCO 1974; UKDEL OECD Paris 1977; Islamabad 1980; FCO 1982; Aden 1983; Canberra 1986; Second Secretary FCO 1989; Second Secretary (Commercial) New Delhi 1992; Bucharest 1995.

Sherar, Paul Desmond; Second later First Secretary FCO since May 1995; born 24.2.53; FCO 1970; Brussels 1973; Africa Floater 1976; Georgetown 1978; FCO 1981; Vice-Consul

(Comm) BTDO New York 1986. Second Secretary (Commercial/Aid) Luanda 1991.

Sherman, Penelope Anne; Cape Town since March 2000; born 29.8.43; Tokyo 1971; Calcutta 1973; Jakarta 1975; Hanoi 1977; Rio de Janeiro 1978; FCO 1980; Algiers 1983; Nicosia 1987; FCO 1989; Harare 1990; New Delhi 1994; FCO 1998; Band B3.

Sherman, Sheila Ann (née Baker); FCO since April 1993; born 6.6.60; FCO 1984; Peking 1985; FCO 1988; Nicosia 1990; Band A2; m 1995 Christopher Sherman.

Sherrington, Simon Richard; SUPL since June 2000; born 27.5.55; FCO 1980; Language Training Kamakura 1982; Tokyo 1983; Second Secretary FCO 1987; Second Secretary (Chancery/Admin) Johannesburg 1987; Second Secretary FCO 1989; First Secretary on loan to the DTI 1994; Deputy Consul General Boston 1996; Band D6.

Shingler, Michael John; Consul (Commercial) Atlanta since September 1995; (First Secretary 1994); born 31.1.47; Post Office 1963; DSAO 1965; Manila 1969; Prague 1973; Dacca 1975; FCO 1979; Dar es Salaam 1981; FCO 1984; Consul (Comm) Casablanca 1984; FCO 1988; Consul (Man) Istanbul 1991; m 1969 Katina Janet Wall (1d 1972; 1s 1975).

Shipster, Michael David, OBE (1990); First Secretary, later Counsellor FCO since November 1994; born 17.3.51; Second later First Secretary FCO 1977; First Secretary (Chancery) Moscow 1981; First Secretary FCO 1983; New Delhi 1986; First Secretary (Chancery) Lusaka 1990; Consul Johannesburg 1991; m 1974 Jacquelynne Mann (2d 1981, 1982; 1s 1987).

Shivers, Marie Louise (née Stone); FCO since October 1999; born 27.8.74; FCO 1992; Singapore 1996; Band A2; m 1999 Gavin John Shivers.

Short, James Walter; Dhaka since September 1999; born 19.10.66; FCO 1986; Calcutta 1989; Shanghai 1991; Third Secretary Tehran 1994; FCO 1997; Band B3; m 1990 Stephanie Sanjukta Ghosh 1s 1998).

Short, Roger Guy, MVO (1971); Consul-General and Director of Trade Promotion Istanbul since April 2001; born 9.12.44; Third Secretary Commonwealth Office (later FCO) 1967; Third later Second Secretary Ankara 1969; First Secretary FCO 1974; Consul (Comm) Rio de Janeiro 1978; Head of Chancery Ankara 1981; Counsellor and Deputy Head of Permanent Under-Secretary's Department FCO 1984; Counsellor, Head of Chancery and Consul-General Oslo 1986; Counsellor FCO 1990; HM Ambassador Sofia 1994; Chief of Staff Sarajevo 1999; m 1971 Sally Victoria Taylor (2d 1978, 1982; 1s 1988).

Shorter, Hugo Benedict; Private Secretary to Minister of State since February 2000; born 11.8.66; FCO 1990; Second Secretary on attachment to ENA Paris 1992; Second, later First

Secretary (Political) UKDEL NATO Brussels 1994; FCO 1998.

Shott, Philip Nicholas; Counsellor Pretoria since November 2001; born 27.11.54; FCO 1980 (Second Secretary 1980); First Secretary Lagos 1983; First Secretary FCO 1986; First Secretary (Chancery) Nicosia 1987; First Secretary FCO 1991; First Secretary (Political) Lusaka 1994; First Secretary FCO 1997; m 1981 Lesley Ann Marsh (1s 1986, 1d 1987).

Shute, Christopher David; First Secretary FCO since March 2000; born 8.10.49; HMIT 1968; FCO 1969; Middle East Floater 1972; Lagos 1974; Cairo 1975; FCO 1979; Rome 1983; Second Secretary FCO 1986; Second Secretary (Comm) Warsaw 1987; Second Secretary FCO 1990; First Secretary (Chancery) Wellington 1995; FCO 1999; Band C5; m 1975 Peta Ann Dewhurst (2s 1987, 1990).

Sidnell, Gail Marilyn; Second Secretary (Commercial) Jakarta since January 1996; born 9.4.53; FCO 1974; Addis Ababa 1975; Monrovia 1977; Gibraltar 1981; FCO 1982; Prague 1983; FCO 1985; Nairobi 1989; FCO 1993; (Second Secretary 1994).

Silva, Ginny Anne (née Kesterton); Luxembourg since November 1994; born 9.7.64; Immig Service Heathrow 1985; FCO 1987; Seoul 1989; Band B3; m 1989 Ronie Silva.

Silverwood, Jane Mary; Muscat since April 1994; born 6.8.60; FCO 1985; Mexico City 1987; FCO 1991; T/D Montevideo 1993; Band B3.

Sime, Charles; First Secretary FCO since 1998; born 11.3.46; CO 1963; FCO 1965; Pretoria/Cape Town 1969; Warsaw 1972; Muscat 1974; FCO 1975; Kinshasa 1978; Perth 1981; FCO 1983; Second Secretary (Management) Dar es Salaam 1986; First Secretary FCO 1992; Istanbul 1995; m1968 Edith Gregg.

Simmons, Belinda-Jayne; Phnom Penh since January 1996; born 12.9.65; FCO 1988; Buenos Aires 1990; Band A2.

Simmons, Ian Paul; Counsellor Nairobi since April 1999; born 5.9.55; FCO 1983; Second Secretary (Inf) New Delhi 1987; First Secretary FCO 1989; Full-time Language Training Point Cook, Melbourne 1992; First Secretary (Political) Hanoi 1992; First Secretary (Regional Affairs) Bangkok 1993; FCO 1996.

Simmons, Timothy Michael John; Assistant Director FCO since June 1999; born 8.4.60; FCO 1982; Third Secretary later Second Secretary Warsaw 1985; First Secretary FCO 1987; First Secretary UKMIS Geneva 1993; seconded to Price Waterhouse Coopers MCS 1997; m 1989 Caroline Mary Radcliffe (2s 1990, 1993).

Simon, Susannah Kate; First Secretary (Political) Bonn since January 1999; born 7.6.64; Third later Second Secretary Bonn 1989; FCO 1988; Second

Secretary Almaty 1992; FCO 1994; m 1994 Mikhail Mnaidarovich Kubekov (1s 1996).

Simpson, Beverley Jayne; UKMIS New York since July 2000; born 11.6.70; FCO 1989; Floater Training 1991; Floater Duties 1992; FCO 1993; Stanley 1994; T/D Mostar 1995; Madras 1997; Band B3.

Simpson, Brian; Vice-Consul Budapest since September 1999; born 8.5.67; FCO 1986; Warsaw 1988; Lagos 1991; FCO 1995; Band B3.

Simpson, Georgina Felicity (née Little); SUPL since March 1999; born 23.2.64; FCO 1986; Language Training 1987; Second Secretary Amman 1989; SUPL 1991; Second Secretary (Comm/Econ/Political) Sana'a 1991; FCO 1994; m 1991 Dominic Mark Simpson.

Simpson, Gordon Grant; Deputy Consul-General and HM Consul (Commercial) San Francisco since September 1998; born 25.8.46; FO 1964; Peking 1968; Lisbon 1970; Ibadan 1972; FCO 1975; Bucharest 1978; Nairobi 1979; Lisbon 1982; Second Secretary FCO 1985; Second Secretary (Comm) Luanda 1987; Second Secretary (Immigration) Islamabad 1990; First Secretary FCO 1992; Deputy Consul-General Rio de Janeiro 1994; m 1970 Jenny Frances Parker (1d 1974; 2s 1975, 1982).

Simpson, Karen Frances (née Thomas); Lagos since June 1998; born 25.8.54; FCO 1975; Islamabad 1976; FCO 1978; UKRep Brussels 1979; Cairo 1982; FCO 1985; Lagos 1987; SUPL 1990; Dhaka 1994; SUPL 1997; Band B3; m 1981 Kenneth Simpson (1s 1990; 1d 1994).

Simpson, Louise Jane; Kampala since November 1998; born 24.6.66; FCO 1986; Lima 1988; SUPL 1990; FCO 1992; Moscow 1993; FCO 1996; Band B3.

Simpson, Scott; Lima since May 1999; born 28.3.70; FCO 1991; Bangkok 1995; Band B3.

Simpson, Timothy John; FCO since September 1998; born 14.9.60; FCO 1988; Band B3; Third Secretary (Political) Budapest 1994; Band B3; m 1985 Lise Margaret Finlay (3d 1986, 1992, 1995).

Sims, Lynda; FCO since September 1977; born 10.11.50; MOD 1968; FCO 1970; Kuala Lumpur 1973; Bucharest 1976; Band B3; m 1981 Richard Ian Taylor.

Sinclair, Fiona Louise; Third Secretary (Political) Zagreb since May 2000; born 13.1.71; FCO 1993; Full-time Language Training 1995; Third Secretary (Political) Strasbourg 1996; Band B3.

Sinclair, Rachel Elizabeth; FCO since August 1994; born 7.2.65; FCO 1984; Harare 1992; Band A2; m 1991 Alexander Field Douse.

Sinclair, Robert Nelson Gurney; on loan to DTI since November 1999; born 10.12.52; FCO 1972; Dacca 1975; Algiers 1978; E Berlin 1980; CG Berlin 1981; FCO 1984; Third later Second Secretary Jakarta 1987; FCO 1991; Second

Secretary (KHF) Sofia 1996; Band C4; m 1975 Diana Sawyer (1s 1986).

Singh, Mala; Buenos Aires since June 2000; born 1.1.73; FCO 1996; Band A2.

Singh, Tracey Michelle (née Chapman); Third Secretary (Immigration) Accra since January 2001; born 30.10.68; FCO 1988; New Delhi 1990; FCO 1994; Dubai 1996; SUPL 1999; FCO 2000; Band B3; m 1995 Jasminder Singh (1d 1999).

Singleton, Jean Patricia; SUPL since January 1990; born 10.3.49; FCO 1987; Band A2.

Sinkinson, Philip Andrew; First Secretary (Commercial) Lisbon since December 1996; born 7.10.50; Inland Revenue 1967; FCO 1970; Warsaw 1973; FCO 1974; East Berlin 1974; Rome 1975; FCO 1976; Rio de Janeiro 1978; Quito 1978; Prague 1979; FCO 1981; Blantyre 1982; Lilongwe 1985; FCO 1986; Second Secretary (Commercial) São Paulo 1991; Olympic Attaché Atlanta 1995; m 1971 Clare Maria Catherine Jarvis (1s 1974).

Sinton, William Baldie; OBE (1999); HM Ambassador La Paz since October 2001; born 17.6.46; Third Secretary FCO 1968; Third later Second Secretary (Comm) Prague 1970; Second later First Secretary UKDEL NATO Brussels 1973; First Secretary FCO 1977; First Secretary (Comm) Algiers 1981; First Secretary FCO 1985; HM Ambassador Panama City 1996; HM Ambassador Algiers 1999; m 1995 Jane S B Aryee.

Sisum, Thomas George; FCO since September 1999; born 16.10.73; Band C4.

Sizeland, Paul Raymond; Consul-General Shanghai since October 2000; born 19.2.52; FCO 1980; UKDEL NATO Brussels 1981; Doha 1985; Second Secretary FCO 1986; First Secretary (Chancery/Aid) Lagos 1988; Private Secretary to Chairman of EC Conference on Yugoslavia 1991; First Secretary later Counsellor FCO 1991; Deputy Head of Mission Bangkok 1996; m 1976 Vasantha Jesudasan (2d 1981, 1982).

Skidmore, Jonathan Richard Llywelyn; Second Secretary UKMIS Vienna since October 2001; born 6.1.70; FCO 1998; Band C4.

Skilton, Christopher Paul; Deputy High Commissioner Kampala since January 2001; born 7.4.54; Bonn 1974; Santiago 1976; FCO 1980; Buenos Aires 1983; Madrid 1986; Resigned 1991; Reinstated 1993; FCO 1993; Madrid 1996; FCO 1998; m 1978 Kathleen Jane (1d 1982; 1s 1980).

Skingle, Diana; Deputy Head of Mission Addis Ababa since February 2001; born 3.5.47; Commonwealth Office (later FCO) 1966; Kampala 1970; FCO 1972; Abidjan 1974; Vila 1975; Prague 1977; Casablanca 1979; Second Secretary FCO 1982; Second Secretary (Aid/Comm) Georgetown 1985; Second Secretary (Dev) Bridgetown 1986; First Secretary (Info) UKDEL NATO Brussels

1988; First Secretary FCO 1993; ptnr, Christopher John Marshall Carrington.

Skinner, Dawn Emma; Sarajevo since April 1997; born 18.5.65; FCO 1985; Prague 1987; UKREP Brussels 1989; Anguilla 1991; FCO 1993; Worldwide Floater 1995; SUPL 1996; Band A2.

Skinner, Gillian (née Smith); FCO since November 1988; (Second Secretary 1992); born 9.1.57; FCO 1976; SUPL 1978; Beirut 1980; SUPL 1980; Beirut 1982; FCO 1982; Brussels 1983; FCO 1984; Kinshasa 1987; Band B3; m (1) 1978 Colin Wynn Crorkin (diss 1991) (2s 1985, 1992), (2) 1996 Graeme John Skinner.

Skyring, Andrea; Dar es Salaam since March 1999; born 1.8.66; FCO 1998; Band A2.

Slade, Caroline Jane; Second Secretary FCO since November 1997; born 13.7.67. Second Secretary (Political) Helsinki 1994; Band C4.

Slater, Angela (née Caldwell); Second Secretary (Consular) New Delhi since January 2000; born 9.3.67; FCO 1986; Washington 1988; Floater Duties 1992; SUPL 1994; FCO 1994; SUPL 1999; Band C4; m 1998 David John Slater (1d 1999).

Slater, David John; Second Secretary (Commercial) New Delhi since July 1999; born 2.3.68; FCO 1987; Abu Dhabi 1989; Accra 1991; FCO 1995; Band C4; m 1998 Angela Caldwell (1d 1999).

Slater, Gina Michelle (née Lambert); Second Secretary FCO since March 1996; born 29.7.54; FCO 1974; Port Stanley 1976; SUPL 1978; Lisbon 1982; FCO 1986; Dhaka 1988; Harare 1992; m 1976 Gordon Slater (diss) (1d 1981).

Slater, Jacqueline (née Brewitt); born 2.8.65; FCO 1985; Dublin 1989; FCO 1989; Beirut 1992; Bonn 1996; Band B3; m 1997 Steven Haigh Slater.

Slater, Judith Mary; SUPL since May 2000; born 26.6.64; FCO 1988; Third later Second Secretary (Political) Canberra 1989; UKMIS New York 1992; First Secretary FCO 1993; Private Secretary to Minister of State 1994; First Secretary (Press & Public Affairs) New Delhi 1997; Band D6; m 1998 Philip Frederick de Waal (1d 2000).

Slater, Karen Elizabeth Sunley; Tunis since August 1999; born 3.7.70; FCO 1988; Lagos 1991; Anguilla 1995; Band B3.

Slaymaker, Caroline Frances (née Grigg); Third Secretary (Political/information) Bratislava since May 1997; born 14.10.64; FCO 1983; Düsseldorf 1986; Third Secretary (Aid) Khartoum 1988; FCO 1990; Vice-Consul Addis Ababa 1992; m 1996 Michael William Slaymaker.

Slinn, David Arthur, OBE (2000); T/D Skopje since June 2001; born 16.4.59; FCO 1981; UKDIS Geneva 1983; Language Training 1986; Second Secretary and Head of Chancery Ulaanbaatar 1987; Second Secretary (Info/Aid) Pretoria/Cape Town 1990; Second Secretary FCO 1993; Chargé d'Affaires T/D Tirana 1995; First Secretary

(Commercial) later (Chancery) Belgrade 1996; Head of British Government Office Pristina 1999; On loan to MOD 2001; T/D Belgrade 2001; m,1982 Melody Sarah Hesford.

Sloan, Kevin Joseph Carnegie; Counsellor New Delhi since July 2001; born 31.8.58; FCO 1984; Second later First Secretary (Chancery) Islamabad 1987; First Secretary FCO 1990; First Secretary Phnom Penh 1992; First Secretary (Economic) Kuala Lumpur 1993; First Secretary FCO 1997; m 1991 Christine Ruth Lowson; (2d 1993, 1994).

Slough, Christopher George James; FCO since July 1996; born 28.11.67; Band B3; m 1993 Angela (1s 1999).

Small, Susan Jane Rosemary; Prague since September 1999; born 23.1.49; FCO 1985; Banjul 1986; UKDEL NATO Brussels 1989; UKMIS New York 1992; FCO 1994; Brussels 1995; Band B3.

Smart, Christopher David Russell; Second Secretary (Commercial) Nairobi since March 1998; born 22.5.52; FCO 1971; UKDEL OECD Paris 1974; Bridgetown 1977; Lilongwe 1980; Third Secretary FCO 1983; Port Moresby 1987; Kingston 1991; Second Secretary FCO 1995; m1980 Patricia Margaret King (2 adopted d 1993, 1998).

Smart, Stephen Brian; Third Secretary (Consular) Karachi since July 1998; born 21.3.58; FCO 1975; UKRep Brussels 1978; Seoul 1980; Karachi 1983; FCO 1985; Warsaw 1988; FCO 1990; Cairo 1991; T/D Moscow 1994; FCO 1995; Band B3; m 1980 Catherine Jane Beard (1s 1986).

Smith, Alan John; HM Consul Palma since March 1999; born 2.10.41; FO 1959; Cairo 1962; Havana 1965; Africa Floater 1966; UK Mission Geneva 1967; Vice-Consul Hanoi 1970; FCO 1971; Casablanca 1975; Second Secretary (Admin) Jedda 1977; Melbourne 1979; First Secretary FCO 1984; First Secretary (Admin) later (Comm) Mexico City 1988; First Secretary (Management) Paris 1991; FCO 1993; m 1975 Susan Melanie Jane Bennett (diss) (1d 1980).

Smith, Andrew Dominic Charles; SUPL since January 2001; born 1.6.67; FCO 1990; Bangkok 1992; Full-time Language Training 1992; Third Secretary (Economic) Warsaw 1993; Third Secretary (Political) Bonn 1996; Band C4.

Smith, Anne; Warsaw since November 1997; born 16.5.60; FCO 1989; Reykjavik 1991; Hong Kong 1994; Band B3; (1d 1998).

Smith, Anthony Donald Raymond; On loan to DfID since October 1996; born 8.11.58; FCO 1986; Second (later First) Secretary Madrid 1988; First Secretary FCO 1991; On loan to the ODA 1996; m 1996 Kerry Jane Rankine.

Smith, Antony Francis; High Commissioner Kingston; born 6.5.42; FO 1959; Phnom Penh 1963; Vice-Consul Luanda 1964; Warsaw 1968; FCO 1970; Tehran 1971; FCO 1974; Second later

First Secretary Accra 1976; UKDEL OECD Paris 1979; Lisbon 1983; First Secretary later Counsellor FCO 1985; Counsellor (Management) and Consul-General Washington 1990; Deputy Head of Mission Lisbon 1994; m 1963 Marion Frances Hickman (2d 1971, 1975).

Smith, Carol Ann; SUPL since January 2000; born 11.11.63; FCO 1987; Cape Town 1989; Budapest 1992; Moscow 1995; Khartoum 1999; Band B3.

Smith, Claire Helen (née Stubbs); Counsellor (Political/Aid) Islamabad since May 1999; born 23.12.56; FCO 1979; Language Training Hong Kong 1981; Second Secretary Peking 1983; First Secretary FCO 1985; SUPL 1990; On Secondment to German MFA Bonn 1994; Bonn 1997; m 1986 Michael Forbes Smith (1d 1989; 1s 1992).

Smith, Colin Anthony; on loan to DfID Sofia since September 1999; born 19.9.69; FCO 1995; Secondment to European Commission Brussels 1997; Second Secretary FCO 1998; Second Secretary (Political) Sofia 1998; Band C4; m2000 Suzanne Hunnewell.

Smith, Deborah Ann (née Connor); SUPL since January 1999; born 10.2.64; FCO 1992; New Delhi 1994; Amman 1998; Band B3; m 1997, (1d 1987).

Smith, David Joseph; First Secretary (Commercial) Tokyo since June 1996; born 12.1.51; FCO 1969; Tokyo 1972; Kuwait 1977; Warsaw 1979; FCO 1981; Osaka 1984; Second later First Secretary (Assistant Trade Commissioner) BTC Hong Kong 1989; First Secretary to T/D Taiwan 1994; First Secretary FCO 1994; m 1975 Hitomi Takahashi (2d 1978, 1982).

Smith, David Leslie Darwin; FCO since December 1976; born 20.4.42; Band B3.

Smith, Derek Moir; SUPL since July 1995; born 12.9.67; Dept of Employment 1986; FCO 1987; Riyadh 1989; Floater Duties Latin America/Caribbean 1993; Band B3.

Smith, Gerald Dominic; FCO since November 1998; born 4.4.70; FCO 1988; Islamabad 1992; Luanda 1996; Band B3; m 1992 Penelope Jane Clifford (1d 1996, 1s 1999).

Smith, Guy William; Rio de Janeiro since July 1991; born 20.4.66; FCO 1985; UKREP Brussels 1987; Sofia 1989; Band A2.

Smith, Hugh Maxwell; New York since January 1992; born 4.4.59; FCO 1981; Brussels 1985; FCO 1988; Band B3.

Smith, James; FCO since August 1998; born 23.2.42; RAF 1962-67; Post Office 1967; FCO 1970; Amman 1972; SE Asia Floater 1977; Tehran 1979; FCO 1980; Kampala 1981; FCO 1982; Hanoi 1983; Atlanta 1984; FCO 1986; Bonn 1990; T/D Zagreb 1993; FCO 1993; Band B3.

Smith, Jason R; Second Secretary (Political) Abu Dhabi since December 2000; born 20.11.70; FCO 1989; Sofia 1991; Dar es Salaam 1993; FCO

1998; Band C4; m 1994 Andreana Vlaeva (1s 1994).

Smith, John Lawrence; Second Secretary FCO since June 1997; born 15.10.65; FCO 1988; Vice-Consul Chicago 1990; Third Secretary Nairobi 1993; m 1990 Gillian Monsen (2s 1993,1997).

Smith, John Stephen; DHM Brussels Embassy since March 1999; born 28.3.57; Third Secretary FCO 1979; Third later Second Secretary (Comm) Seoul 1980; Second Secretary FCO 1985; Second later First Secretary (Chancery) UKMIS New York 1987; First Secretary FCO 1990; First Secretary (Political/Internal) Bonn 1994; m 1984 Wanda Won Min Kim.

Smith, Justine Mary (née Bunn); SUPL since June 2001; born 2.10.64; FCO 1983; Budapest 1986; Doha 1987; FCO 1991; Bangkok 1995; Durban 1999; FCO 2000; Band B3; m2000 Stephen Thomas Smith.

Smith, Katherine Jane; SUPL since April 1999; born 21.5.67; FCO 1990; Third Secretary (Inf) Istanbul 1993; T/D Suva 1997; Band B3.

Smith, Katherine Lucy; UKMIS New York since June 1997; born 10.1.64; FCO 1987; Full-time Language Training 1990; Second Secretary (Chancery/Inf) Athens 1991; First Secretary FCO 1994.

Smith, Lloyd Barnaby; HM Ambassador Bangkok since February 2000; born 21.7.45; Third Secretary FCO 1968; Third later Second Secretary (Chancery) Bangkok 1970; First Secretary FCO 1974; First Secretary (Chancery/Information) Paris 1977; Head of Chancery Dublin 1978; ENA Paris 1981; First Secretary later Counsellor (Press) UKREP Brussels 1982; Deputy Head of Mission and Counsellor (Commercial) Bangkok 1987; Director, (KHF) for Eastern Europe 1990; Counsellor FCO 1993; HM Ambassador Kathmandu 1995; FCO 1999; m(1) 1972 Nicola Mary Whitefield (diss 1982); (2)1983 Mary Sumner (1d 1983; 1s 1985).

Smith, Lynne Marie; Istanbul since March 1999; born 17.2.63; FCO 1982; Peking 1984; Ankara 1987; FCO 1990; SUPL 1994; Band B3; m 1989 Ahmet Kalaycio Fglu.

Smith, Mairi (née Dyer); Helsinki since March 2001; born 3.3.71; FCO 1991; SUPL 1995; FCO 1996; Canberra 1997; Band A2; m 1997 Daniel Beaton Smith.

Smith, Michael Forbes; Deputy High Commissioner Islamabad since November 1999; born 4.6.48; Board of Trade 1966-68; Army 1971-78; FCO 1978; Second, later First Secretary and Head of Chancery Addis Ababa 1979; Deputy to the Civil Commissioner and Political Adviser Port Stanley 1983; First Secretary FCO 1985; Consul (Commercial) Zurich 1990; First Secretary (Press/Information) Bonn 1994; FCO 1999; m(1) 1974 Christian Joanna Kersley (Annulled 1983) (1d 1975); (2)1986 Claire Helen Stubbs (1d 1989; 1s 1992).

Smith, Nicolette Jane; Beirut since July 2001; born 30.4.70; FCO 1989; Kuala Lumpur 1992; SUPL 1995; FCO 1997; Band B3.

Smith, Peter; Muscat since September 1996; born 6.8.51; FCO 1971; Canberra 1974; East Berlin 1976; Khartoum 1978; FCO 1982; Dhaka 1983; Manila 1988; Washington 1989; FCO 1991 (Second Secretary 1994); New Delhi 1994; m 1974 Cynthia Angela Shearn (1d 1975).

Smith, Peter John; CBE (1995); Governor Cayman Islands since May 1999; born 15.5.42; FO 1962; Saigon 1964; Paris 1968; Second Secretary 1969; Commercial Publicity Officer, BIS New York 1970; FCO 1973; Second later First Secretary (Comm) Mexico City 1976; DHC and Head of Chancery Port Louis 1981; First Secretary FCO 1984; Deputy Consul-General Montreal 1987; Deputy Consul-General Toronto and Director of Trade and Investment (Canada) 1988; Royal College of Defence Studies 1992; HM Ambassador Antananarivo, additionally HM Ambassador Comoros (non-resident) 1993; High Commissioner Maseru 1996; m 1964 Suzanne Pauline Duffin (1s 1965; 1d 1967).

Smith, Roland Berkeley; First Secretary (Management/Consul) Kiev since March 1998; born 6.7.55; FCO 1973; Bonn 1975; Karachi 1979; FCO 1981; Nicosia 1985; Manila 1987; Bombay 1991; FCO 1995; m(1) 1978 Shirley Kathleen Sandford (diss 1993) (1s 1988), (2) 1994 Marites Enriquez Garlan (1s 1999).

Smith, Roland Hedley, CMG(1994); HM Ambassador to Kiev since May 1999; born 11.4.43; Third Secretary FO 1967; Second Secretary Moscow 1969; Second later First Secretary UKDEL NATO Brussels 1971; First Secretary FCO 1974; First Secretary (Cultural) Moscow 1978; FCO 1980; Counsellor CDA at IISS 1983; Head of Chancery BMG Berlin 1984; Counsellor FCO 1988; Minister and Deputy Permanent Representative UKDEL NATO Brussels 1992; Director (International Security) FCO 1995; m 1971 Katherine Jane Lawrence (2d 1972, 1975).

Smith, Shirley Kathleen (née Sandford); Second Secretary (Commercial) Dublin since August 1994; born 5.1.56; FCO 1974; Bonn 1977; Karachi 1979; FCO 1981; Nicosia 1985; Manila 1987; Second Secretary FCO 1991; m 1978 Roland Berkeley Smith (1s 1988).

Smith, Simon John Meredith; Counsellor (Commercial, Economic, S & T) Moscow since April 1998; born 14.1.58; Dept of Employment 1981; Second Secretary FCO 1986; Language Training FCO/Kamakura 1987; Second later First Secretary (Econ) Tokyo 1989; FCO 1992; m 1984 Siân Rosemary Stickings (2d 1989, 1993).

Smith, Simon Richard; FCO since July 1988; born 3.10.57; FCO 1974; Peking 1982; FCO 1983; Third Secretary Bucharest 1986; Band B3.

Smith, Stephen Jeremy; First Secretary FCO since February 1998; born 25.10.44; FO later DSAO 1964; Baghdad 1968; Sofia 1973; FCO 1974; Vice-Consul Sydney 1977; FCO (Assistant Parliamentary Clerk) 1982; Second Secretary (Admin) and HM Consul Algiers 1983; FCO 1986; on secondment to the Birmingham Chamber of Industry and Commerce 1989; Second Secretary (Commercial) Dar es Salaam 1991; Deputy Consul General and Consul (Commercial) Shanghai 1994; m 1969 Delyth Morris (2d 1973, 1977; 2s 1975, 1978).

Smith, Stuart Harris; Kiev since September 1998; born 24.4.48; Nicosia 1989; Belgrade 1991; World Wide Floater Duties 1993; Moscow 1996; Band B3; m 1969 Carol Ann (1s 1971; 1d 1974).

Smith, Stuart Vaughan; Rio De Janeiro since January 1999; born 5.7.72; FCO 1991; New Delhi 1995; Band A2.

Smith, Susan Lesley; FCO since January 2000; born 29.12.63; FCO 1983; New Delhi 1985, Belgrade 1988; Kathmandu 1989; FCO 1992; Pretoria 1996; T/D Casablanca 1999; Band B3.

Smith, William John; Peking since December 1998; born 20.2.48; Royal Marines 1964-88; Bonn 1988; Floater Duties 1993; Sofia 1994; Band B3; m 1971 Doreen (1s 1973; 2d 1971, 1976).

Smithson, David; SUPL since November 1997; born 16.4.70; FCO 1988; UKMIS New York 1991; Band A2; Peking 1994; m 1993 Paula Louise Smith.

Smithson, Paula Louise (née Smith) Peking since June 1994; born 13.10.68; FCO 1987; UKMIS New York 1990; SUPL 1992; Band A2; m 1993 David John Smithson.

Smyth, Caroline Ann MBE (1999); FCO since August 1998; born 2.6.61; FCO 1980; Moscow 1982; Strasbourg 1983; Peking 1987; FCO 1989; Washington 1993; Tripoli 1997; Band C4.

Sneddon, Deborah Phillips; FCO since September 1992; born 20.12.63; FCO 1985; UKMIS Geneva 1987; Valletta 1990; Band A2.

Snee, Nicholas James Michael; Vice-Consul Moscow since June 2001; Born 10.7.65; HM Forces Army 1982 – 1994; FCO 1996; Windhoek 1998; Band B3; m2000 Valerie Johr.

Snell, Arthur Gordon; Second Secretary (Political) Abuja since March 2001; born 30.10.75; FCO 1998; Second Secretary (Political/Economic) Harare 2000; Band C4.

Snell, Michael George, MVO (1980); FCO since April 1998; born 9.6.47; FCO 1972; Darwin 1973; FCO 1975; Rome 1978; Banjul 1981; FCO 1982; Sofia 1983; Second Secretary FCO 1985; Second Secretary Washington 1988; Jakarta 1994; m(1) 1973 Diana Mary Powell-Williams (diss 1992); (2d 1977, 1979; 1s 1982); (2)Victoria B Curry (1s 1996).

Snook, Andrew John; Vice-Consul Rio de Janiero since April 1998; born 18.7.72; FCO 1992; World-wide Floater 1995; Full-time language training 1997; m 1999 Priscila de Medeiros Ivo Santos (1d 2000).

Snowdon, Susan Carol; FCO since 2000; born 12.7.65; MOD 1983; FCO 1985; Brussels 1987; Manila 1989; FCO 1993; Accra 1997; Band B3.

Snoxell, David Raymond; High Commissioner Port Louis since September 2000; born 18.11.44; FCO 1969; Islamabad 1972; UKMIS Geneva 1976; Second later First Secretary FCO 1984; Executive Director and Consul (Inf) BIS New York 1986; First Secretary FCO 1991; HM Ambassador Cape Verde, Dakar, Guinea, Guinea Bissau, and Mali 1997; m 1971 Anne Carter (2s 1972, 1977; 1d 1973).

Sommerlad, Alistair Martin; First Secretary (Political) Sarajevo since July 2001; born 15.10.65; FCO 1996; Lagos 1996; First Secretary FCO 1999; Band D6.

Soothill, Deborah Jane; Second Secretary FCO since September 1999; born 22.5.69; FCO 1992; Full-time Language Training Peking 1995; Second Secretary (Chancery/External) Peking 1996; Band C4; m 1996 Brendan Paul Mahoney da Madariaga.

Soper, Andrew Keith; Deputy Head of Mission Brasilia since June 2001; born 6.7.60; FCO 1985; Second later First Secretary (Chancery) Mexico City 1987; First Secretary FCO December 1990; First Secretary Washington 1995; FCO 1999; m 1987 Kathryn Garrett Stevens; (1s 1991, 1d 1993).

Soutar, Samuel Ian; HM Ambassador Sofia since December 2001; born 2.6.45; Third Secretary FCO 1968; Third later Second Secretary UKDEL Brussels (EC) 1970; Saigon 1972; First Secretary FCO 1974; Private Secretary to the Parliamentary Under-Secretary of State for Foreign and Commonwealth Affairs 1976; First Secretary Washington 1977; First Secretary FCO 1981; DHC and Head of Chancery Wellington 1986; On loan to the RCDS 1991; Counsellor FCO 1991; UK Permanent Representative to the Conference on Disarmament in Geneva 1997; m 1968 Mary Isabella Boyle (1s 1971; 1d 1973).

Southcombe, Julie Ann; SUPL since December 1988; born 13.10.57; FCO 1982; Moscow 1983; UKREP Brussels 1984; FCO 1987; Band A2.

Southern, Thomas Andrew Oliver; FCO since September 2000; born 15.1.75; Band C4.

Sowerby, Karen Dorothy Howell; Luanda since October 2000; born 14.6.46; FCO 1991; La Paz 1993; Yaoundé 1997; Band A2.

Sowerby, Lynne; FCO since March 1997; born 17.9.67; FCO 1988; East Berlin 1990; Ankara 1993; Band B3.

Spalding, Thomas James; FCO since November 1990; born 10.11.46; FCO 1970; Lusaka 1971; FCO 1973; New Delhi 1977; FCO 1980; Darwin 1981; FCO 1983; Darwin 1988; Band B3; m 1969 Jenifer Blackburn (1d 1976).

Sparkes, Andrew James; Deputy Head of Mission Jakarta since April 1999; born 4.7.59; FCO 1982; Second Secretary (Chancery) Ankara 1985; First Secretary FCO 1988; First Secretary (Political) Bangkok 1992; First Secretary later Counsellor FCO 1995; on loan to the DTI 1997; m 1985 Jean Mary Meakin; (1s 1988; 1d 1992).

Sparrow, Rosalyn Louise (née Morris) MVO (1999); SUPL since June 2001; born 15.5.61; FCO 1983; Dhaka 1986; UKDEL Brussels 1989; Second Secretary (Economic) Brussels 1991; Second Secretary (Commercial) Singapore 1993; Second Secretary Seoul 1998; m (1) 1986 Richard John Bryant (diss) (1s 1991), (2) David John Sparrow.

Spearman, Richard David; First Secretary (Political) Paris since August 1997; born 30.8.60; FCO 1989; Consul Istanbul 1992; First Secretary FCO 1994; Band D6; m 1987 Caroline Jill Scoones (1s 1992; 2d 1995, 1998).

Speller, Paul Anthony; Deputy Governor Gibraltar since September 1998; born 21.1.54; FCO 1983; Second later First Secretary Bonn 1986; First Secretary FCO 1989; (Private Secretary to the Parliamentary Under Secretary of State 1991); First Secretary (External Relations) UKRep Brussels 1993; FCO 1996; m 1998 Jane Hennessey.

Speller, Susan Barbara (née Arnold); First Secretary (Press/Information) Bonn since June 1996; Berlin from October 2001; born 22.10.56; FCO 1984; Hamburg 1986; Munich 1987; Düsseldorf 1988; Third later Second Secretary FCO 1990; On loan to the ODA 1994.

Spellman, Antoinette Marie (née Mills); Islamabad since October 1999; born 24.5.65; FCO 1988; UKDEL NATO Brussels 1991; Abuja 1993; Kuwait 1996; Band A2; m 1990 Garry James Spellman; (2s 1993, 1998).

Spencer, David Paul, MBE (1988); First Secretary (Political) Dubai since April 1999; born 4.4.59; FCO 1978; Kuala Lumpur 1981; FCO 1983; Aden 1985; First Secretary FCO 1988; First Secretary (Pol) Stockholm 1992; FCO 1996; Band D6; m 1988 Patricia Anne McCullock (2s 1990, 1993).

Spencer, Elaine Joan; FCO since March 1976; born 24.3.49; FO 1966; DSAO 1966; FO (later FCO) 1967; Bonn 1972; Khartoum 1975; Band A2.

Spencer, Sarah; SUPL since November 1999; born 31.5.68; FCO 1988; Kathmandu 1990; FCO 1993; Bucharest 1995; Cairo 1999; Band B3; m 1997 Mark Anthony James Hamilton (1s 2000).

Spiceley, Peter Joseph, MBE (1977); HM Ambassador San José since January 1999; born 5.3.42; FO 1961; Bogotá 1964; DSAO 1967; Lima 1969; Second Secretary (Comm) Yaoundé 1972; Vice-Consul (Comm) Douala 1974; Second later First Secretary Quito 1976; FCO 1982; Consul

Miami 1986; First Secretary FCO 1991; Director of Trade Promotion Sydney 1994; m 1965 Cecilia Orozco (2d 1967, 1970).

Spicer, Haden Richard; Second Secretary (Commercial) Bandar Seri Begawan since April 1999; born 18.6.62; FCO 1985; Abu Dhabi 1989; Moscow 1992; FCO 1995; Band C4; m 1988 Carole E Pymble.

Spindler, Guy David St John Kelso; First Secretary FCO since January 2000; born 9.6.62; Second Secretary FCO 1987; Second later First Secretary (Comm) Moscow 1989; First Secretary FCO 1992; First Secretary (Political) Pretoria 1997; Band D6; m 1999 Laura Jane Brady.

Spires, David Mark, MVO (1992); Second Secretary (Management) Dublin since September 1999; born 18.11.61; FCO 1980; Warsaw 1982; Lima 1985; FCO 1986; Islamabad 1987; Paris 1991; Full-time Language Training 1993; San Salvador 1993; Belgrade 1997; Band C4; m 1987 (2s 1986, 1996; 1d 1990).

Spittles, Cheryl Jean; SUPL since January 1996; born 14.1.50; FCO 1978; Paris 1980; Tunis 1983; Wellington 1985; FCO 1988; Islamabad 1990; FCO 1995; Band B3.

Spivey, Donald; Tokyo since September 1999; born 12.4.68; FCO 1989; Tokyo 1992; FCO 1995; Kamakura 1998; Band B3.

Spoor, Peter Logan; FCO since October 1999; born 4.11.68; FCO 1992; Third Secretary (Commercial) Bangkok 1995; Band C4; m 1998 Joanna M Haydon.

Sprake, Anthony Douglas; Consul-General Melbourne since August 2001; born 16.7.44; Department of Employment 1968; First Secretary (Labour) Brussels 1977; FCO 1980; DHC Freetown 1982; First Secretary later Counsellor FCO 1985; Counsellor (Commercial) The Hague 1990; Counsellor FCO 1994; Minister Peking 1996; FCO 2000; m 1977 Jane McNeill (2s 1980, 1982 dec'd 1989).

Sprod, Caroline; Madrid since November 2000; born 2.3.71; FCO 1993; T/D Kiev 1995; Third Secretary Hong Kong 1996; FTLT 2000; Band B3.

Sprunt, Patrick William; Counsellor (Political Affairs) Tokyo since October 1999; born 13.4.52; Third Secretary FCO 1975; Language Student SOAS 1976; Second later First Secretary Tokyo 1978; FCO 1982; UKREP Brussels 1982; First Secretary Bonn 1983; First Secretary FCO 1986; First Secretary Tokyo 1987; First Secretary (ECOSOC) UKMIS New York 1992; First Secretary FCO since July 1996; m 1979 Haang Ai-Yuan Wong (1s 1985; 1d 1989).

Squibb, Keith Norman; Cairo since October 1999; born 2.9.49; Prague 1989; Tel Aviv 1991; Warsaw 1993; Moscow 1995; Lagos 1998; Band B3; m 1974 Brigitte Pronier (3s 1974, 1978, 1984).

Squire, Richard James; Full time language training since October 1998. born 11.9.74; Band C4; FCO 1996.

Squires, George Thomas; First Secretary (Management) Peking since March 1997; born 20.10.48; FCO 1968; Dacca 1971; Antigua 1973; Warsaw 1975; Jakarta 1976; FCO 1979 (Second Secretary 1983); Vice-Consul later Consul and Administration Officer Sydney 1985; First Secretary (Comm/Dev) Bangkok 1990; First Secretary FCO 1993; m 1979 Helen Mary Thomas (2s 1983, 1985).

Squires, Helen (née Thomas); Second Secretary (Management) Peking since August 1997; born 18.10.51; FCO 1973; Third Secretary (Commercial) Jakarta 1976; Third Secretary FCO 1979; SUPL 1983; Vice-Consul Bangkok 1990; FCO 1993; m 1979 George Thomas Squires (2s 1983, 1985).

Stacey, Christopher Robin; New Delhi since February 1999; born 9.12.47; RAF 1965-74; FCO 1974; Islamabad 1976; Budapest 1980; Singapore 1983; FCO 1984; Manila 1988; Nicosia 1992; FCO 1995; Band B3; m 1977 Coral Jane (2s 1981, 1987).

Stafford, Andrew Jeremy; Counsellor (Political) Stockholm since June 1999; born 1.2.53; Third Secretary FCO 1975; Stockholm 1977; FCO 1979; Second Secretary Accra 1979; Second later First Secretary FCO 1981; First Secretary and Consul Prague 1984; First Secretary FCO 1987; First Secretary (Chancery) Brussels 1991; FCO 1994; m(1) 1977 Felicity Joanna Maria Kelly; (2) 1983 Elizabeth Rosemary Kempston (2d 1985, 1992; 1s 1988).

Stafford, Nina Jeanne; SUPL since February 2001; born 28.9.71; FCO 1991; Buenos Aires 1997; The Hague 2000; Band A2.

Stagg, Charles Richard Vernon, CMG (2001); HM Ambassador Republic of Bulgaria since October 1998; born 27.9.55; FCO 1977; Third later Second Secretary Sofia 1979; The Hague 1982; First Secretary FCO 1985; UKREP Brussels 1987; First Secretary FCO 1988; First Secretary (Info) UKREP Brussels 1991; First Secretary FCO 1993; m 1982 Arabella Clare Faber (3s 1984, 1985, 1990, 2d 1992, 1997).

Standbrook, Timothy William; On loan to British Trade International since June 2000; born 8.6.63; FCO 1988; Language Training Seoul 1990; Third Secretary (Political) Seoul 1992; FCO 1994; ECO Peking 1995; Karachi 1997; FCO 1997; m 1997 Jia Lei (1d 2000).

Stanton, Karen Jane (née Owen); First Secretary (Commercial) Tokyo since July 1999; born 25.1.62; FCO 1984; Language Training Kamakura 1986; Vice-Consul Tokyo 1987; Third Secretary (Chancery) Rome 1991; Second Secretary FCO 1994; First Secretary FCO 1996; m 1990 Graham Stanton.

Stanton, Louise Jane; world-wide Floater Duties since May 1997; born 14.8.68; FCO 1990; Japanese Language Training SOAS 1991; full-time Language Training Kamakura 1993; Third Secretary (Commercial) Tokyo 1993; Band B3.

Stanyer, Julie Grace (née Robins); FCO since February 1992; born 15.3.48; FCO 1984; Bridgetown 1985; UKDEL NATO Brussels 1989; Band B3; m 1988 Patrick Julian Serville.

Staples, Graham Raymond; Vice Consul and Third Secretary Windhoek since December 1997; born 24.1.69; FCO 1988; Dublin 1989; Warsaw 1992; Band B3; FCO 1994; m 1994 Sarah Kathleen Paterson. (1d 1998)

Starkey, Nicholas Andrew; SMO Islamabad since September 1999; born 20.12.52; FCO 1972; SE Asia Floater 1975; Warsaw 1977; Bridgetown 1979; FCO 1981; Kuwait 1985; Second Secretary (Cons) Lagos 1989; Second Secretary FCO 1992; Second Secretary (Management) Bucharest 1995; Band C5; m 1981 Rhodora Corrales Maroto (2s 1983 1999, 1d 1985).

Staunton, Andrew James; Second Secretary FCO since July 1997; born 7.8.67; FCO 1987; Peking 1989; Third Secretary (Chancery/Management) Strasbourg 1991; Third Secretary (Economic) Bucharest 1994; Band D6; m 1990 Rebecca Anne Nixon (1s 1991, 1d 1993).

Stead, Michael; Second Secretary (Commercial) Lisbon since December 1997; born 19.1.58; British Library 1976; FCO 1979; Jedda 1981; Riyadh 1982; LA Floater 1985; Rio de Janeiro 1988; FCO 1991; Second Secretary (Political) Addis Ababa 1994.

Steele, Christopher David; First Secretary (Financial) Paris since September 1998; born 24.6.64; FCO 1987; Second Secretary (Chancery) Moscow 1990; Second later First Secretary FCO 1993; Band D6; m 1990 Laura Katharine Hunt (2s 1996, 1998; 1d 2000).

Steel, Diane Elizabeth; on loan to No.10 Downing Street since December 1999; born 2.8.60; FCO 1978; UKRep Brussels 1982; Dar es Salaam 1985; Doha 1989; St Petersburg 1992; FCO 1995; Band B3.

Steeples, John Charles; Second Secretary FCO since July 1995; born 14.2.45; Army 1966-70; 1972-73; FCO 1973; Dacca 1976; UKDEL NATO Brussels 1978; Prague 1981; FCO 1981; Paris 1985; FCO 1987; Brussels 1988; Vienna 1992; m 1975 Jennifer Maureen Davis (2s 1980, 1983; 1d 1977).

Stein, Gordon; Third Secretary Peking since October 1998; born 20.2.69; FCO 1989; UKMIS Geneva 1991; Rabat 1994; Band B3; m 1994 Deborah Anne Hooper.

Stephen, Ann (née Barbour); UKDEL Nato Brussels since July 1999; born 2.4.66; FCO 1988; Paris 1991; Freetown 1993; Banjul 1998; Band A2; m 1992 Robert Stephen (1s 1995).

Stephens, Adrian Charles; Consul-General Ho Chi Minh City since January 2001; born 19.3.46; DSAO (later FCO) 1964; Karachi 1968; Colombo 1970; Budapest 1972; FCO 1974; Islamabad 1976; FCO 1978, (Second Secretary 1979); Bangkok 1982; Consul Berlin 1986; First Secretary FCO 1990; Seoul 1993; First Secretary (Commercial) Mexico City 1997; m 1968 Susan Jane Everitt (1d 1971; 1s 1973).

Stephenson, John Edmund; First Secretary FCO since March 1998; born 19.12.60; FCO 1986; Second later First Secretary (Inf) Santiago 1989; First Secretary FCO 1992; First Secretary Havana 1994; Band D6; m 1986 Jacqueline Denise Clayton (3s 1990, 1992, 1993).

Sterling, Janice Aeyesha Odonna; UKMIS New York since August 2000; born 8.8.69; FCO 1997; Band A2; m 1994 Dwight Sterling.

Steven, John Young; Floater duties since May 2000; born 21.5.68; FCO 1988; Moscow 1989; Washington 1992; FCO 1995; Band B3.

Stevens, Ian James, LVO (2001); First Secretary (Management/Consul) Oslo since November 1998; born 15.5.66; FCO 1985; UKDEL NATO Brussels 1989; New Delhi 1992; FCO 1996; Band C5; m 1987 Adele Oliver (1d 1989; 1s 1991).

Stevens, Jill Frances; FCO since December 1992; (Second Secretary 1996); born 10.3.57; FCO 1977; Damascus 1979; Bridgetown 1982; FCO 1984; Dar es Salaam 1987; FCO 1989; Moscow 1990; Band C4.

Stevens, Mark; Consul-General Alexandria since May 1999; born 5.7.49; DSAP 1966; FCO 1968; Georgetown 1970; Madrid 1973; East Berlin 1976; FCO 1978; Kingston 1982; New Delhi 1985; Second Secretary FCO 1988; Second Secretary (Management/Vice-Consul) Tunis 1992; FCO 1995; m 1970 Pauline Elaine Graber (2d 1973, 1976).

Stevens, Paul David; Second Secretary Los Angeles since August 1999; born 8.9.59; MOD 1977; FCO 1981; UKMIS Geneva 1983; Kampala 1985; Washington 1988; FCO 1991; Full-time Language Training 1994; Band B3; m 1985 Faye Jaqueline Brand.

Stevenson, Helen Elizabeth (née Dewsnap); FCO since October 1996; born 14.1.66; FCO 1985; Rio de Janeiro 1990; FCO 1992; Paris 1993; Band A2; m 1992 James Richard Stevenson.

Stevenson, William Michael; FCO since July 1997; born 4.9.51; FCO 1971; UKDEL NATO Brussels 1973; Luxembourg 1977; Addis Ababa 1979; Moscow 1983; FCO 1985; Khartoum 1988; Second Secretary Ankara 1993; Band C5; m 1982 Laura Birse Stirton (2s 1986,1987).

Stew, Timothy David, MBE (1996); FCO since May 2000; born 8.10.66; FCO 1988; Language Training 1989; Language Training Cairo 1990; Third Secretary (Chancery) Riyadh 1991; Sarajevo 1995; Deputy High Commissioner Belmopan 1996;

Band C4; m 1991 Michelle Louise Mealor (1d 1996; 1s 1998).

Stewart, Brian Edward; DHM and Counsellor Kuwait since July 1998; born 4.2.50; Third Secretary FCO 1972; MECAS 1973; Third later Second Secretary Amman 1975; on loan to Cabinet Office 1978; (First Secretary 1979); FCO 1980; First Secretary and Head of Chancery Singapore 1982; Head of Chancery Tunis 1986; First Secretary FCO 1989; DHM Damascus 1993; Counsellor FCO 1996; m 1975 Anne Elizabeth Cockerill.

Stewart, Iain Jamieson; World Wide Floater Duties since May 1999; born 3.12.71; UDIS Geneva 1994; Band B3.

Stewart, Roderick James Nugent; SUPL since July 2000; born 3.1.73; FCO 1995; Second Secretary (Economic) Jakarta 1997; Second Secretary British Embassy Office Banja Luka 1999; Band C4.

Still, Jean Margaret (née Wilton); First Secretary (Management) Kuala Lumpur since April 1995; born 16.12.46; FO (later FCO) 1965; Prague 1969; Rio de Janeiro 1971; Nicosia 1974; FCO 1975; Brasilia 1979; Second Secretary FCO 1983; Second Secretary on loan to CAD Hanslope Park 1982; Second Secretary New Delhi 1986; Second later First Secretary FCO 1990; m 1978 Anthony Gerald Still.

Stirling, Sonia Louise; SUPL since June 2000; born 17.6.74; FCO 1994; Paris 1996; Band A2.

Stitt, (Thomas) Clive Somerville; British Trade International since May 1999; born 1.1.48; Third Secretary FCO 1970; Language Student Tehran 1972; Kabul 1972; Third later Second Secretary New Delhi 1974; First Secretary FCO 1977; UKMIS Geneva 1972; First Secretary later Counsellor FCO 1986; Counsellor UKMIS New York 1992; m 1977 Margaret Ann Milward (2d 1982, 1984).

Stokes, Antony LVO (1996); First Secretary (Political) Seoul since April 2000; born 21.1.65; FCO 1994; First Secretary and Head of Political Section Bangkok 1996; FTLT 1999; Band D6.

Stokes, Karen Ann (née Chambers); Tel Aviv since April 1999; born 18.12.67; FCO 1987; Bonn 1989; FCO 1991; Vienna 1993; FCO 1996; m 1998 Paul Terence Stokes.

Stokes, Paul Terence; SUPL since February 1999; born 9.10.63; FCO 1984; Bonn 1988; FCO 1992; UKMIS Vienna 1993; FCO 1996; Band B3; m 1998 Karen Chambers.

Stokoe, Kay; FCO since 1997; born 23.6.69; FCO 1989; Madrid 1992; Floater duties 1995; Band B3.

Stokey, Tracey Joanne Tudor; Luxembourg since November 1993; born 10.3.65; FCO 1988; Bonn 1990; Band A2; m 1988 Brendan Stokey; (1s 1996).

Stollery, Mark Thomas; First Secretary FCO since June 1993; born 8.10.60; Royal Navy 1978-88;

Second Secretary FCO 1988; Second Secretary (EC Affairs) Brussels 1990; Band D6; m 1990 Denise Jekyll, (1s 1995, 1d 1998).

Stone, Jemma Catherine; Moscow since January 1998; born 8.1.70; FCO 1991; Bonn 1994; Band A2.

Stone, Marie Louise; FCO since October 1992; born 27.8.74; Band A2.

Stones, Adrian; First Secretary later Counsellor Harare since October 2000; born 16.10.60; FCO 1986; Second later First Secretary (Inf) New Delhi 1989; First Secretary FCO 1991; First Secretary (Chancery) Washington 1992; First Secretary FCO 1995; m 1990 Gillian Ruth Millman (2s 1992, 1994, 1d ,1998).

Storey, Neil William, First Secretary (Management) and HM Consul Lima since September 2000; born 10.9.61; FCO 1982; Third Secretary Brasilia 1994; FCO 1998; Band C4; m 1992 Oyami Azevedo.

Stott, Adam Paul; UKMIS Geneva since March 2000; born 26.3.71; FCO 1993; Band A2.

Stoves, Margaret; FCO since October 1999; born 3.7.45; FCO 1987; Lisbon 1990; Almaty 1992; UKDEL NATO Brussels 1995; Band A2.

Strain, Scott Robert, Consul General Chongqing since March 2000; born 4.10.70; FCO 1989; Attaché Pretoria/Cape Town 1991; Attaché later Third Secretary Vice-Consul Peking 1995; Band C4; m 1995 Caroline Joanne Ewing (diss 2000).

Stubbings, Graham James; Johannesburg since January 1996; born 17.9.57; DHSS 1974; FCO 1976; UKMIS New York 1979; Kingston 1982; FCO 1986; New Delhi 1989; Band B3; m 1989 Kirsty Alexander (2s 1987, 1994).

Stubbins, Caroline Mary; FCO since April 1991; born 26.2.52; FCO 1972; Prague 1974; FCO 1976; New York 1978; FCO 1981; Canberra 1984; FCO 1987; Washington 1988; Band A2.

Stucley-Houghton, Nicholas John Knight; FCO since June 1996; born 3.10.54; Inland Revenue 1974; Santiago 1976; Mbabane 1979; Warsaw 1982; FCO 1983; Kathmandu 1986; FCO 1988; Copenhagen 1989; Johannesburg 1992; Band C4; m (1) 1976 Beatriz Elvira Sierra-Galindo (1s 1978, 1d 1980) (diss 1990); (2) 1993 Susanna Elisabeth Watkins-Pitchford (diss 1996).

Studham, Clare Nicola; Consul Tokyo since April 1996; born 29.6.58; FCO 1977; Washington 1979; FCO 1982; Floater duties 1983; Brasilia 1984; FCO 1988; Second Secretary (ECOSOC) UKMIS New York 1994.

Sturgeon, Christopher Charles Alexander; Islamabad since November 1998; born 15.3.68; FCO 1988; Floater Duties 1990; Colombo 1993; Sana'a 1996.

Sturgeon, Mary Nicol; FCO since January 1998; born 27.5.48; FCO 1973; Bangkok 1974; Kuwait 1976; Suva 1978; Khartoum 1980; FCO 1982;

Resigned 1985; Reinstated 1988; Nicosia 1991; Amman 1994; Band B3.

Sturgess, Neil; FCO since August 1994; born 13.5.62; FCO 1980; Helsinki 1991; Band C4; m 1988 Wendy Alison (1d 1995).

Styles, Graham Charles Trayton; FCO since August 1998; born 16.4.58; FCO 1977; SUPL 1978; FCO 1981; Port Louis 1985; Paris 1989; FCO 1992; UKDEL Vienna 1995; Band C4; m 1984 Rachael Jane Hopkins (2d 1989, 1991).

Styles, Rachael Jane (née Hopkins); FCO since February 2000; born 14.5.62; FCO 1980; Port Louis 1985; SUPL 1988; Band B3; m 1984 Graham Charles Trayton Styles (2d 1989, 1991).

Sullivan, Janet Ann; Floater Duties since January 1999; born 15.2.58; FCO 1977; Kuala Lumpur 1980; Montevideo 1984; Tel Aviv 1988; Floater Duties 1992; FCO 1996; Band B3.

Summers, David; Third Secretary (Management) Ankara since December 1997; born 13.11.64; FCO 1983; Islamabad 1985; Lisbon 1988; FCO 1991; Lagos 1994; Band B3; m 1987 Anita Cecilia Marsh (2d 1991, 1999).

Summers, Timothy Andrew; Consul Hong Kong since September 1997; born 17.2.72; FCO 1994; full-time Language Training 1995; Band C4.

Sundblad, Emma Louise; Second Secretary (Political/PPA) Stockholm since August 2001; born 28.10.75; FCO 1999; Band C4; m 1998 Morgan Sundblad (2s 1994, 1997).

Surman, Derek Malcolm; FCO since May 1999; born 20.6.47; Commonwealth Office/DSAO 1967; Kinshasa 1969; FCO 1970; Madrid 1971; Dacca 1974; Stuttgart 1976; Beirut 1977; Durban 1978; Salisbury 1980; Khartoum 1982; FCO 1985; Canberra 1990; Second Secretary (Immigration) Bombay 1994; Prague 1999; m 1982 Frances Louise Stapelberg.

Sutcliffe, Nicholas Derek; First Secretary (Commercial) Havana since February 1998; born 9.12.57; FCO 1985; Second Secretary (Economic) Brasilia 1990; Second Secretary FCO 1993; Band D6; m 1985 Carole Ann Hunter (4s 1990, 1992, 1994 (twins).

Sutherland, Elizabeth Victoria (née Myles) FCO since June 1987; (Second Secretary 1988); born 27.4.49; FCO 1971; Havana 1972; Sana'a 1974; FCO 1975; Paris 1984; Band C4; m 1988 Neil Sutherland.

Sutton, Alan Edward; Consul General Tokyo since May 2000; born 21.3.43; FO (later FCO) 1967; Düsseldorf 1970; Istanbul 1972; FCO 1975; Islamabad 1978; FCO 1980; Georgetown 1981; FCO 1985; Second Secretary and Consul Riyadh 1987; Consul Berlin 1991; Second Secretary (Management) Bombay 1993; Band C4; m 1965 Jacqueline Anderson (1d 1966; 1s 1969).

Sutton, Janet (née Christie); FCO since May 1991; born 25.3.64; Dept of Employment 1983;

FCO 1984; Abidjan 1987; Paris 1990; Band B3; m 1986 Andrew Richard Sutton (2s 1987, 1995).

Sutton, Rebecca Claire; FTLT since September 2001; born 25.9.73; FCO 1999; Band C4.

Swainson, Emma Mary Dillwyn; FCO since September 2000; born 28.12.75; Band C4.

Sweeney, Carole Mary (née Crofts); FCO since October 1999; born 24.6.59; MOD 1985; FCO 1987; 1988; Second Secretary Bonn 1989; Second Secretary East Berlin 1990; Second later First Secretary FCO 1991; First Secretary (Economic) Oslo 1997; m 1988 Paul Martin Sweeney (1d 1990; 1s 1992).

Sweet, Kay (née Rose); UKRep Brussels since January 1997; born 11.11.63; FCO 1984; Budapest 1985; Paris 1987; Floater Duties 1991; UKRep Brussels 1993; Paris 1995; SUPL 1996; Band B3; m 1996 Jonathan Charles Sweet.

Sweid, Janice Ann Townsend (née Oldfield); First Secretary (Management) JMO Brussels since October 1998; born 13.6.50; FCO 1970; on loan to Cabinet Office 1973; FCO 1974; Accra 1977; FCO 1979; Washington 1984; Second Secretary (Man) Tel Aviv 1987; FCO 1992; m 1980 Youda Yomtob Sweid.

Swift, Elined Clare (née Evans); First Secretary FCO since April 2001; born 22.2.60; FCO 1988. Second later First Secretary (Economic) Buenos Aires 1990; First Secretary FCO 1993; First Secretary UKDIS Geneva 1997; First Secretary (Regional Affairs) Washington 1999; Band D6; m 1999 Hans Eric Swift.

Swift, Hans Eric; First Secretary FCO since April 2001; born 14.5.58; FCO 1980; New Delhi 1982; Second Secretary FCO 1986; Second later First Secretary (Chancery) Stockholm 1988; FCO 1991; First Secretary (Political) Washington 1998; Band D6; m(1) 1981 Susan Mary Brown (diss 1995) (1d 1988, 1s 1991), (2) 1999 Elined Clare Evans.

Sykes, Graham Leslie; Sana'a since June 1999; born 20.9.60; FCO 1987; New Delhi 1992; FCO 1995; Pretoria 1995; Band B3; m 1995 Wei Li Ming.

Sykes, Roger Michael Spencer; Deputy Head of Mission Karachi since March 2002; born 22.10.50; FCO 1968; Caracas 1971; Freetown 1972; Karachi 1976; Valletta 1978; Lagos 1982; Port Vila 1986; Second Secretary FCO 1990; Amman 1993; First Secretary and Head of British Trade Office Al Khobar 1997-2001; Band D6; m 1976 Anne Lesley Groves-Gidney (3s 1977, 1980, 1988).

Sylvester, Robert Anthony; Johannesburg since June 1999; born 29.12.56; FCO 1996; Band B3; m 1976 Jacqueline Lovely (1d 1986).

Syme, Avril; FCO since 2001; born 13.4.65; FCO 1987; Dublin 1989; Addis Ababa 1992; FCO 1993; Brussels 1994; FCO 1998; Ottawa 2000; Band B3; m2001 Mr Mirrlees Chassels.

Symon, Terence Paul; Vice-Consul Guangzhou since April 2000; born 30.9.56; Army 1973-96; FCO 1997; Band B3; m 1977 Wendy Yuk Wah Leung (2d 1977,1981).

Synnott, Hilary Nicholas Hugh, CMG (1997); High Commissioner Islamabad since May 2000; born 20.3.45; Royal Navy 1962-73; Second Secretary FCO 1973; First Secretary UKDEL OECD Paris 1975; First Secretary Bonn 1978; FCO 1981; Counsellor, Consul-General and Head of Chancery Amman 1985; Counsellor, Head of Western European Department FCO 1989; Security Co-ordination Department 1991; Minister and Deputy High Commissioner New Delhi 1993; Director (South and South-East Asia) FCO 1996; Sabbatical at IISS 1999; m 1973 Anne Penelope Clarke.

Syposz, Shelley Liann (née Mayman); FCO since June 1995; born 2.5.70; FCO 1991; New Delhi 1993; Band A2; m 1996 Julian Jeremy Syposz.

Syrett, Mark Robert; Second Secretary (Political) Oslo since November 1998; born 9.4.69; FCO 1993; Band C4.

Syrett, Nicholas Simon; First Secretary FCO since June 2000; born 7.12.60; FCO 1989; First Secretary (Political) Luanda 1993; First Secretary FCO 1996; First Secretary (Political) Bogotá 1998; Band D6; m 1993 Elena Fircks (1s, 1d 1997 (twins).

T

Tandy, Arthur David; Second later First Secretary FCO since May 1989; born 16.8.49; HO 1974-85; FCO 1985; Second Secretary Riyadh 1987; Band C5; m 1973 Hilary Denise Watson (1s 1978; 1d 1982).

Tansley, Anthony James Nicholas; Counsellor and Deputy Head of Mission Muscat since November 1998; born 19.7.62; FCO 1984; Language Training 1986; Second Secretary (Chancery) Riyadh 1988; Second Secretary (Chancery) Baghdad 1989; First Secretary FCO 1991; Dublin 1994; m 1998 Blaithin Mary Curran.

Tarif, Pamela (née Neave); Second Secretary Yaounde since June 2000; born 3.6.65; FCO 1985; Lagos 1988; Ottawa 1992; FCO 1994; Quito 1997; m 1988 Nacer Tarif (1d 1992, 1s 1995).

Tarry, Stephen Norman; Dublin since January 1993; born 21.1.54; FCO 1971; Washington 1974; Damascus 1977; Brussels 1981; FCO 1983; Islamabad 1983; FCO 1988; Warsaw 1991; Band C4; m(1) 1981 Julie Christine Lawrence (dec'd 1985) (1d (adopted) 1984), (2) 1992 Elzbieta Jaskaczek.

Tarshish, Daniel Morton; Second Secretary FCO since December 2000; born 14.10.69; FCO 1994; Second Secretary UKMIS New York 1998; Band C4; m 1999 Pamela Goddard (1d 1999).

Tasker, Alastair Robin; FCO since July 1984; born 6.4.41; FO (later FCO) 1957; Bonn 1972; FCO 1974; Second Secretary Peking 1976; FCO

1979; Bonn 1982; m 1966 Lesley Mitchell (1d 1975; 1s 1977).

Tatham, Michael Harry; on loan to 10 Downing Street since June 1999; born 2.7.65; FCO since September 1987; Third later Second Secretary (Chancery) Prague 1990; First Secretary FCO 1993; Deputy Head of Mission and HM Consul Sofia 1997; Band D6.

Tauwhare, Richard David, MVO (1983); FCO since August 1999; born 1.11.59; FCO 1980; Third later Second Secretary (Chancery/Inf) Nairobi 1982; Second later First Secretary UKDEL OECD Paris 1986; First Secretary FCO 1989; First Secretary UKDIS Geneva 1994; m 1985 Amanda Jane Grey.

Taylor, Andrea Lynn (née Reid); Abuja since February 1999; born 6.2.70; FCO 1989 Lagos 1992; Banjul 1995; Band A2; m 1996 Charles Richard Taylor.

Taylor, Duncan John Rushworth; Deputy Consul (General Director British Information Services - Press and Public Affairs) New York since April 2000; born 17.10.58; FCO 1982; Third later Second Secretary Havana 1983; First Secretary FCO 1987; Language Training 1991; First Secretary (Commercial) Budapest 1992; On loan to Rolls Royce plc 1997; Counsellor FCO 1997 m1981 Marie Beatrice (Bébé) Terpougoff (3 step d 1972 (twins), 1973; 2s 1984, 1986).

Taylor, Eric Raymond; Third Secretary (Political) New Delhi since April 2001; born 9.1.69; FCO 1994; Vice Consul and Deputy Head of BIS Tripoli February 1999, Vice Consul BE Tripoli July 1999; Band B3; m 1998 Lynn Dudley (1s 2001).

Taylor, Francis; Nairobi since June 1983; born 26.7.56; FCO 1980; Band B3.

Taylor, Helen de Chaville; Strasbourg since 1994; born 15.2.48; FCO 1970; Santiago 1973; Singapore 1974; Second Secretary (Comm) Paris 1978; First Secretary FCO 1984; First Secretary UKMIS New York 1986; FCO 1991; m 1987 Adrian George Ferguson Porter.

Taylor, Hugh Mackay; Consul (Commercial) Munich since November 1999; born 15.5.54; FCO 1972; UKRep Brussels 1975; Brunei 1978; FCO 1981; Munich 1985; Second Secretary (Chancery/Info) Lisbon 1988; Second Secretary FCO 1993; Warsaw 1996; m 1977 Christine Caggie.

Taylor, Ian Stewart; FCO since July 1998; born 27.1.70; FCO 1986; Cairo 1994. Band C4; m 1998 Kim Catherine Higgins.

Taylor, Jeffrey; Second Secretary British Trade International since July 1999; born 15.8.57; FCO 1976; BMG Berlin 1979; Lusaka 1982; Moscow 1984; FCO 1985; Melbourne 1988; Canberra 1990; Second Secretary (Commercial) Helsinki 1992; Second Secretary FCO 1997; m 1981 Janette Anne Hunt (2s 1987, 1990).

Taylor, Karen Ruth (née Nelms); FCO since July 2000; born 23.6.57; FCO 1978; New Delhi 1978; Peking 1982; Washington 1983; FCO 1985; Port Louis 1992; SUPL 1996; Band B3; m 1991 Nigel David Muir Taylor (1d 1994, 1s 1995).

Taylor, Kim Catherine (née Higgins); SUPL since December 2000; born 14.10.66; FCO 1987; Lagos 1989; FCO 1993; Cairo 1994; FCO 1998; Band A2; m 1998 Ian Stewart Taylor.

Taylor, Lisa; FCO since September 2001; born 28.9.73; Band C4.

Taylor, Louis Charles; Consul Oporto since January 2000; born 10.3.54; Home Office 1973; Dhaka 1980; Home Office 1984; Second Secretary Lagos 1990; FCO 1994; Second Secretary (Economic and Trade Policy) New Delhi 1996; Band C5; m 1977 Margaret Ann Price (2s 1984, 1987).

Taylor, Margaret Emily; FCO since September 1997; born 28.8.71; FCO 1994; Kathmandu 1995; Band A2; m2000 Stuart Docherty.

Taylor, Mark Christopher; FCO since September 2000; born 4.6.76; Band C4.

Taylor, Nigel David Muir; Second Secretary FCO since November 1999; born 21.4.61; FCO 1981; Kaduna 1982; Africa/ME Floater 1986; FCO 1989; Port Louis 1992; Second Secretary Grand Turk 1996; Band C4; m 1991 Karen Ruth Nelms (1d 1993, 1s 1995).

Taylor, Robert James; SUPL since October 2000; born 7.4.57; HCS 1987; FCO 1989; Prague 1990; Havana 1992; FCO 1993; Buenos Aires 1996; Band A2.

Taylor, Stephen Andrew; FCO since February 2000; born 15.9.66; Band B3.

Taylor-Tagg, Neil Kevin; SUPL since October 2000; born 29.12.55; FCO 1973; resigned 1974; reinstated 1977; Valletta 1978; Sofia 1981; FCO 1984; Third later Second Secretary Abu Dhabi 1988; Secretary FCO 1993; m 1977 Patricia Anne Lodge (diss 1994).

Teale, Ian Robert McKinnon; T/D Antigua since July 2000; born 28.2.71; FCO 1991; The Hague 1995; Kingston 1996; Sana'a 1999; Band B3.

Tebbit, Kevin Reginald, cmg (1997); On Secondment to the Ministry of Defence since July 1998; born 18.10.46; MOD 1969-1979; UKDEL NATO 1979; First Secretary FCO 1982; First Secretary and Head of Chancery Ankara 1984; On secondment as Directeur du Cabinet, Cabinet of the Secretary-General of NATO Brussels 1987; Counsellor (Pol/Mil) Washington 1988; Counsellor FCO 1992; m 1966 Alison Tinley (1d 1972; 1s 1975).

Teller, Linda Margaret (née Campbell); SUPL since June 1995; born 12.4.61; FCO 1991; Prague 1993; Band A2; m 1995 Nicholas Roy Richard Teller.

Temple, Tracey Joy; Helsinki since December 1998; born 9.8.65; FCO 1993; Buenos Aires 1995; Band A2.

Tench, Gavin Andrew; Second Secretary (Commercial) Kingston since April 1999; born 29.8.68; FCO 1995; Band B3.

Terrett, Nicola; Havana since September 1999; born 2.9.66; HCS 1985; FCO 1994; Band B3.

Terry, Matthew William; First Secretary FCO since March 2001; born 5.10.68; FCO 1992; Second Secretary (Political) Dubai 1994; Second Secretary FCO 1996; Full Time Language Training 1997; First Secretary (Political) Warsaw 1998; Band D6; m 1993 Phillipa Prudence Dunn.

Terry, Raymond Frederick; Deputy Consul-General Melbourne since October 1998; born 18.10.44; MAFF 1961; DSAO (later FCO) 1966; Addis Ababa 1968; Peking 1971; FCO 1974; Islamabad 1976; Second Secretary (Admin) Amman 1980; Second Secretary FCO 1983; Second Secretary (Admin) and Vice-Consul Maputo 1984; Second Secretary (Comm) Jakarta 1988; Second later First Secretary FCO 1993; Deputy Consul-General Melbourne 1998; m 1968 Lois Mary Jones Evans (2d,1970, 1973).

Tesoriere, Harcourt Andrew Pretorius; HM Ambassador Riga since March 2002; born 2.11.50; Royal Navy 1969-73; FCO 1974; Language Student SOAS and Iran 1975; Oriental Secretary Kabul 1976; Nairobi 1979; Second Secretary Abidjan 1981; FCO 1985; First Secretary and Head of Chancery, later Chargé d'Affaires a.i. BIS Damascus 1987; First Secretary FCO 1991; SUPL on secondment as UNOCHA Head of Field Operations (Afghanistan) 1994; HM Ambassador Tirana 1996; UNSMA 1998; FTLT 2001; m 1987 Dr Alma Gloria Vasquez.

Thackstone, Tina; SUPL since April 1997; born 5.2.61; HM Treasury 1980; FCO 1982; Port Stanley 1983; Kingston 1984; Peking 1986; FCO 1989; Harare 1993; Band B3; m 1996 Jürgen Manfred Wicke.

Thain, Robert; Second Secretary FCO since October 1994; born 9.9.52; FCO 1975; Warsaw 1977; Rabat 1979; Zagreb 1982; FCO 1984; Canberra 1986; FCO 1990; Vice Consul Helsinki 1992; m 1977 Susan Mary Nice.

Thiel, Ann Bernadette; Second Secretary FCO since May 1997; born 2.8.52; FCO 1971; Moscow 1973; Kuwait 1975; Düsseldorf 1978; FCO 1981; Floater duties 1984; Moscow 1986; FCO 1988; Second Secretary FCO 1991; HM Consul Johannesburg (later Pristina) 1995.

Thom, Dr Gordon; SUPL since September 1998; born 18.5.53; DOE 1978; FCO 1979; Second later First Secretary Tokyo 1981; FCO 1985; First Secretary (Comm) New Delhi 1989; Counsellor (Econ) Tokyo 1994; m 1977 Margaret Pringle (1s 1982; 1d 1986).

Thomas, Dr Catherine Clare Mitchell; FCO since July 1987; born 3.2.58; Senior Research Officer (DS Band C4) later Principle Research Officer (Band D6); m 1989 Martin Brian Howe. (2d 1990, 1994)

Thomas, Colin Ronald; Third Secretary FCO since October 1987; born 27.3.49; Board of Trade 1967; FCO 1969; Dacca 1971; Havana 1974; Maputo 1975; FCO 1979; Geneva 1984; Rio de Janeiro 1987.

Thomas, David Lloyd; Pretoria since July 2000; born 4.8.70; FCO 1996; Lagos 1997; Band C4.

Thomas, David Roger, CMG (2000); Consul-General San Francisco since July 2001; born 1.1.45; FCO 1968; Third Secretary Cairo 1971; Attaché later Second Secretary UKREP Brussels 1974; Ankara 1978; Second later First Secretary FCO 1982; Consul (Comm) Frankfurt 1986; Consul-General Stuttgart 1990; First Secretary FCO 1993; HM Ambassador Baku 1997; m(1) diss 1977 (2d 1968, 1970); (2) 1978 Fiona Lindsey Tyndall.

Thomas, Graeme Gordon; First Secretary (Commercial) Athens since January 1997; born 26.9.48; FCO 1968; Africa Floater 1971; FCO 1972; Africa Floater 1973; Sana'a 1975; Jedda 1976; Far East Floater 1977; South East Asia Floater 1978; FCO 1980; Victoria 1982; FCO 1986; Second Secretary and Consul Warsaw 1987; Second Secretary FCO 1988; Second Secretary (Commercial) Riyadh 1992; Full-time Language Training 1996; m 1981 Penelope Ann Richmond.

Thomas, Jeffrey MBE (1995); HM Consul-General Madrid Embassy since March 1999; born 13.7.47; CO 1964; FO (later FCO) 1966; Manila 1969; Berlin 1973; FCO 1975; Ibadan 1978; Kaduna 1980; Second Secretary FCO 1984; Second Secretary (Admin/Cons) Muscat 1987; Consul Oporto 1991; First Secretary FCO 1996; m 1969 Lesley Anne Wishart (3s 1973, twins 1975).

Thomas, Martin Hugh Stevenson; First Secretary FCO since May 1993; born 2.7.42; FO 1965; Moscow 1967; Kabul 1969; Ottawa 1971; FCO 1974; Nairobi 1977; Rio de Janeiro 1980; Second Secretary Brasilia 1982; Second Secretary FCO 1983; First Secretary (Comm) Amman 1988; First Secretary (Comm) Belgrade 1991; m 1966 Patricia Saward (2d 1971, 1973).

Thomas, Penelope Ann (née Richmond); Athens since December 1997; born 17.2.50; FCO 1973; UKREP Brussels 1974; Caracas 1977; FCO 1979; Victoria 1982; SUPL 1987; FCO 1988; Riyadh 1992; FCO 1996; SUPL 1997; Band B3; m 1981 Graeme Gordon Thomas.

Thomas, Philip Lloyd, CMG (2001); High Commissioner Nigeria, Ambassador (Non resident) Benin since March 2001; born 10.6.48; FCO 1972; Second Secretary Belgrade 1974; Second later First Secretary FCO 1977; First Secretary (Comm) Madrid 1981; First Secretary (Press) UKREP Brussels 1987; Counsellor on loan to the Cabinet Office 1989; Counsellor (Pol/Mil) Washington 1991; FCO 1996; Consul General Düsseldorf 1999.

Thomas, Simon D; Second Secretary (Political) Warsaw since November 1998; born 24.5.75; FCO 1997; Band C4.

Thompson, Christopher Colin; Port Moresby since November 2000; born 18.5.69; FCO 1989; Floater duties 1992; Tokyo 1995; On loan to the Football Association 1999; Band B3.

Thompson, Clive Vincent; First Secretary FCO since January 1996; born 3.4.47; FCO 1973; MECAS 1975; Islamabad 1976; Tunis 1978; Stuttgart 1981; Second Secretary FCO 1983; Second Secretary (Consul) Moscow 1987; Second Secretary FCO 1990; Consul later First Secretary (Commercial) Munich 1990; m 1969 Carol Knight (2d 1973, 1974).

Thompson, Gillian Hazel; FCO since December 1993; born 8.6.53; FCO 1979; Rio de Janeiro 1980; FCO 1981; Belgrade 1982; FCO 1984; Lisbon 1986; FCO 1989; Berlin 1991; Band A2.

Thompson, Jack Francis; First Secretary (Immigration) and HM Consul Moscow since January 1998; born 10.11.41; HM Customs and Excise 1959; HO 1968; New Delhi 1974; Second Secretary FCO 1980; Vice-Consul Zagreb 1981; Second Secretary (Comm) Santiago 1985; First Secretary FCO 1989; First Secretary (Commercial) Mexico City, 1991; First Secretary (Management) and HM Consul Kuwait 1995; m 1964 Isabel Requena Matallana (2s 1965, 1970; 1d 1967).

Thompson, Jan; FCO since March 2000; born 25.8.65; FCO 1990 (Second Secretary 1991); Second Secretary Bonn 1991; First Secretary FCO 1994; First Secretary UKMIS New York 1997.

Thompson, John, MBE (1975); HM Ambassador Luanda since February 2002; born 28.5.45; FO 1964; DSA 1965; Vice-Consul Düsseldorf 1966; Abu Dhabi 1969; Phnom Penh 1972; Management Studies Polytechnic of Central London 1974; Second Secretary on loan to DOT 1975; FCO 1977; First Secretary and Head of Chancery Luanda 1979; Consul (Comm) São Paulo 1981; First Secretary FCO 1985; High Commissioner Vila 1988; Counsellor and Director of Trade Promotion BTIO New York 1992; Counsellor FCO 1997; m 1966 Barbara Hopper (1d 1967).

Thompson, Lynne Diana; FCO since January 2000; born 20.8.59; FCO 1981; Warsaw 1982; Bandar Seri Begawan 1983; FCO 1986; Vienna 1987; FCO 1988; Istanbul 1996; Band B3.

Thompson, Philippa Ann (née Hadley); Second Secretary (PPA) Paris since August 1999; born 3.8.62; FCO 1980; Brussels 1983; Bridgetown 1985; FCO 1989; Ottawa 1991; Second Secretary UKREP Brussels 1994; FCO 1995; ENA Paris 1998; m2000 Alphaeus Randolph Thompson (1s 2001).

Thompson, Richard Paul Reynier, OBE (2001); First Secretary FCO since January 2001; born 17.8.60; FCO 1989; Second later First Secretary Stockholm 1991; First Secretary FCO 1993; First

Secretary UKMIS Geneva 1996; Band D6; m 1991 Louisa Halliday-Yates (1d 1992).

Thompson, Sarah Jane; FCO since April 1982; born 1.4.58; FCO 1979; Pretoria/Cape Town 1980; Band A2.

Thomson, Adam McClure; Counsellor FCO since September 1998; born 1.7.55; FCO 1978; Third later Second Secretary Moscow 1981; Second later First Secretary UKDEL Brussels 1983; FCO 1986; on loan to Cabinet Office 1989; First Secretary (Chancery) Washington 1991; Counsellor (Head of Chancery) New Delhi 1995; m 1984 Fariba Shirazi; (2d 1991, 1993; 1s 1996).

Thomson, Andrew Robert Hay; Second Secretary (Political) Pristina since September 2000; born 23.6.75; FCO 1998; Band C4.

Thomson, Dick; Consul General Barcelona since October 1999; born 18.12.42; Ministry of Transport 1961; DSAO (later FCO) 1966; Havana 1969; Athens 1970; Warsaw 1972; FCO 1973; San Francisco 1976; Second Secretary 1978; Algiers 1980; First Secretary FCO 1984; First Secretary (Chancery/Inf) Copenhagen 1988; Counsellor FCO 1992; HM Ambassador Santo Domingo 1995; m 1972 Jacqueline Margaret Dunn (1d 1976; 1s 1979).

Thomson, Fergus Russell Cullen; First Secretary FCO since February 1995; born 16.5.44; DWS 1964; DSAO 1967; Peking 1969; Lagos 1972; Second Secretary FCO 1976; BTDO New York 1978; First Secretary (Comm) Addis Ababa 1984; First Secretary FCO 1987; Deputy Head of Mission Lima 1991; m 1970 Jeanette Patricia Louis Mutton (1d 1977).

Thomson, Jonathan Hiroshi Stewart; Second Secretary Tokyo since November 1998; born 13.5.72; FCO 1996; full-time language training 1997.

Thorne, Karen Ann (née Higgins); FCO since March 1984; born 9.3.57; FCO 1974; Lusaka 1978; Grand Turk 1983; Band A2; m 1978 Richard J Thorne (1d 1981).

Thorne, Nicholas Alan; Counsellor (Financial) UKMIS New York since June 1995; born 31.3.48; FO (later FCO) 1965; Yaoundé 1971; UKRep Brussels 1974; Second Secretary FCO 1977; Central London Polytechnic 1977; FCO 1978; Second later First Secretary UKMIS New York 1980; First Secretary Head of Chancery Manila 1983; First Secretary FCO 1987; on secondment to Thorn EMI 1989; Counsellor (Commercial) and Deputy Head of Mission Helsinki 1991; m 1974 Ann Margaret Boorman (1s 1978; 1d 1980).

Thornton, Daniel Vernon; Second secretary FCO since September 1996; born 6.8.69; FCO 1991; Second Secretary (EU Affairs) Brussels 1995.

Thornton, James Sebastian; First Secretary (Chancery) Mexico City since January 2000; born 2.11.64; UKAEA 1986-1989; FCO 1989; Second Secretary (Commercial/Information) Algiers 1992;

Second later First Secretary FCO 1994; Band D6; m 1999 Anne Scrase.

Thornton, John Norris; Third Secretary Berlin since May 1996; born 6.7.59; FCO 1978; BGWRS Darwin 1980; FCO 1982; Beirut 1983; FCO 1984; Third Secretary Tehran 1986; FCO 1987; Third Secretary Geneva 1991; FCO 1993; Band C4; m 1980 Angela Dawn Clarke (1d 1989; 1s 1994).

Thornton, Patricia Ann; First Secretary Islamabad since January 2000; born 11.1.52; FCO 1971; Tehran 1973; Lima 1976; New Delhi 1979; FCO 1982; Guatemala City 1984; FCO 1987; Second Secretary (Comm) Santiago 1988; Consul Johannesburg 1991; FCO 1995.

Thornton, Sarah; FCO since July 2000; born 5.6.72; FCO 1992; Rome 1995; SUPL 1999; Band A2.

Thorpe, Adrian Charles, CMG (1994); HM Ambassador Mexico City since January 1999; born 29.7.42; FO 1965; Language Student Tokyo 1965; Third later Second Secretary (Inf) Tokyo 1968; FCO 1970; Seconded to HCS 1971; FCO 1972; First Secretary Beirut 1973; First Secretary and Head of Chancery Beirut 1975; FCO 1976; First Secretary (Econ) Tokyo 1976; First Secretary FCO 1981; Counsellor Head of Information Technology Dept 1982; Counsellor (Econ) Bonn 1985; Deputy High Commissioner Kuala Lumpur 1989; Minister Tokyo 1991; HM Ambassador Manila 1995; m 1968 Miyoko Kosugi.

Thorpe, Nigel James, CVO (1991); HM Ambassador Budapest since April 1998; born 3.10.45; Third Secretary FCO 1969; Third later Second Secretary Warsaw 1970; Second later First Secretary Dacca 1973; FCO 1975; First Secretary (Econ) Ottawa 1979; on loan to Department of Energy 1981; FCO 1982; Counsellor and Head of Chancery Warsaw 1985; Deputy High Commissioner Harare 1989; Counsellor FCO 1992; Senior Directing Staff at the Royal College of Defence Studies 1996.

Thurlow, John Robert; Second Secretary (Commercial/Industrial Relations) Rome since January 2000; born 28.8.67; HCS 1984; FCO 1988; Algiers 1990; Bridgetown 1992; FCO 1995; On loan to the DTI 1998; Band C4; m 1992 Joanna Welch (1d 1988).

Thursfield, Martin Robert; First Secretary (Political) Vilnius since December 2000; born 8.6.67; FCO 1989; Full-time Language Training Peking 1991; Second Secretary (Inf) British Trade Commission Hong Kong 1993; First Secretary FCO 1995; Band D6; m 1996 Ingrid Katharina Corbyn Hale (1s 1997, 1d 2000).

Thurston, Brenda Pauline; Abuja since April 1998; born 9.11.49; DHSS 1980; FCO 1984; Damascus 1986; Port Louis 1987; Karachi 1990; Pretoria 1994; Band A2; m 1974 John Anthony Thurston.

Tibber, Peter Harris; On loan to British Trade International since September 2000; born 7.9.56;

Second Secretary FCO 1984; Second later First Secretary Paris 1986; First Secretary FCO 1989; PS to the Minister of State 1990; Full-time Language Training 1992; First Secretary (Political) Ankara 1993; Deputy Head of Mission Mexico City 1996; m 1983 Eve Levy-Huet (3s 1986, 1988, 1992).

Tiffin, Sarah Anne; on secondment to the Irish Department of Foreign Affairs since September 2000; born 5.11.65; FCO 1988; ENA Paris 1989; Third later Second Secretary Paris 1990; Second later First Secretary May 1993; First Secretary (Political) New Delhi 1997; m2000 Pádraig Francis.

Tillyard, Barbara Ann (née Levett); Washington since November 1997; born 27.1.46; FCO 1974; UKREP Brussels 1975; FCO 1979; SUPL 1979; FCO 1983; Washington 1985; FCO 1989; Abu Dhabi 1992; Band B3; m 1977 Brian William Tillyard.

Timsit, Milli (née Abbott); Consul/MO Munich since August 2000; born 11.6.56; FCO 1975; Washington 1977; Africa/Middle East Floater 1981; FCO 1982; Islamabad 1984; Tokyo 1986; FCO 1988; Tel Aviv 1991; Casablanca 1995; Band C4; m 1992 Uzi Timsit (1s 1995; 1d 1997).

Tiney, Michael Charles; Kathmandu since December 1998; born 12.9.66; HCS 1989-92; Bucharest 1993; Kampala 1996; Band A2.

Tinline, Robert John; Second Secretary Bogotá since July 1999; born 13.8.76; FCO 1997.

Tiscenko, Julie Maria (née Cooper); FCO since April 1996; born 31.1.65; FCO 1984; Harare 1986; SUPL 1990; Dhaka 1991; SUPL 1994; Band A2; m(1) 1987 Eric Robert Cooper (2s 1989, 1990); m(2) Kenneth Victor Tiscenko.

Tissot, Philip Marius Arthur; Deputy High Commissioner Valletta since April 1999; born 10.2.60; FCO 1978; Africa Floater 1981; Lagos 1983; FCO 1986; Vice-Consul Toronto 1988 (Second Secretary 1989); Second Secretary (Chancery) UKMIS New York 1990; FCO 1994; m 1985 Julie Anne Grant (diss 1999) (1s 1989, 1d 1990).

Tivey, Wendy; Copenhagen since March 1997; born 20.7.61; FCO 1995; Band A2.

Tluczek, Karl Shaun Paul; Prague since September 1999; born 5.1.72; FCO 1991; Band B3.

Tluczek, Mark Joseph; Moscow since October 2001; born 22.3.67; HCS FCO 1987; FCO 1996; Abuja 1998; Band B3; m 1991 Joanne Lindley.

Todd, Damian Roderic; HM Ambassador Bratislava since November 2001; born 29.8.59; FCO 1980; Third later Second Secretary Cape Town/Pretoria 1981; Second Secretary FCO 1984; First Secretary and Consul Prague 1987; First Secretary FCO 1989; First Secretary (Economic) Bonn 1991; HM Treasury 1995; FCO 1997; On secondment to HM Treasury as Head of EU Co-ordination and Strategy Team 1998; m 1987 Alison Mary Digby (1s 1989, 2d 1992,1999).

Tolfree, Alison (née Oxenford); Lusaka since January 1999; born 17.2.66; FCO 1985; Belgrade 1992; FCO 1995; Band A2; m 1991 Mark Tolfree (1d 1997, 1s 2000).

Tollyfield, Caroline Leslie (née Brewer); Second Secretary FCO since September 1998; born 20.6.61; FCO 1994; Second Secretary (Political) Vienna 1995; Band C4; m 1995 Andrew John Tollyfield (1s 2000).

Tomkins, Michael Paul; First Secretary (Management) Jakarta since August 2000; born 23.12.50; FCO 1970; Honiara 1972; Aden 1976; Kingston 1977; Wellington 1980; Warsaw 1982; FCO 1983; Dhaka 1986; UKMIS Geneva 1989; FCO 1992 (Second Secretary 1994); Second Secretary (Commercial) Dubai 1996; m 1979 Eleanor Michelle Ritch (1d 1986; 1s 1989).

Tomkins, Roger James; Moscow since May 1998; born 30.6.48; Royal Navy 1966-88; Prison Service 1988-90; Budapest 1990; Islamabad 1992; Lagos 1994; Band B3; m 1971 Pauline Bennett (1s 1974, 1d 1976).

Tomlinson, Deborah Jane, MVO (1996); SUPL since September 2000; born 16.2.63; FCO 1981; Islamabad 1984; Jakarta 1986; FCO 1990; Third Secretary (Visits) UKREP Brussels 1993; Third Secretary Belgrade 1996; Second Secretary (KHF) Sarajevo 1998; Band C4; m 1992 Mark Hyland.

Tomlinson, Jean Lesley; UKREP Brussels since July 1998; born 14.7.62; FCO 1989; Rabat 1991; FCO 1994; Band A2.

Tomlinson, Thomas Mark; Second Secretary (Chancery) Belgrade since May 2001; born 2.2.63; Third Secretary (Management) and Vice Consul Maputo 1995; Jedda 1998; Band C4.

Tonge, Simon David; Jakarta since July 1989; born 18.9.69; FCO 1996; UKMIS New York 1997; Band C4.

Tonkin, Ramsey Harris; First Secretary (Management) Berlin since May 2001; born 17.4.44; FO 1964; Ankara 1966; Bonn 1969; FCO 1972; Tehran 1975; Second Secretary (Comm) Port of Spain 1978; Second Secretary FCO 1982; Second later First Secretary (Admin/Consul) Bombay 1987; First Secretary (Management) Oslo 1989; First Secretary FCO 1995; First Secretary Bangkok 1997; FTLT 2000; m 1966 Valerie Anne Duff (2d 1967, 1969).

Tonner, Janice Wight (née Taylor) SUPL since March 1995; born 6.11.64; FCO 1985; Rome 1987; Lilongwe 1990; Band A2; m 1987 Gary Campbell Tonner; (1s 1993).

Toothe, Adrian Gerald; Second later First Secretary FCO since August 1989; born 7.1.52; FCO 1972; Jedda 1976; Second Secretary FCO 1980; UKMIS Geneva 1985; Band C5; m 1976 Diane Whitehead (2s 1982, 1985).

Topping, Dr Patrick Gilmer; First Secretary FCO since August 1998; born 5.9.59; FCO 1986; Second later First Secretary (Chancery) Kuala Lumpur 1990; First Secretary FCO 1991; Washington 1994; Band D6; m 1985 Indira Annick Coomaraswamy (1s 1992; 1d 1993).

Torlot, Timothy Achille; Second later First Secretary FCO since May 1992; born 17.9.57; FCO 1981; Muscat 1984; Second Secretary (Chancery) Wellington m1986 Bridie Morton (1d 1990).

Torrance, David John Baillie; Second Secretary (Commercial) Muscat since August 1998; born 29.2.56; FCO 1975; Bangkok 1978; LA Floater 1982; Doha 1984; FCO 1987; Third Secretary and Vice-Consul San Salvador 1990; Third later Second Secretary FCO 1994; Band C4.

Torry, Peter James; HM Ambassador Madrid since October 1998; born 2.8.48; FCO 1970; Third Secretary Havana 1971; Second Secretary (Econ/Comm) Jakarta 1974; First Secretary FCO 1977; First Secretary (Chancery) Bonn 1981; First Secretary later Counsellor FCO 1985; Counsellor Washington 1989; Counsellor later AUSS (Personnel and Security) FCO 1993; m 1979 Angela Wakeling Wood (3d 1980, 1982, 1985).

Totty, Alastair Walton; Rangoon since October 2000; born 24.7.69; FCO 1988; Abu Dhabi 1991; Jerusalem 1994; SUPL 1997; FCO 1998; Band B3; m 1996 Lorraine Helen Fussey.(1s 1997)

Towe, Sheila; Second Secretary (Commercial) Toronto since August 1999; born 26.7.62; FCO 1981; East Berlin 1983; FCO 1985; Baghdad 1987; FCO 1990; On loan to the DTI 1992; Vice-Consul Jedda 1994; on loan to the DTI 1996; Band B3.

Townend, Warren Dennis; Counsellor (Management) Washington since February 2001; born 15.11.45; FO 1964; DSAO 1965; FO (later FCO) 1967; Vice Consul Hanoi 1969; Vice Consul (Comm) Hamburg 1970; Third later Second Secretary (Comm) Dacca 1973; FCO 1976; Second later First Secretary Bonn 1979; First Secretary (Comm) Bangkok 1984; First Secretary FCO 1987; Deputy Consul-General Düsseldorf and Deputy Director-General for Trade Investment Promotion in Germany 1991; HM Consul General Shanghai 1996; m Ann Mary Riddle (1d 1977; twin s 1979; 1s 1980).

Towner-Evans, Louise; Floater Duties since June 2001; born 12.8.71; FCO 1994; Jakarta 1996; FCO 2000; Band A2.

Townsend, David John; Second Secretary (Political) UKDEL Vienna since June 2001; born 31.5.57; ECGD 1984-89; FCO 1989; Vienna 1991; Language Training 1994; Vice Consul Prague 1995; FCO 1997; Band C4; m 1993 Sarah Ann Garry.

Townsend, Stephen Thomas; FCO since February 1997; born 10.7.61; FCO 1980; Caracas 1982; Kinshasa 1986; FCO 1990; Full-time Language

Training 1992; Madrid 1993; Band C4; m 1996 Fiona Maria Kilpatrick.

Townson, Jennifer Caroline; FCO since April 1999; born 22.2.68; FCO 1989; On loan to the ODA 1991; Third Secretary (Chancery) Paris 1992; Vice Consul Port Louis 1995. Band B3.

Towsey, Malcolm John; First Secretary (Commercial) Helsinki since July 1999; born 6.5.47; Ministry of Defence 1963; FO (later FCO) 1965; Baghdad 1969; Warsaw 1972; Rabat 1973; Dacca 1976; FCO 1979; Maseru 1982; Second Secretary FCO 1984; Second Secretary (Commercial) Dublin 1986; Second Secretary FCO 1990; First Secretary (Management) Lagos 1991; First Secretary (Management/Consular) Abuja 1993; First Secretary FCO 1994; m 1976 Erica Pamela Filder (1s 1979; 1d 1981).

Traylor, Owen John; Consul Istanbul since August 2000; born 26.9.55; FCO 1977; Language Student Tokyo 1980; Second Secretary (Econ) Tokyo 1981; First Secretary FCO 1985; First Secretary (Chancery) Berlin 1990; First Secretary FCO 1994; Band D6; m(1) 1981 Angela Carmel Webb (diss 1989) (1d 1985), (2) 1991 Carola Wangerin.

Treadell, Alan; British Trade International since June 1999; born 8.11.51; FCO 1971; Stockholm 1973; Sana'a 1976; FCO 1977; Islamabad 1979; FCO 1983; Kuala Lumpur 1985; Band C4; FCO 1990; m 1985 Victoria Marguerite Jansz.

Treadell, Victoria Marguerite (née Jansz), MVO (1989); First Secretary British Trade International since March 1998; born 4.11.59; FCO 1978; Islamabad 1981; FCO 1983; Kuala Lumpur 1985; FCO 1990; (First Secretary 1998); Band B3; m 1985 Alan Treadell.

Trehearne, Susan Elizabeth (née Morton); SUPL since April 1998; born 25.2.62; FCO 1986; First Secretary (Chancery) Peking 1992; First Secretary FCO 1995; m 1996 Simon Grant Treherne.

Trevelyan, Sarah Frances; FCO since May 1993; born 6.2.65; FCO 1983; Lisbon 1987; Kampala 1990; Band A2; m 1993 Darren Francis Forbes-Batey.

Trott, Angela; Manila since December 1999; FCO 1990; Band C4; m 1996 Jannick Pierre Michel Charpentier.

Trott, Christopher John; First Secretary (Commercial) later First Secretary (Political) Tokyo since July 1996; born 14.2.66; FCO 1991; (Second Secretary 1992); Consul and Deputy Head of Mission Rangoon 1993; m 1992 Sunna Park.

Truelove, Andrew John; New Delhi since October 1997; born 3.4.64; FCO 1991; Band B3.

Truman, Gary Douglas; FCO since March 1994; born 15.10.63; (Home Civil Service 1981); FCO 1990; Bonn 1993; Band A2.

Tucker, Andrew Victor Gunn; HM Ambassador Baku since November 2000; born 20.12.55; Joint

Technical Language Service 1978-81; FCO 1981; Second Secretary Dar es Salaam 1982; First Secretary on loan to the Cabinet Office 1985; First Secretary and Press Attaché Moscow 1987; First Secretary FCO 1991; First Secretary on loan to the German Ministry of Foreign Affairs 1993; First Secretary Bonn 1994; Deputy High Commissioner Nairobi 1997; FTLT 2000; m 1986 Judith Anne Gibson.

Tucker, Ernest; Amman since September 1999; born 16.3.45; Army 1963-1991; Warsaw 1991; Moscow 1993; Lagos 1996; Band B3; m 1965 Ute Elli Wilkelmine (1s 1978).

Tucker, James Philip; First Secretary (Political) Islamabad since October 2001; born 10.1.66; FCO 1990; Second Secretary (Political) Prague 1993; Second Secretary (Political) Bratislava 1994; Second Secretary FCO 1996; Band D6; m 1991 Susie Elizabeth Betts (2d 1994, 1995).

Tucknott, John Anthony, MBE (1990); FCO since August 1998; born 2.1.58; DoE 1975; FCO 1977; Rome 1980; Cairo 1982; FCO 1985; Second Secretary (Admin), later DHM Beirut 1988; Second Secretary FCO 1993 (First Secretary 1994); First Secretary UKMIS New York 1995; m(1) 1980 Susan Jayne Elliott (diss 1992); (2) 1992 Tania Amine Charaf (diss); (3) 2000 Riita-Leena Irmeli Lehtinen.

Tuhey, Claire Elizabeth; FCO since September 1998; born 7.2.57; FCO 1976; SUPL 1976; FCO 1979; Paris 1982; Africa/Middle East Floater 1985; Vice-Consul New York 1987; FCO 1991; Dublin 1994; on secondment to the Glencree Centre on temporary duty 1997; Band C4.

Tuke, Sarah Frances; SUPL since August 2000; born 8.3.63; FCO 1982; Cape Town/Pretoria 1984; Jakarta 1987; Floater Duties 1990; Peking 1993; UMKIS New York 1996; SUPL 1999; FCO 2000; Band B3.

Tully, Colin Nigel; FCO since August 1997; born 15.7.58; FCO 1980; Amman 1982; FCO 1985; New Delhi 1987; FCO 1991; Buenos Aires 1995; Band C4; m 1983 Wendy Joyce Ogden (1s 1985; 1d 1989).

Tunn, Douglas Charles; Tehran since April 2000; born 18.2.68; FCO 1987; UKMIS New York 1989; Port Moresby 1992; Jakarta 1998; Band B3; m 1996 Cecilia Rosemary Tokilala.

Tunn, Rachel Elizabeth; UKMIS New York since January 1995; born 28.5.68; FCO 1989; Bucharest 1991; Hanoi 1993; Band A2.

Tunney, Davina; Washington since June 1999; born 31.7.67; Home Civil Service 1987 to 1989; FCO 1998; Band A2.

Tunnicliffe, Christopher John Robin; Second Secretary (Chancery) Port Louis since May 1999; born 11.11.69; FCO 1989; Prague 1991; FCO 1993; Full-time Language Training 1994; FCO 1995; Riyadh 1995; Band C4; m (1) 1991

Veronica Mary Walters (1d 1989, 1s 1992) (diss 1995) (2) 1996 Zara Louise Chapman.

Turnbull, David Robert; Second Secretary (Finance) UKMIS New York since September 1997; born 25.8.55; MOD 1976; Ankara 1980; FCO 1983; Maputo 1984; The Hague 1988; Third later Second Secretary FCO 1991; Second Secretary (Commercial) Beirut 1995; m 1987 Eva Marianne Persson.

Turner, Alan Roger, Caracas since June 1992; born 9.4.48; Royal Air Force 1965-1968; Band C4; m 1974 Caroline Grace.

Turner , Andrew William; FCO since August 2001; born 8.12.63; FCO 1986; Language Training 1987; Third later Second Secretary (Chancery) Muscat 1989; Second Secretary (Chancery) Damascus 1992 Second later First Secretary FCO 1994; First Secretary (Political) Pretoria 1998; Band D7; m 1992 Angeline Marie Biegler (1d 2001).

Turner, David Harvey; First Secretary FCO since October 1993; born 17.2.45; FO 1966; Bonn 1968; Lagos 1970; Brasilia 1973; FCO 1975; Maputo 1978; Vice-Consul São Paulo 1981; Second later First Secretary FCO 1985; First Secretary (Comm) Lisbon 1989; m 1966 Janet Mary Field (1s; 1d 1975).

Turner, Mark Robin; First Secretary (Commercial) Lisbon since April 2001; born 23.8.55; FCO 1975; Budapest 1977; Maseru 1979; Islamabad 1982; FCO 1984; Los Angeles 1988; Second Secretary FCO 1991; Consul and Second Secretary (Management) Buenos Aires 1994; First Secretary FCO 1998; m 1981 Patricia Louise Brown (2d 1984, 1987).

Turner, Richard Patrick; First Secretary (Information) Moscow since June 2001; born 19.1.63; FCO 1981; UKRep Brussels 1984; Dar es Salaam 1986; Third Secretary (Admin) UKDEL Strasbourg 1988; FCO 1991 (Second Secretary 1993); Sao Paulo 1996; FTLT 2000; Band C5.

Turner, Robert Leigh; Counsellor (EU/Economic) Bonn (now Berlin) since July 1998; born 13.3.58; Department of Transport 1979; PSA 1980; DOE 1981; HM Treasury 1982; FCO 1983; Second Secretary (Chancery) Vienna 1984; First Secretary FCO 1987; Language Training 1991; First Secretary (Economic) Moscow 1992; First Secretary FCO 1995; Counsellor FCO 1997; m 1992 Pamela Ann Major (1s 1992, 1d 1994).

Turner, Stephen Edward; Deputy High Commissioner and Commercial Counsellor Dhaka since March 1999; born 25.3.46; CRO 1963; DSAO 1965; Jakarta 1968; DTI 1972; Third Secretary (Commercial) Kuala Lumpur 1972; Second Secretary FCO 1976; Valletta 1978; Second (Comm) Jakarta 1983; First Secretary (Economic) Jakarta 1986; First Secretary FCO 1988; Consul (Comm) Seattle 1990; Deputy Head of Mission and Consul General Hanoi 1995; m

1966 Maureen Ann Dick (2s 1969, 1971; 2d 1973, 1982).

Turney, Nicholas; FCO since September 1984; born 31.3.53; FCO 1971; Washington 1981; Band C4.

Turunc, Susan Kay (née Powell); Cairo since November 1999; born 27.3.49; FCO 1968; Peking 1970; FCO 1971; resigned 1972; Home Civil Service 1975-79; reinstated FCO 1989; Istanbul 1990; Seoul 1994; FCO 1997; Band B3; m 1991 Gokhan Turunc.

Turvill, Carol May (née Massingham); Accra since July 2000; born 17.6.66; FCO 1985; Pretoria/Cape Town 1988; Havana 1990; FCO 1992; SUPL 1995; Islamabad 1995; FCO 1998; Band B3; m 1994 Stuart Graham Turvill.

Turvill, Stuart Graham; Accra since July 2000; born 18.2.71; FCO 1991; Islamabad 1995; FCO 1998; Band B3; m 1994 Carol May Massingham.

Twigg, Mark Paul; First Secretary British Trade International since July 1999; born 1.3.56 FCO 1975; Beirut 1979; FCO 1980; Harare 1981; Düsseldorf 1983; Tripoli 1987; FCO 1989; (Second Secretary 1991); Full-time Language Training 1994; Second Secretary (Commercial) Prague 1994;

Twyman, Robin Edward; Second Secretary UKMIS Geneva since March 2001; born 27.8.68; FCO 1987; Harare 1989; Africa/ ME Floater Duties 1993; FCO 1996; Band C4.

Tylor, Paul Andrew; Peking since August 1997; born 22.9.64; RAF 1985-1995; FCO 1995; Band A2; m 1988 Yvonne Margaret.

U

Uden, Martin David; Counsellor (Economic) Ottawa since August 1997; born 28.2.55; FCO 1977; Seoul 1978; Second later First Secretary FCO 1982; First Secretary Bonn 1986; First Secretary FCO 1990; Counsellor (Political) and Consul-General Seoul 1994; m 1982 Fiona Jane Smith (2s 1986, 1990).

Underwood, Sheila Bridget; World Wide Floater since September 1999; born 26.11.70; HCS 1995; FCO 1995; Band A2.

Upton, Michael John; HM Consul (Commercial) Seattle since April 1995; born 28.10.51; RAF 1970-76; FCO 1976; Havana 1978; Aden 1982; FCO 1982; Bogotá 1984; Second Secretary UKMIS New York 1986; Vice-Consul (Inward Investment) Los Angeles 1990; First Secretary FCO 1992; m 1978 Susan Marshall (1s 1981; 1d 1983).

Usher, Janet Clare; Cape Town since May 1999; born 23.4.65; FCO 1983; Washington 1986; Prague 1989; Floater Duties 1991; FCO 1994; On loan to the DTI 1996; Band C4.

Usher, Judith; FCO since June 1999; born 14.10.69; FCO 1988; Peking 1991; Zagreb 1993; Lagos 1995; Band A2.

Usher, Seifeldin; Accra since November 1999; born 27.6.69; FCO 1987; UKMIS Vienna 1989; New Delhi 1991; Khartoum 1994; FCO 1997; Band C4; m 1995 Nihad Elnujumi.

V

Van Der Plank, Ian Derek; Second Secretary Islamabad since February 1997; born 21.8.56. Royal Navy 1972-77; FCO 1981; Paris 1987; Third Secretary Lagos 1990; Third Secretary FCO 1992.

Vargas, Emlyn Barry; First Secretary (Technical Management) New Delhi since January 2000; born 2.2.46; HM Forces 1964-86; FCO 1986; Caracas 1989; Helsinki 1992; FCO 1997; Band C5; m 1991 Carmen Rafaela Velazquez.

Vaygelt, Robin (née Maitland); FCO since June 2000; born 14.6.61; FCO 1984; Rio de Janeiro 1986; FCO 1988; Johannesburg 1993; Paris 1996; Band A2; m 1992 Marek Stephen Fernyhough Vaygelt.

Venn, Robert Lawrence; First Secretary (Political) Peking since December 1997; born 15.4.65; FCO 1992; Second Secretary (Economic) Jakarta 1994; Band D6; m 1990 Wendy Ann Wightman (1s 1994, 1d 1996).

Verma, Neeras; SUPL since April 2000; born 21.11.62; FCO 1982; UKDEL NATO Brussels 1984; Luanda 1988; FCO 1992; Vienna 1996; Düsseldorf 1999; Band B3; m 1985 Sarah-Jane Dodman.

Verma, Sarah-Jane (née Dodman) Third Secretary Bridgetown since December 1996; born 31.12.63; FCO 1983; UKRep Brussels 1985; Luanda 1988; FCO 1992; Band B3; m 1985 Neeras Verma (diss 1996).

Very, Donna (née Grant); FCO since January 1999; born 27.7.69; FCO 1988; SUPL 1992; FCO 1994; Tehran 1996; Band A2; m 1994 Steve Jason Very (1s 1997; 1d 1999).

Vickers, David Victor Edwin; Grand Turk since November 1999; born 1.5.53; FCO 1973; Lusaka 1975; Kathmandu 1979; Sofia 1983; FCO 1984; Islamabad 1985; Ankara 1989; FCO 1992; Deputy Head of Mission Tallinn 1996; Band C4; m 1983 Pamela Barron (née Scott).

Vidal, Ruben Joel; FCO since September 1989; born 7.3.41; Royal Marines 1967-72; FCO 1979; Damascus 1981; FCO 1985; Harare 1988; m 1975 Delores Annett (1d 1983).

de Villamizar, Bernadette Teresa (née Edwards); FCO since August 2000; born 2.3.63; FCO 1983; UKREP Brussels 1985; Shanghai 1987; Rio de Janeiro 1988; FCO 1992; Madrid 1993; Caracas 1996; FCO 1999; SUPL 2000; Band B3; m 1999 Igor Antonio Villamizar Rojas.

Vineall, Katherine Patricia (née Jenkins); SUPL since January 1999; born 7.11.63; FCO 1987; (Second Secretary 1989); Second Secretary (Chancery) Madrid 1991; Second Secretary FCO

1992; SUPL 1995; ; First Secretary FCO 1995; m 1992 Nicholas Edward John Vineall (1s 1995).

Virgoe, John; FCO since April 1999; born 1.9.69; FCO 1991; Full-time Language Training 1994; Jakarta 1995; m 1999 Tuti Suwidjiningsih.

Vir Singh, Doris Nefertiti; British Embassy Paris since March 2000; born 3.2.64; FCO 1993; UKMIS Geneva 1996; Band A2.

Voak, Susan; Lilongwe since April 2001; born 2.6.69; FCO 1999; Band A2.

Vosper, Alistair John; FCO since January 2000; born 9.4.70; FCO 1989; Islamabad 1992; Manila 1996; Band B3; m 1995 Lucy Jane Medforth.

Vowles, John Philip, MBE (1994); Havana since April 1999; born 13.8.47; Royal Marines 1962-87; Moscow 1987; Pretoria 1989; Tehran 1991; Kampala 1995; Band C4; m 1968 Maureen Cann.

W

Waddington, Jane Caroline; FCO since July 2001; born 12.10.64; HO 1988; FCO 1998; Stockholm 2000; Band A2.

Wade, Emma Lesley; Second Secretary (Political) since August 1998; born 15.9.73; FCO 1995; Band C4.

Wadvani, Sanjay Mark; Second Secretary (Commercial) Santiago since November 1998; born 6.12.66; FCO 1987; Peking 1989; Damascus 1991; FCO 1995; Band C4.

Wahab, Mohammed Toafiq; Islamabad since July 1998; born 2.4.75; HM Customs and Excise 1993-94; FCO 1997; Band A2; m 1996 Rozmina Muhammad Anwar.(2s 1998, 2000).

Wain, Geoffrey William; Second Secretary (Commercial) Manila since February 2000; born 10.5.65; FCO 1983; Islamabad 1986; Istanbul 1989; FCO 1992 (Second Secretary 1994); Maseru 1995; Band C4; m 1985 Kathleen Anne Lowe (1d 1992).

Wain, Kathleen Anne (née Lowe); Third Secretary (Immigration) Manila since February 2000; born 11.2.63; FCO 1982; Addis Ababa 1984; FCO 1985; Islamabad 1986; Istanbul 1989; FCO 1992; SUPL 1995; Band B3; m 1985 Geoffrey William Wain (1d 1992).

Waite, Timothy Matthew; MO/Consul/ECM St.Petersburg since January 1999; born 21.7.62; PSA 1988-91; FCO 1991; Political/Information/Commercial/Consular/ECO Jedda 1994; Band C4.

Walder, Jacqueline Ann; FCO since October 1998; born 30.8.67; FCO 1989; Abidjan 1992; Almaty 1996; Band B3.

Wales, Lee Anne; Canberra since October 1998; born 7.1.67; FCO 1996; Band A2.

Walford, Thomas Alexander; Second later First Secretary (Management/Consular)Damascus since 1997; born 2.3.49; FCO 1968; Malta 1971; Belmopan 1974; Tunis 1975; FCO 1978; Canberra

1981; The Hague 1983; FCO 1986; Second Secretary and Deputy Head of Mission, Panama City 1989; Second Secretary FCO 1991; m 1974 Mary Thérésa Heafield (1s 1977; 1d 1979).

Walker, Alisdair James; FCO since March 1999; born 14.9.65; FCO 1989; Third Secretary (Chancery) Islamabad 1991; FCO 1995; Assistant Management Officer Moscow 1995; Band C4; m 1992 Susan Mary Ireland (1s 1996, 1d 1998).

Walker, Angela Ruth; on secondment to Ministry of Defence since October 1997; born 7.5.54; FCO 1980; The Hague 1983; Vice-Consul Rio de Janeiro 1986; FCO 1989; Band C4.

Walker, Derek Leonard; Second Secretary JMO Brussels since July 1999; born 28.11.44; FCO 1971; Tripoli 1974; Bucharest 1976; Ottawa 1978; FCO 1980; JAO Brussels 1984; Vice-Consul later Second Secretary (Immigration) Lagos 1988; FCO 1992; Tunis 1995; m 1965 Janice Ann Gamble-Beresford (2d 1968, 1970).

Walker, Helen Mary; First Secretary FCO since January 1999; born 23.7.69; FCO 1991; Full-time Language Training 1993; Athens 1994.

Walker, John Frank; Budapest since January 1998; born 10.2.64; Royal Engineers 1980-85; FCO 1987; Buenos Aires 1991; Band C4; m 1990 Caroline Jane Masters (2s 1985, 1991).

Walker, John Ronald; FCO since March 1985; born 4.5.60; Senior Research Officer Band D6.

Walker, John Stanley; Vice-Consul Damascus since September 1999; born 20.10.66; FCO/HCS 1984; FCO 1988; Bucharest 1989; Doha 1991; FCO 1994; Hong Kong 1997; T/D Bombay 1999; Band C4.

Walker, June; (née Erwin) FCO since June 1997; born 1.6.59; FCO 1992; Dar es Salaam 1996; Band A2; m 1996 Vincent Charles Walker (1s 1997).

Walker, Mary Elizabeth; SUPL since October 1991; born 24.6.68; FCO 1990; Band B3.

Walker, Neil; FCO since March 1997; born 29.4.63; Royal Navy 1979-89; Band A2; m 1992 Angela Seatter (2d 1995, 1997).

Walker, Patricia Arlow; SUPL since May 1997; born 29.9.63; FCO 1988; Berlin 1990; Ankara 1993; Band A2; m 1998 Paul A Bertrand.

Wall, Eric Simon Charles; Counsellor Harare since July 1998; born 4.9.57; Royal Navy 1976-86; Second Secretary FCO 1986; Second later First Secretary UKMIS Geneva 1988; First Secretary FCO 1991; First Secretary (Political) Kampala 1994; First Secretary FCO 1995; m 1983 Elizabeth Anne Gibson (2s 1988,1990, 1d 1994).

Wall, Sir (John) Stephen, KCMG (1996), LVO (1983); On loan to the Cabinet Office since September 2000; born 10.1.47; Third Secretary FCO 1968; Third later Second Secretary Addis Ababa 1969; Private Secretary to HM Ambassador Paris 1972; Second later First Secretary FCO 1974; On loan to

No10 Downing Street 1976; Assistant Private Secretary to the SOS 1977; First Secretary (Chancery) Washington 1979; First Secretary FCO 1983; Counsellor FCO 1985; PPS to the Secretary of State 1988; On loan to the Cabinet Office (at No10 as Foreign Affairs PS to the Prime Minister) 1991; HM Ambassador Lisbon 1993; UK Permanent Representative UKREP Brussels 1995; m 1975 Catharine Jane Reddaway (1s 1979).

Wallace, Euan; Second Secretary FCO since June 1999; born 15.6.63; FCO 1981; Paris 1984; Moscow 1986; Resigned 1988; Reinstated 1990; FCO 1990; UKMIS New York 1993; Vice-Consul New York 1994; UKDEL Brussels 1996; m 1987 Gillian Whittaker (1d 1996; 1s 2000).

Wallace, Gillian (née Whittaker); SUPL since November 1996; born 14.11.63; FCO 1983; Paris 1985; Moscow 1987; FCO 1988; UKMIS New York 1993; Band B3; m 1987 Euan Wallace (1d 1996; 1s 2000).

Wallace, Joanne (née Picton); SUPL since September 1994; born 7.10.69; FCO 1989; Wellington 1992; Band A2; m 1993 Neil Douglas Wallace.

Waller, Mark; Third Secretary (Political) Almaty since July 1999; born 29.9.67; FCO 1987; Kingston 1989; FCO 1992; Abuja 1995; Band B3.

Walley, Martin; Second Secretary (Management) Moscow since March 1999; born 11.6.58; HMIT 1977; FCO 1978; Ankara 1980; Mexico City 1984; FCO 1985; Budapest 1985; Dhaka 1987; FCO 1990; Third Secretary (Commercial) Manila 1992; Bangkok 1995; Second Secretary FCO 1996; On loan to DfID 1997; m 1981 Dilek Sule (2s 1991, 1995).

Wallis, Robin John; First Secretary FCO since June 1997; born 9.7.61; FCO 1986; Second Secretary (Chancery) Buenos Aires 1988; Second Secretary FCO 1990; Vice-Consul (Inf/Aid) Johannesburg 1992; Full-time Language Training 1996; Band D6; m 1989 Janette Staubus (1s 1989, 1d 1992).

Wallis, Victor Charles; First Secretary FCO since April 1999; born 6.2.47; CO 1963; Commonwealth Office (later FCO) 1966; Bermuda 1969; Accra 1972; FCO 1975; Second Secretary Helsinki 1979; Vice Consul (Comm) Sydney 1985; First Secretary FCO 1989; Deputy Consul General Los Angeles 1994; m 1971 Jacqueline Wadhams (1s 1979).

Walmsley, Alan; FCO since July 1998; born 6.9.61; FCO 1981; Abu Dhabi 1984; FCO 1988; Washington 1996; Band C5; m 1992 C. Richardson (1d 1999).

Walmsley, Mark Ronan; Head of Inward Investment Section Taipei since July 1997; born 17.6.58; FCO (HCS) 1978; FCO 1980; Bucharest 1981; African/ME Floater 1983; FCO 1984; Nicosia 1987; Second Secretary (Consul) Bombay 1990; Second Secretary FCO 1994; m 1986 Andrea Elizabeth (1s 1995; 1d 1997).

Walpole, The Hon Alice Louise; UKREP Brussels since June 2000; born 1.9.63; FCO 1985; Third later Second Secretary (Developing Countries) UKREP Brussels 1987; Language Training 1990; Second Secretary Dar es Salaam 1991; First Secretary FCO 1994; First Secretary UKDEL NATO August 1998; SUPL 1999; m 1990 Angel Carro Castrillo (twin d 1990, 1d 1993, 1s 1996, twin s 1999).

Walsh, Nicola Jane; Bridgetown since March 1993; born 24.1.61; FCO 1980; Bahrain 1982; Bridgetown 1985; Kingstown 1986; LA/Caribbean Floater 1988; Band C4.

Walsh, Paul Richard; Third Secretary (Commercial) Warsaw since August 1995; born 15.3.69; DHSS 1987; FCO 1988; Berlin 1990; FCO 1990; Islamabad 1991.

Walsh, Penelope Ruth (known as Penny); FCO since October 2000; born 19.12.66; FCO 1990; Third Secretary (UN) UKMIS Geneva 1991; Third Secretary Tirana 1994; T/D UKMIS Rome 1996; Consul Naples 1996; Consul and Second later First Secretary (Management) Sana'a since July 1998; Band C4; m 1998 Primo Grilli.

Walters, Alison Jane (née Lund); SUPL since February 1996; born 28.8.57; FCO 1976; Yaoundé 1978; FCO 1982; Sofia 1985; Paris 1987; SUPL 1988; Third later Second Secretary (Inf/Chancery) Islamabad 1989; SUPL 1991; FCO 1995; m 1978 Robert Leslie Walters; (2s 1987, 1994).

Walters, David Anthony, MVO (1985); Islamabad since March 2000; born 3.1.57; NSB 1975; FCO 1977, Tehran 1979; Bonn 1980; Port of Spain 1982; FCO 1986; Dhaka 1988; Vice-Consul Atlanta 1991; Band B3; FCO 1994; T/D Abuja 1998; T/D Bogotá 1998; T/D Tirana 1999; Band C4; m 1980 Janis Anne McPhail (3s 1982, 1984, 1991).

Walters, Jonathan Mark; Second Secretary (Political) Berlin since January 1998; FCO 1990; Full-time Language Training 1992; born 28.7.67; Third Secretary (Comm) Bangkok 1993; FCO 1996; Band B3; m2001 Elizabeth Woehr.

Walters, Robert Leslie; SUPL since October 2000; born 23.1.50; FCO 1970; Havana 1972; Kaduna 1973; Valletta 1976; Masirah 1977; FCO 1977; Yaoundé 1978; FCO 1982; Sofia 1985; Paris 1987; Third Secretary (Comm) Islamabad 1989; Second Secretary FCO 1993; T/D Shanghai 1993; Second Secretary FCO 1994; Vice Consul (Commercial) Brisbane 1996; Band C4; m(1) 1973 Mary Elaine Lee (diss 1978); (2) 1978 Alison Jane Lund (2s 1987, 1994).

Walters, Stephen Brett; FCO since January 1985; born 23.8.60; FCO 1981; Peking 1982; Kingston 1983; Band B3.

Walters, Simon Christopher; Second Secretary Riyadh since August 1999; born 3.7.71; FCO 1995; Full Time Language Training 1997; Full time language training 1998; Band C4.

Walton, Derek Antony Ruffel; First Secretary (Legal) UKMIS Geneva since December 1997; born 21.7.66; called to the Bar (Lincoln's Inn) 1989; Assistant Legal Adviser FCO 1991; m 1994 Claire Margaret Hughes (1s 1996; 1d 2000).

Walton, Gillian Mary (née Booth); First Secretary FCO since November 1994; born 16.8.54; FCO 1975; Second Secretary Moscow 1987; Second Secretary FCO 1989; First Secretary Oslo 1992; Band C5; m 1979 (diss 1986).

Walwyn, David Scott; SUPL since June 2001; born 14.4.59; FCO 1985; Second later First Secretary (Chancery) Bangkok 1987; First Secretary FCO 1990; UKDEL OECD Paris 1995; FCO 1999; m 1988 Fiona Cassels-Brown (1s 1997).

Ward, Anthony John; Port Louis since October 1998; born 8.5.47; Royal Marines 1964-88; UKREP Brussels 1988; Moscow 1991; Paris 1992; FCO 1995; Band B3; m 1996 Penelope Joan Walter (3s 1974, 1975, 1977).

Ward, Christine (née Gray); SUPL since May 1997; born 25.12.59; FCO 1978; Budapest 1980; Istanbul 1982; SUPL 1986; Paris 1988; Manila 1992; Band B3; m 1986 Michael John Ward.

Ward, David Gordon; HM Ambassador Santo Domingo since September 1998 and HM Ambassador (non-resident) Port au Prince since January 1999; born 25.7.42; CRO 1961; DSA 1965; Montevideo 1967; Dakar 1970; FCO 1974; Second Secretary (Aid) Victoria (Seychelles) 1977; Second Secretary Luxembourg 1981; First Secretary 1982; Consul Oporto, 1983; First Secretary FCO 1988; First Secretary (Aid) Harare 1990; FCO 1995; m (1) 1966 Rosemary Anne Silvester (2s 1968, 1974; 1d 1972); (diss 1980); (2) 1980 Margaret Martin (1s 1982; 1d 1984).

Ward, Gareth Edward; Second Secretary (KHF) Moscow since November 1998; born 17.1.74; FCO 1996.

Ward, Katherine Georgina Louise (Cathy); Second Secretary Havana since 1998; born 7.4.65; Research Officer FCO 1994; Senior Research Officer 1995.

Ward, Michael David; FCO since June 1995; born 1.6.63; FCO March 1983; New Delhi 1986; Band C4.

Ward, Michael John; Seconded to European Commission since July 2000; born 25.12.58; FCO 1982; Istanbul 1985; Third Secretary (Commercial) later Second Secretary (Science and Technology) Paris 1988; Second later First Secretary FCO 1993; First Secretary UKREP Brussels 1997; m 1986 Christine Gray (2d 1990, 1995; 1s 1991).

Wardle, Mark Thomas; Pretoria since June 2000; born 22.11.62; Royal Navy 1979-89; Police 1990-1995; FCO 1995; Kuala Lumpur 1997; Band B3; m 1994 Julie Anne Russell (1d 1999; 1s adopted 2001).

Wardle, Mark William; Second Secretary (Chancery) Vienna since May 2000; born 25.2.75; FCO 1997; Band C4.

Wardle, Sharon Anne; secondment to Private Sector since August 2000; born 2.3.65; FCO 1985; Moscow 1987; FCO 1989; Ex-Floater Duties 1990; Vice-Consul Beirut 1991; on loan to the DTI then British Trade International since 1996; Band C5.

Ware, Jillian Angela; SUPL since February 1999; born 17.12.62; FCO 1982; UKMIS New York 1984; Africa/ME Floater 1988; FCO 1990; Amman 1994; Band B3; m 1990 David Edward Ware (2d 1991, 1995).

Warr, Martyn John; Second Secretary (Commercial) Lisbon since October 1993; (Second Secretary 1989); born 1.5.59; FCO 1981; Language Training 1983; Jedda 1984; FCO 1988; Band D7; m 1992 Sarah Jane Thompson.

Warren, David Alexander; Director, Business Group, Trade Partners UK since April 2000; born 11.8.52; Third Secretary FCO 1975; Japanese language training 1976-78; Second Secretary and Private Secretary to HM Ambassador Tokyo 1978; Second later First Secretary (Econ) Tokyo 1979; First Secretary FCO 1981; Head of Chancery Nairobi 1987; FCO 1990; Counsellor on loan to the Cabinet Office (Science and Technology Secretariat, later Office of Science and Technology) 1991; Counsellor (Commercial) Tokyo 1993; Head of Hong Kong Department, later China Hong Kong Department 1998; FCO since May 1998; m 1992 Pamela Pritchard.

Warren-Gash, Haydon Boyd; FCO since May 2001; Born 8.8.49; FCO 1971; Language Student, London University 1972; Third Secretary Ankara 1973; Second later First Secretary (Chancery) Madrid 1977; First Secretary FCO 1981; First Secretary (Comm) Paris 1985; First Secretary FCO 1989; Deputy High Commissioner Nairobi 1991; Counsellor FCO 1994; HM Ambassador Abidjan and HM Ambassador non-resident to Liberia, Niger and Burkina Faso 1997; m 1973 Caroline Emma Bowring Leather (1s 1975; 1d 1977).

Warrington, Guy Murray; UKMIS Geneva since July 1997; born 23.9.63; FCO 1986; Third later Second Secretary (Economic/Information) Singapore 1988; Second Secretary UKMIS New York 1992; First Secretary FCO 1993.

Warwick, Sharon Joy; FCO since August 1983; born 31.1.57; FCO 1979; Rangoon 1980; Kuala Lumpur 1982; Band B3; m 1983 Aiden Eustace Warwick.

Watchorn, Kenneth Graham; FCO since April 2000; born 20.9.54; FCO 1971; Washington 1979; FCO 1982; Vienna 1984; FCO 1987; Riyadh 1987; Second Secretary FCO 1992; Paris 1997; Band C5; m 1980 Rossalyn Keen (2s 1983, 1985).

Watchorn, Mark; on loan to the DTI since July 1996 (Second Secretary 1999); born 28.7.65; FCO

1984; Cape Town/Pretoria 1987; Africa/Middle East Floater 1990; FCO 1992; Band C4; m 1996 Christine Jacqueline Holding.(1s 1998, 1d 2001).

Waterhouse, Christine; Athens since October 1998; born 15.9.67; FCO 1987; Nairobi 1991; FCO 1994; Band B3.

Waterhouse, Peter Laurance; FCO since July 1999; born 3.2.58; FCO 1975; Bonn 1987; FCO 1990; Nicosia 1991; FCO 1994; Warsaw 1996; Band C4; m 1985; Clare Rachel Dewar (1d 1993).

Waters, Alan Victor; High Commissioner Solomon Islands since August 1998; born 10.4.42; CO 1958; CRO 1961; Freetown 1963; UKDEL ECSC Luxembourg 1967; Prague 1968; Anguilla 1970; Peking 1971; FCO 1973; Kinshasa 1976; Second Secretary (Comm) Bombay 1980; FCO 1984; First Secretary 1986; First Secretary (Econ) Copenhagen 1987; First Secretary FCO 1991; T/D Tristan da Cunha 1995; First Secretary (Consular) Islamabad 1995; m 1977 Elizabeth Ann Newman (1s 1982; 1d 1984).

Waterton, James, LVO (1995); First Secretary FCO since November 1999; born 25.4.49; FCO 1968; Havana 1970; Valletta 1972; Bonn 1974; FCO 1977; Wellington 1981; Second Secretary and Vice Consul Montevideo 1984; Second Secretary FCO 1987; HM Consul later First Secretary Durban 1991; Deputy Consul General Istanbul 1996; m 1994 Judith Kerwin.

Waterworth, Peter Andrew; First Secretary (Political) Rome since September 1996; born 15.4.57; Assistant later Senior Assistant FCO 1987; Legal Adviser Bonn 1990; First Secretary FCO 1994; Full-time Language Training 1996; m(1) 1981 Hilary Young (diss 1991) (2) 1994 Catherine Finnigan.

Watkinson, Barry; FCO since April 2000; born 22.8.44; FCO 1984; Brussels 1988; FCO 1991; Band C4; Moscow 1996; m 1988 Patricia Rose.

Watson, David James; First Secretary FCO since August 1999; born 4.3.57; FCO 1988; Second later First Secretary Harare 1989; First Secretary FCO 1992; First Secretary (Political) Madrid 1996; Band D6; m 1989 Sheelah McKeown (2d 1989, 1991).

Watson, Gavin Christopher; Assistant Legal Adviser FCO since April 2000; born 21.7.70; Legal Assistant Home Office 1995; Solicitor.

Watson, James Spencer Kennedy; First Secretary FCO since October 2000; born 30.11.64; FCO 1988, Second Secretary (Econ) Kuwait 1991; Second Secretary FCO 1994; First Secretary (Political) Damascus 1997; Band D6.

Watson, Joel Aaron; FCO since June 1998; born 14.9.69; FCO 1989; Belmopan 1991; Islamabad 1994. Band C4; m 1990 Victoria Jane Baxter (1s 1999).

Watson, Nicholas Henry Lewis; Second Secretary (Political) Amman since August 1999; born 12.6.71; FCO 1995; Full Time Language Training 1997; Full time language training Cairo 1998; Band C4; m 1997 Catriona Ann (1s 2000).

Watson, Robert Emmerson; Second Secretary Tel Aviv since November 1998; born 10.8.70; FCO 1996; Band C4.

Watson, Stephen; Chairman DSTUS, FCO since July 2001; born 18.6.57; HO 1975; FCO 1976; Jedda 1979; Hong Kong 1982; Brasilia 1986; FCO 1988; Band C5.

Watson , Terence Paul; Second Secretary (Technical Management) New Delhi since April 2001; born 7.12.48; HM Forces 1964-76; FCO 1988; Band C4; m 1969 Jennifer Margaret (2s 1970, 1972).

Watt, James Wilfrid, CVO; Head of Consular Division since January 2000; born 5.11.51; FCO 1977; MECAS 1978; Second later First Secretary Abu Dhabi 1980; FCO 1983; First Secretary (Chancery) UKMIS New York 1985; First Secretary FCO 1989; Deputy Head of Mission Amman 1992; Deputy Head of Mission Islamabad 1996; SOAS 1999 m1980 Elizabeth Ghislaine Villeneuve (Dec'd)(1s,1981; 1d 1986).

Wattam, John; Second Secretary (Political) UKDIS Geneva since August 1998; born 11.5.63; FCO 1982; Bonn 1984; Karachi 1987; FCO 1991; Third Secretary (Commercial) Lagos 1994; Full time language training 1998; Third Secretary (Political/Information) Lagos 1995; Band B3; m 1991 Anne Michelle Watson (2d 1993, 1998 1s 1995).

Waugh, Linda Alison; FCO since October 1999; born 20.3.65; MOD 1984; FCO 1992; Athens 1996; Band A2.

Waugh, Lisa Helen (née Maley); Director, Americas FCO since August 2000; born 28.8.67; FCO 1988; Brussels 1990; FCO 1992; Hong Kong 1993; Istanbul 1996; RMU Americas Command 1999; SUPL 2000; Band C4; m 1995 Graeme Stewart Waugh (1d 1998).

Way, Lawrence Sidney; Third later Second Secretary FCO since October 1984; born 1.12.49; FO (later FCO) 1967; Washington 1974; FCO 1977; Amman 1978; FCO 1981; Madrid 1982; m 1970 Patricia Margaret Allcock (1s 1975; 1d 1977).

Weale, William Anthony Peter; First Secretary FCO since April 1995; born 26.1.45; HM Forces 1964-70; FCO 1970; Dacca 1971; Jedda 1973; Lagos 1974; FCO 1976; Moscow 1977; FCO 1979; Hanoi 1980; Beirut 1983; Second Secretary FCO 1985; on loan to MOD 1993; Band D6; m 1977 Sheila Ellen Anderson (1d 1985).

Webb, Richard, MBE (1996); First Secretary (Commercial) Jakarta since September 1998; born 20.11.43; Inland Revenue 1962; FO 1965; Peking 1967; Rio de Janeiro 1968; Lagos 1972; FCO 1974; Far East Floater 1978; FCO 1980; Jedda 1981; Second Secretary FCO 1984; Vice-Consul (Comm) Melbourne 1988; Full-time Language Training 1993; Second Secretary (Consular)

Moscow 1993; T/D Montserrat 1995; Second
Secretary FCO 1996; m(1) 1966 Hilary Anne John
(diss 1977) (1d 1970; 1s 1971); (2) 1983 Sandra
Mai Williams (1d 1985).

Webb, Robert OBE (2000); FCO since July 2000;
born 6.6.50; DSAO (later FCO) 1966; Singapore
1971; Guatemala City 1974; FCO 1978; Floater
duties 1982; Hanoi 1984; Second Secretary and
Consul Mexico City 1985; Second Secretary FCO
1989; Deputy Head of Mission Georgetown 1993;
First Secretary Plymouth 1997; Montserrat; m
1989 Maria Del Carmen Colín Irieta (1s 1994).

Webb, Sarah Jane; Floater duties since April 2000;
born 2.12.66; FCO 1987; Budapest 1990; FCO
1992; Kuala Lumpur 1994; FCO 1997; Band A2.

Webber, Barbara Ann (née Leatherbarrow); FCO
since July 1995; born 6.3.66; FCO 1987; Peking
1992; Band B3; m 1996 Martin George Webber.

Webber, Martin George; Third Secretary
(Management) Quito since July 1998; born
19.10.60; HO 1979-81; FCO 1989; UKMIS
Geneva 1990; FCO 1992; Peking 1993; FCO
1995; Band B3; m 1996 Barbara Ann
Leatherbarrow.(1s 1998)

Webster, John Auld; Strasbourg since November
1999; born 6.9.68; FCO 1988; Nicosia 1990; FCO
1992; Port Louis 1996; Band B3.

Weeks, Alan Richard; Deputy Head of Mission
Quito since June 1997; born 29.7.48; FCO 1965;
Tripoli 1970; Sofia 1972; Beirut 1974; Innsbruck
1976; FCO 1979; Second Secretary (Dev) New
Delhi 1984; Second Secretary (Admin) and Consul
East Berlin 1987; First Secretary FCO 1991; m
1971 Penelope Dibb (2s 1974, 1976).

Weeks, Sarah Marguerite; FCO since November
1998; born 15.10.68; FCO 1987; Abidjan 1990;
Floater duties 1993; Paris 1995; Band B3.

Weinrabe, Stephen Michael; First Secretary
(Management) Brasilia since January 2001; born
13.6.50; FO (later FCO) 1967; Bucharest 1971;
Paris 1972; Dublin 1973; Tehran 1975; FCO 1977;
Nicosia 1981; Bangkok 1984; Second Secretary
(Admin) Lagos 1988; Second Secretary FCO
1991; Second Secretary (Commercial) Canberra
1994; Second Secretary (Commercial) Sydney
1994; Assistant Personal Secretary to Minister of
State 1999; FTLT 2000; Band C5; m 1973
Eugenia Del Transito Poppescov Lazo (2s 1975,
1995).

Weldin, Jonathan Michael; First Secretary
(External) Athens since September 1996; born
23.2.59; FCO 1982; Second later First Secretary
(Chancery) Sana'a 1986; First Secretary FCO
1988; First Secretary (Chancery) Tunis 1990; First
Secretary FCO 1993; Band D6; m 1984 Fiona
Jean Nesbitt (1s 1987, 1d 1989).

Weldon, Lawrence John, MVO (1980); Convent
Liaison Officer Gibralter since July 1997; born
6.3.50; FCO 1972; Attaché (Dev) Bangkok 1975;
Attaché (Comm) Tunis 1978; FCO 1981; British

Vice Consul Johannesburg 1983; Second Secretary
FCO 1986; Second Secretary (Comm) Caracas
1989; SUPL 1992; Second Secretary FCO 1995; m
1984 Sarah Helen Burn (1d 1989, 2s 1991, 1999).

Weldon, Paul; Athens since August 2000; born
3.4.59; FCO 1975; Pretoria 1987; FCO 1989;
Band C4; m 1986 Karen Louise Ritchie (2s 1988,
1992).

Wellfare, Ian Bradshaw; Deputy Head of Mission
Tallinn since May 2001; born 13.9.46; FO (later
FCO) 1964; Kinshasa 1969; Guatemala City 1972;
FCO 1975; Peking 1978; Hong Kong 1980;
Second Secretary (Comm) Peking 1981; Vice-
Consul (Comm) Cleveland 1983; Second
Secretary FCO 1986 (First Secretary 1989);
Consul (Comm) Shanghai 1990; Trade
Commissioner (China Trade) BTC Hong Kong
1993; Consul-General Guangzhou 1997; on
secondment to Reading University 1999; Band
D6; m 1968 Ann Palmer (2d 1972 1975).

Wells, Andrew Justin; Third Secretary Amman
since July 1998; born 8.3.68; FCO 1988; Floater
Duties 1991; Zagreb 1993; FCO 1995; language
training Cairo 1997; Band B3; m 1994 Juliette
Swain (2s 1996, 1999).

Wells, Colin Neil; Second Secretary (Political)
Abuja since August 2001; born 29.9.67; FCO HCS
1987; DS 1990; Bridgetown 1992; UKMIS
Geneva 1996 (Second Secretary 1997); FCO 1999;
Band C4; m 1997 Rebekah Wells (2d 1993 1995
1s 1997).

Wells, Daniel; New Delhi since August 2000; born
21.7.70; FCO 1989; Bucharest 1992; FCO 1994;
Lagos 1995; FCO 1998; Band C4.

Wells, David John; Deputy High Commissioner
Nassau since September 2000; born 29.6.63; FCO
1982; New Delhi 1988; FCO 1990; Vice-Consul
Moscow 1995; FCO 1998; Band C4; m 1994
Helen Paula McCarron.

Wells, Helen Paula (née McCarron); SUPL since
September 2000; born 29.6.68; FCO 1986; New
Delhi; 1989; UKMIS Geneva 1992; Moscow
1995; SUPL 1996; FCO 1998; SUPL 1999; FCO
2000; Band B3; m 1994 David John Wells (1d
1996).

Wells, Juliette Elizabeth (née Swain); SUPL since
August 1994; born 12.6.67; FCO 1986; Zagreb
1993; Band A2; m 1994 Andrew Justin Wells.

Welsh, Jolyon Rimmer; First Secretary FCO since
December 1995; born 22.12.67; FCO 1990;
Second Secretary (Chancery/Inf) Colombo 1992.

Welsh, Patricia Angela (née Sherry); Oslo since
January 2000; born 23.8.64; FCO 1985; Madrid
1989; FCO 1992; Brasilia 1994; SUPL 1997; FCO
1999; Band A2; m 1993 James Ormsby Welsh (2d
1996, 1998).

Welsh, Paul Anthony; Deputy Head of Mission,
Tbilisi since March 1998; born 12.10.67; FCO
1986; Harare 1988; Floater Duties 1992; Band C4;

FCO 1994; m(1) 1988 Anne McCoy; (diss 1993), (2) 1994 Emel Elif Icbilen.

Welsted, David Curtis; First Secretary FCO since July 1995; born 17.10.52; FCO 1969; Attaché Warsaw 1975; FCO 1976; Tehran 1978; FCO 1978; Nairobi 1980; FCO 1983; Attaché Amman 1984; FCO 1987; Washington 1992; m 1974 Gillian Mary Harris (1s 1978; 1d 1982).

Wenban, Mark; Lima since July 2001; born 29.5.67; FCO 2000; Band A2.

West, Brian William; Second Secretary (Commercial) Beirut since May 1997; born 4.1.48; FCO 1968; Moscow 1971; Kampala 1972; Strasbourg 1975; FCO 1977; Port Louis 1980; Second Secretary (Commercial) Abidjan 1984; Second Secretary FCO 1988; T/D Athens 1990; Second Secretary (Commercial) Paris 1991; T/D New Delhi 1996; T/D Guangzhou 1997; m 1976 Marie-Odile Gilbert (2s 1977, 1980).

West, Peter Bernard; Deputy Head of Mission Bangkok since April 2000; born 29.6.58; FCO 1977; Ankara 1978; Buenos Aires 1980; Auckland 1984; Second later First Secretary FCO 1986; First Secretary (Pol/Inf) Copenhagen 1992; First Secretary FCO 1997; m 1980 Julia Anne Chandler; (1d 1993, twin s1995).

West, Veronica Frances Bailey; FCO since November 1997; born 16.6.46; FCO 1977; Amman 1978; FCO 1981; Colombo 1983; Kuwait 1987; Sofia 1991; FCO 1993; Bucharest 1995. Band B3.

Westcott, Nicholas James, CMG (1998); Minister-Counsellor for Trade and Transport Policy Washington since August 1999; born 20.7.56; Second Secretary FCO 1982; Seconded to European Commission, Brussels 1984; First Secretary (Agric/Finance) UKREP Brussels 1985; First Secretary FCO 1989; Deputy Head of Mission Dar es Salaam 1993; Counsellor FCO 1996; m 1989 Miriam Pearson (1d 1996; 1s 2000).

Westgarth, Nicholas Philip; Counsellor Peking since August 1999; born 25.11.56; FCO 1980; Third Secretary (Econ) Athens 1981; Second Secretary FCO 1984; Language Training 1985; First Secretary Hong Kong 1986; First Secretary FCO 1989; First Secretary (Chancery) Nicosia 1991; First Secretary FCO 1995; m 1988 Kate Judith Sykes (2s 1989, 1992).

Westmacott, Peter John, CMG (2000), LVO; HM Ambassador Ankara since January 2002; born 23.12.50; FCO 1972; Third later Second Secretary Tehran 1974; FCO 1978; Seconded to EC Commission Brussels 1978; First Secretary Paris 1980; FCO 1984; PS to Minister of State 1984; Head of Chancery Ankara 1987; Counsellor on Secondment to Buckingham Palace as Assistant Private Secretary to TRH the Prince and The Princess of Wales 1990; Head of Chancery Washington 1993; Director (Americas) 1997; DUS (Wider World) 2000; m,1972 Angela Margaret Lugg (diss 1999) (2s 1975, 1979; 1d 1977).

Wetherell, Gordon Geoffrey; HM Ambassador and Consul-General Luxembourg since September 2000; born 11.11.48; FCO (concurrently Third Secretary Vice-Consul British Embassy Chad) 1973; Third later Second Secretary East Berlin 1974; First Secretary FCO (concurrently First Secretary UKDEL CTB at Geneva) 1977; First Secretary UKDEL CTB Geneva 1979; New Delhi 1980; First Secretary FCO 1983; on loan to HM Treasury 1986; FCO 1987; Counsellor and Deputy Head of Mission Warsaw 1988; Counsellor (Political/Military) Bonn 1992; Counsellor FCO 1994; HM Ambassador Addis Ababa and (non-resident) Djibouti and Asmara 1997; m 1981 Rosemary Anne Myles (4d 1982, 1985, 1987, 1989).

Whaanga-Jacques, Lorna (née Jacques); Muscat since November 1999; born 15.9.59; FCO 1985; UKDEL CSCE Vienna 1988; Rangoon 1988; Phnom Penh 1992; SUPL 1993; FCO 1997; Band A2; m 1994 Dean Tamaku Whaanga.

Whale, Geoffrey; Peking since April 1988; born 3.7.52; FCO 1983; Band C4; m 1985 Ingrid Moore (1s 1987).

Whatley, Malcolm George; Second Secretary (Commercial) Hong Kong since November 1999; born 5.9.52; FCO 1973; Washington 1975; Kuwait 1978; Budapest 1982; Dhaka 1984; FCO 1985; Muscat 1986; FCO 1989; Rio de Janeiro 1992 (Second Secretary 1995); Band C4; m 1975 Mary Elizabeth Niven (2s 1979, 1985; 1d 1983).

Wheeler, Bernadette; Kinshasa since April 2000; born 13.2.68; MOD 1986; FCO 1988; Lisbon 1989; FCO 1992; Jakarta 1994; Bucharest 1998; Band B3.

Wheeler, Fraser William; FCO since July 2000; born 23.3.57; FCO 1980; Accra 1982; FCO 1984; UKMIS Geneva 1985; FCO 1988; Language Training 1990 (Second Secretary 1991); Second Secretary (Commercial) Moscow 1991; Deputy Consul General Vancouver 1994; SUPL 1999; Band B3; m 1988 Sarah Humphreys.

Whipp, Kathryn Sarah; SUPL since January 2001; born 1.3.67; FCO 1988; Kiev 1992; FCO 1995; New Delhi 1998; FCO 2000; Band A2.

Whitaker, Giles David Humphrey; First Secretary (Political) Berlin (on attachment to Auswärtiges Amt) since September 1999; born 5.3.62; HM Forces 1980-88; Second Secretary FCO 1988; Second Secretary (Chancery) UKDEL NATO Brussels 1990; First Secretary FCO 1994; Deputy Head of Mission, Berlin 1998; m 1990 Lucy Phyllida Whately Anderson (2s 1992, 1998, 2d 1994, 1996).

Whitby, John Benjamin; First Secretary FCO since November 1997; born 21.2.67; FCO 1990; Language Training 1993; Second Secretary (Political) Tokyo 1994; Band D6; m 1992 Ruth Alexander (1s 1995, 1d 1997).

White, Anthony William; Bridgetown since October 1999; born 29.12.54; FCO 1973; Peking

1980; FCO 1982; Lilongwe 1985; FCO 1988; Third Secretary Kuala Lumpur 1993; FCO 1996; Band C4; m 1996 Rahani Mat Tahir.

White, (Charles) John (Branford); High Commissioner Bridgetown since August 2001; born 24.9.46; Government of Botswana 1968; ODM 1971; Economic Advisers 1977; ODM 1982; CDA at UCL (London) 1983; FCO 1986; First Secretary Lagos 1990; Counsellor, Consul-General and Deputy Head of Mission Tel Aviv 1993; Commissioner for the British Antarctic Territory, Commissioner for the British Indian Ocean Territory and Counsellor FCO 1997; m 1975 Judy Margaret Lewis.

White, Debra; FCO since July 1996; born 28.5.75; Band A2; m 1997 Lee Marcus Crawford.

White, Jacqueline Denise (née Hill); Grand Turk since July 2000; born 24.5.64; FCO 1987; Dar-es-Salaam 1989; FCO 1993; UKMIS New York 1993; SUPL 1996; UKMIS New York 1996; SUPL 1997; FCO 2000; Band B3; m 1990 Jerry Lee White (2s 1996, 1998).

White, Kate Georgina; Taipei since August 2000; born 24.1.73; FCO 1995; Hong Kong 1998; Band C4.

White, Richard Michael, MBE (1983); Assistant Director, Personnel Services since May 2000; born 12.7.50; FCO 1969; UKDEL (later UKREP) EC Brussels 1971; Language Student SOAS and Yazd 1974; Tehran 1975; Second Secretary 1978; APS to the Minister of State 1978; APS to the Lord Privy Seal 1979; FCO 1979; Second Secretary (Comm/Admin) and Consul Dakar 1980; First Secretary (Technology) Paris 1984; First Secretary FCO 1988; Deputy High Commissioner Valletta 1992; First Secretary FCO 1996; Counsellor, Head of Migration and Visa Division 1997; m 1979 Deborah Anne Lewis; (1s 1984; 1d 1986).

White, Tiffany Alexandra; Second Secretary (Political) Rangoon since April 1996; born 10.6.71; FCO October 1994; Full-time Language Training Cairo 1995.

Whitecross, Andrew Ronald; First Secretary (Political) Muscat since February 1998; born 14.4.49; Army 1964-76; FCO 1976; Private Industry 1978; FCO 1980; Sana'a 1981; Baghdad 1985; Second Secretary FCO 1989; Band C5; m 1980 Nancy-Jane Evans (dec'd 1994).

Whitford, Victoria; FTLT Japanese October 2000; born 6.6.74; Hong Kong Desk, CHKD FCO 1999; Head of Hong Kong Section 1999; First Secretary External Relations UKREP Brussels; SUPL 2000; Band C4.

Whitehead, Ian Richard; Counsellor (Management) Paris since December 1999; born 21.7.43; FO 1960; Addis Ababa 1965; Brussels (NATO) 1969; Dubai 1971; Casablanca 1972; FCO 1975; Second Secretary (Comm) Bridgetown 1978; First Secretary (COCOM) Paris 1983; First Secretary FCO 1988; Deputy High Commissioner Dar es Salaam 1991; Head of Mission Skopje

1993; FCO 1994; High Commissioner Georgetown 1998; m 1996 Pamela Denise Mitchison (1d 1996).

Whitehead, Laurence Jeremy; First Secretary (Political) Tirana since December 1999; born 17.4.61; FCO 1984; Second Secretary Jakarta 1987; Second later First Secretary FCO 1990; First Secretary (Political) Vienna 1995; Band D6; m 1995 Marjella Djorghi.

Whitehead, Peter John; First Secretary FCO since July 1999; born 1.4.52; FCO 1978; Rangoon 1980; Manila 1982; Montreal 1985; on loan to ODA 1988; Second Secretary FCO 1990; Second Secretary (Chancery/Information) Abidjan 1992; Second Secretary (Commercial) Calcutta 1995; m 1984 Jesusa Valdez Bueno (1 adopt s 1997, 1 adopt d 1997).

Whitehead, Roger; Second Secretary (Commercial)Singapore since October 1997; born 22.5.54; FCO 1976; Lagos 1979; Kathmandu 1982; FCO 1984; Rangoon 1988; Third Secretary (Management/Consular/Commercial) Toronto 1991; Second Secretary FCO 1994; m 1979 Diane Mann (1s 1987; 1d 1989).

Whitehorn, Caroline Mary; Vice-Consul and Second Secretary (Management) Buenos Aires since March 2001; born 4.10.67; FCO 1992; Mexico City 1992; Second Secretary FCO 1997.

Whiten, Peter Frank, MBE (1991); FCO since August 1998; born 5.12.51; FCO 1974; South East Asia Floater 1976; UKDEL NATO Brussels 1978; Port of Spain 1981; Second Secretary FCO 1986; Second Secretary (Commercial) Madras 1991; Consul Chiang Mai 1995; m 1987 Antonia Ramsaroop (3s 1989, 1991, 1993, 1d 1994).

Whiteside, Andrew John; First Secretary FCO since September 1997; born 21.9.68; FCO 1991; Language Student 1994; Second Secretary (Political) Budapest 1995; Band D6; m 1994 Fiona Elizabeth Bradley (1d 1999).

Whiteside, Bernard Gerrard; MBE (1994); First Secretary on loan to DfID since April 1999; born 3.10.54; FCO 1979; Moscow 1983; UKDIS Geneva 1986; (Second Secretary 1988); Second Secretary FCO 1989; Second Secretary (Chancery/Aid) Bogotá 1991; First Secretary FCO 1995.

Whiteway, Paul Robin; Counsellor and Deputy Head of Mission Santiago since February 2000; born 1.12.54; FCO 1977; Third later Second Secretary (Dublin) 1980; First Secretary FCO 1984; First Secretary Stanley 1986; First Secretary FCO 1987; Seconded to MOD (Navy) 1988; Deputy High Commissioner Kampala 1990; First Secretary FCO 1993; Counsellor and Deputy Head of Mission Damascus 1996; m 1996 Maha Georges Yannieh (1s 1998).

Whitfield, Merle Olene; Nairobi since May 1998; born 6.8.41; FO 1967; Rawalpindi 1968; Lusaka 1969; Luanda 1971; Kuwait 1974; FCO 1976; Dar es Salaam 1978; Kuala Lumpur 1981; Jedda 1984;

Riyadh 1985; FCO 1987; Colombo 1989; FCO 1992; Dar es Salaam 1995; Band B3.

Whitting, Ian Robert; First Secretary (Economic) FCO since July 1997; born 2.4.53; FCO 1972; Moscow 1975; Tunis 1976; Athens 1980 (Second Secretary 1981); FCO 1983; Second Secretary (Chancery) Moscow 1985; Second Secretary FCO 1988; First Secretary (Chancery) Dublin 1990; m 1986 Tracy Anne Gallagher (2d 1990, 1994).

Whittingham, Stephen Arthur; FCO since September 1990; born 29.1.56; FCO 1972; Brussels 1981; FCO 1983; Hong Kong 1988; Band C4; m 1977 Christine Mary Ruth Hodgson (1d 1978).

Whittle, Lesley Elizabeth; SUPL since July 1999; born 4.7.58; FCO 1980; Amman 1981; Cairo 1984; FCO 1987; Paris 1990; Islamabad 1994; Band B3; m 1986 Simon F D Mallett (1s 1995).

Whomersley, Christopher Adrian; Legal Counsellor FCO since 1997; born 18.4.53; Assistant Legal Adviser FCO 1977; Legal Counsellor FCO 1991; Legal Secretariat to the Law Officers 1994; m 1977 Jeanette Diana Szostak (1s 1991, 2d 1993, 1998).

Whomsley, Deborah Jane; UKDEL Vienna since July 1993; born 25.4.67; FCO 1991; Band A2.

Whyte, Michael James; Peking since May 1994; born 24.3.42; Royal Navy 1958-89; Bucharest 1992; Band B3; m 1979 Karen Nina Renée Walters.

Wicke, Tina (née Thackstone); Third Secretary Harare since August 1999; born 5.2.61; HM Treasury 1980; FCO 1982; Stanley 1983; Kingston 1984; Peking 1986; FCO 1989; Harare 1993; SUPL 1997; Band B3; m 1996 Jürgen Manfred Wicke.

Wicks, Graham; Second Secretary (Aid) Khartoum since November 2000; born 2.7.55; FCO 1974; Luxembourg 1976; Islamabad 1976; Peking 1979; Karachi 1981; FCO 1983; Victoria 1986; Vice-Consul Sofia 1990; Third later Second Secretary FCO 1992; Second Secretary (Commercial) Bombay 1995; FCO 1997; m 1978 Genevieve Harriot-Jane McCrossan (2s 1988, 1989).

Wicks, Joanna Ruth (née Collett); Second Secretary FCO since November 1995; born 9.5.56; FCO 1978; Warsaw 1981; FCO 1982; SUPL 1984; Second Secretary FCO 1986; SUPL 1989; Second Secretary FCO 1992; SUPL 1994; Band C4; m 1984 Nigel Earl Wicks (2d 1989, 1994).

Wicks, Nigel Earl; SUPL since March 2000; born 21.3.56; HM Forces 1973-76; FCO 1980; Attaché Damascus 1984; FCO 1986; Lisbon 1989; FCO 1992 (Second Secretary 1994); Second Secretary (Commercial/Economic) Oslo 1995; Band C4; m 1984 Joanna Ruth Collett (2d 1989; 1994).

Wickstead, Myles Antony; HM Ambassador Addis Ababa since November 2000, also HM Ambassador (non-resident) Djibouti; born 7.2.51;

Ministry of Overseas Development 1976; Assistant Private Secretary to Lord Privy Seal (FCO) 1979; Assistant to UK Executive Director IMF/IBRD 1980; Principal, Overseas Development Administration (ODA) 1984; Private Secretary to Minister for Overseas Development 1988; Head of ODA European Community and Food Aid Development 1990; Head of British Development Division in East Africa (BDDEA) 1993; UK Alternate Executive Director World Bank and Counsellor (Development) Washington 1997; m 1990 Shelagh Paterson (1s 1996; 1d 1999).

Wigginton, Christopher James; Second Secretary (Immig/Cons) Bogotá since November 2000; born 23.5.60; FCO 1982; Language Training 1984; Tehran 1984; Stockholm 1988; FCO 1991 (Second Secretary 1992); Islamabad 1994; FCO 1997; FTLT 2000; Band C4.

Wightman, Andrew Norman Scott; Assistant Director Personnel Policy since June 1998; born 17.7.61; FCO 1983; full-time Language Training 1984; Second Secretary Peking 1986; First Secretary FCO 1989; On loan to the Cabinet Office 1989; First Secretary FCO 1991; On secondment to Quai d'Orsay 1994; First Secretary Paris 1995; m 1988 Anne Margaret Roberts (2d 1993, 1997).

Wilbourn, Lillian; Buenos Aires since September 1998; born 27.7.47; FCO 1985; Madrid 1987; Brasilia 1990; Maputo 1994; Band A2.

Wilcox, Juliette Sarah (née Hannah); First Secretary JLG Hong Kong since July 1996; born 29.6.66 FCO 1988; Full-time Language Training Taiwan 1991; Second Secretary (Chancery) Peking 1992; First Secretary FCO 1995; Band D6; m 1996 Wayne Philip Wilcox (1 step s 1984, 1s 1999).

Wildash, Elizabeth Jane (née Walmsley) MVO (1997); Second Secretary (Economic) Kuala Lumpur since August 1999; born 17.10.58; FCO 1978; E Berlin 1980; FCO 1981; Abidjan 1983; FCO 1984; SUPL 1987; FCO 1988; Harare 1989; FCO 1992; Third Secretary (Chancery) New Delhi 1994; SUPL 1998; m 1981 Richard James Wildash (2d 1987, 1996).

Wildash, Richard James LVO (1997); Deputy High Commissioner Kuala Lumpur since July 1998; born 24.12.55; FCO 1977; EBerlin 1979; Abidjan 1981; FCO 1984; Language Training 1986; FCO 1986; Harare 1988; FCO 1992; New Delhi 1994; m 1981 Elizabeth Jane Walmsley (2d 1987, 1996).

Wildman, Richard Hugh; Brasilia since May 1999; born 18.8.54; FCO 1983; Bridgetown 1989; FCO 1992; Band C4; m(1)1989 Fay Dawn Reid (1d 1983); (2)1994 S E Odle.

Wiles, Celia Imogen; SUPL since October 2000; born 23.4.63; FCO 1986; Language Training Kamakuru 1988; Third Secretary (Commercial) Tokyo 1989; SUPL 1993; FCO 1995; On loan to European Commission 1998; FCO 1999; Band D6.

Wiles, Harry; HM Ambassador Managua since September 2000; born 17.6.44; FO 1964; Ankara 1966; Paris 1969; Algiers 1972; FCO 1975; Bilbao 1978; Jedda 1981; Second Secretary (Admin) Riyadh 1983; Second Secretary (Comm) Abu Dhabi 1984; Second later First Secretary on loan to ECGD 1988; Consul (Comm) Barcelona 1990; First Secretary (Commercial) Buenos Aires 1994; First Secretary FCO 1998; m 1966 Margaret Bloom (2d 1967, 1970).

Wilkie, Peter Finlayson; Second Secretary FCO since December 1991; born 30.10.42; FO 1960; Bahrain 1964; Moscow 1966; Athens 1967; FCO 1970; India Floater (Cons1/Imm) 1973; Düsseldorf 1975; Second Secretary (Chancery) Addis Ababa 1978; FCO 1980; Second Secretary The Hague 1984; Second Secretary (Management) Paris 1986.

Wilkie, Robert Andrew; FCO since January 1989; born 9.12.59; FCO 1979; Nairobi 1980; FCO 1983; Darwin 1987; Band B3; m 1986 Sarah Jane Abraham (1d 1987).

Wilkins , John Leslie; Deputy Consul-General Guangzhou since July 1999; born 14.5.45; MPBW 1962; CO 1964; Maseru 1966; FCO 1969; Düsseldorf 1972; New Delhi 1975; FCO 1978; Jakarta 1982; Second Secretary Islamabad 1985; Second Secretary FCO 1990; Deputy Head of Mission Reykjavik 1993; Consul-General Alexandria 1996; m 1967 Margaret Stuchbury (1d 1973).

Wilkinson, Richard Denys, cvo (1992); Director (Americas) FCO since May 2000; born 11.5.46; FCO 1972; Second later First Secretary Madrid 1973, FCO 1977; First Secretary (Econ/Comm) Ankara 1983; Counsellor and Head of Chancery Mexico City 1985; Counsellor (Info) Paris 1988; Counsellor FCO 1993; HM Ambassador Caracas 1997; m 1982 Maria Angela Morris (2s 1983, 1986, 1d 1991).

Wilks, Jonathan Paul; SUPL since October 1999; born 30.9.67; FCO 1989; Full-time Language Training Cairo 1992; Second Secretary (Political/Information) Khartoum 1993; First Secretary (Economic) Riyadh 1996; Band D6.

Willasey-Wilsey, Timothy Andrew; Counsellor (UN Affairs)UKMIS Geneva since August 1999; born 12.9.53; Second Secretary FCO 1981; First Secretary (Chancery) Luanda 1983; First Secretary Head of Chancery (later DHM) and Consul San José 1986; First Secretary FCO 1989; Counsellor Islamabad 1993; Counsellor FCO 1996; m 1983 Alison Middleton Mackie (3s 1986, 1988, 1989).

Williams, Alexander Patrick; Bangkok since July 1996; born 13.2.69; FCO 1986; Band B3.

Williams, Catrin Ceiros; FCO since January 1976; born 22.11.51; FCO 1972; Valletta 1974; Band A2.

Williams , David John; Second Secretary FCO since March 1995; born 6.6.67; FCO 1986; UKMIS Geneva 1988; Bombay 1990; m 1989 Denise Nowak (1d 1991; 1s 1995).

Williams, David Llewellyn; Sofia since March 1999; born 13.12.42; Royal Marines 1961-83; Baghdad 1984; Warsaw 1985; Islamabad 1986; Paris 1987; Peking 1990; Kampala 1991; Kiev 1995; Band B3; m 1969 Gillian Myra James (3d 1961, 1963, 1971, 1s 1966).

Williams, Deborah Mary; Vice-Consul Rome since November 1998; born 30.10.64; FCO 1985; Tokyo 1987; Buenos Aires 1990; FCO 1993; Band B3.

Williams, Douglas James; Second Secretary (Commercial) Madras since May 1998; born 9.2.55; FCO 1978; Suva 1981; UKREP Brussels 1984; New Delhi 1987; FCO 1991; Band B3; Bridgetown 1994; m 1981 Susan Anwen Jones (1s 1984; 1d 1986).

Williams, George (aka Rick), BEM (1975); New Delhi since October 2001; born 6.2.43; HM Forces 1962-84; Prague 1984; Singapore 1985; Moscow 1987; Washington 1988; Dhaka 1991; Colombo 1995; Lagos 1998; Band C4 (CSO); m 1965 Eileen (2s 1965, 1968).

Williams, Jenni; Istanbul since November 1999; born 21.12.70; FCO 1990; Peking 1995; FCO 1999; SUPL 1999; Band B3.

Williams, John; Second Secretary (Political) Gibraltar since September 1996; born 17.6.59; FCO 1978; Moscow 1981; Rabat 1982; FCO 1985; Masirah 1985; LA Floater 1986; FCO 1988; Vice- Consul Johannesburg 1992; m (1) 1981 Jacqueline Peplow (diss 1987), (2) 1994 Cheryl Ann Sim.

Williams, Karen Lesley, MBE (2001); Rangoon since January 1999; born 28.6.63; FCO 1987; Riyadh 1988; UKMIS New York 1991; world-wide Floater Duties 1993; FCO 1995; Band C4.

Williams, Laura Kate Elizabeth; Second Secretary (Political/Information) Addis Ababa since April 2001; born 3.4.74; FCO 1998; First Secretary Paris Embassy 1999; First Secretary UKREP Brussels 2000; FTLT 2000; T/D Second Secretary (Political) UKREP Brussels 2000; Band C4.

Williams, Paul; First Secretary Houston since 1998; born 25.11.48; Immigration Service 1969; Islamabad 1977; Dhaka 1982; Lagos 1987; Second later First Secretary Muscat 1996; m 1969 Barbara Jane Briggs; (2s 1975, 1979).

Williams, Paula Jean; SUPL since August 1994; born 22.10.54; Islamabad 1976; UKDEL NATO Brussels 1976; BMG Berlin 1979; Dakar 1980; Pretoria/Cape Town 1981; FCO 1984; Algiers 1990; Band B3; (1d 1991, 1s 1994).

Williams, Philip George; FCO since July 1988; born 26.7.54; FCO 1972; Nairobi 1985; Band D6; m 1987 Susan Traise McAlden.

Williams, Prue, RVM; FCO since 1998; Bonn 1978; Moscow 1980; FCO 1981; Port of Spain 1983; FCO 1985; Bangkok 1996 (State Visit); The Hague/Luxembourg (Presidency) 1997; Band B3.

Williams, Dr Rhodri Huw; Counsellor Amman since November 2001; born 14.5.59; FCO 1990; First Secretary (Econ) Vienna 1992; First Secretary FCO 1996; m 1986 Hilary Clair Wakeham (1s, 1d twins 1991, 1s 1994).

Williams, Roger Gordon; Jakarta since 1999; born 28.7.48; Army 1963-89; Prague 1989; Washington 1991; Cairo 1993; T/D Cairo 1997; Belgrade 1997; Lagos 1997; Band B3; m 1974 Anne Elizabeth (1d 1974; 2s 1978, 1980).

Williams, Simon John; New Delhi since October 1999; born 22.8.60; FCO 1979; Manila 1981; Mbabane 1984; Kaduna 1986; FCO 1992; Full-time Language Training 1995; Third Secretary (Commercial) Riyadh 1995; Second Secretary Commercial Doha 1998; Band B3; m 1987 Rosemarie Coguntas Diaz.

Williams, Stephen Michael; Counsellor and Deputy Head of Mission Buenos Aires since July 2001; born 20.7.59; FCO 1981; Third later Second Secretary Sofia 1984; Second later First Secretary FCO 1987; on loan to Barclays Bank 1990; First Secretary (Commercial/Economic) Oslo 1991; First Secretary (External Relations) UKREP Brussels 1995; Counsellor FCO 1998; FTLT 2001; m 1983 Fiona Michele Hume (2d 1986, 1989; 1s 1991).

Williams, Steven; Brussels since May 2000; born 30.4.69; FCO 1987; Band C4; m2000 Leah Victoria Cox.

Williams , Tony Scott; Second Secretary (Management) Sofia since August 2000; born 12.9.62; FCO 1981; UKDEL NATO Brussels 1984; Prague 1986; Dhaka 1988; FCO 1989; Athens 1993; Third Secretary (Commercial) New Delhi 1996; m 1985 Denise Tilbrook (1s 1992).

Williamson, Morven Jane; Jedda since October 1999; born 16.4.71; FCO 1991; Hanoi 1994; Band B3.

Willis, Iain Edward; Third Secretary (Political) Valletta since July 1999; born 25.5.71; FCO 1991; T/D Karachi 1995; Vice-Consul Tokyo 1996; Band B3.

Willmer, Nigel Stuart; FCO since September 2000; born 3.7.65; FCO 1983; Madrid 1990; FCO 1993; Lusaka 1997; m 1985 Jackie Mann (1d 1986).

Willock, Oriel; San José since August 2001; born 23.4.68; FCO 1988; Amman 1990; Floater Duties 1994; FCO 1997; T/D Islamabad 1999; T/D Ekaterinburg 2000; Band B3.

Wills, Jane Stirling; First Secretary and Deputy Head of Mission Bratislava since April 1999; born 12.12.46; Commonwealth Office (later FCO) 1964; Prague; 1969; Copenhagen 1971; UKDEL MBFR Vienna 1973; Bombay 1976; FCO 1980; Prague 1983, Ankara 1986; Second Secretary FCO 1989; Deputy Head of Mission Reykjavik 1995.

Wills, Ruth Margaret; Second later First Secretary FCO since December 1991; born 7.11.54; FCO

1977; Rio de Janeiro 1980; Paris 1984; Second Secretary (Press/Info) Bonn 1989.

Willsher, Ian Robert; First Secretary Brussels since September 1998; born 14.4.47; Washington 1974; Vienna 1977; FCO 1979; Accra 1982; Geneva 1985; FCO 1988; Nairobi 1990; FCO 1994; British Forces Germany 1996; m 1976 Amanda Jane (2s 1978, 1979; 1d 1985).

Wilmshurst, Elizabeth Susan CMG (1999); SUPL since March 2001; born 28.8.48; Solicitor 1972; Assistant Legal Adviser FCO 1974; First Secretary later Counsellor on loan to Attorney-General's Chambers 1986; Legal Counsellor FCO 1991; Counsellor (Legal Adviser) UKMIS New York 1994; Legal Counsellor FCO 1998; Deputy Legal Adviser FCO 1999.

Wilson, Allan Richard James; FCO since November 1999; born 11.5.77; Band A2.

Wilson, Caroline Melanie Cherry (née Meath); FCO since July 1999; born 16.9.69; FCO 1990; Canberra 1992; Moscow 1995; SUPL 1998 Band B3; m 1993 James Jeffrey Wilson.

Wilson, Elizabeth Claire; FTLT since October 2000; born 20.9.74; FCO 1998; Band C4.

Wilson, Fraser Andrew, MBE (1980); British High Commissioner Victoria since April 2002; born 6.5.49; Commonwealth Office (later FCO) 1967; Havana 1970; South-East Asia Floater 1971; Seoul 1973; Salisbury 1977; Second Secretary FCO 1980; Language Training 1983; Second Secretary (Comm) Moscow 1984; Second Secretary (Comm) and Vice-Consul (later First Secretary (Comm)) Rangoon 1986; First Secretary FCO 1990; Deputy Consul-General São Paulo 1994; Full time Language training 1998; HM Ambassador Turkmenistan 1998; m 1981 Janet Phillips (2s 1982, 1985).

Wilson, Gillian Grace; Third Secretary (Chancery) Nairobi since April 1995; born 19.4.65; ODA 1981; FCO 1989; Temporary Duty Dhaka 1991; Accra 1991; Band C4.

Wilson, Harry Kenneth BEM (1991); Madrid since November 1999; born 7.5.52; RAF 1971-97; FCO 1998; Band A2; m 1979 Elaine Patrick (1s 1981, 1d 1983).

Wilson, Ian Laurence; HM Consul Beijing since July 2001; born 19.6.44; FO 1962; Moscow 1966; Colombo 1967; FCO 1971; UKDEL NATO Brussels 1974; Banjul 1977; FCO 1981; Canberra 1983; FCO 1987; Second Secretary (Cons/Admin) Calcutta 1987; Second Secretary (Management) Bucharest 1992; First Secretary FCO 1995; Consul and First Secretary (Management) Tehran 1997; HM Consul Riyadh 2000; Band C5; m(1)1970 (diss 1999) (1d 1974; 1s 1976); (2) 1999 Monica Dorri (1s 2000).

Wilson, James Jeffrey (Jeff); FCO since October 1999; born 7.8.67; FCO 1988; Canberra 1992; Moscow 1995; Vice-Consul Ekaterinburg 1997; Band C4; m 1993 Caroline Melanie Meath.

Wilson, Keith Edward; FCO since April 1990; born 18.6.46; CRO (later FCO) 1963; Islamabad 1970; Lagos 1974; Dacca 1977; FCO 1980; Tehran 1983; Johannesburg 1988; Band B3; m 1984 Christine Maria Theresia del Negro (1d 1985; 1s 1988).

Wilson, Patrick John; Counsellor FCO since February 2000; born 16.3.44; FCO 1967; Turin 1968; FCO 1970; MECAS 1971; Jedda 1972; Abidjan 1975; FCO 1982; First Secretary (IAEA) UKMIS Vienna 1985; First Secretary FCO (1989); Rome 1993; Counsellor (Political) Tirana 1998; m 1969 Liliana Rossi (2s 1972, 1974).

Wilson, Peter Michael Alexander; SUPL since March 1999; born 31.3.68; FCO 1992; Full-time Language Training 1993; Full-time Language Training Peking 1994; Peking 1995; Band C4.

Wilson, Robert Thomas Osborne; Deputy Head of Mission, HM Consul Bahrain since September 1998; born 28.1.52; FCO 1982; Senior Research Officer; First Secretary and Head of Chancery Abu Dhabi 1989; Principal Research Officer FCO 1993; m 1979 Susan Ann Watson (2d 1985, 1988).

Wilson, Roy Andrew; First Secretary Banja Luka since October 2000; born 3.12.59; HCS 1978; FCO 1979; Karachi 1982; Seoul 1985; FCO 1987; Bombay 1990; Zurich 1994; Band C4.

Wilson, Simon Charles Hartley; Deputy Head of Mission and Head of Political Section, Bahrain since November 2001; born 9.8.57; FCO 1975; Johannesburg 1978; Helsinki 1981; FCO 1984; Tehran 1987; Riyadh 1987; Second Secretary (Chancery/Info) Lisbon 1992; Second later First Secretary FCO 1997; m 1984 Heather Graine Richardson (2s 1990, 1994).

Wilson, Simon Jules, OBE (1996); First Secretary UKMIS New York since October 1999; born 13.3.66; FCO 1988; Third later Second Secretary (Econ) Athens 1991; Second later First Secretary (Political) Zagreb 1993; First Secretary FCO 1996; Band D6.

Wilson, Susan Jean; Istanbul since November 1997; born 1.2.70; FCO 1989; Bangkok 1994; Band B3.

Wilton, Christopher Edward John; Counsellor FCO since February 1998; born 16.12.51; FCO 1977; MECAS 1978; Second later First Secretary Bahrain 1979; FCO 1981; First Secretary (Chancery) Tokyo 1984; on loan to Cabinet Office 1988; Counsellor (Commercial) Riyadh 1990; Consul General Dubai 1994; m 1975 Dianne Hodgkinson (1d 1981; 1s 1984).

Wiltshire, Terence Keith; Second Secretary (Technical Management) Budapest since February 2001; born 24.12.57; FCO 1981; New Delhi 1983; FCO 1987; Lagos 1994; FCO 1997; Band C4.

Windle, William James; First Secretary FCO since September 1992; born 3.7.52; FCO 1972; on loan to MOD 1975; FCO 1977; Second Secretary (Comm) Muscat 1980; Second later First Secretary

FCO 1984; First Secretary (Chancery) Washington 1989; Band C5; m 1974 June Constance Grimmond (3s 1980, 1982, 1985).

Windsor, Dallas Frederick; FCO since September 2001; born 24.4.74; Band C4.

Winnington-Ingram, Charles Pepys; FCO since 2000; born 6.10.55; Barrister 1977; Export Credits Guarantee Department 1979; FCO 1980; Third Secretary (Commercial) Tokyo 1981; Second Secretary FCO 1985; Second Secretary (Chancery/Information) Oslo 1989; HM Consul (Commercial) and Deputy Head of Mission St Petersburg 1995; HM Consul and Deputy Head of Mission Jerusalem 1996.

Winsley, Marcus Justin; FCO since January 2000; born 1.9.67; ODA 1993; First Secretary Moscow 1996; Band D6; m 1996 Claire Underwood.

Winter, Douglas; Second Secretary (Consular/Management) Sarajevo since April 1999; born 21.1.51; FCO 1969; Mogadishu 1972; Antigua 1974; FCO 1978; Bangkok 1981; Zagreb 1984; Warsaw 1985; Second Secretary FCO 1987; Second Secretary (Commercial) Abu Dhabi 1990; FCO 1994; m 1972 Linda Margaret Harmer (1s 1975; 1d 1978).

Winter, Simon; ECO Accra since November 2000; born 10.4.68; FCO 1990; Tokyo 1995; Budapest 1999; Band A2; m 1993 Alyson Barnett (1s 1994, 1d 1997).

Winterburn, Christine Catherine (née Lowrie); Second Secretary (Political/PPA) Sofia since August 1999; born 20.4.67; FCO 1986; Copenhagen 1987; FCO 1989; Kaduna/Abuja 1992; Lima 1996; Band C4; m 1989 John Winterburn (2s 1995, 2000).

Wise, Graeme Michael; SUPL since October 1999; born 17.6.64; FCO 1984; Addis Ababa 1985; Lagos 1988; Floater Duties 1991; FCO 1992; Second Secretary (Commercial) Buenos Aires 1997; Band C4.

Wise, Patricia (née Donnelly); Nicosia since March 2000; born 24.2.58; FCO 1982; Port Stanley 1983; Lusaka 1983; Rome 1987; Cape Town/Pretoria 1990; FCO 1993; SUPL 1994; Helsinki 1994; SUPL 1996; FCO 1997; Band B3; m(1) 1985 Edward Meredith Leighton (diss 1991); m(2) 1992 David Wise (dec'd 1999) (1d 1994).

Wisker, Rita; FCO since January 1996; born 15.9.51; FCO 1972; Tokyo 1973; FCO 1975; Washington 1977; UKREP Brussels 1980; BMG Berlin 1983; UKMIS New York 1984; FCO 1985; UKDEL Brussels 1992; Band B3.

Withers, John Walter Charles; FCO since August 1994; born 24.11.47; FCO 1975; Moscow 1979; FCO 1982; Lagos 1982; FCO 1985; Ottawa 1986; New York 1987; FCO 1989; Third later Second Secretary Bucharest 1991; m 1970 Vivienne Chater (1d 1976, 1s 1986).

Withers, Matthew Robert; Third Secretary (Political) Buenos Aires since January 2001; born

14.10.67; FCO 1987; Kuala Lumpur 1988; Kathmandu 1992; Lagos 1994; FCO 1998; Band B3; m 1992 Leigh Cooper (2d 1994, 1996).

Witting, Lisa Marie; UKMIS Vienna since January 2000; born 22.2.69; FCO 1988; Dublin 1989; FCO 1993; Berlin 1995; Band A2.

Wolstenholme , Jonathan David; Second Secretary (Chancery) Wellington since August 1998; born 15.1.60; FCO 1980; Baghdad 1982; Moscow 1984; Harare 1986; FCO 1990; (Second Secretary 1992); Second Secretary (Management) UKREP Brussels 1994; m 1986 Karen Suzanne Vivian (2d 1989, 1994; 1s 1992).

Wolstenholme, Karen Suzanne (née Vivian); Wellington since August 1998; born 16.10.62; FCO 1980; Language Training 1983; FCO 1984; Moscow 1984; Harare 1986; Second Secretary FCO 1990; SUPL 1992; Second Secretary FCO 1993; UKREP Brussels 1994; m 1986 Jonathan David Wolstenholme (2d 1989, 1994; 1s 1992).

Wong, Lillian Paterson (née Walker); FCO since February 1976; born 16.2.44; FCO 1970; Second Secretary (Inf/Aid) Yaoundé 1973; Senior Principal Research Officer; (Band D6); m 1979 Robert Puck Keong Wong.

Wood, Christopher Terence; On loan to the Department of Environment since January 1992; born 19.1.59; FCO 1981; SOAS 1982; Language Student Hong Kong 1983; On secondment to Hong Kong Government as Assistant Political Adviser 1984; First Secretary FCO 1987.

Wood, Ian David; SUPL since August 2001; born 14.9.69; FCO 1992; Third later Second Secretary UKDel OECD 1994; Second Secretary (Political) New Delhi 1996; UKDEL NATO 1996; FCO 1998.

Wood, James Sebastian Lamin; Seconded to Harvard since May 2000; born 6.4.61; FCO 1983; Language Student 1984; Second Secretary Bangkok 1986; Second later First Secretary FCO 1989; Full-time Language Training Taiwan 1991; First Secretary and Consul for Macau, BTC Hong Kong 1992; First Secretary UKREP JLG Hong Kong 1994; FCO 1996; On loan to the Cabinet Office 1998; m 1990 Sirihat Pengnuam (3d 1992, 1993, 1995).

Wood, Michael Charles, CMG (1995); Legal Adviser FCO since December 1999; born 5.2.47; called to the Bar, Grays Inn 1968; Assistant Legal Adviser FCO 1970; Legal Adviser Bonn 1981; Legal Adviser later Legal Counsellor FCO 1984; Counsellor (Legal) UKMIS New York 1991; Legal Counsellor FCO 1994; Deputy Legal Adviser 1996.

Wood, Michael John Hemsley; Counsellor Lusaka since September 2000; born 16.9.48; FCO 1972; Third later Second Secretary Athens 1974; FCO 1976; First Secretary Harare 1980; language training 1983; First Secretary and Head of Chancery and Consul Hanoi 1984; First Secretary FCO 1987; Counsellor (Political) Helsinki 1993;

Counsellor FCO 1997; m(1) 1975 Susan Christine Langford, (2) 1983 Wendy Mary Smith.

Wood, Dr Peter Gilruth; Counsellor FCO since September 1998; born 2.11.53; FCO 1982; Language training 1983 (Taiwan 1984); First Secretary (Econ) Peking 1986; First Secretary FCO 1989; Kuala Lumpur 1995; m 1998 Pamela Sue Shookman.

Wood, Richard John; First Secretary FCO since January 1998; born 27.8.67; FCO 1991; Cape Town/Pretoria 1993.

Wood, Richard Lewis; Third Secretary (Commercial) Johannesburg since February 1996; born 7.6.61; FCO 1982; Sofia 1984; Bandar Seri Begawan 1986; FCO 1989; Vice-Consul Riyadh 1992; m 1994 Frances Anne Curley; (2s 1995, 1998).

Woodcock, Andrew; Third Secretary (Economic/Political) Mexico City since July 1996; born 18.9.65; FCO 1988; Vice-Consul Baghdad 1990; AMO/ Vice Consul Brasilia 1991; Third Secretary (Science/Technology) Bonn 1995; Band B3.

Woodham, Mark John; Bangkok since August 1998; born 18.11.67; FCO 1988; Helsinki 1991; Islamabad 1994; Band B3; m 1993 Sari Hannele Hakkarainen.

Woodier, Daniel Robert; FCO since July 1996; born 2.9.65; Band B3; m 1989 Sarah Harmer.

Woodrow, John Peter Gayford; Second Secretary (Consular) Helsinki since June 1997; born 21.11.47; FCO 1972; Barcelona 1975; Quito 1976; FCO 1979; La Paz 1983; Consul Istanbul 1988; FCO 1992; Consul Oslo 1995; m 1977 Yvonne Leffmann.

Woodruff Thomson, Helen; SUPL since January 1994; born 3.8.63; FCO 1985; Washington 1987; Harare 1989; FCO 1992; Band A2; m 1993 Captain Robert John Thomson.

Woodruffe, John Michael; Shanghai since September 1998; born 26.6.57; FCO 1986; Dublin 1989; Amman 1992; FCO 1995; Band C4; m 1989 Marian Barrett.

Woods, David John; Counsellor (Political) Pretoria since October 1997; born 4.8.51; Third later Second Secretary FCO 1976; Second later First Secretary (UNIDO & IAEA) Vienna 1978; FCO 1981; First Secretary (Econ) Bucharest 1981; First Secretary FCO 1985; Counsellor Harare 1992; Counsellor FCO 1995; m 1972 Rachel Haydon White (1s 1977; 1d 1979).

Woods, Harvey John; FTLT since March 2001; born 29.10.70; FCO 1999; Band C4.

Woods, Ian Alexander; Counsellor FCO since September 1998; born 10.6.51; Third Secretary FCO 1976; Second Secretary UKMIS New York 1977; First Secretary FCO 1980; BMG Berlin 1984; Bonn 1986; First Secretary later Counsellor

FCO 1989; Warsaw 1995; m 1978 Stephanie Flett (2s 1982, 1986).

Woodward, Amanda Jane; Muscat since November 1997; born 29.4.56; FCO 1978; Brasilia 1979; New Delhi 1982; Moscow 1985; FCO 1988; Lisbon 1989; FCO 1991; Kuala Lumpur 1993; Band B3.

Woodward, Barbara Janet; Second Secretary Moscow since October 1994; born 29.5.61; FCO 1991.

Woodward, Emma Jane; BCG Jerusalem since May 2000; born 6.6.70; FCO 1996; BTCO Taipei 1997; Band A2.

Woodward, Gillian Yvonne (née Aplin); SUPL since November 1996; born 20.12.46; DSAO (later FCO) 1966; UKDEL OECD Paris 1969; Yaoundé 1972; FCO 1974; Lagos 1979; SUPL 1981; Helsinki 1984; FCO 1987; Mexico City 1990; FCO 1993; Band B3; m 1977 Roger Charles Woodward.

Woodward, Roger Charles; First Secretary (Management) Paris since January 1997; born 15.3.48; Commonwealth Office (later FCO) 1967; Dacca 1970; Caribbean Floater 1972; Doha 1973; FCO 1976; Lagos 1979; Helsinki 1982 (Second Secretary 1984); FCO 1987; Second Secretary (Commercial) Mexico City 1990; Second Secretary FCO 1993; m 1977 Gillian Yvonne Aplin.

Woolley, Lesley Ann; Islamabad since July 1986; born 27.4.64; FCO 1984; Band A2; m 1984 Samuel Patrick David Woolley.

Wooten, Sarah Elisabeth; Consul (Commercial and Investment) Nagoya since August 1999; born 4.2.68; FCO 1989; Third Secretary (Consular) Valletta 1992; Full-time Language Training 1994; Full Time Language Training Tokyo 1995; Osaka 1996; Band C4.

Wootton, Adam Nicholas; FCO since September 1996; born 19.5.60; FCO 1983; Baghdad 1985; FCO 1988; Nairobi 1993; Band C4; m 1984 Adele Wright (2s 1991).

Wordsworth, Ellyse Nichole (née Mingins); SUPL since July 1989; born 12.8.54; FCO 1975; UKREP Brussels 1977; Moscow 1980; FCO 1981; Second Secretary (Comm) Lagos 1984; FCO 1986; m 1981 Stephen John Wordsworth (1s 1987).

Wordsworth, Stephen John; LVO (1992); Head of Eastern Adriatic Dept FCO since August 1999; born 17.5.55; FCO 1977; Third later Second Secretary Moscow 1979; FCO 1981; First Secretary (Econ/Comm) Lagos 1983; on loan to Cabinet Office 1986; First Secretary FCO 1988; First Secretary (Political) Bonn 1990; Counsellor (Deputy International Affairs Adviser) SHAPE Mons 1994; m 1981 Ellyse Nichole Mingins (1s 1987).

Worham, Paul Andrew; Moscow since June 1999; born 15.12.66; HCS 1988; FCO 1997; Band A2; m 1999 Elizabeth Mary Smith.

Workman, Daniel John; FCO since September 2000; born 11.9.78; Band C4.

Worster, Paul Anthony; Third Secretary (Consular) Singapore since May 1999; born 14.5.62; FCO 1983; Warsaw 1985; Washington 1986; Helsinki 1989; FCO 1992; Tehran 1996; Band B3.

Worthington, Ian Alan OBE(1999); FCO since March 1998; born 9.8.58; FCO 1977; Language Training 1978; Moscow 1980; Lusaka 1982; Second Secretary FCO 1985; Second Secretary (Comm) Seoul 1988; Second Secretary (Chancery) Kingston 1992; Head BETO later Consul-General Ekaterinburg 1995; Band D6.

Wotton; Rosaleen Mary (née McManus); ECO Nicosia since June 2000; born 15.1.62; FCO 1987; Oslo 1988; Brussels 1991; FCO 1992; T/D Geneva 1993; Berne 1993; FCO 1996; SUPL 1998; Band B3; m 1997 Alan Leslie Wotton (1s 1998).

Wragg, Ann Desson (née Traill); FCO since August 1992; born 20.3.65; FCO 1983; Paris 1985; FCO 1988; UKMIS New York 1989; Band B3; m 1988 John Wragg.

Wright, Carol; Third Secretary (Management) Baku since August 2001; born 27.6.62; FCO 1988; Pretoria 1992; Johannesburg 1993; FCO 1996; Band B3.

Wright, Clive David; First Secretary UKDEL OSCE Vienna since May 1996; born 14.1.58; Royal Marines 1976; FCO 1977; Ankara 1980; Tripoli 1983; FCO 1984; Doha 1986; (Second Secretary 1989); Vice-Consul (Pol/Admin) Johannesburg 1989; Second later First Secretary FCO 1993; m 1982 Christine Bernadette Caldwell (2d 1986, 1989).

Wright, Cynthia Munro; UKREP Brussels since September 1995; born 17.8.39; FCO 1976; Brussels 1977; Lusaka 1979; FCO 1982; Stockholm 1983; Rome 1986; FCO 1987; UKDEL Paris 1988; FCO 1991; Band A2.

Wright, David Alan, OBE (1984); HM Ambassador Doha since June 1997; born 27.5.42; FO 1965; APS to Minister of State FO 1966; MECAS 1968; Baghdad 1971; Second Secretary (Comm) and Vice-Consul Doha 1973; On loan to DHSS 1976; Second later First Secretary FCO 1978; Consul and Head of Post Durban 1980; First Secretary (Comm) Baghdad 1984; First Secretary later Counsellor FCO 1987; HM Consul General Atlanta1992; m 1966 Gail Karol Mesling (4s 1966, 1968, 1971, 1983; 1d 1978).

Wright, Sir David (John), KCMG (1996), LVO (1990), Grand Cordon of the Rising Sun (1998); Group Chief Executive (Permanent Secretary) British Trade International (Trade Partners UK and Invest UK) from June 1999; born 16.6.44; Diplomatic Service 1966; Third later Second Secretary Tokyo 1966; Second later First Secretary FCO 1972; ENA Paris 1975; First Secretary Paris 1976; Private Secretary to Secretary of Cabinet 1980; Counsellor (Econ) Tokyo 1982; Head of Personnel Services Department FCO 1985; On secondment to Buckingham Palace as Deputy Private Secretary to HRH The Prince of Wales 1988; HM Ambassador Seoul (and Commissioner General, UK Pavilion Taejon EXPO 93) 1990; DUSS (Asia/Americas/ Africa/Trade Promotion) 1994; FCO Non-Executive Director, AEA Technology 1994; HM Ambassador Tokyo 1996; m 1968 Sally Ann Dodkin (1s 1970; 1d 1973).

Wright, David Stephen; First Secretary (Political) Bogotá since February 2000; born 4.2.63; FCO 1989; Second Secretary (Chancery) Mexico City 1991; First Secretary FCO 1993; Band D6; m 1992 Tania Victoria Gessinger (1d 1999).

Wright, Julia Helen; Third later Second Secretary (Chancery) Oslo since July 1997; born 6.2.65; FCO 1991; Full Time Language Training 1993; Amsterdam 1994.

Wright, Nicola (née Daubney); FCO since February 1999; born 31.1.70; FCO 1989; Peking 1992; FCO 1993; Zagreb 1996; Band B3; m 1998 Alan David Wright.

Wright, Stephen John Leadbetter, cmg (1997); Deputy Under-Secretary FCO since October 2000; born 7.12.46; Third Secretary FCO 1968; Havana 1969; Second Secretary FCO 1972; (First Secretary 1975); Director of Policy and Reference Division and Consul (Inf) New York (BIS) 1975; UKREP Brussels 1980; First Secretary FCO 1984; Counsellor 1985; On loan to Cabinet Office 1985; Counsellor and Head of Chancery New Delhi 1988; Counsellor (External Relations) UKREP Brussels 1991; Director (EU Affairs) FCO 1994; Minister Washington 1997. Director (Wider Europe) FCO 1999; m 1970 Georgina Susan Butler (Diss 2000) (1d 1977; 1s 1979).

Wurr, Adam; Second Secretary UKMIS Geneva since January 2000; born 14.12.71; Second Secretary FCO 1995; Band C4.

Wyatt, David; Deputy High Commissioner Lagos since October 2001; born 18.4.46; DSAO 1965; Lusaka 1968; SOAS 1971; Bangkok 1972; (Second Secretary 1975); Second Secretary Yaoundé 1976; Second later First Secretary; FCO 1977; First Secretary 1979; National Defence Course Latimer 1980; First Secretary (Commercial) Athens 1981; First Secretary and Head of Chancery Bangkok 1984; First Secretary FCO 1988; Deputy High Commissioner Accra 1994; FCO 1998; Counsellor (Commercial) Bangkok 1999; m 1969 Rosemary Elizabeth Clarke (1s 1972; 1d 1974).

Wye, Roderick Francis; FCO since 1999; born 13.9.50; Research Officer FCO 1973; PRO 1983; Peking 1985; First Secretary FCO 1988; First Secretary (Chancery) Peking 1995; m 1989 Katelin Rebecca Teller (1s 1994).

Wyeth, Jean; FCO since April 1994; born 13.1.43; Mbabane 1968; Moscow 1971; UKMIS New York 1973; Africa/ME Floater 1976; FCO 1980; Brussels 1983; FCO 1986; On loan to Privy Council Office 1989; FCO 1990; On loan to the DTI 1991; Band B3.

Wyithe, Philip Leslie; Second Secretary (Management/Consular) Seoul since August 1997; born 30.12.64; FCO 1983; Moscow 1987; Floater Duties 1990; Third Secretary (Consular) Sana'a 1992; Third Secretary (Immigration) Valletta 1994; FCO 1995; Band B3; m 1992 Gina Olofernes Daniel (1d 1994).

Wylde, Richard Norman Gordon; First Secretary FCO since October 2000; born 18.10.58; FCO 1985; Second (later First) Secretary (Chancery) and Deputy Permanent Representative ESCAP Bangkok 1989; First Secretary FCO 1992; First Secretary (Political) Rome 1996; Band D6; m 1987 Lesley Tennison (1d 1991; 1s 1995).

Wynburne, Mark Barry; Second later First Secretary FCO since June 1981; born 29.3.45; Army 1963-64; FO 1966; Prague 1967; FCO 1968; Islamabad 1974; FCO 1978; Second Secretary and Vice-Consul Hanoi 1980; Band C5.

Wyver, Wendy Anne; Second Secretary (Political) Tokyo since September 1996; born 26.10.64; FCO 1993; Full Time Language Training 1994; m 1995 Jakob Windfeld Lund.

Y

Yaghmourian, Paul Barkef; Counsellor and Deputy Head of Mission Copenhagen since December 1997; born 14.2.58; FCO 1984; Second later First Secretary Lisbon 1986; First Secretary FCO 1989; First Secretary (Pol) Brasilia 1993; secondment to British Aerospace 1997.

Yapp, John William; High Commissioner Victoria (Seychelles) since January 1998; born 14.1.51; FCO 1971; Islamabad 1973; Kuala Lumpur (Consular) 1975; APS to Minister of State FCO,1978; Dubai (Commercial) 1980; Second Secretary (Economic/Commercial) The Hague 1984; First Secretary FCO 1988; First Secretary (Information/Political) Wellington 1991; Deputy Head of North America Department FCO 1995; m(1) 1973 (1d 1975); (2) 1979 (1s 1981; 2d 1983, 1987); (3) 1997 Petra Jodelis.(1d 1998).

Yarounina, Maggie; FCO since March 2000; born 8.7.72; Band B3; m 1999 Alexandre (Sasha) V Yarounine.

Yarrow, Jon William; Third later Second Secretary (Political/Information) Dubai since July 1998; born 29.1.69; FCO 1987; Washington 1989; Berne 1992; FCO 1995; m(1) 1989 Helen Mugridge (diss 1995) (1d 1992, 1s 1995); (2) 1999 Katherine Ann Short.

Yarrow, Katherine Anne (née Short); SUPL since October 1998; born 19.2.70; FCO 1992; Berne 1994; FCO 1996; Band A2.

Yeadon, Joanne Mary; Budapest since October 1996; born 1.8.65; FCO 1983; Washington 1986; Gibraltar 1989; FCO 1992; Full-time Language Training 1996; Band B3.

York, Jennifer Ann; Second Secretary (Management) since December 1995; born 1.11.60; FCO 1980; BMG Berlin 1982;

Mogadishu 1988; Africa/ME Floater 1985; FCO 1989; Vice-Consul Durban 1992; Band B3; m 1988 Murray Rex Clarkin.(diss 1996).

Young, Amanda Elizabeth (née Mitchell); Dubai since September 1999; born 3.6.59; FCO 1977; Paris 1979; Cayman Islands 1982; FCO 1986; Riyadh 1987; Muscat 1989; FCO 1994; SUPL 1995; Band B3; m2000 Murray Andrew James Young.

Young, Andrew John; SUPL since February 2000; born 2.4.60; Solicitor 1988 (Northern Ireland) and 1990 (England and Wales); Assistant Legal Adviser FCO 1990; Seconded to Hong Kong Government as Deputy Principal Crown Counsel 1994; Assistant Legal Adviser FCO 1997; Legal Counsellor FCO 1999; m, (1) 1991 Lucy Stojak (diss 1996); (2) 1997 Annette Lee (1d 1997).

Young, Helena; FCO since September 1982 (First Secretary 1989); born 8.10.60; Band D6.

Young, Sir (John) Rob(ertson), KCMG (1999), CMG (1991); High Commissioner New Delhi since January 1999; born 21.2.45; Third Secretary FO 1967; MECAS 1968; Third later Second Secretary Cairo 1970; Second later First Secretary FCO 1973; Private Secretary to Parliamentary Under-Secretary later Minister of State FCO 1975; ENA Paris 1977; Paris 1977; FCO 1981; Acting Head of WED FCO 1983; Counsellor and Head of Chancery Damascus 1984; Counsellor FCO 1987; Minister Paris 1991; DUS (ME/FSU/EE) 1994; Chief Clerk 1995; m 1967 Catherine Houssait (2d 1969, 1978; 1s 1971).

Young, Sarah Louise (née Boxall); Cape Town since June 1997; born 16.9.63; FCO 1984; Lisbon 1987; FCO 1989; Band B3; m 1990 Alan Young (diss 1995) (2d 1991, 1992).

Young, Thomas Nesbitt; High Commissioner Lusaka since January 1998; born 24.7.43; FO (later FCO) 1966; Ankara 1969; Madrid 1973; Second Secretary FCO 1977; Ankara 1978; First Secretary and Head of Chancery Ankara 1979. Deputy Director BTDO, New York 1981; First Secretary Washington 1981; First Secretary FCO 1984; Deputy High Commissioner Accra 1987; Counsellor and Director of Trade Promotion Canberra 1990; HM Ambassador Baku 1993; m 1971 Elisabeth Hick (1d 1973; 1s 1975).

Young, Thomas Richard; FCO since September 2001; born 26.4.77; Band C4.

Younger, Alexander William; First Secretary FCO since June 1998; born 4.7.63; Second Secretary FCO 1991; First Secretary (IAEA) UKMIS Vienna 1995; Band D6; m 1993 Sarah Hopkins (1d 1994, 2s 1996,1998).

Younis, Fouzia; Islamabad since September 2001; born 8.7.78; FCO 2000; Band B3.

Z

Ziaullah, Suman Rafique; Second Secretary (Pol/Econ) Jakarta since October 2001; born 27.10.76; FCO 1999; Band C4.

Printed in the United Kingdom by The Stationery Office
667814 C20 12/01 19585